International Directory of

COMPANY HISTORIES

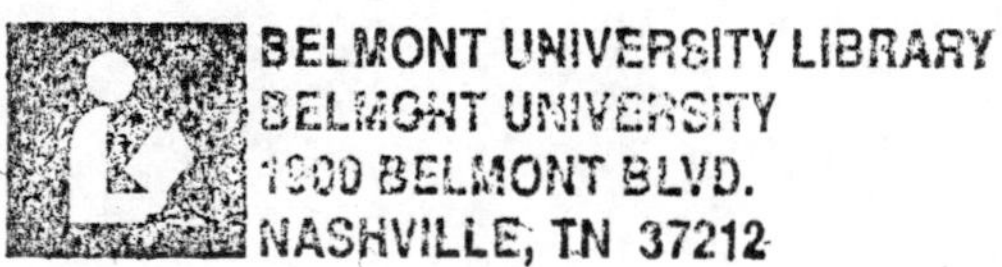

International Directory of COMPANY HISTORIES

VOLUME 68

Editor
Tina Grant

ST. JAMES PRESS
An imprint of Thomson Gale, a part of The Thomson Corporation

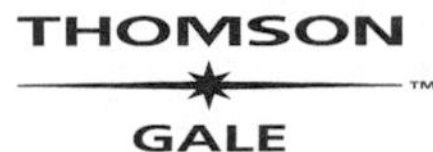

Detroit • New York • San Francisco • San Diego • New Haven, Conn. • Waterville, Maine • London • Munich

International Directory of Company Histories, Volume 68

Tina Grant, Editor

Project Editor
Miranda H. Ferrara

Editorial
Virgil Burton, Donna Craft, Louise Gagné, Peggy Geeseman, Julie Gough, Linda Hall, Sonya Hill, Keith Jones, Lynn Pearce, Maureen Puhl, Holly Selden, Justine Ventimiglia

Imaging and Multimedia
Randy Bassett, Lezlie Light

Manufacturing
Rhonda Williams, Rita Wimberley

Product Manager
Gerald L. Sawchuk

For more information contact
St. James Press
27500 Drake Rd.
Farmington Hills, MI 48331-3535
Or you can visit our Internet site at http://www.gale.com/stjames

LIBRARY OF CONGRESS CATALOG NUMBER 89-190943

ISBN: 1-55862-543-7

BRITISH LIBRARY CATALOGUING IN PUBLICATION DATA

International directory of company histories. Vol. 68
I. Tina Grant
33.87409

Printed in the United States of America
10 9 8 7 6 5 4 3 2 1

CONTENTS

Company Histories

PREFACE

The St. James Press series *The International Directory of Company Histories (IDCH)* is intended for reference use by students, business people, librarians, historians, economists, investors, job candidates, and others who seek to learn more about the historical development of the world's most important companies. To date, *IDCH* has covered over 6,950 companies in 68 volumes.

Inclusion Criteria

Most companies chosen for inclusion in *IDCH* have achieved a minimum of US$25 million in annual sales and are leading influences in their industries or geographical locations. Companies may be publicly held, private, or nonprofit. State-owned companies that are important in their industries and that may operate much like public or private companies also are included. Wholly owned subsidiaries and divisions are profiled if they meet the requirements for inclusion. Entries on companies that have had major changes since they were last profiled may be selected for updating.

The *IDCH* series highlights 10% private and nonprofit companies, and features updated entries on approximately 50 companies per volume.

Entry Format

Each entry begins with the company's legal name, the address of its headquarters, its telephone, toll-free, and fax numbers, and its web site. A statement of public, private, state, or parent ownership follows. A company with a legal name in both English and the language of its headquarters country is listed by the English name, with the native-language name in parentheses.

The company's founding or earliest incorporation date, the number of employees, and the most recent available sales figures follow. Sales figures are given in local currencies with equivalents in U.S. dollars. For some private companies, sales figures are estimates and indicated by the abbreviation *est.* The entry lists the exchanges on which a company's stock is traded and its ticker symbol, as well as the company's NAIC codes.

Entries generally contain a *Company Perspectives* box which provides a short summary of the company's mission, goals, and ideals, a *Key Dates* box highlighting milestones in the company's history, lists of *Principal Subsidiaries, Principal Divisions, Principal Operating Units, Principal Competitors,* and articles for *Further Reading.*

American spelling is used throughout *IDCH*, and the word ''billion'' is used in its U.S. sense of one thousand million.

Sources

Entries have been compiled from publicly accessible sources both in print and on the Internet such as general and academic periodicals, books, annual reports, and material supplied by the companies themselves.

Cumulative Indexes

IDCH contains three indexes: the **Index to Companies**, which provides an alphabetical index to companies discussed in the text as well as to companies profiled, the **Index to Industries**, which allows researchers to locate companies by their principal industry, and the **Geographic Index**, which lists companies alphabetically by the country of their headquarters. The indexes are cumulative and specific instructions for using them are found immediately preceding each index.

Suggestions Welcome

Comments and suggestions from users of *IDCH* on any aspect of the product as well as suggestions for companies to be included or updated are cordially invited. Please write:

The Editor
International Directory of Company Histories
St. James Press
27500 Drake Rd.
Farmington Hills, Michigan 48331-3535

ABBREVIATIONS FOR FORMS OF COMPANY INCORPORATION

AB	Aktiebolag (Finland, Sweden)
AB Oy	Aktiebolag Osakeyhtiot (Finland)
A.E.	Anonimos Eteria (Greece)
AG	Aktiengesellschaft (Austria, Germany, Switzerland, Liechtenstein)
A.O.	Anonim Ortaklari/Ortakligi (Turkey)
ApS	Amparteselskab (Denmark)
A.Š.	Anonim Širketi (Turkey)
A/S	Aksjeselskap (Norway); Aktieselskab (Denmark, Sweden)
Ay	Avoinyhtio (Finland)
B.A.	Buttengewone Aansprakeiijkheid (The Netherlands)
Bhd.	Berhad (Malaysia, Brunei)
B.V.	Besloten Vennootschap (Belgium, The Netherlands)
C.A.	Compania Anonima (Ecuador, Venezuela)
C. de R.L.	Compania de Responsabilidad Limitada (Spain)
Co.	Company
Corp.	Corporation
CRL	Companhia a Responsabilidao Limitida (Portugal, Spain)
C.V.	Commanditaire Vennootschap (The Netherlands, Belgium)
G.I.E.	Groupement d'Interet Economique (France)
GmbH	Gesellschaft mit beschraenkter Haftung (Austria, Germany, Switzerland)
Inc.	Incorporated (United States, Canada)
I/S	Interessentselskab (Denmark); Interesentselskap (Norway)
KG/KGaA	Kommanditgesellschaft/Kommanditgesellschaft auf Aktien (Austria, Germany, Switzerland)
KK	Kabushiki Kaisha (Japan)
K/S	Kommanditselskab (Denmark); Kommandittselskap (Norway)
Lda.	Limitada (Spain)
L.L.C.	Limited Liability Company (United States)
Ltd.	Limited (Various)
Ltda.	Limitada (Brazil, Portugal)
Ltee.	Limitee (Canada, France)
mbH	mit beschraenkter Haftung (Austria, Germany)
N.V.	Naamloze Vennootschap (Belgium, The Netherlands)
OAO	Otkrytoe Aktsionernoe Obshchestve (Russia)
OOO	Obschestvo s Ogranichennoi Otvetstvennostiu (Russia)
Oy	Osakeyhtiö (Finland)
PLC	Public Limited Co. (United Kingdom, Ireland)
Pty.	Proprietary (Australia, South Africa, United Kingdom)
S.A.	Société Anonyme (Belgium, France, Greece, Luxembourg, Switzerland, Arab speaking countries); Sociedad Anónima (Latin America [except Brazil], Spain, Mexico); Sociedades Anônimas (Brazil, Portugal)
SAA	Societe Anonyme Arabienne
S.A.R.L.	Sociedade Anonima de Responsabilidade Limitada (Brazil, Portugal); Société à Responsabilité Limitée (France, Belgium, Luxembourg)
S.A.S.	Societá in Accomandita Semplice (Italy); Societe Anonyme Syrienne (Arab speaking countries)
Sdn. Bhd.	Sendirian Berhad (Malaysia)
S.p.A.	Società per Azioni (Italy)
Sp. z.o.o.	Spólka z ograniczona odpowiedzialnoscia (Poland)
S.R.L.	Società a Responsabilità Limitata (Italy); Sociedad de Responsabilidad Limitada (Spain, Mexico, Latin America [except Brazil])
S.R.O.	Spolecnost s Rucenim Omezenym (Czechoslovakia
Ste.	Societe (France, Belgium, Luxembourg, Switzerland)
VAG	Verein der Arbeitgeber (Austria, Germany)
YK	Yugen Kaisha (Japan)
ZAO	Zakrytoe Aktsionernoe Obshchestve (Russia)

ABBREVIATIONS FOR CURRENCY

$	United States dollar
£	United Kingdom pound
¥	Japanese yen
AED	Emirati dirham
ARS	Argentine peso
ATS	Austrian shilling
AUD	Australian dollar
BEF	Belgian franc
BHD	Bahraini dinar
BRL	Brazilian real
CAD	Canadian dollar
CHF	Swiss franc
CNY	Chinese yuan
COP	Colombian peso
CLP	Chilean peso
CZK	Czech koruna
DEM	German deutsche mark
DKK	Danish krone
DZD	Algerian dinar
EEK	Estonian Kroon
EGP	Egyptian pound
ESP	Spanish peseta
EUR	euro
FIM	Finnish markka
FRF	French franc
GRD	Greek drachma
HKD	Hong Kong dollar
HUF	Hungarian forint
IDR	Indonesian rupiah
IEP	Irish pound
ILS	new Israeli shekel
INR	Indian rupee
ISK	Icelandic krona
ITL	Italian lira
JMD	Jamaican dollar
KPW	North Korean won
KRW	South Korean won
KWD	Kuwaiti dinar
LUF	Luxembourg franc
MUR	Mauritian rupee
MXN	Mexican peso
MYR	Malaysian ringgit
NGN	Nigerian naira
NLG	Netherlands guilder
NOK	Norwegian krone
NZD	New Zealand dollar
OMR	Omani rial
PHP	Philippine peso
PKR	Pakistani rupee
PLN	Polish zloty
PTE	Portuguese escudo
RMB	Chinese renminbi
RUB	Russian ruble
SAR	Saudi riyal
SEK	Swedish krona
SGD	Singapore dollar
THB	Thai baht
TND	Tunisian dinar
TRL	Turkish lira
TWD	new Taiwan dollar
VEB	Venezuelan bolivar
VND	Vietnamese dong
ZAR	South African rand
ZMK	Zambian kwacha

International Directory of

COMPANY HISTORIES

AARHUSUNITED

Aarhus United A/S

PO Box 50
Aarhus C
DK-8100
Denmark
Telephone: +45 87 30 60 00
Fax: 45 87 30 60 12
Web site: http://www.aarhusunited.com

Public Company
Incorporated: 1871 as Aarhus Palmekaernefabrik
Employees: 1,711
Sales: DKK 4.48 billion ($748.4 million) (2003)
Stock Exchanges: Copenhagen
NAIC: 311225 Fats and Oils Refining and Blending

Aarhus United A/S is a leading producer of vegetable oils for the food, confectionery, cosmetics, and healthcare industries. The Aarhus, Denmark-based company produces specialty fats and oils, as well as oleochemicals, derived primarily from palm oils supplied by partner company United Plantations Berhad in Malaysia. Aarhus has played a leading role in developing new oil varieties, such as cocoa butter equivalents (CBEs) and cocoa butter replacements (CBRs), used to reduce the cocoa butter content in chocolate preparations; and oils and margarine with reduced or no trans-fatty acid content. The company also produces bulk oils, a byproduct of its food- and pharmaceutical-grade production. A globally operating company with subsidiaries in 14 countries, Aarhus carries out its own refining operations at its factories in Denmark, Mexico, the United States, the United Kingdom, and in Uruguay. These plants produce more than 800,000 tons of oil per year. Aarhus and its subsidiaries adopted the name Aarhus United in part to unify its operations, and in part to highlight its longstanding relationship with United Plantations Berhad. Aarhus holds a 23 percent stake of United Plantations, which in turn owns 43 percent of Aarhus. In 2003, Aarhus posted revenues of nearly DKK 4.5 billion ($750 million).

Oil Business in the 1870s

Aarhus United's origins lay in the late 19th century, when the Aarhus Palmekaernefabrik was established in 1871. The company's earliest product was cattle feed, in the form of cakes produced using the oil from palm kernels. For the next decade, the young business focused exclusively on cattle feed. Yet in the early 1880s, the construction of another factory in the town of Aarhus—for producing margarine—led the feed cake company to change its direction. In 1883, Aarhus Palmekaernefabrik began refining its palm oil imports as food-grade vegetable oil in order to supply the margarine factory.

Vegetable oils rapidly became the company's focus, leading to the change in name to Aarhus Oliefabrik in 1892. From the start, Aarhus Oliefabrik distinguished itself by a willingness to invest in research and development, which in turn enabled the company to capture a leading share of the Danish vegetable oils market. Leading this growth was Frederik Lausen, who took over as the company's manager at the age of 25. Lausen built a new, modern facility for the company, which then expanded its operations to include the refining of oils from a variety of sources, including sesame, copra, peanuts, and others.

Aarhus rapidly turned to the international market, expanding its reach into the wider Scandinavian market before expanding throughout much of Western and Eastern Europe in the years leading up to World War I. Acquisitions formed a significant part of this expansion, bringing the company to Germany, Russia, and the United Kingdom, and then farther afield, to the United States.

Aarhus's commitment to technical development played a major role in the company's international success. Much of the company's development was attributed to technical manager M.C. Holst, who joined the company in 1896. Under Holst, Aarhus developed a new method for refining coconut oil, eliminating the unpleasant smell and taste from the oil and making it suitable for a variety of foods applications. The new coconut oil made possible the development of the first all-vegetable oil margarine in 1909. Over the next decade, the company added raw materials purchasing subsidiaries in the oil crop producing markets of Southeast Asia and Africa. In this way, the company was guaranteed a steady supply of coconut, palm kernels, and the like, for its steadily growing production levels.

Holst also led the development of another highly significant product for the company, CEBES, in the late 1920s. This was the

Company Perspectives:

We supply customers on selected world markets with vegetable oils processed using advanced technology and formulated to meet specific needs. Within the framework of this mission, we continue to explore a series of opportunities that can lead to growth and an increased income for the group. This has, over the years, taken us into areas regarded as complementary to our main activities.

company's first foray into specialty fats and oils, which became the company's core activity throughout the rest of the century. CEBES represented a breakthrough as one of the first successful cocoa butter substitutes. The new substance, much less expensive than cocoa butter itself, enabled Aarhus to achieve strong growth in the 1920s and 1930s, despite the Depression era. By 1937, Aarhus's raw materials processing levels had topped 300,000 tons annually. The company also had emerged as one of Denmark's largest and most successful enterprises.

Building the Lead in the 1960s

Aarhus continued developing its specialty fats expertise. In the 1950s, the company's attention turned toward the development of a cocoa butter equivalent (CBE) capable of replacing part or even all of the cocoa butter needed for the preparation of chocolate. Supporting this effort was the construction of a modern production facility in the mid-1950s. By 1960, the company had succeeded in developing its first CBE, called Kawex. The new substance represented not only a significant cost savings to chocolate manufacturers, it also offered a greater flexibility for the production of new types of chocolates than cocoa butter itself.

Aarhus then began working with its customers to refine its CBE technology, and by the end of the 1960s had developed its hugely successful ILLEXAO. The success of its efforts led the company to continue its expansion and modernization of its production facilities, including the construction of a continual fractionation plant by the end of the 1970s.

During this period, also, Aarhus rapidly expanded its product range, adding salad oils, frying oils, baking fat and butter replacements, confectionery fats, and other specialty food oils and fats. The company also recognized an extension of its fats technology into nonfood categories, such as oils, lotions, and creams for the cosmetics industry as well as for the pharmaceutical industry. The company developed a range of technical oils for use in the printing and paper industries, as well as for industrial applications, such as hydraulics systems and lubricants. Aarhus's commitment to technical development helped it gain the global leadership in the specialty fats market by the end of the decade.

That period marked a new era of international activity for Aarhus. For one, the end of the 1970s had seen the beginning of a new level of partnership with Malaysia-based United Plantations Berhad. United had been founded at the beginning of the 20th century by a Danish entrepreneur, and had grown into Malaysia's largest oil palm plantation group. Danes remained in control of United despite Malaysian nationalization programs in the 1970s. In the late 1970s, Borge Bek-Nielsen, then head of United, saw strong potential in forming a partnership with Aarhus. In 1978, United acquired a major stake in Aarhus, which remained at 43 percent through the end of the century.

Cementing their relationship, Aarhus then bought a stake in United's holding vehicle, International Plantations and Finance, in 1981. Aarhus later bought a stake in United itself, acquiring 32 percent in 1991. The company later reduced its position to 23 percent.

International Expansion in the 1990s

Aarhus's relationship with United Plantations ensured its supply of raw materials. The company then turned to its own international expansion, adopting a new policy of installing production facilities close to its principal foreign markets. A first step in this strategy was achieved in 1982 with the creation of Anglia Oils Ltd. in the United Kingdom. That company launched production the following year.

The United States became the company's next growth market, with the installation of a new production facility in Port Newark, New Jersey, in 1990. That plant was specialized in the production of lauric oils. In 2002, the U.S. subsidiary began an expansion of the site, building a new and separate production system for the production of nonlauric oils.

Soon after entering the United States, Aarhus turned to Mexico as well, establishing a new production subsidiary there called Santa Lucia. Other international markets followed, including a production facility in Malaysia. By the mid-1990s, Aarhus counted six oil production plants outside of Denmark, including sites in Egypt and Norway, as well as a seventh facility, in Sri Lanka, dedicated to the production of dessicated coconut. In 1996, the company began a new $35 million expansion of its Aarhus site in order to meet the boom in demand for its specialty oils and fats.

Through the 1990s and into the 2000s, Aarhus rapidly expanded its network of purchasing and sales and marketing subsidiaries. As such, the company established offices in such markets as Australia, Hong Kong, Benin, Croatia, Poland, Ghana, and elsewhere.

The year 2000 marked a new opportunity for Aarhus. In that year, the European Commission adopted new rules that enabled manufacturers to include up to 5 percent of CBEs in their recipes and still label their products as chocolate (previous rules in some countries had allowed only the use of 100 percent cocoa butter in chocolate). The new directive promised a boom in the purchase of CBEs, and Aarhus ramped up its production capacity accordingly. After some heel-dragging, the new chocolate directive became enforced in 2003. Yet the market saw little change in the first year after the adoption of the new rules, in part as manufacturers proved reluctant to change their chocolate formulas.

Nonetheless, CBEs remained a promising market for Aarhus. In 2003, Brazil became another country to loosen the ingredients requirement on chocolate, permitting the use of up to 10 percent of approved CBEs in a chocolate recipe. Aarhus

Key Dates:

1871: Aarhus Palmekaernefabrik is founded in Denmark to produce feed cake from palm kernels.
1873: The company begins production of vegetable oil for a local margarine factory; vegetable oils become the company focus.
1892: The company changes its name to Aarhus Oliefabrik and builds a new factory specialized in refining oil.
1909: The company develops a method for refining coconut oil.
1930: The company launches its first specialty fat, CEBES, a cocoa butter substitute.
1960: The first successful CBE, Kewax, is launched.
1978: United Plantation Berhad acquires a stake in Aarhus.
1982: Aarhus opens its first international subsidiary, Anglia Oils, in the United Kingdom.
1990: Aarhus establishes a U.S. production subsidiary in Port Newark, New Jersey.
1991: Aarhus acquires a direct stake in United Plantation.
1996: International expansion gives Aarhus seven production facilities outside of Denmark.
2000: The European Commission adopts new rules governing the use of CBEs in chocolate.
2003: Aarhus changes its name to Aarhus United.
2004: The company begins a partnership in Uruguay in order to increase penetration into the South American market.

quickly moved to position itself in that market, setting up a partnership with Uruguay's Compania Oleaginousa Uruguaya in 2004 in order to gain a foothold in the region.

In the meantime, Aarhus adopted a new identity for the new century. In 2003, the company chose to change its name—and that of its international subsidiaries—regrouping the entire company for the first time under the Aarhus United banner. The name change also underscored Aarhus's longstanding and close relationship with United Plantations. Yet Aarhus remained true to its tradition of technical innovation. In 2004, the company debuted a new range of oils with zero trans-fatty acids. With nearly 135 years of history behind it, Aarhus United had proven itself as a world leader in specialty oils.

Principal Subsidiaries

Aarhus United; Aarhus United Asia-Pacific; Aarhus United Australia; Aarhus United Bénin; Aarhus United Côte d'Ivoire; Aarhus United Croatia; Aarhus United Ghana; Aarhus United Hongkong; Aarhus United Latin America; Aarhus United Mexico; Aarhus United Poland; Aarhus United UK; Aarhus United USA; Aarhus United ZAO (Russia); BSP Pharma (50%); Ceylon Trading Co. (Sri Lanka); Frank Fontannaz (U.K., Malaysia, and Holland); United Plantations (Malaysia; 23%).

Principal Competitors

Itochu Corporation; Cargill Inc.; Unilever PLC; Conopco Inc.; Archer Daniels Midland Co.; Sungai Budi Group; Palmindustrie S.A.; Madhvani Group; Hayel Saeed Anam Group of Cos.

Further Reading

''Aarhus Links Up for Chocolate Formulations in Brazil,'' *Confectionery News,* June 23, 2004.

''Aarhus Olie Celebrates 125th Anniversary Using History to Build for the Future,'' *Candy Industry,* September 1996, p. 62.

''Aarhus Oliefabrik,'' *Chemical Market Reporter,* January 12, 2004, p. 12.

''Aarhus Restructures to Shave Costs,'' *Confectionery News,* July 4, 2004.

''All Change at Aarhus,'' *Confectionery News,* August 18, 2003.

''New Name and Structure for Aarhus,'' *Candy Industry,* September 2003, p. 16.

''Sweet Nothings,'' *Oils & Fats International,* May 2002, p. 32.

''Trans Fat Solution,'' *Candy Industry,* September 2004, p. 40.

'' 'Value-Added' the Way Forward for Aarhus,'' *Confectionery News,* September 3, 2004.

—M.L. Cohen

AEON Co., Ltd.

1-5-1 Nakase
Mihama-ku
Chiba 261-8515
Japan
Telephone: (+81) 43-212-6000
Fax: (+81) 43-212-6849
Web site: http://www.aeon.info

Public Company
Incorporated: 1969 as JUSCO Co., Ltd.
Employees: 44,218
Sales: $32.11 billion (2004)
Stock Exchanges: Tokyo
Ticker Symbol: 8267
NAIC: 452111 Department Stores (Except Discount Department Stores); 442299 All Other Home Furnishings Stores; 443111 Household Appliance Stores; 445299 all Other Specialty Food Stores; 446110 Pharmacies and Drug Stores; 448110 Men's Clothing Stores; 448120 Women's Clothing Stores; 448140 Family Clothing Stores; 448150 Clothing Accessories Stores; 448210 Shoe Stores; 451110 Sporting Goods Stores; 453998 All Other Miscellaneous Store Retailers (except Tobacco Stores); 531120 Lessors of Nonresidential Buildings (Except Miniwarehouses); 551112 Offices of Other Holding Companies; 812921 Photo Finishing Laboratories (Except One-Hour)

Formerly known as JUSCO, AEON Co., Ltd. is the largest retailer in Japan. Through ownership, joint ventures, and investments, AEON controls approximately 4,000 stores worldwide. Under the AEON corporate umbrella are 460 JUSCO superstores, 2,600 Mini Stop convenience stores, 665 supermarket stores, and 1,900 AEON Welcia drug stores. The company owns 60 percent of the women's apparel chain The Talbot and owns all of the U.K.-based apparel chain Laura Ashley.

Origins

The first self-service stores in Japan opened in the 1950s, and the sector grew rapidly despite the hostility of small shopkeepers. Early supermarkets operated on a local rather than a national scale, however, and were ill-equipped to withstand recessions. Many went out of business during the recession of 1964–65, and consequently the late 1960s was a period of consolidation among the survivors, many of which decided to form alliances or merge. It was against this background that JUSCO was formed in 1969 through the business tie-up of three companies—Okadaya, Futagi, and Shiro—in the Chubu and Kansai areas.

Okadaya Co., Ltd. had the longest pedigree of the three, having been founded in 1758. Until World War II, it was a store trading in clothing, including kimonos. After the war, it was restarted by Takuya Okada in a single building built on a devastated site and staffed by five employees. It grew into a chain of 14 department stores in the Mie prefecture but was still very much a regional enterprise in the late 1960s, when Okada, in the light of his observations in both Japan and the United States, decided that, for chain stores, size was becoming a critical issue. Larger chains, he realized, could achieve vital economies of scale in both buying and selling, as well as greater administrative efficiency.

Takuya Okada first broached the subject of a merger to Kazuichi Futagi, the president of Futagi Co., Ltd. This company had been established in 1937 as a clothing store. After the store was destroyed in the war, its proprietor reopened for business in 1945 with a stock of second-hand clothes. So successful was Futagi in rebuilding his business that by 1968, when the foundation of JUSCO was conceived, he had a chain of 26 stores in the Hyogo prefecture.

Shiro Co., Ltd, was a relative newcomer, a chain of 15 stores in the Osaka prefecture dating back to 1955. Its head, Jiro Inoue, learned of the proposed merger between Okadaya and Futagi and let it be known that he, too, would like to participate.

Headquarters for the new company was set up in February 1969, with capital of ¥150 million provided by the three partici-

Company Perspectives:

Customers prefer to shop at ÆON because they believe there is no better source for their daily necessities that so thoroughly addresses very real concerns for product reliability and food safety. Our private-brand TOPVALU products are carefully selected with all of these customer needs in mind, to support a healthy, worry-free and enjoyable lifestyle. The brand encompasses 2,400 products in the food, clothing, recreational, housewares and home-furnishing sectors. For nearly 10 years, ÆON has worked to bring the full force of its buying power and cost efficiency to TOPVALU products so as to deliver consistently low prices at an unswervingly high level of quality.

pants in three equal parts. The actual merger was to follow slightly later, in 1970. The infant company was given the name Japan United Stores Company—soon abbreviated to JUSCO, which became the official name. Futagi was to be chairman and Okada president.

Shortly after the establishment of JUSCO, the vice-president designate, Inoue, died at the age of 41. Inoue's firm of Shiro was heavily indebted, so in the first instance only Okadaya and Futagi merged, keeping Shiro as a separate company called Keihan JUSCO. Okada used Okadaya's profits to help put Keihan JUSCO back on its feet, and it became part of JUSCO proper a few years later.

The foundation of JUSCO coincided with a retail boom, but that did not mean the climate was entirely hospitable to the new enterprise. Along with the economic effects of the oil crises of the 1970s, the company had to contend with stringent building restrictions. In 1973, the persistent lobbying of smaller retailers culminated in the enactment of the Large-Scale Retail Law by the Japanese National Assembly. As a result of the law, further strengthened in the late 1970s, the development of new supermarkets, especially those with floor areas of more than 500 square meters, was made subject to a lengthy planning application process that some said amounted to a veto by the smaller retailers. This legislation naturally put a damper on the internal growth of a company like JUSCO, which nonetheless continued to construct new stores and saw expansion by acquisition the natural course to take.

Throughout the 1970s, more and more local chains came under the JUSCO umbrella. The company acquired a reputation for harmonious cooperation with local businesses and communities, as Takuya Odaka illustrates in his memoirs with the story of the Ezuriko PAL Shopping Center. The citizens of Ezuriko, he recounts, actually sent a deputation to JUSCO's head office to ask for help in constructing a new shopping center.

The internationalization of JUSCO began during the 1970s, particularly with respect to the development of overseas buying operations. In 1973, JUSCO established the Miwon Fishery Co., Ltd., in South Korea, jointly with the local Miwon Co., Ltd. The following year saw the opening of agricultural ventures in Australia and Brazil.

There was a general trend during the 1970s for Japanese retailers to import. To gain leverage, JUSCO's largest competitor, Daiei, formed a buying group with 150 other companies for collective purchasing of overseas merchandise. In 1979, JUSCO, together with other leading retailers, formed a similar retail consortium, the Allied Import Company (AIC). In 1981, AIC would gain exclusive distribution rights in Japan over the products of the world's largest supermarket chain, Safeway of the United States.

In 1980, JUSCO's own-label products, known as White Brand, were launched. White Brand denoted a basic but high-quality product sold in plain packaging at the lowest possible price.

Expansion and Diversification in the 1980s

The 1980s were a period of rapid growth for chain stores. JUSCO was in the forefront of this movement and was usually ranked fourth among the supermarket chains in terms of turnover and second in profitability. Many of JUSCO's acquisitions were allowed to retain their identity as regional chains rather than being absorbed by the parent company. This afforded JUSCO a number of advantages, including cheaper advertising in local media and better levels of cooperation with suppliers.

Increasingly during the 1980s, JUSCO's strategy extended beyond the pursuit of market share in the supermarket sector. The company sought to compensate for government restrictions on the opening of new supermarkets and to cater to an ever more sophisticated Japanese consumer via diversification. It spawned an imaginative range of retail outlets, such as Nihon Direct, a mail-order business; discount store Big Barn; Blue Grass shops for teenagers; and Nishiki, a kimono store. There were also Autorama Life, a car sales company started in 1982, and JUSCO Car Life, which opened five years later to provide automobile maintenance services.

Another JUSCO venture, Mini Stop, was a chain of convenience stores providing not only 24-hour neighborhood shopping facilities but also fast food and some financial services for public utility charges. Appealing particularly to Japan's growing body of working women, Mini Stop, founded in 1980, had 340 stores by 1990.

JUSCO was also beginning to develop a variety of restaurant and fast-food operations to enable it to profit from the growing popularity of eating out in Japan. The first of the Gourmet D'Or Co., Ltd. restaurants, which were to form the company's most important chain, began appearing in 1979 and were originally known as Coq D'Or JUSCO Co., Ltd. These were Japanese-style family restaurants that catered to travelers and shoppers alike.

The 1980s also saw the continued expansion of JUSCO's overseas business. In 1988, the *Financial Times* called it "one of Japan's most internationally-minded retailers." It opened outlets in various parts of Southeast Asia, formed joint ventures with overseas companies to trade both in Japan and elsewhere, and systematically developed foreign lines of supply. It also raised capital abroad, issuing its first Eurobonds in 1976.

JUSCO had opened its first overseas store in Malaysia in 1985. This was operated by Jaya JUSCO Stores SDN. BHD., a

Key Dates:

1758: The earliest predecessor to AEON, Okadaya Co., Ltd., begins trading in kimono fabrics and accessories.
1937: Futagi Co., Ltd. is formed.
1955: Shiro Co., Ltd. is formed
1969: To benefit from economies of scale, JUSCO is formed as a joint purchasing organization through a partnership agreement among Okadaya Co., Ltd., Futagi Co., Ltd., and Shiro Co., Ltd.
1980: JUSCO opens its first Mini Stop shop.
1985: The first overseas store, located in Malaysia, is opened.
1986: Laura Ashley Japan, a joint venture with U.K.-based Laura Ashley, is formed.
1988: JUSCO acquires Talbots Inc., a U.S.-based chain of fashion stores.
1994: JUSCO acquires Claire's Stores, the largest chain of fashion accessories stores in the United States.
1995: JUSCO acquires a stake in the U.S.-based sports-apparel chain The Sports Authority.
2001: JUSCO officially changes its name to AEON Co., Ltd.
2003: The acquisition of Mycal Ltd. makes AEON the largest retailer in Japan.

company originally jointly owned with Cold Storage (Malaysia) and three other local companies. It was the first time that a Japanese company had entered into a significant joint venture in the Malaysian retail industry. JUSCO assumed operational control of Jaya JUSCO in 1988.

Since the latter part of the 1980s, JUSCO's retail operations in Asia have grown to include another Malaysian superstore, four in Hong Kong—including Hong Kong's biggest store, opened in the Kornhill Complex in 1987—and five in Thailand. In 1990, a chain of Mini Stop convenience stores was launched in South Korea under an agreement with the Korean Miwon Group.

One of JUSCO's best-known European joint ventures formed during the 1980s was its partnership with British fashion manufacturer and retailer Laura Ashley. Laura Ashley was Japan's first store opened in Tokyo's Ginza district in 1986. The appeal of the brand's ''traditionally English'' style to Japanese consumers was so strong that by the end of 1990 there were 36 shops, two-thirds of them existing within department stores such as Mitsukoshi, and there were plans to open a further 11 stores in 1991. During 1990, JUSCO increased its share in Laura Ashley Japan from 50 percent to 60 percent, giving it overall control, and also announced the purchase of a 15 percent stake in Laura Ashley UK for £29.9 million, a deal that rescued the British company from a heavily indebted state.

In the United States, JUSCO had made an important acquisition in 1988. The Talbots Inc. was a chain of fashion stores belonging to General Mills Inc., a Minneapolis-based corporation that had decided to focus on its core business in the food industry. JUSCO's purchase of The Talbots for $325 million was the first noteworthy foray by any Japanese firm into the U.S. retail business. JUSCO made a point of leaving the existing management in place and said that it hoped to apply the retailing expertise of its new subsidiary to its domestic operations. The chain grew rapidly in the United States after the takeover. The Talbots stores were also introduced in Japan: the first six establishments opened in 1990, against a five-year plan to open 50. JUSCO and General Mills's relationship predated the Talbot deal. Since 1982, they had been running a joint venture in Japan that proved to be one of JUSCO's most popular catering operations.

In 1990, a wholly owned JUSCO subsidiary, the AEON Forest Co. Ltd., was created to become head franchisee within Japan of The Body Shop. This U.K. company specializing in ''environmentally friendly'' toiletries was an ideal partner for JUSCO, which was increasingly seeking to be seen as a ''green'' enterprise. Japanese consumers had been becoming increasingly environmentally aware during the late 1980s, and the popularity of the first Body Shop in Tokyo solidified JUSCO's plan to open 50 stores in five years.

JUSCO was not just jumping on a ''green'' bandwagon. Cofounder Takuya Okada had always been interested in conservation and had encouraged a range of conservation projects such as tree-planting. The ''JUSCO: in tune with the Earth'' conservation project was launched shortly after the Body Shop tie-up, and JUSCO would soon begin experimenting with recycling of packaging in its own stores.

Throughout the 1980s, JUSCO was expanding its buying activities in the so-called Newly Industrializing Economies (NIEs), following a ''develop and import'' strategy whereby JUSCO would establish links with NIE companies—for example, City Knitting, a knitwear manufacturer in India, in 1988—with the aim of developing products suitable for the quality-sensitive Japanese consumer.

In 1987, *The Economist* noted that although 15 years earlier the top Japanese retailers had been department stores, the five biggest were now supermarket chains, with JUSCO in fourth place. The writer attributed the supermarkets' success in large part to their rapid adoption of information technology. For JUSCO, the second half of the 1980s in particular saw a sustained drive to harness the power of information technology to all aspects of the business. TOMM (Total On-Line Merchandising and Management) was an in-store system implemented in 1986 as part of a corporate information system due to be completed in 1989.

Jusco made great progress in the area of Point of Sale (POS) systems. POS systems automate the management of inventory, making it possible to fine-tune the reordering process and minimize the amount of money tied up in stock. POS also allows detailed analysis of turnover at each outlet, so that stocking policy can be attuned to local tastes. JUSCO had Fashion POS installed at all its outlets by 1990 and showed a marked improvement in turnover rates and profitability as a result. It was rapidly extending POS coverage to non-fashion lines.

On its 20th birthday in 1989, the JUSCO group adopted a new corporate identity. The parent company is still called

JUSCO, and the directly owned superstores continue to bear that name; the group is collectively known as the AEON Group.

In the late 1980s, the group was becoming increasingly eager to propagate its image of a socially responsible ''corporate citizen'' on a global level. The AEON Group 1% Club was one manifestation of this concern. Formed in 1989, the Club collected 1 percent of the pretax profits of 31 member companies and used these funds to promote cultural activities and exchanges. In 1990, the club funded an expedition to Japan for a group of ''young ambassadors'' from Malaysia. In 1991, Takuya Okada—who was chairman and chief executive officer, having been succeeded by Hidenori Futagi as president in 1984—visited London at the time of the Japan Festival to promote a similar scheme for 30 U.K. high-school students.

In 1991, the group created its Environmental Foundation to sponsor academic research on conservation issues as well as such practical work as reforestation in Thailand. Group employees were also being encouraged to undertake environmental work in their local communities through a ''Clean and Green'' campaign.

Benefiting from Deregulation in the 1990s

In the early 1990s, the Japanese retail sector was being deregulated, partly in response to U.S. pressure to lower the barriers to entry that faced would-be overseas entrants. Legislation such as the Large Scale Retail Law was beginning to be relaxed under the Structural Impediments Initiative. As a consequence of the liberalization, the AEON group was likely to have a freer rein in opening new large outlets, as well as in expanding its discount-store activities.

Superstores, however, were becoming less central to the group's plans, since its research found, according to a 1991 company report, that ''Japanese consumers, with more time and money than ever to spend on shopping, are starting to view the generalized superstore as inadequate.'' In response, AEON established what it calls ''new retail formats with specific consumer targets and product categories,'' such as its FORUS fashion centers aimed at the youth market.

AEON also expects that it will increasingly become a developer of shopping centers containing a variety of specialized retail outlets under a single roof. AEON's NOA shopping center was one of the earliest centers of this kind. In 1991, its main development arm, AEON Kosan Co., Ltd., was engaged in the construction of another center. Another development company, Diamond City Co., Ltd., had been started as a joint venture with Mitsubishi Corporation in the year of JUSCO's founding; it, too, was expected to receive a new lease of life after the deregulation. As a retailer, AEON was retooling its specialty chains and restaurants with an eye toward their inclusion in the envisaged large-scale shopping complexes.

Other candidates for inclusion in the complexes include AEON's remarkably wide range of service companies. Nihon Credit Service Co., Ltd. was set up in 1981 to issue credit cards and provide other financial services, including automated teller machines, and insurance. In 1990, it began to operate in Hong Kong as well as Japan. AEON also has a marriage bureau, a travel agency, a tailoring service, and a series of sports and leisure centers.

Interviewed by the *Financial Times* in October 1991, chairman Takuya Okada said, ''Now Japanese retailing companies have the opportunity to grow very significantly because the government's policies have shifted from encouraging manufacturing to encouraging consumer activities. I believe that the changes in retailing in the next 20 to 30 years will be far greater than those in the past 20 to 30 years.''

AEON in the 21st Century

As Takuya Okada predicted, the Japanese retail industry did undergo significant change, but the forces of change arrived earlier than he anticipated. By the end of the 1990s, Japanese retailers faced competitive pressures that they never had to face before. Legislation that barred foreign retailers from entering the Japanese market no longer offered such protection. Foreign competitors such as France-based Carrefour and U.S.-based Wal-Mart Stores began building a presence in Japan, presenting Japanese retailers with a formidable new threat. The threat was met by Okada's son, Motoya Okada, who succeeded his father as president in 1997. The response to the incursion of foreign competitors was aggressive expansion, a plan of action the younger Okada pursued with zeal.

Okada, who earned his MBA at Babson College in Massachusetts, employed a strategy used by his father, one that was uncommon in Japan's retail sector. In 1997, Takuya Okada purchased a financially moribund supermarket company named Yaohan, a purchase that netted the AEON group 36 stores. At the time, Japanese retailers were not known to acquire failing or failed companies, but Motoya Okada followed his father's lead and began increasing the size of the company through the purchase of troubled retailers. AEON, which became the official name of the company in 2001, ranked as the fourth-largest retailer in Japan during the late 1980s. By 2000, the company had risen to the industry's number-two position. In December 2003, after acquiring the financially ailing Mycal Ltd., a combination that gave AEON a total of 1,053 supermarket stores, the company became the largest retailer in Japan, passing Ito-Yokado Co. in the sales rankings.

Through numerous acquisitions and internal expansion, AEON's progress from the number-four position to market dominance was achieved. However, Motoya Okada's ambitions did not end there. The AEON leader intended to make the company one of the ten largest retail concerns in the world by 2010, an objective that promised a slew of acquisitions, mergers, and joint venture partnerships in the coming years. At the start of the 21st century, AEON comprised a collection of companies that together represented considerable financial might. In the future, the company appeared likely to aggrandize its massive stature and rank as one of premier retailers in the world.

Principal Subsidiaries

AEON Stores (Hong Kong) Co., Ltd.; Mycalkyushu Corporation; Guangdong JUSCO Teem Stores Co., Ltd.; Taiwan AEON Stores Co., Ltd.; AEON Kyushu Co., Ltd.; Ryukyu JUSCO Co., Ltd.; Posful Corporation; Qingdao AEON Dongtai Co., Ltd.; AEON Co. (M) Bhd.; MYCAL Corporation; SIAM Jusco Co., Ltd.; Shenzhen AEON Friendship Co., Ltd.; Maxvalu Hokkaido Co., Ltd.; Maxvalu Nishinihon Co., Ltd.; Kasumi Co., Ltd.; Maxvalu

Tohoku Co., Ltd.; Maxvalu Tokai Co., Ltd.; Maxvalu Chubu Co., Ltd.; Maxvalu Kyushu Co., Ltd.; Ministop Co., Ltd.; Bon Belta Isejin Co., Ltd.; Bon Belta Co., Ltd.; Tachibana Department Store Co., Ltd.; The Talbots, Inc.; Talbots Japan Co., Ltd.; Mega Sports Co., Ltd.; Abilities JUSCO Co., Ltd. Mega Petro Co., Ltd.; Blue Grass Co., Ltd.; Laura Ashley Japan Co., Ltd.; Claire's Nippon Co., Ltd.; Book Bahn Co., Ltd.; Cox Co., Ltd.; AEON Forest Co., Ltd.; Nustep Co., Ltd.; Petcity Co., Ltd.; Kraft Inc.; Medical Ikkou Co., Ltd.; IINO Co., Ltd.; CFS Corporation; Takiya Co., Ltd.; Green cross-Coa Co., Ltd.; Welpark Co., Ltd.; AEON Mall Co., Ltd.; LOC Development Co., Ltd.; Diamond City Co., Ltd.; Diamond Family Co., Ltd.; AEON Credit Service Co., Ltd.; AEON Credit Service (Asia) Co., Ltd.; AEON Credit Service (Taiwan) Co., Ltd.; AEON Thana Sinsap (Thailand) plc.; AEON Credit Card (Taiwan) Co., Ltd.; AEON Fantasy Co., Ltd.; Zwei Co., Ltd.; Quality Control Center Co., Ltd.; Jusvel Co., Ltd.; AEON Techno Service Co., Ltd.; Reform Studio Co., Ltd.; AEON Cinemas Co., Ltd.; Gourmet D'Or., Ltd.; MYCAL-IST, Inc.; Certo Corporation; Tasmania Feedlot Pty. Ltd.; Food Supply JUSCO Co., Ltd.; Aic, Inc.; AEON Visty Co., Ltd.

Principal Divisions

General Merchandise Stores; Supermarkets; Convenience Stores; Department Stores; Specialty Stores; Drug Stores; SC Development Operations; Financial Services; Food Services; Food Processing, Distribution, and Other Operations; E-Commerce Business.

Principal Competitors

The Daiei, Inc.; Isetan Company Ltd.; The Seiyu, Ltd.

Further Reading

''Aeon Blames Competition, Weather for Drop in Profits,'' *MMR*, October 20, 2003, p. 15.

''Aeon Denies Acquisition Rumors,'' *MMR*, August 9, 2004, p. 11.

''By February 2004, JUSCO Co., Ltd., the Country's Number-Three Supermarket Operator Expects to Have 30 Freestanding Stores Selling Tommy Hilfiger and Tommy Jeans Clothing,'' *Japan-U.S. Business Report*, December 1999, p. 23.

''Flying High in Japan,'' *WWD*, April 16, 1996, p. 6.

Forman, Ellen, ''New Owner of Talbots Wants to Bring It Home,'' *WWD*, May 23, 1988, p. 8.

Hijino, Ken, ''Ito Yokado, Jusco Data Boost Beleaguered Sector,'' *Financial Times*, October 13, 2000, p. 34.

Katayama, Hiroko, ''The Early Bird Gets. . . . ,'' *Forbes*, March 21, 1988, p. 174.

Nakamoto, Michiyo, ''Japan's Pragmatic Giant Picks off Its Competitors,'' *Financial Times*, April 24, 2002, p. 12.

Pratley, Nils, ''Eternally Yours,'' *Retail Week*, November 1, 1991.

''Wal-Mart's Competition in Japan Looks to Heat Up,'' *DSN Retail Fax*, June 7, 2004, p. 45.

—Alison Classe and John Parry
—update: Jeffrey L. Covell

Alderwoods Group, Inc.

2225 Sheppard Avenue East
Suite 1100
Toronto, Ontario M2J 5C2
Canada
Telephone: (513) 768-7400
Toll Free: (877) 707-7100
Web site: http://www.alderwoods.com/

Public Company
Incorporated: 1987 as Loewen Group International, Inc.
Employees: 8,900
Sales: $740.55 million (2003)
Stock Exchanges: NASDAQ
Ticker Symbol: AWGI
NAIC: 812220 Cemeteries and Crematories; 812210 Funeral Homes; 524113 Direct Life Insurance Carriers; 531210 Offices of Real Estate Agents and Brokers

Alderwoods Group, Inc., is North America's second largest operator of funeral homes and cemeteries. Alderwoods operates 716 funeral homes, 130 cemeteries, and 61 combination funeral homes and cemeteries. With about 9,000 employees, the company provides a full range of funeral services, including prearrangement, family consultation, the sale of caskets and related funeral items, the preparation of the body and removal of the remains, the use of a funeral home for both visitation and worship, various transportation services, and, in addition to the traditional burial items, a cremation service. Funeral operations account for a little over two-thirds of revenues. Besides cemeteries, the company also owns insurance companies that provide pre-need financing services; these are marketed in 35 states and, along with other insurance operations, account for about 10 percent of sales.

Early History

The roots of Alderwoods can be traced to A.T. Loewen, the director of a small funeral home in Steinbach, Manitoba. Opening his business in 1961, Loewen operated a highly successful, but small-volume, operation in a rural area of one of Canada's western provinces. When Loewen fell sick and was unable to continue as director of the funeral home, his son Ray assumed control of the entire business. Ray Loewen had just completed his degree in theology from Briercrest Theological College in Saskatchewan. He had not intended to follow in his father's footsteps; given the circumstances, however, Ray dutifully continued what his father had begun.

Not satisfied with the state of funeral care and services in Manitoba, Ray Loewen came up with an idea of creating a chain of funeral homes that would arrange to share resources such as hearses and services such as body preparation. Unfortunately, not many people were won over by his idea. The young entrepreneur could not find many funeral homes that were willing to become part of a national chain, and the idea of economies of scale was alien to him. Part of Loewen's initial difficulties in establishing a funeral home chain was the result of unusually high barriers to entering the funeral home business. Because of the longstanding reputations and recognition of family-run funeral homes within individual communities, it was almost unheard of for an outsider to arrive in a small town and suddenly open a funeral home. Therefore, the resistance to the idea of establishing a funeral home chain was disappointing to Loewen but not altogether surprising.

Unable to fulfill his dream, in 1969 Loewen decided to move his family to British Columbia, where he operated a funeral home and also delved into real estate and transportation businesses. Although he was able to acquire a number of funeral homes during this time, Loewen became increasingly disillusioned with the funeral home industry. In 1975, Loewen abruptly turned over all responsibility and management of his business holdings to one of his most trusted managers and campaigned successfully as a member of the Conservative Party for a seat in the provincial legislature of British Columbia. Loewen served as a member of the legislature for a period of four years and was much admired by his fellow Conservative Party colleagues for his trustworthiness and knowledge of the political issues of the day. In 1979, Loewen left the political arena as abruptly as he had entered it and set up a major real estate development and management company. When the real estate market began to suffer during the early 1980s, Loewen

Company Perspectives:

Our management team is unique in the industry. We have an operations management team with many decades of experience in the funeral industry and an executive team with leadership experience in multi-unit retailing that brings new perspectives and different ways of doing business to an industry traditionally slow to change. Our 8,900 employees are also distinctive. They are among the best trained in the industry and we work diligently to create an environment that is the best in the industry. In a business that must put a premium on pride and compassion, we are dedicated and committed to our success. Our collective focus is centered on the needs of the families who come to us to help them through their time of need. It is this focus, combined with our new operating initiatives that enabled us to increase the number of services we perform.

thought he would take another chance at fulfilling his dream of building a chain of funeral homes.

Creating a Company During the Mid-1980s

Loewen had more luck the second time around. In the United States, Houston-based Service Corporation International was in the process of an aggressive acquisitions campaign, buying up funeral homes at a rapid pace across the country. When Service Corporation International entered the Canadian market, funeral home owners in Manitoba, British Columbia, and other provinces began to think about selling their businesses. Suddenly, Loewen found himself flooded with acquisition opportunities that consisted primarily of family-run funeral homes in small communities that preferred to sell their businesses to a large Canadian consolidator.

Incorporated as The Loewen Group, Inc. in October 1985, and encompassing funeral services, real estate, and insurance, the company was operating 45 funeral homes throughout the western provinces of Canada within two years. Loewen had also learned the meaning of economies of scale, and he had centralized the firm's purchase of such items as embalming fluid, coffins, advertising, and other essential ingredients to the funeral service industry. During the late 1980s, Loewen's wide range of funeral service offerings, his ability to create economies of scale, and his successful advertising resulted in a phenomenal 65 percent increase in revenue for each funeral service conducted under the auspices of his growing company.

In 1987, The Loewen Group reported earnings of $786,000 on revenues of approximately $14 million. However, this was not enough capital to expand the company as rapidly as Loewen wished. Consequently, the founder decided to sell 10 percent of the company to the public and, as a result, raised $4.6 million to fund his ever-growing list of acquisitions. As it happened, however, the year reflected a very mediocre performance for stock exchanges worldwide, diminishing the inflow of capital that Loewen initially had expected. His ability to make acquisitions was curtailed, and, as he experienced unexpected difficulties turning around the acquisitions he had recently made, Loewen arranged a management conference in Vancouver to discuss the direction of the company. At the conference, Loewen asked how many of the former funeral home owners who were now within The Loewen Group had previous experience managing their business within the framework of a budget. Out of a total of 160 former owners, only four people had such experience. Loewen immediately initiated a comprehensive plan to teach each funeral home director the intricate details of balancing a budget. Loewen's commonsense strategy was that it was much easier to teach a funeral home director how to do accounting than it was to teach an accountant how to run a funeral home.

Acquisition and Expansion During the Late 1980s

At the beginning of fiscal 1988, The Loewen Group owned and operated 98 funeral homes and five cemeteries. One year later, that number had risen to more than 120 funeral homes and ten cemeteries. The focus of Ray Loewen's acquisition strategy during these years was his concentration on small, family-operated funeral homes and cemeteries. His standard operating method was to acquire a funeral home or cemetery, keep the existing management in place, retain the name of the acquired funeral home, and provide funeral directors with generous stock options in the company.

Loewen's unique strategy of ''regional partners'' also proved highly successful. Regional partners were the leading operators of acquired businesses who were allowed to strike a formal affiliation with The Loewen Group and were permitted to retain an interest of approximately 10 percent in the future appreciation of the company's entire regional operation. This arrangement gave the regional partner the ability to benefit from The Loewen Group's financial support, while the parent company benefited from the regional partner's involvement in the local community and ability to identify potential candidates for acquisition. Loewen's regional partner strategy worked so well that within two years nearly 30 percent of all company acquisitions of family-run funeral homes had been identified by regional partners.

The Loewen Group was also able to take advantage of the stability of what had come to be called the ''death care provider'' industry. Beginning in 1983, demographic statistics showed that no fewer than two million people in North America would die each year. As the baby-boom generation reached the age of 65, it was projected that the annual death rate would surpass three million. Thus, regardless of economic conditions, the death rate assured the industry of a regular customer base. By continuing its strategic acquisition policy of family-run funeral homes and capitalizing on the gradual rise in death rates across North America, the company had acquired almost 300 funeral homes and approximately 25 cemeteries by 1990.

Growth During the 1990s

In April 1991, to accommodate the growth of the company and the expansion of its administrative offices, The Loewen Group moved its headquarters to a large, three-story building in Burnaby, British Columbia. Always cognizant of the welfare of its employees, during this period the company established an employee share ownership program for both full-time and eligible part-time employees. By the end of fiscal 1993, The Loewen Group had acquired an additional 83 funeral homes and 33

Key Dates:

1961: A.T. Loewen opens funeral home in Steinbach, Manitoba.
1985: Ray Loewen forms The Loewen Group, Inc.
1991: The Loewen Group moves headquarters to Burnaby, British Columbia.
1996: The Loewen Group settles lawsuit with Jerry O'Keefe, a Mississippi funeral home operator; Loewen acquires Prime Succession Inc., the largest private funeral home business in North America, for $295 million.
1997: The company begins a restructuring program.
1999: The Loewen Group files for Chapter 11 bankruptcy protection in June.
2002: Company reemerges as Alderwoods Group, Inc.
2003: Alderwoods Room concept is introduced.

cemeteries; by the end of fiscal 1994, the company had acquired another 108 funeral homes and 46 cemeteries. The total number of funeral homes and cemeteries owned by The Loewen Group on September 18, 1995 was 764 and 172, respectively, an astounding sixfold increase since 1989.

Along with this phenomenal period of acquisition and expansion, however, came an event that threatened the very existence of the company. The Loewen Group, in the course of its expansion strategy, acquired several local funeral homes in the immediate area of Biloxi, Mississippi. Valued at a cost of $8.5 million, two of the funeral homes belonged to Jerry O'Keefe, a former mayor of the city of Biloxi. The purchase ended O'Keefe's exclusive arrangement to sell his own insurance in the funeral homes that The Loewen Group had purchased. Therefore, O'Keefe decided to sue The Loewen Group for the right to sell his own insurance. Rather than litigate over what management at The Loewen Group regarded as a minor issue, the company agreed to combine funeral-insurance operations in the funeral homes purchased from O'Keefe.

When The Loewen Group backed out of the agreement, O'Keefe returned to court and sued the company for fraud and antitrust violations. O'Keefe had hired an extremely enterprising lawyer who convinced the local jury to award his client between $100 million and $400 million in compensatory and punitive damages. These amounts would have wiped out the net worth of The Loewen Group, and the company decided to appeal the verdict. To make matters worse, however, the Mississippi judge ruled that The Loewen Group would have to post 125 percent of the award within one week, a total of $625 million, if the company wished to continue with the appeal. Company management was understandably stunned. They considered a range of alternatives, from borrowing the money for the bond to declaring bankruptcy under Chapter 11. At the 11th hour, after endless meetings and sleepless nights, management at the company's headquarters in Burnaby, British Columbia, finally agreed to settle out of court for $240 million.

Although the company's stock fell from a high of $41 per share to a low of $8 during the litigation, Ray Loewen was determined not to let this episode prevent him from forging ahead. In early 1995, Loewen acquired the Osiris Holding Company for $103.8 million. Located in Philadelphia, Pennsylvania, Osiris owned and operated 22 cemeteries and four combination funeral home/cemetery facilities, all within the United States. In August 1995, the company purchased MHI Group, Inc., an operator of 13 funeral homes, four cemeteries, and three crematories in the state of Florida and five additional properties in Colorado. One of the most significant properties involved in this transaction was the Star of David funeral home/cemetery facility that served a large Jewish community in Fort Lauderdale, Florida. During late 1995 and early 1996, the company concluded two more major acquisitions, including the Shipper Group and Ourso Investment Corporation. Shipper Group owned and operated a total of seven cemeteries in the New York/New Jersey area, including Beth Israel Cemetery in Woodbridge, New Jersey. Beth Israel Cemetery was the largest cemetery serving the Jewish community in the state of New Jersey. Ourso Investment Corporation, located in Louisiana, was the owner of 15 funeral homes, two cemeteries, and a growing life insurance business. The Loewen Group expected high returns from Ourso, which had annual revenues of more than $70 million, within a very short time.

In addition to aggressive expansion of its network of funeral homes and cemeteries in North America, in the early 1990s the company established The Loewen Children's Foundation, a non-profit organization formed to promote and support hospice care for terminally ill children in both Canada and the United States. The company was also a founding sponsor of Canuck Place, the first freestanding hospice facility to care for terminally ill children and the needs of their families in North America.

The Loewen Group became the second largest provider of death care services in North America, ranked along with the leader in the industry, Service Corporation International, and third place Stewart Enterprises. These three companies, however, represented less than 8 percent of the industry's total properties and less than 15 percent of its total revenues. With more than 85 percent of the funeral homes within the United States still family-owned or under private ownership in the mid-1990s, The Loewen Group felt confident that there would be ample opportunity to continue its growth through acquisition strategy.

Assessing the Damage: The Late 1990s

With the potentially disastrous O'Keefe lawsuit behind it, The Loewen Group was determined to pursue an aggressive acquisition strategy in order to boost profitability. The two most substantial deals were made in conjunction with the New-York-based Blackstone Group. The first acquisition was for Prime Succession Inc. of Chicago, the largest private funeral home operator in North America, for $295 million. Under the terms of the agreement, Loewen would own a 20 percent stake in Prime Succession until the year 2000, when it would have the option to purchase the remaining 80 percent from Blackstone. Ultimately, the merger would give Loewen an additional 146 funeral homes and 16 cemeteries in the United States. Loewen entered into a similar agreement with Blackstone in the buyout of the Rose Hills Memorial Park Association of Los Angeles for $240 million. While such partnerships were unusual for The Loewen Group, the two agreements pushed the total value of the company's acquisitions for 1996 over the $1.4 billion mark, a clear indication that Ray Loewen was intent on expansion.

In the midst of this buying spree came an unexpected—and uninvited—buyout bid from Loewen's much larger American rival Service Corporation International. The terms of the offer were very generous: $2.1 billion, in addition to the assumption of $1.1 billion of Loewen's debt. However, Ray Loewen, who owned a 15 percent stake in the company, valued Loewen's independence above all else, and he urged board members and shareholders to reject the deal. Service Corporation subsequently raised its bid to $3.24 billion. This second offer amounted to $59 a share, significantly higher than Loewen's stock value of approximately $40 per share. Ray Loewen, however, managed to persuade the shareholders that his ambitious acquisition plan would, in the long-term, provide a much higher return on their investment, and once again Service Corporation was rebuffed. In January 1997, Service Corporation officially withdrew its bid, and Loewen was free once again to pursue its independent vision.

Unfortunately, the decision to decline Service Corporation's offer almost precipitated the untimely demise of The Loewen Group. Although profits for 1996 were a respectable $63.6 million, investor confidence in the company was still shaken by the O'Keefe settlement, and the shareholders were beginning to become impatient with the company's sagging share value. Loewen attempted a major restructuring in September 1997, cutting 540 jobs and closing a number of its less lucrative units in an effort to reduce operating expenses by $25 million a year.

However, a series of quarterly losses forced stock prices to fall steadily over the course of 1997 and 1998, and by January 1999 shares had dropped to $5.65, a steep decline from their $40 value only a year earlier.

This downward spiral proved too much for the founder and CEO, and in October 1998 Ray Loewen stepped down as head of the company. He was replaced as chairman by John Lacey. While a merger now seemed like a good idea, interest in the company was no longer as strong as it had been, and by March 1999 the company's creditors were pounding on the doors. After suffering a 77 percent drop in profits for the first quarter of 1999, the company was forced to file for protection in U.S. Bankruptcy Court in June in an effort to restructure its debt and try to stay afloat. This it did, and losses for 2000 were reduced to $72.5 million, compared to $465.2 million in 1999. After relocating to Toronto and selling off over 300 holdings, the company submitted an updated filing in March 2001 and seemed to have some chance of survival.

In late 1998. The Loewen Group had filed suit against the United States government in the International Center for the Settlement of Investment Disputes in Washington, D.C. Loewen sought U.S.$725 million in damages, claiming that in the O'Keefe case the legal system treated the company unfairly and showed an anti-Canadian bias by awarding damages beyond those originally sought by the plaintiff and demanding the company post a 125 percent bond during its appeal. This, said Loewen, violated provisions guaranteeing fair treatment for foreign corporations under the North American Free Trade Agreement (NAFTA). The NAFTA lawsuit took several years to work its way through the tribunal, which eventually ruled against Loewen and its successor company.

Alderwoods Launched 2002

A new company was formed out of the bankruptcy. Before the restructuring, The Loewen Group had, as John Lacey told *Canadian Business,* about 1,300 subsidiaries. The group transferred substantially all of its assets to one of these, Loewen Group International, Inc., which became the basis for the newly named Alderwoods Group, Inc., launched January 2, 2002. Alderwoods, with offices in Cincinnati, Toronto, and Vancouver, was incorporated as a Delaware company. Paul Houston, who became Loewen's CEO in December 1999 and retained the position at Alderwoods, described the new company's strategy: "Our objective is to break the traditional industry barriers between funeral and cemetery services, so that each of our professionals can meet a full range of our customers' needs on a seamless basis."

Alderwoods employed about 10,000 people at the time. Divestitures continued as the company raised cash to pay off debt. Alderwoods was also able to arrange a $325 million credit line to refinance some of its most expensive debt.

Alderwoods sold off its 39 funeral locations in the United Kingdom in October 2003 to a management-led group for $18 million. According to filings with the Securities and Exchange Commission, the company was also aiming to dispose of 148 funeral, 88 cemetery, and four combination locations, as well as the life insurance operations. Alderwoods sold an indirect subsidiary, Security Plan Life Insurance Company, in October 2004.

Revenues for the 53 weeks ended January 3, 2004, were $740.6 million, up from $706.2 million for 2002. The company was able to post net income of $10 million after losing $218 million the previous year. Also, as Alderwoods CEO Paul Houston told Canada's *Financial Post,* the company had been able to reduce its debt from $830 million to $630 million in just two years. Sixty-eight percent of revenues came from funeral operations; the cemetery business provided 22 percent of sales and insurance accounted for the remaining 10 percent.

The Alderwoods Room concept was introduced in 2003 to provide bereaved families a less intimidating setting for considering product options and planning funerals. Rather than rows of open caskets, the new showroom displayed portions of closed caskets only. The new format also allowed more products to be displayed. In addition, Alderwoods introduced an advertising program during the year and was working to build stronger ties to local communities.

Principal Competitors

Carriage Services, Inc.; Service Corporation International; Stewart Enterprises, Inc.

Further Reading

Bailey, Ian, "Loewen Bullish on Expansion: Funeral Chain Earnings Hit $63.9 million," *Toronto Star*, March 6, 1997.

Bohner, Kate, "Tasteless," *Forbes*, July 3, 1995, p. 18.

Brennan, Terry, "Loewen Sells More Assets," *Daily Deal* (New York), September 28, 2001.

Carlisle, Tamsin, "Loewen to Settle Provident Lawsuit for $30 Million," *Wall Street Journal*, February 13, 1996, p. A8(E).

Constantineau, Bruce, "Loewen's Gamble Proves Deadly: Funeral-Chain CEO's Rapid-Growth Strategy Following Lawsuits Leads to His Resignation," *Gazette* (Montreal), October 13, 1998.

"Crisis for a Funeral Giant," *MacLean's*, February 5, 1996, p. 40.

Day, Eileen, "Beyond Breaking Records," *Vision* (Loewen Group), November 1995, p. 5.

Francis, Diane, "Loewen Loses NAFTA Challenge: U.S. Jury's $625M Damage Suit Upheld," *National Post* (Canada), September 14, 2004, p. A2.

"Funeral Home Giants Forced to Retrench: Chains That Spent Freely to Acquire Assets Now Find Themselves in a Cash Crunch," *National Post's Financial Post & FP Investing* (Canada), March 18, 2004, p. FP8.

Hassell, Greg, "SCI Wants to Buy Its Biggest Rival; $2 Billion Bid for Loewen," *Houston Chronicle*, September 18, 1996, p. 1.

Hyndman, Peter, "Closure in Mississippi," *Vision* (The Loewen Group, Inc.), March/April 1996, p. 8.

Joyce, Greg, "Loewen Shares Rocket After Deal; Out-of-Court Settlement in Thorny U.S. Case," *Gazette* (Montreal), January 30, 1996, p. C1.

Kennedy, Peter, "Alderwoods Stock Rejuventated; But Analysts Say the Funeral Industry Is Facing a Period of Slow Growth," *Globe and Mail*, January 19, 2004, p. B13.

"Loewen Group," *Wall Street Journal*, November 7, 1995, p. B4(E).

"Loewen Group Buys U.S. Firm," *Wall Street Journal*, March 20, 1995, p. B4(E).

McMurdy, Deirdre, "Mississippi Blues," *MacLean's*, February 12, 1996, p. 50.

Olijnyk, Zena, "Live and Learn: John Lacey," *Canadian Business*, June 9, 2003, pp. 26-7.

Olsen, Walter, "A Small Canadian Firm Meets the American Tort Monster," *Wall Street Journal*, February 14, 1996, p. A15(E).

Osterman, Cynthia, "Funeral-Home Mogul Loewen Fights Back; Scrambles to Regain Investors' Confidence," *Toronto Star*, January 27, 1997, p. B4.

Schreiner, John, "Loewen Group Regroups: Toronto New Headquarters, Eight Offices Consolidated," *National Post* (Canada), September 7, 2000, p. C4.

Stuart, Scott, "Loewen's Search Could Hit Dead End; Death Care Giant Is Likely Too Late in Its Efforts to Find a Mate," *Mergers & Acquisitions Report*, August 10, 1998, p. 1.

——, "Vultures Pick Over Loewen: Erstwhile Deathcare Giant May Soon Be Digging Its Own Grave," *Mergers & Acquisitions Report*, March 15, 1999.

"Undertaker Lives On," *MacLean's*, February 12, 1996, p. 68.

Valance, Nikos, "NAFTA Effects," *CFO: The Magazine for Senior Financial Executives*, March 2000, pp. 111-13.

Wiley, Elizabeth, "Oklahoma City-Area Funeral Homes Try to Ease Experience of Casket Selection," *Daily Oklahoman*, February 12, 2003.

—Thomas Derdak
—updates: Stephen Meyer; Frederick C. Ingram

Ambassadors International, Inc.

1071 Camelback Street
Newport Beach, California 92660
U.S.A.
Telephone: (949) 759-5900
Fax: (949) 759-5909
Web site: http://www.ambassadors.com

Public Company
Incorporated: 1967
Employees: 121
Sales: $13.7 million
Stock Exchanges: NASDAQ
Ticker Symbol: AMIE
NAIC: 561510 Travel Agencies, 561520 Tour Operators, 541990 All Other Professional and Technical Services, 8741 Management Services, 561920 Convention and Trade Show Organizers

Ambassadors International, Inc., is a leading provider nationwide of strategy, software, and services for meetings and events management and promotional products. The company offers comprehensive hotel reservation and travel services for meetings, conventions, expositions, and trade shows, as well as incentive travel planning and management. Ambassadors has offices in Spokane, Washington, Atlanta, Georgia, Chicago, Illinois, and in Newport Beach, San Diego, and San Francisco, California.

1950s–90s: Promoting Peace through Travel and Education

In 1956, President Dwight D. Eisenhower called a special White House conference of American leaders and asked them to join him in creating the People to People program. Eisenhower hoped to enhance prospects for peace by facilitating contact between nations. He believed that, if ordinary citizens visited each others' homes, attended their schools and places of worship, then the misunderstandings, misperceptions, and resulting suspicions that led to war would disappear. According to his granddaughter Mary Eisenhower, in Ambassadors company literature, Eisenhower held that "the people want peace; indeed, I believe they want peace so badly that the governments will just have to step aside and let them have it."

Eisenhower turned to Mr. Joyce C. Hall, founder of Hallmark Cards, to launch People to People International, Inc. in the private sector, believing that its spirit would be furthered better by private citizens than the government. Hall agreed, and People to People relocated to Kansas City, Missouri. By 1963, People to People had a seven-year history of working toward its mission of personal exchanges and individual, first-hand cultural exchanges among working citizens. That year, Keith Tatham, an active leader in the organization, organized the first delegation of student ambassadors overseas.

Two events occurred in 1967 that shaped the future of People to People. First, the organization became a for-profit business based in Spokane, Washington under Tatham's direction. Second, the Ueberroth brothers, Peter and John, founded International Ambassador Program, Inc., headquartered in California to provide international educational travel programs for students and professionals. People to People plodded along, and by the early 1990s, it was organizing travel for about 6,000 students per year.

1990s: Acquisitions and Partnerships Give Rise to Growth

In 1995, the Ueberroth brothers bought Tatham's business, and the company reincorporated in Delaware under the name Ambassadors International, Inc. Later that year, it went public as a holding company. The Ueberroth brothers drew on their varied experience to expand Ambassadors International. John Ueberroth brought extensive experience in the travel industry to his new business: From 1989 to 1990, he was president of Carlson Travel Group, and from 1990 to 1993, he served as chairman and chief executive officer of Hawaiian Airlines. Peter was a former commissioner of Major League Baseball.

During the second half of the 1990s, Ambassadors International, Inc., opened offices in California, Washington, Illinois, Minnesota; Pennsylvania, Kansas, Massachusetts, Virginia, and Wisconsin and had two operating groups: Ambassadors Education Group and Ambassadors Performance Group. The Educa-

> **Company Perspectives:**
>
> *The company's mission is to deliver outstanding experiences that motivate and inspire customers, partners and employees and innovative event management solutions that cut costs while enhancing performance.*

tion Group, under the direction of Jeff Thomas in Spokane, Washington, offered specialized private-label travel programs for groups such as People to People International, Inc., the Yosemite Institute, and Eddie Bauer. The Performance Group, headed by John Ueberroth, offered an array of performance improvement tools, including travel programs, merchandise award systems, training programs, and marketing communications to businesses.

Beginning in 1996, Ambassadors International engaged in a series of acquisitions. Bitterman and Associates, which developed and managed custom performance improvement programs, and The Helin Organization, a meeting management and incentive travel company, merged into Ambassadors Performance Group that year. Also in 1996, American People to People Ambassador Programs, which along with Ambassadors provided travel services to nonprofit People to People International, Inc., joined the Education Group.

In 1997, the Performance Group acquired Debol & Associates, a marketing incentives company, and in 1998, it acquired Travel Incentives, Inc. and Incentive Associates, Inc.

According to John Ueberroth, president and chief executive officer of the company, in a company-released statement in 1996, the move was part of Ambassador International's expansion efforts into an ''important growth area of the travel industry. We are committed to having a major presence in the segment and plan to accomplish this through additional well thought-out acquisitions.''

The company also engaged in several new partnerships beginning in 1996. It launched an adventure travel program with Eddie Bauer to six destinations: Austria/Switzerland; Australia; India/Nepal; Peru/Galapagos Islands; the Pacific Northwest; and the American Southwest. In 1999, Ambassadors Education Group, Inc., now a wholly owned subsidiary of Ambassadors International, acquired Travel Dynamics International, Inc., a company that specialized in youth travel to overseas sports tours and competitions. That same year, it partnered with Stuart Mill Capital and GE Pension Trust to purchase Sato Travel of Virginia, a leader in providing travel management services to the United States military and government. It sold its share in Sato in 2001.

The Performance Group closed three of its offices in 1999—in Boston, Minneapolis, and one in California—as part of a restructuring effort that included leaving the meetings and incentive merchandising fields and consolidating its conventions services in Georgia. This move led to firing about 30 percent of the Performance Group's staff.

The following year, the company's Education Group acquired a minority interest in Off the Beaten Path of Montana, increasing its access to the baby boomer and adventure travel markets. The year 2000, marked the debut of its travel programs to Cuba when the United States government changed its policy to permit group travel to that country for humanitarian reasons. Ambassadors' programs immediately became one of the nation's chief organizers of sponsored trips to Cuba, sending nearly 50 groups to the island in 2000.

The company as a whole grew steadily throughout the second half of the 1990s. From 1995 to 2001, it enjoyed double-digit growth each year. In 1996, the two operating groups provided services to almost 12,000 students and slightly more than 2,000 professionals. In 1997, student ambassadors totaled a little more than 10,000, with professionals just under 4,000. Programs grew to total 15,500 persons served in 1998 with just under 3,000 professionals. In 1999, the year that the Education Group added its overseas sports programs, that number increased to 17,000 with about 3,000 of these students. The combined total for students and professionals was 25,000 in 2000 and just under 26,000 in 2001, the first of two years that the company was rated one of *Forbes* best small companies.

Early 2000s: The Education Group Spins Off

By 2001, Ambassadors Education Group was the company's largest revenue producing unit, but the precipitous drop in travel following the September 11th terrorist attacks led to 62 lay-offs in Spokane. Ambassadors International also let go another 30 workers in California and Atlanta who dealt with business-based travel.

By 2002, Ambassadors Education Group employed about 130 people at its offices in Spokane, Washington. In March, it spun off from its parent company, Ambassadors International, Inc., and changed its name to Ambassadors Group, Inc. Its services consisted of student travel, adult travel, sports travel, and conference programs. After the spin-off, Ambassadors International, under the direction of Peter Uberroth and his son, Joe, continued to develop, market, and manage meetings and incentive programs for a nationwide roster of corporate clients that utilized travel, merchandise award programs, and corporate meeting management services. It also provided comprehensive hotel reservation, registration, and travel services for meetings, conventions, expositions, and trade shows.

In fact, Ambassadors Group, Inc. fared better after September 11, 2001 than it anticipated, an outcome Jeff Thomas, the spin-off's new president and chief executive officer, attributed to two factors in a company press release: ''... nearly five decades of developing and operating international travel programs, as well as the program equity that has been generated by traveling thousands of delegates in unique educational adventures. More importantly, our delegates know that there is a mission and purpose behind all of our travel programs. Our programs change lives.'' Ambassadors Group introduced domestic conference programs in 2002, serving a combined total of 21,000 students and professionals.

Ambassadors Group continued to grow in the year 2003. In 2003, it served 23,000 individuals, and had gross revenues of $108.6 million compared to $97.1 million in sales for 2002. In 2003, John and Peter Ueberroth sold 12 percent of the com-

Key Dates:

1967: The Ueberroths found International Ambassador Program, Inc.
1995: The company reincorporates as Ambassadors International, Inc. and holds its first public offering.
1996: Ambassadors International acquires Bitterman and Associates and American People to People Ambassador Programs; launches an adventure travel program with Eddie Bauer; acquires The Helin Organization.
1999: Ambassadors International acquires Travel Dynamics International, Inc. and a minority interest in SatoTravel.
2002: The Education Group spins off from the company as Ambassadors Group, Inc.; Jeff Thomas becomes chief executive of the new company.

pany's common stock to Invermed Catalyst Fund, L.P. of New York City. In the first quarter of 2004, Ambassadors Group's new domestic programs generated more than 1,000 delegates, a tenfold increase over the 100 delegates that traveled in the first quarter of 2003. The year's total served came to more than 31,000, making Ambassadors Group the only travel company to improve its business since the terrorist attack on New York. As it looked to the future, Ambassadors Group anticipated further expanding it domestic conference programs.

Ambassadors International continued to develop as well. After losing $1 million in net income in 2001, it gained $2.8 million in 2002. In 2003, the year that Joseph Ueberroth, Peter's son, replaced John as president and chief executive, it purchased Bluedot, an event and exhibition technology firm and upgraded its Event Portfolio Management software. It also formed reinsurance company Cypress Reinsurance, Ltd. In 2004, it began managing its operations as a single brand, Ambassadors, to enable a single team to market and operate its services to its corporate, association, and tradeshow clientele. According to Joseph Ueberroth in a company release in 2004, "Management is actively repositioning the company to better meet the demands of our industry . . . "by realigning and consolidating operations.

Principal Subsidiaries

Cypress Reinsurance, Ltd.

Principal Competitors

WorldTravel BTI; Carlson Wagonlit Travel Inc.

Further Reading

Sowa, Tom, "New York Funds Buys Twelve Percent of Ambassadors Group; Brothers Sell 1.2 Million Shares of Spokane-Based Company," *Spokesman-Review*, July 31, 2003, p. A10.

——, "President Gives Indirect Boost to Ambassadors," *Spokesman-Review*, October 27, 2001.

——. "Spokane, Washington-Based Education Travel Company Offers a Cuban Connection," *Spokesman-Review*, June 21, 2001, p. 23.

——, "Spokane, Washington-Based Travel Company Eliminates 62 Positions," *Spokesman-Review*, October 13, 2001.

—Carrie Rothburd

American Society for the Prevention of Cruelty to Animals (ASPCA)

424 East 92nd Street
New York, New York 10128-6804
U.S.A.
Telephone: (212) 876-7700
Fax: (202) 423-0416
Web site: http://www.aspca.org

Nonprofit Company
Founded: 1866
Employees: 300
Operating Revenues: $10.40 million (2003)
NAIC: 813312 Environment, Conservation and Wildlife Organizations; 812910 Pet Care (Except Veterinary) Services; 541940 Veterinary Services

The American Society for the Prevention of Cruelty to Animals (ASPCA) was the first animal welfare organization formed in the United States. It was created to rescue, care for, and shelter homeless and abused animals, provide humane education programs to the public, and to work with law enforcement agencies to ensure compliance with animal welfare laws. The ASPCA was founded by New York City resident Henry Bergh (1811–1888), who modeled the organization on the British Royal Society for the Prevention of Cruelty to Animals (founded in 1824 by Richard Martin, an Irish Member of Parliament). By the early 2000s, the ASPCA had grown to encompass seven regional offices in four states. It employs more than 300 people engaged in fund raising, veterinary care, lobbying, bill sponsorship, law enforcement, poison control, shelter and adoption programs, and humane education.

Henry and the Horse: 1800s Origins

Henry Bergh was a wealthy New Yorker who had traveled in Europe and served as the US Ambassador to the court of Czar Alexander II in Russia. In the mid-1800s he began a course of activism on behalf of animals, ''these mute servants of mankind,'' that consumed the rest of his life. In 1866, Bergh appeared before the New York State Legislature with a proposed charter for a society to protect animals. The ASPCA was incorporated in April 1866. When an anti-animal-cruelty law was passed that same month, the ASPCA was given the right to enforce it. Shortly thereafter the Society seized newspaper headlines and public notice when Bergh stopped a wagon driver from beating an emaciated, exhausted workhorse. He berated the driver for mistreating the animal and told him about the new anti-cruelty law. According to popular legend, he then unharnessed the horse and led it away to be cared for, cheered on by bystanders. This incident inspired the emblem of the ASPCA, which shows an avenging angel, armed with a sword, stepping between a man and a suffering carthorse.

Initially the organization addressed primarily the plight of the 100,000 to 200,000 workhorses within the boundaries of New York City. Few laws governed the care and well-being of these animals, and the average life span of a working horse in the 1860s and 1870s was between two and four years. Early achievements of the ASPCA included a horse-drawn ambulance for injured horses in 1867, and Bergh's 1875 invention of a sling to lift downed horses and those that had fallen into rivers. The ASPCA put the first motorized horse ambulance into service in 1902; two years before any human hospital had such a vehicle. The Society's first veterinary facility, which opened in 1912, offered free health services for horses, as well as veterinary care for dogs and cats. A basic necessity, clean drinking water, was made available for horses by the ASPCA at public fountains throughout the city that also served cats, dogs, and people.

The Society sought to improve the lives of other animals as well. Bergh invented a mechanical pigeon to replace the live birds that were used in target and sport shooting. In the late 19th century and into the early 20th, dogs were used to power treadmills in small factories and to pull wagons used by ragpickers and itinerant workers. These animals were generally turned loose at night to scavenge food and seek shelter as best they could. They were abandoned when they became too weak, ill, or old to

Company Perspectives:

Our mission is to provide effective means for the prevention of cruelty to animals throughout the United States. We offer national programs in humane education, public awareness, government advocacy, shelter support, and animal medical services and placement. Our New York headquarters houses a full-service animal hospital, behavior center, adoption facility, and Humane Law Enforcement Department.

work. Animal control consisted of rounding up and caging the animals. The cages were lowered into rivers or ponds so that the animals drowned. The ASPCA established shelters, the first in 1894, where animals could be reclaimed or more humanely euthanized. Two other shelters were constructed the following year. The ASPCA sponsored the bill that became a law requiring working dogs to be licensed. The Society also sought to find and confiscate dogs used in dogfighting, and to legally punish people engaged in this activity, which was so commonplace that the outcomes of prominent fights were sometimes reported in newspapers. The city's cat population was more difficult to address. Unknown numbers of cats lived in a semi-wild or completely feral state, difficult to catch or even count.

Early 20th Century: Spreading the Word

Bergh and other members of the growing organization made frequent speeches and appeals to the public on behalf of animal welfare. In 1916, the Society initiated humane education programs in schools, and in 1925 used the new medium of radio to broadcast its message of humane animal treatment in a series of weekly addresses. Bergh told a reporter ''Day after day I am in slaughterhouses, or lying in wait at midnight with a squad of police near some dog pit. Lifting a fallen horse to his feet, penetrating buildings where I inspect collars and saddles for raw flesh, then lecturing in public schools to children, and again to adult societies. Thus my whole life is spent.'' In 1928 the ASPCA aggressively expanded its programs of public education programs in schools and neighborhoods.

The number of horses working or kept for pleasure riding within New York City steadily decreased at the end of the 19th century and the beginning of the twentieth, as machines and engines replaced horse-powered factories and transportation. The ASPCA grew to meet the needs of the relatively new, burgeoning category of house pets. Few animals, with the exception of some exotic birds and songbirds, were kept in homes until the mid-20th century. In the US prior to World War II, dogs were used primarily for hunting, herding, and for protection. Cats were kept for rodent control by businesses and households such as granaries, warehouses, food markets, and farms. Even those cats and dogs that were kept as pets usually lived outdoors or were put outside at night. Public perception was that cats preferred a nocturnal life of hunting that was ''natural'' to them. This resulted in the untimely deaths of millions of them due to animal attacks, disease, accidental and deliberate poisoning, being struck by vehicles, and being deliberately killed by people. Despite educational efforts on the part of the ASPCA and dozens of other animal welfare organizations, this perception has persisted well into the 21st century.

The Mid-20th Century: Pet Ownership and the ASPCA

The ASPCA continually pioneered advances in veterinary medicine, including the use of anesthetic during surgery, the treatment of cancer in animals, perfecting spay and neutering surgery, as well as developing dog obedience training programs, and lobbying for animal welfare bills and laws. In 1954 the Society expanded its New York City animal hospital, and in 1961 ASPCA veterinarians performed the first successful open-heart surgery on a dog. Growing awareness of the traits of different cat and dog breeds, fostered by the efforts of the ASPCA and other animal welfare organizations, contributed to and coincided with their popularity as house pets. Canned pet foods made it easier to keep dogs and cats as pets. The development of absorbent clay cat litter in 1947 by Ed Lowe (1920–) to replace less practical cat box fillers such as ashes, sawdust, and sand, is credited with the increase in popularity of cats as house pets. Vaccines were developed against diseases such as distemper and panleukopenia, which had formerly taken the lives of millions of animals, especially kittens and puppies. Organizations such as the ASPCA were instrumental in informing the public about such advances and the responsibility of the pet owner to obtain health care for companion animals. The ASPCA required that all dogs adopted from its facilities be licensed. Because license tags were easily lost, the Society established the use of the identification tattoo beginning in 1948, and became a proponent of the identifying microchip, a device the size of a grain of rice, that was developed for implantation in adopted cats and dogs in the mid-1980s.

An outcome of the increase in popularity of pet cats and dogs was an increase in the numbers of puppies and kittens. The offspring of uncared-for, undomesticated cats and dogs tended to die in large numbers or were routinely drowned, shot, poisoned, or otherwise killed. Litters born to healthy, well-fed household pets were themselves healthier and likelier to have longer lives. People tended to have an emotional attachment to the litters born to their own animal companions. The ASPCA promoted spay and neuter programs beginning in the 1950s, but met with widespread reluctance on the part of the public. A host of emotional and unscientific responses included the belief that animals were healthier and happier when they were permitted to breed, that ''the miracle of birth'' was an important lesson for children to witness, and the belief that owners would be easily able to find homes for resultant offspring. By mid-century, animal shelters were finding homes for only 20 to 25 percent of the healthy, adoptable pet animals they took in. The remaining 75 to 80 percent were euthanized. In poor and rural areas of the country the percentage of destroyed animals was much higher. The ASPCA countered with more aggressive educational and spay and neuter campaigns beginning in 1963. In that year the Society employed 25 officers full-time to enforce dog licensing laws. In 1973 the Society mandated sterilization for all animals that were adopted from its shelters. Sterilization surgery became increasingly sophisticated and safe, and veterinarians discovered that sterilizing cats and dogs before they had bred actually eliminated some health risks to both sexes. By the end of the 20th century hundreds of veterinarians were trained to perform this delicate operation safely on kittens and puppies as young as six weeks and weighing only a pound.

Key Dates:

1886: Henry Bergh charters the American Society for the Prevention of Cruelty to Animals (ASPCA).
1894: The ASPCA relieves New York City government of responsibility for dealing with stray and unwanted animals.
1912: The first veterinary facility opens; ASPCA veterinarians pioneer the use of anesthesia during surgery on animals.
1916: The ASPCA begins a formal humane education program for school children.
1925: ASPCA begins a series of weekly informative radio broadcasts.
1944: The organization institutes obedience training classes for dogs and their owners.
1952: In New York, the ASPCA inaugurates inspections of laboratory animals used in research.
1966: On the 100th anniversary of the ASPCA, its veterinary hospital in New York is renamed after Society founder Henry Bergh.
1973: The adoption department begins mandatory spay and neuter of all animals in the care of the ASPCA.
1985: A Government Affairs office in Washington, D.C., is opened to monitor, initiate, and lobby for national animal welfare legislation.
1995: The ASPCA returns animal control services to New York City and launches the ASPCA web site.
1996: The ASPCA acquires the National Animal Poison Control Center.
2000: The ASPCA supplies data to support the Safe Air Travel for Animals Act; two of the four provisions of the proposal are signed into law.

The ASPCA has remained in the forefront of advances in animal welfare. The Society pioneered the concept of cage-free shelters, such as Maddie's Pet Adoption Center at the ASPCA shelter in San Francisco, California, where the animals live in home-like settings and their lives are enriched with training and extensive human contact. In 1985 the ASPCA also developed a department of Government Affairs and Public Policy to work toward protecting animals at the state and federal level through new laws and ballot initiatives. This department drafts original bills and analyzes proposals for laws regarding animal welfare. ASPCA attorneys lobby for animal welfare legislation and provide information to lawmakers at the local, state, and national levels. The Department of Government Affairs and Public Policy also runs an Advocacy Center, keeping individual states and communities apprised of animal welfare issues. An early focus of the ASPCA's Government Affairs department was the condition and treatment of laboratory animals. The Society was the first group to push for legislation mandating that laboratory dogs receive adequate socialization and exercise, and to study and seek to improve the psychological welfare of highly intelligent primates used in laboratory research. In 1996, the ASPCA acquired the National Poison Control Center. It has since become the only continuously operating telephone service of its kind, focusing on veterinary toxicology. 1996 was also the year in which the Society launched its Care-a-Van, its first mobile spay and neuter clinic in New York.

The ASPCA entered the field of name and logo licensing in the 20th century as another way to generate revenue to fund its programs. Licensees include Bank One, the official ASPCA credit card; Checks in the Mail, a check and label-printing company that donates a portion of its proceeds to the ASPCA; Chanticleer Press, whose Chronicle Books imprint publishes the ASPCA's informative guides to pet ownership and animal care; Clarke American Checks, Inc., a supplier of checks and bank-related items to financial institutions; Hertz car rental agency, which offers a Hertz/ASPCA credit card; and Pipsqueak Productions, a line of giftware created by artist Mary Badenhop and licensed by the ASPCA.

The ASPCA in the 21st Century

In 2000, the ASPCA was instrumental in lobbying for and helping to pass some provisions of the Safe Air Travel for Animals Act, introduced into the House of Representatives by Representative Robert Menendez (D-New Jersey) and in the Senate by Senator Frank Lautenberg (D-New Jersey). This Act improved safety conditions in the spaces on airplanes in which animals often are conveyed, and it required airlines for the first time to keep records of injuries and fatalities to animals traveling on their craft.

In 2004 the ASPCA was one of the motivating forces behind the October National Feral Cat Summit, the first gathering of its kind devoted to study of managing feral cats. New York City and a number of animal welfare organizations, including the Mayor's Alliance for New York City's Animals, hosted representatives from 25 states, Canada, and the Galapagos Islands.

The organization owned and ran animal shelters, veterinary clinics, animal health care benefits, pet animal adoption events, and a thriving press. The ASPCA produced animal care handbooks for both adults and children under the imprint of Chronicle Books, a division of Chanticleer Press, on the most popular household pets in the United States. Among their best sellers were handbooks on the care of cats, dogs, hamsters, gerbils, rabbits, ferrets, and freshwater fish, as well as more exotic breeds of small animals kept as pets, including chinchillas, hedgehogs, iguanas, other lizards, snakes, saltwater fish, eels, and tarantulas.

The ASPCA's national headquarters and several major centers remained in New York City and state, with branches in New Jersey, Urbana, Illinois, and San Francisco, California. The Society had over 680,000 members and donors in the early 2000s. It remained dedicated to the cause of preventing cruelty and raising awareness of animal welfare issues through education, awareness, and legislative programs. The ASPCA headquarters in New York City housed one of the area's largest full service animal hospitals, an adoption facility, and the Humane Law Enforcement Department, which was responsible for enforcing New York's animal cruelty laws. The ASPCA's Law Enforcement department worked in conjunction with the New York City Humane Law Enforcement (HLE) department and the television station Animal Planet to broadcast *Animal Precinct*, an award-winning reality show that followed the only law enforcement group in New York dedicated to investigating crimes against animals.

Principal Operating Units

ASPCA Member and Donor Services; Animal Cruelty/Law Enforcement; Animal Placement Department, Animal Poison Control Center; Animal Precinct (television show), ASPCA Behavior Center, Communications; Development; Government Affairs & Public Policy; Henry Bergh Memorial Hospital, Humane Education; Humane Law Enforcement Department; Legal Department; Marketing; Media Relations & Advertising; National Shelter Outreach; Public Information; Special Events.

Further Reading

Alexander, Lloyd, *Fifty Years in the Doghouse*, New York: Putnam, 1964.

''ASPCA Animal Poison Control Center Warns Pet Owners: Summer is the Deadliest Time of Year for Companion Animals,'' *Charity Wire*, July 11, 2003.

''Doggone Good,'' *Austin Business Journal*, February 9, 2001, p. A2.

Elvin, John, ''Advocates want Pet-Friendly Skies,'' *Insight on the News*, April 3, 2000, p. 34.

''FAO Schwarz Unites with ASPCA for Animal Causes,'' *Gifts & Decorative Accessories*, November 1999, p. 200.

Harlow, Alvin F. *Henry Bergh: Founder of the A.S.P.C.A.*, New York: J. Messner, 1957.

'' 'Sugar and Champagne' Event Comes to NY, Raises $13K,'' *Nation's Restaurant News*, July 26, 2004, p. 38.

Rooney, Paula, ''Siwel's Pet Project: Fix ASPCA's E-Mail Woes,'' *Computer Reseller News*, August 25, 2003, p. 33.

Saveri, Gabrielle, ''Sheltered Lives,'' *People Weekly*, June 29, 1998.

Stumpf, Elizabeth, ''ASPCA: The American Society for the Prevention of Cruelty to Animals,'' *School Library Journal*, April 2002, p. 141.

Suen, Anastasia, *The American Society for the Prevention of Cruelty to Animals*, New York: Powerkids Press, 2002.

—Marie Lazzari

Andersen

33 West Monroe Street
Chicago, Illinois 60603
U.S.A.
Telephone: (312) 580-0033
Fax: (312) 507-6748
Web site: http://www.andersen.com

Private Partnership
Incorporated: 1918 as Arthur Andersen & Company
Sales: $2.20 billion (2003)
NAIC: 541211 Offices of Certified Public Accountants

Andersen is the name encompassing Arthur Andersen LLP and other international entities that were members of Andersen Worldwide SC, once the massive umbrella organization overseeing Arthur Andersen & Co. and Andersen Consulting. After being convicted in 2002 of obstructing justice in relation to the Securities and Exchange Commission's investigation of Enron Corporation, Arthur Andersen is barred from offering auditing services to publicly traded companies. The company remains in existence to resolve legal problems related to its collapse, a process that is expected to take until the late 2000s to complete.

Early History

The founder and guiding force behind the early years of the accounting firm was Arthur Edward Andersen. Born in Plano, Illinois, in 1885, Andersen was the son of a Norwegian couple who had immigrated to the United States four years earlier. At a young age, Andersen displayed a propensity for mathematics. Upon graduating from high school, he worked in the office of the comptroller at Allis-Chalmers Company in Chicago, while attending classes at the University of Illinois. In 1908, he received a degree in accounting from the university and at 23 years old became the youngest certified public accountant in Illinois.

From 1907 to 1911, Andersen served as senior accountant for Price Waterhouse in Chicago. Following a one-year term as comptroller for the Uihlein business interests in Milwaukee, primarily Schlitz Brewing Company, Andersen was appointed chairperson of Northwestern University's accounting department. Soon thereafter, however, in 1913, Andersen decided to establish his own accounting firm. At the age of 28, he founded the public accounting firm of Andersen, DeLany & Company in Chicago.

Andersen's small company began to grow rapidly, as demand for auditing and accounting services increased dramatically following Congress's establishment of federal income tax and the Federal Reserve in 1913. One of Arthur Andersen's first clients was Schlitz Brewing, and the company's client list soon expanded to include International Telephone & Telegraph, Colgate-Palmolive, Parker Pen, and Briggs & Stratton. The company's primary business, however, consisted of numerous utility companies throughout the Midwest, including Cincinnati Gas & Electric Company, Detroit Natural Gas Company, Milwaukee Gas Light Company, and Kansas City Power & Light Company. Into the 1920s, work for utility companies comprised about 50 percent of Andersen's total revenues, and the company became known as a "utility firm," a dubious distinction in accounting circles. In 1917, Andersen was awarded the degree of B.B.A. from Northwestern University, and, the following year, when DeLany left the partnership, his firm became known as Arthur Andersen & Company.

Licensed as accountants and auditors in many states across the country, the company grew rapidly during the 1920s. The firm opened six offices nationwide, the most important of which were located in New York (1921), Kansas City (1923), and Los Angeles (1926). Serving as auditor for many large industrial corporations, Arthur Andersen also began providing financial and industrial investigation services during this time. In 1927, company representatives testified as expert witnesses in the Ford Motor Company tax case. The company's most important investigation, however, a milestone in the history of Arthur Andersen & Company, involved Samuel Insull's financial empire.

Managing the Insull Empire in the 1930s

Samuel Insull emigrated from England to the United States in 1892. Hired as a secretary by Thomas Edison, Insull would soon prove to be an adept entrepreneur. During this time, the use of Edison's incandescent lights was provided only to licensed utility companies, which became known as "Edison Companies." As many of Chicago's utilities approached bankruptcy early in the

Key Dates:

1913: Arthur Andersen starts his own accounting firm, Andersen, DeLany & Company.
1918: After the departure of DeLany, Andersen's firm changes its name to Arthur Andersen & Company.
1932: Arthur Andersen & Co. is selected to represent Commonwealth Edison, the corporate entity controlled by Samuel Insull.
1947: Arthur Andersen's death passes leadership to Leonard Spacek, who shapes the firm into a genuine international company during his 26-year term as company leader.
1970s: Arthur Andersen & Co. becomes increasingly involved in providing consulting services.
1988: Arthur Andersen & Co. becomes the largest consulting firm in the world, deriving 40 percent of its revenues from the consulting side of its business.
1989: After years of internal discord, the firm is split into two companies, Arthur Andersen & Company (accounting services) and Andersen Consulting (consulting services); these two separate financial entities are governed by Switzerland-based Arthur Andersen Société Cooperative, later named Andersen Worldwide SC, the ruling body of the worldwide Andersen organization.
1994: Arthur Andersen & Co. begins to develop its own consulting business.
1997: The retirement of managing partner and Chief Executive Officer Lawrence Weinbach renews hostilities between the accounting and consulting factions.
2000: The International Court of Arbitration in Paris rules that Andersen Consulting can separate itself completely from Arthur Andersen & Co. and Andersen Worldwide.
2001: Andersen Consulting changes its name to Accenture Ltd.
2002: After becoming embroiled in controversy surrounding the collapse of Enron Corp., Arthur Andersen LLP is convicted of obstructing justice, a ruling that bars the company from offering auditing services to publicly traded companies.
2004: A federal appellate court rules that the 2002 conviction will remain intact.

20th century, Edison sought someone to organize them and keep them solvent. Insull volunteered for the job and immediately began to acquire and manage his own utility companies. In a few years, Insull had built an empire of utility companies, including the first utility to construct a generator with a capacity more than 12,000 kilowatts. In 1907, Insull created Commonwealth Edison, which was formed by the merger of two Insull holdings, Commonwealth Electric and Chicago Edison.

By the early 1930s, Insull's utilities, many of which had suffered during the Great Depression, represented a complicated network of holdings nearly $40 million in debt and badly in need of reorganization. When the Chicago banking community—on which Insull had always relied exclusively—was unable to provide the required cash, Insull was forced to turn to the East Coast banks for help. The East Coast banks refused to extend financial assistance, but, rather than forcing Insull into bankruptcy, they chose Arthur Andersen to act as their representative and manage the reorganization and refinancing of Insull's business holdings.

In 1932, the firm was placed in charge of supervising all the Insull utility companies' income and expenditures and also was involved in the subsequent financial reorganization of all the Edison companies within Insull's empire. To Arthur Andersen's credit, none of the utility companies went bankrupt; the firm maintained a firm control on all the assets during the period of refinancing. Moreover, Arthur Andersen not only increased its gross revenues by 20 percent through the Insull account but also garnered a reputation for honesty and independence that heightened its stature in the business community across the country. Thereafter, the company had no difficulty attracting large corporate clients. The incident also gave rise to the company's self-proclaimed role as watchdog of the accounting industry's methods and procedures.

Andersen not only provided direction for his company and personally approved of all the firm's clients, he remained involved in nearly every aspect and detail of company business. Until the day he died, he paid himself 50 percent of the firm's profits, while the other 50 percent was distributed among the rest of the partners. As he grew older, and as the company grew increasingly successful, Andersen became less tolerant of those within the firm who disagreed with him or began to eclipse his leadership, and he tended to fire or drive out those with whom he was not compatible. Nevertheless, he had an uncanny sense of hiring particularly talented accountants, and many of the individuals hired during the 1920s and 1930s would play prominent roles in the company's development years later.

Under the watchful eye of its founder, Arthur Andersen and Company brought in many new accounts during the 1930s, including Montgomery Ward, one of the most sought-after clients during the decade. By 1928, the company employed approximately 400 people and, by 1940, that figure had increased to 700. To provide greater accessibility to its clients, the firm opened new offices in Boston and Houston (1937) and in Atlanta and Minneapolis (1940).

During World War II Andersen himself reached the pinnacle of his success. His numerous writings on accounting—including "Duties and Responsibilities of the Comptroller" and "Present Day Problems Affecting the Presentation and Interpretation of Financial Statements"—prompted a growing admiration and respect for him in financial, industrial, and academic circles. Andersen served as president of the board of Trustees at Northwestern University and as a faculty member in accounting at the school. In recognition of his contribution to the field of accounting, and also for his devotion to preserving Norwegian history, he was awarded honorary degrees by Luther College, St. Olaf College, and Northwestern.

New Leadership After World War II

During this time, Andersen began grooming his associate, Leonard Spacek, for the company's leadership position. Spacek joined the company in 1928 and was named a partner in 1940, becoming one of Andersen's closest and most trusted confidants. Upon Andersen's death in January 1947, Spacek took over the company, remaining committed to the regimented management style of the founder. During Spacek's tenure, the firm grew from a regional operation located in Chicago with satellite offices across the United States into an international organization with one-stop, total service offices located around the world. Most important, however, Spacek began to focus on Andersen's idea that the company serve the public role of industry policeman.

Until the 1950s, the accounting profession was generally regarded as a club, with its own principles, methods, and procedures that had developed over the years without any standardization. Spacek began a campaign to improve accounting methods and practice by emphasizing the importance of implementing uniform accounting principles that would ensure "fairness." Spacek argued that accounting principles should be fair to the consumer, to labor, to the investor, to management, and to the public. Spacek hoped that his concept of fairness would serve as a foundation for accounting principles that the whole profession would ultimately find acceptable.

Most business historians agree that Spacek did the profession a service by initiating the standardization movement within the industry and by bringing public attention to the fact that existing auditing practices varied with each company. Like Andersen before him, however, Spacek drew considerable criticism from the profession. Unable to change the prevailing attitudes of those within the industry, Spacek focused on his own company, creating Andersen University, with its Center for Professional Education. A training center located in St. Charles, Illinois, the university provided company employees with the opportunity to attend courses in a variety of accounting subjects.

Growing Consulting Services in the 1970s and 1980s

By the time Spacek retired from the company in 1973, Arthur Andersen & Company had opened 18 new offices in the United States and more than 25 offices in countries throughout the world. With a staff of more than 12,000 and an increase of revenues from $6.5 million to more than $51 million during the period from 1947 to 1973, Andersen had grown into one of the world's preeminent accounting firms. The company also featured a profitable consulting service, helping large corporations install and use their first computer systems in the 1950s and branching out into production control, cost accounting, and operations research in the 1960s. Moreover, with audit and accounting revenues reaching a plateau due to the maturity of the industry, the company's consulting services began to represent an increasing share of Andersen's income. In the 1970s, Arthur Andersen became involved in a host of consulting activities, including systems integration services, strategic services, development of software application products, and a variety of additional technological services.

Under the aggressive leadership of Spacek's successor, Harvey Kapnick, the consulting services developed rapidly, and by 1979, its fees represented more than 20 percent of Andersen's total revenues. Anticipating the importance of the burgeoning market for consulting services, Kapnick proposed to split the company into two separate firms, one to oversee auditing and another to focus on consulting as a comprehensive service business. When he presented this proposal to the company's partners, however, he met with protest. The auditors summarily rejected Kapnick's strategy, demanding proprietary control over all aspects of the company's managerial and financial affairs.

Kapnick resigned in October 1979 and was replaced by Duane Kullberg, who had joined the company in 1954 as an auditor. Reassuring the auditors that he would not take any action to split the company along operational lines, Kullberg nevertheless gave more operating control to the consulting side of the business, where employees were becoming increasingly irritated with the centralized control of the auditors. Kullberg's strategy seemed to work; internal discord subsided and both the auditing partners and the consulting principals (who were not called partners until later) devoted themselves to their respective businesses.

Other problems arose for Arthur Andersen, however. In the mid-1980s, the company was the subject of several lawsuits filed by creditors and shareholders of bankrupt companies the firm had audited. These companies—including DeLorean Motors Company, Financial Corporation of American (American Savings & Loan), Drysdale Government Securities, and others—claimed that Arthur Andersen had failed to realize the extent of their financial struggles and, moreover, had failed to inform the public of their findings. In 1984, Arthur Andersen was forced to pay settlements amounting to $65 million within a two-month period.

Nevertheless, Arthur Andersen's business continued to thrive, particularly in the field of consulting services. By 1988, 40 percent of the company's total revenues was generated from consulting fees, making Arthur Andersen the largest consulting firm in the world. During this time, conflict between the auditors and the consultants flared up again, centering on discrepancies in the pay scale and disagreement over the control of consulting operations. Specifically, consultants questioned why they should earn less than auditors, when typical auditing projects brought in $4 million in fees in 1988, and consulting jobs garnered as much as $25 million. Furthermore, consultants took issue with the company's practice of allowing accounting partners to manage the consulting business.

Restructuring in the Late 1980s

Tensions continued to increase; when the firm's disgruntled consulting partners resigned, management filed lawsuits and infiltrated meetings held by the consultants. Finally, in an effort to end the chaos, Kullberg agreed to restructure the company. Under Kullberg's plan, Arthur Andersen was divided into two entities, an auditing and tax firm known as Arthur Andersen & Company and a consulting firm dubbed Andersen Consulting. Each of these firms then became separate financial entities under the Swiss-based Arthur Andersen Société Cooperative, the ruling body of the company's worldwide organization, which would coordinate the activities of the entire firm's operations. In addition, the traditional management hierarchy, in which consultants reported to auditors, was altered, allowing consultants to report to managers in their field all the way up through the level of consulting partner.

In 1989, Lawrence A. Weinbach replaced Kullberg as chief executive officer. Upon graduating from the Wharton Business

School, Weinbach had joined Arthur Andersen and had become a partner after nine years. Known for his diplomacy, Weinbach helped smooth over the harsh feelings among auditing and consulting partners, encouraging everyone to concentrate on increasing business. Under his leadership, Arthur Andersen's revenues skyrocketed. Between 1988 and 1992, Andersen's revenues increased from slightly less than $3 billion to almost $5.6 billion, an increase of nearly 50 percent brought on mostly by the company's burgeoning consulting activities. During these years, revenue from Andersen Consulting grew by 89 percent while revenue from Arthur Andersen & Company's accounting and tax services grew by 38 percent. Clearly, Weinbach recognized the importance of the company's position as the largest management consultant firm in the world.

In the early 1990s, Arthur Andersen was beset with lawsuits from creditors of thrifts that had collapsed during the 1980s. Furthermore, in 1992, the company was sued by the government's watchdog Resolution Trust Corporation for negligence in its auditing of the failed Ben Franklin Savings & Trust. Nevertheless, the company weathered these difficulties, renewing its commitment to high-quality, irreproachable auditing services and focusing on improving and developing both its auditing and consulting services. With a settlement in 1993 Arthur Andersen resolved the lawsuits relating to the failed savings and loans and was released from any further liability.

The firm grew more cautious after this debacle, turning down more clients and even dropping several existing ones. Outstanding lawsuits continued to plague the Big Six accounting firms, however, making insurance coverage more difficult for these firms to acquire. The cost of insurance and settlements for the Big Six was estimated at 12 percent of local fee income in the United States and 8 percent in Britain. Arthur Andersen considered incorporation as a shield for the personal assets of partners not found directly negligent. The Big Six firms also pursued legislative changes that would limit their liability.

Increasing Income in the 1990s

Arthur Andersen's fee income rose steadily in the mid-1990s, as did that of the other Big Six accounting firms. The general accounting prosperity had several causes: an economic boom in the United States, the growth of the accounting firms in Asia and Eastern Europe, and especially an increase in management consulting fees. Total revenues for Arthur Andersen surpassed the $6 billion mark in 1993, rose to $6.7 billion in 1994, and jumped to $8.1 billion in 1995. Half of the firm's $9.5 billion in fees in 1996 came from consulting. Arthur Andersen led the industry in fee income per partner in the mid-1990s.

With the consulting branch enjoying the greatest rise in profits, the accounting branch began offering its own consulting services in the early 1990s to companies with less than $175 million in annual sales. Placing themselves in competition with the consulting partners did nothing to heal the animosity that had led to the division of the company in the first place. Consulting partners argued for total independence from the parent company in the late 1990s, citing the vast disparity in fee contributions between the two subsidiaries. The accounting partners alleged that the consulting business would never have taken off without their initial support, referrals, and subsidies.

Managing partner and Chief Executive Officer Lawrence Weinbach retired in 1997, throwing the divided firm into chaos as a search for a successor led to heated disagreements. One nominee came from consulting, and another came from accounting. Both were rejected in a vote by all company partners. An acting CEO was named by the board: W. Robert Grafton, an accounting partner. Soon thereafter, Andersen Consulting, as the result of a unanimous vote by its partners, sought an arbitrator to gain their firm's complete independence from Andersen Worldwide.

In 1999 Andersen Worldwide continued to oversee its two squabbling operating units and continued to lead the world in providing business consulting services. Its revenues reached almost $14 billion in 1998, and the firm boasted 382 offices in 81 countries around the world.

An Ignoble Exit in the Early 21st Century

The rancor between the consultants and accountants, festering for decades, reached a dramatic climax as Andersen Worldwide entered the 21st century. Andersen Consulting's management wanted to sever completely its ties to the accounting and auditing side of Andersen Worldwide and divorce itself from Andersen Worldwide as well. In August 2000, the war between the consultants and the accountants reached its conclusion when the International Court of Arbitration in Paris separated the two factions. Joe Forehand, chief executive officer of the consulting business, hailed the arbitrator's ruling in an August 8, 2000 interview with the *Chicago Tribune,* exclaiming, "This is a total win for Andersen Consulting. We won. It's over." Jim Wadia, Forehand's counterpart at Arthur Andersen, sounded less enthusiastic. "I think the arbitrator has tried to keep both sides relatively happy, which he has done," Wadia remarked in the same *Chicago Tribune* article. "And he has tried to keep both sides relatively [angry], which he has done as well."

Andersen Consulting went its own way following the ruling. The company was spared having to pay as much as $14 billion to complete the breakup, but it was ordered to drop the Andersen name from its corporate title. In January 2001, the company changed its name to Accenture Ltd. and began to build brand name recognition from scratch. At the time of the ruling, Arthur Andersen's exclusive right to the respected and widely known Andersen brand name was considered an invaluable asset. Within two years of the ruling, the Andersen name was worth nothing.

The scandal that ultimately led to the collapse of the Andersen accounting business erupted in October 2001. Enron, one of Arthur Andersen's biggest clients, disclosed that the Securities and Exchange Commission (SEC) was launching an investigation into the company; the scope of the inquiry included the actions of the company's auditor, Arthur Andersen. Enron filed for Chapter 11 bankruptcy protection in December 2001, the same month Joseph Berardino, chief executive officer of Andersen Worldwide, defended his company's financial accounting practices before the U.S. Congress. The following month, Arthur Andersen LLP, the U.S. arm of Andersen Worldwide, conceded its employees destroyed a substantial number of Enron-related documents, which led to the company's indictment for obstruction of justice. In April 2004, Arthur Andersen

LLP split from its global parent, Andersen Worldwide, two months before a jury deliberated whether or not Arthur Andersen LLP had obstructed justice. The announcement of the jury's guilty verdict in June 2002 spelled the end for Arthur Andersen, forbidding the company from operating as an accountant and an auditor. After nearly a century of existence, the Arthur Andersen name was forever defiled, effectively ending the corporate life of one of the largest and respected names in U.S. business.

In the wake of the 2002 conviction, Arthur Andersen LLP began the long and arduous process of shutting down completely. The company hired a new general counsel—likely the last general counsel the company would employ—in July 2003 to resolve the litigation mess created by the company's downfall and to appeal its conviction. In August 2004, a federal appellate court ruled against the company's appeal, insisting that the conviction remain intact. The court's ruling left Arthur Andersen LLP solely focused on attending to its legal problems, which were expected to be resolved by the late 2000s. After the company's litigation issues were resolved, the Arthur Andersen name was to disappear, finally concluding one of the most spectacular downfalls in U.S. business history.

Principal Operating Units

Arthur Andersen LLP.

Principal Competitors

Ernst & Young International; KPMG International; PricewaterhouseCoopers.

Further Reading

''Accountancy Mergers: Double Entries,'' *Economist,* December 13, 1997.

''Andersen Consulting Announces Its New Name Will Be Accenture,'' *Chicago Tribune,* October 27, 2000, B4.

Bahle, Jane Easter, ''Shred of Evidence: Learn a Lesson from Arthur Andersen; Destroying Documents Makes You Look Bad,'' *Entrepreneur,* December 2002, p. 106.

''British Accountants' Liability: Big Six PLC,'' *Economist,* October 7, 1995.

''Count Down: Andersen,'' *Economist,* March 16, 2002, p. 14.

Crawford, Krysten, ''We're Not Dead Yet!,'' *Corporate Counsel,* September 2003, p. 43.

''A Glimmer of Hope,'' *Economist,* April 1, 1995.

''Finance and Economics: Disciplinary Measures,'' *Economist,* March 6, 1999.

''Out of Control at Andersen,'' *Business Week Online,* March 29, 2002, p. 45.

Randall, Robert, ''The Fall of Arthur Andersen,'' *Strategic Finance,* July 2003, p. 32.

Sachdev, Ameet, ''Andersen Consulting, Athur Andersen Split Signals Industry-Wide Rifts,'' *Chicago Tribune,* August 13, 2000, p. B4.

Schmeltzer, John, ''Arbitrator's Ruling Separates Chicago-Based Consulting, Accounting Firms,'' *Chicago Tribune,* August 8, 2000, p. B2.

Spacek, Leonard, *The Growth of Arthur Andersen and Company, 1928–1973: An Oral History,* New York: Garland, 1989.

Stevens, Mark, *The Big Six,* New York: Simon & Schuster, 1991.

Strahler, Steven R., ''Andersen's Number Is Up: Without a Buyer, Bankruptcy Is Not Firm's Best Option,'' *Crain's Chicago Business,* March 18, 2002, p. 1.

—Thomas Derdak
—updates: Susan Windisch Brown; Jeffrey L. Covell

/\nritsu

Anritsu Corporation

1800 Onna, Atsugi-shi
Kanagawa
243-8555
Japan
Telephone: (+46) 2231111
Fax: (+46) 2258384
Web site: http://www.anritsu.co.jp

Public Company
Incorporated: 1895
Employees: 3,568
Sales: ¥78.40 billion ($742 million) (2004)
Stock Exchanges: Tokyo
Ticker Symbol: 6754
NAIC: 333999 All Other General Purpose Machinery Manufacturing; 333319 Other Commercial and Service Industry Machinery Manufacturing; 334119 Other Computer Peripheral Equipment Manufacturing; 334513 Instruments and Related Product Manufacturing for Measuring Displaying, and Controlling Industrial Process Variables; 334519 Other Measuring and Controlling Device Manufacturing

Anritsu Corporation is a leading global producer of test and measurement devices, equipment, and systems. The Kanagawa, Japan-based company primarily targets the market for wired and wireless telecommunications systems, developing measuring instruments and systems for mobile telephone networks, IP networks, and other ultra-high frequency and infrared-based, general purpose testing applications. The company's Test and Measurement division, which accounted for nearly 61 percent of Anritsu's sales of ¥78.40 billion ($742 million) in 2004, supports the full range of digital, cable, optical, RF/microwave and related transmission systems. Anritsu's Information and Communications division delivers video distribution and monitoring and related systems, primarily for the Japanese government and municipal customers. That division accounted for nearly 16 percent of Anritsu's 2004 sales. The Industrial Automation division, at more than 14 percent of sales, produces automatic weighing systems for industrial applications, while the company's Other Businesses division, accounting for eight percent of annual revenues, produces devices and precision measuring equipment, as well as overseeing the company's logistics, property, employee welfare and related needs. With roots tracing back to 1895 and the founding of Japan's communications industry, Anritsu is listed on the Tokyo Stock Exchange and operates manufacturing and marketing subsidiaries in the United States, England and the rest of Europe, South America, China, and throughout Southeast Asia.

Wireless Pioneer in the 20th Century

The development of the first telephone networks in Japan at the end of the 19th century introduced demand for the production of wire-line and wireless networking equipment and components, as well for the telephones themselves. One of the earliest of the new companies established to meet this demand was Sekisan-sha, founded in 1895. That company represented the earliest component of the later Anritsu.

In 1908, Sekisan-sha merged with another entrant into the country's telecommunications market, Abe Electric Wire Company, and the resulting company was renamed Kyoritsu. By then, Japan's telephone system had begun to develop rapidly, and, with growing penetration in both the public and private sectors, demand for telephones surged. Kyroritsu responded by stepping up its production of telephones, producing both desktop and wall based telephones. By 1925, the company had begun to manufacture public pay phones as well.

Wireless communications technologies had begun to develop concurrently with the deployment of Japan's wire-line telephone grid. One of the pioneers of wireless technologies in Japan was Annaka Electric Company, founded in 1900. In 1903, that company succeeded in developing its first wireless transmitter, which was used for setting off a fireworks display at the Japan Industry Promotion Exposition that year.

Annaka continued building on its wireless transmission technologies, resulting in the introduction of its TYK wireless telephone in 1913. By 1916, Annaka was capable of deploying a full-scale TYK-based telegraph system. Linking Toshijima,

Company Perspectives:

Company Philosophy: Anritsu, with sincerity, harmony, and enthusiasm, will contribute to creating an affluent ubiquitous network society by providing ''Original & High Level'' products and services. Company Vision: To be a shining light by contributing to the development of the global network society. To be a global market leader by transforming our strategy to be market driven and customer focused. Company Commitment: High return for shareholders; win-win relationships with customers; employees who are proud of Anritsu; contribution to society as a good citizen.

Toba, and Kamijima, the TYK system became the world's first wireless telephone network.

Radio became Annaka's major market in the 1920s with the launch of Japan's first radio broadcasts. The company began producing components for the new service, including receivers, headphones, and speakers. Annaka also continued expanding its transmission expertise, and in 1925 the company became the first in Japan to build a 500-watt radio transmitter. This was delivered to Tokyo Central Radio Station. Annaka also began developing its wireless transmission technology for other markets and in 1928 released a 2kW wireless transmitter for ocean-going vessels.

Annaka and Kyoritsu merged in 1931, creating Anritsu Electric Corporation. The enlarged company then turned its attention to developing transmission systems for emerging television technology. By 1922, Anritsu succeeded in building its first television broadcast transmitter. Meanwhile, the company also expanded its telephone systems expertise, launching the first automatic public telephone in 1939.

Testing and Measuring in the 1950s

Communications and related transmission systems remained central to Anritsu's development. The need to ensure transmission over greater distances led Anritsu to develop a coaxial-cable based repeater system in 1943. At the same time, measuring transmission strength, particularly for wireless transmission, became an essential factor in the deployment and development of these networks. This led Anritsu to begin building its expertise in the testing and measuring segment. One of the company's first products in this area, later to become the company's core development focus, was its ARM-6074 field strength meter launched in 1950.

While Anritsu continued developing telephone systems, including a new public telephone system equipped with a credit-based billing system launched in 1953, the company expanded its testing and measuring operations. This effort gained speed with the construction of a new production facility in Atsugi in 1961. The following year, Anritsu entered the industrial automation sector with the release of its first electronic micrometer. The company also began producing automatic weighing systems starting in 1964. In another extension of its technology, Anritsu began manufacturing traffic control systems based on its own hybrid IC technology.

Anritsu went public in 1968, listing on the Tokyo Stock Exchange. The listing enabled the company to expand beyond Japan for the first time, and in 1970 it began exporting its public telephones to Australia.

Testing and Measuring also remained a vital company focus. In the late 1970s, Anritsu had taken a lead in developing optical technologies, while continuing to develop its wireless transmission capacity. In 1977, the company launched an ultra-high-speed error detector, capable of transmitting at speeds up to two gigabytes per second. In that year, also, Anritsu launched the first of its measuring systems for optical instruments. Two years later, an order from the AT&T for measuring systems for microwave circuits brought Anritsu to the United States and put it on the map in the world test and measurement market. The following year, Anritsu entered Europe as well, setting up its first subsidiary there, in Luton, England.

In order to reflect its growth as an international company, Anritsu changed its name to Anritsu Corp. in 1985. Meanwhile, Anritsu remained a leading innovator in its field. In 1986, for example, the company debuted a pulse pattern generator for fiber optics-based communications networks.

Solutions Provider in the 2000s

By the 1990s, Anritsu appeared to have come full circle as wireless telecommunications technologies emerged to become the driving force behind the telecommunications industry as a whole. Anritsu positioned itself early on to capture a central position in both its domestic market and in the United States. This was particularly true following its acquisition of the Wiltron Company in the United States for $180 million in 1990. Wiltron had started out in the 1960s as an electronics outfit operating primarily in the defense sector. With the reduction of defense spending following the collapse of communism in the late 1980s, Wiltron had begun repositioning itself around a core of commercial wireless and wireless test systems. The addition of Wiltron, which was especially strong in the midrange-frequency sector, proved highly complementary to Anritsu's own product range.

Through the 1990s, Anritsu targeted the mobile communications market, particularly the test and measuring sector supporting the roll-out of cellular telephone and related technologies. In 1993, for example, Anritsu supported the emergence of digital mobile communications networks with a launch of a range of new generation measurement systems. The following year, the company launched a new ultra-high-speed error detector capable of operating in the 12.5GHz range.

In the late 1990s, Anritsu stepped up its drive toward building a truly global business. In Europe, the company opened a new European Measurement division in the United Kingdom in order to develop and manufacture test and measurement systems specifically for the European market. That operation launched production in 1997. The same year, Anritsu's U.S. subsidiaries were integrated into the larger structure of Anritsu Corp. The company also entered such key markets as China, Korea, India, Singapore, Taiwan, and Brazil. By the end of the decade, Anritsu was present in more than 50 countries worldwide, with sales topping $1 billion.

Back in Japan, Anritsu invested in its future growth, with special attention to extending its operations to include the pro-

Key Dates:

1895: Sekisan-sha is founded.
1900: Annaka Electric Company is founded and develops the world's first wireless telephone transmitter.
1908: Sekisan merges with Abe Electric Wire Co, forming Kyoritsu, and begins producing of telephones.
1931: Annaka and Kyoritsu merge to form Anritsu.
1950: Anritsu debuts a field strength meter as part of its entry into the testing and measurement sector.
1961: The company opens a new factory in Atsugi and begins producing electronic micrometers.
1967: The company goes public on the Tokyo Stock Exchange.
1970: Anritsu begins exporting telephones to Australia as a first step to entering the international market.
1979: The company wins a large-scale order to produce measuring instruments for AT&T in the United States.
1980: Anritsu establishes a subsidiary in England in order to enter the European market.
1985: The company changes its name to Anritsu Corp.
1990: U.S. company Wiltron is acquired.
1993: Anritsu launches measuring instruments for the mobile communications market.
1997: The company opens a production facility in England to manufacture to European market specifications; enters China, India, Brazil and other countries; and begins manufacturing components and constructs a new $30 million laser diode at its production facility in Japan.

duction of components in addition to its full systems production. As part of this effort, Anritsu spent $30 million building a new laser diode facility in Panasawa. Anritsu also converted a facility that formerly produced electro-mechanical components into one specialized in producing components for optical, RF, and microwave transmission systems.

By 2002, components already accounted for more than 11 percent of Anritsu's annual sales, a percentage held low only because of the group's strong growth in its measurements business. In the early years of the 2000s, Anritsu's sales peaked at $1.3 billion. The ensuing worldwide collapse of the telecommunications market hit Anritsu hard, and sales dropped off accordingly, back to just ¥78 billion ($742 million) in 2004. Nonetheless, Anritsu's strong commitment to research and development had kept the company at the forefront of the industry. As the telecommunications market began to bounce back, with the advent of third-generation mobile telephone technology, Anritsu's product development promised to keep it as a leading figure on the global scene.

Principal Subsidiaries

Anritsu Aktiebolag (Sweden); Anritsu Company (USA); Anritsu Company Incorporated (Taiwan); Anritsu Company Ltd. (China); Anritsu Corporation, Ltd. (Korea); Anritsu Customer Services Co., Ltd.; Anritsu Devices Co., Ltd.; Anritsu Electronics (Shanghai) Co., Ltd. (China); Anritsu Electronics, Ltd. (Canada); Anritsu Eletrônica Ltda. (Brazil); Anritsu Engineering Co., Ltd.; Anritsu GmbH (Germany); Anritsu Industrial Solutions (Shanghai) Co., Ltd. (China); Anritsu Industrial Solutions Co., Ltd.; Anritsu Kousan Kabushiki Kaisha; Anritsu Ltd. (United Kingdom); Anritsu Private Ltd. (Singapore); Anritsu Pro Associe Co., Ltd.; Anritsu Proprietary Ltd. (Australia); Anritsu Real Estate Co.; Anritsu S.A. (France); Anritsu S.p.A. (Italy); Anritsu Techmac Co., Ltd.; Anritsu Technics Co., Ltd.; Anritsu U.S. Holding Inc.; ASIA & PACIFIC Business Description Paid-in Capital Voting Rights; Tohoku Anritsu Co., Ltd.

Principal Divisions

Test and Measurement; Information and Communications; Industrial Automation; Other Businesses.

Principal Competitors

American Meter Company; Fuji Electric Holdings Company Ltd.; ThyssenKrupp Technologies AG; Hewlett-Packard GmbH; Omron Corporation; Nikon Corporation; Andover Controls Corporation; Citizen Watch Company Ltd.; Yokogawa Electric Corporation; Ingram Micro Holding GmbH; Rheinmetall DeTec AG; Ibiden Company Ltd.; Futuris Corporation Ltd.

Further Reading

''Anritsu Expands in European Test,'' *Electronics Weekly*, October 1, 1997, p. 6.
''Cell Master Handheld Analyzer for CDMA and GSM Base Stations,'' November 24, 2004. Available from 3g.co.uk.
Clark, Philip B., ''Going Outside for Expertise,'' *B to B*, October 29, 2001, p. 20.
''Commitment to Research and Development Drives Instrument Innovation,'' *Test & Measurement World*, November 2001, p. S16.
Jones-Bey, Hassaun A., ''Anritsu Builds on Component Investment,'' *Optoelectronics Report*, April 1, 2002, p. 2.
''More Than a Few Japanese Multinationals Experiment,'' *Japan-US Business Report*, March 2000, p. 8.
''100 Best Companies to Work for in 2002,'' *Sunday Times*, March 24, 2002, p. 23.
''Vector Analyzer Measures to 65mhz,'' *Electronics Weekly*, November 4, 2004.
Winkler, Eric, ''Anritsu Agrees to Purchase Wiltron in $180M Deal,'' *Electronic News*, January 22, 1990, p. 1.

—M.L. Cohen

ArQule, Inc.

19 Presidential Way
Woburn, Massachusetts 01801-5140
U.S.A.
Telephone: (781) 994-0300
Fax: (781) 376-6019
Web site: http://www.arqule.com

Public Company
Incorporated: 1993
Employees: 257
Sales: $65.5 million (2003)
Stock Exchanges: NASDAQ
Ticker Symbol: ARQL
NAIC: 541710 Research and Development in the Physical Sciences and Engineering Sciences

ArQule, Inc., is a biotechnology company involved in the research and development of small molecule therapeutics. The company also provides fee-based chemistry services to pharmaceutical and biotechnology companies to produce novel chemic compounds with drug-like characteristics. ArQule's revenue is derived primarily from compound development chemistry performed for its customers and research and development funding.

Origins

ArQule was incorporated in 1993 as one of the first companies to focus on the chemistry aspect of drug discovery. From the beginning, the company pursued a business strategy of raising cash by collaborating with major pharmaceutical companies. In March 1995, ArQule announced a $30 million deal with Pharmacia, the Swedish pharmaceutical company that would use ArQule's technology for making organic compounds to develop new products. This deal was followed by a $35 million agreement with Abbott Laboratories in June for ArQule's technology tools to help find new drugs. The arrangement called for Abbott to pay a significant up-front fee, support ArQule research, and make payments as the work reached certain milestones. Nevertheless, Abbott obtained no ownership stake in ArQule. This was a key business strategy: Unlike other cash-starved biotech companies, ArQule managed to avoid selling itself to big firms with large cash reserves. Instead, the fledgling company sought to negotiate deals in which it did work for larger firms but gave up no ownership control. Following this strategy, in November 1995 ArQule signed its third deal in one year with Solvay Duphar B.V., worth an estimated $50 million.

One major reason for ArQule's success in negotiating favorable deals with leading pharmaceutical companies was its ability to do high-volume testing—1,000 to 5,000 tests—on many compounds using automated assembly line testing methods. What a medicinal chemist might accomplish in two weeks working on a single compound, the company could perform on 1,000 compounds in a single day. Indeed, chemistry had become the chief bottleneck in the drug discovery process. Both pharmaceutical and biotechnology companies had become increasingly anxious to ensure a supply of new chemical compounds suitable for drug screening and to gain access to better technology for optimizing the discovery of new drugs. ArQule's technology offered a revolutionary change in the approach of medicinal chemistry. The company provided a novel modular building block technology that integrated structure-guided drug design, high-speed parallel chemical synthesis, and information technology to accelerate the identification and potential development of new drugs.

Argule's advantageous agreements with other firms also stemmed from larger forces at play. In their formative years, biotech firms were flush with cash for developing breakthrough drugs to challenge the big pharmaceutical companies. In the early 1990s, however, Wall Street investors and venture capitalists began to limit their willingness to gamble on the nation's 1,300 biotech firms after several highly publicized drug failures. Investors also grew impatient with the high cost and extensive time to develop new therapeutics. As these lines of capital began to dry up, the biotech industry turned to major drug firms for new infusions of cash. In addition, biotech companies soon realized that the pharmaceutical sector offered other benefits, including manufacturing capacity, distribution networks, and experience in running human testing trials to meet Food and Drug Administration approval.

In turn, the pharmaceutical companies needed the innovation and creativity of the burgeoning biotech field, which offered new technology to help produce breakthrough drugs in a cost-effective manner. Despite spending billions of dollars a

Company Perspectives:

ArQule is a biotechnology company engaged in research and development of cancer therapeutics. Our mission is to research, develop, and commercialize broadly effective cancer drugs with reduced toxicities compared to conventional cancer chemotherapeutics. ArQule develops cancer therapies based on our innovative and proprietary Activated Checkpoint Therapy (ACT) platform by applying a unique molecular biology approach that leverages automated chemistries and intelligent drug design.

year in research and development, pharmaceutical companies had little to show for their cash layout except for improvements of existing products. In need of innovation, large drug firms began replacing venture capitalists as major sponsors of the biotech industry. While the nature of the deals varied, in the early years cash-strapped biotech firms were often required to turn over product rights, clinical trial testing, marketing and distribution, and sometimes even manufacturing rights in exchange for long-term financial stability. As the biotech industry matured, however, pharmaceutical companies became more willing to share its rewards, offering such incentives as higher royalties and options for manufacturing. Given these trends, ArQule saw its future in becoming the research and development arm of large pharmaceutical firms. Having raised $6.5 million in two capital venture rounds in its first two years, ArQule moved quickly beginning in 1995 to sign multi-year pharmaceutical and biotech partnership deals.

Forming Partnerships for Cash: Mid- to Late 1990s

On October 16, 1996, ArQule made an initial public offering (IPO), raising $34 million at twelve dollars per share. The company expected to use the proceeds for research and development. Also during 1996, ArQule expanded its collaborations with both pharmaceutical companies and other biotech firms. By the end of the year, the company had established a fourth partnership with a multi-national pharmaceutical company, Roche Bioscience, a division of Syntx Inc., worth about $60 million. ArQule also entered the agrochemical area with a five-year deal with Monsanto covering the discovery and development of new agricultural chemicals. ArQule estimated the deal at $12 million plus royalties of the sale of products resulting from the collaboration. In addition, the company signed collaboration agreements with nine biotech firms to leverage their biology with its chemistry capabilities. For 1996, these various collaborations increased revenues to $7.25 million, up from $3.33 million in 1995. In commenting on the company's 1996 fiscal results, president and chief executive officer Eric B. Gordan said that ArQule's plans were to adhere to its novel business model by signing additional pharmaceutical and biotech agreements and increasing the company's presence in the agrochemicals and bioseparations industries.

On April 4, 1997, ArQule announced another IPO of two million shares of common stock, raising $24 million. That July, the company announced a drug discovery collaboration with the Wyeth-Ayerst Pharmaceuticals division of American Home Products. The signing of the sixth pharmaceuticals partnership represented another validation of the company's technology and business strategy. Under the agreement, Wyeth would make a $2 million equity investment and would pay ArQule a minimum of $26 million over five years. In return, Wyeth would get a five-year subscription to ArQule's Mapping Array program, covering about 200,000 new compounds per year. In November, the company also signed a three-year deal with Sankyo worth about $35 million. By the end of 1997, ArQule had established deals with seven leading multi-national pharmaceutical firms, as well as eighteen biotechnology companies, covering diverse therapeutic areas. In addition, the company began collaborating with the University of California San Francisco (UCSF) to develop a new class of HIV protease inhibitors and received a patent covering methods for using compounds called aminimides in the design of polymers with specific functions. According to ArQule, the technology pointed to the potential of combinatory chemistry in uses beyond drug discovery, including agrochemical research and development and materials research.

By the beginning of 1998, ArQule had honed its business strategy to two simple formulas. The agreements with large drug firms involved primarily a pay-as-you-go arrangement, with the company receiving fees for providing access to its novel technology. With the biotech companies, ArQule took a different approach, often trading chemistry know-how for equity in the firms. Under either arrangement, ArQule could apply its technologies in high-throughput automated screening and detection of compounds to a wide variety of pharmaceutical and other life-science applications. In layman's terms, this meant that ArQule's ability to design and produce novel compounds could be used as a starting point for screening programs and perhaps later lead to compounds that were suitable to put into human trials with the aim of discovering new pharmaceuticals. The result was that both the company's technology ventures and its bottom line benefited. For 1997, the company reported total revenues of $17.4 million, up from $7.25 million in 1996. Net income for the year broke in positive territory for the first time, totaling $291,000 compared to a net loss of nearly $3 million in 1996. In addition, as a result of rising revenues and two public offerings of common stock, ArQule built a $51 million war chest that could be used for capital investments for acquisitions.

In 1998, ArQule continued to develop its preeminence as a chemistry services business for drug discovery firms. The company expanded its collaborations with pharmaceutical and biotech companies and academic institutions, including Ontogeny, Sepracor Inc., Immunex, Acadia, Genome Therapeutics, CuraGen, Beth Israel Deaconess Medical Center, and R.W. Johnson Pharmaceutical Research Institute, a Johnson & Johnson affiliate. ArQule also delivered a lead agricultural compound to Monsanto, accomplishing the first major development milestone in the collaboration. In addition, ArQule established its first commercial partnership with Amersham Pharmacia Biotech to develop and market customized bioseparations products for life science and research applications. In addition, the company added new technology relating to a program that would allow exclusive access to specially designed chemistries, received six new patents, and doubled its production capabilities.

Key Dates:

1993: The company is incorporated.
1995: ArQule signs deals with major pharmaceutical firms.
1996: The company makes an initial public offering of common stock, raising $34 million.
1998: ArQule breaks ground on new headquarters and a research and development facility in Woburn, Massachusetts.
2001: The company acquires Camitro Corporation.
2003: ArQule acquires Cyclis Pharmaceuticals Inc.
2003: ArQule announces Phase I human clinical trials for CO-501, an anti-cancer agent.

In July 1998, ArQule broke ground for a 130,000-square-foot headquarters and research and development facility in Woburn, Massachusetts. With 180 employees and collaborations with more than thirty companies and academic institutions worldwide, the new state-of-the-art facility represented the next phase of ArQule's planned expansion. At the same time, ArQule announced a senior management succession plan to guide the company through its next stage of development. The ArQule board of directors, including then current CEO and president Eric B. Gordan, began searching for a new chief executive officer with extensive experience in large scale drug discovery operations. During the transition period, Gordon agreed to hold the position until a new CEO was found, including serving on the board of directors. The change in leadership came on April 1, 1999 with the appointment of Stephen Hill as ArQule's new president and chief executive officer. Hill, a medical doctor, arrived at ArQule after ten years of pharmaceutical experience. Prior to joining ArQule, Hill served as director of Global Drug Development at F. Hoffman-LaRoche in Basel, Switzerland.

In July 1999, ArQule announced a major four-and-a-half–year agreement with Pfizer Inc. worth up to $117 million. The deal was one of the largest in the field of combinatorial chemistry, which enabled pharmaceutical and biotechnology companies to accelerate the search for promising drugs. The agreement provided that ArQule devote its entire Medford facility, including designated technologies, scientists, and its AMAP chemistry operating system, to generating libraries of compounds for Pfizer. ArQule would receive $16 million up front and $20 to $27 million annually over the life of the agreement. ArQule was required to begin providing compounds to Pfizer in the year 2000. In addition, all compounds developed by ArQule would be owned by Pfizer, which would assume control of the Medford facility at the conclusion of the arrangement. The deal came at a fortuitous time as the company had been suffering from steep losses and declining stock prices stemming from a dwindling number of new pharmaceutical collaborations. ArQule signed another agreement in October 1999 with Bayer AG worth $30 million. Under the deal, ArQule would design and develop exclusive chemical compounds for Bayer over a three-year period. In November 2000, the company signed a collaborative drug discovery agreement with SmithKline Beecham for $500,000 to $1 million a year during the term of the contract.

Transformation to Biopharmaceutical Company

Under CEO Stephen Hill's new leadership, the company sought to transform itself from a chemistry services business to a biopharmaceutical drug-discovery firm. In pursuit of this goal, in November 2000 ArQule sold 2.92 million shares of common stock for $65.7 million to help fund its move into the drug-discovery sector. The company, which primarily designed and synthesized molecules for pharmaceutical and biotechnology firms, intended to use proceeds from the stock offering to fund acquisitions in the industry. As a result, in February 2001 ArQule concluded a $95 million merger with Camitro Corporation, a privately held predictive modeling company based in Menlo Park, California. The merger established Camitro as a wholly owned subsidiary of ArQule. Camitro's technology consisted of an integrated platform of predictive models and strategies for the design, selection, and optimization of potential new pharmaceutical drugs. ArQule planned to incorporate these models into its own Parallel Track Drug Discovery program. The company expected the acquisition to be the first significant step in its transition from being a services company to becoming a leading chemistry-based drug discovery firm. Plans for the acquisition failed to materialize, however, as ArQule was unable to commercialize the Camitro's technology, resulting in the layoff of 128 employees. In addition, the company closed its facilities in Redwood City, California, and Cambridge, United Kingdom, to conserve cash and restructure operations.

Despite this setback, on September 8, 2003 ArQule's efforts to reinvent itself as a biopharmaceutical drug and development company hit a milestone with the purchase of Cyclis Pharmaceuticals, Inc., a privately held, development stage cancer-therapeutics company based in Norwood, Massachusetts. The deal was made for $25 million in stock and cash. As part of the deal, ArQule acquired Cyclis's lead clinical candidate for cancer, CO-501, plus its Activated Checkpoint Therapy used to develop the new drug. Shortly after buying Cyclis, ArQule announced the launching of Phase I human clinical trials for CO-501, a product it hoped would reduce and kill tumors via injection by switching on cell ''checkpoints'' that would tell cancer cells of their inherent DNA damage, causing them to self-destruct. ArQule named Chiang Li as chief science officer and vice-president and head of its Biomedical Institute. Li, a former vice-president of research at Cyclis, helped to develop the science behind CO-501. ArQule's future plans included developing products that would combine biology and chemistry to create synthetic versions of CO-501 to treat other cancers. The company also began focusing on inflammation drugs and developing a pill to treat rheumatoid arthritis, which was slated to begin preclinical animal studies by the end of 2003.

Compared with many other small drug-discovery companies, ArQule was well positioned. The company's entry into the drug discovery industry enabled it to negotiate a significant expansion of its 1999 strategic alliance with Pfizer that was worth between $120 million and $345 million depending on whether ArQule attained all milestones in support of Pfizer's efforts to develop new drugs. Moreover, seven months after its acquisition of Cyclis, ArQule leveraged the Activated Checkpoint Therapy technology to conclude an oncology deal with Switzerland's Hoffman-La Roche to discover and develop drug candidates that target a new pathway to selectively kill cancer cells. The alliance included a compound that was in Phase I clinical development. Assuming the successful development and commercialization of the compound under the program, ArQule would receive up to $276 million in predetermined payments, plus royalties based on net sales. By this time, the company also had $83 million in the bank, and second quarter net income for 2003 hit $1 million versus a $4.9 million net loss in 2002. In 2004, Hill believed ArQule was entering its most exciting time in the company's history. The company had much going for it—a clinical-stage compound, growing early-stage portfolio of new drug candidates, promising research and development technology, and cash in the bank.

Principal Subsidiaries

ArQule U.K. Ltd.

Principal Competitors

Albany Molecular Research; Array Biopharma; Pharmacopeia Drug Discovery.

Further Reading

''Cash-Flow Conservation,'' *Med Ad News*, February 2003, p. 16.

Coghill, Kim, ''ArQule Plans $25M Acquisition of Cyclis to Build R&D Program,'' *BioWorld Today*, July 18, 2003, pp. 1–2.

Hollmer, Mark, ''ArQule Continues Transition into Drug Developer,'' *Boston Business Journal*, October 10–16, p. 1.

''Hot Prospects 97: Rich in Promises and Variety,'' *Chemical Week*, December 24, 1997, p. 28.

''Monsanto Extends and Expands Agreement with ArQule,'' *PR Newswire*, January 12, 2000.

Niles, Steven, ''Therapeutic Focus Defined,'' *R&D Directions*, September 2003, p. 16.

''Pharmacia Biotech AB Extends Joint Research Program with ArQule Inc.,'' *PR Newswire*, July 27, 1997.

''Wyeth-Ayerst Hires ArQule,'' *Applied Genetics News*, August 1, 1997.

Rosenberg, Ronald, ''Medford, Mass.-Based Drug Firm Enters Technology Deal with Pfizer,'' *Knight Ridder/Tribune Business News*, July 21, 1999.

Seachrist, Lisa, ''ArQule Assured Most of Money in $117M Pfizer Collaboration,'' *BioWorld Today*, July 22, 1999.

——, ''ArQule Will Deliver Compounds to Bayer in Exchange for $30M.,'' *BioWorld Today*, October 1, 1999.

—Bruce P. Montgomery

Asbury Carbons, Inc.

405 Old Main Street
Asbury, New Jersey 08802
U.S.A.
Telephone: (908) 537-2155
Toll Free: (800) 334-5276
Fax: (908) 537-2908
Web site: http://www.asbury.com

Private Company
Founded: 1896 as Asbury Graphite Mills
Employees: 150
Sales: $18 million (2004 est.)
NAIC: 335991 Carbon and Graphite Product Manufacturing

Based in the small town of Asbury, New Jersey, Asbury Carbons, Inc. is the world's largest independent processor and seller of refined graphite and other carbons. In addition to securing raw material from its mines in Mexico, the company imports from a number of sources around the world. Among the many products Asbury produces are amorphous graphite, natural flake graphite, artificial graphite, graphitized cokes and carbons, metallurgical cokes, graphite specialty lubricants, and carbon fibers. The number of major applications for its products are also numerous, including foundry coatings, fuel cells, aluminum production, bakery lubricants, railroad lubricants, fire retardants, rubber additives, plastic additives, welding, glass manufacturing, cement additives, gaskets and seals, ceramics, batteries, and, not least of all, the common lead pencil. In addition to a plant in Asbury, the company operates processing facilities in Pennsylvania, Michigan, and California. Warehouses are maintained throughout the United States, as well as Canada, South America, Africa, Europe, and Australia. Asbury is owned and operated by the fourth generation of the company's founder, Harry M. Riddle.

1890s Origins

Born in 1865, Harry M. Riddle founded what is today Asbury Carbons, Inc. He became a hard worker at an early age, doing chores on the family farm, then walking some five miles to work at a general store. By the time he was 24, he was part-owner of two general stores, one in Asbury, New Jersey, and another located in the nearby village of Hampton. He was also Asbury's postmaster. However, he had much greater ambitions, and when a friend told him about the wide applications of graphite and its untapped industrial potential he was determined to become involved in the business. Graphite is a mineral in the carbon family whose members include coal, coke, and wood, but it is only one of three pure forms of carbon, the others being diamonds and fullerenes. Unlike diamonds, graphite is soft and because of its construction, comprised of minute platelets, it makes a superior lubricant. In addition, it is an excellent thermal and electrical conductor as well as being heat resistant. Because of these attributes, graphite has a wide range of industrial applicants, more so now than when the imagination of young Harry Riddle became fixed on the mineral.

In 1895, Riddle leased an Asbury flour mill that was owned by a relative and powered by the swiftly flowing Musconetcong River. The mill had been built in 1865 to replace one constructed in the late 1700s. Riddle then hired a miller and transformed the operation so that instead of grist it now milled refined graphite, produced from raw material, some of which he bought from a small Rhode Island mine. Most, however, was imported from Korea and Ceylon by New York City brokers. The barrels of raw graphite came by rail to a nearby New Jersey train station and transported the final miles to the mill by horse and wagon. Riddle called his new company Asbury Graphite Mills. To market his product, Riddle, not surprisingly, relied on the U.S. mail. He wrote letters to potential customers—foundries and manufacturers of such goods as paint and stove polish—and enclosed a sample. It proved an effective technique, as sales grew rapidly, from 36 tons of material to 144 tons during the first three years. Business was so strong that in 1903 Riddle paid $2,000 to buy the mill, and five years later bought another mill across the river. Known as "Plant No. 2," this facility would be continually upgraded and become the hub of Asbury's operation. The original plant, on the other hand, was used only intermittently and was finally closed in the 1970s.

Incorporation in the 1920s

In 1914, Harry M. Riddle, Jr., known as Marvin, joined the company after graduating from high school. At the time, busi-

Company Perspectives:

Asbury Carbons exists to achieve three simple, clear goals: to be increasingly creative in carbons; to be continually global in service; to generate steady growth by responding swiftly to customer needs.

ness had dropped off but it quickly picked up a few months later as Europe became embroiled in World War I. Graphite was in great demand in the mills that made the steel and melted the nonferrous metals needed to manufacture weapons. When the United States entered the war, in fact, all supplies of graphite were commandeered for military use. In 1921, the younger Riddle became his father's partner, and in 1928 the business was incorporated. Also of note, during the 1920s the elder Riddle decided to bypass New York brokers and began importing graphite directly from foreign mines.

Asbury's business was hurt by the Great Depression of the 1930s, but by the end of the decade the demand for refined graphite was beginning to rebound. In the meantime, there was a change at the top. In 1937, Harry Riddle died and was succeeded by his son, who also took over as Asbury's postmaster, with the post office operating out of the company's offices. According to company lore, around lunchtime each day mill employees became postal workers to help get out the mail, then went back to refining graphite. However, when the business grew too large, Marvin Riddle stepped down as town postmaster, thus ending a longstanding family tradition.

With business picking up at the end of the 1930s, Asbury bought a third mill in 1939, a former woolen mill located a few miles upstream on the Musconetcong River in the village of Changewater. However, as the river was no longer able to supply the necessary power, diesel engines were installed to help out, and they eventually replaced the water wheel entirely. (Diesel engines would themselves be replaced in the 1950s by electricity.) In the early 1940s, Asbury expanded its operations to the West Coast, buying a San Francisco distributorship. Later on, a graphite refining operation would be added. The extra production capacity afforded by the Changewater plant would be needed a few years later, during World War II, when once again the need for refined graphite in military applications increased dramatically. During the war, Asbury had all three of its mills in operation. The company also bought a former bakery in town and installed flotation equipment to produce purer blends of graphites required by some munitions.

After the war, in 1948, the Changewater plant was gutted by fire and the company opted not to replace it. The postwar era also saw a major expansion in sources of raw material. Mexico, Madagascar, Germany, and Norway became graphite supplies, and they were later joined by China, which sat on extensive reserves of the mineral. The extra raw material would be much appreciated because commodity prices would drop at a time when Asbury's business reached a plateau. The 1950s would also mark the entry of the third generation of the Riddle family in the business. In 1951, Harry M. Riddle III went to work for Asbury, which at the time was posting annual sales of $1.75 million. "Marv" Riddle had just graduated from Lafayette College with a degree in metallurgy, but he would prove to be a sound businessman and a good salesman as well. Over the course of the next 15 years, he would learn the business thoroughly and be well prepared to carry on the tradition established by his father and grandfather, but at the same time he was instrumental in introducing a new strategy for returning growth to the business. Like his father and grandfather, he eschewed the idea of becoming a value-added manufacturer, believing that Asbury should remain a basic supplier of refined graphite and avoid competing with its customers. Instead, Asbury opted to achieve growth by acquiring strategically located companies in order to expand geographically. The reason was simple yet important: limiting transportation costs was an important factor in maintaining a competitive price.

Thus, in the 1960s Asbury grew on a number of fronts. In 1960, it acquired Cummings-Moore Graphite Company based in Detroit. Not only did it provide Asbury with a Midwest base of operations, Cummings-Moore owned a Mexican mine, Grafitera de Sonora. In 1961, Asbury expanded its West Coast business by launching a joint venture in Oakland, California, called Asbury Graphite Inc. of California. A year later, Asbury completed another acquisition, this one closer to home and slightly older. It bought the Charles Pettinos Graphite Company, established in 1891 some 30 miles west in Bethlehem, Pennsylvania. Although a smaller plant, Pettinos proved to be a perfect place to complete specialty runs for customers. This practice was in keeping with a third principal for growing Asbury and part of a new vision for the company: To meet the need for more complex carbonaceous material, add more sophisticated graphite blends as well as other carbon products.

Harry M. Riddle, Jr., retired in 1965 after heading Asbury for nearly three decades and left a solid record of achievement. When he had succeeded his father, he took over a company with two mills and less than 20 employees generating sales of $400,000. Now he turned over a business to his son that employed more than a hundred people at six plants, with sales approaching $4 million. There was no need for a period of transition, as Harry M. Riddle III had been with the company for 15 years and played a key role in developing Asbury's growth strategy. He merely carried on with the plan.

In 1968, Asbury bought a graphite mill located in Bloomsbury, New Jersey, a purchase that paid immediate dividends when an area company, Joseph Dixon Crucible Company, was destroyed by fire and now required a large, long-term supply of the kind of graphite that Bloomsbury produced. Asbury added to its Mexican mining assets by acquiring a 35 percent stake in Grafitos Mexicanos, the largest graphite mine in the country. All Mexican mining operations were ultimately assigned to the Cummings-Moore division. Asbury grew internationally in 1972 by launching an international sales unit to export refined graphite products: Asbury Cumograph Corporation, based in St. Thomas, Virgin Islands. In 1973, Asbury gained a presence in Canada by acquiring Wilkinson Foundry Facing and Supply Company, which would primarily serve as a distributor of Asbury products. More importantly, Wilkinson provided Asbury with a base of operations from which it could establish a graphite mine near Quebec in 1980.

Key Dates:

1895: Company founded by Harry M. Riddle, Sr.
1928: The business is incorporated.
1937: Riddle dies and is succeeded by his son, Harry M. Riddle, Jr.
1960: Cummings-Moore Graphite Company is acquired.
1965: Harry M. Riddle III succeeds his father as president.
1980: Fluxmaster, Inc. is acquired.
1995: Stephen A. Riddle represents the fourth generation of Riddles to head the family business.
1999: Dixon Ticonderoga Co.'s graphite assets are acquired.

Continuing Expansion: 1970s and Beyond

Asbury also expanded on the West Coast of the United States during the 1970s. The California unit was moved in 1974 to Rodeo, California, where a new plant specialized in producing calcined coke to serve the cast metal and corrosion markets. A year later, Asbury bought a manufacturer of glue and glue extender in the state of Washington, but this attempt at diversification proved to be too far afield from the company's expertise, and it was eventually sold. A few years earlier, Asbury had also attempted to become involved in the production of custom blister packaging for premium graphite products, but this venture was also a poor fit, and in 1976 Asbury Packaging was closed. A more successful attempt at diversification was the 1976 acquisition of Sunbury, Pennsylvania-based Anthracite Industries, which processed nongraphite carbon products—ground anthracite, metallurgical coke, calcined petroleum coke, and amorphous graphite—primarily used by mills to add carbon content to steel. Also of note, in 1977 Asbury reorganized its business under a holding company structure, resulting in the creation of Asbury Carbons, Inc.

Asbury continued to expand and diversify in the 1980s. It acquired Fluxmaster, Inc. in 1980. The Clearfield, Utah-based company made fluxes for the aluminum and foundry markets and became part of Asbury Graphite of California. In 1983, Asbury added lead and colored pencils to the product mix by acquiring The M.A. Ferst Company of Atlanta. (After ten years, however, the unit was closed when it was no longer viable because of cheap foreign competition.) In 1984, Asbury added substantially to its slate of nongraphite carbon products by purchasing a Union Carbide plant near Kitanning, Pennsylvania, just north of Pittsburgh. Although the plant produced some graphite, it primarily processed calcined coke for the cast metal market. In 1989, the company introduced the Asbury Injection Method, which relied on a pneumatic conveyor system designed to handle carbon powders and was especially useful in the steel industry.

Asbury opened a plant in Dequincy, Louisiana, in 1993 to produce natural amorphous graphite, artificial graphite, and calcined coke. The $2 million plant was strategically located to not only serve the southern United States but Central and South America as well. The 1990s would also see Asbury celebrate its 100th anniversary. In addition, 1995 marked a change in leadership as the fourth generation of the Riddle family stepped in. Stephen A. Riddle took over as president, with his father staying on as chairman. Steve Riddle was well groomed to carry on the tradition established by his great grandfather. He was exposed to the family business while growing up, then joined the company full time. He became vice-president of sales in 1987 and executive vice-president in 1995. He now assumed the day-to-day responsibilities for a company that was producing more than 160,000 tons of graphite and other carbon products and generating over $70 million in revenues each year.

Before the 1990s came to a close, Asbury completed another significant acquisition, paying $23.5 million for the U.S. graphite and lubricants division of Dixon Ticonderoga Co., a company that specialized in the production of writing instruments, art supplies, and office products. As a result, Asbury added specialty lubricants to its product mix. Over the next two years, Asbury integrated the Dixon assets, closing down the two plants it inherited and transferring operations to the other Asbury operations. Even as it was shuttering old factories, Asbury was taking steps to preserve the heritage of its first facility, the water-powered flour mill that Harry M. Riddle originally rented to launch his graphite business. Asbury deeded it, along with 3.5 acres of property and two other buildings, to the Musconetcong Watershed Association, which was devoted to preserving the heritage of the 42-mile Musconetcong River and committed to raising money to restore the mill. In the process, the organization would preserve the heritage of the area's most famous company.

Principal Subsidiaries

Asbury Graphite Mills, Inc.; Anthracite Industries, Inc.; Asbury Fluxmaster, Inc.; Cummings-Moore Graphite Company; Asbury Graphite of California, Inc.; Asbury Wilkinson, Inc.; Asbury Louisiana, Inc.

Principal Competitors

Superior Graphite Company; Timcal AG.

Further Reading

Asbury Carbons, Inc., *The Riddles of Graphite*, Asbury, N.J.: Asbury Carbons, Inc., 1995, 24 p.
''Asbury Completes Integration of Dixon Graphite Plants,'' *Industrial Specialties News*, November 26, 2001.
Charlton, Art, ''Asbury Culture and History New Grist for the Mill,'' *Star-Ledger*, February 28, 1999, p. 35.

—Ed Dinger

AT&T Corporation

One AT&T Way
Bedminster, New Jersey 07921
U.S.A.
Telephone: (908) 221-2000
Fax: (908) 532-1675
Web site: http://www.att.com

Public Company
Incorporated: 1885 as American Telephone and Telegraph Company
Employees: 61,600
Sales: $34.52 billion (2003)
Stock Exchanges: New York
Ticker Symbol: T
NAIC: 517110 Wired Telecommunications Carriers; 334111 Electronic Computer Manufacturing; 334210 Telephone Apparatus Manufacturing; 515210 Cable and Other Subscription Programming; 522298 All Other Non-Depository Credit Intermediation; 522320 Financial Transactions Processing, Reserve, and Clearing House

AT&T Corporation organizes its business into two segments, business services and consumer services. AT&T's consumer services business, the bedrock of its existence for more than a century, provides domestic and international long-distance telephone service to roughly 35 million residential customers in the United States, as well as Internet service through AT&T Worldnet and AT&T digital subscriber line (DSL) service to a much smaller portion of the U.S. population. AT&T's business services segment, which the company regards as its future, involves offering global communications services to three million customers, ranging from small businesses to large, multinational corporations. For its corporate clientele, AT&T provides domestic and international voice service, domestic and international data and Internet protocol (IP) services, networking services, and domestic and international wholesale transport services.

Beginnings

AT&T had its origin in the invention of the telephone in 1876 by Alexander Graham Bell. In 1877, Bell and several financial partners formed the Bell Telephone Company, and in 1878 they formed the New England Telephone Company to license telephone exchanges in New England. The two companies licensed local operating companies in Chicago, New York, and Boston. Over the next year, Bell and his backers sold a controlling interest in the companies to a group of Boston financiers.

The companies were soon embroiled in patent disputes with Western Union Telegraph Company, the world's largest telegraph company. During the dispute, the two Bell companies were consolidated into the National Bell Telephone Company, and Theodore J. Vail was named general manager. In November 1879, the patent suit was settled out of court. Western Union left the telephone business and sold its system of 56,000 telephones in 55 cities to Bell. Bell agreed to stay out of the telegraph business and paid Western Union a 20 percent royalty on telephone equipment leases for the next 17 years. Between 1877 and 1881, Bell licensed numerous local operating companies as a way to promote the telephone without having to raise capital. The companies signed five- to ten-year contracts, under which Bell got $20 per telephone per year and the right to buy the licensee's property when the contract expired.

National became the American Bell Telephone Company in 1880 and obtained more capital at that time. Starting in 1881, Bell urged the locals to make the contracts permanent, rescinding Bell's right to buy the respective properties but giving Bell variously 30 to 50 percent ownership of the operating companies. The companies could build long-distance lines to connect exchanges in their territories, but they were prohibited from connecting them with those of other operating companies or independent phone companies. Bell thus became a partner in the local telephone business, allowing it to influence the locals and conserve capital for long-distance operations. American Bell needed large amounts of equipment, and in 1881 it acquired Western Electric, a major Western Union supplier, to serve as its manufacturer. Bell then consolidated into Western Electric several other manufacturers it had licensed to make telephones.

Company Perspectives:

It takes the right technology, the right people, and a bold vision to be the ''The World's Networking Company.'' For more than 125 years, AT&T has been known for unparalleled quality and reliability in communications. Backed by the research and development capabilities of AT&T Labs, our commitment to innovation has made us a global leader in local, long distance, Internet, and transaction-based voice and data services.

More long-distance lines were being built as telephone technology improved. In 1884, Bell built an experimental line between Boston and New York. The next year, it added a Philadelphia-New York line. To construct, finance, and operate its long-distance system, Bell established the American Telephone and Telegraph Company in 1885 to operate as its long-distance subsidiary. At that time, the nascent U.S. telephone system was primarily a series of unconnected local networks. Vail, who was named AT&T president, wanted to get a long-distance network in place before Bell's basic patents expired in 1894. By the time it established AT&T, Bell was in firm control of the telephone business. It regulated the operating companies' long-distance lines and Western Electric, their major supplier. It also had the right to take over their property if they violated their contracts.

In 1888, a huge blizzard in New England knocked most telephones out of service. The company responded by pushing to put more cables underground. Later that year, it became clear that a long-distance network would cost more than planned, and AT&T floated $2 million in bonds to raise capital. The company returned to public investors frequently throughout its history to finance its ever-expanding enterprises. For decades, AT&T stock was the most widely held in the world. In order to attract so many investors, AT&T was forced to be efficient, even though it lacked real competition for much of its history.

Technical advances came regularly. The first coin-operated public telephone was installed in 1889. During 1891, two-party and four-party service was introduced, and the first automatic dial system was patented. A New York-Chicago long-distance line opened in 1892, and Boston-Chicago and New York-Cincinnati lines were initiated in 1893.

Bell initially had a monopoly on the telephone because of its patents, but in 1894 its patent expired. Rather than compete by providing better and less expensive service, Bell often took the growing independent phone companies to court, claiming patent infringements. As Western Electric would not sell equipment to the independents, new manufacturers sprung up to accommodate them. The independents were particularly successful in rural areas in the West and Midwest where Bell did not provide service. By 1898, some cities had two unconnected phone systems, one Bell and one independent. This competition forced Bell to expand faster than it otherwise would have. It jumped from 240,000 phones in 1892 to 800,000 in 1899.

The company needed capital to keep up with this expansion, and Massachusetts, where American Bell was based, presented far more regulatory interference than New York, where AT&T was based. As a result, in 1899 AT&T became the parent company of the Bell System until the breakup in 1984. AT&T's capital jumped from $20 million to more than $70 million. By 1900, AT&T was organizing itself into the vertical structure that characterized it for decades thereafter. It had assets of $120 million compared with a total of $55 million for the independents, but its finances were run overly conservatively and its service was reputedly poor.

Meanwhile, the telephone was having a dramatic impact on the United States, where large numbers of people still lived in the relative isolation of farms or small towns. The telephone lessened their isolation, and the response to the new invention was enthusiastic. The number of rural telephones shot from 267,000 in 1902 to 1.4 million in 1907. The telephone was coming to be viewed as indispensable by virtually all businesses and most private homes.

Fighting the Independents: Early 1900s

Competition from independents continued to mount. Their rates were sometimes half of Bell's, and the United States was in an antimonopoly mood. Many rural communities started their own not-for-profit phone companies that were later sold to independents or Bell. By 1907, the independents operated 51 percent of all phones. AT&T was fighting back, having made the decision to take on the independents when it moved and changed its name. The company's first and most effective action was to slash rates. The arrogance of early company officials was replaced by a desire to please customers. AT&T also bought out independents, set up its own ''independents,'' and used its political and financial clout to strangle competitors. AT&T's greatest advantage was its virtual monopoly of long-distance service, which it refused to let independents use.

The invention of a certain electric device, the loading coil, in 1899 gave long-distance service a push by allowing smaller-diameter wires to be used, which made underground long-distance cables feasible. They were implemented for an underground New York-Philadelphia line in 1906, but long-distance signals remained weak and difficult to hear until the invention of the vacuum-tube repeater in 1912.

Competition had given AT&T a necessary push, forcing it to expand and grow, but it also weakened its finances. Between 1902 and 1906, debt grew from $60 million to $200 million. Through a series of bond purchases starting in 1903, financier J.P. Morgan tried to wrest control of the company from the Boston capitalists, beginning a free-for-all that lasted several years. When the dust cleared in 1907, Morgan and his New York and London backers had won, and they brought back Vail as president. Vail had left in 1887 because of differences with the Bostonians, whose view was focused narrowly on short-term profit. Vail and his backers had a wider vision than the Bostonians, believing they should create a comprehensive, nationwide communications system.

In 1907, AT&T boasted 3.12 million telephones in service, but had a terrible public image, low staff morale, poor service, serious debts, and a bevy of technological problems. Within a decade, Vail turned the company around, making it a model of corporate success. He soon sold millions of dollars in bonds by offering them at a discount to shareholders, which reestablished

Key Dates:

1885: The American Telephone and Telegraph Company (AT&T) is formed, establishing the first national telephone network.
1889: The first coin-operated pay phone is installed in Hartford, Connecticut.
1908: AT&T begins reducing its prices to wrest control away from independent telephone companies.
1922: AT&T establishes WEAF in New York City, marking its entry in the commercial radio business.
1947: Microwave radio becomes the technological basis of long-distance telephone calls.
1962: Telstar, the first AT&T satellite, is launched.
1983: Plans for the breakup of AT&T are approved, leading to the creation of independent, regional telephone companies and freeing AT&T to enter non-telecommunications businesses.
1984: AT&T is organized into two divisions, AT&T Communications and AT&T Technologies.
1991: AT&T acquires NCR Corporation, a computer maker, in a $7.4 billion transaction.
1993: AT&T enters the cellular telephone business with the $12.8 billion acquisition of McCaw Cellular Communications.
1995: AT&T announces it is splitting into three companies, AT&T Corporation, Lucent Technologies, and NCR Corporation.
1999: AT&T acquires cable television giant, Tele-Communications Inc., in a $53.5 billion deal.
1999: AT&T outbids Comcast and Microsoft to acquire MediaOne Inc., making the company the nation's largest operator of cable television.
2001: Comcast acquires AT&T Broadband for $72 billion.
2004: AT&T Wireless is sold for $41 billion to Cingular Wireless.

confidence in the company. He also dramatically increased research and development, hiring talented young scientists and laying the foundation for what would, in 1925, become Bell Labs. Vail concentrated the company's visionaries into central management and left day-to-day network decisions to workers more interested in practical questions. For its first two decades, AT&T had put profits for its shareholders above service for its customers; Vail was one of the first U.S. business leaders to balance profit with customer satisfaction.

At the same time, Vail was a monopolist, believing competition had no place in the telephone industry. He and Morgan set out to make AT&T the sole supplier of U.S. telecommunications services. In 1910, Vail became president of Western Union after AT&T bought 30 percent of Western's stock. For the first time telegrams could be sent and delivered by phone. Telephone and telegraph lines could back each other up in emergencies. AT&T gobbled up independent phone companies at an ever-increasing rate. When Morgan found an independent in financial trouble, he used his power as a leading banker to squeeze its credit, often forcing it to sell to AT&T. By 1911, AT&T had bought so many small independents that Vail consolidated them into a smaller number of state and regional companies. AT&T's ownership was motivated partly by profit but also by the desire to ensure good service.

Antimonopoly pressures from consumers and government began to mount on AT&T well before then. A crucial turning point came in 1913, after Morgan's death, when Vail decided to sell Western Union and allow independents access to AT&T's long-distance lines. The move cost $10 million and ended AT&T's dream of a national telecommunications monopoly, but it won AT&T respect and ended growing pressure to dismember it.

Coast-to-Coast Long-Distance Achieved in 1915

By that time, AT&T was working on the first coast-to-coast telephone line, using loading coils and repeaters. On January 25, 1915, Alexander Graham Bell, in New York, and former collaborator, Thomas Watson, in San Francisco, engaged in a coast-to-coast repeat of the first-ever telephone conversation 39 years earlier. AT&T was also making important progress in automatic switching systems and sent the first transatlantic radio message in 1915. As the telephone became a matter of national interest, pressure for federal regulation mounted, and Vail welcomed it as long as regulators were independent.

During World War I, the AT&T network was used for domestic military communications. AT&T also set up extensive radio and telephone communications lines in France. The war pushed AT&T's resources to the limit, with a $118 million construction budget for 1917. In 1918, a year in which AT&T had ten million phones in service, the U.S. government took over the telephone system. The government set rates and put AT&T under a branch of the post office, although the company continued to be run by its board of directors. One of the government's first decisions was to start a service connection charge. It then raised both local and long-distance rates. Lower rates had been touted as a major benefit of public ownership. When the rates went up, support for government ownership collapsed, and in August 1919 the government gave up its control of AT&T. Vail retired in the same year, leaving the presidency to Harry Bates Thayer, and died in 1920.

AT&T grew rapidly as a regulated monopoly during the laissez-faire 1920s. The Graham Act of 1921 exempted telephony from the Sherman Antitrust Act. The Bell System controlled 64 percent of almost 14 million telephones in the United States in 1921. Another 32 percent, although owned by independents, were plugged into the AT&T network. Commercial radio boomed, and AT&T entered cross-licensing patent agreements with General Electric, Westinghouse, and Radio Corporation of America, with which it was soon embroiled in legal disputes. By the end of 1925, AT&T had a national network of 17 radio stations. AT&T put its first submarine cable into service between Key West, Florida, and Havana, Cuba, in 1921. In 1925, Bell Labs became a separate company, jointly funded by AT&T and Western Electric. The same year, Thayer retired and was succeeded by Walter S. Gifford, who served for the next 23 years. His influence on the U.S. telephone industry was second only to Vail's.

Gifford quickly got AT&T out of radio and other side ventures, although it tried to establish a controlling interest in motion picture sound technology in the late 1920s. He reduced the fee licensees paid from the 4.5 percent of gross revenue established in 1902, to 4 percent in 1926, and 2 percent in 1928. AT&T stockholders grew from 250,000 in 1922 to nearly 500,000 in 1929. In 1929, Bell Labs gave the first U.S. demonstration of color television. By 1932, AT&T had the second largest financial interest in the film industry but sold it in 1936.

The first years of the Great Depression badly hurt AT&T. Many subscribers could no longer afford telephones. AT&T sales for 1929 were $1.05 billion; by 1933, they were $853 million. Western Electric sales in 1929 were $411 million; 1933 sales were $70 million. Western Electric laid off 80 percent of its employees, and AT&T laid off 20 percent.

By 1933, telephone use began growing again, and by 1937 it exceeded pre-Depression levels. During the late 1930s, the newly formed Federal Communications Commission (FCC) conducted a long, damaging investigation of AT&T's competitive practices that reopened the battle over AT&T as a monopoly. In 1939, AT&T had assets of $5 billion, by far the largest amount of capital ever controlled by a corporation up to that time. It controlled 83 percent of all U.S. telephones and 98 percent of long-distance wires. Subsidiary Western Electric manufactured 90 percent of all U.S. telephone equipment. The FCC's final report was initially ignored due to the outbreak of World War II but had significant impact later.

Growth During World War II

Telephone use, particularly long distance, grew tremendously during World War II, with 1.4 million new telephones installed in 1941 alone. Western Electric and Bell Labs devoted themselves primarily to military work from 1942 to 1945, filling thousands of government contracts and making technological innovations. The most important work was in radar, the experience that gave AT&T a huge lead when microwave radio relay became the principal means of transmitting long-distance telephone and television signals in the postwar period.

The FCC forced AT&T to lower rates during the war, and its plants and infrastructure were worn out by wartime production. AT&T's business boomed after the war, as population and prosperity increased, and the habit of long-distance telephoning acquired during the war continued. The company installed more than three million telephones in 1946. Benefits of wartime technology were many. Moving vehicles were brought into the telephone system by radio in 1946. Coaxial cable was first used to take television signals over long distances in 1946. Microwave radio began transmitting long-distance calls in 1947. Bell Labs brought out the transistor, a replacement for the vacuum tube and one of the important inventions of the 20th century, in 1948; its inventors won the Nobel Prize in 1956.

The end of the war brought serious labor trouble. AT&T and the National Federation of Telephone Workers faced off over wages, working conditions, and benefits, producing a nationwide strike in 1947. Public opinion went against the strikers, and the eventual compromise favored AT&T.

Gifford retired in 1948, and Leroy A. Wilson became president. His first task was to push a rate increase past government regulators. He got one in 1949 that helped AT&T sell more stock to raise needed capital. As an outgrowth of the 1930s FCC investigation, the U.S. Department of Justice filed suit in 1949, seeking to split Western Electric from AT&T. AT&T succeeded in delaying the case until the Eisenhower administration, which was not as interested in regulation, took power. In the meantime, the government talked Western Electric into taking over the management of an advanced weapons research laboratory. It formed Sandia Corp. in 1949 to do so. In the 1950s, Western Electric worked on the Nike antiaircraft missiles, making $112.5 million on the venture. Western and Bell Labs worked with others on a huge air-defense radar system. These defense projects gave AT&T a powerful lever against the antitrust suit. In a consent decree in 1956, AT&T agreed to limit its business to providing common-carrier services and to limit Western Electric's to providing equipment for the Bell System, except for government contracts. The antitrust case was settled on this basis.

In 1951, Wilson died and Cleo Craig became president. In the next few years, AT&T made it possible to dial directly to other cities without using an operator. This and ensuing developments enabled long-distance charges to be repeatedly reduced. In 1955, AT&T laid the first transatlantic telephone cable, jointly owned with the British Post Office and the Canadian Overseas Telecommunications Corporation. Craig retired in 1956, and Frederick R. Kappel became president.

AT&T was in enviable financial shape by the late 1950s, although some accused it of getting there by overcharging subscribers. The booming U.S. economy led to unprecedented calling volumes, particularly from teenagers, many of whom were getting their own telephones. Telephones moved from shared party lines to private lines, and telephone services like weather and time announcements became widespread, adding further revenue. AT&T split its stock three-for-one in 1959 and two-for-one in 1964. By 1966, AT&T had three million stockholders and nearly one million employees. In 1954, AT&T began offering telephones in colors other than black. In 1961, it developed Centrex, a system in which an office maintained its own automatic switching exchange; in 1963, it offered the first Touch-Tone service; and in 1968, it brought out the Trimline phone, with the dial built into the handset. By 1965, the Bell System served 85 percent of all households in the areas in which it operated, compared with 50 percent in 1945, and was providing a vast array of services at a variety of rates.

Expanding into Space: Bellcom and Telstar

AT&T formed Bellcom to supply most of the communications and guidance systems for the U.S. space program from 1958 to 1969. Bell Labs worked intensively on satellite communications, and the first AT&T satellite, Telstar, was launched in 1962. Comsat, a half-public, half-private company handling U.S. satellite communications, was founded in 1962, with AT&T owning 27.5 percent at a cost of $58 million.

AT&T worked on an electronic switching system throughout the 1950s and 1960s. The project was more complicated than expected, and by the time the first electronic equipment was installed in 1965, AT&T had spent about $500 million on the project. The speed and automation that electronic switches gave the phone system, however, made possible the vast increases in traffic volume in the 1970s and 1980s, as the United States moved to an information-based society.

In the 1950s and 1960s, other companies began trying to capture specific portions of AT&T's business. The Hush-a-Phone Company marketed a plastic telephone attachment that reduced background noise. Microwave Communications Inc. (MCI) tried to establish private-line service between Chicago and St. Louis. Carter Electronics Corporation marketed a device that connected two-way radios with the telephone system. AT&T responded by forbidding the connection of competitors' equipment to the Bell System. Several FCC investigations followed, with decisions that created competition for terminal equipment and intercity private-line service. AT&T began to face serious competition for the first time in 50 years.

Kappel retired in 1967 and was replaced by H.I. Romnes, a former president of Western Electric. AT&T's earnings were leveling off after tremendous growth in the early 1960s. There also were service problems in 1969 and 1970, with numerous consumer complaints in New York. Similar predicaments followed in Boston, Denver, and Houston. AT&T borrowed money and raised rates to pay for repairs.

More serious problems were beginning for AT&T. In the early 1970s, sales by the interconnect industry were growing, and businesses were buying telephone equipment from AT&T competitors. The U.S. Equal Employment Opportunity Commission accused AT&T of discriminating against women and minorities. AT&T, without admitting it had done so, signed consent decrees under which it agreed to increase the hiring, promotion, and salaries of women and minorities.

MCI claimed AT&T was still preventing it from competing and filed an antitrust lawsuit in 1974. The situation became disastrous when the Department of Justice (DOJ) filed another antitrust suit later in 1974, this time asking for the dismemberment of AT&T. The DOJ charged that AT&T had used its dominant position to suppress competition. The suit dragged on for years.

During the years of the suit, AT&T continued to grow. Both 1980 and 1981 were years of record profits. The $6.9 billion AT&T made in 1981 was the highest profit for any company to that time.

The Breakup of the Bell System in the 1980s

The DOJ suit finally came to trial in 1981. By then, AT&T and the government both wanted to settle the case. AT&T longed to get into computers and information services but was prevented from doing so by its 1956 agreement. In 1982, the FCC required AT&T to set up a separate, unregulated subsidiary called American Bell to sell equipment and enhanced services. In January 1982, AT&T and the DOJ jointly announced a deal to break up the Bell System, while freeing the remainder of AT&T to compete in non-long-distance areas such as computers.

Federal Judge Harold Greene gave final approval for the AT&T breakup in August 1983. At that time, AT&T was the largest corporation in the world; its $155 billion in assets made it larger than General Motors, Mobil, and Exxon combined. After the breakup, on January 1, 1984, AT&T had $34 billion in assets. Its net income dropped from $7.1 billion to $2.1 billion, and its workforce from 1.09 million to 385,000. Its 22 regional operating companies were split off into seven regional holding companies, and AT&T lost the right to use the Bell name. AT&T stockholders received one share in each of the regional companies for every ten AT&T shares they owned. AT&T also lost the highly profitable Yellow Pages, which went to the regional companies.

The new AT&T consisted of two primary parts: AT&T Communications, the long-distance business, and AT&T Technologies, a group of other businesses that mainly involved the manufacture and sale of telecommunications equipment for consumers and businesses. Western Electric was broken up and folded into AT&T Technologies. Long distance was expected to provide the bulk of short-term revenue for the new AT&T, but the unregulated technologies group, backed by Bell Labs, was expected to quickly blossom. AT&T Technologies initially concentrated on switching and transmissions systems for telephone companies. AT&T was losing ground to competitors in that sector and wanted to fight back. The company also worked on telephone-equipment sales, sold through AT&T phone centers and such retailers as Sears. American Bell changed its name to AT&T Information Systems and began pushing computers. AT&T International quickly signed a deal with the Dutch company N.V. Philips to sell switching equipment throughout the world, setting up AT&T Network Systems International.

To help pay for the breakup, AT&T took a fourth-quarter charge of $5.2 billion in 1984, the largest to that time. AT&T, however, was now free to go into computers, a field it had longed to get into since the 1956 consent decree, and the company began spending hundreds of millions of dollars to develop and market a line of computers. James E. Olson became president of AT&T in 1985, cutting 24,000 jobs from the information division later that year to improve its profits. In 1986, Olson became chairman, and Robert E. Allen became president. Olson concentrated on centralizing management and refocusing company strategy around the idea of managing the flow of information.

The company chose Brussels, Belgium, as the site for its regional headquarters serving Europe, the Middle East, and Africa. It also began joint ventures with companies in Spain, Italy, Ireland, Denmark, South Korea, and Taiwan to get its telecommunications products into foreign markets. Still, foreign revenues accounted for only 10 percent of company earnings, compared with 40 percent for many other U.S.-based multinationals. Company earnings declined because of a slumping business equipment market and greater than expected reorganization costs. Earnings also suffered from a drop in rental revenues as more AT&T customers decided to buy their telecommunications equipment outright.

Meanwhile AT&T's computer operations were in trouble. The company had developed a new operating system, Unix, for its computers. While Unix had some advantages, users of personal computers were not familiar with it, manufacturers of larger computers were committed to their own proprietary systems, and buyers stayed away. AT&T computer operations lost $1.2 billion in 1986 alone. At the end of the year, the company restructured its computer operations to concentrate on telecommunications-based computers and computer systems. It custom designed a system for American Express that automatically phoned customers while putting customer information on a terminal screen. At the end of 1986, AT&T cut another 27,400 jobs and took a $3.2 billion charge. Income for the year was only $139 million.

In 1987, the DOJ recommended that the regional operating companies be allowed to compete with AT&T in long distance and telecommunications equipment manufacturing—its two core businesses. The idea was unacceptable to Judge Harold Greene, overseer of the AT&T breakup. Because of fierce competition from MCI and other companies, AT&T retained 76 percent of the long-distance market, down from 91 percent in 1983.

Unix made some gains in 1986 and 1987, and AT&T formed the Archer Group, a consortium of computer makers manufacturing Unix systems. It included Unisys and Sun Microsystems. After nearly $2 billion in losses in computers, the data systems group finally signed a major contract with the U.S. Air Force in 1988. The $929 million contract for minicomputers provided only a slim profit margin, but AT&T hoped that the deal would push its computers over the top, make Unix an industry standard, and lead to further government sales. Olson died in 1988, and Allen became chairman.

More Changes in the Late 1980s

MCI and others continued to erode AT&T's share of the $50 billion long-distance market, which stood at 68 percent at the end of 1988. To fight back, AT&T redeployed 2,500 employees to sales positions and aggressively tackled the business communications market. AT&T also took a $6.7 billion charge to modernize its telephone network and cut 16,000 positions. As a result, the company lost $1.7 billion in 1988, its first-ever yearly loss. Some industry analysts, however, felt the company was finally turning around after four years of confusion and drift. It won two major government contracts that year. One, expected to earn AT&T $15 billion by 1989, was to build a new government telephone system. Competitor US Sprint Communications won a $10 billion contract for a second part of the same system. Regulators finally gave AT&T the right to match the low prices of MCI and US Sprint, leading to the end of the long-distance price wars waged since the AT&T breakup. AT&T showed a $2.7 billion profit for 1989, its largest since the breakup.

In mid-1990, AT&T raised its long-distance rates after low second-quarter earnings. It had been hurt by declining long-distance revenue and slow equipment sales. The company, however, soon made several important sales. It received an extension of a $100 million personal computer sale to American Airlines's Sabre Travel Information Network and signed an agreement to upgrade China's international communications system. AT&T made its first entry into Mexico's communications market, winning a $130 million contract from Mexico's national telephone company, Telefonos de Mexico. It signed a $157 million contract to build an undersea fiber-optic cable between Hawaii and the U.S. mainland, and announced that it planned to build a high-capacity undersea cable between Germany and the United States, with Deutsche Bundespost Telekom. It also won a $600 million contract from GTE Corporation to build cellular network equipment.

Hoping to make money from its financial and information resources, AT&T launched a credit card, Universal Card, in early 1990. By late 1990, it was the eighth leading credit card in the United States, with revenue of $750 million. Wall Street analysts, however, expected the credit card's startup costs to hold back AT&T earnings until at least 1992. Bell Labs announced important breakthroughs in computer technology in 1990, including the world's first computer using light. Products based on the new technologies were years off, but AT&T continued to manufacture computers. AT&T signed an agreement with Japan's Mitsubishi Electric Corporation to share memory-chip technology, and licensed technology from Japan's NEC Corporation to make semiconductors. Late in the year, Philips, under financial pressure, sold back its 15 percent stake in AT&T Network Systems International.

In the early 1990s, AT&T's overseas ventures began bearing fruit. About 15 percent of its revenue, more than $5 billion yearly, came from international calling and sales to foreign buyers of equipment and services. In 1991, AT&T made a major acquisition in the computer industry, buying NCR Corporation through an exchange of stock valued at $7.4 billion. AT&T officials believed the purchase of NCR, which accounted for about 60 percent of its sales in international markets, would put AT&T on the path to becoming a truly global company and a leader in networked computing. NCR had introduced more new products than any other computer company in the preceding year. NCR officials saw advantages of the merger to be an increased customer base, access to the research and development capabilities of Bell Labs, and the addition of AT&T's technical, marketing, and sales resources.

AT&T's fortunes looked solid following the NCR acquisition. The company's stock price was climbing, and several of its previously sluggish operations posted their best earnings figures in years. One area in which AT&T needed market presence was cellular telephone service, even though the company was the largest manufacturer of cell phone system switching devices. In August 1993, the company acquired McCaw Cellular Communications for $12.8 billion in stock. The Kirkland, Washington-based McCaw operated one of the largest cellular systems in the United States, with coverage of one-third of the country.

Division into Three Companies in 1995

Despite these positive developments, AT&T was still having problems. NCR in particular was not earning its keep and lost $600 million in 1994. AT&T's long-distance service profits accounted for the bulk of the corporation's income, but competition was growing ever fiercer. On September 20, 1995, the company announced it was splitting up yet again, this time into three separate entities. The largest would be known as AT&T Corporation and consist primarily of the long distance businesses, AT&T Wireless, the Universal Credit Card, and AT&T Labs. The next largest would be Lucent Technologies, which would consist of the company's consumer and business products operations and Bell Labs. The smallest would be NCR Corporation, consisting more or less of what it had been when AT&T purchased it four years earlier. The breakup, the largest corporate restructuring in history, was accomplished by means of a spin-off of stock to AT&T shareholders. Some 40,000 of the company's employees were also expected to lose their jobs.

Other developments at this time included AT&T's first foray into the world of cyberspace, with the introduction of an array of business and home Internet access services. Also, in February 1996, Congress passed a new telecommunications act which ended monopolies for providers of local phone service. AT&T vowed to become a presence in the local service arena again, though this would entail leasing lines from the largely unfriendly Baby Bells.

In the months following the company's restructuring, corporate morale and investor confidence ebbed as AT&T's efforts to fine-tune the reconfiguration proceeded slowly. CEO Bob Allen, nearing his planned retirement date of January 1998, saw his chosen successor rejected by the board in mid-1997. Finally, on November 1, Hughes Electronics CEO C. Michael Armstrong was approved to take over the reins at AT&T, and Allen stepped down.

Armstrong quickly set about cutting fat and implementing new strategies. He sold the company's credit card unit to Citibank for $3.5 billion, and its communications outsourcing business to Cincinnati Bell for $625 million. He purchased Teleport Communications Group, a local exchange business-service carrier in New York and 65 other cities, for $11.3 billion. International efforts, always a weak point with AT&T, were boosted by the formation of a joint venture with British Telecom. Advertising expenses were cut for a second time in two years, and an additional 18,000 layoffs were announced. Armstrong's biggest move during his first year came in the summer of 1998, when he cut a deal to purchase cable television giant TCI for $53.5 billion in stock.

In October 1998, the company merged its Wireless Services division with Vanguard Cellular Systems, a Northeast U.S.-based cell phone company with 625,000 subscribers. AT&T also started its own "dial-around" service, Lucky Dog. A host of new competitors had emerged who were offering low residential long-distance rates via special 7-digit access numbers. The heavily advertised Lucky Dog was an attempt to tap into this market and was promoted with no mention of its corporate owner. In December, a deal worth $5 billion was reached to buy IBM's Global Network Internet access business, which was expected to provide a starting point for the joint venture with British Telecom.

Restructuring at the Turn of the 21st Century

Armstrong's first year performance was winning rave reviews, and he continued at full throttle in 1999 with the $60 billion acquisition of a second major cable provider, MediaOne. In a heated battle, AT&T had outbid both Comcast and Microsoft. As a sop to the latter, an agreement was reached to sell the computer giant $5 billion in AT&T stock and to use Microsoft products in the company's new cable boxes. Deals with Comcast and Time Warner also brought more cable subscribers to the company. Armstrong's vision for AT&T's future was to offer both telephone and Internet services through the newly acquired cable TV networks, taking advantage of the large data-transmission capacity they offered. This would eliminate the slow download speed experienced by Internet users who connected via telephone line and modem. Billions of dollars would have to be invested to retrofit cable systems for interactivity and telephone use for the plan to succeed.

One constant during AT&T's development was change, particularly during the latter half of the 20th century. As the company prepared for the 21st century, its inconstancy was true to form, as AT&T struggled to find a lasting identity for itself. In October 2000, a little more than two years after Armstrong hailed the beginning of new age for AT&T, the company announced plans to split into four separate companies. Armstrong's vision of using cable-TV networks to deliver broadband Internet access and local phone service to residential customers was abandoned, shelved in favor of creating four distinct businesses: AT&T Consumer, AT&T Business, AT&T Broadband, and AT&T Wireless. "The creation of these four companies," Armstrong remarked in a November 6, 2000 interview with *Business Week*, "is the foundation for a path to value creation. The journey hasn't been simple, but I believe it will be successful."

As the company entered a new decade, the process of stripping itself down to assume a new strategic stance began again, although not according to Armstrong's plan. Major facets of AT&T's business were divested, leaving the company focused on two business areas. In mid-2001, Comcast Corp. offered $40 billion for AT&T Broadband, eventually gaining the assets after it increased its bid to $72 billion at the end of 2001. In early 2004, Cingular Wireless and Vodafone Group launched a bidding war for AT&T Wireless, with Cingular's $41 billion cash offer emerging the winner. The deal was approved by AT&T shareholders in May 2004, leaving AT&T with two business segments, AT&T consumer services and AT&T business services.

By the end 2004, AT&T was preparing for the beginning of a new era. The company's residential telephone business, described by Armstrong in a November 8, 2000 interview with *Knight Ridder/Tribune Business News* as "in systemic decline," offered little opportunity for future growth. In July 2004, the company announced it would stop courting residential customers and instead focus its future on its business services segment. In the years ahead, AT&T planned on providing global voice and data communications services to clients ranging from small businesses to large multinational conglomerates, hoping its expertise in networking, Internet protocol (IP), and e-commerce services would provide a stable foundation for future growth.

Principal Subsidiaries

ACC Corporation; Alascom, Inc.; ATTCapital Holdings, Inc.; ATTCredit Holdings, Inc.; ATTCommunications, Inc.; ATTCommunications of California, Inc.; ATTCommunications of Delaware, LLC; ATTCommunications of Hawaii, Inc.; ATTCommunications of Illinois, Inc.; ATTCommunications of Indiana, Inc.; ATTCommunications of Maryland, LLC; ATTCommunications of Michigan, Inc.; ATTCommunications of the Midwest, Inc.; ATTCommunications of the Mountain States, Inc.; ATTCommunications of Nevada, Inc.; ATTCommunications of New England, Inc.; ATTCommunications of New Hampshire, Inc.; ATTNew Jersey Holdings, LLC; ATTCommunications of New York, Inc.; ATTCommunications of Ohio, Inc.; ATTCommunications of the Pacific Northwest, Inc.; ATTCommunications of Pennsylvania, LLC; ATTCommunications of the South Central States, LLC; ATTCommunications of the Southern States, LLC; ATTCommunications of the Southwest, Inc.; ATTCommunications of Virginia, LLC; ATTCommunications of Washington D.C., LLC; ATTCommunications of West Virginia, Inc.; ATTCommunications Holdings of Wisconsin, LLC.; ATTCommunications Services International Inc.;

ATTGlobal Communications Services Inc.; ATTCommunications Services of Jamaica LLC; ATTSolutions Inc.; ATTGlobal Network Services Group LLC; ATTof Puerto Rico, Inc.; ATTof the Virgin Islands, Inc.; Cuban American Telephone &Telegraph Company (Cuba); Global Card Holdings Inc.; Teleport Communications Group Inc.

Principal Operating Units

AT&T Business Services; AT&T Consumer Services.

Principal Competitors

MCI Inc.; Sprint Corporation; Verizon Communications Inc.

Further Reading

Anderson, Julia, ''Clark County, Wash., AT&T Broadband Subscribers to Become Customers of Comcast,'' *Knight Ridder/Tribune Business News*, December 5, 2002.

''AT&T: Breaking up Is Still Hard to Do,'' *Business Week*, November 6, 2000, p. 173.

Bonamici, Kate, ''Bells and Whistles,'' *Fortune*, April 19, 2004, p. 146.

Brooks, John, *Telephone: The First Hundred Years*, New York: Harper and Row, 1976.

Evans, David S., ed., *Breaking Up Bell: Essays on Industrial Organization and Regulation*, New York: Elsevier Science Publishing Co., 1983.

Faletra, Robert, ''What Is AT&T Thinking with Its Dramatic Shift in Channels,'' *Computer Reseller News*, October 18, 2004, p. 94.

Finneran, Michael, ''The AT&T Breakup: A New Model for a Global Telecom Colossus,'' *Business Communications Review*, November 1995, pp. 78–9.

Goldblatt, Henry, ''AT&T Finally Has an Operator,'' *Fortune*, February 16, 1998, pp. 79–80.

Greenfield, Karl Taro, ''Ma Everything!,'' *Time*, May 17, 1999, pp. 58–60.

Greenwald, John, ''AT&T's Power Shake,'' *Time*, July 6, 1998, pp. 76–8.

Howe, Peter J., ''AT&T Chairman Addresses Boston Audience on Future of Company,'' *Knight Ridder/Tribune Business News*, November 8, 2000.

Kirkpatrick, David, ''Could AT&T Rule the World?,'' *Fortune*, May 17, 1993, p. 54.

——, ''AT&T Has the Plan,'' *Fortune*, October 16, 1995, pp. 84–6.

Kosseff, Jeffrey, ''Comcast, AT&T Merger Will Alter 2 Million E-Mail Addresses,'' *Knight Ridder/Tribune Business News*, December 4, 2002.

Kupfer, Andrew, ''AT&T's $12 Billion Cellular Dream,'' *Fortune*, December 12, 1994, p. 100.

——, ''AT&T: Ready to Run, Nowhere to Hide,'' *Fortune*, April 29, 1996, pp. 116–18.

——, ''AT&T Gets Lucky,'' *Fortune*, November 9, 1998, pp. 108–10.

Loomis, Carol J., ''AT&T Has No Clothes,'' *Fortune*, February 5, 1996, pp. 78–80.

Mehta, Stephanie N., ''Great Balls of Fire,'' *Fortune,* November 13, 2000, p. 44.

——, ''The New AT&T: Not Quite Its Old Self,'' *Fortune*, July 12, 2004, p. 34.

McCarroll, Thomas, ''How AT&T Plans to Reach out and Touch Everyone,'' *Time*, July 5, 1993, p. 44.

Scheisel, Seth, ''AT&T Conjures up Its Vision for Cable, But Can It Deliver?,'' *New York Times*, May 7, 1999, p. 1C.

Sims, Calvin, ''AT&T's New Call to Arms,'' *New York Times*, January 22, 1989.

Slutsker, Gary, ''The Tortoise and the Hare,'' *Forbes*, February 1, 1993, p. 66.

Snyder, Beth, ''AT&T Joins Wave of Marketers Hiding IDs Behind New Brands: Lucky Dog Dial-Around Service Aims for Value-Conscious Crowd,'' *Advertising Age*, November 2, 1998, p. 17.

Trager, Louis, ''AT&T Sticks to Consumer Path,'' *Interactive Week Online*, May 3, 1999.

Villano, Matt, ''Who Ya Gonna Call?,'' *Computer Reseller News*, November 1, 2004, p. 80.

Waserman, Todd, ''AT&T: We're All About Business Now,'' *Brandweek*, August 9, 2004, p. 4.

—Scott M. Lewis
—updates: Frank Uhle; Jeffrey L. Covell

Barr Pharmaceuticals, Inc.

2 Quaker Road
Pomona, New York 10970
U.S.A.
Telephone: (845) 362-1100
Toll Free: (800) 227-7522
Fax: (914) 362-2774
Web site: http://www.barrlabs.com

Public Company
Incorporated: 1970 as Barr Laboratories, Inc.
Employees: 1,400
Sales: $902.9 million (2004)
Stock Exchanges: New York
Ticker Symbol: BRL
NAIC: 32541 Pharmaceutical and Medicine Manufacturing; 325411 Medicinal and Botanical Manufacturing; 325412 Pharmaceutical Preparation Manufacturing

A fast-growing generic drug company, Barr Pharmaceuticals, Inc., develops, manufactures, and markets generic and proprietary pharmaceuticals. The heart of the company and its original focus was on the generic side, a fast-growing segment of the general pharmaceutical industry in which Barr was one of the early pioneers. The company earned notoriety during the late 1980s, when its founder testified before a congressional committee about bribes between generic drug producers and U.S. Food & Drug Administration officials. Barr began to realize phenomenal financial growth during the 1990s, when the U.S. generic pharmaceutical industry grew from a $4-billion-a-year business to an $11-billion-a-year business. By targeting drugs it considered to be covered by weak patents, Barr scored major successes, such as the right to distribute the cancer drug tamoxifen citrate, which accounted for roughly 75 percent of the company's sales during most of the 1990s. During the late 1990s the company's product line was focused on several therapeutic categories, including anti-infectives, cardiovascular agents, hormonal agents, analgesics, oncology, and psychotherapeutic products. At manufacturing facilities in New York, New Jersey, and Virginia, Barr produced more than 60 drug products, including proprietary pharmaceuticals, which the company began manufacturing in 1998.

Industry and Company Origins

Barr was founded in 1970 as a generic pharmaceutical concern based in New York. At the time of the company's formation, the generic drug industry was in its infancy, having first gained legitimacy as a business during the mid-1960s. The catalyst for the industry's emergence was the Drug Efficacy Study Implementation (DESI) program conducted by the National Research Council of the National Academy of Sciences in 1962, which evaluated all drugs that had been approved for use prior to 1962. The DESI evaluation reviewed more than 3,000 products, determining which products were effective and which were ineffective. Those products that gained the DESI stamp of approval paved the way for a new breed of drug makers: generic manufacturers. With a list of products deemed effective by the National Research Council, generic drug companies could manufacture a product according to the prescribed chemical formula and mark the product without additional study, eliminating the need for the costly and time-consuming biostudies conducted by proprietary drug makers. Barr, founded by Edwin A. Cohen and a partner, became one of the early contenders in the generic drug industry when it introduced its first product in 1972.

Initially, Barr concentrated on making antibiotic products, manufacturing generic drugs primarily for other pharmaceutical companies, such as Lederle Standard Products. For more than a decade Barr remained a small enterprise without the ability to realize much financial growth. The restraints on the company's growth stemmed from the immaturity of its industry, which had sprung to life in the wake of the DESI program but retained its fledgling characteristics until the mid-1980s. The turning point in the generic drug industry's evolution occurred when the Drug Price Competition and Patent Restoration Act was promulgated in 1984. Also referred to as the Waxman-Hatch Act, the legislation allowed the production of generic versions of all pharmaceutical products approved after 1962, provided the generic manufacturer could prove the generic version was equivalent to the branded version. The ruling ignited the generic drug industry's growth, ushering in a new era of frenetic expansion and

Company Perspectives:

The people of Barr Laboratories are focused on being first-to-market with quality, off-patent pharmaceuticals in specific therapeutic categories that generate sustainable profitability. Our confidence in our ability to achieve success is based on the skill and dedication of our employees and their commitment to excellence in science, manufacturing and customer satisfaction.

signaling what observers regarded as the beginning of the modern generic pharmaceutical industry. In the first year following the approval of the Waxman-Hatch Act, more than 1,000 applications for new generic drugs were received by the U.S. Food & Drug Administration (FDA), as scores of new generic producers scurried to secure the decisive rights to be the first to market generic equivalents of branded pharmaceuticals. For an industry long held in check, however, the forces that unleashed its potential nearly caused its ruin. Scandal, bribery, and a litany of criminal accusations followed the passage of the Waxman-Hatch Act, staining the image of generic drug producers and the FDA. At the center of the maelstrom of controversy were Barr and its founder, Edwin Cohen.

Crime and Punishment in the Late 1980s

Much of a generic drug producer's success depended on being "first to market," a race that began with the submission of detailed information to the FDA concerning the bioequivalence of a generic alternative, that is, providing proof that the generic drug had the same therapeutic effects as the branded version. Once FDA approval was obtained, a generic producer could introduce its generic alternative into the market, but in the wake of the Waxman-Hatch Act many began to question the FDA approval process, particularly Cohen. Cohen approached the FDA in 1987 and 1988, accusing the agency of favoring his competitors, complaining that other generic producers were securing approval while his applications languished on the desks of FDA officials. Part of Cohen's frustration stemmed from Barr's attempts to market its generic version of erythromycin estolate, an antibiotic. Barr submitted an application for the antibiotic in January 1987 and a short time later the FDA agreed that the company's drug was bioequivalent, but numerous delays followed. By the end of 1987 Cohen still had not received approval for the antibiotic, so he complained to the FDA. By the end of 1988 approval still had not arrived, prompting Cohen to voice his complaints again. The FDA never responded to Cohen's accusations, but in mid-1989 Cohen found someone who would listen. In May 1989 the House Subcommittee on Oversight asked Cohen to testify against the FDA during its investigation of the generic drug industry.

Cohen testified before the congressional committee that FDA officials were accepting bribes from generic drug producers to quicken the approval process. Because of the committee's nearly three-year investigation, more than 40 FDA employees and company executives pleaded guilty to or were convicted of fraud or corruption charges. Of the 52 generic drug producers examined during the investigation, only five, including Barr, were not implicated in the scandal. Although Cohen had helped expose rampant corruption, his triumph did not benefit Barr—if anything, it exacerbated relations with the FDA. By early 1990 Barr still had not received approval for its generic version of erythromycin estolate. Cohen believed the delays were retribution for his testimony in front of the congressional subcommittee and his complaints against the FDA, so he filed a lawsuit against the agency. The antibiotic at last was granted approval in October 1990, nearly four years after the application was submitted, but the end of the long wait did not mark the end of Barr's problems with the FDA. After failing to force Barr to suspend manufacturing and distribution pending the resolution of certain regulatory disputes, the FDA put Barr on its "alert list" of pharmaceutical manufacturers who did not conform to FDA standards. Barr filed another lawsuit in April 1992, contending that its inclusion on the alert list was preventing the company from winning approval on roughly 90 new drugs. Two months later the FDA dropped Barr from its alert list.

There was ample cause for Cohen and other Barr officials to eliminate any impediments to new product introduction as the 1990s began. At stake were billions of dollars of business, business to be won by those generic producers who could identify prime pharmaceutical drugs to produce and then move expeditiously through the FDA approval process. Between 1991 and 1996, patents were to expire on a host of prescription drugs whose aggregate value was estimated at $10 billion in sales. At the time this potentially lucrative five-year period was set to begin, the U.S. generic drug industry was a $4-billion-a-year business and Barr was a $70-million-in-sales company; both were poised for prolific growth. Barr's first major victory during this period was its challenge on the patent for tamoxifen citrate, a breast cancer treatment that became the financial foundation upon which the company rested. Tamoxifen, which Barr distributed but did not produce, accounted for three-quarters of the company's sales during the 1990s and represented an early sign of the company's willingness to dispute the patents of large drug companies. As Barr moved forward during the generic drug industry's decade of opportunity, it focused on drugs that were hard to copy in order to reduce competition and, more notoriously, it earned a reputation for challenging what it considered weak patents. Aggressive and persistent, Barr displayed no reluctance to avoid fiercely contested legal disputes, even on the heels of its fractious battle with the FDA.

Energetic Growth During the 1990s

Beginning in 1993 Barr recorded a five-year period during which annual sales increased an average of 35 percent per year. Much of this growth rested on the shoulders of tamoxifen, which contributed roughly 75 percent of the company's total sales during the period, but the financial success also was attributable to Barr's progress with other drugs, progress achieved after butting heads with some of the country's biggest drug makers. To lead the company forward during this volatile period was Bruce L. Downey, who became Barr's president, chief operating officer, and a member of the company's board of directors in January 1993. Cohen relinquished his title of chief executive officer in early 1994 and was replaced by Downey in February 1994. In Downey, Barr gained a leader well equipped to handle the litigious future it faced. A former

Key Dates:

1970: Barr is founded in New York.
1972: The company introduces its first generic drug.
1994: Bruce Downey is named CEO of Barr and heads up the company during the ensuing period of litigation with the FDA.
2003: Barr Labs is reincorporated, becoming a subsidiary of the Pharmaceuticals holding company.

partner in the law firm of Winston & Strawn, Downey had served as the lead attorney during Barr's legal battle with the FDA, which would serve him well as Barr pursued its strategy of challenging the patents of larger drug companies.

After smoothing over relations with the FDA in 1995, Barr earned FDA approval to sell a generic version of the AIDS drug AZT. Before the company could market its product, however, it had to win court approval to overturn existing patents, held by Glaxo Wellcome. The legal battle over Barr's generic AZT was just one of several ongoing patent challenges that Downey directed during the middle and late 1990s, including the company's 1996 challenge of the patent held by Eli Lilly for Prozac, which collected $6 million in sales daily. Meanwhile, as Barr contested various patents in the courtroom, its success outside the courtroom was solid. Financially, the company had suffered during its long dispute with the FDA, entering the 1990s with $70 million in annual sales and watching that total drop to $58 million by 1993. From 1993 forward, however, sales climbed robustly, swelling to $109 million in 1994, $199 million in 1995, and $232 million by 1996. With managed care organizations growing in number and prominence amid escalating health care costs, generic drugs were becoming more sought after than ever before. Evidence of this rise in demand was illustrated at Barr in 1996 when the company purchased a 65,000-square-foot manufacturing facility in Forest, Virginia, to complement its existing facilities in Pomona, New York, and Northvale, New Jersey.

Downey led the company's charge against DuPont Merck Pharmaceutical Company, which petitioned the FDA in September 1996 for a stay of action against Barr's warfarin sodium, an anti-coagulation agent that was the generic equivalent of DuPont Merck's Coumadin. DuPont Merck fought a state-by-state battle to prohibit the distribution of Barr's generic version of Coumadin, trying to keep the $500 million in sales it collected from Coumadin to itself. Barr received FDA approval in March 1997 and began shipping its warfarin sodium tablets in July 1997, accumulating $15 million in sales during the first month, as DuPont Merck's attempts to stop distribution continued into 1998.

Thanks to its encouraging sales growth, Barr entered 1997 ranked as one of the top ten generic drug makers in the country. Its role as an industry whistle-blower had weakened its stock performance during the late 1980s and early 1990s, but by the late 1990s the company was drawing praise from Wall Street. One stock analyst noted: ''Not every company can do well if the industry is doing well. Barr is a major turnaround company in the industry. They went through some tough times, but have since turned around . . . Barr is getting a reputation of being aggressive in litigation and patent challenging. Barr is willing to take on Goliath.''

Taking on larger pharmaceutical companies continued to be a major focus of the company's strategy as it competed in the late 1990s, but in 1997 it added another facet to its operations by launching a proprietary pharmaceutical development program. Research and development spending increased as a result, jumping 54 percent in 1997 to $10.4 million and another 40 percent in 1998 to $19 million. ''R&D [research and development] spending is the future,'' Downey declared, ''and the last thing we'd cut. It leads to the most earnings and in the fastest way.'' Less than 18 months after launching its proprietary development program, Barr introduced its first product, a contraceptive codeveloped with Gynetics, Inc. Approved by the FDA in September 1998, the product was the PREVEN Emergency Contraceptive Kit, which contained an information booklet, a pregnancy test, and four high-dosage birth control pills. According to the partnership agreement between the two companies, Barr manufactured the pills and Gynetics marketed the product, billing it as a postcoital ''morning-after'' product, the first FDA-approved product specifically designed for such use.

Aside from celebrating its first success in proprietary drug development, Barr officials could point to other favorable developments that suggested a bright future for the company. Financially, Barr was performing admirably, registering a 68 percent increase in net earnings in 1998 to $32.7 million and a 33 percent increase in revenues to $377.3 million, more than six times the total collected five years earlier. With a number of potentially lucrative generic products expected to be introduced once approval was granted, Barr's generic business was as strong as ever, while its new proprietary business, which had four proprietary products in various stages of development in late 1998, provided a promising avenue for future growth. Downey was overjoyed by Barr's success, declaring, ''By all measures, 1998 represents the most successful year in our company's history.''

The 2000s and Beyond

Barr set its sites on acquiring patents for Prozac in 1999, filing suit to gain the mechanism of action patent as well as the use patent, but were defeated in court. The Warfarin legal struggle, however, was settled in Barr's favor, and the company moved forward with its plan to carry the nine different varieties of Warfarin developed by Du Pont Pharmaceuticals. They also won the right to manufacture the drug Tamoxifen when its patent expired in 2002, with market exclusivity for a 180 day period. By year's end Barr had won approval from the FDA to market the generic version of Bristol-Myers Squibb Company's Duricef Capsules, and had received excellent news from the Florida State legislature, who had unanimously approved the use of generic drugs in place of brand-name products, so long as the generics had FDA approval.

Even better news came with January 2000. Drug maker DuPont and Barr announced a termination of their continuing feud over Warfarin and declared an alliance to create and market new drugs. DuPont planned to invest 45 million dollars into a trio of proprietary Barr drugs in exchange for royalties from the products and a share of Barr stock. Things did not remain as rosy in the stock market though. While Barr won the right to manufacture a generic form of Prozac and market it exclusively for 180 days, their stock plummeted some 16 percent in March 2001 when it was announced that a special extension awarded Eli Lilly would be permitted by the FDA to overlap Barr's 180 day exclusivity.

Better news came soon, though, with the release of the joint venture with DuPont to market Trexall, a drug designed to aid rheumatoid arthritis and other ailments. April brought news of the FDA's approval for Barr to market a generic form of the oral contraceptive Ortho Novum. By June 2001 *Business Week* could truthfully report that Barr remained a "hot company," citing its stock prices, which had risen 189 percent above its numbers in 1999. Certainly growth seemed to be in its future, for later in June Barr Laboratories announced that it would be acquiring rival drug firm Duramed Pharmaceuticals Inc. for a $571 million stock swap. This fell in line with CEO Bruce Downey's plans to aim Barr toward branded drugs rather than focusing solely upon generics, an often unpredictable industry. His strategy certainly seemed to pay off: by the third quarter of 2002 company earnings had risen 64 percent. Propelled by its generic version of Prozac, the company achieved its most successful financial investments yet by the fourth quarter of 2002.

In February 2003 Barr made plans to relocate its executive offices to another facility in Bergen County New Jersey. Moreover, the company was reorganized, making Barr Labs a wholly owned subsidiary of the new holding company Barr Pharmaceuticals. Throughout 2003 Barr steadily gained approval for and launched new generic versions of other drugs, among them Accutane, an drug for treating severe acne, Loestrin, an oral contraceptive, Niaspan 1,000 mg extended-release tablets, and the so-called "morning-after pill" Plan B. By December 2003, after another year with strong financial gains, Barr moved to acquire Endeavor Pharmaceuticals Inc. Endeavor was the developer of the synthetic estrogen product Enjuvia. Things were little different in 2004—Barr continued to seek approval for generic versions of drugs from the FDA. Often legal action was required to obtain a patent, and sometimes Barr was challenged but the company remained very competitive and financially sound.

Principal Subsidiaries

Barr Laboratories Inc.; Duramed Research Inc.

Principal Competitors

Watson Pharmaceuticals Inc.; Johnson & Johnson; Wyeth; Mylan Laboratories Inc.

Further Reading

"Barr Laboratories, Inc.," *Insiders' Chronicle,* June 1, 1992, p. 3.

"Barr Laboratories Reports Record Fiscal 1998 EPS of $1.45 Revenues Climb to $377 Million; Net Earnings Jump to $32.7 Million," *PR Newswire,* August 20, 1998, p. 82.

"Barr's First Proprietary Product Receives FDA Approval; Contraceptive Product Co-Developed with Gynetics, Inc.," *PR Newswire,* September 2, 1998, p. 9.

Carrell, Steve, "Firestorm Erupting over Generic Warfarin Release," *Drug Topics,* November 4, 1996, p. 35.

Fleming, Harris, Jr., "Warfarin Vs. Coumadin: Managed Care Joins Battle," *Drug Topics,* November 3, 1997, p. 63.

"Generic Drug Battle Wins Round on List," *Chemical Marketing Reporter,* June 22, 1992, p. 3.

"Indiana Becomes Latest Battleground over a Lucrative Anti-Coagulant Product," *Knight-Ridder/Tribune Business News,* January 20, 1998, p. 12.

Lavelle, Louis, "FDA Approves New Jersey Firm's Morning-After Birth Control Pill," *Knight-Ridder/Tribune Business News,* September 4, 1998, p. 2.

Malone, Bridget, "Generic Drug Firm Offers 'No-Frills' Alternative," *Knight-Ridder/Tribune Business News,* January 2, 1997, p. 10.

Sawaya, Zina, "Getting Even," *Forbes,* April 29, 1991, p. 92.

Zoeller, Janice, "Barr Reissues Warfarin Materials," *American Druggist,* October 1997, p. 24.

—Jeffrey L. Covell
—update: Howard A. Jones

THE BIGFOOD GROUP[plc]

The Big Food Group plc

Second Avenue
Deeside Industrial Park
Deeside CH5 2NW
United Kingdom
Telephone: (+44) 1244-830-100
Fax: (+44) 1244-814-531
Web site: http://www.thebigfoodgroup.co.uk/

Public Company
Incorporated: 1970
Employees: 29,288
Sales: £5.15 billion ($9.49 billion) (2004)
Stock Exchanges: London
Ticker Symbol: BFP
NAIC: 445110 Grocery Stores; 492210 Grocery Delivery Services; 422420 Frozen Foods, Packaged (Except Dairy Products), Wholesaling; 421620 Kitchen Appliances, Household-Type, Electric, Wholesaling

Based in north Wales, The Big Food Group plc (BFG) is one of the United Kingdom's leading food distributors. BFG sells its wares on a wholesale and retail basis and offers Internet shopping. More than 3.4 million consumers shop at BFG's 754 Iceland stores, while 100,000 independent retailers and 370,000 caterers are supplied by BFG's Booker Cash & Carry and Woodward wholesalers. Wholesale accounts for 68 percent of BFG's business. Retail makes up 30 percent, with food service contributing the remaining 2 percent. BFG was known as Iceland Group before 2002.

From Roadside to High Street in the 1970s

Malcolm Walker and Peter Hinchcliffe were in their twenties when they began selling strawberries from the North Wales roadside. Frustrated with their jobs as management trainees with retailer Woolworths, they had begun looking toward starting their own business. Buying up the stock of strawberries from another roadside vendor, the pair set up a stall on the road near Llangollen, selling to passing tourists. While modestly successful, Walker and Hinchcliffe did not see their long-term future in roadside sales. Instead, the pair turned to retail, paying £60 for one month's rent of a storefront in Oswestry, North Wales. Walker and Hinchcliffe filled their small shop with freezers and stock bought on credit and opened for business in November 1970.

Soon to become known as Iceland, the shop offered customers loose frozen foods, rather than packaged foods. The store's foods were displayed on freezer trays, and customers could take as much or as little as they wanted. The shop soon built up a steady clientele, attracted by the store's low prices. Walker's and Hinchcliffe's employers, however, were less impressed with their moonlighting activity and fired them both. The two had no choice but to decide to expand their store concept, creating the new retail food niche of loose frozen food.

From its first shop, Iceland began to expand to new locations, keeping to the North Wales region. After acquiring a second shop and a 20,000-square-foot cold storage facility in Rhyl in 1973, Walker and Hinchcliffe put the Iceland concept into high gear. By 1975, the pair operated a chain of 18 stores and had come a long way toward developing the Iceland look: clean, bright shops featuring a blue and white motif.

The next step in Iceland's evolution was the move away from loose foods to prepackaged frozen foods. As Iceland continued to make acquisitions of other frozen foods shops, struggling in the recession of the mid-1970s, the company also prepared the launch of the first ''mature'' Iceland shop, opened in Arndale Centre, in Manchester, England, in 1977. This was the first Iceland store to abandon loose foods in favor of prepackaged food items. By 1978, the company had begun to expand into a national food store chain, with 28 stores under the Iceland name. As its stores were also growing in size, ranging from 2,000 to 3,000 square feet, Iceland opened a 300,000-square-foot cold store facility in Deeside, Flintshire, in North Wales, where it also moved its headquarters.

Iceland was gaining a reputation among consumers as a low-priced alternative to the major supermarket chains. The company's low prices contributed to a somewhat down-market image, which dogged the company into the 1990s. Nevertheless,

Company Perspectives:

Our strategic objectives are to rebuild and increase shareholder value by: growing sales and improving margins by leveraging the unique strengths of the Group; developing an organisation, processes and people that enable the Group to be both efficient and innovative; building a reputation with our key suppliers as the most constructive and innovative channel to market; integrating and improving Group systems to provide accurate and timely management information and to create a strong platform for e-business development; and creating a capital structure capable of supporting planned growth whether organically or by acquisition.

Iceland continued its rapid growth, boosting its number of stores to 42 by the beginning of the 1980s, while also introducing selected chilled and grocery items for the first time. In 1981, Walker and Hinchcliffe began preparing the next phase of expansion by selling a 16 percent share of the company to the British Rail Pension Fund, giving Iceland a £1.6 million war chest for further growth. The following year, Iceland rolled out its own brand label, the Iceland line of prepackaged frozen foods, which became the basis of the company's success in the 1980s. The large majority of frozen food items sold in the Iceland stores soon featured its own brand. In order to meet the rising demand for the highly successful Iceland brand, the company opened a new one million-square-foot cold store facility at its Deeside location.

Growth in the 1980s

In 1983, the company made its first major acquisition when it bought up the failing 18-store chain of St. Catherine frozen food centers. Iceland was able to turn around the St. Catherine stores and integrate them under the Iceland signage within months. At the same time, Iceland began converting its stores to a new image, abandoning the somewhat chilly blue-and-white color scheme for a warmer red-grey-beige combination. Iceland began looking for more shops to rent and other acquisitions.

Going public in 1984 provided the funding for stepped-up expansion. The company's listing was oversubscribed some 116 times, giving the company the momentum to develop into a nationwide chain. The increase in capital allowed Iceland to continue to expand its stores and also develop its own label lines of chilled foods and grocery items. At the same time, Iceland found it easier to acquire leases for its stores, as landlords were more comfortable renting to a public company. Two years after its initial public offering, Iceland was able to complete its national expansion, moving into southern England with the acquisition of Orchard Frozen Foods. That acquisition had pitted Iceland against larger rival Bejam Group.

Bejam, two-and-a-half times larger than Iceland and in increasing competition as the two chain's operations began to overlap, became Walker and Hinchcliffe's next target. Joining the takeover wars that marked the mid-1980s, Iceland, which had seen its initial acquisition offers rebuffed, turned hostile and launched a takeover battle that lasted some three months. In the end, Iceland won, barely, gaining 50.09 percent of Bejam's shares in 1988. Integrating Bejam's stores, which doubled the Iceland chain to some 275 stores, proved as difficult as acquiring the larger company, especially due to management conflicts. Bejam's operations were moved to Iceland's headquarters, and Bejam storefronts were converted to the Iceland signage. By the start of the 1990s, the integration had largely been achieved. In addition to expanding Iceland's chain of stores, the Bejam purchase also brought the company into home appliance sales for the first time.

Going Green in the 1990s

The faltering economy, with consumers battered by a recession and soaring jobless rates, slowed Iceland's growth at the start of the 1990s. In 1993, however, the company returned to its expansion program, winning an agreement to take over the food halls of the Littlewoods department store chain. The first of the "Iceland at Littlewoods" stores was rolled out in 1993. At the same time, Iceland moved into the Irish market, opening its first stores in Northern Ireland. That year, Iceland attempted a European expansion, buying up the Au Gel chain of frozen foods retail shops in France. That purchase proved untimely, and the company was forced to shut down the Au Gel subsidiary within a year. Efforts to export the Iceland brand's frozen food products were more successful, and the company built a £30 million depot in Swindon to support its domestic business and growing export sales. In 1994, cofounder Hinchcliffe retired to a non-executive position with the company, and Walker took over as chairman and CEO.

After the collapse of the Au Gel subsidiary, Iceland refocused on its core U.K. market. During the mid-1990s, the company stepped up its store opening program, adding some 50 new stores—now with an average store size of more than 4,000 square feet—per year. Nevertheless, Iceland's per-store sales growth—and share price—were affected by the sluggish economy and increasing competition from the major, full-line supermarkets. Iceland turned to expanded services to make the difference. In 1996, the company added home telephone sales and home delivery; while only a small part of the company's sales, these new services nonetheless were quickly profitable.

While the company rebuilt its retail sales momentum, it also began to diversify, purchasing Woodward Frozen Foods, the third largest foodservice provider to the U.K. catering and restaurant markets. Iceland quickly expanded its foodservice division, adding Cold Move, in 1997. In that year, the company renamed its Woodward operations as Wood Foodservice. Within two years, Iceland had built up its food service division to some £50 million in sales per year; Walker made no secret of his plans to extend Woodward's share of the U.K. foodservice market, especially a targeted doubling of Woodward's sales by the end of 2000.

As Iceland faced ever-growing competition from the giant supermarket chains—which were rapidly introducing their own frozen food selections—Iceland sought new ways not only to differentiate itself from its competitors but also to improve its image among consumers. In 1998, catching the spirit of growing public resistance to genetically modified foods (GM foods), Iceland announced its intention to remove all GM food products

Key Dates:

1970: Malcolm Walker and Peter Hinchcliffe open the first loose frozen foods store.
1973: The company opens a second retail store and purchases 20,000-square-foot cold storage facility.
1975: Fifteen Iceland stores are in operation.
1978: The company opens 300,000-square-foot cold store in Deeside, in North Wales.
1981: The company sells a 16 percent share to British Rail Pension Fund for £1.6 million.
1982: Iceland brand frozen foods line rolls out.
1984: The company completes an initial public offering on the London Stock Exchange.
1988: A hostile takeover of Bejam Group is effected.
1993: A roll out of ''Iceland at Littlewoods'' takes place.
2000: Iceland acquires Booker plc.
2002: Iceland is renamed The Big Food Group plc.

from its Iceland-branded foods. The move proved highly successful with British consumers, who were becoming more and more fearful of the possible harmful effects of the so-called ''Frankenstein foods.'' The company further boosted its new-found ''green'' image by introducing its own line of environmentally friendly refrigerators and freezers, replacing Freon and other harmful cooling agents with hydrocarbon based systems. The new appliance line was named ''Kyoto'' after the 1997 environmental summit in Kyoto, Japan. Later that year, Iceland teamed up with U.K. retailer J. Sainsbury to offer home appliances through Sainsbury's DIY (do-it-yourself) superstore subsidiary, Homebase House & Garden Centre.

After boosting its foodservice division in 1999 with the acquisitions of Rossfish and Deep Freeze supplies, which strengthened Iceland's foodservice component in southwestern and northeastern England and brought the company into Scotland, Iceland beefed up its service component, becoming one of the first U.K. grocers to offer free Internet shopping services. On the physical front, Iceland also rolled out a new store concept, Iceland Extra, which offered an extended range of fresh and grocery items, as well as convenience products such as tobacco and newspapers. By mid-1999, the Iceland Extra format began showing its promise—the first eight Extra stores, operating in the London area, had increased their sales by some 40 percent. Iceland began making plans to roll out an additional 20 Extra stores nationwide and saw the potential to convert perhaps 70 more stores of the entire chain's more than 700 Iceland stores to the expanded format.

In 1999, Iceland found a new bandwagon from which to trumpet its health-conscious message. In October of that year, the company made headlines by promising to remove all artificial colors from its branded foods, as well as reducing where possible preservatives and other additives. With more and more studies linking food colorings and other additives to a series of health problems and disorders such as hyperactivity, Iceland's ''clean food'' image continued to impress the British consumer. Iceland had also impressed other retailers. In January 2000, Iceland announced its agreement with Storehouse to create a special line of Iceland products, particularly chilled and fresh food products, for the Storehouse BHS department store chain. The move by BHS to add food products was made to enable that chain to compete head-to-head with rival Marks & Spencer. After a successful prototype run in BHS's Birmingham store, the Iceland-Storehouse agreement called for a rollout of Iceland products in another ten BHS stores, with a possible extension to an additional 90 stores by the end of 2001.

Growth and Competition after 2000

The acquisition mode continued in May 2000 as Iceland bought Booker plc for £373.5 million ($552 million) in stock. Booker's distribution capabilities and storage space were seen as complementary to Iceland's expanding e-commerce trade.

Company co-founder Malcolm Walker stepped down from the chairman's spot in March 2001. An ill-timed foray into organic foods under Walker was blamed for devastating sales results that hammered Iceland's share price. (Walker was investigated, but cleared, of insider trading for selling £13.5 million in BFG stock just before a profit warning was issued.)

Bill Grimsey was named chief executive in January 2001 and tasked with turning the company around. Mergers among giants in the grocery business, such as the takeover of Safeway by Wm. Morrison Supermarkets plc, were making the market even more competitive and, as Grimsey wrote in an editorial in *Grocer,* were threatening thousands of locally owned convenience stores with closure.

In 2001, Iceland combined the finance departments of its three main businesses—Iceland, Woodward Foodservice, and Booker. *Retail Week* reported BFG based the merged finance department at its north Wales headquarters but kept Booker's SAP Financials IT system.

In February 2002, Iceland was renamed The Big Food Group, plc. While the Booker Cash & Carry business had been divesting its foreign subsidiaries, BFG aimed to capitalize on the strength of the Iceland brand of frozen food by increasing overseas distribution. Booker's Chef's Larder brand was also popular among expatriate Brits, noted *Grocer.*

Though 2001 had been something of a bad year for BFG, in the 2001–02 fiscal year the company saw pre-tax profits (before one-off costs) rise from £40.1 million to £42.9 million. The new management team was able to report other positive developments in spite of an extremely competitive environment. A needed £300 million credit line had been obtained. BFG was also raising £250 million in cash in May 2002 by entering into sell and leaseback arrangements on its headquarters and some Iceland stores, reported Liverpool's *Daily Post.*

BFG's Iceland chain relied excessively on promotions to retain customer loyalty during grocery sector price wars. However, it was able to wean itself from the most generous of these margin-eroding incentives.

BFG profits and sales were up in the fiscal year ended March 28, 2004. The group posted a pre-tax profit of £50.1 million, up 35 percent, on turnover of £5.15 billion ($9.49 billion). When these figures were released, BFG had converted 142 of its 754

Iceland stores to a new convenience format and planned to refit another 150 in the coming year. In trials, the new design was found to increase sales at renovated stores by 17 percent.

BFG considered acquiring the Londis food distributor in 2004 but lost interest. The company was attracting takeover interest itself. Iceland's Baugur Group hf built up a 22.11 percent shareholding and made a takeover bid in September 2004 that valued BFG at £378 million. At the time, BFG had a debt of £245 million; neither the Iceland nor the Woodward businesses were making a profit.

Sales were declining at the retail grocery chain despite the continuing renovation program. To increase Booker's marginal profits, BFG was focusing on streamlining the wholesaler's distribution system.

Principal Subsidiaries

Bejam Group plc; BF Ltd.; Booker plc; Booker Cash and Carry Ltd.; Burgundy Ltd.; Iceland Foods plc; Iceland Foods (Ireland) Ltd.; Iceland Foodstores Ltd.; Trans European Insurance Ltd.; Woodward Foodservice Ltd..

Principal Operating Units

Iceland; Booker Cash & Carry; Woodward Foodservice; Expert Logistics.

Principal Competitors

ALDI Group; ASDA Group plc; Brake Brothers; Dixons Group plc; Tesco plc; J Sainsbury plc; Wm. Morrison Supermarkets plc.

Further Reading

Board, Laura, ''Booker Falls to Iceland Group,'' *Daily Deal* (New York), May 25, 2000.

Bruce, Anne, ''Big Food Group Gears up to Grow Export Presence,'' *Grocer*, July 13, 2002, p. 6.

Buckley, Sophy, ''Baugur Set for Takeover after BFG Opens Books: Food Group's Board Positive About Pounds 378m Approach,'' *Financial Times* (London), September 18, 2004, p. 1.

Favell, Andy, ''Solutions Analysis—How Big Food Group Saved Money by Merging Services,'' *Retail Week*, September 17, 2004, p. 23.

Green, Matthew, ''Iceland Continues 10 Pct. Growth,'' *Reuters*, July 20, 1999.

Grimsey, Bill, ''Big Food Group CEO Bill Grimsey Urges the Competition Commission Not to Create a Disastrous Legacy for C-Stores,'' *Grocer*, July 5, 2003, p. 28.

''How Grimsey Will Tackle Sales Falls,'' *Grocer*, July 17, 2004, p. 10.

''Iceland Beats Harrods in Online Shopping Table,'' *Financial Times*, December 1, 1999.

Jones, David, ''Sell-off Wins Big Food Group a Cash Lifeline,'' *Daily Post* (Liverpool), May 14, 2002, p. 21.

McEwan, Alan, ''Big Food Group Reaches Heights as Profits Soar,'' *Evening News* (Scotland), May 27, 2004, p. 3.

Merriman, Jane, ''UK's Iceland Profits from Food Scare,'' *Reuters*, March 23, 1999.

Mesure, Susie, ''Baugur Pounces on Big Food Group,'' *Independent*, September 18, 2004.

Portanger, Erik, ''Big Food Group Execs Mulling Mgmt Buyout,'' *Dow Jones International News*, September 16, 2002.

Pritchard, James, ''Celebrations at Big Food Group,'' *Western Mail*, May 31, 2002, p. 16.

Rankine, Kate, ''Iceland to Drive up Sales through Home Delivery,'' *Daily Telegraph*, September 2, 1997.

''Storehouse Expands Iceland Link,'' *Financial Times*, January 21, 2000.

''UK's Iceland Boosted by Anti-Modified Food Stance,'' *Reuters*, March 23, 1999.

Watson, Elaine, ''Baugur's Big Mystery: The BFG Takeover Strategy Is Hard to Fathom,'' *Grocer*, September 25, 2004, p. 35.

—M.L. Cohen
—update: Frederick C. Ingram

Boddie-Noell Enterprises, Inc.

1021 Noell Lane
Rocky Mount, North Carolina 27802
U.S.A.
Telephone: (252) 937-2800
Fax: (252) 937-2978
Web site: http://www.bneinc.com

Private Company
Incorporated: 1961
Employees: 11,697
Sales: $420 million (2003)
NAIC: 722211 Limited-Service Restaurants

Boddie-Noell Enterprises, Inc., is a privately owned, family-run company based in the small town of Rocky Mount, North Carolina. Primarily involved in the restaurant industry, Boddie-Noell is the largest franchisee of the Hardee's hamburger chain, operating 316 units in North Carolina, South Carolina, Virginia, and Kentucky. Since Hardee's began to lose popularity with consumers in the 1990s, Boddie-Noell has cut back on its Hardee's holdings and added casual dining concepts. The company operates 28 Texas Steakhouse & Saloon restaurants in North Carolina, Virginia, and West Virginia; a pair of BBQ & Ribs Co. restaurants; several Café Carolina & Bakery units; a handful of Moe's Southwest Grill restaurants; and Boddie-Noell's Highway Diner, a 1950s-style silver diner. In addition, the company runs BNE Land & Development, originally set up to purchase land for Hardee's restaurants but now involved in a wide range of commercial and resort real estate projects. Boddie-Noell also runs Rose Hill Conference Center, housed in the founding family's ancestral mansion, built in 1790. Boddie-Noell has a reputation as a tight-knit organization that emphasizes treating employees like family. As a result, the company has established a record of employee retention unmatched in the restaurant industry.

Founding Family Humbled by the Depression

The history of Boddie-Noell Enterprises is very much a riches-to-rags-to-riches story. The lineage of the Boddie family can be traced as far back as William Boddie, a captain in the English navy during the reign of Henry VIII. The Boddies emigrated to America in the 1660s and in 1790 established a sprawling, 10,000-acre plantation in North Carolina called Rose Hill. But with the defeat of the Confederacy in 1865, the family fortunes went into steady decline. By 1926 the property was mortgaged and during the Depression of the 1930s the family could not keep up with the payments on the farm, now reduced to just 700 acres, on which Nicholas Bunn Boddie grew tobacco, corn, and cotton. The property was sold off and the family, on the verge of poverty, was forced to move to a small house owned by his mother-in-law. They scraped by, selling chickens and eggs at the local farmer's markets, until Boddie found work in the Employment Security Commission office, a job he held until his death in 1951. A few years before he died, however, he established a small fuel-oil delivery business. His two sons, Nick and younger brother Mayo, would become the driving force behind the foundation and growth of Boddie-Noell Enterprises.

Both Nick and Mayo Boddie had little use for college, eager to establish themselves in business. Nick dropped out of the University of North Carolina at Chapel Hill in 1949, attracted to the high wages being offered in Alaska. After several months of working in a gold mine, on the railroad, and in a rock quarry, he returned to North Carolina to assume less arduous employment at a hotel his aunt acquired after her husband died. He liked the work and later opened a motel and restaurant, Carleton House. It was named after an Uncle, Carleton Noell, a vice-president at Garrett Tobacco Co., who provided the financing. In the meantime, Mayo, two years younger, also began college at the University of North Carolina, only to find the classroom too stifling, convinced that the world was passing him by. After a year-and-a-half he dropped out intending to join the Navy. Instead, he married his high school sweetheart, joined the reserves, and worked for the railroad until his father passed away and he took over the fuel delivery business. But he soon shut it down, unhappy about working in a business that relied on the extension of credit. He took a number of jobs over the next several years, and then opened a cut-rate gas station, taking advantage of two 6,000-gallon tanks he owned to buy gasoline in volume. By the 1960s he owned three gas stations as well as a pair of laundromats. Both Nick and Mayo Boddie were successful businessmen, big fish in the town of Rocky Mount, North Carolina, with a population significantly less than

Company Perspectives:

Our Mission: To value the people of Boddie-Noell by providing a high quality, successful organization which offers everyone the opportunity to be the best they can be.

40,000. Neither was content, however, to spend the rest of his life doing more of the same. Then, in 1961, a chance arose to become involved with the Hardee's hamburger chain on the ground floor.

In 1960 Wilbur Hardee opened a McDonald's knockoff in Greenville, North Carolina. His accountant was Leonard Rawls, who had attended high school with the Boddies and also did Mayo's books. Rawls teamed up with another high school friend, Jim Gardner, to franchise the Hardee's concept and tried to convince the Boddie brothers to become franchisees. However, they simply could not understand how it was possible to make money by selling hamburgers at 15 cents a piece. When Rawls and Gardner opened a Hardee's in Rocky Mount, the Boddies saw the lines that formed to buy those 15-cent hamburgers, and they became convinced that they could make a profit in fast food.

Early Hardee's Franchisees in the 1960s

The Boddie brothers joined forces with Carleton Noell and bought five Hardee's franchises for $1,500 each. The first opened in January 1962 in Fayetteville, North Carolina. As would be the case with many of their restaurants, the Boddies made a wise choice in location: The restaurant was on the main route leading into the Fort Bragg Army Post. As Mayo had done with his gas stations—where he kept tabs on his managers by nightly checking the pumps and matching up the numbers with the money in the till—he closely monitored his inventory of food and paper products. The store got off to a strong start, but after six months the new restaurateurs were put to the test when a McDonald's opened nearby on Bragg Boulevard, resulting in an immediate 50 percent drop in sales. The Boddies fought back, putting up more signs, contriving promotions and giveaways, and speeding up service. Soon the restaurant won back its market share and the Boddies were ready to launch their second restaurant, located in Kingston, North Carolina, followed by another unit in Fayetteville.

Boddie-Noell grew along with the Hardee's company, which Rawls and Gardner bought from Wilbur Hardee, took public in 1963, and launched an aggressive expansion program. The Boddies developed a simple, risk-adverse, and effective strategy to expand their operations. First, they were smart about site selection. After their run-in with McDonald's in Fayetteville, they decided to concentrate on smaller towns where there was less competition. Although in time they would come to rely on population statistics, traffic flow, and other factors when considering a location, they always made sure to walk the ground, like true farmer's sons, and in the end relied on instinct. Years later a consulting company tried to sell them on a computerized site selection system. To serve as an example the Boddies provided some data on a site, which the consultants after some analysis insisted would not work. It turned out that the site already housed a Boddie-Noell Hardee's restaurant that was doing quite well, and the Boddies decided to continue doing business their own way.

Boddie-Noell built its chain one restaurant at a time, with no goal on a total number. First, Carleton Noell's standing as a tobacco executive was used as leverage with the banks. The company would buy property for a new restaurant, generally with $5,000 as a down payment, and have the deed subordinated. Noell would then use the deed as collateral to borrow the money needed to build and equip the new Hardee's, roughly $100,000. "We'd put $250 in the change fund to open up," Mayo told *Business, North Carolina,* in a 1992 profile. "We had two weeks before we had to pay employees and 15 days before we paid suppliers. So really, in essence, for $5,250 in cash we were able to buy a piece of property, build a building and get into business." By 1965 Boddie-Noell operated 19 Hardee's, and a decade later the chain had grown to 100. The operation was so lean that it was not until the late 1960s that the headquarters finally moved out of a converted laundry room at Carleton House.

Along the way, the partners assumed distinct roles in the organization. Because Nick Boddie was busy running Carleton House when Boddie-Noell was launched, Mayo was the one who headed the new enterprise, a position that suited his personality. He was able to make the tough decisions, while his brother was better dealing with people. As one longtime Boddie-Noell executive expressed it, "Nick's the feeler, Mayo is the doer." Whereas Mayo was aggressive, his uncle, who was more conservative, was present to act as a counterbalance. Although Nick may had been better with people, Mayo was well liked by his employees and he quickly came to understand the value of having good managers and took steps to retain top lieutenants. He often sold store managers a 25 percent stake in a restaurant and instead of charging them $25,000 he asked for just $2,500. As a result, Boddie-Noell's annual turnover of store managers would run at just 10 percent, a far cry from the rest of the fast-food industry. Boddie-Noell also established a top-notch training program, which would serve as an industry model. Nor did management lose touch with the reality of the field workers, as each year everyone in management spent a week working in a Hardee's, wearing the same brown uniform as everyone else.

Boddie-Noell was an innovative franchisee in other ways as well. In the early 1970s a Georgia employee developed a biscuit sandwich to serve for breakfast, an idea that would have a dramatic effect on the Hardee's chain and the entire fast-food industry. After a test run at 22 Boddie-Noell restaurants, the sandwich was rolled out in the mid-1970s to the entire Hardee's chain. Hardee's had resisted the idea at first, but the new item added a day-part to the restaurant, which had formerly been solely a lunch and dinner operation.

The Boddie brothers were so successful with their Hardee's operations that in 1979 they were able to buy back Rose Hill, which they then restored to the glory of its plantation days. The brothers were also smart enough to understand by the mid-1970s that they had grown their Hardee's chain as large as they could hope without bringing in some managers with more sophisticated business skills. Not only were new departments formed and job classifications determined, the company began planning a new headquarters. After five years of effort, a new $3.6 million modern headquarters opened in 1982.

Key Dates:

1962: The company opens the first Hardee's restaurant.
1975: The company owns 100 Hardee's.
1987: A real estate investment trust is launched.
1990: Bill Boddie succeeds his father as president.
1994: The first Texas Steakhouse & Saloon unit opens.
2004: The company acquires an outstanding interest in Café Carolina & Bakery.

Hits and Misses in the 1980s

By 1985 Boddie-Noell was operating nearly 250 Hardee's restaurants, but it also experienced some setbacks during the decade. Efforts to launch a pizza restaurant, a country cooking-inspired restaurant, and a fried chicken concept all failed. A move into the Memphis market with Hardee's restaurants also produced less than spectacular results; 12 restaurants the company opened in Pennsylvania were ultimately closed. But in 1985 the company launched a new fried chicken concept called Skats that caught on. The smaller restaurant format cost much less to launch than a Hardee's and was suitable for small town locations, with populations of 5,000 to 7,000, the kind of markets in which Hardee's was not interested. Once Skats proved successful, however, Hardee's began to open restaurants in some of the same small towns, leading to a 1990 confrontation between Hardee's and Boddie-Noell. It was Mayo's son Bill who brokered a peace between the two parties, leading to the conversion of Skats units to Hardee's restaurants. Another venture launched during the 1980s was BNE Land & Development, a real estate investment trust (REIT) to own restaurant sites in a leaseback program. In 1995 the REIT would extend its activities to apartment and shopping center properties.

Bill Boddie, Mayo's middle son, succeeded his father as president of Boddie-Noell in 1990. Although just 60 years of age, Mayo was determined to effect a smooth succession of power. His choice of Bill was backed by sons Mayo Boddie, Jr., and Mike Boddie, both of whom held prominent roles in the organization. Bill Boddie took over just as the company's chain of Hardee's restaurants was peaking. In 1993 Boddie-Noell's Hardee's portfolio reached its high water mark, with more than 350 restaurants producing revenues of $380 million—sales spurred by the addition of menu items like fried chicken. (The number of Hardee's units topped out at 364 in 1995). But the Hardee's brand was beginning to lose its luster and the chain did not fare well in the discount wars that now flared up with other fast-food restaurants. As the Hardee's business began to tail off, Boddie-Noell began looking to the new casual dining category that was growing in popularity. In 1994 it opened its first Texas Steakhouse in Rocky Mount as a test venture. The concept, launched several years earlier, proved successful and the company soon added three more units in North Carolina. By 2004 another two dozen Texas Steakhouse restaurants would open in North Carolina, Virginia, and West Virginia.

Hardee's changed ownership in April 1997 when CKE Restaurants Inc. bought the ailing chain. Boddie-Noell and the new owners quickly had a falling out over CKE's talk of Hardee's eliminating fried chicken, a major source of income for the Boddie-Noell units. There was, in general, animosity between the franchisee association, formed in 1997 and headed by Bill Boddie, and CKE that took time to recede. CKE had enjoyed success in reviving the Carl's Jr. chain and upon taking over Hardee's insisted that franchisees remodel their stores and add some of Carl's menu items. The attempt to turn Hardee's into Carl's Jr. did not work, however. CKE finally scored a hit in 2001 with the test introduction of the "Six Dollar Burger," a half-pound burger that it claimed would cost $6 at a finer restaurant but less than $4 at Hardee's. In January 2003 the chain began rolling out the new item as the Thickburger, which took some time to catch on but over the course of the next year began to result in increased sales.

While Boddie-Noell struggled to revive the business of its Hardee's restaurants, it continued to delve deeper into the casual dining category. The company launched a concept called The BBQ and Ribs Co., as well as a family dining idea originally called the Shiny Diner, which eventually took on the Boddie-Noell's Highway Diner name. In 2002 Boddie-Noell bought a 60 percent interest in Café Carolina and Bakery, founded in 1995 by Robert Autry, Jr., the son of the former Hardee's Food Systems chairman. The relationship between the two sides soon soured, and Autry sued Boddie-Noell in 2004, claiming that he had been forced out as CEO and Boddie-Noell's interference had hindered his ability to enact the Café Carolina business plan. A few months later a settlement was reached and Boddie-Noell bought out Autry's interest in the business. Another casual dining concept Boddie-Noell pursued was Moe's Southwest Grill. In October 2003 it signed a deal to open 25 of the healthy Mexican food restaurants in North Carolina and Virginia.

Documents that emerged during the Café Carolina suit indicated that Boddie-Noell generated sales of $420 million in 2003. Of that amount, 75 percent came from the Hardee's operations. It was clear that the company's prospects remained very much tied to CKE's efforts in revitalizing the Hardee's brand.

Principal Subsidiaries

BNE Land & Development; Café Carolina and Bakery; Rose Hill Conference Center.

Principal Competitors

Burger King Corporation; McDonald's Corporation; YUM! Brands, Inc.

Further Reading

Bailey, David, "Boddie Language," *Business, North Carolina,* December 1992, p. 22.
Maley, Frank, "Burger Keen," *Business, North Carolina,* October 1, 2004, p. 64.
Seligman, Bob, "Hardee's, Boddie-Noell Lock Horns Over Skats," *Nation's Restaurant News,* February 26, 1990, p. 3.
Waters, Craig R., "Franchise Capital of America," *Inc.,* September 1994, p. 99.

—Ed Dinger

Booker Cash & Carry Ltd.

Equity House
Irthlingborough Road
Wellingborough, Northamptontshire NN8 1LT
United Kingdom
Telephone: (+44) 1933 371-000
Fax: (+44) 1933 371-010
Web site: http://www.booker.co.uk

Wholly Owned Subsidiary of The Big Food Group plc
Incorporated: 1900 as Booker Brothers, McConnell & Co. Ltd.
Employees: 8,212
Sales: £3.50 billion (2004)
NAIC: 422410 General Line Grocery Wholesalers; 424450 Confectionery Merchant Wholesalers; 424480 Fresh Fruit and Vegetable Merchant Wholesalers; 424490 Other Grocery and Related Products Merchant Wholesalers; 424810 Beer and Ale Merchant Wholesalers; 424820 Wine and Distilled Alcoholic Beverage Merchant Wholesalers; 424940 Tobacco and Tobacco Product Merchant Wholesalers

Booker Cash & Carry Ltd. is a leading food wholesaler and distributor in the United Kingdom, operating a network of 173 cash-and-carry branches that serve retailers and caterers rather than end consumers. Though Booker controlled a far broader empire as recently as 1997—with substantial agribusiness, food service, fish processing, and literary enterprises—heavy debt and decreasing profits compelled the company to shed most of these other businesses. Leaner and more focused, Booker committed to bolstering its food distributing division in 1998. In 2000, the parent company, Booker plc, was acquired by Iceland Group, which was renamed The Big Food Group plc. With more than a 35 percent share of the industry in the United Kingdom, Booker provides a key link between independent retailers and caterers and the manufacturing sector. Its retail customers, who number over 400,000, include independent grocers, convenience stores, and news agents, while the more than 20,000 caterers that rely on its cash-and-carry warehouses encompass restaurants, pubs, cafes, hotels, nursing homes, as well as independent caterers.

Booker's Founding and Early Enterprises

Booker's history is inextricably linked to Europe's imperialist past. When the Congress of Vienna divided the northeast coast of South America among Great Britain, the Netherlands, and France in 1815, enterprising merchants from those countries moved quickly to exploit the region's natural resources. The Booker brothers—Josias, George, and Richard—were among these entrepreneurs. Josias was first to make the trip overseas. He arrived in the British colony of Demerara (later British Guyana) in 1815 and obtained employment as a manager of a cotton plantation. Over the next two decades, Josias and his brothers set up several merchant trading houses in Liverpool in anticipation of a flourishing sugar and rum trade. They capped their preparatory activities with the 1834 establishment of Booker Brothers & Co. in British Guyana and the acquisition of their first transport ship the following year. After Richard Booker died in 1838, Josias and George consolidated vertically, purchasing sugar plantations throughout British Guyana.

As is often the case in family firms, generational changes precipitated a dramatic transformation of Booker Brothers. In 1854, Josias Booker II (eldest son of Josias I) and John McConnell (who had worked as a clerk for the Bookers since 1846) created a separate new partnership called the Demerara Company. Upon the deaths of Josias I and George in 1865 and 1866, respectively, Josias II and John McConnell assumed control of all the Booker properties, including the sugar plantations and trading companies in Britain and South America. According to Milton Moskowitz's *The Global Marketplace* (1987), the new generation "became the principal shopkeepers of the colony," building a formidable trade during the late 19th century. Their "Liverpool Line," established in 1887, became one of the top shipping links between South America and Europe.

After Josias II died in the early 1880s, John McConnell inherited control of Booker Bros. & Co., George Booker & Co., and his own John McConnell & Co. McConnell's sons, A.J. and F.V., took possession of the three businesses in 1890 and merged them in 1900 as Booker Brothers, McConnell & Co. Ltd.

Company Perspectives:

Booker provide a professional wholesale service for independent retailers and caterers. We're committed to help make your businesses successful and take an interest in the communities in which you operate.

Guyanan operations had by this time expanded to include sales of food and general merchandise at the retail and wholesale levels.

The company prospered throughout the early 20th century by maintaining its concentration on the sugar and rum trade and limiting its acquisition activities to the Caribbean region. Booker McConnell made its first public stock offering in 1920 and was listed on the London Stock Exchange that same year. (The company name was shortened to Booker, McConnell Ltd. in 1968; in 1986 it would be renamed Booker plc.)

Booker Diversifies in the 1950s–60s

Political unrest in Guyana during the early 1950s prompted John "Jock" Campbell, chairman of Booker from 1952 to 1967, to diversify both geographically and commercially. Diversification became imperative after Guyana won its independence from Great Britain in 1966 and elected a communist government. Booker was eventually compelled to sell its sugar plantations and other businesses in that country to the government. Ironically, Guyanan and other Caribbean officials asked Booker and other British sugar moguls to help manage their struggling operations in the early 1990s. Their request for management advice prompted the formation of Booker Tate, a joint venture with Tate & Lyle, in the early 1990s.

Campbell's "hedge-building" investments in the United Kingdom, Canada, and Central Africa varied widely, from engineering to supermarketing to agricultural consulting. One of the most unusual diversifications made during this era was a division the company called "Authors." This highly unusual sideline developed after the discovery of a loophole in the British tax code that allowed the conglomerate to purchase an author's copyrights, pay him or her a fat fee partly at the expense of the taxpayer, and then collect the royalties. Agatha Christie and Ian Fleming were just two of the bestselling authors in Booker's stable.

The Authors venture soon spawned another celebrated aside. According to Booker's 1994 annual report, Fleming suggested to Campbell over a game of golf that the company pump some of the millions it was earning on the backs of writers back into the literary community. Although Booker was reluctant to give the creator of the James Bond character full credit for the idea, his suggestion influenced the 1969 presentation of the first Booker McConnell Prize for Fiction (now the Booker Prize), bestowed upon the best novel published in Britain by a writer from the British Commonwealth. P.H. Newby's *Something to Answer For* won the first Booker Prize, which became the most coveted and highly esteemed award in British book publishing. The recipient of the honor received a cash award, and the status of the prize was so great that short-listed novels often saw dramatic jumps in sales.

Agribusiness and Food Distribution in the 1970s–80s

Booker's business focus shifted in the late 1970s and early 1980s. The company divested itself of its money-losing engineering interests, sold its last remaining import/export subsidiary, and made several acquisitions in agribusiness and food distribution. Perhaps anticipating increasing demand for low-fat, relatively low-cost sources of protein, the firm's acquisitions included poultry breeding operations and fish breeding and processing businesses during this time.

One of the company's first transitional moves came with the 1978 purchase of 10 percent of International Basic Economy Corporation (IBEC). IBEC had been founded by Nelson Rockefeller and his brothers in 1947 in the hopes of profitably boosting developing countries' economies. Arbor Acres, an American producer of broiler breeder stock that had been operating since before World War II, became part of the IBEC in 1959. Arbor Acres hoped to expand its chicken breeding network from the United States to Latin America, Europe, the Middle East, and Asia. However, when IBEC's sales dropped precipitously in the late 1970s, the Rockefellers elected to liquidate. Booker helped that process along, increasing its share of IBEC to 45 percent in 1980 and a majority interest by 1985. Rodman C. Rockefeller, Nelson Rockefeller's son, served as chairman of Arbor Acres Farms and on Booker's board of directors into the early 1990s.

Infrequent acquisitions of fish breeders and processors in the late 1970s, 1980s, and early 1990s slowly evolved into a significant sector of Booker's business. The company bought W&F Fish Products in 1978, Atlantic Sea Products in 1987, and Marine Harvest International in 1994. By that time, Booker's annual report boasted that it was the largest specialist seafood group in the United Kingdom.

Booker also invested heavily in health foods during the 1980s. The company made at least four acquisitions in this industry in 1986 alone and continued its buying spree in ensuing years. Health food holdings during this period included Britain's largest health food chain, Holland & Barrett; La Vie Claire, a prominent health food company in France; vitamin and nutritional supplement manufacturers in the United States and Great Britain; and several organic food producers.

During the last half of the 1980s, Booker acquired several wholesale food distributors, including E.C. Steed (1986), Copeman Ridley (1987), J. Evershed & Son (1988), Linfood Cash & Carry (1988), and County Catering Co. (1988). By the end of the decade, the company had amassed Britain's largest food wholesaling business. Its customers, which numbered in the hundreds of thousands, included independent grocers, convenience stores, and caterers. It was around this time that the company shifted its business strategy to concentrate primarily on food wholesaling and distribution to the catering trade. Booker sealed its leading position in that industry with the 1990 acquisition of Fitch Lovell plc, a leading processor and distributor of fish and other food products, for £279.7 million.

In keeping with its new focus, Booker divested several peripheral businesses during this period. In 1986, the company sold its chain of Budgen convenience stores, which had been purchased during the 1950s-era diversification. The French

Key Dates:

1834: Booker Brothers & Co. is established.
1900: Booker Brothers, McConnell & Co. Ltd. is formed.
1920: The company makes its first public stock offering.
1966: Guyana wins its independence from Great Britain; this forces Booker to diversify.
1968: The company name is shortened to Booker, McConnell Ltd.
1969: The first Booker Prize is awarded.
1978: Booker acquires International Basic Economy Corporation (IBEC).
1986: The company is renamed Booker plc.
1994: Booker acquires Marine Harvest International.
1996: Booker buys rival Nurdin & Peacock.
1998: Booker commits to focusing on food distribution business.
2000: Booker plc is acquired by Iceland Group, which becomes The Big Food Group plc.

health food interests were divested in 1989, and those in the United Kingdom were sold in 1990 and 1991.

Booker purchased the balance of Arbor Acres' equity (10 percent) from the Rockefellers in 1991 for $22 million. Under its new management, Arbor Acres had grown to become the world's largest broiler breeding company, with customers in over 70 countries worldwide. It had emerged as the cornerstone of Booker's American agribusiness division, which also included North America's leading turkey breeder, Nicholas Turkey Breeding Farms, and CWT Farms International Inc., a producer of broiler hatching eggs.

Restructuring in the Early 1990s

Booker adjusted its organizational structure in the early 1990s by establishing four primary divisions: food distribution, which included wholesaling and food service; food processing, which incorporated operations producing fish and prepared foods; U.S. agribusiness, comprised of the poultry breeding operations; and U.K. agribusiness, which included salmon farming, plant breeding, sugar industry services, and forestry. Food distribution contributed about half of the company's net income in the early 1990s, while the international agribusiness and fish processing chipped in about 20 percent each.

Characterized as a ''dull but worthy'' company, Booker was dragged into the limelight as competition in the British supermarket industry intensified. In 1992, Booker launched its first consumer advertising campaign in support of the ''Family Choice'' branded products it distributed to thousands of independent grocers. These Booker clients were experiencing increased price competition from deep discounters that had entered the market to take advantage of recession-weary Brits.

Booker's sales increased steadily in the early 1990s, from £2.93 billion in 1990 to £3.72 billion in 1994. Net income increased from £49.9 million in 1990 to £59.7 million in 1993, then declined to £45.8 million in 1994. The company blamed the earnings slide on expenses related to the reorganization of the food wholesaling and food service divisions, as well as the acquisition and rationalization of Marine Harvest International, the Scotland-based salmon farming firm. Predictably, Booker chairman Jonathan Taylor expressed confidence that the company's reorganization would begin to pay increased dividends as Great Britain cycled out of recession in the latter part of the 1990s.

Rather than wait, however, Booker sought to remedy its slump through further acquisitions under the leadership of a new chief executive officer, Charles Bowen. In 1996, Booker purchased Nurdin & Peacock, a chain of wholesale cash and carry stores that greatly expanded Booker's food distribution network. As part of its effort to integrate the new stores, Booker launched an 18-month project to form a centralized distribution center the company named Heartland.

Further Changes in the Late 1990s

Despite these measures, Booker did not emerge from its slump. Saddled by enormous debt and sinking profits, the company sold Booker Prepared Foods group, its food manufacturing division, in July 1997. The enterprise, which supplied major U.K. retailers with a range of prepared food products, was bought by Prize Food Group for £57 million. Despite the revenues this transaction brought Booker, the company reported another net loss for 1997. In a unanimous decision, Booker's board of directors ousted Charles Bowen in March 1998.

Booker thereupon commenced a comprehensive review of its operations, a project which one company executive described to *AFX News* as ''wide ranging and all-embracing.'' The process was overseen by Booker's newly appointed CEO, Alan Smith, and its chairman, Jonathon Taylor. In June 1998, the company released its findings. Committing to focusing on its food service operations, Booker pledged to rid itself of businesses outside this newly defined core competency. Booker's agribusiness ventures in the United States and the United Kingdom, its fish processing division, Daehnfeldt seeds business, its stake in sugar-related joint ventures, and its interest in Agatha Christie Ltd. (which held the rights to the author's work) were all being sold off. ''We have decided that a dedicated food distribution group with a new management structure is the right way forward,'' Taylor proclaimed to *AFX News* on June 2, 1998.

Although Booker netted £156 million from initial sales, it was clear by November 1998 that even more cuts were necessary. Stuart Rose, who was named chief executive in October, announced that quarterly earnings were so low that Booker might breach certain covenants with its banks. In response to this announcement, Booker's stock price plummeted over 46 percent, lowering the company's market value by more than £130 million. However, by April 1999 the company had reached an agreement with its creditors. Contemporaneously, as part of an its effort to increase its cash flow, Booker sold Booker Foodservice, Recheio (its Portuguese food wholesaling joint venture), its Spanish cash-and-carry division, and Booker Wholesale Foods.

After pledging that cash-and-carry was to be the company's lifeblood, Rose and new Chairman John Napier instituted a series of measures to boost the division's sales, which had been below expectations in 1998. A sweeping efficiency program led to about 400 job cuts, and the central office strove to improve the appearance, service, and profitability of each branch store. A weekly ''BlockBuster'' promotion held at various branches was intended to drive sales. In addition to expanding the array of goods available at its stores, Booker committed to expanding its private label brands. Both the ''Happy Shopper'' line for retailers and the ''Chef's Larder'' products for caterers offered Booker enhanced margins.

The results of Booker's aggressive reorganizing and pruning could not be immediately determined. Though sales rose in the first months of 1999, company profits were eroded by the cost of restructuring the company. However, Booker remained optimistic about its future. As John Napier told *Dow Jones Business News,* ''We look forward to a significantly better year.''

New Ownership, Sharpened Customer Focus after 2000

After divesting numerous subsidiaries, Booker also made an acquisition in 1999. In November, the company paid an estimated £7.4 million to buy a convenience store chain called Trademarket from the Alldays group. Trademarket owned nine locations in Scotland and northern England and had sales of £128 million.

Booker continued to sell off units in 2000 as it sought to focus on its U.K. cash-and-carry business. Divested were the Foodservice Group, Booker Cash & Carry (Malaysia) Sdn. Bhd., Booker Cash & Carry (Thailand), Marine Harvest McConnel, Sezgingler, Arbo Acres, and Fletcher Smith.

Iceland Group plc, a British frozen foods supplier, acquired Booker plc in 2000 for stock worth £373.5 million ($552 million). Booker's distribution system was an asset to the online division Iceland was developing. The e-commerce business seemed to offer Booker growth prospects in the face of hard times for its customer base of independent retailers. Booker plc head Stuart Rose went on to lead the combined company.

The Booker Cash & Carry business continued as a subsidiary of Iceland, which was renamed The Big Food Group plc (BFG) in February 2002. Booker Cash & Carry got a new chairman, George Greener, and managing director, Jerry Johnson, in 2001 (Iceland founder Malcolm Walker had led the company briefly the previous year).

The Booker Prize also had a change in ownership. BFG transferred the award to a charity, which found a new sponsor for it in the Man investment firm. According to the *Financial Times,* Man agreed to pay £2.5 million over five years; the award was subsequently known as the Man Booker Prize.

Booker also sponsored the Booker Prize for Excellence, a slew of awards in various categories of the catering trade, including Best Restaurant, Best Hotel, Best Ethnic Caterer, Best Pub Caterer, Best Young Catering Business, Best Guesthouse, and Best Young Chef. The winner for each received a £1,000; the Best Young Chef also won a week-long residency with the notoriously demanding Gordon Ramsay. Ramsay had signed on as a consultant with Booker in 2000.

A number of new appointments were made in the marketing department in 2002 as Booker sharpened its focus on customer needs. Booker began testing an online shopping service, which included delivery, at a depot in Wolverhampton in the fall of 2002. This was expanded to 133 of Booker's 173 locations two years later. In addition, the company was expanding its range of Asian grocery items. Booker introduced a loyalty program called Spend and Save in March 2003. Depots were also redesigned to be brighter and more conveniently laid out.

According to *The Grocer,* Booker was aiming for a 34 percent market share by 2004–05. In 2004, Booker was supplying about 440,000 independent retailers, more than 1,700 bearing Booker's Premier brand, and 22,000 caterers. Booker provided members of the Premier retail club with branded signage and monthly promotions. Turnover was £3.5 billion in the fiscal year ended March 31, 2004, up marginally from fiscal 2003 but just under the results for 2002.

Principal Divisions

Booker Own Brands; Premier.

Principal Competitors

ASDA Group plc; J Sainsbury plc; Safeway plc; Somerfield plc; Tesco plc.

Further Reading

Addy, Rod, ''Booker Sharpens Focus,'' *Grocer*, August 31, 2002, p. 12.

''Agatha Christie Helps to Bolster Booker,'' *Financial Times*, September 11, 1998.

Bidlake, Suzanne, ''Booker Boosts Small Stores in Price War,'' *Marketing*, January 23, 1992, p. 6.

Board, Laura, ''Booker Falls to Iceland Group,'' *Daily Deal* (New York City), May 25, 2000.

''Booker Awards Expanded,'' *Catering and Hotel Keeper*, December 6, 2001, p. 59.

''Booker Buys Aquaculture Firm,'' *Wall Street Journal Europe*, October 24, 1994.

''Booker Fish Division Finally Goes on the Block,'' *Frozen and Chilled Foods*, July 1, 1998.

''Booker to Focus on Distribution Business after Strategic Review,'' *AFX News*, June 2, 1998.

''Booker Works to Provide Customers with Winners,'' *Grocer*, June 21, 2003, p. 19.

Bykov, Dimitry, Andrei Nemzer, and Alla Latynina, ''First Booker Russian Novel Prize Awarded,'' *Current Digest of the Post-Soviet Press*, January 13, 1993, p. 16.

''Caribbean Sugar: Come Back, Slavemasters,'' *Economist*, January 23, 1993, p. 83.

Costello, Bernadette, ''Hargrave's Heart Is with Consumers,'' *Off License News*, May 9, 2003, p. 12.

Hollinger, Peggy, ''From Interview to Alliance in Just Four Weeks,'' *Financial Times*, May 26, 2000, p. 24.

Hunt, Julian, ''Collier Unveils Vision of Booker Re-Engineering,'' *Grocer*, April 12, 2003, p. 8.

Jarvis, Paul, ''Booker Chief Confirms Woes; Shares Plunge,'' *Wall Street Journal Europe*, November 11, 1998.

——, ''Booker Reaches Financing Deal With Its Banks,'' Wall Street Journal Europe, April 16, 1999.

''Management-Led Team Buys Booker Food Manufacturers,'' *Frozen and Chilled Foods*, July 1, 1997.

Moskowitz, Milton, *The Global Marketplace*, New York: Macmillan Publishing Company, 1987.

''New Boss at Booker Pledges a Revolution,'' *Grocer*, November 25, 2000, p. 6.

''Premier Recruitment,'' *Off License News*, October 1, 2004, p. 8.

''Radical Retailer Turning over a New Leaf at Booker,'' *Financial Times*, June 6, 1998.

''Ramsay to Advise Booker,'' *Catering and Hotel Keeper*, February 17, 2000, p. 61.

''A Rigorous Ethnic Role at Booker,'' *Grocer*, November 29, 2003, p. 15.

''So Far, So Good,'' *Investors Chronicle*, February 12, 1993, 21.

Thorncroft, Tony, ''New Chapter for the Booker,'' *Financial Times*, May 6, 2002, p. 14.

Voyle, Susanna, ''Booker Buys up Alldays Cash and Carry Subsidiary,'' *Financial Times*, November 30, 1999, p. 26.

Watson, Elaine, ''Booker Delivery Hubs Go Online,'' *Grocer*, October 12, 2002, p. 8.

Wray, Richard, ''Booker Says Chief Executive Bowen Was Asked to Leave,'' *AFX News*, March 17, 1998.

—April D. Gasbarre

—updates: Rebecca Stanfel; Frederick C. Ingram

Bricorama S.A.

21 Avenue du Marechal de Lattre de Tassigny
Fontenay sous Bois
F-94120
France
Telephone: (+33) 1 45 14 72 00
Fax: (+33) 1 45 14 72 10
Web site: http://www.bricorama.fr

Public Company
Incorporated: 1975
Employees: 3,737
Sales: EUR 810 million ($1.1 billion) (2003)
Stock Exchanges: Euronext Paris
Ticker Symbol: BRICO
NAIC: 444130 Hardware Stores

Bricorama S.A. operates the sixth largest retail do-it-yourself (DIY) and hardware store chain in France, with a growing presence in the European market, notably in Belgium and the Netherlands. The company is also the leading independent DIY and hardware retailer in France, as its primary competitors, such as Leroy Merlin, Castorama, Bricomarche, and Mr. Bricolate operate as subsidiaries of a large-scale French retail group. Bricorama targets the mid-sized market, with stores ranging in size from 800 square meters to 4,000 square meters for an average store size of 2,000 square meters. In 2004, however, the company began testing a 10,000-square-meter store concept with an accent on decoration and gardening. Bricorama typically operates near population centers of 35,000 to 40,000 residents but also operates a number of stores in the larger urban markets. Bricorama operates more than 160 stores, including 80 stores in France, 36 in Belgium, and 18 in the Netherlands, as well as 28 franchised stores in France's DOM-TOM possessions and North Africa. The company's stores operate under the Bricorama and Batkor names in France and the Gamma and Karwei names in Belgium and the Netherlands. Together, the company's stores represent more than 475,000 square meters of selling space. Bricorama is quoted on the Euronext Paris Stock Exchange. Founder Jean-Claude Bourrelier nonetheless retains control of 87 percent of the group's stock, with an additional 2 percent held by employees. In 2003, the company posted consolidated sales of EUR 810 million ($1.1 billion). France represents the group's largest market, at 65 percent of sales, while the Benelux market contributes 24 percent to sales.

Do-It-Yourself Hardware Empire in the 1970s

Jean-Claude Bourrelier was just 29 years old when, with a partner, he opened his first hardware store, in Paris's 13th arrondissement on the Place d'Italie, in 1975. From the start, Bourrelier envisioned a larger structure for his store in order better to compete against the fast-growing large-scale DIY groups in France at the time. For this, Bourrelier turned to the ANPF, a DIY store cooperative.

The ANPF roots reached back to the 1960s, at a time when the DIY market—known as ''bricolage'' in France—began its first wave of popularity. France's strong economic growth in the 1950s and 1960s had given people more leisure time, and new industries were appearing that catered to people's hobbies and leisure activities. Bricolage quickly emerged as a French favorite, and by the end of the 1960s the term had come to include everything from simple ''puttering about the house'' to full-scale DIY renovation and construction projects.

In 1964, a number of independent retailers came together to form a cooperative club, the Action Nationale des Promoteurs du Faite-le-vous-même (the French translation of ''do-it-yourself''), or ANPF. The ANPF, initially an informal grouping, developed into a purchasing cooperative by the end of the decade. During the 1970s, the ANPF's role became more and more central to its members. The years of recession in the 1970s had transformed bricolage from a hobby to an economic necessity, and during the decade a number of new large-scale store chains, such as Castorama and Leroy Merlin, had begun to challenge the nation's small hardware shops for control of the market.

The ANPF's members chose to differentiate themselves from their larger competitors, which typically targeted France's larger urban markets, with a focus on the country's mid-sized population centers. The ANPF stores also retained a mid-sized store format in order to provide closer customer service than the

Company Perspectives:

The leading independent group in the medium surface-size market, Bricorama has created stores on a human scale adapted to the needs of a primarily consumer clientele. Focusing on communities of 35,000 to 40,000 residents, the Group is also present in large urban centers with a perfect knowledge of its local markets.

larger stores were able to provide. By the end of the 1970s, the DIY cooperative members, who had continued to operate under their own store names, decided to create a single common name for their network. In 1980, the ANPF cooperative, including Jean-Claude Bourrelier, chose the name Mr. Bricolage.

By then, Bourrelier had already opened his second store, in Nogent-sur-Marne, in 1979. In 1980, Bourrelier bought up a third store, again in Paris. By 1983, Bourrelier had proven himself to be one of the fastest-growing members of the cooperative, with five stores under his control. The purchase of a sixth store, operating under the name Etablissements Wickes, brought Bourrelier into conflict with the ANPF for the first time. After the ANPF refused to allow the Wickes store to be converted to the Mr. Bricolage name, Bourrelier decided to launch a new format for the store, calling it Batkor. Instead of targeting DIY consumers, Batkor adopted a deep-discount approach, with a more limited range targeting the ''hardcore'' DIY segment and the professional trades.

Bourrelier continued adding new stores throughout the 1980s. By 1990, Bourrelier's holding had topped 13 stores. Yet Bourrelier's growing empire had brought him into increasing conflict with the ANPF, and in 1990 Bourrelier broke with the cooperative group. Bourrelier quickly sought a new umbrella structure for his store network, which remained tiny by comparison with the larger networks, and Bourrelier's stores were brought under the DIY arm of the Euromarché supermarket. In 1986, Euromarché had acquired the 16-store Bricorama chain; that store name was then applied to all of Euromarché's large-format stores in 1988. The company maintained a small- and mid-sized store format under the Euroloisirs name.

Bourrelier changed the name of his chain to IDF Bricolage, the IDF referring to the chain's focus on the Ile-de-France region around Paris. In 1990, IDF Bricolage moved beyond its core region with the acquisition of the seven-store Pictoral chain, based in the east of France. The following year, Bourrelier added three Projet stores, this time in the central and western parts of the country, as well as the single Fauvarge store, in Vitry-le-François. With his chain achieving national status, Bourrelier's store then took on the Batkor name. By then, Bourrelier operated more than 20 stores, with sales topping FFr412 million (approximately $70 million).

Independent in the 1990s

The Euromarché group was bought up by Carrefour in 1991. The retail giant sold off its newly acquired DIY operations the following year to the Castorama group. Castorama immediately turned over the 20 small- and mid-sized Euroloisirs stores to Bourrelier and Batkor, as well as the rights to the Bricorama name. Bourrelier then converted his consumer-oriented DIY store network to the Bricorama name, while maintaining the discount and trades-oriented Batkor format. In 1993, Bourrelier changed his company's name to Bricorama S.A.

The second half of the 1990s marked a new phase of rapid expansion for the company. Acquisition fueled much of Bricorama's growth, starting with the purchase of La Bricaillerie, a 15-unit network of small format stores operated by Castorama. The addition of La Bricaillerie boosted the company's total network to 54 stores, for sales of nearly FFr1.3 billion ($150 million).

Bricorama set its sights on a larger target in 1996, the DIY group GIB. In order to fund a takeover offer, the company decided to go public, listing on the Paris Stock Exchange in that year. Bourrelier, however, maintained firm control over his company, holding 87 percent of its shares. An additional 2 percent were held by the company's employees. The public offering helped raise Bricorama's profile; the GIB acquisition failed, however, when a purchase offer made by rival Leroy Merlin was accepted.

Bricorama turned to a new acquisition opportunity in 1997, when the U.K.'s Wickes Plc, reeling from an accounting scandal, announced its intention to sell off its retail holdings in Belgium, the Netherlands, and France. After negotiations with a number of groups, Wickes' choice fell on Bricorama, which acquired the 39 stores for £7.5 million ($11 million). These new stores boosted Bricoram's total to 95, with sales for the year nearly FFr2 billion ($350 million).

International DIY Group in the 2000s

Through the end of the 1990s, Bricorama made a number of smaller acquisitions, such as the six-store Outirama chain, based in the Rhone-Alpes, in 1998. The company also opened a new store in Belgium that year. At the turn of the 21st century, Bricorama implemented a new information technology system linking its stores and moved into new centralized headquarters in Fontenay-sous-Bois. Franchising also contributed to the company's growth, including a new franchised store in Bondy, near Paris. Most of the company's franchise activities took place outside of France, introducing the store name to such places as Réunion, New Caledonia, Wallis et Futuna, Guadeloupe, Guyane, and Saint-Martin in the DOM-TOM (French overseas departments) and in North Africa, including Morocco and Tunisia.

In 2001, Bricorama made a new major purchase, acquiring the more than 25 stores of the Bricostore chain. That purchase pushed Bricorama's network past 130 stores, and its annual sales past EUR 500 ($500 million). The Bricostore acquisition included 16 stores in Belgium that operated as franchises under the Gamma and Karwei brands, held by the Intergamma group. In 2002, Bricorama and Intergamma reached a licensing agreement, and Bricorama began converting its Belgium and Netherlands stores to the Gamma and Karwei formats.

Bricorama continued to progress toward mid-decade, successfully navigating the worst effects of an economic slowdown. The crushing competition for France's DIY market led

Key Dates:

1975: Jean-Claude Bourellier opens his first do-it-yourself store in Paris and joins ANPF.
1979: Bourellier opens a second store in Nogent-sur Marne.
1983: Bourellier opens his first Batkor store.
1986: Euromarche acquires the Bricorama chain.
1990: The company Leaves ANPF and joins Euromarche.
1992: Euromarche is acquired by Castorama; Bricorama is taken over by Bourellier.
1995: La Bircaillerie is acquired.
1996: Bricorama goes public on the Paris Stock Exchange.
1997: Wickes stores in Netherlands, Belgium, and France are acquired.
1998: The company acquires six Outirama stores.
2001: Bricorama installs new information technology (IT) system and acquires 22 stores from Bricostore.
2004: The company launches a 10,000-square-meter store format.

the company to begin developing a new method of differentiating itself to the public. In 2004, the company unveiled a store to test a new format. The new store featured more than 10,000 square meters of floor space, making it far and away the largest in the group. The larger format also emphasized decoration and gardening, two of the fastest-growing ''bricolage'' segments. The success of this store led the company to begin rolling out its new ''Passion'' format, with its base of decoration and gardening. While small among its far larger rivals, Bricorama represented a true DIY success story.

Principal Subsidiaries

Andenne Bricolage BVBA (Belgium); Batkor Finances BV (Netherlands); Boco NV (Belgium); Bouwar N.V. (Belgium); Braine L'alleud Bricolage BV (Belgium); BRICO 1; BRICO 2; Brico St Andre; Bricorama BV (Netherlands); Bricorama France; Bricorama N.V. (Netherlands); CB Bouwmarkten N.V. (Belgium); EPI Services; Gruto BVBA (Belgium); Lansa den Bosch (Netherlands); Lansa Schinjdel (Netherlands); Lokeren Doe Het Zelf B.V. (Belgium); M A G BVBA (Belgium); M A Z BVBA; Maatschap Bouwmarkt (Belgium); Megara Leerdam (Netherlands); Multi Hobby N.V. (Belgium); Robo N.V. (Belgium); Wabo N.V. (Belgium); Zelf Bouwmarkt (Netherlands).

Principal Competitors

METRO AG; Castorama SA; Leroy Merlin S.A.; Praktiker Bau- und Heimwerkermarkte AG; ProMarkt GmbH.

Further Reading

''French DIY Chain Bricorama Is Looking for an Investment Bank to Advise It on a Possible Sale,'' *Sunday Business*, December 9, 2001.

''Un entretien avec Jean-Claude Bourrelier,'' *Observatoire de la Franchise Infos*, June 25, 2002.

''Jean-Claude Bourrelier, PDG de Bricorama,'' September 10, 2004. Available from Canalchat.com.

—M.L. Cohen

Brown Shoe Company, Inc.

8300 Maryland Avenue
St. Louis, Missouri 63105
U.S.A.
Telephone: (314) 854-4000
Toll Free: (800) 766-6465
Fax: (314) 854-4274
Web site: http://www.brownshoe.com

Public Company
Incorporated: 1881 as Bryan Brown Shoe Company
Employees: 11,600
Sales: $1.83 billion (2003)
Stock Exchanges: New York
Ticker Symbol: BWS
NAIC: 316219 Other Footwear Manufacturing; 316213 Men's Footwear (Except Athletic) Manufacturing; 316999 All Other Leather Good Manufacturing; 424340 Footwear Merchant Wholesalers; 448210 Shoe Stores

Brown Shoe Company, Inc., is a retailer, wholesaler, and licenser of men's, women's, and children's footwear. Brown operates 900 retail stores in the United States under the names Famous Footwear, Supermarket of Shoes, Warehouse of Shoes, and Factory Brand Shoes. Naturalizer, the company's flagship brand of women's shoes, supports a chain of nearly 400 retail outlets in North America. The company's wholesale division markets branded, licensed, and private label footwear to mass merchandisers and department stores throughout the country. Buster Brown & Co., which represents the company's children's footwear business, markets Buster Brown shoes as well as other brands geared toward children. Brown operates online through Shoes.com, which features more than 150 footwear brands.

A 19th-Century Shoe Manufacturer

Brown Shoe Company began as a shoe manufacturing concern. George Warren Brown moved to St. Louis from New York in 1873 to work in his older brother's wholesale shoe business. While working as a traveling salesman, Brown came to see great potential in the St. Louis area for shoe manufacturing. At that time, shoes were primarily manufactured on the East Coast. Skilled workers in New England factories made shoes that were then shipped to jobbers at points west. Brown believed that shoes could be made more cheaply in St. Louis than in the established East Coast factories. After working for four years in his brother's wholesale business, Brown had accumulated enough capital to test his idea. With two other investors, Alvin L. Bryan and Jerome Desnoyers, Brown founded Bryan, Brown and Company to make women's shoes. Brown paid five skilled shoemakers from Rochester, New York, to come to St. Louis and start the factory. The company grew rapidly. In its first year, 1878, the company had sales of $110,000. In 1881, the company incorporated as the Bryan Brown Shoe Company. In 1893, Desnoyers retired, and the name was changed to The Brown Shoe Company. In 1885, when Bryan sold his interest, the name was changed to Brown-Desnoyers Shoe Company. Brown shoes were sold all over the Midwest at prices lower than those of the older New England shoe firms. By 1900, the company was growing at a rate of $1 million a year, and St. Louis was becoming known as a major shoe manufacturing center.

Also in 1900, Brown Shoe contributed $10,000 to the St. Louis World's Fair, a gala event that put a spotlight on the Missouri town. The company put up a model shoe plant at the fair, and this exhibit won Brown a grand prize. Another exhibitor at the fair was the cartoonist R. Fenton Outcault, creator of the popular comic strips The Yellow Kid and Buster Brown. A young Brown executive, John A. Bush, made a lasting contribution to his company by buying the rights to the Buster Brown character in 1904. The little blond boy and his dog Tige became the emblem of the Brown Shoe Company children's line. In addition to printing the Buster logo on its shoe boxes, the company hired 20 little people to dress as Buster Brown and tour the country. Buster and Tige played in theaters, shoe stores, and department stores across the country to much popular acclaim.

While some youngsters were applauding the Buster Brown little people, others were at work in Brown Shoe factories under deplorable conditions for extremely low pay. Because the cost of plant equipment and materials was relatively fixed, Brown Shoe had to make its profits by keeping its labor costs as low as

Company Perspectives:

We're Brown Shoe. We're moving forward, growing, forever seeking new ways to delight our customers. We believe our success is the result of continual testing and learning—the kind of disciplined approach that leads to new levels of success. People of integrity, true partners, working together to deliver a remarkable footwear shopping experience to today's consumer. We're always striving to be the best, to be the leader in footwear.

possible. As manufacturing became more mechanized, shoe factory jobs became less skilled. Increasingly, shoe manufacturing jobs were filled by women and children, who could be paid less than men. For example, a 1911 survey of St. Louis shoe workers found more than half to be between the ages of 14 and 19. Some 84 percent of the women and close to 70 percent of the men were under age 24. An average wage for a girl under 16 was less than $10 per week. More shoe manufacturers had followed George Warren Brown's example and set up shoe factories in St. Louis, making the industry extremely competitive. Under these conditions, the wage paid to shoe workers spiraled down.

By 1902, Brown Shoe was operating five factories in St. Louis. In 1907, the company started its first ''out of town'' plant, in nearby Moberly, Missouri. Several St. Louis shoe companies began manufacturing in surrounding rural towns because of the cheaper labor available in those areas.

In response to the poor working conditions at Brown and in other St. Louis-area shoe factories, workers formed unions. The first was the moderate Boot and Shoe Workers Union; the second was the more radical United Shoe Workers of America, associated with the International Workers of the World. Bitter strikes led to increasing militancy among St. Louis shoe workers. George Warren Brown responded by becoming a local leader of the Citizens Industrial Association, a nationwide anti-union propaganda organization that maintained blacklists against union sympathizers. The best way to fight the unions, however, proved to be to leave St. Louis.

The small towns around St. Louis offered many advantages to the Brown Shoe Company. It was standard at that time for a town that wanted a shoe factory to offer to build one for a company and exempt the company from paying taxes. In return, the company would agree to pay out a certain amount of money in wages over a five- or ten-year period. After the stipulated amount of wages had been paid, the company had no more obligation to the town. There were always more towns willing to subsidize a new shoe factory. While Brown's management remained headquartered in St. Louis, the company opened factories in many rural towns in Missouri and Illinois. Each town's economy became dependent on the shoe factory, and pro-company sentiments within the factory towns created a hostile climate for union organizers. The distance between the factories also made union organization more difficult than it had been in the condensed St. Louis shoe district.

Regardless of worker discontent, the Brown Shoe Company grew. In 1907, the company moved its headquarters to a stately building in downtown St. Louis. In 1913, Brown was listed on the New York Stock Exchange. With the entrance of the United States into World War I in 1917, Brown Shoe won profitable army contracts.

The company stumbled in 1920, however, when a sudden change in women's fashions caught Brown by surprise. Hemlines went up, and Brown was left with an overstock of sturdy high-topped shoes that did not go with the new look at all. John Bush, who had bought the Buster Brown logo rights and then worked his way up to president in 1915, when George Warren Brown became chairman of the board, had to go to Boston before he found a bank that would give the company credit. After this crisis, however, Brown Shoe boomed until the stock market crashed in 1929 and the Great Depression set in.

Labor Strife Reaches Peak During Great Depression

During the Depression, Brown Shoe struggled to keep its costs down, which meant that workers' wages suffered. A National Labor Relations Board investigation at Brown's Salem, Illinois, plant found that workers were sometimes drawing checks for as low as $2.50 and $3.00 for a 60-hour week. Workers protested worsening conditions in Brown's factories, but the company's management grew more abusive. President Franklin D. Roosevelt drafted the National Industrial Recovery Act in 1933 to force industries to standardize wages and prices and thus alleviate the workers' downward wage spiral. Two years later, the Wagner Act guaranteed all U.S. workers the right to organize into unions and to strike. Brown's management, however, remained adamantly anti-union. When workers at the Vincennes, Indiana, factory struck for recognition of their union in 1933, Brown closed the plant. William Kaut, the company's general manager in St. Louis, declared that ''The intention of the Brown Shoe Company is to do as much for their help as any shoe industry in the United States . . . and when Brown Shoe Company does its part and even more and if the help are then not satisfied, there is only one thing left to do and that is to close the mill.'' What the Brown Shoe Company was doing for its help, however, reportedly included physical intimidation of union organizers, spying on and infiltrating workers' organizations, and hiring a notorious strike-breaking agency, in addition to its policy of closing down ''troublesome'' plants.

Eventually, Brown attracted national attention when a union representative in Sullivan, Illinois, narrowly escaped being tarred and feathered in September 1935, and the Illinois Federation of Labor forced a grand-jury investigation. No indictments resulted, but the Regional Labor Board in St. Louis later issued a complaint, citing Brown for unfair labor practices and for using officers and agents of the company to intimidate employees. The hearing that followed revealed that John A. Bush had hired the A.A. Ahner detective agency in 1934. Bush testified that he did not know that Ahner was a strike-breaking agency, but Ahner was in fact known as such in St. Louis. In 1929, he had been implicated in an attempted bombing connected with anti-union work. Although Ahner himself claimed he was not hired to break unions, a report in the *Nation* on January 29, 1936 noted that termination of Ahner's connection with the shoe company coincided with the dissolution of most of the locals of the Boot and Shoe Workers' Union in Brown plants.

It was not only physical threats and the economic threat of plant shut-downs that led many union locals to disband. The

Key Dates:

1878: Bryan, Brown and Company is formed, incorporating as Bryan Brown Shoe Company three years later.
1904: The company buys the rights to the Richard Fenton Outcault cartoon character, Buster Brown.
1913: Brown Shoe Company debuts on the New York Stock Exchange.
1950: Brown Shoe Company acquires Wohl Stores, marking its entry into the retail sector.
1969: Brown Shoe Company begins to diversify, changing its name to Brown Group, Inc. in 1972 to reflect the company's variegated interests.
1985: Brown Group announces the divestiture of its recreational products assets.
1986: The acquisition of Pagoda Trading Company, an Asia-based importing firm, signals the company's move away from manufacturing.
1995: The last company-owned shoe factory in the United States is closed.
1999: After changing its name back to Brown Shoe Company, Inc., the company attempts to revitalize its image and brands.
2002: More than 100 Naturalizer stores are closed and 700 Famous Footwear outlets are remodeled as part of the company's sweeping restructuring efforts.
2003: The company signs a licensing agreement to design, source, and market footwear under the Bass label.

Labor Board hearings revealed that Brown had kept a paid spy in its Sullivan factory. The spy turned out to be the former head of the union local. After urging workers into an ill-timed strike, he then incited his union's members to burn the union charter and disband. He was later overheard telephoning Brown headquarters to report his success. Attacked from within and without, most of the Boot and Shoe Workers Union locals at Brown plants folded, because workers were desperate to hang on to their jobs. Brown sometimes closed its plants temporarily, later to rehire only workers who had had no union involvement.

The National Labor Relations Board cited Brown in 1936 for violating the Wagner Act in connection with the dissolution of the Salem local, but the company refused to reinstate strikers and workers who had been fired for union activity. The workers who had not lost their jobs at Brown were finally given some help in their struggle for decent wages when the Fair Labor Standards Act of 1938 established a minimum wage in the United States. The labor shortage during World War II finally gave a boost to union organization, although unrest continued to some degree.

In 1941, Brown opened a new plant in Dyer, Tennessee. A Brown executive, Monte Shomaker, who was later to serve as Brown's fourth president, urged the move south. Shomaker worked to modernize Brown's factories after the war and to relocate many of them in the traditionally nonunion South. At the same time, Brown's third president, Clark Gamble, was taking steps to move the company into retailing.

Expansion into Retailing in the 1950s

Gamble assumed the presidency of Brown from John Bush in 1948, and in 1950 he initiated a merger with Wohl Shoes. Wohl was a 35-year-old wholesale and retail shoe business with headquarters in St. Louis and had annual sales of $33 million, 90 percent of which came from women's shoes. Brown had provided only 10 percent of Wohl's shoes before the merger, which provided a large new market for Brown. Wohl wholesaled shoes through 2,500 stores throughout the United States, Canada, Mexico, and Cuba and operated several hundred retail stores and leased department store shoe salons. With this first major acquisition, Brown took a giant step toward integrating its operations into both manufacturing and retailing.

The Wohl merger was followed by Brown's acquisition of another large retail chain in 1953, Regal Shoes. When Brown acquired G.R. Kinney Corporation in 1956, the company had gone far toward assuring itself of both manufacturing and retailing capabilities. Brown was then the fourth-largest shoe manufacturer in the United States, and Kinney the largest operator of family shoe stores. A U.S. District Court in St. Louis, however, found Brown guilty of antitrust violations in 1959 and ordered the company to divest itself of Kinney. The judge in the case concluded that the Brown-Kinney merger seriously limited the ability of independent retailers to compete with company-owned retail outlets, as well as limiting the market for independent manufacturers. In 1962, the Supreme Court upheld the lower court's ruling. By that year, Brown had taken the number-one spot in the shoe industry. Brown subsequently sold Kinney to F.W. Woolworth.

Monte Shomaker took over the presidency of Brown from Clark Gamble in 1962. Despite the setback of the Kinney ruling, Shomaker was able to continue Brown's expansion. In 1959, the company had acquired Perth Shoe Company, a Canadian firm with wholesale, retail, and manufacturing operations. In 1965, Brown bought the Samuels Shoe Company, a high-fashion women's shoe company, and in 1970 Brown acquired a men's shoe importer, Italia Bootwear, Ltd.

Diversifying in the 1970s

Brown's earnings rose each year in the 1960s, until a flood of imports swamped the U.S. shoe industry in 1968. The company's earnings plunged 25 percent in 1969. A new president, W.L. Hadley Griffin, took over that year. Griffin decided to do what other large shoe companies had been doing for years, that is, to diversify into nonshoe areas. Brown quickly acquired retail fabric chains, the Eagle Rubber Company, Kent Sporting Goods, and a luggage sales company, among others. In 1972, The Brown Shoe Company changed its name to Brown Group, Inc., to reflect the company's diversification. By 1973, close to 20 percent of Brown's sales were coming from its nonfootwear subsidiaries. The Brown Group continued to diversify through the 1970s, buying up companies in two main areas: children's products and sports and recreation.

In 1979, W.L. Hadley Griffin moved up to chairman, and B.A. Bridgewater became the new president. Bridgewater had worked in President Richard Nixon's Office of Management and Budget, where he set fiscal priorities for the State Department, the Defense Department, and the Central Intelligence Agency. Bridgewater introduced cost-cutting measures at Brown, including reductions in the workforce and cutbacks in executive perquisites. Bridgewater's first year set a record for the Brown Group; sales were up 16 percent, earnings up 25 percent, and the company posted a net income of $41 million. Increased costs and foreign competition, however, led Brown to close its St. Louis warehouse in 1980.

Competition Leads to Restructuring in 1980s–90s

Pressure from cheap imports led to more competitive conditions in the U.S. shoe market throughout the 1980s, and Bridgewater had to constantly adjust the Brown Group's business strategy. In the 1970s, diversification into nonshoe areas had proved essential, but in the 1980s, slimming down the company and concentrating on shoe retailing seemed to be the right thing. In 1982, Brown's recreational products division sagged, and Bridgewater ordered a restructuring, which included plant closings and changes in marketing and management. In 1985, after a very poor third quarter, the company announced it would divest itself of all its recreational products operations. The divestiture left Brown with about 75 percent of its business concentrated in shoe manufacture and retailing. The other 25 percent represented various other retail operations, such as Brown's line of fabric stores, specialty women's clothing stores, and the Meis chain of department stores.

In the mid-1980s, Brown bid to keep its shoe business competitive by moving more strongly into shoe importing. Brown acquired Arnold Dunn, Inc., a women's shoe importer, in 1984. That year Brown established an importing division, Brown Group International, and in 1986 it acquired the Pagoda Trading Company, a Far-East importing firm. Importing proved far more profitable than manufacturing. The company closed several U.S. shoe plants but at the same time improved the efficiency of its remaining factories. By 1988, Brown was able to produce almost as many shoes as in 1980, in spite of a 40 percent reduction in the number of plants it operated. The company also opted to concentrate on marketing its well-known brands such as Connie, Naturalizer, and Buster Brown, and discontinue its marginal lines.

Ultimately, over the course of the early and mid-1990s—and under the continuing leadership of Bridgewater—Brown dramatically restructured itself into a footwear retailing and wholesaling company, with shoe manufacturing almost entirely jettisoned and all nonfootwear businesses divested. In 1989, the company sold off all of its remaining nonfootwear specialty retail operations with the exception of the Cloth World retail fabric chain. The following year, the Pagoda International division was formed to market footwear to retailers in Europe, and eventually in Latin America and the Far East. Brown closed six of its fast-dwindling domestic shoe plants in 1991 and 1992. The following year, it began to shutter its troubled Wohl Leased Shoe Department operation, which managed 500 shoe departments in 26 department store chains.

Brown's restructuring efforts reached a peak in 1994 and 1995. All of the company's remaining U.S. shoe factories were closed, leaving Brown with only two manufacturing plants in Canada. More than 100 company-owned Regal and Connie specialty shoe stores and 50 Naturalizer stores were closed. Three of the company's five headquarters buildings were sold, along with its Cloth World chain to Fabri-Centers of America, Inc. for $65.7 million, thereby returning to a pure focus on footwear. More than 8,500 jobs were eliminated as a result of these moves, about 35 percent of the overall workforce.

Freed from several burdensome operations, Brown began to bolster its core businesses through acquisitions and licensing deals. In 1995, the company acquired the Larry Stuart Collection, an upscale women's shoe brand. Brown beefed up its offerings in the hot athletic shoe segment with the 1995 acquisition of the le coq sportif brand (a century-old brand popular in Latin America, Europe, and the Far East) from Adidas AG and with 1996 license agreements through which Brown would market athletic footwear under the Russell and Penn brand names. Pagoda International, meanwhile, built up an impressive list of famous brands that it licensed for use on shoes sold to children outside the United States, including Barbie; Star Wars; Disney's 101 Dalmatians, Hunchback of Notre Dame, and Mickey for Kids; and Warner Brothers' Looney Tunes, Batman, and Space Jam.

By 1996, Brown's extensive and lengthy restructuring had begun to show signs of paying off. The downsized company's sales of $1.53 billion were still well below the levels of the late 1980s and early 1990s, but when adjusted for discontinued operations, sales were on the rise. Profits—$20.3 million in 1996—were recovering as well. In possession of an impressive and expanding assortment of brands, Brown looked to step up its advertising in order to further increase sales with $21 million (8 percent of sales) slated for brand marketing in fiscal 1997. The company was also expected to continue to aggressively pursue overseas sales, which although on the increase still comprised less than 1 percent of overall sales.

Turnaround at the Turn of the 21st Century

The return of Brown's exclusive focus on footwear was reflected in a revival to the company's long-used corporate title. In 1999, the company again began calling itself Brown Shoe Company, Inc. Ronald Fromm, a Brown executive promoted to president in 1998, was appointed chief executive officer and chairman of the company in January 1999. The name change and the appointment of a new leader marked the beginning of a sweeping reorganization program, as Brown sought to revitalize its operations and brands, endeavoring to lose its "reputation for making shoes only grandma could love," as *Knight Ridder/Tribune Business News* noted in a May 18, 2003 article. The company was in dire need of improving both the appeal of its brands and the fundamental way in which it operated. Fromm invested heavily in product design and marketing research, registering notable success with the company's Naturalizer brand. An advertising campaign aimed at attracting younger customers was launched in 1999 that, along with more stylish designs, dramatically increased the brand's popularity. In 1998, Naturalizer ranked as the eighth-largest women's shoe brand sold at department stores. Within five years, the brand ranked as the second-largest seller.

While the Naturalizer brand was making its march up the industry rankings, Fromm initiated a cost-cutting program and revamped the company's retail operations. He implemented stricter control over inventory, closed under-performing stores, and improved efficiency by removing redundant functions with the company's operations. "We looked realistically at the fact that we didn't return a competitive operating margin," Fromm explained in an April 17, 2003 interview with *Business Week Online,* "and we saw a number of things we could do." After two years of restructuring the company, Fromm realized positive results in 2002, when the company's operating profits swelled more than 50 percent. Brown's retail operations also received attention Fromm's salubrious touch. In 2002, Fromm closed 106 Naturalizer stores that were performing poorly. He also remodeled 700 of the company's 921 Famous Footwear stores, adding new lighting, fixtures, and signage. In the future, Fromm intended to open new 8,000- to 12,000-square-foot Famous Footwear shops near retailers such as Target and Wal-Mart.

As Brown prepared for the future, its progress during the early years of the decade offered consumers and investors a more dynamic version of a company that had been in business for over a century. After posting a $4 million loss in 2001, the company registered a $45.2 million profit in 2002, prompting its stock to increase nearly 80 percent in value during the first half of 2003. At the end of 2003, Brown signed a long-term licensing agreement to design, source, and market footwear under Phillips-Van Heusen Corp.'s Bass label. As part of the deal, Brown also gained a new senior executive. Diane Sullivan, a 20-year veteran of the footwear industry who served as vice-president of Phillips-Van Heusen's footwear group, became Brown's president at the end of 2003. Under the leadership of Fromm and Sullivan, Brown continued with its turnaround efforts, attempting to breathe new vitality into one of the country's oldest footwear companies.

Principal Subsidiaries

Brown California, Inc.; Brown Cayman Ltd. (Cayman Islands); Brown Group International, LLC; Brown Group Retail, Inc.; Brown Missouri, Inc.; Brown Retail Development Company; Brown Shoe de Mexico, S.A. de C.V.; Brown Shoe Investment Company, Inc.; Brown Shoe International Sales and Licensing S.r.l. (Italy); Brown Shoe International Sales and Licensing Ltd. (Hong Kong); Brown Texas, Inc.; Buster Brown & Company; CV Missouri L.L.C.; DongGuan Leeway Footwear Company Limited (China); Leeway International Company Ltd.; Maryland Square, Inc.; Maserati Footwear, Inc.; PIC International Corporation (Cayman Islands); Pagoda International Corporation do Brazil Ltda.; Pagoda International Footwear Ltd. (Hong Kong); Pagoda Leather Ltd. (Hong Kong); Shoes.com (91%); Sidney Rich Associates, Inc.; Whitenox Ltd.; Pagoda Trading North America, Inc.; Brown Shoe Company of Canada, Ltd.; Laysan Company Limited (Hong Kong); Brown Group Dublin Ltd. (Ireland).

Principal Divisions

Brown Shoe Retail; Brown Shoe Wholesale; Famous Footwear; Naturalizer.

Principal Competitors

Footstar, Inc.; Payless ShoeSource, Inc.; Wal-Mart Stores, Inc.

Further Reading

Abel, Katie, "Adding to the Sum of Its Parts," *Footwear News*, August 16, 2004, p. 6.

Bess, Alycce, "Fashion Remains a Priority for Brown Shoe," *Footwear News*, June 7, 2004, p. 39.

Brown Group: *The First Hundred Years*, St. Louis, Mo.: Brown Group, Inc., 1978.

Byrne, Harlan S., "Brown Group: Prosperity Following a Shakeout," *Barron's*, March 15, 1993, pp. 46–47.

Feurer, Rosemary, "Shoe City, Factory Towns: St. Louis Shoe Companies and the Turbulent Drive for Cheap Rural Labor, 1900–1940," *Gateway Heritage*, Fall 1988.

Harris, William, "Buster Brown Lives," *Forbes*, July 19, 1982, p. 50.

Heiderstadt, Donna, "Brown Group Puts Growth on Value, Traditional Bases," *Footwear News*, August 9, 1993, p. 24.

Lee, Thomas, "After Years of Troubleshooting, Brown Shoe Captures Top Market Share," *Knight Ridder/Tribune Business News*, May 18, 2003.

Ludington, Callaway, "Brown Group Strides Toward Recovery," *St. Louis Business Journal*, August 6, 1990, pp. 1A, 11A.

Macdonald, Laurie, "Far Reaching Restructuring Under Way at Brown Group," *Footwear News*, January 17, 1994, p. 1.

Owens, Jennifer, "Brown Shoe Signs Bass Licensing Deal with PVH," *Footwear News*, December 29, 2003, p. 2.

——, "Power House," *Footwear News*, December 8, 2003, p. 20.

Quick, Julie, "Bridgewater Shakes Brown's Cobwebs," *St. Louis Business Journal*, January 13, 1992, pp. 1A, 10A.

Sahm, Cathy, "Brown Enters Athletic Shoe Race," *St. Louis Business Journal*, March 25, 1991, pp. 1A, 19A.

Sender, Isabelle, "Brown Factory Closings Lead to $8.4M Qtr. Loss," *Footwear News*, September 11, 1995, p. 1.

Stone, Amey, "Online Extra: Brown Shoe: Still Climbing," *Business Week Online*, April 17, 2003, p. 34.

—Angela Woodward
—updates: David E. Salamie; Jeffrey L. Covell

Bruno's, Inc.

Bruno's Supermarkets, Inc.

800 Lakeshore Parkway
P.O. Box 2486
Birmingham, Alabama 35201-2486
U.S.A.
Telephone: (205) 940-9400
Fax: (205) 940-9568
Web site: http://www.brunos.com

Wholly Owned Subsidiary of Ahold USA
Incorporated: 1959
Employees: 14,500
Sales: $1.74 billion (2004)
NAIC: 445110 Supermarkets and Other Grocery (Except Convenience) Stores

Bruno's Supermarkets, Inc., operates some of the largest supermarket chains in the southeastern United States. One of the nation's most successful supermarket companies, Bruno's operated more than 200 stores, including a variety of retail food stores, pharmacies, and combination food and drug stores in Alabama, Georgia, Florida, Mississippi, and Tennessee. Located in urban and rural settings, these stores comprised Food World, Bruno's Food and Pharmacy, FoodMax, and Food Fair. For years the company had operated dozens of stores under the Piggly Wiggly name but had terminated its franchise agreement allowing it to use the name in 1997. In 2001, Bruno's emerged from bankruptcy and was acquired by Ahold USA, the U.S. presence of the Dutch conglomerate Royal Ahold N.V.

Early History

In 1932 during the Great Depression, Joseph Bruno, the son of Sicilian immigrants, opened his first grocery, an 800-square-foot corner store in Birmingham, Alabama. Using his parent's savings for an initial investment of $600, Joe would achieve the kind of success that young immigrants still dream of. Joe's cash-only policy enabled him to keep prices low, and customers came from all over Birmingham to the first Bruno's store. As they became old enough to work, Joe's three brothers, Anthony, Angelo, and Lee, joined the business. In 1935 the family opened a second store. By April 1, 1959, when the company was incorporated in Alabama as Bruno's, Inc., all four Bruno sons were well established in the business. The company had a firm foundation of 10 stores that year.

A decade later Bruno's began its strategy of opening different chains to target different markets. In 1968 the company opened its first Big B Discount Drug Store, a chain that would grow steadily over the next dozen years. Bruno's Food Stores had also been expanding, reaching a total of 29 stores throughout Alabama by 1970. The following year the family took their business public, although they retained 30 percent of the shares and held on to the management of the company.

In 1972 Bruno's launched its Food World chain. The stores were designed as discount supermarkets, and Bruno's kept prices low with many innovative strategies that would later be widely imitated. More than 40,000 square feet in area, the stores were essentially warehouses that displayed shelves of food in manufacturers' cartons. Their economical store design and no-frills service encouraged high sales volume and low overhead. Food World was the first chain in the region to forgo periodic sales on selected merchandise in favor of everyday low prices.

Expansion in the 1980s

After the success of the Food World chain, Bruno's refined its marketing strategy in the 1980s, more closely targeting different market segments. First, Bruno's divested its Big B Discount Drug Stores in 1980 by offering all stock in the subsidiary to the public. In 1983 the company remodeled its Bruno's Food Stores and renamed the chain Bruno's Food and Pharmacy. Aiming for a higher-end market, these stores stocked gourmet items from the United States and overseas and boasted larger-than-average departments for produce, meat, seafood, deli items, and baked goods. With about 50,000 square feet per store, Bruno's Food and Pharmacy featured one-stop shopping, in-store banks, and specialty items. The combination food and drug stores were committed to customer service, with such amenities as bag boys carrying groceries to customers' cars. The same year Bruno's opened its first Bruno's Finer Foods, and in 1985 it launched its Food Fair chain. Food Fair stores, at only approximately 30,000 square feet, were designed as con-

Company Perspectives:

One company, with one mission: to be the premier grocery retailer in the Southeast, one that understands, anticipates and surpasses customer expectations for value and service.

ventional neighborhood stores with personal service and promotional pricing.

Bruno's also expanded through acquisitions in the 1980s. In 1985 the company bought the Birmingham, Alabama, chain Megamarket. Bruno's changed the new stores' name, adding them to its FoodMax chain, another ''Value Format'' supermarket chain with warehouse-like facilities in the 50,000 to 60,000 square foot range. Bruno's moved into Tennessee in 1987 with the purchase of the Steven's Supermarket chain in Nashville. The company also bought seven BiLo supermarkets in 1988, which moved the company into Georgia.

Also in 1988, Bruno's acquired PWS Holding Corporation, which held Piggly Wiggly Southern, Inc. This purchase helped Bruno's achieve a substantial expansion in northern Georgia and Florida. The acquisition of 58 Piggly Wiggly stores was Bruno's first major competitive purchase. The price was 2.49 million shares of Bruno's common stock. Bruno's retained some of Piggly Wiggly's management, naming the former Piggly Wiggly Southern president, William White, executive vice-president of Bruno's for merchandising and operations. Piggly Wiggly stores were conventional supermarkets typically 28,000 square feet in size. They offered store specials, double manufacturers' coupons, and weekly selected merchandise specials.

In September 1987 Angelo Bruno, cofounder and then chair, signed a joint venture agreement with Kmart. Considered a bold move for Bruno's, the idea was to build hypermarkets of approximately 200,000 square feet all over the country. The hypermarkets would combine groceries and general merchandise, selling everything from vegetables to clothing and featuring up to 50 checkout stands. Such shopping centers already existed in Europe, and this was not the first time hypermarkets would open in the United States. However, this venture represented the first partnership between a grocery chain with the food expertise of Bruno's and a general retailer with expertise in merchandise sales. The management of Bruno's felt that the new sales could boost growth, even in the traditionally slow grocery trade. Three American Fare hypermarkets owned jointly by Kmart and Bruno's opened between 1989 and 1991 in Atlanta, Georgia; Charlotte, North Carolina; and Jackson, Mississippi.

In the late 1980s Bruno's had a reputation in the industry for aggressive, effective management and practices. For instance, it bought most of its food directly from manufacturers rather than from wholesalers. When manufacturers wanted their products sold at Bruno's stores, they made presentations directly to a committee of Bruno's managers, many of whom were part of the Bruno family. If the committee decided to buy the products, they usually bought large quantities and qualified for the largest volume discounts. That way, Bruno's could save money and pass the savings on to their customers. In addition, Bruno's store managers were compensated according to how much money their stores made. This put pressure on them to keep inventories moving, but most Bruno's managers were happy to hustle, especially knowing they could earn as much as $80,000 in a good year. Many of these managers started at Bruno's while they were still in high school and stayed, and this loyalty served the company well.

Always on the lookout for new technology to improve operations in its stores, in the early 1990s Bruno's installed minicomputers connected to the Birmingham mainframe computer in its stores. These computers were used primarily to improve direct store buying and delivery. The system also enabled stores to monitor customer traffic in order to adjust labor needs. They also used the computers to keep track of store employees' attendance and working hours. The warehouse was also highly computerized. Food arrived from manufacturers and was priced, inventoried, and loaded onto Bruno's trucks for delivery to stores. The shipments, arrivals, pricing, and deliveries were also tracked on computer.

A tremendous test to Bruno's organization came in a tragic accident on December 11, 1991, when six Bruno's executives and three others were killed in a crash of the corporate jet shortly after takeoff in Rome, Georgia. The executives, including cofounders Angelo Bruno and his brother Lee Bruno, were on their annual Christmas visit to all of their stores when the crash occurred. Also killed were Sam Vacarella, the senior vice-president for merchandising; Edward Hyde, vice-president for store operations; Randolph Page, a vice-president for personnel; Karl Mollica, produce director; and Mary Faust, an advertising account executive working with Bruno's. The accident took an emotional toll on the family business and required much shifting of personnel. Angelo's son Ronald Bruno, who had been groomed to run the company and who had already been designated president and chief executive officer, was elected to the chair. In August 1992 Bruno's, Inc. bought 3.6 million shares of common stock from the estates of Angelo and Lee Bruno.

Bruno's entered the 1990s in the top 40 of some 270 food stores ranked by sales volume. National competition consisted of such chains as American Stores, Kroger, Safeway, Winn-Dixie, and Jewel, whereas Food Lion, Albertson's, and Giant Food competed with Bruno's mainly in the southeast region. Many of Bruno's competitors in Georgia suffered after Bruno's 1988 acquisition of Piggly Wiggly. However, Bruno's continued to keep watch over its competition as Warehouse clubs and Wal-Mart supercenters began to pose a challenge to Bruno's in several of its larger markets.

Problems in the 1990s

Bruno's, like many food retailers and supermarket operators, suffered during the recession of the late 1980s and early 1990s. Some store sales were slow while consumer spending plummeted. Food prices went down, and consumers were spending less money on food. In addition, competition from Wal-Mart and supermarket chains Winn-Dixie and Publix intensified in the 1990s. In 1992 alone Wal-Mart opened three Supercenters in Birmingham and Publix elbowed into Bruno's territory in Atlanta. Profits for Bruno's, which had more than quadrupled in the last decade, fell 37 percent in 1992. Combined with the loss of the company's leadership in the 1991

Key Dates:

1932: Joseph Bruno sets up a grocery store in Birmingham, Alabama.
1959: Ten stores are incorporated as Bruno's Inc.
1970: Some 29 Bruno's stores are in operation across Alabama.
1985: Company launches is Food Fair chain and acquires the Megamarket chain.
1995: Company is acquired by the buyout firm Kohlberg Kravis Roberts & Co.
2001: Bruno's emerges from Chapter 11 and is acquired by Ahold USA.

plane crash, the lowered profits fed doubts about the company's future on Wall Street. The stock price plummeted from a high of $21 a share in 1991, coming to rest around $12 in 1993. With 256 stores and $2.7 billion in sales in 1992, Bruno's still had a firm foundation on which to rebuild its growth.

Two major changes hurt Bruno's bottom line in 1992 but promised savings in the future. In June 1992 Bruno's announced an end to its joint venture with Kmart. Kmart assumed full ownership of the hypermarkets, taking over Bruno's 49 percent interest in the Atlanta and Charlotte stores and its 51 percent interest in the Jackson store. Bruno's management noted, "We felt it was time to eliminate our loss from the American Fare stores and focus our full attention on our primary store concerns." The company took a charge of $.13 a share, or $10.8 million, for the fiscal year ending in June 1992. Although the one-time charge contributed to the company's lowered profits in 1992, the sale would eliminate the company's $3.5 million annual loss from the joint venture.

Also during fiscal 1992, Bruno's finalized plans to consolidate the Piggly Wiggly division offices from Vidalia, Georgia, to a unit in the Birmingham corporate office. According to Ronald Bruno, savings from the closed Vidalia division offices would be in the vicinity of $5 million. The offices were officially closed in 1992, but the distribution center in Vidalia remained. Bruno's planned to use the facility as a jumping-off point for new operations in that geographic area.

Sales and earnings remained stagnant throughout 1993 and 1994, and despite a reorganization eliminating several layers of management, Bruno's share price continued to fall. Fluctuating between $7 and $10 a share, the low stock price made Bruno's ripe for a takeover. Rumors of a buyout were circulating in 1994, and the following year Kohlberg Kravis Roberts & Co. (KKR) approached Bruno's with an offer to acquire the company for $12.50 a share. The Bruno family held 24 percent of the company in 1995, and Ronald Bruno still ran the company as chief executive officer. Bruno's agreed to the $1 billion offer, which would give KKR 97 percent of the company. Although during negotiations there was talk of Ronald Bruno remaining as chairman of the board for at least three years, he stepped down soon after the buyout. KKR finished the acquisition in 1995, making its subsidiary Crimson Associates L.P. the official owner of the stock.

Optimism was high after the KKR takeover. KKR had made resounding successes of two other grocery chains, Safeway and Stop & Shop, and hoped to do the same for Bruno's. One of the first changes initiated by KKR was moving from every day low pricing at the Bruno's Food and Pharmacy stores to high-low pricing. For example, Bruno's began featuring buy-one-get-one-free offers. In 1996 the company cut costs by closing its distribution center in Georgia and closing or selling 47 underperforming stores.

These efforts did little to slow Bruno's fall: Sales stayed flat at around $2.9 billion, but earnings fell from $33 million in 1995 to a loss of $71 million in 1996. In 1997 KKR brought in Jack Demme, who had helped make a success of supermarket chain Homeland Stores, as president, CEO, and chairman of the board. The same year, Bruno's did not renew the franchise agreement that gave it the use of the Piggly Wiggly name.

Losses for 1997 came in around $50 million, and debt had skyrocketed to approximately $1 billion. Early in 1998 Bruno's filed for Chapter 11 bankruptcy protection. KKR, which owned 82 percent of Bruno's at the time, lost the $250 million in equity it had put up in the 1995 leveraged buyout. Industry analysts, including Bob Lupo of BA Securities, indicated that Bruno's had alienated its customer base with its shift from everyday low pricing to the high-low approach. Major competitors, such as Winn-Dixie Stores, Wal-Mart, and Delchamps, seized the opportunity to move in on Bruno's customer base.

In response Bruno's negotiated a $200 million loan from Chase National Bank, one of its creditors, which allowed the chain to improve its customer service, refurbish older stores, and build new ones. The company's woes were compounded over the next year, however, when both Standard & Poor's and Moody's lowered their ratings of Bruno's bonds. Bruno's was also targeted by the United Food & Commercial Workers Local 1657 in an extensive strike in its hometown of Birmingham, Alabama, which began in September of 1999. In addition, the company was losing sales amounting to more than a billion dollars between 1996 and 1999.

Opening the New Millennium

By January of 2000, however, Bruno's announced plans to emerge from Chapter 11, along with a new name (Bruno's Supermarkets Inc.) and a new chairman (Terry Peets, formerly of PIA Merchandising Services, a food brokerage based in Irvine, California). The new company, owned by the creditors who had owned most of the debt of the company before the Chapter 11 filing, promised to pay unsecured shareholders a cash payment equal to 30 percent of the established value of their claims.

By the end of 2000 Bruno's had already begun to acquire new assets. In November the corporation secured ownership of seventeen stores (including twelve in its home state of Alabama) from rival supermarket chain Delchamps. The acquisitions brought Bruno's into contact with the rising Hispanic population in Alabama, and the company began an outreach intended to attract both Hispanic customers and employees from the local Spanish-speaking population. Local Bruno's stores also stock Spanish-language periodicals and offer job applications in Spanish.

In 2001 Bruno's Supermarkets Inc. was acquired by the international supermarket conglomerate Royal Ahold's U.S. subsidiary Ahold USA, headquartered in Columbia, Maryland, which wished to expand its presence in the southeastern United States. Within two years Ahold launched a corporate restructuring in which Dean Cohagan, head of Ahold's Bi-Lo chain, became head of Bruno's as well. Former Bruno's vice-president Bruce Efird assumed the titles of executive vice-president and general manager. Bruno's also began offering irradiated beef, treating the food with electronic beam technology to kill potentially harmful bacteria.

By the middle of the first decade of the 21st century, Bruno's had began a partial recovery, although its performance came nowhere near what it had been in the 1980s. The process of centralization, bringing logistics, real estate and construction under a single administration, helped bring Bruno's even further into the black. In 2004, as part of that centralization, however, Ahold ordered the closing of 11 stores in Alabama, putting 362 employees out of work. The corporation also put its Bruno's holdings up for sale, so the company's future remained unclear in the mid-2000s.

Further Reading

''Ahold USA Shifts Execs at Two Units,'' *MMR,* January 27, 2003 p. 2.

Bosley, Anita S. ''Breaking the Language Barrier,'' *Birmingham Business Journal,* November 24, 2000, p. 15.

''Brokers Hail Bruno's, Winn-Dixie,'' *Frozen Food Age,* July 1996, p. 14.

''Bruno's After the Crash,'' *Forbes,* July 6, 1992.

''Bruno's Agrees to Be Acquired by KKR for $12.50 Per Share,'' *Corporate Growth Report,* May 1, 1995, p. 7820.

''Bruno's buying 17 Jitney-Jungle Markets,'' *Birmingham Business Journal,* November 3, 2000, p. 10.

''Bruno's Could Protest Too Much,'' *Business Week,* September 26, 1994, p. 112.

''Bruno's Emerges from Chapter 11,'' *Supermarket News,* January 31, 2000 p. 6.

''Bruno's Leaves American Fare Venture with Kmart,'' *New York Times,* June 11, 1992.

Donegan, Priscilla, ''Merchandising the Store,'' *Progressive Grocer,* August, 1987.

''Getting Hyper,'' *Forbes,* January 11, 1988.

Gattuso, Greg. ''Bruno's is Retooling in Bid to Emerge from Chapter 11,'' *Supermarket News,* February 9, 1998, p. 1.

Grossman, Laurie M., and Martha Brannigan, ''Six Bruno's Officials and Three Others Die in Jet Crash During Goodwill Tour,'' *Wall Street Journal,* December 12, 1991.

Kindel, Stephen, ''Bruno's: On the Mend, Slowly,'' Financial World, March 30, 1993, pp. 20–22.

——, ''Rebel Sell,'' *Financial World,* January 9, 1990.

''Newswatch,'' *Supermarket News,* October 4, 1999, p. 2.

Northway, Wally. ''Bruno's Introduces Treated Beef,'' *Mississippi Business Journal,* March 3, 2003, p. 19.

Setton, Dolly, ''Sorry About That,'' *Forbes,* March 9, 1998, p. 130.

Smith, Rod. ''FTC Clears Ahold's Acquisition of Bruno's Stores,'' *Feedstuffs,* December 17, 2001, p. 6.

Smothers, Ronald, ''Crash of Private Plane in Georgia Kills 9,'' *New York Times,* December 12, 1991.

Zwiebach, Elliot. ''Bruno's Sets Chapter 11 Exit, New Chairman,'' *Supermarket News,* January 10, 2000, p. 1.

—Fran Shonfeld Sherman
—updates: Susan Windisch Brown;
Kenneth R. Shepherd

Cabela's Inc.

One Cabela Drive
Sidney, Nebraska 69160
U.S.A.
Telephone: (308) 234-5505
Toll Free: (800) 346-8747
Fax: (308) 254-6102
Web site: http://www.cabelas.com

Public Company
Incorporated: 1965
Employees: 7,600
Sales: $1.39 billion (2004 est.)
Stock Exchanges: New York
Ticker Symbol: CAB
NAIC: 451110 Sporting Goods Stores; 454113 Mail-Order Houses

Cabela's Inc. is a leading retailer of fishing, camping, and hunting equipment, footwear, and apparel. Much of its business is conducted through catalogs, of which it issues some 60 titles annually, as well as via its Internet commerce site. However, Cabela's also operates nine retail outlets known for their vast inventories and museum-quality wildlife displays. Still over 50 percent owned by the founding Cabela family, the company went public on the New York stock exchange in 2004.

Early 1960s Origins

Cabela's historical roots stretched back to quintessential, home-born beginnings. In 1961, Dick Cabela placed a classified advertisement in a Casper, Wyoming newspaper. He had purchased a collection of fishing flies at a furniture show in Chicago, taken the flies back to his home in Chappell, Nebraska, and thought placing a classified advertisement in a small newspaper would be the best way to make a profit from his modest investment. Cabela's advertisement read: ''12 hand-tied flies for $1.'' Unwittingly, Cabela had taken the first step toward creating a half-billion-dollar business, a flourishing mail-order enterprise that would become known as Cabela's, but his intentions at the start were decidedly less ambitious. Orders from the Casper, Wyoming advertisement were filled by Dick and his wife Mary, who worked in their home in Chappell, seated around the kitchen table. As orders for the flies increased, Dick Cabela purchased other outdoor recreational items and mailed a mimeographed list of other products available. For the Cabelas, direct-mail marketing worked quick wonders. The couple's inventory grew rapidly as more and more customers placed orders from the mimeographed lists. By 1962, the growth of their inventory required the establishment of a warehouse. Although the kitchen table still served as the business office, there was now another component to the couple's operations—a small backyard shed that served as their warehouse.

During the first several years of their business, the Cabelas fueled greater demand by continually expanding their mimeographed list of products until it developed into a mimeographed catalogue of merchandise. As the business expanded, its growth created the need for the trappings of a conventional business, but the evolution of the business away from its kitchen-table roots occurred in measured steps. By the fall of 1962, the Cabelas realized their homebound business required greater support, both in terms of personnel and proper facilities. Initially, they had relied on temporary typists to help with catalogue preparation, mailing, and labeling; but not long after devoting their backyard shed to warehouse space, Dick and Mary Cabela knew their business required full-time attention and full-time employees. Dick Cabela convinced his younger brother Jim to join the enterprise in 1963, but neither Jim, Mary, nor Dick received any compensation during the first several years. All the profits were directed toward increasing mailing activities, purchasing a greater selection of merchandise, and paying for bigger facilities. In 1964, after three years of using a kitchen table as their primary office space, the Cabela brothers moved the company's operations into the basement of their father's furniture store in Chappell. By the following year, the business had grown large enough to warrant incorporation and another move to larger facilities. The business was moved across the street into a former U.S. Department of Agriculture building, and then two years later into the American Legion Hall in Chappell. At the Chappell Legion Hall, which housed the company's warehousing operations and its offices, a small retail display was showcased in the corner of one floor. Al-

Company Perspectives:

We are the nation's largest direct marketer, and a leading specialty retailer, of hunting, fishing, camping and related outdoor merchandise. Since our founding in 1961, Cabela's has grown to become one of the most well-known outdoor recreation brands in the United States, and we have long been recognized as the World's Foremost Outfitter. Through our established direct business and our growing number of destination retail stores, we believe we offer the widest and most distinctive selection of high-quality outdoor products at competitive prices while providing superior customer service. We operate as an integrated multi-channel retailer, offering our customers a seamless shopping experience through our catalogs, website and destination retail stores.

though a negligible contributor to the company's financial stature, the retail product display in the American Legion Hall was a precursor to Cabela's grandiose foray into the retail side of the business more than 20 years later.

One year after moving into the Chappell Legion Hall, the Cabela brothers packed up the business and moved again, venturing out of Chappell for the first time. A search for larger quarters had revealed a vacant John Deere building near downtown Sidney, Nebraska. The building, which comprised four stories and 50,000 square feet of space, had been donated to a local hospital as a tax write-off, but the hospital wanted to sell the building before it incurred property taxes. Because of the hospital's predicament, the Cabelas were able to acquire the building at a sharply reduced price, purchasing it in September 1968. The business was moved to the old John Deere building in 1969, and for the first time in its history, the Cabela enterprise occupied a facility that was larger than the company's needs. At first, only one floor—the first floor—of the building was used. Upstairs, above the warehousing, packing, shipping, and retail operations located on the first floor, Cabela employees used a portion of one floor as an archery range, but eventually the needs of the company required the space occupied by the archery range. Gradually, as the 1970s progressed, Cabela's moved up into the empty floors, ultimately occupying the entire building.

By the mid-1980s, more than a decade of steady growth had stretched the company to the physical limits of the building in Sidney, forcing the Cabela brothers to search again for facilities that could accommodate their business's growing needs. The need for more space sprang from the company's ever-growing mail-order operations. As it had from the start, Cabela's produced its catalog on its own, a rarity among direct-mail businesses. The company's employees performed all the work involved in producing the catalog, including the copywriting, typesetting, photography, and merchandising. Aside from the in-house catalog operations, the company also performed all its own warehousing, packing, and shipping duties, as well as staffing its own telemarketing operations, all of which required additional space. In 1986, the Cabela brothers fulfilled their need by acquiring a former Rockwell International plant in Kearney, Nebraska. Into this building, the Cabelas moved their telemarketing operations, which became a source of employment for the community's college students. With a steady supply of college students to operate the telephone lines, Cabela's ran its telemarketing operations 24 hours a day. The Kearney facility also became the home of Cabela's second retail store, a facet of the company's business that attracted nearly all of the attention directed at Cabela's during the 1990s.

Retail a Highlight During the 1990s

During the 1990s, Cabela's opened several new retail stores that managed to transcend the allure of even the most popular retail businesses to become something far more captivating. Cabela's retail stores, all situated in the Midwest, became tourist destinations, attracting weekend crowds that exceeded the population of the communities in which they were located. The stores were massive, intricately and abundantly outfitted with displays that reflected the company's outdoor sporting merchandise. Not surprisingly, when these stores opened to voluminous crowds, the business press focused their attention on the sprawling retail outlets, but at the heart of Cabela's was its mail-order business. Catalog sales propelled the company forward, not the revenue generated by its retail stores. The retail side of the company's business was developed to support the mail-order business, serving the same purpose during the 1990s as it had at its origin in 1967. The difference was in the scale of the company's retail efforts; the difference between a small retail display tucked in a corner of the Chappell Legion Hall in 1967 and the 75,000-square-foot to 150,000-square-foot stores that debuted during the 1990s. The leap in scale between these two eras was in proportion to the enormous growth of Cabela's catalog business, which had grown from a one-line classified advertisement into an operation that mailed millions of catalogs both domestically and abroad each year.

Despite the fact that Cabela's retail stores contributed a small percentage to the company's overall sales, the artistically designed stores were hard to ignore. The first retail store to epitomize Cabela's retail efforts during the 1990s was opened in July 1991, one year after work had begun on the new store. Located on the southern edge of Sidney, the store was situated on a 45-acre plot that included a 450-vehicle parking lot, with a separate lot for semi-trucks and recreational vehicles, a 3.5-acre pond, and a 16-foot tall, bronze sculpture of two bull elk in fighting pose. Inside the store, which measured 75,000 square feet, a 27-foot-tall replica mountain towered at the opposite end of the entryway, decorated with 40 game mounts of North American wildlife in a recreated habitat display. There were also four, 2,000-gallon aquariums stocked with trout, panfish, gamefish, and predator fish; a gun library, featuring a broad collection of firearms; and a travel center, where customers could plan trips to take them across the globe. The merchandise in the store mirrored the product mix found in the company's catalogs, with apparel taking up roughly 50 percent of the retail space, footwear accounting for 30 percent, and the rest of the floor and shelf space filled with hard goods, such as hunting, fishing, and camping equipment.

By all measures, the store was a resounding success, located on the outskirts of a community of 6,000 people, yet capable of attracting more than one million customers a year. Away from the grandeur of the Sidney store, however, the real work of the company was conducted in Kearney, where Cabela's "800

Key Dates:

1961: Dick and Mary Cabela launch a sporting goods catalog.
1965: Company is incorporated.
1969: Operations are moved to a 50,000-square-foot facility in downtown Sydney, Nebraska.
1987: Cabela's opens its first retail outlet.
1998: Operations are moved to a 120,000-square-foot facility.
2004: Cabela's goes public.

Service Center'' was located. In two large rooms, 150 operators stood by the telephones 24 hours a day, seven days a week, receiving an average of two million calls a year during the early 1990s. During peak holiday periods, the 800 center's telephone staff doubled, occasionally taking as many as 35,000 telephone orders in a single 24-hour period. To house and ship the orders generated from the 800 center and to stock the retail stores in Sidney and Kearney, massive distribution centers were needed. At roughly the same time Cabela's was involved in designing and constructing its new Sidney store, the company acquired three buildings on the former Sioux Ordinance Depot grounds in Sidney for warehouse space. In 1992, another five buildings situated at the same location were acquired, making Cabela's warehouse space in Sidney equal to more than ten football fields. The company's distribution capabilities were further enhanced with the construction of a facility in Prairie du Chien, Wisconsin. The 600,000-square-foot distribution center in Prairie du Chien was completed in 1996, positioning the company to better serve its upper Midwestern customers.

Late 1990s Expansion

Physical expansion, both in terms of Cabela's retail business and in the number of facilities that supported its catalog operations, characterized the company's progress during the late 1990s. After more than 35 years of operating in Nebraska, the company had two retail stores in its home state, the massive warehouse in Sidney, its main telemarketing operation in Kearney, which was supported by an additional telemarketing operation in Grand Island, and a customer-service center in North Platte. During the late 1990s, the company's most notable activity took place outside the state of Nebraska, following up on its move into Wisconsin with the Prairie du Chien distribution facility. The one exception was the establishment of a new headquarters in Sidney in January 1998. The company moved out of its original Sidney headquarters building and into a new 120,000-square-foot, two-story building adjacent to the Sidney store. Meanwhile, as employees settled into their new offices in Sidney, the company was preparing for the opening of its largest retail store to date. The store, located in Owatonna, Minnesota, opened in April 1998, by far eclipsing the standard set by the Sidney store seven years earlier. The Owatonna store was twice the size of its Sidney counterpart, comprising 150,000 square feet of space. Half of the retail square footage was devoted to outdoor apparel, including 60 different patterns of camouflage, with the balance divided between footwear and hard goods, nearly identical to the product mix in the company's catalogs. The Owatonna store, a 45-minute drive south from Minneapolis, also contained the eye-catching features and habitat displays found in the Sidney store. Inside, the company built a 35-foot replica mountain, complete with running streams and waterfalls, two dioramas featuring African wildlife, a live-bait shop, a firearms and archery training center, and three aquariums with a combined capacity of 54,000 gallons. Outside the store, there was room for roughly 800 vehicles, including a parking lot for buses and semi-truck trailer rigs, as well as two two-acre ponds. Like the store in Sidney, the Owatonna store was an immediate success, attracting 120,000 customers during its grand opening weekend.

Despite the legions of customers drawn to the Owatonna store, overall retail sales only accounted for between nine and 12 percent of Cabela's total sales during the late 1990s. The balance was generated from catalog sales, which approached $500 million. The company mailed 28 editions of its catalog each year, sending nearly 60 million catalogs to customers in the United States, Canada, and 120 foreign countries. Looking ahead, Cabela's was intent on expanding its retail presence as a strategy to bolster catalog sales. The company was scouting five potential locations for retail stores in late 1998, anticipating its future stores to measure between 75,000 and 80,000 square feet. In October 1998, Cabela's opened its fourth retail store next to its distribution center in Prairie du Chien. A 40,000-square-foot store, the Prairie du Chien outlet was opened to meet the overflow of customers flocking to the flagship Owatonna store.

Millennium Growth

In September 1998 Cabela's announced plans to create its own bank, and add hundreds of people to its call-center (primarily for phone orders and processing credit card orders). Within two years the company had already outgrown its new offices and revealed plans that would almost double the size of Cabela's existing Lincoln Nebraska facility. In the few years after their first expansion Cabela's already found themselves tight on room. They made special arrangements with the community to receive tax breaks for their building projects, widely supported because Lincoln highly valued the company's economic boom. The growth of Cabela's even affected the housing market, where almost all available houses were snapped up by Cabela's employees—the community contractors were called upon to construct new housing developments.

Expansions continued into the next millennium when in 2001 Cabela's announced plans to open a new store in Kansas city, part of a new, $500 million dollar mall. Slated to open in 2003, Cabela's planned to offer 188,000 square feet of sales floor in their eighth store, their second largest. The finished store would feature a 30-foot simulated mountain complete with running streams and a 55,000 gallon aquarium. While this remained the company's sole new building expansion in the early part of the decade, Cabela's management did not sit idle. They signed on with Planalytics, Inc., an Internet-based firm claiming to be able to predict consumer demand for products based on time, location, and, perhaps most importantly, weather. Cabela's expected Planalytics to be especially useful in regards to their outdoor products. They also contracted with ATG, another Internet firm, to spruce up the company's Internet order site, citing concerns that the existing Web site hadn't engaged visitors in an interesting way.

Joining Forces and Going Public

In late 2002 Cabela's partnered with Maiden Mills to launch a new clothing line, Polartec, based on fabric used by the U.S. Special Operations Forces groups for cold weather operations. They then showed such interest in the animal carriers produced by the Avenger Corporation that Avenger doubled its work force to meet product demand. Cabela believed that the special trailers—designed to carry hunting dogs and hunting equipment—would be big sellers with its customers. Early 2003 saw the announcement of two new store locations, one in Wheeling West Virginia, and the first East Coast Cabela's, in Reading, Pennsylvania. More additions were afoot: in April of 2003 the first non-family members rose to top positions within the company. Dennis N. Highby was promoted to Chief executive officer and David A. Roehr to president and chief financial officer. Both had served with the company for many years. Neither Dick nor Jim Cabella planned to step down, declaring that they would remain involved in the day-to-day operations of the company.

Cabela's decided to go public in March 2004, hoping to make at least $230 million on the stock offering. They planned to use the money both to build three additional stores and to pay some $142 million in debt. As they prepared to go public, Cabela's announced plans to open up two Texas stores in 2005, one in Fort Worth and the other some 15 miles south of Austin, in Buda. Once the stock went public, investors flocked to buy Cabela's stock, which opened almost $8.00 higher per share than anticipated (at $27.95). By the end of 2004 Cabela's was looking at Louisiana, New Jersey, and Colorado for additional company locations. Earnings were rising across the board—their stock price remained high, and so did profits. The future continued to look rosy for the company, and while there was some local grumbling about tax incentives given to out-of-state megastores, traffic to the Cabela's franchise remained high, and customers loyal.

Principal Subsidiaries

Cabela's Retail Inc.; Cabela's Catalog Inc.; Cabelas.com Inc.; Cabela's Outdoor Adventures Inc.; Cabela's Ventures Inc.; Cabela's Wholesale Inc.; Van Dyke Supply Company Inc.; Cabela's Marketing and Brand Management Inc.; World's Foremost Bank.

Principal Competitors

Bass Pro Shops Inc.

Further Reading

Brumback, Nancy, "Cabela's, the Mail Animal, Is Pushing the Retail Envelope," *Daily News Record,* July 27, 1998, p. 6.

"Cabela's Bags Strong IPO," *Daily Deal,* June 28, 2004.

"Cabela's Catalog Showroom Set for October Opening in Prairie du Chien, Wis.," *PR Newswire,* August 26, 1998, p. 8.

Cabela's—Unending Progress and Growth Since 1961, Sidney, Neb.: Cabela's Inc., 1998, 7 p.

Duff, Mike, "Cabela's Megastore Masters Sports and Entertainment," *DSN Retailing Today,* November 20, 2000, p. 3.

Gribble, Roger A., "Cabela's Sporting-Goods Mail-Order Center Good News for Platteville, Wis.," *Knight-Ridder/Tribune Business News,* June 22, 1996, p. 6.

Grier, Bob, "Cabela's: A Store with a Story," *NEBRASKAland Magazine,* August 1993, p. 8.

Helliker, Kevin, "Men Who Hate to Go Shopping are Game to Hunt at Cabela's," *Grand Rapids Press,* December 22, 2002, p. F1.

McCartney, Jim, "Giant Sporting Goods Stores Opens 40 Miles from Minnesota's Twin Cities," *Knight-Ridder/Tribune Business News,* April 3, 1998, p. 4.

—Jeffrey L. Covell
—update: Howard A. Jones

Church & Dwight Co., Inc.

469 North Harrison Street
Princeton, New Jersey 08543-5297
U.S.A.
Telephone: (609) 683-5900
Toll Free: (800) 332-5424
Fax: (609) 497-7269
Web site: http://www.churchdwight.com

Public Company
Incorporated: 1925
Employees: 2,266
Sales: $1.05 billion (2003)
Stock Exchanges: New York
Ticker Symbol: CHD
NAIC: 325181 Alkalies & Chlorine Manufacturing; 325611 Soap & Other Detergent Manufacturing; 325612 Polish & Other Sanitation Good Manufacturing

Church & Dwight Co., Inc., is a leading consumer products company that markets numerous brands of deodorizing and household cleaning products, laundry products, and personal care products. Church & Dwight's consumer products, which account for more than 80 percent of annual sales, are sold under the brand names Arm & Hammer, Arrid, Brillo, Mentadent, Pepsodent, Close-Up, Trojan, and Nair. The company is also the world's leading producer of sodium bicarbonate, more commonly known as baking soda. This segment of the company's activities constitutes its specialty products business, which also includes the production of sodium sesquicarbonate, ammonium bicarbonate, rumen bypass fat products, and rumen efficiency enhancers. These products are used in a variety of industrial, institutional, animal nutrition, medical, and food applications. Church & Dwight generates more than 90 percent of its revenue in the United States.

19th-Century Beginnings

The company was founded in New York City in 1846 as John Dwight & Co. by Dr. Austin Church and his brother-in-law John E. Dwight, who had begun processing and packaging baking soda in powdered form in Dwight's kitchen. It was marketed for use in home baking. In 1867, two sons of Church formed Church & Co. to compete with John Dwight & Co. The Arm & Hammer Trademark derives from that year, in which Church & Co. acquired a spice and mustard business named Vulcan Spice Mills that used an arm and hammer—presumably about to descend on an anvil—as its trademark because Vulcan, the Roman god of fire, was associated with the forging of metals.

In 1888, Church & Co. began issuing trading cards bearing the arm-and-hammer trademark to publicize its baking soda and saleratus (potassium bicarbonate) products. In 1896, it merged with John Dwight & Co., which also was issuing trading cards for its ''Cow'' brand of baking soda, to form Church Dwight Co. The merged firm continued to market baking soda under both the Arm & Hammer and Cow trademarks for some time. Arm & Hammer Super Washing Soda was introduced in the 19th century as a heavy-duty laundry and household cleaning product. Around 1915, Church Dwight began suggesting that baking soda could serve as medicine, offering a booklet titled *Home Remedies for Simple Ailments.* Soon it was also advertising baking soda as a tooth cleaner and a cleaner and freshener for laundry and for kitchen surfaces. The firm was incorporated as Church & Dwight Co. in 1925.

Church & Dwight was run by family members in highly conservative fashion for the next four decades—so much so that the company earned more in some years from its investment portfolio than from its operations. the company's methods of producing baking soda eventually became obsolete, and it turned to outside suppliers for the product. When the output of these suppliers proved insufficient, Church & Dwight began to build what soon became the world's largest facility for the production of sodium bicarbonate. The facility was located in Green River, Wyoming, and was completed in 1968.

In that year, Church & Dwight was producing nearly half of the sodium bicarbonate and borax in the United States in collaboration with Allied Chemical Co., a major producer of the sodium carbonate (soda ash) used—along with carbon dioxide—as the raw material for baking soda. Church & Dwight's production plants, in Syracuse, New York (for con-

Company Perspectives:

The combination of a broad and well-balanced product portfolio, well-developed distribution capabilities in the U.S., and a growing international presence will all help the Company continue to meet its growth objectives over the next few years. With the excellent assets at the Company's disposal, our long-term objective is to expand all four of our major businesses—Household Products, Personal Care, Consumer International and Specialty Products, while delivering a return to investors in excess of the industry average.

sumer products) and Green River (for industrial products), were receiving soda ash from Allied's own adjacent plants and turning out about 100,000 tons of sodium bicarbonate a year. Nearly half was going to bulk industrial users, such as baking, pharmaceutical, and fire extinguisher companies. The rest was processed into granules, placed in yellow boxes bearing the Arm & Hammer trademark, and sold to the public. Church & Dwight accounted for least 90 percent of U.S. consumer sales of baking soda. Washing soda (also manufactured by the company) and borax (purchased from suppliers) accounted for about 40 percent of the company's total sales volume.

Exploiting the Arm & Hammer Name through the 1980s

After decades of success, company management ultimately came to realize that housewives who, traditionally, had used Arm & Hammer baking soda as an all-purpose product—to bake bread, clean stains, eliminate odors, relieve indigestion, and alleviate the pain of minor burns and abrasions—had turned to an array of specialized products for all of these uses. Accordingly, under Dwight C. Minton, a fifth-generation descendant of Austin Church who succeeded his father as Church & Dwight's president in 1969, and Robert A. Davies III, vice-president of Arm & Hammer marketing, the company itself began to specialize.

Church & Dwight exploited the venerable Arm & Hammer name to market baking soda tablets for indigestion and mint-flavored ones as a mouth freshener. It also began marketing a phosphate-free laundry detergent based on soda ash and introduced an underarm deodorant (which failed) and oven cleaner, all under the Arm & Hammer name. Net sales rose from $22.4 million in 1969 to $77 million in 1975, and net income increased more than fourfold to $3.8 million during that time period.

In addition, a brilliantly successful advertising campaign begun in 1972 persuaded housewives to open the basic yellow box and place it in the refrigerator for use as a deodorant/freshener. Sales of the product rose 72 percent within three years. To stimulate sales even more, a follow-up campaign advised consumers to remove the box of baking soda after a while and pour its contents down the kitchen drain to deodorize it, too. Yet another ad campaign encouraged consumers to store Arm & Hammer baking soda in the freezer for the same purpose. "There are at least 10 guys running around New York claiming some credit for the refrigerator campaign idea," adman Gerald Schoenfeld told Jack J. Honomichl of *Advertising Age* in 1982. The company also added a bigger box of Arm & Hammer baking soda for heavy-duty applications, such as use in swimming pools and septic tanks, and created new packaging for the product's use as cat litter deodorizer.

Davies became president of Church & Dwight in 1981, while Minton remained chief executive officer. That year, the basic yellow box of baking soda accounted for about one-third of the company's sales volume of $127.1 million. Its main end use now was to deodorize refrigerator air. (In 1970 the main use had been the cleaning of refrigerator surfaces.) The second most important use was general household cleaning. The product's use in home baking now appeared to be negligible. Arm & Hammer had unaided recognition among 97 percent of U.S. female heads of households. Almost all grocery stores stocked the yellow box, and surveys found that, at any point in time, about 95 percent of all U.S. households had one or more packages in use in the home.

Church & Dwight opened another manufacturing plant in Old Fort, Ohio, in 1980. Four years later it purchased the Syracuse plant of Allied Corp. (formerly Allied Chemical Co.) for $14 million. The company's Canadian subsidiary also owned a plant in Ontario. Church & Dwight moved its headquarters from New York City to Piscataway, New Jersey, in the late 1970s, and to Princeton, New Jersey, in 1985.

Church & Dwight reformulated and reintroduced its dry laundry detergent at a lower price in 1981 and introduced a carpet and room deodorizer in the same year. An oven cleaner containing no sodium was marketed in 1982. Liquid detergent was tested in the metropolitan New York City area in 1984. In that year, the company also began testing its own toothpaste and tooth powder, both made with baking soda. In addition, Church & Dwight started marketing a deodorizing spray and a carpet freshener containing baking soda and a bleach and a fabric softener for sheets without baking soda. All of its consumer products, including washing soda, continued to bear the Arm & Hammer name. Although shares of company stock were being traded over the counter, most were held by descendants of the founders or employees.

Church & Dwight's Chemicals Division was producing two-thirds of all sodium bicarbonate sold to U.S. industrial customers in 1986. The division had found a recent customer in the animal feed industry, which applied it as an antacid supplement for dairy cattle. Church & Dwight purchased a 40 percent share of a British firm, Brotherton Chemicals, in 1985, for the industrial sector of its business and increased its stake to 80 percent in 1987. Of the firm's $231.4 million in sales that year, nevertheless, 78 percent came from consumer products marketed by the Arm & Hammer Division.

In 1986 Church & Dwight acquired and absorbed DeWitt International Corporation, a producer of over-the-counter pharmaceuticals and health and beauty aids. Also during that year, the company began a relationship with Armand Hammer, the flamboyant chairman of Occidental Petroleum Corporation. Tired of having to reply in the negative when asked if he was the "baking-soda king" because of the resemblance between his name and the

Key Dates:

1846: Dwight & Co. is formed.
1867: Church & Co. is formed.
1896: Church Dwight Co. is formed through the merger of John Dwight & Co. and Church & Co.
1925: The company is incorporated as Church & Dwight Co.
1968: The modern development of the company begins as it starts to develop a more specialized product line.
1980: The company begins a decade of diversification and growth.
1986: The company diversifies into over-the-counter pharmaceuticals through the acquisition of DeWitt International Corp.
2001: Carter-Wallace Inc. and USA Detergents, Inc. are acquired, adding new brands to the company's consumer products business.
2003: Church & Dwight acquires Unilever's oral care brands.
2004: Church & Dwight acquires Del Laboratories.

Arm & Hammer trademark, Hammer purchased about 5 percent of Church & Dwight's shares for about $15 million and received a seat on the company board so he could reply in the affirmative. As part of the transaction, Occidental and Church & Dwight formed a joint venture to continue the manufacture and marketing of potassium carbonate products at an Occidental-acquired plant in Muscle Shoals, Alabama, whose customers included Church & Dwight. In 1991, after Hammer's death, his successor sold Occidental's stake in Church & Dwight for $19 million, but the joint venture remained in effect.

Church & Dwight in the 1990s

Church & Dwight's net sales of $428.5 million in 1990 was an increase of more than fourfold in a decade, and its net income of $22.5 million was about three times the 1980 figure. The company now had 12 facilities, including three in England and one each in Australia, Malaysia, and Singapore. Its laundry detergent now accounted for one-third of all revenues and ranked third in the United States after Tide and Surf. The company also held 60 percent of the world market for sodium bicarbonate. Arm & Hammer Dental Care toothpaste, introduced nationally in 1988, held 11 percent of the U.S. toothpaste market in 1993. Specialty products included ArmaKleen, a baking soda-based cleanser of computer circuit boards. In 1994, Church & Dwight established a division within its specialty products group to develop industrial cleaning solutions based on baking soda, and two years later it began selling cleaning products to the metal cleaning industry.

Also in 1994, Church & Dwight introduced a line of stick and roll-on deodorants in major U.S. markets under the name Arm & Hammer Deodorant Anti-Perspirant with Baking Soda. It also purchased the remaining share of Brotherton Chemicals. However, sales dipped by $17 million that year, and the company's profits fell 77 percent. Minton attributed the poor results to introducing too many new products. One of these was a liquid detergent more concentrated than other leading brands that fared poorly in the marketplace and had to be reformulated because consumers thought they were being offered less for their money. Another was Peroxicare, a toothpaste with peroxide as well as baking soda that may have been competing, to the detriment of both, with Arm & Hammer Dental Care in the fiercely competitive dentifrice market.

Church & Dwight was still struggling to regain its momentum when Davies, who had left the company in 1984, was renamed president in 1995. He was named chief executive officer, succeeding Minton, in November of that year. Although sales dropped again in 1995, the company took in record revenues of $527.8 million the next year and more than doubled its net income. That year, the company introduced variants of its toothpaste—including sensitive-formula, extra-whitening, and smooth spearmint versions—and its stick deodorant products. Results were even better in 1997, when Church & Dwight acquired a group of five household cleaning brands from The Dial Corporation. Among these was Brillo scouring pads. It also introduced nationally an aerosol deodorant antiperspirant.

In 1998, Church & Dwight acquired the Toss 'n Soft brand of fabric softener dryer sheets from Dial and combined it with Arm & Hammer Fabric Softener Sheets under the Arm & Hammer Fresh & Soft brand name. The company also was offering more differentiated baking soda products, such as Arm & Hammer Super Scoop, an anti-clumping cat litter introduced nationally in 1997, and Arm & Hammer Dental Care Gum, a baking soda-based oral care product introduced in 1998 in three flavors. Church & Dwight had record revenues of $684.4 million and record net income of $30.3 million in 1998.

In 1999, Church & Dwight launched a multimillion-dollar advertising campaign intended to ''reeducate America on the benefits of deodorizing the fridge, and offer added convenience,'' according to a company executive quoted by Christine Bittar in *Brandweek*. Television ads aired in the spring and fall encouraged seasonal replacement of a new baking soda box dominated by the color blue rather than the familiar yellow package. The company also introduced an Arm & Hammer Advance White line of dentifrices in early 1999. Also in that year, Church & Dwight formed a joint venture with Safety-Kleen Corporation called ArmaKleen Company to distribute Church & Dwight's proprietary line of aqueous cleaners.

In 1998, Church & Dwight was still manufacturing sodium bicarbonate at Green River and Old Fort and still retained its partnership agreement with General Chemical Corporation (formerly Allied). The company's liquid laundry detergent, previously contract manufactured, had been moved to the Syracuse plant in 1995. The manufacture of powdered detergent, also being produced in Syracuse from light soda ash, was to move to Green River in 1999. Cat litter was being manufactured in both Green River and Syracuse. A Lakewood, New Jersey, plant acquired in 1998 was manufacturing the underarm deodorant line and was to begin producing dentifrice products in 1999. The Brillo product line and the dryer sheets were being produced at the London, Ohio, plant acquired from Dial Corporation. Other company products were being manufactured by contractors.

Church & Dwight, in early 1999, also owned, through subsidiaries, a distribution center in Ontario, Canada, and a manufacturing facility in Wakefield, England. The Canadian subsidiary was leasing offices in Toronto. A Venezuelan subsidiary was closed in 1998. Church & Dwight still had a half-interest in the Armand Products potassium carbonate manufacturing plant in Muscle Shoals. Its executive offices and research and development facilities, owned by the company, were in Princeton, and it was leasing space in two buildings adjacent to this facility.

Consumer products accounted for 82 percent of Church & Dwight's revenues in 1998. Among these were Arm & Hammer Dental Care toothpaste, tooth powder, gel, tartar-control formula and gel, Peroxicare, and tartar-control Peroxicare. Two underarm deodorants were available in scented and unscented stick, aerosol, and roll-on forms. Its line of specialty products consisted of sodium bicarbonate for commercial baked goods and as an antacid in pharmaceuticals, a carbon dioxide release agent in fire extinguishers, an alkaline agent in swimming pool chemicals, and an agent in kidney dialysis. Sodium sesquicarbonate and a special grade of sodium bicarbonate were being sold to the animal feed market as a food additive for use by dairymen as a buffer, or anti-acid, for dairy cattle.

Acquisitions Fuel Growth in the 21st Century

Church & Dwight recorded strong growth as it exited the 1990s and entered a new century. Nearly all of the company's growth was achieved in the consumer products segment of its business, with several acquisitions adding a handful of well-known brands to its stable of products. In June 2000, Church & Dwight and USA Detergents, Inc. formed a joint venture company, ARMUS LLC, to combine the laundry products businesses of both companies. USA Detergent's brands included Xtra and Nice N Fluffy. Under the terms of the partnership, Church & Dwight, which managed ARMUS, was given the option to buy USA Detergents, an opportunity the company took advantage of in May 2001. The acquisition of USA Detergents was followed by another acquisition in 2001, the purchase of the consumer products business of Carter-Wallace, Inc. The transaction gave Church & Dwight two new brands, the Arrid line of antiperspirants and the Lambert Kay pet care product line. Concurrent with these purchases, Church & Dwight's joint venture company, Armkel LLC, in which it shared a half-interest with a private equity company, Kelso & Co., acquired the rest of Carter-Wallace's consumer products business. The brands acquired by Armkel included Trojan condoms, Nair hair remover, and the First Response line of home pregnancy and ovulation test kits. In 2003, the brands acquired by both Church & Dwight and Armkel were consolidated under Church & Dwight's control.

Church & Dwight's moves on the acquisition front continued in 2002, a year that saw the company eclipse the $1 billion-in-sales mark for the first time in its history. In early 2002, the company turned its attention to its specialty products business and acquired Biovance Technologies Inc. Based in Omaha, Nebraska, Biovance produced Bio-Chlor and Fermenten, two products that bolstered Church & Dwight's animal nutrition product line. The addition of Biovance's products, according to a Church & Dwight executive in a January 14, 2002 interview published in *Feedstuffs*, ''enables us to provide customers with a full lineup of products covering the cow's entire lactation curve as well as the buffer stage.''

Dwight & Church's more significant moves occurred on the consumer products side during the early years of the decade, a business the company resumed expanding in 2003. In the fall of that year, Church & Dwight acquired the oral care brands owned by Unilever, paying $104 million for Pepsodent, Aim, and Mentadent toothpastes, as well as the exclusive licensing rights to Close-Up toothpaste. The acquisition substantially increased the company's existing business in oral care products. ''This transaction,'' Davies announced in the September 26, 2003 issue of *Cosmetics International,* ''strengthens our strategically important oral care business, tripling our unit sales and more than doubling sales in the U.S. oral care section.''

As Church & Dwight neared its 160th anniversary, the company continued to demonstrate a desire to expand its consumer products business. Annual sales in 2003 reached $1.05 billion, 82 percent of which was derived from its portfolio of consumer products brands. The company wanted to increase the size of this mainstay business segment, and in 2004 it appointed a new leader to spearhead such expansion. In June, Davies ended his nine-year tenure as president and chief executive officer, passing the titles to James R. Craigie. Davies, who had been appointed the company's chairman in 2001, continued to serve in this capacity. Craigie, who had spent 15 years at Kraft Foods, joined Church & Dwight after presiding as president and chief executive officer of Spaulding Sports Worldwide for six years. At Spaulding, Craigie was credited for leading the athletic equipment maker's turnaround.

Craigie's tenure began with an acquisition, suggesting Church & Dwight would continue to expand through acquisitions as it plotted its future. In July 2004, the company teamed up with Kelso & Co. again to acquire Del Laboratories in a transaction valued at $465 million. Church & Dwight and Kelso formed a new company, DLI Holding Corp., to serve as the parent company of Del Laboratories, a company whose brands included Sally Hansen Hard as Nails, Cornsilk face makeup, and Naturalistics cosmetics. The transaction was expected to be completed at the end of 2004.

Principal Subsidiaries

Church & Dwight Ltd./Ltee (Canada); C&D Chemical Products, Inc.; Brotherton Speciality Proudcts Ltd. (United Kingdom); Quimica Geral do Nordeste S.A. (Brazil); C&D Technologies, Inc.

Principal Operating Groups

Consumer Products; Specialty Products.

Principal Competitors

The Procter & Gamble Company; Reckitt Benckiser plc; Kimberly-Clark Corporation.

Further Reading

''Arm & Hammer: Taking the Cure,'' *Sales Management*, February 15, 1970, pp. 59–60.

Bittar, Christine, ''C&D Polishing $18M Plan to Brighten Mentadent Sales,'' *Brandweek*, September 6, 2004, p. 5.

——, ''In-the-Box Thinking,'' *Brandweek*, January 25, 1999, p. 3.

''Craigie Named CEO at Church & Dwight,'' *Feedstuffs*, June 28, 2004, p. 6.

Gordon, Mitchell, ''Profitable Pairing,'' *Barron's*, September 6, 1982, pp. 37–8.

Honomichl, Jack J., ''The Ongoing Saga of 'Mother Baking Soda,' '' *Advertising Age*, September 20, 1982, pp. M2–3, M-22.

Howie, Michael, ''Church & Dwight Buys Biovance, Expands Lineup,'' *Feedstuffs*, January 14, 2002, p. 8.

Jacobs, Sanford L., ''And Now We Discover a Miracle Product That's Not So New,'' *Wall Street Journal*, March 21, 1973, p. 1.

Marinelli, Tom, ''A 'Soda' Supplier for 140 Years Is Diversifying,'' *Chemical Week*, May 7, 1986, pp. 78–9.

Montana, Constanza, ''Armand Hammer and Arm & Hammer Finally Arm in Arm,'' *Wall Street Journal*, September 23, 1986, pp. 3, 18.

''The New Face of Arm & Hammer,'' *Business Week*, April 12, 1976, p. 60.

Nulty, Peter, ''No Product Is Too Dull To Shine,'' *Fortune*, July 27, 1992, p. 96.

Prior, Molly, ''Unilever Sells Oral Care Unit to Church & Dwight,'' *Drug Stores News*, September 22, 2003, p. 4.

——, ''Del Labs Acquired in $465 Million Deal,'' *Drug Stores News*, July 19, 2004, p. 4.

''A Smell-Less Story,'' *Forbes*, August 15, 1974, p. 29.

''Sodium Bicarb Expansions Put C&D on the Offensive,'' *Chemical Market Reporter*, July 22, 1996, pp. 3, 18.

Somasundaram, Meera, ''Missteps Mar Church & Dwight's Plans,'' *Wall Street Journal*, April 28, 1995.

Treadwell, T.K., ''The Legacy of . . . Church & Dwight Trade Cards,'' *Antiques & Collecting*, January 1991, pp. 26–8.

''Unilever Brands Under Hammer,'' *Cosmetics International*, September 26, 2003, p. 3.

Weisz, Pam, ''Church & Dwight in Need of Next Big Idea,'' *Brandweek*, November 13, 1995, p. 8.

—Robert Halasz
—update: Jeffrey L. Covell

Clare Rose Inc.

72 Clare Rose Boulevard
Patchogue, New York 11772
U.S.A.
Telephone: (631) 475-1840
Fax: (631) 475-1837
Web site: http://www.clarerose.com

Private Company
Incorporated: 1936
Employees: 250
Sales: $178 million (2003)
NAIC: 424810 Beer and Ale Merchant Wholesalers

Privately owned Clare Rose Inc. is one of the largest beer distributors in the United States, dominating a number of markets: Long Island's Suffolk and Nassau counties and the New York City borough of Staten Island. Domestic beer products include Anheuser-Busch's Budweiser, Busch, and Michelob products, as well as microbrewed products such as Redhook Extra Special Bitter Ale, Ballard Bitter Ale, Blackhook Porter, and Boardy Barn Brew, produced by a popular Hamptons bar. Imports include Amstel, Beck's, Heineken, and those brewed by Anheuser-Busch in the United States: Krinn Lager, Kirin Ichiban, and Kirin Light. Clare Rose also offers Anheuser-Busch's nonalcohol O'Doul's beer. In addition, Clare Rose distributes Tequiza, a beer flavored with Mexican tequila and lime; Bicardi Silver, made with Bicardi rum and citrus; and 180, a carbonated citrus energy drink supplemented with vitamins and natural guarana. Clare Rose is owned by the Rose family and headed by a third generation.

1930s Origins

Clare Rose was founded by Clare F. Rose, who was born in the Long Island hamlet of Patchogue, New York. His father worked as a foreman at a lumber mill, while his mother, of Cherokee descent, worked at a lace mill. Rose quit school at an early age, apparently due to his inability to accept his high school music teacher's criticism of the way he played the cello. He reacted by hurling his instrument into the seats of the auditorium and as a result was asked to leave Patchogue High School. He took a job as a clerk and time keeper at Bailey's Lumber Mill, where his father worked, and later found employment at area grocers. He became involved in the beverage business when a Pepsi bottling plant was opened in Patchogue during the 1930s. Rose became the operation's first salesman and went on to manage the plant. In November 1936 he struck out on his own, forming Clare Rose, Inc. by launching a small distributorship to handle Mission orange soda, a California beverage. He also took on the Plaza brand of soda.

When the United States entered World War II in 1941, Rose became a captain in the Army's Transport Service. Sent home to await deployment to Australia, Rose continued to grow his routes but never received his orders. Instead, he kept working and was able to establish his young business so that by 1944 he was the largest independent soda distributor in Suffolk County. He was also ready to take advantage of the post-war population boom and the buildup of Long Island. In 1947 both Piels and Budweiser beer were interested in entering the market and approached Rose about distributing their products. He took on both companies and began his career as a beer wholesaler. While the Piels brand would fade into obscurity, Budweiser expanded at a rapid clip, and Clare Rose, at first handling just the eastern part of Suffolk County, grew along with it.

Adding Territory in the 1960s

In 1964 Anheuser-Busch asked Clare Rose to add the western half of Suffolk County. Rose called his son Mark, who was about to graduate from college, and told him that if he didn't come to work for him he'd pass on the opportunity. Mark had worked for his father during the summers since he was 15 years of age, but he had been considering the idea of working elsewhere after college, at least for a few years. Eventually Mark gave in to his father's prodding. He told *Long Island Business News* in a 2000 interview, ''After college, the day I walked into the office, my dad walked away from his desk and said he'd never have to sign another check again.'' That gesture was in keeping with Rose's belief that members of the second generation in a family business needed the room to run things as they saw fit. Mark was joined by his brother, Frederick, and they

Key Dates:

1936: Company founded.
1947: Clare Rose become Anheuser-Busch distributor for eastern Suffolk County.
1964: Clare Rose adds western Suffolk County to its territory.
1991: Nassau County added to Anheuser-Busch territory.
1993: Clare Rose becomes Anheuser-Busch wholesaler to Staten Island.
2003: Third generation of Rose family takes charge.

took over the running of the expanded distributorship. Just in case a conflict might arise between the siblings, the elder Rose took care to establish a board of directors, to arbitrate conflicts after he transferred ownership to them. But the board would never be called on to resolve any issues.

Prior to taking over the western half of Suffolk County for Anheiser-Busch, Clare Rose had been a pre-sell operation, meaning that a salesman first visited an account to take an order and a driver later delivered the beverages. For the new territory, the company now adopted a driver-sales approach, with the driver taking his own orders. Not only did it eliminate possible confusion between the salesman and the driver, it proved to be a better fit with many customers—hard working managers who connected better with a blue-collar truck driver than with a white collar salesman who only lifted a pad and pen. The new arrangement worked so well that Clare Rose soon converted the eastern portion of Suffolk County to the driver-salesman model. In the beginning, the drivers earned a base salary and received a commission on all sales exceeding a base level, but at the urging of the union Clare Rose switched to a pure commission system, whereby drivers earned a commission on every sale they made. It was an arrangement that both sides found beneficial. Drivers virtually owned their routes and were more willing to go the extra yard to make another sale.

The driver-salesman practice also encouraged company loyalty, a key to the growth of Clare Rose, which hired individuals with the idea in mind of creating life-long employees. Non-union new hires generally started out with low paying positions, like point-of-sale hangers. Those who proved their commitment to the company would then move to the warehouse and work their way up through the ranks, taking relief sales slots, with the ultimate goal of becoming a driver-salesman. To reinforce the idea that Clare Rose was looking for long-term employees, the company parking lot featured a reserved parking space for everyone in the organization, no matter what their rank, with the name stenciled on the pavement. To boost company morale, Clare Rose also developed the tradition of hosting a black-tie Christmas party each year, as well as an all-expenses-paid five-day ''convention'' at a vacation spot for employees and their spouses. In addition, Clare Rose was willing to invest in technology to help its driver-salesman to produce even better results. For instance, in the early 1980s Clare Rose was one of the first distributors to equip drivers with handheld computer terminals. Despite some initial resistance, the handhelds proved successful and soon drivers became dependent on them.

Under second generation leadership, Clare Rose enjoyed steady growth, which the company continued during the 1980s despite a number of challenges. In the mid-1980s the state of New York enacted a new bottle law that mandated the responsibility for the five-cent deposit on cans and bottles rested with the wholesaler, not the bottler or brewer. The unforeseen problem was that beverages could be shipped into an area and the wholesalers in that market would have to redeem the deposits, whether or not they originated the cans or bottles. Because of its location Clare Rose was put at a decided disadvantage. As explained by *Beverage World* in a 1989 article, ''Almost 80 percent of the beer consumed in New York State is sold in the New York City metropolitan area, including Long Island. Thus, wholesalers in the rural northern parts of the state have an incentive to ship beer into the New York City area by selling to a unique tier of 'home distributors' with both wholesale and retail privileges. By shipping trailer-loads and 'forgetting' to charge a deposit, upstate wholesalers can tempt these home distributors with lower prices than they get from their local wholesaler.'' As a result, an Anheuser-Busch distributor like Clare Rose found itself competing against Miller and Coors distributors as well as fellow Anheuser-Busch distributors from another territory. Moreover, Clare Rose had to absorb the cost of redeeming the empties sold into its market by the upstate Anheuser-Busch wholesalers. The New York State Beer Wholesalers Association failed to address the unfairness of the situation, prompting Clare Rose to withdraw from the organization, which it felt was in the pocket of upstate wholesalers and acting against its interest.

In 1987 Clare Rose also faced new competition in the form of Coors Distributing Company of New York, which now entered the Long Island market. What made the new operation so much of a challenge was that Coors granted it a 14-county territory. This arrangement freed the distributor from the problem of upstate wholesalers shipping in cheaper product. In addition, Coors Distributing of New York was able to handle both distribution and deposits for the entire New York metropolitan region from a single location. While the Coors operation succeeded in taking a major share of the market in most territories, it did not succeed as well on Long Island, however. It hindered Clare Rose's growth somewhat, but did not take away sales. One factor in Clare Rose's ability to maintain its market share was its ability to build brands. The promotion of Busch products was a notable success in the late 1980s. The brand was poorly positioned in the marketplace, hardly a premium beer yet not able to compete with the less expensive brands like Schmidt's and Meister Brau. Clare Rose cut prices, but the resulting growth in sales more than made up for the sacrifice in margin. All told, sales of Busch increased by 66 percent, including a whopping 212 percent in convenience stores.

Territorial Expansion in the 1990s

During the 1990s Clare Rose expanded its territory. In August 1991 it moved closer to New York City, becoming the official Anheuser-Busch wholesaler for Nassau County. Two years later, in May 1993, Clare Rose entered the city itself by acquiring the Staten Island territory for Anheuser-Busch products. The company also expanded beyond Anheuser-Busch products in the 1990s, adding Amstel, Beck's, and Heineken, as well as distributing Boardy Barn Brew to supermarkets. By 2000, as a result, revenues grew to about $110 million, a total that made Clare Rose one of Long Island's largest private companies. But the pace of the company's growth only accelerated over the next few years. In 2002 Clare Rose reached the $150 million mark in annual sales, and a year later reached $178 million.

By now a third generation of the Rose family was working full-time at the wholesaler. Cousins Lisa Rose and Sean Rose both took positions at the company and worked their way up to positions of responsibility. According to Lisa there was no pressure to enter the family business. In fact, she majored in political science at college and thought about becoming a career foreign service officer. She told *Long Island Business News* in 2004, ''I never really thought about going into the family business until I got here and saw what it was all about. . . . It's wonderful working with my family. Sometimes I say I'm the luckiest person in the world.'' Her cousin took a more conventional route to a business career. After graduating from Sienna College he earned a master's degree in management from Webster University in London. He would become general manager of Clare Rose. As was the case with the founder, who was still alive in 2004, responsibility was smoothly passed to a new generation by Mark and Frederic Rose. Sean Rose was named chairman of the board and Lisa Rose became chief executive. Their fathers continued to come into work each day, but like Clare F. Rose they gave their offspring a chance to make their own marks. ''My grandfather set the example,'' Lisa Rose told *Long Island Business News,* ''You can't have too many chefs and run a business successfully.''

Principal Subsidiaries

Clare Rose of Nassau, Inc.; Clare Rose of Staten Island Inc.

Principal Competitors

Brooklyn Brewery; Capital Beverage Corporation; Coors Distributing Company of New York; The Gambrinus Company.

Further Reading

''Busch League,'' *Long Island Business News,* October 27, 2000, p. A5.

Galvin, Andrew, ''Weathering the Storm,'' *Beverage World,* February 1989, p. 33.

Schachter, Ken, ''Many of LI's Successful Ventures Are Family Businesses,'' *Long Island Business News,* November 5, 2004.

—Ed Dinger

Click Wine Group

808 Howell Street, 5th Floor
Seattle, Washington 98101
U.S.A.
Telephone: (206) 443-1996
Toll Free: (800) 859-0689
Fax: (206) 443-2535
Web site: http://www.clickwinegroup.com

Private Company
Incorporated: 1987 as Click Imports
Employees: 18
Sales: $25 million (2003)
NAIC: 424820 Wine and Distilled Alcoholic Beverage Merchant Wholesalers; 312130 Wineries

Click Wine Group markets and distributes a portfolio of wines primarily comprised of Australian brands. The company also distributes wines it has developed or invested in, such as the hugely popular French brand Fat Bastard. Click Wine Group represents approximately 18 brands in the United States, 14 of which are produced in Australia. The company also offers a selection of more than a dozen high-quality brands marketed under the Peter Click Selections banner, which includes wines singled out by the company's founder and chief executive officer, Peter Click. Including the different varieties marketed under a single brand, the company's portfolio comprises more than 50 wines from 15 producers. Click Wine Group's subsidiary, Big Fluke Wine Company, focuses on domestic wines. The company owns a portion of Fat Bastard Wine Co., the producer of Click Wine Group's top-selling wines, Fat Bastard Chardonnay, Shiraz, and Merlot.

Origins

Peter Click's entrepreneurial career began on a road trip. Click trained for a career in the financial industry and started working for a bank, but after two years he realized he had chosen practicality over passion. Click was at a crossroads. While he knew he disliked the banking world, he did not know which direction his professional career should take him. In an attempt to find where his real passion lay, Click took the route followed by many other rudderless young college graduates—he decided to travel. Click bought an All-Asia travel pass and set out on a yearlong adventure. He visited countries around the Pacific Rim but spent most of his time in Australia. Australia, he discovered, was his passion, a country he vowed to somehow make a part of his life.

Click's time in Australia pointed him in a professional direction. The moment happened by chance, occurring at a party Click attended in Sydney. During the course of the evening, he struck up a conversation that landed him a job in a local wine shop. Click was introduced to the country's wine industry and became intrigued, eventually spending six months on a 4,000-mile trek exploring the country's wine country and culture. Click returned to the United States in 1986 intent on using his knowledge of Australian wine to perpetuate his relationship with the country he had grown to love.

When Click returned to America, he found a job as a wine buyer for a restaurant in Colorado. His stint at the restaurant exposed a business opportunity, one that dovetailed neatly with his desires. At the time, there were only several Australian wines available in the country, all less distinguished brands selling for around $5 a bottle. Click decided to give the country what it lacked, a selection of fine Australian wines. He mailed 170 letters to small wineries in Australia, offering to represent the companies in the United States. He received a positive reply from 40 of the wineries, giving him, on paper, the basis for his own wine importing business.

To turn his business idea into a reality, Click, like most entrepreneurs, needed cash. In this all-important area, Click was fortunate, obtaining $50,000 from an investor whose name was never revealed. (Click's only hint at the identity of the investor was that he was a cable-television pioneer). With the capital, Click started his company, which was initially called Click Imports, and began importing boutique, mostly family-owned, Australian wines.

Unimpressive Growth during the Company's First Decade

Importing fine Australian wines proved far more difficult than Click imagined. He spent most of his time shuttling between

Company Perspectives:

We bring high quality wines that represent excellent value to the American table. All our wines are hand selected and exhibit balance and finesse.

Australia and wine wholesalers scattered throughout the United States, attempting to develop an import business that showed few signs of promise. Click's original portfolio of brands included some of the most popular premium wines made in Australia, a roster that included Cullen, Elderton, Grosset, Mitchelton, and Mountadam, but he was able to sell only small quantities of the wines in the United States. Australia, in the minds of U.S. wine buyers, was a viticultural backwater, a perception that held the growth of Click's import business in check.

For Click, the situation worsened before it improved. After a decade in business, Click Wine Group could only claim roughly $2 million in annual sales. Click had earlier tried to expand the business by importing wines from Spain and Bulgaria—regions that were better known to U.S. wine buyers—but the diversification did little to boost the company's revenue volume. In 1997, Click Wine Group's 10th anniversary was pocked by a double blow, setbacks that conspired to make the already limping company stagger. One of the Spanish wineries Click Wine Group represented offered to buy the business. Click refused, and the winery responded by severing its ties with him, stripping Click Wine Group of 40 percent of its sales. At roughly the same time, Mitchelton, Click Wine Group's most important Australian brand, decided to switch its allegiances and sign with a larger importer. The departure of Mitchelton represented another 40 percent cut in sales. Click Wine Group, which had been struggling to increase revenues for a decade, was reduced to a fifth of its size within a year.

Click saw a decade's work unravel within months. He began calling the wineries he represented, informing them that he was closing his business. However, a call made to John Valmorbida, the owner of an Australian winery, ended up saving his business. Valmorbida told Click that the Australian government provided marketing funds to companies that marketed their products abroad. To obtain the subsidy, Valmorbida became Click's partner, enabling Click Wine Group to receive $4,000 a month in promotional funds. The monthly stipend kept the company afloat and in position to make its breakthrough less than a year later. After a decade of struggling, Click was about to enjoy exceptional success.

As Click's business reeled, two winemakers were enjoying the success of a promising new brand. Theirry Boudinaud and Guy Anderson were friends with a history of working together in the winemaking business. French-born Boudinaud was an experienced vintner, having crafted wines in California, France, Chile, New Zealand, and South Africa. British-born Anderson made wines in Italy and France. During the mid-1990s, the pair planned to meet in southern France to sample some wines Boudinaud had made. After spending a week in Burgundy making wine, Anderson joined Boudinaud in his wine cellar in southern France. Boudinaud wanted Anderson to taste an experimental Chardonnay he had made, one made with yeast cells left at the bottom of the barrel, a process known as leaving the wine "one the lees." Both men loved the wine, with Anderson remarking, as quoted in the May 27, 2004 issue of the *Philadelphia Inquirer*, "This is every bit as good as any one of the Batard-Montrachets I was making last week," referring to the rich white Burgundy wine from a village named for an illegitimate son. Boudinaud offered his own assessment, adopting a British descriptive term he had heard Anderson use. "Well, I don't know if it's Batard-Montrachet quality," Boudinaud said, "but it is one fat bastard of a wine." Boudinaud and Anderson agreed they had tasted a quality wine and wrote "Fat Bastard" on the tank.

Boudinaud and Anderson had discovered a name and a wine that appealed to many. For Anderson, who objected to the pretentiousness often on display in the wine industry, the name of the new wine offered a perfect dose of irreverence. The wine's simple white label, decorated with a small gold hippopotamus and "Fat Bastard" emblazoned across it," attracted consumers who purchased the wine because of its quirky name and became repeat customers because of its quality. The first vintage comprised 800 cases, which sold out in the United Kingdom immediately. Production increased in subsequent years and the brand expanded. Boudinaud and Anderson introduced a Fat Bastard Shiraz to complement the brand's Chardonnay. By the late 1990s, the pair was ready to introduce Fat Bastard wines in the United States. Anderson contacted a friend in a position to help export the wine, calling Click in Seattle.

Fat Bastard to the Rescue in 1998

Click was barely keeping his company alive when Anderson approached him. He brokered a deal with Boudinaud and Anderson, taking an equity position in Fat Bastard Wine Co. and becoming the exclusive U.S. distributor of the company's $10-a-bottle wines. Click, for the first time, had firm control over the wine he was importing. Fat Bastard arrived in the United States in 1998, giving Click slightly more than 2,000 cases to test the brand's acceptance. The wines were a stunning success, quickly developing a loyal following. Fat Bastard Wine Co. shipped more than 15,000 cases in 1999 and nearly 46,000 cases in 2000, giving Click Wine Group the revenue-generating engine it had needed for more than a dozen years.

Fat Bastard became the pillar supporting Click Wine Group shortly after Click began importing the brand. Annual sales, which never threatened to substantially eclipse the $2-million mark, grew robustly thanks to the popularity of Fat Bastard, surpassing $10 million in 2001. Fat Bastard, which accounted for between 60 percent and 80 percent of the Click Wine Group's sales, breathed new life into Click's import business, giving the company a growing revenue base and enabling Click to pursue other growth opportunities. The years of struggle taught Click the advantages of having considerable control over the wines he distributed. The sudden flight of a Spanish winery and the Australian brand Mitchelton in 1997 had nearly caused his company's collapse. Fat Bastard, a brand he owned a stake in, delivered his greatest success. Accordingly, while Fat Bastard's sales soared, Click began to build a broader business base for his company, one over which he exerted substantial control.

The development of Click Wine Group's own brands offered the company's chief executive officer the chance to exer-

Key Dates:

1987: Peter Click begins importing wine from Australia.
1997: After losing two major customers, Click Wine Group nearly collapses.
1998: The company begins distributing Fat Bastard wines.
2003: Fat Bastard becomes the top-selling French Chardonnay and Shiraz in the United States.
2004: Big Fluke Wine Co., a Click Wine Group subsidiary, is formed to develop domestic wines.

cise greater control over the fortunes of his company. Click Wine Group introduced its own brand of wine, Buckeley's, made from grapes grown in South Australia. Click's efforts to control his own destiny would go further, but meanwhile his import business was reaping the rewards of consumers' knowledge and tastes dovetailing with Click Wine Group's portfolio of wines. The blank stares confronting Click when he preached the virtues of Australian fine wines during the late 1980s no longer existed. In July 2003, Australia became the second-largest importer of wine in the United States, unseating France. The year also marked a celebratory occasion for Fat Bastard. The brand became the top-selling French Chardonnay and Shiraz in the United States. After years of uncertainty, suddenly everything was coming together for Click.

A sense of confidence emanated from the company during the early years of the 21st century. Click was gleaning the fruits of his commitment to Australian wine and the French-made Fat Bastard, spurring him to push Click Wine Group forward. In the early 2000s, the U.S. wine industry felt the presence of ''Two Buck Chuck,'' an opportunist named Charles Shaw who used a wine glut in California to introduce a brand of wines that retailed for $1.99. Charles Shaw quickly was selling four million cases of wine a year and drawing in new, previously untapped wine consumers. In 2003, believing that Two Buck Chuck customers would move up the price scale, Click offered his response, introducing Jackaroo, an Australian wine retailing for $6.99.

As Click Wine Group prepared for the future, its newfound success encouraged Click to launch new business opportunities. In 2004, when Fat Bastard introduced its third varietal, a Merlot, in April, Click Wine Group formed a subsidiary, Big Fluke Wine Company, to spearhead the company's foray into domestic wines. Through the subsidiary, Click Wine Group intended to form partnerships with vineyard owners and production facilities in the United States. Big Fluke's debut wine, Flying Fish Merlot, produced from Washington state grapes, was introduced in September 2004. Looking ahead, Click planned to introduce one or two premium California wines to flesh out the company's portfolio of domestic wines. In the years ahead, Click was expected to push forward with the development of his own brands, as the import business he had nursed for more than a decade began to exhibit remarkable vitality.

Principal Subsidiaries

Big Fluke Wine Co.

Principal Competitors

Bacchus Wine; Billington Distributors; BRL Hardy Ltd.

Further Reading

''Australian Wine with a Kick,'' *Progressive Grocer*, November 1, 2003, p. 50.
Dietrich, Heidi, ''Click Hopes Jackaroo Helps It Continue to Savor Success,'' *Puget Sound Business Journal*, October 17, 2003, p. 32.
''Duo's Wine Is Going Places,'' *Philadelphia Inquirer*, May 27, 2004, p. E4.
Tice, Carol, ''Click Imports Tastes Success Thanks to One Fat Bastard,'' *Puget Sound Business Journal*, October 18, 2002, p. 45.

—Jeffrey L. Covell

Coleman Natural Products, Inc.

1767 Denver West Marriot Road
Suite 200
Golden, Colorado 80401
U.S.A.
Telephone: (303) 468-2500
Toll Free: (800) 442-8666
Fax: (303) 279-1157
Web site: http://www.colemannatural.com

Wholly Owned Subsidiary BC Natural Foods, Inc.
Incorporated: 1993
Employees: 183
Sales: $150 million (2004)
NAIC: 311611 Animal (Except Poultry) Slaughtering; 311615 Poultry Processing; 311612 Meat Processed from Carcasses

Coleman Natural Products, Inc., is the leading U.S. supplier of natural beef and the first company to ask for and receive a USDA "natural" label. Coleman beef is produced from animals that have been raised from birth without the use of antibiotics or growth-promoting hormones on a 100 percent vegetarian diet. Coleman ranchers, feeders, veterinarians, and truck drivers sign affidavits verifying that the animals have been raised, transported, and handled safely and humanely, according to Coleman's strict guidelines. Humane treatment includes expanded space to reduce stress and prevent disease, as well as special shipping requirements to minimize overcrowding and exposure to vehicle exhaust fumes. Coleman has animal science/meat science Ph.D.s on staff to advise in the areas of animal handling, nutrition, and animal welfare.

1979–90: Steady Growth of the Natural Meat Industry

In 1979, Mel Coleman, Sr., founded Coleman Natural Meat after his daughter-in-law complained that she couldn't find any hormone- and stimulant-free beef in Boulder, Colorado's health food stores. Coleman, a fourth generation rancher whose great grandparents had arrived by covered wagon in Colorado in 1870, had been president and chief executive of Coleman Ranches Inc. since 1968. He and his wife, Polly, had ranched on about 250,000 acres of private, state, and federal lands on both sides of the Continental Divide in the San Luis Valley. Coleman Ranches didn't turn a profit from 1974 to 1979 when Coleman decided to pioneer the production and marketing of natural beef raised humanely and with respect for the environment.

Coleman broke new ground for the beef industry in 1980 when he urged the U.S. Department of Agriculture to develop a new "natural" classification for beef. The following year, Coleman Natural Meats instituted stringent protocols governing every aspect of the company's beef production. That same year, it earned the first "No Antibiotics Used From Birth" USDA-approved label. Later, in 1999, Coleman trademarked its meats with the phrase "No Antibiotics, No Added Hormones . . . Ever."

Coleman's protocols differed markedly from the industry's norm. According to the Union of Concerned Scientists, the majority of conventional beef producers in the United States added sub-therapeutics levels of antibiotics to their animals' feed or administer them through direct injection. Coleman opposed these practices, widely accepted as necessary for disease prevention and to increase growth rate and weight, based on the growing evidence that antibiotics kill off only the weaker, susceptible bugs in animals. This situation, it was argued, left the strongest to reproduce and make their way into human bodies and increase bacterial immunity to drugs used to treat human illness. Coleman's position was supported by the World Health Organization in 1997 and 1998.

Coleman—and later, Coleman Certified Ranchers—practiced sustainable agricultural methods, including rotational grazing, a rangeland management system that Coleman Ranch had utilized since 1960. Rotational grazing employed a series of fenced pastures to prevent overgrazing and allowed for more moisture seepage and germination of grass seed. Coleman's ranchers also promised to practice humane animal care, raising their livestock in low-stress, animal-friendly, ample feedlots with plenty of access to clean water and natural feedstuffs in. Calves spent the first eight to ten months of their life with their mother. After weaning, they fed on a vegetarian diet consisting of grains and

Company Perspectives:

By understanding our customers, we will define and lead in the profitable marketing of superior quality, certified natural and organic meat products, raised and produced using ecologically focused principles.

grasses tested regularly to ensure they were free of prohibited substances. Unlike conventionally ranched cattle, Coleman cattle were raised from birth without antibiotics and growth-stimulating hormones.

All Coleman beef came from the family ranch in Saguache, Colorado until 1984 when the company needed additional ranchers to meet demand for its product. Coleman, who then had about 50 head of cattle, was able to enlist the aid of like-minded ranchers, who agreed to raise animals the ''Coleman Way''—without hormones or feed additives, and the company established the Coleman Certified Rancher and Feedlot Program. With this program, another of Mel Coleman's goals became reality: to provide additional income opportunity for small family farmers and ranchers.

Growth in the 1990s

Throughout the 1990s and especially in the latter half of the decade, the popularity of organic foods soared. Natural and organic products were increasingly available in conventional supermarkets and their sales increased more than 20 percent each year. By 1996, Coleman Natural Meats was distributing its meats through the nation's largest natural food supermarkets, such as Whole Foods Markets, Wild Oats, and Alfalfa's stores, benefiting from the growth of the natural foods industry and increased demand for ''natural'' products. Some conventional grocery stores also carried Coleman's products, contributing to its profits of $620,000 on sales of about $43 million in fiscal 1995. Lee Arst, president and chief executive of Coleman Natural Products since 1994, was quoted in the *New York Times* in 1997 as saying, ''This is not a fad . . . It is a cultural change that is going on. It's a lifestyle . . .''

However, only about half of the states in the country regulated organic food, with standards varying widely, and any producer could label a product organic. After years of ignoring the organic food industry, the USDA stepped in with a sweeping set of proposed regulations in the late 1990s—rules to define exactly which products, whether raw or processed, might be labeled organic. The Department also set standards for the production and handling of organically grown crops and organically raised meat and poultry. Only raw products that were 100 percent organic—grown and manufactured without the use of added hormones, pesticides, and synthetic fertilizers—and processed foods that contained 95 percent organic ingredients—could bear the organic seal. Soil had to be free of unapproved synthetics for three years before a crop could be called organic.

However, the government backed down from its original stance on and ultimately allowed the use of hormones and antibiotics in organic meats and the introduction of genetically altered seeds. Coleman Natural Products and other companies committed to alternative production methods were outraged. Arst and Mel Coleman, Jr., traveled the country speaking out against the proposed regulations for organic farming and food production, which finally became law in October 2001.

Coleman continued to grow at a steady rate through the end of the 1990s. By 1999, Coleman processed all of its own meats at its at own slaughtering facility in Limon, Colorado where lactic acid washes were used to help eliminate bacteria. Animal carcasses were transported to the company's Denver facility for ''fabrication.'' Coleman's protocols required a statistical sampling of incoming as well as finished product for bacteria contamination. The company grossed about $50 million annually by the end of the decade, saw an almost 20 percent increase over its revenues mid-decade. By 2001, it contracted with 700 ranchers and brought in about $70 million a year.

In 2000, while the proposed regulations governing organic meat were being reviewed by federal agencies, the organic and natural products markets were faster growing than ever—a $25 billion a year industry. Coleman's, whose meats still fell in the natural category—cattle raised without hormones or antibiotics, but fed non-organic feed—Coleman, which by then processed about 52,000 head of cattle a year, reported being ready to move into the organic field and began test marketing its organic beef in 39 Food Emporium stores in New York around the turn of the century.

The reason for the company's caution in going strictly organic was that organic feed cost significantly more than non-organic feed: $800 a ton for organic soybean meal, for example, compared to $200 a ton for conventional feed. In fact, it cost more overall to produce organic than non-organic meats. Without the addition of growth-inducing hormones, cattle weigh anywhere from 150 to 250 pounds less at slaughter than their hormone-injected counterparts, and without prophylactic antibiotics, feedlots have to be kept cleaner to reduce the spread of pathogens.

Then in 2001, the federal government passed into law its revised regulations government organic farming and food production. These no longer included ''the big three'' and other inappropriate additions to which Coleman, the Organic Trade Association, and many other advocates of organic foods had objected: genetically manufactured organisms (GMOs), municipal sewage sludge, and antibiotics in livestock production. Commenting on the rules in the *Denver Post* Mel Coleman, Jr., said, ''We're very pleased with the new USDA organic standards . . . It will bring parity to labeling, which will allow us to communicate better with out customers.''

By 2002, Coleman Ranches owned or leased more than 200,000 acres of certified organic rangeland, accounting for almost one-half of the nation's total inventory of organic pasture. And a 2002 study by the Food Marketing Institute showed that about 60 percent of people in the United States had sought out and purchased products labeled natural.

The Early 2000s: A Subsidiary of BC Natural Foods

Mel Coleman, Sr., died in February 2002, and Peter Pappas became interim head of the company. Coleman had been an advisor to the Humane Society, and had served on the boards of the Organic Trade Association, The Nature Conservancy, and

Key Dates:

1979: Mel Coleman, Sr., founds Coleman Natural Meat.
1981: The company becomes the first to receive USDA approval for use of the term "natural."
1984: The company establishes the Coleman Certified Rancher and Feedlot Program.
1985: Coleman begins to sell lamb products.
1994: Lee Arst becomes president and chief executive officer of Coleman; Coleman becomes chairman emeritus of the company.
1999: Coleman trademarks its meats with the phrase "No Antibiotics, No Added Hormones . . . Ever."
2001: Arst leaves his position as president and chief executive officer of Coleman.
2002: Mel Coleman, Sr., dies; BC Natural Foods, Inc. purchases the company; Peter Pappas is hired as interim president for one year; Mel Coleman, Jr., is named chairman.
2004: The company partners with B3R Country Meats to start Angus Beef CAB LLC.

on the Humane Sustainable Agriculture Advisory Board. The governor of Colorado had appointed him to five consecutive terms on Colorado's Brand Board which regulated the state's beef industry.

Coleman's legacy continued to shape the direction of the company. In 2002, Coleman Natural Products launched a line of natural franks, Coleman Natural Uncured Beef Hot Dogs, containing only beef, seasonings, and water, using one of Mel Coleman, Sr.'s recipes. An earlier foray into the beef hot dog market had ended because of the 14-day shelf life of Coleman's wieners. Now new packaging methods allowed the dogs to stay fresh in the refrigerator for 30 days or more, and their popularity grew.

In late 2002, BC Natural Foods purchased Coleman Natural Products. BC Natural Foods owned Petaluma Poultry, and also bought B3R Country Meats LP in 2002. Mel Coleman, Jr., remained at head of the company his father had founded. Coleman's products then sold in more than 1,700 stores across the country with beef sourced from more than 800 ranchers in 17 western states.

In 2003, Coleman offered a full line of beef cuts, a ground beef program, hot dogs, patties, Coleman Natural lamb and pork. The company also launched into the foodservice channel, providing the official ground beef of the Colorado-based quick-serve chain "Good Times Burgers & Custard," which at the time had 35 restaurants. Good Times branded the Coleman logo on their menus, marquees, and packaging.

In 2004, Coleman's foodservice channel continued to expand with CB Potts of Colorado and Lucky 32 chain of North Carolina adding Coleman branded entrees to their menus. Coleman also began its Certified Angus Beef CAB LLC in partnership with B3R Country meats, adding a natural product line to the world's leading beef brand—CAB Natural Products. With demand for natural products steadily on the rise, the company, which had maintained nearly double-digit growth during most of its years, seemed assured a prosperous future.

Principal Competitors

Niman Ranch Inc.; Laura's Lean Beef Company; Cooperative Regions of Organic Producers Pool.

Further Reading

"Antibiotics on the Farm," *New York Times*, January 9, 2001.
Burros, Marian, "U. S. to Subject Organic Foods, Long Ignored, to Federal Rules," *New York Times*, December 15, 1997, p. A1.
James, Barry, "Alarms Over Antibiotics in Food," *International Herald Tribune*, April 16, 2001.
Raabe, Steve, "Coleman Family Sells Natural Beef Company to Gillett, Investors," *Denver Post*, October 13, 2002, p. B2.
——, "Growing Fees, Record-Keeping a Concern," *Denver Post*, October 13, 2002, p. K4.
——, "Vail, Colorado Investor Returns to Agricultural Roots with Buys in Meat," *Denver Post*, October 15, 2002, p. C1.
Voynick, Stephen M., *Riding the Higher Range*, Saguache, Co.: Glenn Melvin Coleman, 1998.

—Carrie Rothburd

Cole's Quality Foods, Inc.

5043 Cascade Road SE
Grand Rapids, Michigan 49546
U.S.A.
Telephone: (616) 975-0081
Fax: (616) 975-0267
Web site: http://www.coles.com

Private Company
Incorporated: 1943
Employees: 150
Sales: $50 million (2004 est.)
NAIC: 311812 Commercial Bakeries

Cole's Quality Foods, Inc. is one of America's leading manufacturers of frozen garlic bread and toast. The Michigan-based firm's products are distributed throughout the eastern half of the United States, as well as to selected markets in the Southwest and West. Cole's other products include bread sticks and low-carbohydrate garlic bread; the company also produces some items for private label and foodservice accounts. CEO Scott Devon owns a controlling interest in the firm.

Beginnings

The roots of Cole's Quality Foods date to 1943, when L. Carroll Cole purchased the Cruikshank Bakery in Muskegon, Michigan. Shortly after assuming control, Cole recruited his brother to open a bakery outlet inside a downtown department store. When World War II ended in 1945, government-imposed sugar rationing ceased, and the bakery was able to expand its offerings to include doughnuts, cakes, and cookies.

Cole's business grew steadily over the next two decades, and he opened additional retail outlets as well as recruiting new grocery store accounts. By the 1970s, the firm was selling more than 100 different varieties of fresh baked goods through its own stores and in 70 Michigan supermarkets.

In 1972, the company hired Wes Devon to serve as vice-president of marketing. To help the firm stand out from its competition, Devon suggested that it create a frozen version of Italian garlic bread. Cole's bakers came up with a one-pound loaf that could be thawed for several hours and then baked to serve hot from the oven. When the firm's retail outlets and a number of grocery stores around Michigan began to stock the product, it caught on with the public and orders for it increased.

At this time large, supermarkets had begun to build in-house bakeries, which took customers away from independent ones, causing many to fold. Cole's frozen garlic bread, a product which no other firms were making, helped to keep it afloat, and in 1978 the company took the gamble of dropping its other products to concentrate on this one item. The firm's Muskegon baking plant was reconfigured to boost production of the bread, and over the next year its remaining retail outlets were closed. Wes Devon, who had for several years been buying out the Cole family, was now the sole owner of the firm.

Growth in the 1980s–90s

The early 1980s saw distribution expand to much of the midwestern and southeastern United States. Between 1984 and 1989, the company's sales tripled, and Cole's Frozen Garlic Bread became the third best-selling frozen bread product in the United States, behind Sara Lee croissants and Lender's bagels.

In 1989, Cole's introduced its first new product offerings in more than a decade. The Home Style bread line consisted of garlic, onion, oregano, cheese garlic, and wheat and honey varieties. After test-marketing the breads in cities such as New York and Chicago, where sales exceeded initial expectations, the line was rolled out throughout the company's sales territory. During 1989, Cole's also spent $5 million to add an 800,000 cubic-foot computerized freezer (the largest at the time in the Midwest) and 20,000 cubic feet of dry storage to its Muskegon plant. The firm was now also considering making baked goods for foodservice customers such as restaurants and hospitals.

During the early 1990s, several competitors began marketing their own frozen garlic bread, and Cole's responded by making changes to its packaging and introducing new items such as frozen bread sticks. New garlic bread varieties like Multi-Grain, Zesty Italiano, and Romano Cheese were also created. In 1994, the company introduced several types of low-

Key Dates:

1943: L. Carroll Cole buys Cruikshank Bakery in Muskegon, Michigan.
1940s–50s: Cole expands his product line and opens several more retail outlets.
1972: The firm introduces frozen garlic bread.
1979: The company's retail shops are closed to focus on garlic bread; Wes Devon buys out Cole.
1980s: Distribution is expanded to the Midwest, East Coast, and South.
1989: The Muskegon baking plant is given a $5 million upgrade.
1995: Wes Devon's son Scott is named president of the company.
1998: Texas Toast is introduced and soon comprises 50 percent of sales.
2001: A Muskegon plant is reequipped to make new flash-frozen garlic bread.
2004: John Sommavilla is named president.

fat, low-cholesterol frozen Focaccia Italian Pan Breads, which could be heated in ten minutes after being thawed. The round, pizza-like breads were distributed to Cole's customers in the Midwest, Southeast, and mid-Atlantic states. During this period, the firm was seeing sales growth of as much as 25 percent per year as more Americans discovered its products.

In 1995, Wes Devon's son, Wesley Scott Devon, Jr. (known as Scott), was made president of the firm, and he hired several other new executives after taking the job. Though the elder Devon continued to hold the posts of CEO and chairman, his health was declining as he entered the early stages of Alzheimer's disease.

French Bakery Restaurant Opened in 1995

In December 1995, Cole's unveiled a new business venture in downtown Grand Rapids, Michigan, about a half-hour from Muskegon. The Saint-Honoré French Bakery and Tea Room was a restaurant which served tea, coffee, authentic French pastries, and French breads, as well as offering educational programs like cooking classes. It was open for breakfast, lunch, and dinner. Located on the first floor of a 1920s bank building, the interior was carefully designed to make use of original architectural features such as brass and mahogany trim, as well as the bank's vault. Executive pastry chef Jean Luc Saint and baker Françoise Sardi had been recruited from Paris, while a second artisan baker was brought in from Seattle. The restaurant was created in part to help Cole's test new products and to identify a wholesale market for others.

In 1996, the company moved Scott Devon's office and its executive sales offices to a new building in Grand Rapids. The firm's official headquarters and all other operations remained in Muskegon.

In January 1997, just over a year after it had opened, the restaurant was closed. Business had not reached the hoped-for levels, and in the face of rising losses it was shuttered. Despite this setback, the company had begun marketing a line of specialty breads under the Saint-Honoré name. Sales of the new products began in western Michigan, with plans to distribute to other areas. The Saint-Honoré baking operation, originally located in Muskegon, later moved to the Detroit suburb of Livonia.

After introducing several varieties of frozen garlic toast in 1997, the following year saw the company's thick-sliced frozen "Texas Toast" line debut. The toast, which was modeled after a competitor's popular product, would go on to become a huge success. Unlike the firm's garlic bread, it could be baked in an oven without thawing and required minimal forethought or preparation time. With the success of Texas Toast, the firm's staff was expanded from 90 to 150.

By 2000, Cole's annual sales stood at $48 million. The company's business was now split evenly between garlic bread and toast. With bread sales about to be eclipsed by the quicker-to-prepare toast, the firm began looking for ways to address the problem. In time, a solution was found: a new method of flash-freezing garlic bread so that it could be prepared in ten minutes, with no pre-thawing required.

Plant Reconfigured in 2001

To prepare for full-scale production of the improved garlic bread, which required different baking equipment, the firm's Muskegon plant was shut down for two weeks in August 2001, gutted, and completely rebuilt. Afterwards, to call attention to the product's changes, the packaging was redesigned. The company had recently won a Gold Taste Award from the American Tasting Institute, and this was touted on the packaging and on the company's Web site. A new slogan, "Cole's Quality Foods: The Clear Choice," was also introduced, based on a quote from the Tasting Institute, which had called Cole's the "clear choice" in taste for its product category. Cole's garlic bread was now priced at $2.29 for a one-pound loaf.

Customer response to the new garlic bread was positive, and sales increased as a result. Consequently, the firm began to expand to new markets, including Phoenix, Salt Lake City, and Buffalo. Its strongest market remained close to home, however—Detroit, Michigan, where some six million loaves of garlic bread were consumed each year. The firm had a loyal customer base, with a repeat purchase rate of 61 percent.

Cole's had seen annual sales increases for a number of years running, which were consistent with the growth in the frozen bread category. Total supermarket sales of frozen bread had risen from $50 million in 1996 to $200 million in 1999 and were approaching $400 million in 2002, according to industry analysts Information Resources, Inc. With this growth had also come the inevitable introduction of supermarket "private label" lines, which accounted for about one-fifth of total sales. For 2002, Cole's had estimated sales of more than $51 million.

The low-carbohydrate diet craze of the early 2000s cut into the sales of many bread products, but, rather than viewing it as a threat, Cole's took up the challenge to create a new product line which could enhance overall revenues. In early 2004, the company introduced Ultra Garlic Bread, which had five grams of carbohydrate per one-ounce slice, less than half of the regular variety. The bread was made by substituting oat fiber and wheat gluten for refined white flour, with no added sugars and a pure butter spread on top. A twelve-ounce loaf was priced at between $2.59 and $3.29, slightly more than a one-pound loaf of the original variety. To produce it, Cole's hired twenty more employees and added a weekend shift at its plant. A few months later, a low-carb Texas Toast was introduced as well. By now, Cole's garlic bread and toast could be found in close to 60 percent of the grocery stores in the United States.

In June 2004, Cole's named a new president. John Sommavilla, age 45, had nearly twenty years in the grocery business, most recently as an executive vice-president at Spartan Stores. Scott Devon would retain the positions of CEO and board chairman.

In August 2004, Betsy Devon, the second wife of ailing company patriarch Wes Devon, filed a $30 million lawsuit against the company, Scott Devon, and the firm's chief financial officer, Cynthia Havard. It alleged that they had unfairly deprived her of the financial resources and companionship of her 65-year-old husband, who had in 2003 been placed in a 24-hour care facility by his son. Betsy Devon also sought to invalidate a prenuptial agreement she had signed. The company's attorneys characterized her suit as being motivated by a desire for money.

After more than sixty years in business, Cole's Quality Foods, Inc. had grown into one of the leading manufacturers of frozen garlic bread and toast in the United States. Having originated the product category, the firm continued to lead with innovations like its new flash-frozen and low-carb varieties.

Principal Competitors

T. Marzetti Company; Pepperidge Farm, Inc.; Joseph Campione, Inc.

Further Reading

Bauer, Julia, "Sliced Out; Cole's Cuts Carbs By Replacing White Flour in Italian Bread," *Grand Rapids Press*, January 20, 2004, p. A6.

Boissoneau, Ross, "Muskegon Bakery Expands Product Mix—To Two," *Grand Rapids Business Journal*, January 30, 1989, p. B5.

Crawley, Nancy, "Cole's Exec Reaches out in New Role," *Grand Rapids Press*, March 9, 2003, p. E1.

Hartnett, Michael, "Home-Baked Profits: Combined, Sales of Frozen Bread Items and Frozen Dough Products Now Exceed Half a Billion Dollars," *Frozen Food Age*, July 1, 2002, p. 30.

Knape, Chris, "Bread Battle: Wife Seeks Millions from Bakery," *Grand Rapids Press*, August 28, 2004, p. A1.

"Product Improvements Speed Coles' Growth," *Frozen Food Age*, February 1, 2002, p. 66.

Radigan, Mary, "Cole's President Acquires Taste for Frozen Garlic Bread," *Grand Rapids Press*, June 28, 2004, p. A6.

——, "Parisian Café Shuts Doors Downtown," *Grand Rapids Press*, January 9, 1997, p. D12.

——, "Paris Style Tea Room Opens Doors," *Grand Rapids Press*, December 11, 1995, p. E1.

Riell, Howard, "Bread and Dough on the Go," *Frozen Food Age*, November 1, 2002, p. 26.

——, "Roll ON! (Frozen Dough Products and Bread)," *Frozen Food Age*, August 1, 2001, p. 36.

"Time Capsule: Bread," *Frozen Food Age*, December 1, 2002, p. 49.

Walsh, Tom, "Cole's Has Fresh Ideas About Bread," *Detroit Free Press*, February 10, 2004.

Wishnow, Sharon J., "Toast of Category: Frozen Bread Rises with Healthy Garlic Flavor," *Quick Frozen Foods International*, April 1, 1998, p. 147.

—Frank Uhle

Constellation Brands, Inc.

370 Woodcliff Drive, Suite 3000
Fairport, New York 14450
U.S.A.
Telephone: (585) 218-3600
Toll Free: (888) 724-2169
Fax: (585) 218-3601
Web site: http://www.cbrands.com

Public Company
Incorporated: 1972 as Canandaigua Wine Company, Inc.
Employees: 7,800
Sales: $4.46 billion (2004)
Stock Exchanges: New York
Ticker Symbol: STZ
NAIC: 312120 Breweries; 312130 Wineries; 312140 Distilleries; 422810 Beer and Ale Wholesaling; 422820 Wine and Distilled Alcoholic Beverage Wholesalers; 312112 Bottled Water Manufacturing; 111332 Grape Vineyards

Constellation Brands, Inc., is the only alcoholic beverage company in the United States involved in all three categories of the industry—wine, beer, and spirits. Constellation markets more than 200 alcohol brands, ranking as the largest wine company in the world, the largest multi-category supplier of beverage alcohol in the United States, and as one of the largest importers of beer in the world. The company's operations, which comprise approximately 45 production facilities in North America, Asia, Europe, Australia, New Zealand, and Chile, are separated into two operating divisions: Constellation Wines and Constellation Beers & Spirits. Through Constellation Wines, the company sells more than 75 million cases of wine each year. Brands sold by the division include Franciscan, Ravenswood, Arbor Mist, Hardys, and Nobilo. Through Constellation Beers & Spirits, the company imports into the United States a portfolio of leading beer brands, including Corona, Modelo Especial, St. Pauli Girl, and Tsingtao. The division also ranks as one of the largest producers and marketers of distilled spirits, offering brands such as Black Velvet, Barton, Fleischmann's, and Skol. Constellation sells its brands in more than 60 countries.

Early History

In 1935, some years after the repeal of the Volstead Act and the end of prohibition, Mack Sands opened the Car-Cal Winery. Located in North Carolina, Car-Cal Winery produced varietal table wines for limited distribution. Mack's son, Marvin, learned about the wine industry from his father and was soon determined to open a winery of his own. In 1945, Marvin's dream materialized when his family purchased a sauerkraut factory-turned-winery located in Canandaigua, New York (in the Finger Lakes region), and he established Canandaigua Industries.

Sands hired eight workers to produce and sell bulk wine in wooden barrels to companies that would bottle them on the East Coast. In just two years, business was so good that Sands decided to significantly change the direction of his company. With a steady flow of cash to deal with unforeseen emergencies, the head of Canandaigua Industries was determined to produce and sell wine using his own name brands. In 1948, the Car-Cal operation run by Mack Sands was closed, and all wine production was transferred to the facility in Canandaigua. In the same year, Marvin Sands purchased the Mother Vineyard Wine Company, located in Manteo, North Carolina, the first in a long line of strategic acquisitions designed to expand Canandaigua's market position.

Primarily concentrating on regional markets, Canandaigua's new brand of wines were moderately successful. In 1951, the younger Sands opened Richards Wine Cellars in Petersburg, Virginia, and asked his father to assume control of the operation. Not long afterwards, the Onslow Wine Company was added to the growing list of regional wine producers owned and operated by Canandaigua. Both Richards Wine Cellars and Onslow Wine Company produced a wine called Scuppernong, made from varietal grapes grown primarily in the southern United States which serve as a popular source of wines throughout the region. In spite of this expansion, sales remained relatively slow and the company's business did not grow rapidly.

In 1954, however, Sands was lucky enough to come up with something most entrepreneurs only dream about—a widely

Company Perspectives:

Constellation's strategy of creating breadth across categories and geographies, and leveraging scale in core markets, delivers long-term profitable growth for shareholders. This strategy allows us more investment choices, flexibility to address changing market conditions and stronger routes-to-market, which result in superior financial performance.

successful product that catapults a company into a future of rapid growth and high profits. This product, which became known as the Richard's Wild Irish Rose brand of dessert wines (named after his son Richard), spearheaded Canandaigua's development for years to come. Quickly realizing the potential of his new product, Sands implemented an extremely innovative franchising system, the very first in the wine industry. The franchising network included an agreement between Canandaigua and five independent bottling companies located in various parts of the United States. These bottlers were given the franchise rights to bottle and distribute Wild Irish Rose brands in their areas. With a minimum capital investment, Sands reaped the rewards of seeing his hot-selling Wild Irish Rose gain a larger and larger part of the dessert wine market.

During the late 1950s, revenues generated from the widespread sale of Wild Irish Rose allowed Canandaigua to concentrate on increasing its own production facilities. As sales of the dessert wine brand continued to grow, the company expanded to meet the explosive demands of the marketplace. People were hired to help extend the company's sales network, and a wholesale distributor operation was also established. During the early and mid-1960s, both the sales staff and the wholesale distributor network was strengthened to meet the ever-growing demand for Wild Irish Rose brands. As sales increased, Sands continued his policy of strategic acquisition by purchasing in 1965 the Tenner Brothers Winery, located in South Carolina, and adding Hammondsport Wine Company in 1969. The acquisition of Hammondsport gave Canandaigua an entry into the sparkling wine market, a direction that Sands had wanted his company to take for years.

Going Public and Expanding Product Lines: 1970s–80s

In 1972, the company was incorporated as Canandaigua Wine Company, Inc., and one year later, it went public. Several important brands of wine were produced at Richards Wine Cellars, but it was the acquisitions strategy that continued to shape the company. The most significant acquisition was made in 1974, when Canandaigua purchased the Bisceglia Brothers Winery in Madera, California. This gave the company access to a large varietal wine market in the western United States. Another milestone in the firm's history was the production of its own brand of champagne, J. Roget, in 1979. This champagne was an immediate triumph and contributed to Canandaigua's seemingly endless string of successful product introductions.

The 1980s were boom years for the company. In 1984, Canandaigua introduced Sun Country Wine Cooler, a carbonated concoction of wine and fruit flavorings. The cooler caught like wildfire across the United States and revenues for the product skyrocketed. During the early 1980s, the firm purchased Robin et Cie, a French producer of high-quality table wine, and renamed it the Batavia Wine Company. Batavia soon began to create different brands of sparkling wines, including champagne. In 1986, Richard Sands, son of founder Marvin, took over as president of the company. The following year, Canandaigua purchased a plant in McFarland, California, in order to produce grape juice concentrate and grape spirits.

The two most important acquisitions in 1987 included Widmer's Wine Cellars and the Manischewitz brands from Monarch Wine Company. Widmer's Wine Cellars, located in Naples, New York, was one of the most successful and popular makers of table wine on the East Coast. Producing a wide range of table wines, from Dry Riesling to California varietals, Widmer had won a host of awards in wine competitions. In the late 1980s, Manischewitz was the best-selling brand name in kosher wines. When Canandaigua purchased the Manischewitz assets, all the production facilities were relocated to the Widmer plant in Naples, New York. Canandaigua's commitment to the production of the Manischewitz brands involved a separate facility which maintained strict supervision for the making of kosher wine under the auspices of the Union of Orthodox Jewish Congregations of America.

Diversification Through Acquisition: 1990s

In 1988, the company added Cal-Products in order to produce grape spirits. During the same year, the company purchased the Cisco brand name products from Guild Wineries, a maker of table wines, dessert wines, and champagnes. Canandaigua was so pleased with the revenue generated by these products that it acquired Guild Wineries in 1991 for $60 million. This purchase brought with it the popular brands of Dunnewood wines, Cribari vermouth, and Cook's champagne. Italian Swiss Colony brand dessert wines were also bought at this time. During the late 1980s and early 1990s, in addition to the acquisition of domestic firms that produced wines, champagnes, and juices, the company began to import the Marcus James brand of table wines from Brazil, the popular Mateus brand from Portugal, the Keller Geister brand of table wines from Germany, and Mondoro Asti Spumante from Italy.

During the 1990s, with Sands heading the company as chairman of the board of directors, and with son Richard serving first as president then as CEO starting in 1993, Canandaigua continued to expand. One of the most significant acquisitions included Barton Inc., which was purchased in June 1993 for approximately $123 million in cash, one million shares of Canandaigua stock, and the assumption of $47.9 million in debt. Barton, located in Chicago, Illinois, was one of the largest producers of distilled spirits and also one of the largest importers of foreign beers. A firm with additional facilities in Carson, California, and Atlanta, Georgia, Barton was in the midst of its own expansion program when acquired by Canandaigua. This purchase provided Canandaigua with an entry into the lucrative distilled spirits market. Barton's brands were already selling well, including Scotch whiskeys such as House of Stuart and Speyburn single malt, Canadian whiskeys such as Canadian Host and Northern Light, and American whiskeys named

Key Dates:

1945: The Sands family purchases a winery located in Canandaigua, New York; Marvin Sands establishes Canandaigua Industries to run the winery.
1948: Sands purchases the Mother Vineyard Wine Company, located in Manteo, North Carolina.
1951: Sands opens Richards Wine Cellars in Petersburg, Virginia.
1954: The company introduces the Richard's Wild Irish Rose brand of dessert wines, which becomes the firm's top brand.
1969: Canandaigua acquires Hammondsport Wine Company, gaining entry into the sparkling wine sector.
1972: The company is incorporated as Canandaigua Wine Company, Inc.
1973: The company goes public.
1974: Bisceglia Brothers Winery, a West Coast varietal wine maker, is acquired.
1979: The company begins production of its own champagne brand, J. Roget.
1984: Canandaigua enters the wine cooler market with the Sun Country brand, leading to skyrocketing revenues.
1986: Richard Sands, son of Marvin, is named president of the company.
1987: Widmer's Wine Cellars, an East Coast table wine producer, and Manischewitz, the best-selling kosher wine brand, are acquired.
1991: The company purchases Guild Wineries, including the Dunnewood and Cook's brands.
1993: The company acquires Barton Inc., a leading producer of distilled spirits and a leading importer of foreign beers, and Vintners International, owner of the Paul Masson and Taylor California Cellars brands.
1994: Canandaigua acquires Almaden Vineyards and Inglenook Vineyards from Heublein, Inc.
1995: The company purchases from United Distillers Glenmore, Inc. 12 distilled spirits brands, including Canadian LTD, Chi-Chi's, Fleischmann's, Inver House, and Mr. Boston.
1997: The company changes its name to Canandaigua Brands, Inc.
1998: The company moves its headquarters to Fairport, New York, and acquires Matthew Clark plc, a leading U.K. producer and distributor of hard cider, wine, and bottled water.
1999: Canandaigua acquires eight Canadian whiskey brands from Diageo plc, including Black Velvet, and enters the premium wine category through purchases of Franciscan Vineyards, Inc. and Simi Winery, Inc.; Richard Sands takes over as chairman following his father's death.
2000: The company changes its name to Constellation Brands, Inc.
2003: Constellation Brands acquires BRL Hardy Ltd., the largest vintner in Australia.
2004: Constellation Brands announces the acquisition of California's The Robert Mondavi Corporation

Corby's Reserve and Kentucky Gentleman. At the time of the acquisition, Barton Vodka was one of the largest selling domestically made vodkas in the United States. The Barton Beer division was just beginning to reap the rewards of importing such popular items as Corona Light from Mexico and Tsingtao from the People's Republic of China.

In October 1993, Canandaigua purchased Vintners International Company, Inc., including Paul Masson and Taylor California Cellars, for $148.9 million in cash. The Paul Masson brand, one of the most popular and respected in the wine industry, was given a new label with a heavy television advertising campaign that included the familiar phrase, ''We will sell no wine before its time.'' Taylor California Cellars brand of table wines, one of the best-selling brands in the country, was given a new price structure. Less than one year after the purchase of the Vintners brands, wholesale orders began to exceed company estimates, and sales steadily increased. In July 1994, Canandaigua became the sole American importer and distributor of Cordorniu sparkling wines. Established in 1972 by the Cordorniu family in Barcelona, Spain, the winery was the first to produce Methode Champernoise sparkling wines on the Iberian peninsula. In 1992, Cordorniu built a facility in Napa Valley where it began to produce the popular Cordorniu Napa Valley Brut Cuvée.

A very significant acquisition for Canandaigua occurred in August 1994, when the company purchased both Almaden Vineyards and Inglenook Vineyards from Heublein, Inc. for $130.6 million. Inglenook Vineyards, founded in 1879 by a sea captain from Finland—Gustave Niebaum—and Almaden Vineyards, established by Etienne Thee and Charles LeFranc in 1852, were two of the oldest and most well-respected wineries in the United States. Together, the two companies sold approximately 15 million cases of wines in 1993, and Almaden ranked fifth while Inglenook ranked sixth in table wine sales within the United States. Almaden alone, before its acquisition by Canandaigua, had captured over 6 percent of the American table wine market. Inglenook had cornered over 5 percent of the domestic table wine market.

With these acquisitions, Canandaigua owned and operated four of the five GAMIT brands (GAMIT is the acronym for the five major wine brands in the United States: Gallo, Almaden, Paul Masson, Inglenook, and Taylor California Cellars). These wineries produced significant amounts of varietal wines, and Canandaigua positioned itself to take advantage of the growing varietal wine market through its acquisition strategy. At the same time, the company also improved upon its ranking as the second leading wine producer in the United States. Under new marketing techniques implemented by management at Canandaigua, Almaden wines such as Mountain Burgundy and Golden Chardonnay grew in popularity, increasing company revenues. A new pricing structure for Inglenook varietal wines, such as Premium Select, Estate Cellars, and Napa Valley, also led to increasing sales.

Double-digit sales growth during the early 1990s catapulted Canandaigua into one of the largest and most popular of the alcoholic beverage producers and importers in the United States. From 1990 to 1994, the company's gross sales shot up from $201 million to $861 million, nearly a fourfold increase. In 1994, net income was recorded at $26 million, a 71 percent increase over the previous year. The acquisition of Barton resulted in a sales increase of $211 million for 1994, while the purchase of Vintners generated $119 million for the same fiscal year. In just one month of sales, the Almaden and Inglenook acquisition added an impressive $17 million to the 1994 year in sales.

That same year, the company announced a comprehensive restructuring program that was estimated to save approximately $1.7 million in 1995 and over $13.3 million by 1996. The acquisition of Barton and Vintners gave rise to an integration of sales staff, improvement of customer services, a marketing campaign with an enhanced focus, greater efficiency in production techniques, an implementation of up-to-date information systems, and more effective finance and administrative operations. During the mid-1990s, Canandaigua consolidated all its facilities already located in California, enabling the company to group three separate bottling operations in one location. The new facility, the Mission Bell plant in Madera, California, began bottling more than 22 million cases annually.

Under the continued leadership of Marvin Sands, Canandaigua in the mid-1990s appeared to be headed for even greater profitability in the future. The company had captured 32 percent of the domestic champagne market, the largest in the industry. By the mid-1990s, the company's Barton Beer Division held 10 percent of the total market share for imported beers in the United States. In 1994, the division's domestic brand, Point Special, increased sales by an astounding 25 percent. The company's Dunnewood brand, a California varietal wine, also increased its sales by 25 percent in 1994. With such popular brands, and astute management that foresaw opportunities and took advantage of trends in the marketplace, it was no surprise that the company's stock price increased by a record 37 percent for fiscal 1994.

Acquisitions continued in the second half of the 1990s, highlighted early on by the September 1995 purchase of 12 distilled liquor brands from United Distillers Glenmore, Inc. for $141.8 million. Among the key brands added to the Canandaigua portfolio were Canadian LTD whiskey; Chi-Chi's cocktails; Fleischmann's gin, vodka, and whiskey; Inver House scotch; and Mr. Boston liqueurs, brandies, and schnapps. This acquisition propelled Canandaigua from the eighth largest distributor of distilled spirits in the United States to the fourth largest.

The company suffered a brief setback during the 1996 fiscal year after running into operational difficulties stemming from the aggressive string of acquisitions of the previous half-decade. Canandaigua subsequently restructured its production, marketing, and distribution operations to cut costs, increase production, and improve profitability. Another key to the turnaround was the beefing up of the company's upper management ranks, including the addition of Daniel Barnett as president of the wine division and Thomas Summer as CFO. Marvin Sands remained chairman of the company, while son Richard continued serving as president and CEO.

The company's 1990s diversification led to the September 1997 company name change to Canandaigua Brands, Inc. The wine division thereupon adopted the Canandaigua Wine Company name, while the spirits and beer operations were organized within Barton Incorporated. In early 1998, the company moved its headquarters from Canandaigua to Fairport, New York (located east of Rochester). For the fiscal year ending in February 1998, Canandaigua Brands reported record net sales of $1.21 billion; the net income of $50.1 million was nearly double the $27.7 million figure for the preceding year.

In the spring of 1998, Canandaigua succeeded with the launch of a new wine brand, Arbor Mist. The new line consisted of fruit-flavored varietal wines with a low alcohol content of 6 percent aimed at first-time and younger wine consumers, particularly women. By the fall of 1998, Arbor Mist had already captured 1.2 percent of the U.S. wine market. With acquisition prospects in the United States dwindling, Canandaigua began seeking international opportunities in 1998. In December that year, the company acquired Matthew Clark plc for $475 million. Founded in 1810, the U.K.-based company was a leading producer and distributor of hard cider, wine, and bottled water in its home country. Among the company's brands were Blackthorn and Diamond White cider, Stowells of Chelsea and QC wines, and Strathmore sparkling water. In April 1999, Canandaigua spent $185.5 million to acquire eight Canadian whiskey brands and production facilities in the provinces of Alberta and Quebec from Diageo plc. The top brand gained thereby was Black Velvet, the number three Canadian whiskey brand in the United States.

A rapidly growing sector of the wine industry in the late 1990s was the premium category, an area in which Canandaigua Brands lacked any presence. That changed in June 1999 when the company completed two separate acquisitions of Franciscan Vineyards, Inc. and Simi Winery, Inc. and began operating them as a separate division called Franciscan Estates. The purchases instantly vaulted Canandaigua into the ranks of the major makers of fine wines, with a portfolio that featured several well-respected brands: Quintessa, Veramonte, Mount Veeder, Franciscan Oakville Estate, Estancia, and Simi.

From the start of its acquisition spree in 1991 through the fiscal 1999 year, Canandaigua Brands achieved a remarkable level of growth, with both net sales and net income increasing at a rate of 33 percent per year. Net sales for 1999 were a shade under $1.5 billion. In August 1999, soon after the company's entry into the premium wine category, Marvin Sands died at the age of 75, after more than 50 years of leading the company. Richard Sands took over as chairman, gaining full responsibility for taking the rapidly growing company through the initial years of the 21st century.

Acquisitions Increase Revenues in the Early 21st Century

Under the leadership of Richard Sands, Canandaigua Brands recorded remarkable growth at the turn of the 21st century, with the 1999 acquisitions of Franciscan Vineyards and Simi Winery signaling a concerted push into middle- and upper-tier wines. The company changed its name again in 2000, adopting the corporate title Constellation Brands, Inc., ''a more apt description of a company that has grown in both breadth and depth of its product line as well as its geographic reach,'' according to a company spokesperson in the September 18, 2000 issue of *Nation's Restaurant News*.

Constellation Brands completed a series of acquisitions during the early 2000s that recast the company's image. Known for years for its portfolio of inexpensive ''jug'' wines, the company broadened its scope to include fine wines, a move that led to robust growth and several massive acquisitions. In early 2001, the company acquired Turner Road Vintners and Corus Brands, purchases that gave it premium wine labels such as Talus, Vendange, Columbia, and Covey Run. In mid-2001, the company acquired Ravenswood, the most popular brand of premium Red Zinfandel in the United States. The most important transaction of the year was concluded in August of that year, when Constellation Brands formed a joint venture company with BRL Hardy Ltd., the largest vintner in Australia. The two companies formed Pacific Wine Partnership, which allowed Constellation Brands to import some of BRL Hardy's Australian and New Zealand wines. The partnership represented an important foray into ''New World'' wines, that is, those produced in Southern Hemisphere countries such as South Africa, Chile, and Australia, a sector of the global wine industry that Constellation Brands would come to dominate. The joint venture with BRL Hardy did not achieve its greatest significance until nearly two years after Pacific Wine Partnership was formed, however, when Richard Sands completed his first massive acquisition.

The relationship between Constellation Brands and BRL Hardy crystallized in early 2003. In April, Richard Sands acquired BRL Hardy in a cash-and-stock transaction valued at $1.1 billion. The purchase made Constellation Brands the largest vintner in the world, enabling the company to overtake E.&J. Gallo. The company's wines sales increased from $1.2 billion to $1.7 billion overnight, while its total revenues swelled to more than $3 billion. Sands, who quickly developed a reputation for being a skilled negotiator, took the company to new heights with the BRL Hardy acquisition, but his appetite for acquisitions was not satisfied after completing the largest deal in the company's history. Roughly a year and a half later, Constellation Brands announced it was acquiring The Robert Mondavi Corp. in a more than $1-billion deal that ranked as one of the largest acquisitions in the history of the California wine industry. The acquisition, announced in November 2004 and expected to be approved by shareholders in late 2004 or early 2005, promised to give Constellation Brands control of approximately 20 percent of California wine production. It also indicated Sands's willingness to acquire, which enabled the company to increase its revenues from $1.5 billion to $4.5 billion during his first five years of leadership. In the years ahead, with the ambitious yet prudent Sands at the helm, the towering presence of Constellation Brands looked set to grow more formidable as the company sought to dominate the production and marketing of wines, beers, and distilled spirits throughout the world.

Principal Subsidiaries

Canandaigua Wine Company, Inc.; Canandaigua Ltd. (United Kingdom); Roberts Trading Corporation; Canandaigua B.V. (Netherlands); CB International Finance S.A.R.L. (Luxembourg); Constellation Brands Ireland Ltd.; Allied Drink Distributors Ltd. (Ireland); Constellation International Holdings Ltd.; Constellation Wines Japan K.K.; Franciscan Vineyards, Inc.; Allberry, Inc.; Cloud Peak Corporation; M.J. Lewis Corporation; Mt. Veeder Corporation; Barton Inc.; Barton Brands, Ltd.; Barton Beers, Ltd.; Barton Brands of California, Inc.; Barton Brands of Georgia, Inc.; Barton Canada, Ltd.; Barton Distillers Import Corproation; Barton Financial Corporation; Barton Beers of Wisconsin, Ltd.; Monarch Import Company; Schenley Distilleries Inc. (Canada); Barton Mexico, S.A. de C.V. (Mexico); Matthew Clark plc (United Kingdom); Avalon Cellars Ltd. (United Kingdom); Constellation Wines Europe Limited (England); Freetraders Group Ltd. (United Kingdom); Matthew Clark Wholesale Limited (United Kingdom); The Gaymer Group Europe Ltd. (United Kingdom); Forth Wines Ltd. (Scotland); CBI Australia Holdings Pty Limited (Australia); Constellation Australia Pty Ltd.; Hardy Wine Company Ltd. (Australia); Vineyards (Australasia) Pty Ltd. (Australia); BRL Hardy Finance Pty Ltd. (Australia); GSI Holdings Pty Ltd. (Australia); BRL Hardy (USA) Inc.; BRL Investments (USA) Inc.; Thomas Hardy Hunter River Pty Ltd. (Australia); The Stanlet Wine Company Pty Ltd. (Australia); Houghton Wines (Western Australia) Pty Ltd. (Australia); The WA Winegrowers Association Pty Ltd. (Australia); International Cellars (Aust) Pty Ltd. (Australia); Walter Reynell & Sons Wines Pty Ltd. (Australia); BRL Hardy (Investments) Ltd. (United Kingdom); Constellation Wines Canada Ltd. (Canada); Nobilo Holdings (New Zealand); Nobilo Wine Group Ltd. (New Zealand); Nobilo Vintners Ltd. (New Zealand); Valleyfield Vineyard Partnership (New Zealand); Mohaka Vineyard Partnership (New Zealand); Selaks Wines Ltd. (New Zealand); National Likquor Distributors Ltd. (New Zealand); Pacific Wine Partners LLC (New Zealand).

Principal Operating Units

Constellation Wines; Constellation Beers & Spirits.

Principal Competitors

E.&J. Gallo Winery; Heineken USA Inc.; The Wine Group, Inc.; Bacardi U.S.A., Inc.; Pernod Ricard; Beringer Blass Wine Estates Limited.

Further Reading

Astor, Will, ''Canandaigua Sets Move of Headquarters,'' *Rochester Business Journal*, December 12, 1997, p. 1.

''Canandaigua to Change Name to Constellation,'' *Nation's Restaurant News*, September 18, 2000, p. 68.

Chao, Mary, ''Canandaigua Brands Aims to Boost 'Undervalued' Stock,'' *Rochester Business Journal*, January 1, 1999, p. 3.

——, ''Canandaigua Capitalizing on New Taste for Wines,'' *Rochester Business Journal*, November 14, 1997, p. 13.

——, ''Canandaigua Eyes Acquisitions,'' *Rochester Business Journal*, October 10, 1997, p. 4.

——, ''Canandaigua Uncorks New Line of Dessert Wines,'' *Rochester Business Journal*, September 18, 1998, p. 14.

——, ''More Canandaigua Brands Growth Projected,'' *Rochester Business Journal*, July 24, 1998, p. 8.

Coffey, Brendan, ''A Vintage Deal,'' *Forbes Global*, February 17, 2003, p. 52.

''Constellation's Star May Be Rising,'' *Business Week*, December 18, 2000, p. 245.

Cowan, Alison Leigh, ''For Smaller Maker, a Rough Fight Just to Survive,'' *New York Times*, October 19, 1987, p. D10.
''Fifty Years Later, World's Largest Vintner Is Born,'' *Long Island Business News*, April 18, 2003, p. 17B.
Fisher, Lawrence M., ''Marvin Sands, Winery's Chairman, Dies at 75,'' *New York Times*, August 31, 1999, p. A18.
Fordahl, Matthew, ''Constellation to Buy Mondavi in $1 Billioin Deal,'' *America's Intelligence Wire*, November 4, 2004, p. 43.
''A 47-Year History of Canandaigua Wine Company,'' *Cellar Echo* (Canandaigua Newsletter), November 1992.
Helman, Christopher, ''Seeing Stars,'' *Forbes*, January 6, 2003, p. 118.
Johnston, David Cay, ''The Wine Maker Canandaigua Is Riding High. But Can It Continue?,'' *New York Times*, March 3, 1995, p. D6.
Khermouch, Gerry, ''Made in the Mist,'' *Brandweek*, July 12, 1999, pp. 18–19.
Kimelman, John, ''Canandaigua Wine: Grape Expectations,'' *Financial World*, February 2, 1993, p. 16.
Lane, Randall, ''Who's Afraid of Big, Bad Gallo?,'' *Forbes*, February 13, 1995, p. 180.
O'Connell, Vanessa, ''A Wine Label with a Bouquet of Controversy,'' *Wall Street Journal*, December 8, 1998, p. B1.
Popp, Jamie, ''Shooting for the Stars,'' *Beverage Industry*, September 2003, p. 33
Prial, Frank J., ''Growing a Giant in the Vineyard,'' *New York Times*, August 22, 1999, Sec. 3, p. 2.
Reflecting on Success, Canandaigua, N.Y.: Canandaigua Wine Co., Inc., 1995.
Roberts, Catherine, ''Analysts Laud Changes at Canandaigua Wine,'' *Rochester Business Journal*, July 18, 1997, p. 6.
——, ''Canandaigua Wine Unit Undergoes Restructuring,'' *Rochester Business Journal,* October 18, 1996, p. 6.
Siwolop, Sana, ''Canandaigua Wine Tries to Get Its Bottles in a Row,'' *New York Times*, February 9, 1997, Sec. 3, p. 4.
Stern, Willy, ''Bottom Fishing in an Empty Pond,'' *Financial World*, March 14, 1995, p. 40.
''Top of the Grape Heap,'' *Business Week Online*, February 5, 2003, p. 54.
Whiskeyman, Dolores, ''Canandaigua Wine Sets New Course,'' *Rochester Business Journal*, January 16, 1989, p. 2.

—Thomas Derdak
—updates: David E. Salamie; Jeffrey L. Covell

Decorator Industries Inc.

18 Industrial Drive
Bloomsburg, Pennsylvania 17815
U.S.A.
Telephone: (570) 752-5644
Fax: (570) 752-8776
Web site: http://www.decoratorindustries.com

Public Company
Incorporated: 1953
Employees: 714
Sales: $41.8 Million (2003)
Stock Exchanges: American
Ticker Symbol: DII
NAIC: 314121 Curtain and Drapery Mills; 314129 Other Household Textile Product Mills

Decorator Industries Inc. designs, manufactures, and sells a wide variety of interior furnishings, primarily draperies, curtains, shades, blinds, bedspreads, valance boards, comforters, pillows, and cushions. The company sells these products to original equipment manufacturers of recreational vehicles and manufactured housing and to the hospitality industry, including hotels and motels, either through distributors or directly to customers. The company's plants are located in Haleyville and Red Bay, Alabama; Lakewood, Florida; Elkhart and Goshen, Indiana; Bossier City, Louisiana; Salisbury, North Carolina; Bloomsburg and Berwick, Pennsylvania; and Abbotsford, Wisconsin.

Company's Founding and Early Development

Decorator was founded and incorporated in Pennsylvania in 1953 under the name of Keck's. In its early years, Decorator prospered as a producer of made-to-measure draperies. In November 1967, the company, which was headquartered in Pittsburgh, Pennsylvania, announced it would split its common stock two-for-one and declare a dividend of 6.25 cents on the split stock. In March 1968, Decorator registered with the Securities and Exchange Commission 160,000 outstanding common shares to be offered for public sale through underwriters headed by Arthurs, Lestrange & Co. of Pittsburg, and Hayden, Miller & Co. of Cleveland, Ohio. The prospectus listed four shareholders who together owned about 58 percent of the company's outstanding common stock and would retain ownership of about 38 percent after the sale. The shareholders said they were selling the stock with the aim of establishing a broad enough market to qualify the shares for daily listing in market reports of National Quotation Bureau, Inc. These moves marked Decorator's rapid growth in the custom made draperies business. By July 1968, the company announced that it expected earnings for the year to be substantially more than the previous year's $330,000, or 41 cents a share. Decorator's president, Earl Rappaport, estimated sales at about $6 million, up from $4.8 million. In November 1968, Decorator declared a 3-for-2 split of its common shares and an increased dividend of four cents on the new shares. The company's robust sales of draperies and bedspreads continued into 1969, boosting Decorator's earnings 25 percent.

In February 1969, Decorator acquired the ill-fated New York-based Melbee Textile Co., a textile converter that specialized in dyes and prints for draperies. The company closed Melbee one year later as some of its products that were considered low markup items were phased out. In 1970, Decorator acquired Cortley Manufacturing Corp., a privately held maker and distributor of draperies headquartered in Hialeah, Florida. Cortley was the first of many such acquisitions to come. Decorator said it was purchasing Cortley with its common stock but declined to state the value of the transaction or to disclose Cortley's sales and earnings numbers. The acquisition complemented Decorator's own business as a producer of medium-priced, custom-made draperies for homes, mobile homes, hotels, and commercial buildings. In 1973, Decorator made two additional acquisitions. In April, it acquired Haleyville Drapery Manufacturing Inc. for $1.8 million in cash and notes, and in June it acquired Drapery Service, Inc. of Hialeah, Florida, for an undisclosed sum of cash and indebtedness. On October 22, 1979, the company acquired Southern Drapery, Inc. of Cullman, Alabama, for cash. In addition, in November 1980 Decorator acquired Qual Fab, Inc. of Hialeah, Florida, for an undisclosed amount of cash and indebtedness. Qual Fab was subsequently merged into the company on January 3, 1981.

Decorator Formulates Growth Strategy in the 1980s

In February 1981, Decorator omitted its quarterly dividend despite showing improved performance for the year. The com-

Company Perspectives:

We manufacture draperies, curtains, bedspreads, pillows, shams, tiebacks, cornices, and related accessories for Recreational Vehicle and Manufactured Housing markets. We take pride in supplying the highest quality products, delivered on time, at a reasonable price.

pany explained that it was omitting the usual March payment because it was the prudent course of action until business conditions improved. For the year, the company's earnings of $247,631, or 18 cents a share, were about double fiscal 1980 net of $122,891, or nine cents a share. However, a charge of $52,946 from settlement of a lawsuit lowered the final net for 1981 to $194,685, or 14 cents a share. In October 1982, Decorator sold its made-to-measure and precision-tailored draperies business, which operated under the names Decorama and Cortley, to Perfect Fit Industries Inc. of Monroe, North Carolina. The sale of the businesses, which was made for an undisclosed sum, included inventory, equipment, trademarks, a manufacturing facility in Hialeah, Florida, and certain other assets. The businesses involved in the sale comprised about 33 percent of Decorator's sales in fiscal 1982. The company sold the businesses to focus efforts on its more profitable Haleyville and Qual-Fab divisions. The company planned to apply the proceeds from the sale toward its indebtedness, with the balance added to working capital.

In July 1984, as the stock market began its historic bull run, Decorator forecast that earnings for the first six months would almost triple the $126,315 of the year earlier. Now headquartered in Hialeah, Florida, the company also projected sales in the six-month period would be about 50 percent higher than the $6.9 million of the previous year. Also in July, the company purchased Taylor Draperies, Inc. of Thomasville, Georgia for $187,400 in cash and $25,000 in treasury stock. The company's rapid growth attracted the interest of Coury Investments Ltd., a Coral Gables, Florida-based investment partnership, which acquired a 5.4 percent stake in the company as an investment for future appreciation. From August to December 1984, the investment concern lifted its stake in Decorator from 8 percent to 15.5 percent on soaring earnings reports. Patrick Bell, who managed Coury, told Decorator chief executive officer Earl Rappaport that the acquisition of the company's stock was strictly an investment, but Rappaport expressed uncertainty about the investment firm's intentions, especially since Decorator did not pay dividends.

By the end of the year, Decorator announced that it expected fourth quarter net income to be 70 percent lower than the year before but still anticipated net income to increase by 13 percent. The company attributed lower earnings in the second half of 1984 to expenses associated with the opening of new manufacturing plants in Lakeland, Florida, and Salisbury, North Carolina, and to training costs associated with new machinery. For the year, however, sales rose to an estimated $20 million from $14.5 million in 1983. In April 1985, Coury Investments, which then held an 18.9 percent stake in the company, filed requests for two seats on Decorator's six-member board. In its Security and Exchange Commission filing, Coury said it wanted board representation to better monitor its investment in Decorator. In addition, on September 1985, Decorator acquired Liberia Manufacturing Co. for $1.13 million in cash.

In the late 1980s and throughout the 1990s, Decorator continued to pursue growth through acquisitions, a strategy that it had begun in the 1970s. In February 1988, it acquired the Bloomsburg, Pennsylvania, business and operations of Keck's Draperies Mfg Co. One year later, however, Decorator sold the business and certain assets of its printing division to QF Industries, Inc. for $2.48 million in cash and a $500,000 promissory note. The division, which operated under the name Qual Fab, underperformed with an erratic earnings history. The sale also allowed Decorator to pay off all short-term bank debt except for a building mortgage. With the sale of the printing division, Decorator planned to pursue internal expansion of its remaining businesses, primarily focusing on its lines for hotels/motels and recreational vehicles.

Growth and Acquisitions in the 1990s

In November 1993, Williams Bassett, Decorator's 56-year-old president and chief executive officer, was named to the additional post of chairman of the company's board of directors. Bassett, who succeeded Earl Rappaport, continued the strategy of building the company through acquisitions. In 1995, the company purchased Paragon Interiors, a producer of draperies and bedspreads for the manufactured housing and recreational vehicle markets located in Goshen, Indiana. The company subsequently established Paragon as a division to design and manufacture draperies, valance boards, bedspreads, and mini-blinds for the recreation vehicle and manufactured housing industry. The company believed the acquisition would provide new growth opportunities in the Indiana market, which comprised almost 60 percent of total U.S. production of all motor homes, travel trailers, and conversion vans. Decorator's strategic moves caught the attention of *Business Week,* which in 1995 listed the company as one of the top small companies in America. In addition, the company was named in a September 1996 *Barron's* article on small cap stocks entitled "Sifting Gems," and in *Forbes Magazine* as one of the 200 best small companies in America in 1996.

Continuing its successful growth strategy, in 1997 Decorator acquired the assets of four companies, including Action Design Interiors, Specialty Window Coverings Corp., Denver Maid, and Southern Interiors, Inc. The purchase of Action Design, located in Elkhart, Indiana, enabled the company to expand its product line to include furniture and cushions for the recreational vehicle industry. The company, which concluded the acquisition on March 4, planned to operate the business under the name Haleyville Manufacturing Co. from the former facilities of Action Design. On March 15, Decorator purchased Specialty Window Coverings Corp., an Elkhart, Indiana-based manufacturer of pleated shades for the recreational vehicle market. The acquisition of Specialty provided initial cash payments of approximately $2.3 million plus conditional payments based on earnings not to exceed $2 million over the following two years. Under the acquisition agreement, Specialty would continue to operate from its existing facilities and would retain its management team. The acquisition, together with Decorator's introduction of an imported mini-blind program for recreational vehicles, allowed the company to extend its reach beyond its core fabric window treatments, valance boards, and bedspreads to provide a full range of window covering prod-

Key Dates:

1953: The company is incorporated in Pennsylvania.
1970: Decorator Industries begins a series of acquisitions with Cortley Manufacturing Corporation.
1988: The company acquires the Bloomsburg, Pennsylvania, business, operations, and assets of Keck's Drapery Manufacturing Company.
1989: Decorator Industries sells the assets of its printing division to QF Industries.
1997: The businesses and certain assets of Action Design Interiors, Southern Interiors, Inc., and Specialty Window Covering Corporation are acquired.

ucts. These acquisitions complemented the company's purchase of Denver Maid, another manufacturer in the markets served by Decorator. In addition, on May 12, 1997 the company completed the acquisition of Southern Interiors, Inc., a Memphis, Tennessee-based producer of window coverings for the hospitality (motel/hotel) market, for $844,313. Under the agreement, Southern Interiors would continue to operate from its existing facilities in Memphis to manufacture draperies from fabric supplied primarily from its customers, principally hotel design and supply firms. Decorator believed the acquisition would enable it to supply the total hospitality market.

As a result of its recent growth, the company's board of directors declared a five-for-four stock split at its meeting on May 16, 1997. After the split, which became effective on June 13, 1997, the company had three million shares outstanding, reflecting the board's confidence in the increased value and future performance of the company. Due to record earnings for 1997 and the first quarter of 1998, the board declared another five-for-four stock split in June 1998 to be effective July 21. Bassett said that it was the intention of the board to continue the regular cash dividend of seven cents per share on the split shares, representing a 25 percent increase in the cash dividend. For fiscal year 1998, the company declared record net income of $3 million compared to $2.9 million for fiscal year 1997 as the company rode a wave of favorable market conditions. Manufactured housing, for example, achieved a 30-year high in the number of homes produced and set a new record for the number of floors produced and shipped. In addition, deliveries by manufacturers of recreational vehicles were the highest in 20 years, buoyed by exceptional growth in both travel trailers and motor homes. However, there were hints that the robust market for the company's products might take a downswing as reports from the hospitality market suggested that construction of new motels and hotels had peaked. Nonetheless, Decorator reported record net sales of $52.5 million for 1999 as market conditions remained favorable. The company also relocated its Goshen, Indiana, window treatment and bedspread plant to a newly constructed 56,000-square foot facility. Despite the company's impressive revenue growth, Bassett stated that Decorator had to address several productivity issues to improve the bottom line, including building new or expanded facilities, investing in new manufacturing equipment, reducing turnover and increasing productivity among employees, and getting the company Year 2000 compliant.

Early 2000s Downturn and Recovery

On September 9, 2000, Decorator announced that it would continue a plan to repurchase its stock. Up to this time, the company had already repurchased more than 300,000 shares of its common stock, leaving approximately 3.27 million shares outstanding after the purchases. One month after the September stock repurchase announcement, however, Decorator reported its profits had fallen 93 percent during the second quarter. In June 2001, Decorator reported its year 2000 earnings had declined 95 percent to $133,198 and that its sales fell 13 percent to $42.6 million. The company attributed declining sales to downturns in the manufactured housing and recreational vehicle markets. The manufactured housing market had experienced excessive levels of inventory, including repossessions, restricted credit availability, and high interest rates. In addition, high gasoline prices and an erosion of consumer confidence affected the market for recreational vehicles.

By 2003, improving but uneven market conditions substantially affected Decorator's sales mix. While Decorator experienced a sharp rise in orders for the recreation vehicle industry, it saw decreased orders for the manufactured housing market. The recreational vehicle market enjoyed one of its best periods in more than 25 years, reporting increased vehicle shipments of 21 percent. As a result, Decorator reported a stronger earnings balance sheet for fiscal year 2002. The company's net income rose 61 percent on a sales increase of 11 percent. As part of its growth strategy, the company continued to look for opportunities to expand its market share though internal expansion and acquisitions. With strong sales of recreational vehicles in the second half of 2003, Decorator saw its sales increase by 8 percent compared with 2002, to $41.8 million. Net income rose even more, by 13 percent, to $1.6 million.

On January 23, 2004, Decorator announced that it had acquired the Douglas, Georgia, drapery operation of Fleetwood Enterprises, Inc. Fleetwood was the nation's leader in recreational vehicle sales and a leading producer and retailer of manufactured housing. Decorator and Fleetwood also entered into a long-term agreement for Decorator to serve as the exclusive supplier of Fleetwood's drapery, bedspread, and other decor requirements. Fleetwood accounted for a substantial portion of Decorator's total sales, amounting to about 23.8 percent in 2002. Decorator said that although it would supply most of Fleetwood's business from its existing plants, it was also planning to open a new facility in the western part of the United States. In addition to serving Fleetwood, the new plant would expand business with other original equipment producers of recreational vehicles and manufactured homes. With robust growth in the recreational vehicle market shoring up Decorator's bottom line, the company also anticipated a turn around in the manufactured home industry.

Principal Competitors

Flexsteel Industries Inc.; Hunter Douglas; Patrick Industries Inc.

Further Reading

"Coury Investments Ltd. Lifts Its Stake to 8% of Decorator Industries," *Wall Street Journal*, August 14, 1984.
"Decorator Earnings Fall," *RV Business*, June 2001, p. 16.

''Decorator Industries Inc.'' *Wall Street Journal*, May 21, 1973, p. 11.

''Decorator Industries, Inc. Announces Acquisitions,'' *PR Newswire*, March 17, 1997.

''Decorator Industries, Inc. Announces Acquisition of Fleetwood Enterprises, Inc.'s Drapery Operation and Signing of Exclusive Supply Agreement,'' *PR Newswire*, January 23, 2004.

''Decorator Industries, Inc. Announces Stock Split and Dividend Increase On Record 1997 and First Quarter 1998 Sales and Earnings,'' *PR Newswire*, June 15, 1998.

''Decorator Industries Inc.: Teamwork and Time Management Result in Quick Turnaround,'' *RV Business*, February 1999, p. 50.

''Decorator Industries Plans to Buy Cortley for Stock,'' *Wall Street Journal*, March 10, 1970, p. 7.

''Decorator Industries Sees Net Up,'' *Wall Street Journal*, September 29, 1969, p. 36

''Decorator Industries Sells Draperies Unit,'' *Wall Street Journal*, October 5, 1982, p. 24.

''Decorator Industries Splits Stock 3 for 2, Lifts Payout,'' *Wall Street Journal*, November 6, 1968, p. 28.

''Decorator Stake Raised to 10% by Investor,'' *Wall Street Journal*, October 23, 1984, p. 1.

''Decorator's Third Quarter Net Income Increases by More Than 75%,'' *PR Newswire*, November 5, 2001.

Dorfman, Dan, ''Heard on the Street,'' *Wall Street Journal*, July 25, 1968, p. 23.

''Fleetwood Enterprises Announces Sale of Drapery Operation,'' *PR Newswire*, January 23, 2004.

Kurowski, Jeff, ''Decorator Buys Fleetwood's Drapery Business as OEM's Revenues Climb 32%,'' *RV Business*, March 2004, p. 12.

—Bruce P. Montgomery

Deutsche Lufthansa AG

Von-Gablenz-Strasse 2-6
D-50679 Cologne, 21
Germany
Telephone: (+49) 69-696-0
Toll Free: (800) 645-3880
Fax: (+49) 69-696-6818
Web site: http://www.lufthansa.com

Public Company
Incorporated: 1926 as Deutsche Luft Hansa AG
Employees: 93,246
Sales: EUR 15.96 billion ($20 billion) (2003)
Stock Exchanges: Frankfurt
Ticker Symbol: LHAG.F
NAIC: 481111 Scheduled Passenger Air Transportation; 481112 Scheduled Freight Air Transportation; 488119 Other Airport Operations; 488190 Other Support Activities for Air Transportation; 722320 Caterers

Deutsche Lufthansa AG (commonly referred to as Lufthansa) is the largest airline in Germany and one of the three largest airlines in the world. More than 45 million passengers take Lufthansa flights each year on a network that is spread relatively evenly around the world. Lufthansa operates a fleet of about 370 planes, most all of them owned rather than leased, and is a founding member of the Star Alliance.

The Lufthansa Group also includes Lufthansa CityLine, a regional airline. Other units, such as data processing specialist Lufthansa Systems and Lufthansa Flight Training, have developed into world-leading businesses. Lufthansa Cargo AG is considered the world's largest carrier of international airfreight, according to the *Journal of Commerce,* while LSG Sky Chefs heads the world's largest alliance of in-flight caterers. Lufthansa also holds a 50 percent interest in Thomas Cook AG, Europe's second largest travel group and majority owner of the Condor Flugdienst GmbH air charter service.

1920s Origins

The history of Lufthansa (LH) parallels the development of aviation in Germany, dating back to a time when the first aviators were just beginning to fly. However, LH was not established as a commercial airline in Germany until the 1920s.

After World War I, the German government favored the development of a national airline system made up of a number of associated regional airlines. One of the largest airline companies, Deutscher Aero Lloyd, was incorporated in 1923 and centered its operations on Berlin's Temple Field. The following year, Junkers Luftverkehr was founded. Junkers built airplanes in addition to operating an airline. Together the two companies dominated German aviation.

The two companies merged with all the other German aeronautic concerns in 1926 to form Deutsche Luft Hansa Aktiengesellschaft (the name ''Hansa'' was taken from the north-German Hanseatic trading league, which had contributed most of the airline's private capital). Luft Hansa was a government-run private monopoly—the chosen instrument for all German air services. The company's logo was taken from Aero Lloyd and its blue and yellow colors were taken from Junkers. By May 1926, Luft Hansa served 57 domestic and 15 international airports.

Intercontinental in the 1930s

In 1934, under the new name ''Lufthansa,'' the company opened an airmail service between Stuttgart and Buenos Aires. As an instrument of state commerce and diplomacy, Lufthansa flew to numerous destinations around the world, including Beijing, New York, Cairo, Bangkok, and Tokyo. Regarded as an instrument of the state, Lufthansa increasingly came under the control of the ruling Nazi Party. Lufthansa began service to destinations in the Soviet Union during 1940. These routes provided the German Luftwaffe (''air force'') with valuable strategic information used in Hitler's surprise invasion of the Soviet Union two years later. In 1941, the Luftwaffe assumed control of Lufthansa's airplanes and converted many of them for military use. As the war continued, many Lufthansa employees were drafted into military service in support of the Luftwaffe, and many lost their lives.

After the war, Germany was occupied by the Soviet Union, the United States, France, and Britain. The Soviet-occupied zone later became the German Democratic Republic (East

Company Perspectives:

Shouldering Responsibility—Keeping a Balance. Service is our vocation. Our staff constitute our most important asset. As an attractive employer of present and future staff, we endeavour to offer our employees job security, good working conditions, career opportunities and convincing corporate ethics. Our staff honour that endeavour with customer-friendly service and thereby underpin future growth. We are committed to creating sustainable value for our investors. The norms are set by the capital market. We aim at a performance level that stands as a benchmark for the European airline industry. Business success does not rule out a corporate policy geared to sustainable development and care for the environment. We are fully committed to keeping a balance between them. Protecting the environment is therefore a prime corporate objective, to which we subscribe with total conviction.

Germany), and the American, French, and British zones became the Federal Republic of Germany (West Germany). A general state of belligerency between the Soviet Union and the western allies further divided East and West Germany. Under the conditions of the occupation, both East and West Germany were forbidden to establish their own airline companies. British, French, and American airlines had a monopoly on air service in West Germany, while the Soviet airline Aeroflot assumed all air services in East Germany.

Lufthansa Reborn in the 1950s

By 1951, the reestablishment of a national airline for West Germany was proposed. The following year, the West German government in Bonn set up a preparatory airline corporation, and on January 6, 1953, Luftag (Aktiengesellschaft für Luftverkehrsbedarf) was created in Cologne. Hans Bongers, who joined Lufthansa in 1926, was reinstated as director of the national airline. Luftag began service with four Convair 340s, later joined by three DC-3s and four Lockheed Constellations.

Luftag's airplanes were piloted by foreign airline personnel while former Lufthansa pilots were retrained in the United States. The Germans later flew as copilots until 1956, when all-German crews were assigned. In 1954, Luftag instituted its old name, Lufthansa (Deutsche Lufthansa Aktiengesellschaft), and in the following years reestablished its services to North and South America and the Middle East.

Jet-Powered Expansion in the 1960s

Lufthansa began flying Boeing 707 passenger jets on its international routes in 1961. The introduction of jets marked the beginning of an equipment rotation at Lufthansa. The older propeller-driven airplanes were slowly phased out and replaced by passenger jets. With this new equipment, Lufthansa had firmly reestablished itself as one of the world's premier air carriers.

The expansion of Lufthansa continued with the reintroduction of services to Africa. The airline established service to Nigeria in 1962 and later that year began service to Johannesburg, South Africa. Despite the heavy investment required for the airline's expansion, Lufthansa was able to declare its first profitable year in 1964. Previously the airline had charged its losses to the federal government.

Lufthansa joined a maintenance pool called ATLAS in 1969. As a member of ATLAS, Lufthansa cooperated with Air France, Alitalia, Sabena, and Iberia in the repair and maintenance of aircraft and other equipment. Lufthansa's Hamburg facility was designated to perform repairs for the pool's B-747s, DC-10s, and A-300s.

The updating of equipment at Lufthansa continued over the next few years as the airline introduced Boeing's 737 for short distance shuttle routes, and a 747 jumbo jet for heavily traveled long-distance services. In addition to the 747, Lufthansa purchased several McDonnell Douglas DC-10s. The new aircraft replaced the older propeller-driven airplanes, the last of which was removed from the fleet in 1971. During this period, Lufthansa developed its air freight services with a fleet of 747s specially designated to haul cargo. The airline constructed automated freight handling facilities in a number of destinations across the world. Lufthansa recognized the importance of cargo services before most of its competition. The company established one of the most modern freight handling systems in the world, and cargo services became a major source of revenue for Lufthansa.

Challenges in the 1970s

Being a European airline, Lufthansa was dangerously exposed to terrorist activities during the 1970s. Security was inadequate at many airports served by the company, which made it easy for terrorists to board and later commandeer an airplane. However, not one Lufthansa passenger lost his life despite numerous hijackings on the airline. The chairman of the company during the 1970s, Rolf Bebber, must be credited for Lufthansa's success in ending the hijacking peacefully. He established a crisis management procedure which enlisted the diplomatic influence of the West German government. Through this procedure, the company could respond quickly to terrorist demands in order to resolve a crisis. In addition, security at all Lufthansa airports was significantly upgraded.

The airline experienced considerable problems with German air traffic controllers who staged a "go-slow" from May to November 1973. Lufthansa estimated that it lost $71 million due to flight cancellations during that period. The controllers, who were civil servants, had been demonstrating their displeasure with working conditions in this manner since 1962. Lufthansa tried to persuade the federal government to change the status of the controllers in an effort to avoid future slowdowns but was unsuccessful.

Lufthansa received its first A-300 jetliner in 1976 from Airbus, the French-German-British-Spanish aircraft consortium. The A-300 was the first commercial aircraft to be built primarily by Germans in over 30 years. The German member of the Airbus group, Messerschmidt-Bolkow-Blohm (MBB), continued to contribute to the development of more advanced Airbus jetliners and Lufthansa continued to add them to its fleet. In 1983, the airline commissioned its first A-310 and later purchased the consortium's A-319, A-320, A-321, and A-340 jumbo jets.

Key Dates:

1926: Deutsche Luft Hansa is formed from consolidation of German aviation interests.
1934: Lufthansa launches airmail service to Buenos Aires.
1941: Luftwaffe assumes control of LH's aircraft.
1945: Germany banned from operating its own airlines after World War II.
1953: A new airline is launched in West Germany as Luftag.
1954: Luftag, renamed Lufthansa, reestablishes intercontinental routes.
1964: LH posts its first postwar profit.
1976: First Airbus A300, a mostly German-made airliner, enters the company's fleet.
1990: LH flies to Berlin after German reunification.
1995: MRO division Lufthansa Technik is spun off as independent subsidiary.
1997: Star Alliance is formed with LH as a founding member.
2001: LH undergoes a comprehensive "D-Check."

MBB was particularly willing to involve Lufthansa in the Airbus projects. Since both companies were German, they were encouraged by the Federal government to coordinate and serve each other's economic interests. As a result, Airbus was especially sensitive to Lufthansa's design requirements. Moreover, because Lufthansa was a highly respected modern air carrier, the jetliners built to its specifications were, in turn, more marketable to other airline companies.

A World Leader in the 1980s

In 1982, 80 percent of Lufthansa's stock was owned by the West German government. The board of directors, however, was appointed by Lufthansa's private investors. On June 22 of that year, the board of directors narrowly elected a new chairman to succeed Herbert Culmann. Culmann was a popular chairman, but he retired two years early to save his company embarrassment over allegations of kickbacks to travel agents.

The new chairman was Heinz Ruhnau, a career bureaucrat with strong affiliations with the West German Social Democratic Party. His appointment generated an unusual amount of concern because many feared the ruling Social Democrats were attempting to politicize the airline. Ruhnau was an undersecretary in the Transport Ministry and a former chief assistant to the head of West Germany's largest trade union, IG Metall. He did not, however, have experience in private enterprise, and Lufthansa was being prepared for a further privatization of its stock. In 1985, the federal government held 74.31 percent of Lufthansa, 7.85 percent was held by government agencies, and the remaining 17.84 percent was held by private interests.

Ruhnau assumed his post on July 1, 1982, in a smooth transition of leadership. Ruhnau's immediate tasks were to improve Lufthansa's thin profit margin and win the support of the company's 30,000 skeptical employees. The company's performance in 1982 was impressive and resulted in its selection as airline of the year by the editors of *Air Transport World.*

Weathering Change in the 1990s

The early to mid-1990s was a period of enormous change in Europe, change that proved extremely challenging for Lufthansa. Most obvious was the 1990 reunification of Germany, a difficult process that nonetheless afforded Lufthansa the opportunity to fly to Berlin under its own colors for the first time since the Allied occupation. The period also featured steadily increasing competition which forced down ticket prices worldwide and cut into Lufthansa's market share. The company was particularly vulnerable because of its cumbersome bureaucracy and its relatively high-wage workforce, with the workers traditionally protected by the company's state-run status. Other forces reshaping the operating environment for Lufthansa included the gradual deregulation of the airline industry in Europe, the trend toward privatization sweeping the continent, and the planned economic integration of Europe during the 1990s. By the turn of the 21st century, Lufthansa had made numerous changes in response to these challenges, emerging as a very different company.

Leading Lufthansa through most of the 1990s was Jurgen Weber, who became chairman in September 1991. The company was hemorrhaging at the time amid fierce competition and the first decline in European air travel in history in 1991—with the Gulf War a major catalyst for the drop. For the first time since 1973, Lufthansa lost money, posting a net loss of DEM 425.8 million in 1991, followed by another loss of DEM 391.1 million in 1992. Starting in mid-1992, Weber began working feverishly to bring the company's costs in line. By 1994, job cuts totaling 8,400 had been made, and Weber got workers to agree to an unprecedented one-year wage freeze in 1993. He also dumped unprofitable routes and cut some services, such as first class within Europe. Through these measures, $1 billion in annual cost savings were realized, leading Lufthansa back into the black by 1994, when it made DEM 302 million.

Not everything went smoothly, however. A new low-cost domestic shuttle service, Lufthansa Express, was launched in 1992 but caused confusion among customers and was eventually scrapped. Meantime, Lufthansa faced a new and potentially formidable competitor in its home market when in 1992 British Airways plc acquired a 49 percent interest in a Berlin-based carrier, newly dubbed Deutsche BA. The regional airline offered high-quality service to business travelers and competed directly with Lufthansa's regional airline, known as Lufthansa CityLine, which also catered to business travelers and which Lufthansa gained 100 percent control over in 1993. By the mid-1990s, Deutsche BA had firmly established itself as Germany's number two scheduled airline, with a market share of 14 percent.

By 1993, the German government still held 51.6 percent of Lufthansa. A rights issue soon reduced the stake to 35 percent, giving company workers less government protection. In July 1993, Weber began restructuring Lufthansa. With a vision of Lufthansa as a holding company for several separately operated units, he spun off Lufthansa Cargo as a stand-alone, but wholly owned, business, the largest specialized air cargo carrier in the world. In succeeding years, several additional operations were similarly spun off, creating Lufthansa Technik in the maintenance area, Lufthansa Systems in data processing, LSG Lufthansa Service in catering, and Lufthansa Flight Training. Lufthansa CityLine and air charter specialist Condor Flugdienst also operated autonomously. The culmination of this process came in April 1997 when Lufthansa's flagship scheduled passenger business was made independent as well, under the name Lufthansa German Airlines. Deutsche Lufthansa had thereby evolved into a holding company for what was referred to as the Lufthansa Group.

Star Alliance Formed 1997

Another key goal of Weber's was to seek out international partnerships, as alliances became increasingly common and vital for survival in the 1990s. In October 1993, Lufthansa and United Airlines, the leading U.S. airliner, began a code-sharing arrangement whereby a single flight number in a reservation system could involve a journey consisting of a Lufthansa leg and a United leg. This partnership eventually led to the May 1997 formation of the ''Star Alliance,'' which initially involved Lufthansa, United, Air Canada, Scandinavian Airlines System (SAS), and Thai Airways International. The Star Alliance included not only code-sharing but also reciprocal frequent flyer programs, reciprocal lounge access agreements, and scheduling and pricing coordination efforts. In October 1997, the Brazilian airline Varig joined the alliance. In 1997 and 1998, Lufthansa also entered into separate bilateral partnerships with Singapore Airlines and All Nippon Airways of Japan. In May 1998, Air New Zealand and Ansett Australia agreed to join the Star Alliance during 1999. Regulators in Europe, however, were taking a close look at this and other alliances and were likely to require that changes be made before granting final regulatory approval.

In October 1997, Lufthansa was fully privatized with the sale of the government's remaining 37.5 percent stake in the airline, raising about DEM 4.7 billion ($2.77 billion). The company was now free of its government ties, operating within a new group structure, and was considered one of the most profitable airlines in the world (net profits for 1997 were DEM 834.7 million), an amazing turn of events from the depths of the early 1990s. With the airline industry fully open to competition throughout the European union, Lufthansa at the turn of the 21st century was presented with new challenges—even greater competition—as well as additional opportunities. In the globally competitive industry environment, it seemed likely that the company's future depended heavily upon that of the Star Alliance.

In 1999, Lufthansa subsidiary GlobeGround GmbH acquired Hudson General Corp., the world's largest publicly traded airport services company. The deal was worth $132.6 million. GlobeGround had been formed in 1990 as Lufthansa Airport and Ground Services. A subsidiary of Lufthansa Commercial Holding, it was renamed in January 1999 and was acquired by Penauille PolyServices of France in 2001.

Profits rose 9 percent to $620 million in 2000, even in the face of rising fuel costs. Revenues were about $14 billion. Nearly 47 million people flew the airline during the year. Lufthansa had about 250 planes, plus another 60 operated by CityLine. Operationally, LH was developing a second hub at Munich as its Frankfurt base became crowded.

Lufthansa Cargo AG was considered the world's largest carrier of international airfreight, according to the *Journal of Commerce,* carrying more than 1.6 million tons of cargo a year among 450 destinations. The unit operated a fleet of 22 dedicated freighters and utilized cargo capacity on the passenger flights of Lufthansa and partner Spanair. Its revenues were $2.64 billion in 2000, when it had 5,000 employees.

A ''D-Check'' in 2001

In April 2001, chairman Jurgen Weber, a former maintenance head, announced a ''D-Check'' for the entire company (the name refers to an aircraft's most comprehensive inspection). D-Check hoped to generate an additional $1 billion a year in cash flow by 2004. The next month, a pilot's strike cost the airline more than $50 million.

In the Future European Operations initiative, LH reorganized its regional services. A new commuter subsidiary, Lufthansa CityLine, was formed, while PrivatAir of Switzerland was contracted to handle certain business routes. These were both low-cost operations, unfettered by traditional collectively bargained wage agreements. Lufthansa also acquired a 25 percent stake in budget startup Eurowings.

The airline also upgraded its business class service and made plans to provide a broadband Internet connection on flights. The Star Alliance continued to attract new members among the world's airlines, bringing Lufthansa additional feeder traffic sources from abroad.

Following the September 11, 2001 terrorist attacks on the United States, LH coped with the general downturn in aviation by reducing capacity while retaining employees. The company's SkyChefs catering business was particularly hard hit, an executive told *Airfinance Journal,* leading to layoffs of 30 percent of staff.

The world's aviation industry reeled from the effects of 9/11 in 2002. *Forbes Global* remarked at how well Lufthansa was able to fare, given Germany's reputation for high social costs. By November, the airline was planning to add 2,000 jobs while some of the biggest airlines in the United States were trying to stave off bankruptcy. Analysts credited Lufthansa's survival to its quick and flexible responses to the crises of the previous decade, as well as its ability to forecast future business conditions. Net profit was EUR 717 million for 2002.

Lufthansa made a couple of key divestments in 2002, selling its 25 percent holding in DHL World Wide Express for $514 million to Deutsche Post World Net, and disposing of its Start Amadeus GmbH travel package company for $95 million.

In 2003, a very difficult year, LH posted a net lost of EUR 984 million ($1.2 billion) on sales of EUR 15.96 billion ($20.03 billion). Like other airlines, Lufthansa struggled with the SARS crisis in Asia and the war in Iraq; the economy was also slow, particularly in Germany. The year also saw some significant changes. Wolfgang Mayrhuber, formerly head of Lufthansa Technik, then the passenger business division, replaced Jurgen Weber as Lufthansa Group's new chairman and CEO. The airline had a fleet of about 370 planes and more than 93,000 employees. Lufthansa was again tweaking its regional operations and searching for cost-cutting opportunities. It was also looking for places to grow, as with a new non-stop route from Frankfurt to Portland, Oregon.

The airline was aiming to grow its capacity to China by 50 percent, a company source told *China Daily,* after a new 2004 bilateral agreement increased access to the country's skies. Lufthansa finally hammered out a new pay agreement with the pilots' union Vereiningung Cockpit in December 2004. The pilots agreed to a pay freeze and extra hours.

Principal Subsidiaries

LSG Sky Chefs, Inc. (USA); Lufthansa Cargo AG; Lufthansa CityLine GmbH; Lufthansa Flight Training; Lufthansa Systems Group GmbH; Lufthansa Technik AG; Thomas Cook AG (50%).

Principal Divisions

Passenger Business; Logistics; Maintenance Repair Overhaul; Catering; Leisure Travel; IT Services; Service and Financial Companies.

Principal Competitors

Air Berlin GmbH & Co Luftverkehrs KG; Air France; AMR Corporation; British Airways plc; Deutsche BA; FedEx Corporation.

Further Reading

''Airline of the Year: Lufthansa,'' *Air Transport World*, February 1995, p. 39.

Bowley, Graham, ''Lufthansa Opens the Throttle,'' *Financial Times*, August 25, 1998, p. 21.

Braunburg, Rudolf, *Die Geschichte der Lufthansa: vom Doppeldecker zum Airbus*, Hamburg: Rasch und Rohring, 1991, p. 335.

Bruch, Heike, and Thomas Sattelberger, ''Lufthansa's Transformation Marathon: Process of Liberating and Focusing Change Energy,'' *Human Resource Management*, Fall 2001, pp. 249ff.

Carey, Susan, ''Lufthansa Jettisons Bureaucratic Baggage,'' *Wall Street Journal*, September 30, 1996, p. 36.

''Crash Marriage,'' *Economist*, October 9, 1993, pp. 75–76.

Davies, R.E.G., *Lufthansa: An Airline and Its Aircraft*, New York: Orion Books, 1989.

Fisher, Andrew, ''Pilot for the Open Skies,'' *Financial Times*, April 1, 1997, p. 16.

Flint, Perry, ''Friends Again (Lufthansa Technik as a Standalone Subsidiary of Lufthansa),'' *Air Transport World*, August 2001, p. 24.

Flottau, Jens, ''German Makeover: Lufthansa Plans to Slash Costs, Restructure European Operations in Ongoing Effort to Restore Profitability,'' *Aviation Week & Space Technology*, October 27, 2003, p. 39.

French, Trevor, ''Low Marks: The German Flag Carrier Lufthansa Is Grappling with Heavy Losses, Major Aircraft Investment Commitments, and a Deteriorating Home Economy,'' *Airline Business*, January 1993, pp. 54ff.

Gill, Tom, ''The Devil's in the Detail,'' *Airline Business*, September 1998, p. 2.

Grube, Lorri, ''Network Dogfight,'' *Chief Executive*, January-February 1996, pp. 24–26, 28.

Hill, Leonard, ''Banking on Acronyms,'' *Air Transport World*, November 1995, pp. 71–73.

——, '' 'Leaner, Meaner' Lufthansa,'' *Air Transport World*, January 1992, pp. 82–84.

——, ''Lufthansa's Bitter Pill,'' *Air Transport World*, July 1993, pp. 68–71.

——, '' 'Same Mountain, Different Angle',,'' *Air Transport World*, June 2001, p. 42.

——, ''Training (R)Evolution,'' *Air Transport World*, April 2002, p. 64.

''Hudson General Sells to Competition,'' *Long Island Business News*, February 19, 1999, p. 8A.

Josselson, Steven, ''Reality Check from Germany,'' *Airfinance Journal*, May 2002, pp. 34f.

''Jurgen Weber,'' *Business Week*, June 11, 2001.

''Lufthansa Finally Reaches Pay Deal with Pilots (Lufthansa legt Tarifstreit mit Piloten bei),'' *Die Welt*, December 7, 2004.

''Lufthansa Plots Strategy for More Market Share in China,'' *Asia Pulse*, November 29, 2004.

Morrison, Murdo, ''Agile Lufthansa Looks Near and Far,'' *Airline Business*, January 1, 2002, p. 18.

Odell, Mark, ''Germany's Perfect Union,'' *Airline Business*, September 1994, pp. 34ff.

——, ''Reid All About It,'' Airline Business, November 1997, pp. 24ff.

Reed, Arthur, ''Congestion, Competition Crimp Lufthansa's Growth,'' *Air Transport World*, July 1989, pp. 38+.

Reichlin, Igor, Andrea Rothman, and Stewart Toy, ''Even Lufthansa Is Carrying Too Much Baggage,'' *Business Week*, September 7, 1992, p. 80.

Rivera, Dylan, ''New Lufthansa Executive to Bring Change in Style to Airline,'' *Oregonian* (Portland), April 7, 2003.

Skapinker, Michael, and Bethan Hutton, ''Lufthansa and United Extend Alliance to Japanese Airline,'' *Financial Times*, March 10, 1998, p. 6.

''State Ends Link with Lufthansa,'' *Financial Times*, October 14, 1997, p. 31.

Steinborn, Deborah, ''The Crane Keeps Aloft,'' *Forbes Global*, February 17, 2003, p. 37.

Templeman, John, ''A Crack Navigator—And Lufthansa Is on Course,'' *Business Week*, July 18, 1994, p. 78F.

——, ''Just When Lufthansa Was Gaining Altitude. . . . ,'' *Business Week*, July 1, 1996, p. 44.

Wachtel, Joachim, *The Lufthansa Story*, Cologne: Lufthansa German Airlines, 1980, p. 135.

''Weber Keeps Lufthansa Flying,'' *Wall Street Journal Europe*, October 15, 2001, pp. 25f.

Whitaker, Richard, ''In Transition,'' *Airline Business*, August 1991, pp. 58+.

——, ''Lufthansa's Standard Bearer,'' *Airline Business*, November 1991, pp. 58+.

Woodruff, David, ''Rivals Are Buzzing All around Lufthansa,'' *Business Week*, March 3, 1997, p. 48.

—updates: David E. Salamie; Frederick C. Ingram

Dillard's Inc.

1600 Cantrell Road
Little Rock, Arkansas 72201
U.S.A.
Telephone: (501) 376-5200
Fax: (501) 376-5917
Web site: http://www.dillards.com

Public Company
Incorporated: 1964
Employees: 53,598
Sales: $7.59 billion (2004)
Stock Exchanges: New York
Ticker Symbol: DDS
NAIC: 452110 Department Stores

Based in Little Rock, Arkansas, and located throughout suburbs and secondary markets in 24 states in the South, Southwest, and Midwest, Dillard's Inc., operates hundreds of stores selling brand-name goods in the middle to upper-middle price ranges. Key product lines include home furnishings and fashionable clothing. Dillard's stores rarely run discount promotions, preferring an everyday pricing strategy based on local competition, aided by a sophisticated computerized inventory and sales system.

Early 20th Century Beginnings

Dillard's was founded by William Dillard, who also headed the company until his death in 2002. Born in 1914, Dillard was raised in a merchandising family in tiny Mineral Springs, Arkansas. He worked in his father's hardware store and later studied at the University of Arkansas and the Columbia University School of Business. After earning his master's degree at Columbia and completing a Sears training program, Dillard borrowed $8,000 from his father and in February 1938 opened T.J. Dillard's in Nashville, Arkansas, near his home town.

From the first, business was good. His father's wholesalers extended him credit, and customers reacted positively to his well-known father's name, ''T.J.'' Dillard and his wife, Alexa, stocked the store with name-brand merchandise they had bought at low prices. With heavy advertising, first-year sales reached $42,000.

With the onset of World War II, Dillard volunteered for service in the U.S. Navy. He sold his merchandise to another store but kept his store open to collect on credit accounts. While Dillard was waiting for his naval commission, his father died. Family responsibilities called him home, and when the commission came through, he declined it.

In 1944, Dillard and his wife reopened their store. Despite the war, retail sales hit $300,000 in 1945. Business was so good, in fact, that in 1946 Dillard added an 80-foot-long addition. Considering the following year's $340,000 in sales an absolute maximum, Dillard sought new opportunities elsewhere. He invested $50,000 in the proposed expansion of Wooten's Department Store in Texarkana, a town split down the middle by the Texas-Arkansas border. After commuting between Nashville and Texarkana for six months he decided to settle in Texarkana. In March 1948, Dillard sold T.J. Dillard's and upped his stake in Wooten's to 40 percent, changing its name to Wooten & Dillard Inc.

With Wooten's consent, Dillard decided that, instead of expanding the existing store, Wooten & Dillard should open a new store featuring name brands and revolving credit. Despite strong sales, Wooten & Dillard lost money during its first six months, and Wooten asked Dillard to buy him out. To assemble the needed $100,000 in capital, Dillard collected investors and obtained a loan from the Federal Reconstruction Finance Corporation. By March 1949, he controlled the company. Dillard then began a massive newspaper advertising campaign, developing a relationship with the media that was to become his trademark. Within three months the store was profitable.

Expansion in the 1950s–60s

Ready to expand again in 1955, Dillard bought a 7,500-square-foot Magnolia, Arkansas, store from a family friend. Magnolia, a town of 7,000 located 55 miles from Texarkana, proved a lucrative market. The following February, Dillard added appliances and furniture to his line of products.

Dillard's next opportunity came in 1956. Mayer & Schmidt had long been Tyler, Texas's most successful store. A failed

Company Perspectives:

At Dillard's, respect for our customers is paramount. Building enduring relationships with customers has, in large measure, accounted for our steady growth and continued financial success. Experience has shown that we can best earn their trust by always emphasizing value.

attempt at expansion, however, had left it financially vulnerable. In April 1956, Dillard and a group of investors bought it. Dillard completely remodeled the place, expanding into the basement and leasing some departments. When he reopened in September, he advertised heavily in the local papers; the store soon set records for one-day sales.

Dillard's astute financing and smooth turnarounds caught the attention of the region's bankers. In 1959, Fred Eisman, a director of the First National Bank of St. Louis, asked Dillard to buy a failing Tulsa, Oklahoma, department store, Brown-Dunkin. Dillard jumped at the idea. Tulsa was bigger than Tyler, and Brown-Dunkin was bigger than Mayer & Schmidt. With the help of friends, bankers, and other investors, Dillard raised $325,000 and in February 1960 bought the store.

Turning Brown-Dunkin around was difficult. Within 24 hours of the purchase, disgruntled union members began picketing the store, protesting a previous dismissal of maids and elevator operators. A week later, Dillard discovered a cigar box filled with $150,000 in unpaid bills. Struggling with the situation, Dillard sold his Texarkana and Magnolia stores to Alden's for $775,000. In three months, the union gave up picketing, and with a loan from the National Bank of Tulsa Dillard paid off Brown-Dunkin's debts. After launching a newspaper campaign, Dillard had the store back in the black.

In 1961, as Dillard was consolidating Brown-Dunkin, he formed Dillard Investment Company, Inc. With bank loans, Dillard Investment bought Dillard's credit accounts. As customers paid their bills, the subsidiary repaid the banks. This gave Dillard stores the benefit of credit sales while remaining free of debts.

In 1962, Dillard wanted to return with his family to Arkansas. At the time, there were two leading stores in Little Rock, the Gus Blass Department Store and the Joseph Pfeifer Department Store. Rebuffed in his bid for Blass, Dillard turned to Pfeifer. After extensive negotiations, Pfeifer president Sam Strauss accepted Dillard's bid of more than $3 million.

Dillard was again creative with capital. He collected investors, sold $325,000 worth of stock to Mayer & Schmidt shareholders, and convinced Sperry & Hutchinson, makers of S & H Green Stamps, to invest $1.5 million in exchange for issuing its stamps in his stores. In the fall of 1963, the Mayer & Schmidt store bought the Pfeifer store.

In January 1964, shareholders reincorporated Mayer & Schmidt in Delaware, where laws were more favorable. They changed the name of the company to Dillard Department Stores, Inc. but retained the names of the individual stores until 1974.

In February 1964, Gus Blass Co. allowed Dillard to buy the 192,000-square-foot Little Rock store and a 61,000-square-foot store at Pine Bluff, Arkansas. Since the main Blass store was just two blocks from Pfeifer, Dillard concentrated on remodeling the Pine Bluff store. By year's end, total corporate sales reached $41.2 million.

Two other key events occurred in 1964: the company installed its first computer system and opened its first mall store. The computers were the start of one of the industry's most advanced tracking systems. The mall store, on the west edge of Little Rock, marked the beginning of a move to the suburbs. Under various names, Dillard opened six more mall stores during the years from 1964 to 1968.

The year 1968 also marked the next turning point in corporate organization. For better administration, Dillard divided his 15 stores into three divisions: Arkansas, Oklahoma, and Texas. He also formed Construction Developers, Inc., a wholly owned subsidiary, to manage the company's real estate holdings.

In 1969, Dillard turned to the stock market. He divided the stock into two classes. Class A would raise money. Class B, the voting stock, would remain under Dillard's control. Listed on the American Stock Exchange, the first offering sold 242,430 shares worth $4 million.

Acquisitions in the 1970s–80s

Dillard opened three mall stores in 1970, and in August 1971 he purchased five Fedway stores from Federated Department Stores. Though not unprofitable, Federated considered the Fedway stores less than successful. After restocking the stores with name brands, Dillard renamed the stores Dillard's in 1972. By the end of that year, Dillard had 22 stores and sales of more than $100 million. Three of that year's four new stores had a regional rather than a metropolitan focus. As such, they were placed at the convergence of major highways.

The year 1973 marked the beginning of Dillard's border operations. To attract the inhabitants of nearby Matamoros, Mexico, the recently opened Brownsville store accepted the peso and extended credit to Mexican citizens.

The following year, Dillard bought five Leonard's stores from the Tandy Corporation for stock and cash. Leonard's provided an instant saturation of the Dallas-Fort Worth market. Saturation was an important factor as it allowed the company to spread advertising costs over many stores. By year's end, company-wide sales reached $173.4 million. More mall stores opened through the mid-1970s. Two stores came on line in 1975, including the first in Kansas, and in 1976 Dillard opened a record six stores in Texas, Oklahoma, and Louisiana.

In 1977, William (Bill) Dillard II, William Dillard's son, was named president and chief operating officer. William Dillard remained chief executive officer and chairman of the board, while E. Ray Kemp was named vice-chairman and chief administrative officer. By year's end, there were 38 Dillard's with sales of $269 million.

While sales had doubled from 1973 to 1977, debts had also doubled. By the end of 1977, the company lacked expansion

Key Dates:

1938: William Dillard opens a retail store in Nashville, Arkansas, and expands his business through acquisitions.
1964: The company is incorporated.
1968: The company now has stores in Arkansas, Oklahoma, and Texas.
1969: Dillard's goes public on the American Stock Exchange.
1975: The company expands into Kansas.
1984: The company pays the Dayton Hudson Corporation $140 million for 18 John A. Brown stores and 12 Diamond stores in the southwestern United States.
1985: Twelve stores are acquired from the R.H. Macy Company.
1989: New Orleans-based D.H. Holmes Company, a chain of 17 stores located in Louisiana, Mississippi, Alabama, and Florida, is acquired.
1990: The company purchases J.B. Ivey & Company's 23 stores in the Carolinas and Florida.
1993: For a period, the company begins opening new stores rather than acquiring existing businesses.
1998: Dillard's purchase of Mercantile Stores for $2.9 billion signals the beginning of financial difficulties for the company.
2003: Dillard's begins selling off operations as part of a strategy to recover lost financial ground.

capital. Searching for money, William Dillard met A.C.R. Dreesmann, chief executive officer of Vroom en Dreesmann B.V., the Netherlands' largest retail company. Dreesmann agreed to become Dillard's largest stockholder and to stay out of management. In February 1978, the board approved the sale of $24 million worth of Class A stock to Vroom en Dreesmann's subsidiary, Vendamerica B.V. The sale took place in three annual installments and gave Vendamerica 55 percent of the Class A shares. In 1979, Dillard used Vendamerica's first installment to build four new stores and remodel several older ones.

In 1980, rising interest rates checked Dillard's profits growth. Higher rates meant bigger payments on borrowed money and also hurt Dillard's own credit sales. Nevertheless, in 1980, Dillard added six stores in Texas and Oklahoma.

By contrast, 1981 was a banner year. The booming oil industry fueled sales growth, and management shifted its emphasis toward fast moving soft goods and away from less profitable home furnishings. Sales increased 26 percent to $470.7 million, profits vaulted 91 percent to $16.3 million, and earnings per share surged 85 percent to $5.35.

In 1982, new Dillard's stores opened in Dallas and Memphis. The success of the Memphis store prompted Dillard to lease three former Lowenstein stores and saturate the Memphis market. The three Memphis stores were a part of the record 11 new Dillard's opened in 1982. In the early 1980s, Dillard's grew at twice the department store average. Although the devaluation of the peso had a negative effect on border operations, 1982 profits still rose to $21.95 million.

As profits skyrocketed, so did stock prices. High stock prices reduced the company's financial flexibility, and in 1983 it embarked on a series of stock splits. With new capital available, Dillard acquired 12 St. Louis-area Stix, Baer & Fuller stores from Associated Dry Goods. The purchase came about through a chance meeting. While waiting for a flight at New York's LaGuardia Airport, William and Bill Dillard spotted mall developer Ed DeBartolo's corporate jet. They stopped for a visit and by chance met Bill Arnold, Associated's chairman. Arnold mentioned the possibility of selling Stix, Baer & Fuller, and months later, when new mall space became difficult to find, Dillard bought the stores.

The company had yet another year of massive expansion in 1984, when August Dillard agreed to pay the Dayton Hudson Corporation $140 million for 18 John A. Brown stores and 12 Diamond stores in the southwestern United States. Though not unprofitable, the stores performed below the Dayton Hudson average. Dillard immediately changed the John A. Brown stores to Dillard's. The Diamond stores went through a longer process in order to acquire the Dillard's name. In response to the needs of these western stores, Dillard added a new division based in Phoenix.

By the end of 1984, Dillard's sales had increased 50.7 percent to $1.27 billion. Net profit had jumped $15 million to $49.5 million, and the number of stores had increased from 66 to 93. Indeed, the only stain in the company's performance that year came through some poor publicity generated when Dillard's failed to feature any minority models in a major advertising supplement. The National Association for the Advancement of Colored People (NAACP) complained and the next year protested the company's treatment of minorities, announcing a boycott of the stores. In 1986, William Dillard agreed to hire more African-Americans and include more of them in management, a move that resolved the dispute.

The middle and late 1980s were marked by a shrewd reading of other department stores' finances. In 1985, after a management-led buyout of the R.H. Macy Company, Dillard went to New York, hoping that Macy's management would sell stores for needed capital. Within three months he closed a $100 million deal for 12 Macy's stores in Kansas City, Missouri, and Topeka and Wichita, Kansas.

Also during this time, Campeau Corporation, a Canadian company that had acquired Allied Stores Corp., needed cash to defray expenses. For $225 million, Campeau sold Dillard's 27 Joske's department stores and three Cain-Sloan department stores in 1987. Joske's gave Dillard what some described as a monopoly in Texas and pushed the retailer into the Houston market, while Cain-Sloan gave Dillard's a presence in Nashville, Tennessee. In 1989, in a joint venture with The Edward J. DeBartolo Corporation, Dillard's acquired the Higbee Company, a chain of 12 Ohio department and specialty stores, in a $165 million deal.

While continuing to open new stores in Missouri, Oklahoma, and Texas, Dillard's 1989 focus was again on acquisitions. Dillard acquired New Orleans-based D.H. Holmes Company, a chain of 17 stores located in Louisiana, Mississippi, Alabama, and Florida. Although Holmes was a consistent money-loser, Dillard was confident of a turnaround and was hungry for Holmes's New Orleans and Baton Rouge properties. In 1989, Dillard also moved its stock listing to the New York Stock Exchange and offered two million shares of Class A common stock as well as two sets of debentures.

1990s and Beyond

Dillard's continued its acquisition campaign in 1990, paying BAT Industries $110 million for J.B. Ivey & Company's 23 stores in the Carolinas and Florida. The price of $109 million, or one-third of annual sales, compared favorably with rates others were paying for BAT assets. The purchase also provided Dillard's a base from which to expand in such lucrative markets as Jacksonville and Daytona Beach, Florida, and Raleigh-Durham, North Carolina.

While for many retailers, 1990 was a disastrous year, Dillard's experienced some unique gains. Some estimated that Dillard's enjoyed an 18 percent same-store sales gain over 1989. In 1990, every expense item on the company's income statement dropped as a percentage of sales. Because the company's ratio of debt to capital is lower than that of competitors, interest was less of a problem for Dillard's than for its competition.

By 1992, Dillard's acquisitions program was winding down. In 1991, the company gained eight Maison Blanche Department Stores located in central and western Florida. The following year the company bought four more stores in Ohio from Joseph Horne Co. to add to its Higbee's chain but only after Horne sued Dillard's over its backing out of a deal to acquire Horne in the late 1980s. Horne officials claimed the failed deal ruined the company's finances by disrupting its operations and leading to the departure of key executives. Dillard's received the first significant battering of its clean reputation as a result, but seemed to emerge otherwise unscathed. Also in 1991, Vendamerica sold all of its shares in Dillard's in a public offering.

By 1992, Dillard's had failed to turn around the Higbee's stores in Ohio, but nonetheless increased its exposure by buying out its partner, DeBartolo, for about $90 million. The company also announced that year that it would enter the Mexican market through the development of Dillard's anchors for five planned regional department stores. By mid-1996, the venture had not borne fruit, the apparent victim of the Mexican economic crisis of 1994.

Starting in 1991, the company significantly increased the number of new stores it was opening each year—ten added in 1991 and 11 the following year. Indeed, 1993 saw the beginning of an official shift in the company's growth strategy away from acquisitions and to the opening of new stores. From 1993 to 1995, 26 new stores were opened, while none were added through acquisition. A record 16 new stores were planned for 1996. One advantage of this growth strategy was that Dillard's could carefully choose the locations for its new stores, and it moved into such desirable areas as Louisville, Atlanta, Denver, and Colorado Springs.

By 1993, sales at Dillard's had grown to $5.13 billion, a sixfold increase over a ten-year period, while profits were also multiplying from $34.1 million to $241.1 million. Signs of a downturn, however, were evident even in the 1993 results as sales increased only nine percent, following year after year of growth in the 12 to 19 percent range. Profits, meanwhile, had increased only 2 percent over 1992. This slowdown continued through 1995 as sales increased 8 percent in 1994 and 7 percent in 1995, while profits increased only slightly to $251.8 million in 1994 before falling dramatically to $167 million in 1995, which even without a $78.5 million charge for impairment of long-lived assets would still have totaled only $245.6 million.

Analysts reasoned that Dillard's was in part a victim of weak sales of women's apparel industrywide, which could be devastating for a company that generated about 40 percent of its sales from this sector. However, the company's marketing strategies were also identified as contributing to the difficulties, in particular its longstanding everyday pricing policy; some observers noted that Dillard's lack of promotions caused it to lose customers to other department stores, which lured people through their doors by running sales on an almost constant basis.

Although it was sticking with its marketing policies as of mid-1996, Dillard's reorganized its operating divisions along geographic and climatic lines in March 1996 in order to improve operating results. The company's Cleveland and San Antonio divisions were merged into the company's other divisions, leaving the company with a more streamlined operation with five divisional buying offices.

By the end of the 1990s, however, Dillard's had begun to expand its operations to compete against new competitors in retailing, including giant Wal-Mart. Early in 1998, Dilard's announced plans to purchase rival retailer Mercantile Stores for $2.9 billion, acquiring 103 separate locations in the transaction. Later in the year, Dillard's announced plans to sell off twenty-six of the newly acquired locations—in places as diverse as Duluth, Minnesota and Spartanburg, South Carolina—to avoid competing with itself. The acquisition of Mercantile caused Dillard's expenses to nearly double, cutting deeply into the year's profits. Nevertheless, the addition of the Mercantile stores also boosted sales by more than 25 percent in the third quarter of 1998.

The dip in Dillard's sales following the Mercantile acquisition caused angst for stock market analysts. Early in 1999, following a weak second-quarter report, Wall Street traders reduced their valuation of Dillard's stock. The corporation responded by announcing a plan to repurchase $250 million of its common stock, partly for use in boosting employee retirement plans. Heading into the end of the century, the question facing Dillard's was whether it could turn itself around from the difficult period of the mid-1990s and reestablish its formerly lofty position, which just a few years earlier had it placed at the forefront of the department store industry.

The outlook did not look bright as Dillard's entered the new millennium. By the middle of 2000, the company had posted losses for five consecutive quarters. Business picked up toward the end of the year, however, and by March of 2001 the company reported fourth-quarter net income of $66 million, more than twice what it had been a year before. By the following March, business had increased even further, bringing in net profits of $102 million despite a decline in sales. Dillard's spokespersons credited the early retirement of debt and cost-cutting measures as important steps in the recovery program.

Dillard's sales continued to fall into 2003, driven downward by a difficult economy that hit the business and other full-price retailers hard. Despite adopting new accounting practices, cutting operating expenses by a further 1.9 percent, and tax credits left over from its acquisition of Mercantile, the company continued to lose money and sales. Dillard's responded with a program to slough off six underperforming stores and cutting prices to reduce inventory. Losses continued to mount, however, and at the end of 2003 the Wall Street investor service firm Moody's downgraded Dillard's rating. In 2004, Dillard's also suffered a setback when Hurricane Charley ripped through the southeast, forcing the closing of at least fourteen stores for at least a day.

Despite these setbacks, Dillard's continued to improve performance by cutting operating costs, interest expense, and average gross margin. The company also divested itself of some of its non-core operations. In June 2004, the corporation sold its ticket-sales operation, Dillard's Box Office, to EMT Entertainment Network of California. In September of 2004, Dillard's sold its credit card business to GE Consumer Finance.

From a small department store in Arkansas, the late William Dillard built one of the fastest growing department store chains in the United States. Expanding first by acquisition and later by placing stores in suburban malls and buying underperforming assets from debt-burdened competitors, Dillard's has grown without burdening itself with crushing debt.

Principal Subsidiaries

Cain Sloan, Inc.; Construction Developers Inc.; Dillard Investment Co. Inc.; Dillard Travel, Inc.; D.H. Holmes Company, Limited; J.B. Ivey & Company.

Further Reading

Brown, Susan, ''Dillard: Acquiring for the Future,'' *Financial World*, October 30, 1990, p. 19.

Caminiti, Susan, ''A Quiet Superstar Rises in Retailing,'' *Fortune*, October 23, 1989, pp. 167–69.

——, ''The New Champs of Retailing,'' *Fortune*, September 24, 1990, pp. 85–100.

Creno, Glen. ''Dillard's Negotiates to Sell Arizona-Based Box Office Operations,'' *Knight Ridder/Tribune Business News*, June 18, 1999.

''Dillard's Inc.: Quarterly Loss Narrowed, But Sales Dropped by 2.9%,'' *Wall Street Journal*, August 19, 2004, p. B8.

''Dillard's Sells Its Bank for $1.25 Billion,'' *Chain Store Age*, September, 2004, p. 151.

Fisher, Christy, and Laura Loro, ''May, Dillard Hot, but All Watch Specialty Inroads,'' *Advertising Age*, January 28, 1991, p. 23.

Forest, Stephanie Anderson, ''Dillard's Has a Dilly of a Headache,'' *Business Week*, October 3, 1994, pp. 85–86.

Hogsett, Don. ''Dillard's Pushes Profit up in 1Q,'' *Home Textiles Today*, May 26, 2003, p. 20.

——. ''Dillard's Doubles Profits,'' *Home Textiles Today*, May 17, 2004, p.33.

——. ''Dillard's Inc. Narrows Loss,'' *Home Textiles Today*, August 30, 2004, p. 16.

Krim, Jonathan. ''Dillard's Swings to a Q2 Loss on Lower Same-Store Sales,'' *The America's Intelligence Wire*, August 20, 2003.

Maile, Matt. ''Large Retailers Adapting to Changing Environment,'' *Journal Record* (Oklahoma City, OK), November 6, 2002.

Morgenson, Gretchen, ''A Midas Touch,'' *Forbes*, February 4, 1991, p. 42.

Much, Marilyn. ''Recession's Been Kind To Stores, But Retail Casualties May Climb: K-Mart Teeters on Brink; Though in Better Shape, Dillard and Gap Struggle,'' *Investor's Business Daily*, January 18, 2002, p. A01.

Rosenberg, Leon Joseph, *Dillard's: The First Fifty Years*, Fayetteville: The University of Arkansas Press, 1988, 141 p.

Schroeder, Michael, and Wendy Zellner, ''Hell Hath No Fury Like a Big Store Scorned: Horne's Department Store Is Suing Dillard, the Suitor That Balked,'' *Business Week*, September 23, 1991, pp. 39–40.

Sutor, Ruthanne, ''The Friends of Bill Dillard,'' *Financial World*, September 6, 1988, p. 22.

Talley, Karen. ''Dillard's, Ross Rise Amid Merger Talk,'' *Wall Street Journal*, June 11, 2004, p. C3.

——. ''Rising Oil Prices Depress Blue Chips; Industrials, Tech Stocks Dig Deeper Into Lows for 2004; Dillard's Rises 5.7% on Pact,'' *Wall Street Journal*, August 10, 2004, p.C4.

—Jordan Wankoff
—updates: David E. Salamie; Kenneth R. Shepherd

Dole Food Company, Inc.

One Dole Drive
Westlake Village, California 91362
U.S.A.
Telephone: (818) 879-6600
Fax: (818) 879-6615
Web site: http://www.dole.com

Private Company
Incorporated: 1894 as Castle & Cooke Co., Inc.
Employees: 59,000
Sales: $4.77 billion (2003)
NAIC: 11121 Vegetable and Melon Farming; 111211 Potato Farming; 111219 Other Vegetable (Except Potato) and Melon Farming; 111310 Orange Groves; 111320 Citrus (Except Orange) Groves; 111331 Apple Orchards; 111332 Grape Vineyards; 111333 Strawberry Farming; 111334 Berry (Except Strawberry) Farming; 111335 Tree Nut Farming; 111336 Fruit and Tree Nut Combination Farming; 111339 Other Noncitrus Fruit Farming; 111422 Floriculture Production; 311411 Frozen Fruit, Juice, and Vegetable Manufacturing; 311421 Fruit & Vegetable Canning; 311423 Dried and Dehydrated Food Manufacturing; 311520 Ice Cream and Frozen Dessert Manufacturing; 311911 Roasted Nuts and Peanut Butter Manufacturing

Best known for its pineapples, Dole Food Company, Inc. promotes its Dole brand of fresh and packaged food and nonfood products through what it calls its 'Dole Standard.' With its fully integrated operations of sourcing, growing, processing, distributing, and marketing, it is the world's largest producer and distributor of fresh fruits and vegetables. Specifically, the company is one of the world's leading producers of bananas and pineapples, along with being a major marketer of apples, grapefruit, oranges, pears, plums, table grapes, other tropical and citrus fruits, dried fruits, canned fruits, fresh-cut flowers, and nuts. In recent years, Dole has added value-added products, such as packaged salad mixes, fresh vegetables, and novelty-canned pineapple shapes. As of 2004, Dole became one of the largest importers and marketers of fresh-cut flowers in the United States. The Dole brand, which was introduced in 1933, is one of the most recognized brands for fresh and packaged produce in the United States. In all, Dole sells or sources over 200 products in more than 90 countries around the world.

Company Origins

In 1851, Samuel Northrup Castle and Amos Starr Cooke established in Hawaii the company that eventually became Dole Food Company, Inc. Cooke and Castle set up business to sell wholesale goods, and in 1858 the pair entered the food business, investing in Hawaii's sugar industry. The business continued to grow, and in 1894 the company was incorporated as Castle & Cooke Co., Inc. A few years later, James Drummond Dole, a 21-year-old graduate of Harvard, arrived in Hawaii. With degrees in business and horticulture and a keen interest in farming, Dole hoped to make a living by growing the exotic pineapple. His cousin, Sanford B. Dole, an influential politician who became governor of the newly acquired territory of Hawaii, encouraged James's ambition to market pineapple commercially.

By 1901 James Dole had acquired 60 acres of land 18 miles north of Honolulu, in Wahiawa, and had formed the Hawaiian Pineapple Company. His groves of smooth Cayenne pineapples were ready to be harvested two years later. Rather than trying to export the fresh fruit, Dole decided to market his pineapple in cans. He established a cannery near the pineapple groves, which allowed him to achieve the best results by canning soon after the ripened produce was harvested. The Hawaiian Pineapple Company packaged and marketed nearly 2,000 cases of canned pineapple in 1903.

Two years later Dole was shipping 25,000 cases of canned pineapple. The company's success was facilitated by a new railroad constructed between Wahiawa and Honolulu, and the availability of ample, cheap labor allowed the company to keep its costs low. In addition, Dole persuaded the American Can Company to establish a manufacturing plant next to his cannery. For Dole this eliminated the expense of importing cans from the mainland and allowed vast quantities of pineapple to be pro-

Company Perspectives:

Dole Food Company, Inc. is committed to supplying the consumer and our customers with the finest, high-quality products and to leading the industry in nutrition research and education. Dole supports these goals with a corporate philosophy of adhering to the highest ethical conduct in all its business dealings, treatment of its employees, and social and environmental policies.

cessed quickly and cheaply. The company's increasing supply, however, required a corresponding growth in demand, but few Americans outside those living on the California coast had ever seen, much less tasted, a pineapple. Thus, the company's existing market was approaching saturation.

The Mainstreaming of Pineapple in the United States: 1910–30

In 1911 engineer Henry Ginaca, an employee of the Hawaiian Pineapple Company, invented a machine capable of processing 100 pineapple cylinders a minute. Such production facilities enabled the company to market its produce across a large portion of the United States. Developing a successful marketing strategy became a high priority for the company during this time, particularly important if Dole was to attain his goal of making pineapple available throughout the country.

Together with several smaller companies that were also involved in the processing of pineapple, Dole financed an advertising blitz in magazines and newspapers on the mainland, promoting canned pineapple products under exotic, foreign brand names such as Ukelele and Outrigger. As a result, demand increased significantly. Toward the end of World War I, in 1918, Dole's Hawaiian Pineapple Company was producing one million cases annually and had gained a reputation as the largest processor of pineapples in the world. During this time Dole purchased more land in order to expand his business and in 1922 purchased the island of Lanai for a pineapple plantation. To finance the purchase, Dole sold a third interest in his company to Waialua Agricultural Company, which was a division of Castle & Cooke. By the mid-1920s Castle & Cooke had evolved into a Hawaiian real estate and land development company.

Surplus supply in the 1920s compelled Dole and other pineapple growers to pool their resources to mount an even bigger national advertising campaign. Using the new medium of radio, the company aired advertising using slogans such as "It Cuts with a Spoon like a Peach" and "You Can Thank Jim Dole for Canned Pineapples." As a result, sales and profits increased dramatically.

New Products and Continued Growth: 1930–70

With the onset of the Great Depression, the company's sales declined, and its advertising budget was depleted. The introduction of a new product, pineapple juice, was unsuccessful when the company could not promote it. In the first nine months of 1932, Hawaiian Pineapple lost more than $5 million, and the principal stockholders, Castle & Cooke, took over Dole's company by acquiring an additional 21 percent. Thereafter the Hawaiian Pineapple Company became Castle & Cooke's principal business, and beginning in 1933 the Dole name was affixed to the company's products.

The new owners managed to reverse the downward trend of the Hawaiian Pineapple Company. With greater financial resources at its disposal, the company launched a major advertising campaign for pineapple juice, boosting sales and putting the company back on a profitable footing by 1936. The end of Prohibition also facilitated sales of pineapple juice, as the company promoted pineapple juice as a mixer for liquors, particularly gin.

The company continued to report healthy profits over the next two decades. By the 1950s Americans were spending more on food than the people of any nation on earth, and food companies were quickly expanding their markets to accommodate demand. In 1961, three years after the death of James Dole, Castle & Cooke purchased the remainder of Hawaiian Pineapple. Dole products retained the Dole name because of its strong brand image.

Castle & Cooke introduced several new pineapple products during the 1950s and 1960s, including both fresh and canned pineapple processed in chunks and slices or crushed, in addition to expanding its markets to include citrus fruits, macadamia nuts, vegetables, and even tuna. Particularly noteworthy was Castle & Cooke's entrance into the banana business. The company established pineapple and banana farms in the Philippines in 1963 to serve markets in East Asia. A year later the company bought 55 percent of the Standard Fruit & Steamship Company, one of the largest U.S. producers and importers of bananas. In 1968 Castle & Cooke bought the remainder of Standard Fruit.

Given the tremendous diversification of Dole products, advertising became critical to ensuring the company's dominance in the marketplace. In order to capitalize on public recognition of the Dole brand name, Castle & Cooke decided to use it on the labels of several of its non-pineapple food products. In addition, television became an important medium for the company's advertising, and by the 1960s James Dole's dream of making pineapple as familiar as apples and oranges had been realized.

Expansion and Sustained Success in the 1970s–80s

During the 1970s Dole continued to diversify and grow. In 1972 Standard Fruit's bananas began carrying the Dole label, and in the same year all food activities except sugar were organized into a single division—Castle & Cooke Foods. The company branched into mushrooms in 1973 with the acquisition of West Foods, Inc., the biggest producer of mushrooms in the western United States. Also in 1973 Castle & Cooke became the nation's leading banana producer, adding two large banana plantations to its roster. In addition, the company took advantage of the increasing demand for nutritious foods, advertising its products as healthy additions to the diets of adults and children.

Despite the company's accelerated growth, Castle & Cooke suffered financial setbacks in the early 1980s. The company was heavily in debt and had barely escaped two hostile takeover attempts. Its problems were largely resolved when it merged with Flexi-Van Corporation, a business that leased transportation

Key Dates:

1851: Castle and Cooke obtain licenses to sell wholesale products in Hawaii.
1858: Castle and Cooke enter the food business with an investment in Hawaii's sugar industry.
1894: Castle & Cooke Co. is incorporated.
1901: James Dole begins growing pineapple and incorporates his company as the Hawaiian Pineapple Company.
1932: Castle & Cooke acquires a 21 percent ownership of Hawaiian Pineapple Company.
1961: Castle & Cooke and the Hawaiian Pineapple Company merge.
1964: Castle & Cooke enters the banana business.
1986: The Dole brand enjoys a worldwide recognition rate of 98 percent.
1991: Castle & Cooke changes its name to Dole Food Company, Inc.
1996: Dole pioneers packaged fresh salad mixes.
2003: CEO David Murdock completes deal that converts Dole to private company.

equipment, in 1985. Flexi-Van's owner, David H. Murdock, became the chairman and CEO of Castle & Cooke, and the company continued to expand and build equity in the Dole brand.

In 1986 Dole's logo was redesigned. The resulting yellow sunburst logo was intended to convey quality, freshness, and wholesomeness. The Dole brand name came to be used to promote additional products as Dole Fresh Fruit operations extended its line to include table grapes, strawberries, nuts, raisins, cherries, and strawberries. In 1988 Dole introduced a new line of dried fruits and nuts. The following year, Dole Fresh Vegetables began marketing produce under the Dole name, dropping the Bud of California name it had been using since 1978, and the company purchased two apple growers in Washington State. By the late 1980s Dole had a global recognition factor of 98 percent.

Innovation in the 1990s

In the early 1990s Dole launched a major multimedia advertising campaign accompanied by the slogan ''How'd You Do Your Dole Today?'' The campaign was designed to encourage consumers to eat more vegetables and fruits, including pineapple, regularly. As a result of its effective advertising, Dole maintained the largest market share of pineapples and bananas in North America. The company also continued its tradition of diversification and innovation, introducing a line of packaged fresh vegetable products in 1990. The convenience of precut vegetables and salads appealed to consumers and soon became the fastest-growing division in grocery stores.

In 1991, under the direction of Murdock, Castle & Cooke's stockholders voted to use the Dole name to represent all of the company's fruit and vegetable operations, reorganizing under the name Dole Food Company, Inc. The Castle & Cooke name was retained solely for the company's real estate business, which became a subsidiary of Dole Food Company. In the early 1990s ice cream bars were added to the list of Dole products. The company also retained interests in beer processing in Honduras, sugar refining in Hawaii, and tropical flower marketing in the Philippines. In addition to the individual consumer, Dole's market expanded to include other food processors, which used Dole products as ingredients.

Dole began to expand more aggressively into international markets in the 1990s. While Dole products had the leading market share in the United States, Canada, Mexico, and Japan, the company began to gain a significant share of the European market. In 1989 a division of Dole Food Company was established in London, poised to take advantage of imminent changes in the integrated European market. Dole's international growth strategy included expansion into eastern Europe, South Korea, and the Middle East. In 1992 Dole bought SAMICA, a dried fruits and nuts firm in Europe, and in 1994 acquired an interest in Jamaica Fruit Distributors. A year later the company purchased the New Zealand operations of Chiquita Brands International, Inc. Dole's international expansion continued in 1996 with the purchase of Pascual Hermanos, the largest grower of fruit and vegetables in Spain, and in 1998 with the acquisition of 60 percent of SABA Trading AB, a Swedish importer and distributor of fruits and vegetables. Dole also established operations in South Africa following the deregulation of that country's fresh fruit industry.

In 1995 Dole sold its juice and beverage business, except for pineapple juice, to the Seagram Co. Ltd., which planned to market the juices under its Tropicana brand. In the same year Dole separated its food and real estate business, and Castle & Cooke began to operate independently of Dole as a real estate development firm. Dole was thus focusing solely on its operations as a producer and distributor of food products. By the end of 1995 the company served more than 90 countries, and its product line included more than 170 food products.

Taking advantage of the growing interest in packaged fresh produce, Dole introduced packaged salad mixes in 1996 and set off a major trend. Dole's salad operations plant in Soledad, California, received Food Engineering Magazine's Plant of the Year Award in 1996 for its design quality. The salad business grew rapidly, and Dole founded a processing plant in Ohio to service states in the Midwest and the East. Plans for new salad products were implemented to ensure continued growth through the first few years of the 2000s. The company also established a salad plant in Japan in 1998 to introduce the packaged product to Japanese consumers.

To further diversify its product line, Dole entered the fresh flower market through several major acquisitions in 1998. The company bought Sunburst Farms, Inc., the largest U.S. importer and marketer of fresh cut flowers, as well as Finesse Farms, an importer and marketer of roses, Four Farmers, Inc., a bouquet company, and CCI Farms, a Miami-based producer, importer, and marketer of fresh-cut flowers. Dole hoped that its new flower division would generate revenues of more than $200 million a year in the United States, which, with sales of about $7 billion, was the largest floral market in the world. The floral industry's growth was attributed in large part to the increased availability of fresh-cut flowers in supermarkets, an arena in which Dole already held a commanding position.

Although the company moved forward in its acquisitions and innovations in 1998, Dole faced numerous challenges, some presented by unpredictable weather conditions and others by unstable economic conditions in key markets. The economic crisis afflicting East Asia significantly affected Dole, as the Asian market had played an important role in Dole's growth in the 1990s. Russia accounted for about 8 percent of the global banana business, and when the Russian economy collapsed in late 1998, Dole lost an important market for its bananas. El Niproduce market grew at a rate that was above the rate of population growth, which was due primarily to increased retail emphasis on attracting customers with fresh produce; consistent trends in greater consumer demand for healthy, fresh, and convenient foods; and increased retailer area devoted to produce. However, during this same period of time, Dole continued to suffer from adverse weather and worldwide economic shifts. Its revenues only slightly increased from 1999 to 2003.

Net revenues in 2000 were less than in 1999 due to a reduction in banana profits caused by a deterioration in the euro-to-U.S. dollar exchange rate; a large price increase in fuel rates; an oversupply of bananas; and a longer-than-expected time period to achieve profitability of its consolidated flower operations. As a result, performance improvement and cost reduction plans were enacted in the Fresh Fruits and Fresh Flower segments. These activities helped to improve net income. Dole's other segments—Fresh Vegetables, Packaged Foods, and Beverages—performed well in 2000. Fresh Vegetables announced record earnings as a result of reliable growth in the fresh-cut salads business and favorable pricing in the commodity vegetables business. The canned pineapple business—within Packaged Foods—maintained its 50 percent market share in North America with the introduction of ''Fruit Bowls'' plastic cups. The beverage business in Honduras returned to normal after Hurricane Mitch. To better concentrate on its primary businesses of fruits, vegetables, packaged foods, and flowers, Castle & Cooke, Inc., a diversified real estate company within Dole, was privatized in 2000.

In 2001, Dole began a concerted effort to reduce operating costs and to liquidate non-core and/or under-performing businesses. As a result, Dole discontinued its Beverages segment when it sold its 97 percent stake in the Cerveceria Hondureña S.A. beverage operations. Cash proceeds of $537 million from the sale were used to reduce its debt. In December, Dole's Florida-based fresh-cut flowers distribution operation was transferred into a new 328,000 square-foot building. Net revenues for 2001 were much higher in most of Dole's core businesses primarily as a result of higher prices and volumes for its Premium Select pineapples in North America and Europe; increased volumes for its North American packaged salads business; higher prices and volumes for North American bananas; and increased volumes of its ''Fruit Bowls'' and ''Fruit-n-Gel Bowls'' in North America. These increases were offset by the negative impact on revenues from asset sales and business shutdowns.

In 2002, Dole continued its efforts to reduce costs and to eliminate undesirable businesses. Financial results in 2002 were somewhat improved over 2001, with net revenues up while net income went down, being adversely effected by a one-time business reconfiguration charge. Dole's Fresh Fruit segment received strong returns especially in North America, Europe, and Asia, primarily due to its programs in Premium Select pineapple and organic banana. In Dole's Fresh Vegetables segment, its packaged salads increased its market share by 1 percent, to 38.2 percent. Overall, weaker commodity prices were balanced by continued growth in its packaged salads business. In Dole's Packaged Foods segment, financial results improved, gaining market share in canned pineapple and Fruit Bowls (up 4.2 share points from the previous year, to 43.9 percent). Dole's Fresh Flowers segment reduced its operating loss as a result of an improved cost structure. Dole completed its selling activities of non-core and/or unprofitable businesses, when it sold its Pascual Hermanos vegetable business in Spain and its Saman dried fruit and nut business in France.

Cost-cutting measures in the early 2000s, including job deductions and sale of non-core/unprofitable businesses, helped to increase Dole's earnings so that net revenues grew to $4.77 billion in 2003. In order to maximize future long-term growth and to minimize uncertain short-term exposure to the public equities market, CEO David Murdock and his management partners took the company private in 2003. Murdock and his partners acquired 76 percent of the company's shares as part of a buyout valued at about $2.4 billion ($1.4 billion in stock, plus debt assumption of $1 billion), which gave them total ownership. Subsequently, the company expanded with increased 2003 sales of nearly 9 percent and increased earnings of about 18 percent. In addition, Dole repaid over $200 million in bank debt. Also, in 2003, Dole opened its Dole Nutrition Institute, a group dedicated to educating the public about the health benefits of fruits and vegetables. Dole also broke ground on the new Dole Wellness Center, Spa, and Hotel, which will consist of medical facilities with state-of-the-art diagnostic services, 267-room hotel, conference center, full-service spa and fitness center, and television production facility.

As of 2004, Doles' primary business segments were: Fresh Fruits, Fresh Vegetables, Packaged Foods, and Fresh Flowers. During 2004, Dole purchased J.R. Wood, Inc., a manufacturer and marketer of fresh frozen fruit products, and Coastal Berry Co. LLC, one of the largest producers of strawberries in the United States.

By holding the number one or number two position within its industry with regards to many of its major products, Dole has positioned itself to meet the future requirements of retailers through the delivery of high-quality and innovative produce, competitive product pricing, and reliable service. The company has also diversified globally so that its operations in 28 countries now distribute products to more than 90 countries; a plan that helps Dole reduce losses from natural disasters and political problems. Dole has built a state-of-the-art production, processing, transportation, and distribution structure and has become among the lowest cost producers within many of its major product lines. Over many decades, Dole has built a strong global brand that is easily recognized by consumers worldwide. Over the last few years, the company has begun to focus its operations on identifying to consumers why fruits and vegetables are beneficial to good nutrition.

Principal Subsidiaries

Dole Fresh Fruit Company; Dole Fresh Vegetables; Dole Packaged Foods; Royal Packing Co.; CCI Farms; Finesse Farms;

Coastal Berry Co. LLC; Four Farmers Inc.; Floramerica Co.; J.R. Wood, Inc.; Sunburst Farms Inc.; Beebe Orchard Co.; Wells & Wade Fruit Co.; SABA Trading AB (60%; Sweden).

Principal Operating Units

Dole Latin America; Dole Asia; Dole Europe; Dole Worldwide Packaged Foods; Dole Worldwide Fresh Vegetables; Dole Fresh Flowers; Dole North America Tropical Fresh Fruit; Dole Chile.

Principal Competitors

Chiquita Brands International, Inc.; Fresh Del Monte Produce Inc.; Del Monte Foods Company; Fyffes plc.

Further Reading

Booth, Jason, "Not a Fruitful Year at Dole As Banana Prices Plummet," *Los Angeles Business Journal,* November 2, 1998, p. 50.

"David H. Murdock Acquires Dole Food Company, Inc.," *Canadian Corporate News,* March 29, 2003.

"Dole Food Company, Inc. Announces Additional Duties for Its Chairman and CEO, and Early Retirement of Its President and COO," *Business Wire,* February 4, 2004.

"Dole Food Company, Inc. Announces the Acquisition of Coastal Berry Company, LLC.," *Business Wire,* October 15, 2004.

Dole, Richard, and Elizabeth Dole Porteus, *The Story of James Dole,* Aiea, Hawaii: Island Heritage Publishing, 1999, 120 pp.

Facts On: Dole Fresh Pineapple, Westlake Village, Calif.: Dole Food Company, Inc., 1992.

Fairclough, Gordon, and Darren McDermott, "Fruit of Labor: The Banana Business Is Rotten, So Why Do People Fight over It?," *Wall Street Journal,* August 9, 1999, p. A1.

The History of Dole, Westlake Village, Calif.: Dole Food Company, Inc., 1992.

Koeppel, Dan, "Dole Wants the Whole Produce Aisle: Branded Fruits and Vegetables Are Turning the Nation's Supermarkets into Dole Country," *Adweek's Marketing Week,* October 22, 1990, p. 20.

Kravetz, Stacy, "Retailing: King of Pineapples Tiptoes to Tulips for Faster Growth," *Wall Street Journal,* July 6, 1998, p. A17.

Lynch, Russ, "Dole Net Slips on Banana Woes," *Honolulu Star-Bulletin,* November 6, 1998, p. B1.

Martinez, Carlos, "Largest Producer of Fruits, Vegetables has Huge Reach. (Best Companies in the Valley—A Special Report)," *San Fernando Valley Business Journal,* June 23, 2003, p. 24.

Petruno, Tom, "Why Dole Offers More Than Just a Bit of Appeal," *Los Angeles Times,* October 11, 1991, p. D3.

Taylor, Frank J., Earl M. Welty, and David W. Eyre, *From Land and Sea: The Story of Castle & Cooke of Hawaii,* San Francisco: Chronicle Books, 1976, 288 pp.

Weiss, Jeff, "Dole to Put Focus on Health at Hotel, SPA near Headquarters," *San Fernando Valley Business Journal,* March 15, 2004, p. 10.

Zwein, Jason, "Pineapples, Anyone? (Dole Food Operations)," *Forbes,* November 27, 1989, p. 286.

—Sina Dubovoj
—updates: Mariko Fujinaka; William Arthur Atkins

DriveTime Automotive Group Inc.

4020 E. Indian School Road
Phoenix, Arizona 85018
U.S.A.
Telephone: (602) 852-6600
Toll Free: (800)TO-DRIVE
Fax: (602) 852-6686
Web site: http://www.drivetime.com

Private Company
Incorporated: 1977 as Ugly Duckling Rent-A-Car System, Inc.
Employees: 2,049
Sales: $729 million (2003)
NAIC: 441120 Used Car Dealers; 52222 Sales Financing; 551112 Offices of Other Holding Companies

DriveTime Automotive Group Inc. is a leading independent retailer of used automobiles in the United States. Using a ''buy here/pay here'' financing model, the company caters to buyers with subprime credit and finances the sales itself. The group has about 80 lots in eight states; it was formerly known as Ugly Duckling. Traditionally based in the Sun Belt, the chain's operations are located in 11 major metropolitan areas as diverse as Los Angeles and Richmond, Virginia.

Origins

The Ugly Duckling story began in 1977 when Ugly Duckling Rent-A-Car System, Inc. was formed in Tucson by 63-year-old Thomas S. Duck, Sr., a retired insurance salesman. Just to keep busy, he started his company by using $10,000 of his savings to buy a few used cars to sell. Soon his franchise business expanded into other states.

Ugly Duckling Rent-A-Car entered a growing industry dominated by the Big Three: Avis and Hertz, both started in 1947, and National. In the 1970s all rental car firms struggled with the energy shortage. In the 1980s price wars engulfed the industry, encouraged by the success of low-cost rental companies like Budget Rent-A-Car and, of course, Ugly Duckling. By 1985 Ugly Duckling was the nation's fifth largest car rental company. Its sales reached $65 million from 550 franchises at the end of 1985, but in 1989 the company declared bankruptcy, thus ending phase one of this story.

Acquired by Garcia in 1990

A transition period began in 1990 with the involvement of Ernest C. Garcia II. Born in Gallup, New Mexico, in 1957, Garcia studied business at the University of Arizona in Tucson before working in real estate, banking, and securities. In 1990 he formed a company called Duck Ventures, Inc., which purchased the assets of Ugly Duckling Rent-A-Car. Meanwhile, Garcia had to work through some major financial and legal difficulties before moving on.

In October 1990 Garcia pled guilty to felony bank fraud related to the savings-and-loan crisis of the 1980s. In 1987 Garcia had obtained a $20 million loan from Charles Keating's Lincoln Savings & Loan. That gave Garcia's real estate development company the funds it needed to buy back some stock from an investor. Garcia also agreed at the time of the loan, however, to buy land from a Lincoln subsidiary. The Resolution Trust Company found that the two transactions were improperly linked, without directly blaming Garcia. In December 1993 the U.S. District Court for the Central District of California sentenced Garcia with a $50 fine and a three-year probation, a light penalty due to Garcia's full cooperation with the authorities. Meanwhile, his real estate company had declared Chapter 11 bankruptcy and he had filed personally for Chapter 7 bankruptcy.

In 1992, while his case was still in the district court, Garcia incorporated Ugly Duckling Holdings, Inc., an Arizona firm that purchased Duck Ventures, Inc. and made it a subsidiary. He started out by buying a small used car dealership in Phoenix and later in 1992 purchased a second dealership in Tucson.

Garcia could have changed the company's name, but he stuck with Ugly Duckling. ''We have enormous fun with the duck and we go with the name tongue in cheek,'' said Garcia in the August 25, 1996 *Arizona Tribune.* ''We're just using it to have fun. We're not saying our cars are ugly or anything else, because if you look at our facilities, if you look at the automobiles . . . we're clearly selling a very competitive and clean product.''

Company Perspectives:

Mission Statement: To be the auto dealership and finance company of choice for people with less than perfect credit. DriveTime means Innovative Credit Solutions, Quality Vehicles and Outstanding Customer Service.

Ups and Downs from 1993 to 1995

In 1993 Garcia acquired three Ugly Duckling dealerships. The next year the company built four brand new dealerships with an improved upscale look. Although the firm still catered to those with lower incomes, it wanted to do so in a more positive atmosphere, compared with the dirty and dusty lots of some subprime dealerships.

Ugly Duckling closed one dealership in 1994 because it did not measure up to the firm's high standards. In addition, in late 1995 it closed its dealership in Gilbert, Arizona, because the firm's experiment to sell later model used cars there failed. The Gilbert dealership had tried to sell cars two to seven years newer and often twice the cost of those at other Ugly Duckling dealerships, but the company's infrastructure and financing programs could not accommodate those kinds of vehicles. Ugly Duckling sold the land and dealership building for $1.7 million.

By the mid-1990s Ugly Duckling was gaining popularity in its Arizona home base. ''You go to Tucson or Phoenix and people know The Duck,'' said William Gibson, Cruttenden Roth's senior investment analyst in the October 14, 1996 *Investor's Business Daily.* ''It's an icon in those cities.''

To help its customers buy a used car and establish a positive credit rating, Ugly Duckling offered several innovations. From January through March, it offered to help customers prepare their income tax returns and even pay preparation fees. In return, a customer could use his or her forthcoming tax refund for credit toward a car down payment, instead of waiting extra weeks for the government to send a refund check.

Another program was established as an incentive to make installment payments on time. If customers paid all or almost all of their payments when due, they were refunded their down payment when the contract was completed. Down payments accounted for 10 to 15 percent of the purchase price, so this was a substantial refund.

Third, Ugly Duckling offered qualified customers the chance to gain a Visa credit card. The company actually secured those cards by paying a $250 deposit to the credit card firm. This demonstrated a great deal of confidence in Ugly Duckling customers and gave them an opportunity to rebuild positive credit histories.

Fourth, the company dealerships had onsite repair facilities to service the used cars it sold. Broken-down cars were a major reason for customers no longer making their car payments, so Ugly Duckling offered repair contracts to their used car customers. Not surprisingly, these optional contracts were financed.

Since many Ugly Duckling customers did not have credit cards, the company allowed them to pay cash for their monthly installments at their dealerships. Most car dealers did not give customers that option.

In 1994 Ugly Duckling acquired Champion Financial Services from Steve Darak. Champion became a subsidiary and Darak became Ugly Duckling's chief financial officer. Acquired mainly because of its management's skills and its contract servicing software, Champion Financial became Ugly Duckling's second source of making money. When it was purchased in 1994, Champion had subprime contracts worth $1.9 million.

Through a network of branch offices, the first one opening in April 1995, Champion Financial Services purchased subprime car installment contracts from third-party used car dealers. Those contracts generally were with customers with more resources than those who purchased a used car from an Ugly Duckling dealership.

At the end of 1995, after four years in business, Ugly Duckling's financial picture was quite mixed. The good news was that total revenues, of which used car sales comprised the bulk, had consistently increased, reaching $58.2 million ($47.8 million from car sales alone) at the end of 1995. In three of those four years, however, the company lost money, including losses of $2 million and $4 million in 1994 and 1995, respectively.

Growth and Competition in 1996 and 1997

In April 1996 the Arizona firm of Ugly Duckling Holdings, Inc. reincorporated in Delaware under the new name of Ugly Duckling Corporation. As Ugly Duckling expanded its used car sales, it simultaneously reduced its rental car business. By August 1996 it had closed more than 100 rental franchises, leaving about 40 still in operation. The firm planned to completely end that type of business when its last franchise contracts expire within ten years.

In June 1996 Ugly Duckling became a public corporation. On the NASDAQ under the symbol ''UGLY,'' its initial public offering consisted of 2.3 million shares of common stock sold at $6.75 per share. It was underwritten by Cruttenden Roth Inc. of Irvine, California. Later in the month more stock was sold for a total of 3.1 million shares. That month's offerings raised $17.8 million in additional equity, including $14.8 million in cash and the conversion of $3 million in subordinated debt to common stock. The firm raised $65 million in its secondary stock offering at $15 per share in November 1996, underwritten by Cruttenden Roth and also Friedman, Billings, Ramsey & Company of Arlington, Virginia. Ugly Duckling used funds from these stock offerings to open a new Arizona dealership but mainly to reduce its total debt from $49.8 million in 1995 to $26.9 million at the end of 1996.

In 1997 Ugly Duckling continued to raise money through stock sales and other means. In February 1997 it announced that it had sold to institutional investors five million shares of common stock at $18.625 per share. The investors included Boston's Wellington Management Company and Fort Lee, New Jersey's Kramer Spellman L.P., the owner of 5 percent of Ugly Duckling's shares. Some stock analysts were surprised by the success of this offering, since many stocks in the subprime auto sales and financing industry had declined recently by about 30 percent. In the February 12, 1997 *Wall Street Journal,* one of Kramer Spel-

Key Dates:

1977: Ugly Ducking is formed.
1990: Ernest Garcia II acquires the assets of bankrupt Ugly Duckling.
1994: Ugly Duckling buys Champion Financial Services.
1996: Ugly Duckling goes public on the NASDAQ.
1997: The company undergoes aggressive expansion in Florida, Texas.
2002: Ugly Duckling is taken private in a management buyout, becoming DriveTime Automotive Group.

lman's managers stated, "There are good companies and bad companies and I think we're seeing some of the shakeout."

That same article described how Ugly Duckling was taking advantage of the problems in other car financing companies. In early 1997 Mercury Finance admitted to "accounting irregularities." Chairman Garcia said that 30 of his 35 managers formerly worked for Mercury, adding, "Up until last week it [Mercury Finance] was a great thing. Whatever their problems . . . for 12 years they were the leader in the industry and we consider their people to be the best trained."

In May 1997 GE Capital increased its line of credit available to Ugly Duckling Corporation from $50 million to $100 million. Under the terms of that Revolving Credit Facility, GE Capital had the power to limit Ugly Duckling's decisions such as incurring more debt, making loans or cash advances to company leaders, paying dividends, and merging with another firm.

Ugly Duckling announced in July 1997 that it had signed an agreement with First Merchants Acceptance Corporation to provide it up to $10 million in "debtor in possession" financing. Earlier First Merchants had filed a Chapter 11 bankruptcy petition, so the Bankruptcy Court had to approve any financing provided by Ugly Duckling to First Merchants.

Ugly Duckling aggressively opened several used car dealerships in 1997. It started in January by purchasing five subprime car dealerships and $35 million in finance contracts from Seminole Finance Corporation in the Tampa/St. Petersburg, Florida area. In April 1997 it completed its acquisition of some of the assets of E-Z Plan, Inc., a subprime sales and finance firm based in San Antonio, Texas. For $26.3 million, Ugly Duckling purchased seven "Red McCombs EZ Motors" used car dealerships, including vehicle inventory and finance contracts. The same week it also opened its first dealership in Las Vegas. Later in the year it added two other dealerships in New Mexico.

By August 1, 1997, Ugly Duckling operated a total of 24 dealerships in Arizona, New Mexico, Florida, Texas, and Nevada, which made it the largest public "buy here, pay here" chain in the nation. Most dealerships included 100 to 300 used vehicles of all kinds, ranging in age from five to ten years old with an average price of about $7,100.

In addition, Ugly Duckling by August 1, 1997, operated a total of 64 branch offices in 17 states. These offices had purchased finance contracts from about 2,710 third-party dealers through Champion Financial Services, Inc. The finance contracts purchased by Ugly Duckling from third-party dealers usually required customers to buy casualty insurance within 30 days of purchasing a vehicle. Most bought insurance on their own, but Ugly Duckling was able to purchase a policy for them and then charge them the premiums. The firm through its Drake Insurance Agency subsidiary contracted with American Bankers Insurance Group to force customers to get their car insurance. By the end of December 1996 Ugly Duckling had signed up through this process about 1,200 customers. Although not a major part of Ugly Duckling operations, the firm was considering expanding its services to cover life, disability, and unemployment insurance.

In September 1996 Ugly Duckling announced that it was adding a third revenue generator to its portfolio, to supplement its used car sales and Champion Financial income. It formed Cygnet Finance, Inc. as a subsidiary to offer a source of alternative credit to buy-here pay-here independent used car dealers. Ugly Duckling's leaders felt that many of the nation's independent dealers were undercapitalized and had trouble gaining access to more traditional sources of financing, so Cygnet could bridge that gap. By the end of 1996 Cygnet had hired a former GE Capital employee to be Cygnet's vice-president, tested its proprietary software used to closely monitor participating dealers, and enrolled its first independent dealer in its finance program.

To promote these various services, in November 1996 Ugly Duckling hired two new advertising firms. First, it replaced Moses & Anshell of Phoenix with the Riester Corporation of Phoenix to conduct its general marketing. Second, it hired the Dallas firm Dieste & Partners to start Ugly Duckling advertising in Spanish. With the number of Spanish speakers rapidly growing in the Southwest, that last move was indeed timely.

Since loan defaults were an obvious problem in Ugly Duckling's industry, the firm used its Champion Acceptance Corporation to verify loan application data and use collection techniques for both owned and serviced loans.

Ugly Duckling's overall financial performance showed definite improvement in 1996, when total 1996 revenues increased almost 30 percent to $75.6 million. Instead of losing money as it had in 1992, 1994, and 1995, Ugly Duckling in 1996 had net earnings of $5.9 million. The company's first quarter 1997 report showed revenues of $30.6 million, up 58 percent from first quarter 1996, and net earnings reached $3.3 million, compared with $1.1 million in first quarter 1996.

This 1997 expansion was reflected in the number of company employees. From 652 employees on December 31, 1996, the firm had increased to 1,776 employees by early September 1997.

Although Ugly Duckling had made major strides in just a few years, it faced some tough competitors in the late 1990s. The used car business really boomed in the 1990s, with many players entering this volatile industry. The basic incentive was that used cars earned about a 10 percent profit per car, compared with just 2 percent for each new car sold. Many new car dealers and rental car agencies began selling their good used cars. In addition, several large companies entered the used car market. For example, Circuit City started CarMax, a huge chain of used car dealerships. Another player was AutoNation, USA, which purchased Alamo-Rent-a-Car to have a ready source of more than 100,000 used cars every year. Of course, many of these operations sold newer cars to more affluent customers than those targeted by Ugly Duckling.

Although Ugly Duckling gained most of its revenue from used car sales, that percentage dropped significantly from 82 percent in 1995 to 71 percent in 1996. The firm in 1996 saw major increases in its revenues from interest income, gain on sale of loans, and servicing and other income. Since the company financed almost all the cars it sold, one analyst in the November 11, 1996 *Washington Post* said Ugly Duckling was "a bank masquerading as a used-car lot." That was a good way of describing what seemed to be Ugly Duckling's strategy: to continue to sell used cars but also strive to be a major player in the financial and credit aspects of the subprime used car retail industry.

Still Expanding in the Late 1990s

As the chain expanded across the Sun Belt to 46 dealerships, Ugly Duckling's sales continued their impressive growth, rising 150 percent to $191 million in 1997. Net income rose from $5.9 million to $9.4 million.

The group's buying power meant it could stock its lots with more vehicles than the Mom & Pop's that made up most of the country's 58,000 independent car dealers. "And as far as we know, there's not a significant regional or national competitor," Chief Financial Officer Steven T. Darak told Knight Ridder's *Dallas Morning News.* Ugly Duckling also could afford to buy much more advertising, CEO Gregory Sullivan told the *Wall Street Transcript* in 2000.

In 1999, Garcia made a brief takeover run at an Ohio rival, troubled National Auto Credit Inc. After building up a 10 percent holding and gaining voting control from one of National's majority owners, Garcia sold his shares back to the company at a premium.

Ugly Duckling closed its Champion Financial Services branches in early 1998 to focus on lending operations at its own dealerships. At the time, the company was providing financing or collections assistance to two bankrupt auto lenders, First Merchants Acceptance Corp. of Deerfield, Illinois and Reliance Acceptance Group Inc. of San Antonio.

Garcia bought Ugly Duckling's Cygnet Deal Finance unit for about $37.5 million in late 1999, about a year after its planned spinoff was canceled. CEO Greg Sullivan told the *Arizona Republic* that Cygnet, which provided financing to other dealers, was sold off to make Ugly Duckling more of a pure player in used car sales for investors. Garcia soon formed the Zoomlot.com e-business venture to attract independent dealers to Cygnet. Ugly Duckling's other businesses, apart from the dealership chain, were divested by December 1999.

Ugly Duckling also was embracing the Internet as a way to connect to its own customers. According to Sullivan, many were leery of applying for a car loan in person due to the potential embarrassment of rejection. Around the beginning of 1999, the company installed its proprietary "CLASS" Car Loan Accounting and Servicing Software, Sullivan told the *Wall Street Transcript.* This allowed the transaction, from car purchase through the life of the loan, to be managed through one source. Ugly Duckling sold 46,120 used vehicles in 1999. Profits rose from $3.5 million to $8.7 million. The Ugly Duckling company itself also made two acquisitions in 1999, in Orlando, Florida and Richmond, Virginia. According to Sullivan, it was the only dealer actively acquiring others that year.

By the beginning of 2000, the chain had 72 dealerships, making it one of the largest of the country's 60,000 independent car dealers. Ugly Duckling had annual sales of $541.7 million in 2001, when it employed 2,200 people. According to Sullivan, the subprime auto market was a $100 billion-a-year industry.

The company's corporate headquarters was moved to a former Mega Foods grocery store in 2001. The abandoned big box location may have seemed like an unusual choice but the *Business Journal* of Phoenix praised its economical approach and clever renovation.

In January 2002 Garcia and Sullivan bought Ugly Duckling for $15.5 million. Garcia owned 65 percent of shares before the deal and 92 percent afterward. The company name was changed to DriveTime Automotive Group Inc. Seeking to publicize its new name and expand its client base, the company hired the advertising firm O'Leary and Partners in 2003, dedicating some $10 million for radio and television advertising. Management of the newly restructured DriveTime also sought to computerize and streamline its inventories, investing in new business intelligence software for those purposes.

Principal Competitors

AutoNation Inc.; CarMax; Ricart; Sonic Automotive Inc.; United Auto Group Inc.

Further Reading

Box, Terry, "Dallas Dealership's Low-End Car Sales Rake in High-End Profits," *Knight Ridder/Tribune Business News,* June 2, 1998.

Byrne, John A., "Keeping Out of Mischief Now," *Forbes,* October 8, 1984, p. 238.

Cecil, Mark, "Chairman Garcia: Gimme All of Ugly; Ugly Chairman Needs Someone to Show Him the Money, However," *Mergers and Acquisitions Report,* September 25, 2000.

"Chain of Used Car Dealers Is Bought by Its Chairman," *New York Times,* December 11, 2001, p. C4.

Croft, Nancy L., "It's Never Too Late," *Nation's Business,* September 1986, p. 18.

Dunaj, Diana, "Ugly: Tucson Car Rental Firm Turns Beautiful Profits," *Arizona Business Gazette,* December 30, 1985, p. A1.

Eldridge, Earle, "Ugly Duckling Fits Bill for Drivers with Bad Credit; Car Chain Charges High Interest to Fill Buyers' Needs," *USA Today,* August 17, 2000, p. 6B.

——, "Ugly Duckling Officers See Beauty of Going Private," *USA Today,* January 22, 2002, p. 10B.

Elliott, Alan R., "Swan-To-Be," *Investor's Business Daily,* October 14, 1996.

Flass, Rebecca, "O'Leary Invites 'Credit-Challenged' to DriveTime," *ADWEEK,* Western ed., January 28, 2004.

"Gauger + Santy Rebrands Ugly Duckling," *ADWEEK,* Western ed., September 2, 2002, p. 6.

Giblin, Paul, "Ugly Duckling Looks to Turn into a Swan with Expansion," *Arizona Tribune,* August 25, 1996.

Gregory, Michael, "Duckling Works Subprime Niche," *Private Placement Letter,* August 7, 2000.

Knight, Jerry, ''Dealing in Stock Cars, Both New and Used,'' *Washington Post,* November 11, 1996, p. WB27.

Miller, Joe, ''Ugly Duckling Keeps Cygnet in the Fold,'' *Automotive News,* October 12, 1998, p. 44.

Murray, Teresa Dixon, ''National Auto Credit Agrees to Buy Out Major Shareholder,'' *Plain Dealer* (Cleveland), May 14, 1999, p. 2C.

Nickell, Naaman, ''Phoenix, Ariz.-Based Used-Car Dealership Continues to Grow,'' *Arizona Republic,* January 24, 2000.

''Prizes Found in Empty Boxes,'' *Business Journal—Serving Phoenix & the Valley of the Sun,* October 19, 2001, p. 62.

Pulliam, Susan, ''Ugly Duckling, Subprime Auto Lender Run by Convicted Felon, Manages to Raise Money,'' *Wall Street Journal,* February 12, 1997, p. C2.

Root, Kim O'Brien, ''Newport News, Va., Used-Car Dealership Is Sued Over Name,'' *Daily Press* (Newport), October 21, 2004.

Sawyers, Arlena, ''Ugly Duckling Thriving in Subprime Pool,'' *Automotive News,* June 12, 2000, p. 40.

Serres, Christopher, ''Nat'l Auto Interests Rival CEO: Ugly Duckling Exec Owns 7% of Car Lender,'' *Crain's Cleveland Business,* September 21, 1998, p. 5.

Swafford, Michelle, ''Two Arizona-Based Auto Businesses Battle Over 'Drive Time' Name,'' *East Valley Tribune* (Mesa, Arizona), September 17, 2002.

Teichgraeber, Tara, ''Garcia's Latest Venture Puts Car Lots on Superhighway,'' *Business Journal—Serving Phoenix & the Valley of the Sun,* May 12, 2000, p. 10.

''Ugly Duckling Corporation CEO Discusses Product Line,'' *Wall Street Transcript,* June 12, 2000.

''Ugly Duckling Offering Shareholders a Way Out,'' *Arizona Republic,* December 20, 1998, p. D1.

Vandeveire, Mary, ''Sub-Prime Auto Lending Expanding Operations Here,'' *Business Journal—Serving Phoenix & the Valley of the Sun,* March 13, 1998, p. 4.

—David M. Walden
—update: Frederick C. Ingram

Dynea

Snellmaninkatu 13
Helsinki
FIN-00170
Finland
Telephone: +358 10 585 2000
Fax: +358 10 585 2001
Web site: http://www.dynea.com

Private Company
Incorporated: 2001
Employees: 3,200
Sales: EUR 1.1 billion ($1.32 billion) (2003)
NAIC: 325211 Plastics Material and Resin Manufacturing; 322222 Coated and Laminated Paper Manufacturing; 325520 Adhesive and Sealant Manufacturing

Dynea is a world-leading producer of industrial adhesives and adhesive resins. The Helsinki, Finland-based company, formed from the merger of Neste Chemicals, part of Scandinavian oil giant Fortum, and the specialty chemicals business of explosives maker Dyno Nobel in 2001, produces a wide range of adhesives, resins, hardeners, and overlays. Dynea's products include panel board resins used for forming particle board, medium density fiberboard (MDF), oriented strand board (OSB), and laminated veneer lumber (LVL), as well as plywood. The company produces a variety of wood and specialty adhesives, with applications such as parquet flooring, doors, wood panels, I-beams, windows, cabinets, and kitchen and other furniture, as well as specialty adhesives for bookbinding, shoes, packaging, labels, and the like. In response to stricter environmental emissions legislation, Dynea has introduced a formaldehyde-free adhesive in 2004. Dynea's industrial resins business provides the support for such applications as insulation backing, laminates, impregnated papers, abrasives, and others. The company also produces industrial and decorative paper overlays for diverse applications, including home furnishings. Dynea is an internationally operating company with manufacturing sites in 26 countries, including much of Europe and in North America, while Asia represents its fastest-growing market in the early 2000s. Privately held Dynea is controlled by Swedish investment group Industri Kapital. In 2003, the company reported sales of approximately EUR 1.1 billion ($1.32 billion).

Finnish Oil Origins in the 1950s

Dynea grew out of Finland's efforts to develop its own oil industry during the years following World War II. The country's total dependence on oil imports had left it vulnerable at the outbreak of war, and prompted the creation of a fuel reserve body, the PVA, which was placed under the Ministry of Defense. The PVA launched its first oil company, NKV, which developed storage facilities for the country's fuel oil and lubricants reserves in the coastal caves near Naantali.

At the end of the war, the NKV was incorporated as a state-owned company and placed under the oversight of the Ministry of Trade and Industry and extended its operations to include importing, wholesaling, and transporting oil and derivatives. The company's charter also called for it to develop its own refining and production capacity. The company, which remained controlled by the Finnish government throughout the rest of the century, was then incorporated as Neste (the Finnish word for ''liquid'') in 1948.

Neste's start was rocky—its first oil tanker proved financially ruinous, then a fire broke out in its cave-based storage facilities. Neste also met with resistance from the government, close to the major oil companies, for its plans to build its own refinery. Neste only received permission to construct its first refinery in 1954. Built in Naantali, the first Finnish refinery launched initial production in 1957. At its inauguration, Neste confirmed its intention to extend its refining operations into petrochemicals in the near future.

The Naantali site quickly ramped up capacity from 700,000 tons to 1.2 million tons per year, then doubled capacity again in the early 1960s. At the same time, Neste began designing a second refinery, to be based in Porvoo, near Helsinki. The new refinery was designed from the outset for the production of petrochemicals as well.

With the launch of refinery operations at the Porvoo site in 1967, Neste moved ahead with its plans to build petrochemicals

> **Company Perspectives:**
>
> *Dynea's strategy for global growth includes strengthening our presence in Asia for all our businesses. Investments in both China as well as Thailand show Dynea's commitment to meeting the needs of our fast-growing customer industries in these markets.*

capacity. In 1968, the company launched a plan to construct two production units, the first for ethylene and the second, in a joint venture, for polyethylene and polyvinylchloride (PVC). Production at both units began in 1972.

Neste's success encouraged the development of other petrochemicals operations in Finland, while petrochemicals production emerged as a major part of Neste's own business in the 1980s. Neste began extending its operations through acquisitions during the late 1970s. Neste took over the joint venture formed to produce PVC in 1979. By then, it also had acquired another petrochemicals business, Priha, which developed as an important Finnish adhesives manufacturer. That company had been formed in nearby Hamina in 1968 by the Priha family as a producer of adhesive resin. In 1981, Neste restructured its operations, creating a number of individually operating business units, including Neste Chemicals.

Creating an Adhesives and Resins Specialist in the 1990s

Through the 1980s, Neste's chemicals division represented the company's fastest-growing operation. By the end of the 1980s, Neste Chemicals was not only the leading petrochemicals company in Finland, but represented a major player in the European and world petrochemicals markets as well. Although plastics remained the division's core market, Neste also grew strongly in the adhesives and industrial resins market. In the early 1980s, the division had success with the development of a plastic-impregnated wood, Neswood, used for flooring.

Neste Chemicals strengthened its adhesives business through acquisitions in the late 1980s and early 1990s, such as that of Chembond in the United States in 1988, and of MCN, in The Netherlands, in 1991. The company returned to North America the following year, buying up the resins business of Reichold's in Canada.

The Finnish government began preparations for the privatization of Neste in the early 1990s. In 1994, the company launched a new and further-reaching restructuring program. As part of that process, the company broke up its chemicals division, spinning off its main petrochemical and plastics operations into a new joint venture formed with Sweden's Statoil called Borealis A/S. Neste Chemicals now regrouped around a core of adhesives and industrial resins. The company continued looking for growth opportunities, and particularly for acquisitions beyond Finland. In 1997, for example, Neste Chemicals acquired Krems Chemie in Austria—for which the company went head to head with Norwegian rival Dyno Industrier—and the resins operations of Condea in Germany.

That year marked the next stage in Neste's privatization program, as Neste merged with the state-owned Finnish electric power group Imatran Voima Oy (IVO). The merged company later was renamed as Fortum Oil and Gas Oy in 1999. Meanwhile, Fortum had continued its restructuring around newly defined core operations. As a result, Fortum sold off Neste Chemicals to Swedish investment group Industri Kapital that year. Scandinavia-oriented Industri Kapital had been formed in 1989 to acquire and develop investments in the region. Among the companies in Industri Kapital's ownership portfolio were Noviant of Finland and Alfa Laval of Sweden. Soon after its acquisition of Neste Chemicals, Industri Kapital made another strategic purchase, of Denmark's Dyno Industrier. That company was then renamed as Dyno Nobel.

The new name highlighted Dyno's dual core of adhesives on the one hand, and explosives on the other—including its link to the company founded by Alfred Nobel in 1865. Nobel invented dynamite in 1876, and explosives were to remain a major component of the company through the next century. Yet in the mid-20th century, Nobel expanded into the specialty chemicals field as well, establishing Dyno Kjemi Norge in 1949.

Dyno's expansion into adhesives started in the mid-1970s, with the acquisition of The Netherlands' Methanor. The company also established a foothold in China in the early 1980s, when it produced four turnkey plants for the production of formaldehyde and panelboard resins for the Chinese government. In 1989, the company's adhesives business took a step forward with the purchase of the formaldehyde operations of Ciba-Geigy, based in the United Kingdom. Formaldehyde was a primary ingredient used in a number of adhesives applications, such as in the preparation of parquet flooring.

Dyno looked to the Far East for further expansion in the 1990s. In 1991, for example, the company acquired an adhesives business in Indonesia. At mid-decade, the company made a number of acquisitions in the regions, adding operations in Vietnam and Thailand, and a representative office in Shanghai, in 1996. Closer to home, the company also acquired Sweden's GlueStick AB. In 1999, after losing out to Neste Chemicals in the battle for Krems Chemie, Dyno acquired fellow Danish adhesives group Nordcoll. Under Industri Kapital, Dyno was renamed as Dyno Nobel in order to emphasize its roots as an explosives pioneer.

Leading Adhesives Group in the New Century

Industri Kapital moved quickly to merge Dyno's specialty chemicals business with that of Neste Chemicals, creating Nordkemi in 2000. The new company represented one of the world's leading adhesives and industrial resins groups, with some EUR 1 billion ($900 million) in sales per year. By 2001, however, Nordkemi had settled on a new identity: Dynea.

That year marked a turning point for Dynea. On the one hand, parent company Industri Kapital had acquired Perstop, based in Sweden, earlier that year—with an eye on folding part of Perstop's operations into Dynea as well. On the other hand, Dynea itself made an important acquisition, buying up Finnish rival Kemira, a EUR 2.5 billion per year company controlled by the Finnish government. The addition of Kemira, which cost Dynea about EUR 1 billion, gave Dynea a leading position in the specialty resins market, particularly for the pulp and paper market. The following year, Dynea took over Perstop's resins operations.

Key Dates:

1865: Alfred Nobel founds an explosives company (later Dyno) in Denmark.
1948: Neste Oy is created as a state-owned petrochemicals group.
1949: Dyno begins specialty chemicals development.
1968: The Priha family founds an adhesives business in Hamina, Finland.
1971: Neste launches petrochemicals production.
1976: Dyno buys The Netherlands' Methanor.
1978: Neste acquires the Priha company.
1981: Neste Chemicals is established as an independent division of Neste.
1988: Neste Chemicals acquires Chembond in the United States.
1989: Dyno expands to the United Kingdom with the purchase of Ciba-Geigy's formaldehyde business.
1992: Neste enters Canada with the acquisition of the resins business of Reichold.
1994: Neste spins off most of its specialty chemicals business into Borealis joint venture; Neste Chemicals regroups around a core of adhesives and resins.
1997: Neste merges with IVO and becomes Fortum.
1999: Industri Kapital acquires Neste Chemicals and Dyno (renamed as Dyno Nobel).
2000: Neste Chemicals and Dyno's specialty chemicals operations are merged as Nordkemi.
2001: Nordkemi is renamed as Dynea; the company acquires Kemeri of Finland.
2002: The company opens a new plant in Shanghai; the Perstop resins business is acquired.
2003: The company builds new plants in Thailand, Indonesia, and China.
2004: A MetaDynea joint venture is formed in Russia; plans are launched to build a new plant in Thailand; formaldehyde-free resin is launched.

With the consolidation of its Scandinavian and European interests mostly completed, Dynea turned its attention to its fastest-growing market, the Far East. By the early 2000s, Dynea operated production subsidiaries in a number of countries in the Asia Pacific region, including in Australia and New Zealand, Malaysia, Singapore, Thailand, Pakistan, Vietnam, and Indonesia. The company's early presence in China at last resulted in the creation of the company's own production subsidiary for that market, in Beijing in 1999. The company next boosted its operations in China with the construction of a water-based resins production facility in Shanghai in 2002.

Dynea began construction of a new panelboard resins plant in Thailand that year as well, forming a joint venture with local partners to build a facility with a capacity of 60,000 tons per year. That plant launched production in 2003. By the end of that year, Dynea had opened two more plants in the region. The first, in Indonesia, provided an annual capacity of 4,800 tons per year of water- and solvent-based adhesives. The second added to the group's Chinese presence with a panelboard and industrial resins facility capable of producing 60,000 tons per year.

Dynea continued its expansion into 2004. The company's attention turned to Russia that year, with the launch of the MetaDynea joint venture, in partnership with JSC Metafrax. The partnership began building its first resins plant in Gubakha, launching production by the end of the year. The company also began formulating plans to build a second unit serving Western Russia by 2006. Meanwhile, the company had announced a plan to extend its presence in Thailand with the construction of a large-scale formaldehyde and resins plant, with a total production capacity of 100,000 tons per year. Dynea's strong growth placed it among the top producers of adhesives and industrial resins entering the new century.

Principal Subsidiaries

Dynea ASA; Dynea Austria GmbH; Dynea B.V. (Netherlands); Dynea Chemicals Oy (Finland); Dynea Erkner GmbH (Germany); Dynea Ireland Ltd.; Dynea NV (Belgium); Dynea Finland Oy; Dynea UK Ltd.; Dynea Resins France SAS; Dynea Canada Inc.; Dynea Overlays Inc. (USA); Dynea U.S.A. Inc.; Dynea NZ Ltd.; Dynea Singapore Pte. Ltd.; PT Dyno Indria Indonesia (51%).

Principal Competitors

Borden Chemicals Inc.; Georgia-Pacific Corporation; BASF AG.

Further Reading

''Dynea Opens a Plant in Southern China,'' *Forest Products Journal,* July-August 2004, p. 6.
''Dynea Targets Formaldehyde-Free Resin Tech,'' *Chemical Market Reporter,* September 20, 2004, p. 6.
Milmo, Sean, ''IK Seeks to Buy Dyno and Unite It with Neste,'' *Chemical Market Reporter,* November 15, 1999, p. 8.
''Neste Chemicals Will Go It Alone,'' *Chemical & Engineering News,* October 18, 1999.
Preteepchaikul, Veera, ''Adhesives Maker Dynea Plans Second Plant in Southern Thailand,'' *Bangkok Post,* November 22, 2004.
Short, Patricia, ''Dynea Takes a Giant Step,'' *Chemical News & Engineering,* September 10, 2001, p. 10.
Young, Ian, ''Industri Kapital Merges Dyno and Neste,'' *Chemical Week,* August 16, 2000, p. 21.
——, ''Spin-Off Considered for Neste Chemicals Following Energy Megamerger,'' *Chemical Week,* August 26, 1998, p. 23.

—M.L. Cohen

The Echo Design Group, Inc.

10 E. 40th Street
New York, New York 10016-0200
U.S.A.
Telephone: (212) 686-8771
Toll Free: (800) 331-3246
Fax: (212) 686-5017
Web site: http://www.echodesign.com

Private Company
Incorporated: 1923 as Echo Scarfs, Inc.
Employees: 200 (est.)
Sales: $75 million (2002 est.)
NAIC: 315999 Other Apparel Accessories and Other Apparel Manufacturing

Long known as a print scarf maker, New York City-based The Echo Design Group, Inc., is an emerging lifestyle brand, involved in a range of fashion accessories as well as paper goods and homewares. Drawing inspiration from its extensive archives of patterns, some of which date to the 1800s, Echo continues to produce women's scarves under the Echo name and through licensing agreements with Ralph Lauren, Laura Ashley, Gloria Vanderbilt, and Adrienne Vittadini. Echo also makes private-label scarves for Ann Taylor, Ann Taylor Loft, Coach, Talbots, and several museums, including the Metropolitan Museum of Art, the Museum of Modern Art, the Smithsonian Institution, and Boston's Museum of Fine Arts. In addition, Echo offers women's wraps, gloves, hats, and raincoats, and men's ties. Home products manufactured under license include wallpaper, decorative fabrics and trim, bedding, bath coordinate ensembles, decorative pillows, and area rugs and throws. Echo also has taken steps to enter retailing. The company has operated a freestanding store in Hong Kong since 1999 and more recently opened an in-store location in Marshall Field's State Street store in Chicago. Sales offices are maintained in New York, Atlanta, Chicago, Dallas, Los Angeles, Toronto, Montreal, London, and Como, Italy. Echo is privately owned and operated by the family of its founders, Edgar C. and Theresa Hyman.

Launching the Company in the 1920s

After Edgar Hyman worked for two veiling companies that failed he decided to strike out on his own. According to family lore, on September 27, 1923, the day he married Theresa, he founded Echo Scarfs, Inc. He chose "Echo" because it was an acronym for Edgar C. Hyman & Co. The company set up shop in New York, eventually moving to 485 Fifth Avenue, where it would stay for 45 years. The couple's only child, Dorothy, joined the company in 1950 along with her husband, Paul Roberts. When her parents died, ownership passed to an aunt, and later to her husband. Along the way, Echo began building up its impressive archive of patterns that would form the backbone of its design unit. During the 1950s most of its manufacturing was moved offshore. In 1968 a museum commissioned the company to create a commemorative scarf, and out of this assignment emerged a customer design division. In 1973 the company began to do some private-label work. It would be the start of a strong period in the scarf industry. But it was a cyclical business and the good times came to an end in 1978, followed by an equally long period of poor sales.

Echo also was affected in 1978 by the death of Paul Roberts. Dorothy now took over the running of the company. In a 1998 interview with *Daily News Record,* she recalled, "Right after my husband died, I had one of our closest resources come to me and offer to teach me the scarf business. I had to count to 10. I grew up in this business and know it as good as anyone else." Her knowledge would be put to the test, as the scarf category endured a fallow period that lasted until 1983. She attempted to diversify the company, which now produced capes, ponchos, vests, bags, and fabric belts. But only the belts sold well, prompting Echo to beat a quick retreat. It discontinued all the new items, with the exception of belts, but even they proved a difficult sale. Although fabric belts fit in with Echo's expertise, to be a true player in the category a company needed to offer leather belts, which required a better understanding of the leather market and a different design approach. Nevertheless, belts moved the company beyond scarves, prompting a name change from Echo Scarfs to The Echo Design Group.

After surviving a tough patch, Echo resumed its growth in 1983, when it began selling in Europe. The company also

Company Perspectives:

At ECHO, we believe in four defining principles that set our products apart from the rest: design, quality, value, and integrity.

looked to build up its business through licenses. One of the most important deals struck in company history was the licensing agreement reached with Ralph Lauren. The Echo and Ralph Lauren labels used different quality fabrics and designs, allowing the scarf lines to peacefully coexist. In 1986 the company reorganized its marketing approach by creating three product groups, each targeting a different customer with a separate marketing campaign. The Ralph Lauren collection was not affected much by the change. The company now offered the Echo collection, distributed through department and specialty stores and wholesale from $4 to $30. The Club 7 line, wholesaling from $4 to $25, focused on department and career-oriented stores. (The name was meant to connote traditional styles as embodied by the Seven Sisters schools.) Finally, Echo offered its Signature collection, sold to higher quality specialty shops and department stores, wholesaling from $15 to $110. Later in the 1980s Echo would create an even more expensive line of scarves under the Ralph Lauren Collection banner. With a wholesale price ranging from $120 to $300, these were the most expensive scarves ever offered by Echo. They were made in Italy using high-grade silk, wool, and cashmere. In 1987 Echo also added a lower price point to the mix through a licensing agreement with Sarah Coventry, Inc. The new collection, wholesaling from $2 to $4, was aimed at mass merchandisers such as Kmart and marketed solely by Sarah Coventry.

Adding Belts in the 1980s

Echo enjoyed strong growth in the second half of the 1980s, despite some disappointment with belts. In 1987 the company signed a licensing agreement with Albert Nipon Co. to produce belts, small leather goods, and other accessories under the Nipon label, but there was little demand for the line. When Nipon changed ownership later in the year, its new owner indicated that it was in the market to acquire an accessories company, presenting a potential conflict of interest with Echo. Because Echo had no interest in selling out, it took the opportunity to terminate the licensing agreement. In the late 1980s, nevertheless, belt sales began to pick up for Echo.

According to *WWD,* company sales totaled $8 million in 1984 and grew to the $50 million range by the end of the decade. The company was positioning itself for further growth by gearing up to apply its design, print, color, and fabrication skills to areas beyond scarves and, for that matter, accessories. To help facilitate this move, the company began investing in computer-aided design (CAD), installing a lone work station in 1989. Major proponents of applying high-technology to the old-line business of making scarves was a new generation of family leadership eager to take an increasing level of responsibility in running Echo.

Echo hired Werner Management Consultants to help realign management responsibilities and help the company to reach the next level in its growth, which had already prompted Echo to double its showroom and office space in Manhattan. Although Roberts remained CEO and chairman, she eventually turned over the presidency and more day-to-day operational responsibilities to Charles Williams, who was not related but had been with the company for 14 years. Her son, Steven, on the other hand, had worked at Echo for the past 11 years. He was promoted to a new post, executive vice-president of marketing. A daughter, Lynn, also worked for the company, serving as vice-president of advertising, and Steven's wife, Meg Roberts, was a designer. In many respects Williams and Steven Roberts were on equal levels, but with the reorganization there was a clearer demarcation of responsibilities, with Williams overseeing operations and accounting and Steven in charge of sales and marketing. In 1993, in fact, Roberts and Williams would become co-presidents of the firm, although blood would in the end win out and Roberts ultimately emerged as the firm's lone president.

The scarf business again revealed its cyclical nature in the 1990s when minimalism took hold in the fashion industry, resulting in a drop in the sales of jewelry and accessories. Echo had no choice but to become far more aggressive in its approach to business. It beefed up its private-label segment, winning work from major retailers such as Gap, Ann Taylor, and Talbots. Echo's next major effort to diversify its product offerings came in 1992 with the launch of a men's tie division. It was a natural fit, given that the company was already well known in the silk industry and over the years had purchased large amounts of silk. Also not to be overlooked was Echo's name recognition among women, who not only bought scarves for themselves but the majority of men's ties as well. Echo went after a high price point and it took some time before the unit established itself, but after a few years of adjusting the design and presentation, the company found its place in the market. In 1998, it added a more expensive, handmade neckwear line called Echo By Hand.

Licensing Agreements Fueling 1990s Growth

During the 1990s Echo achieved much of its growth through licensing agreements. In 1993 Echo transferred its expertise to the home textile industry through several licenses. It began producing bed and bath ensembles under a Revman Industries Inc. license, upholstery fabrics under Greef Fabrics Inc., and coordinated wallcovering prints under Imperial Fabrics and Décor. Echo signed a pair of licensing deals in 1994. For the Laura Ashley name it developed a line of scarves and jewelry. The company also licensed its own name to Manetti Farrow for a line of handbags, belts, and small leather goods. In 1996 Echo applied its design capabilities to paper products, including stationery, photography albums, paper plates and napkins, and giftwrap, available through C.R. Gibson. The company also grew through acquisition in 1997, when it acquired Schertz Umbrellas, a 50-year-old company that focused on men's umbrellas under the names Tundara, Travelaire, Jewels, and Weather Original. The business was renamed the Echo Umbrellas division and its line of women's umbrellas expanded. In 1998 Echo secured a licensing agreement with leather goods maker Coach to make scarves and other accessories. Also of note in the 1990s, Echo took its first steps into retail, opening a freestanding store in Hong Kong's Harbour City Mall, selling scarves, rainwear, umbrellas, and cold-weather items. The store

Key Dates:

1923: The company is founded.
1950: Dorothy and Paul Roberts come to work for the family company.
1978: Dorothy Roberts heads the company following her husband's death.
1983: The company begins selling in Europe.
1992: The men's tie division is launched.
1996: Paper products are added.
1999: A retail store in Hong Kong opens.
2003: Homeware products are expanded through the Creative Bath Products license.

had the potential to serve as a prototype for future Echo retailing operations in the United States. Coinciding with its 75th anniversary in 1998, the company also tried its hand at publishing. It released a coffee table-sized home design book, *A Home for All Seasons,* authored by Meg and Steven Roberts. The book proved so successful that it was followed up in 2001 by a second title, *Time at Home.* Retailers were especially pleased to see Echo grow its own brand name, which to customers embodied an enduring sense of style and fashion and could be more fully exploited to the benefit of both Echo and its retail partners.

With the start of the new century, Echo continued to build on its brand and broaden its product offerings. The company took an interest in gloves, an item it felt had been long neglected. It launched a line under its own name and one under Ralph Lauren. Echo added to its leather goods line in 2000 by acquiring Monsac Corp., which offered luxury handbags, accessories, and travel-related items. In 2001 Echo licensed its name to Kravet Fabrics Inc., a major decorative textile distributor, to produce a line of fabrics and trimmings. The next product area to which Echo felt it could effectively transfer its design capabilities was rugs. Echo's vice-president of marketing, Tracey Nelson, told *Home Textiles Today,* "We're known for our patterns and colors, so what better vehicle for pattern and color than area rugs. It's a natural extension and category for us." The company signed a licensing agreement with Trade Am, a home textile manufacturer, to create a line of area and accent rugs, as well as throws and decorative pillows. In 2003 Echo added to its home textile product offerings through a licensing agreement with Creative Bath Products, which would produce shower curtains, towels, bathroom accessories, and decorative pillows under the Echo Design Collection.

In 2003 Echo opened its first in-store shop in a Chicago Marshall Field's, a move that might lead to similar retail operations and perhaps, one day, freestanding stores. Although Echo had been in business for 80 years, it appeared to be on the verge of embarking on a new era, as it steadily evolved into a lifestyle brand. There remained plenty of room for growth in its existing product lines and licenses, but the company also looked to new categories, such as hats, socks and legwear, giftware, furniture, and table top. Whatever direction the company chose to take, it would remain privately owned and family-run for the foreseeable future. Over the years, the Roberts family had made it clear that it had no intention of selling despite an abundance of offers, and no interest in going public, a change that would likely interfere with the company's long-term approach to business. Steven Roberts called the buyout offers flattering, but explained to *Daily News Record,* "We don't live a grand lifestyle, but none of us need more cars or bigger houses."

Principal Operating Units

Design; Product Development; Sales and Marketing; Operations.

Principal Competitors

Burberry Limited; Emilio Pucci S.R.L.; Hollander Home Fashions Corporation.

Further Reading

Botton, Sari, "Echo Design: Sounding Out the Future," *WWD,* February 19, 1989, p. 4.
Brill, Eileen B., "The Marketing Genius of Echo Design," *WWD,* October 25, 1985, p. L30.
McKinney, Melonee, "Feedback from Its Women's Scarfs Helps Sell Echo's Ties," *Daily News Record,* June 5, 1998, p. 18.
Parr, Karen, "Echo Celebrates 75 Years," *WWD,* May 4, 1998, p. 8.
Paul, Cynthia A., "Echo of an Interesting Company," *HFD—The Weekly Home Furnishings Newspaper,* February 22, 1993, p. 33.

—Ed Dinger

Edward Hines Lumber Company

1000 Corporate Grove Drive
Buffalo Grove, Illinois 60089
U.S.A.
Telephone (847) 353-7700
Fax: (847) 353-7891
Web site: http://www.edwardhineslumber.com

Private Company
Founded: 1892
Employees: 100
Sales: $73 million (2003 est.)
NAIC: 321113 Sawmills

Edward Hines Lumber Company is a private company owned by the Hines family and based in the Chicago suburb of Buffalo Grove, Illinois. The company has deep ties to the lumber industry in the United States; its founder, a true pioneer in the field, was responsible for a number of innovations taken for granted today. While the company once owned forests in Wisconsin, Oregon, and Mississippi, along with the railroads that served these regions and interests in coal and natural gas, Hines is now focused on its lumberyard operation. The company is one of the largest building materials suppliers in the Chicago area, operating 13 full-service yards. It also maintains six specialty centers for precision components, precision staining, cabinets, millworking, woodworking, and windows. The president and chief executive of the company is Edward Hines, grandson of the founder.

19th-Century Origins

Company founder Edward Hines was born in Buffalo, New York, in 1863, the son of a ship carpenter and eldest of seven children. When he was only two years old, the family moved to Chicago, where he would attend public school. However, like many children during that period, he left school early to begin working. He was a grocer's errand boy for a spell, but soon found a position as tally boy for a Chicago lumber commission firm. Then, at the age of 14, he became an office boy for S.K. Martin & Company, a prominent Chicago wholesale lumber firm. He now learned the lumber business, mostly on the road as a traveling salesman, before returning to the home office to become a bookkeeper and general office man. He was a natural salesman and possessed the potential to become an outstanding executive. He was 21 years old when he was named secretary-treasurer of S.K. Martin, and over the next eight years he assisted Martin in the running of the firm. In 1892, Hines decided to strike on his own and start his own lumber company.

Hines raised $200,000 to launch Edward Hines Lumber Co. and recruited two of his former colleagues at the Martin Company to help him run it: L.L. Barth, vice-president, and C.F. Wiebe, secretary. In the first year of operation, Hines bought the T.R. Lyon operation and turned out 98 million feet of lumber. The second year, however, was to prove more difficult, as the United States was gripped in one of the era's periodic economic meltdowns: the Panic of 1893. Hines held on, due in large part to the help provided by Jesse Spalding, one of Chicago's legendary lumbermen.

Chicago had emerged as a major wholesale lumber market shortly after the Civil War in the 1860s because it possessed a number of natural and manmade advantages. Because it was located on Lake Michigan, it could receive raw material by boat from the region's teeming forests. In Chicago, the lumber would be milled and then delivered by train to the major eastern cities, as well as to Minneapolis and the Dakotas and as far west as Denver. As the railroad expanded into the treeless prairie states, the Chicago lumbermen were able to serve these growing populations with the building materials they needed. Trainloads of Chicago lumber were also delivered to such growing Texas cities as San Antonio and Houston. While Hines served his apprenticeship at Martin Company, there were approximately 125 lumberyards in Chicago, most of which were involved in the wholesale shipping business. As a result of its lake location and excellent railroad facilities, Chicago became the largest lumber receiving and shipping center of the world.

Acquiring Vast Tracts of Timber in the Early 1900s

Hines became the driving force among a new generation of lumbermen. In 1896, he bought out his old firm, Martin Company. A year later, the company began acquiring mills and tracts

Company Perspectives:

The integrity of Edward Hines Lumber Co. can never be compromised. Honest, fair dealings are essential with our various constituent groups, our customers, our people, our vendors, our communities and our stockholders.

of northern pine. In that year, it acquired 200 million feet of Wisconsin timber from Weyerhaeuser & Rutledge. The legendary Frederick Weyerhaeuser would become a part owner of Hines after buying out Spalding and another investor. The so-called Lumber King, who by the end of the 1800s owned more timberland than any other American, served on the Hines board of directors until his death in 1914. He and Edward Hines became devoted friends as a result of their business association. In 1898, Hines added another 150 million feet of timber by acquiring Wisconsin's McCord & Company. Another 60 million feet of Minnesota standing timber was purchased in 1900 from Chatfield & Company, which a year later sold Hines an additional 300 million feet of Wisconsin timber. Hines bought more forests, as well as a saw mill and a railroad, in a deal with Washburn, Wisconsin-based Bigelow Brothers. In 1905, Hines spent what was then the considerable sum of $3 million to acquire the White River Lumber Company in Wisconsin, adding vast tracts of timber and the town of Mason, Wisconsin. Over the next 20 years, the company continued to acquire large tracts of northern pine in Wisconsin and Minnesota. Around 1906, Hines purchased a massive tract of southern pine spread across northern Minnesota and into Canada, containing some three billion feet of timber.

Realizing that the supply of northern pine was being depleted at a fast rate, in the early 1900s Edward Hines began turning his attention to other regions of the country. He established the Edward Hines Yellow Pine Company, based in Mississippi, which became one of the largest southern pine operations in the country. He also bought large tracts of timberland in Oregon and built one of the largest mills in the Pacific northwest, located in the company-owned town of Hines, Oregon. These assets formed the basis of the Edward Hines Western Pine Company. By the end of his career, Edward Hines owned tracts of timber that stretched from Canada to the Gulf of Mexico and as far west as the Pacific. He also owned sawmills, railroads, and entire towns.

In addition to building a business empire, Edward Hines was also responsible for some important innovations in the lumber industry. He began the practice of contracting for lumber a season ahead, which allowed him to provide a reliable delivery schedule to customers. He created the car card certificate system, whereby lumber was graded at the mill by inspectors and a record was placed in a sealed envelope in the railcar. Furthermore, he started the practice of trademarking each piece of lumber along with an indication of its grade, so that consumers could be certain of what they were receiving. He also developed the branch-yard system to better distribute lumber locally, leading to multiple retail outlets where both contractors and small consumers could inspect the lumber before buying it. By 1930, Hines operated 27 of these outlets in the Chicago area. In addition to bringing much needed changes to the lumber industry, Edward Hines served on the boards of a number of other lumber companies and banks. He served two terms as the president of the National Lumber Manufacturers' Association and remained a member of the executive committee for several years. He also served as the president of the Lumbermen's Council of the National Union, the president of the Lumbermen's Association of Chicago, and was a board member of the Northern Hemlock & Harwood Manufacturers' Association. Moreover, he was engaged in many philanthropic activities.

A New Generation Takes the Helm in the Early 1930s

In June 1930, Edward Hines suffered a severe heart attack. Although he recovered, his participation in running his business and in other activities was now limited. He contracted a case of pneumonia in November 1931, and after lapsing into a coma he died on December 1, 1931. His sons, Charles and Ralph Hines, took over the Edward Hines Lumber Co. An elder son, Edward Hines, Jr., had died in combat during World War I. Charles, the second son, dropped out of Yale University because of illness and in 1923 went to work for some of his father's companies. Ralph, the youngest, earned a degree at Yale and also studied at Oxford before going to work for the Edward Hines Lumber Co.

Upon the death of their father, Charles joined Ralph at Hines and helped to guide the company through the difficult Depression years. Hines benefited from the need for construction supplies in the building of the 1933 Chicago's World Fair and the rebuilding of the Chicago Stockyards, destroyed by a fire in 1934. When the United States entered World War II, Ralph joined the U.S. Navy and Charles became president of Hines. During the war, the company did a great deal of business resulting from the construction of the Great Lakes Naval Depot and other military bases and camps. After the war, Hines thrived as returning servicemen began raising families, resulting in the Baby Boom generation and spurring the rapid growth of housing developments in the Chicago suburbs. During the 1950s, Hines continued to display an innovative spirit. It claimed to be the first Chicago-area lumber dealer to open a millwork facility and by the middle of the decade was offering builders such items as pre-hung doors and glazed windows to help them speed up the construction process.

A Public Company in the 1980s

Charles Hines retired in 1979, and a year later the company went public. Although the company had a float of just 1.8 million shares, traded on an over-the-counter basis, Hines began to attract the attention of major investors by 1984, due in large part to the value of its underlying assets. From the sale of timber properties and sawmills, the company had nearly $12 million cash in the bank. It was also overly conservative in the reserves it held as well as owning a Louisiana gas exploration and drilling company and a 34.5 percent interest in Southern Mineral Corp., a firm that leased oil-and-gas drilling right. Finally, Hines operated ten Chicago wholesale lumber yards, another 15 do-it-yourself stores, and 11 warehouses spread throughout the Midwest and Southwest.

To some observers, the lumber business could produce much better results if new management were brought in to

Key Dates:

1892: Edward Hines starts a lumber company.
1905: White River Lumber Company is acquired.
1931: Edward Hines dies and is succeeded by his sons Charles and Ralph.
1980: The company goes public.
1985: Edward Hines III takes the company private as a retail operation.
1997: The company is restructured to focus on lumber.

replace the Hines family, which controlled an estimated 40 percent of the company. Edward Hines III now served as president and CEO. New York and Connecticut investors with a 23 percent stake hired the New York banking firm of Rothschild Inc. to advise them on how to force the company to maximize the value of their investment. In response, Hines hired Salomon Brothers Inc. to help it consider what steps to take in the best interests of shareholders, including a possible sale of assets or a merger. In reality, there was little chance of a merger because of the variety of assets the company held. Consequently, in 1985 the company formulated a plan of liquidation under which Edward Hines purchased the wholesale lumber yards and the do-it-yourself centers and the rest of the assets were sold off.

Strategies New and Old in the 1990s and Beyond

The stripped-down version of the Hines company, generating some $100 million in annual revenues, carried on under the leadership of the founder's grandson. In 1992, the 26-unit business celebrated its 100 anniversary, taking the opportunity to launch a year-long promotional campaign. The goal was to build on customer loyalty, the erosion of which, according to Edward Hines III, was a serious trend. He told *Building Supply Home Centers,* "Some retailers neglect quality in the equation. Price is important, but too many focus only on that and ignore quality. You've got to provide the right product, for the right job, at the right price." To bolster its relations with the all-important contractor market, Hines added a number of improvements, including a second component plant, a new millwork plant, and a scanner-based purchasing system. The company also extended its reach to the southern part of the Chicago-area market by acquiring a contractor-oriented yard in Mokena, Illinois, located some ten miles from the nearest Hines yard. In 1996, Hines added another area yard when it acquired Moser Lumber Inc., a well-established business that had been operating in Naperville, Illinois, for 50 years.

At the same time, Hines also closed some of its operations as it faced increased competition from national big-box do-it-yourself retailers like Lowe's and Home Depot. Hines instituted a restructuring plan in 1997. Four stores were closed while two others were expanded. The commercial division was also expanded and relocated, and the company decided to focus on its core lumber business, targeting contractors with its remaining 16 stores and eliminating plumbing and electrical supplies. By the close of the decade, Hines would be reduced to 13 units.

At the beginning of the 21st century, Hines turned to the Internet to boost business. It launched a Web-enabled procurement program that was able to track job quotes and accept orders. The Internet hardly revolutionized the lumber business, however, but was just another tool to communicate with customers, who were still just ordering material from a lumberyard. The company's online purchasing system was slow to catch on with customers, bringing in only a modest amount of sales, and few of the customers that logged on took advantage of the system's full capabilities.

In some respects, the lumber business had not changed since a teenaged Edward Hines learned the business traveling throughout the Midwest. Nevertheless, there were changes in the business. In order to continue to thrive, the company employed a new formula to better serve the professional market, supplementing conveniently located full-service lumberyards with a number of specialty centers offering millworking, cabinets, windows, doors, decking, and staining capabilities.

Principal Subsidiaries

Hines Precision Components; Hines Precision Staining; Muench Woodworking, Inc.

Principal Competitors

The Home Depot, Inc.; Lowe's Companies, Inc.; Seigles's, Inc.

Further Reading

"Anniversary Promo Woos Customers for Hines' 2nd Century," *Building Supply Home Centers*, April 1992, p. 32.
"A Great Lumberman Called by Death," *American Lumberman*, December 5, 1931, p. 1.
"Hines-Fitzgerald Retire Following Distinguished Careers With Company," *Update: A Quarterly Newsletter Published by The Edward Hines Lumber Co.*, spring 1979, p. 1.
Jaffe, Thomas, "Oh, What a Lovely War," *Forbes*, July 16, 1984, p. 163.

—Ed Dinger

Enodis

Enodis plc

Washington House, 40-41 Conduit Street
London W1S 2YQ
United Kingdom
Telephone: (+44) 20-7304-6000
Fax: (+44) 20-7304-6001
Web site: http://www.enodis.com

Public Company
Incorporated: 1910 as S&W Berisford Plc
Employees: 6,015
Sales: £679.4 million ($1.3 billion) (2003)
Stock Exchanges: London; NYSE
Ticker Symbol: ENO
NAIC: 333415 Air Conditioning and Warm Air Heating Equipment and Commercial and Industrial Refrigeration Equipment Manufacturing; 333294 Food Product Machinery Manufacturing; 333319 Other Commercial and Service Industry Machinery Manufacturing

Enodis plc is a leading manufacturer of commercial kitchen equipment. The company, which derives its name from the Latin for ''solutions,'' produces food preparation equipment such as choppers, grinders, mixers, shredders; storage and handling equipment, including dish carts and utility carts, counter tops, dispensers, bins, and boxes; serving equipment ranging from buffet stations, salad bars and equipment, beverage dispensers, deli display cases, and beer coolers; refrigeration installations and systems, including ice machines; sanitation and environmental systems, including ventilation, fire suppression, and washing machine systems; and cookware and kitchen tools. Enodis makes its products under a variety of brand names, including Garland, Frymaster, Lincoln, Cleveland, Welbilt, Scotsman, Vent-Master, and Belshaw. Many of the company's brands and operations hold world-leading positions in their product categories. Enodis stems from the former Berisford conglomerate, which originated in the mid-1950s. The company is listed on the London and New York Stock Exchanges. Although based in England, Enodis and its CEO operate out of the company's headquarters in Florida in order to be closer to its primary North American market. In 2003, the company posted sales of £679.4 million ($1.3 billion).

Mid-19th Century Origins

Samuel and William Berisford founded a small grocery and pharmacy in Manchester, England, in 1851. That company later grew into one of the United Kingdom's largest commodity trading groups with a variety of diversified manufacturing interests before transforming itself into the commercial kitchen equipment specialist Enodis at the turn of the 21st century.

This transition began with the arrival of William Berisford, grandson of one of the company's founders, as the head of the family business near the end of the 19th century. The company launched a secondary business in sugar wholesaling, which soon grew into the company's primary operation. S&W Berisford bought a new facility in Manchester to house its sugar business, and by the beginning of the 20th century had grown into one of the United Kingdom's largest sugar merchant houses.

S&W Berisford went public in 1910. Following World War I, the company began expanding, acquiring other sugar merchants, while also adding new activities. Such was the case with its 1926 purchase of Henderson and Liddell Ltd., another prominent sugar wholesaler. Henderson and Liddell also operated a strong canned goods wholesale business. In order to supplement that operation, Berisford acquired Liverpool-based JF Turner & Co. The company then moved its headquarters to London and focused its foods business on imports of canned goods and dried fruits.

Berisford began a drive to increase its scale following World War II, launching a new acquisition drive that added some 20 new companies to the group's scope before the beginning of the 1960s. One of the company's earliest and most important acquisitions of this period came was of Joseph Travers and Sons Ltd., a public company with interests ranging from sugar and spices to coffee, canned goods, wine, citrus fruits, and cereals.

In the 1950s, Berisford, which previously had focused on supplying England's small grocers, now recognized the potential of the new supermarket format then being introduced into

> ## Company Perspectives:
>
> *Our strategy continues to be to gain profitable market share through: passion for customer service before, during, and after the sale; focus on major markets, leading products and brands, and key accounts; and excellence in products, distribution and service.*

the country. Berisford began marketing a number of packaged foods under the Haven Protected Foods label. In 1958, the company created a dedicated subsidiary for that operation, Haven Foods Ltd., in order to roll out a more extensive line of Haven-branded products. As part of that effort, the company also built a new manufacturing facility. By the end of the 1970s, the Haven brand had grown into the United Kingdom's second-largest producer of dried currants, raisins, and sultanas, as well as a leading producer of packaged dried beans and rice.

Growing Conglomerate: 1970s and 1980s

Berisford's attention remained fixed on the British market until the late 1960s. In 1968, however, the company acquired JH Rayner Ltd, a company with trading operations throughout the world. Rayner added strong business in the cocoa and coffee trade and added to Berisford's own sugar portfolio, while extending the company into the metals trading market for the first time. The Rayner acquisition helped transform Berisford from a wholesaler into one of the world's major commodities trading groups. A large part of that transformation was credited to former Rayner chief Ephraim Margulies, who took over as head of Berisford and guided it until the early 1990s.

Through the 1970s, Berisford continued to develop its wholesale and branded foods operations. In 1970, the company created The British Pepper and Spice Company, transferring these operations from its other subsidiaries in order to group them under a single structure. Also in 1970, Berisford established a subsidiary for importing and packaging citrus fruit juices.

At the same time, Berisford began extending its manufacturing side. In 1968, the company acquired Matthew Walker Ltd., based in Heanor, Derbyshire, which produced Christmas puddings and mincemeat. Under Berisford, the Matthew Walker label was expanded to include fruit cakes for the foreign market. This extension was supported by the building of a new factory in 1979.

In 1973, Berisford acquired Berlin-based Kascho Kakao und Schokoladenwerke, a manufacturer of cocoa and chocolate products. This purchase was complemented by the addition of the Netherlands-based Wessanen Cacao in 1980. Other acquisitions made by Berisford during the 1970s including Smithfield and Swanenberg, a meat trading, slaughtering, and wool merchanting group (1973); Jarmain & Sons, a wool scourer; Tom Martin Metals Group (1976), adding that company's metal reprocessing business; Turner Curzon, a timber broker with a farm machinery distribution business (1978), and British Tanners Products (1979), acquired principally for its Gelatine Products subsidiary.

By the beginning of the 1980s, Berisford had transformed itself into a highly diversified conglomerate with sales of more than £2.17 billion. Yet merchanting and commodity trading remained the group's primary business, accounting for nearly 92 percent of its revenues and more than 66 percent of its profits.

Rebuilding in the 1990s and Beyond

Berisford gained headlines in the 1980s for its battle to take control of British Sugar. After nearly five years, including scrutiny from the British Monopolies and Mergers Commission, Berisford at last succeeded in acquiring British Sugar—only to find that the sugar market itself, faced with competition from a new generation of artificial sweeteners, was shrinking dramatically.

More difficult for the company was its attempt to diversify beyond its core foods businesses into the financial services and property markets. The company invested heavily in real estate into the late 1980s, particularly in the United States. Yet the global crash of the real estate market at the end of the decade left Berisford extremely exposed. With a debt of about £1.2 billion, the company was forced to begin a sell off some of its holdings, including British Sugar in 1990. That sale, to Associated British Foods for £880 million, helped pull the company back from the brink of bankruptcy.

Yet the sale of British Sugar also left the company without a strategic focus, as its remaining operations proved too small to carry it into the future. At this time, the company brought in a new chief executive, Alan Bowkett, in order to lead its transformation. Bowkett at first targeted the footwear industry, making a takeover offer for privately owned British shoe giant C&J Clark. However, the company's offer was rejected by the Clark family shareholders.

Bowkett then went scouting for a new direction for Berisford. In 1994, he turned to the consumer kitchen sector, paying £56 million in order to acquire Magnet, a maker of kitchen cabinetry and operator of a 200-store retail kitchen furniture and joinery chain.

The following year, Berisford found its purpose. In January 1995, the company acquired Connecticut-based Welbilt, a leading manufacturer of commercial kitchen equipment. Founded in 1929, Welbilt had expanded into the commercial foodservice industry with the purchases of Frymaster, Belshaw, and others in the early 1980s. In 1989, Welbilt added a number of other operations, including Cleveland Range, Dean Industries, Merco Products, Savory Equipment, and the Food Service Equipment Group of Alco Standard. Welbilt was particularly active in the fast food sector, which was undergoing enormous growth in the 1990s. Berisford's position as an international company provided a means for Welbilt to follow the ambitious global expansion programs of its clients, which included MacDonald's, PepsiCo (owner of KFC, Taco Bell, and Pizza Hut), and Burger King.

As Bowkett described the company's prospects to the *Sunday Times:* "The decisions on what equipment they use are taken in America and not Moscow or Peking. A feature of the industry is working with these customers to develop a product which they will apply across all their chains." Nevertheless, the United States remained a major market for Welbilt, as Bowkett explained: "Where we see further growth possibilities in America is in developing litigation-avoidance equipment. If you sell an undercooked burger to someone in California, you face a

Key Dates:

1851: Samuel and William Berisford found a small grocery and pharmacy in Manchester; under their grandson, William Berisford, the store begins dealing in the sugar merchant business.
1910: S&W Berisford incorporates as a public company.
1926: The company acquires sugar merchant Henderson & Liddell.
1945: S&W Berisford launches an expansion drive, acquiring 20 companies over next 15 years, including Joseph Tavers & Sons.
1958: The company begins manufacturing canned and other foods and establishes Haven Foods Ltd. as a subsidiary.
1968: Berisford acquires JH Rayner and becomes a leading commodities trading group.
1985: The company succeeds in acquiring control of British Sugar and expands into real estate and financial services.
1990: On the brink of bankruptcy, Berisford sells off British Sugar for £880 million.
1994: The company begins a reorientation, acquiring Magnet, a maker and retailer of kitchen furniture and joinery.
1995: Berisford acquires Welbilt in the United States and enters the commercial foodservice equipment market.
1999: The company acquires Scotsman Industries in the United States, expanding its foodservice range to include refrigeration technologies.
2000: Berisford changes its name to Enodis.
2001: Enodis sells off Magnet and refocuses as a specialized foodservice equipment group.
2002: The company sells off its non-core operations in order to focus on its core business in the U.S. foodservice market.
2004: The company launches a new range of equipment to meet the fast-food industry's attempt to introduce ''healthier'' foods.

million-dollar lawsuit. A great many of these restaurants have 100 percent turnover in their staff, and a lot of them are low-skilled people or high-school kids. They need equipment that is foolproof so that they are not going to serve up potentially hazardous food.''

By the end of the decade, foodservice equipment emerged as the clear focus of Berisford, which adopted the name Berisford Plc in 1995. In the second half of the 1990s, Berisford adopted a new strategy of providing full-service and even turnkey ''solutions'' for its customers, and the company began acquiring companies in order to flesh out its range of products. The United States, where the kitchen equipment market remained highly fragmented, became the company's main strategic focus.

In 1999, Berisford acquired Scotsman Industries Inc., paying £442 million ($700 million) in a deal later described by some observers as ''disastrous.'' Indeed, although Scotsman enabled Berisford to complete its range into the refrigeration and refrigerated equipment sector, it also exposed the company to high debt levels.

The economic slump in the early 2000s exacerbated the company's debt problems, and at the turn of the 21st century Berisford once again found itself struggling with losses. The company's share price, as investors responded only slowly to the company's transformation from the former commodity training group, also suffered. In order to highlight its makeover from a conglomerate to focused manufacturer, the company changed its name to Enodis in 2000.

Enodis added a number of small kitchen equipment manufacturers in the early 2000s. Among them was Merrychef, which produced commercial-grade microwave ovens, for £17 million in 2000. The company also began shedding its non-core businesses, including, in 2001, the Magnet kitchen business. Enodis's sell-offs continued into 2002 with the sale of Austral Refrigeration, based in Australia, and Alladdin/Temp-Rite, a Nashville-based maker of meal-delivery systems.

In 2003, Enodis briefly put itself up for sale. However, after entering talks with a number of potential buyers, the company proved unable to find a suitable purchase price and dropped the plan. Instead, Enodis turned to a new CEO, Dave McCulloch, already active in the company as its COO. In recognition of the company's strength in the United States, McCulloch moved his office to Florida to be closer to Enodis's main customers. Enodis itself remained headquartered in the United Kingdom.

Enodis continued to be hurt by the global economic slowdown that saw its core client base scale back their own expansion efforts. The trend toward healthier foods brought new concerns for the company, as customers began to shy away from the fat-rich foods offered by the fast food industry. Yet that same trend brought new hope for Enodis, as companies such as MacDonald's sought to introduce new food items in order to cater to the trend toward healthier foods. The new foods required new equipment solutions, and Enodis positioned itself to provide them. As a leading foodservice equipment producer, Enodis had performed a remarkable transformation from its grocery roots and its long history as a commodities trader.

Principal Subsidiaries

Castel MAC S.p.A. (Italy); Cleveland Range Ltd. (Canada); Cleveland Range, L.L.C. (United States); Convotherm Elektrogerate GmbH (Germany; 91%); Convotherm Ltd. (United Kingdom; 91%); Convotherm Singapore Pte Ltd. (Singapore; 91%); Enodis Corporation (United States); Enodis Deutschland GmbH; Enodis France SA; Enodis Group Ltd. (United Kingdom); Enodis Iberia SA (Spain); Enodis UK Ltd.; Frimont S.p.A (Italy); Frymaster L.L.C. (United States); Garland Commercial Industries, Inc. (United States); Guyon Productions SA (France); Hartek Beverage Handling GmbH (Germany); Jackson MSC Inc. (United States); Kysor Industrial Corporation (United States); Lincoln Foodservice Products, Inc.(United States); Linea.net, Milano SrL (Italy; 95%); Merco/Savory, Inc. (United States); Merrychef Ltd. (United Kingdom); Mile High Equipment Company (United States); New Ton Food Equipment Co. Ltd (Thailand); Scotsman Group Inc. (United States); Scotsman Ice Systems SA (PTY) Ltd (South Africa; 51%); The

Delfield Company (United States); Vent Master (Europe) Ltd. (United Kingdom); Viscount Catering Ltd. (United Kingdom); Welbilt Manufacturing (Thailand) Ltd.; Welbilt Walk-Ins, L.P. USA; Whitlenge Drink Equipment Ltd. (United Kingdom).

Principal Competitors

Robert Bosch GmbH; Aco-Service A/S; Swidnicka Fabryka Pomp Sp zoo; FMC FoodTech; Wanbao Electrical Appliance Group Corp; CIR S.p.A; Fenaco; Premark International Inc.; Stork N.V.

Further Reading

Aldrick, Philip, ''Steer Clear of the Enodis Diet,'' *Daily Telegraph*, May 12, 2004.

Davoudi, Salamander, ''Enodis Lifted by US Restaurant Demand,'' *Financial Times*, August 4, 2004, p. 21.

''Enodis Lists Its Future in the U.S.,'' *Foodservice Equipment & Supplies*, August 2000, p. 11.

''Enodis Sells Units, Changes Execs,'' *Foodservice Equipment & Supplies*, July 2002, p. 13.

''Equipment Manufacturer Changes Name to Enodis,'' *National's Restaurant News*, December 4, 2000, p. 50.

Hobday, Nicola, ''Enodis to Stay Independent, Rejects Bidders,'' *Daily Deal*, ''August 21, 2001.

Minton, Anna, ''Latin Solution at Transformed Berisform,'' *Financial Times*, May 23, 2000, p. 27.

Murray-West, Rosie, ''Enodis' Fat Business is Getting Thinner,'' *Daily Telegraph*, November 19, 2003.

Saigol, Lina, and Peter Smith, ''Four Approaches for Enodis,'' *Financial Times*, August 2003, p. 1.

Waples, John, ''Bowkett Touch Gets Berisford Back on Its Feet,'' *Sunday Times*, January 22, 1995, p. 6.

—M.L. Cohen

Environmental Power Corporation

1 Cate Street, 4th Floor
Portsmouth, New Hampshire 03801
U.S.A.
Telephone: (603) 431-1780
Fax: (603) 431-2650
Web site: http://www.environmentalpower.com

Public Company
Incorporated: 1982 as Cresci Associates
Employees: 13
Sales: $41.2 million (2003)
Stock Exchanges: Over the Counter
Ticker Symbol: EVPW
NAIC: 221119 Other Electric Power Generation

Environmental Power Corporation is a New Hampshire-based company that develops, owns, and operates electrical generating facilities using renewable energy sources and non-commodity fuels. Since its founding in the early 1980s Environmental Power has been involved in a dozen clean energy projects, using hydro, resource recovery, and waste-coal power generation facilities to produce more than 200 megawatts of electricity. Most of the company's efforts are now focused on two subsidiaries: Buzzard Power Corporation and Microgy Cogeneration Systems. Since 1993 Buzzard has operated the Scrubgrass facility in Venango County on a leasehold basis. Scrubgrass uses waste coal from abandoned mines in the area to power an 83-megawatt generator, capable of providing electricity to 83,000 homes. Moreover, Scrubgrass has saved the public an estimated $10 million in waste-coal cleanup costs, local groundwater has improved in quality, and over 500 acres of land has been reclaimed and converted into habitat sanctuaries. Environmental Power's other major operation, Microgy, uses a licensed technology to convert manure produced by dairy and hog farms and other large animal operations into a safe, renewable energy source. Environmental Power is a public company trading on an over-the-counter basis.

Industry Grows Out of 1970s Legislation

In response to the energy crisis of the 1970s and America's dependence on foreign oil, the United States enacted the Public Utility Regulatory Policy Act (PURPA) in 1978, opening the way for the alternative energy industry. Until this time only utilities could own and operate electric generating plants, but PURPA now required them to buy power from independent companies capable of producing cheaper electricity. Studies also indicated that within ten to 15 years, the United States would face a energy shortage due to the aging of power plants and the lack of new facilities ready to come online. Environmental Power was founded by two men—Joseph E. Cresci and Donald A. Livingston—neither of whom had a background in the energy industry, but they recognized that PURPA offered an opportunity to form an alternative energy company.

After earning an undergraduate degree from Princeton University and a law degree from Cornell Law School in the 1960s, Cresic practiced law in Philadelphia, Pennsylvania, before becoming the chief operating officer of Garden State Racing Association in 1969. He used that experienced to become president of Ogden Recreation Inc., where he was involved in running a resort, a parking operation, and a promotions company. In 1976 he became chief executive of G.E. Stimpson Company, Inc. and Stimpson Systems, Inc, distributors of commercial office supplies and printing products. After selling the company in 1982 Cresci began looking for a new business to become involved in. He decided to join forces with Donald Livingston to enter the alternative energy field. Livingston had a background in financial services from his days at Capital Resources, Inc. In addition, from 1974 to 1982 he served as the chief executive of Green Mountain Outfitters, Inc., maker of industrial plastic parts. Like Cresci, Livingston was seeking a new challenge after selling his company. The two men decided that Cresci's legal experience and Livingston's banking background, as well as their mutual understanding of tax-advantaged investing, made a good combination for launching an alternative energy company, which would have to face complicated regulatory and fiscal hurdles. In 1982 they founded Cresci Associates, Inc.

Cresci and Livingston initially set up shop in Boston, although they would soon open a Vermont office and ultimately relocate the corporate headquarters to Portsmouth, New Hampshire. They were hardly the only businessmen who saw PURPA as an opportunity to become involved in the energy field, but Cresci and Livingston were much both suited to deal with

Company Perspectives:

For more than two decades, Environmental Power Corporation has been 'Doing Well by Doing Good'.

bureaucratic hurdles in obtaining licenses, gaining local and state governments to approve projects, and putting the necessary financing in place. During the first several years in operation, Cresci Associates developed a successful strategy to succeed in an industry fraught with impediments. The company embraced community involvement and looked to find a balance between generating power and protecting the environment. After winning over a community with a responsive approach, Cresci Associates then had to obtain a license from the Federal Energy Regulatory Commission in order to obtain the right to develop a site. Before it actually began to build a power plant, however, the company also made sure it had in place a long-term power contract to ensure there was a market for the energy. Next, it hired the best available contractors to design and build the plant, coupled with community input to make sure the facility fit in with its surroundings. The company was also responsible for arranging the financing. For organizing and supervising a project, whether it was the upgrading of an existing facility or the building of a new plant, Cresci Associates received a supervisory developer's fee. The company would then make money when the operation was sold.

Late 1980s: A Flurry of Projects

During its first five years, Cresci Associates was involved in several projects. In Maine it upgraded and sold a 0.6 megawatt hydroelectric facility in Dover-Foxcroft. The company developed and built a 2.4 megawatt hydroelectric plant in Quechee, Vermont, and after the facility was sold off, Cresci Associates continued to run it for the new owners. Also during this period, the company upgraded a hydroelectric plant in Hartland, Vermont, to 1.8 megawatts. In 1986 it acquired Texas-based Environmental Protection Resources, which was developing plants in Lubbock and Texas City that burned municipal wastes in combination with limestone to eliminate pollutants. Cresci Associates also opened an office in Camp Hill, Pennsylvania, to develop power facilities that used coal waste. It was during this time that the company began developing the Scrubgrass plant that relied on the burning of tailings from coal mines to generate power. The company also set up a pilot program to use coal mine fires as a source of energy. Abandoned mines often produced smoldering fires that might last for decades, virtually impossible to extinguish, and were hazardous in a number of ways: The carbon monoxide they threw off made surrounding acreage uninhabitable, and the fires also caused surface cave-ins and ignited forest fires. Cresci Associates' idea was to install vents to draw hot gases from the fire that could be used to drive steam turbines and produce electricity. Moreover, by introducing oxygen, the fires burned quicker, dramatically cutting down on how long the mine fire would last. By the end of the 1980s the company had the technology in place and signed contracts with Virginia Electric & Power Co. to sell electricity generated by two coal mine fires in Virginia.

In 1986 Cresci Associates was reincorporated in Delaware and became Environmental Power Corporation, a name its founders chose to emphasize the company's dual purpose: generating power in an environmentally sensitive way. In 1987 the company was taken public and completed a $7 million stock offering. Also during that year it paid $5.4 million to West Penn Power Company to acquire Milesburg Energy Inc., which owned a decommissioned oil-fired power plant in Pennsylvania that Environmental Power wanted to upgrade, and it signed a 20-year agreement to sell the electric output of its Scrubgrass Power Station, which would come online in the 1990s. In 1988 Environmental Power paid $1.3 million for a waste-coal project in Sunnyside, Utah, and the rights to build a $96 million power plant.

Despite its promising start, Environmental Power struggled in the late 1980s to turn a profit. It lost $4.7 million on revenues of $514,341 in 1988, followed by a loss of $4.2 million on revenues of $583,026 in 1989. As a result, the company was no longer able to fund development projects, such as the Milesburg facility. The money crunch became so severe that by the spring of 1990 its auditors expressed concerns about the company's ability to "continue as a going concern." Environmental Power managed to survive as it waited for cash flow to pick up as the Scrubgrass and Sunnyside facilities became operational and could sell electricity to buyers already contracted. In July 1993 Environmental Power signed a letter of intent to be purchased by KFX Inc., a Denver environmental technology company, for approximately $36 million. A month later, however, KFX backed out of the deal, leaving Environmental Power to scrape by on its own.

The company was finally able to realize some electricity sales from its power plants in 1993, when revenues totaled $1.6 million because of the Sunnyside plant coming on line. After Scrubgrass became operational sales jumped to $30.7 million in 1994 and the company was able to post a profit of $670,000. At this point Environmental Power sold its interest in Sunnyside for approximately $6 million and its only source of income, other than investments, was the Scrubgrass plant. The company held on to the Milesburg property, which remained in the developmental stage, but in light of cheap oil and gas prices that prevailed during this period, there was little if any investor interest in backing new alternative energy projects.

A New Century and a Hard Look

Power generation revenues totaled $40.7 million in 1995, and grew to $47.9 million in 1996, when Environmental Power posted a net profit of $1.6 million. In 1997 the Milesburg project was sold for $15 million in a buyout agreement with West Penn Power Company after two years of negotiations. Sales from power generation fell off in the late 1990s but reached $48.3 million in 1999 and improved to $54.3 million in 2000. At this point management decided to take a hard look at the company and determine what course of action was in the best interest of shareholders. After considering the possibility of selling the business or simply liquidating it, Cresci and Livingston decided to use its Scrubgrass revenues to back an effort to grow the company through external means.

In 2001 Environmental Power acquired privately held Microgy Cogeneration Systems Inc. What made Microgy so attractive as a development stage company was the exclusive license it held on a Danish technology called anaerobic digestion to extract methane from animal wastes. Such systems had been in

Key Dates:

1982: Company founded as Cresci Associates.
1986: Name changed to Environmental Power Corporation.
1987: Company taken public.
1995: Sunnyside, Utah, power plant sold.
2001: Microgy Cogeneration Systems, Inc. acquired.
2003: Kam Tejwani named CEO.

use in Europe for 15 years where land was more scarce and energy prices higher. Essentially, manure was heated to hasten the release of methane gas, which was captured, stored in large bladders, and burned off to generate electricity during times of peak demand. The mostly liquid wastes were reduced during the process and could then be used for compost, fertilizer, or animal bedding. Using manure as a power-generating fuel was hardly a new concept. During the 1980s many of these projects were launched, but they were built and operated by the farmers, whose expertise was in raising animals not generating electricity. What Microgy offered was a new approach. The company would build and maintain the digesters, allowing the farmers to concentrate on their own businesses while enjoying the benefits of using a natural byproduct. Aside from the money the units brought in, they eliminated the smell and the chore of periodically cleaning up lagoons of animal waste. It was an attractive concept and easy to sell to farmers. Microgy signed contracts with Wisconsin farms, followed by an agreement with the Vermont Public Power Supply Authority. The company also began to make inroads in California, the largest dairy producer in the United States and a potentially major market for the Microgy technology.

In 2003 Cresci stepped down as CEO and Livingston as president in favor of Kam Tejwani who they recruited to take over both posts. The company's founders, however, remained very much involved in the business. Cresci stayed on as chairman of the board and Livingston as chairman of the executive management committee. Tejwani had a background in investment banking and also served as the chairman and CEO of Air-Cure Technologies, Inc., maker of air pollution control systems. Tejwani was successful in raising funds to invest further in Microgy and in order to attract greater attention to Environmental Power from the investment community, he engineered a seven-for-one reverse split of the company's stock in November 2004. As a result, the share price increased significantly, and the hope was that investors would give the company a closer look and ultimately Environmental Power would move beyond its over-the-counter status and gain a listing on a national stock exchange.

After a decade of lying dormant, Environmental Power appeared well positioned to experience strong growth in the years to come. The upside for Microgy was enormous, with the market for its equipment estimated to be $14 billion. Although other companies were also becoming involved in this form of renewable energy, there was an opening for Environmental Power to stake a significant claim in the market. Under new leadership, the company was also actively looking for acquisition opportunities to complement Microgy's business or pursue other alternative energy sources, in particular wind and solar.

Principal Subsidiaries

Buzzard Power Corporation; Microgy Cogeneration Systems, Inc.

Principal Competitors

Covanta Energy Corporation; AES Corporation; PPM Energy, Inc.; U.S. Energy Systems, Inc.

Further Reading

Barna, Ed, "Environmental Power Goes Public," *Vermont Business,* July 1987, p. 76.

Fujii, Reed, "Companies Hope to Produce Energy, Animal Feed, Compost From California Manure," *Record,* (Stockton, Calif.), September 7, 2004.

Johnson, Jim, "N.H. Firm Turns Farm Waste into Energy," *Waste News,* October 28, 2002, p. 21.

Stipp, David, "Fires in Coal Mines That Burn for Years Might Have a Use," *Wall Street Journal,* January 30, 1989, p. 1.

—Ed Dinger

Etablissements Franz Colruyt N.V.

Wilgenveld, Edingensesteenweg 19
Halle B-1500
Belgium
Telephone: (+32) 2 360 10 40
Fax: (+32) 2 360 02 07
Web site: http://www.colruyt.be

Public Company
Incorporated: 1925
Employees: 11,906
Sales: EUR 3.85 billion ($4.79 billion) (2004)
Stock Exchanges: Euronext Brussels
Ticker Symbol: COLR
NAIC: 445299 All Other Specialty Food Stores; 323119 Other Commercial Printing; 541512 Computer Systems Design Services; 551112 Offices of Other Holding Companies

Etablissements Franz Colruyt NV is one of Belgium's top three supermarket and retail companies. The company's flagship network of large-surface, deep discount Colruyt stores offers a broad range of food and non-food items. The more than 170 stores in the Colruyt network are characterized by their no-frills appearance. Items are displayed on metal shelves, the lighting is dimmed, and the company does not provide shopping bags to customers. These and other cost-cutting measures allow the company to guarantee its customers prices lower by seven to 15 percent than its competitors. The company also grinds and roasts its own coffee, under the Graindor brand. In addition to its supermarket chain, Colruyt has been building a network of convenience stores under the Okay format and is also a supplier to the Spar supermarket group in Belgium. Since the 1990s, Colruyt has diversified its retail operations, adding the DreamLand chain of toys and seasonal items, and its offshoot, DreamBaby, specializing in products for infants. Colruyt launched its organic food supermarket concept, Bioplanet, in 2001. The company has also entered France, extending into that country's cash-and-carry and catering supply markets through a series of acquisitions in the early 2000s. Colruyt is also developing plans to enter the Dutch market. In addition to its distribution activities, Colruyt controls publicly listed information technology company Dolmen and printing and packaging subsidiary Druco. Listed on the Euronext Brussels Stock Exchange, Colruyt remains controlled by the founding Colruyt family, including chairman Jef Colruyt.

Bakery to Wholesale in the 1920s

Franz Colruyt began his career as a baker in Lembeek, near the city of Halle in Belgium. In the 1920s, Colruyt recognized the potential for developing a new line of business supplying wholesale goods to local grocers. Colruyt began importing goods such as coffee, sugar, and spices, and by the mid-1920s had expanded his clientele base to include the larger Brussels area as well. In 1925, Colruyt incorporated his wholesale operation as Etablissement Franz Colruyt.

Over the next decades, Colruyt continued expanding its range of goods and emerged as one of the region's prominent wholesale groups. By the early 1960s, the company already counted some 800 independent grocers among its clientele. Coffee became a prominent Colruyt product; in 1937, Franz Colruyt established the company's own roasting house and began offering blends under its own brand, Graindor. Also during this period, Colruyt began sourcing grape varieties for bottling and selling under his own wine labels. Colruyt gained a reputation for two other product groups packaged under the company's name, sliced cheese and oils and vinegars.

Franz Colruyt was joined by his sons, one of whom, Jo Colruyt, emerged as head of the company in the mid-1960s. The younger generation led the extension of the family business into the supermarket and cash-and-carry sectors. In 1964, Colruyt began developing its store concepts under the names Super Boni, a small format store which adopted the self-service concept just then being introduced to the Belgian market.

Colruyt's focus quickly turned to exploring the larger potential of the cash-and-carry concept. Where traditional grocery stores and the new supermarkets required substantial investment in design, layout, and interior furnishing, cash-and-carry stores tended to be sparsely furnished and undecorated. Colruyt recognized that it could exploit this feature within the retail

Company Perspectives:

Colruyt is a Belgian family company that has become one of the major players in the Belgian retail network, with a unique sales strategy. With more than 170 shops throughout the country, Colruyt's aim is to enable clients to shop efficiently, at the Lowest Prices.

sphere as well. By 1965, Colruyt had extended its cash-and-carry format into the creation of a new ''discount'' supermarket open to the public.

The cost-savings generated from the stripped down format—with products displayed on metal shelves, wiring and plumbing fixtures left exposed, and customers required to supply their own shopping bags—were passed onto customers. Colruyt was able to guarantee lower prices than its competitors, with savings as high as 15 percent. In order to ensure this, the company put together a dedicated team whose job was to make the round of local grocers and report back on prices. Colruyt then adjusted its own prices accordingly; in the event that the company was unable to offer a significant discount, it often chose simply to drop the product.

Computer technology became a central part of the company's cost-saving efforts. Colruyt became one of the first supermarket groups in the world to incorporate computer technology as part of its cashier checkout process, with an IBM 360-20 in its headquarters linked to a tabulating machine in its store. Information technology was placed at the heart of the group's retail operation, enabling inventory tracking and unit pricing some 20 years and more ahead of most of its competitors. It also allowed the company to avoid the expensive retrofitting process that its competitors were later required to undertake.

Colruyt's computer department grew along with its supermarket chain, which began adding stores through the 1960s and into the 1970s. By 1976, the company had converted all of its discount retail stores to the Colruyt name. The following year, Colruyt went public on the Brussels Stock Exchange. Control of the company nevertheless remained within the Colruyt family.

The public offering encouraged Colruyt to reorganize parts of its operations. In 1979, the company regrouped its printing operations into a dedicated subsidiary, Druco. The computer department, meanwhile, had gained sufficient scale to begin providing its services to other businesses. By 1982, the computer department's scale enabled it to be reformed as a separate subsidiary, Dolmen NV. Dolmen was later spun off in a public offering in 1997.

Diversification in the 1990s

Developing its discount network remained a priority for Colruyt throughout the 1980s. The company began an ambitious expansion program to build up a national network. In 1987, Colruyt became the first retailer in Belgium to convert its stores to new bar code systems, allowing the company to achieve full automation of its restocking, ordering, and warehousing systems.

Colruyt's expansion left it in a weak financial position as recession hit Belgium at the end of the decade. The company found itself clawing its way back from near collapse, and the period encouraged the company to adopt a more cautious expansion strategy. As Jef Colruyt, who took over as company chairman from his father Jo in 1994, told *Trends:* ''We have learned the lesson that it's dangerous to grow rapidly if your financial base is weak. Since then, our strategy has been to grow step by step.''

One step in that strategy was to diversify the company's operations retail holdings beyond the supermarket sector. In 1994, the company moved into toys and seasonal goods with the acquisition of Droomland, a chain of five stores founded in 1979. Droomland featured a year-round assortment of toys, school and offices supplies, infant needs, and gifts, as well as a constantly revolving assortment of items linked to the different seasons and holidays.

Droomland originally focused on the Flemish-speaking region of Belgium. Under Colruyt, the operation extended into the French-speaking Walloon region, adopting the name Dreamworld. By 2002, with 14 Droomland stores and four Dreamworld stores in operation, the company decided to simplify the chain, converting all stores to the single DreamLand format. At the same time, the company launched an offshoot of the DreamLand concept, the infant and toddler-oriented DreamBaby. The new store format specialized in baby care articles, including nursery furnishings, car seats, clothing, and strollers.

Returning its focus to its grocery operations, Colruyt launched a number of new initiatives at the turn of the 21st century. In 1998, the company created a new subsidiary, Collect & Go, that offered Internet-based grocery shopping. Accompanying that launch was the creation of home delivery service, Collivery. Yet Collect & Go's main focus was on the development of collection sites permitting customers to pick up their own order. Starting with two sites in 1999, the company extended its network, with some 70 sites by 2002.

International Ambitions in the 2000s

Colruyt had also begun testing a new retail format, a small convenience store format under the Okay name. These stores featured just 400 square meters of selling space, with locations close to town and city centers. By the end of 2004, the company had already opened 15 Okay stores, with plans to expand the network to 150 and more through the rest of the decade.

At the same time, Colruyt began testing another supermarket format, Bioplanet, focusing on the fast-growing organic foods and alternative health products market. Featuring a large-scale supermarket format, the first Bioplanet opened in Kortrijk in 2001.

By the mid-2000s, Colruyt had gained a position as the third-largest retail distribution group in Belgium, with a respectable 17 percent share of the market. The company's strategy called for it to increase its market share to as much as 25 percent in the near future.

Belgium's small size, however, led Colruyt to begin eyeing the international market. Colruyt turned first to France, buying up Ripotot, based in Dole in the Dijon region, in 1996. That purchase brought a network of 30 Coccinelle groceries in France's eastern region, as well as the ten-store Codi cash-and-carry chain. Ripotot also gave the company a strong business serving the

Key Dates:

1925: Franz Colruyt, a baker, launches an import business for coffee, spices, and other products.
1937: The company begins coffee roasting, wine bottling, cheese slicing, and oil and vinegar bottling operations.
1950: The company enters the wholesaling sector.
1964: The company's first supermarket opens.
1965: A discount cash-and-carry supermarket format is used by the company.
1976: The cash-and-carry stores are converted to the Colruyt name.
1977: Colruyt lists stock on the Brussels Stock Exchange.
1982: The company spins off its information technology subsidiary, Dolmen.
1987: Bar coding in stores is rolled.
1994: The Droomland store chain is acquired.
1996: Ripotot, in France, is acquired.
1997: Dolmen goes public.
1998: Collect & Go Internet shopping service is launched.
2000: Doumenge, in the south of France, is acquired.
2001: Colruyt acquires BLIN, in the Brittany region of France.
2002: The company renames its Droomland and Dreamworld stores as DreamLand and launches DreamBaby.
2003: Colruyt acquires Laurus supermarket and its cash-and-carry holdings in Belgium.
2004: The company acquires France-based Galland and Mallet.

group and institutional sector. The company then began converting the larger Coccinelle stores to the Colruyt format.

Colruyt expanded its French holdings again in 2000, acquiring Doumenge Group. That company focused on supplying the group and institutional sector in the south of France, including the regions centering on Toulouse, Perpignan, and Marseilles. Moving north, the company next purchased Etablissements BLIN, based in Renne, in the Brittany region. The addition of BLIN enabled Colruyt to position itself as a nationally operating food services provider in France.

Back in Belgium, Colruyt's took a major step closer to its market share goals when it agreed to purchase the Belgian operations of the Netherlands' Laurus in 2003. That agreement brought Colruyt 21 new supermarkets under the Battard name, five new cash-and-carry stores, and a supplier commitment to 350 Spar supermarkets in Belgium. The addition boosted Colruyt's annual sales by some 16 percent; by 2004, the company sales had topped EUR 3.8 billion ($4.79 billion).

While formulating plans to enter the Netherlands in the mid-2000s, Colruyt continued to build its French presence. In 2004, the company acquired Group SA Mallet, a wholesale supplier of dry foods and fresh food products. That purchase was followed soon after by the October 2004 acquisition of Galland, based in Gap, in the Haute-Alpes region, which operated as a food distributor and retailer. By the end of 2004, international sales represented eight percent of Colruyt's total sales. While still a tiny player among such European retail giants as Carrefour, Ahold, and Delhaize, Colruyt had built a solid base for further growth in its discount supermarket and wholesale supplier operations.

Principal Subsidiaries

Ceatech Engineering; Colruyt Export; Dolmen NV; Dreambaby; Dreamland; Druco; Infoco NV; Okay; Ripotot (France).

Principal Competitors

Carrefour SA; Ahold NV; Delhaize NV.

Further Reading

Bilefsky, Dan, "Making the Cuts," *Wall Street Journal*, September 22, 2003.

Killemaes, Daan, "Colruyt: the Art of the Simple," *Trends*, vol. 58.

Osborn, Andrew, "Belgian Supermarket Starts Car Sales," *Guardian*, January 22, 2002, p. 22.

—M.L. Cohen

F. Korbel & Bros. Inc.

13250 River Road
Guerneville, California 95446-9593
U.S.A.
Telephone: (707) 824-7000
Fax: (707) 869-2506
Web site: http://www.korbel.com

Private Company
Founded: 1862
Employees: 537
Sales: $130 million (2002)
NAIC: 312130 Wineries

Based in Sonoma County, California, F. Korbel & Bros. Inc. has been known for its champagnes since the 1880s, produced through subsidiary Korbel Champagne Cellars. In addition to producing more than a dozen varieties of champagne from its vineyards and winery located along Sonoma's Russian River, Korbel also bottles less expensive sparkling wines, brandies, and sherries. The 2000-acre Korbel estate is open to the public for tours, as is the Korbel Champagne Cellars operation. Tourists can also visit the Korbel Wine Shop and Tasting Room, eat at the Korbel Delicatessen, and enjoy the Antique Rose Gardens featuring more than 250 varieties of antique roses and more than 1,000 varieties of other plants and flowers. In addition, the company runs Korbel Media, located in Beverly Hills, to handle product design, advertising, product placement, and media in house. Korbel is owned by the Heck family, which bought the business from the Korbels in the 1950s.

Origins of Champagne in the 1600s

Legend holds that a blind French Benedictine monk with heightened tasting abilities named Dom Perignon invented champagne, named for France's Champagne region. The key to making a sparkling wine was the *methode champenoise,* which allowed a second fermentation to take place in the bottle, resulting in champagne's distinctive tiny bubbles. Upon his first taste of champagne, Dom Perignon—who was most likely not blind—supposedly called out to another monk, ''Come quickly, I'm drinking stars.'' It is also likely that the first fermented sparkling wine was produced more than 100 years before Dom Perignon's birth in 1640. Much of his fame, in fact, is due to 20th century marketing than his own winemaking ability. Nevertheless, he was a skilled and influential winemaker, well ahead of his time in terms of cultivating grapes and probably the first to successfully bottle and seal champagne using Spanish corks. However, it would be other French winemakers in the 1700s and 1800s who perfected the *methode champenoise.* Champagne production in California dates to the late 1800s, when two groups—Almaden Vineyards the Korbel brothers—offered their first bottles for sale.

The Korbel brothers—Francis, Anton, and Joseph—were born in Bohemia in what is today the western region of the Czech Republic. Francis was the driving force behind the champagne business that would emerge in the United States. According to family lore, Francis was in Prague in 1848 and fired the shot that started a revolution against the monarch of the Austrian Empire. The attempt to overthrow the ruling Hapsburgs failed, and the world would have to wait almost 70 years more before another gun shot mortally wounded Arch Duke Ferdinand, the heir to the throne of what had now become the Austro-Hungarian Empire, an act that led to World War I and the downfall of the Hapsburgs. For his part in revolutionary activity, young Korbel landed in Daliborka Prison. He managed to escape, however, reportedly with the help of his grandmother who provided civilian clothes that allowed him to stroll out an unlocked gate to freedom, casually smoking a cigar. He fled to New York City, where cigars would once again play a part in his colorful story. Francis Korbel learned the craft of cigar making, a difficult way to make a living due to the trade's notorious sweatshop conditions. In fact, it was because of these conditions that the labor movement in America emerged, as cigar-maker Samuel Gompers would one day found the American Federation of Labor—the AFL of the later AFL-CIO.

Francis Korbel now left the crowded conditions of New York City for the less populated and less settled locale of San Francisco, making his way there through the Isthmus of Panama. He arrived in 1860. Korbel now turned his attention to cigar boxes, opening up a repair shop. In order to manufacture his own cigar

Company Perspectives:

Korbel Champagne Cellars has continued its pursuit of excellence for more than 120 years as America's number one selling premiere champagne.

boxes, he asked his brothers back in Bohemia to join him in San Francisco to assist in his enterprise, even though Joseph and Anton Korbel had developed skills that were not necessarily applicable to their brother's business. Joseph was a trained metallurgist, while Anton was a forger. In 1862, they formed a partnership, F. Korbel & Bros., and opened the first cigar box factory in San Francisco. It was an immediate success, and it was not long before they owned their own schooner, aptly named The Bohemia, to import veneers from around the world. They acquired more ships and became involved in the export of hardwood. They also bought timber for shipping and opened sawmills to produce lumber for use in San Francisco's booming building industry.

It was the timber that first attracted the Korbel brothers to the Russian River Valley of Sonoma County in 1872. They took on a partner to buy timber land and build a pair of sawmills. A fourth brother, Winsel, was brought in from Bohemia to run this part of the business, but he died from an illness shortly upon his arrival. The Korbel brothers elected to buy out their partner and run the lumber operation themselves. When the building boom subsided, however, they found themselves holding a lot of timber for which there was little demand. Forever resourceful, they researched what could be done with the cleared acreage and decided the land was ideal for any number of agricultural purposes. They began to grow alfalfa, beets, corn, prunes, and wheat and used some of the crops to feed cows and start a dairy.

Turning Timber into Wine in the 1880s

The Korbel brothers also began to plant vineyards on their Russian River property. They experimented with different varieties of grapes, including Pinot Noir, the favorite of winemakers in France's Champagne region. As the Korbels were supplying their grapes to California winemakers, other growers emerged, the market became too crowded, and the brothers shifted gears once again. They kept their grapes and became winemakers themselves. According to company records, the brothers were producing as much as 30,000 gallons by 1882. The winemaking operation was so promising that over the next two years they devoted all their attention to it, converting their farmland to vineyards and shutting down the diary. Again they turned to their native land for help, bringing in an experienced Prague winemaker named Frank Hasek to become their champagne master in 1884. At the time, it was believed that a suitable champagne could not be produced in California.

Hasek used the *methode champenoise* approach to making champagne and spent the next decade blending the results of different grape harvests to produce a distinctive house style for Korbel champagne. By 1894, the Korbel brothers began to sell their champagne, and the people who doubted that California could produce excellent champagne were silenced. By the end of the 1800s, Korbel was an award-winning, internationally recognized label.

The Korbel brothers' winery business was interrupted by the advent of Prohibition in 1919, forcing them to turn to other business interests. None of them would be alive to see the repeal of Prohibition in 1933 and the resumption of champagne making at the family estate. Ownership of the winery passed to a second generation, seven cousins in all, who continued the family tradition by planting more vineyards and expanding the winery building. Then, in the early 1950s, the cousins decided among themselves that the time had come to sell the business. They were careful about making sure the winery passed into the hands of someone who respected its family tradition and was committed to the *method champenoise*. The Korbels found their man in Adolf L. Heck, a young winemaker who had already made his mark.

Heck was a third generation winemaker whose family had roots in the winemaking area of Alsace Loraine straddling France and Germany. Heck's father immigrated to the United States at the turn of the 20th century, and like the Korbel brothers his winemaking career was interrupted by Prohibition. After the repeal of Prohibition, he became manager of the American Wine Company in St. Louis and succeeded in reestablishing the Cook's Imperial Champagne Cellars and the Cook's label. The younger Heck returned to Germany to study at the highly regarded Gelsenheim Institute, receiving a degree in Enology in 1938. He managed to return to the United States before war broke out in Europe in 1939. He first took a job with Sweet Valley Wine Company in Ohio, then ran a number of wineries before moving to California in the early 1950s to take over as the president of the Italian Swiss Colony Winery. Under his leadership, Swiss Colony developed one of the most successful marketing campaigns in the history of spirits, using "the little old winemaker, me" tagline for its advertisements. After four years at the helm, Heck had transformed Swiss Colony into the largest American winery. Despite this success, however, Heck's harbored a dream of owning his own cellar where he could pursue his "California Style" of cuvee, a blend of wines used to produce champagne. He believed that by cutting back on the yeast so favored by European champagnes and accentuating the fruit he could produce a champagne more suited to the American palate.

When Heck heard that the Korbel family was putting its champagne cellar on the block, he mortgaged his home, took on his brothers Ben and Paul as partners, and raised additional funds to put together an offer. Supposedly he made his bid to the Korbel family just after midnight struck preceding the day the business was put up for sale. The Korbels happily accepted the offer and placed in his hands the fate of the business their fathers had founded some 70 years earlier. When the Hecks took over, Korbel was producing just 6,000 cases a year.

Korbel under Adolph Heck: 1950s through Mid-1980s

Adolph Heck pursued his vision for California-style champagnes. In 1956 he reintroduced Korbel Brut, making it much lighter and drier than other American champagnes. He developed his own champagne yeasts and introduced Korbel Natural, Korbel Blanc de Blancs, and Korbel Blanc de Noirs. He also made innovations on the production end, inventing and patenting the industry's first automatic riddling machine in 1966. The purpose of riddling was to remove dead yeast, *remuage,* after the second fermentation. Done by hand, it was a time-consuming process

Key Dates:

1862: F. Korbel & Brothers is founded to make cigar boxes.
1884: Frank Hasek is hired as a champagne master.
1954: The Korbel family sells the company to Adolph Heck and his brothers.
1965: Adolph Heck's son, Gary, joins company full time.
1984: Adolph Heck dies and is succeeded by Gary Heck.
1997: Three Sonoma Valley wineries are acquired.
2002: Korbel sells Russian River Brewing.

that was open to a great deal of human error. The bottles had to be gradually tipped to a vertical position and turned daily over the course of a four-to-five week period to allow sediment to work its way to the cap for removal. Heck's automated process had the bottles placed upside down in racks that vibrated and rocked periodically so that the yeast was guided to the neck. Once riddling was completed, the bottles were dipped in a freezing brine solution, thus creating a frozen plug of yeast that would pop out when the temporary cap was removed. A small amount of sugar and wine was then added in a process called dosage and the bottle capped. All told, between the time the temporary cap was removed and corking took place, the champagne was exposed to the air for only approximately 25 seconds. The champagne would then sit in the winery for a month to allow the cork to soften and the dosage to blend properly.

Champagne Consumption Peaks in 1980s

Adolph Heck ran Korbel and served as its champagne master until his death in 1984. His son, Gary, took over as chairman of the board and Robert Stashak became Korbel's champagne master. Gary Heck grew up in the business. He joined Korbel on a full-time basis in 1965 and worked in almost all capacities at the winery, from working in the vineyards to acting as assistant officer manager. He became executive vice president in 1974 and was named president in 1982. He took over the company just as champagne consumption in the United States was reaching a peak in the mid-1980s after a decade-long run of success. At a time when sales of liquor, beer, and table wines were sluggish, demand for champagne and other sparkling wines was growing at an incredible clip, a 34 percent increase between 1983 and 1984 alone. In 1986, Korbel was shipping one million cases of champagne, an increase of 13 percent over the previous year. Revenues were estimated to be $76 million, a 9 percent increase. However, the good times would come to an end and champagne consumption began to slip. Moreover, the business was problematic because it had become so seasonal, with most of the product purchased during the year-end holidays.

Challenges in the 1990s and Beyond

In 1990, champagne sales in the United States declined by 7 percent. Only because of hard work was Korbel able to beat the industry average, losing just 4 percent of sales. Korbel increased it advertising and went upscale, introducing more expensive products and even limited edition bottles from fashion designer Nicole Miller and singers Frank Sinatra and Tony Bennett. It spent money on promotions in an attempt to spur non-holiday sales. Korbel sponsored a boat in the America's Cup yacht race and in 1996 became an official licensed product of the Atlanta Olympic games. In addition to champagne, Korbel also sold brandies, but it looked to diversify further in the still wine market. After launching a still wine program with a 1991 vintage, Korbel supplemented the operation through acquisition. With no debt, Korbel was able to borrow the money needed in 1997 to acquire three Sonoma County wineries. It also bought Russian River Brewing to add a line of beer and ale.

The champagne industry held out great hopes for increased sales from millennium celebrations. Shipments were strong. In fact, Korbel shipped out the last of 1.6 million cases of champagne in mid-November 1999. Unfortunately for champagne makers, many consumers were too afraid to venture to parties, fearful of Y2K computer meltdowns or terrorist attacks. As a result, hotels and restaurants cancelled parties, and it would take a year or so for the world to work through the oversupply of champagne. By the end of 2001, Korbel was back on track with an inventory of 30 to 40 days. Korbel sold Russian River Brewing to its head brewmaster in 2002 and continued to pursue its still wine program. Nevertheless, the company was still very much known for, and dependent upon, its champagne. Korbel continued to actively promote the product, hoping to grow non-holiday sales. The company, for example, began sponsoring the "Perfect Proposal Contest," in which contestants proposed marriage in unique ways. How well Korbel would succeed in convincing consumers to drink more champagne was debatable, but there was little doubt that the company would remain privately owned and family run. Gary Heck's son Aaron was already heavily involved in the business and was being groomed to one day become the third-generation of the Heck family to lead what the Korbel brothers had begun in the 1800s.

Principal Subsidiaries

Korbel Champagne Cellars; Korbel Media; Master Cellars Inc.; Kenwood Winery; Valley of the Moon; Lake Sonoma.

Principal Competitors

Heaven Hill Distilleries, Inc.; Marne et Champagne SA; Taittinger S.A.

Further Reading

Ball, Deborah, and Isabella Lisk, "After a Two-Year Dry Spell, Champagne Gets Its Fizz Back," *Wall Street Journal*, December 24, 2002, p. B1.

Howie, Millie, "Korbell . . . Millenium and More," *Wines & Vines*, December 1998, p. 54.

Koepp, Stephen, "The Corks are apoppin'—For Wine Makers, Everything That Sparkles Is Gold," *Time*, December 31, 1984, p. 50.

Walker, Larry, "A Sparkling Chat with Gary Heck," *Wines & Vines*, December 2001, p. 16.

—Ed Dinger

Fat Face Ltd.

P.O. Box 1
Havant
PO9 2UA
United Kingdom
Telephone: (+44) 870 6000 090
Fax: (+44) 23 9248 5550
Web site: http://www.fatface.com

Private Company
Incorporated: 1968
Employees: 500
Sales: £45 million ($60 million) (2003)
NAIC: 448150 Clothing Accessories Stores; 315228 Men's and Boys' Cut and Sew Other Outerwear Manufacturing; 315999 Other Apparel Accessories and Other Apparel Manufacturing; 339920 Sporting and Athletic Good Manufacturing

Fat Face Ltd. is one of the United Kingdom's fastest-growing retail sportswear companies. Targeting the active lifestyle, outdoor sports enthusiast, Fat Face produces a full range of functional sportswear fashions, including clothing and outerwear and related accessories. Fat Face traditionally targets the complementary skiing/snowboard and surfing/windsurfing and sailing markets as well as enthusiasts of mountain biking, hang gliding, tennis, and other sports. This strategy enables the company to build steady sales year round. Fat Face has long resisted distributing its products through traditional third-party wholesale and retail channels, preferring to maintain tight control of its retail sales—and brand image. Since 1993, the company has built up an extensive network of retail shops through the United Kingdom and Ireland, with more than 80 shops in operation at the end of 2004. The company also operates four shops in the French Alps ski resort region and has plans to boost its total network of shops to more than 150 at mid-decade. While founders Jules Leaver and Tim Slade retain 60 percent control of the company (the remaining is held by investment group Isis), Fat Face is preparing to launch a public offering, perhaps as early as 2005. As part of that process, the company has boosted its management with the 2003 appointment of Louise Barnes, formerly with Monsoon, as CEO, and Stephen Sunnucks, former CEO of retail rival New Look, as non-executive director in 2004. Fat Face's revenues, growing at an average of 50 percent annually since the mid-1990s, topped £45 million ($60 million) in 2004.

Ski Bums in the 1980s

Like many of their peers in England, Jules Leaver and Tim Slade were avid skiers who went to work in the French Alps in order to finance their passion for the sport. Leaver had graduated from Plymouth University with a degree in business, then took off for France in the late 1980s. There, he met Tim Slade, who had completed a three-year stint as a policeman before hitting the slopes himself.

Slade and Leaver met in 1988 while tending bar at Meribel and discovered that they shared the same predicament. Both had been trying to earn enough money to support their skiing activities, and both found their schedule of waking early to ski and tending bar late in the night too exhausting. They began discussing ways of earning a living on the slopes and hit upon the idea of selling T-shirts and other clothing.

Rather than sell existing T-shirt designs, the pair decided to create their own. They hit on the idea to create so-called "Been There Done That" apparel—or, as Leaver himself described it: "We printed some T-shirts and sweat-shirts with messages pertinent to certain resorts and sports." The pair found a manufacturer in Leicester, England, willing to produce short runs of T-shirts according to their design and another company to print the slogan "Meribel 88" on the back.

Slade and Leaver literally began hawking their shirts on the slopes at Meribel and quickly sold out of their initial order. The money they earned enabled them to place larger and larger orders. Before long, Leaver became the pair's salesman, remaining in Meribel and selling the shirts from a backpack behind the bar where he continued working. Slade meanwhile went back and forth between England and France to retrieve and deliver new orders for their merchandise. As Leaver admitted: "Initially we were surprised at the demand for this kind of kit. But the demand

Company Persepctives:

1988 . . . Meribel, French Alps . . . Two ski bums . . . Jules and Tim . . . money's running short . . . design a few sweat-shirts . . . sell them from a rucksack . . . ski until Spring . . . head for the beach . . . Fat Face is born. Well guys . . . a few years later and we're still around. The kit remains true to those early days—designed for lifestyle and made to last. So if you ski, surf, sail, climb, fly, mountain bike, play tennis or just love getting amongst it, then Fat Face gear is for you. Remember . . . life is out there. . . .

quickly started to out-strip the supply, and it became obvious that there was a good business opportunity there.''

Still in their early 20s, Leaver and Slade seized on the opportunity for travel that their new business afforded them. At the end of the 1988 ski season, the pair decided to travel around the world rather than return to England. Sales of their T-shirt and sweatshirt designs, adapted to each new location, provided funding for Leaver and Slade's travel and sports interests for some five years.

By 1993, Leaver and Slade had begun to look more seriously at their business. ''Once we began to understand our marketplace—it was about affluent and aspirational people—then we realised that if we could tap into it, the business would probably catch fire. That was when we began to think seriously about it.''

Founding a Retail Business in the Early 1990s

Returning to England, Leaver and Slade decided to open a retail shop for their ski apparel designs and founded Fat Face Ltd. Named after the Le Face ski slope in France's Val d'Isere, the company was financed with £12,000 raised by the sale of Leaver's Volkswagen van and a number of stock shares held by Slade. The partners quickly recognized that if they limited their inventory to the ski market, they would be in business only six months per year. Instead, Fat Face soon added a line of clothing targeting the summer-oriented surf and windsailing markets.

The company's first store opened on London's Fulham Road in 1993. Before long, Fat Face developed into a concept embracing a wider variety of active lifestyle and outdoor sports apparel. ''Having a mixture of High Street and activity-based portfolio has worked very well for us,'' Leaver told startups .co.uk, especially as it appealed to a specific clientele. ''The average age is early 30's, with an even split between men and women. Because people at this sort of age are often into a profession, coupled with the fact that watersports and snowsports are generally enjoyed by people with more disposable income, it has kept us in good stead.''

Another important factor in Fat Face's rising sales was the enthusiasm Leaver and Slade shared with their customers for the active, outdoor lifestyle. Recognizing this, Fat Face's adapted its hiring policies to recruit sports enthusiasts to staff their stores. As Leaver pointed out to the *Sunday Times:* ''When you buy a Fat Face product, you're not just buying the fleece, you're buying the chat in the shop about the quality of the snow in Val d'Isere or the surf in Cornwall. We can't afford to compromise customer service with growth.''

Indeed, even as Fat Face began expanding its retail network, adding stores close to the United Kingdom's ski resorts and surfing areas, Leaver and Slade remained highly accessible to their customers, often taking phone calls and suggestions. The partners also recognized the importance of maintaining their brand's integrity as they steered the company's growth through the mid-1990s.

Fat Face rejected wholesale expansion, at least for the short-term, refusing to make distribution deals to place their brand in the larger national and international retail market. As Leaver explained: ''We could wholesale the hell out of it and be in every ski or surf shop in Europe in a year. Within two years we'd have trashed the brand.''

Instead, the company chose to roll over its steadily growing profits and cash flow into expanding its own retail store network. By 1995, sales had already risen to £750,000 pounds. Over the next three years, the company posted an impressive average annual growth of 85 percent, reaching £4.8 million in annual sales. The launch of a mail order business and the company's e-commerce Web site provided a new boost to its growth, and by 1999 the company's revenues had topped £9 million. By then, its store network stood at 31, including three stores in the Alps.

Expanding Lifestyle Brand in the 2000s

Fat Face now began preparations to expand. The company remained committed to its policy of avoiding wholesale distribution deals, emphasizing Fat Face as a lifestyle brand, as opposed to a fashion brand. As Leaver pointed out to the *Sunday Times:* ''If you make the connection with lifestyle, not fashion, there is no reason why you can't sell for life, from toddler to grandpa.''

Fat Face took a step toward that goal, launching a new line of children's clothing under the name ''Brat Face'' in 2000. The company then turned to outside investors to fuel the next phase of its expansion effort, selling a 40 percent stake to Friends Ivory & Sime Private Equity (later Isis) in exchange for £5 million in expansion capital.

The new funds enabled Fat Face to step up its store opening schedule. By the end of 2002, the group operated nearly 50 stores. The company's sales grew accordingly, and by the end of 2003, as the company's retail network topped 70 stores, Fat Face posted annual revenues of more than £30 million.

The appointment of former Monsoon executive Louise Barnes as company CEO in 2003 represented a new milestone for the company. Leaver and Slade had begun to distance themselves from the day-to-day operations of their company in order to make way for a more professional management structure. Barnes' arrival fueled speculation that the company was preparing a public offering in the near future.

Under Barnes, Fat Face launched a more aggressive store expansion drive, with plans to top 100 stores by the end of 2004 and expectations of reaching 150 stores soon after. Barnes also

Key Dates:

1988: Tim Slade and Jules Leaver begin selling T-shirts in order to fund their skiing season at Meribel.
1993: Slade and Leaver open the first Fat Face store on Fulham Road in London.
1995: Company sales top £750,000 as Fat Face expands its retail network.
1999: The launch of mail order and Internet sales spur growth to £9 million; the company's retail network tops 30 stores.
2000: Slade and Leaver sell 40 percent of the company to Isis in exchange for £5 million in capital funding.
2003: Louise Barnes, formerly of Monsoon, is appointed as CEO and plans to expand the company's retail network to 150 stores.
2004: Fat Face appoints former New Look CEO Stephen Sunnucks to its board of directors, sparking expectations of a public offering.

led the development of a larger store format. The company had also taken its first steps toward developing a global position, registering its trademark in a number of foreign markets, including North America, Australia, and New Zealand. By the end of 2003, the company's sales had topped £45 million.

Fat Face's public offering appeared increasingly imminent in late 2004, especially after the appointment of former New Look chief executive Stephen Sunnucks to the company's board of directors. Analysts now expected the company to list its shares by 2006, and possibly as early as mid-2005. Having literally grown from rags to riches, Fat Face had positioned itself as one of the world's fastest-growing lifestyle brands for the 2000s.

Principal Competitors

GUS PLC; Arcadia Group Ltd.; Coats Ltd.; JJB Sports PLC; Top Shop/Top Man Ltd.; Mr Price Group Ltd.

Further Reading

Adams, Richard, ''Riding a Wave,'' *Guardian*, February 2, 2004, p. 22.
Conway, Edmund, ''Fat Face Rides High on Record Profits,'' *Daily Telegraph*, August 31, 2004.
''Cult Firm Stays in Touch with Followers,'' *Sunday Times*, November 18, 2001, p. 15.
Ellson, Andrew, ''Retailer That Started from a Rucksack,'' *Times Online*, August 31, 2004.
Gracie, Sarah, ''Leisurewear Firm Tailors Its Ambitions Globally,'' *Sunday Times*, February 27, 2000, p. 13.
Jameson, Angela, ''Fat Face Gets Plump Returns as Sales Grow,'' *Times*, October 13, 2003, p. 23.
''New face at Fat Face,'' *Daily Post*, September 1, 2004, p. 11.
Prynn, Jonathan, ''The £70m Fat Face Pair,'' *Evening Standard*, February 9, 2004.
Skorecki, Alex, ''Fat Face Outlines Growth Prospects,'' *Financial Times*, August 31, 2004, p. 21.
Smith, Alison, ''Fat Face Looks for European Lift,'' *Financial Times*, May 4, 2004, p. 24.
''Sunnucks' Arrival Prompts Float Talk for Fat Face,'' *Guardian*, August 31, 2004, p. 12.
West, Karl, ''Fat Face to Double Its Stores in Scotland,'' *Herald*, October 15, 2003, p. 24.

—M.L. Cohen

Feed The Children, Inc.

P.O. Box 36
Oklahoma City, Oklahoma 73101-0036
U.S.A.
Telephone: (405) 942-0228
Toll Free: (800) 627-4556
Fax: (405) 945-4177
Web site: http://www.feedthechildren.org

Nonprofit Company
Incorporated: 1979
Employees: 160
Sales: $575.9 million (2003)
NAIC: 624230 Emergency and Other Relief Services

Feed The Children, Inc., is an international relief agency founded and run by televangelist Larry Jones of Oklahoma City, Oklahoma. The organization provides food, medical care, and day-to-day necessities to needy people in the United States, and also responds to humanitarian crises, disasters, and wars around the world. Feed The Children provides short-term emergency relief as well as working toward long-term improvements in quality of life. Donations of surplus goods and money come from corporations, viewers of Jones's television broadcasts, and through the efforts of other parties including celebrities like actress Melanie Griffith and country singer Garth Brooks.

Beginnings

Feed The Children (FTC) grew out of an Oklahoma City-based Christian organization called Larry Jones International Ministries. Jones, an evangelical minister since 1964, had over the years become well known through appearances on religious television programs. The inspiration for FTC came in January 1979, when he was in Port-au-Prince, Haiti to speak at a church. One night, as he was walking back to his hotel following a sermon, a small boy named Jerry approached him, arm outstretched, and asked for a nickel. Jones gave it to him, then paused to ask what he needed it for. The boy said that the nickel would buy him a roll to eat, and another three cents would let him buy butter to put on it. Jones then asked what it would cost for a Coke to wash it down, and gave the boy 20 cents for everything. When he discovered that this was Jerry's only meal of the day, Jones remembered a verse of scripture, "I was hungry and you gave me food" (Matthew 25:35), which he used as the basis for his next sermon.

After he returned to Oklahoma, the plight of the poor in Haiti, and the boy Jerry in particular, kept coming back to his mind. Jones decided to do some research, and soon found out that the U.S. government had a surplus of 35 million metric tons of wheat stored in grain elevators. Along with his wife Frances, he began to appeal to groups wherever he spoke, and on television, to donate money to feed the people of Haiti. Although he had not specifically asked for donations of wheat, farmers offered to give him 50 truckloads of it.

Not sure how to get it to its destination, Jones soon found a volunteer willing to drive the wheat to the shipyard, and another who donated and set up grinding equipment in Haiti. With this success Jones decided to build an organization that he called Feed The Children, which branched out to offer aid to the hungry in Africa as well. In 1981 an office was also opened in El Salvador, and the organization began to offer child sponsorships.

The early 1980s saw FTC offer assistance in the wake of several humanitarian crises around the world, helping famine victims in Ethiopia with food, as well as citizens of Romania with medical needs after the fall of that country's dictator. In 1984 the organization received a prestigious DOVE award for humanitarian work.

Forming a Trucking Subsidiary in 1986

The year 1986 saw the founding of a for-profit trucking subsidiary, Feed The Children Transportation, Inc. During the year the country music group The Oak Ridge Boys approached Jones and offered to donate the proceeds from a concert they were giving in Nice, France. Having just returned from a visit to Africa, Jones told them he would use the money to help drill four wells in the drought-ridden area he had visited, and offered to name one well after each member of the group. Many other celebrities also would pitch in to help the organization over the years, including country singer John Conlee, famous for a hit

Company Perspectives:

Feed The Children is a nonprofit, Christian, charitable organization providing physical, spiritual, educational, vocational/technical, psychological, economic and medical assistance and other necessary aid to children, families, and persons in need in the United States and internationally.

song called ''Busted.'' When concert-goers one night began putting small amounts of money on the edge of the stage in joking response to the song's lyric about being broke, leaving a total of $58, Conlee got the idea of offering it to FTC to help feed poor Americans in Appalachia. Although Jones was initially nonplussed by Conlee's phoned-in offer of help, when the singer next called he reported that the donations had reached $10,000, and later, after appearances on the Grand Ole Opry and on a television show with Jones, he presented FTC with a check for $150,000. A few years later country superstar Garth Brooks would give FTC $1 from the sale of each copy of his Christmas album, in conjunction with collections at concerts and record stores. Other performers who became involved with the organization over the years included actress Melanie Griffith, actor John Ritter, comedian Sinbad, and politicians from both halves of the political spectrum including Ronald Reagan and Hillary Rodham Clinton.

Although donations fell off by as much as one-quarter in the wake of the non-FTC related 1987 scandal involving televangelists Jim and Tammy Faye Baker, the organization took in $41 million during that year, and its outreach continued to grow with activities including helping Mother Teresa distribute aid to Armenia following an earthquake there in 1988. By that year, the organization had shipped food and other goods to 34 countries and 44 U.S. states. Jones was now producing a weekly television program that appeared on more than 100 stations in the United States, and 15 FTC trucks were typically on the road at a given time, picking up and delivering donations like grain from Kansas or pasta from Puerto Rico.

By 1991 the organization was taking in $86.3 million worth of donated goods and $25.7 million in cash, and was operating throughout the United States and in dozens of countries abroad, with three-fourths of its assistance distributed at home. FTC reported that it devoted 79.1 percent of its donations to direct relief, 12.1 percent to ministry and education, and the remainder to administrative and fund-raising expenses. It now had 110 employees. During 1991 FTC had distributed goods to victims of an Iranian earthquake and U.S. troops in Operation Desert Storm. Americans hit by Hurricane Andrew were helped the following year when FTC sent 58 truckloads of supplies to Florida.

Controversies in the 1990s

Despite its established record of good works, Feed The Children was not without controversy. In 1991 a 60-year-old organization called Save The Children sued over its similar name and logo, citing copyright infringement, and a year later an article in the *Chronicle of Philanthropy* charged that FTC was exaggerating its efficiency and the amount of funds it spent on charitable giving. Specifically, it was asserted that the donated books that comprised almost 40 percent of the $86.3 million in commodity giving had been valued at their wholesale price, rather than a ''charity value'' of approximately one-fifth that amount. FTC also was accused of falsely claiming that the radio and television programs it produced, at a cost of nearly $10 million per year, were ''educational,'' when they were actually devoted almost entirely to fundraising. Jones responded to the accusations by saying, ''I'm not trying to pad my books. I'm trying to help people.''

Continuing to follow its mission in spite of such distractions, FTC's relief efforts of the 1990s included sending food to Somalia to help children orphaned in the war there, and giving assistance to citizens of Jones's own home town following the April 19, 1995 bombing of the Murrah Federal Building. FTC provided thermal underwear and steel-toed boots for rescue workers, meals for police, and funeral expenses for some of the families of the victims. Due to Jones's visibility on CNN and network television programs, donations to the organization shot upward, and it took in $6.7 million in extra goods and cash in the aftermath of the bombing.

FTC's international relief efforts continued in the latter half of the 1990s, and included providing aid in 1999 in Kosovo to victims of the war there, and in Turkey to victims of an earthquake. New controversy erupted that same year when the chief of FTC's 274,000-square-foot Nashville warehouse and six of his staff were videotaped by a local television station taking boxes of donated goods home with them. The items included clothing, shoes, blankets, food, and videos. Jones subsequently fired the entire staff of the facility and installed surveillance cameras and other safeguards. The next year FTC also discovered that its chief financial officer had forged signatures and supplied inaccurate financial documents, and he too was dismissed, with the organization's 1998 and 1999 years subsequently re-audited. At this time, FTC was taking in more than $200 million in donations.

Abandoned Baby Center Opening in Kenya in 2001

Once again moving beyond the controversy, in August 2001 FTC opened its first Abandoned Baby Center in Nairobi, Kenya, to provide a home for babies and toddlers left homeless by the AIDS epidemic. On September 11, 2001, following the attacks on the World Trade Center and Pentagon, Jones (who happened to be in New York City that fateful morning) provided relief for survivors as he had during the Oklahoma City bombing. A few months later, after the U.S. invasion of Afghanistan, FTC supplied food, blankets, tents, and sleeping bags to citizens of that country who were living in refugee camps.

In 2003 FTC launched a partnership with the National Basketball Association Players Association, in which players would participate in food distribution events. Also during the year, the organization received the largest donation of powdered milk ever given by the U.S. government, and purchased a distribution warehouse in Elkhart, Indiana, which was FTC's fifth such facility, along with others in Oklahoma, Tennessee, California, and New Jersey. In addition to warehouse space, it would house administrative offices and a nutrition research center, and generate at least 100 jobs. The building had been sold to FTC for $1 by Bayer Diagnostics.

Key Dates:

1979: Larry Jones founds Feed The Children after sending wheat to Haiti.
1981: The second international office is opened in El Salvador.
1986: Feed The Children Transportation is formed.
2001: The first Abandoned Baby Center is established in Kenya; aid is sent to 9/11 victims.
2004: Boxes of supplies are sent to soldiers in Iraq and their families.

During the 2003 fiscal year, FTC distributed 54 million pounds of food and 15 million pounds of other items to agencies in all 50 U.S. states, in both urban and rural environments. Subsidiary FTC Transportation operated 55 semi tractor-trailers to distribute goods around the country. FTC now operated field offices in more than a dozen foreign countries including Romania, Ethiopia, Kenya, South Africa, Thailand, Japan, El Salvador, Haiti, and Nicaragua. During the year they distributed more than 14 million pounds of food and other supplies to children and families in 62 countries. FTC's medical teams treated almost 46,000 patients in medical, eye, and dental clinics, and dispensed more than 58,000 prescriptions for medicine and eyeglasses. Other FTC activities abroad over the years, which had reached a total of 109 countries, included constructing fish hatcheries, protecting fish breeding grounds, building model farms and agricultural training centers, establishing micro-loan programs, and initiating water sanitation projects.

Working with many major corporations, in 2003 FTC received donations of more than $480 million worth of surplus food, medicine, clothing, and other goods. An additional $80 million came in the form of cash, which when added to more than $11 million in other donations totaled more than $575 million in funding. FTC gave out $333 million worth of child-care, food, and medical services, $5.4 million in disaster relief, and $165.5 million in education and community development. An additional $52.1 million was spent on fundraising, along with $15.1 million that went to administration and general overhead. A total of 88 percent of expenditures went to program services, according to FTC.

In 2004 the organization's work continued with distribution of care boxes and food to soldiers in Iraq, in the wake of the U.S. war that drove Saddam Hussein from power. Families of soldiers in the United States also were offered assistance.

After a quarter-century in operation, Feed The Children, Inc. had grown into the 19th largest charity in the United States, supplying some of the world's neediest and most vulnerable citizens with food, medical care, and other basic necessities. Despite several controversies, the organization's donations and assistance continued to increase each year.

Principal Subsidiaries

FTC Transportation, Inc.

Principal Competitors

Save The Children; Christian Children's Fund; Second Harvest.

Further Reading

Belsie, Laurent, "One Man's Battle to Feed Hungry," *Christian Science Monitor,* June 15, 1988, p. 4.
Clolery, Paul, "Feed The Children Beats Nashville Solicitation Ordinance," *Non-Profit Times,* May 1, 2002, p. 4.
"Feed The Children Battles Controversy," *Christianity Today,* December 6, 1999, p. 23.
Ford, Brian, "CPA Faces Fraud Allegations," *Tulsa World,* July 19, 2001.
"Garth Starts Charity Drive," *Billboard,* August 29, 1992, p. 29.
Gubernick, Lisa, " 'I Can't Be Everywhere,' " *Forbes,* September 26, 1994, p. 124.
Herrick, Thaddeus, "Oklahoma City Tragedy; Charity's High Visibility, Tactics Debated," *Houston Chronicle,* May 21, 1995, p. 21.
Kissell, Margaret Rutledge, "Feed The Children Helps Feed Hundreds of Valley's Hungry," *Dayton Daily News,* September 30, 2004, p. B1.
McCall, Ashley, "Michiana Welcomes Feed The Children," *South Bend Tribune,* January 6, 2004, p. A1.
Schultheiss, Sally, "Melanie's Care Packages," *In Style,* July, 1998, p. 124.
Sinclair, Matthew, "Mismanaged Financials," *Non-Profit Times,* December, 2000, p. 1.
Spohn, Gustav, "Charity Faces Scrutiny Over Budget Claims," *St. Petersburg Times,* December 26, 1992, p. 4E.
Stevenson, Douglas, "One Million Pounds of Food Trucked Here for the Hungry," *Washington Post,* September 6, 1987, p. C1.
Yarrow, Andrew L., "2 Charities for Poor Children Battle Over a Name," *New York Times,* January 2, 1992, p. 5B.

—Frank Uhle

The Finish Line, Inc.

3308 North Mitthoeffer Road
Indianapolis, Indiana 46236
U.S.A.
Telephone: (317) 899-1022
Fax: (317) 899-0237
Web site: http://www.finishline.com

Public Company
Incorporated: 1976
Employees: 12,066
Sales: $985.9 million (2004)
Stock Exchanges: NASDAQ
Ticker Symbol: FINL
NAIC: 448210 Shoe Stores; 448150 Clothing Accessories Stores; 451110 Sporting Goods Stores

The Finish Line, Inc., is an athletic specialty retailer, carrying men's, women's, and children's brand name footwear, apparel, and accessories. The company operates roughly 550 primarily mall-based stores in 46 states. The average size of a Finish Line store is more than 5,000 square feet, which is substantially larger than its competitors and which allows for a broader and deeper merchandise mix. Sales of footwear bring in approximately 70 percent of the company's total revenue, with apparel and accessories making up the remainder. Brand names carried by the company's stores include Nike, adidas, Reebok, K-Swiss, Phat Farm, New Balance, Timberland, Asics, and Saucony.

Franchise Beginnings: 1976–86

The Finish Line's founders, David Klapper and Alan Cohen, first became involved in athletic retailing in 1976 when they opened an Athlete's Foot franchise on Monument Circle in downtown Indianapolis. The Athlete's Foot was a Pittsburgh-based athletic footwear retailer that had begun franchising in 1972. By 1976, when Klapper and Cohen signed their ten-year franchise agreement, there were almost 100 Athlete's Foot stores located in malls throughout the country. Although athletic wear was not a major retail force at the time, Cohen and Klapper, longtime friends and fervent athletes, both believed in the potential of the nascent market.

Under the terms of the franchise arrangement, the duo had a ten-year license with the Athlete's Foot for the state of Indiana. Within four to five years, Klapper and Cohen had added nine more stores, located in the state's larger malls, to their operation. It was at that point they decided it was time for a change. As franchisees, Cohen and Klapper were constrained by the dictates of the Athlete's Foot on every front—from product mix to store size to merchandise presentation. The partners, however, believed that the athletic specialty business was taking a new shape, and they wanted the latitude to respond to the changing market. They decided to start their own company—the Finish Line.

To begin the new venture, Cohen and Klapper brought in two more full partners: Larry Sablonsky and David Fagin. Sablonsky, who was also from Indiana, had a department store background, and Fagin had previously been a sales rep for an athletic wear manufacturer. From its first days, the Finish Line was conceptually different from the Athlete's Foot. Whereas the standard Athlete's Foot store was fairly small—between 1,500 and 2,000 square feet—and located in an enclosed mall, the early Finish Line stores were located in strip malls and outlet centers and, at 3,000 to 4,000 square feet, were substantially larger than the norm. While the smaller Athlete's Foot stores had focused almost exclusively on athletic shoes, the Finish Line's extra space allowed for a much broader mix of merchandise, specifically sports apparel and accessories. This broader product mix let Finish Line target a broader market, offering shoes and apparel for the whole family, whereas athletic retailing had catered traditionally to young males aged 12 to 24.

Another difference between the Finish Line and the Athlete's Foot was the type of merchandise they carried. The Athlete's Foot focused on new, high-profile merchandise from big-name athletic vendors. As an unproven entity, the Finish Line could not always stock the latest, hottest products carried by its competitor and instead often carried value or closeout merchandise. Although begun out of necessity, this merchandise mix proved to be serendipitous, as it mirrored a trend toward closeout and outlet shopping that was just then taking shape in the United States.

Although the partners continued to operate their existing ten Athlete's Foot stores through the term of their ten-year agreement, the lion's share of their energies were focused on growing their

> **Company Perspectives:**
>
> *Finish Line will provide the best selection of sport inspired footwear, apparel and accessories to fit the fast culture of action addicted individuals.*

Finish Line chain. By 1986, when Klapper and Cohen's franchise with the Athlete's Foot expired, they already had established between 25 and 30 Finish Line stores. The stores were concentrated in areas where the outlet shopping craze was most deeply rooted, such as North Carolina, Texas, and upstate New York.

Gathering Speed: 1987–93

With the expiration of the Athlete's Foot franchise agreement, the partners had to decide whether to renew the contract or to convert their existing Athlete's Foot stores into Finish Line stores. They opted for the latter. Applying what they had learned from operating the two types of stores, the foursome determined to combine the best of both concepts for future expansion. They believed that the Athlete's Foot's strongest points were its high-profile products and its mall-based location strategy. The Finish Line's strengths lay in its larger store size and its combination of new and value merchandise. Blending the concepts, Klapper, Cohen, Sablosky, and Fagin decided to take their stores back into the malls, but to make them much larger and to carry a wider variety of merchandise, including both the latest, high-profile products and discounted, value items. Little by little, the company began closing its strip and outlet mall stores, becoming ever more entrenched in enclosed malls.

Meanwhile, the U.S. market for athletic footwear was booming. From 1982 through 1991, retail sales of athletic footwear had climbed from $3.88 billion to $10.73 billion. Much of this growth was directly attributable to an Oregon-based athletic shoe manufacturer named after a Greek goddess—Nike, Inc. Throughout the 1980s, the popular Nike shoes—characterized by the signature ''swoosh''—took the nation by storm, showing up on the feet of every age group. When its footwear proved so wildly popular, Nike built a line of apparel and accessories that met with a similar consumer response. Soon, Nike was the Finish Line's largest vendor.

By 1991, there were 105 Finish Line stores operating primarily in Midwest and Southeast states. In June of the following year, with 120 stores up and running and sales at $98 million, the four partners took the company public. Then, using the capital generated by the initial public offering and a concept that was proving highly successful, the company expanded rapidly for the next several years. With the steady addition of more stores, revenues rose predictably each year, climbing to $129.5 million in 1993 and $157 million in 1994.

Bigger Is Better: 1994–96

By the end of fiscal 1994, Finish Line had 164 stores located in 22 states stretching from New York to Texas. Not only was the company growing the number of its stores—it was also growing its store size. Of the 30 new stores opened in the company's fiscal 1995 (February 1994 to February 1995), the average size was 4,100 square feet. This brought the overall average store size up to 3,641 square feet, a 5.6 percent increase from the previous year's average. ''Our stores are getting bigger, a strategy we believe will allow us to maintain a competitive edge against our mall competition, and better position us to compete against large box athletic retailers located outside of malls,'' wrote Alan Cohen in the company's 1995 annual report. These larger stores were laid out with a ''track'' around the perimeter, which served to draw customers through the various categories of shoes. Apparel and accessories were displayed inside the track.

The company also rolled out three new large-format stores for testing. Sprawling over 7,000 to 9,500 square feet, the monster stores were divided into separate departments for men's, women's, children's, licensed product, and activewear. The flashy new stores also incorporated new color schemes, lighting, signage, and video and audio screens. Aside from the three new formats, all Finish Line stores were formatted as either ''rack'' or ''backroom'' stores. The 33 rack stores, which ranged in size from 3,000 to 5,500 square feet, were the older store designs, with stock stored on the sales floor in original boxes. The more common backroom format had a sales floor with display and try-on areas and an adjacent stockroom used to store inventory. The stores became known for their trademark ''wall of shoes,'' a large, often curving wall display holding hundreds of shoe styles.

Cohen's team followed through on the larger store strategy in fiscal 1996 and 1997, opening 69 stores over the course of the two years, with an average square footage of almost 5,000. At the end of fiscal 1997, the company's 251 stores had an overall average size of 4,336 square feet, as compared with 1994's average of 3,449 square feet. In addition to the overall jump up in size, the company unveiled a ''large format'' store in fiscal 1996, which dwarfed virtually all of its other stores. Located in downtown Indianapolis, the 20,000-square-foot behemoth was stocked with approximately 1,300 styles and 30,000 pairs of athletic shoes, as well as large lines of apparel and accessories. The store was an immediate success, reaffirming the partners' belief in their superstore concept. Based on the encouraging performance of the Indianapolis store, the company began to plan for a 1997 opening of three more large-format outlets—in Buffalo, New York; Denver, Colorado; and Memphis, Tennessee.

Because the larger stores cost $1.7 million, as opposed to the $375,000 needed to build an average-sized store, the company needed extra capital. It raised it in a 1996 secondary stock offering, selling 1.3 million newly created shares and grossing more than $35 million. In addition, Cohen, Klapper, Sablosky, and Fagin together sold 1.3 million shares of their own stock.

For categorization purposes, the company began to characterize its stores by size. Stores smaller than 10,000 square feet, which included the majority of locations, were classified as ''traditional format'' stores. These stores generally carried 600 to 700 shoe styles. ''Medium format'' stores were those ranging from 10,000 to 15,000 square feet, stocked with approximately 1,000 shoe styles. Stores that were larger than 15,000 square feet were designated as ''large format'' stores.

Size and quantity were not the only points of focus for the Finish Line during the mid-1990s. The company also was work-

Key Dates:

1976: David Klapper and Alan Cohen open an Athlete's Foot franchise.
1981: Klapper and Cohen form The Finish Line.
1986: After their franchise agreement with The Athlete's Foot expires, Klapper and Cohen convert all their Athlete's Foot stores to Finish Line stores.
1992: The Finish Line completes its initial public offering of stock.
1995: The company opens its 200th store.
1999: The Finish Line records its first online sale.
2003: Following a spat between Nike and Foot Locker, Finish Line receives a greater allocation of top-selling Nike footwear, boosting the company's business.

ing to improve efficiency in its warehousing and distribution systems. In 1995, the Indianapolis distribution center was expanded to more than double its previous size. Shortly thereafter, new management software was implemented in the center to allow for more accurate tracking of inventory.

Market Downturn: 1997–99

For most sports retailers, the second half of 1997 and all of 1998 were somewhat less than ideal. Sales growth of both athletic footwear and apparel slowed industry wide, resulting in overstocked inventories and collapsing profits for both retailers and wholesalers. Many of the Finish Line's mall retail competitors lost ground. Even the superpower Nike, which by that time accounted for more than 60 percent of the Finish Line's merchandise, had disappointing numbers.

The Finish Line initially fared better than most of its competitors, closing its fiscal year in February 1998 with a 32 percent increase in total sales and a 42 percent increase in net income. While the Woolworth Corp., the operator of the Foot Locker, Lady Foot Locker, and Champs retail chains, posted a 4 percent drop in same-store sales, the Finish Line reported a six percent gain. The company's management believed that their larger store sizes allowed them to prosper while other athletic retailers hit the skids. Whatever the reason, investors responded favorably, and the company's stock price skyrocketed—climbing more than 100 percent between February and July 1998.

The company maintained its momentum through the spring of 1998 but stumbled during the summer months and was unable to recover. Same-store sales declined throughout the remainder of the year, as did net income. Finish Line's CEO Alan Cohen pointed to a sharp drop off in apparel and accessories sales as the culprit. ''During this period, apparel fashion trends appear to have moved away from the athletic brands to other contemporary brands, which is evident by the recent sales strength of many non-athletic specialty retailers,'' he said in a September 29, 1998 press release. With approximately one-third of Finish Line's total sales coming from apparel and accessories, the company was harder hit by this particular decline than some of its competitors, who carried only 12 to 20 percent apparel and accessories.

Despite disappointing sales, the company continued to expand, opening 59 new stores in the fiscal year ending February 27, 1999, and remodeling or expanding 26 existing stores. At fiscal year-end, there were 358 Finish Line stores—a 19 percent increase over the previous year's total. In addition, the company's total retail square footage jumped up 32 percent to 2,095,000 square feet, as opposed to fiscal 1998's 1,587,000 square feet.

Despite its slump, the Finish Line entered 1999 determined to move ahead with expansion plans, which were to include opening between 40 and 60 new stores and remodeling another 20. The company planned to continue with its strategy of opening larger stores and carrying broader and deeper product lines than most athletic specialty retailers. This, management believed, would allow them to continue reaching a broader demographic market and to maintain operating margins that were larger than traditional stores. Although apparel sales were in a slump, management expected them to rebound. ''We feel apparel is in a down cycle. It will not remain down forever,'' stated Steven Schneider, the company's vice-president of finance, citing the cyclical nature of sports clothing retailing.

Finish Line Surges Ahead in the Early 21st Century

The decline in apparel sales, which plummeted when consumers—teens mostly—no longer found licensed-sports apparel fashionable, hobbled Finish Line at the end of the decade. Several days before the end of 1999, the company's stock dipped below $5 a share, triggering concern at company headquarters. Schneider was right, however. The downturn did not last forever. When Finish Line mounted a comeback, its return was marked by resounding success.

A change in fashion trends was credited partly with Finish Line's resurgence. Teens began clamoring for retro apparel that featured out-of-business sports franchises, a trend that sent consumers back to sports apparel retailers such as Finish Line for fashionable apparel. The company's strong showing during the early years of the decade stemmed largely from another factor, however. Finish Line benefited significantly from a feud between its largest competitor, Foot Locker, and Nike. In 2002, Foot Locker informed Nike that it wanted to reduce orders on some of the sporting-goods manufacturer's products, a demand that angered Nike. Nike responded by not making available its most high-end tier of footwear to Foot Locker, a retaliatory blow that worked in Finish Line's favor. Finish Line received a greater allocation of Nike's shoes, giving the retailer a substantial boost to its business. In a September 15, 2003, interview with *Indianapolis Business Journal,* an analyst from Oppenheimer described Finish Line's good fortune. ''Having Nike's key products, when Foot Locker does not, has enabled Finish Line to become the place to go in shopping malls for shoppers who want the latest styles of premier products.''

As the relationship between Nike and Foot Locker soured, Cohen used the opportunity to improve his relationships with his other suppliers. Finish Line had quickly become the destination of choice for a substantial percentage of shoppers, giving the company the strength to expand its business with vendors such as K-Swiss, Reebok, and adidas. ''We got aggressive with a lot of our vendors,'' Cohen explained in an October 19, 2003 interview with *Investor's Business Daily.* ''We told them we wanted to do more business with them—and that the Nike situation showed that if they come to us with the right programs and products, we could do great things.''

By the fall of 2003, Finish Line's stock value had increased remarkably from the company's low point at the end of the 1990s. Shares that had traded for less than $5 were trading for more than $30, giving the company's management cause for celebration. Cohen and his team worked to use the company's well-regarded reputation to expand the chain further. In early 2004, the company attempted to purchase stores from Footstar Inc., which filed for bankruptcy protection in March 2004. Foot Locker bid $160 million for 353 of Footstar's Footaction stores, and Finish Line countered by offering to pay $195 million for 192 Footaction outlets. Foot Locker increased its bid to $225 million in April 2004, eventually gaining control over the Footaction stores, but the rivalry between the two retailers did not end there.

Foot Locker was roughly six times larger than Finish Line, but it was evident that the much larger company feared the advances of its smaller pursuer. In May 2004, Finish Line filed a lawsuit against Foot Locker, alleging that the rival company was trying to convince Finish Line executives to join Foot Locker with the intention of gaining confidential information from the executives and harm Finish Line. While the battle between the two retailers dragged on, Finish Line management did its best to push forward with expansion plans and further intensify the rivalry between the two companies. In fiscal 2004, Finish Line opened 58 new stores, giving the company a total of 545 stores by April 2004. The total represented a more than five-fold increase from the store count a dozen years earlier, when the company converted to public ownership. In fiscal 2005, Finish Line intended to open approximately 60 stores in both new and existing markets. As the company moved forward with its expansion plans, its increasingly combative relationship with Foot Locker promised to provide drama in the months ahead. The stakes were high, and Finish Line was not content to let Foot Locker reign as the industry's dominant retailer forever.

Principal Subsidiaries

Spike's Holding, Inc.; Finish Line Transportation Company, Inc.

Principal Competitors

Foot Locker, Inc.; The Sports Authority, Inc.; The Athlete's Foot Group Inc.; Wal-Mart Stores, Inc.; Dick's Sporting Goods, Inc.

Further Reading

Andrews, Greg, ''Finish Line Says Top Rival Spreading 'Misinformation,' '' *Indianapolis Business Journal*, May 31, 2004, p. 4.

——, ''Finish Line Shares in Step with Hot Sector,'' *Indianapolis Star/News*, July 6, 1998.

——, ''Finish Line's Sales Surge Helps Bring Retailer Full Circle,'' *Indianapolis Business Journal*, September 15, 2003, p. 4A.

Bora, Madhusmita, ''Finish Line Profit Climbs 19 Percent,'' *Indianapolis Star*, September 24, 2004, p. B3.

''Finish Line Bets on Mega-Stores,'' *Indianapolis Business Journal*, June 3, 1996, p. 8A.

''Indianapolis-Based Sporting Goods Retailer to Stay Put, Expand Headquarters,'' *Knight Ridder/Tribune Business News*, February 14, 2003.

Linecker, Adelia Cellini, ''Finish Line Inc.,'' *Investor's Business Daily*, December 19, 2003, p. A6.

Maurer, Katie, ''Retailer Feeling Blue: Finish Line Has High Hopes for Private Apparel Label,'' *Indianapolis Business Journal*, August 12, 2002, p. 3A.

McFeely, Dan, ''Finish Line Hits Stride as Olympics Approach,'' *Indianapolis Business Journal*, February 13, 1995, p. 5.

Murray, Shanon D., ''Finish Line Submits Footaction Bid,'' *Daily Deal*, April 22, 2004, p. 34.

Owens, Jennifer, ''Finish Line's New President Races to Keep Competitive Edge,'' *Footwear News*, November 3, 2003, p. 6.

Retting, Ellen, ''Coaxing Women to the Finish Line,'' *Indianapolis Business Journal*, July 13, 1998, p. 1A.

Wall, J.K., ''Foot Locker Outbids Finish Line for Struggling Shoe Store Chain,'' *Indianapolis Star*, April 23, 2004, p. B6.

——, ''Sporting-Goods Retailer Finish Line Ends Year Strongly,'' *Indianapolis Star,* March 5, 2004, p. B4.

—Shawna Brynildssen
—update: Jeffrey L. Covell

Foot Locker, Inc.

112 West 34th Street
New York, New York 10120
U.S.A.
Telephone: (212) 720-3700
Fax: (212)720-4397
Web site: http://www.footlocker-inc.com

Public Company
Incorporated: 1905 as F.W. Woolworth & Co.; 1998 as Venator Group Inc.
Employees: 40,298
Sales: $4.77 billion (2004)
Stock Exchanges: New York
Ticker Symbol: FL
NAIC: 448210 Shoe Stores; 448110 Men's Clothing Stores; 448120 Women's Clothing Stores; 448130 Children's and Infants' Clothing Stores; 448150 Clothing Accessories Stores; 551112 Offices of Other Holding Companies

Top athletic shoe retailer Foot Locker, Inc., was known until 1998 as the Woolworth Corporation and until 2001 as Venator Group Inc. Foot Locker is a multinational retailer of athletic shoes with stores and support operations in North America, Europe, Australia, and Asia. The company's holdings include the chains Foot Locker (and its Kids and Lady store concept versions), Footaction USA, and Champs Sports. Since Woolworth's establishment in 1879, the business has been involved in general merchandising; in its incarnation as Venator, however, the company focused on the retailing of athletic footwear and apparel. In 2001 Venator renamed itself after its best-performing specialty chain, the Foot Locker athletic footwear shops.

Origins as the First Five-and-Ten Store

The history of Foot Locker may be traced through that of Woolworth and that company's founder, Frank Winfield Woolworth, who parlayed the idea of the five-and-ten cent store into an international retailing empire. Born in 1852, in Rodman, New York, Woolworth moved to Watertown, New York, in 1873 where he apprenticed and then clerked with Augsbury & Moore, a wholesaler and dry goods store. Wanting more money, Woolworth soon left Augsbury & Moore for A. Bushnell & Company, a local dry goods and carpet store. His new employer, however, found him a poor salesman and lowered his wages from $10 to $8 a week. In response, Woolworth overworked himself, had a complete breakdown, and spent six months convalescing.

When Woolworth recovered in 1876, he returned to his former employer William Moore, whose business was now called Moore & Smith. There he concentrated on window displays. In 1878, Moore & Smith found itself with high debt and excess inventory. To raise money, the store held a five-cent sale. Smith and Woolworth laid a group of goods such as tin pans, washbasins, button-hooks, and dippers, along with surplus inventory, on a counter over which they hung a sign reading: ''Any Article on This Counter, 5¢.'' After the sale, Frank Woolworth was convinced a five-cent strategy could work on a broader basis.

In 1879, Woolworth left Moore & Smith. On February 22nd of that year, he opened his first ''Great 5¢ Store'' in Utica, New York. At first business was good, but as the five-cent novelty faded, the store's poor location became a handicap and he closed it in early June. Still, he had repaid Moore & Smith's loan of $315.41, which he had used for his initial inventory, and had made $252.44 in new capital.

On June 21, 1879, Woolworth opened his second Great 5¢ Store in Lancaster, Pennsylvania. This time he had three windows on a main street and $410 worth of goods. The store was a success. The first day he sold 31 percent of stock. In succeeding months, he changed the store's name, first to Five-and-Ten, and later to Woolworth's. The additional ten-cent items allowed him to search out further bargains.

Woolworth soon began opening new outlets. Some stores succeeded, while others failed. By the mid-1880s, there were seven Woolworth's in New York and Pennsylvania. Most were run by partner-managers. These men—Woolworth's brother, Charles Sumner Woolworth; his cousin, Seymour Horace Knox;

Key Dates:

1879: Frank Woolworth opens his first ''Great 5¢ Store'' in Utica, New York.
1905: Woolworth incorporates his business as F.W. Woolworth & Co.
1912: F.W. Woolworth & Co. becomes the publicly traded F.W. Woolworth Co.; the company moves into the Woolworth Building.
1926: Woolworth inaugurates its German operating subsidiary.
1960: Sales surpass the $1 billion mark.
1962: Woolworth's opens the first Woolco.
1965: The company purchases G.R. Kinney Corporation.
1972: Woolworth and Woolco are consolidated in one division.
1974: The Kinney shoe division opens the first Foot Locker stores.
1982: Kinney's Canadian operation starts Lady Foot Locker.
1993: Woolco's operations are sold to Wal-Mart.
1997: Woolworth's closes the last of its five-and-dime stores in the United States.
1999: Woolworth's changes its name to Venator Group.
2001: Company closes its Northern Reflections chain and renames itself Foot Locker Inc.

former employer, W.H. Moore; and Fred M. Kirby—ran the stores in which they held a 50 percent interest. Frank Woolworth ran the initial store and took care of purchasing.

In succeeding years, these partner-managers bought out Frank Woolworth's shares and began opening chains on their own. Woolworth continued opening stores. After 1888, he did so completely with his own capital. In these new stores, he entered into a profit-sharing agreement with managers.

While Woolworth owed much of his success to low prices, his treatment of the customer was also important. In the 1870s and 1880s, patrons usually had to ask for goods held behind the counter, and prices varied according to the customer; it was considered impolite to enter a store without buying. Woolworth changed all that. His merchandise sat on counters for everyone to see. His price was the same for everyone. He encouraged people to enter the store even if they were just looking.

Another reason for Woolworth's success was the decline in wholesale prices during the first 12 years of Woolworth's existence. This led to wider availability of goods in the five and ten cent price range, wider margins, and higher profits. As operations grew, Woolworth found he needed a New York City office from which he could govern his stores. In July 1886, he took an office on Chambers Street. Soon after, he began writing a daily letter that went out to all store managers.

In 1888, Frank Woolworth contracted typhoid. Until then, he had handled everything from accounting to ordering to inspecting stores; however, after two months in bed, he realized the importance of delegating authority. With that in mind, he chose Carson C. Peck to run day-to-day operations. Peck had been a fellow clerk at A. Bushnell & Co. and a partner-manager in Woolworth's Utica, New York, store. He became Woolworth's first general manager.

Freed of day-to-day operations, Woolworth made his first European buying trip in 1890. On his return, U.S. consumers flocked to his stores to obtain pottery from England and Scotland, Christmas decorations from Germany, and other goods from the great commercial fairs of Europe.

The same year, Woolworth established the ''approved list.'' On the approved list were goods that Woolworth would reorder for his managers. This system allowed managers the leeway to adjust stock for local preferences while at the same time benefiting from the chain's buying power. In 1897, Woolworth opened his first Canadian store, in Toronto, Ontario. Three years later, there were 59 Woolworth's with sales of $5 million.

Tremendous Growth in Early 20th Century

By 1904, Woolworth was opening stores at a fantastic rate. He opened some stores from scratch. Others he converted from small chains he bought. In 1905 he incorporated as F.W. Woolworth & Co. At this point, Woolworth had $10 million in sales and 120 stores. In 1909, Woolworth sent three associates overseas to open the first of what was to be a hugely successful group of English stores, known as Three and Sixpence stores. In 1910, he appointed the first resident buyer in Germany, and, in 1911, he opened his first overseas warehouse at Fuerth, Germany.

At this point competition began to increase from such retailers as J.G. McCrory and S.S. Kresge Company. Also, many former partner-managers had chains of their own. In 1912, Woolworth saw the opportunity to create a huge new entity. He merged with five other retailers: W.H. Moore, C.S. Woolworth, F.M. Kirby, S.H. Knox, and E.P. Charlton. All were former partner-managers except for Earle Perry Charlton, who had built a chain of his own west of the Rocky Mountains. F.W. Woolworth & Co. became the publicly traded F.W. Woolworth Co., a nationwide retailer with 596 stores and $52 million in sales. Frank Woolworth was chief stockholder and president. The new retailing behemoth took residence in the 60-story neogothic Woolworth building in New York City. Frank Woolworth's office, within the $13.5 million ''Skyline Queen,'' was a replica of Napoleon Bonaparte's Empire Room.

In 1915, Carson Peck died. Peck had been supervising day-to-day operations since 1888. Woolworth assumed Peck's duties, but the strain proved to be too much. On April 8, 1919, Woolworth himself died. To succeed him as president, the board named Hubert T. Parson, Woolworth's first bookkeeper and later a company director and secretary-treasurer. The board also named Charles Sumner Woolworth, F.W. Woolworth's brother, chairman of the board.

Expansion continued under Parson. The company sent its first buyers to Japan in 1919. In 1924, it opened stores in Cuba. Woolworth inaugurated a German operating subsidiary in 1926, and, in 1927, opened its first German store. By the company's 50th anniversary in 1929, there were 2,247 Woolworth stores in the United States, Canada, Cuba, England, and Germany. Sales topped $303 million. In the United States, F.W. Woolworth was far and away the biggest five-and-ten retailer. Its 2,100 U.S.

stores had 1929 sales of $273 million. By comparison, J.G. McCrory had about 220 stores with $40 million in sales, and S.S. Kresge had about 500 stores with $147 million in sales.

The Great Depression caused the first decline in the company's sales since 1883, reaching a low of $250 million in 1932. In 1931, the company sold off part of its British operations, allowing that subsidiary to become a public company.

In 1932, Hubert Parsons retired and Byron D. Miller became the company's third president. Miller had worked his way up in the company and had helped start Woolworth's U.K. operations. Among Miller's first acts was to raise the ten cent price ceiling to 20 cents. Woolworth was the last five-and-ten chain to raise its prices. After three years in office, Miller retired and Charles Deyo became president. On taking office in 1935, Deyo and the board of directors removed all arbitrary price limits.

Sales turned upward during the late 1930s, but World War II posed new problems. Nearly half of Woolworth's male employees entered the Armed Forces, as did many female employees. During the war, women managed 500 stores. Demand expanded. Supplies were limited, but consumers tolerated substitutions, and because the war meant labor shortages, consumers also tolerated less service.

Prolonged Slump Following World War II

In 1946, Alfred Cornwell succeeded Deyo as president, while Deyo remained on as CEO. Under Deyo and Cornwell, Woolworth had difficulties adapting to the postwar rush of discount houses, supermarkets, and shopping centers. According to a 1965 Dun's Review article, "Woolworth was mired in a depression mentality. It was keeping costs down and prices low at a time when customers wanted service and when prosperity made prices a secondary consideration."

The situation began to deteriorate, and, in 1953, earnings hit a five-year low of $29.8 million. Concerned with what was happening, three board members—Allan P. Kirby, Seymour H. Knox, and Fremont C. Peck—forced Woolworth to create a new forward-looking finance and policy committee to combat what they saw as the management's overly conservative tendencies. Woolworth's British operation was having similar problems. Consumers were abandoning the stores for supermarkets and rivals such as Marks & Spencer, British Home Stores, and Littlewoods. In response, Woolworth increased the number of stores in England but did little to upgrade the existing outlets.

In 1954, James T. Leftwich became president. Leftwich addressed some of Woolworth's problems and spent $110 million to expand, modernize, and move stores. In 1956, Woolworth opened two stores in Mexico City, and, in 1957, began operations in Puerto Rico. Much was left to be done, however, under the leadership of Robert C. Kirkwood, who took over as president in 1958.

Under Kirkwood, Woolworth raised price limits and added profitable soft goods such as clothing and fabrics. Kirkwood also introduced self-service, opened hundreds of new stores, enlarged or relocated hundreds of others, and pushed Woolworth into shopping centers. Further, he increased advertising, instituted formal job training, and shortened hours and improved benefits for traditionally underpaid sales people, a move that reduced costly employee turnover from 43 percent to 19 percent.

Yet while Kirkwood was rejuvenating Woolworth, competitors such as Kresge and W.T. Grant had already overhauled their stores and were moving into new lines and new locations. Each was able to surpass Woolworth in earnings growth. In fact, while Woolworth sales surpassed $1 billion for the first time in 1960, U.S. earnings dropped from $14 million in 1960 to $12.6 million in 1963. It was only the return from British Woolworth that enabled consolidated earnings to keep moving upward. British stockholders later accused the U.S. board of milking the English operation without infusing the proper amount of capital.

Diversifying in the 1960s and 1970s

Woolworth and Kresge both sought new types of stores that would better fit the changing retail environment. In 1962, Woolworth opened the first Woolco, and S.S. Kresge opened the first Kmart. Each offered the services of a full-line department store and was very large—in some locations, more than 100,00 square feet. Woolworth had 17 Woolco stores by 1965, and as the 1960s continued, Woolworth expanded, diversified, and modernized. In 1965, it acquired the G.R. Kinney Corporation for $39 million. Founded by George Romanta Kinney in 1894, Kinney had 584 family shoe stores in 45 states. The same year, Lester A. Burcham became president of Woolworth. Under Burcham, Woolworth expanded operations into Spain and established a buying office in Tokyo. Two years later, it opened the first Woolco in England.

In 1968, sales topped $2 billion, and, in 1969, Woolworth acquired Williams the Shoemen, an Australian shoe store chain that has since become a dominant force in Australian shoe retailing with more than 460 stores ranging from high fashion to athletic and family footwear. Also in 1969, Woolworth acquired Richman Brothers Company, a manufacturer and retailer of men's and boys' clothing. Finally, as part of a 90th anniversary celebration, Woolworth replaced the old "Diamond W" logo with a modern looking white "W" on a light blue field.

Yet Woolworth was still not growing at the rate of its competitors. By 1970, sales at Kresge were running essentially neck and neck with Woolworth. One problem was British Woolworth. In 1965, Woolworth's 52.7 percent-owned subsidiary, F.W. Woolworth Ltd., had contributed 50 percent of the parent company's profits, but during the late 1960s it began a steep decline. The reasons included a lack of investment, a devaluation of the pound, and an increase in employment taxes. By 1969, the British subsidiary was contributing just 30 percent of profits. In an effort to gain market share, British management cut prices. Sales grew, but profits fell.

John S. Roberts, who became Woolworth's president in 1970, also needed to address problems at Woolco, which was performing at nowhere near the rate of Kmart. His solution was to consolidate Woolworth and Woolco in one division in 1972. Rather than providing economies, however, the consolidation only blurred the identity of each chain. Woolworth's 1973 sales were $3.7 billion; Kresge's were $4.6 billion, 90 percent of which was generated by Kmart. A positive event occurred, however, in 1974, when the Kinney shoe division opened the first two Foot Locker stores, athletic-shoe retailers that would later prove highly profitable.

With stock prices on the wane, the board recognized the need for change, and, in 1975, named outsider Edward F. Gibbons president. Gibbons in turn named W. Robert Harris the first president of the U.S. Woolworth and Woolco Division. In 1978, consolidated annual sales topped $6 billion, of which Kinney, growing at a rate of 18 to 20 percent a year, contributed $800 million. Also in 1978, Harris became president and Gibbons became chief executive officer.

Juggling of Store Lineup in 1980s and Early 1990s

While Woolco continued its sluggish growth and Woolworth stores suffered neglect, F.W. Woolworth Co. continued diversifying. In 1979, Woolworth opened the first J. Brannam, a men's clothing store whose name stood for ''just brand names.'' J. Brannam was a quick moneymaker and often stood within or beside otherwise lackluster Woolco department stores. No matter how much the management tinkered, the problems of Woolco refused to go away. After the stores lost $19 million in 1981, Harris and Gibbons hired Bruce G. Albright to revive the ailing chain. Albright, who had come from competitor Dayton Hudson's Target stores, had a plan to revive Woolco, but company projections still saw the stores losing money. After Woolco lost $21 million during the first six months of 1982, Gibbons decided to shut down all 336 Woolcos in the United States, shrinking the $7.2 billion company 30 percent and laying off 25,000 employees. Closing costs were estimated at $325 million.

In the fall of 1982, Woolworth disclosed plans to sell its interest in British Woolworth to a syndicate of English investors, for $279 million. One analyst, quoted in Business Week, October 11, 1982, blamed British Woolworth's failure on the U.S. parent, saying, ''The American Woolworth has been milking the British unit for years, insisting on high dividend payout that has forced it to scrimp on investment and to take on more and more debt.''

Analysts, however, were pleased with the company that remained. Left were the profitable, but shaky, 1,300 variety stores, Richman Brothers, and Kinney Shoe Corporation—a $1.1 billion division that had done well with Kinney, Foot Locker, a women's clothing store known as Susie's Casuals, and the newly created and profitable J. Brannam. Woolco's closing, however, left 28 of the 41 J. Brannam outlets homeless.

Edward F. Gibbons died suddenly in October 1982. Contrary to expectations and much to the chagrin of younger talent, the board named company veteran John W. (Bud) Lynn chief executive officer. As a variety store man, Lynn paid close attention to Woolworth's. He changed merchandise, reducing the number of high-priced items such as appliances and dresses and expanding basic lines like candy, and health and beauty aids. He arranged stores in arrow patterns to cut down on unprofitable corners.

Lynn pushed the company to adopt a set of strategic priorities that angled Woolworth away from money-losing businesses and toward specialty retailing. Kinney's Canadian operation had started the remarkably successful Lady Foot Locker in 1982, and in 1983 Woolworth paid $27 million for Holtzman's Little Folk Shop, a full-price children's clothing merchandiser and its subsidiary, Kids Mart, a discount operation.

Lynn retired in 1987, and the board named Harold Sells as the new chief executive officer. Sells continued to push Woolworth's profitable mall-based specialty operations. Managers sought out new ideas for stores, and those that the company liked were tried. If the stores were profitable, Woolworth's opened more. If they were not profitable, the company tried another idea at the same location.

In 1990, Woolworth opened 896 stores and closed 351. Many of the new ventures were specialty stores, such as Kinneys, Kids Marts, Foot Lockers, and Lady Foot Lockers. The latter two sold a full 20 percent of all brand-name athletic footwear in the United States in the late 1980s. The 40 types of specialty stores included After Thoughts, seller of costume jewelry and handbags; Champs, seller of athletic goods and apparel; and Woolworth Express, seller of the fastest-moving goods of a traditional Woolworth.

In 1993, Sells retired and was replaced as by CFO William Lavin, who quickly made moves toward the elimination of the company's general merchandise stores in favor of an exclusive focus on specialty formats. Four hundred Woolworth's were closed in the United States, and 122 Woolco stores in Canada were sold to Wal-Mart, terminating Woolco altogether. Woolworth also sold 300 underperforming Kinney outlets and liquidated the 286-store Richman Brothers/Anderson-Little men's and women's clothing stores. Along with the nearly 1,000 stores, about 13,000 jobs were eliminated. As a result of these moves, the company recorded a $558 million charge resulting in a net 1993 loss of $495 million.

These radical moves were barely complete when an accounting scandal arose in early 1994, revolving around alleged false reporting of quarterly results during 1993. Several lawsuits were filed which were eventually combined into a class-action lawsuit. This suit appeared to be settled by mid-1997 when Woolworth agreed to make undisclosed cash payments to affected shareholders. Later in 1994, Lavin was forced out, and Roger Farah became chairman and CEO in December 1994.

Rebuilding in the Late 1990s

Farah, a longtime department store manager who had most recently been president of R.H. Macy & Co., took over a Woolworth in shambles. Thanks to dwindling profits, by early 1995, the company was nearly out of cash, and short-term debt had swelled to $853 million. Consequently, Farah's first task was to improve cash flow in 1995. To do so, he broke Woolworth's string of 83 straight years of dividends; restructured company debt, reducing total debt by $475 million and shifting $290 million of short-term debt to longer-term financing; reduced operating spending by $100 million; wrote off $241 million of inventory; and began to sell off nonstrategic chains and real estate. Early in 1995, Woolworth sold the Rx Place chain of pharmacies for $37 million and the 331 Kids Mart/Little Folks children's clothing stores to the LFS Acquisition investor group for $15 million. Two other Canadian chains, Karuba and Canary Island, were also closed during the year.

The various charges incurred as a result of these actions led to a net loss of $164 million.

In 1996, Woolworth continued to restructure. Short-term debt was eliminated altogether, and total debt was reduced an additional $116 million. Another $100 million in operating spending was eliminated, and $222 million in cash was generated from the disposal of additional nonstrategic chains and real estate. Among the divestments were the Accessory Lady chain in the United States; the Silk & Satin lingerie chain in Canada; the Lady Plus apparel chain, the Rubin jewelry chain, the Moderna shoe store chain, and the New Yorker jeans business, all in Germany; and the Gallery shoe store chain in Australia. All told, 1,443 unproductive stores were disposed of in 1995 and 1996.

In the midst of these moves, institutional investor Greenway Partners forced to a vote a shareholder proposal to spin off Woolworth's Athletic Group, which included the profitable and growing Foot Locker and Champs chains. However, the plan was soundly defeated. Unlike his predecessor, Farah was not ready to give up on the neglected Woolworth's chain. To better monitor and plan sales, point-of-sale equipment was installed at all locations in 1995, and purchasing, pricing policies, and promotional strategies were all centralized. He assembled a management team of veterans of successful high volume specialty stores and streamlined merchandising systems.

In 1996, the chain began testing new formats featuring higher-quality (and higher-priced) merchandise, with more brand names. Based on customer surveys, the prototype stores were aimed at the time-pressed and budget-minded working woman looking for products for herself, her home, and her family. So, rather than carrying everything from hamsters to beach chairs, the product mix included more cosmetics and housewares. The antiquated lunch counters were replaced by small coffee bars. The three-store 1996 test was successful enough to justify an expansion of the test to 13 more stores in 1997.

Overall, Woolworth's fortunes improved in the late 1990s, as the company posted a net profit of $169 million in 1996. The company appeared to be on track with the paring back of its unwieldy portfolio of retail formats. Farah began piecing together a sporting goods conglomerate on the foundation of Foot Locker and Champs Sports, acquiring the operations of Sporting Goods, Athletic Fibers, and Eastbay Inc., a Wausau, Wisconsin-based catalog company specializing in athletic footwear. Woolworth and Eastbay planned to develop catalogs for such Woolworth retail brands as Foot Locker and Champs.

Nevertheless, in a telling psychological blow, Woolworth was replaced by Wal-Mart on the Dow Jones Industrial Average in 1997. The chain experienced a $24 million operating loss for the first quarter as compared to a loss of $37 million for all of 1996. Unable to withstand such hemorrhaging long enough to turn the chain around, Woolworth announced on July 17, 1997, that it would close its more than 400 five-and-dime stores in the United States, lay off about 9,200 Woolworth's workers (about 11 percent of the company's workforce), and take a $223 million charge for the discontinued operations. The company planned to convert about 100 of the Woolworth's locations to Foot Locker, Champs Sports, and other specialty formats. Although the Woolworth's chain had seen the final chapter written on its history in the United States, the chain's saga would continue in Mexico and Germany, where about 70% of the five-and-dimes still operated. The German stores were sold off in 1998.

The company also announced that it planned to change its name, according to company literature, "to better reflect its global specialty retailing formats." The new corporate name, the Venator Group, inspired by the Latin word for sportsman, was intended to describe "a global team of retailers . . . invigorated by the challenge of winning in the world's marketplace." In preparation for the change, the company spent more than $130 million to streamline merchandising and back office operations. Over the next three years, it went on to spend another $149 million to redesign the architecture of its information systems for the development of an integrated global retailing approach. In the United States, the Venator Group established 719 such stores and remodeled 582 in 1998. It simultaneously debuted its web site, which featured virtual stores selling athletic footwear, equipment, apparel and accessories from the various Foot Lockers, Champs Sports, and Eastbay lines.

Unfortunately the retailing environment for athletic footwear had become difficult during this time, as consumer tastes shifted to street shoes, fleece, and denim. Foot Locker, as the largest athletic specialty store, while not alone in missing the shift, was more affected by it than its smaller competitors. The Venator Group, under the direction of president and chief executive officer Dale Hilpert since late 1999, responded by expanding its catalog and e-commerce interests, by exiting eight of its non-core businesses, and by closing stores and slashing jobs. The cutbacks continued into January 2000 when Venator announced the closing of 123 Foot Locker, Lady Foot Locker, and Kids Foot Locker stores, 27 Champs Sports units, and 208 Northern Group stores. Venator also began to consolidate the managements of Kids and Lady Foot Lockers concepts into one organization and to reduce expenses and workforce.

By the second half of 1999, Venator Group began to generate significant same-store sales gains, fueled by growth in the high-end footwear category. The company experienced a small increase in comparable-store sales, and its athletic stores gained in market share in 1999. In addition, the direct-to-customer business enacted via Footlocker.com enjoyed a 21.9 percent increase in business that year. By spring 2000, shoe sales throughout the industry were showing signs of rebounding. With 17 percent of the $14 billion U.S. athletic footwear market, 3,700 athletic retail stores in 14 countries, $3.8 billion in annual sales, and significant opportunities in the global market, the Venator Group anticipated gaining market share through increased productivity at its retail stores and through its catalog and Internet businesses.

Into the New Millennium

The beginning of the 21st century was marked by a change in management at Venator. President Roger Farah resigned in 2000 to take over the top slot at Polo/Ralph Lauren. Chairman and CEO Dale Hilpert resigned soon after to become CEO of Williams-Sonoma. Venator's board named COO Matthew Serra to replace both men in 2001. Although Hilpert and Farah had shared responsibility for refocusing the former discount store toward athletic apparel, Serra was the one responsible for bringing Foot Locker to prominence in its field of retail. Soon after Serra took over management of the corporation Venator announced that it was closing its Northern Reflections stores in the United States in order to concentrate exclusively on athletic apparel. In the fall of 2001, this change was reflected when the Venator board voted to change the name of the corporation to Foot Locker Inc.

The newly refocused company began to expand beyond its traditional mall-focused retail model early in 2002, introducing stores in areas outside malls near movie theaters, restaurants, gaming outlets, and other areas that attracted a younger clientele. Management explained that this was due partly to the fact that Foot Locker had already established stores in malls across the United States, and partly because the chain wanted to capture sales from people who were out looking for entertainment.

During the 2002 Christmas season, Foot Locker squabbled with Nike, one of its major brands, over the restrictions Nike was placing on sales outlets that carried its products. Some top-of-the-line Nike products, such as the Air Jordan athletic shoes, sold very well in Foot Locker stores and brought the retailer a nice profit. In order to carry the high-end ''marquee'' products, however, Nike required retailers to purchase a certain number of less-popular lines. If those lines didn't sell well, the retailer lost money. In order to improve its sales performance, Foot Locker announced that it would not carry Nike products unless it received better pricing and product from the vendor. Both businesses suffered as a result of the decision, but by the end of 2003 they had negotiated an agreement and were looking forward to placing Nike products in Foot Locker stores once again.

In mid-April 2004 Foot Locker significantly increased its market share in the rival Footaction retail chain from the bankrupt retailer Footstar Inc.. Within a few weeks, however, Finish Line countered with a larger bid for about half of Footaction's stores. Foot Locker responded by raising its initial bid of $160 million to $225 million. The competition between the two intensified the following month when Finish Line filed a corporate espionage suit against Foot Locker, claiming that the retailer was actively recruiting management from its stores.

The suit was perhaps less significant for its claims than for highlighting the extent to which Foot Locker had come to dominate the U.S. athletic apparel market. In the six years following Matthew Serra's arrival at Venator, he had led a team that turned the company around, from a money-losing, diverse corporation to a lean, focused retail powerhouse. ''Foot Locker has been very successful during this time frame in terms of growing sales and profits and our shareholders have been nicely rewarded,'' Serra told Katie Abel of *Footwear News*. ''As a result, I believe the morale of our organization is high and our 44,000 worldwide associates come to work each day with a winning attitude.''

Principal Operating Units

Foot Locker; Kids Foot Locker; Lady Foot Locker; Footaction USA; Champs Sports; Eastbay.

Principal Competitors

The Sports Authority, Inc.; The Finish Line, Inc.

Further Reading

Abel, Katie, ''Athletic Chains Aim for Diversity; in 2002, Major Retailers Foot Locker and Footstar Are Moving Beyond the Traditional Mall,'' *Footwear News,* May 6, 2002, p. 2.

——, ''Extreme Makeover; Top Executive Matt Serra Has Cleaned House and Rebuilt the Company from the Ground Up,'' *Footwear News,* June 28, 2004, p.16.

——, ''Foot Locker, Nike Seeking Detente,'' *Footwear News,* July 21, 2003, p. 6.

''Arsenal Mall in Watertown,'' *Chain Store Age Executive,* July 1998, p.1.

Berman, Phyllis, and Caroline Waxler, ''Woolworth's Woes,'' *Forbes,* August 14, 1995, pp. 47–48.

Biesada, Alexandra, ''Dumping on the Dime Store,'' *Financial World,* October 30, 1990, p. 62.

Bird, Laura, ''Hamsters Get Heave-Ho in New Five-and-Tens,'' *Wall Street Journal,* September 26, 1996, pp. B1, B10.

——, ''Woolworth Corp. to Post a Charge and Cut 9,200 Jobs,'' *Wall Street Journal,* July 18, 1997, p. C16.

——, ''Woolworth Is Hoping to Score in Sportswear,'' *Wall Street Journal,* March 12, 1997, pp. B1, B6.

Bongiorno, Lori, ''Lost in the Aisles at Woolworth's,'' *Business Week,* October 30, 1995, pp. 76, 78.

Carofano, Jennifer, ''Antitrust Review Next for Foot Locker,'' *Footwear News,* April 26, 2004, p. 2.

Currier, Al, ''Woolworth's: The Prototypical Small-Town Store; Store Founder Credited with Launch of Low-Cost, Large-Scale Retailing,'' *Bellingham Business Journal,* May, 2002, p. C12.

''Foot Locker: The Prince of Retail,'' *DSN Retailing Today,* September 3, 2001, p. 4.

Gill, Penny, ''Sells: Key Player in Woolworth Renaissance,'' *Stores,* May 1991, p. 24.

Karr, Arnold J., ''Serra Takes CEO Slot at Venator,'' *WWD,* February 13, 2001, p. 2.

Miller, Annetta, ''A Dinosaur No More: Woolworth Corp. Leaves Dime Stores Far Behind,'' *Newsweek,* January 4, 1993, pp. 54–55.

Nichols, John P., *Skyline Queen and the Merchant Prince,* New York: Pocket Books, 1973.

''100th Anniversary, 1879–1979,'' New York: F.W. Woolworth Co., 1979.

Ryan, Thomas, ''Foot Locker Steps Toward Greater Profits,'' *Sporting Goods Business,* February, 2003, p. 42.

——, ''Hot off the Shelf: The Nike/Foot Locker Squabble over Marquee Product Produces a Windfall for Their Competitors,'' *Sporting Goods Business,* November, 2002, p. 20.

Saporito, Bill, ''Woolworth to Rule the Malls,'' *Fortune,* June 5, 1989, p. 145.

Weitzman, Jennifer, ''Venator Earnings On Target,'' *WWD,* January 29, 2001, p. 24.

Winkler, John K., *Five and Ten: The Fabulous Life of F.W. Woolworth,* Freeport, N.Y.: Books for Libraries Press, 1970 (reprint of 1940 edition).

Woolworth's First 75 Years: The Story of Everybody's Store, New York: F.W. Woolworth Co., 1954.

Young, Vicki M., ''Venator Accused of Ageism,'' *HFN,* July 12, 1999, p. 8.

Zinn, Laura, ''Why 'Business Stinks' at Woolworth,'' *Business Week,* November 25, 1991, pp. 72, 76.

—Jordan Wankoff
—updates: David E. Salamie, Carrie Rothburd, Kenneth R. Shepherd

FORTUNE BRANDS

Fortune Brands, Inc.

300 Tower Parkway
Lincolnshire, Illinois 60069
U.S.A.
Telephone: (847) 484-4400
Fax: (847) 478-0073
Web site: http://www.fortunebrands.com

Public Company
Incorporated: 1904 as The American Tobacco Company
Employees: 30,988
Sales: $6.21 billion (2003)
Stock Exchanges: New York
Ticker Symbol: FO
NAIC: 551112 Offices of Other Holding Companies; 312140 Distilleries; 337110 Wood Cabinet and Countertop Manufacturing; 323116 Manifold Business Forms Printing; 332116 Metal Stamping; 333313 Office Machinery Manufacturing; 339920 Sporting and Athletic Goods Manufacturing; 332913 Plumbing Fixture Fitting and Trim Manufacturing; 332919 Other Metal Valve and Pipe Fitting Manufacturing; 422340 Footwear Wholesalers

Fortune Brands, Inc., is a widely diversified conglomerate with principal businesses in distilled spirits, home products, hardware, office supplies, and golf equipment. Most of its brands are either number one or number two in their market categories. Fortune's brands include Jim Beam, the world's best-selling bourbon, Swingline staplers, Acco paper clips, Master Lock padlocks, Moen faucets, and Titleist and Pinnacle golf balls. Fortune was a major player in the tobacco industry until the late 1990s, when it sold its domestic and foreign tobacco interests and got out of that business entirely. Nearly 20 of the company's brands generate more than $100 million in sales.

Early History

Fortune Brands traces its origin to the remarkable career of James Buchanan (Buck) Duke, founder of The American Tobacco Company. Duke was born in 1856 on a small farm outside Durham, North Carolina, where his father, Washington Duke, raised crops and livestock. The Duke farm was ravaged by armies of both North and South at the end of the Civil War, and upon his release from a military prison Washington Duke found that his sole remaining asset was a small barn full of bright leaf tobacco. Bright leaf, so called because of its golden color, had been introduced only recently, but its smooth smoking characteristics were already making it a favorite, and its fame was soon spread by the returning war veterans. Duke set out to peddle what leaf he had, and, pleased with the response, he quickly converted his land to tobacco culture, selling his wares under the name Pro Bono Publico, meaning "for the public good" in Latin. In its first year of operation, W. Duke & Sons sold 15,000 pounds of tobacco and netted a very handsome $5,000.

Along with his father, his brother Benjamin, and half-brother Brodie, Buck Duke labored to make the family business succeed, working long hours from childhood and learning every aspect of the tobacco business from crop to smoke. Duke's timing was fortuitous—bright leaf tobacco became the most prized of all U.S. varieties, and Durham was the epicenter of bright leaf country. By far the best-known brand of bright leaf was Bull Durham, the label of William T. Blackwell & Company. Blackwell gained a long lead on the rest of the Durham tobacco merchants, including the Dukes, who did not establish their first true factory in Durham until 1873. The Dukes chose to concentrate their energies on the manufacture and sale of tobacco rather than on raising the crop, which was notoriously erratic in quality and quantity. Buying their leaf from local farmers, the Dukes cured and then shred or compressed the tobacco to form, respectively, smoking or chewing tobacco. As cigarettes were hardly yet known, tobacco smoking was accomplished with a pipe or in cigars, the latter not being made by the Dukes.

Buck Duke attended a business school for six months in 1874, when he was 18, and became an increasingly dominant figure in the family business. Intensely ambitious, single-minded, and aggressive, Duke had no interest in anything less than mastery of the tobacco business. In 1878, Buck, Washington, and Ben Duke formed a partnership with businessman George Watts of Baltimore, Maryland, each contributing equally to the capital base of $70,000. Richard H. Wright joined the partnership two years later. The company was profitable and

Company Perspectives:

Behind our brands is a heritage of innovation few can match. In 1795, a grain mill operator named Jacob Beam filled his first barrel of bourbon . . . and more than two centuries later, the bourbon that bears his great-grandson's name remains true to its unsurpassed authenticity. In 1904, a company founded by a jewelry repairman improved the workplace with the invention of the ring binder . . . and Wilson Jones still sells hundreds of millions of them year after year. In 1924, Master Lock founder Harry Soref invented the laminated padlock . . . and it remains the ''Tough Under Fire'' market leader today. In 1935, two college class-mates, Phil Young and Fred Bommer, set out to create a superior golf ball; they named it Titleist and began the longest-running success story in golf. In 1937, a young inventor named Al Moen created the single-handle faucet; billions of dollars in sales later, Moen is a household name and our single largest brand. The same spirit of innovation that inspired these pioneers runs through our operations today. We see building our brands for internal growth as our best investment. So to leverage the imagination of our inventors, researchers and developers, we invest heavily in product development to deliver next-generation innovations to consumers.

expanding, but Buck Duke was dissatisfied with its role in second place to Blackwell's Bull Durham, and in 1881 he decided to enter the new and relatively small field of cigarettes. At the time, there were only four major producers of cigarettes in the United States, and none of them had yet understood the potential importance of mechanized rolling machines and widespread advertising. Duke appreciated the power of both, and he set out to catch the four leaders.

Duke located and leased two of the new automatic rollers invented by James Bonsack of Virginia, who agreed to give Duke a permanent discount in exchange for taking a chance on the untested machines. After some adjustments, the machine proved capable of rolling about 200 cigarettes per minute, or 50 times the production of the best hand-rollers. Duke next revamped his packaging, devising the slide and shell box to offer better protection against crushing. He then marketed his Duke of Durham cigarettes at ten for five cents, or half of the usual price. This combination of excellent bright leaf tobacco, smart packaging, and a discount price was an immediate success, and to these tangible virtues Duke soon added the intangible power of advertising. He very early recognized that advertising would determine success in the cigarette business and throughout the 1880s spent unprecedented amounts of money on promotional gimmicks of every stripe, much to the astonishment, ridicule, and—later—regret of his rivals.

While Richard Wright handled marketing overseas and Edward F. Small built up the western U.S. trade, Duke himself decided in 1884 to meet his competitors head on in New York City, the largest market and manufacturing center of the cigarette business. He moved to the city, established a local factory, and commenced an all-out war against the four leading companies—Allen & Ginter, Kinney Brothers, and Goodwin, all of New York City, and Kimball of Rochester, New York. The Big Four sold 80 percent of the nation's 409 million cigarettes in 1880. After a few years of Duke's relentless campaign, the total market had swollen to 2.2 billion, and W. Duke & Sons owned 38 percent of it. The Duke name appeared on billboards, storefront windows, and the sides of barns around the country, as well as on some 380,000 chairs Duke distributed free of charge to tobacconists. By 1889, company sales reached $4.25 million and net income was one-tenth of that. Duke had grown to dominance of the cigarette business in a single decade and, shortly, was to duplicate the feat worldwide.

Though triumphant, Duke was faced with the prospect of continuing bitter competition and restricted profits. The 32-year-old veteran thereupon proposed a solution that was startling in scope: to merge all five of the competitors and, by joining forces, bring to an end the wasteful price warfare. His fellow manufacturers at first balked at the initiative, but they eventually agreed and in January 1890 formed The American Tobacco Company, its $25 million in capital divided among ten incorporators, with J.B. Duke named president. The new company, one of the first true combinations in the history of U.S. business, controlled 80 percent of the nation's cigarette business and showed a net profit of $3 million in its first year.

Whereas American Tobacco was a large concern, it was by no means the entire tobacco industry, and having once captured the cigarette business Duke set to work on the rest of the tobacco world. In 1891, American Tobacco bought out 80 percent of the relatively minor snuff business; four years later, Duke launched what has come to be known as the ''plug wars.'' Between 1895 and 1898, American Tobacco waged a prolonged struggle to enter the field of plug, or chewing, tobacco, the largest of the various tobacco markets. With this move Duke made clear the extent of his ambitions, and a number of the original American Tobacco incorporators saw fit to sell their stock rather than join him in what they saw as a foolhardy battle against superior odds. Duke's ambition proved to be realistic, however, and after three short years of price wars and buyouts he had secured more than 60 percent of the vast plug market, including such later giants as Lorillard, Liggett & Meyers, and Drummond. Duke's methods in doing so were much like those he used in the snuff, smoking tobacco, and cigar segments of the industry. Selective price wars were followed by acquisitions, followed by the return of prices to a more profitable and unchallenged level. Many of these practices were in violation of the Sherman Antitrust Act, one of whose more spectacular victims would later be J.B. Duke. For a long time the extent of American Tobacco's holdings was not obvious, as many of Duke's 250 acquisitions managed to maintain secrecy about their new affiliation; neither Congress nor the executive branch of government became interested in taking on the combinations until the first decade of the next century.

At the conclusion of the plug wars in 1898, Duke united his various plug companies into a new holding company called Continental Tobacco Company, most of whose stock was in turn owned by American Tobacco. In 1901, American Tobacco bought itself the largest share of the cigar industry, which, however, frustrated all efforts at monopoly because of the difficulty and variety of cigar manufacture; in the same year, American Tobacco acquired a controlling interest in what would become

Key Dates:

1890: The American Tobacco Company is formed.
1911: The U.S. Supreme Court orders the dissolution of the American Tobacco Company.
1969: After diversifying into alcohol, office products, and other non-tobacco businesses earlier in the decade, American Tobacco changes its name to American Brands.
1979: American Brands acquires The Franklin Life Insurance Company.
1991: American Brands greatly increases its distilled spirits business by acquiring seven brands from Seagram Company.
1994: American Brands exits the tobacco business.
1996: American Brands changes its name to Fortune Brands, Inc.
1999: Fortune Brands acquires Schrock Cabinet Co.
2002: Omega Holdings, Inc., the fourth-largest cabinet maker in the United States, is acquired.
2003: Fortune acquires Therma-Tru Holdings, Inc., the leading brand of residential entry doors in the United States, in a $924 million transaction.

the dominant retailer of tobacco in the country, United Cigar Stores Company. Having thus finished off nearly the entire domestic tobacco industry, Duke tightened his grip on his family of holdings, in 1901 forming and retaining the largest shareholding in Consolidated Tobacco Company, which in turn bought up the assets of the former American and Continental companies in a transaction that netted him a tidy profit while also providing more direct corporate control. Finally, Duke began to expand internationally. After a nationwide price war in England against a coalition of the leading British tobacco men, the two sides agreed not to compete in each other's countries and to pursue jointly the rest of the world's markets through a company called British-American Tobacco Company, two-thirds of which was won by James Duke and his allies. Even at this early date, the overseas retail trade was significant. British-American soon employed some 25,000 salesmen in Asia alone, all of them working under Duke's director of foreign sales, James A. Thomas.

Duke's control of United Cigar Stores' more than 500 outlets gave the public a clearer picture of the extent of Duke's domain, and his company soon faced rising criticism and opposition, some of it violent. Those in both the industry and the public had reason to dislike Duke and his cartel; Kentucky tobacco growers, for example, their prices repeatedly lowered by the single large buyer in town, banded together in 1906 to burn down a number of the trust's large tobacco warehouses. More serious was the increasing pressure brought to bear by the U.S. Department of Justice, which took heart under the administration of President Theodore Roosevelt and began a series of antitrust actions against the industrial combines. In 1907, the department filed suit against Duke's creation, now once again called American Tobacco Company, and in 1911 the Supreme Court agreed that the trust must be dissolved to restore competition to the tobacco industry. Total corporate assets were estimated at more than $500 million.

From the complex dissolution of American Tobacco, designed and overseen by James Duke himself, came the elements of the modern tobacco industry. Spun off as new corporate entities were Liggett & Meyers, Lorillard, R.J. Reynolds, and a new, smaller American Tobacco Company. With the exception of Reynolds, these companies were given assets in all phases of the tobacco business, and Reynolds, the youngest and most aggressive of the companies, soon acquired what it lacked. Control of British-American Tobacco was lost to the British, where it has remained. Duke turned over direction of American Tobacco to Percival S. Hill, one of his veteran lieutenants, and himself went with British-American as chairman and one of its directors. The founder retained large holdings of stock in each of the newly formed spin-offs and, upon his death, left a great deal of money to the eponymous Duke University and a score of other charitable causes.

Growth during World War II

At the time of its dissolution, the tobacco industry still exhibited two characteristics soon to be swept aside by modern advertising and changing tastes. The business continued to be dominated by chewing tobacco, and it featured a plethora of brands. In 1903, for example, no fewer than 12,600 brands of chewing tobacco were listed by an industry catalog, along with 2,124 types of cigarettes. In 1913, Joshua Reynolds, founder of R.J. Reynolds, introduced the era of nationally known cigarette brands with his new Camel, a blend of bright leaf and sweet burley tobacco that took the country by storm. Camel was probably the most successful cigarette ever launched, and in 1916 American Tobacco answered with Lucky Strike, while Liggett & Meyers pushed its Chesterfield. The blitz of advertising that followed caused an enormous upsurge in national consumption, from 25 billion cigarettes in 1916 to 53 billion three years later. By 1923, cigarettes had passed chewing tobacco as America's favorite form of nicotine, an evolution helped immeasurably by the growing acceptance of women smokers, for whom the cigarette was the only fashionable form of smoking.

Under the leadership of Percival Hill and, after 1926, his son George Washington Hill, American Tobacco battled Reynolds for decades in the race for cigarette dominance. Each of the Big Four manufacturers settled on one or, at most, a few brands and spent inordinate amounts of money on advertising in both print and radio formats. The Great Depression years were not as bad for the tobacco companies as they were for many industries. Consumption in 1940 was nevertheless no higher than it had been ten years before, with Lucky Strike sales hovering at around 40 billion cigarettes annually. World War II and its attendant anxieties provided an instant sales boost, however, pushing Lucky Strike totals to 60 billion by 1945 and 100 billion a few years later. American Tobacco also found a winner in Pall Mall, which ushered in the "king size" era of 85-millimeter cigarettes in 1939 and soon was challenging Lucky Strike and Camel for the top spot. So complete was the triumph of the cigarette that when American Tobacco's sales reached $764 million in 1946, fully 95 percent of it was generated by cigarettes.

Postwar Years

The immediate postwar years were good for American Tobacco, which upped its overall share of the domestic tobacco market to 32.6 percent in 1953. However, that would prove to be the high-water mark for the company's cigarette business. The year before, R.J. Reynolds introduced Winston, the first filtered cigarette, and inaugurated the trend toward lighter and less harmful smokes. American Tobacco replied with its Herbert Tareyton Filters in 1954, but with both Lucky and Pall Mall among the top three sellers overall it felt no urgency about the filter business and did not spend the money and effort needed to establish its brands in the new category. This failure would be crucial in determining the subsequent development of American Tobacco, which never did catch up to its competitors and eventually assumed a minor role in the cigarette world. While Reynolds and later Philip Morris reaped fortunes with Winston and Marlboro, American Tobacco belatedly pushed losers such as Hit Parade, a cigarette so unpopular that the company was reportedly unable to give away free samples.

In the long run, however, American Tobacco's relative failure in cigarettes may have been a blessing. Beginning in the mid-1960s, the company used the steady cash flow from its remaining tobacco business to make a number of promising acquisitions. Chief among these were Gallagher Ltd., one of the United Kingdom's largest tobacco companies; James B. Beam Distilling Company; Sunshine Biscuits; Duffy-Mott; and several makers of office products. In recognition of the company's changing profile, it was renamed American Brands in 1969, by which date its share of the domestic tobacco market had slipped to 20 percent and continued to decline. After a handful of other minor acquisitions, American Brands made its largest purchase in 1979, buying The Franklin Life Insurance Company, the tenth largest life insurer in the United States. By that time, non-tobacco assets were generating one-third of American Brands' operating income of $364 million, and the company's diversification program generally was regarded as a modest success.

American Brands, however, was weakest in the most lucrative of its markets, domestic tobacco. The increasing stigma attached to tobacco sales and the threat of government restrictions have ensured immense profits for those few companies still in the U.S. tobacco business, as no new potential competitors are willing to venture into such troubled waters. Even as the cigarette makers diversify, therefore, domestic tobacco continues to pay up to 35 percent on every sales dollar, providing cash needed to diversify further out of tobacco. In domestic tobacco, American Brands' share of the market eventually fell to the neighborhood of ten percent. The $1.6 billion in sales generated there in 1990, however, returned more operating income than did the company's $6.4 billion in overseas tobacco business, where margins were much tighter and equaled the return of all of the non-tobacco divisions taken together.

American Brands fought off a takeover bid by E-II Holdings in the late 1980s and significantly strengthened its position in liquor and office products. Its liquor division was the third-largest seller of spirits in the United States, its office products division was billed as the world's largest, and Gallagher Limited had grown into the leading U.K. tobacco company, far outstripping its parent company's tobacco sales. Earnings growth had been steady for years at American Brands, whose balanced revenue structure rendered the company relatively immune to sudden downturns in any one area.

Without Tobacco in the 1990s

In 1991, American Brands strengthened its hold on the distilled spirits market by acquiring seven brands from the Seagram Company. American spent $372.5 million for the brands, which represented approximately one-quarter of giant Seagram's sales in the United States. In the midst of a down turn in liquor consumption, Seagram had decided that those who were drinking less should drink better. Thus, it wanted to unload some of its less prestigious brands. American, however, was deliberately pursuing the opposite tack, aiming for more budget-conscious consumers. The brands it took over from Seagram were the American whiskies Calvert Extra and Kessler, Canadian whisky Lord Calvert, Calvert gin, Ronrico rum, Wolfschmidt vodka, and Leroux liquor. The acquisition made American's subsidiary Jim Beam Brand Company the third largest spirits company in the United States. American's strategy seemed profitable. Though its new liquor brands and its tobacco brands lacked both snob appeal and great market share, they did make money. Profits rose to record levels in 1991, with a rise of almost 40 percent for the year. Liquor sales, bucked by the Seagram acquisition, rose 12 percent, and tobacco sales rose all of 1 percent. This small rise, however, was the first increase for American since 1965.

By mid-1992, American Brands was confident that it had found a way to hang onto its tobacco business despite hard times for the industry. The threat of lawsuits and overall decline in smoking made conditions harsh domestically, and U.S. tobacco sales overall were declining by about 3 percent annually. However, American energetically pursued a low-price strategy. It introduced several new brands, all priced at several dollars less per carton than leading brands like Marlboro and Winston. Though American's Pall Mall was fading, with sales dropping almost 20 percent in 1991, its new Misty and Montclair racked up sales. Extensive advertising trumpeted the new brands' principal virtue: they were cheap. Similarly, in its spirits division, American's marketers claimed that its brands were just as good as the ones that cost more. The company seemed to have hit on a winning strategy, so it was somewhat of a surprise when in April 1994 American sold off all its American tobacco business. B.A.T. Industries, long ago the British sister of Duke's American Tobacco, bought up American Brands' tobacco holdings for $1 billion. Tobacco had made up 58 percent of revenues and 66 percent of profits for American in 1991. Now it was out of tobacco altogether except for one British cigarette manufacturer, Gallagher.

Six months after B.A.T. bought the tobacco division, American also sold off its profitable insurance subsidiary, Franklin Life Insurance Co. Franklin was bought by American General Corp. in a deal estimated to be worth $1.2 billion. Franklin had assets of $6.2 billion and had a strong market share, principally in small towns and with middle-income blue-collar customers. The company was a money-maker for its parent, yet it was American's only financial service unit, and in many ways American looked better without it. After divesting Franklin, American focused on consumer goods, which were still were fairly mixed, from golf shoes to gin.

The company then changed its name in 1996, from American Brands to Fortune Brands. This came after the company sold the last vestige of its tobacco business, its British unit, Gallagher. The company was concerned that investors still associated its old name with a tobacco company. For example, when a smoker in Florida won a substantial jury award against another tobacco company in August 1995, American's stock suffered. The newly named company's CEO, Thomas Hays, explained the rationale behind the choice, saying, ''People talk a lot about something being fortunate or making a fortune, which is certainly what we want to do for our shareholders'' (from a December 9, 1996 interview in *Fortune* magazine).

By the late 1990s, Fortune was rather different from what it had been ten years earlier. After getting rid of its tobacco holdings, Fortune began buying up companies in the home and office products area, such as Schrock Cabinet Co. and Apollo Presentation Products, a maker of overhead projectors. It also bought in the liquor segment, picking up Geyser Peak Winery in 1998 and entering an agreement in 1999 with two European liquor companies to jointly distribute their spirits worldwide. Fortune also vowed to better manage the brands in its portfolio, and in 1999 took a charge of $1.2 billion to restructure and write down goodwill. The company also announced it would cut costs by reducing its corporate staff by one-third and moving its headquarters to Lincolnshire, Illinois, where its office products division already was located.

Acquisitions Fuel Growth in the 21st Century

Fortune's impressive collection of leading brands performed admirably at the turn of the century, encouraging management to expand even as the economy slipped into a recession. The company completed nearly a dozen acquisitions during the early years of the century's first decade, focusing its most significant efforts on expanding its home and hardware segment, the company's fast-growing business and the source of nearly half of its annual revenues. In 2002, Fortune spent $538 million to acquire Omega Holdings, Inc., a leading manufacturer of cabinetry. Omega ranked as the fourth-largest cabinet maker in the country, with its addition to Fortune's operations adding custom and frameless semi-custom lines to the company's cabinetry offerings. In 2003, the company's acquisitive activity intensified considerably, as it bolstered its brand holdings in both the home and hardware segment and the spirits and wine segment. In April, Fortune acquired American Lock Company, a manufacturer of commercial locks. In June, it acquired Capital Cabinet Corporation, which supplied cabinets to the construction market in the Southwest. In July, the company acquired Wild Horse Winery, a producer of ultra-premium California wines. By far the largest acquisition of the year was completed in November, when Fortune spent $924 million to acquire the leading manufacturer of residential entry doors in the United States, Therma-Tru Holdings, Inc.

After a half-century of diversifying beyond tobacco, Fortune's reinvention of itself proved to be a highly successful accomplishment. Between 2000 and 2003, the company's annual revenue increased nearly $500 million, reaching $6.21 billion after the more than $1 billion spent on acquisitions in 2003. Profits were increasing robustly, with the nearly $580 million in net income posted in 2003 testifying to the strength of the company's market leading brands. As the company prepared for the future, it was expected to leverage the strength of its existing brands to acquire other leading brands in its four sectors of operation. As it did so, the assiduous brand management and marketing that made its past a success was expected to deliver equal success to the company's endeavors in the years ahead.

Principal Subsidiaries

Acco World Corporation; Acco Brands, Inc.; Masterbrand Industries, Inc.; Jim Beam Brands Worldwide, Inc.; Acushnet Company.

Principal Divisions

Home and Hardware; Spirits and Wine; Golf; Office Products.

Principal Competitors

Brown-Forman Corporation; Diageo PLC; Masco Corporation.

Further Reading

''American Brands' Net Fell 93% in 4th Period,'' *Wall Street Journal,* January 28, 1991, p. C8.

''American Brands Profit Sets Record,'' *New York Times,* January 25, 1992, p. 39.

Barrett, Amy, and Ernest Beck, ''Fortune in Pact with Remy and Highland,'' *Wall Street Journal,* March 31, 1999, p. B4.

Choe, Howard, ''Fortune Brands: More Than Just Lucky,'' *Business Week Online,* June 7, 2003, p. 6.

''Consumers Enjoy Lap of Luxury,'' *Investor's Business Daily,* October 27, 2003, p. A7.

Fairclough, George, ''Fortune Brands To Take Charge of $1.2 Billion,'' *Wall Street Journal,* April 28, 1999, p. C24.

''Fortune Brands Inc.,'' *Wood & Wood Products,* January 2004, p. 16.

Lieber, Ronald B., '' 'What? Fortune Makes Golf Balls?,' '' *Fortune,* December 9, 1996, p. 40.

MacFadyen, Kenneth, ''Kenner Remodels Portfolio,'' *Buyouts,* November 17, 2003.

Rice, Fay, ''How To Win with a Value Strategy,'' *Fortune,* July 27, 1992, pp. 94–95.

Saporito, Bill, ''Who'll Drink What Post-Recession?,'' *Fortune,* December 2, 1991, p. 13.

Scism, Leslie, ''American General Corp. Seeks To Buy Life-Insurance Unit of American Brands,'' *Wall Street Journal,* November 29, 1994, p. A3.

Shapiro, Eben, ''Seagram Is Selling 7 Liquor Brands,'' *New York Times,* November 1, 1991, p. D1.

''Sold American!''—The First Fifty Years, New York: American Tobacco Company, 1954.

Steinmetz, Greg, ''B.A.T. To Buy Rival American Brands Division,'' *Wall Street Journal,* April 27, 1994, pp. A3, A4.

Thomaselli, Rich, ''Fortune Smiles on Increased Ad Spending: Defies Sour Economy to Boost Brands,'' *Crain's Chicago Business,* July 15, 2002, p. 7.

''U.S.: Fortune Brands Raises Targets after Q1,'' *Just-Drinks.Com,* April 26, 2004, p. 35.

Winkler, John K., *Tobacco Tycoon: The Story of James Buchanan Duke,* New York: Random House, 1942.

—Jonathan Martin
—updates: A. Woodward; Jeffrey L. Covell

Fry's Electronics, Inc.

600 East Brokaw Road
San Jose, California 95112
U.S.A.
Telephone: (408) 487-4500
Fax: (408) 487-4741
Web site: http://www.frys.com

Private Company
Founded: 1985
Employees: 5,650
Sales: $2 billion (2002 est.)
NAIC: 443112 Radio, Television, and Other Electronics Stores.

With its headquarters located in San Jose, California, Fry's Electronics, Inc., is a private company that runs a chain of 28 electronics superstores, ranging in size from 50,000 square feet to more than 180,000 square feet. Each stores offers about 30,000 items and exceeds the competition in breadth of choice. The stores are also known for cheap prices and notoriously poor customer service. The first Fry's, located in Silicon Valley, was frequented by hi-tech professionals who did not require, nor welcome, assistance from salespeople. These customers liked Fry's unique one-stop approach to buying electronic products and components. Not only could they buy little-found items at a reasonable price, they could also stock up on junk food, No-Doz, and men's magazines while preparing to work all night. They could also talk shop, gossip, and network while they were at it. As Fry's has become more mainstream, however, the chain's disinterest in customer service has become more of a problem. Nevertheless, the stores remain popular. Part of Fry's idiosyncratic charm involves the stores' often bizarre theme-based decor. For instance, the Campbell, California, site features an ancient Egypt theme, complete with a two-foot sphinx and King Tut tombs. The Fremont, California, store pays tribute to the electricity exhibits from the 1893 Chicago World's Fair. In Woodland Hills, California, shoppers are treated to an Alice in Wonderland motif, while the Las Vegas store features the world's largest slot machine. All told, Fry's operates 15 stores in California, six in Texas, two in Arizona, and single units in Georgia, Illinois, Oregon, Nevada, and Washington. In addition, Fry's sells merchandise on the Web through Outpost.com. The company is owned and operated by three Fry brothers—John, Randy, and David—and a former girlfriend of CEO John Fry, Kathryn Kolder. The Frys are private by nature and do not grant press interviews.

1950s Origins

John, Randy, and David Fry's father was Charles Fry, a highly competitive person who was an all-state high school basketball player in Oklahoma. After earning a college degree in mathematics, he opened a supermarket in Contra Costa County, California, in 1954. Throughout the 1960s, he grew a chain of 41 Fry's Food Stores in the San Francisco and Phoenix, Arizona, markets. He sold the business in 1972 for approximately $14 million to Modesto, California-based Save Mart Supermarkets, but he stayed on to manage the chain until 1983. His eldest son, John, took after him in a number of ways. He was also a star athlete, a quarterback with professional promise. He was recruited by Santa Clara University to play football but due to injuries was never able to realize his potential. Like his father, he also earned a math degree, graduating from Santa Clara in 1978. He then went to work for his father's supermarket chain, managing the computer system. Thus, he not only learned the techie mindset but also the low-margin grocery business that would later serve him well in selling electronics.

After the Fry family discontinued managing the supermarket chain, John Fry envisioned a new retail operation, one that would be a variation on grocery retailing: an electronics supermarket. According to people interviewed by the *San Jose Mercury News* for a 1997 company profile, Fry thought through the idea in his own fashion: ''He measured the ratio of low prices to high sales. He multiplied the prototypical engineer's basic needs times a variety of sundries. And he found the intersection between a sales clerk's level of expertise and a customer's level of tolerance. The result was a retail operation that has helped define Silicon Valley.''

After selling his chain of supermarkets, Charles Fry reportedly gave each of sons $1 million. John Fry now convinced his

Company Perspectives:

Fry's has been keeping hi-tech professionals supplied with products representing the latest technological trends and advances in the personal computer marketplace for over 18 years.

younger brothers to pool their money and launch Fry's Electronics. Also joining as a partner was his former girlfriend, Kathryn Kolder, who would become an executive vice-president. David Fry would be put in charge of the computer systems, while brother Randy was charged with handling day-to-day operations, freeing up the eldest brother to concentrate on the big picture. True to his roots, John Fry conducted business supermarket style. The company opened its first electronics superstore in Sunnyvale, California. Once foot traffic was high enough, he began selling shelf space and charging a premium for the freestanding placements located at the end of aisles. The money was then used to buy newspaper advertisements, which, like supermarket ads, lured in customers with specials. Because Fry's sold snacks to its clientele of high-tech workers, it would even use the old supermarket ploy of loss-leaders—for example, selling Coca-Cola at a loss—to get customers in the door. Once inside, they would face a shopping situation similar to that of a supermarket: Should they buy the name-brand product or the cheaper no-name product offering more features sitting next to it? In the case of the latter, of course, Fry's stood to make a higher profit.

The Sunnyvale store became, in the words of *U.S. News & World Report,* a "geek paradise" where electronic components, computer peripherals, as well as TV sets and stereos were sold along with candy bars, high-caffeine soft drinks, razors, toothpaste, and adult magazines. "Buses of tourists would come to gawk at shelves that seemed to have anticipated every electronic, caloric, and hormonal need of nerds who wanted to lay in fresh provisions with one-stop shopping." High-tech savvy customers were also attracted to Fry's because of its assortment of hard-to-find components and bargains. An entire computer could be pieced together cheaply from parts available at Fry's. In the early days, Fry's featured a "blow out" table where items that needed a little fixing could be bought for pennies on the dollar.

Even as Fry's was becoming an institution among Silicon Valley techies, it was also establishing a personality that either did not bother its core customers or was something they were willing to overlook. Fry's hired people with little technological knowledge at rock-bottom wages, and, not surprisingly, they were not much help on the sales floor. Then again, there was simply no one the store could hire who could match the technical expertise of Fry's customers, so why bother? Returning merchandise was also problematic, as customers found themselves bouncing from the cashier to the returns desk and back again. Receiving a refund instead of a credit check required the persistence of the truly dedicated, since Fry's employees received a bonus based on their ability to get customers to take store credit. Even after a customer accepted the latter, weeks would pass before a customer received a credit check in the mail. Insiders called this policy "the double H," which stood for "hoops and hurdles." One ex-employee told *Forbes* in 1997 that the point was to wear customers down until they gave up.

Because the pay was low, employee turnover was high, but that did not matter to management as long as there was someone waiting to fill the position. Fry's instituted strict security measures, fearful that its employees or its customers might steal the merchandise—and with good reason. It was estimated that the computer electronics industry, which produced a lot of small expensive items that could be easily fenced, lost about 10 percent of revenues each year due to theft. Employees were virtually frisked at the end of the day, while customers had to run a gauntlet of security guards before leaving the premises. Instead of stock rooms, inventory was stacked in the open, and the stores were laid out so that blind spots where merchandise could be tucked away were eliminated. A multitude of security cameras, generally hidden from view, surveyed the floor. Eventually, even dumpsters were randomly sent to headquarters where they were checked to make sure someone on the inside was not attempting to smuggle out merchandise.

From a customer's perspective, the positives outweighed the negatives at Fry's. After a bad experience, customers might vow to never shop again at Fry's, but the great prices or the vast selection would cause them to break down and return at the next opportunity. A second store was added in Fremont in 1988, followed by a Palo Alto location in 1990. Unlike other big-box retailers, Fry's sought less expensive, out-of-the-way sites in office and industrial parks, rightly believing that its customers would be willing to go out of their way to shop at Fry's. The company, however, was not parsimonious when it came to decor. Fry's began adding entertainment to the mix, hiring a former designer from Lucas Films to create fantasy settings. Sunnyvale's haphazard shelves of products was replaced with neat aisles and a presentation of the history of Silicon Valley; Fremont explored the origins of electricity the way it was presented at the World's Columbian Exhibition, better known as the Chicago World's Fair of 1893; and Palo Alto offered a vision of Wild Bill's Wild, Wild West. Fry's would spend $1 million on each store, and as the number of stores mounted, so did the unusual nature of the motifs, from Alice and Wonderland to an Industrial Revolution-era factory, from the ruins of Ancient Rome to the history of cattle ranching, from the lost city of Atlantis to the history of the Las Vegas strip.

The 1990s and Beyond

Fry's moved outside the San Francisco Bay area in 1992 with the opening of a store in the Los Angeles suburb of Manhattan Beach. A year later, Fry's returned to northern California, where it opened a store in Campbell only after the city came up with $2 million in tax concessions. Within three years, the chain would double in size, operating ten stores located in northern and southern California, making Fry's the 13th largest computer retailer in the country. In 1997, Fry's expanded beyond the state by acquiring the six-store Incredible Universe electronics superstore chain from Tandy Corporation at the cost of $118 million. Incredible Universe, launched in 1992, attempted to emulate Fry's success by opening massive stores averaging 185,000 square feet. The idea was to make the spectacle of sheer size a drawing card and make shopping there a form of entertainment. However, sales were essentially the

Key Dates:

1954: Charles Fry opens his first supermarket.
1985: Fry's sons—John, Randy, and Dave—open their first electronics superstore.
1992: The company opens its first store outside of the San Francisco Bay Area.
1997: Six Incredible Universe stores are acquired.
2001: Cyberian Outpost acquisition provides the company with a Web business.

same as what could be expected at a smaller store, and Tandy struggled to find the right blend of computer products and white goods such as washers and dryers, stove, and refrigerators. Unable to make the concept work, Tandy sold the operation to Fry's, which in addition to a store in Sacramento, now added units in Texas, Arizona, and Oregon. In one stroke, as a result, Fry's became a regional enterprise, but it also found itself moving into markets that might be less forgiving of its disregard to customer service. No longer could the chain depend on catering to professionals. In addition, more people were turning to direct marketers like Dell and Gateway to buy their computers. In 1997, for the first time, direct marketers sold more computers than retailers, and with an increasing number of people shopping on the Internet—which Fry's traditional customer would be the first to exploit—the company faced a number of challenges. On the positive side, however, the general public was becoming increasing knowledgeable about computer and electronic products, and were willing to put up with Fry's ''double-H'' approach if it meant a vast array of choices and cheap prices.

The Fry's formula continued to work, as customers lined up hours before a new store opened and were willing to endure long lines and frustrating service. Throughout the rest of the 1990s the chain added just one store, a second location in the Phoenix area. In the early 1990s, the company experienced a major growth spurt, opening another 11 stores, adding units in Texas and California, while also entering new states: Georgia, Illinois, Nevada, and Washington. Fry's was late to embrace the Internet but finally became involved in online retailing. In 2001, it paid $8 million to acquire Cyberian Outpost, a struggling online software and electronics retailer based in Kent, Massachusetts. Fry's renamed it Outpost.com.

Although there was no way to be certain, due to the private company's policy of remaining closed-lipped about its affairs, Fry's annual sales were estimated at more than $2 billion. Business must have strong enough to warrant the fast pace of store openings in the early years of the 21st century. In 2004, the family-run company came full circle with the opening of a store in Concord, California, the first to be located in Contra Costa County, where 50 years earlier Charles Fry opened his first supermarket. One of his sons, Randy Fry, was on hand to greet customers as they entered the new 146,500-square-foot store. When a newspaper reporter requested an interview, he received the same one word offered to everyone: ''Welcome.'' Nevertheless, what was found inside spoke volumes about Fry's Electronics.

Principal Subsidiaries

Outpost.com

Principal Competitors

Best Buy Co., Inc; CompUSA Inc.; Good Guys, Inc.

Further Reading

Bajarin, Tim, ''Fry's: A One-Stop Shopping Emporium and Cultural Icon,'' *PC WEEK*, July 2, 1990, p. 110.
''Fry's Retains Bargain Prices Despite Theme-Park Glitz,'' *PC/Computing*, March 1991, p. 274.
Harris, Pat Lopes, ''Fry's Mystique: Timing, Focus, Frugality—and Lots of Advertising,'' *Business Journal*, January 14, 2000, p. 52.
Lanberg, Mike, and Larry Slonaker, ''Expansion Will Test Fry's Spotty Customer Service Record,'' *San Jose Mercury News*, September 3, 1997.
Marsh, Ann, and Scott Woolley, ''The Customer Is Always Right? Not at Fry's,'' *Forbes*, November 3, 1997, p. 86.
Slonaker, Larry, ''Founder of Fry's Electronics Plays Hardball and Is Driven to Succeed,'' *San Jose Mercury News*, August 25, 1997.
Stross, Randell. ''A Nerd's Paradise,'' *U.S. News & World Report*, January 13, 1997, p. 42.

—Ed Dinger

The Gillette Company

Prudential Tower Building, Suite 4800
Boston, Massachusetts 02199
U.S.A.
Telephone: (617) 421-7000
Fax: (617) 421-7123
Web site: http://www.gillette.com

Public Company
Incorporated: 1901 as American Safety Razor Company
Employees: 29,400
Sales: $9.25 billion (2004)
Stock Exchanges: New York London Frankfurt Zurich
Ticker Symbol: G
NAIC: 325620 Toilet Preparation Manufacturing

The Gillette Company is the world leader in the men's grooming product category as well as in certain women's grooming products. Although more than half of company profits are still derived from shaving equipment—the area in which the company started—Gillette has also attained the top spots worldwide in writing instruments (Paper Mate, Parker, and Waterman brands) and correction products (Liquid Paper), toothbrushes and other oral care products (Oral-B), and alkaline batteries (Duracell products, which generate almost one-fourth of company profits). Gillette maintains 64 manufacturing facilities in 27 countries, and its products are sold in more than 200 countries and territories, with more than 60 percent of sales occurring outside the United States.

Entrepreneurial Beginnings

One summer morning in 1895, an ambitious traveling salesman found that the edge of his straight razor had dulled. King Gillette later said that the idea for an entirely new kind of razor, with a disposable blade, flashed into his mind as he looked in irritation at his dull blade. King Gillette had been searching for the right product, one that had to be used—and replaced—regularly, around which to build a business. His innovation in shaving technology was just such a product. Another safety razor, the Star, was already on the market at the time but, like the straight razor it was meant to replace, its blade needed stropping before each use and eventually had to be professionally honed. Gillette envisioned an inexpensive, double-edged blade that could be clamped over a handle, used until it was dull, and then discarded.

Gillette spent the next six years trying to perfect his safety razor. Scientists and toolmakers he consulted were pessimistic, and thought the idea impractical. Gillette, 40 years old at the time and a successful salesman, inventor, and writer, did not give up. In 1901 he joined forces with William Nickerson, a Massachusetts Institute of Technology-educated machinist. Nickerson developed production processes to make Gillette's idea a reality, while Gillette formed the American Safety Razor Company to raise the estimated $5,000 they needed to begin manufacturing the razor. Gillette became president of the company and head of a three-man directorate. Production of the razor began early in 1903.

The renamed Gillette Safety Razor Company began advertising its product in October 1903, with the first ad appearing in Systems Magazine. The company sold 51 razor sets at $5 each and an additional 168 blades—originally at 20 for $1—that first year.

In 1904 Gillette received a patent on the safety razor; sales rose to 90,884 razors and 123,648 blades that year. The following year the company bought a six-story building in South Boston. By 1906 the company had paid its first cash dividend. During the years before World War I Gillette steadily increased earnings through print advertisements, emphasizing that with his razor men could shave themselves under any conditions without cutting or irritation.

At the same time, Gillette was expanding abroad. He opened his first foreign office, a London sales branch, in 1905. By 1909 he had established manufacturing plants in Paris, Montreal, Berlin, and Leicester, England, and offices in France and Hamburg, Germany. By 1923, foreign business accounted for about 30 percent of Gillette's sales.

In 1910 King Gillette decided to sell a substantial portion of his controlling share of the company to the company's major investor, John Joyce. Gillette had succeeded in fighting off

Company Perspectives:

The Gillette Company is a globally focused consumer products marketer that seeks competitive advantage in quality, value-added personal care and personal use products. We are committed to building shareholder value through sustained profitable growth.

challenges for control of the company from Joyce in the past, but this time he took approximately $900,000 and bowed out. Gillette retained the title of president and frequently visited foreign branches, but he no longer played an active role in company management. Joyce was made vice-president, a position he used to manage day-to-day operations. When Joyce died in 1916, his longtime friend, Edward Aldred, a New York investment banker, bought out the Gillette shares left to Joyce's estate and took control of the company. Aldred remained on Joyce's management team.

Wartime Production

During World War I the U.S. government ordered 3.5 million razors and 36 million blades to supply all its troops. In order to meet military supply schedules, shifts worked around the clock and Gillette hired over 500 new employees. Gillette thus introduced a huge pool of potential customers to the still-new idea of self-shaving with a safety razor. After the war, ex-servicemen needed blades to fit the razors they had been issued in the service.

In 1921 Gillette's patent on the safety razor expired, but the company was ready for the change. It introduced the ''new improved'' Gillette razor, which sold at the old price, and entered the low-priced end of the market with the old-style razor, renamed the Silver Brownie razor, priced at only $1. Gillette also gave away razor handles as premiums with other products, developing customers for the more profitable blades. Expansion and growth continued.

The company also continued to expand abroad. In 1922 Gillette became royal purveyor to the prince of Wales and in 1924 to King Gustav V of Sweden. More favorable publicity followed when the Paris office gave Charles Lindbergh a Gillette Gold Traveler set the day after he completed the first transatlantic flight.

By the end of the decade, Gillette faced its first major setback. Auto Strop Safety Razor Company, owned by Henry J. Gaisman, filed suit for patent infringement after Gillette produced a new blade using a continuous-strip process similar to one originally presented to Gillette by Gaisman.

Gillette resolved the suit by merging with Auto Strop, only to face another problem. When Gaisman checked the company's financial records, he found that Gillette had over-reported its earnings for the past five years by about $3 million. Confidence in Gillette fell, as did its stock. From a high of $125 early in 1929, the stock bottomed out after the disclosure, at $18.

The crisis led to management reorganization. King Gillette resigned as nominal president, and died 14 months later at age 77. Gaisman became the new chairman of Gillette and Gerard B. Lambert, son of the founder of the Lambert Pharmacal Company—makers of Listerine—and a former manager there, came out of retirement to become president of Gillette. Lambert agreed to work for no salary with the guarantee of company stock if he could bring earnings up $5 per share.

Under Lambert, the Gillette Company made a bold advertising move: it admitted that the new blade it had brought out in 1930 was of poor quality. The company then announced what became its most recognizable product, the Gillette Blue Blade. Made under Gaisman's strip-processing method, the Blue Blade promised uniformly high quality.

The Blue Blade kept Gillette the leader in the field, but profits remained disappointing throughout the Great Depression, as men increasingly turned to bargain blades. Lambert resigned in 1934 without meeting his goal of improving earnings and without receiving compensation from the company. He was replaced by a former Auto Strop executive, Samuel C. Stampleman, who had no more success. With profits at their lowest since 1915, the board of directors appointed Joseph P. Spang Jr. president in December 1938 in an effort to invigorate the company.

Spang immediately restored the company's advertising budget, which had been cut to save money. Under this policy, Gillette's trademark sports advertising developed. Spang purchased radio broadcast rights to the 1939 World Series for $100,000. Despite a short series, in which the Cincinnati Reds lost four straight games to the New York Yankees, sales of Gillette's World Series Special razor sets were more than four times company estimates.

This success encouraged more sports advertising. By 1942 the events Gillette sponsored were grouped together as the ''Gillette Cavalcade of Sports.'' Although it eventually included the Orange Bowl, the Sugar Bowl, and the Kentucky Derby, in addition to the World Series and the All-Star game, the ''Cavalcade of Sports'' became best known for bringing boxing to American men. Spang attributed Gillette's continuing success to the sports advertising program, and sports programs remained an important vehicle for Gillette advertising.

During World War II foreign production and sales declined, but domestic production more than made up for those losses. Almost the entire production of razors and blades went to the military. In addition, Gillette manufactured fuel-control units for military-plane carburetors. The backlog of civilian demand after the war led to consecutive record sales until 1957.

Postwar Diversification

During the profitable postwar period Spang began to broaden Gillette's product line. The company had introduced Gillette Brushless shaving cream, its first, nonrazor, nonblade product, in 1936. In 1948 Spang began to diversify by acquiring other companies when he bought the Toni Company, a firm that made home permanents. In 1955 Spang purchased Paper Mate Company, a manufacturer of ballpoint pens.

When Spang retired in 1956, Carl Gilbert became CEO. During the 1960s Gillette faced a threat to its bread-and-butter

Key Dates:

1901: American Safety Razor is founded by King C. Gillette.
1904: King Gillette's safety razor is patented.
1918: Gillette manufacturers razors and blades for soldiers during World War I.
1942: The Cavalcade of Sports program is formed to oversee the company's various advertising and promotional activities in athletics.
1967: Braun AG is acquired.
1971: Company is organized into four domestic divisions: the Safety Razor Division; the Toiletries Division (featuring Right Guard antiperspirant); the Personal Care Division; and the Paper Mate division.
1991: Gillette ranks 20th among the Fortune 500.
1996: The company acquires battery manufacturer Duracell.

product, the double-edged blade. In 1962, the English Wilkinson Sword Company began to export stainless-steel blades to the United States. Wilkinson had developed a polymer coating that made it possible to put an edge on stainless steel, which resists corrosion, increasing the number of shaves from a blade.

Two of Gillette's domestic competitors—Eversharp, which made Schick blades, and American Safety Razor—rushed versions of the stainless-steel blade onto the market. Gillette, the market leader, was left behind without a stainless-steel blade of its own to compete, and profits slumped in 1963 and 1964. Gillette recovered much of its market share through a simple strategy: developing a better blade and initiating an aggressive advertising campaign that emphasized quality. After its own blade hit the market, Gillette's market share stabilized at 60–65 percent, compared to 70–75 percent before the challenge.

Vincent C. Ziegler, head of the company's North American razor operation, had developed the razor-marketing strategy, and when Gillette reorganized on a product line basis in July 1964, Ziegler was named president. He took over as chairman of the board in 1965. The stainless-steel blade controversy taught Ziegler not to rely on one product. He saw Gillette as "a diversified consumer products company," and promoted both internal development of new product lines and acquisition of other companies.

During the later 1960s Gillette pursued this strategy actively, but with mixed results. A new line of Toni hair-coloring products failed, as did Earth Born shampoos, luxury perfumes, and a line of small electronic items such as digital watches, calculators, smoke alarms, and fire extinguishers. Many of the companies Gillette acquired, such as Eve of Roma high-fashion perfume, Buxton leather goods, Welcome Wagon, and Hydroponic Chemical Company—which produced Hyponex plant foods—never found the fit with Gillette comfortable. The acquisitions led to shrinking profit margins.

Gillette did have some successes. The Trac II twin-blade shaving system introduced in 1971 was a success, and the 1970 acquisition of the French S.T. Dupont gave Gillette the disposable Cricket lighter, which Gillette introduced to the U.S. market. By 1971 Gillette had four domestic divisions: the Safety Razor Division; the Toiletries Division, which featured Right Guard deodorant and antiperspirant; the Personal Care Division; and the Paper Mate division.

By the mid-1970s Ziegler was ready to retire, and began to groom outsider Edward Gelsthorpe to succeed him, but Gelsthorpe left Gillette to join United Brands, now Chiquita Brands, 15 months after his appointment as president. Ziegler next tapped Colman M. Mockler Jr. to replace him when he retired in 1975. Mockler had been at Gillette since 1957 and had an entirely different background and style than Ziegler. He had come up from the financial end of the business rather than through sales.

Diversification Moderated Starting in the Mid-1970s

Mockler moderated Ziegler's diversification policy. He concentrated on a limited number of promising markets, particularly high-volume, repeat-purchase consumer items, selling Ziegler's least successful acquisitions—including Buxton in 1977, Welcome Wagon in 1978, and Hyponex and the Autopoint mechanical pencil business in 1979—and pumping money into promising companies compatible with already-existing manufacturing or distribution capabilities. Mockler stuck with the Cricket disposable lighter even though high introductory marketing costs and a costly price war with the Bic Pen Corporation, owned by the French Société Bic, kept it from showing a profit.

Mockler also held on to the West German Braun company. Ziegler had bought the family-owned business in 1967 to gain entry to the European electric-shaver market and for the quality and style of its small-appliance designs. Mockler pared Braun's less profitable lines and rode out a Justice Department antitrust suit against the acquisition. The suit eventually prevented Gillette from introducing Braun shavers in the U.S. market before 1984. Mockler also increased Gillette's advertising budget and undertook companywide cost-cutting measures in all other divisions. Before the results of those policies could be seen, Mockler faced other problems. Growing fear of fluorocarbons, which deplete the earth's ozone layer, affected sales of products in aerosol cans during the 1970s.

Gillette eventually developed new product-delivery systems to replace aerosol cans, such as nonaerosol pumps and roll-ons, for Gillette's already-established product line, and he put advertising dollars behind the products, which included Right Guard and Soft & Dri deodorants and Adorn and White Rain hair sprays. He also started development of a new deodorant product, Dry Idea, which feels dry when applied. Dry Idea was launched in 1978 after two years of development at a cost of $118 million. It quickly recovered a quarter of the deodorant market for Gillette.

Gillette faced a more serious threat from Bic. In the 1960s Bic came to the United States with a 19¢ disposable pen, which made dramatic cuts into sales of Gillette's 98¢ Paper Mate pens. In the 1970s Bic attacked Gillette's Cricket disposable lighter with its own disposable lighter. Since the Cricket was more expensive to make—it had more moving parts than the Bic—Gillette was losing the price war. Lighters and pens, however, produced only 15 percent of Gillette's pretax profits; razor blades accounted for 71 percent of profits. When Bic began producing disposable razors and purchased American Safety Razor, with its 13 percent of the blade market, from Personna and Gem blades, Gillette had to respond. Gillette countered by competing with Bic on price while emphasizing the higher quality of its products. Gillette brought out the Eraser Mate pen despite marketing studies that questioned demand for an erasable pen, and sales soared. By 1980 Gillette had improved profitability despite the attack by Bic.

Takeover Threats in the 1980s

Mockler's policies led to a higher profit margin and a surplus of cash. Some of this cash was used in 1984 when Gillette added oral care products to its product mix with the $188.5 million purchase of Oral-B Laboratories, Inc.—the leading maker of toothbrushes in the United States—from Cooper Laboratories, Inc. The excess cash, however, also led to a new threat in the mid-1980s: the threat of takeover. In 1986 Ronald O. Perelman, head of Revlon, offered $4.1 billion for Gillette. He was attracted by Gillette's well-known personal-care brands, the possibility of combining the sales and distribution systems of the two companies, and Gillette's expertise in marketing abroad.

Gillette rejected Revlon's offer of $65 a share and bought back stock from Perelman at $59.50 a share and paid some expenses, for a total of $558 million. Revlon made two other unsolicited requests to buy the company in 1987, both of which were refused by the Gillette board of directors.

In response to the takeover threats, Gillette reorganized top management; thinned out its workforce through layoffs; modernized its plants while shifting some production capacity to lower-cost locations; and sold many smaller and less profitable divisions.

That was not the end of the takeover threats. In early 1988 Coniston Partners announced that it had acquired approximately 6 percent of the company and was determined to replace four members of Gillette's 12-member board so it could influence company policy. Members of the partnership said they would actively seek offers to sell or dismantle Gillette if they managed to get representation on the board. Coniston Partners' battle to get shareholders' proxy rights was intense, but in 1988 Gillette came out on top with 52 percent of the votes for directors to Coniston's 48 percent. The matter was finally resolved when Gillette instituted a stock repurchase for all shareholders, which included 16 million of Coniston's 112 million shares at $45 a share.

Finally, in August 1989, Warren Buffett's Berkshire Hathaway bought $600 million of Gillette convertible preferred shares. The deal potentially placed 11 percent of Gillette's stock with Buffett, who had agreed to give the company the right of first refusal on the block, should he wish to sell it. The friendly agreement decreased the threat of takeover, though it tightened up cash flow at the company. Buffett's dividend was $52.5 million a year.

With takeover threats behind it and restructuring completed, Gillette returned to emphasizing its powerful brand names and its bread and butter, shaving products. While toiletries and cosmetics represented low-margin items and profitable stationery products accounted for only 9 percent of the company's total profits, razors and blades still accounted for a little over 70 percent of profits. Gillette brought in a new head of shaving operations, John W. Symons, formerly head of European operations, and developed new ad campaigns to emphasize the more profitable shaving systems over disposable shavers such as its own Good News.

In October 1989, Gillette unveiled the Sensor shaving system, which featured thinner blades mounted on springs by lasers so they could follow contours. The blades, to be used in a permanent shaving system, cost close to $200 million to develop and were launched simultaneously in the United States and Europe, backed by a $100 million advertising budget. Sensor's touted superior shave was a huge success with consumers, and the product garnered several awards. The Lady Sensor soon followed in 1992, with sales for both products exceeding $500 million that year.

Early to Mid-1990s

Gillette made another effort to expand its presence in shaving when it attempted to buy the U.S. and non-European operations of its old competitor, Wilkinson Sword, early in 1990. The Justice Department blocked the sale of Wilkinson's U.S. interests since Gillette controlled about half the U.S. market and Wilkinson was number-four in the market with about 3 percent. Also in 1990, as part of a realignment of its shaving and personal-care units in North America and Europe, Gillette sold its European skin and hair care operations to Nobel Consumer Goods AB, a division of Nobel Industries of Sweden, for $107 million.

Despite the Wilkinson setback, the 1990s proved to be extremely fruitful years for Gillette thanks to an aggressive program of new product development coupled with the pursuit of targeted acquisitions. Mockler, who had had a very successful term as CEO and chairman and who planned to retire at the end of 1991, died unexpectedly in January of that year. Alfred M. Zeien, Mockler's heir apparent who was president and chief operating officer, replaced Mockler in both of his positions. Also in 1991 Gillette launched another award-winning product, the Oral-B Indicator toothbrush, which had bristles that change color to show when a new toothbrush is needed. This popular feature was added to all Oral-B toothbrushes the following year.

Significant new product introductions and a major acquisition highlighted 1992. Gillette's personal-care product division launched the Gillette Series line of men's toiletries, which included 14 "high-performance" products in the deodorant/antiperspirant, shaving cream, and aftershave categories. The company announced the acquisition of Parker Pen Holdings Ltd. for £285 million ($484 million), with the deal being consummated in May 1993. The addition of the Parker brand to Gillette's Paper Mate and Waterman brands moved the company into the top position worldwide in writing instruments.

Late in 1993 Gillette took an after-tax charge of $164 million for a reorganization of its overseas operations, including the integration of Parker Pen facilities into Gillette's structure. About 2,000 jobs were eliminated as a result of the reorganization.

Just four years after the debut of Sensor, Gillette in late 1993 launched in continental Europe and Canada its next-generation shaving system, SensorExcel, which promised even closer and more comfortable shaving based on its skin guard made of ''five soft, flexible microfins.'' After its successful debut, SensorExcel was rolled out in Japan, England, and the United States in 1994. Other 1993 and 1994 product introductions included Braun's FlavorSelect coffeemaker; the Oral-B Advantage toothbrush, which was designed to remove plaque better than other toothbrushes; and Custom Plus men's and women's disposable razors with pivoting heads.

Gillette returned to acquisition mode in 1995 and 1996. In late 1995 Oral-B's position in Latin America was bolstered with the purchase of the Pro oral care line. Near the end of the year Gillette acquired Thermoscan Inc., a leader in infrared ear thermometers. Thermoscan promised to provide a base for Gillette to expand into the rapidly growing personal home diagnostic products area. Then in late 1996 the company made its largest acquisition ever when it paid $7.1 billion for Duracell International Inc., the world leader in alkaline batteries. Gillette thus added its first major product line since the purchase of Oral-B; in fact, batteries immediately became the company's second-leading product line in terms of sales, trailing only razors and blades. Duracell batteries had been underdistributed outside the United States, so Gillette planned to achieve sales growth by leveraging its existing marketing channels, which reached more than 200 countries by the mid-1990s. More immediately, the Duracell merger led Gillette to record a fourth quarter 1996 charge to operating expenses of $413 million to eliminate overlap between Gillette and Duracell operations.

In 1996 the company also launched more than 20 new products, including SensorExcel for Women. That year, a whopping 41 percent of Gillette sales came from products that debuted during the previous five years, a testament to the company's new product development strength. And an improvement on the SensorExcel was already in the works. Sales neared the $10 billion mark, as 1996 revenues were $9.7 billion, and net income—despite the Duracell charge—was a healthy $949 million.

Razor Wars: Late 1990s and Beyond

Gillette introduced a significant innovation in shaving technology—the first major innovation in safety razors since the beginning of the 1970s—with the Mach 3 in 1998. The new safety razor system introduced a third blade into the twin-blade system that had dominated the wet-shaving market for the previous quarter-century. The blades were set at an angle so that each blade shaves closer to the skin, allowing shavers to use fewer strokes to get the same close, comfortable shave. The shaving cartridge was set on a pivot, allowing the head of the razor to move with the angle of the jaw and skin. In addition, the cartridge itself was designed to facilitate cleaning, and the handle was ergonomically designed to make the razor more comfortable in the hand.

The entire Mach 3 system, protected by 35 patents, cost Gillette $35 billion just to bring to market. As a result, the corporation set the price for replacement cartridges about 35 percent more than its previous best-selling razor, the SensorExcel. Marketing strategy was slanted to persuade current Gillette product users to trade up their previous equipment in favor of the newer, more expensive models because of their improved performance, offering a closer shave with fewer nicks and cuts.

Despite (or perhaps because of) the expense of introducing the new razor, Gillette saw its worst economic performance in almost a decade in 1998. Sales during the third quarter of the year alone dropped 15 percent. In October, Gillette management announced staff cuts of 4,700 jobs, about 11 percent of its total workforce. Lowered sales in key markets such as Brazil, Germany, and Russia also contributed to the loss of income, and share prices dropped by 11 percent virtually overnight.

Gillette's underperformance continued in 1999 and 2000, in large part because of currency-exchange differences. Its stationery and small-appliance businesses showed the greatest losses and the battery and toiletries businesses provided most of the profits. In October 2000 Gillette's managing board responded by firing CEO Michael Hawley and announcing a world-wide restructuring effort that would be led by former Nabisco CEO James M. Kilts, who joined the firm during its centennial year, in January 2001. Kilts, who had earned a reputation as a fixer of troubled companies, needed all his skills. Gillette's battery business, which had dominated the top of the market, lost market share to other brands (Energizer and Rayovac) that offered similar performance at a lower cost. In addition the company lacked fiscal discipline and used an antiquated quarterly tracking system. As a result of these and other expensive practices, Gillette's earnings continued to perform below expectations. Stock prices fell by about 60 percent in the months between early 1999 and late 2001.

Gillette's control of the toiletries market was threatened early in 2003 when rival Schick-Wilkinson Sword introduced the Quattro, the world's first four-blade shaving system. Gillette claimed that the Quattro illegally infringed on Gillette's patents for the Mach 3. The violence of the company's reaction was explained in part because the Quattro actually increased Schick's market share from about 14 percent to about 17 percent. At the same time Gillette's market share slipped by a similar amount—although the Boston-based firm still held a commanding 63 percent of the total wet-razor market. Although Gillette lost its attempt to ban sales of the Quattro in court, it nonetheless saw sales of its products increase. By the end of the first quarter of 2004, Gillette was able to report a 43 percent increase in profits, much of which was provided by its mens' and womens' wet razors, the Mach 3 and Venus systems. The company's grasp of its core businesses—toiletries and oral care—remained strong.

Principal Operating Units

Blades & Razors; Duracell; Oral Care; Braun; Personal Care.

Principal Competitors

Colgate-Palmolive Company; The Proctor & Gamble Company; Société BIC; American Safety Razor Company.

Further Reading

Adams, Russell B. Jr., *King C. Gillette: The Man and His Wonderful Shaving Device*, Boston: Little, Brown, 1978.

Brooker, Katrina, ''Jim Kilts Is An Old-School Curmudgeon. Nothing Could Be Better for Gillette,'' *Fortune,* Dec 30, 2002, p. 94.

Bulkeley, William M., ''Duracell Pact Gives Gillette an Added Source of Power,'' *Wall Street Journal,* September 13, 1996, pp. A3, A4.

Chakravarty, Subrata N., ''We Had to Change the Playing Field,'' *Forbes,* February 4, 1991, p. 82.

Clark, Chapin, ''Gillette Is Set to Make Noise with Mach 3,'' *Supermarket News*, May 4, 1998, p. 172.

Donlon, J.P., ''An Iconoclast in a Cutthroat World,'' *Chief Executive*, March 1996, pp. 34–38.

''Gillette: Simply the Best,'' *European Cosmetic Markets*, October, 1999, p. 413.

''The Gillette Company, 1901–1976,'' *Gillette News*, 1977.

''Gillette Profit Rises 26% on Strong Sales,'' *New York Times*, July 30, 2004, p. C3, col 01.

''Gillette's Billion-Dollar Baby,'' *Marketing Magazine*, June 22, 1998, p. 38.

Grant, Linda, ''Gillette Knows Shaving—and How to Turn out Hot New Products,'' *Fortune*, October 14, 1996, pp. 207–208, 210.

Koselka, Rita, '' 'It's My Favorite Statistic,' '' *Forbes*, September 12, 1994, pp. 162–72.

Levine, Joshua, ''Global Lather,'' *Forbes*, February 5, 1990, p. 146.

Maremont, Mark, ''How Gillette Is Honing Its Edge,'' *Business Week*, September 28, 1992, pp. 60–61.

——, ''How Gillette Wowed Wall Street: It Structured the Duracell Buy to Juice Up Earnings Immediately,'' *Business Week*, September 30, 1996, pp. 36–37.

Miller, William H., ''Gillette's Secret to Sharpness,'' *Industry Week*, January 3, 1994, pp. 25–26, 28, 30.

Newport, John Paul Jr., ''The Stalking of Gillette,'' *Fortune*, May 23, 1988, p. 99.

''Razor Burn at Gillette,'' *Business Week*, June 18, 2001, p. 37.

Reidy, Chris, ''Boston-Based Gillette to Sell Stationery Product Lines,'' *Boston Globe*, June 2, 2000.

Ricardo-Campbell, Rita, *Resisting Hostile Takeovers: The Case of Gillette*, Westport, Conn.: Praeger, 1997.

Teather, David, ''It's Mach 3 Versus Quattro as Gillette Crosses Swords with Schick,'' *Guardian*, August 15, 2003, p. 16.

—Ginger G. Rodriguez
—updates: David E. Salamie; Kenneth R. Shepherd

Golden Krust Caribbean Bakery, Inc.

3958 Park Avenue
Bronx, New York 10457
U.S.A.
Telephone: (718) 655-7878
Fax: (718) 583-1883
Web site:

Private Company
Incorporated: 1989
Employees: 75
Sales: $16 million (2003)
NAIC: 311412 Frozen Specialty Food Manufacturing

Based in the borough of the Bronx in New York City, Golden Krust Caribbean Bakery, Inc., operates a chain of company-owned and franchised Golden Krust Caribbean Bakery restaurants. All told, there are some 75 units located in New York, New Jersey, Philadelphia, Atlanta, and Florida. Stores were also slated to open in Boston, Chicago, and California. Golden Krust's signature product is the Jamaican beef patty, but the pocket pastry also is offered with chicken and vegetable fillings. In addition to patties, the restaurants offer jerk chicken, stewed chicken, curried chicken, curried goat, escoveitch fish, sliced fish, and ox tail. Baked goods include coconut cake, sponge cake, spice bun, Antiguan bread, gizzarda, fruit cake, and tuti fruiti. Golden Krust is owned and operated by the Hawthorne family.

Company's Founding by a 1980s Immigrant

Golden Krust was founded by Lowell Hawthorne, one of 11 siblings born in St. Andrews, Jamaica. His parents, Mavis and Ephraim, ran a successful bakery, Hawthorne & Sons Bakery, which they started in St. Andrews in 1949 and where Lowell learned the business. But the bakery could employ only so many children and the 1970s brought difficult economic conditions to Jamaica, prompting nine of the Hawthorne children to immigrate to the United States. Lowell arrived in New York in 1981, determined to one day run his own business. In the meantime, Hawthorne earned a degree from Bronx Community College and took a job as a junior accountant with the New York City Police Department, a position he would hold for eight years. Like his siblings Hawthorne saved his money diligently. All of them bought homes. One of his brothers, Lloyd, worked for Royal Caribbean, the largest West Indian bakery in New York, and had a feel for the local retail situation. He realized that Royal Caribbean and the other bakeries were interested in doing business with wholesalers only and they failed to realize how large the Caribbean population in the city had become. Moreover, West Indian baked goods were not sold close enough to where the customers actually lived.

Sensing an opening in the market, Hawthorne took a leave of absence from the Police Department to start his own bakery. He would never return to the job. Nevertheless, launching the business did not come easily. With so many restaurants failing in the 1980s, banks were not interested in loaning money to someone who wanted to open an eatery in a working class section of the Bronx targeting West Indians. Undeterred, Hawthorne called a family meeting, and his eight brothers and sisters agreed to mortgage their homes and deplete their savings to raise the funding for the new business, $107,000 in all. "We recognized the idea's profitability," Hawthorne told *Emerge* in a 1997 profile. "We knew it was a risk, but it was a calculated risk."

The first Golden Krust Caribbean Bakery opened in 1989 on East Gunhill Road in the Bronx, in the heart of a major West Indian neighborhood. With ovens and racks in the basement and a coffee shop on the ground floor, the store was an immediate success. In the first year, the business rang up $100,000 in sales and the company was already expanding. It opened another bakery next door to handle delivery routes and expanded beyond the Hudson River to open another store in New Jersey. The Hawthornes also paid attention to where their customers came from, the ones who ordered patties in bulk, and began scouting out new locations in the city. By the end of the second year, Golden Krust was operating five stores and sales had grown to $1 million.

Steady Growth in the Early 1990s

As Golden Krust proved successful, it was able to secure a $1 million bank loan and contribute a portion of earnings to build a new plant. In keeping with a desire to help bring

Company Perspectives:

In 1989 the Hawthorne family had a dream, that is, to offer the most sought after Caribbean cuisine in New York.

opportunities to minorities, the facility, which opened in 1992, was located in one of the most disadvantaged sections of the Bronx. Whereas Ephraim Hawthorne was able to produce only a few hundred meat patties each day in Jamaica, the new Bronx plant could turn out as many as 300 each minute. They were then flash-frozen, distributed, and heated at the stores for serving. The extra production capacity would be needed, not only to supply the needs of the growing chain of Golden Krust restaurants, which spread to the other New York boroughs, but to meet large orders. Inmates at the Rikers Island prison were served Jamaican patties, consuming more than 50,000 each month. In 1995 New York City schoolchildren would start eating the patties as part of the school lunch program. Later city hospitals, Mount Vernon, New York-Schools, Rockland County jails, and supermarkets in some 30 states also would be added as customers.

By the end of 1996 Golden Krust was generating sales in excess of $10 million from 13 company-owned stores. The chain also had established a beachhead in Florida and opened a production plant in Fort Lauderdale. In addition, the company was taking steps to grow the Golden Krust chain through franchising, something that Hawthorne had not envisioned originally. As he explained to *Black Enterprise* in 2002, ''Suddenly, calls started coming in from all over; people were interested in the concept. So we sought information on franchising.'' It was a move few minority business owners were willing to make, due to the expense and time it took to set up a viable franchising structure and the danger of losing focus on running the core business. But Hawthorne once again displayed his business acumen by putting together a program. Golden Krust licensed franchises for $20,000 and received 5 percent of profits, with 2 percent earmarked for cable television advertising.

In 1997 the first handful of franchised operations began to open. An early success story was Jamaican-born Hillary D. Hurbs, an acquaintance of Hawthorne. She already had experience at the Pepsi-Cola Company and with a consulting firm before deciding to become a Golden Krust franchisee and going to work for herself. Most Golden Krust outlets were small affairs, some as small as 600 square feet, located in enclaves of West Indian immigrants. But Hurbs's restaurant was 4,350 square feet in size and capable of seating 74. It was located in lower Manhattan on Chambers Street, much closer to Wall Street than to the Bronx or Brooklyn. She also would provide catering to nearby City Hall, as well as the mayor's residence at Gracie Mansion.

With a business background, Hurbs was an unusual Golden Krust franchisee. A large number of other women launched Golden Krust restaurants, but many of them were nurses. It was an understandable connection on a number of levels. Many West Indians worked in hospitals, leading Golden Krust to locate many of its units close by. As a result a lot of registered nurses became regular customers, and some took an interest in going into business for themselves. Moreover, many nurses developed strong leadership skills and brought other attributes to the table. In a *New York Times* profile of the company, Jeffrey E. Kolton, a lawyer specializing in franchising, explained why nurses made ideal candidates: ''Good franchisees are people who want to follow systems. Nurses take pride in their work, are good at following orders and manuals, and they're customer service oriented.''

By mid-1999 the Golden Krust chain was 35 units strong, 24 of which were franchise stores. The company also had a new 60,000-square-foot Bronx plant, funded by $1.2 million in city-backed business development loans. The chain was now moving well beyond its base of Caribbean customers and appealing to the general public. In an effort to reach everyone, the chain modified its menu to meet the tastes of a neighborhood. For instance, it offered soy protein patty fillings for vegetarians and halal patties for Muslims. In Hurbs's Chambers Street outlet, customers could find cold cuts as well as curried goat. Golden Krust's success did not go unnoticed. In 1999 Ernst & Young named the company its Entrepreneur of the Year in New York City.

Continued Expansion in the 2000s

Golden Krust continued to make strides in the new century. It entered the Philadelphia market, where it hoped to open more than 20 stores within five years. The first Philadelphia outlet also would introduce the chain's jerk chicken dish and be the first to use the Golden Krust Caribbean Bakery & Grill name. The management of the company to this point had been dominated by members of the Hawthorne family, but in early 2003 Golden Krust hired experienced outside management help to take the business to the next level. Brought in were a vice-president of franchising; director of research, development, and training; director of marketing and public relations; and a director of franchise sales and development. The immediate goal was to better promote the Golden Krust brand and grow the franchise operation. The chain also was improving its advertising program with the signing of a spokesperson, Tiki Barber, star football player of the New York Giants.

Later in 2003 Golden Krust demonstrated that it had reached a new level of credibility when it signed a seven-year agreement with Pepsi USA. Pepsi would install soda fountains in all of the Golden Krust stores, help the chain redesign its menu boards, provide assistance in marketing, and also help in analyzing demographics for use in selecting new store locations. The chain was also in line to receive rebates based on the volume of Pepsi products it sold. Several months later Golden Krust, in conjunction with Pepsi, introduced combo meals to drive sales for both parties. To support the program, the company launched a major advertising campaign, making full use of Tiki Barber in all media, including radio, television, newspapers, billboards, and buses.

As Golden Krust entered 2004, the chain consisted of 73 stores located with five states. Another 12 units were under construction. But management was aiming at a much loftier goal: 250 stores in operation within the next five years. Essentially, this meant opening three units each month. Because

Key Dates:

1989: The first Golden Krust Caribbean Bakery opens.
1992: The Bronx manufacturing plant opens.
1997: The first franchised units open.
2003: An alliance is forged with Pepsi USA.
2004: Golden Krust expands to the West Coast.

Florida, with its large Caribbean population, held great potential for the Golden Krust concept, the company conducted one-day ''Franchise Opportunity Seminars'' in Fort Lauderdale and Orlando. The hope was to land area developers, people willing to open five or more stores, rather than just individual franchisees. Not only did people receive a presentation about the concept, they also had a chance to meet individually with top Golden Krust officials.

Later in 2004 Golden Krust granted territorial rights to a franchisee for the first time in its history. Moreover, the ten-store deal was slated for the Los Angeles, California, market, in effect giving Golden Krust a coast-to-coast presence. These new units would also be the first to employ a drive-through window for takeout. The new franchisees were partners Donald Royes, June Royes, and Carl Ashman, who collectively had a great deal of experience in marketing and restaurant management. Earlier in the year they had become aware of the Golden Krust concept, and after conducting some research into the company and its leadership, decided to sign on.

The company also launched a variation on its original concept. In partnership with the Mid Bronx Senior Citizen Center it made plans to open a Golden Krust Café, a true sit-down restaurant that would offer a seafood grill in addition to the chain's traditional fare. Golden Krust had come a long way in 15 years; the American appetite for Jamaican food appeared to be the only limiting factor in determining the company's long-term potential.

Principal Subsidiaries

Golden Krust Patties, Inc.; Golden Krust Franchising Inc.

Principal Competitors

Caribbean Food Delights; Royal Caribbean Bakery; Tower Isles.

Further Reading

Block, Valerie, ''Eatery Chain Hopes Spice Is Right,'' *Crain's New York Business,* October 20, 1997, p. 26.
Kramer, Louise, ''For Ex-Nurses, Real Money's in Takeout,'' *New York Times,* April 4, 2004, p. 10.
Millman, Joel, ''Imported Entrepreneurs,'' *Forbes,* November 6, 1995, p. 232.
Rouse, Deborah L., ''Making Dough,'' *Emerge,* November 1997, p. 13.
Salaam, Yusef, ''A Golden Fixture Among Manhattan Eateries,'' *New York Amsterdam News,* August 14, 1997, p. 27.
Waldman, Amy, ''From a Flaky Foundation, a Food Empire,'' *New York Times,* April 26, 1998, p. 14.

—Ed Dinger

Gristede's Foods Inc.

823 11th Avenue
New York, New York 10019-3535
U.S.A.
Telephone: (212) 956-5803
Toll Free: (877) GRI-XPRESS; (877) 474-9773
Fax: (212) 247-4509
Web site: http://www.gristedes.com

Private Company
Incorporated: 1913 as Gristede Brothers, Inc.
Employees: 2,180
Sales: $279.69 million (2003)
NAIC: 422410 General Line Grocery Wholesalers; 42248 Fresh Fruit & Vegetable Wholesalers; 44511 Supermarkets & Other Grocery (Except Convenience) Stores; 44611 Pharmacies and Drug Stores; 446199 All Other Health & Personal Care Stores; 551112 Offices of Other Holding Companies

Gristede's Foods Inc., owns and operates 46 supermarkets in the New York City metropolitan area. It also sells groceries online via amazon.com and its own web site, XpressGrocer .com. The company also owns and operates a warehouse that supplies these supermarkets with groceries and fresh produce and sells wholesale fresh produce to third parties. Gristede's is 92 percent owned by John A. Catsimatidis, in part through the Red Apple Group, Inc. holding company.

Gristede Brothers: 1891–1987

Charles Gristede and his brother Diedrich came to the United States from Germany in 1888, found work in grocery stores, and in 1891 opened a tiny gaslit store at 42nd Street and Second Avenue in Manhattan. This site was then far uptown from the central shopping area but close to housewives who walked or rode in private carriages to the store. A second store opened in Harlem—then a middle-class white neighborhood—in 1896. The business flourished and expanded, reaching suburban Westchester County in 1920 and Connecticut in 1926. Gristede Brothers also opened a wine and liquor store in Manhattan in 1933. When Charles Gristede died in 1948, the chain consisted of 141 stores in Manhattan, the Bronx, Westchester, and Connecticut. In 1956 it opened its first Long Island store, in Garden City.

In Manhattan, Gristede Brothers remained concentrated on the more affluent East Side, where it specialized in personal service and gourmet items and charged premium prices. It shipped items to customers around the world, including, for example, a Greek who wanted melons sent to him in Paris by air freight. The company had annual sales of about $60 million and 115 stores in all—including six liquor stores in Connecticut—when it was sold in 1968 to The Southland Corporation, owner of the 7-Eleven convenience store chain, for Southland stock valued at $11.5 million.

Southland retained the prior Gristede Brothers management and for more than a decade left the chain to its own devices. In 1977 Gristede's consisted of 120 stores, mostly ranging in size from 6,000 to 11,000 square feet and carrying 7,000 to 8,000 gourmet items, including size 23 grapefruit (about the size of a large cantaloupe), strawberries picked in California only 36 hours earlier, large Idaho potatoes already wrapped in tin foil, quiche Lorraine, and Beluga caviar.

By the early 1980s, however, Gristede's, as well as other supermarket chains with outlets in New York City, was reeling from a number of adverse conditions, including the small size of the stores, the high cost of delivery in the city, escalating rents, and competition from gourmet shops and specialty food stores. In 1980 the chain still consisted of 100 outlets, including 24 Charles & Co. sandwich shops, but by 1983, when Gristede's fell into the red, there were only 84. During 1983-84 Gristede's concentrated its operations in Manhattan, closing 36 stores and its warehouse. In 1985 there were 18 conventional supermarkets; 17 generally smaller service stores featuring telephone ordering, home delivery, and charge accounts; ten Charles & Co. sandwich shops and one gourmet shop; and one liquor store. Sales came to about $105 million in 1985.

Southland sold the Gristede's and Charles & Co. stores to Red Apple Co. in 1986 for an estimated $50 million. Red Apple, owned by John A. Catsimatidis and operating in the Bronx as well as Manhattan, now became the largest supermarket chain in New

Company Perspectives:

Gristede's has been feeding New Yorkers for over 100 years. Our stores offer fresh meats, produce, dairy products, baked goods, frozen foods, gourmet foods, and nonfood items. We at Gristede's strive to make every shopping experience a great shopping experience. Our customers have come to expect the best products at the lowest prices in town.

York City. Gristede's and Red Apple remained distinct, however. Red Apple had completed 14 Gristede's remodels by the fall of 1987, including adding in-store delicatessens, bakeries, salad bars, hot takeout foods, and upscale cheese, prime-meat, and seafood sections. The Charles & Co. stores were closed.

Sloan's Supermarkets: 1956–97

Born in the Bronx and reared by foster families after his mother died, Max Sloan left school after the eighth grade to sell fruit and vegetables from a pushcart. A small vegetable and fruit store he opened in 1940 with $500 grew into the Orange Grove chain. Sloan and his partner, Lou Meyer, also ran a wholesale produce operation supplying fruits and vegetables to many grocery stores in Manhattan and the Bronx. They entered the supermarket business in 1956 with two Manhattan stores. There were 25 Sloan Supermarket Stores—mostly on Manhattan's West Side—in 1973, when the chain purchased seven more from Bohack Corporation. By this time Sloan had annual sales of $42 million.

Meyer died in 1969, and Sloan retired in 1977. His successor was a son-in-law, Jules Rose. By 1982 the 42-store Sloan's Supermarkets Inc. chain had estimated sales of $150 million a year. Its viability, Rose said, rested on seeking to market items with the greatest profit margin, such as meat, frozen items, produce, and gourmet foods. The city's consumer affairs agency had consistently listed Sloan's as one of the most expensive food chains in Manhattan. Sloan's success also rested on careful monitoring of the borough's ethnically diverse clientele. A store on the Lower East Side, for example, had a large line of Goya-brand products for Hispanics and kosher products for Orthodox Jews. Another, close to the United Nations, had full international foods sections. Located in a high-income area, it also had a higher proportion of frozen food and dairy products sales and included health and natural foods sections.

Sloan's Supermarkets had 38 stores in early 1990, when it was first reported on the auction block. Cynthia Rigg of *Crain's New York Business* wrote, "Over the past decade Sloan's reputation for quality has fallen dramatically. The privately held chain has done little to upgrade its stores while [its competitors] have undertaken extensive expansion and modernization programs." She also reported that industry sources said the four principals of Sloan's were "often at loggerheads, which stymies decision making." Despite its problems, Sloan's was said to hold a 20 percent share of Manhattan's grocery business.

After selling three stores to various companies in 1990, Sloan's Supermarkets sold 21 more to Red Apple during 1991–92. One observer explained to Richard Turcsik of *Supermarket News,* "Gristede is definitely considered upscale. Sloan's is somewhere in between and Red Apple is considered low-end. By keeping the Sloan's name, Red Apple will be able to service all three segments of the customer base from one distributor." The acquisition had its hazards, however, because three of Sloan's owners were, in 1993, being charged with fraudulently redeeming at least $3.5 million of discount coupons clipped from newspapers, an action that threatened 15 of the acquired units with forfeiture to the federal government. The three Sloan's partners—Rose, Max Sloan's other son-in-law, and Meyer's son—eventually went to jail.

Despite these problems, Red Apple bought the remaining 11 Sloan's supermarkets—ten in Manhattan and one in Brooklyn—in 1993 for $8.8 million plus certain accounts payable. This purchase was not assigned to Red Apple itself but to Designcraft, Inc., a publicly owned shell corporation whose main stockholder was Catsimatidis. Following the sale the federal government agreed to withdraw all claims against Sloan's Supermarkets. Designcraft then took the Sloan's Supermarkets name and continued operations under Red Apple Group management.

This transaction raised the number of supermarket stores in the New York area controlled by Red Apple to 75. In 1994 the Federal Trade Commission filed a complaint, seeking the sale of ten Red Apple-controlled stores in four Manhattan neighborhoods because of possible anticompetitive effects, such as higher food prices and lower quality and selection. Supermarkets under the Red Apple, Gristede's, and Sloan's names were serving 37 percent of Manhattan's food shoppers on a regular basis, according to a survey. Catsimatidis agreed later in 1994 to divest six stores in order to settle the complaint. In 1997, however, he and three of his firms agreed to pay a $600,000 penalty for failing to comply with the FTC order. Only one of the stores had been divested, according to the agency.

The Red Apple name virtually disappeared during this period, its outlets sold to Rite Aid Corporation or converted to Gristede's or Sloan's supermarkets. Sloan's acquired three more supermarkets from a subsidiary of Red Apple Group in 1995 for $5 million plus the cost of inventory. It also opened an additional supermarket and a Brooklyn health and beauty aids store in 1996.

Gristede's Sloan's: 1997–99

In 1997 Sloan's Supermarkets acquired 19 Gristede's and ten Sloan's supermarkets, plus a produce distribution center, from Red Apple for $36 million worth of stock plus the assumption of $4 million in debt. The company was then renamed Gristede's Sloan's, Inc. During fiscal 1998 (the year ended November 30, 1998), Gristede's Sloan's acquired another supermarket from an affiliate of Catsimatidis and remodeled ten stores at a cost of $10 million. The company also closed four stores and combined two adjacent ones into a single store. Company sales came to $157.5 million, with a net loss of $288,339. Gristede's Sloan's had a long-term debt of $21.6 million at the end of the fiscal year. Catsimatidis, the chief executive officer, owned or controlled 91 percent of the company in February 1999.

Of the 40 Gristede's Sloan's stores in 1998, 35 were in Manhattan, one was in Brooklyn, three were in Westchester

Key Dates:

1891: Charles and Diedrich Gristede open their first store.
1956: Max Sloan opens his first supermarket.
1968: Gristede Brothers is sold to The Southland Corporation.
1986: Southland sells Gristede's to Red Apple Co.
1993: Red Apple completes the purchase of Sloan's begun in 1991.
1997: The two chains are combined as Gristede's Sloan's, Inc.
1999: The stores are renamed Gristede's; cafés and pharmacies are introduced.
2002: "Mega Stores" debut.
2003: XpressGrocer.com is launched.
2004: The company is taken private; the company begins fulfilling amazon.com orders.

County, and one was on Long Island. They ranged from 3,200 to 23,000 square feet in selling space, with an average of 9,000, and were all leased. City Produce Operating Corp., on leased premises in the Bronx, was a warehouse operation supplying the company's supermarkets with groceries and fresh produce and selling fresh produce wholesale to third parties.

Gristede's Sloan's supermarkets were offering broad lines of merchandise, including nationally and regionally advertised brands and private-label and generic brands. Their food items included fresh meats, produce, dry groceries, dairy products, baked goods, poultry and fish, fresh fruits and vegetables, frozen foods, delicatessen items, and gourmet foods. Nonfood items included cigarettes, soaps, paper products, and health and beauty aids. The company also was operating an in-store pharmacy in one of its supermarkets. Check-cashing services were available to qualified customers, and groceries were being delivered to apartments for a small fee. The stores were open 16 hours a day, seven days a week, and on holidays. At least one was open around the clock.

Gristede's Sloan's was planning to remodel 12 more stores in fiscal 1999 and to open two new stores and four in-store pharmacies. Of the 11 stores operating under the Sloan's name, four had been converted to Gristede's by May 1999, when the company announced that the remaining seven would also take the Gristede's name by the end of the year. Catsimatidis told *Supermarket News* that the Gristede's banner "is a better name, with better marketing potential."

Expanding for the New Millennium

In the late 1990s, Gristede's began experimenting with a lunch counter called The Café at two of its Manhattan stores. Fare included hot dogs and sandwiches, as well as more prepared entrées. In 1999 one of the Cafés began testing a sushi bar concept through a joint venture with HMC Sushi of Plainfield, New Jersey (the sushi was prepared on the premises).

The first pharmacies were installed in two Gristede's stores in 1999. They were operated under license from Legend Pharmacies, Inc., a cooperative based in Melville, New York.

The company celebrated openings of new and renovated stores through a special promotion with the *New York Daily News*. Gristede's gave shoppers free copies (as many as 5,000 in all) of a specially printed version of the paper, which had a full-page ad for the store on the front and back.

Gristede's had about 1,500 employees in 2000. Sales were $216.3 million. Losses were narrowed from $2.9 million to $191,000. Sales rose to $230 million in 2001 as the company managed a net profit of $275,000.

In 2002, A&P (The Great Atlantic & Pacific Tea Company) sold Gristede's three Food Emporium stores for $5.5 million. These were soon reopened under the Gristede's banner. The company was developing some of its own locations as "Mega Stores," which, at 20,000 square feet, were almost twice the size of the company's traditional buildings.

After a 20-year absence, Gristede's reentered the New Jersey market by opening more than ten supermarkets there beginning in 2002. According to *The Record*, Catsimatidis was attracted to the market after researching a potential acquisition, Kings Super Markets Inc. Both chains had a similar customer base and similar approach. Gristede's was bidding against rival D'Agostino Supermarkets, Inc. to acquire Parsippany, New Jersey-based Kings Super Markets from Marks & Spencer PLC (M&S). Neither company was able to secure the necessary financing to buy the 28-unit chain, and in August 2003, M&S pulled Kings off the market.

Gristede's also opened its first store in the Bronx in November 2002. According to the *New York Times*, Catsimatidis was encouraged to open a supermarket in a Latino neighborhood there following the success of a store in the Washington Heights area.

To keep up with the evolving e-commerce side of the grocery business, the company launched its XpressGrocer.com site in December 2003. Gristede's also began filling orders taken through amazon.com in November 2004. The amazon orders were available to be shipped anywhere in the United States, not just New York.

After losing nearly $1 million in fiscal 2002, the company posted a net loss of $11.6 million on sales of $279.69 million in fiscal 2003. The loss was attributed in part to opening seven new stores during the year. The blackout on August 14–15, 2003 resulted in the loss of some perishables.

In 2004, Chairman John Catsimatidis, who owned more than 90 percent of Gristede's, was taking the company private. According to *BusinessWeek*, cumbersome and expensive new regulatory burdens and the hassle of trying to drum up investor interest for such a small company (valued at just $16 million) were behind the move.

Principal Subsidiaries

City Produce Operating Corporation; Gristede's Delivery Service, Inc.; Gristede's Foods NY Inc.; Namdor Inc.

Principal Operating Units

XpressGrocer.com.

Principal Competitors

D'Agostino Supermarkets, Inc.; FreshDirect.com; A&P Food Stores and The Food Emporium; Key Food Stores Co-Operative Inc.; Pathmark Stores, Inc.; Pioneer Supermarkets.

Further Reading

''Charles Gristede, Grocer 77, Is Dead,'' *New York Times,* October 31, 1948, p. 88.

Clark, Chapin, ''Ex-CEO of Sloan's Begins Prison Sentence,'' *SN/ Supermarket News,* March 9, 1998, pp. 1, 73.

Collins, Glenn, ''Red Apple to Sell Up to 20 Stores,'' *New York Times,* November 30, 1994, p. D3.

Croft, Tara, ''Gristede's Shops for Kings,'' *Daily Deal,* July 21, 2003.

DeMarrais, Kevin G., ''Gristede's Market Prepares to Enter New Jersey, Challenge Kings Supermarket,'' *The Record* (Hackensack, N.J.), August 9, 2002.

Evans, Matthew W., ''Red Apple Becomes Legend Operator,'' *Supermarket News,* June 7, 1999, p. 97.

Finklea, Robert W., ''The Gristede's Link in Southland's Chain,'' *New York Times,* July 17, 1977, Sec. 3, p. 3.

Ghitelman, David, ''Gristede's Boss Wants C-Stores Taxed,'' *Supermarket News,* March 8, 2004, p. 8.

——, ''Gristede's Settles Delivery-Worker Case for $3.25 Million,'' *Supermarket News,* December 22, 2003, p. 7.

''Gristede's Flag Will Fly Over Remaining Sloan's,'' *SN/Supermarket News,* May 3, 1999, p. 8.

Harper, Roseanne, ''Gristedes Opens New NYC Store with Café,'' *Supermarket News,* May 31, 1999, p. 19.

——, ''Sushi-Bar Test Goes Swimmingly at Gristede's,'' *Supermarket News,* November 22, 1999, p. 19.

''Holders Approve Purchase of Stores from Chairman,'' *Wall Street Journal,* October 31, 1997, p. B4.

Kugel, Seth, ''Gristede's Arrives in the Bronx, But Does Not Forget the Rice,'' *New York Times,* November 10, 2002, p. 8.

Mesure, Susie, ''M&S Scraps US Supermarkets Sale,'' *Independent,* August 15, 2003.

Murray, Barbara, ''Gristede's: Bigger Is Better,'' *Supermarket News,* December 30, 2002, p. 7.

Nagle, James J., ''Gristede-Southland Merger Set,'' *New York Times,* October 16, 1968, pp. 59, 64.

Pace, Eric, ''Max Sloan, 83, Whose Pushcart Grew into a Supermarket Chain,'' *New York Times,* August 7, 1995, p. B10.

Paikert, Charles, ''Jules Rose: Manhattan's Food Market Maven,'' *Chain Store Age Executive,* January 1982, pp. 48, 55–56, 59.

Reckert, Clare M., ''Bohack Sells 7 Units,'' *New York Times,* August 14, 1973, pp. 43, 47.

Rigg, Cynthia, ''At Sloan's, the Specials for Investors Are Stakes,'' *Crain's New York Business,* December 6, 1993, p. 4.

——, ''Fraud Case Threatens Sloan Sale,'' *Crain's New York Business,* March 22, 1993, pp. 3, 36.

Schmitt, Eric, ''Red Apple Buying Gristedes,'' *New York Times,* February 6, 1986, p. D4.

Springer, Jon, ''Gristedes Sales Fall; Web Deal Set,'' *Supermarket News,* September 6, 2004, p. 8.

Strupp, Joe, ''New York Daily News Goes to Market,'' *Editor & Publisher,* August 14, 1999, p. 27.

Tanner, Ronald, ''How Jules Rose Nourishes His Broadway Baby,'' *Progressive Grocer,* February 1983, pp. 105, 108, 110, 112.

Thornton, Emily, ''A Little Privacy, Please; More Small Outfits Are Deciding That Being a Public Company Isn't Worth the Hassle,'' *BusinessWeek,* May 24, 2004, p. 74.

Tsai, Michelle, ''Amazon to Offer Gourmet Food Via Gristede's Partnership,'' *Dow Jones News Service,* June 17, 2004.

Turcsik, Richard, ''Red Apple Starts Sloan's Store Buyout,'' *Supermarket News,* July 2, 1991, pp. 1, 34.

''Washington Briefs,'' *Supermarket Business,* February 1997, p. 9.

Zwiebach, Elliot, ''Chairman Planning to Take Gristede's Private,'' *Supermarket News,* April 19, 2004, p. 8.

—Robert Halasz
—update: Frederick C. Ingram

GROZ-BECKERT®

Groz-Beckert Group

Parkweg 2
D-72458 Albstadt
Germany
Telephone: (49) (7431) 10-0
Fax: (49) (7431) 10-2777
Web site: http://www.groz-beckert.com

Private Company
Incorporated: 1937 as Theodor Groz & Soehne
Employees: 7,500
Sales: EUR 452.4 million ($561.2 million) (2003)
NAIC: 339993 Fastener, Button, Needle, and Pin Manufacturing; 333512 Machine Tool (Metal Cutting Types) Manufacturing; 333513 Machine Tool (Metal Forming Types) Manufacturing; 332618 Other Fabricated Wire Product Manufacturing

Groz-Beckert Group is among the world's leading manufacturers of high-precision industrial needles used in the cloth making, textile, and shoe manufacturing industries. The company's product range includes about 60,000 different needles and related accessories, including knitting and hosiery machine needles and parts, sewing and shoe machine needles, felting and structuring needles for the production of non-woven materials and tufting needles and modules for carpet manufacturers. In addition to developing and manufacturing this broad range of industrial needles, Groz-Beckert builds the machines to produce the needles in-house. The company's Swiss subsidiary Grob Horgen AG is the world's leading supplier of weaving machine accessories. Groz-Beckert also makes high-precision ceramic punching components which are used to manufacture multilayer microchips used in computers, mobile phones and other high-tech products. Groz-Beckert products are manufactured in Germany, Switzerland, the Czech Republic, Portugal, Canada, India and China. Headquartered in Albstadt, southwestern Germany, the family-owned company exports more than 80 percent of its output to over 150 countries.

Early Roots Go Back to 1850s

The history of the Groz-Beckert Group began in the middle of the 19th century in Ebingen, a small town in Swabia, Germany. In a region where hosiery knitting was the dominant way to make a living, Theodor Groz, the son of a pharmacist who died prematurely, decided to leave his home town to learn the craft of needle making. After apprenticeships in Germany and Austria he returned to Ebingen in 1852, got married and opened a store for fashion accessories and toys. At the same time he began to make warp-knitting needles on the side, which were used in stockings manufacturing. Groz took this ''side business'' very seriously. Driven by the idea to make better needles than anyone else, he invested most of his financial resources into refining the needle making process. Needle-making was time consuming and complicated. Each needle was made from iron wire, which had to be bent, stretched, drilled, pressed, cut, filed, hardened, polished and finally straightened out. Although needles constituted only a fraction of a knitting factory's cost, they played a decisive role in the end product. Poorly made needles could break after being used only for a short time or—even worse—stain or cut the thread, and thereby ruin the product. Therefore, high-quality needles were a concern of foremost importance for every knitting factory owner.

In 1864 the warp loom needle output of the better part of a year turned out to be of such a low quality that they could not be used, due to the low-quality of the wire used to make them. This serious threat to the existence of his enterprise encouraged the company founder even more to invest his time in quality improvement. By 1867 Groz had created detailed ''How-To'' manuals for the production of steel needles, hosiery frame needles and latch needles that exceeded the quality standards of the time. One of the main factors that determined the quality of the needles was the hardening of the iron, and later steel wire, to make the material as durable as possible. For ten years Groz experimented with different technologies, using high-quality piano wire imported from England, and finally succeeded in developing a process that yielded outstanding results.

With the onset of the industrial revolution in the late 19th century more and more steps of the manufacturing process were mechanized. Groz realized that—to keep ahead of the

Company Perspectives:

Ready to meet any challenge related to tools for the textile industry—that's Groz-Beckert. Today, tomorrow, and in the future.

competition—he had to develop his own needle-making machines that were not available on the market. The company's engineers pioneered the field with a number of innovations, including the so-called bearded forming machine in 1883 and the Shanking machine in 1890.

Soon Groz's needles gained a reputation for outstanding quality. By 1861 Groz's needle-making workshop employed 25 workers, putting out some 10,000 bearded needles a week. After a few years Groz decided to add latch needles to his product range, a new type of needle which gained a growing market share at the time, and the workshop produced between 1,000 and 2,000 latch needles weekly. In 1874 his son Daniel together with a friend made a significant improvement in the design of the latch needle, mechanizing the latch fastening process.

The arrival of the steam engine in the 1870s boosted productivity to new heights. At the same time, mechanization of the knitting industry resulted in a higher demand for knitting machine needles. The growing number of incoming orders stretched the workshop's capacity to its limits. In 1884 production was moved to a factory building near Ebingen's train station. By 1892 the factory's work force reached 400. At the turn of the century the 550 workers at Theodor Groz produced 40 million bearded needles and 15 million latch needles a year in one of the industry's most modern production facilities.

Merger Creates World Market Leader in 1937

The late 19th century was a period of change in leadership at the Theodor Groz company. In 1879 Theodor Groz's oldest sons Theodor and Daniel became partners in their father's business, which was renamed Theodor Groz & Sons. Thirteen years later the company founder as well as his son Theodor died. In 1897 Daniel Groz passed the management reins on to his younger brother Oskar and brother-in-law Heinrich Cless. However, only four years later they left, and Adolf Groz, the company founder's youngest son, took over the family firm.

In the early years of the 20th century Theodor Groz & Soehne enjoyed a period of continued growth. Adolf Groz continued his predecessors' efforts to expand into new markets outside of Germany. At the time, France, Great Britain and the United States were the major markets for industrial knitting needles. As early as 1884 Theodor Groz had started to export the company's new latch needles to the United States. When World War I erupted in 1914 it interrupted the company's further growth. Exports came to a sudden halt. However, right after the war the company established a joint sales office in New York City with another leading German knitting needle manufacturer—Ernst Beckert, Nadelfabriken Commandit-Gesellschaft, based in Chemnitz, Saxony.

Similarly to Theodor Groz, company founder Ernst Beckert grew up in an area where hosiery knitting was the usual way of making a living. Growing up in Eibenberg in Saxony, he was used to helping his family turn the hand wheel of the knitting loom. However, Beckert was more interested in machines rather than textiles. He became a mechanic and worked in one of the region's numerous mines until he broke both his legs in an accident at work. During the several months he was unable to work and had to lay in bed, Beckert became interested in the needles his father used for hosiery knitting. He spent not only hours and hours, but also all his money, experimenting with different ways to manufacture knitting needles. After studying the needle-making craft for over a decade, Ernst Beckert began to manufacture needles in his hometown in 1871, the year when a new German Empire was proclaimed. At first, Beckert made his needles under the most primitive conditions. However, with industrialization picking up speed in a thriving economy, Beckert realized that his needles would be needed in large numbers and consequently focused on industrial mass production. Beckert's enterprise took off immediately and soon grew into Saxony's biggest knitting needle factory. A second production site was established in nearby Stollberg in 1885. At the turn of the century Beckert's enterprise employed more than 200 workers. In the following decades the company kept growing. Before World War I, Ernst Beckert Nadelfabriken exported up to half of their total output to the United States. In addition, Beckert's knitting needles were shipped as far as Central and South America, the Far East, Japan, India and even Australia.

The establishment of a joint sales office in 1918 in the United States marked the beginning of a cooperation between the Groz and Beckert companies. While the isolation from the world markets during World War I caused a temporary setback, the two German needle makers soon caught up again with their competitors from France, England and the United States after the war. Due to a number of technological innovations, such as the first automatic rotary table latching machine, productivity reached new heights at the Ebingen and Chemnitz plants. However, in the aftermath of the lost war, the German currency collapsed in 1923. After the new *Reichsmark* was introduced, nine leading needle manufacturers from Saxony, including Ernst Beckert Nadelfabriken, and Theodor Groz & Sons, entered merger negotiations. However, when the German economy went back into growth gear, the merger plans were abandoned. Nevertheless, in 1928 Ernst Beckert's grandson Fritz Seelmann-Eggebert bought a minority stake in Theodor Groz & Sons. Nine years later the leading knitting needle manufacturer in Swabia finally merged with the largest knitting needle producer in Saxony. In 1937 the Theodor Groz & Sons and Ernst Beckert companies became Theodor Groz & Soehne & Ernst Beckert, Nadelfabriken Commandit-Gesellschaft, Ebingen und Chemnitz—in short Groz-Beckert.

The merger created Germany's largest manufacturer of knitting needles with a large market share. The new firm remained in the hands of the two founding families. From the Groz family, the sons of Alfred Groz, Hans and Walther, joined the Groz-Beckert company. The Beckert family was represented by Fritz Seelmann-Eggebert. Meanwhile, Adolf Hitler and his National Socialist Party seized political power in Germany. Two years after the merger, Germany went to war again. The result was disastrous for Groz-Beckert. In the last months of the war the company's factory in Chemnitz was destroyed, while a

Key Dates:

1852: Theodor Groz opens a needle-making workshop in Ebingen, Swabia.
1871: Ernst Beckert founds a needle factory in Eibenberg near Chemnitz, Saxony.
1918: The two companies establish a joint sales office in the United States.
1937: The Theodor Groz & Sons and Ernst Beckert companies merge to become Groz-Beckert.
1945: The company's factory in Chemnitz is destroyed and machines are dismantled by Russian Allied Forces.
1960: A production subsidiary is established in India.
1980: Groz-Beckert brings sewing, felting, structuring and shoe machine needles into its product range.
1996: The company is renamed Groz-Beckert Kommanditgesellschaft.
1997: The company enters the market for ceramic punching components.
1998: Groz-Beckert acquires tufting needle manufacturer Josef Zimmermann.
2000: The company takes over Swiss weaving accessory maker Grob Horgen AG.

burning ammunition train exploded near the Ebingen factory, shattering roofs, doors and windows.

New Geographical and Product Markets

After the end of the war the old Beckert factory in Chemnitz fell under the rule of the Russian occupation forces. While the finished goods warehouse was completely destroyed, most of the machines were usable again after minor repairs. However, the Russian Aliied Forces dismantled anything that was left in the factory and shipped it to Russia. Fritz Seelmann-Eggebert, one of the company's directors, was arrested and held in custody for four years. While the Chemnitz plant was lost for the company, the former Groz-factory in Ebingen, which was governed by the French occupation authorities, was rebuilt and resumed production after lobbying efforts by the French knitwear industry had successfully prevented its dismantling. In the beginning, the needle output of the factory was traded for food, which was in short supply right after the war. The company not only helped feed its remaining and newly hired workers, but also helped them find a new home by building several hundred apartments. By the late 1940s the reconstruction of the buildings was completed and state-of-the art equipment had been developed and installed. In 1950 the company's output in Swabia alone reached prewar production levels for both Ebingen and Chemnitz. Within only two more years that output doubled again. As the German economy entered the postwar economic boom, Groz-Beckert enjoyed a long period of sustained growth.

Right after the company was up and running again, Groz-Beckert revived its prewar contacts with customers in other countries. By 1948, almost two thirds of the company's output was shipped to 39 foreign countries again. However, the international expansion did not stop there. As early as in the 1950s Groz-Beckert began to move parts of its production abroad. In 1957 the company established its first production facility in the United States. Three years later a production subsidiary was set up in India. In 1969 a Groz-Beckert production plant went on stream in Portugal, which was followed up by the acquisition of the Portuguese needle manufacturer Euronadel in 1980. In the 1990s the company added production subsidiaries in the Czech Republic and China.

In the 1980s Groz-Beckert began to venture into new product markets. For almost 130 years the company had successfully occupied the niche market for knitting machine needles. However, in the long run that market was too small to sustain further growth. Beginning in 1980, Groz-Beckert added sewing, felting, structuring and shoe machine needles into its product range. A further expansion into new product markets was established by acquisitions. In 1998 Groz-Beckert acquired the tufting needle manufacturing unit from Aachen-based Josef Zimmermann GmbH & Co. KG, including the rights to the ''Eisbär'' brand name. Two years later the company took over Swiss tufting and weaving accessory maker Grob Horgen AG. In addition to these new markets within the textile industry, Groz-Beckert ventured into an unrelated product market which, however, allowed the company to utilize its know-how in making high-precision parts from hardened metal. In 1997 the company began to manufacture ceramic punching components that were used to make multi-layered microchips used in computers, mobile phones and other electronic devices. In 2003 the company was still managed by descendants of the founders: Dr. Thomas Lindner, a member of the Beckert family and Florian Groz from the Groz family's side.

Principal Subsidiaries

Groz-Beckert KG; YANTEX (Yantai) Precision Textile Accessories Co. Ltd. (China); Groz-Beckert Asia Private Ltd. (India); EURONADEL-Indústrias de Agulhas Lda. (Portugal); Groz-Beckert Portuguesa, Lda. (Portugal); Groz-Beckert Czech s.r.o. (Czech Republic); Sinotech Asia Ltd. (Hong Kong); Groz-Beckert Singapore Pte. Ltd. Groz-Beckert Korea Co. Ltd.; Groz-Beckert Japan K.K.; PT Groz-Beckert Indonesien (Indonesia); Groz-Beckert USA, Inc.; Groz-Beckert Canada; Groz-Beckert de México, S.A. de C.V.; Groz-Beckert U.K. Ltd.; Groz-Beckert Verkaufsstelle (Switzerland); Groz-Beckert Española, S.A. (Spain); Groz-Beckert Italia S.r.L. (Italy).

Principal Competitors

Ferd. Schmetz GmbH; Haase + Kühn Group; Fukuhara Needle Company, Ldt.

Further Reading

''Auftragsbelebung bei Groz-Beckert,'' *Frankfurter Allgemeine Zeitung,* November 25, 1996, p. 23.

''Bestechende Geschichte,'' *Frankfurter Rundschau,* May 4, 2004, p. 30.

Kumar, Rahul, ''Groz Beckert to export industrial needles to Europe,'' Asia Africa Intelligence Wire, April 3, 2004.

Langer, Karsten, ''Nadeln im Goldhaufen,'' *manager magazine online,* April 28, 2003.

150 Years Groz-Beckert: 1852–2002. Albstadt, Germany: Groz-Beckert KG, 2002, 10 p.

—Evelyn Hauser

Guess, Inc.

1444 South Alameda Street
Los Angeles, California 90021
U.S.A.
Telephone: (213) 765-3100
Toll Free: (800) 22-GUESS
Fax: (213) 744-7838
Web site: http://www.guessinc.com/

Public Company
Incorporated: 1981
Employees: 4800
Sales: $636.6 million (2003)
Stock Exchanges: New York
Ticker Symbol: GES
NAIC: 315224 Men's and Boys' Cut and Sew Trouser, Slack, and Jean Manufacturing; 315228 Men's and Boys' Cut and Sew Other Outerwear Manufacturing; 315239 Women's and Girls' Cut and Sew Other Outerwear Manufacturing; 315999 Other Apparel Accessories and Other Apparel Manufacturing; 448110 Men's Clothing Stores; 448120 Women's Clothing Stores.

Once known primarily for its denim jeans, Guess, Inc. designs, manufactures, and licenses a wide variety of men's and women's denim, cotton, and knit apparel. Guess products are available primarily in factory and retail stores in the United States and Canada, as well as through its Internet store at http://www.guess.com. Its apparel lines, which are designed in classic yet trendy and upscale styles, include jeans, pants, overalls, dresses, skirts, shorts, shirts, blouses, jackets, and knitwear. Its accessories, which complement its apparel lines, include eyewear, footwear, fragrances, handbags, jewelry and watches, leathers, swimwear, and kids' and infants' apparel. The company's products are marketed under trademarks including GUESS, GUESS, GUESS U.S.A., GUESS Jeans, GUESS and Triangle Design, Question Mark and Triangle Design, BRAND G, a stylized G, GUESS Kids, Baby GUESS, and GUESS Collection. Guess' advertising campaigns are well known for their innovative and creative images, having been highlighted in international ad campaigns in nearly every major magazine, on television, and other such mediums. Guess advertising has been awarded nearly every distinguished design award, and The Metropolitan Museum of Art chose the Guess Press Book and Nashville catalogue for its Permanent Library Collection.

Origins in Early 1980s

In 1981, Georges Marciano and his brother Maurice arrived in Los Angeles and opened a clothing store in Beverly Hills. Born in Morocco and raised in Marseilles, the Marcianos—who would be joined the following year by brothers Armand and Paul—had previously owned and operated a chain of twelve retail stores in France, but had left that country in order to avoid a tax bill of approximately FF 9 million. (The bill was finally settled in 1986.) Among the merchandise sold in the Marcianos' store were jeans designed by Georges Marciano. These jeans—named Guess, because it was easy for the brothers to pronounce—were meant to fit tightly and featured zippers at the ankles. Innovative for the time, the jeans were stone-washed, giving them a softer feel and lighter colors than typical denim jeans. They also featured what would soon become the distinctive Guess triangle on the back pocket. By then, however, the 1970s boom in designer jeans had faded. It seemed unlikely that a new entry into this tapped-out market could be successful.

Georges Marciano flew to New York in December 1981. Despite his limited English, he convinced Bloomingdale's to display on consignment 30 pairs of his European-style jeans in Bloomingdale's flagship New York store. Within three hours, Bloomingdale's sold out of every pair, despite a $60 sales tag. Guess jeans sales took off spectacularly the following year when Paul Marciano arrived in California to direct the company's advertising campaign. Although he had no previous advertising experience, Paul Marciano devised a campaign that revolutionized the way jeans—and clothing—were sold. Instead of adopting the typical studio design, Paul brought his brother's jeans, and the models wearing them, outdoors, using grainy black-and-white photography and provocative poses described by Forbes as ''catering to teenage cravings for sex, power, attention and self-love . . . electric not only with sexual-

Company Perspectives:

At GUESS?, we are committed to being a worldwide leader in the fashion industry. We deliver products and services of uncompromising quality and integrity consistent with our brand and our image. We are committed to listening and responding to the needs of our customers, associates, and business partners, and to honoring their individual value. We are dedicated to personal and professional enrichment through an environment of open communication, teamwork, trust, and respect. We continue to give back to the community, support humanity, and protect the environment as part of our responsibilities. We remain committed to an entrepreneurial spirit that fuels the growth of our company and increases shareholder value. Through principled leadership, we embrace diversity, and we cultivate strength, pride, and passion to align our personal lives with our professional lives.

ity but with an implicit brutality and exhibitionism as well.'' The controversial ads and their sexy Western look swiftly created household names not only of the Guess brand, but also of its models, in effect starting the supermodel trend that would make many of the ''Guess Girls''—including Carre Otis, Claudia Schiffer, Naomi Campbell, Eva Herzigova, and Anna Nicole Smith—international stars. By the end of 1982, the Marcianos had sold some $12 million worth of their jeans.

Demand for their product soon overwhelmed the Marcianos. Searching for the capital to expand and access to cheaper foreign labor, the Marcianos signed a deal in July 1983 with the Nakash brothers of the company Jordache, giving Jordache 50 percent ownership of Guess in exchange for $4.8 million and use of Jordache's Hong Kong manufacturing plants. Under the deal, Jordache was also licensed to set up a new line of jeans, called Gasoline, to use parts of Guess designs in a lower-priced line. The Guess-Jordache deal neglected, however, to provide for written assurances against copying each others' designs, a common garment industry practice called ''knockoffs.'' Instead, the Marcianos relied on the Nakashes' assurances that, given the success of their own clothing designs, they had no need to knock off Georges Marciano's designs. This lack of written agreement would soon come to haunt the company.

Like the Marcianos, the Israeli-born Nakashes manufactured designer jeans, starting their company in 1977 from a single store in Brooklyn, New York and building a $280 million business by 1983. Jordache's fortunes, however, had already begun to slip, as the designer jean market fizzled and the Jordache name increasingly became known as a mass merchandise label. The Marcianos, on the other hand, sought to establish the Guess name as exclusively high-end. Throughout the company's growth, distribution of Guess clothing was limited largely to upscale department stores and the Marciano's own growing chain of MGA (for Maurice, Georges, and Armand) retail stores.

By the time of the Jordache deal, the Marcianos had already begun to expand their line beyond jeans. In 1982 they entered the menswear market through a licensing agreement with Jeff Hamilton, Inc., which marketed a line of men's clothing under the Guess name in exchange for a 7 percent royalty fee. Between 1983 and 1984, sales of Guess menswear rose from $2.5 million to $27 million. However, Guess soon sought to terminate the Hamilton license agreement and bring the menswear line in-house, maintaining that Hamilton's Guess line was oriented too strongly toward the young men's market, and that Hamilton's ''dumping'' (according to Maurice Marcian in the Daily News Report) of Guess merchandise in Kmart and other discount stores was hurting the label's high-end image. This led to a legal battle with Hamilton that slowed growth in menswear, which Guess brought in-house in 1986.

Court Battles Later in 1980s

The Marciano's largest legal battle, however, was with Jordache. By 1984, sales at Guess had reached $150 million, with the price of Guess jeans climbing as high as $85 per pair, but the partnership between the two sets of brothers had already soured. The Marcianos sued the Nakash brothers and Jordache in 1984, charging that company with unfair competition and claiming that the Nakash brothers were using their position on the Guess board of directors and their access to Guess designs in the Hong Kong plant to produce knockoffs of Guess clothing in their Jordache line. The Marcianos' suit asked the court to undo the 1983 agreement that had given the Nakashes control of half of Guess.

The battle for control of Guess continued for the next five years. Along the way, both sides leveled charges of corporate espionage and document shredding; the Nakashes weathered an investigation by the Internal Revenue Service into Marciano-alleged tax evasion and customs quota fraud, and the Marcianos faced allegations of improper dealings with the IRS. At one point, the Marcianos hired Israeli commandoes to patrol their offices; the Nakashes, for their part, hired security experts to sweep their offices for bugging devices. Meanwhile, the judge overseeing the suit ordered the Marcianos to repay more than $1.5 million of an alleged $1.8 million in unauthorized fees taken out of the company (including the Marcianos paying themselves double their salaries). Estimated attorney fees ran as high as $10 million per year for each side. As one attorney involved in the case told Forbes: ''This is not just war, this is total war. Take no prisoners. There is not an issue that has not been filed. This is litigation at its worst.''

Despite Guess' legal distractions, sales continued to grow, reaching $350 million in 1987, with profits of $100 million. While much of its sales continued to be in jeans, Guess had successfully entered the women's market, with its upscale Georges Marciano label, as well as children's, leatherwear, and footwear. Relaunching its menswear line in 1986, Guess began to make inroads in that market as well, placing its products in men's departments of most major department stores. Licensed products, including Guess watches, eyewear, and a Guess women's fragrance line produced by Revlon, also contributed to overall sales: in 1990, Guess watches alone sold an estimated $60 million. Meanwhile, Guess' chain of retail stores, renamed Guess and averaging 2,000 square feet, grew to 19 locations. The company also moved its Los Angeles operations to a 14-acre site encompassing six buildings, where it manufactured 93 percent of its products. By 1990 sales reached an estimated $575 million.

Key Dates:

1981: Georges and Maurice Marciano open clothing store in Beverly Hills, California.
1982: Paul Marciano begins to direct revolutionary advertising campaign.
1983: Guess expands with help of Nakash brothers of Jordache.
1984: Marcianos and Guess sue Nakash brothers and Jordache, charging unfair competition.
1990: Court battle returns full control of Guess to Marcianos.
1996: Guess becomes publicly-traded company.
1999: Guess establishes an e-commerce retail store with launch of web site: http://www.Guess.com.

Marciano Control Returns in Early 1990s

The legal battle between the Marcianos and the Nakashes finally ended in early 1990, when a jury agreed with the Marcianos and returned 100 percent control of Guess to them. A second trial was set for May 1990 to determine damages. However, as the jury in that case was deliberating, the Marcianos announced that they had reached a settlement with the Nakashes for an undisclosed amount. This development occurred over the objections of their attorney, who pushed them to continue the case to full victory. The Marcianos stated, however, that they feared seeing the case continue through the appeals process and still more years of litigation. The Marcianos' attorney then sued them for $17 million in damages.

But with the battle with Jordache over, the Marcianos set about expanding their business. The years of litigation and the enormous attorneys' fees had limited their growth: the company believed that it would have topped $1 billion in sales by its tenth anniversary had it not been for the court case. With their resources freed up, the Marcianos increased their advertising budget to $22 million in 1991. The company also expanded its retail chain, to 33 stores by the end of 1991, including its European flagship store in Florence, Italy. While the recession of the early 1990s slowed growth somewhat, to 7 percent in 1991 compared to double-digits throughout the 1980s, Guess menswear took off, with a 41 percent sales growth in 1991 alone. By the end of that year, menswear accounted for just under 40 percent of company sales. International sales were also becoming more important to overall revenues. Licensing arrangements brought Guess clothing to more than a dozen countries, with sales particularly strong in Canada and Japan.

In 1993 Guess and its licensees registered an estimated $700 million in sales. In that year, Georges Marciano stepped down as the company's chairman, chief executive officer, and designer, citing differences of opinion with his brothers over the direction of the company. Georges, who had left the company briefly in 1988, sold his 40 percent share of the company to his brothers for an estimated $200 million. The year before, Maurice Marciano had also left the company, but he returned shortly before Georges Marciano's departure. Maurice was named chairman and chief executive officer and took over direction of design; Paul Marciano remained president and chief operating officer, and Armand continued to act as senior executive vice-president. After leaving Guess, Georges Marciano sued Guess and his brothers for allegedly infringing on the Georges Marciano trademark. Meanwhile, Georges opened a new company, Go USA Surfwear, and purchased 80 percent of Yes Clothing Company.

With Guess ads now featuring Maurice's name instead of Georges Marciano, Guess looked to its overhauled junior's line and international distribution, along with a stepped up promotional campaign, to fuel its further growth. Advertising spending reached $28 million in 1993; international sales were expected to reach 25 percent of total sales by the end of 1995. Licensing also continued to be an important source of revenue, with products now including home furnishings, infant wear, and junior knitwear. Sales of Guess watches topped $100 million in 1994, and Guess footwear sold more than $60 million. Meanwhile, Guess stores had also been growing, to an average of 3,500 square feet, and to 61 stores by the end of 1995, including a 7,000 square-foot store in Hawaii's Ala Moana Center and an 8,400 square-foot store in the Woodfield Mall in Schaumburg, Illinois. In less than fifteen years, the Guess label had grown from 30 pairs of jeans to a diversified, billion-dollar branded empire.

Competitive Pressures in Late 1990s

In 1996, Guess became a publicly traded company when it made its initial public offering in July. At about this same time, Guess continued with its earlier expansion plans. However, the next year was a disappointment to Guess due to weak performance in its retail stores, weaknesses in its wholesale division, slower-than-expected non-core Asian licensing revenues, and discontinued licenses. However, three areas were stronger: its international operations, mostly in Latin America and Europe; certain core licensed product lines, such as handbags and accessories; and women's knitwear.

In 1998, Guess launched its new line of high-end ring-spun denim jeans called Premium Denim for both men and women. However, the company lost market share in 1998, mostly due to competitive pressures in the branded basic jeans business and a terrible retail environment. Guess started, in early 1999, its first virtual retail (e-commerce) store at its web site, http://www.Guess.com. The web site, since its inception, had consistent interactive success in combining fashion images, information, and technology.

Guess reduced its expansion plans in 2000 in order to concentrate more on improving investment returns, regaining business strength, and strengthening capital structure. Even so, Guess was still able to open 56 new stores in critical locations throughout the U.S. and Canada, while closing three underperforming stores. Guess also opened a new distribution facility in Louisville, Kentucky. In the fall, Guess introduced G Brand, a complete line of high-quality women's and men's jeanswear that used premium quality Italian ring-spun denim in its European designs. Annual retail and wholesale sales increased by more than 32 percent. However, the company's profitability declined greatly because of higher retail occupancy costs due to less productive stores along with additional expenses for new stores; large inventories due to excessive buying and slowing sales trends; low productivity in its new Kentucky distribution facility; increased consulting fees; increased expenses with Guess Canada; and higher advertising expenses. At the end of 2000, Guess had 212 stores in the United States and Canada.

Decline Spurs New Strategy in 2000s

The popularity of Guess clothing peaked in the spring of 2000 with its advertising campaign that featured the wearing of sexy jeans and short-shorts on such models as Naomi Campbell, Claudia Schiffer, Anna Nicole Smith, and Eva Herzigova. However, the company's fortunes began to plummet near the end of 2000 when sales declined over increased competition. With sluggish sales, Guess' inventories became quite high. In 2001, in response to its problems, Guess began to implement a strategy to improve its profitability and maximize shareholder returns by reinvigorating its past successes at attracting fashionable and trendy men and women. Carlos Albertini was hired as chief operating officer and Frederick G. Silny was hired as chief financial officer in order to coordinate this new strategy, which included using creative new merchandising techniques, retail expansion plans, and strong marketing methods.

While the majority of its previous business was selling wholesale products to department stores, Guess began to make its retailing sector its main activity in 2001. With increased competitors, Guess decided to emphasize what other companies could not offer customers: the complete Guess lifestyle of jeans, accessories, and image. However, Guess and the ailing retail industry experienced poor sales due to the economic recession that fell upon the United States and the devastating reactions to the September 11 attacks. Thus, net earnings plummeted from $20.4 million in 2000 to $9.4 million in 2001. However, Guess was still able to reduce its cost structure and inventory levels. In fact, inventory levels were reduced by over 33 percent. It was, unfortunately, forced to reduce the number of new store openings from 60 to 25. This same year, Guess debuted its online outlet at its web site, http://www.Guess.com/outlet. The company also purchased the remaining 40 percent of Guess Canada with the intention of benefiting from its growth potential.

Guess continued to be hurt in 2002 with decreasing consumer confidence and continuing negative economic and political developments. However, the company was able to effectively manage its inventories and costs while product lines were enlarged, which increased customer interest. The style of the Guess men's line was improved in order to create products that were more appealing to customers and more consistent with the Guess brand. Extra money was injected into marketing and advertising programs in order to reinforce the brand's appeal. As a result, independent surveys showed that Guess was ranked as one of the top five brands in total U.S. spending by teenage girls. In November, Guess.com partnered with Amazon.com in order to give the Guess brand wider online (Internet) exposure. The company opened a total of 24 new stores consisting of 21 new full-price retail stores and three factory-outlet stores and closed two underperforming stores in the United States and Canada.

At the end of 2002, Guess operated a total of 249 stores in the United States and Canada, consisting of 171 full-price retail stores, 11 kids stores and 67 factory outlet stores. Its leading domestic wholesale customers included Federated Department Stores, Inc., Dillard's, Inc., The May Department Stores Company, and Marshall Field's. Guess' retail store in Florence, Italy, was an integral part of its European design activities, and its international licensees and distributors operated 222 Guess stores in 37 countries.

Guess' retail, wholesale, and licensing business segments showed mixed performance results in 2003. The company made progress within its retail stores as the economy improved overall for the industry. The company's actions and investments began to show positive returns when comparable store sales for the year grew 9.3 percent as compared with 2002. The retail segment provided the largest gains due to improvement of its women's and men's lines as well as growth in its accessories line; strong results from its U.S. specialty stores; and a strong record for its Canadian stores. However, its wholesale business within department stores hit hard times when Guess products appeared in only 950 department store and specialty shop locations, after an all-time high of 2,400 locations only a few years earlier. In 2003, inventory levels declined 12.7 percent from 2002, having been cut in half within the last three years. In the fall of 2003, Guess announced a development and distribution partnership with Parlux Fragrances, Inc. in which a new Guess fragrance collection would be tied in with the company's image and its customers' sexy and casual lifestyle.

The next Guess girl, Paris Hilton, was hired in 2004 to help recapture business along with the company's glamorous image. The company's web site showed Hilton in various sexy poses. In the summer of 2004, Guess launched the Marciano chain, an extension of its brand Marciano that was designed in the style of sexy, yet sophisticated apparel and accessories. Stores in Los Angeles, California; McAllen, Texas; and Toronto, Canada were opened to serve slightly older customers interested in higher-end clothes and accessories such as glitzy evening dresses and fancy jeans. Additional Marciano stores were planned to open in the United States later in the year. Guess also began opening several Accessories boutiques, a mall-based chain that carried only accessories such as handbags and hats, but no clothes. Besides these two new store concepts, Guess was also planning on 100 store openings over the next 12 months.

Now a billion-dollar multinational retailer, Guess was one of the most widely recognized brands in the world. Known for quality, marketing creativity, and popularizing new trends and styles, the company had seen increased competition throughout its markets during the first few years of 2000. While jeans remained the foundation of Guess style, the company continued to expand its lines to include comfortable, casual clothing and accessories for women, men, children, and babies to meet every lifestyle. Guess possessed licensees and distributors in 232 retail stores in 77 countries throughout North America, South America, Europe, Asia, Africa, and Australia. Guess' wholesale business was represented in over 846 establishments in the United States. Guess owned and operated a chain of over 180 retail and factory stores, and over 1,000 in-store shops in other retailers in the United States. Guess had more than 30 stores in Mexico and about 46 stores in Canada.

Principal Subsidiaries

Guess Retail; Guess.com Inc.; Guess Licensing Inc.; Guess Canada.

Principal Divisions

Retail; Wholesale; Licensing.

Principal Competitors

Diesel SpA; Gap Inc.; Levi Stauss & Co.; bebe stores, inc.

Further Reading

Behar, Richard, ''Does Guess Have a Friend in the IRS,'' *Forbes,* November 16, 1987, p. 147.

Belgum, Deborah, ''Guess Recovery Mode Starting with Better Control of Inventory,'' *Los Angeles Business Journal*, January 20, 2003, v. 25, i. 3, p. 9(1).

Burrows, Dan, ''Guess Issues Soar as CEO Ups Stake,'' *WWD,* June 2, 2003, p. 19.

Lipke, David, ''Paris Hilton Says 'Oui' to Guess,'' *Daily News Record,* July 12, 2004, p. 3.

Marlow, Michael, ''Guess Back on Track with Ambitious Plans for Global Expansion,'' *Women's Wear Daily*, February 16, 1995, p. 1.

Rozhon, Tracie, ''Guess Tries to Regain Its Fabulousness,'' *New York Times,* September 25, 2004.

Slutsker, Gary, ''The Smoking Bun,'' *Forbes,* March 25, 1985, p. 210.

Socha, Miles, ''Guess Revisited,'' *WWD,* 0149-5380, March 19, 1998, p. 7.

——, ''Guess Who's 10'' *Daily New Report,* December 20, 1991, p. 4.

——, ''Marcianos Go Full Time Now at Guess,'' *Women's Wear Daily,* July 16, 1990, p. 1.

—M.L. Cohen
—update: William Arthur Atkins

Guitar Center, Inc.

5795 Lindero Canyon Road
Westlake Village, California 91362
U.S.A.
Telephone: (818) 735-8800
Fax: (818) 735-4923
Web site: http://www.guitarcenter.com

Public Company
Incorporated: 1964
Employees: 5,520
Sales: $1.27 billion (2003)
Stock Exchanges: NASDAQ
Ticker Symbol: GTRC
NAIC: 451140 Musical Instrument and Supplies Stores

Guitar Center, Inc., is the leading retailer of musical instruments in the United States, selling guitars, amplifiers, percussion instruments, keyboards, and professional audio and recording equipment. The company operates a chain of 122 stores, maintaining a presence in 45 major markets and in 15 secondary markets. Guitar Center operates online through Musician's Friend, a mail-order and e-commerce retailer of musical instruments. The company also operates a chain of approximately 20 musical instrument stores called American Music, a purchase made in 2001. The company's operations are served by a 500,000-square-foot distribution center near Indianapolis, Indiana, the largest facility in the company's industry. Management foresees Guitar Center eventually developing into a chain of 160 large, ''big-box'' stores and 160 smaller stores.

1960s Origins

Guitar Center was born, almost by accident, in 1964. Wayne Mitchell was managing the Organ Center, a 21-store chain of music stores in Southern California. The store specialized in keyboards, organs in particular, the instrument that dominated music sales at the time. In 1964, the Thomas Organ Company acquired Vox, a manufacturer of guitars and amplifiers. Unfortunately, its sales representatives knew next to nothing about the new products and had no idea how they should be sold. The Thomas representative approached Mitchell at Organ Center and—possibly through the application of subtle or outright pressure—persuaded him to take on the Vox line. A deal was reached: Mitchell would rent a storefront in Hollywood and Thomas would provide the sign. When it arrived it read ''Vox Guitar Center,'' which later was shortened to Guitar Center.

Mitchell quickly discovered that his new store was a gold mine. Rock and roll music was taking off, the British Invasion was at its height, and bands like the Beatles, Rolling Stones, and Kinks had sparked an unprecedented demand for guitars and amps. When Mitchell realized how much better guitars were selling than organs, he started closing his Organ Centers to concentrate on the new business.

Not all of Guitar Center's early success can be explained by Mitchell's remarkably good timing. By all accounts, he was a born salesman and a charismatic personality. He brought the savvy and technique he had developed as an automobile salesman and put it to work at Guitar Center. He knew, for example, that auto dealerships rely on their parts and service departments to pay the bills, enabling salesmen to cut margins on car sales to a minimum and offer customers the best deal possible. Mitchell decided that the equivalent at Guitar Center was the accessories department. Its products—cords, straps, picks, and effects, for example—helped stores cover their expenses. Mitchell cut costs to the bone and invested little in the look of his store, an expense he considered not directly linked to profits. The early Guitar Center stores showed it: old carpets mended with duct tape and racks purchased at closeout or bankruptcy sales gave them a bargain basement look.

One point that Mitchell insisted on was that Guitar Center pay all bills promptly. It used the reputation it developed, one unusual in music retailing, to win price concessions from manufacturers. Mitchell also created a hungry, aggressive sales atmosphere by putting his sales staff on straight commission. ''If you didn't work,'' Chief Operating Officer Marty Albertson later recalled, ''you didn't eat.'' While a ''hustle'' atmosphere was created that helped fuel Guitar Center's early growth, this policy was consciously abandoned in the mid-1970s.

Mitchell used a series of gimmicks, described in company literature as ''Barnum & Bailey-style sales promotions,'' to

Company Perspectives:

Our goal in the retail stores business is to continue to expand our position as the leading music products retailer in the United States. We plan to increase our presence in existing markets and open new stores in strategically selected markets. We will continue to pursue a strategy of clustering stores in major markets to take advantage of operating and advertising efficiencies and to build awareness of our Guitar Center and American Music brand names in new markets.

draw customers into his new store. He set a record for keeping a store continuously open (11 days), which made it into the Guinness Book of World Records. He created the world's largest Les Paul guitar cake. He mounted 36-hour-long sales extravaganzas in which the store opened at ten in the morning one day and did not close until ten in the evening the following day. He continued to rely on those events throughout Guitar Center's first 20 years.

By the end of the 1960s, Mitchell's combination of low prices, attention-grabbing promotions, and timely paying of suppliers had made Guitar Center one of the most profitable stores in southern California. In contrast to the staid, old-fashioned department store style of the established music stores, the Guitar Center on Sunset Blvd. had a distinctly counterculture feel. Its salespeople were usually musicians themselves who, while making their hard-sell pitch, encouraged customers to handle the merchandise, to pick it up and play it.

Expansion in the 1970s

Mitchell had the ultimate vision of 50 Guitar Center stores across the country. He opened a second store in San Francisco in 1972 and a third in San Diego the following year. To cut overhead, Mitchell kept Guitar Center decentralized as it expanded. The new stores were semi-autonomous and were run as a partnership, with Mitchell serving as the majority partner to the store manager. Mitchell instilled all his employees with a sense of what Guitar Center could become. The positive attitude that he created manifested itself in the group that later evolved into the company's senior management. Mitchell began hiring them as salesmen in the mid-1970s: in 1975, Ray Scherr, who later took over the company; in 1977, Larry Thomas, later president and CEO; in 1979, Marty Albertson, later executive vice-president and COO. Historically, Guitar Center has had more than average staff turnover at the entry level but nearly no turnover at the management level. Store managers remain an average of eight years. By the late 1990s, most senior management had been with Guitar Center from 10 to 15 years.

Ray Scherr moved rapidly from the sales floor, became a store manager, and then became a sort of junior partner to Wayne Mitchell. Scherr became a major force for innovation at the company in the 1970s and 1980s. It was Scherr's idea, for example, to centralize Guitar Center operations and thereby increase the company's buying power with vendors. Initially, Mitchell resisted the added expense of central administration until he could be shown that the money saved in vendor discounts would pay for it. Scherr also instituted the direct mail campaign that is still an important element of Guitar Center marketing. The Guitar Center of the early 21st century embodies the vision of both men. ''Wayne Mitchell built a lot of the value culture of Guitar Center,'' Albertson said, ''while Ray Scherr built the operating structure.''

In 1979, the company received information that a bank was about to foreclose on a music store in Chicago. Guitar Center moved quickly and later that year opened a store in that city, the company's first outside California. Moving into the Chicago market forced Guitar Center to confront its weaknesses and to rethink its entire approach. It discovered it could not simply enter the Chicago market and conquer it. Chicago, Guitar Center learned, was dominated by local independent retailers who commanded fierce loyalty from their customers. What was more, Chicagoans were put off by the company's hard sell tactics as well as its radio ads, which had worked well in California for five years or more. ''Chicago was where we cut out teeth on expansion,'' said Larry Taylor. ''It changed the way we did business.'' The experience led Guitar Center to become more customer service oriented, working to win consumer confidence and earn repeat business, a goal that hitherto had not been a high priority.

Changes and Continued Growth in the 1980s

In 1980, Mitchell inaugurated an Employee Stock Ownership Plan (ESOP), a stock-sharing program for Guitar Center workers. The ESOP transformed the company from a sole proprietorship to one owned jointly by management and employees and helped increase employee commitment to company growth. Because of the transient nature of the company's entry-level sales force, however, the ESOP was later converted to a profit sharing plan.

For a short period around 1980, Guitar Center became involved in guitar manufacture when it purchased Kramer Guitar. Kramer eventually produced a full range of guitars for beginners to professionals, and its popularity was increased substantially at the time by its association with guitarist Eddie Van Halen. Kramer's head Dennis Berardi was, in Larry Thomas's words, ''a very young, inspirational, undisciplined kind of guy.'' Berardi's management style clashed with Mitchell's, which was considerably more conservative. Running Kramer came to be so stressful for Mitchell that Guitar Center decided to pull out. Mitchell already had heart problems and other members of senior management were afraid he would suffer a heart attack.

In 1983, at the age of 57, Wayne Mitchell did die of a heart attack. Mitchell's family sold half of his share of the company to the ESOP and half to Ray Scherr. Scherr, who had been Guitar Center president for several years, became the majority shareholder and took over the running of the company. The Guitar Center chain had, in the meantime, grown to nine stores and under Scherr the chain continued to grow, adding an average of one store a year for the next decade.

In 1985, the Hollywood store inaugurated the ''Rock Walk,'' where the greats of popular music have pressed their hand prints in the sidewalk. It went on to become a popular tourist attraction in Los Angeles. More important, the chain was

Key Dates:

1964: Wayne Mitchell opens his first store, initially called "Vox Guitar Center."
1972: Mitchell's second store opens in San Francisco.
1979: Guitar Center's first store outside California opens in Chicago.
1993: The 17-store chain reaches the $100 million-in-sales mark.
1997: Guitar Center completes its initial public offering of stock, becoming the first publicly traded company in the music retail industry.
1999: Guitar Center acquires Musician's Friend, the largest mail-order and e-commerce retailer of musical instruments.
2001: Guitar Center acquires the 19-store musical instrument chain American Music Group.
2002: A 500,000 square-foot distribution center is opened near Indianapolis, Indiana, the largest facility in the industry; sales surpass $1 billion for the first time.
2004: The GCP Pro sales division is formed to serve the commercial recording market.

operating 12 stores by that year, and it had become obvious that an effective infrastructure was urgently needed that would enable the company to effectively control inventory and sales. As a result, Guitar Center interrupted its expansion drive for a couple of years to concentrate on computerizing its existing stores and introducing bar coding for its entire line of merchandise. The work lasted a year and a half, but when it was completed the company had a state-of-the-art system that was far ahead of its competitors in the music retail industry. Once in place, the system laid the foundation for Guitar Center's explosive growth during the 1990s.

Becoming a Public Company in the 1990s

Guitar Center engaged in another short-lived involvement in manufacturing when it acquired amplifier producer Acoustic Amplification in 1987. It sold Acoustic only two years later. In 1991, Larry Thomas—after working as a salesman, a store manager, a regional manager, corporate general manager, and chief operating officer—became Guitar Center president. By 1993, the company had 17 stores across the United States, with annual sales of approximately $100 million.

In 1996, Ray Scherr decided to leave Guitar Center. As a result, senior Guitar Center management, led by Larry Thomas and Marty Albertson, borrowed $100 million and, together with three California venture capital companies, bought most of Scherr's stock in the company. Not long afterward, the company made a high yield bond offering to convert the $100 million loan to long-term debt. The added burden of that large debt, together with the new involvement of the venture capitalists who were counting on stepped-up, national growth, led to the decision to make an initial public offering (IPO) in March 1997. The company had a scare the day the stock was priced when the market plunged 157 points and some of the banks involved almost pulled out. The stock, however, after being offered at $15, closed the first day of trading at $18, and about $90 million was raised. Guitar Center became the first publicly traded company in the music retail industry.

Going public raised some difficult issues for Guitar Center. The stock offering was predicated on the assumption that the company would expand quickly. It was accustomed, though, to opening one store at a time, then closely monitoring developments before opening another store. Suddenly it had to move efficiently at a much faster pace. In 1997, the company opened five new stores; in 1998, it opened 12 more stores and planned 12 more for 1999 and 16 for 2000. At the time, the company foresaw a network that would ultimately number 150, including a new smaller store format in small- and middle-sized markets across the United States. Another important question was whether manufacturers would be able to supply a much larger Guitar Center with the large volume of products it required. Most suppliers were able to adapt to Guitar Center's new needs. Nevertheless, a common complaint of smaller music retailers is that they are often not able to take shipment on items because most have been allotted to Guitar Center. Overall, Guitar Center's first year as a public company was a successful one. In the spring of 1998, it reported that sales had increased 39 percent and net income increased 60 percent to $11 million.

In May 1999, Guitar Center acquired Musician's Friend in a stock transaction valued at approximately $50 million. Musician's Friend, based in Medford, Oregon, was the world's largest mail-order and e-commerce retailer of musical instruments, with $97 million in revenue in 1998. Its acquisition made Guitar Center the leader in Internet as well as traditional musical instrument retailing. The Internet business was to remain headquartered in Medford under the name Musician's Friend. Most of its music stores were converted into Guitar Center stores. Guitar Center intended to use the stores, located in smaller markets, to create its new smaller store format.

Vibrant Growth in the 21st Century

Guitar Center embarked on the most prolific period in its history as it entered the 21st century, expanding physically and recording enormous sales growth. Perhaps most remarkable, the company's robust development occurred while the rest of the retail industry—not just musical instrument retailers—suffered from recessive market conditions. Guitar Center was one of the few success stories in the entire retail industry during the early years of the century's first decade, demonstrating strength that was acknowledged by an impressed financial community. The stock market reached its lowest point in four years early in the decade, but Guitar Center's stock increased in value, doubling between September 2002 and September 2003. Wall Street was watching the next "category killer," a company like Wal-Mart or Home Depot that silenced competitors through sheer might, and it approved of the strategy. The company's growth led an editor of an industry trade magazine to remark to the *Los Angeles Business Journal* on September 30, 2002, "They have taken market share and they've pounded a lot of other businesses. What everyone asks is, 'How big can they get?' "

Guitar Center, prodded by its IPO to expand more aggressively, did not disappoint investors following the acquisition of Musician's Friend in 1999. The company opened its 100th store in early 2002, a shop located in Little Rock, Arkansas. A year earlier, the company acquired a new vehicle for expansion, purchasing American Music Group, a Liverpool, New York-based chain of 19 musical instrument shops that sold and rented band instruments to schools and colleges. The company planned to open between eight and ten new stores, focusing on markets with a ''strong educational environment,'' according to Albertson in a November 25, 2002 article in the *Los Angeles Business Journal*. In 2002, when 20 new Guitar Center stores were established, the company opened a 500,000-square-foot distribution center near Indianapolis, Indiana, to service its rapidly expanding chain. With the distribution center, Thomas and Albertson hoped to secure price reductions from instrument manufacturers, arguing that Guitar Center should receive some of the savings realized by shipping and billing to one location instead of myriad locations. It was the stuff of Home Depot and Wal-Mart, giving Guitar Stores an advantage over smaller retailers who were not in the position to ask for discounted prices.

By the end of 2002, Thomas foresaw Guitar Center as chain of 160 large stores and 160 smaller stores. That was the goal the company was pursuing as it enjoyed enormous increases in its revenue volume. Sales, which neared $400 million in 1998, leaped to nearly $800 million in 2000 before reaching $1.1 billion in 2002. The company opened 14 new Guitar Centers in 2003 and announced plans to open between 16 and 18 new stores in 2004. In March 2004, the company formed a new division to broaden its already comprehensive customer base. GCP Pro was established to serve the commercial recording market by offering services that included analyzing a professional musician's recording studio and installing equipment and upgrades on-site.

As Guitar Center celebrated its 40th anniversary, the company held sway in the musical instrument industry. The company was the dominant player in the industry by far. Few industry observers doubted that Guitar Center would cede its overwhelming lead in the years ahead, particularly given its intention to eventually establish more than 300 stores in major and secondary markets throughout the United States. The task of blanketing the nation with ''category killer'' units fell largely to Albertson, who became sole chief executive officer and chairman of the company in late 2004. Thomas, who had served as co-chief executive officer and chairman, became Guitar Center's chairman emeritus. As the company pressed ahead with Albertson dictating its strategy, competitors and industry observers waited for the answer to the question: ''How big can they get?''

Principal Subsidiaries

Musician's Friend, Inc.; Guitar Center Stores, Inc.

Principal Divisions

GCP Pro; Musician's Friend.

Principal Competitors

Sam Ash Music Corporation; American Music Supply; Sweetwater Sound Inc.

Further Reading

Belgum, Deborah, ''Guitar Center Will Strike up the Band with a New Brand,'' *Los Angeles Business Journal*, November 25, 2002, p. 10.

Booth, Jason, ''Guitar Center Earnings Are Music to Ears of Analysts,'' *Los Angeles Times*, December 14, 1998, p. 40.

''California Guitar Center Agrees to Buy Musician's Friend Mergers,'' *Los Angeles Times*, May 14, 1999, p. C2.

Fox, Jacqueline, ''Guitar Center Gets Boost as It Turns up Volume on Growth,'' *San Fernando Valley Business Journal*, May 12, 2003, p. 7.

''Guitar Center Celebrates 35 Years,'' *Musical Merchandise Review*, January 1999.

''Guitar Center Expands with Stores in Chicago, Northern California,'' *Music Trades*, November 1996, p. 69.

''Guitar Center Launched,'' *Chain Store Age*, May 2004, p. 26.

''Guitar Center Looks to Target Commercial Recording Market,'' *DSN Retail Fax*, March 22, 2004, p. 45.

''Guitar Center Merges with Musician's Friend,'' *Los Angeles Times*, June 8, 1997.

''Guitar Center of Westlake Village, Calif., the Nation's Largest Music Instrument Retailer, Is Opening 100th Store,'' *Arkansas Business*, February 18, 2002, p. 13.

''Guitar Center Strums Deal Strongs,'' *Mergers & Acquisitions Report*, August 18, 2003.

''Guitar Center's Profits to Miss Estimates,'' *Los Angeles Times*, June 5, 1999.

''Inside Guitar Center: A Look at the Financial Workings of the Nation's Largest Music Products Retailer,'' *Music Trades*, August 1996, p. 198.

''Is Guitar Center Worth $251.0 Million?,'' *Music Trades*, July 1996, p. 169.

''Meltdown in Miami: Showdown Between Guitar Center and Sam Ash Music,'' *Music Trades*, July 1997, p. 102.

Palazzo, Anthony, ''Guitar Center Finds Growth Resonates with Wall Street,'' *Los Angeles Business Journal*, September 30, 2002, p. 30.

Proctor, Lisa Steen, ''Wall Street, Get Ready to Rock,'' *Los Angeles Business Journal*, March 17, 1997, p. 17.

''Record Sales at Guitar Center,'' *Music Trades*, April 1997, p. 50.

Relly, Jeannine, ''Los Angeles-Based Guitar Retail Chain Eyes Tucson, Ariz., Market,'' *Knight Ridder/Tribune Business News*, August 29, 2001.

''Revenge of the Store,'' *Music Trades*, August 1997, p. 168.

Scally, Richard, ''Guitar Center Packs Coffers in 97,'' *Discount Store News*, May 25, 1998. p. 8.

Strauss, Neil, ''Coddling Musicians' Dreams: Selling the Stairway to Heaven, and Instruments Too,'' *New York Times*, February 3, 1999, p. 1E.

''The Top 200,'' *Music Trades*, August 1998.

Vrana, Debora, ''Ready To Rock Guitar Center Going Public, Cranking Up for Nationwide Expansion,'' *Los Angeles Times*, March 14, 1997, p. D1.

Winters, Rebecca, ''A Store Strikes a Chord: Wannabe Rock Stars—and a Few Real Ones—Are Driving Guitar Center's Crescendo,'' *Time*, September 15, 2003, p. A15.

—Gerald E. Brennan
—update: Jeffrey L. Covell

Hoss's Steak and Sea House Inc.

170 Patchway Road
Duncansville, Pennsylvania 16635
U.S.A.
Telephone: (814) 695-7600
Toll Free: (800) 621-0270
Fax: (814) 695-3865
Web site: http://www.hoss.com

Private Company
Incorporated: 1983
Employees: 3,700 (est.)
Sales: $80 million (2002)
NAIC: 722211 Limited-Service Restaurants

With its headquarters located in Duncansville, Pennsylvania, Hoss's Steak and Sea House Inc. is a privately owned chain of more than 40 family-style restaurants in a territory that encompasses parts of Pennsylvania, Virginia, and West Virginia. All but three of the units are found in Pennsylvania, with a pair located in West Virginia and another restaurant in Winchester, Virginia. The Hoss's menu centers around steaks, seafood, and a salad bar. Steaks are aged, hand-selected, and fresh cut at the chain's beef facility—part of Hoss's Fresh Xpress, a warehouse and distribution unit that supplies all of the restaurants. Hoss's offers a wide range of steaks from 6-ounce sirloins, the Little Hoss, geared toward youngsters, to 28-ounce Porterhouse cuts. Seafood offerings include baked cod, salmon, haddock, whitefish, lobster tail, crab cakes, clam strips, and shrimp. Hoss's also offers chicken dishes and ham steak. Included with entrees is Hoss's salad bar, which offers more than 100 items, including homemade soups, breads, desserts, and soft-serve frozen yogurt. Also on the menu are hamburgers, Philly cheese steak, ham and Swiss cheese, and other sandwiches. A children's menu includes grilled cheese, hot dogs, hamburgers, popcorn chicken, popcorn shrimp, and pizza. In keeping with its efforts to appeal to seniors and families, Hoss's has never served alcohol, and early on it became a smoke-free environment. Hoss's décor features memorabilia appropriate to its location. Corporate advertising is handled by an in-house agency, Image Advertising. In addition, the company operates Hoss's Fresh Food Market in Duncansville where cuts of meat and other ingredients used in the restaurants are available for sale. The company has begun testing a second concept, Marzoni's Brick Oven & Brewery, with a single location in Duncansville. Hoss's is headed by its founder and chief executive Willard E. "Bill" Campbell.

1980s Origins

After growing up on a farm, Bill Campbell sampled a wide variety of jobs before becoming involved in restaurants. He dug ditches, he drove a truck, he learned how to cook while serving in the National Guard, and he started his own general construction company. Always wanting to run his own restaurant, Campbell in 1979 became a franchisee of the Augusta, Georgia-based Western Sizzlin' Steak House chain. Campbell opened his first unit in Duncansville, Pennsylvania, in 1979. It became profitable quickly, prompting Campbell to open a second restaurant in Johnstown, Pennsylvania. In 1983 Campbell wanted to buy a third Western Sizzlin' franchise, to be located in Chambersburg, Pennsylvania, but according to him the parent company "sold it out from under us." In response, Campbell decide to start his own steak house, one like Western Sizzlin' that would fill a niche between fast-food and full-service restaurants. Western Sizzlin' used a cafeteria approach to family dining. Patrons pushed trays through a serving line and then carried them to open tables. For a name Campbell and his family sat around their dinner table searching for something that was evocative of the Old West. They came up with five possibilities but only Hoss's was not trademarked.

In late 1983 Campbell opened his first Hoss's in DeBois, Pennsylvania. In the beginning, this restaurant, and a second Hoss's, continued to follow the Western Sizzlin' cafeteria-style concept. Campbell then began to tweak the operation. He eliminated the tray, creating a format in which customers placed their orders at the counter and were then seated and received full service. In order to appeal to families, Campbell diversified the menus to avoid losing business simply because someone in the group did not want steak. In addition, he recognized that more customers were becoming increasingly more health-conscious and cutting back on red meat. He added seafood to the mix as

Company Perspectives:

Hoss's Steak and Sea House is family dining featuring fresh-cut steaks, savory seafood, and tender chicken entrees . . . all cooked to order!

well as chicken dishes and a full salad bar. There was also an emphasis placed on offering fresh steaks. All the cuts came from western grain-fed beef, USDA Choice or better, delivered fresh to Hoss's, never frozen, and cut by the chain's own butchers in a controlled environment. The meat was then seasoned in a natural marinade before preparation. The restaurants also began making their own soup and crab cakes. In spite of this improvement in quality, Hoss's was able to keep prices low and attractive to the family trade. Another factor in appealing to this market was the decision to forgo the sale of alcohol. ''If you want a good steak and want nothing to do with alcohol, where are you going to go?,'' Campbell told *Restaurants & Institutions* in a 1994 company profile. ''That's a huge niche. We just decided to fill it.''

Campbell eventually converted his Western Sizzlin' operations to the Hoss's format and began opening three or four new restaurants each year, taking full advantage of his contracting background to have his Campbell Enterprises unit construct all the new buildings. Each featured a homey fireplace, wagon-wheel chandeliers, Americana paintings, and knickknacks. Also lining the walls was local memorabilia like old advertising signs and framed pictures devoted to the history of the local town, items that proved to be of great interest to many customers. Hoss's also emphasized friendly service and made an effort to become a significant part of the community. Drawing on his own farming background, Campbell encouraged restaurant managers to get the units involved in the activities of local 4-H chapters and the Future Farmers of America. Each year Hoss's visited dozens of 4-H fairs, buying many of the top-prize steers. The restaurants also became involved in a number of other charitable activities, such as raising money for the Multiple Sclerosis Society. In addition, the restaurants bought ads in high school yearbooks and other area publications and sponsored youth sports teams. As Campbell told *Nation's Restaurant News* in 1997, ''We pump a lot of money into the community.'' All told, it was a winning combination, so that by the end of 1988 Hoss's was doing $1.6 million in business and operated 21 restaurants located in small- to medium-sized towns in western Pennsylvania.

Hoss's also gained a reputation for treating its employees well. Tuition assistance was provided, and there were opportunities for advancement in the organization. Much of his management team, in fact, would rise through the ranks. His human resources vice-president, for instance, started out as a laborer in the construction business. All managers received eight weeks of training at ''Hoss University'' at the corporate headquarters. Moreover, management structure was kept lean and responsive, with very few layers separating Campbell from his store managers. At the top was Campbell and his president, followed by a director of operations who had a five-person team to work directly with unit managers. As a result, Hoss's was able to maintain tight quality control standards. Another key element was the creation of Hoss's Fresh Xpress, a combination commissary and warehouse located in Claysburg, Pennsylvania, to service the stores and ensure consistency in what the chain served. Campbell was also careful to open new units within a small radius to make sure his influence was felt.

Expansion in the Early 1990s Beyond Pennsylvania

In the early 1990s Hoss's expanded into West Virginia and Virginia and continued to add restaurants in Pennsylvania, but management made sure that all units were located within a four-hour drive of company headquarters to keep a tight rein on quality control. Sales increased steadily as Hoss's refined its formula. In 1993 the company enjoyed a 33.3 percent increase in systemwide sales over the previous year, growing to $60 million. A factor in this growth was the chain's ability to attract seniors through an early-dinner program, which from 1 p.m. to 4 p.m. featured entrée specials priced at just $4.99. In 1994 the chain looked to spur sales by adding variety to the menu, but it did so by simply repackaging current items that could then be promoted in TV and newspaper advertising. Crab cakes that cost $10.99 were now offered in ''light portions'' half the size of the regular but still costing $7.99. Chicken fillet and sirloin tips were combined to make a $10.99 entrée. Hoss's also added scampi sauce, vegetables, and potato to the 8-ounce portion of langostinos on the menu to create a lobster-pot special.

By the end of 1994, Hoss's had 36 units in place with plans to add several more in 1995. One of those units was located in New York State in Binghampton, one of the few locations that did not work out for the chain. Ultimately Hoss's closed down the unit. Although the formula for Hoss's success continued to center around fresh food, a family friendly atmosphere, and developing strong ties to its small town customers through active participation in the community, Hoss's also was willing to use technology to improve its service. At peak times during the week, lines of customers often stretched out the door. Menu boards were placed outside for customers to look at, as well as signs indicating that the wait to the register at one juncture was 15 minutes and at another ten minutes. But unlike many restaurants, customers were able to place their orders sooner rather than later. The key was a computer system and headsets worn by the waiters and waitresses, allowing them to communicate with the hostess. As soon as a table came free, the hostess would be informed and with the help of a computer that kept track of available tables and servers she was able to make decisions on which parties to seat. The system was especially useful in handling large groups, a situation that often caused significant delays at other restaurants. Moreover, orders placed at the registers were relayed electronically to the kitchen, rather than having a waiter or waitress hand-deliver the order after accomplishing other tasks on the way to the kitchen. As a result, lunch orders could be ready in ten minutes and dinner around 15 minutes. Hoss's use of technology caught the eye of *Inc.* magazine, which in the mid-1990s named it one of its ''Positive Performers.''

Hoss's had clearly developed a winning formula in the increasingly competitive restaurant field, but Campbell at this stage made it clear that he was not interested in franchising the concept, fearful he might lose the tight control that was key to Hoss's success. ''At this point, we are going to be a regional

Key Dates:

1979: Willard Campbell becomes a Western Sizzlin' franchisee.
1983: Campbell opens his first Hoss's Steak House.
1988: Hoss's chain grows to 21 Pennsylvania units.
1990: Hoss's enters West Virginia.
2002: Franchising plans are announced.
2004: The first Marzoni's Brick Oven & Brewery opens.

chain,'' he told *Restaurants & Institution* in 1994. ''We don't want really fast growth. Along the eastern seaboard, there is quite a lot of population, so we can stay and grow here for quite a while.''

New Marketing Approach in the Late 1990s

In the late 1990s Hoss's hired a Pittsburgh advertising agency, The Kaiser Group, to handle its marketing. After a year a consumer study was conducted to help in positioning the chain for future growth. What the research revealed was that Hoss's main selling points were its homestyle food and service. To focus attention on the food and ''hoss-pitality,'' the chain introduced a new tag line, ''Welcome to a good, honest meal,'' and centered its advertising around a new slate of daily specials. To encourage repeat business, customers' favorite dishes were consistently offered as a special on the same day of the week. For instance, Monday was stuffed steak night and Friday was baked haddock night. Television spots also relied on employees rather than actors to make the pitch. In one, a server said, ''It's all about what's on the plate,'' a comment that epitomized the new approach. Radio spots also featured employees' comments edited together in a documentary style. The success of the new marketing program was evident in the increasing sales Hoss's enjoyed in 2000.

By 2002, when the Hoss's chain numbered 41 units and annual sales were estimated at $80 million, Campbell and his president, John Brown, felt the time had come to explore the possibility of franchising the Hoss's concept. As Brown explained to *Nation's Restaurant News* in 2002, ''We've tried to grow from a central point in small radii so we could keep control. New we believe we're well enough established that we can maintain those controls even with franchisees.'' Campbell and Brown were not ruling out any part of the country, open to turning Hoss's into a national chain but intending to ''play it by ear.'' As of late 2004 the company had not yet announced any franchised operations. But in the meantime it launched a new concept, Marzoni's Brick Oven Brewery, offering wood-fired pizza and pasta along with a microbrewery providing specialty beers. Whether the Marzoni's concept would be introduced elsewhere or the Hoss's chain might grow beyond its regional roots through franchising remained to be seen.

Principal Subsidiaries

Hoss's Fresh Xpress, Inc.; Hoss's Restaurant Operation; Hoss's Franchise Corp.; Hoss's Enterprises Inc.

Principal Competitors

Denny's Corporation; Eat'n Park Hospitality Group; Friendly Ice Cream Corporation.

Further Reading

Hamstra, Mark, ''Hoss's Steak & Sea House Shuns Glitz for Small-Town Style,'' *Nation's Restaurant News,* March 10, 1997, p. 160.

King, Paul, ''Hoss's Family Steak and Sea House: Family-Owned Steak and Seafood Concept Plans to Beef Up Presence Outside Home Region Through Franchising,'' *Nation's Restaurant News,* January 28, 2002, p. 94.

McDowell, Bill, ''Hoss's Steak and Sea House,'' *Restaurants & Institutions,* August 1, 1994, p. 70.

Molyneaux, Jeanne, ''Campbell's Hoss's Restaurant Chain Captures Niche in Pa.,'' *Pittsburgh Business Times & Journal,* June 12, 1989, p. 3SS.

—Ed Dinger

Hummel International A/S

Kraftcentralen
Sonderhoj 10
DK-8260 Viby J, Aarhus
Denmark
Telephone: +45 87 34 48 00
Fax: +45 87 34 48 29
Web site: http://www.Hummel.dk

Private Company
Incorporated: 1923
Employees: Not available.
Sales: DKK 500 million ($140 million) (2004)
NAIC: 339920 Sporting and Athletic Good Manufacturing; 315228 Men's and Boys' Cut and Sew Other Outerwear Manufacturing; 315291 Infants' Cut and Sew Apparel Manufacturing; 315999 Other Apparel Accessories and Other Apparel Manufacturing; 316211 Rubber and Plastics Footwear Manufacturing; 316219 Other Footwear Manufacturing

Hummel International A/S is one of the world's oldest sportswear designers and manufacturers. Viby, Denmark-based hummel (the company prefers the lower case) has focused traditionally on designing uniforms, footwear, and accessories for the team sports segments, particularly for soccer (football), handball, volleyball, ice hockey, and basketball teams. Much of hummel's team sports sales are promoted through its sponsorships with teams all over the world. The company's sponsorships range from the Aston Villa football club in England, to the Grassroots soccer team in the United States, and, in addition to teams throughout most of Western and Eastern Europe, include far-flung places such as Japan, Korea, Greenland, Armenia, South Africa, and even Tibet. Hummel supplements its teams sports sales with its leisurewear collection, which includes the labels Kick 'N' Rush, Express, h-line, and Frontrunner. Yet hummel's fastest-growing business is represented by its newest division, Hummel Fashion. Guided by Christian Stadil, son of the company's owner Thor Stadil (who controls hummel through his Thorinco holding company), Hummel Fashion has emerged as one of the mid-2000s hottest labels, sported by celebrities ranging from Jennifer Lopez and Priscilla Presley to Nicholas Cage. The strength of the somewhat exclusive hummel label—featuring its bumblebee logo—has helped the private company's sales grow to about $140 million in 2004.

Fitting Footballers in the 1920s

Although hummel later became synonymous with Danish sportswear, the hummel company was originally founded in Hamburg, Germany in 1923. The company's early success was founded on an important innovation that was to have a dramatic impact on the world soccer scene as well. Until the 1920s, soccer players wore flat shoes. But hummel added a number of studs, similar to the cleats found on baseball shoes, enabling players to achieve a greater grip on the playing field. Hummel's studded shoes caught on quickly, and before long cleats became standard fixtures on the world's soccer fields as well.

Hummel focused primarily on its soccer footwear for the next decades, flushing out that product with a limited range of sports uniforms and clothing. The company's clothing, like its footwear, was geared toward athletic performance, rather than fashion. In the 1950s, the company moved to Denmark. There, the company set up a factory in the town of Viby, near Aarhus.

The 1970s marked an important milestone for the company. Into the 1970s, professional sports remained relatively free of sponsorships, and sports sponsoring was certainly nowhere near the extremes reached by the early 2000s. This was especially so in the realm of professional soccer.

Hummel had by then come under the ownership of star Danish handball player Jorgen Vodsgaard, who, together with fellow handball player Max Nielsen, began approaching a number of Danish athletes with an offer to outfit them with hummel footwear and clothing. One of the first of the company's sponsorship deals was with start soccer player Hendrik Jensen, then with Real Madrid, in 1976. The following year, the company struck another important deal, this time with Danish football team Vejle Boldklub. Vodsgaard and Simonsen had met while both were competing for the Danish Olympics team at the 1972 Munich Games. Simonsen, a former Vejle Boldklub player who

Company Perspectives:

A brand with a clear stand. At hummel we work as a team for teams in order to fulfil our mission: To become the most exciting teamsport brand in the world.

Key Dates:

1923: Hummel launches production of footwear in Hamburg, Germany, and develops a studded soccer shoe.
1950s: Hummel moves to Viby, Denmark.
1974: Under ownership of Danish star handball player Jorgen Vodsgaard, hummel launches sponsorship operations, and begins producing sports apparel.
1979: Hummel wins a sponsorship contract with the Danish national soccer team, then expands into a variety of other sports.
1992: On the verge of bankruptcy, hummel is acquired by Thor Stadil.
1993: New CEO Soren Schriver begins restructuring hummel's apparel range.
1997: Christian Stadil establishes the Hummel Fashion division to begin marketing retro designs based on hummel fashions from the 1970s and 1980s.
2001: Hummel agrees to sponsor the Tibetan national soccer team.
2003: Hummel establishes a U.S. subsidiary.
2004: Hummel opens a U.S. showroom in New York City.

was named European Player of the Year in 1977, acted as a middleman for hummel in its negotiations with Vejle Boldklub. The sponsorship deal worked out for the company and the soccer team remained a central part of hummel's sponsorship roles into the next century.

Hummel rapidly expanded its range of sponsorships, and began outfitting players and teams throughout Denmark, Europe, and as far away as Japan. A key moment for the company came in 1979, when it was named the outfitter for the Danish national soccer team. The company retained that contract into the late 1990s.

Fashion Focus for the New Century

Hummel capitalized on its growing range of sponsorships by developing a strong catalog of sportswear and related apparel. The company's sales now extended beyond the athletic world to include the general consumer market. The company then began a push to expand into new international markets, entering the United States, among others.

During the 1980s, hummel—which had gained an advance in the sponsorship race on larger rivals such as Nike and adidas—began broadening its athletic interests beyond its core soccer focus. The company began signing up sponsorships in a variety of sports, including golf, boxing, cross-country running, volleyball, handball, basketball, and ice hockey. Yet this effort spread the company too thin, and also served to dilute its brand image.

Meanwhile, competitors such as Nike, Reebok, adidas, and others launched a veritable sponsoring frenzy, and by the beginning of the 1990s, prices on sponsorship deals had skyrocketed beyond tiny hummel's reach. By 1992, hummel was on the verge of bankruptcy. In that year, Thor Stadil, a powerful Danish investor with a number of companies under his control, bought up 100 percent control of hummel.

Stadil placed Soren Schriver in charge as hummel's CEO in 1993. Under Schriver, hummel scaled back its range of sponsorships and apparel. The company also exited a number of its international markets, including the United States. During the 1990s, hummel worked to revitalize its range, and narrowed its focus to just a handful of sports. Although soccer remained the company's most active market, it also retained sponsorship positions in handball, and to a lesser extent, in volleyball, basketball, and ice hockey.

A new turning point for the company came with the arrival of Christian Stadil, son of the company's owner. The younger Stadil had been studying law at the University of Aarhus in the late 1990s when he noticed a trend: that people were scouring the local thrift shops for old hummel fashions from the 1970s and 1980s. Stadil recognized similar trends in other markets, with retro fashions blooming in such capitals as Paris and London. Skipping classes, Stadil went to hummel's headquarters and began going through its old catalogs. By 1997, Stadil had convinced hummel to establish a new division, Hummel Fashion.

Stadil used a selection of the company's older designs as the basis for the launch of the company's first fashion-oriented clothing collection. The new collection was dubbed ''Bumble Bee,'' from the company's long-held logo. From the start, Stadil sought to maintain the collection's exclusive aura, shunning advertising and restricting sales to a select range of boutiques. Word-of-mouth provided the division with sufficient momentum. By 1999, with the division's briskly building sales propelling the rest of hummel, Christian Stadil took over the direction of the company itself. By the early 2000s, hummel was growing by more than 50 percent per year.

A major component of the company's growth was the adoption of its fashions by a growing number of international celebrities. Adding to the company's cachet was its agreement to act as sponsor to the first Tibetan national soccer team in 2001—which had been turned down previously by Nike, adidas, and Reebok. Hummel embraced the project, and profited from its political overtones, as a number of celebrities, including Richard Gere and U2's Bono began wearing the Tibetan team's tee-shirt in a gesture of solidarity.

With people like Jennifer Lopez, Priscilla Presley, Robbie Williams, and Jon Bon Jovi wearing the company's clothing, hummel's expansion into the international fashion market was considerably eased. Japan represented an important new market for the company. By 2002, the company had re-entered the United States as well. At first, hummel returned to the United States through an agreement with a licensee. By 2003, however, the company decided to take control of its U.S. expansion, setting up an American subsidiary and establishing its U.S. headquarters in Burlington, Vermont—which the company's

U.S. CEO called the "Denmark of the United States." In 2004, the company opened its first U.S. showroom in New York City.

Hummel Fashion's edgy designs began to rub off on the group's sportswear in the 2000s. In 2002, the Danish national soccer team chose hummel to design its uniforms for the 2002 World Cup, taking to the field in the company's retro styling. In the United States, the company launched a new line of women's soccer apparel, including pink cleats.

By the end of 2004, hummel's sales had soared to more than $140 million—compared with approximately $60 million just two years earlier. Nonetheless, hummel resisted investing in advertising, preferring to maintain its brand's exclusive appeal. At the same time, the company's growing profile enabled it to score a major sponsorship contract, with the United Kingdom's Aston Villa soccer club. Meanwhile, the company continued to seek out unusual sponsorship opportunities. In 2004, for example, the company became the sponsor of the first female athletes to participate as part of the Afghan Olympic team. The company's efforts for the women's sports segment earned it the Best Athletic Women Award from Sportswear International that same year. Under Christian Stadil, hummel definitely appeared to have caught a second wind for the new century.

Principal Subsidiaries

Hummel America Inc.; Hummel Austria; Hummel Denmark; Hummel España; Hummel Finland; Hummel France; Hummel Germany; Hummel Greece; Hummel Holland; Hummel Hungary; Hummel Iceland; Hummel International A/S; Hummel Italia; Hummel Japan; Hummel Korea B/D; Hummel Portugal; Hummel Russia; Hummel Switzerland; Hummel UK.

Principal Competitors

Nike Corporation; adidas Salomon AG; Reebok Inc.; Kappa S.p.A.; Umbro Ltd.; New Balance Shoe Corporation.

Further Reading

Bailey, Lee, "Soccer Punch: Denmark's Hummel Ramps Up Its Efforts to Score a Goal with fashion-Conscious Young Men in the US," *Daily News Record,* January 12, 2004, p. 21.

Funder Larsen, Paul, "Good Sport," *WWD,* August 18, 2003, p. 19.

Griffin, Cara, "Hummel Builds a Buzz," *Sporting Goods Business,* March 2004, p. 18.

"Hummel Signs Sales Agreement with UK Sports Chain All Sports," *Nordic Business Report,* May 21, 2004.

Kletter, Melanie, "Hummel, New Balance Stake New Ground," *WWD,* May 27, 2004, p. 11.

Scharbau, Stefanie, "Coole Menschen, coole Orte," *Die Zeit,* April 1, 2003.

"Villa Get Shirty," *Coventry Evening Telegraph,* February 11, 2004, p. 23.

—M.L. Cohen

Irkut Corporation

30/7, Building 2, B. Molchanovka Street
Moscow 121069
Russia
Telephone: (+7) 095 290-34-04
Fax: (+7) 095 290-34-04
Web site: http://www.irkut.com/en/

Public Company
Incorporated: 1932
Employees: 22,000
Sales: RUB 13.07 billion ($522 million) (2003)
Stock Exchanges: RTS MICEX
Ticker Symbol: IRKT
NAIC: 336411 Aircraft Manufacturing; 541710 Research and Development in the Physical, Engineering, and Life Sciences

Irkut Corporation is a leading developer and producer of aircraft and aviation products. In March 2004, Irkut became Russia's first publicly traded defense company. Originally the Irkutsk Aircraft Factory, one of the Soviet Union's major manufacturers of combat aircraft, including the MiG-23, MiG-27 and Su-27 fighters, the company became known as Irkut Corporation after its 1992 privatization.

As part of its bid to become a vertically integrated aircraft producer, Irkut acquired a controlling interest in the Beriev Design Bureau in 1997. A 76 percent holding in the famous Yakovlev Design Bureau was acquired after Irkut's initial public offering in 1994.

As it sought to increase the proportion of civilian-related work, Irkut was focused on three primary niches: trainers and light fighter aircraft; UAVs (unmanned aerial vehicles), and military cargo and amphibious planes. Irkut was also manufacturing Russia's most advanced fighter, the Sukhoi Su-30, for export.

Origins

The Irkutsk Aircraft Factory was established in Siberia in 1932. Located more than 3,000 miles east of Moscow, the plant was as secretive as it was remote. Over the years, it came to fill five dozen buildings at its complex to the southwest of Lake Baikal.

While Western aircraft companies had their own design and production facilities, under the Soviet system design bureaus and factories were independent.

In the mid-1930s, Irkutsk manufactured a stubby little fighter aircraft called the I-14. During World War II, the plant built heavy fighters and bombers. These included thousands of the Pe-2/Pe-3 series designed by the V.M. Petlyakov design bureau. Ilyushin's Il-4/Il-6 series of long-range bombers was also built in vast numbers. The Yermolaev Yer-2 was a twin-engine bomber built by Irkutsk in the last years of the war.

Production of bombers continued after World War II, including jets such as the IL-14 and Il-28 and later the Yak-28. The factory also built Antonov's An-12 and An-24 series of transport aircraft.

From 1970 to 1983, Irkutsk cranked out thousands of the MiG-23 and MiG-27 fighters, which were the workhorse of the Soviet fleet during most of the Cold War. The MiGs were followed by variants of the Sukhoi Su-27 and its successor, the Su-30, Russia's most advanced fighters of the 1990s. According to the *Financial Times,* Irkutsk was producing two dozen Suhkoi jets every year at the height of production.

Privatized in 1992

Irkut Corporation was established in 1992 as the factory was privatized. Irkut was led by Alexei Innokentyevich Fedorov, who served as chief engineer and director general of the factory from 1989 to 1997 and as Irkut Corporation's president after that. Fedorov had joined Irkut as a design engineer in 1974 and earned an MBA at Oklahoma State University in 1994.

The successor to the Sukhoi Su-27, the Su-30 was first built for export. The cash-strapped Russian military bought none of the company's aircraft between the time Irkut went private in 1992 and its 2004 initial public offering (IPO), according to the *Financial Times.*

The Sukhoi Su-30 was considered equivalent to the U.S.-made F/A-18E/F Super Hornet, but priced about 25 percent

Company Perspectives:

Our key business objective is to maintain and develop the Russian civilian and military aircraft industry. To this end, more than 15,000 dedicated employees of IRKUT are at work each day delivering advanced aerospace solutions for both our civilian and military customers.

less, at $40 million. With thrust-vectoring engines, it was probably the most maneuverable fighter aircraft in the world at the time; some of its state-of-the-art avionics had been sourced from Israel and France.

In 2000, Irkut signed a deal with Hindustan Aeronautics Ltd. (HAL) to build 140 Sukhoi Su-30 fighters in India. The next year, the People's Republic of China ordered 40 Su-30s worth $2 billion. Another large order worth $2.2 billion followed in 2002, when Malaysia ordered 18 planes.

HAL of India was also collaborating on the development of a new military transport aircraft called MTA. The Ilyushin Aviation Complex was assisting with design in the venture, which was a smaller version of the firm's Il-76 airliner.

A $50 million, three-year modernization of the factory's equipment was begun in 2001. The AviaSTEP design bureau was acquired in 2002. It had been created six years earlier to specialize in computer-assisted design and manufacturing.

In 2003, according to *Business Week,* Irkut had pretax profits of $94 million on estimated sales of $522 million (according to international accounting standards), and a backlog in excess of $4.3 billion—enough to keep production lines busy for eight years. *Vedomosti,* as quoted in the *Russian Business Report,* reported the company's revenues as $368 million for the year, with a net loss of $4.86 million.

Besides producing Su-30s, Irkut was also upgrading an earlier version, the Su-27, as well as Mi-8 helicopters. The company performed systems integration using equipment from sources inside and outside Russia. Irkut raised its interest in Russian Avionics (or ZAO Russkaya Avionika, formerly Ramenskoye Instruments) from 26.6 percent to 51 percent in 2001.

Irkut accounted for 10 percent of Russia's military production, and military aircraft accounted for 90 percent of its output, but the company was eager to raise the proportion of civil aircraft to 45 percent. In late 2003, Irkut won a contract to build floor panels for the Airbus A320.

Buys Beriev in 2002

Irkut had acquired a 40 percent holding in the Beriev Design Bureau, or Taganrog Scientific-Technical Complex, in 1997. This was raised to a controlling interest in the summer of 2002. Beriev had been formed by Georgei Beriev in the early 1930s and was best known for its hydroplanes.

While the West had stopped building large amphibious aircraft at the end of World War II, the Soviet Union's Beriev Design Bureau had developed a range of planes, including small jet airliners, that could land on water.

Key Dates:

1932: Irkutsk Aircraft Factory is established in Siberia.
1970: Irkutsk begins making thousands of MiG-23 fighters.
1986: Suhhoi Su-27 fighters enter production at Irkutsk.
1992: Irkut Corporation is privatized.
2002: The company acquires a controlling interest in Beriev Design Bureau.
2004: Irkut launches the first Russian defense sector initial public offering and acquires control of Yakovlev.

The Beriev Be 200 was one of the world's most capable firefighting aircraft. Powered by two Rolls-Royce jet engines, it could scoop up 12 tons of water in seconds. Beta-Air was established to market the Be-200. Before Irkut's 2004 IPO, Hawkins & Powers Aviation Inc. of Greybull, Wyoming, announced it was buying eight Be-200 aircraft for $200 million.

Other projects under development at Beriev included a land-based commuter airliner called the Be-32R and the huge A-40 ''Albatross'' amphibian, as well as the A-42PR search and rescue aircraft.

2004 IPO

Irkut launched its initial public offering in March 2004 on the Russian Trading System (RTS) and Moscow Interbank Currency Exchange (MICEX). Irkut became the first Russian defense firm to be publicly traded. It floated 23.3 percent of shares, raising $127 million for the company.

Irkut's top ten managers owned 70 percent of the company before the IPO, after which their holding fell to 50.3 percent. The Russian government owned 14.7 percent of shares before the offering and 13.4 percent after.

The company acquired a 75.46 percent holding in the venerable A.S. Yakovlev Design Bureau with the proceeds from its public offering. One source put the price of this acquisition at more than $50 million.

The Yakovlev buy helped build Irkut into a vertically integrated company. A new military jet trainer, the Yak-130, was already being developed to both Russian and world markets. Yakovlev was also working on unmanned aircraft and had designed a mid-range, 120-seat airliner called the MS-21.

Vedomosti reported in July 2004 that company officials were hoping to team up with Bombardier, the Canadian producer of regional jets, on the CSeries mid-size airliner it was developing. Irkut was also forming a joint venture with EADS, the European defense conglomerate, to market the Be-200 in the West. The first of these was delivered to Italy, which was considering buying up to ten of them for its civil defense department.

In September 2004, EADS polled the Russian government for permission to acquire a 10 percent interest in Irkut. At that time, foreigners were limited to owning 25 percent of a Russian aerospace company's share capital.

The Russian government designated Irkut president Alexei Fedorov as the head of RSK MiG, furthering plans to create a unified national aerospace company in Russia. MiG was famous for light fighter aircraft. The Unified Aircraft-Building Corporation, which had the Russian acronym of OAK, was also to include Tupolev and Ilyushin. Fedorov followed a string of seven general directors at state-owned MiG in eight years.

By 2014, said Irkut president Alexei Fedorov in 2004, Irkut aimed to have sales of $1.6 billion, with nearly half of that from the commercial aviation market.

Principal Subsidiaries

Beriev Aircraft, JSC (38.6%); BETA AIR CJSC (66.15%); Gidroaviasalon Ltd. (30%); IRKUT AviaSTEP Design Bureau JSC; Irkutsk Aviation Production Association; ITELA, CJSC (51%); Russian Avionics Design Bureau CJSC (51%); Techserviceavia, CJSC (51%).

Principal Competitors

McDonnell Douglas; Northrop Grumman Corporation; OAO Sukhoi.

Further Reading

''Arms Maker Irkutsk Is Flourishing,'' *Country ViewsWire*, January 7, 2004.

Arvedlund, Erin E., ''Russian Plane Maker Embraces Capitalism,'' *New York Times*, Sec. W, March 11, 2004, p. 1.

''Capitalism Takes off at Fighter Jet Factory,'' *Europe Intelligence Wire*, September 17, 2002.

''Defense Plant Enters Stock Market,'' *Economic Press Review*, March 29, 2004.

Doyle, Andrew, ''Russia Set for Industrial Revolution; Irkut's Alexey Fedorov Leads Way as Consolidation of Outdated Soviet-Style Infrastructure Gathers Pace,'' *Flight International*, May 18, 2004, p. 35.

''EADS Requests Russian Government about a Permit for Buying into Irkut,'' *Russian Business Monitor*, September 24, 2004.

''IAPO to Change Its Name to Irkut,'' *Europe Intelligence Wire*, September 23, 2002.

''Irkut Corporation Disclosed Information about Its Owners,'' *WPS: Russian Finance Report*, March 26, 2004.

''Irkut Corporation to Increase Production of Civil Airplanes,'' *Russian Business Monitor*, July 23, 2004.

''Irkut Exported the First Be-200 Amphibian Airplane,'' *Russian Business Monitor*, August 25, 2004.

Karnozov, Vladimir, ''United Front,'' *Flight International*, August 12, 2003, p. 29.

Kukushkin, Mikhail, ''Irkut Plane-Maker Buys 75-Per-Cent Stake in Yakovlev Design Bureau,'' *BBC Monitoring International Reports*, May 9, 2004.

——, ''The Baykal 'Yak,' '' *Vremya Novostey*, April 22, 2004

Moxon, Julian, ''Moscow Picks Fedorov to Prepare 'Single Entity'; Irkut President to Head RSK MiG as Plansto Unify Aerospace Industry Progress,'' *Flight International*, October 5, 2004, p. 27.

Ostrovsky, Arkady, ''Irkut Looks to Lighten Its Military Load: Company Hopes to Use IPO Proceeds to Fund Civilian Aircraft,'' *Financial Times* (London), March 1, 2004, p. 25.

Pronina, Lyuba, ''Irkut Becomes MiG's Wingman,'' *St. Petersburg Times*, October 5, 2004.

——, ''Irkut Chief Is Happy with IPO Numbers,'' *Defense News*, April 5, 2004, p. 24.

——, ''MiG Chief Fired, Head of Rival Irkut Takes Over,'' *Moscow Times*, September 28, 2004.

''A Russian Planemaker's Daring Maneuvers; Irkut Is Aiming High with an IPO and Ambitions in Overseas Markets,'' *Business Week Online*, March 15, 2004.

''Russia's Irkut Aircraft Producer Boasts Full Order Book for Next Eight Years,'' *BBC Monitoring International Reports*, September 21, 2004.

Wastnage, Justin, ''Irkut Eyes Separate Business Units; New Factory Will Help Company to Cut Production Costs and Expand Into Broader Market After Flotation,'' *Flight International*, March 9, 2004, p. 23.

——, ''Irkut to Establish Systems Integration Division,'' *Flight International*, March 16, 2004, p. 18.

—Frederick C. Ingram

KAMAN

Kaman Music Corporation

20 Old Windsor Road
Bloomfield, Connecticut 06002
U.S.A.
Telephone: (860) 509-8888
Fax: (860) 509-8891
Web site: http://www.kamanmusic.com

Wholly Owned Subsidiary of Kaman Corporation
Incorporated: 1966 as Ovation Instruments, Inc.
Employees: 370
Sales: $145.4 million (2003)
NAIC: 339992 Musical Instrument Manufacturing; 423990 Instruments, Musical, Merchant Wholesalers

Kaman Music Corporation manufactures Ovation, Adamas, and Hamer guitars and is also the largest independent distributor of musical instruments and accessories in the United States. Created by pioneering helicopter designer Charles Kaman in the mid-1960s, the firm's revolutionary ''roundback'' fiberglass composite body Ovation guitar has been embraced by such musicians as Paul McCartney, Glen Campbell, and Jon Bon Jovi.

Roots

Kaman Music's origins date to the mid-1940s and a young aerospace engineer named Charles H. Kaman. Kaman had grown up in Washington, D.C., the son of a German immigrant who worked as a construction supervisor on projects like the U.S. Supreme Court building. Though his hopes to be a pilot were dashed because he was deaf in one ear, Charles Kaman studied aerodynamics at Catholic University in Washington, where he graduated in 1940. He then took a job at the Hamilton Standard division of United Aircraft, where famed helicopter inventor Igor Sikorsky worked. Although Kaman was made head of aerodynamics in 1943, he left the firm two years later when his suggestions for improvements to helicopter rotor systems were ignored.

The 26-year old Kaman then decided to form a helicopter company of his own, Kaman Aircraft, with $3,000 in savings and $1,000 each from two friends. Starting out with a test rig in his mother's West Hartford, Connecticut, home that he built from scavenged parts, Kaman and a team of eager young inventors soon moved into a World War II gymnasium, where they worked seven days a week to develop the K-125 helicopter using Kaman's ''servo-flap'' rotor principles. The design proved a success, yielding a more stable and easy-to-fly helicopter, and the company went on to create and build a number of innovative models over the next several decades, including the first gas turbine powered helicopter in 1951 and the first remote-controlled helicopter in 1957. Kaman's rugged HH-43B ''Huskie'' model proved durable in a range of uses including in the Vietnam war, where it was used to rescue downed pilots. It would prove to be the first helicopter to go through its service life with no accidents or loss of life attributed to the helicopter itself.

Over the years, Charles Kaman found time to pursue a number of different interests, including breeding German Shepherd dogs (he helped create a line which was virtually unaffected by debilitating hip dysplasia) and playing the guitar. In the late 1930s, he had in fact won a contest that gave him the opportunity to play with the Tommy Dorsey Orchestra, whereupon the duly impressed Dorsey offered him a $75-a-week contract, which Kaman respectfully declined.

Diversification in 1960s Leads to Guitars

In 1964, after Kaman Corporation had lost an important defense contract, the company's board began seeking ways to diversify away from government work. While considering the manufacturing of boats, golf clubs, and tennis racquets, Charles Kaman happened to take an acoustic Martin guitar he owned to that company's factory in Pennsylvania for repair. After seeing the labor-intensive, old-world techniques Martin used to create its legendary instruments, Kaman began thinking of ways to harness modern technology to make the process more efficient and made an offer to purchase Martin.

When the offer was rejected, Kaman turned his attention to designing a guitar of his own which would sound natural but be made of modern composite materials. While creating a successful helicopter involved eliminating vibration, a successful guitar

Company Perspectives:

The mission of Kaman Corporation is to achieve long-term growth for our investors by building on our core competencies in manufacturing and distribution in a fiscally responsible manner. Kaman's deep experience in aerospace manufacturing and reputation for technical pre-eminence will continue to provide a strong foundation for our future growth. We are committed to providing world-class products and services that we continually strive to improve through ''lean thinking'' and careful attention to the needs of our global customers. We believe that providing a work place where talented people are rewarded and inspired to creative problem solving, technical excellence and leadership is key to creating long-term benefits for our shareholders, customers, employees, suppliers and the communities in which we do business.

design had to create attractive musical tones, and Kaman pursued this logic as he worked with a team of engineers on a design that would produce what he described as a ''clean, uninterrupted sound'' to the *New York Times*. The resultant guitar combined a round-backed (rather than flat-backed) fiberglass body (the same material used for helicopter blades) and a laminated sprucewood top, along with strong bracing and a warp-proof neck. When Kaman played the first prototype instrument for a group of friends and co-workers to an enthusiastic response, one commented that it deserved an ''ovation.'' The word stuck in his mind, and in 1966 Kaman Corp. formed a new company called Ovation Instruments, Inc. to market the guitar.

With endorsements from renowned performers like folk singer Josh White and pop singer Glen Campbell, who used an Ovation on his popular weekly television show beginning in 1968, sales took off. To manufacture the guitar, Ovation set up a production facility in a former textile mill in New Hartford, Connecticut, and some time later added a second in Moosup, Connecticut. Over the next decade, a maker of guitar strings and several musical instrument distribution companies were purchased, including Coast Wholesale Music Co. in 1968 and C. Bruno & Sons, Inc. in 1971. An international sales unit, Kaman Music International, was established as well. The company also began making solid-body electric guitars and came up with an important technical advancement in creating a high-quality built-in microphone that allowed Ovation acoustic guitars to be played through an amplifier with good results. Within a few years, this option would be added to 90 percent of the firm's guitars. In 1977, the company introduced another new product, the graphite-faced Adamas acoustic guitar, which also drew acclaim from musicians.

By 1981, Kaman Music was taking in estimated revenues of $20 million, about 3 percent of the total earned by parent Kaman Corp. More than 100 workers were employed at the firm's two plants, who turned out a total of 72,000 guitars per year. Ovation now had approximately 60 percent of the U.S. acoustic guitar market, and the company's products were also sold in Canada, Europe, Asia, and South America. Charles Kaman's son, 30-year old William Kaman II, was now serving as vice-president in charge of research and development, while Fred L. Smith had been named president.

In the early 1980s, the acoustic guitar industry hit a severe slump. Although some suggested selling the unit, Charles Kaman (who owned 73 percent of the voting stock of Kaman Corp.) refused, citing the fact that similar problems with his helicopter business had resolved themselves. His foresight proved correct, and business began to pick up during the decade with such new developments as improved microphones for acoustic guitars that enabled their use in a rock band context, and the popularity of the ''MTV Unplugged'' television program and acoustic spin-off albums by the likes of Eric Clapton.

In 1986, Kaman Music was reorganized into two divisions. One would contain the fretted instruments operations (guitar and strings manufacturing and distribution), while the other would consist of percussion, sound electronic, and general music products. Both divisions' products were distributed through six regional centers. The entire operation was placed under a single corporate umbrella called Kaman Music Corp. Soon after these changes were made, William Kaman II was named president of the company.

Purchase of Hamer Guitars in 1988

In 1988, Kaman Music bought premium electric guitar maker Hamer Guitars of Chicago. Former Hamer executive Frank Untermeyer moved to the Ovation factory, where he helped improve manufacturing by soliciting the input of factory workers for new ideas. Ones that the firm incorporated into production models included an on-board guitar tuner and a touch-sensitive pre-amp to adjust volume. For some customers, Kaman made also made custom instruments such as a nine-string model made for an Indian musician and a triple-neck guitar made for musician Richie Sambora.

In 1991, the company began making ''roundback'' mandolins and mandocellos, and the following year saw Kaman Music acquire Trace Elliot, a British guitar amplifier manufacturer with sales of approximately $5 million. In 1994, the company boosted its distribution business again with the purchase of Hornberger Music Ltd. of Canada, which operated a musical instrument distribution company called B&J Music of Toronto. The 63-year-old company had revenues of about $8 million CAD and distributed a full line of musical instruments and accessories to all of Canada's provinces. That same year saw Kaman Music Corp. move into a new 43,000-square-foot headquarters building in Bloomfield, Connecticut. Annual sales were now in excess of $100 million, up from $40 million in 1986.

Kaman Music had by now firmly established itself as the largest independent distributor of musical instruments in the United States. Sales of expensive guitars were also soaring, as middle aged baby-boomers sought to reclaim their youth by indulging in luxurious ''adult toys.'' New models were continually being designed and produced, including the black ''Q'' Adamas model introduced in January of 1997. That same year saw production of Hamer instruments move from the Chicago area to the Ovation factory in Connecticut. While the company's high-end guitars, which started at $850, were still manufactured in the United States, Kaman had some time earlier shifted production of its entry-level models to Korea.

Key Dates:

1945: Kaman Aircraft is founded by Charles Kaman to build helicopters.
1966: Kaman begins making composite-material guitars through Ovation Instruments.
1988: Hamer Guitars is bought.
1992: British amplifier maker Trace Elliot is purchased.
1994: Canadian distributor Hornberger Music is acquired.
1997: Trace Elliot is sold.
2002: Latin Percussion, Inc. is purchased.
2003: Speaker cabinet/amp maker Genz Benz Enclosures is acquired.

In June 1997, the company sold its Trace Elliot amplifier business to that firm's senior management. Kaman Corp. took a $10.4 million pre-tax charge after the sale, whose terms were not made public. A year later, in August 1998, William Kaman II stepped down as head of Kaman Music and was replaced by Robert H. Saunders, Jr., who had been serving as senior executive vice-president of the company. During the transition period, founder Charles Kaman stepped in to offer assistance.

The late 1990s saw Kaman streamline its distribution operations, adding sophisticated new software systems and consolidating distribution centers in Illinois and Georgia into a new 100,000-square-foot facility in Goodlettsville, Tennessee. In February 2000, the first Adamas signature guitar was introduced, a 12-string Melissa Etheridge model that retailed for $2,300. That year also saw the company introduce an e-commerce Web site and sign an exclusive global deal with Fred Gretsch Enterprises to distribute its renowned line of drum products. Kaman had already successfully marketed beginner-level drums under its own CB imprint, and Latin percussion instruments under the Toca name, for some time. Sales for 2000 hit $128.5 million, up from $118.4 million in 1999.

In 2001, the firm added a distribution warehouse in Ontario, California, that was similar to the new Tennessee site. It replaced one half its size in Compton, California. Both new facilities were designed to support the company's ''same day shipping'' policy.

Latin Percussion Bought in 2002

In the fall of 2002, Kaman acquired ownership of Latin Percussion, Inc. of Garfield, New Jersey. Latin Percussion had been founded in 1964 by Latin music fan Martin Cohen and had made a name manufacturing and distributing conga drums and other hand percussion instruments under the brand names LP, LP Aspire, and Matador. It employed 75 people and had revenues estimated at $20 million. After the acquisition, it would operate as a separate entity within Kaman Music, though some operations were folded into established Kaman units. By now, Kaman was distributing more than 10,000 products of all types for musicians of all skill levels. It continued to make the Ovation, Adamas, and Hamer guitar lines, as well as distributing Japanese Takamine models, to which it had gained rights some years earlier. Other brands Kaman distributed included Sabian and Gibraltar percussion products.

In the fall of 2003, the firm acquired Genz Benz Enclosures, Inc., a maker of speaker cabinets, Tube Works brand amplifiers, and other sound reinforcement equipment. Helped by the addition of Latin Percussion and a strong Christmas season, Kaman Music recorded sales of $145.5 million for the year. Operating profits reached $9.5 million, up from $7.2 million a year earlier.

In the summer of 2004, Kaman opened a new 156,000-square-foot distribution center in Portland, Tennessee. It replaced the Goodlettsville site, which had been opened just a few years earlier, and allowed for expansion of another 150,000 square feet if needed, as well as offering 24 loading docks.

Approaching its 40th year in business, Kaman Music had grown from a pioneering manufacturer of composite-body guitars into one of the world's leading guitar makers and the largest independent distributor of musical instruments and accessories in the United States.

Principal Subsidiaries

KMI Europe, Inc.; B&J Music Ltd. (Canada); Latin Percussion, Inc.

Principal Competitors

Yamaha Corp.; C.F. Martin & Co., Inc.; Fender Musical Instruments Corporation; Gibson Guitar Corporation; Taylor Guitars.

Further Reading

Cruice, Valerie, ''From the Ratcheting of Helicopters to a Guitar's Hum,'' *New York Times*, December 8, 1996, p. 2.
''How to Bring Aerospace Know-How to the Guitar Industry,'' *Business Week*, June 26, 1978, p. 74.
''Kaman Music Sales up 17%,'' *Music Trades*, June 1, 2004, p. 41.
''Kaman Opens New Hdq.,'' *Music Trades*, May 1, 1994, p. 108.
''Kaman: Safely Diversified and Back into Helicopters,'' *Business Week*, July 30, 1984, p. 88.
''Kaman Steps up Service with Expanded Warehouse,'' *Music Trades*, October 1, 2001, p. 72.
Marks, Brenda, ''Connecticut Firm Makes Guitars, Helicopter Blades from Same Fiberglass,'' *Waterbury Republican-American*, May 31, 1999.
O'Neill, Laurie A., ''A Guitar Developed by Space-Age Ideas,'' *New York Times*, December 6, 1981, section 11, p. 4.
''Retooling for the Millennium,'' *Music Trades*, June 1, 1999, p. 68.
Rosenberg, John S., ''A Lesson in Diversification,'' *New York Times*, July 5, 1981, section 11, p. 21.
Smart, Tim, ''What Do Dogs, Guitars, and Choppers Have in Common?,'' *Business Week*, July 26, 1993, p. 64.

—Frank Uhle

kate spade LLC

48 West 25th Street
New York, New York 10010-2708
U.S.A.
Telephone: (212) 739-6650
Fax: (212) 739-6544
Web site: http://www.katespade.com

Private Company
Founded: 1993
Employees: Not available.
Sales: $125 million (2003 est.)
NAIC: 316992 Women's Handbag and Purse Manufacturing

Based in New York City's garment district, kate spade LLC nurtures the emerging Kate Spade lifestyle brand. Originally focusing on handbags, Kate Spade is now also involved in stationery, shoes, raincoats, pajamas, eyewear, beauty products, and homewares. In addition, the company has branched into book publishing and music. Kate Spade products are sold in upscale department stores as well as 15 company-owned boutiques. The people behind the Kate Spade vision are wife and husband, Kate and Andy Spade. The company is majority owned by The Neiman Marcus Group, Inc.

1980s Origins

Kate Spade was born Katherine Noel Brosnahan in 1962 in Kansas City, Missouri. Her father owned a construction company and her mother was a housewife. She was not especially interested in high fashion growing up, preferring, rather, to visit a vintage shop to pick up items that her mother might have worn in the 1950s or 1960s. These styles she would eventually emulate when she became a designer. In the meantime, she went to college at Arizona State University in the early 1980s and majored in journalism. At school she found part-time work in a men's clothing store, where she met another Arizona State student, Andy Spade. They began to date and soon became a couple. He had grown up in Arizona, encouraged by his parents to be creative and follow his own path. Even in college he displayed an entrepreneurial spirit, launching a successful advertising agency with a friend. In 1986 *Phoenix Magazine* named it one of the top 50 new Arizona businesses.

After graduating from college in 1985 Kate, Andy, and a friend, Elyce Arons, planned to tour Europe together. But Andy had to stay in Phoenix to run his business and Arons opted to move to New York to begin her career. Kate traveled on her own and when she returned to the United States she had just a few dollars in her pocket. She stopped to visit Arons in New York and applied at a temp agency to make some quick cash. The next day she was called in to work at Conde Nast, where she was assigned to the fashion department at *Mademoiselle* magazine. After the assignment was over, she elected to stay on as assistant to the senior fashion editor. Andy then sold his share in the advertising agency and relocated to New York to move in with Kate, and he quickly found work in advertising as a copywriter. He worked for a number of agencies, ultimately becoming a creative director. At *Mademoiselle,* after six years, Kate rose to the position of Senior Fashion Editor/Accessories, but she began to have misgivings about the career track she was on. The couple, still not married, began thinking about starting a business together. Because Andy was regarded as the creative one, Kate assumed that he would come up with a product and her task would be to sell it. But because they would need to depend on his income from advertising, they could not afford to have him quit his job. According to Kate, as told to *Fortune Small Business,* Andy said, "What about handbags? You love them."

The idea clicked with Kate, who during her years involved with accessories at the magazine had become disenchanted with the over-designed handbags of the day. Her vision was to design a functional bag that still displayed an air of sophistication and style. In 1992 she quit her job at *Mademoiselle,* but not before asking if the magazine would take her back if her scheme failed, and then cashed in her $6,000 401k to help finance the new venture. Andy contributed $35,000 from his savings. In the couple's apartment she began designing a handbag, using tracing paper and scotch tape and choosing a simple

Company Perspectives:

Always searching for the quintessential handbag, Katherine Noel Brosnahan thought it would be easier and definitely more interesting to create her own.

square shape. The shape was different from what was on the market, and it presented Kate with a blank canvas on which to explore fabrics, colors, and patterns. After she completed six prototypes, she turned to a contact at *Women's Wear Daily* to get the name of a manufacturer to make a technical pattern and samples. The company wanted nothing to do with a start-up, suggesting she would be better off starting a family than a business, but gave her the name of a Brooklyn company, which agreed to take on the assignment. Before she could show her sample bags to prospective customers, however, she needed a guarantee that the fabric would be available. Again, she overcame her start-up status and the need to commit to buying a large run of fabric before she had any sales by using the Yellow Pages to track down a company that made potato sacks and required no minimum order size. Although she was now able to purchase burlap to sew bags, she now faced the problem of procuring webbing for the handles. She found no way around buying this material in bulk, but was reluctant to pay out the $1,500 required. It was Andy who now stepped in and convinced her to spend the money and forge ahead. He also played a key role in the naming of the new company. Rejecting outright the idea of ''Kate Brosnahan'' as her label, she considered ''Olive'' and ''Alex Noel,'' then turned to Andy, who suggested they combine their names: Kate Spade. Moreover, he simply liked the sound of it.

Debut of Kate Spade Bags in the Early 1990s

Kate Spade bags made their debut at a 1993 trade show in New York's Jacob Javits Center. The fledgling company was granted space in a far corner of the building, and rather than spending money on commercial displays, Kate trucked in furniture from the couple's apartment. Despite these limitations, she was able to attract the attention of a buyer from a pair of influential New York department stores, Barney's and Charivari, who bought the bags. Even then, Kate did not recover the cost of the show. But it was an important start as the stores quickly sold the bags and ordered more. At the next accessories show where she presented her next collection, Kate simply used the same shape with different fabric. The Barney's buyer considered the new bags to be no different from the first bags, and Kate had to explain that retaining the shape was the concept—it was her signature. The most distinctive change from the first collection was the presentation of the logo, ''kate spade new york,'' attached to the bag's exterior as an accent. In fact, on a whim the day before the show, she removed the tags from the interior and stayed up all night sewing them on front. Barney's agreed to buy 18 of the bags, but only if the tags were returned to the interior. In a stroke of good fortune *Vogue* covered the show and featured the bags in an accessories layout. Customers came into Barney's looking for the Kate Spade bags with the logo on front, quickly forcing the store to reverse course and insist that Kate Spade return the tags to the exterior. As a result, the bag's accent began to build the Kate Spade brand name.

Kate Spade stuck with the square shape, a consistency that helped the new label to differentiate itself until it caught on with the public. The company grew slowly but steadily, at a pace with which the couple felt comfortable. In 1993 they brought in a partner, Pamela Bell Simotas, who helped in locating materials and producing the bags, and a year later their old college friend, Elyce Arons, became a partner to head sales and public relations. Kate and Andy also became more than business partners, marrying in 1994. In 1993 the company generated less than $100,000. Two years later that number grew to $1.5 million. During shipping season, the couple's apartment was packed to the ceiling with inventory, but the company soon was able to move into a 2,800-square-foot space on 29th Street, which combined a showroom with manufacturing capabilities. Andy quit his job in 1996 to devote his energies full time to the company. After Neiman Marcus and Saks each ordered 3,000 bags that year, sales jumped to $6 million and Kate Spade was able to turn a profit for the first time. Also in 1996 Kate Spade opened its first boutique, a 400-square-foot shop located in Manhattan's trendy SoHo district, and moved its headquarters into a 10,000-square-foot space in West 25th Street. The spaces were designed by Rogers Marvel Architects, a firm that lacked retail experience. But like Kate Spade, it believed in simplicity and the use of unusual materials. The fact that Rogers Marvel lacked retail experience, in fact, was a plus as far as Kate and Andy Spade were concerned. It would be a collaboration that would continue with the opening of additional boutiques. Just a year after opening its first shop, Kate Spade outgrew the Thompson Street space and moved to a new Soho location, with a number of other shops in the planning stages in Los Angeles and elsewhere.

Kate Spade bags had become trendy enough that the company now had to begin worrying about copies and knockoffs. In 1997 the company sued Gap Inc.'s Banana Republic subsidiary for selling a copy of a Kate Spade nylon tote bag, forcing the retailer to drop the item. Other retailers also would be forced to stop infringing on Spade's designs, including Dayton Hudson and Kmart, as well as manufacturer Accessory Network. Kate Spade also began expanding beyond fabric totes, introducing a collection of leather handbags and other small leather goods in August 1997. The company looked overseas as well, signing a manufacturing, distribution, and licensing agreement with Itochu Fashion System and Sanei International, with the goal of creating 29 in-store shops in Japan and another ten freestanding shops. In addition, Kate Spade began advertising on a national level, as it began taking steps to elevate itself from mini-brand to major label status.

In keeping with the company's unusual approach to business, Kate Spade's first licensing deal, signed in 1998 with the Willard Group, was for stationery items, for which the designer had a personal passion. The Kate Spade Paper collection included formal stationery as well as journals, address books, organizers, agendas, pencils, and erasers. The stationery products were covered in fabric to compliment the current handbag collection. In July 1998 Kate Spade brought in the former

Key Dates:

1992: Kate Brosnahan quits her job to design handbags.
1993: Kate Spade handbags are first shown.
1996: The first Kate Spade boutique opens.
1999: Neiman Marcus acquires a controlling interest.
2004: Kate Spade style books are published.

president at Donna Karan, Stephen Ruzow, to serve as chief executive and oversee expansion. He wanted to accelerate store openings and greatly enlarge the licensing program, but Kate and Andy Spade had second thoughts about growing so quickly. They put on the brakes, and after just three months Ruzow departed. Ruzlow called them ''great kids'' but ''extremely conservative.'' From the perspective of Kate and Andy Spade, however, it was a matter of properly cultivating the brand and not doing anything that would cheapen it.

Changing Directions in the Late 1990s

Other companies recognized the potential of the Kate Spade brand, which embodied simplicity and elegance, and several attempted to buy all or part of the company. Neiman Marcus became a suitor and won over Kate and Andy Spade by assuring them creative control of the company they founded. In February 1999 Neiman Marcus paid $33.6 million to acquire a 56 percent interest in the company. The Spades and their two partners continued to own the rest of the company and handle day-to-day operations. Later in the year, Kate Spade found the right executive to bring professional managerial experience to the business. The company hired as its new president Robin Marino, a Donna Karan executive who had been the couple's first choice before hiring Ruzow. She had instead taken a position at Burberry Ltd., but now agreed to take on the challenge of growing Kate Spade, which generated some $25 million in sales in 1998 and $50 million in 1999. Andy Spade remained the company's chief executive officer, however.

The company made additional licensing deals in 1999, but only in areas where it felt it could offer something different. It licensed raincoats, after concluding that there was a market for something more exciting than Burberry beige. It signed a licensing agreement with GFW Group Inc. to create footwear, a category that Kate had wanted to pursue but waited until she could find the right partner. New York-Based GFW did the footwear business for Adrienne Vittadini and Isaac Mizrahi. Also in 1999 Kate Spade teamed up with The Estee Lauder Cos. to develop beauty and related products. Another development in 1999 was the launch of the Jack Spade line of tote bags for men, which were initially sold in a hardware store. The one area in which Kate showed no interest was designing a clothing line, although she would later design a uniform for the new Delta Song airline.

At the start of 2000, Kate Spade operated five stores: three handbags boutiques located in New York, Boston, and Beverly Hills, and Kate Spade Paper and Jack Spade stores in Manhattan. Two other stores, located in Greenwich, Connecticut, and Chicago, also were set to open. The company signed another licensing deal in 2000, this one in upscale women's eyewear, frames, and sunglasses, a category it had been researching for some time. Its partner was Safilo Group, the major Italian eyewear firm. In 2001 Kate Spade became involved in another area of personal interest to Kate: home goods, including fabric, wallpaper, bedding, and tabletop items. The company teamed up with Platform LLC, a design service company headed by two men experienced in the home category. Troy Haterman founded the Troy design store and Stephen Werther was the former president of Ralph Lauren Home and the founder of the Portico chain of upscale home retail stores. But the two parties had a falling out and turned to the courts to settle their differences. Although delayed by a season, Kate Spade would ultimately launch its homewares line.

Kate Spade signed a deal in 2002 with Simon & Schuster to publish a series of three style books. Published in 2004 the books were titled, ''Occasions,'' ''Manners,'' and ''Style.'' According to the *New York Times,* the books adopted a somewhat haughty tone: '' 'Occasions,' the book on home entertaining, insists that plastic flatware never be used, 'not even for a picnic,' 'Manners' presents some of its advice in the form of a hypothetical quandary: 'You're a bridesmaid in your brother's summer wedding in Nantucket. His fiancée has chosen dresses that are vaguely nautical, but your personal style is Comme des Garcons.' And 'Style' tell us to combine navy and pink.''

Whether the Kate Spade books were an accurate reflection or not of the Kansas City-born designer's view of proper behavior, there was no doubt that Kate Spade was evolving from a handbag brand to a full-fledged lifestyle brand. It even branched into music, offering a CD of eight ''60s cocktail songs'' performed by U.K. band Beaumont. Nevertheless, the company was picky about the categories into which it moved. Kate Spade continued to open boutiques in the United States, adding stores in Boca Raton, Atlanta, Houston, Dallas, Charlotte, Chicago, Georgetown, San Francisco, and Manhasset and Central Valley, New York. There were also plans to open additional boutiques in Las Vegas, Palo Alto, and King of Prussia, Pennsylvania. In addition, in 2003 Kate Spade signed a distribution deal with a Hong Kong company to open 15 stores in the Asian market.

Kate Spade continued to fight vigorously to protect its designs, aggressively pursuing individuals that produced knockoff Kate Spade handbags or sold them on the street or at ''purse parties.'' There was some talk in the press that the demand for Kate Spade bags had cooled somewhat, and the company was faulted for not recognizing the resurgence in leather and failing to come up with a competitive product. In July 2004 the company hired an executive search firm to recruit a new chief executive officer to replace Andy Spade, who would remain as creative director, fueling speculation that the move was made at the behest of Neiman Marcus, which was reportedly disappointed with the growth of the company and believed more executive talent was needed to help take the business to the next level. Andy Spade replied to these criticisms by admitting to the press that while the company endured a rough patch in 2001, along with most retailers, it remained profitable. He explained his decision to step down as CEO: ''We grew so quickly, but Kate and I had to stop for a moment, as you do, and build your team, and really focus on the infrastructure.'' With revenues from the licensing agreements beginning to contribute to the balance sheet, as well as the company's growing string of boutiques, he estimated that the company would reach the $200 million mark in sales in fiscal 2005.

Principal Subsidiaries

Kate Spade; Kate Spade Paper; Jack Spade.

Principal Competitors

I Pelletieri d'Italia S.p.A.; Kenneth Cole Productions, Inc.; Salvatore Ferragamo Italia S.p.A.

Further Reading

Bumiller, Elisabeth, "A Cautious Rise to a Top Name in Fashion," *New York Times,* March 12, 1999, p. B2.

Conlin, Michelle, "It's in the Bag," *Forbes,* December 28, 1998, p. 86.

Hessen, Wendy, "The Spade Ascent," *WWD,* October 20, 1997, p. A10.

"Kate Spade: Kate & Andy Spade," *Fortune Small Business,* September 2003, p. 51.

Karimzadeh, Marc, "Kate Spade Sets a New Course," *WWD,* August 16, 2004, p. 18.

—Ed Dinger

Kennametal Inc.

1600 Technology Way
Latrobe, Pennsylvania 15650
U.S.A.
Telephone: (724) 539-5000
Fax: (724) 539-7835
Web site: http://www.kennametal.com

Public Company
Incorporated: 1938 as McKenna Metals Company
Employees: 13,700
Sales: $1.97 billion (2004)
Stock Exchanges: New York
Ticker Symbol: KMT
NAIC: 333512 Machine Tool (Metal Cutting Types) Manufacturing; 333131 Mining Machinery and Equipment Manufacturing; 333515 Cutting Tool and Machine Tool Accessory Manufacturing

Kennametal Inc. ranks as the largest manufacturer of metal-cutting tools in North America and as the second-largest competitor worldwide. Kennametal also ranks as the world's leading manufacturer of tools used by the mining and highway construction industries. Kennametal's tools and tooling systems utilize complex metallurgy and materials science in tungsten carbide powders, high-speed steels, ceramics, industrial diamonds, and other materials resistant to heat, abrasion, pressure, and wear. The company markets its products under various brand names, including Kennametal, Hertel, Rubig, Widia, Cleveland Twist Drill, Greenfield, Hanita, Circle Machine, and Disston. Kennametal markets its products in more than 60 countries, deriving nearly half its sales from outside the United States. Overseas, the company's European operations are based in Furth, Germany, and its Asian operations are based in Singapore. Kennametal operates 28 manufacturing plants in the United States and 25 production facilities overseas.

Background of the McKenna Family

In 1832 a coppersmith named Robert McKenna traveled from Ireland to Pittsburgh, Pennsylvania. McKenna established his own copperworks and, after he died in 1852, the business was reorganized by his three sons—Alexander, John, and Thomas—as A. & J. McKenna. The name was later changed to the A. and T. McKenna Brass and Copper Works. By 1899 all the brothers had died, and the firm was once again reorganized, this time under the name McKenna Brothers Brass Company. The seven sons of Thomas McKenna continued the brass and copper works, and also struck an agreement with Firth Sterling Steel Company to become its sole agent for selling cutting tools in the cities of Pittsburgh and Cincinnati, Ohio.

In 1900 one of the seven brothers, A.G. McKenna, developed an alloy tool steel that contained about 18 percent tungsten. A.G.'s development was a milestone in cutting medium steel. Prior to that time, the cutting speed of steel had been only about 16 feet per minute in 1800 and 26 feet per minute in 1860. The 18 percent tungsten alloy, however, increased the cutting speed to 99 feet per minute. Yet this was not the final development. When A.G. added 1 percent vanadium, the cutting speed nearly doubled. As a result, in 1910 the McKenna clan organized a new company. The offices for the new venture, Vanadium Alloys Steel Company (VASCO), were established in Latrobe, Pennsylvania. The McKenna family was the majority stockholder, and McKenna Brothers Brass Company became the new firm's sales agent in the United States.

A.G. McKenna was the single largest stockholder and the impetus behind the firm's metallurgical developments, although he was never officially an officer of the company. Men of A.G.'s acquaintance at Firth Sterling ran the company until brother Roy McKenna became president in 1915. VASCO grew rapidly under the able management of Roy, especially during World War I. The company manufactured most of the ferro-tungsten alloy needed for the American war effort. Near the end of the war, VASCO was producing half as much ferro-tungsten as tool steel sales. It is at this point in the history of Kennametal that Philip M. McKenna begins to play a prominent role.

Philip was exposed to the finer points of metallurgy at a very young age by his father, A.G. McKenna. Born in 1897, by the age of seven Philip was given the responsibility of stoking the fire for his father's blacksmith forge, where he carefully watched the heating of drill steels. In 1907 Philip learned how to operate a lathe and, when he later entered high school, was knowledgeable enough to manufacture a true-tempered hunting

Company Perspectives:

Kennametal's aspiration is to be the premier tooling solutions supplier in the world with operational excellence throughout the value chain and best-in-class technology.

knife on his own. Trained in pattern-making, drafting, and mechanical drawing in high school, in 1914 he worked as an assistant in the Iron Division of the U.S. Bureau of Standards. His duties there included cleaning electroplating and other equipment. By 1915 Philip was employed as a professional chemist and had secured two registered patents, one for an efficient process to extract tungsten values from ores, the other for a method of separating cobalt from nickel.

An ambitious young man, Philip convinced his father to help him start Chemical Products Company in order to market some of his patents. Chemical Products began to provide cobalt, based on the process patented by Philip, for VASCO to use. When the supply of tungsten became more urgent with the advent of World War I, Philip patented a highly efficient method of producing ferro-tungsten. This process was not only used by his own company but also employed by VASCO. After the war, Philip engaged in a number of activities. He attended Columbia University, searched for tantalum and niobium ores in the American west, closed down the Chemical Products Company, and started an analytic laboratory in San Leandro, California, for the purpose of conducting more intense research on tooling materials.

In 1928 Philip moved to Latrobe, Pennsylvania, to become research director at VASCO. At VASCO, Philip began to work with tantalum alloys in order to produce better steel-cutting tools than the tungsten carbide tools manufactured by other companies. In 1936 an agreement was reached to create a new company, Vascoloy-Ramet, for the manufacture of tantalum carbide tools. Participants in the venture included Ramet Corporation of America, General Electric Company, Carboloy Company, and Fansteel Metallurgical Corporation. Sales in 1936 amounted to $450,000, but the new company was plagued with mismanagement and complaints from customers about tools that were poorly made. At one point, Chevrolet Auto Body rejected 1,200 tools made by Vascoloy-Ramet. Dissatisfied with the direction of the new company, Philip resigned from Vanadium Alloys in early 1938.

McKenna Metals Birth in 1938 Leads to Kennametal

Just a few months later, Philip was busy forming a new company based on the tungsten-titanium carbide composition he had patented while working for VASCO. The denseness of this metal, known by its trade name Kennametal, led to an easier machining process. As a result, tools could be made more quickly than ever before. Although the firm was initially set up as a sole proprietorship to develop and manufacture tool materials, in 1940 Philip convinced his cousin Alex, his brother Donald, and other McKenna family members to join him as partners in the new company. Philip's development of hard carbide tools produced results immediately—tools manufactured by the new McKenna Metals Company were soon recognized as the highest quality products in the entire metal cutting industry. During the first year of operations, the company's sales amounted to $30,000. By the end of fiscal 1941, however, sales had skyrocketed to $999,000.

The coming of World War II provided McKenna Metals Company with just the outlet it needed to market its tools. In 1941 the firm received its first order based on the Lend-Lease agreement between the United States and Britain. Orders also arrived from United States Steel Export Company and Chrysler Tank Arsenal. Due to the rapid growth of the firm and the burgeoning administrative responsibilities, in 1943 Philip decided to conclude the partnership and incorporate under the name of Kennametal, Inc. Throughout the war, the company helped machine the enormous quantities of steel required to produce war materials for the U.S. armed forces. It improved tooling for shell production at the same time that it developed a process that increased the production of tungsten carbine penetrators (the outer core of a shell casing made to pierce German tank armor). Kennametal's revenues increased to $7.55 million by the end of fiscal 1943.

The end of the war in 1945 triggered a decrease in orders from the U.S. government, and Kennametal's revenues suddenly dropped. To compensate for this loss of business, Philip McKenna began to develop tools for the mining industry. A new plant was built in Bedford, Pennsylvania, for the production of these mining tools.

In 1946 the company started a virtual revolution in the metal cutting industry. Philip and the men working for him at Kennametal developed indexable carbide insert systems (which included thermal strain-free assemblies and precision-ground "throw-away" inserts) and a carbide designed specifically for all-purpose, high-speed tooling. It was not long, however, before the company was once again in the employ of the U.S. government.

When the Korean War started in 1950, the U.S. Department of Defense contracted Kennametal to manufacture the anti-tank penetrators that it had become famous for producing during World War II. With 190,000 of these items produced for use in Korea, sales increased to $24 million by the end of 1954.

The mid- and late 1950s were a period of expansion and growth for the company. Kennametal opened a tungsten mining venture in Nevada, with the accumulated stockpile sold to the American government. When mining was halted in 1957, the company patented an original process to reduce tungsten ore concentrates into tungsten carbide. This revolutionary process formed the basis of Kennametal's tungsten powder business for the future. In 1958 the company expanded overseas with the creation of Kennametal Overseas Corporation. It also established an affiliation with an Italian firm to sinter Kennametal's carbide in Europe. A joint venture was established in Britain just a few years later.

During the 1960s, revenues for the company continued to increase. In 1962 sales were 31 percent higher than the previous year, while net income was up 58 percent; 1963 revenues increased more than 12 percent, while net profits rose 29 percent. Major technological developments were also introduced by Kennametal during the decade, including the produc-

Key Dates:

1938: McKenna Metals Company is organized.
1943: McKenna Metals is incorporated as Kennametal Inc.
1958: Company expands abroad, forming Kennametal Overseas Corporation.
1977: Kennametal completes its initial public offering of stock.
1990: Kennametal acquires J&L Industrial Supply.
1991: Kennametal spends $27 million to build its Corporate Technology Center.
1993: Kennametal acquires German toolmaker, Hertel AG.
1997: Kennametal acquires Greenfield Industries Inc.
1999: Markos Tambakeras is appointed president and chief executive officer.
2000: After spinning off JLK Direct Distribution Inc., Kennametal purchases all the company's outstanding shares.
2002: Kennametal acquires Widia (India) Ltd.
2004: Revenues reach a record high of $1.97 billion.

tion of high-purity tantalum powders for electronic applications and tool materials, the production of heavy tungsten alloy materials under the trade name ''Kennertium,'' and the manufacture of Kengrip tire studs. Three rock bit firms were purchased, new warehouses were opened in Illinois and West Virginia, a powder preparation plant was built in Fallon, Nevada, and sales offices were established in West Germany and Australia. Sales over the period from 1961 to 1969 more than doubled, and net income was five times greater at the end of the decade than it had been at the beginning. Philip McKenna died in 1969, but the company remained under the management of family members. Alex McKenna retained his position as president and chief executive officer, and Donald McKenna assumed the position of chairman of the board.

Kennametal's success continued into the 1970s as the new generation of family members supervised the development of innovative products and manufacturing techniques. In collaboration with its Italian affiliate, the company developed a clamping system that provided more stable and accurate holding of metal cutting tools. Kennametal also introduced a revolutionary line of ceramic tooling materials, such as ceramic inserts and holders. By the end of the decade, Kennametal was the undisputed leader in metal cutting tooling throughout the United States. The company had grown into the largest producer of cemented carbide products, bypassing such industry giants as General Electric.

1977 IPO Fuels Expansion

Kennametal made its first public stock offering in 1977, a move that triggered a dramatic surge in interest in the company. By the end of fiscal 1979, sales had more than tripled, net income and earnings per share had quadrupled, and dividends had more than doubled. With the influx of new capital, management expanded the company's West German and Australian operations and acquired the oldest carbide producer in Canada, A.C. Wickman.

The 1980s began auspiciously for the company, with record sales of $389.9 million by 1982. In 1983, however, sales dropped 31 percent due to the worst recession since World War II. Nonetheless, management initiated a comprehensive expansion and acquisition strategy. Two new plants were built in North Carolina, and construction was completed on a new headquarters near Latrobe Airport, in Pennsylvania. Consolidation of operations in Ohio led to the construction of a new steel products plant in Cleveland. A new plant was also built in Neunkirchen, West Germany. In addition, Kennametal purchased all the holdings of Lempereur (Belgium, The Netherlands, and France), Craig Bit Company (Canada), and Bristol-Erickson (England). During this time, a joint venture was started with Kobe Steel in Japan to market the company's metalworking and construction products in that country. By the late 1980s, the company had completely recovered from the recession of the early and mid-1980s. It posted record sales of $420 million in 1988.

In 1991 Kennametal created a $27 million Corporate Technology Center in order to remain at the forefront of technological developments in the metalcutting industry. New products and manufacturing techniques in metalcutting inserts, toolholding systems, carbide-tipped bits for mining machines and road planers, and other metalcutting tooling applications of carbides, ceramics, and artificial diamonds are the focus of engineers at the center. The center, located near company headquarters at Latrobe, Pennsylvania, also provides consulting services in tooling management and productivity to meet the unique and rapidly changing needs of Kennametal customers.

Acquisitions Highlight the 1990s

With a revitalized cash flow, Kennametal entered the 1990s determined to surpass its previous success. Management's first move was the acquisition of J&L Industrial Supply, a catalog supplier of metalwork tooling located in Detroit, Michigan. Kennametal's purchase of J&L provided the company with the ability to respond more quickly than ever before to satisfy customer needs for metalwork equipment and supplies. In 1993 Kennametal purchased an 81 percent interest in Hertel AG, a German manufacturer of tooling systems. This acquisition was made to give Kennametal greater access to the growing Eastern European markets. In 1994 Kennametal purchased W.W. Grainger (an American distributor of industrial equipment and supplies), thus improving upon its fast-growing marketing base already established with J&L. These acquisitions boosted Kennametal to a position as the second largest metalworking products manufacturer in the world, and the leader in mining and construction tooling. Nearly 35 percent of the company's total sales were from outside the United States.

As Kennametal bolstered its operations during the first half of the 1990s, it did so under the leadership of Robert McGeehan, the first non-McKenna family member to head the company. McGeehan, who joined the company in 1973 as a metalworking service engineer, was appointed president in 1989 and chief executive officer two years later. His acquisition of J&L Industrial Supply, completed at the beginning of his leadership term, was a masterstroke, giving the company a mail-order operation that served as a one-stop source for cutting tools, abrasives, machinery and accessories, precision measuring instruments, and industrial supplies. The company, which became known as JLK Direct Distribution Inc., was spun off as a separate public company toward the end of McGeehan's decade-long tenure, a period of great activity for the company.

JLK Direct was spun off from Kennametal in early 1997, roughly two years before McGeehan's retirement. His last years were busy years, particularly during the period when JLK Direct was spun off. During the year, the company moved 270 workers from its metalworking division in Raleigh, North Carolina, to its headquarters facility in Latrobe. The most significant event of the year—and perhaps during the decade—was the announcement in October that the company was acquiring Augusta, Georgia-based Greenfield Industries Inc. in a staggering $1 billion deal. Greenfield, which generated $510 million in sales in 1996, obtained slightly more than half its revenues from cutting tools, drill bits, and related tools. The company also manufactured tools used in oil and gas drilling and circuit board manufacturing, as well as saw blades for builders, contractors, and consumers. Greenfield served as the exclusive supplier of drill bits for Sears' Craftsman line of tools. The acquisition was completed in November 1997, a move applauded by analysts who praised McGeehan's success in adding a new dimension to Kennametal's product line. ''Strategically,'' one analyst remarked in the February 6, 1998 issue of *Pittsburgh Business Times*, ''this makes sense because Greenfield makes round cutting tools, like drill bits, whereas Kennametal is strong in carbide inserts.''

The acquisition of Greenfield was McGeehan's last major contribution to Kennametal's development. He announced his retirement in mid-1998 and stepped aside in July 1999. His replacement was Markos Tambakeras, who left his post as president of Honeywell Industrial Control to take charge of Kennametal. Born in Egypt, raised in Greece, and educated in South Africa, Tambakeras arrived at Kennametal with a sterling reputation. ''Markos is innovative, hard driving, a big motivator,'' an analyst noted in an October 22, 1999 interview with *Pittsburgh Business Times.* ''He definitely does not shy from a challenge.'' The challenge facing Tambakeras was renewing the financial community's faith in both Kennametal and JLK Direct (Kennametal owned more than 80 percent of JLK Direct after its spin off). Both companies' stock performance was lackluster in the months leading up to Tambakeras' arrival, with Kennametal's woes related to the enormous debt incurred from the Greenfield acquisition.

Kennametal at the Turn of the Century

One of Tambakeras' first accomplishments was gaining full control of JLK Direct. In November 2000, Kennametal paid $36 million to purchase all the outstanding shares of JLK Direct, returning the company to its role as a wholly-owned, private subsidiary. At the turn of the century, Tambakeras guided the company through a difficult period, as recessive economic conditions dampened demand in Kennametal's key markets. In November 2001, the company announced it was closing three manufacturing plants in an attempt to cut costs in the face of declining sales.

The anemic market conditions prevalent during the early years of the decade gave way to more prosperous times, as Kennametal entered the mid-2000s on a high note. The company strengthened its position in its Asia Pacific territory with the 2002 purchase of Widia (India) Ltd., a India-based maker of carbide-tipped, metal-cutting tools that primarily served the automotive and defense industries. Kennametal completed the integration of Widia into its operations in 2004, a year which sales increased 12 percent to a record high of $1.97 billion. The company, by this point, held a firm grasp on markets throughout North America, Europe, and Asia, ranking as the second largest metals company in the world. In the years ahead, Kennametal was expected to fortify its position and purse global dominance, a lofty objective that provided the impetus for future expansion.

Principal Subsidiaries

Kennametal Australia Pty. Ltd.; Kennametal Exports Inc.; Kennametal Foreign Sales Corporation; Kennametal (Canada) Ltd.; Kennametal (Shanghai) Ltd.; Kennametal (Thailand) Co., Ltd.; Kennametal (Xuzhou) Company Ltd.; Kennametal Hardpoint Inc.; Kennametal International S.A. (Panama); Kennametal Japan Ltd.; Kennametal (Malaysia) Sdn. Bhd.; Kennametal de Mexico, S.A. de C.V.; Kennametal SP. Z.o.o.; Kennametal (Singapore) Pte. Ltd.; Kennametal South Africa (Pty.) Ltd.; Kennametal Korea Ltd.; Kennametal Holding (Cayman Islands) Limited; Kennametal Financing I; Kennametal Financing II; Kennametal Holdings Europe Inc.; Adaptive Technologies Corp.; Circle Machine Company; Conforma Clad Inc.; Greenfield Industries, Inc.

Principal Operating Units

Metalworking Solutions and Services Group; Mining and Construction Division; Engineered Products Group; Energy Products Group; Industrial Products Group; Electronics Products Group; J&L Industrial Supply; Kennametal Europe; Kennametal Asia Pacific.

Principal Competitors

Atlas Copco AB; Gildemeister AG; Sandvik AB.

Further Reading

Antonelli, Cesca, ''Kennametal Must Fix Debt-Laden Finance, Standard & Poor's Claims,'' *Pittsburgh Business Times,* February 6, 1998, p. 4.

Boselovic, Len, ''Kennametal of Latrobe, Pa., Announces Purchase of Georgia Firm,'' *Knight Ridder/Tribune Business News,* October 14, 1997.

——, ''Pennsylvania's Kennametal Inc. to Spin Off Industrial-Supply Unit,'' *Knight Ridder/Tribune Business News,* April 30, 1997.

Green, Leslie, ''Kennametal Finishes Buying JLK Direct, Settles Suit,'' *Crain's Detroit Business,* November 20, 2000, p. 6.

Guerriere, Alison, ''Iraq War Shoots Down Kennametal Outlook,'' *American Metal Market,* March 31, 2003, p. 2.

''Head To Head With Robert McGeehan, President, Kennametal, Inc.,'' *Cutting Tool Engineering*, October 1991, pp. 21–24.

Jaffe, Thomas, ''Capitalist Cutting Tool,'' *Forbes,* June 8, 1992, p. 164.

''Kennametal Eyes Three Paths to Profits,'' *Industrial Distribution,* October 1992, p. 10.

''Kennametal Inc.,'' *Industrial Distribution,* August 2003, p. 18.

''Kennametal Inc. to Run Planned Weapons Center in Pittsburgh Area,'' *Knight Ridder/Tribune Business News,* December 17, 2002.

''Kennametal Keen on Acquisitions,'' *Asia Africa Intelligence Wire,* April 10, 2003, p. 43.

''Kennametal Sees Wildia as Sourcing Hub for Asia-Pacific,'' *Asia Africa Intelligence Wire,* September 17, 2002, p. 32.

''Kennametal to Acquire Greenfield,'' *Industrial Distribution,* November 1997, p. 19.

''KenTip Drills with Changeable Tips,'' *Industrial Distribution,* March 2004, p. 60.

Lott, Ethan, ''Kennametal Inc.,'' *Pittsburgh Business Times,* October 22, 1999, p. 13.

McKenna, Donald C., *The Roots of Kennametal, or Philip McKenna and How He Grew,* Latrobe: Kennametal, Inc., 1974.

Sacco, John E., ''Honeywell Executive Takes Kennametal Helm,'' *American Metal Market,* May 12, 1999, p. 3.

——, ''McGeehan to Retire as Kennametal Chief,'' *American Metal Market,* March 25, 1999, p. 3.

——, ''Kennametal Stock Sales Reduces Debt,'' *American Metal Market,* March 30, 1998, p. 3.

''The Shopper's Edge: Kennametal's Changing Marketing Strategy,'' Pittsburgh High Technology, Pittsburgh High Technology Council, reprint.

Tomich, Jeffrey, ''Latrobe, Pa.-Based Metalworking Company to Close Pine Bluff, Ark., Plant,'' *Knight Ridder/Tribune Business News,* November 16, 2001.

—Thomas Derdak
—update: Jeffrey L. Covell

Kerr-McGee Corporation

Kerr-McGee Center
123 Robert S. Kerr Avenue
Oklahoma City, Oklahoma 73102
U.S.A.
Telephone: (405) 270-1313
Fax: (405) 270-3123
Web site: http://www.kerr-mcgee.com

Public Company
Incorporated: 1932 as A&K Petroleum Company
Employees: 3,915
Sales: $4.19 billion (2004)
Stock Exchanges: New York
Ticker Symbol: KMG
NAIC: 211111 Crude Petroleum and Natural Gas Extraction

From its beginning as a small drilling company during the Great Depression, Kerr-McGee Corporation has grown to become one of the country's more successful medium-sized energy and chemical companies. Kerr-McGee's operations focus on three areas: oil and natural gas production, production and marketing of inorganic industrial chemicals, and coal mining and marketing.

Company Origins in Oil Drilling Contracting

The Great Depression was just around the corner when Anderson & Kerr Drilling Company was founded near Oklahoma City, Oklahoma, in July 1929. The company's assets amounted to three boilers and two steam rigs, and the company was one of many small oil-related firms vying for drilling contracts in a city that was booming. The local newspaper, the Daily Oklahoman, in October 1929, mentioned the October stock market crash briefly under the headline, ''Business Men are Unnecessarily Troubled by Crash of Stocks.'' This town wasn't feeling the depression—there was oil here and plenty of it.

While James L. Anderson handled the equipment end, Robert S. Kerr sought drilling contracts, operating from a hotel room and going home only on weekends. Anderson was said to have ''a nose for oil'' and the ability to drill more economically than others, and Kerr was a talented capital raiser. Financing the young company was a constant challenge. It faced rising debt, strong competition, and the need to keep busy, when Kerr, still relatively unknown, met with Frank Phillips, founder of Phillips Petroleum Company. Kerr wanted to drill some of Phillips's leases in the area, and he eventually won a contract. As Kerr's longtime associate, Rex Hawks, told John Samuel Ezell, in *Innovations in Energy: The Story of Kerr-McGee,* ''As Kerr was about to leave, he turned and said, ''By the way, Mr. Phillips, there's one little item I was about to forget.' When asked what that was Kerr replied that he would have to borrow $20,000 to sink the well. Phillips then ''cussed a little while and exclaimed, 'You spend all this time wanting the job and haven't the money to drill it with.' Kerr 'hemmed and hawed,' but in the end Phillips called [his office] . . . and said, 'Let this damn man have $20,000 to drill this lease with.' '' Kerr's bold drive and inexhaustible belief in his company kept the company moving forward through times when the speculative nature of the business and the tough competition would have folded a less determined company.

In 1932 the company opened an office for its staff of 11 in Oklahoma City and was incorporated as A&K Petroleum Company. In 1935 its first public offering of 120,000 shares of common stock was made available at $5.00 per share. In 1936 when the company was negotiating a second stock offering, Anderson decided that the company was growing to a size he no longer felt comfortable managing, and he opted to sell his interest in the A&K.

The year 1937 was a critical time. The economy was in recession, oil prices were decreasing, and there was no money to finance drilling. The company's directors recognized a need for leadership at the executive level to move the company's exploration and production into the black. They were willing to bank a large part of their holdings on two men from Phillips Petroleum, offering them salaries that dwarfed their own by comparison. Robert Lynn became executive vice-president of the company which, in these formative years, restructured and renamed its operations several times. He played a prominent role in the company, then called Kerlyn Oil Company, for five years. Dean A. McGee, the second man from Phillips, was to

Company Perspectives:

At Kerr-McGee, our values influence everything we do. We are committed to quality, safety, environmental responsibility and ethical conduct.

direct the company on a new course almost immediately. His presence was felt until his death in 1989.

McGee, who had been Phillips's chief geologist, relied heavily on credit, faith, and hard labor. Within a year the company made its first major oil discovery—the Magnolia field in Columbia County, Arkansas. The revenues from the Magnolia discovery fueled further expansion.

Demand for oil was rising dramatically as a result of wartime needs, however the company struggled under debt, taxes, government restrictions, and a shortage of capital and manpower, as well as continuing low prices for its products. Kerr and his workers continued making deals, leveraging assets, and using their talents to keep operating. Kerlyn was chronically short of capital in its early years and often had to stop drilling until money could be raised to continue. Much of its capital came from small contributions of $1,000 to $3,000. In 1943 a deal was struck in which Phillips Petroleum put up 75 percent of the cost for half a share in any Kerlyn venture in which it participated. That year, the company's exploratory drilling, or wildcatting, led to discovery of oil to the northwest of Oklahoma City, setting off the west Edmonton boom. The U.S. Bureau of Mines categorized this find as the year's ''greatest addition of new oil.''

In 1942, confident that the company was in capable hands and certain that his primary role was to be played out in public office, Bob Kerr made a long-desired move into politics. That year he was elected governor of Oklahoma, and throughout successive political roles, including U.S. senator, Kerr remained an active member of the company's board until his death in 1963.

When Kerr made his move into politics Robert Lynn decided to leave the company. From the time he joined the firm, McGee had acted as a key figure in the company. He was the logical choice to move into Lynn's leadership role, and in 1946 the company changed its name to Kerr-McGee Oil Industries, Inc. McGee became executive vice-president in 1942 and was made president of Kerr-McGee in 1957.

Expansion into Downstream Operations in 1945

Exploration activities continued to increase as Kerr-McGee expanded its drilling operations to the Gulf of Mexico. Seeking to capitalize on the increased need for refined oil products, the company also moved into ''downstream'' operations with the purchase of its first refinery in 1945. Downstream activities generally include transportation, refining, storage, marketing, distribution, and slop disposal—in short, all activities that follow the upstream activities of exploration and production.

In the postwar 1940s the energy needs of the United States were rising dramatically. The country was using as much oil in one year as did the entire world in 1938. Kerr-McGee responded to this trend with many firsts in oil exploration and production, including in 1947, the completion of the world's first commercial oil well that was out of sight and safety of land, 11 miles off Louisiana's shore. This marked the beginning of the nation's offshore drilling industry. The company added natural gas processing with the purchase of three plants in Oklahoma in 1951, and a fourth in Pampa, Texas, in 1952.

Diversification in the 1950s–60s

As the cold war escalated, the government's need for uranium to fuel the atomic bomb program also grew. Kerr-McGee was the first oil company to enter the uranium industry when it acquired mining properties on a Navaho reservation in Arizona in 1952. Mills were needed to process the materials, and Kerr-McGee soon moved into this area, completing its first mill in the fall of 1954. Soon thereafter the company began construction of the country's largest uranium-processing mill, which was brought onstream in 1958.

In 1955 the company moved into major retailing with its purchase of the Deep Rock Oil Corporation. Building upon an established base of service stations in the midwestern states, Kerr-McGee formed a subsidiary, Deep Rock Oil Company, to continue this aspect of expansion. During this period, Kerr-McGee also expanded its refining capabilities, with the purchase of Cato Oil and Grease Company, and Triangle Refineries, a major wholesaler of petroleum products. Transworld Drilling Company Ltd. was formed to handle Kerr-McGee's domestic and overseas contract drilling in 1958.

The company remained strong in a very competitive industry by making use of innovative methods in its oil production. In 1961 the company was making use of drilling devices that eventually were used to complete the largest vertical shaft successfully drilled by rotary methods in North America at the time. In 1962 the company commissioned the world's largest submersible offshore drilling unit, and in 1963 it built a new research center in Oklahoma City.

In its drive to become a total energy company, Kerr-McGee continued to push into other energy-related areas, entering the forestry business in 1963 with its purchase of two suppliers of railroad cross-ties, and acquiring several fertilizer-marketing companies in the early 1960s, which in 1965 were consolidated into Kerr-McGee Chemical Corporation.

In 1965 Kerr-McGee Oil Industries, Inc. became Kerr-McGee Corporation, a name that better represented the company's diversified holdings. Growth and expansion continued. Although Kerr-McGee had begun doing business in industrial chemicals, its 1967 merger with American Potash and Chemical Corporation marked the company's major entry into the market. This gave the company control of 13,000 acres of a dry lake bed in Searles Valley, California, from which it began extracting brine to produce soda ash, boron products, sodium sulfate, and potash. Two industrial chemical plants were also included in the acquisition, making Kerr-McGee a major processor of a number of industrial chemicals, including the company's most profitable chemical product, titanium dioxide, a white pigment used mainly in the manufacture of paint and plastics.

In 1970 Kerr-McGee was a major player in six of the eight parts of the nuclear fuel cycle, including exploration, mining,

Key Dates:

1929: The Anderson & Kerr Drilling Company is founded.
1945: Seeking to diversify, the company buys a refinery in Oklahoma.
1946: The company changes its name to Kerr-McGee.
1956: The company goes public on the New York stock exchange.
1967: Company enters the industrial chemical industry, buying a pigment plant in Mississippi.
1983: Frank A. McPherson is elected CEO and chairman.
1990: The company begins streamlining its activities, divesting its offshore drilling contracts.
1999: Kerr McGee merges with Oryx Energy.
2004: Company celebrates its 75th anniversary.

milling, conversion of uranium oxide into uranium hexafluoride at a new Sequoya facility in eastern Oklahoma, pelletizing of these materials, and fabrication of fuel elements at its Cimarron Facility in Oklahoma.

At this time the oil industry was undergoing major change. The Organization of Petroleum Exporting Countries's oil embargo in 1973 sent the price of gasoline and energy soaring, and the U.S. public was forced to begin conserving. It was a time of opportunity for energy companies; revenues were increasing and the government was bending over backwards to encourage exploration and production by deregulating and offering hefty tax credits. Despite these favorable conditions, however, Kerr-McGee's performance slipped in a number of areas, as the company lost its lead in offshore drilling and suffered from a lack of managerial direction. Chairman since 1963 and CEO since 1967, Dean McGee instigated an organizational restructuring that, among other changes, established two new subsidiaries, Kerr-McGee Coal Corporation led by Frank McPherson, and Kerr-McGee Nuclear Corporation led by R.T. Zitting. The restructuring was meant to give the company the strength needed to compete in the increasingly complex, turbulent world market.

Kerr-McGee's oil exploration and production operations grew substantially through the mid-1970s. In 1974 the company increased its refining capabilities significantly with the acquisition of the Southwestern Refining Company, Inc., in Corpus Christi, Texas. In 1976 the company expanded its production activities into the Arabian Gulf and the North Sea, and participated in the discovery of the Beatrice oil field, off Scotland's shore.

Coal operations began proving lucrative when the first commercial deliveries of steam coal—coal used to produce steam—were made from surface mining operations in Wyoming in 1978. In the same year, soda ash production began at the company's Argus, California, facility, significantly increasing the company's industrial chemical output.

The Silkwood Case and Other Controversies in the 1970s

The concerns of environmentalists began to loom large in the 1970s, and litigation took up more of the company's time and money. Although there had been previous charges made against Kerr-McGee involving worker safety and environmental contamination, the highly publicized case of Karen Silkwood, which began in 1974, highlighted the hazardous nature of nuclear energy and raised important questions regarding corporate accountability. The Oil, Chemical and Atomic Workers Union alleged that Kerr-McGee's Cimarron River plutonium plant near Oklahoma City was manufacturing faulty fuel rods, falsifying product inspection records, and, in certain cases, risking the safety of its employees.

Silkwood, a 28-year-old lab technician at Cimarron and one of the union's most active members, was involved in substantiating the charges before the Atomic Energy Commission. Silkwood had suffered radiation exposure in a series of unexplained incidents and had then been killed in an automobile crash while on her way to meet with an Atomic Energy Commission official and a *New York Times* reporter. Although never confirmed, her untimely death led to speculation of foul play and prompted a federal investigation into safety and security at the plant. Following additional problems with worker contamination and a National Public Radio report alleging the misplacement of a significant quantity of plutonium, the company finally shut down the Cimarron plant. In 1986 Karen Silkwood's family settled an $11.5 million plutonium-contamination lawsuit against Kerr-McGee for $1.38 million with Kerr-McGee admitting no liability in the case.

Creating further negative publicity for the embattled company, Kerr-McGee's nuclear-fuel processing plant in Gore, Oklahoma, was cited by the Nuclear Regulatory Commission for 15 health and safety infractions between 1978 and 1986. In 1986 an overfilled cylinder of uranium hexafluoride exploded, releasing a toxic cloud of radioactive hydrofluoric acid. One employee died, and 110 people were hospitalized. This fueled public outcry and set in motion a number of legal proceedings. The controversy surrounding the incident was further exacerbated when the Nuclear Regulatory Commission accused Kerr-McGee of giving a false statement during the commission's investigation.

Kerr-McGee's uranium mining, milling, and processing operations accounted for 2 percent of its revenues, while costing $72 million in losses between 1982 and 1986. Aside from the environmental problems, demand had fallen off significantly. Kerr-McGee's leadership was still confident that the slump in demand would reverse itself and that its substantial uranium reserves would pay off in the 1990s.

Aside from the problems associated with uranium production, the company's oil operations were not expanding satisfactorily. Kerr-McGee's failure to pay scientists competitive salaries through the tumultuous, highly competitive 1970s proved especially harmful to the company's bread-and-butter oil exploration and production. A market-research firm estimated that between 1980 and 1984 Kerr-McGee's oil reserves fell 21 percent and gas reserves fell 10 percent. In 1986 an estimate by Morgan Stanley & Company put Kerr-McGee's average cost for finding a barrel of oil at $13.03; the average cost for 12 competitors was $7.35 per barrel.

After years of expanding to fulfill its goal of becoming ''the total energy company,'' Kerr-McGee was involved in a wide variety of resource enterprises, including uranium and plutonium mining, milling, and processing; chemicals and coal; contract drilling; refining; gasoline retailing; and timber. Many analysts felt that Kerr-McGee suffered from too much diversification. Earnings dropped from $211 million in 1981 to $118 million in 1983. In 1983 Dean McGee stepped aside as chairman and Frank A. McPherson was named his successor.

Era of Restructuring: 1983–97

Soon after taking over, McPherson embarked on a long-term slimming down of Kerr-McGee's operations. When the fertilizer market began to suffer in the 1980s, McPherson sold off the company's potash operations to Vertac Chemical in 1985 and divested its phosphate mines in the following year. In 1988 McPherson finally decided to sell the company's troublesome uranium interests, which were divested by the end of 1989. In late 1990 and early 1991, Kerr-McGee severed its remaining tie with the company's roots by selling off its contract drilling operations as well as divesting its soda products operations; together, the contract drilling and soda products sales brought in $340 million after taxes.

By the end of 1991 Kerr-McGee was focused exclusively on oil and natural gas, chemicals, and coal, but McPherson was not finished cutting. The company's petroleum refining and marketing unit was losing money, leading to the mid-1992 decision to explore the sale, merger, or restructuring of this troubled operation. After failing in an effort to sell the unit as a package—which included four refineries, several terminals, a 1,300-mile pipeline, and 51 service stations in Oklahoma, Kansas, and Texas—Kerr-McGee succeeded in divesting them piecemeal in 1995. Of the approximately $400 million brought in through the sales, about $300 million was used to buy back company stock, with the remainder going to pay down debt, which had dropped to $632 million in 1995 compared to $886 million in 1991.

Meanwhile, Kerr-McGee was working to beef up its remaining core businesses. In 1991 production started at titanium dioxide plants in Western Australia and Saudi Arabia, helping to establish the company as a global producer and marketer of pigment. In the area of oil and gas exploration, three major North Sea fields came onstream in 1993, with one of them setting a record for fast-track development through the use of the first permanently moored floating production, storage, and offloading facility in the North Sea. Kerr-McGee was also achieving success through exploration ventures in Indonesia (onshore), the Gulf of Mexico (the deepwater Pompano project), the South China Sea (through a partnership with Amoco Corp.), and China's Bohai Bay. Overall, the company's proven crude-oil reserves in 1996 stood at 170 million barrels, 45 percent more than in 1989.

At the same time that the company was drilling around the globe, however, Kerr-McGee was pulling back from its North American onshore oil and natural gas exploration and production operations, in what the company called ''part of the effort to further focus our operations.'' After divesting some of its North American onshore fields in late 1995 and 1996, Kerr-McGee merged what remained into Devon Energy Corporation in exchange for a 31 percent stake in Devon.

As a result of the McPherson-led cuts, Kerr-McGee was a much smaller company ($1.93 billion in 1996 sales, compared to $3.68 billion in 1990 and $3.15 billion in 1985) but also a much more profitable one (net income was a record $220 million in 1996, compared to $150 million in 1990 and $137 million in 1985). The restructuring behind it—and with the nightmarish memories of its ill-fated venture into the nuclear industry finally beginning to recede—the company could now focus on growing its three core businesses. It did so, however, under new leadership. McPherson retired in early 1997, and Luke R. Corbett, who had been named president and chief operating officer in 1995, became the company's fourth chairman and CEO.

Into the New Millennium

In the late 1990s Kerr-McGee continued its recovery from its dip into nuclear power production by refocusing its aims on its core businesses and rationalizing its approach to its side interests. In 1998 the company began acquiring titanium dioxide plants in Europe from Bayer, a major producer of the compound. The following year a merger with Oryx Energy Company increased Kerr-McGee's exploratory prospects and reserves. In 2000 Kerr-McGee purchased plants in Savannah, Georgia and Botlek in the Netherlands from the Kemira Corporation. Although the deal made Kerr-McGee the third-largest producer of the compound in the world, with 16 percent of total market share, it was not without its drawbacks. The Savannah plant, for instance, had a record of environmental violations. Later that year, Kerr-McGee sold its interest in some TiO_2-producing plants in Saudi Arabia in an effort to focus its business on assets in Europe and the United States.

Natural gas was another area in which Kerr-McGee expanded its interests, concentrating on sites in Europe and the Americas. In the spring of 2002 the company and its partner in the operation, Ocean Energy, announced that they had uncovered large natural gas deposits at a deep-water well in the Gulf of Mexico. At the same time Kerr-McGee expanded its interests in natural-gas drilling in the North Sea, off the coast of the British Isles. According to a report in ''Offshore,'' the company had committed almost half of its annual budget for exploration and production to develop sites in the area. Kerr-McGee also took advantage of an opportunity to divest itself of some natural-gas interests in Indonesia. But that year the company ventured into new areas in petroleum exploration, including sites in northeastern China.

Principal Subsidiaries

Kerr-McGee Chemical Corporation; Kerr-McGee China Petroleum Ltd. (Bahamas); Kerr-McGee Coal Corporation; Kerr-McGee Credit Corporation; Kerr-McGee Oil (U.K.) PLC; Westport Resources.

Further Reading

Barrett, Amy, ''Kerr-McGee: New Tricks for an Old Dog?,'' *Financial World,* October 15, 1991, p. 18.

Ezell, John Samuel, *Innovations in Energy: The Story of Kerr-McGee*, Norman: University of Oklahoma Press, 1979.

Fan, Aliza, ''Kerr-McGee Focuses on Production After Losing Downstream Burden,'' *Oil Daily*, March 25, 1996, p. 3.

''Kerr-McGee (50% and Operator) and Ocean Energy (50%) Have Announced a Natural Gas Discovery at the Merganser Prospect on

Atwater Valley Block 37 in the Deep-Water Gulf of Mexico,'' *Petroleum Economist*, May, 2002, p. 44.
''Kerr-McGee Sells TiO_2 Stake,'' *Chemical Market Reporter*, October 16, 2000, p. 3.
''Kerr-McGee to Buy Westport Resources,'' *Chemical Week*, April 7, 2004, p. 9.
''Kerr-McGee Unveils Measures to Strengthen its TiO_2 Business,'' *Chemical Market Reporter*, January 20, 2003, p. 2.
Kohn, Howard, *Who Killed Karen Silkwood?*, New York: Summit Books, 1981.
Mack, Toni, ''Playing with the Majors,'' *Forbes*, November 13, 1989, p. 92.
McGee, Dean A., *Evolution into Total Energy: The Story of Kerr-McGee Corporation*, New York: Newcomen Society in North America, 1971.
Rashke, Richard L., *The Killing of Karen Silkwood: The Story Behind the Kerr-McGee Plutonium Case,* Boston: Houghton Mifflin, 1981.
Reifenberg, Anne, ''Publicity-Shy Kerr-McGee Draws Unwelcome Spotlight,'' *Wall Street Journal,* September 8, 1995, p. B4.
Seewald, Nancy, ''Kerr-McGee Confirms Plans to Buy Two Kemira Plants,'' *Chemical Week,* February 23, 2000, p. 7.
Wood, Andrew, ''Fixing Up a Big Mess Down in Savannah,'' *Chemical Week*, October 25, 2000, p. 51.

—Carole Healy
—updates: David E. Salamie; Kenneth R. Shepherd

Koor Industries Ltd.

14 Hamelacha Street
Park Afek
Rosh Ha'Ayin 48091
Israel
Telephone: 972 3 900 8333
Fax: 972 3 900 8334
Web site: http://www.koor.co.il

Public Company
Incorporated: 1944 as Koor Industries & Crafts Co., Ltd.
Employees: 6,328
Sales: ILS 7.69 billion ($1.76 billion) (2003)
Stock Exchanges: Tel Aviv New York
Ticker Symbol: KOR
NAIC: 325310 Fertilizer Manufacturing; 325311 Nitrogenous Fertilizer Manufacturing; 325312 Phosphatic Fertilizer Manufacturing; 325320 Pesticide and Other Agricultural Chemical Manufacturing; 334210 Telephone Apparatus Manufacturing; 334220 Radio and Television Broadcasting and Wireless Communications Equipment Manufacturing; 334290 Other Communications Equipment Manufacturing

Koor Industries Ltd. is a leading industrial holding company in Israel. The company made ambitious investments in telecommunications start-ups and venture funds just before the tech bubble burst. Publicly traded, Koor's primary shareholder is The Claridge Group, the investment management company of Charles R. Bronfman (co-chairman of Seagram Company) and his family, which holds almost 29 percent of Koor stock.

Even after divesting certain noncore holdings in 1999, Koor's array of businesses is diverse. It has telecommunications and electronics operations, through ECI Telecom, Telrad Networks, and the Elisra Defense Group. It also owns a venerable agrochemicals business, Makhteshim-Agan Industries. An investment arm, Koor Corporate Venture Capital, finances high-tech start-ups. Koor is also a partner in the Sheraton-Moriah hotel chain, Israel's largest.

The Early Years: Labor Union Roots

Koor's predecessor was Solel Boneh Construction, founded in British Palestine in 1924 by the Histadrut (the General Federation of Labor) to construct roads and buildings. Through Solel Boneh, the Histadrut provided a livelihood for settlers in an attempt to found a Jewish state in Palestine.

Solel Boneh began planning for independence as early as 1944, when it created an industrial arm called Koor Industries. Koor employed 500 workers at its two plants, Phoenicia Glass and Vulcan Foundries, both in Haifa. Many of Koor's early employees were immigrants who had escaped Europe. After World War II Koor employed many concentration camp survivors and refugees from Arab nations, providing much-needed job training and employment for these immigrants not just in cities but also in remote villages.

Koor formed Nesher Cement in 1945 as a joint venture with private investors. Koor's first exports, Vulcan car batteries, were sold to Syria in 1947. In 1951 Koor entered the telecommunications field through another joint venture called Telrad, which was located in the town of Lod, near Tel Aviv. From this facility and another built at Ma'alot in 1965, Telrad manufactured telephones, PABX switching terminals, and a variety of other electronic devices.

Shortly after Israeli independence was declared in 1948, the state was attacked by Arab nations. In repelling the attack, Israel took additional land and doubled in size. The war, however, left Koor economically isolated within the Middle Eastern region. Without local export markets, the company instead concentrated its sales efforts in Europe, North America, and Africa. But with continuing tensions between Israel and its Arab neighbors came the need for Israel to develop a domestic arms industry. In 1952 Koor, in conjunction with the Finnish company Tampella, established the Soltam artillery manufacturing plant. Koor's arms manufacturing grew over the years as Israel's Arab neighbors acquired increasingly sophisticated weaponry.

Koor opened the Harsah Ceramics plant in Haifa in 1953, and the following year built a steel processing complex in partnership with German interests. In conjunction with American interests, Koor established the Alliance Tire and Rubber

Company Perspectives:

Koor Industries is a leading investment holding company, focusing on high-growth, internationally-oriented, Israeli companies. Koor actively invests in telecommunications through its holdings in ECI Telecom and Telrad Networks; in agrochemicals through Makhteshim Agan Industries; and in defense electronics through the Elisra Defense Group. The company also invests in tourism and aviation through its holdings in Knafaim Arkia Holdings (TASE: KNFM) and the Sheraton-Moriah hotel chain. Koor's portfolio companies' strategy is to offer products and solutions that are best of breed, capturing international markets through innovation, quality and service. Koor Corporate Venture Capital, Koor's venture capital arm, promotes growth in innovative Israeli high-tech companies that can benefit from Koor's technological intellectual capital and management know-how.

Company in 1955. Through these ventures, Koor not only contributed significantly to Israeli import-substitution efforts, but generated valuable foreign exchange, too.

Gaining Independence in 1958

By 1958 Koor had grown to 25 plants with 6,000 employees and overshadowed its parent company, Solel Boneh. That year Hevrat Ha'Ovdim, the economic arm of the Histadrut, decided to make Koor a separate entity specializing in industrial products, management and financial services, and foreign trade.

In 1962 Koor created an electronics company called Tadiran, jointly owned by Koor and the Israeli Defense Ministry until 1969. A year after creating Tadiran, Koor entered the chemical industry by purchasing Makhteshim. Israel's largest manufacturer of herbicides, pesticides, and insecticides, Makhteshim became an important exporter and source of foreign exchange.

Because it was so closely tied to the Histadrut labor organization, Koor often made business decisions according to workers' welfare rather than profit potential. One of the company's innovations in industrial relations was a joint labor-management committee to discuss production problems. This committee, introduced in 1964 at the Phoenicia Glass plant, raised productivity and minimized labor disputes and was copied later at other plants.

Israeli borders were expanded again in 1967 after another war with its Arab neighbors. The West Bank, formerly a part of Jordan, the Syrian Golan Heights, and Egypt's vast Sinai Peninsula came under Israeli control. Israeli economic influence spread into these occupied territories with the establishment of communal settlements. The development of these predominantly agrarian frontier regions represented an expansion of the domestic economy and increased demand for many of Koor's industrial and commercial products.

The Israeli Defense Ministry sold its 50 percent interest in Tadiran to America's General Telephone and Electronics Corporation (GTE) in 1969. The new ownership gave Koor access to superior technologies developed by GTE and helped Tadiran to become Israel's largest electronics manufacturer and one of its largest employers. In 1970 Koor purchased Hamashbir Lata'asiya, an integrated food manufacturer that produced edible oils and processed, canned, and frozen foods under the Telma brand name. In consumer goods, the company began manufacturing footwear and later added cosmetics, toiletries, cleaning products, and paper goods.

Foreign Expansion in the 1970s

In 1971 Koor took over the government-owned Elda Trading company and renamed it Koortrade. This new subsidiary promoted Koor products in export markets and represented other manufacturers who could not afford to establish their own trade promotion groups.

Koor also built its international reputation through turnkey projects in developing countries. The first of these was a cotton farm established in Ethiopia in 1972. Additional Koor projects in Nigeria, Togo, and other African nations improved Israeli relations in Africa and elsewhere in the Third World—especially important in light of continued Arab hostility toward Israel.

In 1973, when Israel was attacked by its Arab neighbors, it severely damaged its enemies' air forces in defending itself. Koor now was a more important strategic resource than ever before. The company was called upon to develop new weapons, help increase armament stockpiles, and raise military preparedness. In 1974, as part of an effort to promote more even geographical industrialization, Koor established the Agan Chemical plant in the Negev Desert in southern Israel.

Through peace and war, the company remained highly supportive of its workers, establishing a profit-sharing plan in 1973 and a worker-discount center in 1978. Recognizing the importance of skilled managers, the company also opened a management training school in 1981.

Koor's Telrad subsidiary was awarded the Industrial Development Prize in 1983 for a multiline telephone system it had developed. The award generated greater interest in the system and bolstered both domestic and international sales for the company. Telrad devoted a disproportionately high percentage of earnings to research and development, which led to more sophisticated battle management systems and communication devices as well as ''smarter'' weapons. In another defense-related project that year, Koor formed a partnership with Pratt & Whitney to build jet engine parts at Carmel Forge in northern Israel.

Despite a lasting peace agreement with Egypt in 1979, Israel endured numerous financial crises that often resulted in a high inflation rate. This in turn compromised the ability of Israeli exporters to remain competitive in world markets. Indeed, because it was in large part an instrument of Israeli labor, Koor devoted much of its excess capital to job creation, leaving it few resources to draw upon in times of economic hardship. Worse yet, a 1986 campaign to attract capital in American markets failed, resulting in losses of $253 million during 1987.

Difficulties in the Late 1980s

A new management team, headed by Benjamin Gaon, took over in May 1988 when Gaon's predecessor resigned in protest over interference from the Histadrut. Gaon's first task was to

Key Dates:

1924: Solel Boneh Construction is formed.
1944: Solel Boneh creates an industrial arm, Koor Industries & Crafts Co., Ltd.
1947: Telrad telecommunications joint venture is launched.
1952: Koor creates the Soltam munitions plant with Finland's Tampella.
1953: The Harsah Ceramics plant is opened.
1955: Alliance Tire and Rubber Company is created with American investment.
1958: Koor Industries is spun off from Solel Boneh.
1962: Koor creates the Tadrian electronics joint venture.
1963: Makhteshim chemical company is acquired.
1969: The company name is shortened to Koor Industries, Ltd.
1970: Hamashbir Lata'asiya food producer is acquired.
1971: Elda Trading Company is acquired, renamed Koortrade.
1974: Agan Chemical factory is established.
1988: A new management team leads the company through restructuring.
1995: The Disney family's Shamrock Holdings buys out Histadrut's holding.
1997: Shamrock sells its stake to the Bronfman family's Claridge Group.
2001: Koor posts a record $575 million loss after the tech bubble bursts.
2004: Koor announces the sale of the majority of its shares in Knafaim Arkia Holdings Ltd., an Israeli airline operator.

reorganize the company. Several factories were closed and others were combined. Koor's operations were reorganized into five groups, plus one division for international trade. Each group became an individual profit center, placing the burden of performance on individual group heads, while deep cuts were made in management staff.

But like the economy of which Koor was so much a part, the company's difficulties could not be sorted out overnight. Saddled with a $1.2 billion debt, a third of which was owed to foreign banks, Koor neared bankruptcy in late 1988. In fact, Bankers Trust Co. of the United States tried to force the company into liquidation when it failed to make a $20 million payment on a $175 million loan. After a Tel Aviv court granted the company a temporary stay, Gaon moved quickly to save the company.

Reborn in the 1990s

Gaon responded with an American-style restructuring, slashing the company's workforce by 40 percent, from more than 32,000 to 20,000, undeterred by fierce protests from Israeli workers. He also jettisoned numerous noncore subsidiaries, reducing the number of holdings from 100 to less than 30. Three key sectors were retained as the core of the new Koor: telecommunications and electronics, agrochemicals, and building and infrastructure. In 1991 the company's $1.1 billion in debt was restructured. A return to profitability in 1992 signaled the culmination of the turnaround, which also was aided by an influx of Russian immigrants into Israel, who provided a sharp boost to the economy resulting in increased demand for numerous Koor goods and services.

Underlying the restructuring was a fundamental shift in company philosophy away from the pro-labor stance of the past toward a focus on profitability and competitiveness. But perhaps more important, Koor's financial ties to the Histadrut were considerably weakened by the debt restructuring agreement, in which lenders traded debt for equity stakes in Koor. An outgrowth of this deal was that Israeli banks gained significant stakes in Koor. Bank Hapoalim held almost 23 percent by the mid-1990s and Bank Leumi Le-Israel held barely more than 6 percent. The Histadrut saw its stake decline to only 22.5 percent by 1993. This was reduced to zero in 1995 when Shamrock Holdings, a private investment vehicle of Roy Disney (vice-chairman of Walt Disney) and his family, bought the labor federation's stake. Later in 1995 Koor held a successful international public offering in New York, raising about $120 million in American depository receipts.

By 1997 Shamrock was pushing for a breakup of Koor to enhance shareholder value. Both Gaon and Bank Hapoalim objected to such a move, resulting in Shamrock selling its Koor stake to The Claridge Group, the investment management company of Seagram Company co-chairman Charles R. Bronfman and his family, in mid-1997. Bronfman became chairman of Koor, with Jonathan Kolber, a Claridge Group executive, becoming deputy chairman. In July 1998 Gaon retired as president and CEO and was succeeded by Kolber. With Gaon having successfully established Koor as the largest and most profitable industrial concern in Israel, the stage had been set for the new management team to build upon this solid framework.

Betting on High Tech: 1999–2002

Kolber attempted to direct the firm into more profitable, export-oriented businesses. Koor bought into ECI Telecom in 1998 and merged it with Tadiran the next year. Makhteshim Chemical Works Ltd. and Agan Chemical Manufacturers Ltd. also were merged. Noncore holdings in software, cable television, and energy were divested in 1999, as was Koor's 50 percent share in the Mashav cement venture.

At the same time, Koor was increasing its investments in the tourism industry. In April 1999, it joined U.S.-based Starwood Hotels and Resorts in a $76 million acquisition of Radisson Mariah Hotels. This made their existing hotel interests, the Sheraton Israel, Israel's largest hotel chain.

In 1999, Tadiran Communications, a division of Tadiran, was sold to the Shamrock group, First Israel Mezzanine Investors, and a group of managers. Five years later, in 2004, Koor bought back a 33 percent stake with the intent of merging its business with Elisra, reported *Defense Daily International.* The $140 million to $150 million Koor paid for its one-third stake was equal to the value of the whole company when it had been sold off five years earlier.

Koor joined Canada's Nortel Networks in launching a local joint venture in early 2000. Nortel Networks Israel, 72 percent owned by its Canadian namesake, produced high-bandwidth

Internet equipment. As part of the deal, Koor was acquiring the Canadian company's 20 percent shareholding in Telrad for $45 million. Three years later, in November 2003, Nortel Networks bought out Koor's 28 percent holding in Nortel Networks Israel.

Koor's investment focus had shifted from established companies to start-ups, observed the *Daily Deal.* The company launched its own $250 million fund in January 2000. Koor Venture Capital (KVC) invested exclusively in Israeli companies. By November of the year, it had made investments in 16 firms, some of them spinoffs of Koor subsidiaries. This helped retain scientists who wanted to start their own companies. KVC also invested in other venture capital funds, including those of Polaris Venture Capital, Carmel, Genesis, Star, BRM, and Delta, reported the *Jerusalem Post.*

Like many investors, Koor suffered when the high-tech bubble burst. After making net income of $60 million in 2000, it posted a heart-stopping net loss of $575 million (ILS 2.5 billion) for 2001. Nir Goldberg, writing for *Israel's Business Arena,* characterized the results as ''one of the worst reports ever published by an Israeli company.'' ECI Telecom and Telrad Networks accounted for 80 percent of the loss.

The ECI Telecom Ltd. unit lost a record $256 million in 2001 and subsequently terminated 1,400 employees. In January of the year, ECI's five divisions (optical networks, broadband access, transport networks, fixed wireless, and next generation telephony) became independent companies. The wireless networking business was sold off in 2002.

There were two bright spots for Koor, noted *Business Week.* Makhteshim-Agan Industries Ltd., the pesticide producer, had become its ''cash cow.'' Koor's Elisra Electronic Systems Ltd. unit boasted an $800 million backlog. Government-owned Israel Aircraft Industries (IAI), through its Elta Systems Ltd. unit, acquired a 30 percent stake in Elisra in 2002. Elisra's subsidiaries supplied Control, Communication and Computer Intelligence systems, training simulators, and other defense electronics.

A Glimmer of Hope in 2003

After losing $71.6 million before taxes (and $175.1 million net) in 2002, Koor managed a pre-tax profit of $102.4 million (and a net profit of $10.6 million) in 2003. Sales were $1.76 billion (ILS 7.69 billion) in 2003. The largest business sector was agrochemicals, with 68 percent of sales. Defense electronics accounted for 17 percent while telecommunications contributed 10 percent. Most of Koor's sales came from abroad; Europe was the largest region, accounting for 32 percent of the total. South America contributed 22 percent.

In September 2004 Koor announced that it was selling 19 percent of the 28 percent of shares it owned in Knafaim Arkia Holdings Ltd., an Israeli airline operator. A group of investors paid $33 million for the shares.

Principal Subsidiaries

ECI Telecom Ltd. (31%); Elisra Electronic Systems Ltd. (70%); Koor Corporate Venture Capital; Koor Trade Ltd.; Makhteshim-Agan Industries Ltd. (41.3%); Sheraton Moriah (Israel) Hotels Ltd. (55%); Telrad Networks Ltd.

Principal Divisions

Telecom; Agrochemicals; Defense Electronics; Venture Capital; Other Holdings.

Principal Competitors

Cisco Systems; Dow AgroSciences; DuPont Agriculture & Nutrition; Federmann Enterprises Ltd.

Further Reading

''Blimey: Koor,'' *Economist,* April 3, 1993, p. 66.

''Claridge Israel Buys Shamrock's Shares in Koor Industries,'' *Israel Business Today,* July 31, 1997, p. 1.

Dempsey, Judy, ''Koor Appoints Kolber as New Chief Executive,'' *Financial Times,* March 13, 1998, p. 27.

——, ''Koor Net Hit by Telecoms Revamp,'' *Financial Times,* March 31, 1998, p. 33.

——, ''Shamrock To Push for Spin-Offs at Koor,'' *Financial Times,* July 5, 1997, p. 17.

''Gold Fleeced? Israeli Business,'' *Economist,* July 26, 1997, p. 56.

Gordon, Buzzy, ''Koor Launches $250m. Corporate VC Fund,'' *Jerusalem Post,* November 9, 2000, p. 17.

''Kato to Buy 'Substantial Holdings' in Koor,'' *Israel Business Today,* January 31, 1997, p. 14.

''Koor Blimey,'' *Economist,* October 22, 1988, p. 77.

''Koor Together with Starwood Hotels Make Sheraton Israel the Country's Largest Hotel Chain,'' *Israel Business Today,* April 1999, p. 17.

Landau, Pinchas, ''Koor Giant Back on Its Feet,'' *Israel Business Today,* May 15, 1992, p. 1.

Machlis, Avi, ''Koor Held Back by Restructuring,'' *Financial Times,* May 25, 1999, p. 28.

Machlis, Avi, and Judy Dempsey, ''New Owners to Widen Koor's Horizons,'' *Financial Times,* January 13, 1998, p. 27.

Marcus, Amy Dockser, ''Big Israeli Firm and Palestinians Go into Business,'' *Wall Street Journal,* October 6, 1993, p. A12.

''Nortel Networks, Koor Industries to Adjust Ownership in Israeli Operation to Better Leverage Key Business Strategies,'' *Canadian Corporate News,* November 10, 2003.

''One-Third of Tadiran Communications' Stakes Sold to Koor,'' *Defense Daily International,* September 17, 2004.

Ozanne, Julian, ''Koor Reveals New Strategy for Growth,'' *Financial Times,* March 29, 1996, p. 30.

——, ''Koor's Mr. Turnaround Builds Bridges in the Middle East,'' *Financial Times,* February 13, 1995, p. 14.

——, ''Offering from Koor Draws in Almost $120m,'' *Financial Times,* November 14, 1995, p. 33.

——, ''State Near Completion of Koor Sell-Off,'' *Financial Times,* December 29, 1993, p. 15.

——, ''US Investment Group Agrees to Buy Koor Industries Stake,'' *Financial Times,* March 8, 1995, p. 25.

Sandler, Neal, ''A High-Tech Makeover That Didn't Make It,'' *Business Week,* June 11, 2001, p. 66.

——, ''Koor's Tech Strategy Comes into Focus,'' *Daily Deal* (New York), March 7, 2000.

Silver, Robert, ''Koor Industries: Israel's Conglomerate Restructured,'' *Multinational Business,* Spring 1989, pp. 28–29.

Steinberg, Jessica, ''A Victim of Bad Timing,'' *Jerusalem Post,* June 7, 2001, p. 15.

Waldman, Peter, ''Big Brother Is Shown the Door at Koor, Giving Israel's Largest Company a Boost,'' *Wall Street Journal,* July 3, 1991, p. A4.

—updates: David E. Salamie; Frederick C. Ingram

Kuwait Airways Corporation

Kuwait International Airport
PO Box 394
Safat 13004
Kuwait
Telephone: 965 434 5555
Toll Free: (800) 458-9248
Fax: 965 431 6581
Web site: http://www.kuwait-airways.com

State-Owned Company
Incorporated: 1954 as Kuwait National Airways Company
Employees: 5,044
Sales: KWD 215.96 million ($732.8 million) (2004)
NAIC: 481111 Scheduled Passenger Air Transportation; 481112 Scheduled Freight Air Transportation; 488119 Other Airport Operations; 488190 Other Support Activities for Air Transportation; 722320 Caterers; 722213 Snack and Nonalcoholic Beverage Bars

Kuwait Airways Corporation (KAC) is the flag carrier of Kuwait. The airline had a fleet of 17 aircraft, all but two of them Airbuses, when it celebrated its 50th anniversary in 2004. KAC also has catering and aircraft maintenance organizations that serve airlines passing through Kuwait. These were to be spun off. The carrier itself has been under consideration for privatization since 1996. The country's Persian Gulf location has been both a liability—as during the Iraq invasion—and advantage for the airline. The Indian subcontinent, the source of much of Kuwait's guest work population, is KAC's busiest market.

Origins

Kuwait Airways dates its founding back to 1954, when two local businessmen launched the Kuwait National Airways Company. Start-up capital was KWD 150,000, the equivalent of $500,000 in 2004, reports *Airliner World.* The fleet consisted of three Douglas DC-3s. Flight operations began on March 16, 1954, connecting Kuwait City with Abadan, Iran; Beirut, Lebanon; Damascus, Syria; and Jerusalem.

The company was renamed Kuwait Airways Corporation the next year as the government acquired a half interest. The route network was expanded throughout the Gulf region with the addition of leased, four-engined Vickers Viscount aircraft in 1958.

The government of Kuwait, which became independent from Great Britain in 1961, bought the remainder of KAC's shares in May 1962 after the launch of rival Trans Arabian Airways made the competitive situation difficult. The government acquired a controlling interest in Trans Arabian in April 1964 and folded its Douglas DC-6 aircraft into the KAC fleet.

In the meantime, KAC had begun operating its first jet aircraft, de Havilland Comets, in 1962. This allowed the company to venture into Europe with a six-hour nonstop to London. The Comets were soon supplemented with a handful of newer planes, Hawker Siddeley Tridents and BAC One-Elevens. The One-Elevens were leased off within a couple of years, but the Tridents were very successful plying routes in the Middle East.

KAC bought its first Boeing aircraft when it acquired three 707 airliners in November 1968 at a cost of about $25 million. By 1976, the airline had retired its earlier jets and turboprops and was flying a fleet of eight 707s. These were supplemented with midsize Boeing 737s and widebody 727s, one of which was operated exclusively for the government. KAC received its first of four Boeing 747 jumbo jets in August 1978. These long-range giants allowed the airline to begin extending the London service to New York City as well as start service to Manila in the Philippines.

Mixing It Up in the 1980s

Although the 747 service proved popular, KAC elected to replace its short- and medium-range fleet with A300 and A310 aircraft from the European consortium Airbus. The first of these were added to the fleet in September 1983. The 11 A300s were valued at about $1 billion.

The Iran-Iraq war and political instability in the Middle East were blamed for a 10 percent fall in annual revenues in the mid-1980s. The airline stepped up its marketing efforts to compensate for a drop in traffic. KAC also had to contend with hijackings in 1984 and 1988.

Company Perspectives:

Kuwait Airways aims to re-establish its network to reach more than 46 countries around the globe with a firm commitment to providing the finest service and comfort to passengers while continuing to rank safety as one of its highest priorities.

Boeing was able to win back some of KAC's business when it sold the airline three Boeing 767s, which were delivered in 1986. KAC ended the 1980s with about two dozen aircraft in all. It was ferrying about 1.5 million passengers a year among 42 destinations in 35 countries. The airline had been profitable since the mid-1980s and posted income of KWD 11.62 million ($40 million) in 1989–90. It had about 5,500 employees.

1990 Iraqi Invasion and Aftermath

Kuwait was invaded by Iraq on August 2, 1990. In the seven months that followed, notes *Airliner World,* more than 85 percent of KAC's assets were destroyed or stolen. Company Director-General Ahmad al-Zabin told the *Financial Times* the airline suffered $1.6 billion in losses due to damage to its fleet, computer reservations system, and lost revenues.

A dozen of the airline's 20 planes, and another three owned by the Kuwaiti government, were seized by Iraq. Several of these planes were destroyed in the war. The Iraqis also absconded with KAC's entire $150 million spare parts inventory, reported the *Financial Times.* Six of its Airbuses were flown to Iran during the occupation. KAC filed an insurance claim for $694 million for loss of the planes; however, Lloyd's of London limited its payout to $300 million, its maximum for a single event. Litigation against Iraq's national airline, which had repainted seized planes in its own colors, stretched on for years.

As the *New York Times* reported, KAC carried on operations from a temporary base in Cairo even while its homeland was occupied. Half of its employees, including Chairman Ahmad Hamad al-Mishari, had been out of the country during the invasion.

The aftermath of the Persian Gulf War produced a global recession that affected airlines around the world. No other carrier had to endure what KAC did, however. The airline posted a loss of KWD 38.67 million ($133 million) in the 1990–91 fiscal year.

KAC was operating a fleet of nine aircraft immediately after the war; all but one of these planes, reported the *Financial Times,* had been out of the country during the invasion. Reservations and maintenance operations were shifted to outside facilities. The airline ordered 17 new aircraft worth $1.44 billion to be delivered by 1996. These included two new Boeing 747s to replace the old ones.

KAC lost buildings as well as aircraft during the occupation. Construction of a new, $37 million, two-story headquarters began in 1993 (the airline moved into it in 1998). New hangars also were erected. The cost of rebuilding the ground infrastructure was reported at up to $250 million by *Airline Business.*

The Mideast air travel market became more competitive in the mid-1990s as capacity growth exceeded demand (which was nevertheless increasing faster than in other markets). To cope, KAC developed limited alliances with other carriers in the region such as Syrian Airlines, Middle East Airlines, Cyprus Airways, and Thai International. It helped bankroll two new start-ups, India's Jet Airways and Shorouk Airways of Egypt. Shorouk (''sunrise'') was a charter joint venture with Egyptair. While Shorouk consistently lost KAC money, Jet Airways, also backed by the Gulf Air, became India's leading independent domestic carrier and an important source of feeder traffic for KAC. Both KAC and Gulf withdrew from Jet in 1997, however, in order to meet an Indian government mandate barring foreign ownership of domestic airlines.

In 1994, KAC began implementing a five-year plan to man technical positions with Kuwaitis. At the time, the airline employed about 160 Kuwaiti pilots and 60 foreign ones. The Kuwaitization policy also was extended to nonflight crew positions. By this time, the company was completing about 60 percent of its own aircraft maintenance.

The route network was expanded as the fleet was rebuilt. New destinations in the mid-1990s included Kuala Lumpur, Malaysia. This was cut after six months due to losses, however. Frequencies were increased on routes within the Middle East region.

The Kuwaiti government instituted an open skies policy in 1996, opening KAC up to increased competition at home and eroding its market share from 60 percent to 52 percent, noted *Airline Business.* The government also was considering privatizing KAC.

KAC joined Trans World Airlines (TWA) of the United States in a code-sharing agreement in late 1999. The allowed KAC to list TWA's flights to St. Louis, Los Angeles, and San Francisco under its own reservation code.

Revenues were KWD 168.30 million ($570.83 million) in 2000. The Indian subcontinent was the source of most of its business, reported the *Hindu Business Line.* There were about 375,000 Indians living in Kuwait, attracting competition from Air-India and Indian Airlines (the latter eventually joined KAC in operating a cargo route). KAC had about 5,000 employees.

The airline maintained a reputation for excellent in-flight service. As the flag carrier of a Muslim country, KAC did not offer alcoholic drinks, and meals were prepared according to *halal* dietary principles. The airline removed one more vice from its cabins in 2001, when it banned smoking on all flights.

50th Anniversary in 2004

KAC began 2004 with a fleet of 17 aircraft. The Kuwaiti government was restructuring the airline as a shareholding company to allow for its eventual privatization. The airline had considered spinning off its cargo operations and creating a separate regional carrier.

Kuwait Aviation Services Co. (KASCO), a catering subsidiary formed in 1981, was expected to be spun off on the Kuwait Stock Exchange. The operation had grown to operate airport restaurants as well as Kuwait's Costa Coffee shops, licensed from a British company. KASCO also had formed an overseas joint venture with Al-Bateel Trading Company of Qatar. KASCO provided ground handling services at Kuwait International Airport as well.

Key Dates:

1954: Kuwait National Airway Company (KNAC) is formed.
1955: The company is renamed Kuwait Airways Corporation (KAC) as the government acquires a half interest.
1962: The Kuwaiti government buys the remainder of KAC's shares; the first jets enter the fleet.
1978: KAC receives its first Boeing 747 jumbo jet.
1983: Airbus jets replace Boeings in the short- and medium-range fleet.
1990: Most of KAC's assets are lost in the Iraqi invasion; operations continue from the Cairo base.
1995: The Oasis frequent flyer club is introduced.
2004: KAC is restructured in preparation for privatization.

KAC lost KWD 28.96 million ($98.3 million) on revenues of KWD 215.96 million ($732.8 million) in the 2003–04 fiscal year. Losses due to the war in Iraq were less than expected, although in both conflicts the need to fly around controlled airspace added considerable expense. Fuel prices, a major expense for any airline, skyrocketed as well. According to *Airline Business,* KAC, which flew the first relief flight to Baghdad after the fall of Saddam Hussein, was poised to benefit from business traffic related to the rebuilding of Iraq. The carrier had accrued losses of KWD 530 million since 1990.

The airline was shopping for new planes to replace its Airbus A300, A310, and A320 airliners. KAC was planning to have a total fleet of about 25 aircraft to meet anticipated growth, reported *Flight International.* A new airport was being constructed in Kuwait City for KAC's exclusive use. It was to be completed by 2015.

Principal Subsidiaries

Kuwait Aviation Services Co. (KASCO); Alafco; Shorouk Airways (49%).

Principal Competitors

Air-India; Emirates Airlines; Indian Airlines Ltd.; Saudi Arabian Airlines (Saudia).

Further Reading

Abrahams, Paul, ''Rebuilding an Airline,'' *Airline Business,* October 1991, pp. 46ff.

——, ''Rebuilding Kuwait; Phoenix Rises from the Ashes of Iraqi Destruction,'' *Financial Times* (London), July 8, 1991.

''AI, IA Operating Scheduled Flights to Kuwait,'' *The Hindu* (Madras, India), March 27, 2003.

''Anatomy of a Hijacking,'' *Reader's Digest,* October 1985, pp. 71ff.

''Assembly Panel Opens Talks on national Airline KAC Privatisation Taking Off,'' *Kuwait Times,* December 14, 2003.

Bray, Roger, ''Kuwait Airways to Ban Smoking,'' *Financial Times,* March 20, 2001, p. 18.

Cameron, Doug, ''Struggle from the Rubble,'' *Airline Business,* January 1997, pp. 36ff.

Colodny, Mark M., ''Kuwait's Planeless Airline Chief,'' *Fortune,* April 8, 1991, p. 91.

Feazel, Michael, ''Kuwait Maintenance Plant Designed to Cut Losses,'' *Aviation Week & Space Technology,* April 18, 1993, pp. 44ff.

Fernandes, Frankie, ''Kuwait Airline Plans Major Expansion with New Planes,'' *Moneyclips,* April 1, 1995.

Greenwald, J., ''Nightmare on Flight 422,'' *Time,* April 25, 1988, pp. 46ff.

''Homeless, But Still Flying,'' *Time,* November 26, 1990, p. 71.

''KAC Financial Situation Sound, Strong—Al-Zubin,'' *Kuwait Times,* May 1, 2000.

''KAC Is Still Recovering from the Last Iraqi Conflict,'' *Middle East Economic Digest,* February 28, 2003, p. 6.

''KASCO Shares May Go Public; KAC Plans Flights to Trivandrum,'' *Moneyclips,* April 19, 1994.

''Kuwait Airways Corporation (KAC) Is Facing a 6–10% Decline in Revenue in Its 1985/86 Budget,'' *Textline Multiple Source Collection (1980–1994),* April 22, 1986.

''Kuwait Airways Corp Reports $98.3 Mln Loss FY 2003,'' *Kuwaiti News Digest,* June 15, 2004.

''Kuwait: Construction of $37 Million Airline Headquarters,'' *ESP—Report on Engineering Construct & Operations in the Developing World/The Export Sales Prospector (ESP),* December 1, 1992.

Lenorovitz, J.M., ''Egyptair, Kuwait Form Joint Carrier for Chart Passenger, Cargo Flights,'' *Aviation Week & Space Technology,* April 20, 1992, pp. 40ff.

Maslen, Richard, '' 'Baghdad This Is Kuwait 104'; Flying in Iraqi Airspace with Kuwait Airways,'' *Airliner World,* October 2004, pp. 79–81.

——, ''Kuwait Airways,'' *Airliner World,* September 2004, pp. 53–58.

——, ''Rebuilding an Airline,'' *Airliner World,* October 2004, pp. 76–78.

''*MEED* Special Report on Kuwait—KAC—New Carrier Rises from the Ashes,'' *Middle East Economic Digest,* February 20, 1995.

Murali, Janaki, ''Kuwait Airways Plans Divestment,'' *Business Line (The Hindu),* September 13, 2001.

''No Decision Yet on Privatisation—KAC Plans to Reduce Number of Employees,'' *Kuwait Times,* September 7, 2000.

''Passenger Safety, Security Top KAC Agenda,'' *Kuwait Times,* June 25, 2001.

Pinkham, Richard, ''Time to Take Control,'' *Airline Business,* August 1, 2003, p. 54.

''Plan to Privatise Airline Grounded; 'KAC Making Profit,' '' *Moneyclips,* August 10, 1994.

Rahman, Saifur, ''Kuwait to Construct New Airport,'' *Asia Africa Intelligence Wire,* March 4, 2003.

Shadi, Hisham Abu, ''KAC Launches 5-Year Kuwaitisation Plan; 'Pilots Being Trained at Own Expense,' '' *Moneyclips,* May 2, 1994.

Vandyk, Anthony, ''Bold, New Spirit,'' *Air Transport World,* June 1995, pp. 196ff.

Wagland, Maria, ''Kuwait Airways Set to Renew Fleet,'' *Flight International,* August 19, 2003, p. 9.

Weiner, Eric, ''With Few Planes, Kuwaitis Try to Revive an Airline Without a Country,'' *New York Times,* October 15, 1990, p. A13.

—Frederick C. Ingram

Lassonde Industries Inc.

755 rue Principale
Rougemont, Quebec
J0L 1M0
Canada
Telephone: (450) 469-4926
Toll Free: (888) 477-6663
Fax: (450) 469-1366
Web site: http://www.lassonde.com

Public Company
Incorporated: 1918
Employees: 800
Sales: CAD 247.54 million (2003)
Stock Exchanges: Toronto
Ticker Symbol: LAS.A
NAIC: 311411 Frozen Fruit, Juice, and Vegetable Manufacturing; 311421 Fruit and Vegetable Canning; 311941 Mayonnaise, Dressing, and Other Prepared Sauce Manufacturing

Lassonde Industries Inc. is Canada's second largest producer of juice and fruit drinks. The company also has operations in China and Tunisia. Its products are marketed under its own Rougemont, Oasis, Fruité, and Graves brand names, and others under license (Nature's Best, Tetley, Allen's, Mitchell's, Sunkist, Sun-Maid, and Canadian Club). Although family owned for the most part, the company prides itself on its entrepreneurial culture and has developed several innovations in processing and packaging. Corn processor Produits Ronald was added to the company's holdings in 1981. Europe, where fresh corn is relatively scarce, is a big market for the company's canned corn-on-the-cob. Lassonde also produces sauces and marinades.

Origins

Aristide Lassonde opened a cannery in Rougemont, Quebec in 1918. After working for a time in Massachusetts as a baker, he had begun farming strawberries and raspberries on a plot of land southeast of Montreal in 1903. The cannery's earliest products included tomatoes and beans. First distributed in the surrounding countryside, by 1925 its products were being sold in Montreal itself.

Lassonde's son Willie took over the family business upon the death of his father in 1944. Under his direction, the cannery expanded into the production of apple juice in 1959. The Rougemont area was full of orchards.

Innovation and Acquisition in the 1970s–80s

Fruit drinks were added in 1970. Sales passed CAD 1 million in 1971, according to *Marketing Magazine*. By 1977, they were up to CAD 5 million. That year, Lassonde bought the assets of nearby juicer Coopérative Montérégienne. Four years later, Lassonde diversified into corn products with the purchase of Produits Ronald, based in Saint-Damase, Quebec. Produits Ronald also developed a line of sauces and marinades.

Troubled by the six hours needed by the batch method to clarify apple juice, Lassonde introduced its own continuous clarification system in 1979. The proprietary Clarifruit process was eventually licensed to other companies around the world.

Sales were CAD 20 million in 1979. That year also saw the introduction of Lassonde's Oasis brand juice packaged in one-liter laminated containers.

On September 3, 1981, the holding company Lassonde Industries Inc. was created, with A. Lassonde, Inc. and Produits Ronald as the operating subsidiaries.

The acquisition drive continued with the purchase of Vac-O-Nut in 1983. The company, which packaged and marketed imported nuts and dried fruit, was sold off nine years later. Another short-lived subsidiary was pastry products supplier BHR Bakers Specialties Ltd. Acquired in 1986, it was shut down in 1993.

Public in 1987

In 1987, Lassonde acquired Montreal-based Effex Marketing Inc. to sell its own products as well as those of others. The same year, Lassonde underwent a public offering on the Montreal Exchange.

Company Perspectives:

The mission of Lassonde Industries Inc. is to be a global leader in developing, producing, and marketing a distinctive, innovative range of fruit and vegetable juices and drinks as well as certain specialty food products and other products compatible with the production activities of the Lassonde Group.

By 1990, the company was processing 30,000 tons of apples each season. In 1991 Lassonde bought the juice and beverage unit of Cobi Foods and renamed it Greatvalley Juices Inc. It was the leading juice company in the Maritime Provinces. Lassonde's sales were nearly CAD 126 million in 1991; net income was a little less than CAD 5 million. According to Toronto's *Financial Times,* Quebec accounted for about 70 percent of business.

Expanding in the Mid-1990s

Lassonde expanded abroad in the mid-1990s through joint ventures and alliances. A Thai venture was created in 1993; the following year, the company invested in a Chinese nectar business. The company started a citrus juice business in China in 1995 in collaboration with its Thai partner, Tipco Foods. It soon became the majority owner in the two Chinese juice plants. By 1996, Lassonde had the third-leading brand of juice in China, noted the *Financial Post.*

Known for its shelf-stable beverages, in 1994 Lassonde began selling refrigerated drinks. The company also began producing Tetley tea under license for sale in both the United States and Canada. It also entered a reciprocal marketing alliance with U.S. cranberry juice producer Clement Pappas & Co.

Lassonde posted net earnings of CAD 13.8 million on sales of CAD 128 million in 1995. In 1995, the company formed a refrigerated storage business, followed by a dry storage business the next year.

In 1996, the company acquired Ruthven, Ontario-based Mar-Brite Foods Co-operative Inc., supplier of Martin, Bright, and Olinda brands of apple juice and nectars. The deal was worth about CAD 5 million. Mar-Brite, which had annual sales of about CAD 10 million, was renamed Lassonde Juices. The acquisition greatly increased Lassonde's profile in Ontario and gave it a production facility there to support further expansion to the west and into the United States, where the company was selling about CAD 3 million dollars worth of canned juice to the institutional market.

In 1996, Lassonde's Fruité (a jellied fruit drink) and Oasis brands began to be distributed by retail chains in Massachusetts and Florida. This brought the company into competition with juice giant Tropicana on its home turf.

Lassonde also was trying to win market share up north. Southern Gardens Citrus, a subsidiary of United States Sugar Corp., worked out an exclusive supply deal with Lassonde, shipping fresh, not-from-concentrate orange juice from Florida in refrigerated, 5,000-gallon tanker trucks (up to a dozen deliveries per week). Lassonde marketed this juice under the Oasis Florida Premium brand. Its Effex Marketing Inc. unit also secured private-label contracts for Southern Gardens. According to *Food in Canada,* the Southern Gardens deal was three years in the making.

Key Dates:

1918: Lassonde opens a cannery in Rougemont, Quebec.
1944: Willie Lassonde takes over the company after the death of his father.
1959: The company begins making apple juice.
1970: Fruit drinks are added.
1971: Sales exceed CAD 1 million.
1977: The company buys the assets of nearby juicer Coopérative Montérégienne.
1979: The Clarifruit process for quickly clarifying juice is introduced.
1981: St.-Damase corn processor Produits Ronald is acquired.
1982: The holding company formed.
1987: Lassonde goes public on the Montreal Exchange; Effex Marketing is acquired.
1991: The juice and beverage unit of Cobi Foods is bought, renamed Greatvalley Juices.
1993: A Thai venture is formed.
1994: The company invests in a Chinese nectar venture.
1995: A China citrus juice venture is started.
1996: Mar-Brite Foods is bought, renamed Lassonde Juices.
1998: Southern Gardens of Florida agrees to supply fresh orange juice.
1999: Lassonde acquires share of Tunisian juice company Phytoflora Lassonde; a Nova Scotia plant and Allen's juice brand also are acquired.
2001: A. Lassonde becomes the Sunkist licensee for eastern Canada.
2003: The Sun-Maid license for Canada is acquired.

According to the Canadian Press, Lassonde's 18 percent share of the fresh orange juice market in Canada was second only to Tropicana's 60 percent. Revenues were more than CAD 158 million in 1997, with a profit of CAD 8 million. There were about 400 employees. An apple storage warehouse was acquired during the year. One new product in the late 1990s was Vegetable Delight, a refrigerated vegetable juice.

New Brands, New Geography for 2000 and Beyond

The company explored in a new compass direction when it bought a 35 percent share in Tunisian juice company Phytoflora-Lassonde in 1999. About CAD 3 million was spent to upgrade the factory, which employed 70 people. By this time a third plant had been added in China, where the company's joint venture employed 200 people. Lassonde had another 575 employees in Canada.

A Nova Scotia plant and the Allen's juice brand were acquired in 1999. Revenues reached CAD 236 million in 2000, up more than 15 percent from the previous year. This growth was from eastern Canada, not from the United States, where sales were flat, or from China, where local competition was taking a toll. In 2003, Lassonde sold off its China assets, but continued development of the Rougemont brand there through licensing.

Lassonde cautiously entered the organic foods market in 2002, growing and vacuum packing small batches of organic corn-on-the-cob. Golden Town Apple Products Ltd. of Ontario was acquired in September 2002.

A. Lassonde became a Sunkist licensee for eastern Canada in 2001. The Canadian license for Sun-Maid brand was picked up two years later. The company introduced a line of barbeque sauces in spring 2003 under the licensed Canadian Club brand name.

Net sales were CAD 248 million in 2003. At CAD 21.8 million, net earnings had doubled since 2000. Canada's growing fruit juice consumption and interest in nutrition bade well for the company, reported Montreal's *Gazette*. The firm extended the Oasis brand into a line of healthy snacks.

In April 2004, the *Gazette* reported that Lassonde was on the prowl for acquisitions. The company preferred to have bottling facilities near its suppliers and would need to acquire plants to support geographical expansion.

Principal Subsidiaries

A. Lassonde Inc.; Produits Ronald Inc.

Principal Competitors

Minute Maid Company; Mott's Incorporated; Tropicana Products, Inc.

Further Reading

Barcelo, Yan, ''Industries Lassonde: L'innovation, condition de survie,'' *Les Affaires,* September 5, 1998, p. T4.

Beauchamp, Dominique, ''Differenciation dans un marché encombré sert bien Industries Lassonde,'' *Les Affaires,* May 25, 1991, p. 28.

——, ''Industries Lassonde reprend sa courbe de rentabilité,'' *Les Affaires,* September 2, 1989, p. 21.

Burn, Doug, ''Think Positive: It's Worked for These Fruit and Vegetable Processors,'' *Food in Canada,* May 1992, pp. 12f.

Clark, Campbell, ''Juice-Maker Expanding Abroad,'' *Gazette* (Montreal), June 7, 1995, p. D9.

Dougherty, Kevin, ''No Squeeze on Quebec's Top Juice Maker: Lassonde Industries Boasts Solid Profits and Not Enough Debt to Call for New Equity,'' *Financial Post* (Toronto), July 20, 1992, p. 24.

Dunn, Brian, ''Orange Juice Business Crosses the Border,'' *Supermarket News,* March 30, 1998, p. 22.

——, ''Taking on Tropicana: Quebec Juice Maker Lassonde Is Out to Become a Major North American Player,'' *Marketing Magazine,* November 2, 1998, p. 16.

Eagle, Sandra, ''Taking On the Big Boys,'' *Food in Canada,* May 1998, pp. 72f.

Gibbens, Robert, ''Lassonde Blossoms Outside Quebec,'' *Financial Post* (Toronto), October 26, 1995, p. 31.

''Lassonde Concentrates on Exports: Juice-Maker's Revenues Grow As It Tackles Chinese, Tunisian Markets,'' *Gazette* (Montreal), July 31, 1999, p. F3.

''Lassonde Targets Ontario with Purchase,'' *Financial Post Daily,* July 3, 1996, p. 8.

Le Blanc, Guy, ''Industries Lassonde: Une croissance tranquille, mais solide,'' *Les Affaires,* February 2, 1991, p. 45.

——, ''Industries Lassonde: Vers de nouveaux marches,'' *Les Affaires,* November 25, 1989, p. 69.

Lingle, Rick, ''Juice Products with a Twist,'' *Prepared Foods,* February 1990, pp. 108ff.

Litchfield, Randall, ''Quebec's Noisy Revolution,'' *Canadian Business,* October 1990, pp. 70ff.

MacDonald, Don, ''Liquid Assets: Lassonde Healthy Despite Being Squeezed by Multinational Fruit-Juice Competition,'' *Gazette* (Montreal), February 7, 2004, p. B1.

MacDonald, Jason, ''Fruitful Endeavors (Success Hasn't Made Lassonde Complacent),'' *Canadian Packaging,* June 1999, pp. 15, 17.

McGovern, Sheila, ''Lassonde Squeezes Juice Competitors; Its Philosophy: Have Plants Near Suppliers,'' *Gazette* (Montreal), May 5, 2004, p. B3.

Makely, William, ''Juice Bottler Delights Customers with Easy Twist-Off T-E Closure,'' *Food & Drug Packaging,* March 1999, p. F1.

Melnbardis, Robert, ''Lassonde: An Apple in Investors' Eyes,'' *Financial Times of Canada,* November 21, 1992, p. 15.

Nadeau, Jean-Benoit, ''Fruits de l'innovation: Jean-Paul Barre a assuré la croissance des Industries Lassonde,'' *Revue Commerce,* February 1991, pp. 18–20, 24ff.

Paquin, Guy, ''Transformer le secteur (de recherché et developpement) en eventuelle source de profits,'' *Les Affaires,* September 5, 1998, p. T5.

Shalom, François, ''Lassonde Expands in U.S.: Quebec Juice-Maker Thirsty for a Larger Share of Retail Market,'' *Gazette* (Montreal), December 16, 1997, p. E3.

''Will This Idea Jell?,'' *Prepared Foods,* March 1998, p. 13.

—Frederick C. Ingram

LDC

Zone Industrielle Saint Laurent
Sablé sur Sarthe
F-72300
France
Telephone: (+33) 2 43 62 70 00
Fax: (+33) 2 43 92 34 18
Web site: http://www.ldc.fr

Public Company
Incorporated: 1869
Employees: 10,000
Sales: EUR 1.49 billion ($1.86 billion) (2004)
Stock Exchanges: Euronext Paris
Ticker Symbol: LOUP
NAIC: 311615 Poultry Processing; 311612 Meat Processed From Carcasses; 311412 Frozen Specialty Food Manufacturing; 311611 Animal (Except Poultry) Slaughtering

LDC is now Europe's leading poultry processor after edging out fellow French rival Doux Père Dodu in 2004. Moreover, LDC has long held the leading position in France's poultry market, slaughtering more than 500,000 tons of chicken, turkey, and duck, as well as rabbit, per week. LDC markets poultry products under a number of brand names, including national brands Loué and Le Gaulois and regional brands Bourgogne, Bretagne, Landes, Ardèche, Normandie, Gascogne, which reflect the group's nationally operating network of slaughtering and processing facilities. Since the 1990s, LDC has extended its operations to include a variety of prepared foods and is the fifth-largest company of this kind in France. In this segment, the company produces pizza, deli meats, sauces, ready-made sandwiches and snacks, and cooked dishes. These products are distributed through its own range of brands, including Loué and Le Gaulois, as well as under private label and distributor brands. The company is also one of France's leading producers of prepared ethnic foods, notably Chinese-style food products under the Chip Long brand. Long focused on France, LDC has begun extending its successful growth strategy to the international market, focused for a start on Spain and Poland. The company also has two production partnerships in China. Altogether, the company operates 28 production sites supplied by more than 6,000 poultry farmer partners. In 2004, international sales already represented some 16 percent of the group's nearly EUR 1.5 billion ($1.8 billion) in sales. LDC is led by Denis Lambert, son of the company's founder. The Lamberts remained the publicly listed company's largest shareholder, with nearly 42 percent of shares.

Joining Forces in the 1960s

Auguste Lambert led a group of Loué-area poultry farmers in building a poultry slaughtering facility in 1959. That company, SA Lambert, based in Sablé sur Sarthe, grew into a strong regionally operating business throughout the next decade. The rise of France's first generation of regional and national supermarket groups during that period offered new possibilities for expansion. In 1968, Lambert joined up with another poultry processed, SA Dodard Chancereul, which operated in the Mayenne region in the village of Saint Denis d'Anjou.

The combined company was called Lambert-Dodard-Chancereul (LDC). With its extended geographic reach and strong production capacity, LDC was able to develop a strong relationship with the growing distribution groups. The combined operation was also able to raise financing for the construction of a new, larger, and modern slaughtering facility in the Saint Laurent zone of Sablé sur Sarthe. The company continued to expand that site and by the turn of the century was processing more than 500,000 chickens, turkeys, ducks, and rabbits there each week.

LDC's production remained focused on its traditional segment of dressed poultry through the 1970s. By the end of that decade, however, LDC moved to expand into the market for conditioned poultry and expanded its site to include processing lines for packaged wings, breasts, and thighs.

LCD reached a significant milestone in 1980, the year it created its first subsidiary, SA Cavol, and built a new production site dedicated to slaughtering and processing Loué poultry. The Loué brand quickly gained a reputation for high quality and grew into France's leading poultry brand.

Company Perspectives:

A strategy built on three key points:

Poultry in France: increasing the value of our products in order to respond to new consumer habits. Poultry International: duplicate the strength of the French model by associating integrated supply lines and value-added products. Prepared Foods: develop this pole and achieve profitability by modernizing and specializing sites, and by building positions in promising and complementary segments.

The creation of the Loué brand led to a decade of fast growth for the company. The rapid dominance of France's retail scene by the large-scale distribution groups provided LDC with a ready market for its products. In order to meet the demand, the company launched a drive to expand its national coverage. LDC made its first acquisition in 1984, acquiring SA Mathey, in Louhans, in Saône-et-Loire, which was subsequently renamed LDC Bourgogne. Four years later, LDC targeted the Brittany region, acquiring a stake in SA Serandour, based in Lanfains, in the Côtes d'Armor department. LDC's initial stake stood at 35 percent; by the end of the 1990s, LDC had acquired full control of what became known as LDC Bretagne.

Diversifying in the 1990s

LDC continued acquiring scale into the 1990s. In 1989, the company added operations in Maine-et-Loire with the purchase of SA Guillet. The following year, the company added poultry processor Bidou, based in Bazas, which formed the foundation of its subsidiary LDC Aquitaine. In 1991, the company acquired SA Plamid'or, based in Saône-et-Loire. That acquisition boosted LDC's slaughtering and processing capacity for its duck and rabbit segments. Also in 1991, LDC established a new logistics subsidiary, SA CEPA (Centre d'Expédition de Produits Alimentaires) in Sablé sur Sarthe. This gave the company a distribution platform capable of serving all of France.

The changing food habits of French consumers and their growing adoption of prepared and ready-to-eat foods led LDC into diversifying its operations in the 1990s. In 1990, the company decided to invest in developing the capacity to produce breaded poultry products and other prepared foods, constructing a new production facility in Sablé sur Sarthe that specialized in both cooked and uncooked prepared foods. LDC then launched its Le Gaulois brand, which quickly conquered the French market and became the country's leading poultry-based prepared foods brand. As a result, LDC was forced to make several expansions to its latest facility, tripling its production volume from the initial 10,000 tons per day.

LDC continued seeking new diversification opportunities. In 1991, for example, the company launched a new 50–50 joint-venture, SA Bressane de Production, for the breeding of poultry livestock. The company also branched out into the slaughtering and processing of turkeys with the construction of a dedicated facility in 1993. In that year, the company also joined in the launch of a new joint venture for the production of foie gras, SA Foie Gras de Maine. The company raised its initial stake of 24.5 percent to 75.5 percent in 1997.

Key Dates:

1959: August Lambert establishes a poultry slaughtering and processing facility for Loué poultry farmers.
1968: Lambert SA merges with Dodard-Chancereul to form Lambert-Dodard-Chancereul (LDC).
1970: LDC constructs modern slaughtering and processing facility in Saint-Laurent in Sablé sur Sarthe.
1980: LDC creates subsidiary Cavol to take over the processing of Loué poultry and begins processing chicken parts.
1984: Mathey, renamed as LDC Bourgogne, is acquired as part of national expansion strategy.
1988: Serandour, renamed as LDC Bretagne, is acquired.
1990: LDC purchases Bidou, renamed as LDC Aquitaine, and builds a new facility for the preparation of fresh and cooked prepared foods.
1993: The company begins the production of turkey products.
1994: La Toque Angevine is acquired as part of LDC's diversification in the prepared foods market.
1995: LDC goes public with a secondary market listing on Euronext Paris and acquires a stake in Hermanos Saiz (Spain).
2000: The company enters Poland with the acquisition of 97 percent of Drosed.
2001: LDC acquires Huttepain SA, a producer of live poultry with five slaughtering and processing sites.
2003: Regalette, a producer of crepes, and Spain's Avilaves Gredos are acquired.
2004: LDC becomes the leading European poultry products producer.

Into the mid-1990s, LDC sought to extend its operations beyond the poultry market. In 1994, the company acquired La Toque Angevine, based in Maine et Loire, which specialized in fresh pizzas and other deli products. LDC now sought to establish itself as a leading producer of prepared foods in France. The acquisition of Atlantic Traiteur Innovation in Herbignac in the Loire Atlantique in 1997 brought LDC closer to that goal. In the same year, LDC purchased of a stake in SOPRAT, which held a leading position in France for prepared Chinese and other ethnic foods under the Chip Long brand name. In 2000, the company boosted its prepared foods unit with the purchase of Européenne de Plats Cuisinés, based in the Sarthe region, adding to the company's range of fresh foods and sauces.

European Leader in the 2000s

LDC had already begun to explore new horizons for the new century. In 1995, the company went public, listing its stock on the Paris Bourse's secondary market. By then, the company's sales neared FRF 2.5 billion (approximately $450 million). The public offering enabled the company to make its first international acquisition with the purchase of a 40 percent stake in Madrid-based Hermanos Saiz, a poultry products processor. LDC raised its stake in its Spanish subsidiary to 98 percent in 1999.

In 1997, LDC's international strategy brought it to China, where it launched two joint ventures in Shandong Province and oversaw construction of a new slaughtering and processing facility with a capacity of 10,000 tons per year. In that year, the company also acquired the poultry slaughtering operations of France's Fléchard group. That acquisition alone added nearly FRF 800,000 to the LDC's sales. By the end of 1998, the company's sales had nearly doubled, topping FRF 4.6 billion ($900 million).

LDC next turned its attention to raising its profile in Europe. In 2000, the company turned to Poland, the largest of the next round of countries slated to join the European Union. LDC acquired a 97 percent stake in Drosed, that country's leading poultry processor.

Back in France, the company acquired another family-controlled company, Huttepain SA, in 2001. Huttepain's primary business involved producing live poultry livestock. The company also owned five slaughtering and processing facilities, and an egg distribution business. The acquisition also strengthened LDC's position in Poland, where Huttepain controlled a company producing poultry feed. The addition of Huttepain helped boost the company's total sales from EUR 1.05 billion in 2001 ($900 million) to nearly EUR 1.35 billion ($1.1 billion) in 2002.

Already the poultry leader in France, LDC was rapidly gaining on its chief rival, Doux Père Dodu, which, with its own international expansion, had become Europe's leading poultry group. LDC continued to grow through acquisitions, buying control of Avilaves Gredos, based in Avila, Spain. In that year, also, the company acquired Regalette, a producer of crepes and crepe-based prepared foods.

By the end of 2004, LDC had overtaken Doux Père Dodu, claiming the spot as Europe's number one producer of poultry and poultry products. Led by Denis Lambert, son of the company's founder, LDC announced its intention to pursue its international expansion, especially in Europe, while continuing to diversify its line of prepared foods products. LDC expected to join the ranks of the world's major food groups in the 21st century.

Principal Subsidiaries

Groupe Drosed (Poland); La Gamme (Poland); S.A. Huttepain Aliments; S.A. Toque Angevine; S.A.S. Cavol (96.59 %); S.A.S. Foie Gras Du Maine (75.52 %); S.A.S. Guillet; S.A.S. Guillot Cobreda; S.A.S. Ldc Aquitaine; S.A.S. Ldc Bourgogne; S.A.S. See Guillot Cobreda; S.A.S.U. Alimab; S.A.S.U. Ardevol; S.A.S.U. Atlantic Traiteur Innovation; S.A.S.U. Bressane De Production; S.A.S.U. Cepa; S.A.S.U. Europeenne De Plats Cuisines; S.A.S.U. Ldc Bretagne; S.A.S.U. Ldc Traiteur; S.A.S.U. Les Fermiers De L'ardeche; S.A.S.U. Palmid'or; S.A.S.U. Regalette; S.A.S.U. Servais; S.A.S.U. Société Normande De Volaille; S.A.S.U. Sovopa; S.A.S.U. Stam; S.A.S.U. Volabraye; Sarl Tom'pain; Sasu Ldc Sable; Sasu Ldc Volaille; Shandong Fengxiang L.D.C. (China; 35%); Shandong Ldc Fengxiang Food Ltd (China; 45%); Sl. Aves Ldc España; Sl. Avilaves Gredos (Spain); Sl. Hermanos Saiz (Spain).

Principal Competitors

Cargill Inc.; Tyson Foods Inc.; Romsilva RA Regia Autonoma a Padurilor; ConAgra Foods Inc.; Smithfield Foods Inc.; Agricola Super Ltda.; Protinal/Proagro C.A.; Perdigao Agroindustrial S.A.; Orkla ASA; Lambert-Dodard-Chancereul Doux S.A.

Further Reading

"Le bon choix avec Huttepain pour Le Gaulois," *Filières Avicoles*, January 2003, p. 6.

Deschamps, Johan, "Nous attendons une amélioration de nos bénéficies au second semestre," *Investir*, June 6, 2003.

"LDC confirme son ambition au traiteur," *Linéaires*, July/August 2003, p. 64.

"LDC en Espagne," *RIA*, January 2003, p. 16.

"LDC résiste," *Télégramme*, June 4, 2003.

"LDC: No. 1 du palmarès des volaillers," *Fiilère Avicoles*, May 2004, p. 1.

—M.L. Cohen

Loganair Ltd.

St. Andrew's Drive
Glasgow Airport
Paisley PA3 2TG
United Kingdom
Telephone: (+44) 141-848-7594
Fax: (+44) 141-887-6020
Web site: http://www.loganair.co.uk

Private Company
Incorporated: 1962
Employees: 210
Sales: £48 million (2004 est.)
NAIC: 481111 Scheduled Passenger Air Transportation

Loganair Ltd., known as "Scotland's Airline," provides remote island communities in the region with a commercial lifeline, making trade and tourism feasible, and in some cases provides air ambulance service as well. Once owned by British Midland, the carrier operates regional routes on behalf of British Airways.

Loganair is known for operating the world's shortest scheduled flight—the two-minute hop between Westray and Papa Westray in the Orkneys. Another unique service, the daily flight from Glasgow to the remote island of Barra in northwest Scotland, was the only known scheduled route to land on a beach, according to *Airliners World.* The airline operates a fleet of Britten Norman Islander piston engine planes, two de Havilland Twin Otter turboprops, and seven Saab 340 34-passenger turboprop aircraft.

Air Taxi Origins

Loganair's origins can be traced to February 1, 1962, when Logan Construction Company Ltd. (or Duncan Logan Contracts, according to one source) started a small air taxi service in Edinburgh. The only equipment was a single Piper Aztec, the company reports.

Scheduled services were soon added to meet a readily apparent demand. In 1964, a route network was established centering on the island community of Orkney. The Shetland Islands received similar attention beginning in 1970. The company began providing air ambulance services for several remote locations in 1967. Loganair also began operating the eight-seat Britten Norman Islander that year. In addition, the airline picked up other public service contracts such as carrying mail and received government subsidies to keep some routes open.

The Royal Bank of Scotland acquired Loganair in 1968. Future company chairman Scott Grier later told *The Herald* the story of how one bank employee, Maisie Munn, took more than 8,500 flights visiting island communities as a kind of traveling teller. Grier also passed on tales of "Shetland ponies being stuffed into sacks" and other livestock conveyed on Loganair's earliest flights.

After British Airways (BA) was formed by the merger of British Overseas Airways Corporation (BOAC) with British European Airway (BEA) in the mid-1970s, Loganair picked up some of BEA's less traveled feeder routes in the area. One of these was a unique Glasgow-Barra service that had been operated by various airlines since June 1936, according to *Airliner World.* The only suitable landing spot at Barra, in Scotland's northwestern isles, was on the beach.

Expansion then moved to Northern Ireland, with services between Glasgow and Derry introduced in 1979. The next year, Loganair took over British Airways' Belfast-Edinburgh route.

The fleet was subsequently upgraded to Shorts 360 and Fokker Friendship aircraft. Loganair was Scotland's largest independent airline, with two dozen aircraft, reported *The Guardian* in January 1981. Manchester was added to the route network in the early 1980s as the company catered to increasing numbers of business travelers.

Loganair posted an annual loss of £1 million in 1982, its fourth losing year in a row. Turnover was £10 million. The airline was plying about 20 routes at the time with 15 aircraft.

Acquired by British Midland in 1983

British Midland Group acquired control of Loganair in September 1983 for less than £1 million. The purchase was part of British Midland's challenge to British Airways following

Company Perspectives:

Loganair's growth has stemmed from the rightful return of the Scottish internal routes to Loganair's ownership, and from a steady and watchful eye on new opportunities. Loganair continues to hold a British Airways franchise, conforming to the high standards of service quality set by British Airways and expected from us by our passengers. The airline's unique pattern of operation and current success is based on the skill and dedication of the professionals who have been involved in the services for many years. Loganair looks forward with confidence to the future as it continues to provide the lifeline community services and develops further the business routes, which have enabled Loganair to stake its claim as an independent airline of significance. Loganair is not an ''overnight'' success; it is the product of years of work and dedication. The qualities, which have brought the company this far—skill, service, enthusiasm—shall ensure Loganair's future.

BA's withdrawal of transatlantic service from Scotland. British Midland was part of the Airlines of Britain Group led by Michael Bishop.

By the late 1980s, Loganair was a leading player at the Manchester, Belfast City, and Southampton airports. The company was profitable through most of the decade and posted record income of £808,000 in 1988. In 1988, Loganair began flying its first jets: two 101-seat BAe 146 ''Whisper Jets'' from British Aerospace. These first saw service on the Edinburgh-Manchester route.

In 1990, Loganair was operating 18 aircraft of five different types. The carrier employed 520 people. The scheduled route network stretched as far south as Brussels. The airline also had charter operations based in Manchester for tours to southern Europe. Loganair operated the shortest scheduled air route, a 90-second trip between Westray and Papa Westray in the northern Orkney Islands, as managing director Scot Grier told the *Sunday Times.*

The Glasgow-Manchester route was cancelled in March 1990 after six years due to severe competition from BA. Interestingly, in taking over Loganair's schedule on this route, British Airlines simply leased the same jet Loganair had been using. Loganair was able to pick up the Glasgow-Leeds route in July 1990 after Capital Airways folded.

Around this time, Loganair invested £22 million in new aircraft to bolster its fleet. Loganair was the launch customer for a turboprop airliner made in Scotland. The Jetstream 41, built by British Aerospace at its Prestwick plant, seated 29 passengers. The first of the initial order of three was delivered to Loganair in November 1992.

The early 1990s were devastating years for civil aviation around the world. Nevertheless, Loganair was able to post a pre-tax profit of £500,000 million in 1990 while most airlines (including sister carrier British Midland) were posting losses. However, Loganair was unable to outmaneuver the aviation

Key Dates:

1962: Loganair is established as an air taxi service.
1968: Royal Bank of Scotland acquires Loganair.
1983: British Midland acquires a controlling interest in the company.
1988: The company acquires its first jets.
1994: Loganair becomes a British Airways affiliate in Scotland.
1997: Loganair is acquired by management.
2002: More than 300,000 passengers fly Loganair in its 40th anniversary year.

industry's recession, posting losses in 1991 and 1992. The loss of some Royal Mail contracts added to the airline's problems. A number of carriers operating in the region saw their operations restructured in the wake of the financial crisis.

Loganair cut 170 jobs. Another 80 employees were transferred to sister carrier Manx Airlines, along with eleven of its turboprop aircraft, as Airlines of Britain assigned Manx all of Loganair's routes outside the ''Highlands and Islands'' of Scotland.

In 1996, Airlines of Britain moved Loganair's headquarters to the Isle of Man to share an accounting department with sister company Manx Airlines. Both carriers retained their own accounts and identities.

Loganair had begun operating internal Scottish routes on behalf of British Airways in July 1994. As a BA franchisee, Loganair painted its aircraft in BA colors and began operating as British Airways Express. Though popular in America, franchise arrangements between major carriers and regional feeder airlines were relatively new to Britain, observed the *Sunday Times.*

Acquired by Management in 1997

A group of Loganair managers led by managing director Scott Grier completed a buyout of the company in March 1997. Grier had attempted a similar deal twice in the previous four years. The buyout did not include the carrier's heaviest routes, which former owner British Regional Airlines retained. Loganair continued flying as British Airways Express. Grier, who had first come to the airline in 1975 as an accountant, became the company's chairman and largest shareholder with a 25 percent shareholding that was eventually increased to 70 percent, according to *The Herald.* Former Loganair executive Trevor Bush returned from a job at British Midland to replace Grier as managing director.

The company continued to update its fleet. It began acquiring 34-seat Saab 340 turboprops in 1999 to replace its aging Shorts 360s.

Loganair carried 250,000 passengers in 2001. The company posted a pre-tax profit of £368,664 on turnover of £25 million in the fiscal year to March 31. Scotland's *Business a.m.* noted this was the company's best performance since its 1997 management buyout. Surviving to its fortieth anniversary was another reason for celebration. ''Since we started in 1962, more than 30 airlines have come and gone,'' Scott Grier told *Business a.m.*

In 2002, Loganair's regional network expanded outside of Scotland as it took over feeder routes from British Airways. The routes connected Glasgow and Manchester to destinations in Ireland.

The expanded scheduled meant a dramatic increase in business. Loganair carried 315,000 passengers in 2003 and had a turnover of £30 million. The airline expected to have 585,000 passengers in 2004 while taking in £48 million, as Loganair acquired seven routes from BA's CitiExpress operation. Leases and pilots for four of BA's turboprops were transferred to Loganair, whose BA franchise had been extended another four years, to 2008. In April 2004, Loganair also launched service between Glasgow and Galway, the largest city on Ireland's west coast.

Principal Competitors

EasyJet Airline Company Ltd.; Highland Airways; Ryanair Holdings plc; ScotAirways.

Further Reading

Allan, Richard, ''Low-Cost Strategy Doesn't Work for Us, Says Loganair,'' *Business a.m.* (Scotland), December 3, 2002.

Buxton, James, ''Highland Link by BA and Loganair,'' *Financial Times*, April 25, 1994, p. 16.

——, ''Loganair and Dan-Air Apply for BCal Routes,'' *Financial Times*, November 17, 1987, p. 11.

Calder, Colin, ''Loganair Birthday Marked by Cuts,'' *Sunday Times*, January 30, 1994.

——, ''Loganair in Fresh Battle Against BA,'' *Sunday Times*, April 1, 1990.

——, ''Loganair Posed to Swoop on BA Routes,'' *Sunday Times*, June 16, 1991.

——, ''New Jetstream Takes Off in Record Time,'' *Sunday Times*, November 22, 1992.

Clark, Ron, ''Still Flying High for Scotland,'' *Herald*, February 14, 2004, p. 18.

Clayton, Nick, ''Loganair Buyout Hits Trouble,'' *Sunday Times*, July 10, 1994.

Crump, Eryl, ''On the Beach: A Unique Air Service,'' *Airliner World*, September 2004, pp. 78–80.

Dalton, Alastair, ''Loganair in Major Expansion by Taking over Seven of BA's Routes in Scotland,'' *Scotsman*, November 28, 2003, p. 21.

Doyle, Peter, ''Cheaper Flights Hailed—But There Is a Sting in the Tail,'' *Aberdeen Press & Journal*, December 11, 2003, p. 1.

Dunn, Graham, ''FI2002: Loganair Adds Two More Saab 340s,''*Air Transport Intelligence*, July 24, 2002.

''Get Your Career off to a Flier; Airlines Bring Back Apprentices,'' *Sunday Mail*, June 20, 2004, p. 56.

''The Guardian Has Taken a Look at the Scottish Regional Airline Situation,'' *Guardian*, January 22, 1981, p. 17.

Harrison, Michael, ''Airlines of Britain Expects Turnaround after £12m Loss,'' *Independent* (London), July 15, 1991, p. 20.

''Layoffs at Loganair after Loss of Mail Contracts,'' *Commuter Regional Airline News*, August 17, 1992.

''Loganair Cuts Fares to Attract Passengers,'' *Aberdeen Press & Journal*, June 1, 2004, p. 9.

''Loganair Moves Its Headquarters to the Isle of Man,'' *Herald*, December 16, 1995, p. 9.

''Loganair: Scotland's Airline,'' *Airliner World*, September 2004, p. 81.

McLain, Lynton, ''British Midland Takes over Loganair,'' *Financial Times*, September 24, 1983, p. 3.

Meredith, Mark, ''Fitting Services to the Market,'' *Financial Times*, April 12, 1983.

Murray, Graeme, ''Boost for Airport as New Flights to Galway Unveiled,'' *Evening Times*, April 13, 2004, p. 16.

O'Connell, Dominic, ''Management Buyout of Loganair Finalised,'' *Travel Trade Gazette UK & Ireland*, March 19, 1997, p. 19.

Sarrett, In, ''Carrier Celebrates 25 Years of Service from City of Derry,'' *Belfast News Letter*, April 3, 2004, p. 23.

Stewart, Graeme, ''Exploit European Market, Advises Head of Loganair,'' *Scotsman*, October 30, 1992, p. 5.

Stokes, Rob, ''Loganair Set to Spread Its Wings after Steady Start,'' *Scotland on Sunday*, October 18, 1998.

Taylor, Robert, ''British Airways and Loganair Resist Public Subsidies for Island Flights,'' *Business a.m.* (Scotland), May 22, 2002.

''World's Shortest Flight in for a Bumpy Ride,'' *Herald*, October 28, 2000, p. 3.

—Frederick C. Ingram

MTA Long Island Rail Road

The Long Island Rail Road Company

Jamaica Station
Jamaica, New York 11435-4380
U.S.A.
Telephone: (718) 558-7400
Web site: http://222.mta.nyc.ny.us/lirr

Wholly Owned Subsidiary of Metropolitan Transportation Authority
Founded: 1834
Employees: 6,424
Sales: $372.7 million (2002)
NAIC: 482112 Short Line Railroads

A subsidiary of the Metropolitan Transportation Authority (MTA), The Long Island Rail Road Company (LIRR) is the most traveled commuter railroad in the United States and the oldest in the country to operate under its original name. The LIRR is also the only railroad in America more dependent on passengers than freight. Each workday, the LIRR carries an average of 274,000 passengers on 730 trains. The system stretches from Pennsylvania Station in the heart of Manhattan to the eastern tip of Long Island at Montauk, 120 miles away. All told, the system is composed of 700 miles of track on 11 different branches. In New York City the LIRR connects to MTA buses and subways to accommodate the hundreds of thousands of Long Island residents that commute into the city for work. The LIRR has been the source of humor over the years, especially in the 1970s, due to neglect that caused excessive delays and breakdowns. The line also has been the site of tragedy, as evidenced by the 1993 shooting spree that occurred on one of its trains, leaving six people dead and 19 wounded.

One of the Early American Railroads in the 1800s

The LIRR was chartered by the State of New York on April 24, 1834, less than ten years after the first railroad in the world was started in Great Britain. France followed suit in 1828, Austria in 1829, and in the United States the first true railroad, the Baltimore and Ohio, opened in 1830. The LIRR was intended to form part of a rail and ferry combination that would transport passengers from New York City to Boston. At the time, railroad engineers declared that building a railroad from New York to Boston was impossible because of the hills of southern Connecticut. Under the LIRR scheme, passengers would travel by train to Greenport on Long Island's North Shore, where they would then travel by ferry to Stonington, Connecticut, the terminus of the Old Colony Railroad, to pick up a train for the final leg to Boston by way of Providence. In fact, this rail-ferry connection was part of an all-rail route that stretched from Charleston, South Carolina, to Boston.

The first railroad chartered on Long Island was actually the Brooklyn and Jamaica Railroad in 1832. Within two years a ten-mile track from Brooklyn to the Long Island town of Jamaica was completed. The LIRR charter allowed the LIRR to absorb the Brooklyn and Jamaica road, which it did in 1836 by signing a 45-year lease. In 1836 the LIRR began using the line, even as it began laying new track down the center of Long Island where the terrain was more level. Because the purpose was to move people from Manhattan to the North Shore ferry, little thought was given to serving the Long Island population by building the road closer to population centers, which lay on the north and south shores and not in the center of the island. The LIRR tracks reached Hicksville in 1837, Farmingdale in 1841, Deep Park in 1842, Yaphank in 1843, and finally Greenport in 1844. It was on July 27, 1844, that the first train traveled the length of the line, from Brooklyn to Greenport, and launched the much anticipated "all rail" line to Boston. The trip took three and a half hours. More important, the trip from New York to Boston, which took 16 hours by steamer, was cut in half by using the LIRR link.

The LIRR prospered for several years carrying passengers and mail from Brooklyn to Greenport on their way to Boston. By 1850 the road operated 15 locomotives, 22 passenger coaches, 12 mail and baggage cars, and 128 freight cars. Five trains ran each day, making two stops for fuel and water. The Brooklyn to Greenport passenger fare was $1.75, $2 for the Boston Express. But the "all rail" dream of the LIRR came to an end in 1850 when a true all-rail line was built from New York to Boston through the hills of southern Connecticut, proving the engineers wrong. The Boston business evaporated overnight, and it appeared that LIRR investors had a white elephant on their hands.

Company Perspectives:

Always maintaining close ties to the region it serves, the growth of the Railroad went hand-in-hand with the growth of Long Island as the thriving center of suburban life it is today.

Ownership of the LIRR was passed onto receivers and new management tried to make the best of a poor situation.

Second Half of the 1800s: Struggling to Find Its Place

Because the island was scarcely populated, and most of the people who lived there were located far from the railroad, the LIRR had no choice but to help grow Long Island in order to build up traffic while extending lines to the north and south communities. Other railroad companies were launched to fill in the gaps on Long Island, and the LIRR either leased these lines or bought them outright. The situation also was complicated by the City of Brooklyn banning steam locomotives from operating within its limits, forcing the LIRR to build a terminal in Hunter's Point, now Long Island City. The most western part of Long Island, Brooklyn, had 90 percent of the island's population, so that being denied a terminal was a major setback for the railroad. Starting in 1860, LIRR's major trains ended their journeys at Hunter's Point, where ferries made connections to 34th Street in Manhattan. Ten years later Brooklyn would relent, but by then it was too late—the line that had run from Flatbush Avenue to the East River ferry terminal had been abandoned and the LIRR would never do significant business in Brooklyn. There would be a stop where Flatbush and Atlantic Avenues converged, but essentially LIRR was linked to Manhattan, and it was the trolley cars and the subway system that emerged in the early years of the 20th century that would build the rail lines that served Brooklyn.

In the populated areas where it did operate, the LIRR met with increasing competition from a number of new lines, including the Flushing and North Side Railroad owned by Conrad Poppenhusen. Because there was not enough business to support all of these lines, they were either abandoned or bought out by the survivors. In 1976 Poppenhusen bought out the LIRR, and he was able to consolidate all the railroad operations on Long Island for the first time since the 1850s. But fixed costs proved too high and the LIRR took on too much debt, so that in 1879 it again went into receivership, taken over by its lender, Drexel, Morgan & Co.

In December 1880, Drexel, Morgan sold the LIRR to Austin Corbin and a group of Boston and London investors, the latter of which were interested in building a number of major resort hotels on Long Island and wanted the railroad to service them. Corbin had made a success of the Philadelphia & Reading Railroad, and he also had the backing of the most powerful financier of the era, J.P. Morgan. Under Corbin's leadership over the next 17 years the LIRR enjoyed something of a golden era. The line had fallen into disrepair, prompting wags of the period to call the LIRR "a right of way and two streaks of rust." Not only did Corbin make sure that the roadbeds and right-of-ways were made safe and iron rails replaced with steel, he also bought more powerful locomotives and new passenger cars. He had the new Westinghouse air brakes installed and adopted an improved signaling system. In addition, he filled out the LIRR's network of track. In 1881 the company built the Patchogue to Eastport link and a year later bought the New York, Brooklyn and Manhattan Beach Railroad. Other lines built during his tenure included Locust Valley to Oyster Bay in 1889, Bridgehampton to Montauk and Port Jefferson to Wading River in 1895, and Great Neck to Port Washington in 1898. Corbin died on June 4, 1896. He had done much to improve the LIRR, but he failed to achieve his dream for the railroad, akin to the one that launched the line in the first place. Corbin wanted to build a great international port at the eastern end of Long Island and use the LIRR to transport passengers bound by ship to England. In this way, some 4 to 12 hours could be saved. Unfortunately, he was unable to convince the U.S. Congress to pay for the necessary harbor improvements.

In 1900 the Pennsylvania Railroad (PRR) acquired the LIRR to use as a major link in its extensive network of railroad lines, connecting the resorts and Long Island beaches and the residential sections of Long Island to the cities of New Jersey. Moreover the PRR wanted to connect the 1.5 million people who lived in Queens and Brooklyn to the rest of the United States. With PRR's backing, the LIRR invested liberally on improvements. In 1905 the first third-rail electric service began. In 1907 the Flatbush terminal at Atlantic Avenue opened. From 1903 to 1910 construction of the East River Tunnels were completed into Manhattan. Also in 1910 the Holban Yards were completed after five years of labor. More important, Pennsylvania Station opened in Manhattan in 1910, the crown jewel of the Pennsylvania Railroad, connected to Long Island by the East River Tunnels and to New Jersey by Hudson River tunnels, the construction of which was one of the largest railway projects in history as well as one of the world's greatest engineering accomplishments. Pennsylvania Station also would become, in essence, the home of the LIRR. Of today's 730 daily trains, 500 originate or terminate at the new Pennsylvania Station. (The original ornate facility was torn down in the 1960s, despite civic protests, leading to the landmark preservation movement in New York City.) The other major LIRR station, the Jamaica Station, was built from 1910 to 1913.

The LIRR grew steadily during the first two decades under PRR control. In 1905 it accommodated 18 million passengers and hauled nearly 2.8 million tons of freight, while in 1923 the number of passengers increased to more than 86 million and the amount of freight approached 8 million tons. But already another mode of transportation was growing rapidly and preparing to eclipse the usage of the railroad: the automobile.

Postwar Decline in Rail Usage

Railroad usage reached it culmination during World War II. Cars and trucks had begun to cut into the business of the railroad, but with wartime rationing limiting the number of tires and amount of gas available to the public, the railroads were relied on more than ever to move war materials and commercial freight, as well as soldiers and everyday passengers. With the end of the war and a booming economy that emerged in the late 1940s, however, Americans moved to the suburbs and bought cars at an accelerated pace. The result was a severe drop in rail

Key Dates:

1834: Long Island Rail Road is chartered by New York State.
1844: The entire line is completed.
1900: Pennsylvania Railroad acquires the line.
1910: Pennsylvania Station opens.
1966: New York State acquires LIRR.
1968: Metropolitan Transportation Authority begins running LIRR.
1990: Industry veteran charles Hoppe is hired as president of LIRR.
1993: LIRR suffers the greatest tragedy of its history when a shooting spree on a train during evening rush leaves six people dead and 19 wounded.
2002: The first M-7 electric cars enter service.

usage across the country. With the rise of a national highway system in the 1950s, a Cold War defense initiative, freight also would be transported increasingly by truck. The LIRR countered with improvements like air-conditioned cars, which first went into service in 1955. It also upgraded its locomotives, as the last of the steam engines also were retired in 1955.

The LIRR remained a vital part of the transportation system of Long Island, prompting the state of New York to acquire the line from PRR in 1966. Two years later the MTA, which had been established in 1965 as the Metropolitan Commuter Transportation Authority, turned over the running of the LIRR. Over the next 20 years the system would go electric, but this and other improvements were costly and took time to implement. In the meanwhile, the LIRR deteriorated on a number of fronts. Passengers were forced to endure constant delays, resulting in frayed tempers and contention interactions with train personnel. The LIRR's reputation was such that it became the butt of jokes from Johnny Carson (''Tonight Show'') and countless comedians.

In the early 1980s the MTA began investing in capital improvements in the LIRR to bring the line into good repair. But the LIRR remained a troubled line, one that faced ''a peculiar set of circumstances,'' in the words of *Long Island Business News* in a 1990 profile: ''It has a monopoly on a vital business in a lucrative landlocked area, but its control by a net of bureaucratic rules and regulations severely limits its ability to perform as a profitable business. . . . The railroad is buckling under recessional economic times that are causing ridership to decline and its costs to surge.'' Moreover, the LIRR's freight system declined steadily, losing 58 percent of its business from 1975 to 1990. It also lost much of its federal funding during this period, and almost all of its top executives were ultimately purged, leaving the line in a perilous state. In 1990 railroad industry veteran Charles Hoppe, who brought with him global experience, was hired as the president of the LIRR.

Hoppe was credited with removing the homeless from Pennsylvania Station in a sensitive manner. He also oversaw the upgrading of 15 important stations, making them fully accessible to the disabled. Hoppe made great strides in revitalizing the freight business, which lost money in 1991 but turned a profit in 1992. On-time performance improved and funding was arranged to replace an aging fleet of diesel locomotives with new diesels and add 114 bi-level coaches. Moreover, he oversaw the $190 million on-budget and on-time renovation of the LIRR terminal at Pennsylvania Station. But also during his watch, the LIRR suffered the greatest tragedy in its history. On December 7, 1993, a man named Colin Ferguson calmly walked through an evening rush hour train, firing a gun at passengers, only stopping when he had depleted his cache of 30 bullets and was subdued by three passengers. He left six people dead and another 19 wounded. His trial would become an international sensation, due in large part to his decision to defend himself. After three weeks of testimony and often bizarre cross-examination, followed by ten hours of deliberations, the jury in February 1995 found him guilty on six counts of second-degree murder and 19 counts of attempted murder.

In light of the Colin Ferguson murder case, the events that led to Hoppe's resignation from his post at the LIRR were trivial. In February 1994 New York City and Long Island was hit with a major blizzard that left thousands of LIRR riders stranded as the line was unable to cope with the conditions and ceased to function. Unfortunately for Hoppe, he was out of town attending a labor relations meeting in Washington, D.C., and was unable to return to New York to personally deal with the problem because of an ice storm. He chose instead to handle the situation by telephone from his Virginia home. In the media feeding frenzy that ensued, he became the ready target for public rage, blamed personally for the paralysis that struck the system. Ironically, before he resigned in July 1994, Hoppe developed new snow emergency plans to prevent a recurrence of what had happened that winter.

After Hoppe's departure, the LIRR continued to upgrade its system. The last of the 1950s-era diesel locomotives was retired in 1999, and in 2002 the first M-7 electric cars came into service. The line's on-time performance also improved significantly. Going forward, the LIRR planned to fill out its locomotive fleet with the M-7 cars. A new Jamaica hub was to be added, as was a new Atlantic Terminal in Brooklyn. In addition, a long cherished plan to gain access to Manhattan's east side was in the works. LIRR trains would now be able to use Grand Central Station, thus relieving congestion at Pennsylvania Station, which was designed to accommodate 200,000 passengers but now serviced 500,000 each day. Steps were taken to build a new Pennsylvania Station across the street. In any event, the use of Manhattan's two major train stations would mark a new and promising era in the history of the LIRR.

Further Reading

Demery, Paul, ''The Long and Short of the LI Rail Road,'' *Long Island Business News,* November 26, 1990, p. 23.
Jochum, Glenn, ''LIRR's Human Face: The Hoppe Years,'' *Long Island Business News,* August 22, 1994, p. 29.
McQuiston, John T., ''Jury Finds Ferguson Guilty of Slayings on the L.I.R.R.,'' *New York Times,* February 18, 1995, p. A1.
Reifschneider, Felix, ''Felix Reifschneider's 1925 Long Island Rail Road History,'' *The Third Rail,* April 2001.
Smith, M.H., *Early History of the Long Island Railroad, 1834–1900,* Uniondale, Long Island: Salisbury Printers, 1958.

—Ed Dinger

MABUCHI MOTOR

Mabuchi Motor Co. Ltd.

430 Matsuhidai
Matsudo
270-2280
Japan
Telephone: +81 47 384 1111
Fax: +81 47 389 5299
Web site: http://www.mabuchi-motor.co.jp

Public Company
Incorporated: 1954
Employees: 51,796
Sales: ¥ 105.74 billion ($983.80 million) (2003)
Stock Exchanges: Tokyo
Ticker Symbol: 6592
NAIC: 335312 Motor and Generator Manufacturing

Mabuchi Motor Co. Ltd. is the world's leading manufacturer of small electric motors, with a global market share of more than 50 percent. The company designs and manufactures a broad range of motors for the audiovisual, telecommunications, automotive, office equipment, precision instrument, home appliance, and industrial equipment industries. The company's motors—ranging from tiny to miniscule—are literally ubiquitous, finding applications in such products as DVD players, CD players, video cameras, VCRs, and the like; portable telephones and pagers; automobile features such as window lifters, rearview mirror actuators and door lock mechanisms, cruise controls, antenna lifters, navigation systems, and dozens of others; computers and related devices, such as printers, fax machines, copiers, computer cameras, CD-ROM and DVD-ROM drives, and other computer components and peripherals; appliances such as electric toothbrushes, vacuum cleaners, hair dryers, clippers, and shavers, as well as power tools such as drills, sanders, grinders, and the like; and a wide variety of toys—including model slot-car racers. Founded in 1954 from technology developed by Kenichi Mabuchi, the company has long focused its manufacturing operations outside of Japan, with production facilities centered on China, Taiwan, Malaysia, Singapore, Vietnam, and Hong Kong. Mabuchi is listed on the Tokyo Stock Exchange but remains controlled by the Mabuchi family, including the founder and his younger brother and current chairman Takaichi Mabuchi.

Making Things Move in the 1950s

Kenichi Mabuchi founded a research institute, Kansai Rika Kenjyusho, in 1946 and in no small way changed the world. Mabuchi began work on developing a miniaturized, electrically powered motor, and by 1947 had succeeded in designing a small horseshoe-shaped magnet-driven motor capable of being powered by both electricity and batteries. Mabuchi's invention was to have an enormous impact on virtually every industry. One of the earliest markets for the Mabuchi motor came from the toy industry. Whereas toys had long been driven by rubber bands and wind-up spring motors, they could now be battery operated—and seem to run forever.

Mabuchi continued developing and improving his motor design over the next several years. By the early 1950s, with the motor perfected, Mabuchi launched his own company, Tokyo Science Industrial Co. Ltd. Financial backing for the new company was provided through a ¥1 million loan from a Japanese toy maker. Tokyo Science's initial goal was to begin the manufacture of toys, models, appliances, and other end products, in addition to its motor production. In support of that effort, the company established a subsidiary, Japan Science and Industry Co. Ltd., in 1955.

Yet motors quickly became the company's primary focus. A major step forward in the later Mabuchi Motor's growth came in 1955 as well, when Mabuchi developed an automatic winding machine, used for wrapping the motors' copper wire armature. The new machine enabled Mabuchi to achieve a significant boost in production capacity. Another significant moment in the company's history came in 1958 with the launch of a new motor based on a ferrite magnet. The new material permitted still smaller, more lightweight motor designs.

By then, Mabuchi had established a dedicated export sales business, Mabuchi Shoji Co., which began operations in 1957. In 1959, the two earlier companies were merged together, at first renamed as Mabuchi Industrial Co., but then becoming Tokyo Science Co. Ltd. The development of the company's

Company Perspectives:

In the 21st century, a time when the field of competition will change dramatically, Mabuchi Motor promises to solidify our value as a corporation and become a staple enterprise to the world.

next generation of motors, the miniature, high-precision RM and FM types, in 1960, marked the début of the company's growth into the world's leading small electric motor manufacturer. The company now began supplying a wider variety of customers. In addition to the toy industry, Mabuchi began supplying motors to audio equipment manufacturers—especially makers of turntables and reel tape machines—and watch and clock manufacturers.

In 1962, Mabuchi built a new factory in Tatabayashi in order to meet the demand. The following year, the company launched its new, powerful FT motor type—which quickly revolutionized the slot-car racing market. Another high-power motor, the RS, launched in 1963, enabled the company to enter the market for home appliances as well.

The following year, Mabuchi took the unusual step of opening a production plant in Hong Kong, then a source of ready, cheap labor. As such, the company was able to cut manufacturing costs by as much as two-thirds. Yet Mabuchi continued to invest in its production capacity in Japan, building a new factory in Matsudo City, near Tokyo, in 1965. In that year, also, the company opened a sales office in the United States, which emerged as one of Mabuchi's most important markets.

Mabuchi released several more successful motor designs through the late 1960s, including the compact RE type, the low-cost FA type, and a ''submarine'' motor for the toy and hobby market. The company also entered the European market, establishing a sales subsidiary in Frankfurt, Germany in 1969.

Public Offering in the 1980s

Mabuchi continued building up its international manufacturing base through the 1970s and into the 1980s. The company turned next to Taiwan, founding Mabuchi Taiwan Co. in Taipei in 1969 in a 50–50 partnership. That company quickly began construction of a new, modern facility, which opened in 1973. By then, Mabuchi had officially changed its name, to Mabuchi Motor Co. Ltd., in 1971. That year, also, the company moved into a new headquarters in Matsudo City, combining its production and sales operations. In 1972, the company created a new company, Mabuchi World Trade Co, combining its domestic and export sales divisions.

During the 1970s, Mabuchi expanded its operations to include the production of high-precision machine tools, needed for its motor production. The company also began producing more of its components, including motor shafts. For this, the company established a new subsidiary, Mabuchi Precision Industries, in 1974.

The 1970s also were marked by a rapid expansion of the company's motor technologies into a variety of new areas. In 1974, the company introduced a new motor for the model airplane market. More significant was its launch of a motor with built-in governor, which permitted the development of new home audio and electronics products, such as cassette decks and eight-track tape players. The release of a geared motor in 1975 brought the company a new range of customers among vending machine manufacturers, among others. That same year, Mabuchi launched its first automobile mirror motors, marking the company's entry into the automotive market. Mabuchi also became an early entrant in the promising market for videocassette recorders, developing its first motors for those appliances in 1980. Similarly, the following year, the company's development of an electric drill motor prompted its full-scale entry into the market for power tools and industrial equipment.

The rising costs of business in Japan led the company to increase its investment in Hong Kong in the mid-1970s, with the construction of a new production plant in Tsuen Wan in 1976. The company also built a new factory in Taiwan, in Hukou, in 1978. The following year, in order to respond to dramatic increases in demand, Mabuchi built a third plant in Taiwan, in Kaohsiung. Part of the driving force behind the rising demand was the company's decision to establish a dedicated local sales and service subsidiary, Mabuchi Motor America, in the United States in 1977.

Mabuchi constructed a new factory in Katsushika, Tokyo in 1982, and built a new factory as well as expanded its existing Hukou plant, in Taiwan in 1984, in order to keep pace with the surging demand for its motors worldwide. In 1984, also, Mabuchi made its first move into the public market, listing its shares on the Tokyo over-the-counter market. Two years later, Mabuchi joined the Tokyo Stock Exchange with a full listing on the exchange's secondary market. Just two years after that, Mabuchi's stock moved to a listing on the primary board. By then, the company's sales neared $320 million, producing net profits of $45 million. The company's production totaled more than 600 million motors per year. Kenichi Mabuchi, then entering his 70s, had taken on the role of company chairman, while younger brother Taikaichi guided the company as president.

The late 1980s marked a significant shift in Mabuchi's manufacturing focus. The company opened its first processing facility in mainland China, in Guangdong in 1986, becoming one of the first Japanese manufacturers to shift part of its production there. One year later, the company became the first Japanese company to set up a fully owned subsidiary in China, Mabuchi Motor Dalian Ltd. The company opened a second subsidiary in China in Shenzhen the following year, to produce machine tools and provide maintenance services for its main Guangdong subsidiary.

Mabuchi turned its attention toward expansion in the fast-growing ASEAN region as well. In 1989, the company opened a manufacturing subsidiary in Malaysia, following by a subsidiary in Singapore. These moves helped the company shift the largest part of its manufacturing base outside of Japan. By the early 1990s, the company already operated ten manufacturing sites overseas, and by the beginning of the next decade, fully 98 percent of the company's production took place outside of Japan. In this way, Mabuchi was able to slash operating costs by as much as two-thirds, and avoid the worst effects of the rapid inflation of the Japanese yen.

Key Dates:

1946: Kenichi Mabuchi founds the research center Kansai Rika Kenkyusho to develop small electric motors.
1954: Tokyo Science Industrial Co. is created to produce electric motors.
1955: The company builds an automatic winding machine, enabling large-scale production.
1962: The company builds a new factory in Tatebayashi.
1964: The company builds its first foreign manufacturing plant in Hong Kong.
1969: The company invests in its first manufacturing plant in Taiwan.
1971: The company changes its name to Mabuchi Motor Co. Ltd.
1977: The Mabuchi Motor America Corp. is founded in the United States.
1984: The company lists stock on the Tokyo Stock Exchange's over-the-counter market.
1986: The company moves its shares to the Tokyo secondary market; its first production and processing plant in China is opened.
1988: The company's shares are listed on the Tokyo main board.
1989: The company launches a manufacturing joint venture in Malaysia and a subsidiary in Singapore.
1993: A European sales subsidiary is established in Frankfurt, Germany.
1996: The company establishes a manufacturing subsidiary in Vietnam.
2004: Mabuchi controls 54 percent of the world market for small electric motors.

At the same time, Mabuchi strengthened its sales and marketing operations in the West. After opening a new sales office in Detroit in 1989, the company shifted its U.S. subsidiary's headquarters to that city in 1997. Meanwhile, Mabuchi installed a full subsidiary to support its European sales in Frankfurt, Germany, replacing the representative office originally opened there.

Global Leader for the New Century

China's position as Mabuchi's primary manufacturing base was reinforced through the late 1990s and into the 2000s with a series of new plant openings, including in Wafangian and Jiangsu in 1994, and a new sales office in Shanghai in 2002. The company completed a new bearings factory in Dalian in 2003, as part of its effort to gain tighter control of its components needs. In the meantime, Mabuchi continued to seek new manufacturing opportunities in the greater Southeast Asia region. In 1996, the company entered Vietnam, establishing a wholly owned manufacturing operation there.

Mabuchi continued to expand its range of operations through new product development as well. In the mid-1990s, the company began developing motors for pagers. That activity led to the development of motors for portable telephones in 2001. In 2002, the company strengthened its operations in the automotive industry with the launch of a new power unit motor department dedicated to developing actuator applications. The following year, Mabuchi moved into the optical disk segment with the launch of a new class of brushless motors for CD and DVD players.

By 2004, Mabuchi's sales had topped ¥105 billion ($983 million). The company celebrated its 50th anniversary as the world leader in small electric motors, with a global market share of more than 50 percent. The company's history of innovation and strategic expansion underscored its growth prospects for the new century.

Principal Subsidiaries

Dongguan Mabuchi Motor Equipment Co., Ltd. (China); Mabuchi Industry Co. Ltd. (China); Mabuchi Industry Co. Ltd. (Hong Kong); Mabuchi Motor (Europe) Gmbh (Germany); Mabuchi Motor (Jiangsu) Co., Ltd. (China; 88%); Mabuchi Motor (Malaysia) Sdn. Bhd. (86%); Mabuchi Motor (Shanghai) Co., Ltd.; Mabuchi Motor (Singapore) Pte. Ltd.; Mabuchi Motor America Corp. (U.S.A.); Mabuchi Motor Taiwan Ltd.; Mabuchi Motor Vietnam Ltd.; Mabuchi Motor Wafangdian Ltd. (China); Mabuchi Precision Industries Hong Kong Ltd.; Mabuchi Precision Industries Ltd.; Mabuchi World Trade Co. (Malaysia).

Principal Competitors

VA Technologie AG; ABB Inc.; Siemens AG; Elgin Maquinas S.A.; Elektrodvigatel Plant; Elma EAD; United Technologies Kft.; Rockwell Automation Inc.

Further Reading

Do Rosario, Louise, and Hamish McDonald, "Offshore Revolution," *Far Eastern Economic Review,* February 13, 1992, p. 46.

"Japan's Mabuchi to Buy Back 5.74% of Own Shares," *Reuters,* May 26, 2004.

Katayama, Hiroko, "Making It Abroad," *Forbes,* November 30, 1987, p. 240.

Konaga, Yoko, "Mabuchi Motor a Prime Example of How to Do Business in Asia," *Tokyo Business Today,* February 1994, p. 26.

"Mabuchi Motor Ready to Post Highest Profits," *Comline Transportation,* February 20, 1998.

"Mabuchi Ups Dividend Sharply Despite 7% Profit Fall in FY 2003," *Japan Weekly,* February 23, 2004.

"Mabuchi Motor Group Earnings Down in Fiscal Year to Dec. 31," *Japan Weekly Monitor,* February 18, 2002.

"Profits Rise for Japan's Mabuchi Motor," *Knight Ridder/Tribune Business News,* August 19, 2003.

—M.L. Cohen

MacGregor Golf Company

1000 Pecan Grove Drive
Albany, Georgia 31701
U.S.A.
Telephone: (229) 420-7000
Toll Free: (800) 841-4358
Fax: (800) 455-1220
Web site: http://www.macgregorgolf.com

Wholly-Owned Subsidiary of The Parkside Group
Founded: 1897
Employees: 200 (est.)
Sales: $50 million (est.)
NAIC: 339920 Sporting and Athletic Goods Manufacturing

MacGregor Golf Company makes golf clubs, balls, bags, clothing, and accessories, with a focus on premium quality equipment. The firm was once the highest-regarded golf club maker in the world, but in recent years has suffered from repeated ownership and management turnover. CEO Barry Schneider's Parkside Group now owns the company, and he has pledged a return to form during his tenure.

19th Century Beginnings

MacGregor Golf Company's origins date to the end of the 19th century and a company called Crawford, MacGregor and Canby, which manufactured wooden shoe lasts in Dayton, Ohio. The firm, which had been founded in 1822 as the Dayton Last Company, was co-owned by the Crawford brothers, John MacGregor, and Edward Canby. On a trip to Europe, Canby was introduced to the sport of golf, which had originated there and was especially popular in Scotland. Sensing a business opportunity if it became popular in the United States, he put his company's woodworking expertise to use and began manufacturing golf clubs with persimmon wood heads and hickory shafts.

Because much of the firm's output would initially be shipped to Great Britain, the brand was given the Scottish-sounding name "J. MacGregor," after Canby's partner. At a time when most club heads were carved by hand, the company took advantage of the lathe copying process with which it made shoe lasts, where a replica of a metal original was mechanically carved in wood, and within a few years the firm was producing 100,000 clubs per year. Over time, Canby became sole owner of the company.

In the 1920s MacGregor was one of the first to offer steel-shafted clubs, and 1927 saw the first "Harmonized" club set, which included both wood and steel shafts. In the 1930s, the company's name was officially changed to MacGregor Golf Co., and the "J." was dropped. That decade saw a number of innovations under the leadership of Toney Penna, who worked with such legendary players as Ben Hogan and Byron Nelson to create new club designs. Successes of the era included the "Neutralizer," a wooden dowel of spring hickory that was inserted in the shaft where it joined the head of the club, and a grip made of rubber and cord—previous ones had been made of leather. This "All-Weather" grip was soon adopted by most of the game's top players. MacGregor later created a soft rubber grip called the "Tri-Tac," which went on to be even more popular. Another innovation of the period, the "Four-Way Roll," improved the performance of wooden clubs by softening the edges of the club face, yielding a better result from off-center shots.

Industry Leadership in the 1940s

By the 1940s MacGregor had become the sport's dominant club maker, with more than half of the players in Professional Golf Association (PGA) events using its clubs. Many top players of the era also signed on to the company's Advisory Staff. By now the firm had come under the control of Charles H. Rickey, who was serving as president. Tragically, in May 1945 he was killed in an automobile accident, after which his place was taken by Henry P. Cowen.

The late 1940s saw MacGregor find success with the Tommy Armour line, which outsold all other professional clubs on the market. In 1949 the company introduced its first matching set of four "woods" (for long shots) and nine "irons" (for shorter shots). The so-called MT line was sold in a special display box which housed the 13 clubs as a single unit. Included with the irons was a sand wedge, the first time this type of club had been sold as part of a set. The MT line was enthusiastically accepted by golfers, and was credited with changing the way clubs were marketed from that point forward.

Despite a drop in the number of golf courses immediately following World War II (when some were converted to housing

Company Perspectives:

All great companies ''rewrite the rules'' in some way which requires dedicated leadership, that through commitment, talent, and ''will'' takes people where they would otherwise not go. Such leadership and commitment is MacGregor's collective priority for 2004 and beyond. Not just with big customers, not just on important occasions . . . MacGregor strives to exemplify this type of inspired leadership every single day in everything that we do, large and small. In practical terms, this means we will continue to innovate with ideas that are new and different. We will continue to develop patented technologies and equipment that is easy-to-hit, forgiving and high performing. We will strive to deliver to golfers of every level handicap tangible performance and forgiveness advantages, not marketing hype. And we will only make equipment for which we are unbelievably proud.

developments), the post-war years saw the public at large embrace golf as never before. By 1952 MacGregor's sales had increased eightfold from a decade earlier.

In the 1950s MacGregor became one of the first golf firms to offer sponsorship to African-American professionals, at a time when the PGA had a ''Caucasians only'' clause in its constitution (which was not removed until 1961). Company president Bob Rickey was a nephew of the Brooklyn Dodgers' Branch Rickey, who had broken baseball's color barrier in 1947 by hiring Jackie Robinson. During the decade MacGregor also introduced the popular ''Eye-O-Matic'' woods, which featured a red and white fiber insert on the club face that helped visually frame its ''sweet spot.''

Sale to Brunswick in 1967

In 1967 the Rickey family sold MacGregor to Brunswick Corporation. The sporting goods firm held onto the company until 1979, when it was sold to retailer Wickes Corporation of San Diego, whose chairman, E.L. McNeely, was reportedly an avid golfer. In 1982, with Wickes strapped for cash, Jack Nicklaus and a MacGregor executive led a group that bought controlling interest in the company for $17 million. Nicklaus was one of the game's legends, and had endorsed MacGregor for nearly 20 years.

Once in charge of the company, Nicklaus poured himself into improving it. The firm had been in a slump since the 1960s, both creatively and financially, and he involved himself in all aspects of the operation, helping bring MacGregor back into the black for the first time in 26 years.

In 1984 the company sold a 75 percent stake in a Japanese subsidiary it had launched in 1979 to whisky distiller Suntory, and by 1986 its annual sales stood at a reported $39 million. That year, when Nicklaus used a new MacGregor putter to win golf's prestigious Masters tournament, the company took orders for 5,000 of the clubs before noon the next business day.

In late 1986, Nicklaus and his partners sold 80 percent of MacGregor to Amer-Yhtymae OY, a Finnish company with holdings in consumer products, sporting goods, and tobacco. The price was a reported $30 million. MacGregor was now operating subsidiaries in Ireland, Britain, and Hong Kong, along with the Suntory-owned Japanese affiliate. Three years after acquiring the company, Amer Sport bought major American sporting goods firm Wilson for $200 million. MacGregor's Finnish parent now began looking to boost sales by remaking the firm in the more broad-based Wilson mold, and introduced less-expensive lines of clubs in pursuit of mass sales.

In November 1991 David M. Gibbons was named president and chief operating officer of MacGregor, replacing Robert Forbush who had held the job for just over a year. It was hinted that the firm would be merged into Wilson, but the plan was not carried out. MacGregor, now headquartered in Albany, Georgia, would remain there, with its corporate offices moved to that location from North Palm Beach, Florida.

Nicklaus Sells Stake in 1992

In January 1992 Jack Nicklaus sold his remaining 20 percent stake in MacGregor to Amer Sport. He was reportedly frustrated with the direction the company had been taking, and announced plans to form a club manufacturer of his own through his Golden Bear International firm.

The year 1992 also saw MacGregor introduce the new T920 club, a ''wood'' made of titanium metal that was reportedly the first golf club designed with the help of a computer. Featuring an oversized head and a graphite shaft, a single club was priced at $500. The company also licensed the right to make golf pull carts and golf gloves to unrelated firm MacGregor Sports and Fitness, Inc. during the year.

The mid-1990s saw MacGregor's financial picture deteriorate. Amer put out word that it would consider any offers to buy, while also again looking at the possibility of combining its operations with Wilson or even shutting the company down. In October 1996 it was announced that MacGregor would be sold to Masters International Ltd. of the United Kingdom and a consortium of investors for $19.6 million. The deal was finalized early the next year, after which William Marsh, formerly of the Breco Group of Companies, was named president and CEO.

In 1997, to celebrate its 100th anniversary, MacGregor brought out limited edition Centennial reproductions of some of its most celebrated club designs, consulting with retired company craftsmen to get the details right. New models were introduced under the Excentury name, including a titanium wood that was available with four different shafts, priced at between $772 and $947. The company also offered a trade-in deal in which golfers could get a discount on new MacGregor clubs if they brought in an old set, which the company would donate to youth organizations.

At the same time that it was announcing these promotions, MacGregor's new owners were formulating aggressive plans to revitalize the brand, which included a $10–15 million ad campaign, almost ten times what had been spent annually in recent years. In addition to clubs, the company was also marketing golf bags, balls, Gore-Tex outerwear, and accessories.

Sale to Parkside Group in 1998

In August 1998, however, MacGregor was again sold, this time for a reported $42 million. The buyer was The Parkside

Key Dates:

1897: Crawford, MacGregor, and Canby begin making wooden golf clubs.
1920s: Introduction of steel-shafted clubs, matched sets.
1930s: Name of company changed to MacGregor Golf Co.
1940s: MacGregor's Tommy Armour line becomes top-selling club; MT line debuts.
1950s: Eye-O-Matic clubs are introduced.
1967: Brunswick Corporation buys MacGregor.
1979: Brunswick sells company to Wickes Corporation.
1982: Jack Nicklaus-led group buys control of the firm.
1984: Majority stake in Japanese subsidiary is sold to Suntory.
1986: Finnish conglomerate Amer Sport buys MacGregor.
1997: Sale to consortium led by Masters International of the United Kingdom.
1999: Barry Schneider's Parkside Group buys the company.
2003: MacGregor buys back Japanese subsidiary and acquires Bobby Grace Putters.

Group, a newly-formed investment firm headed by Barry Schneider, who took the position of MacGregor's chairman. Schneider had previously run floor covering distributor MSA Industries, which he had sold to DuPont in 1997. After the sale William Marsh continued in the roles of president and CEO of the company, which now employed 200 and had estimated annual sales of $50 million.

In March 1999 MacGregor's first television ads since the mid-'90s were run on The Golf Channel, complemented by print ads in several leading golf magazines. They were aimed at weekend golfers, and used light humor to tout the new line of Tourney clubs. Since the sale to Parkside, the company's product line had been almost completely revamped to emphasize classic, understated good looks and feel. Offerings ranged from sets of irons for under $1,000 to the one-of-a-kind Tourney Forged Personals, unique to each player, which were priced at $5,000. The company's low-end lines were simultaneously phased out in a bid to help re-position the brand as a premium product.

The fall of 1999 saw MacGregor switch ad agencies, the eighth such change in the previous 15 years. New television ads debuted in early 2000, and featured more humor, a rock music soundtrack, and an emphasis on the hand craftsmanship of the firm's clubs.

In July 2000 the company was once again put up for sale, but this time there were no takers. During that year and into 2001, MacGregor's advertising spending was curtailed, and in April 2001 a new president, John McNulty, was named. He had previously served as vice-president of marketing at Brunswick.

After spending just over $1 million on advertising in 2001, which saw the worsening U.S. economy hit makers of luxury goods hard, the firm decided to boost its ad spending to $10 million in 2002. In conjunction with this move, owner and now CEO Barry Schneider published an open letter in several sports publications that addressed the firm's problems and laid out his plans for the future. The company was now working on grassroots efforts such as in-store marketing, sponsoring college golf teams, holding 1,200 demonstration days nationwide, and boosting its presence on the PGA tour and with golf pros at clubs. 2002 also saw the firm name a new president, Dana Shertz, who had previously worked for industry leader Callaway Golf.

In the fall of 2003, MacGregor bought back control of MacGregor Golf Japan from Suntory. The profitable Japanese unit had successfully marketed its own MAC TEC brand of clubs since 1992, which the parent company now planned to sell worldwide. The lower-priced line was manufactured in China, and would be modified to meet U.S. golf rules before its introduction there in early 2005. The fall also saw the acquisition of Bobby Grace Putters, whose products would henceforth be made in MacGregor's Albany, Georgia plant.

After more than 100 years, MacGregor Golf Company was seeking to build on the legacy of its storied past to create a profitable future. With the commitment of owner and CEO Barry Schneider to turning the company around, hopes were high that its position of industry leadership could be restored.

Principal Subsidiaries

MacGregor Golf (U.K.) Ltd.; MacGregor Golf Japan.

Principal Competitors

Callaway Golf Company; Nike, Inc.; Acushnet Company; Karsten Manufacturing Corporation; TaylorMade-adidas Golf; Mizuno Corporation; The Top-Flite Golf Company.

Further Reading

Albers, Bucky, ''Links to History: Exhibit Features MacGregor, Golf Mementos,'' *Dayton Daily News*, April 1, 2001, p. 7D.
Carnegy, Hugh, ''Masters Hooks Amer's MacGregor Golf Arm,'' *Financial Times*, October 16, 1996, p. 36.
Cushman, Tom, ''A Sad Chapter: The PGA Tour's 'Caucasians Only' Clause Excluded Deserving Players at 1952 San Diego Open,'' *San Diego Union-Tribune*, February 7, 2001, p. 3.
Dunn, Robert, ''Parkside Tees Up MacGregor Deal,'' *Buyouts*, September 14, 1998.
''MacGregor Golf to Bring Japan-Designed Clubs to U.S.,'' *Asia Pulse*, March 3, 2004.
Moore, Stephen D., ''Finland's Amer Group Earnings Plunge Amid Woes at U.S. Sporting Goods Units,'' *Wall Street Journal*, May 13, 1991, p. A9E.
Osterman, Jim, ''MacGregor Golf on Comeback Trail with Howard, Merrell & Partners,'' *Adweek Southwest*, October 13, 1997, p. 3.
Panczyk, Tania D., ''Magnani Teams With KS&M for MacGregor Golf,'' *Adweek Midwest Edition*, December 17, 2001, p. 5.
''Suntory to Sell Golf Equipment Subsidiary to MacGregor,'' *Kyodo News*, September 17, 2003.
Sweda, George, ''Nicklaus Ends Ties with MacGregor,'' *Plain Dealer Cleveland Ohio*, January 6, 1992.
Wilson, Catherine, ''Golf's 'Golden Bear' Is Also a Business Fox,'' *St. Petersburg Times*, December 9, 1991, p. 6.

—Frank Uhle

Mercury Marine Group

W6250 West Pioneer Road
Fond du Lac, Wisconsin 54935
U.S.A.
Telephone: (920) 929-5000
Fax: (920) 929-5060
Web Site: http://www.mercurymarine.com

Division of Brunswick Corporation
Incorporated: 1939
Employees: 6,000
Sales: $2 billion (2003 est.)
NAIC: 333616 Other Engine Equipment Manufacturing

Mercury Marine Group is a leading global manufacturer of marine propulsion systems. Its products include the Mercury Outboard lineup of motors, which range from 2.5 to 300 horsepower; Mercury MerCruiser gas sterndrives and inboards; high-performance Mercury Racing engines; Mercury Precision Parts and Accessories; and Mercury Propellers. In addition to its world headquarters, manufacturing, and distribution base in Fond du Lac, Wisconsin, Mercury Marine operates manufacturing sites in Stillwater, Oklahoma; Juarez, Mexico; Petit-Rechain, Belgium; and Newton Abbot, United Kingdom. Mercury Marine also has U.S. distribution centers in Cranbury, New Jersey; Dallas, Texas; Hayward, California; and Suwanee, Georgia. The company is a division of Brunswick Corporation.

Birth of a Pioneer: 1906–39

Mercury Marine originated from the efforts of Elmer Carl (E.C.) Kiekhaefer. Born on June 4, 1906, in Mequon, Wisconsin, to Arnold and Clara Wessel Kiekhaefer, Carl Kiekhaefer became familiar with the workings of gas-powered engines at a very young age, while working on his family's farm.

After graduating from Cedarburg High School, Kiekhaefer spent one year attending the Milwaukee School of Engineering, and later took extension courses from the University of Wisconsin that prepared him for a career in electrical engineering. Kiekhaefer first worked as a draftsman for Nash Motors Body Division in Milwaukee in 1926, and later for Evinrude. In 1928, he was hired as a draftsman at Stearns Magnetic, a Milwaukee-based electrical products manufacturer. Within ten years, Kiekhaefer had been promoted to the position of chief engineer.

During his eventual career as a marine industry pioneer, Carl Kiekhaefer was often compared to legendary Green Bay Packers football coach Vince Lombardi because of his temper, an obsession with winning, and his ability to motivate others. For example, during the 1950s Kiekhaefer would host inspirational sales meetings in the woods outside of Fond du Lac, Wisconsin. In addition to providing food, drink, and entertainment from polka bands, the eccentric company leader would often hang a competitor's outboard motor from a tripod and set it on fire, with talk of ''killing the enemy.''

In the June 21, 1992, issue of the *Milwaukee Journal*, David I. Bednarek said: ''Kiekhaefer hated his competitors. He spied on them. And, ever suspicious that they were doing the same things, he ran much of his company, as well as a secret testing lake and grounds in Florida, like a military installation, complete with armed guards and workers confined to base during tests.''

In addition to his paranoid obsession with competitors, Kiekhaefer had a legendary temper. Beyond throwing a mechanic's tools from a factory window, other stories tell of him firing executives and then reprimanding them when they did not report back for work. On several occasions, he ''fired'' truck drivers and other non-employees for sitting around on company time, unwittingly giving them a final week's pay. Nevertheless, Kiekhaefer was fiercely devoted to his company, working Sundays, holidays, and even while his wife gave birth to his children.

A Difficult Start: 1939–44

In partnership with his father, Carl Kiekhaefer started what he intended to be an electrical products company in 1939. That year he founded the Kiekhaefer Corporation, using $25,000 to acquire the assets of Cedarburg Manufacturing Company, an outboard motor manufacturer that had declared bankruptcy. Cedarburg's facility contained leftover Thor outboard engines that the company had been manufacturing for Montgomery Ward. Of 500 total engines, 384 had been rejected for quality

Company Perspectives:

The company's mission is to enhance the consumer's positive boating experience by providing the finest marine propulsion systems and services, integrated electronics and parts and accessories.

problems. To generate capital, Kiekhaefer convinced Montgomery Ward that he could improve the engines. This ultimately led to more orders from Montgomery Ward and Western Auto, and cemented Kiekhaefer's fate as an outboard motor manufacturer.

One year after establishing his enterprise, Kiekhaefer unveiled a new line of outboard motors that carried the Mercury name, inspired by the Roman god of speed. By the end of 1940, the company had produced 9,401 engines. The company's forthcoming ''Mystery Motor,'' the Thunderbolt, was mentioned to dealers at the New York Motor Boat Show in 1941. Although things seemed to be progressing well, World War II quickly hampered progress. In February 1941, U.S. Government restrictions on the use of aluminum essentially brought all outboard motor production to a standstill.

Faced with this challenge, within a few months Kiekhaefer was working on a prototype for a two-man chainsaw engine. Although he was hopeful that wartime production efforts would save the company, by November Kiekhaefer Corporation had reduced its workforce from 110 workers to a mere 18. In March 1942, more bad news came in the form of an outright ban on the use of aluminum for recreational products.

A blessing came in May 1942, when Kiekhaefer Corporation received a desperately needed order for 3,300 chainsaw engines. In 1943 Kiekhaefer Corporation shipped more than 10,000 engines to the military, in a total of six different configurations. That October, the company was recognized with the Army-Navy ''E'' Award for excellence in defense production. Military contracts totaled $4 million in 1944 and $5 million in 1945. In addition to chainsaws, the company produced engines for water pumps, generators, compressors, and target aircraft.

Marine Evolution: 1945–69

As the war neared its end, Kiekhaefer received an order for 15,000 outboard motors from Western Auto, to be labeled under the ''Wizard'' brand name. When government restrictions on the use of aluminum ceased, Western Auto upped its order to 33,000 engines. These were needed no later than January 1946. However, Kiekhaefer Corporation was still engaged in defense production and was in dire need of more production space.

The former Corium Farms in Fond du Lac, Wisconsin—acquired at a cost of only $25,000—became the company's new home in February 1946. Towering nearly five stories high, a massive 300-foot-long barn that once housed a dairy operation was converted into Kiekhaefer's new production plant. In addition to 38 acres of surrounding land, the farm included four silos that were converted into a variety of uses, from testing aircraft engines to spray-painting. Shortly after the move, the new production plant grew rapidly. A 25,000-square-foot addition came first, followed by a subsequent 40,000-square-foot expansion.

By September 1946, Kiekhaefer shipped more than $3.0 million worth of engines for chainsaws, generators, and other industrial equipment, along with $1.5 million in outboard engines. That year, an affiliate corporation named Kiekhaefer Aeromarine Motors was established.

More than 55,000 outboard engines were produced in 1947. Learning from his manufacturing experience during the war, Kiekhaefer began making outboards that were more durable and reliable. With the introduction of the 10-horsepower Mercury Lightning, he also gave his motors a new look. Finally, in 1948 Kiekhaefer Corporation unveiled the 25-horsepower Thunderbolt, its so-called ''mystery motor.'' It was around this time that the company began underrating the true horsepower performance of its engines, in order to ensure they would outperform rivals in the same class.

After the war, a flood of outboard engine manufacturers entered the market, increasing competition. In addition, the Korean War resulted in another round of aluminum restrictions at Kiekhaefer. This disappointing news came around the same time that Arno C. Kiekhaefer, president of Kiekhaefer and chairman of Kiekhaefer Aeromarine Motors, died in October 1950. A contract valued at $3 million for chainsaw engines, as well as the prospect of more drone aircraft engine production for the military, were factors that prevented Carl Kiekhaefer from selling the company during the early 1950s.

Challenges and setbacks continued during the early part of the decade, including cash flow problems that endangered the company's ability to meet payroll on several occasions and hindered the ability to expand and invest in research and development. Despite revenues of $16 million in 1954, the company lost $200,000 that year. By the decade's end, Carl Kiekhaefer was considering potential mergers with two bowling industry players, Brunswick Corporation and American Machine and Foundry Company (AMF), as well as Chrysler.

In 1961 Kiekhaefer sold his company to Brunswick for approximately $34 million in stock, and the company became known as Kiekhaefer Mercury. Although the sale gave Mercury the capital it needed for expansion, Carl Kiekhaefer suffered a tremendous financial loss from the deal when Brunswick's stock price fell from $63 to $6. Kiekhaefer also was saddened by the loss of his own company, even though he remained in a leadership role.

Throughout the 1960s, tension increased between Carl Kiekhaefer and Brunswick management. In the June 21, 1992 issue of the *Milwaukee Journal*, writer David I. Bednarek explained that, according to Jeffrey Rodengen's book, *The Legend of Mercury*, Carl Kiekhaefer decided to leave Mercury Marine in 1970 upon the urging of company executives, namely Brunswick President Jack Hanigan. At the time of his departure on January 31, 1970, the company had annual sales of $175 million, and 5,000 employees. Mercury products were available in 118 countries through a network of 8,000 dealers.

New Beginnings: 1970–88

Following Kiekhaefer's departure, Brooks Abernathy was named as Kiekhaefer Mercury's president. Rather than retire,

Key Dates:

1939: Carl Kiekhaefer establishes the Kiekhaefer Corporation.
1940: Kiekhaefer unveils outboard motors carrying the Mercury name.
1941: War production includes engines for chainsaws, water pumps, generators, compressors, and target aircraft.
1946: Kiekhaefer relocates to Fond du Lac, Wisconsin.
1950: The Korean War results in another challenging round of aluminum restrictions.
1961: Kiekhaefer sells his company to Brunswick and it becomes known as Kiekhaefer Mercury.
1970: Mercury products are available in 118 countries through a network of 8,000 dealers.
1971: Kiekhaefer Mercury's name is changed to Mercury Marine.
1982: Efforts to consolidate and decentralize operations improve bottom line.
1983: Carl Kiekhaefer dies at age 77.
1991: Brunswick lays off more than 8,000 workers, as sales for its Marine Group register a 60 percent decline following economic recession.
1992: As demand increases from boat dealers, Mercury begins recalling workers.
2004: Mercury benefits when Brunswick acquires three aluminum boat companies—Lowe, Crestliner, and Lund—from Genmar Holdings of Minneapolis.
2004: Mercury closes its legendary Lake X testing facility in central Florida, replacing it with Watson Bayou, a larger test lake in Panama City, Florida.

Kiekhaefer sold his stock in Brunswick and used the proceeds to fund Kiekhaefer Aeromarine Motors, a company that he still owned. After receiving permission to compete with Brunswick in September 1971, Kiekhaefer's new company began producing high-performance marine engines.

In November 1971, Brooks Abernathy changed Kiekhaefer Mercury's name to Mercury Marine. When Abernathy was elevated to president and chief operating officer of Brunswick the following year, Jack Reichert was named as Mercury's president.

In addition to European expansion, 1972 also saw the formation of a relationship with Yamaha in which Brunswick and Yamaha jointly owned Sanshin Kogyo Co., a Yamaha subsidiary that made outboard motors. By 1974, the Yamaha arrangement allowed Mercury to introduce a second line of engines under the Mariner brand name.

In 1975, Mercury Marine was realigned under four divisions: the Mercury Division (outboard motors), the MercCruiser Division (stern drives and inboard motors), the Quicksilver Division (parts and accessories), and the Mariner Division that stemmed from the company's venture with Yamaha. Other noteworthy developments at Mercury during the mid-1970s included the opening of a plant in Stillwater, Oklahoma, to produce MercCruiser stern drives, as well as a seven-week strike involving 3,200 workers who were at odds with management over incentive pay.

Charlie Alexander was named Mercury Marine's president in 1977, replacing Jack Reichert, who was promoted to president and COO of Brunswick. However, before Reichert left he mended relations between Brunswick and Kiekhaefer, and would stay in contact with Mercury's founder until his death.

Following efforts to consolidate and decentralize operations, Mercury Marine's net earnings skyrocketed to $192 million in 1992, up from $24 million in 1980. One example was the trimming of management staff from 500 to 240, which resulted in savings of $25 million. Mercury suffered a setback in 1983, when the Federal Trade Commission halted Mercury's joint venture with Yamaha, leaving the Japanese manufacturer with a significant presence in the North American market.

In 1983, the marine industry mourned the loss of a legend and pioneer when Carl Kiekhaefer died at the age of 77. In the October 5, 1983, issue of the *Reporter* (Fond du Lac), Brunswick President Jack Reichert paid tribute to Kiekhaefer, remarking: "Carl Kiekhaefer was described many times as an engineering genius. Clearly he was that, but he was a great deal more. He had the imagination and the courage to try new ideas, and he was constantly searching for a better way to do things. Consequently, more than any individual of his generation, he was responsible for building the recreational boating industry into what it is today. He will be missed by his friends at Brunswick and by the entire marine industry."

In 1984 Mercury Marine announced it would devote $100 million to a five-year manufacturing efficiency initiative that included $23 million to upgrade the skill base of the company's workforce. The following year, Richard Jordan was named as Mercury's president. In an effort to increase the company's responsiveness and efficiency, Mercury's divisions were consolidated to form the Marine Power Group.

By 1985 Mercury Marine had estimated annual sales of $790.8 million, accounting for about half of Brunswick's total sales, along with net income of $126.5 million. The following year, Brunswick made waves throughout the marine industry by purchasing Bayliner Marine Corporation and Ray Industries (Sea Ray), the world's two largest boat companies, giving it the ability to market complete packages of trailers, boats, and motors. Bayliner was acquired for about $425 million, including $375 million in cash, while Ray Industries was obtained for $350 million, $300 million of which was cash.

In 1986, Mercury contributed $949 million to Brunswick's total $1.7 billion in sales, and achieved net income of $153 million. The following year, Mercury Marine's sales increased 24 percent. At that time, the company agreed to acquire BMW Marine, the marine engine operation of German automobile manufacturer BMW AG.

In mid-1987, progress continued as Mercury announced record contracts for 1988 model year MerCruiser stern drives and inboard engines. This record pace continued for the 1989 model year, as orders for MerCruiser stern drives and inboards climbed 8 percent, reaching $1.3 billion. Another key development during the late 1980s was Mercury's 1988 agreement with General Motors to manufacture high-performance V8 engines for certain 1989 Corvettes at the company's plant in Stillwater, Oklahoma. In November 1988, Mercury President Richard Jordan announced his retirement. Replacing him was Thomas R. Weigt, president of the Brunswick division who had previously spent 21 years working at Mercury Marine.

Troubled Times in the Late 1980s

Mercury Marine ended the 1980s on a sour note. In January 1989, concerns were raised by the Wisconsin State Department of Natural Resources concerning carbon monoxide emission problems at Mercury's Fox River engine testing facility. This led the company to install a $250,000 exhaust control system to rectify the problem. Then, a recession that resulted in falling sales and rising retail inventories led to massive layoffs that would continue into the early 1990s. The first layoffs came in April 1989, when more than 200 of Mercury's 3,500 workers were laid off. Amidst these difficult times, Mercury Marine named David Jones as its new president.

In 1990, Kiekhaefer Aeromarine Motors was acquired by Brunswick and named as its high-performance division. In addition, Mercury Powerboats was reorganized as Brunswick Fishing Boats that year. In addition to recessionary conditions, Mercury faced other difficulties, including resistance from boat builders to buy motors from Mercury Marine, which had become a competitor. The layoffs of the late 1980s also continued. Some 1,000 employees had been laid off by January 1990. Overall, Brunswick laid off more than 8,000 workers in 1991, as sales for its Marine Group registered a 60 percent decline.

Number One on the Water 1990s and Beyond

Conditions finally started to improve at Mercury in 1992. As demand increased from boat dealers, the company recalled 200 workers, increasing total employment to approximately 2,700. From this point forward, the company worked diligently to strengthen its leadership position within the industry. By 1992, Mercury Marine accounted for an estimated 35 to 40 percent of Brunswick's sales, according to industry analysts. This amounted to between $800 million and $900 million in revenues. At this time, Mercury was organized into five business units: Outboards, MerCruiser, Quicksilver, Hi-Performance, and International.

Mercury President David Jones was responsible for improving the company's performance during the 1990s. His efforts included initiatives to boost morale, including training and development programs and a family medical center for Mercury employees. More specifically, an article in the June 26, 1994 *Milwaukee Journal* explained that Jones led a Brunswick management team that ''established a five-point strategy for the company: Satisfy customers, inside and outside the company; improve quality; motivate employees; cut engine emissions; and diversify into non-marine businesses to cushion the ups and downs of the highly cyclical boating business.''

By 1993 Mercury's employee base had grown to 3,230, up from a low of 2,600 in 1991 and just shy of a record 3,500 during the 1980s. This improvement came in the wake of a contract to offer engines to Tracker Marine, a fishing boat builder than formerly worked with Mercury competitor OMC. In addition, Mercury introduced a 225-horsepower outboard engine to boaters.

After an eight-year tenure as president of Mercury Marine, David Jones was succeeded by George Buckley, a marine industry newcomer who previously worked for Emerson Electric Co. Buckley remained at the head of Mercury until June 2000, when he was named CEO of Brunswick. Buckley increased Mercury's sales 14 percent during his three years as president.

In fall of 2000, Pat Mackey was named as Mercury's president. Late that year, the company received a boost when competitor OMC declared bankruptcy. OMC was later sold to Bombardier. Despite this, Mercury announced the elimination of 166 jobs in July 2001, citing restructuring efforts and slack demand for boats.

In 2003, Mercury Marine acquired a minor interest in New Zealand-based Rayglass Sales and Marketing Limited, a manufacturer of fiberglass and inflatable boats. In early 2004, Mercury benefited when Brunswick acquired three aluminum boat companies—Lowe, Crestliner, and Lund—from Genmar Holdings of Minneapolis. With combined 2003 sales of $311 million, the addition of the three companies made Brunswick the world's largest recreational boat company, and provided Mercury with new sales opportunities.

In response to a petition filed by Mercury that accused Japanese marine companies of ''price dumping,'' or selling engines at below market prices in the United States, the International Trade Commission upheld a ruling by the Commerce Department supporting a 22.52 percent anti-dumping tax on motors made by the likes of Yamaha Motor Co., Honda, and Suzuki.

In addition to the price dumping situation, Mercury filed a lawsuit over the pricing of engine components, alleging that Yamaha was in violation of an agreement the two companies had made. According to the September 28, 2004, *Milwaukee Journal Sentinel*, Yamaha raised prices of the components it supplied to Mercury by 92 percent, even though the companies had previously agreed to other terms. Yamaha claimed the move was necessary in light of anti-dumping measures. Although the competition within the marine industry remained tough, Mercury was positioned as a strong competitor—a point that would have made Carl Kiekhaefer proud.

Principal Competitors

Yamaha Motor Company.

Further Reading

Barrett, Rick, ''Fond du Lac, Wis., Firm Closes Boat Engine Testing Facility in Central Florida,'' *Milwaukee Journal Sentinel*, March 27, 2004.

——, ''Mercury Marine Parent Brunswick to Buy Three Boat Companies,'' *Milwaukee Journal Sentinel*, March 9, 2004.

——, ''Wisconsin Governor to Visit Japan to Discuss Trade Issues,'' *Milwaukee Journal Sentinel*, September 28, 2004.

Bednarek, David I., ''Brunswick to Lay Off State Workers,'' *Milwaukee Journal*, July 29, 1989.

——, ''Fiery Genius,'' *Milwaukee Journal*, June 21, 1992.

——, ''Motor Giant Nearly Sank Golden Idea. Bilious Founder Derided Stern Drive, Author Says,'' *Milwaukee Journal*, December 22, 1991.

Behm, Don, ''Mercury Marine Agrees to Curb Pollution in Tests,'' *Milwaukee Journal*, January 27, 1989.

''Brunswick Adding Another Boat Company,'' *Milwaukee Sentinel*, November 29, 1986.

Curtis, Alvin L., "Brunswick Corp. to Purchase Bayliner Marine for $425 Million," *Milwaukee Sentinel*, November 4, 1986.

——, "Productivity Boosts Mercury Marine," *Milwaukee Sentinel*, November 4, 1983.

Engel, Larry, "Big Swing Outlined at Mercury Marine," *Milwaukee Sentinel*, February 18, 1988.

Gores, Stan, "Kiekhaefer Was Brilliant Star in Industry and Created Jobs," *Reporter* (Fond du Lac, Wisc.), October 6, 1983.

Gunn, Erik, "Mates: New Cooperation Restarts Mercury Marine. Fond du Lac Firm and Union Each Gave a Little—and Gained a Lot," *Milwaukee Journal*, June 26, 1994.

Leon, Tony, "Kiekhaefer Dead at 77," *Reporter* (Fond du Lac, Wisc.), October 5, 1983, p.1.

"Long-Range Plan Set at Mercury," *Milwaukee Sentinel*, December 13, 1984.

"Mercury Engines to be Built in China," *Milwaukee Sentinel*, May 1, 1986.

"Mercury Marine Adding BMW Link," *Milwaukee Sentinel*, May 8, 1987.

Rodengen, Jeffrey L., *The Legend of Mercury*, Ft. Lauderdale, Fla.: Write Stuff Enterprises Inc., 1998.

Sandberg, Steve, "Kiekhaefer Services Planned," *Reporter* (Fond du Lac, Wisc.), October 6, 1983, p. 1.

"U.S. Rules against Japanese Outboard Engines on Dumping Charges," *International CustomWire*, August 8, 2004.

Wahl, Melissa, "Lake Forest, Ill.-Based Boat Company Elects New CEO, Divests Three Units," *Chicago Tribune*, June 28, 2000.

Wright, Jim, "Carl Kiekhaefer. The Eccentric Emperor of Marine Engines Is Still Kicking," *Biography News*, July/August 1975.

—Paul R. Greenland

MIGROS

Migros-Genossenschafts-Bund

Limmatstrasse 152
Zurich CH-8005
Switzerland
Telephone: +41 1 277 21 11
Fax: +41 1 277 25 25
Web site: http://www.migros.ch

Cooperative
Incorporated: 1925
Employees: 81,600
Sales: CHF 83.15 billion ($16.02 billion)(2003)
NAIC: 452910 Warehouse Clubs and Superstores

Migros-Genossenschafts-Bund (also known as Federation of Migro Cooperatives) is Switzerland's leading retailers and one of the top retailing concerns in Europe. As it name implies, Migros operates through 12 cooperative groups with some 580 supermarkets located throughout Switzerland. Migros supermarket offering is distinguished by a heavy reliance on private-label goods. More than 95 percent of the items on the company's shelves come from its own brands, and many of which are manufactured by the company itself. The company also operates supermarkets in Austria, and to a lesser extent in France. In addition to its primary Migros supermarket brand, the company operates a number of other retail formats, including Do It + Garden Migros; Micasa; Migros Melectronics; OBI and SportXX. The company also controls the Globus department store group, which includes 11 Globus department stores, the Oviesse clothing store chain, Interio, and Office World. Migros has long been a diversified group, and includes its own newspaper publishing and printing wing, with titles including Bruckenbauer and Construire. The company's Hotelplan subsidiary is a European leader in the travel and accommodations industry, through such subsidiaries as Hotelplan, Belair, Dornbierer Reisen, Esco, Interhome, Royal Tours, and others. Migros's cultural/social/entertainment division operates a number of subsidiaries, including Eurocentres, FitnessPark, Golfpark, Migros Kulturprozent and Monte Generoso. Founded by Gottlieb Duttwiller in 1925, Migros converted to a cooperative structure in the early 1940s. The company remains controlled by its owner-shareholders, who have a strong degree of influence over corporate decisions. The company employs nearly 82,000 people. In 2003, the company posted sales of CHF 83.15 billion ($16.02 billion).

Breaking the Mold in the 1920s

Born in 1888, Gottlieb Duttwiller started his professional career as an apprentice at the wholesale trading firm of Pfister & Sigg. Duttwiller later became a partner in the business, which took the name of Sigg & Duttwiller. Working as a wholesaler gave Duttwiller an insight into the pressures facing Switzerland's small grocers at the time. More or less forced to make their purchases through wholesalers and other intermediaries, grocers struggled to earn a profit on their sales.

The reliance on intermediaries brought other problems: the often long delivery times meant that products lacked freshness. The traditional system of weighing out and packaging individual purchases, which varied widely in size, was also judged by Duttwiller to be inefficient and time-consuming. Stores were also required to purchase and maintain relatively expensive weighing and packaging equipment, which further cut into store profits.

Duttwiller began developing an idea for a new retail model for Switzerland. In 1923, after the Sigg & Duttwiller partnership wound down, Duttwiller and wife Adèle moved to Brazil in order to manage a coffee plantation. Within a year, however, the couple had abandoned that effort and returned to Switzerland.

Duttwiller now decided to put his retail model to the test. Together with a group of four friends, Duttwiller founded a new company, Migros SA (formed from the prefix "mi," meaning 'half,' and the word "gros," meaning 'wholesale'). Duttwiller put up 100,000 Swiss francs in order to purchase five Fort T delivery vans, which were converted into mobile stores. The stores featured a limited range of goods—coffee, rice, pasta, coconut oil, soap and sugar—which Duttwiller purchased in bulk and stored in his own warehouse. Goods were then packaged in standard measurements, eliminating the need to weigh and package goods in the stores.

The Migros stores first took to the streets of Zurich in August 1925. With prices as much as 40 percent lower than

Company Perspectives:

Pioneers in the market, we want to reinforce our position as leader, improve our performance in favor of our clientele. We equally want to be the reference point in terms of cultural, social and ecological engagement.

competitors, the mobile stores quickly attracted a strong clientele. Yet Migros also attracted a number of powerful enemies—including retailers, wholesalers and food manufacturers. By 1926, the local government joined the battle against Migros, raising taxes on mobile stores by 500 percent.

In response, Migros opened its first fixed-site store that same year. The larger premises enabled the company to raise the number of goods sold, to nearly 50 products. One feature that was to remain a company hallmark throughout the century was its refusal to sell tobacco and alcohol product. Another feature of the early Migros store model was the use of rounded pricing, rather than rounded measurements, which made making change easier for store clerks.

Duttwiller had meanwhile begun planning to expand the Migros concept beyond Zurich, setting his sights on Aargau. When that city moved to ban the use of mobile stores, Migros instead opened its second fixed-site store that year.

Continued pressure from wholesalers and manufacturers, which instituted a boycott against Migros, provided a new phase in the company's growth. In 1928, Migros bought up Alkoholfreie Weine AG Meilen, which was renamed as Produktion AG Meilen, and which provided the company with its first entry into food manufacturing. The company was now equipped to provide for its own product need, and Migros' quickly expanded its production capacity. The company also adopted a policy of featuring primarily its own label products—by the turn of the century, private label products represented some 95 percent of the group's sales.

Converting to Cooperative in the 1940s

Migros continued its expansion, entering Bern, Basle and Lucerne in 1930. By 1932, the company had opened stores in western Switzerland as well, giving it a presence in all of the Switzerland's regions. Migros began opening a larger number of stores over the next year. Yet the company once again faced government-backed pressure, with the passage of a ban on branch store openings in 1933. The inclusion of a retroactivity clause forced Migros to close four of its newest stores.

Duttwiller found a way around the branch store ban in 1937, when he formed a new company, Waren-Giro-Genossenschaft. The new company grouped 30 independent retailers, who agreed to sell Migros products. Four years later, Duttwiller, who had no children, went a step further. In 1941, Migros was converted into a group of nine regional cooperatives, under the umbrella organization Migros Genossenschafts Bund (or Federation of Migros Cooperatives). The company's customers were granted the right to acquire membership in the cooperative, at CHF 30 per share. At its start, the company already boasted more than 75,000 paid members.

By then, Migros had entered publishing, launching the Italian-language weekly newspaper, Azione, in 1938. In 1942, the company introduced a German-language weekly, Wir Bruckenbauer. This newspaper became the company's flagship, espousing Duttwiller's views concerning 'social capitalism.' An offshoot of this company philosophy was the creation of the Migros Club Schools, which offered adult education programs in a variety of subjects, in 1944. In that year, the company launched a French-language weekly, originally called *Le Pionnier Migros,* and then renamed as *Construire* in 1947.

The company's acquisition of a canning factory, Konservenfabrik Tobler & Co, in 1945 enabled the company to skirt new boycotts. Yet opposition to the company's retail model remained strong. The opening of the company's 11th regional cooperative in Geneva in 1945, for example, was greeted with anti-Migros demonstrations. Nonetheless, Migros by then had succeeded in winning strong support from a growing number of shoppers—and Migros members—and in 1946 the ban on branch store openings was repealed. The company immediately expanded, adding 19 new stores, as well as 10 new mobile shops.

In 1948, Migros became one of the first in Europe to test the relatively new self-service supermarket concept that had been introduced in the United States. While Duttwiller himself remained skeptical of the new retailing model, he agreed to open the company's first self-service store in Zurich in 1949. The store was an instant success, and before long Migros began converting its other stores into modern self-service supermarkets.

Expansion and Diversification in the 1950s

Migros rapidly expanded its supermarket concept in the 1950s. The larger self-service format enabled the company to expand the range of goods sold in its stores, and in 1950 Migros began offering non-food items for the first time. In 1952, the company expanded the supermarket format again, launching the first Migros Markts (MM) in Basle and Zurich. These stores featured in-house butcher and flower shops, as well as a restaurant.

Migros also expanded its network of production facilities, acquiring baked goods manufacturer Saverma, soap and perfume producer Rumpf, and the Birrfeld bakery in 1951. The following year, Migros added an interest in book club Ex Libris, which expanded in 1952 with a record club, Grammoklub Ex Libris. Migros also ventured into fuel oil, launching Migrol, which acquired its first gas station in 1954. Two years later, Migros opened a new conserves plant, Conserves Estavayer, for canned peas and dairy products. This was followed by the acquisition of Riseria Curti, in Taverne, then the largest rice mill in the country, in 1957. Migros also made its first attempt to export its mobile retail concept during the 1950s, launching Migros Turk in Istanbul in 1954.

Migros growing clout in Switzerland's retail sector, and in the country's overall economy, was underscored by its entry into the banking and insurance markets. The company established Migros Bank in 1957, followed by the launch of automobile insurance group Secura AG, in 1959. Closer to its retail base was the construction of the group's own meat processing facility, Micarna, in 1960.

By the time Gottlieb Duttwiller died in 1962, Migros already represented one of Switzerland's major retail groups, with sales

Key Dates:

1925: Gottlieb Duttwiller and four friends launch Migros, providing mobile grocery store service in Zurich.
1926: Migros opens its first fixed store in Zurich.
1928: Boycotts prompt company to begin manufacturing its own goods with acquisition of Produktion AG Meilen.
1930: New stores in Bern, Lucerne, and Basle are established.
1933: Government imposes a ban on branch store openings.
1937: Migros forms Waren-Giro-Genossenschaft, skirting branch ban.
1941: Migros converted into association of nine cooperatives, Migros-Genossenschafts-Bund (Federation of Migros Cooperatives).
1946: The branch ban ends, and company opens 19 stores and ten mobile stores.
1948: Launch of the 'American' self-service format at Migros store in Zurich.
1966: Sales top CHF 2 billion.
1970: Launch of the MM department store format.
1975: Sales top CHF 10 billion.
1977: Company launches a life insurance subsidiary, Secura-Leben.
1989: The hotel and tourism subsidiary acquires Interhome AG.
1991: First MM department store opens in France along Swiss border.
1993: Migros forms joint-venture to acquire 112 Familia supermarkets in Austria.
1997: Co-op acquires Globus department store group for CHF 200 million.
2004: An online supermarket featuring 6,000 products is launched.

topping CHF 1 billion. Less than five years later, the group's sales, spurred by the buoyant economy of the period, had already doubled. By then, the company's network included nearly 450 stores, as well as 134 mobile stores. The mobile stores remained in operation until 1976. By then, the company had already introduced its latest large-scale retail concept, the MMM department store, the first of which had opened in 1970.

Migros decided to withdraw from the Migros Turk operation in 1975 after that company proved unwilling to convert to cooperative status. Migros then entered a long period of relatively conservative growth, as members—now numbering more than one million—voted against further international expansion.

Instead, Migros focused on further expansion and diversification. In 1977, the company moved into the life insurance market, then added health insurance products two years later. In the mid-1980s, the group launched its own computer software subsidiary, M-Informatic. Hotels and tourism, through the Hotelplan subsidiary, were also fast-growing segments of the group, which posted sales of more than CHF 10 billion in 1984. In 1989, the company acquired Interhome AG, the world's largest holiday home broker.

International Outlook for the New Century

By 1990, Migros' sales had topped CHF 15 billion. The company now represented some 16 percent of Switzerland's total retail market. Migros, by then with more than 530 stores, began to recognize that its further expansion within Switzerland appeared limited. In 1990, therefore, permission was granted to Migros cooperatives operating near the country's borders to open stores in their neighboring foreign markets. France was a natural market for the company. Yet, because another company already owned the Migros name in France, the Swiss group's expansion there faced a major obstacle. Nonetheless, the company opened an MMM department store in France's Val Thoiry in 1993, followed by a second MMM store in Etrembieres in 1994.

In 1993, Migros entered the Austrian supermarket sector, forming a joint-venture with Konsum Osterreich to acquire the 112 store Familia supermarket chain from the Zumtobel Group. Migros' share of the joint venture stood at 75 percent. The stores, later converted to the Metro name, provided an outlet for a rapidly growing parallel market for the company—private label products. In 1994, the company entered Germany as well, aded a store in Lorrach.

In addition to supplying its own stores with a wide range of products, Migros began supplying its own-label products to smaller, primarily independent grocers. By the early 1990s, Migros had already signed up nearly 60 grocers, who agreed to buy a minimum of 80 percent of their products from Migros. The company's success as a private label supplier led it to develop this activity further. By the late 1990s, this activity had become one of the group's most international, with supply contracts to Belgium and Holland, as well as the United Kingdom, starting in 1997.

That year market the company's largest acquisition—and the largest-ever among Switzerland's retailer—when Migros paid CHF 200 million to acquire the Globus department store group. That company, founded in the late 19th century, added 11 large-scale department stores to Migros' retail portfolio.

Into the new century, Migros continued to seek out new growth opportunities. With its leadership position in Switzerland protected—in part because the country's high real estate prices made such large-scale competitors as Wal-Mart and Carrefour wary of entering the market—Migros turned to a new, if virtual, market. In 2003, the company announced its joint-venture agreement with Swiss online grocer LeShop to launch Switzerland's largest online retail supermarket. That project got off the ground in 2004, with the launch of the Migros online shop featuring a range of some 6,000 products. With more than 75 years of success, Migros had become a true retailing institution in Switzerland.

Principal Subsidiaries

Fitness Parc; Globus; Golfparc; Migros Aar (Schönbühl); Migros Bâle; Migros-Genève; Migros Lucerne (Dierikon); Migro Neuchâtel-Fribourg (Marin); Migro Suisse orientale (Gossau); Migro Ticino (Antonino); Migro Vaud (Ecublens); Migro Valais (Martigny); Migro Zurich.

Principal Competitors

Carrefour S.A.; Metro AG; Co-op Suisse; Casino S.A.

Further Reading

Der Migros-Kosmos, Zur Geschichte eines aussergewöhnlichen Schweizer Unternehmens, Migro, Zurich 2004.

Hauser, Claude, ''At 75 Migros Looks to Its Laurels,'' *Swiss News*, May 2000, p. 12.

Klinner, Gerd, *Chronik der Migro: Portrat eines dynamischen Unternehmens*, Zurich: Migros-Genossenschafts-Bund, 1995.

''Migros to Launch Own Label in UK,'' *Grocer*, March 15, 1997, p. 4.

''Switzerland's Leading Retailer, Migros, and Online Grocer LeShop Will Join Forces to Create the Country's Biggest Online Supermarket,'' *Food Institute Report*, September 29, 2003, p. 8.

''The Migros Alternative,'' *UNESCO Courier*, September 1993 p. 30.

The Migros Story, Zurich: Migros-Genossenschafts-Bund.

—M.L. Cohen

Miquel y Costas Miquel S.A.

Tuset 10, Apartado Postal 629
Barcelona
E-08006
Spain
Telephone: (+34) 93 290 61 00
Fax: (+34) 93 290 61 26
Web site: http://www.miquelycostas.com

Public Company
Incorporated: 1929
Employees: 923
Sales: EUR 165.4 million ($205.4 million) (2003)
Stock Exchanges: Madrid
Ticker Symbol: MCM.MC
NAIC: 322110 Pulp Mills; 322121 Paper (Except Newsprint) Mills; 424130 Industrial and Personal Service Paper Merchant Wholesalers

Miquel y Costas Miquel S.A. (MCM) is a manufacturer of specialty papers and one of only four cigarette paper manufacturers in the world. The Barcelona, Spain-based company is also one of the oldest Spanish paper companies, with a continuous history dating back to 1725. MCM is known throughout the world for its flagship Smoking brand rolling papers, and exports accounted for 78 percent of the group's sales of EUR160 million in 2003. Altogether, MCM ships its products to more than 70 countries worldwide. Roll-your-own cigarette papers account for just 2 percent of the group's revenues, however. Papers for the cigarette industry is the group's largest segment, generating 45 percent of its sales. The company also produces a range of specialty papers, including filter paper for vacuum cleaner bags; decorative overlay paper; filter papers for preventing insects from attacking fruit; grid pasting tissue for automotive batteries; and adhesive papers for transfers. Most of these products were developed by the company's own research and development efforts. MCM's specialty papers operations are carried out by subsidiary MB Papeles Especiales. Specialty papers add 13 percent to the group's sales. MCM also operates its own pulp production, some 50 percent of which is sold to third parties, representing 23 percent of sales. The company also grows its own hemp and sisal for its specialty papers. MCM has been listed on the Madrid Stock Exchange since the late 1970s.

Rolling Papers in the 19th Century

Christopher Columbus introduced tobacco to Europe, bringing the first tobacco leaves into the Spanish port of Barcelona. The earliest cigarettes, however, were rolled in corn leaves. It was only toward the beginning of the 18th century that thin papers began to be used as cigarette paper, and Spain took credit for originating the ''roll-your-own'' cigarette market. By the middle of the 18th century, cigarette papers had become quite common, although many preserved the yellow color of corn leaves. The Barcelona area and the Catalan region in general became a noted center for paper production, and the many cigarette paper producers introduced a number of innovations, such as glue lines and the use of rice paper, that later became industry standards.

One of the earliest and oldest of Spain's paper producers was the Miquel family, which started manufacturing paper by hand in 1725. The family later built a mill in Capellades, outside of Barcelona, taking advantage of the river there and the abundant supply of water. The Miquel (later Miquel y Costas) family launched its own cigarette paper production in 1752, establishing their business as the world's oldest continuously operating producer of cigarette and roll-your-own papers.

The growth of the cigarette paper industry in Spain also gave rise to one of the earliest examples of consumer product packaging. During the 19th century, paper producers began to distinguish their products, sold in booklets of cigarette-sized papers, with highly illustrated covers. The booklets in turn stimulated demand and also gained consumer brand loyalty, foreshadowing the mass-produced, consumer culture of the late 20th and early 21st centuries.

The Miquel y Costas family emerged as a leading innovator and producer of cigarette papers into the second half of the 19th century. The company began to specialize in thin rolling papers in 1820. In 1879, brothers Llorenzo, Antonio, and Pau Miquel y Costas incorporated the family business as Miquel y Costas Hermanos. The brothers aimed at developing new technologies to enhance the quality of their papers, as well as to increase the

Company Perspectives:

From the outset the principal line of business has been the manufacture of fine and specialty lightweight papers, with the main specialisation being hi-tech cigarette papers. . . . The company's state-of-the-art technology, developed in house, enables it to be present in the major world markets, including those that are most demanding when it comes to total quality. Consequently, customers and their requirements have always been the focal point of the company's business.

efficiency of the production process. In support of this, the company built a new factory in La Pobla de Claramunt that year.

From the outset, Miquel y Costas left the door open for an extension into other paper categories, noting in its articles of incorporation its intention to produce and market various types of paper. Yet cigarette papers remained at the heart of the family business. The company also foresaw the development of the international paper trade, taking advantage of Spain's presence in Latin America to begin exporting its cigarette paper booklets there by the early 1880s. By the end of the century, Miquel y Costas had developed an international network of sales agents spanning South American, Mexico, Cuba, and New York. In 1901, the company added a new shareholder, and the company's name was changed to Miquel y Costas & Miquel, or MCM.

Branding in the 1920s

The invention of the first industrial cigarette making machines transformed the tobacco industry in the late 19th century. Whereas cigarette smoking had remained relatively minor in comparison to pipe and cigar smoking, the ability to mass produce cigarettes led to their eventual dominance of the tobacco market. The new tobacco product also represented an opportunity for specialty paper producers such as MCM, which quickly began producing papers to be used in the new cigarette production machinery.

Yet the original coarse quality of the manufactured cigarettes providing MCM, like many of its competitors, with a dual opportunity. During the late 19th century and early 20th centuries, the custom rose among Spanish smokers to unroll the mass-produced cigarettes in order to roll the tobacco into roll-your-own paper. In this way, companies like Miquel y Costas often doubled their sales, selling once to the manufacturer, and again to the consumer.

MCM earned a place among the majors in 1924 with the launch of its Smoking brand. Smoking quickly became the company's flagship brand and helped expand the company's exports worldwide. This development took off especially after the company's participation in the International Exhibition in Barcelona in 1929. In that year, the company converted its status to a limited liability company. Before long, Smoking had become one of the world's strongest selling rolling paper brands.

In the 1930s, cigarette manufacturers had begun to use higher-quality papers for their cigarettes, thereby putting the end to the re-roll market. MCM, which retained a tradition of innovation, was able to respond to demands for higher quality paper and quickly asserted itself as an important partner to the world's tobacco companies. At the same time, the company continued to supply the roll-your-own market. In 1935, the company established a subsidiary, Sociedad Espanola Zig Zag, using overlap production technology developed by the French Zig Zag company at the turn of the 20th century.

The Spanish Civil War devastated the Spanish cigarette paper industry. Already hit hard by the end of their re-roll sales, most of the companies in the industry were forced out of business by the time the war ended. MCM also suffered during the war, which saw it lose its export markets. The end of the war in 1939 enabled the company to recapture some of its export sales, yet full recovery would have to wait until the period following World War II.

Specialty Paper Development in the 1970s

As it worked to rebuild its international sales, MCM also moved to expand its operations. In 1952, the company established a new subsidiary, Cellulose de Levante, also known as Celesa, and built a rice pulp mill in Tortosa, Tarrogona, near the Ebro river. The pulp mill enabled MCM to control the quality of its pulp and also gave the company a strong secondary activity. Before long, the company had begun to sell off some 50 percent of its pulp production.

MCM's pulp capacity provided it with further expansion opportunities as demand for specialty papers grew during the 1960s. In the mid-1960s, the company began to receive request for higher-grade papers. The company responded by importing raw flax in order to produce flax pulp at the Celesa site, launching production in 1967. In that year, also, MCM added a new component to its operations when it began planting hemp on its own plantations near the Celesa site. The company began production of hemp pulp soon after. At the same time, the company began producing high quality flax- and hemp-based cigarette papers.

Miquel y Costas sold off majority control of MCM in 1968 as the company prepared to expand beyond cigarette papers. In 1970, MCM established a new subsidiary, Papeles Anoia, which began producing a wide range of specialty papers and fabrics, including artificial leathers, technical fabrics, and specialty filters. In 1975, the company further expanded its operations with the acquisition of SA Paya Miralles.

Leading RYO Producer in the 20th Century

MCM went public in 1979, listing on the Barcelona Stock Exchange, following the death of dictator Francisco Franco and the creation of a Spanish democracy. The public offering enabled the company to invest in developing its technologies and production processes, as well as expand its production capacity.

Until the mid-1980s, MCM's production had been based exclusively in Spain. In 1985, however, the company moved closer to Latin America, one of the major tobacco markets, establishing Miquel y Costas Argentina. The company further boosted its Argentinean presence with the acquisition that year of Paperleras Reunidas's operations in Buenos Aires.

Back at home, the company's Celesa subsidiary launched production of sisal pulp in 1989. The following year, MCM

Key Dates:

1725: Miquel family begins producing paper by hand in Barcelona, Spain.
1752: The family begins producing cigarette rolling papers.
1820: The company decides to specialize in cigarette papers.
1879: Miquel y Costas Hermanos is incorporated and a new factory is constructed in La Pobla de Claramunt; the company begins exporting.
1901: The company changes its name to Miquel y Costas & Miquel.
1924: Smoking brand of rolling papers is launched.
1935: Miquel establishes the Sociedad Espanola Zig Zag.
1952: The company creates pulp production subsidiary Celesa.
1967: The production of flax pulp is added to the company's operations.
1968: Hemp plantations are planted and production of hemp pulp begins.
1970: Specialty paper subsidiary Papeles Anoia is established.
1978: Miquel lists on the Spanish Stock Exchange.
1985: The company forms a subsidiary in Argentina.
1989: Miquel begins producing sisal pulp.
1990: MB Papeles Especiales joint venture begins operations.
1996: After a takeover, the company lists its stock on Mercado Continuo.
2002: The company acquires full control of MB Papeles Especiales.
2003: Miquel y Costa Tecnologias is formed.

joined with Papelera del Besos, a specialty papers maker, to establish the 50–50 joint venture MB Papeles Especiales. As part of the joint venture, Papelera del Besos bought a share in two of MCM paper mills. Located in a facility in Pobla de Claramunt, the joint venture began producing specialty filter papers.

Yet MCM was struggling with losses as it entered the 1990s. In 1991, the company put into place a thorough restructuring, which including modernizing its plants, improvement in quality, and a shift into higher-margin product categories. In this way, the company was able to return to profitability by 1992. Into the middle of the decade, the company came under new ownership, although members of the Miquel y Costas family nonetheless remained prominent shareholders. The company subsequently added a listing on the Madrid Stock Exchange's Mercado Continuo in 1996.

MCM meanwhile had begun working on what it called the next generation of cigarette papers. The company's commitment to research and development enabled it to release a new type of fine hemp cigarette paper. In 2002, the company introduced another new rolling paper product, the Smoking King Size Deluxe, featuring a long slim format and luxury paper. The company hoped to establish a new market for ''slim'' cigarettes with this product. Also in 2002, MCM payed EUR3.6 million ($3.1 million) to its joint-venture partner Papelera del Beso in order to acquire full control of MB Papeles Especiales.

By 2004, MCM's sales had topped EUR165 million ($205 million). The company had firmly established itself as one of the world's leading cigarette papers manufacturers. MCM was by then one of just four producers of papers for the tobacco industry and had also emerged as one of the world leaders in roll-your-own papers. The company remained committed to its history of innovation and in 2003 created a new subsidiary for new product development, Miquel y Costas Tecnologias. MCM appeared set to move into its fourth century as one of Spain's leading specialty paper producers.

Principal Subsidiaries

Celulosa de Levante, S.A.; Desvi, S.A.; M.B. Papeles Especiales, S.A.; Miquel y Costas Argentina SA; Papeles Anoia, S.A.; Payá Miralles, S.A.; Sociedad Española Zig Zag, S.A.

Principal Competitors

Bollore SA; Zaklady Celulozy i Papieru CELULOZA SWIECIE S.A.; VENEPAL SACA; Krasnoyarsk Pulp and Paper Mill JSC; Tsepruss JSC; International Paper Company; Petrocart S.A.; Stora Enso Oyj; Frantschach Pulp and Paper Czech A.S.; UPM-Kymmene Corporation; Svenska Cellulosa AB.

Further Reading

Bell, Jonathan, ''In Search of the RYO, First Stop . . . Barcelona,'' *Tobacco International*, October 1, 1989, p. 10.
Marcus, Amanda, ''MCM: No Smoke without Success,'' *Pulp & Paper International*, May 1992, p. 128.
''Miquel y Costas Makes Special Purchase,'' *Paperloop*, March 4, 2002.
''Miquel y Costas (RYO),'' *Tobacco Europe*, May-June 2002, p. 16.

—M.L. Cohen

MORNINGSTAR®

Morningstar Inc.

225 West Wacker Drive
Chicago, Illinois 60606
U.S.A.
Telephone: (312) 696-6000
Toll Free: (800) 735-0700
Fax: (312) 696-6001
Web site: http://www.morningstar.com

Private Company
Incorporated: 1984
Employees: 830
Sales: $139.5 million (2003)
NAIC: 511120 Periodical Publishers; 511210 Software Publishers; 516110 Internet Publishing and Broadcasting

Based in Chicago, Morningstar Inc. provides a wide range of independent investment research to more than three million individual investors, some 100,000 financial advisors, and 500 institutional investors, including banks, brokerage firms, insurance companies, mutual fund companies, and retirement plan providers, in 16 countries. The company's information products cover approximately 100,000 different investment options and are distributed in a variety of print and electronic formats, including CD-ROM, software applications, and the Internet. According to Morningstar, its reports provide coverage of closed-end funds, college savings plans, exchange-traded funds, mutual funds, separate accounts, stocks, and variable annuities. In addition, the company offers asset management, indexes, investment consulting, and retirement planning services.

Start-Up Success in the Mid-1980s

As with many successful companies, Morningstar is the product of one individual's idea. Joseph Mansueto, the son of an Indiana physician, developed the desire to start his own company while pursuing an MBA at the University of Chicago. His interest in securities analysis was formed after reading about legendary investor Warren Buffett in John Train's book, *The Money Masters*.

In the June 1, 1998, issue of *Crain's Chicago Business*, Mansueto explained: ''I went back and read all the Berkshire Hathaway annual reports and got very interested in securities analysis. I would look at all the Buffett holdings throughout the '70s and try and figure out why he purchased certain companies, why he found them attractive. Sparked by Buffett, I started contacting other talented fund managers, and I began collecting all these shareholder reports. And once I had all of these annual reports scattered across my kitchen table, I thought it would be neat to try to compile all of this into one book, to see how outstanding investors thought and what kind of stocks they invested in.''

After graduating with his MBA in 1980, Mansueto and college roommate Kurt Hanson started a market research firm that served the radio industry. Mansueto later went to work for the Chicago venture capital firm Golder Thoma, where his responsibilities included applying for cellular licenses. His next job was a stint with the investment firm Harris Associates.

In April 1984, Mansueto left Harris at the age of 27 to establish Mutual Fund Sourcebook Inc. from his one-bedroom apartment in Chicago's Lincoln Park. He used $70,000 of his own money from savings and stock sales to compile and publish *The Mutual Fund Sourcebook*, a quarterly mutual fund survey for individual investors. The 500-page survey, which sold for $32.50, contained complete portfolios for 400 mutual funds. Mansueto initially printed 800 copies of the survey, which then resembled a photocopied computer printout.

In the same *Crain's Chicago Business* article, Mansueto recalled the days when Morningstar was a fledgling start-up: ''I just put all the furniture from the living room into the bedroom, bought some cheap tabletops, some PCs and started going. I wrote to all the fund companies and asked them for their literature. I wrote programs to manage data and had help key-punching in portfolios.

''Fortunately, technology helped me out. The IBM PC had been introduced, and it made it affordable for someone without a lot of capital to get into a business like this. Ten years earlier, it would have been a lot more costly. In fact, I spent a couple of months researching computer platforms. It sounds crazy today, but then I thought I would have to do timesharing on a mainframe or lease mid-range IBM or DEC computers.''

Company Perspectives:

Whether investors, advisors, or institutions are using our services, our goal is to produce high quality, well-designed offerings that help improve the overall investing experience. Since Morningstar was founded more than 20 years ago, we've continued to evolve and expand our products, and we remain committed to leading the industry in delivering world-class investment research and services to people around the globe.

Mansueto's enterprise received a big boost after he shelled out $6,000 for a large advertisement in the investment magazine *Barron's*. The ad resulted in 600 orders worth $78,000. First-year sales reached $100,000, and doubled to $200,000 in 1985, when the company unveiled its Star Rating system for mutual funds.

In 1986 Mansueto loaned $200,000 of his own money—and a similar amount from his father—to Morningstar, which used the capital to launch a fortnightly publication called *Mutual Fund Values* (later re-titled *Morningstar Mutual Funds*).

That year, Mansueto chose a more flexible name for his company, changing it to Morningstar Inc. after the ending of Henry David Thoreau's *Walden*. In the June 1, 1998, issue of *Crain's Chicago Business*, Mansueto explained that he was first influenced by the author's themes of independence, thrift, and self-reliance as a college student, and that they remained important to him during his business career: ''I thought those were good qualities for a company to embody. And I still remembered that last line of Walden: 'The sun is but a morning star.' ''

Morningstar evolved rapidly during the 1990s, introducing a host of new offerings. This was especially evident during the first half of the decade. In 1991 a new bi-weekly publication called *Morningstar Mutual Funds* was introduced, providing coverage of 1,700 mutual funds. That year, the company also unveiled its first CD-ROM-based product. Called Mutual Funds OnDisc, the software was later renamed Morningstar Principia. The *5-Star Investor*, which eventually became *Morningstar FundInvestor*, came in 1992. The *Morningstar Mutual Fund 500*, an annual publication summarizing 500 carefully selected funds, was unveiled in 1993. Morningstar's 1994 acquisition of MarketBase added stock coverage to its offerings. The following year, Mutual Fund Documents OnDisc, a set of 30 CD-ROMs with 14 gigabytes of data for researchers and institutional investors, was introduced. The product included annual and semi-annual reports, prospectuses, and other Morningstar reports.

After reducing its work force by 5 percent and scaling back some offerings in 1996, Morningstar migrated to the World Wide Web. The development of Morningstar.net in 1997 ushered in a new era in the company's history, in which the Web played a key role in content distribution.

International Expansion in the Late 1990s

Several important developments occurred in 1998. In January the company announced a joint venture with Tokyo's Softbank Corporation that resulted in the formation of Morningstar Japan K.K. In the wake of deregulation it became possible for Japanese banks to sell mutual funds at retail, and Japanese consumers gained the ability to directly hold foreign assets. The new venture was established to provide existing Morningstar products, as well as new offerings, to a new segment of Japanese investors.

Donald Phillips also was named as Morningstar's CEO in 1998. Phillips had joined the company as its first analyst in 1986, after answering an ad in the *Chicago Tribune*. In his first job at Morningstar Phillips provided coverage of 111 different mutual funds every two weeks. By 1992 he had been promoted to publisher of *Morningstar Mutual Funds*, with a 70-person staff that included 12 analysts.

In March 1998, Timothy K. Armour was named Morningstar's chief operating officer. Prior to joining the company, Armour was president of Stein Roe Mutual Funds. His career also included work as senior vice president and director of marketing for Citibank's Chicago office, along with stints in product management and strategic planning for General Foods Corporation.

A monthly individual investment newsletter called *Morningstar StockInvestor* was introduced in April 1998, with the aim of helping personal investors identify and analyze undervalued stocks. The company also introduced a premium membership service on Morningstar.net. For a monthly fee of $9.95, investors were able to access analyses of 500 mutual funds, as well as the leading 25 portfolio holdings for funds, historical stock prices, and more. By October, the entire Morningstar.net site included 250,000 registered users, with 12,000 new users added monthly. The Web site, which was praised by leading financial publications and included free fund news and portfolio analyses information, was redesigned the following year and renamed Morningstar.com.

By 1999 Morningstar was quickly becoming an international company. That year, Softbank Corp.—the company's partner in the Morningstar Japan venture—secured a 20 percent stake in Morningstar. This came in the form of a $91 million investment that provided Morningstar with capital to expand its Internet business, which already provided financial content to the likes of AOL, Bloomberg, Intuit, Microsoft, and Netscape. The move was a departure from Mansueto's strategy of growing the business exclusively from the company's own pool of cash.

In 1999 Morningstar also expanded into Canada and opened offices in New Zealand and Australia. An arrangement with FPG Research allowed the company to provide information in the latter two countries. Morningstar ended the 1990s with the introduction of Morningstar Stock Grades.

Armour assumed the role of president in 1999, and the company restructured a number of executive responsibilities. This included Armour taking control of publication marketing, which the company wanted to better separate from its editorial division. Armour also was tasked with building relationships with financial advisors. In part, this was accomplished by developing a Web version of Morningstar's financial planning software, Principia.

With the dawning of the new millennium, Morningstar continued to increase its international scope with the establishment

Key Dates:

1984: Joseph Mansueto leaves Harris Associates to establish Mutual Fund Sourcebook Inc. and publish the *Mutual Fund Sourcebook.*
1986: The company changes its name to Morningstar Inc.
1991: The company unveils Mutual Funds OnDisc, its first CD-ROM product.
1997: Morningstar migrates to the World Wide Web with its first Web site, Morningstar.net.
1998: A joint venture with Tokyo's Softbank results in the formation of Morningstar Japan K.K.
2000: The company establishes Morningstar Asia, Morningstar Europe, Morningstar Korea, and Morningstar Norge AS.
2004: The company prepares for an initial public offering of its stock.

of Morningstar Asia, Morningstar Europe, and Morningstar Korea. Morningstar Japan also made its initial public offering in 2000 on NASDAQ-Japan. The formation of Morningstar Norge AS—a joint venture involving Storebrand subsidiary Finansbanken and Morningstar Europe—filled an information void in Norway, where data on mutual funds was hard to come by. In addition, the company's content was carried by Finland's leading business daily newspaper.

New product offerings also continued to appear. In 2000 a service for the 401(k) market called Morningstar ClearFuture provided online investment education, guidance, research, and advice to plan participants. In addition, investment advisors were offered their own Web portal called MorningstarAdvisor.com that included both free and subscription-based content. In addition to offering information from Morningstar, the new portal was designed to facilitate direct communication between advisors themselves, and between advisors, fund companies, and institutions.

Focused on the Future

Morningstar ended 2000 by reorganizing its company structure into seven decentralized business units. In doing so, the company sought to increase accountability and more closely measure revenues and profits in the wake of the NASDAQ plunge. In a move that some saw as controversial, 44-year-old founder and chairman Joe Mansueto took the CEO reins back from Don Phillips. Along with Tim Armour and Tom Florence, Phillips was named one of three managing directors. Tao Huang, a Chinese native who had joined Morningstar in 1990 to develop its CD-ROM products, was named chief operating officer. In the December 18, 2000, issue of *Mutual Fund Market News*, Mansueto cited his desire to put Morningstar on the fast track to profitability by reducing expenses. This included cutting the marketing budget for Morningstar.com, which had amassed some 80,000 registered users.

New offerings in 2001 included an online institutional research platform called DataLab, along with the Morningstar Rating for stocks. Two services for financial advisors also were unveiled in 2001. These included a Web-based investment planning offering called Morningstar Advisor Workstation, as well as a fee-based investment management service named Morningstar Managed Portfolio.

Don Phillips saw Morningstar Managed Portfolio—which was available only through the professional financial community and not to individual investors—as a natural progression for the company. Nevertheless, it angered some within the investment community, who argued that Morningstar was infringing upon their turf by pursuing the same clients. In the September 3, 2001, issue of *Crain's Chicago Business*, Rick Miller wrote: "Many financial advisors, likely to be major targets of Morningstar Managed Portfolios' marketing, are looking askance at the research company's new direction, citing concerns about competition and the potential damage to Morningstar's objectivity in fund analysis."

By 2001 Morningstar had firmly established its international presence, with Web sites for investors in Australia, Canada, Denmark, Finland, France, Germany, Hong Kong, Italy, the Netherlands, Norway, Spain, Sweden, and the United Kingdom. At the year's end, Morningstar had reduced its domestic work force by 14 percent, to 525 employees, while its overseas employee base had skyrocketed 50 percent, to 300 employees. Morningstar's annual revenues reached $91.2 million in 2001.

In 2002 Morningstar enhanced its Star Rating system. As opposed to using four broad asset classes to rank and rate funds, the new approach used 50 categories and took more factors into consideration. That year, Morningstar.com moved beyond 100,000 premium members, and the company first published *Morningstar Stocks 500*. The company's world-wide Internet presence was bolstered when MSN Money added Morningstar data to nine of its international sites.

Other new offerings in 2002 included the Morningstar 529 Advisor, which helped financial advisors select the best college savings plans, as well as a retirement advice initiative involving Morningstar Associates and Nationwide Retirement Solutions.

In 2003 Morningstar's revenues reached $139.5 million, up from $109.6 million in 2002. That year, the company's acquisition of mPower, a privately held investment advisory firm located in San Francisco, increased the base of retirement plan participants to whom it provided online advice. Following the acquisition, Morningstar served 9.1 million participants, up from 7.5 million.

Other developments in 2003 included the expansion of Morningstar's equity research staff, improvements to the company's system for classifying mutual funds, the publication of *The Morningstar Guide to Mutual Funds: 5-Star Strategies for Success*, and the introduction of new offerings such as Morningstar Managed Retirement Portfolios and the Morningstar Advice Statement.

Confirming what some observers had anticipated for several years, in May 2004 Morningstar prepared for an initial public offering (IPO) of its stock by filing a registration statement with the U.S. Securities and Exchange Commission (SEC). The company indicated that its IPO would hopefully generate $100 million.

At the time of Morningstar's IPO announcement, the company indicated that stock analysis for the institutional investment community would be a major source of future growth. Helping matters was the $1.4 billion Global Research Settlement between the SEC and 10 leading securities firms that were charged with issuing biased reports to investors. As part of the settlement, $432.5 million was earmarked for the securities firms to purchase independent research and provide it to their customers over a five-year period. Following the settlement, Morningstar was tapped to provide investment research to Citigroup's Smith Barney, Goldman Sachs, J.P. Morgan Chase, Merrill Lynch & Co., and Piper Jaffray.

In August 2004 Morningstar announced a new ranking system that pertained to the governance of mutual funds. The system initially evaluated 500 funds on such subjective criteria as corporate culture, regulatory compliance, and the quality of an organization's board. It was designed for investors to use with other tools and rankings as part of their overall decision-making process.

Also of note in 2004 was Morningstar's development of a hedge fund database, the acquisition of Pensions & Investments' ePiper separate account database, and the Morningstar Rating for separately managed accounts. In addition, Morningstar published Pat Dorsey's book, *The Five Rules for Successful Stock Investing*. Twenty years after its humble start in a one-room Chicago apartment, Morningstar had firmly established itself as an information leader within the investment world.

Principal Subsidiaries

Morningstar U.S.A.; Morningstar Canada; Morningstar U.K.; Morningstar Spain; Morningstar Benelux; Morningstar Norway; Morningstar France; Morningstar Denmark; Morningstar Germany; Morningstar Italy; Morningstar Finland; Morningstar Asia (Hong Kong); Morningstar China; Morningstar Korea; Morningstar Japan; Morningstar Australia; Morningstar New Zealand.

Principal Competitors

Bankrate Inc.; Bloomberg L.P.; The Motley Fool Inc.; Thomson Corporation; MarketWatch Inc.; Value Line Inc.

Further Reading

Arndorfer, James B., "Morningstar Going Online with Advice for 401(k)ers," *Investment News*, September 20, 1999.

——, "People: Marketing Pro Leads Push at Morningstar," *Crain's Chicago Business*, July 12, 1999.

——, "Tao Huang 38; Chief Operating Officer, Morningstar Inc.," *Crain's Chicago Business*, November 19, 2001.

Chase, Tammy, "Morningstar to Provide Stock Research to Merrill Lynch," *Chicago Sun-Times*, May 20, 2004.

Dale, Arden, "Morningstar Debuts New System for Fund Governance Ratings," *Lincoln Journal Star*," August 27, 2004.

Greene, Andrew, "Morningstar Reorganizes, Shifts Phillips," *Mutual Fund Market News*," December 18, 2000.

"Joe Mansueto: Top of the Morningstar," *Business Week*, December 25, 2000.

Kosnett, Jeffrey R., "Morningstar's Next Stop," *Kiplinger's Personal Finance Magazine*, September 2001.

McEachern, Cristina, "Morningstar Enters Portal Arena," *Wallstreet & Technology*, May 2000.

Miller, Rick, "Morningstar Clients Become Rivals; Money Management Entry Angers Some Customers," *Crain's Chicago Business*, September 3, 2001.

"Morningstar and Dataware Create Mutual Fund Documents OnDisc," *Information Today*, November 1995.

"Morningstar Buys Advisory Firm," *New York Times*, June 1, 2003.

"Morningstar Buys ePiper," *Accounting Technology*, October 2004.

"Morningstar Revises Star Ratings," *Financial Planning*, June 1, 2002.

"Morningstar Unveils Stock Investing Publication," *Business Wire*, April 28, 1998.

"New Day Dawns for Morningstar; IPO Tests Fund Rater's Star Power with Institutional Investors," *Crain's Chicago Business*, May 17, 2004.

Slutsker, Gary, "Watch Out, Value Line," *Forbes*, May 25, 1992.

"Softbank and Morningstar Launch Joint Venture," *Business Wire*," April 21, 1998.

Strahler, Steven R., "Star System," *Crain's Chicago Business*, June 1, 1998.

"Timothy Armour Named Morningstar Chief Operating Officer," *Business Wire*, March 11, 1998.

Warshaw, Michael, "Mr. Morningstar Stocks Up," *Inc.*, December 1, 2001.

—Paul R. Greenland

Neenah Foundry Company

2121 Brooks Avenue
Neenah, Wisconsin 54956-4756
U.S.A.
Telephone: (920) 725-7000
Toll Free: (800) 558-5075
Fax: (920) 729-3661
Web site: http://www.nfco.com

Private Company
Incorporated: 1872
Employees: 975
Sales: $165 million
NAIC: 331511 Iron Foundries; 332198 Gray & Ductile Iron Foundries; 332811 Metal Heat Treating; 332997 Industrial Pattern Manufacturing; 509901 Exporters; 671901 Holding Companies (Non-Bank)

With headquarters in Neenah, Wisconsin, and distribution and sales locations in 13 states, Neenah Foundry Company is a leading manufacturer of iron castings and steel forgings. In addition to serving industrial customers with custom casting work, Neenah Foundry has a strong presence in the municipal products market. The company's many offerings include tree grates; drainage grates; manhole frames/covers; catch basin frames/grates; gutter inlets; airport castings; catch basin traps and hoods; bridge scuppers; median, subway, and building drains; sign bases; downspouts; floor drains; curb and wheel guards; slab-type castings; and electrical boxes and ballast screens.

A Simple Beginning: 1872–1927

Neenah Foundry's roots stretch back to 1872, when the United States was recovering from the Civil War. William Aylward, who had moved to Neenah, Wisconsin, from Corning, New York, around 1859, foresaw the need to provide farmers with quality plows. With experience gained during his employment at the Moore Brothers Foundry, where he served as foreman, Aylward established the Aylward Plow Works with two employees.

Aylward made regular treks via oxcart to Green Bay, Wisconsin, some 40 miles away, to buy the Swedish pig iron that his enterprise used for manufacturing. Aylward's plows were well received by farmers, and the company branched out to produce other cast iron products including bean pots, barn door rollers, sleigh shoes, and sugar cauldrons.

In *From Plowshares to . . .*, a publication detailing Neenah Foundry's first 100 years, the company explained: ''Bill Aylward's early foundry operation was very basic. The melting furnace was called a cupola, but burned coal rather than coke. Automation, such as it was, came in the form of a horse walking a circle on a windlass, pumping the huge bellows necessary for draft. The rest of the shop was hand operation. The hours were long, the work hard, the output limited.''

Between 1875 and 1880 the Aylward Plow Works was able to steadily increase its capacity as William Aylward's sons (William, Jr., Edward Charles, and John) joined the business. This ultimately prompted the company to expand its physical infrastructure for the first time in 1881. By this time, production had grown to include cast iron stoves.

Following the dawn of a new century, the Aylward Plow Works continued to expand its product line. Manhole covers and sewer grates, which eventually became ''flagship'' products, were first produced in 1904. When William Aylward died three years later, the company was appropriately renamed as the Aylward Sons Co.

In 1918 several noteworthy changes occurred when Edward Charles Aylward renamed the company as E.C. Aylward Foundry Co. and relocated operations to a rural area in southwestern Neenah. The foundry continued operations in a 50-by-80-foot structure with clay floors, which was heated by coke-fired salamanders and molten metal. Administrative facilities consisted of a small, one-room office adjacent to the railroad tracks.

A final name change came in 1922, when the enterprise adopted the name Neenah Foundry Co. When E.C. Aylward died in 1926, his son Edmund John ''Ed'' Aylward, who had joined the company in 1919 after returning from World War I, was appointed manager and senior partner.

Company Perspectives:

Neenah Foundry has been producing quality castings in Neenah, Wisconsin, for over 125 years. The commitment to quality and service that started in 1872 is still the driving force behind Neenah Foundry being recognized as the quality and service leader in the industry.

At this time, the company employed about 18 workers. After about 50 years of operation, foundry life continued to be grueling. As the company explained in *From Plowshares to . . .*: ''Most of our early operations were powered by the muscles of men. Coke was unloaded from boxcars with pitch forks. The cupola was charged by hand, piece by piece. Sand was stored in a small wooden shed next to the tracks. Hot metal was carried in ladles by the molder who 'poured off' his own work. Casters were rolled or carried to the cleaning yard for hand painting and shipment. These methods were common because power tools were unheard of. Yet, our men took much pride in producing quality castings and being part of a closely-knit group.''

Surviving Difficult Times: 1928–45

In 1928 Neenah Foundry began to manufacture industrial castings in support of a growing regional printing industry. The following year, however, brought the Great Depression and a period of dire economic struggle for the United States. To avert disaster and maintain operations, Ed Aylward took out a second mortgage on his home. During the 1930s, projects from the Works Progress Administration—an employment relief program that was part of President Franklin Delano Roosevelt's New Deal—resulted in heightened demand for municipal castings like manhole covers. This prompted the company to focus heavily on the sale of construction castings.

In *From Plowshares to . . .*, former Neenah Foundry Vice-President Jim Keating recalled how difficult the 1930s were for the company, explaining: ''During the depression years, our selling prices became quite ridiculous. We were selling grate bars and miscellaneous castings to the paper mills for less than 3 cents a pound and a 540 lb. manhole cover and frame was machined and delivered to Chicago for $8.50 per set during the period 1929–1934.''

Despite the difficult years of the Great Depression, Neenah Foundry managed to achieve growth. By 1942, the company was able to open a credit union as a benefit for its employees, and other improvements were on the horizon.

Automation and Expansion: 1946–71

The advent of World War II brought wartime production business to Neenah Foundry. This was followed by the introduction of automated molding lines in 1946 that expanded capacity and supported growth of the company's employee base, which had risen to 320 by 1950.

More than 75 years after William Aylward established the company, his descendants remained actively involved in its daily operations. Ed Aylward's son, Edmund William ''Bill'' Aylward, came on board in 1948, followed by Richard John ''Dick'' Aylward in 1953. A metallurgist who received his education from the University of Wisconsin, Dick Aylward became a vice-president at Neenah in 1959 after making many valuable contributions. In 1960, the company suffered a loss when he died following a short illness.

Developments began to unfold at a steady clip around this time. In addition to gray iron, the company began using ductile iron in 1957, which was stronger than gray iron and more suitable for certain applications. This development allowed Neenah to better meet the needs of its customers.

Ed Aylward became company chairman in 1959, and his son Bill was named president. With a workforce that had grown to 565 employees, Neenah Foundry expanded the following year with the opening of Plant 2, which it described as the world's largest and most automated facility for the manufacture of construction castings. At this time, Neenah Foundry also introduced its own truck fleet. As additional evidence of the company's growth, sales increased some 400 percent between 1950 and 1960. Although Neenah Foundry had served international customers for more than 20 years, in 1966 the company began to formally market its products abroad by sending catalogs around the globe.

The addition of Plant 3, dedicated to industrial castings, followed in 1967. In July of 1969, Ed Aylward celebrated a 50-year tenure with the company his grandfather started. Sadly, he died on September 30, 1970. His leadership had been important to the company's success. In fact, between 1960 and 1970, Neenah Foundry's sales increased 300 percent.

A Second Century: 1972 to the Present

Upon the occasion of its 100th anniversary, Neenah Foundry had much to celebrate. Over the course of a century the company had grown from three employees to more than 1,200. In addition, its three plants had a combined daily production capacity of 800 tons. Plant 2, where the lion's share of Neenah Foundry's construction castings were made, generated 50,000 tons of construction castings annually alone.

In *From Plowshares to . . .*, Neenah Foundry explained that it produced some 24,000 different kinds of construction castings, which were used throughout the world. In addition to a seemingly endless number of municipal and military locations, the company's castings were used at such well-known locations as Disney World, the Empire State Building, the Golden Gate Bridge, Kennedy International Airport, and the St. Lawrence Seaway.

Along with a vast array of construction castings, Neenah Foundry's Industrial Division offered an equally impressive lineup of 82,000 products. These castings were used in the manufacture of different kinds of motors and equipment, including trucks, cranes, air conditioners, electric motors, transmissions, farm machinery, and even motor housings for U.S. Navy ships.

In addition to its headquarters and production facilities in Neenah, Wisconsin, Neenah Foundry operated regional sales offices and distribution yards. The company employed sales people in major U.S. cities, and also worked with independent representatives and jobbers to market its products. By 1972

Key Dates:

1872: William Aylward establishes the Aylward Plow Works in Neenah, Wisconsin, with two employees.
1875: The company steadily increases its capacity as William Aylward's sons, William, Jr., Edward Charles, and John, join the business over the next five years.
1904: Manhole covers and sewer grates are first produced.
1918: Edward Charles Aylward relocates operations to a rural area in southwestern Neenah.
1922: The name Neenah Foundry Co. is adopted.
1930s: Projects from the Works Progress Administration drive demand for municipal castings and allow the company to grow during the Great Depression.
1946: Neenah Foundry introduces automated molding lines to support expanded capacity.
1957: The company begins using ductile iron, stronger than gray iron.
1960: The company opens Plant 2, the world's largest and most automated facility for the manufacture of construction castings.
1966: Neenah Foundry begins to market its products internationally.
1987: Operations within Plant 3 are completely rebuilt to enable high-production ductile iron casting for industrial customers.
1992: E. William Aylward, Sr., dies.
1997: After 125 years and five generations of family involvement, the Aylward family sells its enterprise to NFC Castings Inc.
1998: Following its acquisition by NFC Castings Inc., Neenah Foundry begins acquiring other companies at a rapid pace.
2001: Neenah Foundry's use of technology to maximize efficiency and control emissions results in a Foundry of the Year award from *Modern Casting.*
2003: Neenah Foundry reorganizes under Chapter 11 bankruptcy protection, and emerges in October after reaching an agreement to repay its creditors.

Neenah Foundry's international reach had grown to include locations such as Bombay, Guam, Haiti, Honduras, Hong Kong, Iraq, Jamaica, Kuwait, Lebanon, Libya, Nigeria, Pakistan, Puerto Rico, South Africa, and the Virgin Islands.

E.W. ''Bill'' Aylward remained Neenah Foundry's president in 1972, marking 100 years of family involvement with the company. At this time, the company's workers were represented by the Pattern Makers Association of Milwaukee and Vicinity, as well as the Allied Workers Union, and the A.F.L.-C.I.O. Workers were kept abreast of company news via a bimonthly employee newsletter called the *Iron Worker.*

During the early 1980s, Neenah Foundry weathered a period of great difficulty within the foundry industry, during which hundreds of foundries either shut down or were acquired by other firms. Even though the company continued to hold a virtual monopoly on municipal castings in the Midwest, it faced heightened competition from foreign firms. By 1985 Bill Aylward estimated that Japanese firms had cost American foundries 25 percent of their industrial market share, according to the January 27, 1985 *Milwaukee Journal.*

In response to these conditions, Neenah Foundry tightened security by banning cameras from its production plant. The company also invested millions of dollars in new equipment throughout the decade, in order to increase efficiency and productivity. These improvements included the complete rebuilding of operations within Plant 3 in 1987, which supported high-production ductile iron casting for industrial customers.

The 1990s were both eventful and challenging for Neenah Foundry. After the death of E. William Aylward, Sr., in 1992, the company shuttered Plant 1 the following year. The facility, which had been constructed in the early 1900s, was closed because it could not keep pace with modern production demands. The closure resulted in the elimination of 350 jobs. By this time, Neenah Foundry was the nation's third largest castings producer.

The most significant development in the company's history came in May 1997. After 125 years and five generations of family involvement, the Aylward family sold its enterprise to NFC Castings Inc., an investment group composed of Citicorp Venture Capital Ltd. (a subsidiary of Citibank N.A.) and Metropolitan Life Insurance Co. The Aylward family's sale of Neenah Corp. included Neenah Foundry Co., as well as two related businesses: Hartlet Controls Corp. and Neenah Transport Inc. At the time of the sale, Neenah Foundry's annual revenues were estimated at between $150 and $200 million. E. William Aylward's three sons—E. William, Jr., Andrew, and Richard—were the last family members involved with the company.

In 1997 Neenah Foundry continued advancing with the addition of a bar coding/automatic data collection system. According to the July 2001 issue of *Modern Casting,* the system provided ''the ability to track work-in-process cast components from molding to shipping. A portion of this system provides real time information to employees for cleaning parts on the shop floor. The automatic data collection systems provide Neenah management the ability to track and monitor department backlogs and product flow. Production bottlenecks are identified and can be traced to specific jobs.''

After it was acquired by NFC Castings Inc., Neenah Foundry began acquiring other companies at a rapid pace. This began with the April 1998 acquisition of Deeter Foundry. Based in Lincoln, Nebraska, the company was one of the largest manufacturers of tree grates and manhole covers in the United States.

Neenah Foundry acquired Advanced Cast Products Inc. of Meadville, Pennsylvania, in September of 1998. The merger resulted in the formation of a nine-company group that provided forging and casting services. According to the same July 2001 issue of *Modern Casting,* this created ''one of the largest municipal construction casting suppliers in North America and provided a larger foundation in other industrial component markets such as heavy truck, compressors, automotive/light truck, railroad and mining.''

Neenah Foundry made a number of subsequent acquisitions through the end of the 1990s, including Mercer Forge Co. of Mercer, Pennsylvania; Warsaw, Indiana-based Dalton Corp.; Cast Alloys Inc. of Carlsbad, California; and El Monte, California-based Gregg Industries.

In 2001 Neenah Foundry continued to evolve with the addition of robotic cells in its cleaning and finishing area. That year, the company's use of technology to maximize efficiency and control emissions resulted in a Foundry of the Year award from *Modern Casting.*

Neenah Foundry was honored again in June of 2002 when the Wisconsin Environmental Working Group, an affiliate of Wisconsin Manufacturers and Commerce, gave it the Business Friend of the Environment award. The award recognized Neenah Foundry's use of a special process to curb pollutants from air emissions. According to the June 11, 2002 issue of the *Post-Crescent,* hydrogen peroxide, water, and ozone were combined with dust during the production process, which was then reused to produce sand molds for castings. This resulted in a lower level of combustible materials.

In the wake of a sour economy that was especially dire for the nation's manufacturing sector, Neenah Foundry was forced to lay off 74 of its workers in late 2002, bringing its Neenah, Wisconsin workforce to 960. For the fiscal year ending September 30, 2002, the company's sales totaled $405 million, while its debt totaled $454.6 million that December.

Neenah Foundry reorganized under Chapter 11 bankruptcy protection in June 2003 and emerged that October after reaching an agreement to repay its creditors. Heading into the mid-2000s, Neenah Foundry had proved its resilience through more than 130 years of continuous operation.

Principal Competitors

Crescent Foundry Company Pvt. Ltd.; Washington Street Castings, Inc.

Further Reading

"Appleton, Wis., Foundry's Layoffs Continue," *Post-Crescent* (Appleton, Wis.), December 10, 2002.

Bach, Pete, "Two Companies with Wisconsin Presence Win Environmental Awards," *Post-Crescent* (Appleton, Wis.), June 11, 2002.

Boardman, Arlen, "Wisconsin's Neenah Foundry Sold to East Coast Investors," *Post-Crescent* (Appleton, Wis.), May 6, 1997.

From Plowshares to . . . , Neenah, Wisconsin: Neenah Foundry Co., 1972.

Martin, Chuck, "Neenah Foundry to Cut 350 Jobs," *Milwaukee Journal,* March 5, 1993.

Mulholland, Megan, "Neenah, Wis., Iron Castings Maker Buys Warsaw, Ind., Foundry," *Post-Crescent* (Appleton, Wis.), September 30, 1998.

Murray, Shanon D., "Neenah Ends Short Bankruptcy," *The Deal,* October 20, 2003.

"Neenah Foundry Buys Manhole Cover Maker," *Milwaukee Journal Sentinel,* April 9, 1998.

"Neenah Foundry Purchases Gregg Industries," *Modern Casting,* January 2000.

"Neenah Foundry to File for Chapter 11," *Milwaukee Journal Sentinel,* June 4, 2003.

"Neenah Foundry Urges Restructuring of Debt," *Milwaukee Journal Sentinel,* May 3, 2003.

Spada, Alfred T., "2001 Foundry of the Year: Neenah Foundry Co.," *Modern Casting,* July 2001.

Zahn, Michael O., "Neenah Foundry: A Sweating Giant," *Milwaukee Journal,* January 27, 1985.

—Paul R. Greenland

New Balance Athletic Shoe, Inc.

20 Guest Street, Brighton Landing
Boston, Massachusetts 02135-2088
U.S.A.
Telephone: (617) 783-4000
Toll Free: (800) 343-1395
Fax: (617) 787-9355
Web site: http://www.newbalance.com

Private Company
Incorporated: 1906 as The New Balance Arch Company
Employees: 2,400
Sales: $ 1.3 billion (2004 est.)
NAIC: 316210 Footwear Manufacturing

New Balance Athletic Shoe, Inc., manufactures running, hiking, tennis, basketball, and cross-training shoes, offering its footwear in a broad range of width sizes. New Balance, in contrast to its larger competitors, manufactured nearly all of its footwear in the United States, as opposed to manufacturing its merchandise overseas. The company's five company-owned manufacturing facilities during the late 1990s were all located in Massachusetts and Maine. In addition to its lines of footwear, New Balance also produces a variety of athletic apparel.

Early 20th Century Origins

New Balance was founded in 1906 in Belmont, Massachusetts, where the company began operations as The New Balance Arch Company. Initially, the company manufactured arch supports and orthopedic shoes and, in fact, for much of the 20th century it continued to focus on this narrow, niche-oriented business line, rarely expanding and never moving beyond the boundaries of its native state. Like its physical growth, The New Balance Arch Company's financial growth occurred at a crawling pace as well, inching nearly imperceptibly forward as the decades passed. About the only notable achievement during the company's first half-century of existence was the establishment of a solid reputation, a renown forged by the quality of its specialty shoes and buttressed by decades of consistent high-quality craftsmanship. Though the work of the company was held in high regard, there was only a small circle of customers who could profess to the quality of New Balance's footwear. Beyond this tight circle, the company was unknown; it was a small, Northeastern enterprise blanketed in anonymity.

Widespread notoriety and a worldwide customer base eventually would come New Balance's way, but it would take roughly 70 years before the New Balance brand name stormed onto the national stage. One important step in this direction was taken in the 1930s, when New Balance began manufacturing specially designed orthopedic footwear for baseball players and track and field athletes. The foray into the athletic market was a pivotal one, moving the company into a business area that years later would provide plenty of fuel to drive its financial growth upwards. It also was an entry most likely forced upon the company by special requests from the athletes themselves, rather than arising from management's own initiative, but however the diversification originated, its occurrence planted the seed for further involvement. In 1961 the seed flowered, this time under management's directive, when New Balance applied its experience in producing specially designed athletic footwear to a new shoe dubbed "Trackster," a ripple-soled running shoe for men. The Trackster was unique, manufactured in a range of widths ranging from AA to EEEE, which set it apart from all other competing brands. Like its predecessor New Balance models, the Trackster gained a loyal following, winning over wearers who admired the workmanship and tailored fit of the shoes. However, like all New Balance models before it, the Trackster enjoyed only a limited customer base. The majority of Trackster sales were made through mail order purchases from local high schools and colleges. No other attempt was made to market the shoe. Although New Balance had moved into a promising market, one that offered a greater potential for growth than the market for orthopedic shoes and arch supports, the personality of the company had not changed. New Balance remained tied to its demure roots, preferring a corporate existence in the shadows rather than a more ambitious life as an innovative trendsetter with mass-market appeal. New Balance's mellow and staid existence persevered for years after the introduction of the Trackster, but in the early 1970s an abrupt change took place, sparked by the arrival of a new owner, James S. Davis.

Company Perspectives:

Which would you prefer? Athletic shoes built around the belief that the marketing prowess of an NBA superstar can sell anything? Or athletic shoes built around the belief that better fit and technology mean better performance?

We prefer the latter; that's why we adhere to a unique "Endorsed By No One" philosophy. Instead of paying celebrities to tell you how great our products are, we invest in research, design, and domestic manufacturing and let our products speak for themselves. By adhering to this philosophy, we are able to celebrate the true stars: every day athletes who choose New Balance footwear and apparel because they fit and because they perform.

New Ownership in the 1970s

A 1964 graduate of Middlebury College, Davis was 28 years old when he acquired New Balance in 1972. Academically, Davis's interests were in biology and chemistry, but he only pursued these disciplines tangentially as a professional. His chief interests were in marketing and sales, and he learned these skills while working as a sales representative for a high-technology medical electronics company. After two successful years in sales, Davis was promoted to sales manager, but he did not linger long in his new position. By the beginning of the 1970s Davis was ready to fulfill his next dream: owning and managing his own business. A friend of Davis's suggested that he talk to Paul Kidd, who wanted to retire and sell his company, New Balance Shoes. Davis talked with Kidd and spent some time investigating the company by canvassing New Balance's small band of customers. His findings piqued his interest. "I felt that leisure-time products would be a high-growth market," Davis remembered, recalling his thoughts prior to purchasing the company, "and I found that New Balance had a good product. After running in them myself, I was very impressed with the shoe. I got the same reaction from other runners. The company had relied entirely on word-of-mouth advertising and I was confident that with some marketing, sales could be expanded substantially." Using his savings and money obtained from a long-term bank loan, Davis bought New Balance in 1972 for $100,000, the same amount the company was collecting in sales per year.

When Davis acquired New Balance, the company employed five workers who worked in a Watertown, Massachusetts, garage producing approximately 30 pairs of Tracksters per day. Davis was intent on dramatically magnifying the scale of the company's operations, but first he needed to establish a nationwide sales distribution system to support such growth, and he spent much of his first year establishing a network of geographically based sales representatives. After doing this, forces beyond Davis's control swept the company toward prolific growth, making his tenure of ownership overwhelmingly successful soon after he took control. The era of recreational jogging exploded with widespread excitement in 1973 and 1974, as vast multitudes took to the streets and parks and began logging miles in earnest. In a matter of months, running was transformed from an activity that attracted only serious racers and physical fitness enthusiasts into major leisure-time activity. The timing of Davis's acquisition had proved superb. Amid the sweeping passion for running appeared a collection of new magazines that catered to the jogging enthusiast, one of which was Runner's World, which in 1975 published its first annual supplement that rated the leading running shoes. In the first issue, New Balance placed third, an encouraging result in itself, but the following year, in October 1976, the New Balance 320 was judged to be the best running shoe in the world, with two other New Balance entries placing third and seventh. The notoriety received from being billed as the best tied New Balance to a rocket; at company headquarters in Watertown the telephone did not stop ringing with urgent requests for the New Balance 320. "Our biggest problem," Davis noted, "was getting enough of them out the door."

Energetic Growth Begins in the Mid-1970s

Quickly, Davis found himself marketing a highly popular product, the success of which forever altered the face of the once sleepy New Balance. As the company struggled to meet demand by increasing production, an order backlog swelled with each passing month. Annual sales leaped upward, jumping from $221,583 in 1973 to more than $1 million by 1976 and eclipsing $4.5 million in 1977. Everything was changing at the company that labored 70 years to achieve a sales volume of $100,000, but there were aspects of the company that did not change and, in the years ahead, would stand as hallmarks of New Balance. Chief among these qualities that tied the company to its 1906 origins were its attention to craftsmanship (something Davis continued to preach as his staff frenetically endeavored to meet demand) and to making shoes for a wide range of width and length sizes. Marketing shoes with widths stretching from AA to EEEE and lengths up to size 20 was something no other athletic footwear manufacturer did, either in the 1970s or 20 years later when the athletic footwear industry represented a nearly $10 billion business. Another thread of continuity was the company's long-time presence in New England. As the athletic footwear industry grew by leaps and bounds from the early 1970s forward, registering robust growth through the 1980s and into the 1990s, nearly all of the manufacturers moved their production overseas where labor costs were an infinitesimal fraction of labor costs in the United States. New Balance did not make such a move. Davis, through the years, was steadfast about his refusal to establish manufacturing operations in Asia, preferring to keep his production operations close to home where he believed he could exert greater control over manufacturing quality. As New Balance moved forward from the early 1970s on, its domestic production operations and width-sizing choices would stand as two of the most distinctive qualities describing the company.

The massive surge in the popularity of running that began in the early 1970s and swept up New Balance in late 1976 pressed forward into the 1980s, never losing much of its energy. Though the intensity of the running craze suggested it might be a fleeting fad, the athletic footwear industry recorded numbing growth throughout the 1980s, distinguishing itself as a legitimate multibillion-dollar business. As the industry expanded at an annual pace of roughly 20 percent, New Balance shared in the riches, registering great gains in its revenue volume. By 1982, a decade after Davis acquired a $100,000-a-year-in-sales company, New Balance was collecting $60 million a year in

Key Dates:

1906: The New Balance Arch Company is founded in Massachusetts.
1961: New Balance introduces the Trackster running shoe.
1972: The company is acquired by James Davis for $100,000.
1975: A new model, the 320, is worn by Tom Fleming during his winning run in the Boston marathon.
1982: Sales reach $60 million.
1991: Sales reach the $100 million mark.
1997: A new manufacturing facility in Maine is constructed.
2004: New Balance becomes a sponsor of major league lacrosse and purchases a manufacturer of lacrosse equipment.

sales, with its future prospects as bright as they had been during the previous six years. Three years later the company was generating $85 million a year in sales, but it was at this point that the perpetually growing athletic footwear industry and New Balance parted company. Though the industry continued to expand at an exhausting rate, New Balance no longer was sharing in the riches. The company faltered, and Davis blamed himself. ''We lost our focus,'' he later mused, recalling the years when industrywide growth pushed the company forward. ''Growing that dramatically, you're behind the eight ball all the way. It was out of control. We didn't execute well . . . we tried to chase Nike and Reebok in terms of design, which we never should have done. The result was a lot of closeouts, a lot of selling below the recommended wholesale price.'' Between 1986 and 1989, New Balance's prolific financial growth all but vanished, leaving Davis searching for answers.

New Balance Falters During the Late 1980s

The bleakest point during the anemic late 1980s occurred in 1989 when Davis's leading executives urged him to shutter the company's domestic manufacturing operations and move production overseas. The benefits of such a move were easily identifiable. Instead of paying $10 an hour plus benefits to its U.S. workers, New Balance could conduct its manufacturing in Asia and pay manufacturing workers $1 dollar a day or less. Moreover, all of New Balance's biggest competitors had made the move overseas years before and were realizing startling financial growth—companies such as Nike, which was hurtling past the $1 billion sales mark while New Balance was beginning to flounder below the $100 million sales mark. Despite the overwhelming evidence, Davis could not be swayed. He insisted on keeping his production facilities close to the company's headquarters and, in fact, did the opposite of what his management team was prodding him to do. Davis began pouring money into his U.S. manufacturing facilities, entrenching his position as others persuaded him to move abroad. ''The sizzle of the 1980s is gone,'' Davis proclaimed, ''and the steak of the 1990s is here. We've never made sizzle. We've always made steak.''

Davis reasoned that New Balance's strength was its attention to quality and the company's ability to respond quickly to retailers' needs, both of which would diminish if the company began subcontracting manufacturing thousands of miles away across the Pacific Ocean. His goal, as the 1990s began, was to shorten significantly the time required to roll out a new shoe model, slashing development time from one year to four months. Toward this objective Davis began investing heavily in capital improvements to increase efficiency and lift capacity. ''What always sold,'' he remarked, ''were our core running products and our tennis shoes. But we never had enough of them because we had spread ourselves too thin in all these peripheral areas.'' Accordingly, Davis narrowed the company's focus and began funneling money into its manufacturing facilities in Massachusetts and Maine. In 1991, as sales approached $100 million and profitability returned, Davis set aside $2 million for new equipment, spreading the investment over two years. In 1993 $3 million was earmarked for high-technology equipment such as automated cutting and vision-stitching machines. By the end of 1994 $6 million had been spent during the previous three years on new equipment, including a new computer-assisted design system that, along with other new machinery, enabled New Balance's research-and-development team to cut the required time for new product introduction from one year to four months. In addition, the investment in new equipment helped boost New Balance's gross profit margins from the mid-20 percent range averaged in the 1980s to the mid-30 percent range by 1993, a figure that compared favorably to the 38 percent reported by Nike, whose labor costs were much lower.

Flourishing in the 1990s and Beyond

By the mid-1990s New Balance was again a thriving enterprise recording encouraging financial gains. Revenues in 1995 were up to $380 million and successful forays into apparel and a variety of athletic footwear niches had been completed. At the company's five, company-owned manufacturing facilities in Massachusetts and Maine, running, walking, cross-training, tennis, basketball, and hiking shoes were assembled, giving the company wide exposure to a variety of popular recreational activities during the 1990s. When annual sales jumped to $474 million in 1996 and New Balance ranked as one of the top six best-selling footwear brands in the world and one of the top five domestically, Davis set his sights on reaching the $1 billion sales mark by 2000. Toward this end, the company made encouraging progress in 1997, when sales increased to more than $550 million. During the year, as many of the company's competitors recorded lackluster growth, New Balance exuded confidence that years ahead would bring continued success. The company established a new factory in Norway, Maine, and opened a $15 million distribution center in Lawrence, Massachusetts. To reach its goal of $1 billion in sales by the beginning of the new century, the company intensified its advertising efforts, setting aside $13 million for advertising in 1998 compared with the $4 million spent in 1997. On this ambitious note, the company prepared its plans for the future, confident that the awareness of the New Balance brand name would increase as sales climbed toward the $1 billion goal.

By the end of 1998 New Balance had transformed into one of the top five players in athletic footwear. Demand for New Balance shoes had increased such that in order to fill demand, the company had subcontracted a good portion of its manufacturing work overseas. Chairman and CEO James Davis planned to more than triple the amount of money put in to advertising New Balance shoes, focusing the ads on lifestyle and still steering clear of celebrity endorsements. In June 1998 New Balance made its first offering in the private placement market. Interest was so pronounced that the transaction rose from $50 million to $65 million. Come September 1998 New Balance purchased the Dunham brand name and prepared to launch into the business of boots, specifically outdoor, hunting, work, and sports boots. Davis announced that Dunham would become a new brand under the New Balance umbrella. Dunham would continue to manufacture their product, but New Balance would increase its distribution. All of Dunham's 33 boot models would endure.

Throughout 1998 athletic shoes were in a near universal slump, and all companies that produced them except adidas and New Balance were losing money. New Balance was up 15 percent from their profits in 1997. While they enjoyed fiscal health, New Balance, like other show manufacturers during this time, found itself accused by the Union of Needletrades, Industrial, and Textile Employees (Unite) of contracting out to Chinese workers employed in sweatshop-like conditions, in direct contrast to the claims of New Balance. A spokesman for New Balance countered that the company employed consultation firms to ensure that human rights were not violated in any of their production plants, that many of the shoes made overseas were sold overseas, and that some 70 percent of its manufacture still occurred in the United States, a comparatively high rate.

During this time, New Balance surged forward to become the fourth largest athletic shoe company. In March 1999 the company launched a new marketing campaign for their kid's line of athletic shoes on Nickelodeon. Ground was broken on the company's new corporate headquarters in May 1999, although the company remained in Boston. By August 1999 it relaunched the Dunham boot brand with variable widths, one of the company's most successful features in its athletic shoe line. January 2000 saw two important additions to the company: a California manufacturing plant employing 250, and a new president and chief operating officer, Jim Tompkins, a vice-president with New Balance, who reported directly to CEO Davis. In fall of 2000 New Balance seemed poised to achieve some success with a new line of apparel. The market for apparel had been universally soft, but New Balance remained optimistic.

New Balance announced in April 2001 that a newly created division, Aravon, would specialize in the production of orthopedic shoes, product to be available by spring of 2002. As part of expansion efforts, CEO Davis also signed several licensing agreements for the New Balance logo, though, unlike Nike and other popular rivals, he and his company declined to sign sports stars to multi-million-dollar endorsement deals. Instead, Davis stayed the course that had built the company, emphasizing the quality and design of New Balance shoes rather their stylistic appeal. Nor did New Balance target young consumers with the same zeal of its rivals. By 2003, the company was ranked third among athletic shoe manufacturers, capturing an 11 percent share of the market. In February 2004, the company acquired lacrosse equipment manufacturer Warrior and became a sponsor of major league lacrosse in the United States.

Further Reading

Abel, Katie, ''A Balancing Act: Jim and Anne Davis Have Always Had More on Their Minds, and Hearts, than Athletic Shoes,'' *Footwear News,* December 9, 2002, p. 44.

Finegan, Jay, ''Surviving in the Nike/Reebok Jungle,'' *Inc.*, May 1993, p. 98.

Fonda, Daren, ''Sole Survivor: Making Sneakers in America is So Yesterday. How Can New Balance Do It–and Still Thrive?,'' *Time,* November 8, 2004.

Gatlin, Greg, ''New Balance Stepping Out from Its Sole Business, *Boston Herald*, April 1, 2004, p. 41.

Kurlantzick, Joshua, ''New Balance Stays a Step Ahead,'' *U.S. News & World Report,*'' July 2, 2001, p. 34.

Melville, Greg, ''Balancing Act; Bolstered This Year by Innovative New Products New Balance Continues To Buck the Odds in the Flagging Athletic Industry,'' *Footwear News*, December 15, 1997, p. 9.

''New Balance is Running Around Asia,'' *AsiaPulse News*, October 8, 2002.

Tedeschi, Mark, ''New Balance Looks To Double Sales,'' *Footwear News,* January 28, 1991, p. 73.

——, *''New Balance Targets $200 Mil. Sales,'' Footwear* News, June 29, 1992, p. 15.

——, ''The SGB Interview,'' *Sporting Goods Business*, February 4, 1998, p. 38.

—Jeffrey L. Covell
—update: Howard A. Jones

New Belgium Brewing Company, Inc.

500 Linden Street
Fort Collins, Colorado 80524
U.S.A.
Telephone: (970) 221-0524
Toll Free: (888) 622-4044
Fax: (970) 221-0535
Web site: http://www.newbelgium.com

Private Company
Incorporated: 1991
Employees: 185
Sales: $45 million (2003 est.)
NAIC: 312120 Breweries

New Belgium Brewing Company, Inc., is one of the largest regional specialty brewers in the United States, producing about a dozen distinctive beers which are distributed to fifteen states in the West. Its brands include top-seller Fat Tire Ale, Sunshine Wheat Beer, and Abbey Belgian Style Ale, as well as seasonal offerings like Biere de Mars, Transatlantique Kriek, and Two Cherry Ale. The environmentally-friendly firm uses wind-generated electricity as well as heat and energy derived from byproducts of the brewing process. Founders Kim Jordan and Jeff Lebesch hold controlling interest in the company, which is partly owned by their employees.

Beginnings

The New Belgium Brewing Company (NBB) was founded in 1991 in Fort Collins, Colorado by the husband-and-wife team of Jeff Lebesch and Kim Jordan. Lebesch, an electrical engineer, had taken up the hobby of brewing beer at home a decade earlier, and had later volunteered at breweries in California to sharpen his skills. He became interested in founding his own brewery after going on a bicycle tour of Belgium, where he visited a number of breweries and acquired a special strain of yeast to bring home.

Although Belgian beer was not as well known in the United States as its German and English cousins, the country had its own distinctive approach to brewing, with a long tradition akin to that of winemaking in France. Belgians were particularly fond of adding flavors, like spices or fruit, to their brews, and also produced barrel-aged beers with a higher alcohol content.

After working up a business plan during an Easter Sunday hike in the mountains, Lebesch and Jordan, a social worker, decided to start a brewery in the basement of their home, and took out a $60,000 second mortgage to finance the endeavor. The company's initial offerings were the flavorful Abbey Trappist Style Ale and the lighter Fat Tire Ale, which was named after the bike Lebesch had toured Belgium on. The first bottles were capped in June 1991, and featured a neighbor's watercolor paintings on the labels.

Having persuaded a few local stores to carry their beer, Jordan, who handled the marketing, delivered it in the family station wagon. During their first year, the couple turned out 3,300 cases of 22-ounce "bomber" size bottles. Lebesch's Fat Tire Ale was especially well-received, and as its popularity grew its size was switched to the more standard 12-ounce bottles.

With sales climbing steadily upward, Lebesch and Jordan quit their day jobs to brew beer full time. In the fall of 1992 the company's operations were moved into a former rail freight warehouse in Fort Collins, and distribution was gradually expanded to cover much of the state of Colorado and a few outstate metropolitan areas. By 1994 NBB's annual output had grown to 28,000 31-gallon barrels, and the firm had begun offering public tours of its plant.

A New Brewery Opens in 1995

In November 1995 NBB opened a new $5 million brewery down the street from its existing location. By now the firm's beers included several additional varieties, including Old Cherry Ale, which was flavored with fresh berries. The company employed 50, with Lebesch serving as vice-president and head of brewing operations, and Jordan as president and CEO.

The so-called "microbrewery" segment of the marketplace was now experiencing tremendous growth. In 1994 Colorado had less than forty breweries and brewpubs (bars or restaurants which brewed beer on the premises), but just two years later the

Company Perspectives:

Long before New Belgium had a marketing department, it was just Kim and Jeff traveling to festivals, sampling out beers and talking to folks. These days it's the same idea but a little further flung. Now we have Beer Rangers who travel throughout the west talking to people, hosting events, and generally ensuring that all our beers are top quality from the draft line to your glass.

number had increased to more than sixty. Fort Collins was a hot spot, with one brewery per 12,000 residents, more than four times the statewide average of one per 51,000. In addition to NBB and several other small breweries and brewpubs, the city was also home to a major Anheuser-Busch plant.

In 1996 NBB experienced a minor controversy when it received a cease-and-desist letter from a small group of Belgian and Dutch Trappist Abbeys that objected to the use of the term ''Trappist'' in one of its beers' names. The firm complied with their request and changed the name to Abbey Belgian Style Ale. For the year, NBB brewed 57,000 barrels of beer and had sales estimated at $11 million. Jeff Lebesch had recently decided to step back from overseeing brewing operations, and the firm hired Peter Bouckaert from Rodenbach Brewery of Belgium to serve as its head brewer. NBB was now brewing a total of nine beers, which were distributed to Colorado, Wyoming, Kansas, New Mexico, and Arizona.

At this time the micro- and craft brewing industry was entering a long-anticipated period of retrenchment. Although the number of brewpubs continued to increase, fewer small breweries were opening and some were going out of business. Distributors and stores had begun limiting their stock to only the more popular craft beers, and the industry was also impacted by the newly-aggressive marketing campaigns of beer importers, the declining beer consumption of Americans (from 23.7 gallons per capita in 1985 to 22.1 in 1995, according to the Beer Institute), and the successful efforts of the distilled spirits industry to rekindle interest in their products, which took market share away from beer.

NBB was largely able to transcend these obstacles, however, as it had by now grown beyond the ranks of tiny microbreweries or mid-size craft brewers to the level of established regional brewer. Its output was dominated by Fat Tire Amber Ale (75 percent of sales), with other popular varieties including Abbey Belgian Style Ale, Trippel Belgian Style Ale, and Saison Belgian Style Farmhouse Ale.

The firm was already beginning to outgrow its new plant, and a two-year, $4.2 million expansion program was undertaken to add an additional 12,000 square feet of warehouse space, 8,000 feet of fermentation space, and 5,000 feet of utility space. Eight additional $100,000 fermentation vessels were also added to boost capacity to 150,000 barrels per year. NBB was now ranked among the top 25 beer-makers in the United States.

The company's rapid success was attributed in part to Lebesch and Jordan's systematic approach to the business and their focus on maintaining quality and consistency. Lebesch had created computer programs that monitored brewing processes, temperature, and ingredient flow, and the company also took such measures as using metal pipes rather than hoses to transport beer through the brewery, which yielded greater efficiency and sanitation. Six teams of laboratory testers were employed to ensure that each batch of beer met quality standards.

Growth in the Late 1990s

Over time NBB had gradually expanded its distribution area, and by 1998 its beers were available in ten states. Recent additions included Montana, Idaho, Washington, Texas, and Missouri. The firm's offerings were increasing as well, with new varieties including Sunshine Wheat, flavored with coriander and orange peel; 1554 Brussels Style Black Ale, based on a recipe from the sixteenth century; and Blue Paddle Pilsener, a lighter Czech-style beer. To help promote these brews, the company had expanded its marketing department to eighteen people, whose work included meeting with store owners and attending promotional events and beer festivals. For 1998 production jumped to 104,000 barrels, nearly a third higher than the year before.

1999 saw NBB make headlines when it signed a contract with the city of Fort Collins to buy only wind-generated electricity to operate its plant for a ten-year period. As a result, a new wind turbine was installed near Medicine Bow, Wyoming to produce the 1.8 million kilowatt-hours of electricity the plant consumed per year. The company would pay a 26 percent higher rate for the power, which would reduce emissions of carbon dioxide associated with coal-fired electricity. NBB's 105 employees had voted in favor of the move, which was financed in part by reducing their annual bonuses.

In the fall of 2000 NBB sponsored a promotional six-city ''Tour de Fat,'' a traveling festival that offered community bike rides, a Cruiser Bike Olympics, and a children's activity area. Proceeds were donated to local non-profit and bicycling organizations. The year also saw the introduction of the citrusy Biere de Mars, which was sold in the late winter and spring.

In 2001 the company introduced a new cherry-flavored beer. It had discontinued Old Cherry Ale in 1998, but enough requests for another cherry brew came in that the firm decided to re-formulate it. Two Cherry Ale was lighter than its predecessor, but contained the flavor of whole cherries added during the fermentation process. The seasonal brew was made available from late summer through fall. A dark, wood-aged French-style beer, La Folie, was also introduced during the year and sold on a seasonal basis. 2001 proved another record year for the firm, with production increasing to more than 230,000 barrels. In the fall, NBB began another expansion of its brewery to triple production capacity.

Dealing with rapid growth in a small business could sometimes be difficult, and Lebesch and Jordan developed several creative strategies to increase worker satisfaction. When the owners' salaries became the subject of speculation and rumors, they opened the books so employees could see what they earned along with the firm's expenses and profits. They also decided to place a third of the company in a trust which would dispense shares to workers' retirement accounts. Every employee was

Key Dates:

1991: Jeff Lebesch and Kim Jordan begin brewing beer in their basement.
1992: New Belgium Brewing's operations move to renovated freight warehouse.
1995: Company moves into a new $5 million brewery.
1996: A Belgian brewmaster hired.
1998: Production tops 100,000 barrels for the first time.
1999: Firm begins to use wind-generated electricity.
2001: Expansion of plant to triple capacity begins.
2004: Distribution is expanded to Southern California; New Belgium beer is now sold in 15 states.

given a case of beer a week, and after a year they received a $400 fat-tired cruiser bicycle. After five years, a trip to Belgium was awarded. The firm's plant included many ''fun'' touches as well, like a playground slide connecting the third- and second-floor offices for those wishing to descend in a hurry.

In addition to taking care of its employees, the company continued to be a conscientious steward of the environment. Along with using wind-generated electrical power, the firm recycled heat from brewing to warm parts of its plant, lit its warehouse with sunlight, had a comprehensive recycling program, and built a $4 million wastewater treatment plant, from which methane gas was extracted to generate additional electricity, and solid wastes were sold to farmers for use as fertilizer. NBB also gave $1 for each barrel it brewed to charitable organizations. The company, which employed a ''sustainability outreach coordinator,'' saw its environmental efforts highlighted on NBC television's *Today Show* in July 2002.

Increasing Emphasis on Seasonal Beers in Early 2000s

NBB was now making six year-round beers and four seasonal varieties. The latter were proving increasingly popular, and a new one was introduced every few months. The light, kaffir leaf-flavored Loft was introduced in August 2002, and early the next year the company announced that it would import a two-year aged Belgian beer to be blended 50/50 with a brew of its own. The result, Transatlantique Kriek, was issued in the fall.

NBB was also selling products emblazoned with its logo including hats, t-shirts, beer glasses, frisbees, and even a Sunshine Wheat lip balm. Over the years the company had won many awards for its beers, and it had been named the best mid-sized brewery in the United States at the Colorado-based Great American Beer Festival for several years running.

By now, half of NBB's production was sold in Colorado, with the rest shipped to a dozen neighboring states, including the recently-added Nebraska. Explaining the firm's regional focus, in 2003 CEO Kim Jordan told *Mother Earth News*, ''we're not looking at aggressive marketing strategies right now because quality of life—for ourselves and our employees—is important, too. If sales become the only focus of a business, and you're constantly hiring new staff, you may lose track of the original goals: to have some fun, maintain a great working environment and produce an excellent product that doesn't have [negative] impacts on the environment.'' While she continued to lead the firm, her husband Jeff Lebesch now served on its board of directors and as a technical consultant. Jordan was a well-respected leader within the industry, and had recently served as chairman of the Brewers Association of America.

In 2003 output increased yet again, to 285,000 barrels. NBB was producing half the amount that leading craft brewer Sierra Nevada did, but its distribution was more limited, and it had a higher annual growth rate than the larger firm. The company was now one of the top ten employers in the Fort Collins area, and also hosted 80,000 visitors to its plant during the year.

In 2004 NBB was awarded an Environmental Achievement Award by the U.S. Environmental Protection Agency for the firm's efforts to reduce energy and water consumption at its plant. Ten percent of its power was now being supplied by methane derived from waste, and this amount was expected to increase over time.

The fall of 2004 saw distribution expand to Southern California, two years after sales had begun in the northern part of the state. NBB introduced its beers into a new market only after establishing a solid foothold in the last one, starting with the popular Fat Tire Ale and gradually adding the rest of its line. The company's beers were now available in fifteen states west of the Mississippi, with Iowa and Minnesota slated to be added next.

In just over a decade, New Belgium Brewing Company, Inc., had grown from a home-based brewery into one of the largest regional ''craft'' brewers in the United States. The firm's success was built on quality products, strong leadership, a dedication to its employees, and a deep respect for the environment. With more than two-thirds of the United States still untapped, its growth looked assured for years to come.

Principal Competitors

Sierra Nevada Brewing Co.; Boston Beer Co.; Odell Brewing Co.; Flying Dog Brewery; Breckinridge Brewery; Rockies Brewing Co.; Left Hand & Tabernash Brewing Co.

Further Reading

Bastian, Kristen S., ''Fat Chance,'' *Northern Colorado Business Report*, October 1, 2004, p. 1.
Berta, Dina, ''With Microbrew Chic Fading, Industry Turns to Bottom Line,'' *Denver Rocky Mountain News*, October 3, 1999, p. 1G.
Brand, Rachel, ''Reaching the Peak: New Belgium Brewing Co. Goes From Basement to 3rd Largest in State,'' *Rocky Mountain News*, November 17, 2001, p. 1C.
Bronikowski, Lynn, ''There's No Cap on Microbreweries; Colorado Has More Suds Factories Per Person Than Any Other State,'' *Rocky Mountain News*, March 24, 1996, p. 8W.
Bunn, Dina, ''Fat Tire Brewer Getting Fatter,'' *Rocky Mountain News*, November 5, 1997, p. 20B.
——, ''Fat Vats—New Belgium's Tanks Teeming With Business,'' *Rocky Mountain News*, November 8, 1997, p. 2B.
Cada, Chryss, ''Brewing Company CEO Keeps Focus on Products, Workers,'' *Northern Colorado Business Report*, October 3, 2003, p. 23.
——, ''New Belgium Founders Have Success Bottled Up,'' *Northern Colorado Business Report*, November 3, 2000, p. 9C.

Doehrman, Marylou, ''Brewing Beer and an Ideal Business Model,'' *Colorado Springs Business Journal*, April 18, 2003, p. 1.

''First Wind Powered Brewery in America,'' *Environment News Service*, March 22, 1999.

Katz, Alan, ''Trappist Monks Shove Cork in Copycat Beers,'' *Denver Post*, July 7, 1997, p. A1.

Kreck, Dick, ''Fort Collins Breweries Friendly Rivals,'' *Denver Post*, December 21, 1994, p. E1.

''New Belgium to Use Methane for Power,'' *Modern Brewery Age*, October 28, 2002, p. 2.

O'Keefe, Brian, ''Something's Brewing—Beer Buzz: World Famous? Maybe Not, But These Five Microbreweries Are World Class,'' *SmartMoney*, August 1, 2000.

Wann, Dave, ''Peddling Sustainable Brews,'' *Mother Earth News*, April 1, 2003, p. 15.

—Frank Uhle

The NPD Group, Inc.

900 West Shore Road
Port Washington, New York 11050
U.S.A.
Telephone: (516) 625-0700
Fax: (516) 625-2347
Web site: http://www.npd.com

Private Company
Founded: 1953 as Home Testing Institute
Employees: 705
Sales: $117.6 million (2003)
NAIC: 541910 Marketing Research and Public Opinion Polling

The NPD Group, Inc., is a global market research firm operating out of Port Washington, New York. Long reliant on the use of diaries to track consumer behavior, NPD now focuses its efforts on electronic cash register information—which is drawn from 230 retail partners—to determine product movement and online panels of consumers to track consumer behavior. NPD samples 600,000 people out of a pool of 2.5 million registered members in its online panel to conduct most studies, supplemented by follow-up surveys. Not only are panelists afforded an opportunity to have their opinions count, they are also enticed to participate by drawings of cash and prizes. NPD serves a wide range of industries, including apparel, appliances, automotive, beauty, consumer electronic, food and beverage, housewares, information technology, music, toys, travel, and video games. Data is available online to clients through Internet portals. The firm also offers clients in-depth analysis, topical reports, and proprietary research. In addition to consumer industries, NPD offers information products geared toward investment professionals to help them answer similar questions: Who is buying their products, where, why, and at what price? All told, NPD works with more than 1,000 clients, many of which are Fortune 500 companies such as Dell, General Electric, Mattel, Nike, Unilever, and Warner Brothers. Aside from its Long Island headquarters, NPD maintains offices in New York City; Chicago; Greensboro, North Carolina; Houston; and Reston, Virginia. International offices are located in Toronto, London, Madrid, Mexico City, Milan, Nuremberg, Paris, and Tokyo. NPD is owned by its chairman and CEO, Tod Stuart Johnson.

1950s Origins

NPD was founded in 1953 as Home Testing Institute by a pioneer in the market research industry, Henry Brenner. Born in New York City in 1914, Brenner grew up in Mount Vernon, New York, the son of East European immigrants. He was an ambitious youngster who grew up wanting to attend medical school in order to one day find a cure for cancer. In a 1984 *Advertising Age* profile, Brenner described himself as ''a little fat kid completely too smart for my peers; good at math and sciences but terrible in languages.'' During the early years of the Depression, when money was tight, he attended college at night, including classes at Columbia University, City College of New York, and Pace Institute, but he never earned a degree. To scrape by, he took a series of day jobs, which included stints slicing bread at a Wonder Bread factory, helping a surveyor, and writing freelance sports stories for a Mount Vernon newspaper.

It was not by design that Brenner became involved in the advertising field, and in truth he showed no particular aptitude for it. By his own count he was fired by five companies in five years, including Standard Brands, Inc., where he would later return as the director of market research. ''I was a lousy employee,'' Brenner told *Advertising Age*. As he also recalled, ''Things were so desperate that I put an anonymous situations wanted ad in the *Times* and my boss answered it.'' Nevertheless, out of this experience, Brenner drew a valuable lesson that later served him well: instead of criticizing, pose questions. During World War II, Brenner took a break from his frustrating advertising career, serving from 1943 to 1946 in the U.S. Maritime Service, where he was able to use his penchant for science by teaching meteorology at the U.S. Merchant Marine Academy in Kings Point, New York.

When he was discharged from the service, Brenner became involved in the new market research field, starting out as a freelance field interviewer on grocery sales. He found full-time employment in 1946 with Standard Brands, and now having found his niche, he rose through the ranks to become the firm's

Company Perspectives:

Many of the world's most successful companies rely on us for insight on what is selling, where and why so that they can understand and leverage the latest trends.

director of market research. In 1951, he left to become merchandising manager for Columbia Broadcasting System in New York City, a position he held for two years before deciding to strike out on his own and start Home Testing Institute, which initially he ran out of the basement of his Long Island home.

Using panels of representative consumers who recorded their buying habits and other information in diaries, Home Testing began to build an extensive database of marketing information. Out of this grew the National Purchase Diary Panel, which in 1965 used the initials to become NPD Research, Inc. Aside from running these businesses, which formed the core of what was loosely called the NPD Group, Brenner also founded or bought several other market research companies, including McCullom/ Spielman Research in Great Neck, New York; Marketing Evaluations in Port Washington; OPOC Statistics in New York City; Acker Retail Audits in Lyndhurst, New Jersey; Hart Systems in Garden City, New York; and Grocery Laboratory in New York City. Brenner had a major influence on the market research field and is credited with developing such important techniques as monadic product testing, in which a single product is evaluated by respondents over a certain period of time to provide a detailed analysis of its effectiveness and appeal. Brenner was also highly regarded for his willingness to help others in the field. A ''one-man personnel agency,'' he helped scores of acquaintances to find market research jobs and he offered career advice to hundreds. Not only did he make friends in the field, he developed loyal customers. General Foods honored his 25 years of service to the company, as did Philip Morris for 30 years of market research. In 1976, the Advertising Research Foundation named Brenner one of the founding fathers of the research industry, along with the likes of George Gallup and A.C. Nielsen.

New Leadership in 1980s

Brenner was hard working and competitive, traits that led to the development of ulcers. In 1975, he suffered a heart attack. Thereafter, he made an effort to cut back on his work load and during the winter months worked from his Florida home. He retired in 1986 and sold NPD to Tod Johnson, who had been active in running this and other Brenner businesses for some 15 years. Born in Minneapolis in 1944, Johnson earned undergraduate and graduate degrees from Carnegie Mellon University, then started his business career in 1967 with Market Science Associates, Inc, in Des Plaines, Illinois. He became a vice-president, then left the company in 1971 to join Brenner. Johnson was named the president and chief executive officer of NPD Research. In 1980, he took over the same roles at Home Testing Institute, followed by the same arrangement at OPOC Computing two years later. In 1989, NPD Research, Home Testing Institute, and OPOC Computing were merged to form The NPD Group Inc., with Johnson owning the business and serving as president and chief executive officer.

Under Johnson's leadership, NPD enjoyed strong growth and continued the legacy of innovation established by its founder. One of Johnson's greatest contributions was to recognize how NPD's research could be leveraged as a marketing tool for the firm. People liked to read about their own spending habits, and NPD became adept at packaging its data into factoids that hundreds of newspapers and magazines either reprinted or used as the basis for feature articles. During Johnson's first 20 years at the helm, NPD also accomplished a number of firsts. In 1978, it launched the first point-of-sale tracking system for toys. Also during that year, it expanded the concept of syndicated databases beyond packaged goods to other consumer products. In 1981, NPD revolutionized market research in the packaged goods area by introducing the handheld scanner. The company then licensed its scanner technology to A.C. Nielsen in 1987. Along the way, NPD expanded the number of industries it served. It added foodservice in 1975, apparel and toys in 1978, and consumer electronics in 1987. NPD became involved in athletic footwear in 1990, cosmetics and fragrances in 1996, cookware and bakeware in 1996, and fashion footwear in 1997.

The 1990s saw NPD in the vanguard of measuring Internet usage and, more importantly, using the Internet as a tool to conduct market research. In 1995, NPD created the PC Meter (the first tool capable of measuring consumers' Internet usage), created the first online consumer panel, and conducted the first online research. PC Meter grew out of work NPD was doing in tracking computer software sales. Company researchers realized that it was possible to follow the activity of America Online subscribers, leading NPD to develop the PC Meter to monitor users' mouse clicks and plot their Internet activity. A panel of 40,000 representative consumers was formed and the PC Meter was employed to determine how many and what kind of people were turning to cyberspace, measuring traffic on America Online as well as on Web sites throughout the Internet. A subsidiary was formed using the PC Meter name, and data was compiled on a daily, weekly, and monthly basis, provided online to Internet, technology, media, and finance companies who subscribed to the service. Like most startups, it was a money-losing proposition, but because NPD was a private company it was free of the pressures a public company would face in taking a hit to the bottom line over an extended period of time. Johnson and his management team sensed the potential impact of the Internet, in general as well as on the future of market research, and were determined to become involved at an early stage. In 1997, PC Meter changed its name to Media Metrix and merged with its main rival RelevantKnowledge.

Media Metrix made an initial public offering in May 1999 at the height of the demand for Internet-related stocks and within a matter of months the price of its shares increased to the point that the company was worth an astounding $1 billion, this for a company that had yet to make any money and had lost some $20 million since its founding. In 2000, Media Metrix, which Johnson also headed, merged with Jupiter Communications, Inc., becoming Jupiter Media Metrix, which Johnson claimed was ''poised to redefine the landscape of Internet information services.'' Despite the company's ambitious goals and technical expertise, it soon fell victim to the dot-com meltdown that claimed so many Internet ventures during this period. The company was dismantled in September 2002, with the Media Metrix

Key Dates:

1953: Henry Brenner founds Home Testing Institute.
1971: Tod Johnson is named CEO of NPD Research.
1986: Brenner retires and sells NPD Group to Johnson.
1995: PC Meter is introduced.
1999: Media Metrix is spun off.
2001: Custom Research is business sold.

Internet Audience Measurement service that grew out of NPD's PC Meter venture being sold to com-Score Networks for just $1.5 million.

During the rise and fall of Media Metrix, NPD made progress on other fronts. In 1996, it entered into a joint venture with two market research companies, GfK of Germany and SOFRES of France, to combine their existing consumer panels to help clients who needed to examine consumer behavior across countries. The company also began offering marketing research for e-commerce ventures and in 2000 offered online tracking services for the apparel, foodservice, and footwear industries. In that same year, it aligned itself with Information resources to bolster its retail sales tracking capabilities for the U.S. automotive aftermarket.

A Break with the Past in the 21st Century

Even as the price of Internet stocks were beginning to tumble, NPD made a greater commitment to cyberspace. It had become increasingly difficult to find enough statistically representative consumers willing to serve as diary panelists whose online behavior NPD tracked and recorded for little or no compensation. In 2001, the company decided to make a break from the past, electing to use the Internet for both consumer sampling and the delivery of its product. In keeping with this new approach, NPD sold off its custom research operation—testing clients' concepts, brands, and advertisements—to a French research firm, Ipsos, for $120 million. The business accounted for about $65 million of NPD's total revenues of $160 million in 2000, but Johnson was confident that NPD would be better off in the long run if it concentrated on its new approach to business. By leveraging the power of the Internet, NPD hoped to collect even more market information across more industries, allowing it to attract more clients and provide even greater detail because of the increased size of the sample. In addition, by putting the data online, it would be available more quickly to clients. The first of its portals soon opened, NPD Foodworld and NPD Fashionworld. They would be followed by NPD Funworld, NPD Techworld, and NOPD Houseworld. To support this new direction, NPD invested some $40 million in technology. The company had clearly reached a major turning point in its history, but there was every reason to believe that even with its new sampling and delivery mechanisms it would remain a major market research company in the years to come.

Principal Competitors

Information Resources, Inc.; Taylor Nelson Sofres plc; VNU N.V.

Further Reading

Griess-Glabman, Maureen D., "One Entrepreneur's Legacy," *Advertising Age*, May 17, 1984, p. M.
Sanger, Elizabeth, "A Major Shift for the NPD Group," *Newsday*, January 25, 2001, p. A50.
——, "Media Metrix Ready for IPO Riches," *Newsday*, May 6, 1999, p. A65.
Strugatch, Warren, "Sultans of Stats," *Long Island Business News*, November 12, 1999, p. 1A.

—Ed Dinger

Odakyu Electric Railway Co., Ltd.

1-8-3 Nishi-Shinjuku
Shinjuku-ku
Tokyo 160
Japan
Telephone: (+81) 3-3349-2526
Fax: (+81) 3-3346-2447
Web site: http://www.odakyu-co.com

Public Company
Incorporated: 1923 as Odawara Express Railway Co., Ltd.
Employees: 14,062
Sales: ¥624.92 billion ($5.89 billion) (2004)
Stock Exchanges: Tokyo
Ticker Symbol: 9007
NAIC: 482111 Line-Haul Railroads; 236116 New Multi-Family Housing Construction (Except Operative Builders); 237990 Other Heavy and Civil Engineering Construction; 445110 Supermarkets and Other Grocery (Except Convenience) Stores; 452111 Department Stores (Except Discount Department Stores); 485111 Mixed Mode Transit Systems; 485310 Taxi Service; 485410 School and Employee Bus Industry; 541810 Advertising Agencies; 561510 Travel Agencies; 561599 All Other Travel Arrangement and Reservation Services; 713990 All Other Amusement and Recreation Industries; 721110 Hotels (Except Casino Hotels) and Motels; 722110 Full-Service Restaurants

Odakyu Electric Railway Co., Ltd. is one of the major private railroad companies in Japan, responsible for carrying 13 percent of the 34.5 million rail passengers who travel throughout the Tokyo metropolitan area each day. Odakyu's railway consists of three lines that travel a total of 120.5 kilometers. The core of the company's operations is the Odakyu Line, which connects Shinjuku Station—the largest terminal in Japan, with 3.4 million passengers per day—with Fuji-Hakone National Park, which lies at the foot of Mount Fuji, and also with Shonan, Japan's most famous seaside resort. Together, the company's railways serve an average of 1.82 million passengers each day. Nearly five million people live alongside the Odakyu Line, a population Odakyu serves by developing a variety of businesses, including leasing large-scale commercial buildings, developing residential housing areas, and operating leisure facilities, retail stores, and hotels. The Odakyu Group, of which Odakyu is the core, comprises 116 companies with 27,000 employees.

Origins

Japanese society is increasingly concentrated in large cities and centered on railroad stations. The rapid growth of the Japanese economy has accelerated the trend, and there is continuing demand for space in or within easy access of a city for both residential and business purposes.

As Tsutomu Shimizu, one of Odakyu's top executives, has stated, "Just as the ancient civilizations flourished in the basins of big rivers, modern civilization develops alongside railways." Private railroad companies in Japan usually build their railroads on undeveloped and unused sites with easy access to city centers and construct supermarkets and department stores in the station buildings, thus establishing their stations as centers for distribution and commercial activities. Railroad companies acquire massive amounts of land around their stations and diversify into businesses such as real estate, construction, leisure and tourism, and information services.

Tsurumatsu Toshimitsu, the founder of Odakyu, was a lawyer and then a member of the National Diet before he became involved in the management of the railroad business. In 1911, he founded the Kinugawa Hydro-Electric Co., Ltd., which was eventually to develop into Odakyu Railway Company Limited. In 1921, Toshimitsu applied on behalf of Tokyo High Speed Railway Co., Ltd. for a license to build a railroad linking the southwestern part of Tokyo with the central region of Kanagawa Prefecture. The license was granted in 1922, and the company was renamed Odawara Express Railway Co., Ltd. after Odawara City, which lies at the foot of Mount Fuji. The official inauguration of the company took place on May 1, 1923. Nearly four months after Toshimitsu had embarked on this difficult project, which required enormous initial investment, the Great Kanto Earthquake struck, reducing Tokyo and Yoko-

Company Perspectives:

Odakyu aims to ensure autonomous growth in the future, even in an era of declining population, by quickly responding to changes in markets, customers and business conditions through strategic market-oriented management. While using selection and concentration in allocating management resources, Odakyu is making every effort to realize the Best Way Integrated Business Concept, the Group's business vision. Under the Best Way Integrated Business Concept, the Odakyu Group is leveraging its strengths and management resources in developing a variety of businesses that are tailored to local communities and center on transportation operations. The Odakyu Group aims to ensure future growth by expanding its market share and further developing its operational areas, while maintaining Group markets by attracting people to its areas even as the national population declines due to low birth rates and an aging society.

hama to ashes. However, this disaster worked to the advantage of the newly established Odakyu, because many people whose homes had been destroyed began to want to move into the less-affected suburbs, boosting new land development and construction work. As the development of suburban Tokyo was an important social issue at that time and a great number of investors were willing to invest in this project, there was no difficulty in securing funding for the construction of the railroad. In 1925, government permission was given for the execution of the whole project and an 82-kilometer-long railroad between Shinjuku and Odawara was built in one and a half years, the fastest completion period recorded in the history of Japan's railroads. Business went well until Japan was hit by the Depression in the 1930s.

Odakyu's business started to recover again in the mid-1930s, but in 1937 the Sino-Japanese War broke out and there was every sign that it would be long and hard. As part of the wartime emergency measures, the Japanese government decided that the power industry should come under the control of the state. As a result, Kinugawa Hydro-Electricity Company, the parent company of Odawara, had to close down and merge with its subsidiary to form Odakyu Electric Railway Company (Odakyu) in 1941. As the war continued and its ferocity intensified, the government took further steps to establish the land transport infrastructure. In 1944, Odakyu was merged with three other railroad companies, now known as Keio Electric Co., Ltd., Keihin Express Electric Railway Co., Ltd., and Tokyu Corporation. The new company, Tokyo Express Electric Railway Co., Ltd., was headed by Keita Grotoh, previously the third president of Odawara Express Electric Railway Company, who had had experience in many other electric railroad companies and was to become Minister of Transport and Communications. The unification of private railways in the southwestern suburbs of Tokyo was thus completed by the newly named Tokyo Express Electric Railway Co., Ltd.

The end of World War II made it possible for those railroad companies that had been forced to amalgamate during the state of emergency to become independent again, and in June 1948 they started to go their separate ways. In October 1948, the newly born Odakyu introduced a non-stop special express between Shinjuku and Odawara, and in 1950 it fulfilled its long-cherished dream by opening a new direct line to Hakone-Yumoto, one of Japan's best-known hot spa resorts. In 1957, it launched the epoch-making Romance Car SE, which set the world speed record on the narrow-gauge track. In 1960, it completed the Golden Course, a round-trip route around the Hakone area. In order to strengthen the company's grip on tourist transport, it put new strategies into practice.

Diversification Begins in the 1960s

Until the mid-1960s, Odakyu's main strategic task was to expand its flagship line connecting the western gateway of Tokyo with Japan's most famous tourist resort, Hakone. However, since the mid-1960s the strategy of Odakyu has developed into a second phase, directed toward enhancing the quality of life of the residents along its lines. Odakyu's strategy in the second phase was, as is the case in other major private railway companies, to further promote affiliated divisions and subsidiaries through diversification, and thereby to reinforce the overall strength of the Odakyu Group. The Odakyu Group comprises many diversified divisions and subsidiaries, with Odakyu Electric Railway Company as its core. Their business activities are classified into seven fields: public transport, leisure, distribution, real estate, construction, information services, and overseas business.

In 1967, Odakyu completed the rebuilding of Shinjuku Terminal Building, and in 1975 it opened a branch line, the Tama Line, to Tama New Town for the commuters among the town's 300,000 inhabitants. In 1978, a direct route into all areas of Tokyo was opened by way of the agreement with the Underground Chiyoda Line, enabling trains of both companies to use the same track, dramatically enhancing the function of Odakyu in providing urban transport networks.

However, as the population of the areas along its lines has been growing rapidly, Odakyu's transport capability is increasingly unable to cope with the growing number of passengers. During the rush hours, Odakyu runs one ten-carriage train every two minutes or so, yet the trains are filled to more than twice their capacity, so that the passengers often find it difficult even to read magazines on their journey.

With an increasing number of high-tech industries and universities either newly set up or moving out from the city center, and with population expected to increase further in the areas along the Odakyu Line, the consensus of management is that the only way to solve the problem is to build a four-track line as soon as possible. Odakyu attempted to raise finance for this project in various ways such as obtaining government grants and issuing warrant and convertible bonds as well as foreign bonds in 1978, the first such attempt made by a Japanese railroad company. Having successfully secured such financing, Odakyu began to build a four-track line in the early 1990s. In 1991, Odakyu achieved the extension of its operations to Nishi-Izu, a fashionable seaside resort particularly popular among young people, and developed its business activities into the new area.

In the leisure industry, Odakyu has always had the advantage of running a railroad between Shinjuku and Fuji-Hakone.

Key Dates:

1911: Tsurumatsu Toshimitsu establishes the Kinugawa Hydro-Electric Co., Ltd.
1923: The company changes its name to Odawara Express Railway Co., Ltd.
1941: Odakyu Electric Railway Co. is formed after the Japanese government demands the merger of Kinugawa Hydro-Electric Co. and Odawara Express Railway.
1962: Odakyu Electric enters the retail business with the establishment of a department store.
1980: In a joint venture with Hyatt Hotels, Odakyu Electric opens the Hotel Century Hyatt.
1987: The company enters the cable television business through the formation of Odakyu Cable Vision Company.
1998: The Best Way Odakyu management plan is introduced.
2004: Odakyu announces long-term plan to construct multiple double tracks in all its regions by 2014.

In spite of this, Odakyu was rather late in establishing a comprehensive leisure business. However, since it started its operations in the field of international travel services as an authorized International Air Transport Association (IATA) agent in 1972, and especially since it set up Odakyu Service Co., Ltd. in 1976, it has begun to develop a complete range of travel services.

In the early stages of its entry into hotel-related business, Odakyu ran mainly resort hotels. However, since it opened the Hotel Century Hyatt, in conjunction with Hyatt International of the United States in 1980, it has been progressing into the urban hotel business and has built chain hotels in many local cities. It also runs approximately 220 restaurants and coffee shops in these hotels and around the Odakyu line. Moreover, it has recently entered the field of sport and leisure facilities and the health industry. In 1979, it opened Seijo Tennis Garden, and since then it has added a great number of swimming pools, skating rinks, bowling alleys, and athletic clubs in the Tokyo and Kanagawa areas. Furthermore, it has stepped up its operations by opening Nishi-Fuji Golf Club in 1989, and Naka-Izu Club in 1990.

Odakyu's involvement in the retail business dates back to 1962, when the Odakyu Department Store was opened at the west exit of Shinjuku Station. Since the reconstruction of Odakyu Station building in 1967, it has become the jewel in the company's crown. At present, the task of the Shinjuku Odakyu Department Store is to respond to changes in the type and increasing number of customers resulting from the move of the municipal government offices into this area. It is estimated that the daytime population has increased by 25,000. Odakyu Shoji Co., Ltd, which is another significant part of the group, has moved into variety stores, supermarkets, and convenience stores. The first store was opened in Sagami-Ohno in 1963, and in the early 1990s the company had more than 38 stores. In the face of intense competition, Odakyu has achieved good results, making full use of its prime locations by stocking high-quality goods and thoroughly training employees in customer service. In 1976, the Odakyu Department Store opened a branch in Machida, Tokyo's most rapidly developing satellite town. Subsequently, it has expanded its operations in Fujisawa and has recorded steady growth in the sector.

The real estate department of a railroad company tends to focus only on the land close to its lines. In order to overcome this tendency, Odakyu Real Estate Co., Ltd. was established in 1964 with the aim of providing general real estate services and developing related businesses. Its operations cover the sale and leasing of land and properties as well as other intermediary services throughout the Kanto area.

The redevelopment plan for the area along the Odakyu Line is already under discussion by the interested parties, including local authorities looking ahead to the 21st century. The real test of the company's ability will be how effectively it can play its part in the long-term plan. Odakyu has concentrated its energies on renting out office buildings. Its leasing business has shown steady growth since its reorganization in 1975. It has utilized the open spaces in unused railroad land, station buildings, and hotels by letting them to tenants. In this field, Odakyu has shown remarkable growth, and its future prospects are highly promising.

Since about 1982, the phrase the "Era of New Media" has been frequently used in Japanese mass media. Cable television has become very popular and its future is promising, but it requires major investment in plant and equipment as well as in software development. Odakyu's management was initially cautious but eventually decided to enter into this business.

First, Odakyu set up a subsidiary, Odakyu Cable Vision Co., Ltd, in 1987, and then in 1988 it joined in the management of International Cable Network Co., Ltd. The viewers' chief motives for subscribing were the desire for clearer TV pictures, satellite transmission, and special local programs. Technical research is under way to establish a service network through which the customers can make payments automatically to participating shops from their own homes. In its effort to enhance its services, Odakyu Computer System Co., Ltd. and Odakyu CAP Agency Co, Ltd.—CAP stands for Communication And Promotion—were set up in 1989 and in 1990 respectively.

Approaching the 21st century, the most important project in the company's third phase was the enhancement of cooperation within the Group in its search for new business both in Japan and abroad.

Beginning in the second half of the 1980s, Odakyu saw overseas markets as fertile ground for new business opportunities. In 1989, the Odakyu Group opened its representative office in London, and it also established Odakyu Hawaii Corp. through the acquisition of Outrigger Hobron, Condominium Hotel, in Hawaii, which has 600 rooms. In 1990, the Odakyu Department Paris Office was renamed Odakyu France S.A.R.L., and Odakyu Tours U.S.A. Inc. was established to provide better services for overseas tourists.

Group Management Structure Emerges in the 1990s

As Odakyu progressed through the 1990s, its found itself operating in a business environment whose dynamics were changing. Industry deregulation and the globalization of business, coupled with an aging population and declining birthrate, forced Odakyu's leadership to adapt to the times. As the company worked on practical matters—for instance, extending the Tama Line by 1.5 kilometers in 1990 and completing one section of multiple double tracks in 1997—it also worked on more philosophical issues. The result of management's discussion on how Odakyu could best respond to the changes surrounding it was formulated in a long-term management plan introduced in 1998. Known as the ''Best Way Odakyu'' plan, the approach adopted by management centered on increasing value along the company's railway lines. Perhaps the most readily obvious manifestation of Best Way Odakyu was a component of the broadly defined management plan called ''Best Way Integrated Business Concept,'' introduced in 2001. The concept focused on taking a market-oriented approach to the various business sectors along the company's railway lines. Each sector, or enclave of constituents, had its own special market characteristics that the company tailored its services toward. Accordingly, the company divided its service area into the Shinjuku Region, a commercial business area; the Railway Line Region, an upscale residential area; and the Hakone Region, a leisure area. These three regions were subdivided, such as with the Railway Line Region, which was separated by the Setaga Region and the Tama Region. By organizing its railway lines in distinct markets, Odakyu could provide services targeted to the specific characteristics of each area.

As Odakyu moved forward under the guidance of its Best Way Odakyu plan, the company continued to expand, building on its already towering size. In 2002, the company established Odakyu Hotels and Resorts Co., Ltd. as the core entity of its hotel business. On the restaurant side of its business, a subsidiary company, Giraud Restaurant System Co. Ltd., acquired a pasta restaurant company and, together with Odakyu Restaurant System Co., opened 11 new restaurants in 2004. As the company prepared for the future, it had bold plans for its railway business, the essence of Odakyu. The company was working on the construction of a more than ten-kilometer section of multiple double tracks in the greater Tokyo area. The majority of the section was expected to open by the beginning of 2005. Looking further ahead, Odakyu planned to complete construction of multiple double tracks in all its regions by 2014.

Principal Subsidiaries

Hakone Tozan Railway Co., Ltd.; Hakone Kankosen Inc.; Kanagawa Chuo Kotsu Co., Ltd. (44.2%); Odakyu Bus Co., Ltd. (97%); Tachikawa Bus Co., Ltd. (38%); Tokai Jidosha Co., Ltd. (33.1%); Odakyu Kotsu Co., Ltd.; Odakyu Hotels Co., Ltd. (30%); The International Tourist Corporation (94.2%); Odakyu Restaurant System Co., Ltd.; Odakyu Department Store Co., Ltd. (58.5%); Fujisawa Odakyu Co., Ltd. (30%); Giraud Restaurant System Co. Ltd.; Odakyu Real Estate Co., Ltd. (47.8%); Odakyu Construction Co., Ltd. (45.9%); Odakyu Building Service Co., Ltd.; Odakyu Hotels and Resort Co., Ltd.

Principal Competitors

West Japan Railway Company; East Japan Railway Company; Central Japan Railway Company; Hokkaido Railway Company; Shikoku Railway Company; Tokyo Kyuko Electric Railway.

Further Reading

''American Companies in Japan: Construction and Real Estate,'' *Japan-U.S. Business Report,* May 31, 1998, p. 13.

''American Malls Plans Store in Odakyu Station,'' *Comline-Tokyo Financial Wire,* March 30, 1998, p. 41.

''Odakyu Railway to Aid Retail Unit Restructuring,'' *Japan Transportation Scan,* December 20, 1999, p. 16.

—Norimasa Satoh
—update: Jeffrey L. Covell

Owens & Minor, Inc.

4800 Cox Road
Glen Allen, Virginia 23060
U.S.A.
Telephone: (804) 747-9794
Fax: (804) 273-0232
Web site: http://www.owens-minor.com

Public Company
Incorporated: 1927 as Owens & Minor Drug Company, Inc.
Employees: 3,245
Sales: $4.24 billion (2004)
Stock Exchanges: New York
Ticker Symbol: OMI
NAIC: 423450 Medical, Dental, and Hospital Equipment and Supplies Merchant Wholesalers

The second-largest wholesale distributor of medical and surgical supplies in the United States, Owens & Minor, Inc. owns distribution centers across the nation that serve hospitals, primary care facilities, healthcare systems, and group purchasing organizations. Originally founded as a wholesale drug company in 1882, Owens & Minor first entered the medical and surgical supply business in 1966 and then, through a series of acquisitions completed during the ensuing three decades, entrenched its position in its new business, divesting its wholesale drug business in 1992 to operate exclusively as a medical and surgical supply distributor during the mid-1990s.

Origins

The corporate history of Owens & Minor charts the history of the Minor family, tracing the roots of a family tree that stretch back more than a century before the company was founded. Four generations before a Minor family member founded the company that would employ generations of Minors, Dr. George Gilmer spent his life working as an apothecary-surgeon, attending to patients in colonial Williamsburg until his death in 1751. Dr. Gilmer was the first in a long line of family members who would spend their professional careers working in the pharmaceutical or medical fields, beginning a legacy that would continue on two centuries later and inspire his son to enter the medical profession as well.

Dr. Gilmer's son and namesake followed his father's footsteps and received training in the medical field. The younger Gilmer, who would earn distinction as Thomas Jefferson's personal physician, practiced medicine in Charlottesville, Virginia, working there as a doctor before and after the Revolutionary War. His sister, Lucy Gilmer, lived in Charlottesville as well, where she married Dr. Peter Minor, also a Charlottesville physician. The married couple's son, George Gilmer Minor, took to the seas and studied medicine abroad, then returned to the United States and began practicing medicine in New Kent County, not far from Williamsburg. Following the conclusion of the Civil War, George Gilmer Minor, the first of many generations to bear that name, moved his family to the newly reconstructed and burgeoning city of Richmond, Virginia, where his son, George Gilmer Minor, Jr., cofounded what would become one of the oldest family-operated companies in the country. It was in Richmond and through the efforts of George Gilmer Minor, Jr., that Owens & Minor was first established.

Before entering into the business world on his own, George Gilmer Minor, Jr., worked as a salesman for a Richmond wholesale drug firm called Powers Taylor Drug Company. The introduction to the wholesale drug business would have a lasting effect on the youngest of the Minor family, as would the fortuitous meeting between Minor and another salesman, Otho O. Owens. Owens, who worked for a rival drug company named Purcell Ladd and Company, and Minor presumably met through the course of their business, as each plied his trade in and around the Richmond area. Any competitive fire between Owens and Minor was forever snuffed in January 1882, when the two salesmen entered into business together and established a company that a century later would dominate its industry as Owens & Minor, Inc.

The company was founded as Owens & Minor Drug Company and operated as a wholesale and retail business, with the wholesale side of the enterprise conducted behind the retail space that faced Richmond's Main Street. From these quarters, Owens & Minor sold patent medicines, cosmetics, prepared prescrip-

Company Perspectives:

Owens & Minor's mission is to provide our customers and suppliers with the most responsive, efficient and cost-effective distribution system for the delivery of healthcare products and services in the markets we serve; to earn a return on our invested capital consistent with being an industry leader; and to manage our business with the highest ethical standards in a socially responsible manner with particular emphasis on the welfare of our teammates and the communities we serve.

tions, and a wide range of other goods, including window glass, paints, oils, and dyes. Otho Owens served as the company's president, heading the operation for the first five years, until Owens & Minor Drug Company was reorganized as a limited partnership comprising 24 investors, and for the ensuing 19 years, until his death in 1906. George Gilmer Minor, Jr., then took the reins of command, picking up where Owens left off and guiding the company for five years until his death in 1911.

The next leader of the company came from neither the Owens nor the Minor family, but instead from inside the organization itself. Conway M. Knox, a former stock boy for the company who had worked his way up Owens & Minor's ranks, received the ultimate promotion in 1911, when he succeeded George Gilmer Minor, Jr., as president. Under Knox's watch, Owens & Minor moved to a larger location, occupying in 1913 what would serve as the company's headquarters for more than the next 50 years. Knox superintended the company's fortunes for a commensurate amount of time, serving as the president from 1911 to 1941, successfully bringing the company through World War I, a devastating, decade-long economic depression, and to the dawn of World War II. During his tenure at Owens & Minor, Knox was assisted by two sons of the company's founder, George Gilmer Minor, III, and William Y. Minor, who were with the company when it was incorporated in 1927, the year the Owens family sold their stake in the company and brought to an end a 45-year business relationship between the two families. George Gilmer Minor, III, succeeded Knox as president of the company in 1941, but his term was cut tragically short, ending just 15 months after it began with his death in 1942.

To fill the leadership void, the company once again turned to someone outside the Minor family, naming James B. Bowers president in 1942. Bowers had joined the company in 1902 and served as its president for five years before retiring in 1947, ending his career after 50 years of involvement with Owens & Minor. The next Minor to take charge of the company would be the company's most influential leader in its first century of business, a man who represented the third generation of the Minor family to head Owens & Minor and who would direct the company into a new line of business that would predicate its existence during the 1990s.

In 1934, George Gilmer Minor, IV, joined the family business directly from the Virginia Military Institute, starting with Owens & Minor as an office boy and eventually gaining experience in every facet of the company's operations before succeeding Bowers in 1947. Grandson of the company's founder, George Gilmer Minor, IV, would play as pivotal a role in the company's history as his grandfather had played, and like his grandfather, he went by the name George Gilmer Minor, Jr.

In a presidency that would span 29 years, George Gilmer Minor, Jr., waited until 1955 to make his first major move. At the time, the number of competitors in Richmond's drug wholesale business community had been whittled down to three major companies: Bodeker Drug Company; Powers Taylor, which had purchased Purcell Ladd in 1910, the company Otho Owens had worked for; and Owens & Minor. In 1955, however, that number was reduced to two when Owens & Minor acquired the accounts and the name of Bodeker Drug Company. Bodeker Drug Co. was well-known to generations of Richmond citizens, having been established in 1846, nearly two decades before Owens & Minor Drug Co. was founded. Bodeker Drug was also twice as large as its new owner, giving Owens & Minor a considerable boost to its business and lending the company a new name: Owens, Minor & Bodeker Drug Co.

1966 Entry into a New Business

In the wake of the 1955 acquisition of Bodeker Drug Co., the company expanded, establishing its first distribution center outside of Richmond in 1959 in Wilson, North Carolina, and another in Norfolk, Virginia, in 1962. The company's acquisitive pace picked up under George Gilmer Minor, Jr.'s presidency as well, accelerating Owens, Minor & Bodeker's growth appreciably. The company completed ten acquisitions between 1964 and 1981, but none was as important as the purchase of A&J Hospital Supply in 1966. From 1966 forward, Owens, Minor & Bodeker would gradually become a different kind of company entirely.

Up until 1966, the company had always operated as a wholesale drug firm, devoting 84 years to the sale of pharmaceutical goods, but with the acquisition of A&J Hospital Supply, Owens, Minor & Bodeker Drug Co. entered the medical and surgical distribution business for the first time. The move into a new business area, a move spearheaded by George Gilmer Minor, Jr., began to steer the company in a new direction, one that would completely reshape the company and define its existence during the 1990s. From 1966 forward, all major acquisitions would add to the company's presence in the medical and surgical distribution field, not its storied wholesale drug business. Owens, Minor & Bodeker Drug Co. did not abandon the wholesale drug business by any means, but it would be another 18 years before the company acquired a company whose business was related to the wholesale drug business.

Further acquisitions in the medical and surgical distribution business followed the 1966 purchase of A&J Hospital Supply, as the company, with George Gilmer Minor, Jr., still leading the way, strove to expand its new business. In 1968, the company acquired the Richmond, Norfolk, and Washington, D.C., operations belonging to Powers & Anderson, Inc., then the following year purchased Powers & Anderson's operations in Charleston, South Carolina. With the properties gained from this two-year buying spree, Owens, Minor & Bodeker gained strategically valuable product lines for the medical and surgical distribution market. Next, in 1970, the company acquired Augusta, Georgia-

Key Dates:

1927: The Owens & Minor Drug Company is established.
1955: Bodeker Drug Company is acquired.
1966: Owens & Minor enter the surgical supply business.
1992: The wholesale drug business is divested, making Owens & Minor solely a medical and surgical supplier.

based Marks Surgical, another strategically important move that helped Owens, Minor & Bodeker eclipse $20 million in sales by the end of the year and widen its geographical scope to comprise a four-state territory.

Growth in the 1970s

The company went public the following year, in 1971, offering stock for the first time on the over-the-counter exchange, then embarked on another acquisition spree, entrenching its position in the medical and surgical distribution market. In 1972 the company acquired Murray Drug, based in Norfolk, Virginia, then two years later purchased White Surgical of Knoxville. In 1976 the company increased its geographic territory, gaining four locations in Texas and Louisiana through the acquisition of Southern Hospital, and securing a foothold in Florida fours years later with the purchase of Jacksonville, Florida-based Medical Supply.

These acquisitions were completed during a decade that saw Owens, Minor & Bodeker Drug Co.'s sales volume increase sixfold and its geographic scope broaden considerably. The company entered the 1970s generating slightly more than $20 million a year, and exited the decade with annual sales exceeding $130 million. Geographically, the acquisitions completed by Owens, Minor & Bodeker helped extend its service territory from six to ten states during the 1970s, as year by year the magnitude of the company's medical and surgical distribution business grew.

Aside from exponential growth, the 1970s also marked the end of an era when George Gilmer Minor, Jr., ended his nearly 30-year presidency in 1976. George Gilmer Minor, Jr., who had been instrumental in the company's diversification into the medical and surgical distribution business, stayed on as chairman and chief executive officer after 1976, but from that year until 1981 another individual from outside the Minor family, William F. Fife, assumed the duties of president. When Fife, in turn, vacated the post of president in 1981, the next Minor in line, George Gilmer Minor, III, stepped in, beginning a term of office that would carry the company through the mid-1990s and would span the complete transformation his father had initiated in 1966.

George Gilmer Minor, III, fifth by generation and the fourth Minor to head the company, joined the family business at age 15, beginning his career as a schoolboy before assuming a more influential role in the company's operation after his graduation from Virginia Military Institute in 1963 and his graduation from the Colgate Darden School of Business Administration at the University of Virginia in 1966. Following his education, George Gilmer Minor, III, went on to become the division manager of the company's wholesale drug division and general manager of all three drug divisions. Continuing his rise through the company's ranks, George Gilmer Minor, III, eventually was named vice-president of operations for Owens, Minor & Bodeker, gaining more and more responsibility until he was ultimately selected as the company's president in 1981, a year during which he had played a leading role in the company's acquisition of eight locations belonging to the Will Ross division of G.D. Searle, the second-largest distributor of medical and surgical supplies in the country.

In January 1982, at the beginning of the company's centennial year, a name change was effected and Owens, Minor & Bodeker Drug Co. became Owens & Minor, Inc. Acquisitions continued to drive the company's growth during the 1980s, including the purchase of Oklahoma City-based S&S Hospital Supply in 1983, a year in which medical and surgical supplies as a percentage of total sales doubled. Florida Hospital Supply was purchased the following year, representing the first wholesale drug acquisition in nearly two decades, but the most momentous development in 1984 occurred in Owens & Minor's other business segment. For the first time, medical and surgical sales eclipsed the total generated by the company's 102-year-old wholesale drug business, marking a milestone in Owens & Minor's history that foretold the direction the company was headed toward.

Sales reached $367 million in 1985, the year George Gilmer Minor, III, announced his ambitious goal of reaching $1 billion in sales by 1990. Toward this lofty goal, the company made an important step in 1985 when it signed a three-year contract with the Voluntary Hospitals of America, the largest nonprofit hospital system in the United States, which was renewed in 1988 in perpetuity. The company expanded beyond the Sunbelt in 1987 with the acquisition of Bridgeton, New Jersey-based Leon Stotter Company, then expanded westward in 1989 through the purchase of National Healthcare, which operated in California, Arizona, Texas, Oregon, Utah, and Colorado.

1992 Divestiture of Wholesale Drug Division

In 1990, the year George Gilmer Minor, III, had hoped to reach $1 billion in sales, Owens & Minor recorded $1.2 billion in sales, exceeding earlier expectations. Two years later, after 110 years in the business, Owens & Minor exited the drug wholesale trade, divesting nearly all the assets composing its drug wholesale division. From 1992 forward, Owens & Minor executives would focus exclusively on the business the previous generation had first entered in 1966, devoting their energies and resources toward positioning the company as one of the country's preeminent surgical and medical supply distributors. In 1994, two years after selling its drug wholesale business, Owens & Minor completed a gigantic leap toward becoming one of the country's elite medical and surgical supply competitors when the company acquired $890 million-in-sales Stuart Medical, Inc., the third largest distributor of medical and surgical supplies in the nation.

On the heels of this major acquisition, Owens & Minor recorded $2.4 billion in sales, then the following year, in 1995, generated $2.97 billion in sales, more than eight times the figure posted ten years earlier. Owens & Minor was growing at a robust pace during the 1990s, and as management, with George Gilmer Minor, III, leading the way, looked toward the late 1990s and the beginning of the 21st century, further acquisitions in the medical and surgical supply field were expected.

The New Millennium Begins with a Bang

However, the late 1990s did not altogether live up to the expectations it had set in the middle of the decade. A major sign of trouble came in May 1998, when the corporation lost its largest account (Columbia/HCA Healthcare Corp oration) to a rival firm. The loss of the account meant the loss of more than 10 percent of Owens & Minor's annual revenues. The corporate stock dropped like a stone, collapsing 23 percent in value virtually overnight.

This impending disaster required extensive damage control—including laying off about 250 employees. Fortunately, foresight by Owens & Minor executives had already begun to put the solutions in place. A new extranet IT system, designed to allow both customers and supplies share product data online, went live in 1997. It replaced an older, outmoded mainframe system that could only present customers with usage reports on a quarterly basis. The new system, which allowed customers to interact with the data almost in real time, allowed hospitals to judge their inventories of supplies more accurately and to order new supplies on a more timely basis.

By the end of fiscal 1998 Owens & Minor's new system had changed the loss of the Columbia/HCA account from what could have been a major disaster into a much less troubling hiccup. Even as early as the end of the third quarter of 1998, analysis showed that, while sales had dropped (as compared with the same period in the previous year), profits had actually increased and earning per share had gone up by as much as 25 percent. The company's use of IT systems—rare in the pharmaceutical and healthcare supply industry—brought it an estimated $100 million in new business over the next three years. The system also allowed Owens & Minor to shave their operating margins to a tremendously lean 2.3 percent. In 1999, Owens & Minor introduced OM Direct, an online service that allows customers and suppliers to interact directly over the Internet. The new system was set up to permit customers to log their inventory directly into the online database using a handheld computer and an infrared scanning bar-code reader.

These innovations allowed Owens & Minor to remain at the top of the medical supply industry during the early years of the 21st century. Between 1999 and 2002, company profits increased by 37 percent, while stock price increased about 150 percent during the same period. At the end of the first quarter of 2004, dividends paid to shareholders of record had increased 38 percent over what they had been the previous year. Owens & Minor's performance demonstrates that the corporation remains a major player in the medical supplies industry well into its second century.

Principal Subsidiaries

A. Kuhlman & Co.; Koley's Medical Supply, Inc.; Lyons Physician Supply Company; National Medical Supply Corporation; Owens & Minor Medical, Inc.; Owens & Minor West, Inc.; Stuart Medical, Inc.

Further Reading

Campanella, Frank W., ''Wholesale Health,'' *Barron's,* October 7, 1995, p. 57.

Condon, Bernard, ''Unhealthy Prognosis,'' *Forbes,* August 12, 1996, p. 20.

''Enron Corp., Owens & Minor a Study in Contrasts,'' *Knight Ridder/Tribune Business News,* May 4, 2002.

Gold, Jacqueline S., ''Owens & Minor: No. 2 in Health—and Loving It,'' *Financial World,* May 11, 1993, p. 20.

Larson, Julie, ''Distributor Buys Into Market for Columbia,'' *Denver Business Journal,* May 26, 1995, p. 3C.

Lee, Carrie, ''Owens and Minor: Heal Thyself,'' *Financial World,* November 7, 1995, p. 18.

''Medical-Surgical Supply Distributor Owens & Minor Said it Is Laying off about 250 Employees,'' *Modern Healthcare,* July 20, 1998, p. 4.

Owens & Minor, Inc. 1882 and Beyond, Glen Allen, Va.: Owens & Minor, Inc., 1992.

''Owens & Minor,'' *Hospital Materials Management,* March, 2002, p. 18.

''Richmond, Va.-Based Medical Supplier Raises Its Dividend,'' *Richmond Times-Dispatch,* April 25, 2003.

Rublin, Lauren R., ''For Whom Old Age Is More Than a Consolation,'' *Barron's,* December 7, 1987, p. 70.

Stanley, Bonnie Newman, ''Richmond-Based Owens & Minor Inc.,'' *Richmond Times-Dispatch,* May 1, 1996, p. 50.

Teach, Edward, ''A Shot in the Arm for Owens & Minor,'' *CFO,* December, 1998, p. 75.

''Texas Hospital System Selects Owens & Minor as Medical-Surgical Distributor,'' *Hospital Materials Management,* August, 2001, p. 5.

—Jeffrey L. Covell
—update: Kenneth R. Shepherd

PHOENIX

Phoenix AG

Hannoversche Strasse 88
D-21079 Hamburg
Germany
Telephone: (+49) 40 7667-01
Fax: (+49) 40 7667-2211
Web site: http://www.phoenix-ag.com

Public Company
Incorporated: 1856 as Gummiwarenfabrik Albert & Louis Cohen
Employees: 9,722
Sales: EUR 1.15 billion ($1.43 billion) (2003)
Stock Exchanges: Frankfurt
Ticker Symbol: PHO
NAIC: 326291 Rubber Product Manufacturing for Mechanical Use; 32622 Rubber and Plastics Hoses and Belting Manufacturing; 336399 All Other Motor Vehicle Parts Manufacturing; 313320 Fabric Coating Mills

Phoenix AG is a major supplier of sound and vibration control systems, technical hoses, and rubber components to the German automotive industry. The company's Comfort Systems division includes Stankiewicz, the German market leader in automotive sound isolation systems, and Vibracoustics, a joint venture with the German Freudenberg Group that develops vibration control systems for passenger and commercial vehicles. Phoenix's Automotive Comfort Systems subdivision serves German automakers DaimlerChrysler, BMW and Volkswagen, among others, while its Traffic Technology subdivision develops similar systems for trucks, trailers and rail vehicles. Phoenix's Fluid Handling division makes hoses and hose systems for vehicles and industry. The company's third business division, Conveyor Belt Systems, makes large conveyor belts for the worldwide mining industry. Other business units produce waterproof sheeting, rubberized fabrics, and profiles and roofing membranes for the construction industry. Comfort Systems generates almost half of Phoenix's revenues. Fluid Handling contributes roughly 30 percent to total sales while conveyor belts and other products add about 10 percent each to the total. Headquartered in Hamburg, Germany, the company has production facilities in Germany, Belgium, France, the United Kingdom, Spain, Romania, Poland, the Czech Republic, Hungary, Turkey, India, China, Canada, and the United States. In 2004, Germany's largest tire manufacturer Continental AG acquired a controlling interest in Phoenix.

Rubber Boots and Rubberized Fabrics in 1856

In 1856, two French brothers, Albert and Louis Cohen, established a rubber products factory in the northern German city of Harburg, near Hamburg. They hired 280 workers who started manufacturing rubber boots and rubberized fabrics 24 hours a day. Within a year, the two entrepreneurs almost doubled their workforce and expanded production capacity. The Albert & Louis Cohen rubber factory took on the production of rubber articles used in medicine, industry, and transportation as well as of rubber balls and sponges. Eight years later, the brand name was born that eventually became the company's name: Phoenix. However, for the time being, the company was renamed Vereinigte Gummiwaaren-Fabriken Harburg-Wien in 1872, after it was merged with Europe's oldest rubber factory—Vienna-based J.N. Reithoffer. The company was then transformed into a public corporation. Riding the wave of the economic boom following the foundation of the German Empire in 1871, the enterprise became a huge success within a few years.

With the rise of the automobile as a means of transportation, new uses for rubber products abounded. In 1894, the company started making tires for bicycles. Eight years later it began manufacturing tires for automobiles. In 1907, Vereinigte Gummiwaaren-Fabriken entered another new product market that became on of the company's mainstays for almost a century: conveyor belts. World War I, which began in 1914, suddenly confronted the company with serious problems, since it was completely cut off from the world market where it had bought its natural rubber. However, as early as 1904 they had set up a separate production line for a synthetic rubber-like material called ''Galalith.'' After the war, the company's plant in Austria was transferred to Semperit AG. In 1922, the Phoenix brand became part of the company name when it was renamed Harburger Gummiwaren Fabrik Phoenix Aktienge-

> **Company Perspectives:**
>
> *High quality rubber products and acoustic systems have established our competence in technology and made us an international leader in systems, technology and expense in many domains.*

sellschaft. In the years preceding World War II, Phoenix ventured into synthetic materials such as thermoplastic and KERIT phenol and patented a bonded metal rubber compound which they branded ''METALLGUMMI'' (metal rubber). The new material was used in automobiles and airplanes. During the bombing raids on Hamburg during World War II, Phoenix lost 60 percent of its production plant and shut down operations in the last months of the war.

Emphasizing Technical Rubber Products in the 1970s–80s

The introduction of a new currency in postwar Germany in 1948 ignited the economic boom that became legendary as the German Economic Miracle. Three years later, Phoenix entered an agreement of technical and marketing cooperation with the Firestone Tire and Rubber Company, then the world's second-largest tire manufacturer. The North American company, hoping to penetrate the German market, acquired 25 percent of Phoenix's raised share capital and Phoenix agreed to market tires for automobiles under the brand name ''Firestone PHOENIX'' in Germany. In 1971, Firestone, which had not been able to gain a controlling influence over Phoenix, withdrew from the agreement and from the German market and sold its share in Phoenix to Deutsche Bank. The bank, which also owned a share in northern German tire manufacturer Continental, developed a plan for the reorganization of the German rubber processing industry and—together with Continental's major shareholders—made plans for a merger with Phoenix. However, due to difficulties in financial evaluation as well as to high resistance and from workers, the deal was postponed.

The end of the cooperation with Firestone initiated Phoenix's transition from a manufacturer of rather simple, low-margin rubber and plastics products to a technology-partner of the vehicle manufacturing industries, including automobiles, commercial vehicles, trains, and airplanes. In 1973, Phoenix began to scale down its tire business. Ten years later, the company ceased its tire production completely. Instead, the company began to focus on technical rubber products with a higher profit margin. The production of rubber boots was phased out while its sports shoe business under the Palladium brand was spun off into the new subsidiary Palladium SA. Phoenix focused on manufacturing rubber parts for cars, technical hoses, large conveyor belts for the mining industry, car body parts made from molded polyurethane, rubber parts for commercial vehicles, and rubber-metal vibration damping components. In 1972, the company began to work with German car maker Mercedes-Benz on the development of the first air bags for passenger cars. Eight years later, Phoenix began the serial production of airbags. In 1987, the company won a contract to deliver waterproof sheeting for the Eurotunnel that connected France and Britain.

Expansion and Reorganization in the Early 1990s

From the 1950s until the late 1980s, Phoenix grew through a number of mostly national acquisitions. By 1989, the company had become Europe's eighth-largest manufacturer of rubber products. With about 6,850 employees, Phoenix generated $560 million in revenues. Roughly three-quarters of that total derived in Germany while most of the remaining sales came from Western Europe. Major car makers had become the company's single most important revenue source, contributing 57 percent of total sales. Setting its sight on the liberalized Western European market of the 1990s, Phoenix began to expand internationally. Sales subsidiaries had already been set up in Belgium, the Netherlands, the United Kingdom, and France. However, as Germany's large car makers began establishing assembly lines all over Europe, they required their suppliers to follow suit.

In 1989, Phoenix acquired a majority stake in Societa Manicotta Gomma, an Italian manufacturer of hoses for the automotive industry. In 1990, the company took over a Spanish supplier of technical rubber products for cars. In that same year, Phoenix set up two marketing subsidiaries—one in Sweden for the Scandinavian market and one in Cartered, New Jersey, to market industrial rubber products such as tunnel seals and railroad goods. In 1991, Phoenix acquired another Italian company and founded a marketing subsidiary in Austria.

In 1992, with European economies slowing down, Phoenix entered a period of radical internal reorganization. To stay competitive in an increasingly consolidating global market, the company initiated a restructuring program under the name ''P/3S.'' A synonym for ''Phoenix slim-speedy-strong,'' the program was aimed at creating a leaner, more efficient and customer-oriented organizational structure. The number of levels of hierarchy was reduced from eight to six. Phoenix's workforce was reduced by roughly one-fifth. The remaining staff was trained in the Japanese concept of Kaizen—collectively improving things one step at a time. Then, employees from different divisions, locations, and even companies worked together in teams to solve often complex problems. One of them was the issue of how to meet automakers' demand to cut costs by one-fifth while at the same time staying profitable. Together with engineers from Mercedes-Benz—one of Phoenix's most important customers—one such team reduced the number of engine bearings used in various Mercedes models from three to one. The new bearing was not only 40 percent cheaper but also lighter than its predecessors. Many such teams were assigned similar tasks. As a result of these efforts, Phoenix shrunk its inventory of raw materials by 40 percent, cut production times in half, increased the equipment utilization by roughly one-third and reduced the annual electricity bill by DM 10 million.

A second step in the company's restructuring efforts was the reorganization of Phoenix's broad range of products and many subsidiaries under the umbrella of three market-oriented business divisions: automotive and non-automotive elastomers and plastics. The reorganization did not prevent Phoenix from going through a severe slump in sales in 1993, caused by a contracting market for the automotive and non-automotive elastomers and by increasing pressure on costs by car manufacturers. For the first time in fifteen years, Phoenix reported a net loss of over DEM10 million. However, due to the company's concerted effort to streamline operations and cut costs, Phoenix pulled itself out of the red within two years.

Key Dates:

1856: Albert and Louis Cohen set up a rubber factory in Harburg.
1864: The PHOENIX brand is introduced.
1872: The company goes public.
1902: Phoenix starts making tires for automobiles.
1907: Production of conveyor belts for the mining industry begins.
1935: The company develops bonded metal rubber compounds under the brand name METALLGUMMI.
1972: Together with Mercedes-Benz, the company pioneers air bags for passenger cars.
1978: The company is renamed Phoenix Aktiengesellschaft.
1983: Phoenix ceases tire production to focus on technical rubber products.
1989: The establishment of a global production infrastructure begins.
1992: Phoenix' management initiates an internal restructuring program.
1994: The company acquires German vehicle-soundproofing specialist Stankiewicz.
1995: Phoenix begins to cooperate with the Freudenberg Group in the area of sound and vibration control for vehicles.
1999: Joint venture Vibracoustics is founded.
2004: German tire manufacturer Continental AG acquires a majority stake in Phoenix.

From Parts Supplier to Systems Provider: Mid- to Late 1990s

Another aspect of Phoenix's strategy for the 1990s was to focus on product lines in which the company was capable of gaining a competitive advantage by becoming the market leader. The year 1994 was an important milestone in that direction. With the acquisition of Stankiewicz GmbH, Phoenix entered the market of sound proofing parts for vehicles, which soon became one of the company's main income sources. Stankiewicz, a leading manufacturer of sound insulation mats for the passenger cabin with about 800 employees, had four production plants—two in Germany, one in the United States, and one in the Czech Republic. In the second half of the 1990s, Stankiewicz added two more plants, one in Belgium and one in the United Kingdom. In 1995, Phoenix entered a strategic partnership with the German Freudenberg Group. The two companies agreed to cooperate in the development, production, and marketing of complete vibration control and sound proofing systems for vehicles. With this strategic decision Phoenix evolved from a mere auto parts manufacturer to become a provider of whole systems, often developed in close cooperation with the company's customers. Freudenberg's own acoustics unit Dichtungs- und Schwingungstechnik KG was integrated into Stankiewicz in exchange for a 10 percent share in Stankiewicz.

A second step in the same direction followed four years later when Phoenix and Freudenberg established a joint venture for vibration control systems. This venture was named Vibracoustic and began operations in 2001. Phoenix was experienced in the development and production of bushings and air springs. Freudenberg completed the new venture with its hydro mount know-how. Together with Stankiewicz, Vibracoustic became one of Phoenix's three newly defined core business divisions: Comfort Systems. Besides passenger cars, the division was geared towards the commercial and rail vehicle markets. The other two core business divisions formed in 2000 as part of the company's ''Strategy 2005'' program were Conveyor Belt Systems and Fluid Handling. The latter focused on manufacturing technical hoses and hose modules for various applications in vehicles, including hoses for fuel, water, and air, as well as for a variety of uses in the mining, construction, chemical, and food processing industries, among others. The new divisions were strengthened by acquisitions while business activities that did not fit into the new strategic focus, such as plastics, molded plastic parts, airbags, and offset blankets were sold.

In the area of vibration control, air springs—which in the past had been used only in trucks—made their way into passenger cars to raise driving comfort to a new level. In 1998, Vibracoustic pioneered this emerging market when the company created an innovative design for air springs. Developed in cooperation with Krupp Hoesch Automotive and DaimlerChrysler, the new air springs were used for the first time in the Mercedes S-Class series and later adapted for other Mercedes models as well as for other upscale cars, including BMW and Jaguar. The new air springs were reinforced by individual strands of polyamide fibers, which were precisely laid along—instead of crisscrossed over—the rubber cylinder that constituted the spring body. The new design allowed the rubber to expand more easily, enabled the production of more compact air springs for passenger cars, and reduced the weight of a vehicle by roughly one-third. More advantages included smaller movement of the springs and less heat build-up. Phoenix set its sights on further lowering the cost for air spring vibration control systems, hoping that they would eventually be used in mid-sized passenger cars.

Global Player after the Fall of the Soviet Union

The opening of the Iron Curtain coincided with Phoenix's efforts to move low-tech and low-profit production to lower wage countries. Although the company's products had been marketed around the world, most of its manufacturing plants were still in Germany. Beginning in the early 1990s, as much as 30 percent of the company's production was moved abroad through acquisitions, joint ventures, or the establishment of brand-new factories. At first, production was moved mainly to Eastern European countries such as the Czech Republic, Poland, Hungary, and Romania. Later, Phoenix had factories in Turkey, India, and China. By 2000, about one-third of Phoenix's 9,200 employees worked outside of Germany. Besides cutting costs, the company was hoping to conquer new markets with this step, mainly in Eastern Europe and Asia.

Despite the company's efforts to cut costs and introduce innovative products with above-average profit margins, Phoenix slipped into the red in 2001. Increasing oil prices made rubber, the company's main raw material, more expensive, while the fierce competition made it impossible to raise prices for Phoenix's products. Restructuring costs and higher taxes contributed to the negative result. While the company was making plans for new strategic ventures, such as new product development and acquisitions, and took steps to decrease its high debt, major changes in ownership occurred.

After the company's share value plunged in response to Phoenix's negative results, Deutsche Bank, a major shareholder, sold its Phoenix shares to German textile entrepreneur Claas Daun, who had already gained an 11.14 percent stake in the company. Phoenix's new single biggest shareholder, who became president of the company's advisory board in mid-2003, relieved concerns over the possibility of breaking up the company to sell its most profitable units to the highest bidder.

At the end of 2003, Phoenix's CEO of ten years, Konrad Ellegast, who had successfully repositioned the company as a specialized systems provider in well-defined markets in the 1990s, retired. Under Ellegast's leadership Phoenix's sales more than doubled, reaching EUR 1.13 billion in 2002, while the company's workforce grew to 10,000 and its network of subsidiaries in Germany and abroad expanded to about 50. The percentage of sales generated abroad increased by one-third between 1994 and 2000. Ellegast predicted that the number of suppliers to the automotive industry in Europe would shrink dramatically in the long run. While there were 8,000 such firms in the late 1990s, Ellegast expected that number to shrink to some 200 to 300 in the future. Only a few months later, the merger that did not come through in the early 1970s finally came to pass some thirty years later. In March 2004, Continental AG, one of the world's largest tire manufacturers with some 69,000 employees worldwide, announced its intention to buy Phoenix AG. Three months later, Continental announced that it had gained more than three-fourths of Phoenix's shares. In October 2004 the European Commission approved the deal under the condition that Phoenix sell its stake in the Vibracoustics joint venture and its air springs plant in Hungary. Continental was also obliged to sell Phoenix's wide steel cord conveyor belt production to its competitor Sempertrans. Continental was planning to integrate Phoenix into its technical rubber products division Conti Tech, which was to be taken public some time in the future.

Principal Subsidiaries

Phoenix Automotive GmbH; Stankiewicz GmbH; Vibracoustic GmbH & Co. KG; Eddelbüttel & Schneider GmbH; Mündener Gummiwerke GmbH; Phoenix Fluid Handling Industry GmbH; Phoenix Conveyor Belt Systems GmbH; TGB Transportgummi Bad Blankenburg; Phoenix Compounding Technology GmbH; Phoenix Dichtungstechnik GmbH; Phoenix Traffic Technology GmbH; Conseo GmbH; Phoenix Service GmbH & Co. KG; IPM GmbH; Phoenix Romania S.r.l.; MACFI S.A., Cornellá (Spain); Vibracoustic Iberica, S.L. (Spain); Vibracoustic Polska Sp.zo.o. (Poland); Stankiewicz Polska S.p.zo.o., Swarzedz-Jasin (Poland); Vest-Izol a.s. (Czech Republic); Vibracoustic CZ s.r.o. (Czech Republic); Gumimüvek Phoenix Hungária Kft. (Hungary); Phoenix Rubber Industrial Ltd. (Hungary); Conveyor Belt Systems Phoenix Ltd. (Hungary); Phoenix Airsprings Kft. (Hungary); Stankiewicz Belgium N.V.; BELTAN A.S. (Turkey); Phoenix Sigma Vibracoustic Pvt., Ltd. (India); Phoenix Yule Ltd. (India); Shanxi Phoenix Conveyor Belt Co. Ltd. (China); Phoenix France S.a.r.L.; Phoenix Industries S.a.r.L. (France); Stankiewicz UK Ltd. (United Kingdom); Phoenix Beattie Ltd. (United Kingdom); Dunlop Oil & Marine Ltd. (United Kingdom); Phoenix Vibracoustic Ltd. (United Kingdom); Beattie Industrial Ltd. (Canada); Phoenix North America Inc. (U.S.); Stankiewicz International Corporation (United States); Phoenix Beattie Corporation (United States.).

Principal Divisions

Comfort Systems; Conveyor Belt Systems; Fluid Handling.

Principal Operating Units

Vibracoustics.

Principal Competitors

The Goodyear Tire and Rubber Company; Bridgestone Corporation; Compagnie Générale des Établissements Michelin; Dana Corporation; ZF Friedrichshafen AG; Paulstra CRC; Tokai Rubber Industries, Ltd.; Sempertrans Nirlon Ltd.

Further Reading

"Continental bietet fuer den kleineren Mitbewerber Phoenix," *Frankfurter Allgemeine Zeitung*, March 30, 2004, p. 15.

Davis, Bruce, "Phoenix Rises in Spain, France; Automotive Manufacturers to Make Acquisitions," *European Rubber Journal*, July-August 1989, p. 6.

——, "Running a Born-again Phoenix," *European Rubber Journal*, September 1989, p. 60.

——, "Phoenix Reveals Plans for '90s'—Concentrates on Hose Mouldings," *European Rubber Journal*, March 1990, p. 14.

——, "Phoenix Reports Loss for '93," *European Rubber Journal*, March 1994, p. 10.

"Phoenix-Vorstand beurteilt das Continental-Angebot skeptisch," *Frankfurter Allgemeine Zeitung*, April 28, 2004, p. 16.

Thiede, Meite, "Ohne P/3S stünde es heute schlimm um Phoenix," *Süddeutsche Zeitung*, August 25, 1994.

"Transport: Clearance for Continental Acquisition of Phoenix," *European Report*, October 27, 2004, p. 301.

Reed, David, "Phoenix Continues to Rise as Focus on Core Pays Off," *European Rubber Journal*, February 1999, p. 6.

Shaw, David, "Phoenix Ready for 21st Century," *European Rubber Journal*, January 2000, p. 13.

——, "Vibracoustic to Operate on Three Continents," *European Rubber Journal*, January 2000, p. 12.

White, Liz, "Phoenix Buys Dunlop Oil and Marine Hose Unit," *European Rubber Journal*, September 2000, p. 3.

——, "Phoenix Expects Conti to Make Structural Changes," *European Rubber Journal*, September 2004, p. 12.

——, "Phoenix Optimistic Following Record 2001," *European Rubber Journal*, March 2002, p. 6.

——, "Phoenix's Profiles Unit to Move to Thuringen," *European Rubber Journal*, December 2002, p. 9.

——, "Phoenix Revolutionizes Airspring Design," *European Rubber Journal*, June 2002, p. 21.

—Evelyn Hauser

Plantation Pipe Line Company

1435 Windward Concourse
Alpharetta, Georgia 30005
U.S.A.
Telephone: (770) 751-4000
Fax: (770) 751-4050
Web site: http://www.plantation-ppl.com

Wholly Owned Subsidiary of Kinder Morgan Energy Partners
Founded: 1940
Employees: 279
Sales: $156.4 million (2002)
NAIC: 486910 Pipeline Transportation of Refined Petroleum

Majority owned by Kinder Morgan Energy Partners, Plantation Pipe Line Company is an Alpharetta, Georgia-based company that operates a 3,100 mile pipeline system in the southeastern United States, stretching from Louisiana to Washington, D.C. Plantation's lines range in size from 6 to 30 inches in diameter. Each day, Plantation delivers over 20 million gallons of gasoline, diesel, heating fuels, kerosene, and commercial and military jet fuels originating from nine refineries in Mississippi and Louisiana, or fed into the network from other pipeline systems or Mississippi River Marine facilities. All told, the system includes 130 shipper terminals and 29 delivery points located in eight states. A minimum batch of one million gallons is required to use the system, and a typical 1,000-mile journey takes about 20 days. The cost of a typical delivery from Baton Rouge to Washington, D.C., is approximately two cents per gallon. Kinder Morgan owns 51 percent of Plantation and for years has made it known that it would like to buy the rest of the company, owned by Exxon Mobil.

Origins in a World War II Defense Initiative

Plantation was founded in 1940 and authorized by the United States Congress to build a national defense pipeline from Baton Rouge, Louisiana, to Greensboro, North Carolina, one of several pipelines to be constructed for the same purpose during this time. Although the United States was not yet involved, World War II had already begun in Europe and in the Pacific the Japanese Army had invaded China. The U.S. government, while officially taking a neutral position on the war, was rapidly preparing the country for war. A vital consideration was the protection of the petroleum products that a modern army depended on. Given the success of German submarines in the disruption of shipping during World War I, it was prudent to create a pipeline system to deliver fuels underground. The idea of establishing a pipeline system in the southeastern United States had been in the exploratory stages during the 1930s, but the prospect of war was the key factor in making the concept a reality. Plantation quickly laid eight-inch pipe and became operational in January 1942 at an important moment in the history of the country. Only a month earlier, the Japanese Navy conducted a surprise attack on the U.S. Naval base at Pearl Harbor. The United States declared war on Japan and Germany, Japan's ally, followed suit by declaring war on the United States. Over the course of the next year, German submarines had a field day sinking allied tankers and freighters. Moreover, the U.S. railways were overburdened moving troops and material. Therefore, the availability of the Plantation pipeline system was of strategic importance in America's war effort.

Major Upgrades in the 1960s

In the beginning Plantation delivered 48,000 barrels of petroleum products each day, serving just four customers. By the end of the war, however, delivery increased to 86,000 barrels per day and the number of customers grew to nine. Following the end of World War II in 1945, Plantation retained its military value, especially in light of the ideological conflict between the Soviet Union and the United States that would endure for the next half-century. However, the pipeline system now primarily served commercial interests in the postwar world. It also played an important role in the growth of the economy in the southeastern United States. To keep pace, Plantation expanded beyond its original Baton Rouge to Greensboro route. In 1964, a spur was built into Virginia. Then, in 1968, a major expansion program was launched. A larger mainline, 26 inches in diameter, was laid between Collins, Mississippi, and Greensboro. A 12-inch diameter loop was built between Pascagoula, Mississippi, and

Company Perspectives:

We safely and profitably transport petroleum products throughout the Southeast, on-spec, on-time and on-volume because a reliable and economical supply of energy is vital to our society.

Collins, a ten-inch diameter spur was added in Alabama that ran from Helena to Birmingham, and an eight-inch diameter spur was laid in Georgia that ran from Bremen to Macon. In addition, the main line from Baton Rouge to Greensboro was supplemented with parallel pipelines, some smaller lines were replaced with larger pipes, and larger pumping stations were installed throughout the system.

Aside from the need to expand the pipeline system to meet the growing needs of the South, some of the work Plantation undertook during the 1960s was to correct hasty work done in laying pipeline before World War II, when the movement of fuel was of vital importance to the security of the nation. During the 1960s, a section of steel pipe began to leak gasoline under several farms in Marion County, Mississippi. It was discovered only when one farmer became suspicious after he was unable to grow cotton for a number of seasons. Plantation repaired the leak, conducted a cleanup, and made settlement payments to the landowners affected. However, tracking technology at the time was not very sophisticated, and Plantation had no firm idea how much gasoline had leaked. Moreover, it was a substance that could leach into the groundwater and years later become a problem for another community hundreds of miles away. As a result, the leak of the 1960s would return to trouble Plantation decades later.

In the meantime, Plantation continued to upgrade its network, making it less likely to have future containment problems. Starting in 1973, Plantation initiated a program to modernize and expand the pipeline system, an endeavor that would continue on an ongoing basis. Service was added to airports at Charlotte, North Carolina, and Atlanta, Georgia, as well as to Richmond, Virginia. As a result, the network grew to about 3,500 miles by the 1990s.

The problems that resulted from the gasoline leak of the 1960s returned to trouble Plantation in 1993. Close to the initial spill site, a homeowner attempted to dig a well only to find the water was contaminated with gasoline. Because there were no new leaks discovered in the pipeline, the conclusion was that the contamination was the result of the leak from some 30 years earlier. Plantation faced a new round of lawsuits and paid approximately $10 million in settlements, cleanup costs, and legal fees. It filed claims with the company's main insurer during the 1960s, Royal Indemnity Co., which management felt was still liable because the claims were the result of events that occurred during the time of coverage. When the insurer refused to pay for any of the new costs, Plantation sued. After some years of litigation, a Superior Court judge ruled in 1999 that Plantation had failed to notify Royal in a timely manner. A second insurance company, Continental Casualty Co., which covered Plantation with excess coverage from 1963 to 1969, also refused to pay the company's claims. Continental bided its time and after the 1999 Royal ruling took the position that Plantation's late notice also applied to it and freed the insurer from the obligation of paying any claims related to the leak. Plantation disagreed and in September 2003 filed suit in U.S. District Court in Atlanta alleging breach of contract. Another drawn-out legal battle was likely to follow.

Plantation was owned jointly by affiliates of four energy giants—Shell, Texaco, Chevron, and Exxon—but in 1998 the ownership composition changed. Equilon Enterprises LLC, a joint venture between Royal Dutch/Shell Group and Texaco, sold its 24.4 percent stake in Plantation to a new company, Kinder Morgan Energy Partners LP, for $110 million. Shell had been forced to sell because of a Federal Trade Commission order. In a short period of time, Kinder Morgan had emerged as the largest pipeline master limited partnership in the country, operating more than 5,000 miles of pipeline and maintaining more than 20 terminals.

Kinder Morgan was founded in February 1997 by Richard Kinder and William Morgan, friends from their law school days at the University of Missouri in the early 1960s. Later, they became colleagues at Enron Corporation, whose chairman, Kenneth Lay, they also knew from Missouri. Enron's roots were actually in the pipeline business. Lay was employed by Florida Gas Transmission and hired Morgan, who in turn hired Kinder. Houston Natural Gas acquired Florida Gas in 1984 and a year later merged with InterNorth to create Houston-based Enron. Both Kinder and Morgan stayed on to work for what would become one of the most notorious companies in American history. Morgan ran some of Enron's pipelines before leaving in 1987 to manage private energy investments, while Kinder took on increasing levels of responsibility at Enron. By the mid-1990s, it was widely assumed that Kinder was in line to succeed Lay as Enron's chairman, whose contract was about to expire, but in 1996 Lay agreed to a new five-year term. Kinder, now 52 years old, realized that it was highly unlikely that he would ever reach the top spot at Enron. He opted to resign, a fortuitous decision in light of what was to occur at Enron.

It was Morgan who convinced Kinder to forgo any thought of early retirement and to start a business together—Kinder Morgan, Inc.—devoted to the fee-based pipeline business. With backing from Charlotte, North Carolina-based First Union Capital Markets, they bought Enron Liquids Pipeline, L.P. for $40 million. They then took the partnership public as Kinder Morgan Energy Partners, employing the little-used Master Limited Partnership (MLP) structure, which was similar to the Real Estate Investment Trusts (REITs) that had become popular in the 1990s. Units in these entities could be bought and sold like stock, but 95 percent of taxable income had to be distributed to unit holders each year. Investors paid income taxes on the distribution, making the MLP exempt from corporate taxes. As a result of being an MLP, therefore, Kinder Morgan was able to acquire assets that traditional corporations, subject to both investor and corporate taxes, would not touch. During his days at Enron, Kinder rejected any properties that offered anything less than a 15 percent return after taxes. Now he was able to make acquisitions at a much lower threshold: an 8.5 percent pretax return on investment. Kinder Morgan's first major acquisition after the Enron deal was Santa Fe Pacific Pipeline Partner, L.P., a $1 billion transaction in October 1997 that brought with it

Key Dates:

1940: Plantation Pipe Line is founded.
1942: Plantation becomes operational.
1964: Pipeline is extended to Virginia.
1973: Modernization program is launched.
1999: Kinder Morgan become the company's majority owner.
2002: A $116 million upgrade project is launched.

3,300 miles of pipeline and a major West Coast presence. This deal was followed by the purchase of a stake in Plantation Pipe Line. Kinder Morgan Inc. then refined its structure by engineering a reverse merger with publicly traded KN Energy, followed by a reverse initial public offering of stock. In this way, not only did Kinder Morgan add KN Energy's pipeline assets, it added what the partners called ''the second barrel of the shotgun,'' a publicly traded corporation to own the MLP. In this way, Kinder Morgan was able to combine the tax benefits of an MLP with the ability of a corporation to use stock to buy assets. After completing the acquisition, Kinder Morgan sold off KN Energy's non-pipeline assets.

New Ownership in the Late 1990s

Kinder Morgan made no secret that it wanted to acquire the rest of Plantation Pipe Line and believed that the major oil companies that owned it and other pipelines would be open to selling, given that the ownership of a common carrier no longer offered a competitive advantage. In May 1999, one of Plantation's owners, Chevron Corp., agreed with that assessment and sold its 27 percent stake in the pipeline for $124 million in cash. As a result, Kinder Morgan held a controlling 51.2 percent stake, with Exxon Pipeline Co. owning the balance. While it continued to lobby Exxon to sell its share of the pipeline network, Kinder Morgan was at least free to cut costs, add capacity to both the mainline and lateral lines, and make other changes to grow Plantation's business.

By the start of 2000, Plantation launched a $40 million project to increase the system's gasoline capacity by approximately 10 percent. Under Kinder Morgan control, Plantation also initiated a two-year $116 million project in 2002 to upgrade the system, supported by contracts from major oil companies. The plan called for 190 miles of 1940s-era, eight-inch pipe stretching from Bremen, Georgia, to Knoxville, Tennessee, to be replaced by new 20-inch pipe. As a result, the pipeline would be able to double its capacity and better serve the high-growth areas of eastern Tennessee and northwestern Georgia.

In February 2004, Exxon Mobil agreed to sell to Kinder Morgan seven refined petroleum products terminals connected to the Plantation system. Exxon Mobil then signed a long-term agree to use the facilities. Whether Exxon Mobil would ever agree to sell its 48.6 percent stake in Plantation to Kinder Morgan, however, remained to be seen.

Principal Competitors

Colonial Pipeline Company.

Further Reading

Credeur, Mary Jane, ''Pipeline Company, Insurer in Court Over Costs of Leak,'' *Atlanta Business Chronicle*, September 26, 2003, p. A8.
Flessner, Dave, ''Atlanta-Based Companies to Upgrade Tennessee Fuel Pipelines,'' *Chattanooga Times/Free Press*, July 17, 2002.
Shook, Barbara, ''Kinder Adds New String to Liquids Pipeline Bow,'' *Oil Daily*, June 19, 1998.
Spencer, Starr, ''Kinder Morgan Takes Major Stake in Plantation'' *Platt's Oilgram News*, May 4, 1999.

—Ed Dinger

Printpack, Inc.

4335 Wendell Drive
Atlanta, Georgia 30336
U.S.A.
Telephone: (404) 691-5830
Toll Free: (800) 241-9984
Fax: (404) 699-7122
Web site: http://www.printpack.com

Private Company
Incorporated: 1956
Employees: 3,906
Sales: $1 billion (2003)
NAIC: 323112 Commercial Flexographic Printing

Printpack, Inc., is one of the largest manufacturers of flexible packaging products in the United States. The firm's offerings, which typically conform to the shape of their contents, include packages for snacks, beverages, frozen foods, pet foods, cheese, produce, and personal care and diaper products. Printpack's client list includes a host of well-known names like Frito-Lay, Kraft, and Coca-Cola. The company is owned and run by the family of founder J. Erskine Love, Jr.

Early Years

The origins of Printpack date to 1956, when Atlanta native J. Erskine Love, Jr., decided to found a printing company. Love, 28, had studied at Georgia Tech, and then worked at Westinghouse as an engineer before switching to a small Atlanta-based food company. Married with one child and a second on the way, he struck out on his own after gathering the needed capital by mortgaging his home and borrowing money from relatives and friends. While awaiting delivery of a four-color Kidder stack printing press, he initially produced blank cellophane bags for vegetables in the basement of an office building with a used machine he had bought for $500. In June 1957, Love moved into new quarters, and in July the newly delivered press began operation. At this time Printpack's payroll was expanded to ten.

The firm's client base soon began to grow, and in 1958 Love hired an art director so he could develop in-house the graphic designs he believed were key to successful packaging. In 1960, the growing Printpack hired a Midwest sales representative to help it expand beyond its southern stronghold, and in 1963 the firm moved into a new 30,000-square-foot space, which would remain its headquarters for decades to come. The company had by now firmly established its niche in the field known as "flexible packaging conversion," in which raw materials like polypropylene were made into packages that conformed to the shape of a product such as potato chips or candy.

By 1964, Printpack employed sixty-five, and the firm was performing work for more than fifty different clients including Frito-Lay, Murray Biscuit, The Arkansas Rice Growers Co-Op, and Crackin' Good Bakeries. By the time the company celebrated its first decade in business just two years later, its payroll had more than doubled to 150.

Acquisitions Begin in 1969

In 1967, Printpack established a research and development group to help create new types of products, and in 1969 the company's first manufacturing facility outside Atlanta was constructed in Grand Prairie, Texas. The firm also made its first acquisition, Southeastern Packaging, Inc., which was soon followed by Standard Packaging, Sigmadyne Corporation, and Daniels Packaging.

The company's efforts at research and development paid off in 1970 with the creation of extrusion laminating, a new process for making potato chip bags. In 1972, Printpack added a quality control laboratory to enable it to more efficiently perform standardized tests on materials.

The printing industry was presented with a new challenge in the early 1970s with the introduction of the Universal Product Code (UPC). Because an incorrectly printed UPC could cause scanning (and pricing) errors, printers had to rigorously monitor consistency and quality to ensure that retailers were able to scan all products correctly. Producers of flexible packages were particularly challenged, because they generally relied on flexographic printing, which used photographically created plates that were less precise than the older etched-metal rotogravure plates. Printpack rose to the challenge, and the company's employees took special care to make sure print runs conformed

Company Perspectives:

Printpack is a family-owned company with old-fashioned family values. We believe that cooperation, honesty, and an active adherence to high moral and ethical standards results in the highest quality flexible packaging products for our customers. We feel it is our responsibility to build strong, long-term relationships with our customers so we can meet and exceed their expectations. But while our values may be old-fashioned, our methods certainly are not. We are constantly seeking ways to provide greater value to our customers. Printpack is a place where trust, respect and teamwork are highly valued; this environment fosters a great deal of innovation and encourages continuous process improvements. We know this dedication to progress gives us and our customers a competitive advantage in the marketplace.

to the new higher standards after UPC use began in 1975. That same year the firm introduced its new logo, a small round swirl that looked like a camera shutter and was referred to by insiders as "the bug."

By 1976, when Printpack celebrated its 20th anniversary, the company's employment ranks had grown to 469. In 1978, the firm added another feather to its cap when it became the first manufacturer of all-plastic labels for PET plastic bottles. Printpack was now recognized as the largest independent flexible packaging converter in the United States, the largest supplier of flexible packaging materials to the snack food industry, and the country's largest converter of cellophane.

In 1980, Printpack opened a new technical center, which offered materials testing, chemical and physical analysis, research and development, and engineering services. It also had a pilot plant to do sample print runs. In 1983, the company expanded further with the purchase of a Richmond, California, printmaking facility that made co-extruded plastic film for high density polyethylene products. The year 1985 saw the firm win a prestigious packaging industry award for its pressurized plastic tube for Wilson tennis balls.

By 1985, Printpack's major accounts included Frito-Lay, Tom's, Lance, Golden Flake, and Wise Foods. It was making bags for their salty snacks like potato and corn chips, as well as wraparound plastic labels for two-liter bottles of Coca-Cola and Pepsi, luncheon meat packages for Swift, Hormel, and Eckrich, boiler bags for Stouffer's frozen entrees, and wrappers for cookies, candy, and granola bars. The company was now operating plants in Atlanta (where its original location had been expanded to 250,000 square feet); Grand Prairie, Texas; Elgin, Illinois; Fredricksburg, Virginia; and Richmond, California. It had 930 employees and revenues of more than $100 million.

In the three decades since the firm was founded, many new flexible packaging materials and processes had been developed. Having started out with cellophane, by the mid-1980s Printpack was using a variety of plastics, papers, films, adhesives, and inks to produce its packaging, with most items made from two or more materials laminated together. Some 95 percent of Printpack's output consisted of flexible packaging that conformed to the shape of the food it held, with most of the remainder comprised of wraparound plastic labels for two-liter soda bottles. The company's products performed two basic but important functions: preserving the freshness of food and providing an eye-catching design to win the attention of customers.

In an interview with *Business Atlanta* magazine in 1985, Erskine Love attributed the company's success to the quality of its employees and to its dedication to customer service. Love himself took calls at any time, day or night, and frequently visited with major clients to be sure he was closely attuned to their needs. He also took pride in his involvement with a variety of charitable organizations in Atlanta, serving as president of the United Way, Rotary Club, and Boy Scouts. He was on numerous boards of directors, as well, and was a trustee of several educational and religious organizations.

Sudden Death of Founder in 1987

On February 21, 1987, 58-year-old Erskine Love suffered a massive heart attack and died while jogging near his home. The company had no clear succession plan, but Love's widow Gay quickly assumed the title of chairman of the board, and their oldest son, Dennis, was named CEO. Dennis Love, age 32, had earned his MBA from Harvard before joining Printpack's marketing department. Though he was not yet experienced enough to take the firm's top position, his mother felt he would "grow into the job" while maintaining the family's leadership role.

Dennis Love proved to be an able leader, and over the next several years undertook an aggressive campaign of expansion. By 1992 Printpack had more than 2,000 employees and a total of eleven plants in the United States and Ireland. In May 1993, the firm acquired Flexpack U.K. Ltd. of Bury, England, which was renamed Printpack Europe Ltd. Less than a year later the company bought U.C.B. Packaging Ltd. with operations in St. Helens and Gainsborough, England, and merged them into the former Flexpack operation. Printpack later sold the U.C.B. plant in Gainsborough to EPL Technologies. The U.C.B. purchase doubled the firm's European sales to $120 million, while also giving it the ability to make flexible medical product packaging.

In 1994, the company sold a 51 percent stake in its Forest Park, Illinois facility to Oscar Robertson's Orchem, Inc. The jointly owned venture would be known as Orflex, Inc., and would continue to produce flexible packaging for the food industry. The plant had been slated to close, but under the leadership of former basketball star Robertson, who was African American, it would benefit from the growing numbers of businesses that were pledging to support minority-owned concerns. By now, Printpack had total annual revenues of more than $500 million and employed 2,700.

In 1995, Printpack opened a new 206,000-square-foot manufacturing facility adjacent to its plant in Grand Prairie, Texas, which would be equipped with six- and eight-color flexographic printing presses, adhesive and extrusion laminators, and new ink mixing and control systems. It would also have a 1,000-square-foot quality assurance laboratory. Some operations from Printpack's Villa Rica, Georgia, plant were shifted to Grand Prairie, though no jobs were lost.

Key Dates:

1956: J. Erskine Love, Jr., founds Printpack in Atlanta, Georgia.
1960: An outside sales representative is hired to seek Midwest business.
1963: The company moves to larger quarters.
1969: A new plant is built in Texas; acquisitions begin with Southeastern Packaging.
1970: Extrusion laminating process is introduced.
1975: The company begins producing packages with UPC codes; a new logo is unveiled.
1978: The first all-plastic labels are created for plastic bottles.
1980: A new technical center is opened for testing and analysis of products.
1987: J. Erskine Love dies; his wife Gay is named board chairman and his son Dennis becomes CEO.
1993: U.K. firm Flexpack is acquired.
1996: The acquisition of James River flexible packaging unit doubles the company's size.
2002: Sales top $1 billion.

Company Doubles Size with 1996 James River Purchase

In August 1996, Printpack completed its biggest acquisition to date—the Flexible Packaging Group of the James River Corporation. The deal, valued at $372 million, gave Printpack four lamination and coating plants in Missouri, Ohio, Louisiana, and California; five film and converting plants in Delaware, Texas, Indiana, Tennessee, and Mexico; a rigid plastics container facility in Virginia; and pilot plant equipment from James River's technology center in Ohio. The James River operations, which employed a total of 2,200 people, had accounted for approximately $490 million in sales in 1995. The deal brought Printpack several major new accounts, including Georgia-Pacific and Kraft. The move was made as food companies sought to reduce the number of packaging suppliers they dealt with, and the acquisition strengthened Printpack's ability to offer a diverse range of products.

Following the purchase Printpack closed two plants and consolidated several other operations, with a total of 4,100 employees remaining afterwards. The integration process was not always smooth, with problems like a twelve week strike at the former James River plant in Greensburg, Illinois, that caused Printpack to lose some accounts.

While this was in process, Printpack also acquired a patented flat-bottom food pouch developed by a company called Jebco, which had gone bankrupt. The pouch, and new aseptic juice boxes, would bring additional business for Printpack as these formats were embraced by food companies.

For the fiscal year ending in June 1998, the company reported annual sales of $850 million. At the same time that the kinks from the James River merger were being worked out, serious difficulties with Printpack Europe were also being dealt with. The company closed its U.K. plant at St. Helens, consolidated operations at Bury and Saffron Walden, and reduced its client base from 140 to 50 by eliminating unprofitable contracts. By 2000 the unit was back in the black, earning £1.7 million on sales of £62 million.

The turn of the 21st century saw the company continuing to innovate, with successes like a special Harry Potter label for plastic Coca-Cola bottles which revealed a prize symbol only after the beverage had been consumed. In February 2002, Printpack formed another minority-owned joint venture with Woodrow A. Hall called Diversapack. Hall would own 51 percent of the operation, which included the former Orflex plant in Ohio and two others in Indiana and Illinois. By now, Printpack's annual revenues had risen above $1 billion.

Over time, each of the six children of company founder Erskine Love and his wife Gay became involved with the company. In addition to CEO Dennis Love, his brothers Bill, Keith, Jimmy, and David and sister Carol Anne had all joined the firm. Each had first worked in the shipping department, then returned after college to take higher-level positions.

On July 19, 2003, tragedy struck when a chartered plane carrying Bill Love, his wife Beth, the eldest of their four daughters, and nine other members of Beth Love's extended family crashed into a mountaintop in Kenya, killing all aboard. They had been scheduled to move back to Atlanta from the firm's European division just a month later so that Bill Love could take the position of director of business development at Printpack.

In September 2003, the company bought a 105,000-square-foot thin-wall container thermoforming facility in Newport News, Virginia, from competitor Amcor, Inc. The new plant would expand its capabilities in this product area, which were already served by a similar operation in Williamsburg, Virginia. Revenues for the fiscal year reached $1.053 billion, down slightly from the record $1.1 billion of 2002.

After nearly a half-century in business, Printpack, Inc. had grown into one of the largest flexible packaging manufacturers in the United States, while contributing a number of innovations to the industry. The firm, which was still family-run and owned, continued to serve many long-term clients like Frito-Lay and Coca-Cola.

Principal Subsidiaries

Printpack Europe (U.K.); Printpack Mexico.

Principal Competitors

Bemis Co., Inc.; Alcan, Inc.; Reynolds Food Packaging; Amcor, Ltd.; Pliant Corporation.

Further Reading

Ford, Tom, "Printpack Buys Packaging Unit for $365 Million," *Plastics News*, April 15, 1996, p. 1.
Grillo, Jerry, "That's a Wrap: Printpack Keeps Brand Products Looking Good," *Georgia Trend*, May 1, 2001, p. 56.
Larkin, Patrick, "Oscar Gets an Assist for Saving Plant," *Cincinnati Post*, November 22, 1994, p. D5.
Lauzon, Michael, "Amcor Sells Thin-Wall Unit to Printpack," *Plastics News*, September 15, 2003, p. 1.

Neuberger, Christine, ''Virginia Label Maker Is on a Roll,'' *Richmond Times-Dispatch*, March 29, 1992, p. E1.

Pidgeon, Ron, ''Printpack Plans Ahead,'' *Packaging Magazine*, February 8, 2001, p. 24.

Smith, Faye McDonald, ''Printpack's Erskine Love: Making Service the Standard,'' *Business Atlanta*, October, 1985, p. 66.

Smith, Sarah S., ''Printpack Battles Setbacks,'' *Plastics News*, March 8, 1999, p.95.

Van Dusen, Christine, ''Tragic Deaths Hit Home at Company,'' *Atlanta Journal-Constitution*, July 29, 2003, p. D1.

—Frank Uhle

Psychiatric Solutions, Inc.

113 Seaboard Lane, Suite C100
Franklin, Tennessee 37067
U.S.A.
Telephone: (615) 312-5700
Toll Free: (800) 848-9090
Fax: (615) 312-5711
Web site: http://www.psysolutions.com

Public Company
Incorporated: 1988 as PMR Corporation
Employees: 6.780
Sales: $293.66 million (2003)
Stock Exchanges: NASDAQ
Ticker Symbol: PSYS
NAIC: 541611 Administrative Management and General Management Consulting

Psychiatric Solutions, Inc. (PSI) is a leading provider of behavioral health programs through hospitals owned or leased by the company and through management programs offered at acute-care facilities owned by other companies. PSI owns or leases 34 freestanding psychiatric inpatient facilities with more than 4,000 beds in approximately 20 states. The company derives roughly 75 percent of its revenue from the inpatient facilities it manages. The remaining 25 percent of the company's revenue is generated through management contracts with government agencies and medical surgical hospitals. Under the terms of the management contracts, PSI develops, organizes, and manages behavioral health care programs. PSI is one of three companies competing for national dominance in inpatient psychiatric care, employing a strategy underpinned by acquiring inpatient facilities and leading the consolidation of a fragmented industry.

Origins

The 2002 merger between PSI and PMR Corporation joined two companies with different strategic approaches to providing mental health care. The merger also created a company with two branches of history. Of the two companies, PMR was the older enterprise, established in 1988 to provide outpatient psychiatric services, although it later expanded into other areas of the behavioral care business. The company operated its outpatient programs under management contracts with local health care providers, forging agreements with acute-care hospitals and community mental health centers. PMR focused on providing care to individuals diagnosed with what it classified as "serious mental illness," an often chronic condition afflicting just over 1 percent of the U.S. population. The majority of the patients treated under PMR's outpatient programs were diagnosed with schizophrenia and bipolar disorder (manic depression). As the company matured, it delved into other facets of the mental health care industry, taking its direction from its chairman, chief executive officer, and president, Allen Tepper. Tepper, a graduate of Temple University, where he earned his undergraduate degree, and Northwestern University, where he earned his Masters of Business Administration degree, joined PMR in October 1989. Before taking the helm at PMR, Tepper founded Consolidated Medical Corp., a company that provided outpatient clinic management services to acute care hospitals in the Philadelphia area.

During his tenure, Tepper shepherded PMR into other areas of the mental health care market. Perhaps the most significant diversifying move was made in 1993, when the company began offering case management services. PMR's case management services relied on a proprietary service system for managing the treatment and rehabilitation of patients, one that used detailed plans for delivering and managing their care. The company's case management program enabled its users—typically case management agencies and community mental health centers—to assess and to manage the financial risk associated with providing health care treatment. PMR initially operated its case management programs in Tennessee, deriving the majority of its business from the Nashville and Memphis markets. By 1996, the company had begun to extend its case management services to clients in Arkansas.

By the time PMR began to open case management programs in Arkansas, it also had a third line of business it was developing. Through a wholly owned affiliate, the company offered programs to treat chemical dependency and substance abuse,

Company Perspectives:

We strongly believe that our long-term success in expanding revenues through increased market share will depend on our providing the highest quality of services. We are fundamentally committed to providing this level of quality to each of our patients, and we believe this commitment is reflected by the tremendously dedicated and talented employees, physicians and other health care professionals treating patients in our facilities every day. In addition to the positive impact of increased revenues, we focus on enhancing the profitability of each facility through increased operating efficiencies. Among other steps, we bring each facility into our group-purchasing cooperative to reduce supplies expenses, and we consistently review operations to optimize staffing ratios and total compensation expense, our largest operating cost. As a result of this overall process, we expect to operate not only high quality but also highly efficient facilities that provide a consistent and significant contribution to the company's profitable growth.

selling its services to managed care organizations in southern California. PMR also offered ambulatory detoxification programs in Arkansas, catering its services to patients covered by Medicaid and other government-funded programs.

PMR Struggles in the Late 1990s

As PMR prepared for the late 1990s, it regarded its outpatient and case management business lines as its two primary growth engines, with its chemical dependency programs playing a subsidiary role in future plans. As the company progressed through the late 1990s, however, neither its outpatient programs nor its case management programs proved to possess sufficient strength to deliver financial vitality. To blame were the ills of the industry the company served, as conditions within the mental health care market conspired to hobble PMR's financial growth. The negative affect of the market conditions eventually led PMR to look to PSI as its savior, resulting in the 2002 merger that brought PMR and PSI together.

PMR's problems in the late 1990s stemmed from events in the 1980s. During the 1980s, a plethora of new hospitals were opened in the United States, the establishment of which sent hospital rates spiraling upwards. At the time, reimbursement rates—the amount paid by Medicare, Medicaid, and other insurance providers—were based on the cost structure of new facilities. As the number of costly, new hospitals proliferated, the construction costs caused a sharp increase in the fees to treat patients, eventually escalating to the point that traditional payers such as Medicare and Medicaid balked at paying the fees. Business was lost as a result, causing many of the facilities to shut down, leaving PMR in a precarious position as its sources of revenue dried up. PMR posted $3.1 million net income in 1997, $1.8 million the following year, and afterward fell into a pattern of losing money every year, racking up more than $22 million in losses by the beginning of the 2000s.

PMR's management searched for a solution to the company's financial woes. New sources of revenue needed to be discovered to compensate for the unwillingness of traditional payers to reimburse the company for treating individuals with serious mental disorders. In 2000, PMR launched a proprietary, Web-based pharmaceutical and prescription system called InfoScriber that suggested the beginning of a new era for the company. Instead of operating as an administrator of outpatient services for the mentally ill, PMR began to fashion itself as a pharmaceutical and health care marketing company. The metamorphosis was never completed, however. In July 2001, one year after the introduction of InfoScriber, PMR licensed the Web-based system to Conundrum Communications Inc. and returned to focusing on mental health services. Some analysts perceived the move as a prelude to courting a suitor; by licensing InfoScriber, PMR cut its costs and made itself more appealing to a potential buyer. PMR's board of directors, in fact, was exploring such strategic alternatives during the first half of 2001. Board members discussed the possible sale of the company, with PSI's name coming up frequently during discussions. PMR and PSI had talked before about forming an alliance or merging, signing a five-year confidentiality agreement in June 1999 to pursue such possibilities. By the end of 2001, the two companies began to make concrete plans about joining forces.

PSI occupied a stronger position than PMR as discussions evolved at the turn of the 21st century. PSI was founded in September 1996, starting its corporate life as provider of inpatient and outpatient behavioral health care services. The company was led by one of its founders, Joey Jacobs, who had spent two decades at Hospital Corporation of America, holding various executive titles during his stay. Initially, Jacobs and his management team were involved in psychiatric physician practice management, outpatient treatment facilities, employee assistance plans, and psychiatric contract management. PSI changed the nature of its business, however. In 1999, the company began to focus on inpatient hospital settings, adopting a business strategy that turned it into an owner and operator of freestanding, acute-care facilities. The company discontinued its physician practice management unit in 2001 and sold its employee assistance plan division the following year, choosing to keep its contract management services business. As PSI shed its unwanted businesses, it also established itself in its new line of business by acquiring four freestanding specialty hospitals in 2001. Accordingly, as the company entered 2002, its operations comprised two divisions: one focused on owning and operating freestanding psychiatric inpatient hospitals and the other focused on managing psychiatric units within hospitals owned by third parties.

Essentially, PSI was exploiting the same industry conditions that afflicted PMR. When PSI aimed its efforts at acquiring psychiatric hospitals, the number of facilities was diminishing, creating an opportunity for Jacobs to capture market share in markets abandoned by other hospital operators earlier in the decade. In Houston, for example, PSI owned two of the five freestanding psychiatric hospitals in existence at the turn of the 21st century. At one time, there were 28 freestanding psychiatric hospitals serving the Houston market. Although the company devoted much of its attention to providing behavioral health programs for critically ill children, adolescents, and adults, the core of the company's strategy was acquiring psychiatric hospitals. The prospect of merging with PMR represented

Key Dates:

1988: PMR Corporation is established.
1996: PSI is formed.
1999: PSI begins to focus on acquiring psychiatric hospitals.
2002: PSI and PMR Corp. merge.
2003: PSI acquires The Brown Schools, Inc. and Ramsay Youth Services, Inc.

a chance for PSI to broaden the spectrum of health care services it could provide at its facilities, the number of which was expected to increase substantially during the 2000s. For PMR, the merger offered potential revenue enhancement and significant value to its shareholders.

PMR and PSI Merge in 2002

In May 2002, the merger between PSI and PMR was announced, an all-stock transaction valued at an estimated $60 million. Jacobs, who used the merger as means to make privately held PSI a publicly traded company, commented on the deal in the May 7, 2002 issue of *Knight Ridder/Tribune Business News*. "After many years of contraction," he stated, "the psychiatric inpatient market now has favorable supply and demand fundamentals and we will now have the only public company focused on consolidating this market." The merger was completed in August 2002 in a multi-step transaction designed to integrate the two companies to make PSI a publicly traded company. On August 5, 2002, a new subsidiary of PMR called PMR Acquisition Corp. merged with PSI. Next, PSI changed its name to Psychiatric Solutions Hospitals, Inc., which became the surviving corporation of the merger. This company was made a wholly owned subsidiary of PMR. Concurrently, PMR Corporation changed its name to Psychiatric Solutions, Inc., or PSI. On August 6, 2002, the shares of PSI were approved for listing on the NASDAQ.

When the merger was announced, PSI owned and operated four freestanding psychiatric hospitals in Texas and North Carolina, and it managed 44 psychiatric units for third-party hospitals in 14 states. During the next several years, the stature of the company grew substantially, particularly in terms of the number of hospitals it owned, as Jacobs, who was appointed to lead the new merged entity, applied PSI's corporate strategy of consolidating the industry through acquisitions.

Following the merger, Jacob's priority was to acquire inpatient psychiatric facilities. The company looked at both small and large acquisition candidates, intent on becoming one of the leading consolidators of a fragmented industry. In 2003, PSI completed two large acquisitions that substantially increased its stature. The company's first major acquisition following the merger was completed in April 2003, when PSI paid $63 million for six inpatient behavioral health care facilities from The Brown Schools, Inc. The acquisition gave the company 895 additional licensed beds and three hospitals in Texas, one in Virginia, one in Colorado, and one in Oklahoma. A larger acquisition followed two months later, when PSI purchased Ramsay Youth Services, Inc. PSI paid $81 million for Ramsay, obtaining 11 psychiatric hospitals with nearly 1,300 beds and ten contracts to manage inpatient psychiatric facilities for government agencies.

PSI also completed smaller acquisitions as it expanded its national portfolio of behavioral health care facilities. In November 2003, the company acquired the 109-bed Alliance Health Center in Meridian, Mississippi. In March 2004, PSI acquired two hospitals from Brentwood Behavioral Health, which gave the company an additional 311 beds. By targeting both small and large properties, PSI grew robustly, quickly emerging as one of the most powerful psychiatric care companies in the nation. In the 12 months leading up to August 2004, PSI completed eight acquisitions, paying slightly more than $200 million to assert itself as a contender for national dominance. During that same 12-month period, the number of beds owned or leased by the company leaped from 2,800 to more than 4,000. The financial community liked what it saw, noting that PSI was the only publicly held company exclusively focused on consolidating the fragmented inpatient psychiatric care industry. The company's stock value reflected Wall Street's enthusiasm, as PSI's share price increased 189 percent during the first eight months of 2004.

As PSI entered the mid-2000s, the company ranked as the third-largest company of its kind, trailing Universal Health Services and Ardent Health Services, both private companies. "These three large players will continue to get bigger," an analyst said in a July 27, 2004 interview with *Investor's Business Daily*. Industry pundits did not expect PSI to acquire psychiatric facilities at the pace shown during the first years following the merger of PSI and PMR, and further acquisitions were on the horizon. Observers expected PSI to acquire between four and six behavioral health care facilities annually for the remainder of the decade.

Principal Subsidiaries

Aeries Health Care Corporation; Aeries Health care of Illinois, Inc.; Bountiful Psychiatric Hospital, Inc.; Brentwood Acquisition, Inc.; Brentwood Acquisition-Shreveport, Inc.; Collaborative Care Corporation; Cypress Creek Real Estate, L.P.; East Carolina Psychiatric Services Corporation; Great Plains Hospital, Inc.; Gulf Coast Treatment Center, Inc.; Havenwyck Hospital Inc.; H.C. Corporation; H.C. Partnership; Holly Hill Real Estate, LLC; HSA Hill Crest Corporation; HSA of Oklahoma, Inc.; InfoScriber Corporation; Laurelwood Center, Inc.; Michigan Psychiatric Services, Inc.; Neuro Institute of Austin, L.P.; Neuro Rehab Real Estate, L.P.; Premier Behavioral Solutions, Inc.; Premier Behavioral Solutions of Alabama, Inc.; PSI Cedar Springs Hospital, Inc.; PSI Cedar Springs Hospital Real Estate, Inc.; PSI Community Mental Health Agency Management, Inc.; PSI Hospitals, Inc.; PSI Surety, Inc.; PSI Texas Hospitals, LLC; PSI-EAP, Inc.; Psychiatric Management Resources, Inc.; Psychiatric Practice Management of Arkansas, Inc.; Psychiatric Solutions Hospitals, Inc.; Psychiatric Solutions of Alabama, Inc.; Psychiatric Solutions of Arizona, Inc.; Psychiatric Solutions of Florida, Inc.; Psychiatric Solutions of North Carolina, Inc.; Psychiatric Solutions of Oklahoma, Inc.; Psychiatric Solutions of Oklahoma Real Estate, Inc.; Psychiatric Solutions of Tennessee, Inc.; Ramsay Managed Care, Inc.; Ramsay Treatment Services, Inc.; Ramsay Youth Services of Florida, Inc.; Ramsay Youth Services of Georgia, Inc.; Ramsay Youth Services of South Carolina, Inc.; Ramsay Youth Services Puerto Rico, Inc.; RHCI San Antonio, Inc.; Riveredge Real Estate, Inc.; Solutions Center of Little Rock, Inc.; Sunstone Behavioral Health, Inc.; Texas Cypress Creek Hospital, L.P.; Texas Laurel Ridge Hospital, L.P.; Texas Laurel Ridge Hospital Real Estate, L.P.; Texas Oaks Psychiatric Hospital, L.P.; Texas Oaks Psychiatric Hospital Real Estate, L.P.; Texas San Marcos Treatment Center, L.P.; Texas San Marcos Treatment Center Real Estate, L.P.; Texas West Oaks Hospital, L.P.; The Counseling Center of Middle Tennessee, Inc.; Therapeutic School Services, L.L.C.; Transitional Care Ventures, Inc.; Transitional Care Ventures (Texas), Inc.; West Oaks Real Estate, L.P.

Principal Competitors

Horizon Health Corporation; Magellan Health Services, Inc.; Universal Health Services, Inc.

Further Reading

Block, Donna, ''Psychiatric Solutions Plans $78 Million Deal,'' *Daily Deal*, April 10, p. 32.

Heilman, Wayne, ''Tennessee Psychiatric Care Firm to Purchase Colorado Springs, Colo. Center,'' *Knight Ridder Tribune Business News*, March 13, 2003, p. ITEM03072024.

''PSI Buys More Facilities,'' *Mississippi Business Journal*, March 15, 2004, p. 11.

''Psychiatric Solutions Completes $16 Million Acquisition of Riveredge Hospital of Illinois,'' *Health Care Strategic Management*, August 2002, p. 3.

''Psychiatric Solutions, Inc., a National Behavioral Health Company, Acquired The Brown Schools' NeuroRehabilitation Center in Austin, Texas,'' *Behavioral Health Business News*, November 22, 2001, p. 7.

''Ramsay Youth Services Stock Surges 37% on News Tennessee Company Will Acquire It for $78 Million,'' *Miami Daily Businss Review*, April 10, 2003, p. A3.

—Jeffrey L. Covell

Qantas Airways Ltd.

ABN 16 009 661 901
Qantas Centre
Level 9, Building A
203 Coward Street
Mascot NSW 2020
Australia
Telephone: (+61) 2 9691 3636
Toll Free: (800) 227-4500
Fax: 61 2 9691 3339
Web site: http://www.qantas.com

Public Company
Incorporated: 1920 as Queensland and Northern Territory Aerial Services Ltd.
Employees: 35,000
Sales: AUD 11.35 billion (2004)
Stock Exchanges: Australian
Ticker Symbol: QAN
NAIC: 481111 Scheduled Passenger Air Transportation; 481112 Scheduled Freight Air Transportation; 488119 Other Airport Operations; 48819 Other Support Activities for Air Transportation

Qantas Airways Ltd. is Australia's number one domestic airline and a leader in the Asia-Pacific region. It is one of the ten largest airlines in the world and is considered to be the second oldest (after KLM of the Netherlands). Qantas connects Australia to 81 destinations in 40 other countries worldwide and operates extensive domestic services in both Australia and New Zealand. In addition to its flagship Qantas line, the company also operates several regional airlines in Australia and is a partner in a budget start-up based in Singapore. Qantas and its regional subsidiaries carry more than 30 million passengers a year. Qantas maintains a number of alliances and code share arrangements; it is a member of the oneworld global airline alliance led by American Airlines and British Airways plc, which is Qantas's largest shareholder with an 18 percent interest.

Early History

Qantas was founded by two World War I veterans, William Hudson Fysh and Paul McGuiness, who had served with the Australian Flying Corps. In March 1919, they gained the support of a millionaire industrialist to enter a competition for a prize of AUD 20,000 offered by the Australian government for the first Australians to fly from Britain to Australia within 20 days. Unfortunately, their patron died before the arrangements for their flight had been made. They accepted a related task from the Australian Chief of General Staff to survey the air race route from Longreach in Queensland to Katherine in the Northern Territory and to lay down supplies along the route for the competitors.

After the completion of their overland survey in August 1919, Fysh and McGuiness were convinced that aircraft could play an important role in transporting passengers and freight over the sparsely populated areas of western and northern Queensland and northern Australia, and they decided to form an airline. The pair had insufficient capital to launch their new venture, but a chance meeting between McGuiness and Fergus McMaster, a prominent Queensland grazier, led to the latter's involvement in the project. McMaster, together with his fellow grazier Ainslie Templeton, agreed to provide financial backing for Fysh and McGuiness's proposed air service for western Queensland.

On November 16, 1920, Queensland and Northern Territory Aerial Services Ltd. (Qantas) was registered in Brisbane with an initial paid-up capital of AUD 12,074. McMaster became the first chairman of the airline; he was to prove anything but a silent partner. Without his constant efforts on behalf of Qantas, it is doubtful whether the airline would have survived.

In 1921, the airline's head office was moved from Winton to Longreach, another small Queensland outback town. During its early years, the airline encountered serious problems in obtaining suitable aircraft, as most of the British-manufactured aircraft were inappropriate for the Australian outback and the country's hot climate. Eventually, in 1924, the company found an aircraft up to the challenge: the de Havilland DH50. In the early days, passengers were few in number and most of the airline's revenue came from joyriders and air taxi work.

Company Perspectives:

Going forward, Qantas will strive for greater efficiency, continue to invest in new aircraft and product, grow operations and job opportunities and protect its reputation as Australia's national carrier and one of the world's leading airlines. We aim to compete effectively across all sectors of the aviation marketplace and in a growing number of markets.

It soon became clear that Qantas would need a government subsidy to survive. In late 1921 Qantas won the contract for a weekly subsidized mail service between Charleville and Cloncurry in Queensland, and the airline's first scheduled service was inaugurated on November 2, 1922. Later in that year, McGuiness left the company, leaving Fysh as the sole employee from what John Gunn described in *The Defeat of Distance: Qantas 1919–1939* as the airline's ''dreamtime days.'' In February 1923, Marcus Griffin, the airline's first professional manager, resigned. With McMaster's support, he was replaced by Fysh.

In 1924, the subsidized mail service was extended from Cloncurry to Camooweal, and three years later another subsidized mail service was started from Cloncurry to Normanton. The following year, the Australian Medical Service—renamed the Flying Doctor Service in 1942—was formed, and Qantas was contracted to operate medical flights on demand. On April 17, 1929, Qantas inaugurated the 710-kilometer Charleville-Brisbane service on the first direct link to the coast, bringing its total route network to nearly 2,380 kilometers. In 1930, the airline's headquarters were moved to Brisbane, the capital of Queensland.

QEA Formed in 1934

The original link with Britain's Imperial Airways took place in 1931, when Qantas assisted in carrying the first official airmail as part of an experimental Australia-Britain route. Qantas carried the airmail between Darwin, the capital of the Northern Territory, and Brisbane. On January 18, 1934, Qantas Empire Airways Ltd. (QEA) was formed as a 50–50 joint venture between Imperial Airways and Qantas to enable the Australian airline to participate in the new airmail service. QEA secured subsidized airmail contracts for the Brisbane-Singapore via Darwin and also Cloncurry-Normanton services. The new weekly transcontinental service began on December 10, 1934. In 1936, a second weekly service was begun between Brisbane and Singapore.

On June 10, 1938, the route between Australia and Britain was upgraded to a thrice-weekly subsidized service with the introduction of Short Brothers Empire Flying Boats, extending the route to Sydney. Imperial Airways and QEA's flying boats were flown directly across the whole route, with the British crews taking over the aircraft in Singapore. During the same year, QEA's headquarters were moved to Sydney.

During the 1930s, KLM emerged as a major competitor with its Amsterdam-Batavia (Jakarta) service. In July 1938, its partner airline, KNILM, started a service between Batavia and Sydney. QEA regarded KLM's service as superior to that of Imperial Airways, partly because of KLM's use of American aircraft. In the earliest days of air travel, British aircraft had been superior to those built in the United States, but with the development of a major commercial airline industry in the 1930s American planes gained dominance. Pan American Airways (Pan-Am) also emerged as a strong competitor to the Imperial Airways-QEA Sydney-London service with the inauguration of a United States West Coast-Honolulu-Auckland service in 1940 after an abortive start in 1938.

World War II Efforts

After the outbreak of World War II, the Sydney-London route over which the flying boats operated became a vital line of communication. QEA continued to fly to Singapore. After the occupation of Singapore by Japan, however, all QEA aircraft eventually were recalled to Broome in Western Australia as Japanese forces advanced ever closer to Australia. QEA continued a token domestic service, but it ceased to be an overseas commercial passenger airline until the end of the war. More than half of the QEA fleet was commissioned for war service by the Australian government. Later in the war, QEA crews served alongside the Royal Australian Air Force in the battle zones of New Guinea.

In 1943, an agreement was signed between QEA, the British Air Ministry, and British Overseas Airways Corporation (BOAC—formerly Imperial Airways) to reestablish an air link between Britain and Australia. Using Catalina flying boats—obtained from the United States and leased from the Australian government—regular flights were carried out between Perth, the capital of Western Australia, and Ceylon. The single ocean route of 5,600 kilometers was the longest ever undertaken. Between July 10, 1943, and July 18, 1945, 271 flights were completed.

Postwar Rebuilding and Expansion

Having survived World War II, QEA was left with virtually no aircraft. Hence, it immediately began the task of rebuilding and modernizing its fleet. Against bitter opposition from the British government, BOAC, and their friends in Australia, QEA refused to consider seriously the purchase of what it regarded, correctly as it later transpired, as inferior and unairworthy British aircraft not even off the drawing board. Instead, in October 1946 an order worth AUD 5.5 million was placed with Lockheed for four Constellation aircraft. The DC3 aircraft also was introduced by QEA for use on the Australia-New Guinea and on internal New Guinea and Queensland routes.

QEA had been the national overseas airline of Australia since 1934. The nationalization of Imperial Airways in 1940 by the British government, however, had led to pressure in Australia for the nationalization of QEA. In 1947, the Australian ALP government purchased BOAC's 50 percent share of QEA and later in the year also purchased Qantas's 50 percent share as well. In October, McMaster retired as the result of persistent ill health, and Fysh became chairman of the newly nationalized QEA in addition to his role as managing director.

The first L749 Constellation arrived in October 1947, and in December QEA began its first regular weekly service right through to London via Singapore on the famous ''Kangaroo

Key Dates:

1920: Qantas is formed.
1947: ''Kangaroo Route'' to London via Singapore is initiated.
1967: A koala becomes the airline's famous TV mascot.
1979: Qantas flies the world's first all-Boeing 747 fleet.
1982: New aircraft types are acquired in fleet modernization program.
1989: The first nonstop Sydney-London route is flown.
1992: Qantas takes over Australian Airlines.
1993: British Airways buys a 25 percent shareholding in Qantas.
1995: Qantas shares floated publicly.
2001: Qantas dominates its domestic market as competitors struggle.
2003: Qantas begins investing in several regional airlines.

Route.'' The Douglas DC4 Skymaster was introduced to the fleet in June 1949 on the new Hong Kong service. In 1949, Qantas handed over its services in Queensland and the Northern Territory and the Flying Doctor Service to Trans-Australia Airlines (TAA). TAA had been formed in December 1945 as a state-owned domestic airline. It was government policy that TAA should operate only domestic routes and that Qantas should confine itself to overseas routes. In 1950, a commercial service to Japan was inaugurated, followed in 1952 by a fortnightly service to Johannesburg, South Africa. In October 1953, QEA received permission to operate its first scheduled service to North America with the transfer of this service from the previous operator, British Commonwealth Pacific Airways (BCPA). QEA eventually took over BCPA.

In 1954, QEA began taking delivery of Lockheed Super Constellation aircraft and was able to inaugurate its new twice weekly transpacific service to North America on May 15. One service flew on to San Francisco, and the other to Vancouver, BC. During 1957, Qantas moved to new headquarters in Sydney. The following year, QEA inaugurated its first round-the-world service with the establishment of the ''Southern Cross Route'' via San Francisco and New York. An agreement had been signed in 1957 for QEA to operate between Britain and Australia via the United States. In mid-1958, despite Qantas's weak financial position, the government decided that both its internal operations in New Guinea and Sydney were domestic in nature. Hence, it decided that Qantas's New Guinea services would be taken over by TAA, which was done in 1960.

Entering the Jet Age in 1959

In 1959, ahead of all of its non-U.S. competitors, QEA took delivery of seven Boeing 707-138 jet aircraft. These were introduced in turn on both the Southern Cross and Kangaroo Routes during the same year. The Boeing 707 fleet was expanded rapidly and frequencies increased. By 1964, 13 707 jetliners were operating on most of the Qantas routes, and the airline had begun selling off its aging propeller-driven aircraft. By March 1966, Qantas's Boeing fleet had reached 19 jets, six of which were the larger 707-338C series, with five more on order.

In June 1966, Sir Hudson Fysh retired as chairman of Qantas because of his ill health. His retirement was soon followed by that of the man most responsible for the postwar Qantas expansion, Sir Cedric Turner, who had been general manager since 1951 and chief executive since 1955. Captain R.J. Richie, who had taken a leading role in building up the company's fleet and airline network after World War II, was appointed general manager; Sir Roland Wilson, a Qantas Board member, was appointed as the new chairman.

The same year, Qantas made the decision to standardize its fleet with the larger Boeing 338C series and to dispose of its 138B aircraft. It also considered purchasing an even larger, innovative aircraft: the Boeing 747. As a result of the high costs involved, it was decided that Qantas would hold on to its 21-strong 707 fleet to protect its immediate position and would wait for the more advanced ''B'' series of the 747. An initial order for four Boeing 747Bs was placed in August 1967. Although this meant that Qantas's competitors would have been operating the wide-bodied jet for nearly two years before it took delivery, the B series had features and refinements particularly suited to long-haul operations. The airline also changed its name on August 1, 1967, to Qantas Airways Limited. At the end of the 1960s Qantas came under government pressure to cut its airfares because the Australian Tourist Commission and some government ministers felt that lower fares were essential for the development of the Australian tourist industry. Qantas, which was facing rising costs and falling revenue yields, did not want to cut its fares.

In 1970, Qantas again decided to standardize its fleet with Boeing aircraft when it rejected the option of purchasing cheaper DC10s in favor of 747s. In the early 1970s, the airline was facing strong competition, particularly on the Pacific, where it had excess capacity and one of its principal rivals, Pan-Am, was already using 747s. Qantas was forced to eliminate some of its air crew. Qantas also experienced problems with the United States Civil Aeronautics Board (CAB), which banned its 747 operations even though Pan-Am used 747s on its flights to Australia. As a result, Qantas introduced its 747s on routes to Singapore and London instead of on transpacific services to the West Coast of the United States. The Australian government was forced to allow more American airline services between the United States and Australia. In return, the CAB allowed Qantas to begin 747 services to the United States in January 1972.

Low Fare Policy Debuts in the Early 1970s

In the early 1970s, Qantas formed a charter subsidiary, Qantair Ltd., with the strong support of the Australian government and with the intention of recovering the traffic it had lost to charter services on the Europe-Far East part of the journey to Australia. At the same time, Qantas decided to embark upon a low fares initiative in late 1971. On April 1, 1972, subject to British government approval, it cut the one-way fare between London and Sydney from £276 to £169. Single fares between Australia and four other European cities were cut similarly. The British government deferred approval for the new fare, but Qantas sold unapproved tickets in the face of bitter opposition to the new low fare from its rivals. In late May, Britain approved the new fare. Britain's liberal line earned it a good deal of anger from other countries and non-British airlines. Qantas offered travelers charter-level fares while still retaining the benefits of scheduled services. As a result, the airline's passenger traffic and revenue grew dramatically, despite the huge increase in the price of aviation fuel.

In August 1972, the Australian government authorized Qantas to go ahead with the construction of the International Centre, the new headquarters located in downtown Sydney. In December, the ALP replaced the Liberals as Australia's governing party. The new government confirmed its predecessor's decision that Qantas would replace the two domestic airlines Ansett and TAA on the highly profitable route between Port Morseby and Australia after Papua New Guinea (PNG) became independent on December 1, 1973. Qantas had been forced to surrender this route to TAA in 1960.

After the introduction of its low fare policy in 1972, Qantas embarked upon a major rationalization of its route network. Margins were extremely tight and the airline could not afford to spread its operations over wide areas of the world for reasons of prestige alone. Hence Qantas decided to discontinue its ''Southern Cross Route'' to London as it had done earlier in the case of operations between Hong Kong and London.

During the late 1970s, Qantas readopted its policy of offering bargain fares between Britain and Australia, beginning with fare cuts of up to £79 in 1977. Further fare cuts of up to one-third were made in February 1979 as a means of meeting the potential threat of cheap advance booking charter fares proposed by Laker Airways of Britain. Qantas's policy was opposed by members of the Association of South East Asian Nations (ASEAN). Singapore especially opposed it because the policy excluded stopovers in their countries, cutting tourism and airline profits. At a meeting in Kuala Lumpur in May 1979, however, Australia succeeded in forcing ASEAN to accept its new policy.

With the sale of its last Boeing 707 in 1979, Qantas became the world's first airline to operate a fleet composed entirely of Boeing 747s. The final roundtrip 707 flight operated between Sydney and Auckland at the end of March. Over the next few years, Qantas took delivery of several 747 variations. In 1980, the chairman since 1975, Sir Lenox Hewitt, retired. He was replaced by Jim Leslie, who was initially only a part-time chairman as well as continuing temporarily to be chairman and managing director of Mobil Oil Australia.

Fleet Modernized in the Early 1980s

In the early 1980s, Qantas suffered from large operating losses. After the election of the new Labor (ALP) government in 1983, one of its first actions was to increase Qantas's capital base from AUD 89.4 million to AUD 149.4 million. The airline had been denied adequate capital by the previous government and had been obliged to borrow heavily to maintain its aircraft fleet in a modern, efficient, and competitive form. The government hoped that the injection of new capital would assure the future of Qantas as a wholly owned government enterprise.

The new government approved Qantas's largest-ever aircraft order, an AUD 860 million fleet modernization program involving the purchase of three stretched upper-deck Boeing 747s and six of the Extended Range Boeing 767 twin-engine jets. The latter would help service airports such as Adelaide, which joined the Qantas network in November 1982, and Cairns, Darwin, and Townsville. The twin-engine jets also were to be used on the New Zealand routes and expanded to Asian and Pacific destinations. Qantas was to sell its six oldest 747s progressively as the new aircraft were delivered.

Qantas returned to profitability in 1984, making a record pretax profit from airline operations of AUD 58 million in the year to March 31. This was a particularly strong performance given the depressed state of world aviation at that time. Qantas was able to sustain its strong recovery throughout the mid-1980s. Leslie felt that there was now more optimism because of depressed fuel prices and cost-cutting by airlines; he felt the main opportunity in Australia lay with tourism. Although the introduction of large, long-range aircraft could affect Australia's neighbors, Leslie reasoned, tourist traffic from the Asian region itself could be increased.

In 1987, Qantas embarked upon the next stage of its fleet modernization program with an order for four fuel-efficient Boeing 747-400s, which the company hoped would keep it competitive with British Airways (the successor to BOAC) and Singapore Airlines on its Britain-Australia and transpacific routes. The record profits made in 1986–87 of AUD 63.4 million showed that the airline had become one of Australia's top export earners.

In 1988, the governments of Australia and New Zealand decided to merge and partially privatize their state-owned airlines, Qantas, Australian Airlines (formerly TAA), and Air New Zealand. This plan was abandoned after it met with strong opposition in New Zealand. The New Zealand government decided to privatize Air New Zealand in its existing form. In December, Qantas was part of a consortium led by Brierley Investments of New Zealand (BIL) that purchased Air New Zealand, defeating a consortium led by British Airways. As a result, Qantas acquired a 19.9 percent stake in the airline. The following year, it was revealed that Qantas had reached a secret financial agreement with its partners in the consortium consisting of BIL, American Airlines, and Japan Air Lines to prevent control of Air New Zealand going to British Airways. The subsequent disclosure of this agreement damaged the reputation of Qantas.

At the same time, it was revealed that AUD 5.4 billion was to be spent on aircraft by 1992 and that the company would need a capital injection of AUD 600 million by the Australian government unless shares were sold to private investors. In 1989, the Australian government proposed the complete privatization of Qantas because in order to remain competitive it needed substantial capital injections, which the government was unable to fund. This new proposal led to a bitter argument in the ALP. During the year, Qantas took delivery of the first of its ten long-haul Boeing 747-400s and flew it nonstop from London to Sydney. It was the first airline to do so and, at 17,850 kilometers, it was the longest single distance any commercial aircraft had ever flown.

Transformative 1990s

In 1990, Qantas reported a loss as a result of its fleet expansion program and the five-month-long domestic pilots' dispute. These losses increased during 1990 as a result of the Persian Gulf crisis, and by early 1991 the airline was facing its worst financial situation since its foundation, including the Great Depression. It was decided to lay off 5,000 employees, sell nine Boeing 747s earlier than planned, and cut flying hours by 14 percent in the year to June 30, 1991.

In early 1990, Leslie was succeeded as chairman by Bill Dix, with John Ward continuing as chief executive, a position he attained in the late 1980s. In September 1990, the ALP had been persuaded to support the privatization of 49 percent of Qantas. The Australian government abandoned plans to float the airline in early 1991, however, and decided on a trade sale instead.

Change came swiftly and dramatically for Qantas in the mid-1990s. In June 1992, the Australian government approved Qantas's purchase of 100 percent of Australian Airlines' shares for AUD 400 million; in October 1993, the operations of Qantas and Australian Airlines were merged under a single brand: ''Qantas—The Australian Airline.'' It was also announced in June 1992 that later that year 49 percent of Qantas would be sold through a trade sale, and the remaining 51 percent would be floated publicly during the first half of 1993. Foreign interests were to be allowed to invest up to 35 percent, with the Australian government retaining a ''golden share.'' These plans were soon altered, however, when British Airways in late 1992 stepped in with an offer that was accepted—and completed in March 1993—to buy a 25 percent stake in Qantas for AUD 665 million ($470 million). The move was part of British Airways' push to create a global airline by forming a series of alliances, and it followed previous British Airways deals for 49 percent of TAT of France, 49 percent of Deutsche BA, and 31 percent of Air Russia. British Airways soon added a 25 percent stake in American carrier USAir. Meanwhile, in March 1993 the Australian government pumped AUD 1.35 billion into Qantas to enhance the company's competitive position ahead of privatization.

For Qantas, the deal with British Airways created management turmoil, as it was reported that both Dix and Ward opposed the alliance. By mid-1993, both had departed the company, replaced by Gary Pemberton, former chief executive of Brambles Ltd., a transport and industrial services group, in the chairman's slot, and James Strong, who had previously served as chief executive of Australian Airlines, in the chief executive's chair.

The new management team immediately faced the challenge of completing the privatization, as well as improving upon the dismal results of fiscal 1993—an after-tax loss of AUD 376.8 million ($250 million) incurred in part as a result of difficulties encountered integrating the operations of Australian Airlines. A plan for a September 1993 public offering of the remaining 75 percent of Qantas still owned by the government was pushed back because a spate of privatizations were hitting the Australian market at about the same time. The long-anticipated initial public offering (IPO) finally took place in July 1995, and the company's shares were listed on the Australian Stock Exchange; the foreign ownership limit was set at 49 percent. Qantas thus celebrated its 75th anniversary in 1995 as a public company.

From 1993 through 1997, the alliance between Qantas and British Airways evolved into a comprehensive collection of code-sharing arrangements, reciprocal frequent flyer programs, reciprocal lounge access agreements, and scheduling and pricing coordination efforts. The core of this alliance—and most airline alliances—was the code-sharing, whereby a flight operated by one carrier would also be listed in computer reservation systems under another airline's code. During this period, Qantas developed or enhanced several other alliances, including ones with American Airlines, Canadian Airlines International, Air Pacific, Asiana, Japan Airlines, Emirates, and Reno Air.

In March 1997, Qantas sold its 19.9 percent stake in Air New Zealand to ANZ Securities for NZD 425 million ($295 million), using the after-tax profits of AUD 66.8 million to reduce debt. This move was made in anticipation of Air New Zealand's purchase of an equity stake in Qantas's Australian rival, Ansett Australia. Later that year, Qantas began a AUD 560 million ($430 million), three-year fleet modernization program, including the refurbishment of all of its international 747s and 767-300ERs with new seats featuring seat-back personal video screens.

By fiscal 1997, Qantas was solidly in the black, achieving net profits of AUD 252.7 million ($190.1 million) on revenues of AUD 7.83 billion ($5.89 billion). In early 1998, however, the Asian financial crisis forced the company to cut back on some of its Asian service, including destinations in Indonesia, Malaysia, and Thailand. The crisis threatened to derail, at least temporarily, what had been a fairly successful start to Qantas's public company era.

Nevertheless, Qantas, known for its conservative fiscal management, weathered the Asian financial crisis much better than its rivals, noted *Air Transport World.* Still, competition was strong. While working to cut costs, Qantas revamped its customer service and installed in-flight entertainment systems. Celebrated Aussie chef Neil Perry was brought in to develop a new menu.

The mascot in Qantas's U.S. TV ads, a talking koala, was pulled out of an eight-year retirement in 1999. While the original, who made his debut in 1967, had grumbled about being ignored by the tourists Qantas was bringing Down Under, the newer koala was depicted as a savvy traveler himself who enjoyed the airline's improved business class amenities. The new commercials piggybacked on Australia's visibility as host country of the 2000 Summer Olympics, though Qantas was not an official sponsor.

More than 20 million passengers flew the airline in 2000. Qantas posted revenues of AUD 6.98 billion in the fiscal year ended June 30, 2000; sales rose to AUD 7.94 billion in 2000–01, while net income slipped from AUD 517 million to AUD 415 million.

Domestic Dominance after 2001

While the September 11, 2001 terrorist attacks on the United States had a strong negative effect on international operations, at home the situation for Qantas was becoming very favorable. Rival Ansett Airlines collapsed in September 2001, nearly forcing its parent Air New Zealand Ltd. (ANZ) into bankruptcy as well. Qantas was allowed to buy struggling low-cost startup

Impulse Airlines Pty Limited, leaving Qantas with an 80 percent share of the domestic Australian aviation market.

In 2002, Qantas proposed acquiring a large (22.5 percent) interest in ANZ and developing a strategic alliance with the Kiwi carrier. However, the suggested linkup aroused antitrust concerns from the Australian Competition and Consumer Commission.

Qantas posted a net profit of AUD 428 million ($230 million) on revenues of AUD 11.3 billion (up 11 percent) in the fiscal year ended June 30, 2002. The airline underwent a AUD 800 million share offering in part to help raise money for a AUD 2.46 billion capital improvements program, which included aircraft replacement, cabin renovations, and upgraded airport facilities.

Profit before tax reached a record AUD 964.6 million in fiscal 2003–04, up 92 percent from the previous year, though revenue slipped 0.2 percent to AUD 11.4 billion. Qantas carried more than 30 million passengers in 2003–04. Fifteen new aircraft were added to the fleet during the year, ranging from Dash 8s to Boeing 747s. Qantas was *Air Transport World*'s ''Airline of the Year'' for 2004.

Qantas teamed with Australia Post to acquire Star Track Express, a 30-year-old freight carrier, in late December 2003. Five months later, Qantas also started a new budget airline, Jetstar Airways Pty Limited. It was originally focused on Eastern Australia. Geoff Dixon, Qantas CEO since March 2001, told *Aviation Week* the company was aiming to let domestic market share slip no lower than 65 percent in the face of new competition, including Richard Branson's Virgin Blue entrant.

Qantas was also a partner in a new low-cost regional carrier based in Singapore called Jetstar Asia. Qantas invested SGB$50 million for a 49.9 percent share in the venture, reported *Aviation Week & Space Technology.* According to *Aviation Week,* Qantas was looking for growth outside of Australia in order to maintain its place in a consolidating global aviation industry. In addition to being a code-share partner with a long list of carriers, Qantas was a member of the oneworld alliance led by American Airlines and British Airways, whose shareholding in Qantas had by then been diluted to 18.25 percent.

Principal Subsidiaries

Airlink Pty Ltd; Australian Air Express Pty Ltd. (50%); Australian Airlines Ltd.; Eastern Australia Airlines Pty Ltd.; Impulse Airlines Pty Ltd.; Jetstar Airways Pty Ltd.; Jetstar Asia (Singapore; 49.9%); Qantas Flight Catering Holdings Ltd.; Qantas Holidays Ltd.; Sunstate Airlines Pty Ltd.; Star Track Express Pty Ltd.

Principal Divisions

International Flying Businesses; Domestic Flying Businesses; Flying Services; Qantas Freight.

Principal Operating Units

Qantas International; Australian Airlines; Qantas Domestic; QantasLink; Jetstar; Engineering Technical Operations and Maintenance Services; Airports and Catering; Qantas Freight; Qantas Holidays; Qantas Defence Services.

Principal Competitors

Air New Zealand Ltd.; Virgin Blue Airlines Pty Ltd.

Further Reading

''Aircraft Sale Underlines Qantas Rise,'' *Financial Times*, December 13, 1991.

''Australian Airlines Joins the Rat Race,'' *Financial Times*, April 26, 1991.

''An Australian View,'' *Flight International*, February 22, 1973.

''Australia Set for Airline Shake-up,'' *Flight International*, June 10, 1992.

''BA Defeated in Bid for Air New Zealand,'' *Financial Times*, December 22, 1988.

Ballantyne, Tom, ''A Step in the Dark: Australia's New Aviation Policy Is a Gamble Designed to Help Smooth the Privatization of Qantas and Australian Airlines,'' *Airline Business*, May 1992, pp. 44+.

——, ''Qantas: Hard Times,'' *Airline Business*, May 1991, pp. 16+.

——, ''Flying Doctor,'' *Airline Business*, December 1993, pp. 30+.

——, ''Global Horizons: The Linkage with British Airways Should Open Up New Opportunities for Qantas,'' Airline Business, April 1993, pp. 32+.

Beyond the Dawn: A Brief History of Qantas Airways, Sydney: Qantas Public Affairs, 1997.

''Canvassing for Qantas,'' *Flight International*, August 28, 1971.

Deans, Alan, ''Flight to a Merger: Australia's Main Airlines to Form Mega-Carrier,'' *Far Eastern Economic Review*, June 25, 1992, pp. 51+.

Dennis, William, ''As It Profits, Qantas Plans Share Offering,'' *Aviation Week & Space Technology*, August 26, 2002, pp. 42f.

Donoghue, J.A., ''Approaching Privatization,'' *Air Transport World*, July 1995, pp. 54+.

Eastway, Jocelyn, ''Quantum Leap in Service for the Flying Kangaroo,'' *BRW*, October 22, 1999, pp. 104ff.

Flottau, Jens, ''New Horizons; Qantas Eyes Growth Outside of Its Home Market to Take Part in Industry Consolidation,'' *Aviation Week & Space Technology*, July 12, 2004, p. 42.

''Flying in Formation: Airline Alliances,'' *Economist*, July 22, 1995, pp. 59+.

Fysh, Hudson, *Qantas at War*, Sydney: Angus & Robertson, 1968.

——, *Qantas Rising: The Autobiography of the Flying Fysh*, London: Angus & Robertson, 1966.

——, *Wings to the World: The Story of Qantas 1945–1966*, Sydney: Angus and Robertson, 1970.

Gallagher, Jackie, ''The World's Favourite Jigsaw?,'' *Airline Business*, December 1993, pp. 50+.

Goetzl, David, ''Qantas' Cranky Koala Returns to Bask in New TV Campaign,'' *Advertising Age*, March 22, 1999, pp. 3f.

——, ''Qantas Lands Olympic Presence; Airline Goes for Glory Despite Losing Sponsorship Bid,'' *Advertising Age*, August 21, 2000, pp. 1f.

Gottliebsen, Robert, and Lucinda Schmidt, ''Fight for the Skies,'' *BRW*, October 12, 1998, pp. 76ff.

Goyer, Robert, ''Qantas Marks 50 Years of Kangaroo Route,'' *Flying*, April 1998, p. 38.

Gunn, John, *Challenging Horizons: Qantas 1939–1954*, St. Lucia: University of Queensland Press, 1987.

——, *High Corridors: Qantas 1954–1970*, St. Lucia: University of Queensland Press, 1988.

——, *Pioneers of Flight: An Abridged History of Qantas Airways Limited*, The Company, 1987.

——, *The Defeat of Distance: Qantas 1919–1939*, St. Lucia: University of Queensland Press, 1985.

Hall, Timothy, *Flying High: The Story of Hudson Fysh, Qantas, and the Trail-Blazing Days of Aviation*, Sydney: Methuen of Australia, 1979.
''Hard Time for Qantas Too,'' *Flight International*, April 22, 1971.
Hill, Leonard, ''Re-Creating Qantas,'' *Air Transport World*, May 1994, pp. 74+.
Leonard, Bruce, *A Tradition of Integrity: The Story of Qantas Engineering and Maintenance*, Sydney: UNSW Press, 1994.
''Many Happy Returns,'' *Airline Business*, September 1995, pp. 84+.
Mathews, Neelam, and Michael Mecham, ''Qantas Proposed ANZ Stock Deal,'' *Aviation Week & Space Technology*, December 2, 2002, pp. 25f.
''NZ Backs Qantas Bid for Stake in Airline,'' *Financial Times*, September 20, 1988.
Phelan, Paul, ''Adventurous Analyst,'' *Flight International*, August 12, 1992, p. 36.
''Qantas' Airline Loss Doubles,'' *Financial Times*, December 2, 1983.
''Qantas: Airline of the Year,'' *Air Transport World*, February 1996, pp. 30+.
Qantas Empire Airways and Q.A.N.T.A.S.: Chronological History, Sydney: Qantas Empire Airways, 1946.
''Qantas Faces Financial Crisis,'' *Financial Times*, March 18, 1991.
''Qantas on the Move,'' *Interavia Aerospace World*, September 1993, pp. 44–46.
''Qantas Renews Drive for Airline Link-up,'' *Financial Times*, June 29, 1988.
''Qantas Soars to Record Results,'' *Financial Times*, July 28, 1987.
''Shake-up in Australia,'' *Flight International*, December 21, 1972.
''Sir Lenox Hewitt Leaves Qantas,'' *Flight International*, July 5, 1980.
Skapinker, Michael, ''UK Stays Qantas ''Flagship' Route,'' *Financial Times*, July 18, 1997, p. 23.
Stackhouse, John, *From the Dawn of Aviation: The Qantas Story, 1920–1995*, Double Bay, New South Wales: Focus Pub., 1995.
Tait, Nikki, ''Qantas Finds Privatisation Route Far from Smooth,'' *Financial Times*, April 28, 1995, p. 26.
Thomas, Ian, ''Sure-Footed Kangaroo,'' *Air Transport World*, September 2002, pp. 24–28.
——, ''The Quiet Roar,'' *Air Transport World*, September 1998, pp. 40ff.
''Threat to Airline,'' *Daily Telegraph*, January 12, 1979.
''USAir: BA's American Dream,'' *Observer*, July 12, 1992.
Westlake, Michael, and Jacqueline Rees, ''Birds of a Feather,'' *Far Eastern Economic Review*, July 6, 1995, pp. 69–70.
Woolsey, James P., ''Qantas Changing Course to Capture New Growth Possibilities,'' *Air Transport World*, May 1986, pp. 24+.
——, ''Qantas Is Trying to Rise from 1989 Turmoil,'' *Air Transport World*, June 1990, pp. 32+.

—Richard Hawkins
—updates: David E. Salamie; Frederick C. Ingram

Quintiles Transnational Corporation

4709 Creekstone Drive
Riverbirch Building, Suite 200
Durham, North Carolina 27703-8411
U.S.A.
Telephone: (919) 998 2000
Fax: (919) 998 9113
Web site: http://www.quintiles.com

Private Company
Incorporated: 1982 as Quintiles, Inc.
Employees: 16,000
Sales: $2.04 billion (2003)
NAIC: 541710 Research and Development in the Physical Sciences and Engineering Sciences; 541910 Marketing Research and Public Opinion Polling

Quintiles Transnational Corporation is a comprehensive provider of contract research, marketing, and sales to the global biotechnological, pharmaceutical, and medical device industries. Quintiles also provides a full range of policy consulting and disease-and-health information management services to the international healthcare industry. The services offered by the company include centralized clinical trial laboratory management, data management and biostatistics, regulatory toxicology, pharmaceutical sales and marketing, health economics and healthcare policy consulting, and the development and packaging of clinical trial materials. With offices in more than 49 countries, Quintiles operates through three major groups: Commercialization, which is responsible for strategic marketing services and sales force deployment; Product Development Services, which is responsible for all phases of clinical research and outcomes research consulting; and PharmaBio Development, which is responsible for creating unique alliances that help customers obtain Product Development and Commercialization services. Quintiles has access to unique patient-level healthcare information and data products from Verispan LLC, a joint venture co-founded by Quintiles and McKesson Corporation.

Early History

The founder of Quintiles Transnational Corporation is Dennis B. Gillings, a native of London, England. Having received a diploma in Mathematical Statistics from Cambridge University, and a Ph.D. in Mathematics from the University of Exeter, in 1971 Gillings decided to leave England and accept a research and teaching position at the University of North Carolina at Chapel Hill. As a professor in the Department of Biostatistics, Gillings published extensively in academic, scientific and medical journals. In 1974, looking for a way to apply his research to a practical problem, Gillings signed his first consulting contract with a large European pharmaceutical company to compile data about, and analyze the performance of, one of its newest products. Gillings was soon providing statistical consulting for clients throughout the world on a regular basis.

From 1974 to 1982, Gillings and a growing part-time staff provided contract services in the field of statistical consulting for a large number of firms in the pharmaceutical industry. It was during that time that the ''contract research organization'' (CRO) industry began to develop. Initially, contract research organizations were formed to provide the pharmaceutical and biotechnology industries with independent product development services. In order to manage the drug development process more efficiently, and to lower costs and maximize profit, the large pharmaceutical firms and biotechnology companies began to outsource product development to contract research organizations. Deriving all of their revenues from the research expenditures set aside in the research and development budget of pharmaceutical and biotechnology companies, the contract research organizations grew rapidly. Early on, the CROs primarily provided pre-clinical trial services but during the late 1970s and early 1980s, CROs developed into full-service providers, offering not only pre-clinical trial services but clinical and post-clinical marketing services for the introduction of new drug therapies.

Because of the direction of his research, and his extensive European contacts, Gillings was poised to take advantage of the emergence of the contract sales industry during the early 1980s. Originating in the United Kingdom, where regulatory cost containment pressure was brought to bear by the British government, pharmaceutical firms were forced to search for more cost-

Company Perspectives:

Quintiles Transnational Corp. strives unceasingly to exercise strong LEADERSHIP in our industry and to be the unquestioned FIRST CHOICE Contract Pharmaceutical Organization in an increasingly competitive marketplace. We will DELIGHT our CUSTOMERS worldwide with the fullest range and highest quality of information and services, and with a spirit and a DEDICATION that bring professional esteem and admiration. We demand the utmost level of EXCELLENCE, CREATIVITY, and SKILL from all our staff and management so that we add value to our customers by driving to PERFORMANCE goals in ways that are quantifiable. We thrive on continuous IMPROVEMENT and QUALITY enhancements through attention to detail, consistent feedback, state-of-the-art systems, TRAINING and TEAMWORK. We seek unendingly to bring our customers' PRODUCTS and SERVICES to MARKET ever sooner and to play a creative role in their achievement of earlier and greater commercial SUCCESS. Throughout our commercial pursuits, we will respect and hold in esteemed honor our EMPLOYEES, to whom we owe our very existence. We will maintain and enhance our reputation and integrity by demanding the highest possible ETHICAL STANDARDS and demonstrate by example an unyielding dedication to employees, customers, vendors, and shareholders. A SHARED VISION of success among these stakeholders will enhance the quality of life for all people of the world as we vigorously pursue our mission in an era of unprecedented OPPORTUNITY.

effective methods to introduce and market new drug products. As a result, pharmaceutical companies throughout the United Kingdom started to outsource all of the sales and marketing activities related to the introduction of a new product.

Recognizing the trends in the marketplace, and knowing his own talent for providing statistical consulting to pharmaceutical companies at a cost-effective price, Gillings decided to establish his own firm. Incorporated as Quintiles, Inc. in North Carolina in 1982, the small firm was staffed by Gillings himself and a few part-time employees, mostly those whom he had already worked with at the University of North Carolina. Gillings correctly predicted the worldwide spending increase on the development and introduction of pharmaceutical products. As the competition among pharmaceutical companies became more intense during the early and mid-1980s, he created a firm with a focus on innovation, highly focused research and development, rapid product introduction, and cost-effectiveness. These attributes were valued by pharmaceutical firms which were looking to maintain or increase their market share. By 1985, Quintiles, Inc. had arranged to provide contract services worth millions of dollars to a number of large pharmaceutical firms in the United States.

Expansion and Development in the Mid- to Late 1980s

During the mid- and late 1980s, under the leadership of Gillings, Quintiles embarked on a major expansion plan, both within the United States and in Europe. In January 1987, Quintiles Ltd. began operations to serve clients in the United Kingdom. Originally established in London, the company's office moved to Reading in 1989 to take advantage of greater office and laboratory space, a move that resulted in considerable expansion of Quintiles' British operations. In 1988, the company opened an office in Cambridge, Massachusetts to provide contract services to pharmaceutical and biotechnology firms located in the northeastern section of the United States.

By the end of the 1980s, Quintiles was providing a range of contract services to assist companies in converting a laboratory discovery into a product that was ready for sale in the marketplace. Before a new drug can be marketed, it must undergo extensive testing and approval by the appropriate regulatory agencies in the country where it will ultimately be marketed and sold. The initial stage of the drug development process is pre-clinical research. During a period of one to three years, the new drug is tested on animals. After this period, if the drug is determined to be safe for human consumption, it undergoes a series of clinical tests on human beings. Tests on human beings usually are conducted in four phases including: phase I, in which the drug's safety is monitored and its pharmacological data is gathered over a period of six months to one year, having been tested on between 20 to 80 individuals; phase II, in which the drug is tested on approximately 100 volunteer patients in order to determine its effectiveness and dosage response; phase III, in which the drug is tested on thousands of people in order to determine its safety and efficacy on a large scale; and finally phase IV, which takes place only after a country's regulatory approval, in which the drug is tested once again to prove its safety, to determine new dosage strengths, to confirm its cost-effectiveness, and to analyze data on its long-term safety when used by patients under normal circumstances.

Quintiles specialized in contracting clinical trial services, including pre-clinical research and the four phases of a drug's testing in areas such as endocrinology, gastroenterology, and genitourinary and musculoskeletal diseases. Quintiles provided such services as: study design, in which the company designed and prepared the initial drug study; investigator recruitment, in which the company arranged physicians to administer the drug to patients; study monitoring, in which the company made an investigational site analysis, assisted in patient enrollment, and collected data from the test; and clinical data management and biostatistical services, in which Quintiles employees created customized databases in order to meet the specific needs of client formats. By the end of the 1980s, Quintiles was one of the fastest growing and most respected of all of the contract research organizations.

Early to Mid-1990s

The growth of Quintiles during the first half of the 1990s was truly remarkable. As its reputation grew, the company began to expand at an unbelievable rate. In August 1990, Quintiles Pacific, Inc. was established to provide contract services for the biotechnological and pharmaceutical firms in the western United States and around the Pacific Rim. In November of the same year, Quintiles Ireland Ltd., was established in Dublin, and a joint venture was formed with CRC Research Institute to market the company's contract services to pharmaceutical firms in Japan. As

Key Dates:

1974: Dennis Gillings signs first contract to provide statistical and data management consulting for pharmaceutical clients.
1982: Quintiles, Inc., is incorporated in North Carolina.
1997: Quintiles completes successful secondary stock offering.
1999: Quintiles is the first company in industry to break the $1 billion mark, when it reports net revenues of $1.19 billion.
1999: Company joins the S&P 500 Index.
2003: Board of Directors agrees to merge with Pharma Services Holdings Inc; Quintiles becomes a private company.

the activity of the company grew, management decided to form a holding company, Quintiles Transnational Corporation, located in North Carolina, to provide a headquarters for the coordination of all of its offices worldwide.

In 1991, Quintiles GmbH was established in Germany to augment the company's contract services to European clients, and Quintiles Laboratories, Ltd. was created in Atlanta, Georgia to provide contract clinical trial laboratory services to companies that were developing healthcare products. In 1992, the company established Quintiles, S.A. in Paris to augment its contract services to clients in southwestern Europe, and also acquired Toxicol Laboratories, Ltd., a British-based international contract toxicology laboratory. Quintiles Australia Pty., Quintiles Asia, Inc., Quintiles Belgium, S.A., and Quintiles S.r.l., located in Milan, Italy, were also formed to expand the company's operations worldwide.

In 1995, in addition to opening an office in Copenhagen, Denmark, and establishing Quintiles East Asia Pte Ltd. in Singapore to provide contract research services to firms in that region of the world, management implemented a highly aggressive acquisitions policy. In March of that year, the company acquired Syntex Pharmaceuticals Ltd., a well-known pharmaceutical and biotechnology product development firm based in Edinburgh, Scotland. Combining the pre-clinical services of the company's operation in Ledbury, England with Syntex Pharmaceuticals, Quintiles was able to provide its worldwide customers with an extensive range of pre-clinical and toxicology contract services. Syntex, one of Quintiles most important acquisitions, specialized in identifying, quantifying, and evaluating the risks to human beings that result from the production or use of biotechnology or pharmaceutical products. In addition, the company purchased Benefit, a health economics firm with offices in France, Germany, Italy, France, and The Netherlands, and San Diego Clinical Research Associates, a world-renowned clinical research organization that concentrated on the regional monitoring of allergies and of infectious and respiratory diseases.

Continuing its frenetic pace of growth and expansion, in 1996 the company opened offices in Pretoria, South Africa; Vienna, Austria; Helsinki, Finland; Madrid, Spain; and Buenos Aires, Argentina. Acquisitions included The Lewin Group, Inc., a Fairfax, Virginia-based healthcare policy research and consulting company with a global reputation, and PMC Contract Research AB located in Uppsala, Sweden, giving the company the ability to provide contract drug development services to all of the Scandinavian countries. Quintiles' two most important acquisitions in 1996 were BRI International and Innovex Ltd. BRI International, based in Arlington, Virginia, is a leading international contract research company specializing in regulatory compliance consulting and medical device development. Innovex Ltd., located in Marlow, England, is one of the world's leading contract pharmaceutical firms that specializes in the sale and marketing of drugs for international pharmaceutical companies. The acquisition of Innovex made Quintiles the world leader in providing contract services to pharmaceutical, biotechnology, and healthcare companies around the globe.

With such a worldwide network of companies and offices, Quintiles management thought it best to reorganize the company in order to integrate its holdings and take advantage of the synergies that each acquisition and office provided. Company operations were organized into three operating divisions: The Contract Research Division, which provides services such as those involved in clinical trials, regulatory affairs, and medical device consulting; The Innovex Division, which provides the company's marketing and sales services; and The Lewin-Benefit Division, which provides services in the areas of health economics and healthcare policy consulting, and disease and health information management contract services. This reorganization enabled the company to provide full-service, vertically integrated, product development, sales, and marketing services to all of its clients worldwide.

Through the mid-1990s, company revenues increased at a phenomenal rate, making Quintiles one of the most highly regarded firms in the contract research services industry. The company's stock became the darling of Wall Street as stock brokers and analysts saw its future promising even more success than its past.

In 1996, Quintiles provided services to 11 of the world's largest biotechnology firms, and 49 of the world's 50 largest pharmaceutical companies. Perhaps most impressive of all the company's achievements is its average net revenue growth rate which exceeded 50 percent from 1992 to 1997.

Late 1990s to Early 2000s

Quintiles announced in February 1997 that it had become a publicly traded company. Quintiles decided to use its new funds for geographic expansion, service additions, acquisitions, capital expenditures, and other working capital. As a result, acquisitions became one of the company's major activities over the next several years. In fact, in February, the company began its acquisition activities when it acquired Debra Chapman Consulting Group Pty Limited and Medical Alliances Australia Pty Limited, located in Sydney and Melbourne, Australia (respectively). The acquisition helped the company to provide additional contract sales and healthcare recruiting services in Australia and New Zealand. Mid-year, Quintiles bought CerebroVascular Advances, Inc., of San Antonio, Texas, a clinical research company dealing in stroke clinical trials; Butler Communications Inc., of Raleigh, North Carolina, a company that specialized in communication programs to help patient recruitment for clinical trials; and Medical Action Communications Limited, of Egham, United Kingdom, a leading international medical communications consultant. Near year-end, Quintiles acquired Intelligent Imaging, Inc., of Plymouth Meeting, Pennsylvania, an information management company that specialized in digital medical imaging services for clinical trials and the healthcare industry; Clindepharm International Limited and Rapid Deployment Services, both of South Africa, which were the country's leading contract research and contract sales organizations (respectively). Quintiles also opened up offices in Hong Kong; Beijing, China; Moscow; and Mexico City. Quintiles' purchases helped to increase demand for its global services and, as a result, improved its financial statistics.

In early 1998, Quintiles continued its string of acquisitions, which had now made it the world's largest contract researcher, when it acquired Belgium's leading contract sales organization Pharma Networks N.V.; San Francisco, California-based Technology Assessment Group, an international health outcome assessment company; Taiwan's leading contract research organization More Biomedical Contract Research Organization Ltd.; and French T2A S.A., a leading contract sales organization. Midyear, Quintiles opened a clinical trials and product distribution facility in Singapore; acquired a clinical trial materials production and warehouse facility in Scotland; bought South Africa-based ClinData International Pty Ltd.; and acquired British Cardiac Alert, a provider of a centralized electrocardiogram monitoring service. Near the end of the year, Quintiles acquired The Royce Consultancy plc, a leading British pharmaceutical sales representative recruitment and contract sales organization; New Jersey-based Data Analysis Systems Inc., a major pharmaceutical company specializing in sales force planning and territorial optimization systems; New Jersey-based Simirex Inc. and Simirex International Ltd, which operated clinical packaging services; Paris, France-based Serval, a contract sales and marketing company that expanded Quintiles' ability to provide contract sales services across Europe; and New York City-based Q.E.D. International Inc., a provider of product marketing and communication services. Quintiles also opened offices in Shanghai, China; Bulgaria; Hungary; Israel; and Sao Paulo, Brazil. With numerous major purchases of core businesses and expansions into new strategic areas during the year, Quintiles reported that it made $1.19 billion in net revenues during 1998, becoming the first company in its industry to break the $1 billion mark.

In early 1999, Quintiles acquired a drug development facility from Kansas City-based Hoechst Marion Roussel; Oak Grove Technologies Inc., a major provider in Good Manufacturing Practice compliance services; Scott-Levin, a major provider of U.S. pharmaceutical and managed-care market information and research services; ENVOY Corporation, a provider of healthcare electronic data interchange and data analysis services; and South Africa-based Medlab Pty Ltd., a clinical trial laboratory. During the last half of the year, Quintiles acquired Scotland-based Minerva Medical plc, a clinical research organization that specialized in patient recruitment and management of primary-care clinical trials involving chronic diseases; SMG Marketing Group, Inc., a leading healthcare market information company with healthcare facility databases; New Jersey-based Medcom, Inc., a provider of physician meetings and educational events; MediTrain, the Netherlands' leading multimedia pharmaceutical sales representative training company; and Medicines Control Consultants Pty Ltd., South Africa's leading pharmaceutical regulatory consulting company. Quintiles opened an office in Warsaw, Poland. In November, Quintiles joined the Standard & Poor's 500 (S&P 500) Index, a leading U.S. stock market index, as a healthcare services leader in product development, commercialization, and electronic healthcare transaction processing.

Quintiles realigned its operating units, early in 2000, due to recent changes in the development of drugs and the introduction of new medicines and their impacts to the healthcare industry. Quintiles added two new units—Early Development and Laboratory Services (which dealt with worldwide preclinical, clinical trial materials, manufacturing and packaging, laboratory, and Phase I operations) and Quintiles Integrated Strategic Solutions (which dealt with services and strategies and that helped Product Development, Commercialization and Informatics)—to its current four operating units (Clinical Development Services, Commercialization, ENVOY Corporation, Quintiles Informatics). In April, CEO Dennis Gillings purchased over 390,000 company shares with the hope of a turnaround with his struggling company that had been plagued over the past year or so with poor performance and badly run units. Gillings, who founded the company, now owned about 5.5 percent of the shares. During the year, Quintiles acquired the clinical development unit of Pharmacia Corporation, a Stockholdm, Sweden-based company. Quintiles opened offices in Norway; Greece; Czech Republic; Romania; Thailand; the Philippines; Chile; and Kobe, Japan. As an industry turndown was occurring, Quintiles made a major reduction in staff positions, along with numerous layoffs, with the hope to help its bottom line.

Pamela Kirby took over as chief executive officer of Quintiles, in April 2001, with Dennis Gillings named as Chairman. Kirby concluded that Quintiles was moving in basically the right direction but was concerned about the company's decline in stock price during the previous year and into 2001. As a result, Kirby began to slowly transfer Quintiles to a more lucrative business, that of contract sales. In addition, after acquiring so many companies over the past few years, Quintiles had become a very large organization when compared to its competition. As a result, its revenue growth had lagged somewhat when compared to its major competitors, especially as the industry emerged from its recent financial slump. In particular, Kirby saw Quintiles struggling with weak demand due to the result of consolidation in the pharmaceutical industry and a reduction in the number of new (developmental) products. During the year, Quintiles opened the Japan International Desk in Princeton, New Jersey in order to expand the Japanese pharmaceutical market. In addition, Quintiles bought Swiss-based OEC SA, a company that provided drug safety services to the pharmaceutical industry, and Pretoria, South Africa-based Ungerer Laboratory and Bavaria pd CC in order to expand its network of centralized clinical laboratories.

In early 2002, Quintiles bought certain assets of Bioglan Pharma Inc., the U.S. subsidiary of U.K.-based Bioglan Pharma Plc. During the middle of the year, Quintiles and McKesson Corporation formed Verispan, an informatics joint venture that became the leading U.S. provider of patient data delivered. Within the year, Quintiles Chairman Gillings announced his intent to buy Quintiles for $1.3 billion. A lawsuit ensued stating that the offer was unfair and inadequate. The board of directors for Quintiles ultimately rejected the offer, but then put the company up for auction.

In April 2003, Pharma Services Holding Inc.—the team formed by Gillings and One Equity to bid for Quintiles—won the auction with a $1.75 billion offer. Later in the year, the Quintiles board of directors agreed to merge with Pharma Services, which resulted in Quintiles becoming a private company led by its founder and chairman Dennis Gillings. As a private company, Gillings promoted the idea that the company could better concentrate on being more long-term oriented rather than being tied down to the uncertainties of short-term quarterly reports. Gillings also vowed to continue to grow the company by purchasing key companies and partnering with drug development firms.

As the largest company in the pharmaceutical outsourcing services industry, Quintiles saw good growth in the first year of being a private company. In the first six months of 2004, Quintiles saw an increase of almost a billion dollars in new business. As a wholly owned subsidiary of Pharma Services, Gillings continued to promote increased business development efforts and to increase its margins in order to maintain its market lead in providing a full range of integrated products and services to the pharmaceutical and biotechnological industries.

Principal Subsidiaries

Butler Clinical Recruitment, Inc.; The Lewin Group, Inc.; Medical Technology Consultants; Quintiles, Inc.; Quintiles Canada, Inc.; Quintiles Laboratories, Ltd.; Quintiles Latin America, Inc.; Quintiles Pacific, Inc.; Benfit B.V.; Innovex (Spain) S.L.; Medical Action Communications, Ltd.; Quintiles AB; Quintiles England, Ltd.; Quintiles Ireland, Ltd.; Quintiles Scotland, Ltd., Quintiles S.r.l.; Quintiles Laboratories, Ltd.; Quintiles Asia, Inc.; Quintiles East Asia Pte. Ltd.; Quintiles Pty. Ltd. (Australia); Quintiles Hong Kong, Ltd.; Verispan LLC (43%).

Principal Divisions

Contract Research; Innovex; Lewin-Benefit.

Principal Operating Units

Product Development Services; Commercialization; PharmaBio Development.

Principal Competitors

Covance Inc.; IMS Health Inc.; PAREXEL International Corporation.

Further Reading

''Big Doses of Capital Cure Cash Deficiency,'' *Business North Carolina,* February 1998, p. 95.

''Focused on Increasing Margins: One Year after Going Private, Quintiles is Recording New Business Wins and Service Revenue Growth,'' *R & D Directions*, September 2004, p. 66.

Freudenheim, Milt, ''High-Flying Quintiles to Buy Innovex in $747.5 Million Deal,'' *New York Times*, October 8, 1996, p. 7D.

''The Joys of Going Private: So Far, So Good for Quintiles, Whose Founder Couldn't Stand the Public Markets,'' *Investment Dealers' Digest,* December 8, 2003.

Leo, John, ''From 'No Man's Land,' He Returns to the Helm,'' *Triangle Business Journal*, April 9, 2004, p. 5.

Marcus, David, ''One Equity Partners Dennis Gillings Quintiles,'' *Corporate Counsel*, August 2003.

Nilsen, Kim, ''CEO UPS His Stake in Quintiles,'' *Triangle Business Journal* (Raleigh, N.C.), June 23, 2000, p. 4.

''Quintiles Transnational's Chairman's Plan to Buy Company Criticized,'' *Mergers & Acquisitions Report*, October 21, 2002.

''Quintiles Transnational Corporation,'' *Wall Street Journal,* August 1, 1996, p. 4B.

''Quintiles Transnational Plans to Buy BRI International,'' *New York Times*, August 1, 1996, p. 4D.

''A Season of Growth,'' *Economist*, February 25, 1995, pp. 5–9.

Smith, Lisa, F., ''Durham, N.C., Marketing Services *Firm Reports Record Earnings,'' Knight* Ridder/Tribune Business News, January 26, 1999.

Vollmer, Sabine, ''New Strategy by Quintiles May Pay Off,'' *Triangle Business Journal* (Raleigh, N.C.), April 13, 2001, p. 1.

Weber, Joseph, ''Turning Genes into Vaccines,'' *Business Week*, June 24, 1996, p. 154.

—Thomas Derdak
—update: William Arthur Atkins

Rally's

14255 49th Street North
Clearwater, Florida 33762
U.S.A.
Telephone: (800) 872-5597
Fax: (727) 519-2001
Web site: http://www.checkers.com

Business Unit of Checkers Drive In Restaurants Inc.
Incorporated: 1984
Employees: 5,500
Sales: $144.9 million (1997)
NAIC: 722211 Limited-Service Restaurants

A unit of Checker's Drive-In Restaurants Inc., Rally's is a chain of limited-menu, fast-food establishments featuring double drive-thru order and pickup service but no indoor seating except at five experimental locations. One of the largest chains using this arrangement, Rally's has always placed its emphasis on delivering a quality hamburger more cheaply and quickly than its competitors. It features the original signature Rallyburger and Big Buford (a double-patty cheeseburger), two other, newer signature burgers, and a chicken breast sandwich, plus uniquely seasoned fries and onion rings, and soft drinks and milkshakes to complement its entrees. Its menu has remained simple, originally consisting of 11 basic items, all of which are readied within 45 seconds after a customer places an order. In 1997, the Rally system operated 477 restaurants in 18 states, predominantly in the Midwest and the South. By the close of the decade, amid mounting financial losses, Rally's merged in a stock swap that formed Checkers Drive-In Restaurants, Inc., which continued to operate both its own Checkers restaurants as well as the Rally's restaurants.

1980s Origins

Rally's was founded and incorporated in Tennessee in 1984 and opened its first restaurant in January 1985, but did not offer franchises until November 1986. It waited an additional three years, until 1989, to go public, the same year in which it created its first subsidiary, Rally's of Ohio, Inc.

At the outset, Rally's adopted its double drive-thru system, basing it on the fact that about half of all fast-food hamburger service is takeout or drive-thru. Rally's restaurants do provide outside patio benches and tables, but, except for the five experimental units, no interior seating, hence the emphasis has always been on quick takeout service and quality food. The arrangement has a 1950s drive-in ambiance, providing a bit of nostalgia that sets it apart from giant chains like McDonald's, Burger King, and Wendy's and giving it a distinct identity.

In 1990, one year after Rally's went public, the company's management reins passed to Burt Sugarman, a film and television producer and major investor in the business. To attract new owner-managers, Sugarman began reducing royalty costs for franchise holders, and, in 1992, after two very promising and profitable years, Rally's even rebated $700,000 to franchisees. These moves and the company's quick expansion prompted analysts to note that Rally's had become a serious contender in the fast-food chain market.

Sugarman oversaw the expansion. It included the buyout of Maxie's of America and Snapps Drive-Thru in 1991 and Zipps Drive-Thru in 1992, purchases which added an additional 100 units to Rally's chain. In that same year, Rally's organized MAC 1 to purchase Beaman Corporation, after that company became insolvent and was forced into bankruptcy. Rally's bought all of Beaman's common stock for about $200,000. Beaman, located in Greensboro, North Carolina, had been the contracted fabricator of Rally's modular restaurant units.

Challenges in the Early and Mid-1990s

The expansion continued in 1993, when Rally's bought West Coast Restaurant Enterprises in a stock exchange agreement and acquired three franchised Rally's restaurants in Bakersfield, California. However, the expansion was becoming too rapid, and in that same year the company lost money, primarily from a $12 million outlay to cover the cost of closing 26 units. It also opened only half the number of its projected 100 new units. Rally's management responded to the losses with attempts to improve efficiency through streamlining its operations. Among other things, it installed computers in each of the company-owned

Company Perspectives:

Rally's: You Gotta Eat!

units. Networked to the main office, these point-of-sale computers gave the company logistical control of the day-by-day operation of its restaurants. They also provided a means of monitoring the progress of the various units and making better-informed decisions about market strategies. Still, losses worsened, increasing by 100 percent between 1993 and 1994.

A managerial shake-up followed. Sugarman, who had earlier stepped down, returned as chairman. Losses continued, however, largely because the company's overexpansion and discount-pricing strategy was not advancing Rally's share of the fast-hamburger market. It was reeling under the impact of the ''margin-eroding 99-cent sandwich wars'' being conducted by giant competitors. Thus, in 1994, the company was forced to abandon some planned expansion projects, including additional real estate purchases and infrastructure investments. It made alternative plans to dispose of up to 60 company-owned units. However, the drastic reduction was modified the following year, despite the fact that the company suffered a net loss of $47 million. Alternative financial strategies helped planners limit downsizing to the closure of 16 of the 60 selected units and an additional nine units that had been performing poorly at core market sites.

In 1995, Rally's introduced some new sandwiches and price points in an effort to outflank the value-meal strategy adopted by Wendy's and McDonald's that was deeply undercutting the 99-cent signature hamburger market of the double drive-thru chains. It also bought out Hampton Roads Food, Inc. and divested itself of the Beaman Corporation, selling all common stock in the module-fabricating company for about $3.1 million. However, it still lost ground. Its stock, once valued at $20 a share, dropped to about $2.50 in the last quarter of 1995, and the company was suffering losses at 55 underperforming units outside its core market. In addition to a frustrating failure to make gains in its tough market, mostly out of its control, in its worst years the company also faced problems of its own devising. For example, its 1996 advertisements were found by industry analysts to be extraordinarily inept, ''adolescent, brainless, and offensive,'' full of appetite-suppressing sexual suggestiveness. Nevertheless, Don Doyle, the new president and CEO of Rally's remained convinced that value and convenience were the keys to a financial turnaround, and despite repeated losses, Rally's was not ready to abandon its basic double drive-thru scheme. What it needed was some new marketing strategies and restructuring.

Late 1990s Troubles

At the end of 1996, Rally's shifted its brand positioning strategy partly away from price towards even better quality. The changes resulted in an increase in the size of its basic hamburger patty from 2.8 to 3.2 ounces and the addition of two new signature hamburgers to its core product line—the Barbecue Bacon Cheeseburger and the Super Double.

Other, more essential changes began in 1997. In response to its financial reversals, Rally's began negotiations with a projected buyout of its chain by Checkers Drive-In Restaurants, partly owned by CKE Restaurants, but financial obstacles imposed by the Securities and Exchange Commission prompted the two companies to withdraw from a full merger.

However, both companies saw potential benefits in a close affiliation. In fact, they had actually entered agreements as early as November 1994, when Rally's, through an exchange of property and a waiver arrangement, acquired some leases for Checkers restaurants and converted five existing units into Rally's restaurants. New negotiations were started in November 1997, when Rally's entered a management agreement with Checkers. Under its terms, Checkers began providing various administrative services for Rally's. That move was followed by a stock exchange agreement in December. Rally's purchased over 19 million shares of Checkers common stock, including 14.4 million shares owned by CKE and Fidelity National Financial (FNF), a California-based title insurance underwriting firm headed by William P. Foley, II, who was then chairman of both CKE and Checkers. Also involved in the arrangement was the Giant Group, a masonry and portland cement company headed by Sugarman and holder of a large block of Rally's stock. In the exchange, Rally's issued shares of its common stock and a new series of preferred stock. The purchase made Rally's, with 27 percent of the outstanding shares, the largest holder of Checker's common stock. When converted, the two major investors, CKE and FNF, would own about 44 percent of the outstanding shares of Rally's common stock.

Although it was not an official merger, the stock-exchange plan allowed Rally's and Checkers to restructure and consolidate their managerial staffs. Foley replaced Sugarman as Rally's chairman. Corporate headquarters also moved from Louisville, Kentucky, to Clearwater, Florida, into the same building housing the headquarters of Checkers. This was a cost-saving move that combined the operational and administrative functions of the two companies. It thereby allowed for the benefits of a merger without obligating either company to undertake the costly accounting procedures required by the Securities and Exchange Commission. Among the benefits was a reduction in food costs made possible by the fact that the 5,000 restaurants in the CKE family were in a better position to leverage prices than was possible for the individual companies comprising the cooperative group.

The cooperative managerial team also sought to develop a new ''positioning'' strategy designed to counter the low-price promotional strategy employed by other major chains like McDonald's and Burger King in their special ''value'' packages and low-price promotions. As part of the new strategy, Rally's began experimenting with indoor seating, responding to the fact that about 50 percent of fast-food customers want to dine in. Beginning in 1997, as a test, it remodeled five double drive-thru units into restaurants with indoor dining, with encouraging but inconclusive results. In addition, it has permitted a few franchisees to open Rally's restaurants in some empty buildings that had formerly housed restaurants using concepts incompatible with a double drive-thru arrangement. In 1998, Rally's also sought to enhance its public face by negotiating a $12 million ad campaign with M&C Saatchi, replacing the agency that prompted the harsh criticism of its earlier Rally's ads. The new spots with the keynote motto—''Make me a burger. Hold the

Key Dates:

1984: Rally's is founded in Tennessee.
1986: The Rally's concept is franchised.
1989: The company goes public.
1998: Headquarters moves from Kentucky to Florida.
1999: Rally's and Checkers merge in a stock swap.

hype.''—began airing on national television in March. The company also entered into an agreement with the North Carolina-based Fresh Foods, Inc. (formerly named WSMP, Inc.) that resulted in the placing of Rally's brand products in retail stores and clubs. Fresh Foods, comprised of wholly owned subsidiaries, packages and markets branded sandwiches in its prepared food division. Its tie-in with Rally's as well as CKE and Checkers was strengthened with the addition of Foley and Andrew F. Puzder, executive vice-president of both CKE and FNF, to its board of directors in May 1998.

Nonetheless, Rally's continued to face problems. In 1997, its revenues dropped to $144.9 million, off about 11 percent from the previous year. Its slide in a very difficult market needed to be reversed, but the following year there was no indication of an imminent turnaround. The company's original strategy of offering a good hamburger at a low price was still losing to the marketing strategies of much larger competitors. In addition, Rally's remained a defendant in putative class-action lawsuits originating in 1994 which were yet to be resolved and could prove costly.

Late 1990s: Striving To Reach New Markets

In 1999, Rally's and Checkers announced that they would merge operations in a stock swap. The merger was complete in the summer of 2000, and thereafter the two operated as brands of the Checker's Drive-In Restaurants holding company. In a bid to reach new markets, Rally's management announced an alliance with WSMP Inc., a food processor and restaurant operator, in March 1998. WSMP planned to work with Checkers and Rally's to create a new line of sandwiches available in supermarkets and had the capacity to produce four million microwaveable burgers a week. This move was followed by a partnership with Canteen Vending Services in late June, a company that planned to make Rally's, Hardees', and Blimpie's sandwiches available through vending machines west of the Mississippi in over 7,000 locations. July saw the introduction of Rally's' new USA combo meal, which included a chili-cheese hot dog, french fries, apple-pie turnover, and a soft drink. It was launched at the same time as new 10- and 30-second ads promoting the product.

In August 1998 Rally's left Saatchi for Crispin Porter & Bogusky, a Miami-based ad firm already producing ads for Checkers. September saw an even more momentous change: Rally's and Checkers merged at last, picking up a Rally's investor company Giant Group Ltd. in the process. The management of all three companies was pleased with the deal, stating that they hoped to save money and use the increased cash flow to add more sit-down dining to Rally's and Checker's drive-through restaurants, and to remodel Rally's exteriors to be more welcoming to customers. Sugarman, owner of Giant Group, remained the largest stockholder, and those next in line were controlled by California entrepreneur William P. Foley II, who owned several restaurant chains through his holding companies. It was announced that Foley would become the new company chairman, although Sugarman would remain involved in day-to-day operations as vice-chairman.

Third quarter financial news improved slightly in 1998, but was still a loss of over $1 million dollars for Rally's; nor was there good financial news for Checkers, which posted a third-quarter loss of $1.47 million. The new company remained hopeful, however; Rally's and Checkers jointly launched a new 99-cent Chicken Sandwich in January 1999. In late 1999 Rally's and Checkers teamed with NFL Alumni to promote a new Superbowl Weekend Sweepstakes and a Kid of the Year essay contest, the winner of which would get a trip for four to the Superbowl. The year 2000 opened with a different kind of ad campaign. Following months of discussion about launching something edgier a new Japanimation style character burst onto the scene, a busty gal in a hotrod and in a hurry, running on empty. The new tagline: ''High performance, human fuel.'' Rally's management expected the new ads to appeal to the all-important 18 to 25 demographic. By mid-July an important debt restructuring program was underway, and new CEO Daniel Dorsch was confident that company debt had been reduced to a level that allowed refinancing to begin. Over 150 restaurants had been sold to franchises, and plans were on to build some 80 new stores. When asked about the Rally's downslide, Dorsch had this to say to *Restaurant Hospitality* magazine: ''What happened was the chain got very successful very quickly. So, everyone pulls their money out, the guys with all the passion left, and they pulled in managers. Managers who, maybe, didn't have the passion I'm bringing. I'm bringing the passion back.''

Innovation followed, including a 2001 campaign to award a car to managers of each of the top-performing Rally's or Checkers chains, and a new series of hip-hop ads with the tagline ''You Gotta Eat!'' Innovation seemed to produce results; same-store sales rose 11.2 percent for December 2001, the first time the company had been out of the red in several years. CKE Restaurants divested its interest in Checkers during this time in order to focus on the Hardees' chain. By the end of 2002 same store sales at Checkers/Rally's had risen another 10.8 percent, and by the middle of 2003 Rally's had secured the rights to be the ''exclusive hamburger provider'' at the Indianapolis 500 and Brickyard 400 auto races. Under the auspices of the Checkers parent company, the Rally's brand was rebounding.

Principal Competitors

McDonald's Corporation; Wendy's International Inc.; Sonic Corporation.

Further Reading

Carlino, Bill, ''Doyle Sets Course to Steer Rally's into Less 'Troubled' Seas,'' *Nation's Restaurant News*, April 8, 1996.
''Checkers Passionate C.E.O.,'' *Restaurant Hospitality*, May 2000, p. 148.

Garfield, Bob, "Rally's Touts Taste, Though It Has None," *Advertising Age,* March 4, 1996, p. 37.

Hamstra, Mark, "CKE Crafts Merger of Checkers, Rally's," *Nation's Restaurant News,* April 7, 1997, pp. 1, 6.

Hayes, Jack, "Drive-Thru Players Rev up for Test of Indoor Seating," *Nation's Restaurant News*, September 1, 1997, pp. 3, 79.

——, "Seeking New Weapons to Defuse the Price Wars," *Nation's Restaurant News,* May 2, 1994, p. 11.

Hein, Kenneth, "Checkers Plans $20 Million Moves to Jump Over the Burger Competition," *Brandweek*, April 7, 2003, p. 4.

Howard, Theresa, "Double-Drive-Throughs Tuning Engines: Big 3 Shift Gears to Stay on Course," *Nation's Restaurant News*, April 11, 1994, pp. 1, 37.

——, "Rally's Shifts Gears with New Chief Exec Laney Howard," *Nation's Restaurant News*, February 14, 1994, pp. 1, 80.

Kim, Hank, "Rally's Makes Its Pick," *Adweek,* November 24, 1997, p. 4.

Martin, Richard, "CKE Adds Checkers to Rally's Effort Fix," *Nation's Restaurant News*, November 25, 1996, pp. 1, 56.

Papiernik, Richard L., "Goliath Slams David: Rally's Takes a Tumble in QSR Value Wars," *Nation's Restaurant News*, September 25, 1995, pp. 9, 22.

——, "Rally's Clears Nasdaq Hurdle with $10.8m, Posts 2q Profit," *Nation's Restaurant News*, October 14, 1996, p. 12.

Pollack, Judann, "Rally's Big Buford Ads Stir Small Controversy," *Advertising Age*, March 4, 1996, p. 12.

"Rally's into Major Change As Losses Mount in 3rd Q," *Nation's Restaurant News,* November 27, 1995, p. 12.

Welling, Kathryn M., "1994 Roundtable (Part 2): Pick of the Portfolio," *Barron's,* January 24, 1994, pp. 12–37.

—John W. Fiero
—update: Howard J. Jones

RFC Franchising LLC

12400 North Meridian Street, Suite 190
Carmel, Indiana 46032
U.S.A.
Telephone: (317) 819-0700
Fax: (317) 819-0261
Web site: http://www.ritters.com

Private Company
Incorporated: 1989
Employees: not available
Sales: not available
NAIC: 533110 Lessors of Nonfinancial Intangible Assets (Except Copyrighted Works); 311520 Ice Cream and Frozen Dessert Manufacturing; 445299 All Other Specialty Food Stores

RFC Franchising LLC operates the Ritter's Frozen Custard chain of premium ice cream shops. Nearly sixty Ritter's outlets are located in seven U.S. states, two-thirds of which are in the firm's home state of Indiana. Each offers a half-dozen freshly made flavors of frozen custard (which is like ice cream but denser and richer) for cones, dishes, smoothies, and shakes, along with frozen custard cakes and pies. The firm is headed by Bob Ritter, son of the firm's founder.

Beginnings

Ritter's Frozen Custard was founded by a Chicago-based movie animator named John Ritter, who, though nearing retirement age, decided to seek a new career when the animation industry began turning to computers in the 1980s. While discussing the idea with his family, one of his sons reminded him that he had often said he wanted to open his own ice cream shop. He had fond memories of the fresh ice cream he had made at a high school job in the late 1940s and also of family trips to neighboring Wisconsin for frozen custard, which was extremely popular there. Ritter decided to open a frozen custard shop of his own and spent several years researching different formulas until he had created one that satisfied him.

Similar in many ways to ice cream, frozen custard includes a small amount of egg yolk and has less butterfat. It is also much denser, as it contains less added air: ice cream is typically 50 percent air, while Ritter's custard is just 11 percent. Because of this, and because it is served at a warmer temperature than most ice cream (18 degrees), its flavor is noticeably more intense and rich.

Once Ritter was satisfied with his custard formula, he and his wife Bonny began looking for a site to open a shop. Initially hoping to locate in Bloomington, Indiana, they had difficulty finding the right property. On a drive through of the Indianapolis suburb of Franklin, however, Ritter came upon a site that looked good, and he quickly arranged to acquire it. In 1989, the first Ritter's Frozen Custard shop was opened.

Frozen custard was not well-understood in mid-Indiana, and at first the shop attracted few customers. Some who did try it, Ritter later told the *Indianapolis Star and News,* "thought it was mom's chocolate pudding." Business got a boost at the end of the 1992 sales season, when Ritter's Frozen Custard was voted best dessert in a poll of *Indianapolis Star and News* readers. The next spring, traffic picked up noticeably, with some customers driving in from as far away as Kentucky for the frozen treat.

RFC Franchising Formed in 1994

Ritter subsequently opened a second shop, and in 1994, after his son Bob had joined the company, began making plans to franchise the idea. Saul Lemke, who had many years of franchise experience, was hired to help run the newly named RFC Franchising. In 1995, the first franchise outlet was opened in Bedford, Indiana.

Ritter's Frozen Custard shops featured a round blue roof and patio seating covered by blue-and-white umbrellas, which encouraged families to sit and enjoy their ice cream outdoors. John Ritter believed strongly in the value of family, and he wanted his customers to enjoy their frozen custard together in a pleasant setting where they could socialize with friends and neighbors while waiting in line. Because demand for frozen desserts dropped during the winter, the stores were only open for eight months of the year.

Ritter was highly selective when choosing franchisees, turning down the vast majority of those who inquired about opening

Company Perspectives:

Our Mission: To delight each guest with the very best premium ice cream treats. To have our treats enthusiastically served by knowledgeable, caring, well-groomed Ritter's team members. To serve our guests in a relaxed, sparkling-clean environment.

a shop. The company kept strict control over its franchise outlets and issued detailed guidelines on how each should look and what they could sell. The initial franchise fee was $15,000, and RFC also collected a royalty of 5 percent of sales.

By early 1998, the chain had grown to seven shops, and during the year seven others were opened, six in Indiana and one in Texas. By now, the company was gaining a reputation within the industry for its quality, cleanliness, and service. True to his original inspiration, Ritter's shops served only custard that had been freshly made on the premises each day, and the firm's outlets made their own fresh waffle cones as well. Custard unsold at day's end would be packed into pints or quarts and frozen for take-out sale. Though Ritter had created more than eighty flavors, only five were offered at a time. Vanilla and chocolate were always available, along with one nut flavor, one fruit flavor, and one special flavor. Prices ranged from 99 cents to $3.59 for a range of items that included cones, dishes, shakes, floats, sundaes, and the "Glacier," which had mixed-in toppings and was thick enough to be served upside-down.

Florida Expansion Rights Sold in 2001

By the start of 2000, more than twenty locations were open, and a year later the total stood at twenty-eight. Ritter's outlets were now in Arizona, Florida, Kentucky, Texas, Ohio, Michigan, and Indiana. In June 2001, the company sold the rights to expand in Florida to two Ritter's franchisees for $175,000. They formed Ritter's of Florida Franchising, which would split the franchise fees and royalties from every store they opened with the parent firm. Plans were soon announced to open 100 stores there over the next decade. Florida outlets could bring in revenues year-round, unlike those in the Midwest, which were closed during the winter months. The move was reportedly made because RFC did not have the systems in place to handle such rapid growth itself.

By this time, the company was also working on a redesign of its stores, which featured some interior seating (earlier stores had only offered outdoor seating) and a drive-through window. The design would allow all of the chain's new stores to be open year-round, instead of just during the warmer months. The first prototype opened in Indianapolis in early 2002.

In the summer of 2002, Ritter's suffered a brief round of negative publicity when one of its franchisees, Peter Loomis, cancelled a scholarship program for his young employees. His promise of $3 per hour in scholarship money, to be paid out when employees had worked for 500 or more hours for three consecutive seasons, was fulfilled by company founder John Ritter, who stepped up with more than $20,000 to help pay five former employees' college expenses. Loomis blamed the policy change on the deteriorating business climate that came on the heels of the September 11, 2001 terrorist attacks against the United States. The economic downturn was also slowing expansion, with only a handful of the projected Florida outlets actually opening.

In September 2002, the company announced that all future stores would be built with the square-shaped, indoor-seating format. Existing stores in the older round-shaped design would retain their eight-month seasonal schedule, while the newer outlets would remain open for eleven months (all except January). The move would help the chain increase sales in the colder months as well as on rainy days, when the outdoor seating only stores had difficulty attracting customers.

In November 2002, Ritter's granted an exclusive license to J. Beard Franchising to franchise Ritter's shops to casinos and riverboat gambling operations. Five locations were expected to open over the next two years, with the first being the Horseshoe Casino in Hammond, Indiana, and the Flamingo Hilton and Las Vegas Hilton in Las Vegas. J. Beard was also granted a nonexclusive license to sell Ritter's franchises at other nontraditional venues like airports, sporting arenas, and concert halls.

For some time, Ritter's had been offering a low-calorie vanilla frozen yogurt for its customers who were dieting, but it accounted for less than 1 percent of the firm's sales. The company decided to reformulate the product to make it tastier, and sales soon improved to more than 2 percent of total revenues. The new light vanilla custard had five grams of fat and 110 calories per serving, as compared with nine grams of fat and 180 calories for the standard custard. Other light flavors, including raspberry, caramel, chocolate, and espresso, were also created.

In 2003, the company introduced a new "inline center" shop, designed for use in strip malls. The first was built in Hendersonville, Tennessee, near Nashville. It featured a larger indoor ordering and seating area, and was set up to allow customers to watch the frozen custard being made. Display freezers were installed, stocked with pre-packaged pints, quarts, frozen custard cakes, and ice cream sandwiches, to encourage take-out sales.

Garfield Celebrated in 2003

The year 2003 also saw Ritter's introduce a line of smoothies, priced at $3 to $4.50, as well as a frozen custard cake that commemorated the twenty-fifth anniversary of the "Garfield" comic strip, produced by Indiana native Jim Davis. Davis, who had approached Ritter's with the anniversary idea, created four comic strips featuring the cantankerous cat that promoted the company's products, which were made available in limited-edition color prints at Ritter's shops to customers who bought five smoothies. A second promotion gave free Garfield-themed birthday parties to winners of drawings in each of the chain's fifty-four shops. The parties, for the winner and ten friends, would be hosted by a live Garfield-costumed character and included food, decorations, and party favors. Other promotions included a Garfield-themed summer safety program on the company's Web site, and a summer reading challenge for five to nine-year-olds, who received a free sundae if they read five books. Cats were not the only animal RFC used to promote its treats. Some company outlets featured "Dog's Night Out" on the first Monday of each month, offering free bowls of ice cream for dogs, whose owners responded enthusiastically to the idea.

Key Dates:

1989: The first Ritter's Frozen Custard shop opens in Franklin, Indiana.
1994: The company forms RFC Franchising to sell franchise opportunities.
1998: Seven new stores open, doubling the chain's size to fourteen locations.
2001: Rights to expand in Florida are sold to Ritter's of Florida Franchising.
2003: Smoothies are introduced, ''Garfield'' promotion debuts, and the company's 50th store opens.
2004: A retail line is test marketed; Bob Ritter is named CEO.

In March 2004, Ritter's began to test-market retail packages of custard in pints and quarts, as well as custard cakes and pies, at a South Bend, Indiana grocery store. The move was motivated in part by a desire to make Ritter's products available year-round in areas where the stores operated for only eight months. The company had also begun promoting the low-carbohydrate light version of its custard to customers who were following the Atkins and South Beach diets, which emphasized foods low in carbohydrates as a way to lose weight.

The spring of 2004 saw a dramatic increase in the price of RFC's raw materials of milk, vanilla, and chocolate, and the company was forced to raise prices slightly to compensate. In September 2004, Bob Ritter, son of the company's founder, was named CEO of RFC Franchising. He had started out making custard and serving customers in the company's first stores and had in recent years been groomed by departing CEO Saul Lemke to take over the top spot. Ritter, age 34, announced that he would spend much of the next year focusing on building up the systems, communications, and training programs needed to produce quality franchisees who would build the firm into a national brand. He anticipated opening six to seven new stores by the end of 2004.

After just fifteen years in business, RFC Franchising, LLC had grown into a chain of nearly sixty frozen custard shops, which featured the company's distinctive line of scooped treats, along with smoothies, shakes, cakes, and pies. Ritter's Frozen Custard shops were in seven states, and the company was planning an ambitious national expansion in the years ahead.

Principal Competitors

Culver Franchising System, Inc.; Shake's Frozen Custard, Inc.; CoolBrands International, Inc.; Allied Domecq Quick Service Restaurants; International Dairy Queen, Inc.

Further Reading

''The Blue Chip Enterprise Award: Ritter's Frozen Custard Shoppes,'' *Indianapolis Business Journal*, August 14, 2000, p. S10.

Bradford, Ken, ''Workers Scoop up Family Spirit at Ritter's,'' *South Bend Tribune*, August 23, 2000, p. D7.

Dempsey, Eileen, ''Refreshing Paws; Shops Offer Frozen Summer Treats for Canine Visitors,'' *Columbus Dispatch*, May 31, 2004, p. 1B.

Horgan, Sean, ''Central Indiana Frozen Custard Company Plans National Expansion,'' *Indianapolis Star and News*, April 12, 1999.

Knight, Dana, ''Indianapolis-Based Frozen Custard Franchise Ready to Dip into New Markets,'' *World Reporter*, March 14, 2001.

——, ''Franklin, Ind.-Based Custard Shop Chain Leaves Quirky Building Design Behind,'' *Indianapolis Star and News*, September 28, 2002.

——, ''Indianapolis-Based Frozen Custard Chain Feels Lucky about Casino Sites,'' *Indianapolis Star and News*, November 12, 2002.

——, ''Competition Heats up in Indianapolis Ice-Cream Market,'' *Indianapolis Star*, July 29, 2003.

Maurer, Katie, ''Ritter's Rival Targets Indiana for Expansion,'' *Indianapolis Business Journal*, August 26, 2002, p. A3.

McCall, Ashley, ''Indianapolis-Based Franchiser Intervenes in Frozen Custard Tuition Imbroglio,'' *South Bend Tribune*, September 27, 2002.

Nagengast, Kate, ''Tuition Meltdown at Ritter's; Ex-Workers Say They've Lost Earned Money With Scholarship Plan Changes,'' *South Bend Tribune*, August 16, 2002.

Prescott, Heidi, ''Frozen-Custard Franchisee Builds Business a Customer at a Time,'' *South Bend Tribune*, March 18, 1998, p. C10.

——, ''Old-Fashioned Custard Shops Enter 'Expansion Mode,' '' *South Bend Tribune*, April 13, 2001.

''Ritter's Expanding in Midwest and Florida,'' *Ice Cream Reporter*, March 20, 2001, p. 1.

''Ritter's Gets Garfield License,'' *Ice Cream Reporter*, June 20, 2003, p. 1.

''Ritter's Introduces Inline Shop Design for Strip Malls,'' *Ice Cream Reporter*, May 20, 2003, p. 3.

''Ritter's Offers Its Frozen Custard to Retail,'' *Ice Cream Reporter*, April 20, 2004, p. 4.

Schoettle, Anthony, ''Ritter's Ready to Capitalize on Custard Craze,'' *Indianapolis Business Journal*, April 12, 1999, p. 3A.

Walkup, Carolyn, ''Frozen Custard Heats up Sales for Growing Number of Shops,'' *Nation's Restaurant News*, April 16, 2001, p. 8.

Wall, J.K., ''Frozen Custard Chain Dishes up Expansion Plan for 100 Florida Stores,'' *World Reporter*, June 23, 2001.

——, ''Son of Founder to Lead Indianapolis-Based Custard Shop Franchiser,'' *Indianapolis Star*, September 4, 2004.

—Frank Uhle

Rock Bottom Restaurants, Inc.

248 Centennial Parkway, Suite 100
Louisville, Colorado 80027-1675
U.S.A.
Telephone: (303) 664-4000
Fax: (303) 664-4199
Web site: http://www.rockbottomrestaurantsinc.com

Private Company
Incorporated: 1994
Employees: 6,500
Sales: $264 million (2004 est.)
NAIC: 312120 Breweries; 551112 Offices of Other Holding Companies; 722110 Full-Service Restaurants; 722410 Drinking Places (Alcoholic Beverages)

Rock Bottom Restaurants, Inc. (RBR) owns or operates more than 100 dining and entertainment establishments under several brands; its namesake brewpub chain, with 29 company-owned locations, is one of the largest in the United States. Other brands are Old Chicago (54 units), The ChopHouse (4), The Walnut Brewery (1), as well as three Sing Sing piano bars and the Axiom nightclub. There are also eight Old Chicago restaurants owned by franchisees. The company's Old Chicago restaurants feature deep-dish pizza and a trademark 110-brand beer list. The Rock Bottom Brewery units feature an eclectic menu and microbeers brewed on the premises. The company's upscale dining and beverage concept is its ChopHouse & Brewery. The first publicly traded restaurant-brewery company in the United States, RBR was taken private in a 1999 management buyout. The company was looking to franchises to deliver growth in 2004 and beyond.

Origins

The central personalities responsible for Rock Bottom's rapid expansion during the 1990s first met in 1973, roughly 20 years before they joined forces to create a chain of combination restaurant-breweries. One of the pair, and the junior of the two, was Thomas A. Moxcey, who was working in Boulder, Colorado, as a waiter at a restaurant named Cork & Keg during the early 1970s. Moxcey proved to be in the right place at the right time because in 1973 he was recruited by a restaurateur named Frank Day, who was putting his academic training as a Harvard MBA to the test. Day was opening his first restaurant, an establishment called The Walrus, and hired Moxcey to help him run the Boulder-based business. Day and Moxcey spent two years working together, then went their separate ways, beginning a 15-year period that saw Day continue as an entrepreneur and Moxcey embark on a career in restaurant management. Day opened a restaurant named Old Chicago in 1976 and developed it into a small chain, while Moxcey climbed the managerial ranks at two restaurant chains, Cork & Cleaver and Village Inn. When Day and Moxcey reunited in 1990, they brought together their experience to launch a new concept in the food service industry, one designed to appeal to the interest in microbrewed beer. The result of their efforts would become known as Rock Bottom Restaurants, Inc.

The idea behind the new establishment was a restaurant that featured an open kitchen and a prominently displayed brewing operation, complete with shining steel vats in which premium beers were produced. Specialty beers as an instrument to lure dining patrons was not a new idea for Day. His Old Chicago restaurants featured more than 100 different types of imported beers and used bottled beers and keg taps as an integral part of their decor. What Day and Moxcey had in mind with the new concept, however, was distinctly different from Day's Old Chicago units. The brewery-restaurant they opened in 1990, named Walnut Brewery, was slightly more upscale than Old Chicago, and the new concept was underpinned by the onsite brewing facilities. The ability to brew their own beer enabled them to realize hefty profit margins, as much as 94 percent of the $3 per pint price they charged, giving the two entrepreneurs much to hope for with their new concept.

When Moxcey and Day opened their second brewery, they struck upon the name for the holding company that would be created to superintend the operation of the restaurant-breweries and Day's chain of Old Chicago restaurants. The second restaurant-brewery was opened in Denver in the Prudential Plaza, which was owned by the giant insurance company of the same name. Day and Moxcey came up with a twist on Pruden-

Company Perspectives:

Our Mission: To run great restaurants . . . for the benefit of our Guests, our Community, and Ourselves. Our mission is embedded throughout our company and our people. It is the foundation for all of our decisions. We believe in it and strive to live it, everyday.

tial's long-standing advertising theme of "A Piece of the Rock" and dubbed their new restaurant-brewery "Rock Bottom Brewery," thereby lending a permanent name to their enterprise. After the opening of the second restaurant-brewery, Day and Moxcey opened another with the idea of expanding the concept into other regions set in their minds. At the time, it was an unusual strategic objective to pursue: There were many independently owned brewery restaurants scattered throughout the country, but there were only a limited number of companies operating multiple, full-service restaurant-breweries. The number of companies operating multiple, full-service restaurants in multiple states—as Day and Moxcey would do—was lower still. Day and Moxcey's few competitors would be wiped away completely once they executed their next strategic move. They were going to take their business public, something no other restaurant-brewery operator had ever done before.

Initial Public Offering in 1994

Before converting to public ownership, Day and Moxcey needed a single corporate entity to offer to Wall Street. Rock Bottom Restaurants, Inc. was formed in April 1994 to serve such a purpose, combining what previously had been a number of "S" corporations under the umbrella of a holding company. From its first day of existence, Rock Bottom comprised the three restaurant-breweries operating under the names Rock Bottom Brewery and Walnut Brewery and eight Old Chicago restaurants. A majority of the restaurants were located in Colorado, but the geographic scope of the company was expected to broaden after its initial public offering (IPO), which was completed in July 1994. The IPO netted Day and Moxcey nearly $16 million, a total drawn from the two million shares of stock that debuted at $8 per share, giving them the financial wherewithal to move forward with their expansion plans. Rock Bottom's development program, funded by the slightly more than $10 million set aside from the IPO, called for the establishment of five Rock Bottom Brewery units and 14 Old Chicago restaurants by the end of 1994. Expansion plans for 1995 projected the establishment of three or four Rock Bottom Breweries and eight Old Chicago restaurants.

By February 1995, Day and Moxcey had opened eight new restaurants during the previous 12 months, giving them a total of five Rock Bottom Breweries and 16 Old Chicago restaurants. On the heels of this ambitious effort, they continued to stick to their plans for opening four Rock Bottom Breweries and eight Old Chicago restaurants in the coming year. To finance the expansion, the company needed additional capital, having essentially exhausted the funds gained from the July 1994 IPO. Once again, Day and Moxcey turned to Wall Street for financial help, announcing a second public offering in February 1995 that found a receptive audience more than willing to invest its cash in the fortunes of an aggressive restaurant-brewery operator. Investors' interest was piqued by Rock Bottom's sound management, its attention to food quality and service, and by the profit margins the company was realizing from the sale of its microbrewed beers. When the second public offering was completed in March 1995, 2.1 million shares had been purchased at $18 per share, grossing $37.8 million for Rock Bottom's future expansion efforts. With this cash, Rock Bottom pushed ahead into new geographic areas, building on its presence in Colorado, Minnesota, Texas, and Oregon.

The second public offering resolved the financing problems for Rock Bottom's immediate expansion, but there was another nagging issue with which Day and Moxcey had to contend in the early months of 1995. Both of the executives knew there was a finite number of urban markets capable of supporting a Rock Bottom Brewery and that they could not expect to rely heavily on the Rock Bottom Brewery concept as a vehicle for expansion. More Rock Bottom Breweries could be established in new markets, to be sure, but for greater market penetration the pair felt a need for a third concept to drive future sales and earnings growth. In March 1995, the same month the second public offering was completed, they celebrated the debut of their new, third concept, the Denver ChopHouse & Brewery. Expected to generate $4 million a year in sales, the Denver ChopHouse provided Rock Bottom with an entry into the top tier of the restaurant-brewery industry, giving Day and Moxcey a more upscale concept to flesh out their restaurant business. As the company moved forward from this point it could wage a three-pronged attack, with Old Chicago units competing for business in the low-end segment of what insiders referred to as the "brew and chew" market, while Rock Bottom Breweries competed in the middle tier and the new ChopHouse formula competed in the upper tier.

Troubles Arise in 1996

By the beginning of 1996, Rock Bottom was a $70-million-in-sales company deriving nearly half of its revenue volume from the sale of its high-profit-margin beverages. Scattered throughout the country were 28 Old Chicago restaurants, ten Rock Bottom Breweries, and the company's lone ChopHouse & Brewery in Denver, with more restaurant openings in the offing. Much had been achieved since Day and Moxcey began developing new restaurant-breweries in earnest in 1994, but by the beginning of 1996 problems began to surface that were related directly to the ambitious efforts of the two long-time partners. The aggressive expansion undertaken by Day and Moxcey had produced prodigious leaps in sales, driving the company's revenue volume upward as more and more restaurant-breweries joined Rock Bottom's operational fold. Consistently rising sales, however, did not represent the only ingredient for a company's success. Profitability, important to any company's vitality, was particularly important for a publicly traded company such as Rock Bottom, which had made a tacit agreement with investors to give them a meaningful return on their investments. In this area, Rock Bottom was suffering. Sales for the first fiscal quarter of 1996 jumped more than 60 percent, but the increasing cost of opening new restaurants began to hobble earnings growth, engendering a nearly 6 percent decline in profits for the quarter. Although the decline in

Key Dates:

1976: Frank B. Day opens the first Old Chicago restaurant in Boulder, Colorado.
1991: The first Rock Bottom restaurant opens in Denver.
1994: Rock Bottom makes an initial public offering.
1999: The firm is taken private in a management buyout.
2004: RBR opens its 100th restaurant.

earnings did not represent a staggering loss, it was sufficient to set off alarms both inside the company and in the minds of industry observers. An analyst from the underwriting firm for Rock Bottom's public offerings offered his riposte to the company's anemic earnings growth, remarking, "The company committed one of those rookie mistakes—they got a little ahead of themselves." Moxcey admitted as much, saying, "The development side became distracting." The ensuing months were spent trying to lessen the sting delivered by Rock Bottom's growing pains.

Despite the financial ills stemming from the company's rapid expansion, Rock Bottom officials reiterated their intention to move forward with the expansion of the ChopHouse concept, although no particulars were offered. Moxcey, whose promotion to chief executive officer in 1995 conferred upon him the responsibilities of curing the problems Rock Bottom faced, handled the more pressing concerns regarding slipping earnings. As president of the company, Moxcey had earned the reputation of a "hands-on" leader, devoting considerable time to visiting each restaurant-brewery, meeting with employees and managers, and overseeing day-to-day issues. In 1996, as Rock Bottom began to reel from fundamental problems, Moxcey had to check his desire to know everyone and everything on an operational level and blossom into a genuine chief executive officer, that is, less of an in-the-field leader and more of a tactician in the realm of strategic planning. Along these lines, Moxcey realigned Rock Bottom's businesses into two divisions in late 1996, organizing a Brewery Restaurant Division and an Old Chicago Restaurant Division.

Despite the menacing cloud that loomed in Rock Bottom's future, the company opened 16 new restaurants in nine new markets in 1996, exceeding its own projections for the year by two units. In 1997, the company opened its second ChopHouse in Washington, D.C., at last moving forward with its expansion plans for its third dining concept, but optimism at Rock Bottom's headquarters did not eliminate the problems that arose in early 1996. Financial losses continued to pile up, particularly in the company's fourth fiscal quarter when it registered a numbing $4.25 million loss as it shuttered unprofitable units. For the year, sales were up because of continued expansion, swelling from $109 million to $150 million, but $4.7 million in losses were racked up, intensifying the need for righting the floundering company. Rock Bottom's precarious but not fatal financial position was compounded in December 1997 when the company lost its primary caretaker. Moxcey resigned from the company in December 1997, leaving to pursue other business interests. His departure left Day in charge and as the holder of Rock Bottom's three top executive positions of president, chief executive officer, and chairman. (Day was also founder and president of Concept Restaurants Inc.)

By 1998, several strategic options had been explored, including the possible sale of Rock Bottom in its entirety or in parts, but as the company looked to its future from the vantage point of early 1998 it was pressing ahead with the pace of expansion that had characterized its growth throughout the mid-1990s. With Day at the helm, Rock Bottom planned to open five Rock Bottom Brewery units, a third ChopHouse, and three restaurants through Trolley Barn Brewery Inc., a joint venture partner. Whether the financial troubles resulting from the company's mid-1990s expansion were temporary or indicative of a more serious flaw was a question to be answered by the future progress of Rock Bottom. To Day fell the responsibility for making his creation an unequivocal success.

Day later told the *Rocky Mountain News* that he had unsuccessfully tried to find a buyer for the company during its lowest point, when it was almost sold to Landry's Seafood. RBR's stock fell to $6 a share in December 1997 (it had peaked at $30 in June 1995). With bad weather and increased competition in the brewpub sector eating into earnings, RBR brought in consultants to spice up its menu and streamline its kitchen management.

Rock Bottom sold its 50 percent interest in Trolley Barn Brewery Inc. towards the end of 1998, fetching $7 million. Sales were $160.1 million for the year.

Private in 1999

RBR was taken private in an August 1999 buyout by Day and company co-founders Bob Greenlee, Arthur Wong, and David Lux. The cost of meeting cumbersome regulatory requirements was one strong disincentive for a business of Rock Bottom's size to remain a public company, one analyst told the *Denver Post.* (Consolidated Restaurants Cos., owner of El Chico and other chains, and ConQuest Partners, both based in Dallas, had also bid for the company.) The deal was worth about $80.6 million, according to the *Denver Post.*

At the time, Rock Bottom had annual sales of $190 million. The company was growing even though some observers thought the brewpub concept was tapped out. Sales were estimated at $204 million for 2000, with net income of $26 million, as noted in the *Boston Business Journal.*

Ned R. Lidvall became RBR's president and CEO in October 2001. Once president and COO of Brinker International's On the Border Cafes Corporation, Lidvall had held a number of executive posts at RBR since 1995. Frank Day remained with RBR as chairman. Day had opened more than 100 restaurants in the previous 30 years, noted the *Denver Post.*

No other brewpub chain sold more beer than Rock Bottom in 2001, according to the Institute for Brewing Studies. It sold 39,342 barrels of beer in all. During the year, the company acquired four Northeast units of bankrupt Brew Moon Enterprises Inc., plus one Hops and one Cougan's location in Arizona.

By 2003, sales were up to $250 million a year. RBR expanded its headquarters to accommodate the growth. It had been occupying more than half of a 39,000-square-foot building in Louisville, Colorado, and leased the remainder of it to increase administrative space by almost 80 percent. The company owned and operated 90 restaurants in all and was beginning to franchise its Old Chicago concept.

A franchised Old Chicago location in St. Cloud, Minnesota, became RBR's 100th restaurant in April 2004. Old Chicago was RBR's only franchise concept. The company was preparing for an aggressive expansion plan that would open more than 100 new Old Chicago Restaurants, ten of them by 2008, reported the *Denver Business Journal.* Many of the new Old Chicago locations were being opened by multi-unit franchise partners.

There was more to the Rock Bottom story than the numbers, suggested CEO Ned Lidvall. ''We're in a business that is all about people, and we believe that there is a greater purpose than simply running great restaurants,'' he said.

Principal Operating Units

Axiom; Chophouse; Old Chicago; Rock Bottom Restaurant and Brewery; Sing Sing; Walnut Brewery.

Principal Competitors

Brinker International, Inc.; Gordon Biersch Brewery Restaurant Group, Inc.; Hops Grill and Bar Inc.; Uno Restaurant Holdings Corporation.

Further Reading

Accola, John, ''Rock Bottom Chain Aims for Rebound,'' *Rocky Mountain News*, February 19, 1998, p. 5B.

''A Brand New Day: Rock Bottom Restaurants 'Very Strong' After Founder Buys Back In,'' *Rocky Mountain News*, October 17, 1999, p. 4G.

''Back at Rock Bottom; Founders of Restaurant Chain Regain Ownership,'' *Denver Post*, July 24, 1999, p. C1.

''Changes Brew at Rock Bottom's Top,'' *Denver Post*, September 6, 2001, p. C1.

''Eateries Accept Buyout; Rock Bottom Set to Go Private in Deal,'' *Denver Post*, March 20, 1999, p. C1.

Goodman, Donna L., ''Brew Moon Hits 'Rock Bottom,' Pubs Are Sold,'' *Boston Business Journal*, December 18, 2000.

Howard, Theresa, ''Rock Bottom Brewery,'' *Nation's Restaurant News*, May 22, 1995, p. 136.

Kirchen, Rich, ''Rock Bottom Fashions a Law to Allow Its Expansion,'' *Business Journal of Milwaukee*, April 21, 1997.

Liddle, Alan, ''Rock Bottom Accelerates 'Brew-n-Chew' Growth,'' *Nation's Restaurant News*, October 3, 1994, p. 4.

Papiernik, Richard L., ''Rock Bottom Hits Rocky Road; Day Back as Chief,'' *Nation's Restaurant News*, March 9, 1998, p. 3.

''Rock Bottom Chief Bids to Buy Back Chain,'' *Rocky Mountain News*, January 28, 1999, p. 1B.

''Rock Bottom Expands Headquarters,'' *Rocky Mountain News*, November 11, 2003, p. 10B.

''Rock Bottom Names Day Prexy, Chief Executive,'' *Nation's Restaurant News*, December 22, 1997, p. 4.

''Rock Bottom Plans 110 New Locations by 2008,'' *Denver Business Journal*, February 18, 2004.

''Rock Bottom Profits Rise 23% in Fiscal Year 1996,'' *Nation's Restaurant News*, February 17, 1997, p. 12.

''Rock Bottom Raises $38M in 2nd Offering,'' *Nation's Restaurant News*, March 13, 1995, p. 14.

''Rock Bottom Rests. Forms into Two Operating Divisions,'' *Nation's Restaurant News*, December 9, 1996, p. 2.

Ruggless, Ron, ''Rock Bottom Fuels Growth with Second Stock Offering,'' *Nation's Restaurant News*, February 27, 1995, p. 14.

Smith, Brad, ''Rock Bottom Serves Up ChopHouse Concept; Popular LoDo Eatery Considering Expansion Sites in Chicago, D.C.,'' *Denver Business Journal*, May 31, 1996, p. 15A.

Walkup, Carolyn, ''Rock Bottom Expansion Takes Its Toll,'' *Nation's Restaurant News*, May 20, 1996, p. 11.

—Jeffrey L. Covell
—update: Frederick C. Ingram

Royal Ten Cate N.V.

Postbus 58
Almelo
NL-7600 GD
The Netherlands
Telephone: +31 546 54 49 11
Fax: +31 546 81 41 45
Web site: http://www.tencate.com

Public Company
Incorporated: 1957 as Nijverdale Ten Cate
Employees: 3,278
Sales: EUR 570 million ($680 million) (2003)
Stock Exchanges: Euronext Paris
Ticker Symbol: 375731
NAIC: 325991 Custom Compounding of Purchased Resin; 313210 Broadwoven Fabric Mills; 313312 Textile and Fabric Finishing (Except Broadwoven Fabric) Mills; 315999 Other Apparel Accessories and Other Apparel Manufacturing; 325211 Plastics Material and Resin Manufacturing; 325212 Synthetic Rubber Manufacturing; 326113 Unsupported Plastics Film and Sheet (Except Packaging) Manufacturing; 326130 Laminated Plastics Plate, Sheet, and Shape Manufacturing; 551112 Offices of Other Holding Companies

Royal (Koninklijke in Dutch) Ten Cate N.V. is one of the world's leading producers of technical textiles. The Nijverdal-based company is also the Netherlands' oldest industrial firm, tracing its history back to 1704. Since the early 1990s, Ten Cate has transformed its operations from traditional textiles to become a specialist in advanced and technical textiles including artificial grass fibers, used to replacement natural grass playing fields; antiballistic and flame resistant materials for personal and vehicle protection; fabrics for tents, awnings, protective clothing, construction fabrics, and fabrics, textiles and components for the environmental, agricultural, and other industries. The company is also a leading producer of caps and covers, such as those used on aerosol cans, tissue boxes, and the like, through subsidiary Plasticum. Ten Cate also produces rollers for printers and copiers. Although based in the Netherlands, Ten Cate has a strong international presence, particularly in North America, which with 24 percent of sales is Ten Cate's largest market. At the mid-2000s, the company has been making an effort to expand its presence in the Asian region as well. Royal Ten Cate is listed on the Euronext Amsterdam stock exchange. In 2003, the company posted sales of EUR 570 million ($680 million).

18th Century Textile Origins

Although Ten Cate dated its origins from 1704, the Ten Cate family was likely already active in the textiles trade for some time—in 1691, for example, several members of the Ten Cate family had a signed a petition relating to trade duties, indicating that they were already established in business. The first mention of an involvement by the Ten Cate family in the Netherlands' textiles industry appeared only in 1704, however. More than half a century later, another Ten Cate, Hendrik Ten Cate, founded a new business in Almelo trading in textiles. By 1766, H. Ten Cate was operating as a commercial agent, buying yarn, which was then distributed among peasants in the Almelo area. The peasants fashioned the yarn into fabrics, which Ten Cate then sold.

H. Ten Cate grew into a prominent regional linen supplier. In the early 19th century, the company began seeking to export its fabrics, notably to the Dutch colonial possessions in Indonesia. Unable to gain permission from the Dutch Trading Company to enter Indonesia, H. Ten Cate bought up an existing weaving mill, which already acted as a fabrics supplier to Indonesia, in Almelo in 1841. That year also marked the company's first shift toward industrial production techniques.

Over the next century, H. Ten Cate grew into one of the Netherlands' most prominent textile concerns. The company's first expansion came in 1860, when it built its first steam driven mill. That business was operated under the name of Steam Weaving Mill Holland, and became a central part of the company. Ten Cate continued to expand its capacity through the turn of the century. In 1924, the company added its first spinning machinery.

Company Perspectives:

Royal Ten Cate seeks to achieve international leadership in niche markets on the basis of technological commitment and innovative capacity. The company focuses on the production of advanced materials offering specific functionalities. In so doing it draws on the high level of expertise available in the organisation in both textile technology and the chemical processes related to the manufacture of technical textiles.

The German occupation of the Netherlands during the Second World War caused severe hardships to the country's textiles industry. Emerging from the war, Ten Cate began seeking a partner for its future growth. In 1949, the company entered into a talks with the Koninklijke Stoomweverij (KSW) based just 15 kilometers away in Nijverdal.

That company had its origins at the beginning of the 19th century, when Gottfried and Heiman Salomonson began a business importing and selling cotton yard from England in 1916. G&H Salomonson remained a trading house until mid-century, when, at mid-century, they decided to enter manufacturing and located a site in Nijverdal, on the road between Almelo and Zwolle The site had originally been constructed Thomas Ainsworth, an Englishman, in 1836, in order to store and trade machinery for the Dutch Trading Company. Ainsworth built a warehouse, but died in 1841, leaving behind a spinning mill, a yarn sizing machine, and a weaving mill.

The Salomonson brothers bought the site in 1851, then decided to raze the existing structure. In its place the company built a larger steam-driven weaving mill, the first in the Twente region. The site was impressive, featuring more than 450 weaving looms, representing a major investment at the time. The following year, the company was granted the right to use the royal seal, and the site became known the Koninklijke Stoomweverij.

From the start, production at the Royal Stoomweverij was oriented toward the international market, and especially the Dutch colonial possessions. In order to support its export business, the company particiapted in establishing the Internationale Crediet en Handelsvereeniging ''Rotterdam'' N.V. in that important port city in 1863.

Heiman Salomonson's son Godfried joined the family business in 1859. The younger Salomonson played a decisive role in the company's growth and expansion over the next fifty years. An important moment for the company came with its incorporation as a limited liability company in 1872, as the Koninklijke Stoomweverij N.V. te Nijverdal (KSW). Part of the reason for the change in the company's status was a need to clarify the company's leadership among Godfried Salomonson and his cousins and nephews. Salomonson soon emerged as the company's sole leader and was credited with leading the company through an extended period of expansion. By the time of Salomonson's death in 1911, KSW had tripled its weaving capactiy.

KSW had also expanded its range of operations. In 1889, the company inauguarated its own bleaching plant. Through the 1920s, KSW, now led by Hein Salomonson, continued its expansion. In 1926, for example, the company established its own spinning mill. Two years later, KSW added a dye facility as well.

From Textiles to Plastics in the 1980s

KSW's talks with Ten Cate led to a cooperation and profit-sharing agreement as early as 1952. Over the next several years, the two companies moved closer to a full-scale merger, which took place in 1957. The new company, which became Nijverdal-Ten Cate, was granted the right to use the royal seal the following year.

Nijverdal Ten Cate remained focused on traditional textiles into the 1970s. In 1974, however, the company acquired fellow Dutch company Nicolon N.V. In the early 1950s, Nicolon had played a crucial role in the development of a new generation of dikes to protect the Netherlands' coastlines. For this project, Nicolon developed a highly resistant industrial textile, which was put in place as a mean to retain and protect the dike walls. The addition of Nicolon marked an important phase in Nijverdal Ten Cate's later transition from traditional to technical textiles.

Nicolon also became a spearhead of the company's international expansion. In 1980, the company set up a new subsidiary, Nicolon Corporation, in the United States, in order to begin producing and distributing its industrial textiles to this market. Over the next two decades, the North American market emerged as Ten Cate's single largest market, accounting for some 25 percent of its sales by the beginning of the 21st century.

Much of Ten Cate's growth during the period came through a series of acquisitions. In 1987, for example, the company acquired a 60 percent stake in Dutch specialty fabrics producer Kayser, which made fabrics for the medical market, but also outerwear and jeans fabrics. That purchase was followed by the acquisition of the European operations of the United States' Burlington in 1988.

Another 1987 acquisition, however, pointed the way toward Ten Cate's later transformation. The purchase of a 80 percent stake in Florida-based Bradley Materials not only boosted the group's U.S. presence, it also gave it control of a line of specialty industrial and geotextile fabrics used in civil engineering projects. The growing strength of Ten Cate's technical textiles sales was reflected in the expansion of its production capacity through the end of the decade.

Yet in the late 1980s and early 1990s, Ten Cate appeared to have lost interest in textiles. Instead, the company had made an entry into plastics, making a series of acquisitions that brought it operations including the production of pipe systems, polystyrene products, and, through its Plasticum unit, plastic packaging such as caps for aerosol sprays and other cans. Closer to home, Ten Cate also invested in a building capacity in a rang of plastic fabrics as well.

By 1994, the change in Ten Cate appeared nearly complete. In that year, plastics represented some 80 percent of the group's sales. The company had also shifted from producing traditional textiles, and now technical textiles stood at the core of the company's remaining textiles operations. Yet in that year, the company appeared prepared to exit technical textiles altogether.

Key Dates:

1704: First historical mention of the Ten Cate family being involved in textiles trade.
1766: Hendrik Ten Cate founds a textile trading company.
1816: Founding of G&H Salomonson, a textile trading company.
1851: G&H Salomonson establishes Koninklijke Stoomweverij te Nijverdal (KSW).
1872: G&H changes its name to KSW.
1888: KSW installs a bleaching unit.
1924: Ten Cate installs a spinning mill.
1926: KSW installs a spinning mill.
1928: KSW installs a dyeing unit.
1949: KSW and Ten Cate begin talks to merge.
1952: KSW and Ten Cate reach cooperation and profit-sharing agreement.
1957: The KSW and Ten Cate merger is finalized.
1974: Company acquires Nicolon.
1980: Nicolon Corporation is established in the United States.
1995: Company changes name to Royal Ten Cate.

In January of 1994, for example, Ten Cate sold off a 75 percent stake in its Ten Cate Technical Fabrics division, which manufactured tent fabric, sailcloth, and other technical fabrics. Instead, the group, through a 50–50 joint venture with Shell, acquired France's Isobox, a maker of polystyrene-based packaging products.

Technical Textiles Focus in the New Century

Ten Cate adopted a new name in 1995, becoming Koninklijke Ten Cate. In the second half of the 1990s, the company abandoned its effort to transform itself into a plastics-focused company. The lingering recession in its core European markets—which continued to account for some 80 percent of the company's sales in the early 1990s—had convinced Ten Cate to shift its focus to technical textiles production. At the same time, the company shifted its plastics production to more specialized areas as well, such as the production of specialized rollers for printers and photo-copiers. Another key area for the group was the development of advanced anti-ballistics plastics. In 1999, the company expanded that segment through its purchase of Bryte Technologies, based in San Jose, California.

Ten Cate's shift toward advanced plastics led to the sale of its Plasticum caps business in the United States. The company also began plans to sell off its European plastics packaging operations as well, a strategy confirmed by the company in 2004. In the meantime, Ten Cate's momentum was carried forward by its technical textiles operations, and particularly its development of a new artificial grass fiber used for sports playing fields. In 2004, the company received an important boost when the UEFA, the European soccer federation, announced that it would permit playing on artificial grass for the first time in the 2005 season. After 300 years in operation, Ten Cate maintained a world leading position in the textiles industry.

Principal Subsidiaries

Ares Protection Sas (France); Bryte Technologies Inc (USA); Landscape Solutions BV; Multistiq International Coating BV; Ten Cate Advanced Composites BV; Ten Cate Advanced Spinning BV; Ten Cate Advanced Textiles BV; Ten Cate Advanced Weaving BV; Ten Cate Nicolon Asia Sdn Bhd (Malaysia); Ten Cate Nicolon Australia Pty Ltd (Australia); Ten Cate Nicolon BV; Ten Cate Nicolon USA; Ten Cate Permess BV; Ten Cate Permess Interlinings Hong Kong Ltd; Ten Cate Permess Italia Spa; Ten Cate Permess UK Ltd; Ten Cate Permess Xishan (China); Ten Cate Protect BV; Ten Cate Technical Fabrics BV; Ten Cate Thiobac BV; Ten Cate Thiolon BV; Ten Cate Thiolon USA Inc;

Principal Competitors

Sekisui Chemical Company Ltd.; Daikin America Inc.; PolyOne Corporation; A. Schulman Inc.; Shintech Inc.; Goldschmidt AG; TPI Polene PCL; Gamma Technologies; Reliance Industries.

Further Reading

''Bryte Technologies Bought by Royal Ten Cate USA,'' *Advanced Materials & Composites News*, May 17, 1999.
''Dutch Company Acquiring Southern Mills,'' *bizjournals.com*, March 8, 2004.
''300 years of Ten Cate,'' *Future Materials*, October 26, 2004
White, Liz, ''Ten Cate Seeks Partner for Globalisation,'' *European Rubber Journal*, April 2000, p. 10.
Wilson, Adrian, ''Protective Action,'' *Textile Month*, July 1996, p. 8.

—M.L. Cohen

Ryan's®

Ryan's Restaurant Group, Inc.

405 Lancaster Avenue
Greer, South Carolina 29650
U.S.A.
Telephone: (864) 879-1000
Fax: (864) 877-0979
Web site: http://www.ryansrg.com

Public Company
Incorporated: 1977 as Ryan's Family Steak Houses, Inc.
Employees: 22,600
Sales: $805 million (2003)
Stock Exchanges: NASDAQ
Ticker Symbol: RYAN
NAIC: 722110 Full-Service Restaurants; 533110 Owners and Lessors of Other Non-Financial Assets

Ryan's Restaurant Group, Inc., operates more than 300 restaurants in the southern and midwestern United States. The company operates restaurants in 23 states. The majority of Ryan's restaurants operate under the name Ryan's Grill, Buffet & Bakery. The restaurants, which cater primarily to families, feature a menu that changes daily, offering a selection of steaks, chicken, seafood, hamburgers, side dishes, and vegetables. The restaurants are best known for their signature offering, the Mega Bar buffet, a collection of self-service buffets scattered throughout the dining area. Ryan's also owns roughly two dozen restaurants that operate under the name Fire Mountain. The Fire Mountain units, designed to look like a lodge, are more upscale than the Ryan's Grill, Buffet & Bakery chain, featuring a display grill where patrons can watch their meals being prepared. The Fire Mountain units, like the larger chain, also allow unlimited visits to food bars scattered throughout the dining area.

Origins

Ryan's founder, Alvin A. McCall, Jr., was born in 1927, ninth in a family of 11. His parents worked at a mill in Pelzer, South Carolina, and he and his siblings grew up poor. His entrepreneurial bent showed itself at an early age as he recruited his sister Martha to help him raise chickens, peppers, and tomatoes for sale. As a teenager McCall delivered newspapers and also cleaned a movie theater and worked in a couple of grocery stores, including a Dixie Home Store, one of the forerunners of the Winn-Dixie chain.

After graduating high school, McCall served a stint at a mortuary owned by the father of a friend. After serving a year in the Navy at the end of World War II, he studied business and accounting at schools in Greenville, South Carolina, and Johnson City, Tennessee. He also moonlighted as a bookkeeper for a restaurant and a gas station, both of which provided practical perks. When he returned to Greenville, he joined an accounting firm and married. He continued his habit of moonlighting, which earned him more than his regular salary.

The restless McCall next began to build houses. His initial success prompted him to quit his accounting job to form McCall Construction Co., which, according to McCall, showed a $43,000 profit its first year, 1958. This led to property development; eventually he built and ran a Volkswagen dealership in Sumter, South Carolina.

McCall's search for interesting businesses to run brought him to restaurants. In 1970, inspired by the successful Ponderosa chain, he started his own, Western Family Steak House, most of which took the name Quincy's in 1976. The first restaurant was on Wade Hampton Boulevard in Greenville, built by employees from his contracting business. After the hired manager lost $50,000 in three months, McCall took the reins and developed a formula based on principles of quality he had learned as a contractor. Quality at his steak house began with using fresh meat, not frozen.

In 1977, McCall sold his interest in Quincy's to what would become Trans World Corporation, but he retained the freedom to compete. He started Ryan's the same year and the first restaurant opened in 1978 on Laurens Road in Greenville. Sales for the first year were $568,000. Although the restaurants, which numbered seven by 1981 (including one franchisee), were successful, growth was limited by the structure of the company, which put profits back in the hands of the partners, not into the business. At the end of 1981 (when sales were $8.1 million) the partnerships were consolidated; Ryan's first public stock offering raised $4 million.

Company Perspectives:

Since 1978, the Company has offered high quality food at affordable prices with exceptional friendly service in a family-oriented atmosphere to millions of hungry patrons who always leave well satisfied. From our delicious grill selections, our vast array of hot vegetables, our fresh salad ingredients to our sumptuous dessert bar, only the highest quality products are presented to our customers.

Beginning Life As a Public Company in 1982

Unfortunately, there was initially a small obstacle to expansion and the stock offering. The name ''Ryan's'' had been chosen because it was short and recognizable, with a wholesome and frugal Irish ring to it. The registration of the trademark was opposed, however, by John Rian, owner, through Rian's Inc., of ten restaurants in the metropolitan Portland area of Oregon. In order to speed its 1982 initial public offering, McCall agreed not to use the name ''Ryan's'' west of the Mississippi except for in Texas, Oklahoma, and Louisiana. In 1987, to clear the way for westward expansion, Ryan's paid Rian $150,000 for use of the name in the remaining United States.

Once these hurdles were cleared, Ryan's growth was impressive. A share of stock, worth $9.25 originally, rose to more than $30 at its peak. Ryan's never paid dividends and was thus able to use all of its profits for expansion. Fred Grant, a finance officer, explained in 1991 that issuing a 25-cent dividend would cost $13 million, enough to start six restaurants. The company maintained that its policy helped secure stock prices in a highly leveraged industry. In the 1990s, Ryan's opened approximately 20 new restaurants each year, peaking at 30 in 1993. This performance flew in the face of emerging concerns over the health risks related to the animal fat and cholesterol in beef, or the ''beef scare'' of the 1980s. The variety found in the Mega Bar helped satisfy wider crowds; the restaurants also sold a few à la carte fish and poultry dishes.

McCall relied on conservative methods to maintain control of the restaurant's destiny. Although he tinkered with franchising in the beginning, McCall found that it left him unable to ensure consistent quality from store to store. Franchises did come to contribute a significant portion of company revenues, however, though not without some difficulties. When Family Steak Houses of Florida, Inc., Ryan's largest franchisee, fell behind in royalty payments in 1993, Ryan's restructured its agreement. Family Steak Houses, based in Neptune Beach, lost $2.1 million in 1993, in large part due to the closure of unprofitable stores. The company, which went public in 1986, was founded by Eddie Ervin, Alvin McCall's brother-in-law, owner of Margate, Florida's Rustic Inn Crabhouse. The first Ryan's in a foreign country was a franchised restaurant, which opened in Ballarat, Australia, in 1994.

Borrowing also surrendered control of the company, and Ryan's developed a habit of relying on cash, not credit. In fact, it gained a reputation for extraordinary promptness in paying its vendors. In the late 1980s the company did begin to borrow to fund expansion. Inside the restaurants, Ryan's did not accept credit cards until 1991.

In some ways, the company took an unconventional approach. In addition to its lukewarm embrace of franchising, at least in the early days, it disdained advertising, even for store openings. The company did not run a significant advertising campaign until 1994, when it bought television and radio spots in Charleston. By 1996 the company planned to support one-third of its stores with $1.7 million of advertising, a great deal for a chain that for years relied exclusively on word of mouth.

While most restaurants invested 3 to 4 percent of sales in advertising, Ryan's, according to company officials, preferred to apply the money toward what it stated were the highest food costs in the business, hoping that would bring back customers. The high costs made high volumes critical to the success of the restaurants. Ryan's stores also boasted twice the volume of others in its segment, about $2 million each in the 1980s.

In May 1986, McCall's son T. Mark McCall was named president of the company, after shepherding the introduction of the ''Mega Bar.'' These offered salads, entrees and vegetables, and desserts. After just one year, the buffet bars accounted for nearly half of Ryan's total sales, and pushed same-store sales up 50 percent to 2.5 times the industry average. At the same time, bread-baking ovens were installed, allowing the chain to offer fresh rolls made from scratch (the recipe was developed with help from General Mills). In 1986, annual sales were up 99 percent to $103.3 million; profits rose 92 percent over the previous year.

Mark McCall faced difficult times in his tenure as president. In October 1987, the company's stock fell, as did the stock of just about every other company in the wake of the stock market crash. The average restaurant stock fell 42 percent during this time. This prompted company officials to think about the possibility of a takeover for the first time. The success of the Mega Bars drew many imitators, which flattened sales.

In June 1988 Alvin McCall resumed his role as CEO as his son Mark left the post to start a restaurant chain in Texas. Greenville accountant Charles Way took over as CEO in 1989 after serving as controller since the company was only two years old. Way, whom Alvin McCall described as his protégé, had already been serving as president. In 1992, he became board chairman as well.

Maturing in the 1990s

In 1990, a Restaurants & Institutions survey named Ryan's the best steak house in the United States. Nevertheless, the company slowed its expansion temporarily around this time and hired more staff to improve service. It also made retention of managers (who typically worked 14-hour days) a top priority, feeling that consistency in management helped reduce employee turnover. The pay of managers and supervisors was heavily tied to performance, and generally exceeded the industry average, although high volumes made payroll consume a lower portion of sales.

In 1991, ''Bakery Bars'' were added to Ryan's restaurants, offering desserts baked in the store. They were successful in

Key Dates:

1970: Ryan's founder, Alvin McCall, Jr., enters the restaurant business by opening the Western Family Steak House.
1977: After selling Western Family, McCall establishes Ryan's, opening his first restaurant the following year.
1982: Ryan's completes its initial public offering of stock.
1986: Ryan's introduces the Mega Bar, a self-service buffet bar.
1993: The Mega Bar concept is revamped, turning one central buffet bar into six buffet stations.
1997: Ryan's celebrates its 20th anniversary by generating nearly $600 million in revenue.
2000: Some of the company's restaurants begin to cook entrées in view of diners.
2003: The display cooking restaurants are given their own name, Fire Mountain.

boosting sales, but start-up costs and a poor economy prevented them, at least initially, from increasing earnings. The Mega Bar concept was revitalized in 1993, when it was changed from one central station to six buffet stations, known as "scatter bars," which reduced traffic congestion and increased variety. Expanded installation of the scatter bars in 1995 helped Ryan's turn around sales declines. In 1993, the company experimented with a higher priced weekend buffet bar, which featured seafood, prime rib, and Virginia ham. The new bar, which cost $11 per plate—nearly double the usual check average—was an attempt to increase declining same-store sales.

In order to create tax savings and in preparation for more growth, Ryan's created three subsidiaries in 1993. Ryan's Properties would manage Ryan's trademarks and service marks. Ryan's Family Steak House East operated the restaurants. Ryan's Capital Holding Corp. would deal with debt financing. Another subsidiary, Big R Procurement Co., had already been created in 1992 to purchase supplies.

In the mid-1990s Ryan's searched for ways to diversify in light of fierce competition in the family dining segment. In 1994, it began talks with Frankie's Food, Sports, and Spirits, an Atlanta sports bar. The company also built its own Caliente Grill, a Tex-Mex restaurant, in Greenville and operated it on a test basis. Another casual dining concept being tested in 1994 was an upscale Western-style steak house, the Laredo Grille, which opened in Plano, Texas, at the site of an existing Ryan's. Both of these casual dining restaurants offered alcoholic beverages, unlike Ryan's steak houses, and featured full-service dining as opposed to Ryan's order line and buffet tables. Observers cited these forays into casual dining as evidence of Ryan's mature management team.

A New Look for the Future

Ryan's management's search for a new twist to the company's dining concept ranked as a primary objective during the second half of the 1990s. The development of new concepts during the mid-1990s failed to take hold, but Way and his team persisted in exploring new opportunities for growth. The introduction of the Mega Bar, particularly the revision of the concept in 1993, had delivered significant sales growth, breathing new life into the chain and convincing its executives of the importance of finding new ways to attract diners. By the time the company's 20th anniversary arrived, a year in which sales reached $599 million, it had yet to find a new growth vehicle, either through developing an entirely new concept or revamping its existing concept. The company was successful, nonetheless, having adding roughly 50 new restaurants to the chain during the previous two years, giving it a total of 277 units by the beginning of 1998.

Ryan's found the new wrinkle it was looking for at the end of the 1990s, and the source of inspiration was its closest rival, Golden Corral Corporation. In 1999, Golden Corral began displaying the preparation of vegetables and bakery products to its patrons. The following year, Ryan's adopted a single-price format and began carving meat in view of its customers, a move that marked the beginning of the development of the company's display cooking concept. Ryan's soon began cooking steak and other items on a grill in view of its diners, which led it to remodel some of its Ryan's Grill, Buffet & Bakery units. These revamped units, designed to look like a lodge, featured a more upscale décor, new signage, and new lighting. By 2001, the company had introduced display cooking in 30 of its 300 restaurants, recording a 15 percent increase in sales at the remodeled units. As the company prepared for the decade ahead, much of its focus was on incorporating its open-grill format into the chain.

When Ryan's first began remodeling its units, the open-grill restaurants were referred to as "lodge" restaurants, but as the remodeling program evolved, the "new" units were given their own identity. At the end of 2003, 31 of the company's 352 restaurants were lodge models, seven of which were newly constructed restaurants (the rest were conversions of the company's traditional stores). These newly built units began operating under the name Fire Mountain, giving the company, after years of searching, a new restaurant concept to fuel its future growth. Ryan's planned to open as many as 25 Fire Mountain restaurants in 2004, with more units planned for the years ahead.

Principal Subsidiaries

Big R Procurement Co. LLC; Ryan's Properties, Inc,; Fire Mountain Restaurants, Inc.; Rymark Holdings, Inc.; Fire Mountain Properties, LLC.

Principal Competitors

Golden Corral Corporation; Metromedia Restaurant Group; The WesterN SizzliN Corporation.

Further Reading

Basch, Mark, "Neptune Beach, Fla.-Based Steak House Company Drops Affiliation," *Knight Ridder/Tribune Business News*, December 18, 2003.

Brammer, Rhonda, "What's the Beef?," *Barron's*, January 2, 1995, pp. 23–24.

Carlino, Bill, "Despite Rebound, Ryan's Still Feels January Chill," *Nation's Restaurant News*, May 9, 1994.

——, "Ryan's Explores Upscale All-You-Can-Eat Format," *Nation's Restaurant News,* January 4, 1993.

——, "Ryan's to Test Tex-Mex with Caliente Grille," *Nation's Restaurant News,* July 11, 1994.

Cebrzynski, Gregg, "Ryan's Anniversary Promotion Rewards Loyal Customers," *Nation's Restaurant News,* August 10, 1998, p. 36.

Feldman, Rona, "Steak: Nutritional Concerns Have Not Hurt Segment Profits," *Restaurant Business,* June 10, 1992, p. 176.

Festa, Gail, "Ryan's Express," *Restaurant Hospitality,* August 1987.

Fleet, Lee Ann, "Cutting No Corners: Alvin McCall Built Ryan's His Way," *Greenville News,* August 31, 1992.

——, "Ryan's Officials See Business Rebounding," *Greenville News,* April 25, 1991.

Hayes, Jack, "Christman Takes Helm at Family Steak Houses," *Nation's Restaurant News,* May 2, 1994, pp. 3, 123.

——, "Ryan's Making a Pitch for High-Volume Sports Bar," *Nation's Restaurant News,* March 7, 1994, p. 4.

——, "Ryan's Posts Record Earnings with Cost Controls, Growth," *Nation's Restaurant News,* February 10, 2003, p. 11.

——, "Ryan's Ramps Up Media Blitz with $1.7M Radio, TV Push," *Nation's Restaurant News,* April 22, 1996, p. 21.

——, "Steak Rivals Sell Sizzle of Image Upgrades," *Nation's Restaurant News,* August 1, 1994, pp. 140, 148.

Little, Loyd, "Alvin McCall Had Hunger to Succeed," *Upstate Business,* May 23, 1993.

——, "McCall's Successor Charting Way for Ryan's Family Steak Houses," *Upstate Business,* May 23, 1993.

Mamis, Robert A., "Meat and Potatoes," *Inc.,* July 1986, pp. 53–63.

Marcial, Gene G., "Steak Houses That May Soon Sizzle," *Business Week,* July 22, 1991, p. 62.

Mehegan, Sarah, "Ryan's Hope," *Restaurant Business,* September 1, 1995.

Netzer, Baie, "Regional Brokers Pick Them from Their Own Backyards," *Money,* November, 1991, p. 84.

Palmeri, Christopher, "The Two Hundred Best Small Companies," *Forbes,* November 9, 1992, p. 210.

Patterson, Pat, "Southern Steak-House Chain Finds Flexibility Spells Success," *Nation's Restaurant News,* January 15, 1990, p. 47.

Person, Sarah, "Ryan's Stake in Budget Beef Segment," *Restaurant Business,* October 10, 1995.

Rogers, Monica, "Steakhouses Looking to Add Sizzle," *Restaurants & Institutions,* July 15, 1994, pp. 144–46.

——, "Steakhouses Say Adios to Big-Menu Strategies," *Restaurants & Institutions,* July 15, 1993, pp. 124–34.

"Ryan's Earnings Fall in 2nd Q with Higher Food Costs," *Nation's Restaurant News,* August 2, 2004, p. 34.

"Ryan's Ends Relationship with 16-Year Fla. Franchisee," *Nation's Restaurant News,* January 5, 2004, p. 78.

Spielberg, Susan, "Ryan's Gets More Upscale with New Look, Name," *Nation's Restaurant News,* February 16, 2004, p. 4.

"Starting to Sizzle at Ryan's," *Business Week,* August 6, 2001, p. 87.

Werner, Ben, "Bad Weather, Higher Costs Eat Away Sales at Ryan's Restaurant Group," *The State,* October 24, 2004, p. B2.

—Frederick C. Ingram
—update: Jeffrey L. Covell

Sanlam Ltd.

2 Strand Road
Bellville, Western Cape 7532
South Africa
Telephone: (+27) 21-947-9111
Fax: (+27) 21-947-3670
Web site: http://www.sanlam.co.za

Public Company
Incorporated: 1918
Employees: 10,700
Total Assets: ZAR 10 billion ($1.5 billion) (2003)
Stock Exchanges: Johannesburg
Ticker Symbol: SANLAM
NAIC: 523120 Securities Brokerage; 524113 Direct Life Insurance Carriers; 524114 Direct Health and Medical Insurance Carriers; 524126 Direct Property and Casualty Insurance Carriers;

Sanlam Ltd. is South Africa's second-largest life insurance and financial services group, behind Old Mutual. Sanlam is organized into four primary business clusters: Life Insurance is the group's largest component, with a full range of life insurance, pension plans, and savings and investment products through subsidiaries that include Sanlam Personal Finance. Short-term Insurance is conducted largely through the company's 53 percent stake in Santam, South Africa's leading short-term insurer with operations in the corporate, commercial, and personal sectors. The Investment cluster groups Santam's asset management, stockbroking, and related operations, including the company's Gensec subsidiary and stockbroker Hichens, Harrison & Co., acquired in 2003. Lastly, the Independent Financial Services markets Sanlam products for sale through independent agents and includes the group's Sanlam Capital Markets. Unlike many other South African financial groups, Sanlam has chosen to focus its operations primarily on the South African market. Nonetheless, the group is also active in Namibia through its Life Insurance cluster and has investments in Namibia, Malawi, Zimbabwe, and Zambia through Santam. In 2003, Sanlam extended its life insurance business into the United Kingdom as well, acquiring that country's Merchant Investors Insurance Company. Sanlam, formerly the insurance arm of the Afrikaner National Party, has taken the lead in the Black Enterprise Empowerment (BEE) initiative. In 2004, the company sold 10 percent of its shares to the Ubuntu-Botho empowerment consortium. Sanlam is listed on the Johannesburg Stock Exchange.

Post-World War I Afrikaner Empowerment

Following its defeat in the Boer War, South Africa's Afrikaner population found itself impoverished and generally treated as second-class citizens. Although the Afrikaners managed to regain control in the years leading up World War I, the country's economy lay firmly in the hands of its English-speaking population. The transition of the South African economy from a largely agrarian, Afrikaner-dominant basis to an industrialized economy dominated by English interests had led to the marginalization of huge segments of the Afrikaner population.

By the end of the first decade of the 20th century, many Afrikaners had been forced from their land and into the urban regions. With industry dominated by the English-speakers, however, Afrikaners found themselves shut out from skilled labor jobs, as well as from jobs in the commercial sector. The English-controlled banks also refused to lend to most Afrikaners. Among the only jobs open to the Afrikaner population were dangerous, unskilled jobs in the growing number of South African mines. Large portions of the Afrikaner population sank into poverty.

The country's decision to enter World War I on the side of the Allies led to the opening of a new schism in South Africa. Many Afrikaners favored the Germans—who had given them support during the Boer War—over the British. In opposition, a number of Afrikaners split from the government and formed a new political party, the Nasionale Pers (''National Party''). A failed coup, meant to topple the government led by Louis Botha, led to an armed uprising among Afrikaners.

The suppression of that uprising by the South African army exacerbated the Afrikaner population's economic misery. Yet the need to come to assistance of the rebels and their families gave rise to a new initiative among the Afrikaners, the informally adopted idea of ''helpmekaar'' (literally ''help each other''), giving rise to new mutual aid efforts.

Company Perspectives:

Our vision: To be the leader in wealth creation. The vision clearly defines the ultimate goal of Sanlam to be a group of businesses focused on building, preserving and growing wealth for all our clients. Building wealth is about providing our clients with access to savings and credit products.

Preserving wealth is our traditional business of providing guaranteed products for investment market risks and contingency risks such as life, health, property, casualty and liability.

Growing wealth comprises investment management through various investment vehicles. Our values: At Sanlam, we . . . Grow shareholder value through innovation and superior performance . . . Lead with courage . . . Serve with pride . . . Care because we respect others . . . Act with integrity and accountability.

As World War I began to wind down, a number of prominent Afrikaners, for the most part wealthy vineyard owners living in the western Cape region, launched more formal efforts to raise the status of the Afrikaners. In December 1917, a group of men, including National Party founders Willie Hofmeyr, Fred Dormehl, and Pieter Malan, joined together to establish a new mutual aid society. The group decided to create a short-term insurance business in order to provide loans and credits to Afrikaners shut out by the country's English-controlled banks.

The new business was to be entirely funded by Afrikaners, and its operations restricted to the Afrikaner population. Called Suid-Afrikaanse Nasionale Trust en Assuransie Maatskappij, or Santam, the new company was formally registered in March of 1918. The new credit association was initially intended to include life insurance products. However, the company's backers soon decided to establish a second company for those operations. In June 1918, the life insurance business was incorporated as The Suid-Afrikaanse Nasionale Lewens Assuransie Maatskappij Beperk (''South African National Life Insurance Company Limited''), or Sanlam.

Sanlam faced a crisis from the start as the outbreak of Spanish Flu in 1918 brought a huge number of claims against the new company. Nonetheless, Sanlam managed to remain profitable that year and by the beginning of the 1920s was ready to expand its operations. Originally focused on the rural Afrikaner population, Sanlam soon moved to cover the growing number of Afrikaans-speaking city dwellers. In 1928, the company extended its reach to include South West Africa, then a protectorate of South Africa and later to be known as Namibia. In 1943, a formal independent branch office, which became Sanlam Namibia, was established there.

Investment Driven in the 1940s

By the mid-1930s, Sanlam had become the dominant partner of the Sanlam-Santam tandem. This fact was recognized by the transfer of Santam's own life insurance operation, African Homes Trust, later renamed Metropolitan Life, to Sanlam. Santam meanwhile remained Sanlam's majority shareholder.

Sanlam also expanded its scope of operations in order to fulfill its mission of providing jobs and economic empowerment to the Afrikaner population. In 1940, Sanlam launched the Federale Volksbeleggings (FVB), which used the funds generated through the company's policy holders to invest in the country's industrial and commercial sphere. As such, Sanlam built up significant stakes in most of South Africa's major Afrikaner-backed corporations, including the creation of mining giant Gencor in the 1950s. In 1946, Sanlam created a second investment vehicle, Bonuskor, which used policy bonuses as the basis for providing capital for establishing and expanding Afrikaner-led businesses. Another company possession was the National Party newspaper *Die Burger,* founded by Hofmeyer in 1915.

The National Party gained control of the South African government in 1948, sparking a new era of growth for Sanlam. The company became still more closely associated with the National Party (and with its apartheid politics). As such, Sanlam built up a significant assets management operation, which included the Volkskas, as a banking vehicle for the South African government. Sanlam also gained control of the government's pension funds. Other Sanlam investments included Gencor and the distribution vehicle Tradegro. The latter company oversaw one of Sanlam's largest and most profitable investments, the Checkers retail empire.

The Sanlam-Santam relationship was turned upside down in the mid-1950s. In 1954, the two companies entered negotiations in order to convert Sanlam to the status of a mutual life insurance company. As a result of the negotiations, Sanlam became Santam's majority shareholder.

The growth of Sanlam's Bonuskor business led it to create a second investment vehicle in 1960. The new company, Sankor, targeted large-scale developments for its investments. The company remained a player in the funding of major developments, and in 1985 launched a new business, Sankorp, in order to extend its development investments. At its height, Sankorp's investment portfolio was worth some ZAR31 billion and included the company's shares in Gencor, Billiton, Murray & Roberts, Sappi, and Genbel, to name a few.

De-Mutualized Financial Services Group in the 1980s and 1990s

By the early 1980s, Sanlam had begun an effort to expand its business beyond the Afrikaans-speaking population. This effort, however, was only mildly successful. The company had by then entered into a period of decline. The company's Tradegro group crashed after the Checkers chain was crushed by rival Pick n' Pay. In the 1980s, also, Sanlam's Bankorp collapsed, requiring a government bailout that cost the company's policyholders more than ZAR1 billion. Following the bailout, Sanlam sold Bankorp to ABSA in exchange for a 25 percent stake in the South African bank.

Sanlam, with its close ties to the government, appeared to have sunk into complacency throughout the 1980s. The end of apartheid and the collapse of the Afrikaner government soon provided a wake up call for Sanlam. With the end of its political patronage, Sanlam was forced to reinvent itself in order to shake

Key Dates:

1918: Founding of Suid-Afrikaanse Nasionale Lewens Assuransie Maatskappij Beperk, or Sanlam, as a life insurance and investment group in order to fund economic development of Afrikaner population in South Africa.
1928: The company establishes a branch office in South West Africa (Namibia).
1935: Sanlam acquires African Homes Trust (renamed Metropolitan Life) from parent company Santam.
1940: The company forms Federale Volksbeleggings investment operation.
1946: Bonuskor investment vehicle is created.
1954: Sanlam converts to a mutual life insurance company and becomes a majority shareholder of Santam.
1960: Sankor development arm is formed.
1985: Sankorp, which becomes Sanlam's central investment holding company, is created.
1993: Control of Metropolitan Life is transferred to NAIL.
1998: Sanlam de-mutualizes and lists stock on the Johannesburg Stock Exchange.
2003: Merchant Investors, a life insurance and assets management business based in Bristol, England, is acquired.
2004: Sanlam sells a 10 percent equity stake to Ubuntu-Botho, a black empowerment consortium.

its image as the financial wing of the National Party. When the new ANC-led government switched its pension fund deposits, Sanlam's Volkskas, once one of the country's major financial institutions, suddenly ceased to exist.

Throughout the 1990s, Sanlam continued reinventing itself as a financial services group. As part of this process, the company began unbundling many of its investments, such as Gencor, which were split off as separate companies. The company divested Tradegro, broke apart Federale Volksbeleggings, and dismantled another of its major ''pyramid'' holdings, Malbak, which had controlled the company's stakes in Foodcorp, SA Druggists, Tedelex, Ellerines, Haggie, Kohler, and other concerns. As then chairman of Sanlam told *The Business Times:* ''We will gradually unbundle our non-financial service interests but in a way which will add value to stakeholders and our policyholders.''

As it shed these holdings, Sanlam began to build up new areas of operations in the assets management, estate and trust planning, unit trusts, and other financial services. In 1998, the company moved to simplify its structure, transferring its assets management business to Genbel Securities, or Gensec. The move raised Sanlam's stake in Gensec to more than 66 percent.

That deal came ahead of a more significant milestone in the company's history. In October 1998, Sanlam voted to demutualized and list as a public company on the Johannesburg Stock Exchange. That step was completed in November of 1998 in what was then South Africa's largest ever initial public offering.

Combining Social and Business Concerns in the 2000s

Sanlam's restructuring continued as it began a reorganization to regroup its operations around its four primary clusters in the early 2000s. That restructuring was largely completed by 2004. At the same time, Sanlam had also been undergoing a more surprising transition.

Starting in the early 1990s, Sanlam—the former financial and investment wing of the South African apartheid government—emerged as one of the spearheads of the country's Black Economic Empowerment (BEE) scheme. The company became one of the first to participate in the initiative, which was meant to shift a share of the country's wealth to its black population. In 1993, the company transferred a controlling stake in Metropolitan Life to Metlife Investment Holdings, a black-controlled vehicle. The transfer resulted in the creation of a new company, New Africa Investments Limited, or NAIL, which remained a partner in Sanlam's BEE initiatives through the turn of the 21st century.

Sanlam's embracing of the BEE appeared surprising. Yet a number of observers pointed out the similar circumstances of the Afrikaners at the turn of the 20th century and the country's black population at the turn of the 21st century. For these observers, it seemed only fitting that Sanlam, founded as an empowerment initiative for the country's Afrikaners, should now do the same for the country's blacks.

While most of Sanlam's competitors, including Old Mutual, had turned to the international market for the growth in the 1990s and early 2000s, Sanlam focused on developing its operations in its newly expanded domestic market. The company's international move remained largely limited to its acquisition of Merchant Investors, a Bristol, England-based life insurance and asset management group.

Meanwhile, as part of its domestic expansion, Sanlam became one of the first companies in the country to meet the government's black ownership guidelines, which called for all companies to achieve minimum black ownership levels of 10 percent by the end of the first decade of the century. In 2004, the company sold a 10 percent stake in itself to the empowerment black consortium Ubuntu-Botho. Sanlam hoped to reestablish its place a central figure in South Africa's economy in the new century.

Principal Subsidiaries

Fundamo; Gensec Bank; Gensec Property Services; Hichens Harrison Ltd; Innofin; Io investors; Merchant Investors; Punter Southall; Sanlam Collective Investments; Sanlam Employee Benefits; Sanlam Investment Management; Sanlam Life; Sanlam Multi Manager Portfolios; Sanlam Namibia; Sanlam Personal Portfolios; Sanlam Private Investments; Sanlam Property Asset Management; Sanlam Trust; Santam.

Principal Competitors

J.P. Morgan Chase and Co.; Fortis N.V.; General Electric Capital Services Inc.; Prudential Financial Inc.; AEGON N.V.; CDC IXIS Capital Markets; Westpac Banking Corp.;

Landesbank Berlin-Girozentrale; Northwestern Mutual Life Insurance Co.; Power Corporation Of Canada; Lincoln National Corp.; DnB NOR ASA; Standard Chartered Bank Singapore; Td Securities Inc.; Citigroup Inc.

Further Reading

Bolger, Andrew, ''Sanlam Buys UK Life Office,'' *Financial Times*, October 8, 2003, p. 26.
Degli, Nicol Innocenti, ''Sanlam Sells Stake to Black Consortium,'' *Financial Times*, December 5, 2003, p. 30.
''Fashioning the New Sanlam,'' *CBN*, October 1998.
Formby, Heather, ''Leaner Sanlam to Focus on Financial Services,'' *Business Times*, December 8, 1996.
Hogg, Alec, ''Afrikaners No Longer Dominate Sanlam Boardroom,'' *Moneyweb*, May 28, 1999.
Klein, Marcia, ''Reluctant Sanlam Forced into the Market Spotlight,'' *Business Times*, December 7, 1997.
Lamont, James, ''Boardroom Coup at Sanlam,'' *Financial Times*, December 10, 2002, p. 13.
——, ''Hands Across the Ocean but Not the Land,'' *Financial Times*, July 18, 2001, p. 14.
Mallet, Victor, ''Sanlam Announces SA's Largest IPO,'' *Financial Times*, October 29, 1998, p. 26.
''Sanlam a Hungover Giant,'' *CBN*, April 1998.
Seeger, Dina, ''Sanlam Makes Moves to Grow Market Share,'' *Business Times*, February 28, 1999.

—M.L. Cohen

School Specialty, Inc.

W6316 Design Drive
Greenville, Wisconsin 54942
U.S.A.
Telephone: (920) 734-5712
Toll Free: (888) 388-3244
Fax: (920) 882-5863
Web site: http://www.schoolspecialty.com

Public Company
Incorporated: 1950 as Universal Paper and School Supply
Employees: 2,800
Sales: $907.5 million
Stock Exchanges: NASDAQ
Ticker Symbol: SCHS
NAIC: 424120 Stationery and Office Supplies Merchant

School Specialty, Inc., is a publicly traded, direct marketing education company based in Greenville, Wisconsin. It offers more than 80,000 products, essentially anything other than textbooks, serving the pre-kindergarten through high school market through catalogs and the Internet. Product offerings are split between general school supplies and specialty products. Offerings include art supplies, classroom supplies, school furniture, instructional materials, educational games and software, academic calendars, audiovisual equipment, physical education equipment, and indoor and outdoor equipment. School Specialty sells to schools as well as individuals. It mails more than 40 million catalogs each year, and its online operation offers both an educational portal and an e-commerce web site.

1950s Origins

School Specialty was established in 1950 by Ed Schrede as Universal Paper and School Supply. The company changed hands in 1968 and the new owners changed the name to Valley School Supply. Because selling school supplies was a seasonal business—with virtually all net income earned from May to October—Valley over the course of the next 20 years attempted to diversify by opening retail stores and selling to churches. Unfortunately, the noncore businesses all lost money, so that by 1988 the company was losing a million dollars a year and its debts exceeded assets. In essence Valley was bankrupt, although it did not yet need protection from creditors. It was at this point that Dan Spalding, the man instrumental in the growth of School Specialty, entered the picture.

Spalding's father was one of Valley's owners and he convinced the other investors to hire his son to attempt a turnaround. It was hardly an act of nepotism, his son having already demonstrated great skill as an executive. While just a high school student, Spalding in 1975 bought an apparel company called Downers—the name referring to the business's basement location in an Appleton, Wisconsin theater. Here, Spalding and partner Kim Vanderhyden produced T-shirts with school logos that they sold to college bookstores and sporting goods stores. The small company built its own sales force and began mailing a catalog, so that within five years sales grew from less than $200,000 to $20 million. Spalding now took a pivotal step, paying $5 million in 1980 to acquire Jansport, which produced outdoor equipment like tents, sleeping bags, and backpacks. It was the backpacks that interested Spalding, because they were popular with high school and college students who used them as book bags. He dropped the other lines, turned the sales focus from sporting goods stores to mass merchants, and hired a new advertising agency to target a younger market. The improvement in business was dramatic, as Jansport's sales grew to $20 million by 1985. The company attracted the eye of V.F. Corporation, known for Wrangler and Lee jeans, which offered to buy the business for more than Spalding and Vanderhyden thought it was worth. They accepted and Spalding stayed on as chief executive officer until 1988 when he received the call from his father at Valley School Supply.

In a move reminiscent of what he had done at Jansport, Spalding upon taking over at Valley began to cast off the money-losing parts of the business. Over the course of the next two years he sold or closed down seven businesses, resulting in employment being trimmed from 180 to 80 and revenues dropping from $35 million to $22 million. Although smaller, the company was focused on the education market and once again a profitable concern. Spalding was now ready to grow the company through acquisitions. His first deal came in 1991 with the purchase of Western School Supply, followed by two more

Company Perspectives:

School Specialty is forging an exciting era in the educational resources market as a family of brands focused on helping educators to help students succeed.

acquisitions that year and another three in 1993. Annual sales reached the $100 million mark by 1994.

A New Name and an Acquisition Spree in the 1990s

In 1995 Valley acquired a Salina, Kansas-based company called School Specialty, and Spalding elected to adopt that name for his rapidly growing business. It was also in that year that the company made an important change in strategy. For years it had sold its product lines to school districts, but now there was a trend developing in education called site-based management, which allowed teachers to begin making some purchasing decisions. To tap into this movement, School Specialty established an initiative called Classroom Direct to sell directly to teachers through a catalog. At the same time, Spalding sold the company's string of 40 Valley School Supply stores, which no longer fit into the new business model. To enter the pre-kindergarten market the company bought Childcraft from Disney Co. in 1997, and to add art supplies it acquired Sax Arts and Crafts in the same year. School Specialty also gained a presence in the British market in 1997 through the acquisition of Don Gresswell, Ltd. As a result of these transactions, revenues increased to $120 million. Spalding and his team sensed that they could achieve even more, however, and established a sales goal of $300 million. Reaching that target required an infusion of new capital, but just as Spalding began scouting private equity firms he was approached by U.S. Office Products (USOP) with a buyout offer, which was accepted.

USOP was a new company, founded in 1994 to create a national office products supplier. It went public in February 1995, and within two years completed 35 acquisitions. USOP took a hands-off approach to School Specialty, allow Spalding to grow the business as he saw fit. As it turned out, School Specialty would be part of the USOP fold for only two years. During that time, it used USOP's resources to make 15 acquisitions worth $200 million. Then, in January 1998, USOP decided to change course. It had expanded in any number of directions, owning such diverse interests as a print management company, a computer networking company, and a business travel agency. Management now decided to focus on its core office products business and as part of a restructuring effort elected to spin off four of its divisions as separate public companies: Aztec Technology Partners Inc., Navigant International Inc., Workflow Management Inc., and School Specialty Inc. As its share of a June 1998 public stock offering, School Specialty emerged with $34.2 million, earmarked to help the company expand its geographic reach, especially into California, Texas, and Florida, the biggest states in education expenditures.

Although it now lacked the deep pockets of USOP, School Specialty did not let up in its drive to achieve growth through acquisitions. To run the business on a day-to-basis, Spalding brought in David VanderZanden, former president of Ariens Company, an outdoor lawn and garden equipment manufacturer, to serve as president and chief operating officer. Shortly before the spin-off, School Specialty bought the catalog division of Education Access, Inc., and afterward completed two significant acquisitions. The first was the $16.5 million purchase of Hammond & Stephens, Co., a 100-year-old company that made educational forms, including school gradebooks, teacher plan books, student assignment books, school year calendars, and award certificates. The second deal added a much younger company, two-year-old Teacher DeskTop, which offered planning software for teachers in formats such as calendars, scheduling forms, grade books, teacher lesson plans, student communications, and parent communications. The most significant acquisition of the year, however, took place later in the summer when School Specialty bought its largest competitor, cataloger Beckley-Cardy Group, for $78.1 million in cash and the assumption of $56.6 million in debt. Duluth, Minnesota-based Beckley-Cardy was generating annual sales in the $175 range, compared with School Specialty's sales of $310 million. Aside from the significant boost to the balance sheet, the addition of Beckley-Cardy got School Specialty involved in science materials though the pickup of Frey Scientific and fulfilled a goal of increasing market penetration in two key regions, the South and Southwest. Moreover, School Specialty grew its customer base, resulting in greater buying power and other efficiencies.

In 1999 School Specialty continued its aggressive pursuit of external growth while launching important initiatives from within. The company paid $23 million to add Sportime, LLC, which offered four catalogs: *Sportime,* targeting elementary and middle school students; *Chime Time,* for the pre-school and early childhood market; *Abilitations,* devoted to products for physically challenged children; and *Active Minds,* which offered a range of creative movement-oriented products for preschool and grade school children. Next, School Specialty acquired SmartStuff Development Company, a developer of security software limiting children's computer access, followed by the addition of a pair of California-based school supply companies: Holsinger Inc., which had been selling school furnishings in northern California for 50 years, and Audio/Graphics Systems, seller of school furnishings and audiovisual equipment in southern California. To support its growth, School Specialty also paid $2.6 million in 1999 to acquire a combined warehouse and distribution facility in Appleton, Wisconsin.

Turning to the Internet in the Late 1990s

School Specialty also launched a pair of Internet-based operations in 1999. the first, Classroom Direct.com, was launched in January to sell school supplies to school districts, as well as targeting teachers and parents. Management hoped the online approach would cut the cost of processing orders by 20 percent. It set a goal of doing a third of its business online, which if met would greatly lower the company's costs. In June 1999 School Specialty launched an online purchasing portal called JuneBox.com devoted to teachers and school districts, but after 11 months in operation it was expanded into a business-to-business portal, linking school supplies vendors to the United States' 16,000 school districts. The site allowed the parties to place bids and grant approval electronically.

In fiscal 1999 School Specialty recorded sales of $521.7 million and net income of $8.9 million. Fiscal 2000 would bring

Key Dates:

1950: The company is founded as Universal Paper and School Supply.
1968: The name is changed to Valley School Supply.
1988: Dan Spalding takes over the failing company.
1995: The company assumes the School Specialty name.
1996: The company is acquired by U.S. Office Products.
1998: The company goes public in a spin-off.
2002: Dan Spalding dies of a heart attack at age 47.
2004: McGraw-Hill's children's publishing unit is acquired.

a continuation of the company's robust growth, fueled by further acquisitions. School Specialty paid $34.3 million in cash to add Global Video, LLC. An even larger deal was completed later in 2000 with the $82.5 million acquisition of a major stake in wholesaler J.L. Hammett Company, a company producing $100 million in annual revenues. Revenues in fiscal 2000, which ended in April 2000, grew to $639.3 million and net income more than doubled over the previous year to $18.5 million, all without the benefit of the J.L. Hammett deal, which was completed after the close of the fiscal year. To support its rapid growth and build a national distribution system, the company began construction on a 330,000-square-foot warehouse and distribution center in Appleton that also would house the company's headquarters. Earlier in the year the company opened a 167,000-square-foot distribution center in Fresno, California, and expanded facilities located in Massachusetts and Texas.

School Specialty remained active on the acquisition front in 2001. For $6.7 million in cash and stock it acquired Envision, Inc. It paid $1.2 million for Premier Science, and another $156 million to add Premier Agendas, the largest provider of academic agendas in the United States and Canada. The company also sold off a pair of businesses that no longer fit its mix: U.K. subsidiary Don Gresswell, Ltd., and SmartStuff Software. In fiscal 2001 School Specialty posted revenues of $692.7 million and net income of nearly $12 million. But a recession was taking hold, the effects of which would lead to cutbacks in state spending on education. The company continued to expand but was unable to match its recent pattern of growth. Despite School Specialty's ability to prosper in difficult times—it would increase revenues to $767.4 million in fiscal 2002 and report net income of $21.8 million—Wall Street lost faith in the company's stock at the first hint of a setback. All along, Spalding had been disappointed in a languishing stock price, as the company was upstaged by high-tech ventures.

Although the 47-year-old Spalding had no apparent health concerns, he did report chest pains in 2001. Then in March 2002, on a skiing vacation to Colorado with his wife and VanderZanden and his wife, he collapsed in his condominium, stricken by a heart attack. He was rushed to a hospital but was soon pronounced dead. School Specialty's management team was shocked and distraught, but there was no disruption in the running of the business. Spalding had left behind a strong team and a sound corporate structure. VanderZanden took over as CEO on an interim basis as a search for Spalding's replacement was launched. The job was offered to VanderZanden, but he quickly turned it down, maintaining that he was comfortable with his current role in the company. Several months later, however, VanderZanden was finally persuaded to change his mind and he took the CEO position on a permanent basis. At the same time, interim chairman Leo C. McKenna assumed his post permanently. A New Hampshire-based financial consultant, McKenna became the first outside director to become chairman of the company, a move that was made with corporate governance issues in mind.

Little changed with VanderZanden in charge. The company continued to grow through acquisition. In 2002 School Specialty added ABC School Supply, which made products for the kindergarten to eighth grade market. School Specialty also bought the rest of J.L. Hammett in 2002. In February 2003 the company acquired Sunburst Video, a division of Sunburst Technology Corp., which made DVDs and videos on health, guidance, and other topics for the kindergarten through high school market. In May 2003 School Specialty acquired Select Agendas, a Canadian producer of student agendas. Early in 2004 the company added Calfone International, Inc., maker of multimedia and audiovisual systems.

Although School Specialty still declined to enter the textbook market, in which purchasing decisions were made at a state level and did not fit in with the company's sales approach, it did decide to become involved in educational book publishing. In early 2004 School Specialty bought the children's publishing unit of McGraw-Hill Cos., thereby adding supplementary materials such as literature books, workbooks, and manipulatives. The unit published as many as 700 books each year and possessed a backlist of some 5,000 titles. Not only did the acquisition of the unit add another niche to the School Specialty portfolio, it brought a new customer base the company could approach with its many other product offerings.

Revenues topped $870 million in fiscal 2003 and net profits soared to $39.6 million. Those numbers would show only modest improvement the following year, to $907.5 million in sales and $40.8 million in profits, but School Specialty remained on track to become a $1 billion company and enjoy even greater success in the coming years.

Principal Subsidiaries

ClassroomDirect.com, LLC; Childcraft Education Corp.; Frey Scientific, Inc.; Sax Arts & Crafts, Inc.

Principal Competitors

American Education Products, Inc.; Educational Insights, Inc.; Excelligence Learning Corporation.

Further Reading

Boardman, Arlen, "Wisconsin's School Specialty Inc. Overcomes Void Left by CEO's Death," *Post-Cresent,* July 28, 2002.

Del Franco, Mark, "Specialty Acquisitions," *Catalog Age,* August 1996, p. 6.

Kroll, Karen M., "Head of the Class," *Catalog Age,* February 1999, p. 1.

Mullins, Robert, "Appleton School Supply Firm Take Acquisition Course," *Business Journal-Milwaukee,* May 28, 1994, p. 12A.

Prestegard, Steve, "Everything But the Textbooks," *Marketplace,* August 15, 2000, p. 12.

—Ed Dinger

ServiceMASTER®

The ServiceMaster Company

3250 Lacey Road, Ste. 600
Downers Grove, Illinois 60515-1700
U.S.A.
Telephone: (866) 663-2000
Toll Free: (888)937-3783
Fax: (630) 663-2001
Web site: http://www.servicemaster.com

Public Company
Incorporated: 1947
Employees: 40,000
Sales: $3.63 billion (2004)
Stock Exchanges: New York
Ticker Symbol: SVM
NAIC: 561720 Janitorial Services; 561730 Landscaping Services; 561710 Exterminating and Pest Control Services

The ServiceMaster Company serves some 10 million households and businesses annually through 5,400 company-owned, franchised service centers overseeing Merry Maids housecleaning, Terminix pest control, and TruGreen and ChemLawn landscaping services. For many years the company's primary business was the cleaning of hospitals, but as growth in that field slowed in the 1980s, the company diversified its service offerings and geographic reach. By the late 1990s, however, the company was overextended and debt-laden. Efforts to streamline and refocus lead by CEO Jonathan Ward helped stabilize ServiceMaster in the early 2000s.

1930s Origins

ServiceMaster was founded by Marion Wade, who was born in 1898 and had worked as a minor league baseball player, a life insurance salesman, and a door-to-door peddler of pots and pans before getting into the business of cleaning and moth-proofing carpets in 1937. In 1942 Wade sold his first franchise license for his residential and commercial on-site carpet cleaning business.

Two years later Wade underwent an ordeal that would become a turning point in his personal life and in his business. After he was badly burned in an explosion of cleaning chemicals, Wade nearly lost his sight. While recovering from his accident, Wade experienced a religious conversion. ''I closed my eyes and I prayed,'' he wrote in The Lord Is My Counsel, his autobiography. ''I told the Lord I would turn everything over to Him. I said: ''I don't expect any miracles. I don't intend to sit back and expect You to run everything, but I want You to tell me how to run things and send my way the men I will need to do the job.' ''

Those men, it soon transpired, came from Wheaton College, a Bible college outside Chicago. Chief among them was Kenneth Hansen, a Wheaton graduate who was the acting rector of a small congregation in Chicago. Together, Wade and the bow-tied Hansen incorporated the company that would become ServiceMaster in 1947. In 1954 Hansen recruited a second Wheaton graduate, Kenneth T. Wessner, who had worked previously as an advertising salesman. In 1958 the three named their carpet-cleaning company ServiceMaster. The name they chose ''struck us as perfect in every area. Masters of service, serving the Master,'' Wade explained in his autobiography. At that time ServiceMaster franchised residential and commercial cleaning businesses. The following year the company sold its first franchise license in Great Britain, an operation that would form the core of ServiceMaster International.

Postwar Expansion into Hospital Maintenance

The business in which ServiceMaster would become best known and which it would eventually come to dominate was an outgrowth of the company's commercial cleaning operations. ServiceMaster got its start in the hospital housekeeping business when Wade gave a speech in the Chicago area. After the speech, he was approached by a nun, who suggested that Wade's company should offer its services to health care facilities. Hansen and Wessner were enthusiastic about the idea; after some research they learned that there was a company in New Zealand that had a large hospital cleaning business in Britain, Australia, and New Zealand. ServiceMaster formed a joint venture with Crothall, the firm from down under, to gain expertise in the field and help ServiceMaster break into the American market. Eventually, however, the joint venture fell apart.

Company Perspectives:

The company's objectives are to honor God in all we do; to help people develop; to pursue excellence; and to grow profitably.

Crothall took away a share in the American company, and ServiceMaster took away enough information about hospital cleaning to strike out on its own.

The company got its first contract to clean hospitals in 1962, when the Lutheran General Hospital in Park Ridge, Illinois signed on. With this move, ServiceMaster became a pioneer in the industry of contracting to clean institutions, also known as outsourcing. The company offered its clients lower costs, higher productivity, and better employee morale. In that same year ServiceMaster also sold stock to the public for the first time.

Rapid Growth in the 1970s

In 1970 ServiceMaster sold its first nonhospital cleaning franchise in Japan. Eventually, ServiceMaster would franchise operations in 30 countries around the world.

By 1971 ServiceMaster had contracts with more than half the hospitals that looked to outsiders for their cleaning and the company had notched record profits of $1.2 million. Its arena for growth looked unlimited, since nine-tenths of all U.S. hospitals still handled cleaning themselves and, indeed, throughout the decade of the 1970s ServiceMaster would average an increase in earnings of more than 25 percent a year.

ServiceMaster's founder Marion Wade died in 1973, and his two associates, Kenneth Hansen and Kenneth Wessner, moved up to chairman and president/chief executive officer, respectively. By the following year the company had sold more than 1,000 franchise licenses in its consumer cleaning division, and by 1975 ServiceMaster's health care division had signed contracts with 466 hospitals to clean their premises. The company added another 42 medical clients in the first six months of 1976.

By 1979 earnings had reached $11 million and ServiceMaster had developed a method of doing business that was sensitive to the special needs of hospitals and also worked to its own advantage. The company provided cleaning equipment and supplies, as well as management and supervision of a hospital's own workers. The ServiceMaster system meant that hospitals got more efficient labor from their employees and also did not have to replace their own worn-out or outdated janitorial equipment. ServiceMaster ensured that their facilities stayed spotless, thereby bolstering public confidence in their care and preventing infections caused by improper cleaning.

Long-Range Plan Guides the 1980s

In 1980 ServiceMaster began the process of planning for the future by initiating the formation of a long-range growth plan, called ServiceMaster Industries 20, abbreviated and pronounced ''SMIXX.'' The company set up more than 50 committees of three to seven employees each to set goals for the next two decades. As one part of this process the company vowed to reach $2 billion in revenues by 1990, from just $400 million in 1980.

Also in that year ServiceMaster branched out from its franchising of commercial and residential cleaning services and its health care management activities to add management services to educational institutions such as universities and school districts to its roster. Within three years the company had 90 academic customers signed up. In 1981 ServiceMaster also began offering its services to industrial customers with more than 1,000 employees and factories larger than one million square feet. Its first customers in this division were Appleton Electric in Chicago and Motorola in Franklin Park, Illinois. Both of these moves helped to broaden the company's potential customer base and insulate it somewhat from factors that might affect the health care industry. By 1987 these two new areas were providing nearly a third of ServiceMaster's revenues, but a much smaller percentage of its profits, because high start-up costs, for things such as training and equipment, ate up excess revenue.

By 1983 ServiceMaster's health care management offerings included laundry and linen services, physical plant operations and maintenance, clinical equipment maintenance, materials maintenance, and a fledgling food services sector, in addition to its traditional housekeeping services. Of the six divisions, housekeeping, laundry, and plant operations provided the bulk of the company's revenues. Most of the company's clients contracted for one or two of the services offered, and initial contracts were set for two years, to make the company's initial investment in a project worthwhile.

In May 1983 ServiceMaster signed its first contract to supervise home health care, in which hospital patients were discharged before their care was entirely complete as a cost-reducing measure. Also in that month the company signed up a large hospital chain, Voluntary Hospitals of America, for its standard management and housekeeping services, adding 135 new locations to its tally. Fees from contracted services, primarily to hospitals, made up about 97 percent of the company's revenues, with the remainder being derived from franchisees, who paid the company a monthly fee and purchased equipment and supplies from ServiceMaster.

Acquisitions in the Late 1980s

ServiceMaster's leadership underwent a shift in 1983, as Chief Executive Officer Kenneth Wessner moved up to chairman and former Wheaton College 45-year-old administrator C. William Pollard took over the helm. Within several years of Pollard's move to the top spot, ServiceMaster found that its core business of hospital cleaning had started to suffer, as strict controls on health care costs, some federally mandated, were implemented. As overall tighter hospital budgets cut into profits, ServiceMaster's growth in earnings rate slowed from its accustomed 20 percent to around 5 percent. In an effort to rejuvenate itself and return to its previous high rate of growth, ServiceMaster looked to expand the scope of its operations through acquisitions. Although the company traditionally had hewed to extremely conservative financial policies, taking on no debt whatsoever, its managers now began to consider the use of borrowed capital to finance the purchase of other companies.

Key Dates:

1942: Co-founder Marion Wade begins franchising his carpet cleaning business.
1947: ServiceMaster is incorporated by Wade and partner Kenneth Hansen.
1962: The company wins its first contract for cleaning hospitals.
1970: International expansion begins with franchise sold in Japan.
1986: Terminix pest control business is acquired.
1988: Merry Maids franchise is purchased.
1992: Chem-Lawn is acquired.
2001: ServiceMaster sells its management services division for $800 million.

In April 1986 the company moved to acquire a one-third interest in American Physicians Service Group, Inc., which marketed office machines and financial services to doctors and dentists. ServiceMaster agreed to advertise and sell American's products to medical personnel. In November 1986 ServiceMaster announced an agreement to purchase Terminix International, the country's second largest pest control concern, with 164 company-owned outlets and 150 franchised branches nationwide. ServiceMaster paid $165 million for the business, which reported annual sales of about $150 million. ServiceMaster hoped that Terminix would prove a good match with its residential and commercial cleaning businesses, as both operations could be used to generate clients for the other.

Another way that the company looked to compensate for its slowing growth was through financial restructuring. To maximize its returns to investors, ServiceMaster reconfigured itself as a publicly traded master limited partnership. In addition to freeing up cash for the company's acquisitions activities, this allowed ServiceMaster to avoid paying federal taxes and made it possible for owners of the company's stock to avoid double taxation, paying only a lower personal tax rate on their earnings. On the last day of 1986 the business of ServiceMaster Industries, Inc. was transferred to ServiceMaster Limited Partnership. In response to this move, the company's stock made some of the largest gains in the market in the first days of 1987, when it first moved from over-the-counter trading to the Big Board of the New York Stock Exchange.

ServiceMaster made a second large acquisition when it spent $40 million on American Food Management, a company that ran cafeteria facilities in educational institutions. In an effort to make its hospital operations more profitable, ServiceMaster began to market compound contracts to its clients, in which they signed up for several of the company's services all at once, increasing efficiency. These "Support Service" contracts were slow to gain popularity, enticing just 12 of ServiceMaster's 1,300 hospital customers by early 1987, but the company remained confident that the program would eventually win converts. By the end of 1987 company revenues had reached $1.4 billion.

As the hospital services sector, which made up 60 percent of ServiceMaster's revenues, grew more competitive in the late 1980s, ServiceMaster's market share became more and more dependent on the company's ability to provide quality service at a low price. The company relied on its extensive employee training programs and ongoing product and equipment development to maintain its competitive edge. ServiceMaster used videotapes, audiotapes, and thick training manuals that broke tasks, such as washing a floor, down into detailed five-minute steps to assist its workers. To remind employees at all levels that the most humble tasks lay at the core of the company's success, each employee invested at least one day every year performing a company service. In addition, ServiceMaster worked to keep its equipment state-of-the-art, developing new and more effective germicides, a battery-powered vacuum cleaner, and a longer-lasting, easier-to-use fiberglass mop handle. Training and innovation were designed to keep productivity and profits high.

Despite these efforts, however, the amount of money generated by the company's hospital cleaning operations continued to drop and revenues crept up just 7 percent in the first nine months of 1988. At the end of that year ServiceMaster reported that changes in the ways medical services were provided and paid for had resulted in smaller markets for services at the company's existing clients and delays in signing contracts with new clients. In addition, for the first time ServiceMaster had to terminate some clients for failing to pay their bills. Given these factors, the company's food service, clinical equipment maintenance, and home health care contracting operations had stronger returns in 1988 than its housekeeping services.

Expansion into Residential Services in the Late 1980s

In response to this situation, ServiceMaster continued its policy of diversifying its operations to arenas other than health care facilities. Following its purchase of Terminix, which primarily handled residential pest control, the company acquired another home-based business, "Merry Maids," in 1988. Founded in Omaha, Nebraska, in 1980, Merry Maids had built up a franchise network that specialized in cleaning customers' homes once a week, twice a month, or for special occasions. The company hoped that this purchase would further cement its standing in the home services industry and increase the amount of synergy generated by its different parts.

In June 1988 the company took another step in this direction when it purchased a Memphis-area home appliance maintenance and plumbing service, with about 400 customers. ServiceMaster renamed the company the ServiceMaster Home Systems Service. For $500 a year, the company promised to unclog toilets, fix leaky faucets, and handle any other necessary home repairs. After a big marketing push, the company was able to sign up customers at the rate of 40 a month. ServiceMaster made a much larger commitment to this field in April 1989, when it purchased American Home Shield, a California company that had been providing home warranties since 1971. ServiceMaster paid $120 million for the company, which had 200,000 home service contracts to its credit by 1990.

In that year ServiceMaster's health care operations provided just 40 percent of the company's earnings, down from 90 percent a decade earlier. One aspect of the health care business that did show potential for growth was the home health care subsidiary. ServiceMaster had 60 programs in place by the end of the 1980s, many of them joint ventures with a number of hospitals. Since home health care was so different from normal hospital operations, administrators were more willing to bring in outside specialists to assist in managing their programs.

Early 1990s Acquisitions

Acquisitions paced ServiceMaster's annual growth in the early 1990s as the company sought profitable new service niches. As traditional sectors matured, they comprised an ever-smaller slice of ServiceMaster's operating income, shrinking to barely one-third by 1996. The company augmented its home services division with the November 1990 purchase of two divisions of Waste Management, Inc.: a pest control business, and TruGreen, a lawn care service with commercial and residential customers. TruGreen's lawn operations complemented ServiceMaster's own exclusively residential lawn care division, which it had inaugurated in 1984.

The company branched out into another field it considered ripe for significant growth when it entered the child care business in 1990 by purchasing the GreenTree Preschool in Wheaton, Illinois. Using this facility as a base, ServiceMaster then opened additional child care centers in corporate settings in the Chicago area, providing benefits to employers and their workers.

ServiceMaster also purchased a 22 percent interest in the privately held Norrell Corporation in December 1991. Norrell provided temporary office and light industrial employees through a network of 250 company owned and franchised temporary agencies and also augmented ServiceMaster's home health care operations with 95 agencies that provided medical workers for residential settings. By the end of 1996 ServiceMaster affiliates were providing management support to more than 2,500 clients.

The acquisition-hungry company purchased its largest lawn care rival, ChemLawn, from Ecolab for $104 million in 1992. The 1996 purchase of Barefoot Inc. for $232 million further solidified ServiceMaster's leading position in this market. The company also added an inspection service and an in-home furniture repair company to its roster of residential offerings in the 1990s.

International growth was achieved through joint ventures and subsidiary companies. In the 1990s ServiceMaster focused on penetration of Europe, forming operations in Germany, Austria, Switzerland, and the United Kingdom. The conglomerate also hoped to expand into Asian and Pacific Rim countries by the end of the decade.

In 1993 Carlos H. Cantu succeeded William Pollard as CEO. Pollard, who had transformed ServiceMaster from a maturing company into a fast-growing, highly profitable leader of the service industry, continued as chairman. By this time it had become clear that ServiceMaster's corporate structure, the limited partnership, which had provided marked tax benefits when it was instituted, subsequently had made the company unattractive to institutional investors. The company, therefore, began to search for a way to restructure itself that would eliminate the barriers to investment by other companies. The partnership's shareholders approved a plan of reorganization that would reincorporate ServiceMaster as a corporation in December 1997.

Returning its attention to the health care industry mid-decade, ServiceMaster purchased VHA Long Term Care, a nursing home management company, in 1993 and formed Diversified Health Services through the union of its hospital and home health divisions in 1994. This division enjoyed a comeback during the 1990s, chalking up seven consecutive years of 40 percent plus increases in profits.

Overall revenues increased from $1.8 billion in 1990 to nearly $3.5 billion in 1996, and net income more than doubled from $94.4 million to $245.1 million. ServiceMaster appeared poised to take advantage of several social, demographic, and economic trends in the late 1990s. As Cantu and Pollard wrote in their 1996 letter to shareholders, "The need for time-saving home services and the increase in the number of elderly Americans, coupled with fiscal pressures which are forcing institutions to 'do more with less,' create ongoing demand for our services."

Changes in the New Millennium

Despite their optimism, however, the end of the 20th century proved a difficult time for ServiceMaster. In 1999 Carlos Cantu developed cancer and stepped down, turning the reins over to his predecessor, C. William Pollard. Pollard continued to run the country until 2001, when he turned it over to Jonathan Ward, who came to the company from R.R. Donnelley & Sons Co. Ward confronted a significant challenge: how to integrate the different parts of the company and ensure their work smoothly together while helping the company get out from under debt.

Ward's difficulties were compounded by two acquisitions ServiceMaster had made in 1999. LandCare USA, a landscaping business, and American Residential Services (ARS), an amalgamation of heating, cooling, plumbing, and electrical services, initially boosted ServiceMaster's revenues by 20 percent. However, both businesses proved difficult to integrate into the ServiceMaster family of companies. They were both originally loose conglomerations of relatively independent firms whose central business functions needed to be brought together in a single system to eliminate inefficiencies. LandCare USA proved especially difficult because the hundred little independent landscaping businesses that comprised the organization had never been integrated in the first place. As a result of LandCare's chaotic organization, ServiceMaster had to dedicate a lot of resources to restructuring. Profits slipped as a result, and ServiceMaster's stock dropped precipitously for the first time in almost 30 years.

Between 1998 and 1999 the difficulties posed by LandCare and ARS—as well as other problems experienced by the company—caused profits to slip. Wall Street responded by downgrading ServiceMaster's stock from buy to hold. Between 1999 and 2000 the company's stock dropped 50 percent in value. In the third quarter of 2000, ServiceMaster announced that its profits fell by 29 percent. In October of that year stock prices for the company were near a 12-month low; around $8 a share as opposed to $25.50 a share at its highest point in 1998. Sales for the year remained virtually flat.

As a result Ward began taking ServiceMaster in different directions. Instead of acquisitions, the new CEO turned toward e-commerce as a way to bring the company back to profitability. Early in 2001 he introduced WeServeHomes.com, a way for customers to book ServiceMaster services online, twenty-four hours a day, seven days a week. It also introduced customers to other corporate services; if a customer booked for pest control, for instance, the website could also introduce house-cleaning services or lawn care without high-pressure sales tactics. Company executives announced that over 90 percent of existing customers who used the website also signed up for additional services.

Ward also introduced other incentives to help attract both customers and investors. Customers received warrantees on work performed and better customer service. Investors received high dividend payments. Perhaps Ward's most important move, however, was in selling the company's Management Services division to Aramark in 2001 for $800 million. Funds from the sale could then be used to pay down debt.

One sign of ServiceMaster's continuing standard of performance lay in the fact that investor Warren Buffet bought up large quantities of ServiceMaster shares through his company Berkshire Hathaway between 2003 and 2004. Buffet was attracted to the stock, a spokesperson for his company explained, because of its high dividend yield. Despite the fact that profits remained relatively flat, ServiceMaster stock continued to trade at higher than the market average in comparison to its projected income.

Principal Operating Units

TruGreen ChemLawn; TruGreen LandCare; Terminix; American Mechanical Services; ARS Service Express/Rescue Rooter; American Home Shield; ServiceMaster Clean; Merry Maids; AmeriSpec; Furniture Medic.

Further Reading

''Aramark Buys ServiceMaster Unit,'' *Plumbing & Mechanical,* November 2001, p. 18.

Arndorfer, James B., ''Eternal Rewards at ServiceMaster,'' *Crain's Chicago Business,* May 19, 2003, p. 1.

''As ServiceMaster's Chairman, Mr. Wessner Combined His Faith in God with a Strong Work Ethic,'' *Modern Healthcare,* September 14, 1992, pp. 32–33.

Dubashi, Jonathan, ''God Is My Reference Point,'' *Financial World,* August 16, 1994, pp. 36–37.

Garza, Melita Marie, ''Illinois-Based Building Maintenance, Services Firm's Income Plunges 29 Percent,'' *Chicago Tribune,* October 26, 2000.

Gelfand, M. Howard, ''Growing ServiceMaster Industries, Inc. Thrives by Calling on God and Hospitals,'' *Wall Street Journal,* January 23, 1973.

Henkoff, Ronald, ''Piety, Profits, and Productivity,'' *Fortune,* June 29, 1992, pp. 84–85.

Murphy, H. Lee, ''Trugreen's Poor Results Leave ServiceMaster Blue,'' *Crain's Chicago Business,* May 14, 2001.

Oneal, Michael, ''ServiceMaster: Looking for New Worlds To Clean,'' *Business Week,* January 19, 1987.

Ozanian, Michael K., ''ServiceMaster: Gearing Up For a New World,'' *Financial World,* November 27, 1990, p. 16.

Pollard, C. William, ''The Leader Who Serves,'' *Strategy & Leadership,* September–October 1997, pp. 49–51.

Puente, ''Against the Odds,'' *Hispanic Business,* September 1997, p. 16.

Rudnitsky, Howard, with Christine Miles, ''. . . Who Help Themselves,'' *Forbes,* March 3, 1980.

''ServiceMaster: Focus on Employees Boosts Quality,'' *Business Marketing,* April 1988.

Siler, Charles, ''Cleanliness, Godliness, and Business,'' *Forbes,* November 28, 1988.

Skolnik, Rayna, ''Marketing Cleanliness with Godliness,'' *Sales & Marketing Management,* December 5, 1983.

Tice, Carol, ''The Lean, Clean Service Machine,'' *National Home Center News,* August 10, 1998, p. 40.

Wade, Marion E., and Glenn D. Kittler, *The Lord Is My Counsel: A Businessman's Personal Experiences with the Bible,* Englewood Cliffs, N.J.: Prentice Hall, 1988.

Wagner, Mary, ''Surviving Through Diversity: C. William Pollard Won't Let ServiceMaster Become Extinct,'' *Modern Healthcare,* January 15, 1988, p. 64.

—Elizabeth Rourke
—updates: April D. Gasbarre; Kenneth R. Shepherd

Smith & Hawken, Ltd.

4 Hamilton Landing, Suite 100
Novato, California 94949-8256
U.S.A.
Telephone: (415) 506-3700
Toll Free: (800) 940-1170
Fax: (415) 506-3900
Web site: http://www.smithandhawken.com

Wholly Owned Subsidiary of The Scotts Company
Founded: 1979
Employees: 850
Sales: $145 million (2004 est.)
NAIC: 444220 Nursery and Garden Centers

A subsidiary of The Scotts Company, Smith & Hawken, Ltd. is a Novato, California-based company best known for its upscale gardening catalog. Over the course of 25 years, it has added retail outlets, a wholesale operation, and a web site where customers can shop and seek gardening advice. In addition to the specialty garden equipment that made the company famous, Smith & Hawken now offers plants, bulbs, housewares, work apparel, books, and furniture. The company operates 56 stores located in 21 states and the District of Columbia, as well as a number of store-within-a-store locations in high-end gardening centers. Under Scotts ownership, Smith & Hawken is taking steps to further position itself as a lifestyle brand.

Paul Hawken, a Child of the 1960s

Smith & Hawken was cofounded by Dave Smith and Paul G. Hawken, but it was the latter who was the driving force behind the foundation and early growth of the company. Born in 1946, Hawken was a young man during the 1960s when he became an entrepreneur by happenstance. Troubled by asthma, he found relief by changing the food he ate. He avoided the typical American diet in favor of natural foods, but found it overly difficult to shop. As he wrote in a 1987 article in *Inc.*, pursuing his diet meant ''spending 10 hours a week shopping at ethnic food stores, farm stands, Seventh-Day Adventist flour mills, and other distant vendors.'' Believing he was not the only one frustrated by the lack of natural foods in the marketplace, he decided in 1967 to start the first natural food store in Boston, one of the first in the entire country. With just $500 he established Erewhon Trading Company. (''Erewhon'' is ''nowhere'' spelled backwards, the name of Samuel Butler's 1872 novel of social commentary.) The store started slowly, taking in about $300 a day, but Erewhon tapped into a trend and within a few years Hawken opened more stores and became a wholesaler to supply his own outlets as well as others. His network of farmer-suppliers spread across 37 states, and his impact was felt across the country.

When Hawken sold Erewhon in 1973, it was doing $25,000 a day in sales. He spent the next couple of years out of the country, living in England and Japan. When he returned to the United States and began looking for a job, he quickly discovered that despite having started a successful business, employers did not care for his resume, which lacked a college degree or any salaried positions. By default, Hawken would have to become self-employed. He set himself up as a consultant, and trading on his success with Erewhon, he landed consulting jobs with several companies and helped in completing three turnarounds. Hawken was also an organic gardener by now, along with his friend Dave Smith. One day, another friend, John Heavons, complained about the difficulties of finding in the United States a certain heavy digging device made in England, where gardening was a passion and many garden tools were available. To fill this need, Hawken and Smith started a specialty garden tool catalog in 1979.

By one account Smith & Hawken started out with $40,000 in capital, by another $100,000. In any event, it was a shoestring affair, especially because Hawken, the chief executive, as a matter of principle, refused to borrow additional funds or take a salary, determined to make do with his seed money. He was also an iconoclast in his approach to the mail-order business. He rejected the strategy of renting a large number of lists and sending off hundreds of thousands of initial catalogs to do a sampling. From there, the best performing lists would be chosen and a much larger mailing done. But Hawken eschewed the use of rented lists in the beginning, preferring instead to build Smith & Hawken's own list by buying one-inch ads, costing $90 a piece, placed mostly in gardening and horticulture magazines.

Company Perspectives:

At Smith & Hawken, we believe in the beauty of the garden, whether five acres or one plant.

Only people who requested a catalog received one, and from this response, and orders from people who happened upon a catalog and purchased from Smith & Hawken, the company began to build its own list.

Smith & Hawken also took a different approach in putting together a catalog. Hawken explained in his *Inc.* article his misgivings about the current state of catalogs: "The copy was designed to make me feel that my life would be bereft if I didn't buy an electronic mail detector for my rural mailbox . . . Nor did I appreciate the come-ons about discounts and the 'surprise gift' to be included with my order, or photography so overdone that the actual looked a little shabby . . . And then there were the 800 numbers that reached a contract phone-service clerk who knew absolutely nothing about the products I was ordering." Instead, Hawken and his partner developed the kind of catalog that they would buy from. It was a simple black-and-white affair, and rather than mail out 500,000 to mostly uninterested consumers, it sent just 487 catalogs to people who requested them. In an industry where a 2 or 3 percent response rate was considered a success, Smith & Hawken received 283 orders from its initial mailing, a success rate well over 50 percent. The company kept placing its tiny magazine ads, which "didn't amount to much in themselves," Hawken wrote in *Inc.*, "but their persistence proved that we were still around and still doing business. People began to wonder, 'Well, what are these tools?' Slowly, ever so slowly, our list grew, and so did our revenues."

Fending Off the Competition in the 1980s

After it was in business for four years, Smith & Hawken was generating $1 million in annual sales. It had built its own list to 200,000 names, and only now did the company rent its first outside mailing list. Because the company had achieved some prominence, the mailing produced good results. By this time Smith & Hawken also had opened its first retail store in Mill Valley, California. The company's success in the gardening market did not go unnoticed, however. Brookstone Company, backed by the deep pockets of its corporate parent, Quaker Oats, took aim at Smith & Hawken. With 20 years of experience in the mail-order business selling tools, some of them garden-related, Brookstone, which had 400,000 mail-order customers compared with Smith & Hawken's 25,000, appeared to be a formidable challenger. But after testing out three different company names and mailing catalogs to one million customers, Brookstone failed to break through. According to Hawken, "Brookstone didn't have the permission of the marketplace. Zeal, experience, and tons of money were simply not a substitute." But Brookstone was not alone in its desire to take away Smith & Hawken's business. Several competitors arrived on the scene and over the course of a year and a half, gardeners were inundated by mailings from Smith & Hawken imitators. Smith & Hawken replied by dropping prices and tripling the number of catalogs it mailed. The strategy worked and within two years sales grew to $10 million and by 1987 Smith & Hawken was generating $30 million in annual sales.

All the while it was fending off upstart competition, Smith & Hawken recognized that gardening tools pitched to avid gardeners was a limited market, and the company took steps to expand into other areas without sacrificing its hard-earned identity. It added general gardening merchandise, bulbs, and furniture. Hawken himself designed the highly popular Monet garden bench. In 1988 the company began offering work clothes after a designer named Gib Mann, who had worked with outdoor manufacturers Sierra West and North Face, convinced Smith and Hawken that they should offer apparel. In the main catalog in 1988, the company tested the waters with a pair of gardening pants, which sold out. In the next catalog, the company added gardening shorts and a gardening smock. These items also sold out and Mann was brought in to become director of clothing. The company now offered a more extensive line of clothing, with the emphasis on practicality and only a secondary regard for fashion. Smith & Hawken offered cotton dresses and shorts, chambray shirts and jackets, fleece jackets, canvas shirts, denim jeans, Japanese farmer pants, clogs, canvas high-top boots, handkerchiefs, scarves, and Panama hats. The items were also moderately priced, with most costing under $50 and none more than $100.

Hawken used his success at Smith & Hawken as a platform to advance his ideas about socially responsible enterprises. He wrote a book, *Growing a Business,* published in 1987 and later turned into a public television series. He advocated environmentally sound business practices. In 1990 he launched an initiative that challenged the practices of the mail-order industry. Smith & Hawken catalogs would now rely on recycled paper and no longer would a new cover adorn a catalog that had not changed inside. Moreover, each catalog contained a postcard that consumers could use to have their names removed from the Smith & Hawken mailing list. Hawken's goal was to cut down on the amount of junk mail in America, and as a consequence reduce the number of trees used to make paper and slow the pace of landfills.

By the end of 1991 sales at Smith & Hawken were about $55 million. A second retail store had been opened in Palo Alto, and a warehouse store in Berkeley became the first outlet to offer the entire Smith & Hawken line. In addition, the company began building up its executive staff, bringing in veterans from LL Bean, Banana Republic, and Toys 'R Us to fill roles in operations, fulfillment, and marketing. At the start of 1992, Hawken relinquished the presidency to Mark Fasold, who also took on a newly created chief operating officer position. Hawken stayed on as CEO and chairman, but by March he decided to quit completely, saying he wanted to devote his time to public speaking and writing books to champion his views on business and the environment. With hindsight, it appeared that Hawken had been preparing for his departure for some time, and given his reputation for candor, most took him at his word, unlike many parting executives, when he said he was leaving for personal reasons.

Although it appeared that Hawken left the company he cofounded well positioned for future growth, in truth Smith & Hawken was losing money, due to disappointing sales in

Key Dates:

1979: The company is founded by Dave Smith and Paul Hawken.
1982: The first retail store opens.
1992: Paul Hawken leaves the company.
1993: CML Group acquires Smith & Hawken.
1999: DDJ Capital buys the company.
2004: The Scotts Company becomes the new owner.

clothing. In September 1992 Smith & Hawken discontinued its clothing catalog. The company was put on the block and in January 1993 direct marketer CML Group, best known for its NordicTrack fitness equipment subsidiary, bought the business for $15 million and incorporated it into one of its units, The Nature Company Group, which also sold nature-related books, compact discs, and gifts. The hope was for Smith & Hawken to achieve cost efficiencies by using the group's more advanced fulfillment and communications system. CML also wanted to grow sales through the retail side. Within the year Smith & Hawken opened two new stores in Los Gatos and San Diego, California.

Change in Ownership in the Late 1990s

By the end of 1997, Smith & Hawken was operating 25 retail stores and had established a presence on the East Coast, where the company had six outlets. During this period Smith & Hawken also branched into publishing, releasing a series of gardening books with Workman Publishing Co. Unfortunately for CML, the success of Smith & Hawken was the only bright spot in what had become a gloomy picture. NordicTrack had fallen out of favor in the home-exercise market, leading to the 1996 sale of assets: Britches of Georgetowne, a men's clothing retailer, and The Nature Company. CML lost more than $40 million in fiscal 1997 and in January 1998 announced that it had hired Lehman Brothers to help weigh strategic alternatives. In November CML sold the NordicTrack division, leaving only Smith & Hawken, which now had sales of $88 million, as its remaining property. Then in December 1998, CML filed for Chapter 11 bankruptcy protection, indicating that it planned to sell Smith & Hawken. The subsidiary was sold in February 1999 to Wellesley, Massachusetts-based DDJ Capital, along with the State of Wisconsin Investment Board.

With the change of ownership the executive ranks at Smith & Hawken were turned over. DDJ looked to cut back on the circulation of the company's catalog and to refine the merchandise mix. Clothing was cut back in order to better position the company's brand within the gardening market. Like CML, the new owners were also eager to expand Smith & Hawken's chain of retail stores. By early 2000 the company was operating more than 40 units. As the economy began to soften, however, business tailed off, leading to no new store openings and prompting a major overhaul in 2001. A new chief executive, Barry Gilbert, was hired to revive the fortunes of Smith & Hawken. He brought 25 years of experience to the task, having held executive and management positions at Warner Bros. Studio stores, May Department Stores, Federated Department Stores, and Sharper Image, where as the No. 2 executive he was instrumental in building up it profits and stock price.

Under Gilbert, Smith & Hawken enjoyed success on a number of fronts. It bolstered its online business, so that holiday sales in 2002 improved by 40 percent over the previous year. The company opened four stores in 2002 and another ten in 2003. In addition, in May 2002 Saks Inc. opened 20 in-store Smith & Hawken shops in 20 of its department stores. Also in 2002 Smith & Hawken took steps to begin licensing its name, hiring New York Licensing Agency COP Corp. to pursue opportunities. The first licensed Smith & Hawken product, in keeping with its heritage, was an environmentally friendly wood flooring and decking made from reconditioned teak. In 2003 the company entered into the wholesale business, arranging to sell its products to the 300-unit The Home & Garden ShowPlace chain.

After five years of ownership by DDJ, Smith & Hawken changed hands once again. The Scotts Company, the largest supplier of lawn care products in the world, known for such products as Miracle-Gro plant food, Scotts Turf Builder, and Ortho Bug-B-Gone, agreed to pay $72 million and assume $14 million in debt to acquire Smith & Hawken. To some observers the marriage of upscale Smith & Hawken to mass market Scotts Co. seemed incongruous, but to Scotts's management the deal provided the parent with an opportunity to move beyond ''grow and kill'' garden products, soften its image—especially important in wooing women who comprised three-quarters of all gardeners, and claim a significant share of the steadily growing $21 billion garden-lifestyle industry in the United States. At the same time, Scotts planned to take advantage of its mass market contacts to beginning selling Smith & Hawken merchandise at retailers such as Home Depot, Lowe's, and Wal-Mart—Scotts's three largest customers. With Gilbert staying on as CEO, the plan was to add more retail outlets, continue to build on the wholesale business, and grow revenues from the $145 million projected for 2004 to the $500 million level.

Principal Competitors

Brookstone, Inc.; The Home Depot, Inc.; Williams-Sonoma, Inc.

Further Reading

Dworkin, Peter, ''A 'New Age' Look at Business,'' *U.S. News & World Report,* November 30, 1987, p. 51.

Ellison, Sarah, ''Scotts to Add Smith & Hawken in Bid for Upscale Garden Turf,'' *Wall Street Journal,* August 9, 2004, p. B3.

Hawken, Paul, ''Truth or Consequences,'' *Inc.,* August 1987, p. 48.

''Smith & Hawken: A Bumper Crop,'' *WWD,* September 17, 1990, p. 6.

Tate, Ryan, ''How Its Garden Grows,'' *San Francisco Business Times,* November 14, 2003, p. 3.

—Ed Dinger

Spectrum Organic Products, Inc.

5341 Old Redwood Highway, Suite 400
Petaluma, California 94954
U.S.A.
Telephone: (707) 778-8900
Toll Free: (800) 995-2705
Fax: (313) 782-3333
Web site: http://www.spectrumnaturals.com

Public Company
Incorporated: 1980 as Spectrum Naturals, Inc.
Employees: 59
Sales: $40.6 million (2003)
Stock Exchanges: Over the Counter (OTC)
Ticker Symbol: SPOP
NAIC: 311421 Fruit and Vegetable Canning; 311422 Specialty Canning

Spectrum Organic Products, Inc., comprises three major business segments: natural and organic foods under the Spectrum Naturals brand, essential fatty acid nutritional supplements under the Spectrum Essentials brand, and industrial ingredients for use by other producers sold under the Spectrum Ingredients name. The company is a leading producer of high-quality culinary oils and essential fatty acid products and has positioned itself as ''The Good Fats Company.'' The company's natural and organic foods products consist of olive oils and other culinary oils, salad dressings, condiments, and butter substitutes, such as Spectrum Organic Margarine and Spectrum Spread. All of the company's culinary products comprise healthy fats, contain no hydrogenated or trans fats, and are provided in a variety of sizes and flavors in both organic and conventional non-GMO (genetically modified organisms) offerings. The nutritional supplement products under the Spectrum Naturals brand include organic flax oils, evening primrose oil, borage oil, Norwegian fish oil, and other essential fatty acids in both liquid and capsule forms. The Spectrum Ingredients segment produces organic and conventional non-GMO culinary oils, organic vinegar, condiments, and nutritional oils offered to other manufacturers. The company sells its products either directly or through distributors to health food and specialty food stores, club stores, and retail chain and independent grocery stores in the United States, Canada, Europe, and the Far East. The company changed its name to Spectrum Organic Products following its merger with Spectrum Naturals in 1999.

Company Founding

Spectrum Organic Products, Inc. is the result of a 1999 merger between Spectrum Naturals, Inc., founded by Jethren Phillips in Petaluma, California, in 1980, and S&D Foods, Inc., which was incorporated in 1987. Jethren Phillips founded Spectrum Naturals, Inc. to bring nutrition and quality into the vegetable oil market. After launching the Spectrum Naturals brand in 1986 to produce quality vegetable oil, Phillips gradually expanded its product line to include condiments and salad dressings. At the same time, he created the Spectrum Essentials brand to produce and market nutritional supplements. Both brands were marketed as premium, healthy alternatives to conventional products stemming from the use of organic raw ingredients and the chemical-free extraction of the oils utilizing mechanical (expeller) pressing techniques. As a result, Spectrum Naturals became a leading innovator in the development and marketing of expeller-pressed and certified organic vegetable oils. The company also became a leading proponent of testing and verifying the absence of genetically modified organisms in its culinary oils.

Beginning in 1987, Spectrum Naturals introduced a series of new products, first marketing natural mayonnaise, then adding organic vinegar in 1989 and healthy fat salad dressings in 1996. Spectrum Spread, a healthy alternative to butter or margarine in baking, was introduced in 1993. Expanding into the market for nutritional supplements, Spectrum Naturals began a program of nutritional research and development, becoming the first company to market organic flax oil in the United States. In 1989, Spectrum also instituted its proprietary technology known as SpectraVac, which constituted an organic method of fresh oil extraction from seed without the use of chemicals that also minimized the impact of oxygen, light, and heat. The SpectraVac system employed micron filtration technology, which eliminated impurities without stripping out the beneficial compounds in the oil.

Company Perspectives:

Simply put, we're passionate about healthy fats. Our founder, Jethren Philips, started Spectrum over twenty years ago wit the purpose of making healthy oils available to the American public. That commitment and vision hasn't dimmed one bit. Whether artisan olive oils and trans-fat free spreads, or supplements like Flax Oil and other essential lipids, we're committed to bringing you the best there is.

In 1995, the company formed Spectrum Commodities, Inc. to serve other natural food producers with similar bulk ingredient needs. Spectrum Commodities' mission was to improve the integrity of the ingredients used in food manufacturing by offering, for example, expeller-pressed oils instead of those made with petroleum solvents. Spectrum Commodities also obtained exclusive distribution rights to new products such as organic palm and coconut oils and entered a distribution network that had rail car pumping stations and warehouses on both coasts. With this distribution network in place, Spectrum Commodities could provide industrial quantities of organic and expeller-pressed culinary and nutritional oils and organic vinegar to manufacturers, co-packers, and private label and food service accounts throughout the country.

Merger Sets New Course: Late 1990s

The company's current manifestation as Spectrum Organic Products, Inc. was formed on October 6, 1999 by the merger of Spectrum Naturals and Organic Food Products, Inc., based in Morgan Hills, California. The merger also included Spectrum Commodities, Inc., an affiliate of Spectrum Naturals, and Organic Ingredients Inc., an affiliate of Organic Food Products. Organic Food Products was incorporated in 1987 as S&D Foods, and changed its name to Garden Valley Naturals in 1995. The company operating as Garden Valley Naturals from 1987 to 1995 specialized in producing and marketing pesticide-free (''organic'') and preservative-free (''all natural'') pasta sauces, salsas, and condiments under the brand names ''Garden Valley Naturals'' and ''Parrot.'' In June 1996, Garden Valley merged with Organic Food Products, which also marketed a line of organic food products, including pasta sauces and salsas, together with dry cut pastas and organic children's meals. The surviving merged entity operated under the Organic Food Products Inc. name. In February 1998, Organic Food Products acquired the natural fruit juice and water bottling operations of Sunny Farms Corporation for cash and 566,667 shares of common stock. In addition, in 1997, Organic Food Products went public and was traded on the NASDAQ small cap market until being delisted in May 1999 due to non-compliance with the net tangible assets requirement. The company's common stock thereafter traded on the OTC Bulletin Board System until the October 1999 merger, upon which the two companies adopted the name Spectrum Organic Products, Inc.

The merger agreement was a change from the original plan, in which Organic Food Products was slated to acquire Spectrum's food division in May 1998. The acquisition collapsed, however, because the company was losing money and could not complete the takeover before an August 1998 deadline to conclude the agreement. The two companies continued discussions over the following year as Organic Food Products' stock plunged, dropping from $3.75 a share in August 1998 to 38 cents in December. As a result, Spectrum took the lead in the negotiations with its stronger finances and in a reverse acquisition bought Organic Foods in the form of a stock for stock exchange. Under the merger agreement, Jethren Phillips became chief executive officer and chairman of the board of the merged company. John Battendieri, president of Organic Food Products, would lead the new product and business development efforts and serve as a member of the board. The merger was expected to produce consolidated annual revenues of about $50 million in branded products and industrial ingredients for the organic and natural products industry. The terms of the agreement also provided management and board members with ownership of almost 88 percent of the company. The merger was designed to open new channels of distribution for both companies in an industry that was growing 20 percent a year as natural food products were spreading from health food stores to mainstream grocery chains.

Following the merger, the new company obtained an $11.6 million loan from Wells Fargo Bank to consolidate accounts, reduce debt, and provide capital for growth and began trading on the NASDAQ Bulletin Board under the trading symbol ''SPOP.'' Further, the merger had strengthened the positioned of the new company as a leading producer and marketer of organic foods, culinary oils, vinegar, and condiments under the Spectrum Naturals, Millina's Finest, Garden Valley Organic, Parrot Brand, and Grandma Millina's Kids Meals labels. In addition, Spectrum was a leading manufacturer and marketer of essential fatty acids nutritional supplements under the Spectrum Essentials label.

Strategic Alliances, Spin-offs, and Litigation in the 21st Century

In October 2000, Spectrum signed an exclusive agreement with Venice Maid Foods of Vineland, New Jersey, the first of many strategic alliances it planned to make to become the leading organic foods and nutritional supplements company in the industry. Under the agreement, Spectrum's industrial division, Organic Ingredients, would supply Venice Maid with all of its organic raw materials. In addition, Spectrum would serve as the exclusive master distributor for all of Venice Maid's organic products. In June 2001, however, Spectrum sold its tomato-based products and children's meals marketed under the Garden Valley Naturals, Parrot, and Millina's Finest brand to Acirca, Inc. to raise additional working capital to invest in its core businesses of essential fatty acids and supplement products. The sale made Acirca the nation's second-leading producer and marketer of organic pasta sauces with a 22 percent market share. Also in 2001, the company announced a series of new products, including organic omega-3 mayonnaise, organic hemp oil supplements, and nutritional supplements based on omega-3 rich flaxseed oils, GLA rich borage oil, and selected Chinese herbs such as black cohosh, wild yam, and black haw bark. The supplements based on traditional Chinese medicinal theory were packaged and offered under the marketing names Flax Relax, Cycle Balance, and Menopause Balance. Despite the introduction of new products, the company reported a net

Key Dates:

1987: Jethren Philips founds Spectrum Naturals, Inc.
1989: Spectrum Naturals introduces a new proprietary technology known as SpectraVac.
1995: The company establishes Spectrum Commodities, Inc.
1999: Spectrum Naturals purchases Organic Food Products, Inc. in a reverse acquisition.
2001: The company sells its tomato-based product lines to Acirca, Inc.
2002: An industrial accident results in the death of two employees; the company sells Organic Ingredients division to Acirca, Inc.
2004: Spectrum opens a new flaxseed production facility in Iowa.

loss of $5.2 million for 2001 versus a net loss of $2 million for the prior year. The increased loss stemmed primarily from the sale of the company's tomato-based product lines. Spectrum CEO Jethren Phillips explained the loss as reflecting several non-recurring write-offs associated with restructuring efforts to rid the company of underperforming assets.

In April 2002, the company experienced an industrial accident at its Petaluma manufacturing and bottling plant when two men died after being found unconscious in a stainless steel tank filled with deadly gas. Police investigators concluded that one man fell in while cleaning the tank and the other man followed while attempting a rescue. The tank was empty of oil at the time of the accident but was filled with argon. The inert gas, like nitrogen or carbon dioxide, is used to clean industrial vats by purging them of oxygen to eliminate bacteria. As a result of an investigation, the California workplace safety agency cited the company for multiple safety violations, concluding that Spectrum failed to provide proper training and safety equipment to employees who clean tanks to process flaxseed oil for use in a variety of nationally retailed organic food and health products. Spectrum subsequently appealed the $137,895 in fines proposed by the state Occupational and Safety and Health Administration, but in February 2004 Spectrum pleaded no contest to two counts of violating the California Labor Code Section 6425, requiring employers to provide, maintain, and ensure employees use required confined space equipment. As part of the terms of settlement, the company agreed to pay $375,000 in fines, restitution fees, and reimbursements to various state and county law enforcement and health and safety agencies. The settlement also imposed a probationary period during which Spectrum was required to ensure that all worker safety and health laws were upheld within its facilities. A large portion of the restitution payments went to the state of California to assist in the prosecution of other worker safety cases.

In May 2002, Spectrum sold its Organic Ingredients division to Acirca, Inc. The division included the company's industrial sales of organic fruits, vegetables, concentrates, purees, and certain private label products. Philips said that after the sale of Spectrum's tomato-based product lines to Acirca in June 2001, it became clear that Organic Ingredients no longer complemented the company's other operations. The sale of the business was anticipated to improve the company's working capital and allow Spectrum to focus funds on its core business of natural and organic fats and nutritional supplements business.

Return to Profitability under New Leadership

On September 1, 2002, Spectrum appointed Neil G. Blomquist as its new Chief Executive Officer. Blomquist had served as president of the company's branded divisions since Spectrum was formed in a 1999 four-way merger. Spectrum founder Jethren Philips, who stepped down as CEO, continued to serve as the chairman of the board. Under Blomquist's leadership, the company returned to profitability, earning a record net income for 2002 of $1.1 million compared to a net loss for the prior year of $5.2 million. Leading the way were increased industrial ingredient sales of culinary oils and vinegars, which rose by 30 percent over the previous year. Sales of consumer products also rose significantly for the company's culinary products and nutritional supplements. At the same time, Spectrum continued to diversify its product lines, introducing new varieties of organic salad dressings, dips, non-stick cooking spray, and toasted hazelnut and toasted pumpkin seed oils. The company's robust sales continued through 2003, increasing to a record $45.7 million compared to $40.5 million for 2002, an increase of 13 percent. Net sales for the company's Spectrum Ingredients Division rose by 31 percent, benefiting in part from mass media attention to the link between hydrogenated oils and obesity and cardiovascular disease. During 2003, several food companies issued press releases promising to reduce or eliminate hydrogenated oils from their packaged consumer products, which helped to direct attention to Spectrum's ingredient product lines. In addition, the trend toward healthy oils benefited the company's Spectrum Naturals line of packaged culinary oils, dressings, and butter substitutes, contributing to increased sales for these products by 19 percent over the previous year.

In March 2004, Spectrum provided an educational grant to support the first annual Nutrition and Health Conference. The conference, which was held March 11-13 by the University of Arizona Program in Integrative Medicine in conjunction with the Columbia University College of Physicians and Surgeons in Tucson, represented the first initiative on behalf of the company to further nutrition-based education to health care professionals. The company sponsored the conference with the aim of providing clinical relevance to nutrition and its role in health.

Spectrum Looks to the Future

The company also began a major commitment to and investment in a new Iowa-based future in flaxseed farming and processing. As a result, Spectrum entered into a joint venture with BIOWA Nutraceuticals, an Iowa-based company, with the aim of opening the world's largest production facility dedicated to organic, plant-based EFA oils. The joint venture signified a "back-to-the-future" business scenario with flaxseed formerly a leading Iowa crop five generations ago. In 2004, only a handful of farmers were growing flax again due to successful organic agriculture research trials conducted at Iowa State University. However, Spectrum anticipated this statistic would rise dramatically over the next decade to include hundreds of Midwest farms growing flax organically if its plans for regionalized flax production were achieved. The company believed this new marriage of agriculture with manufacturing would plant a new sustainable economy for the future. By relocating its 15-year-old processing operations to the Midwest, Spectrum planned to pay a 50 percent premium to flax farmers who converted to certified organic practices.

The new $4 million, 10,000-square-foot plant opened on October 12, 2004, after a ribbon-cutting ceremony featuring keynote speaker and Iowa Lieutenant Governor Sally Pederson. The company expected that the relocation of its production facility to Iowa would enable Spectrum and BIOWA Nutraceuticals to work directly with local farmers, including testing new flaxseed varieties. The move also meant that Spectrum could better meet the growing demand for its line of more than 20 certified organic flaxseed oil-based products sold nationally at natural and specialty product retail stores. The new plant, which was certified organic by Quality Assurance International according to USDA standards, would have the capacity to produce 60 tons of flax per day with the ability to expand to 120 tons per day. Because most flaxseed was produced by farmers in Canada or overseas, Spectrum and BIOWA believed their Midwest-based operation also would reduce transportation time and costs. After having positioned itself as the leading producer and marketer of organic and natural oils and condiments in North America with more than 175 products under its brand names, Spectrum's aggressive pursuit of new growth opportunities seemed to have assured that it would continue to prosper into the future.

Principal Divisions

Spectrum Naturals; Spectrum Essentials; Spectrum Ingredients.

Principal Competitors

ConAgra, Inc.; Hain Food Group, Inc.; H.J. Heinz Company.

Further Reading

''Acirca Acquires Millina's Finest Sauces; Second Largest Organic Pasta Sauce Joins Growing Portfolio,'' *Business Wire*, June 12, 2001.

Allday, Erin, ''Spectrum Loses $776,000 in 4-Way Merger,'' *Press Democrat*, August 18, 2000, p. E1.

——, ''Spectrum Organic Sales Improve,'' *Press Democrat*, March 15, 2002, p. E1.

Appel, Ted, ''Spectrum Naturals Buys Suitor Petaluma; Firm Ends Long Courtship,'' *Press Democrat*, October 9, 1999, p. E1.

——, ''Spectrum Organic Founder Steps Down,'' *Press Democrat*, September 3, 2002, p.E1.

Benfell, Carol, ''Petaluma Natural Food Merger Firm in Merger,'' *Press Democrat*, March 23, 1999, p. E1.

Del Rio, Javier, ''Police Search Insurance Files in Spectrum Probe,'' *Press Democrat*, June 20, 2002, p. B3.

Estrella, Javier, ''Petaluma Tank Deaths: Investigators Believe Second Man Died Trying to Rescue Friend: Probe of Tragic Accident Could Take Six Months,'' *Press Democrat*, April 27, 2002, p. A1.

Ginn, Mike, ''2 Die in Petaluma Tank Gas Accident,'' *Press Democrat*, April 26, 2002, p.A1.

Hay, Jeremy, ''Company Cited in Deaths of 2 Workers: Spectrum Organic Products to Appeal $137,895 Fine Levied by Cal-OSHA,'' *Press Democrat*, October 19, 2002, p. B1.

Lash, Steve, ''FDA Alerts Companies to Improper GM-Free Labels,'' *Food Chemical News*, December 24, 2001, p.11.

Lauer, George, ''Organic Food Producer Buying Petaluma Company,'' *Press Democrat*, May 16, 1998, p. E1.

''Organic Food Products, Inc./Spectrum Naturals, Inc. to Merge,'' *Business Wire*, February 18, 1999, p. 1.

''Spectrum Organic Products Partners with Venice Maid Foods,'' *Business Wire*, October 30, 2000.

''Spectrum Organic Products, Inc. Appoints New CEO,'' *Business Wire*, August 29, 2002.

''Spectrum Organic Products, Inc. Reports Settlement with Sonoma County District Attorney,'' February 4, 2004, p.1.

''Spectrum Organic Products Reports Fourth Quarter and Full Year Results,'' *Business Wire*, March 14, 2002.

''Spectrum Organic Products Reports Record Profits for 2002,''*Business Wire*, March 10, 2003.

''Spectrum Organic Products Reports Sale of Organic Ingredients,'' *Business Wire*, May 1, 2002.

''Spectrum Organic Products Responds to FDA Letter Regarding Use of Non-GMO Seal on Canola Oil Label,'' *Business Wire*, January 3, 2002.

—Bruce P. Montgomery

The Stop & Shop Supermarket Company

1385 Hancock Street
Quincy Center Plaza
Quincy, Massachusetts 02169
U.S.A.
Telephone: (781) 380-8000
Fax: (781) 770-6033
Web site: http://www.stopandshop.com

Wholly Owned Subsidiary of Ahold USA
Incorporated: 1925 as Economy Grocery Stores Corporation
Employees: 57,000
Sales: $11.17 billion (2003)
NAIC: 445110 Supermarkets and Other Grocery (Except Convenience) Stores; 551112 Offices of Other Holding Companies

The Stop & Shop Supermarket Company runs the largest grocery chain in the New England area of the United States; with more than 340 supermarkets and combination supermarket-general merchandise stores in Connecticut, Massachusetts, New Hampshire, New York, New Jersey, and Rhode Island. In 1996, Stop & Shop was acquired by Ahold USA, the largest grocery retailer on the eastern coast, itself a subsidiary of Dutch retail giant Royal Ahold N.V. Growing from a single corner grocer to a multi-billion dollar supermarket chain, Stop & Shop has offered its customers a wider variety and selection, along with better quality and value, in food and nonfood items than traditional grocery stores for more than 85 years.

Origins as Economy Grocery Stores

When Sidney R. Rabb went into his uncle Julius's business, it was a small chain of stores known as the Economy Grocery Stores Company, founded in Somerville, Massachusetts, specializing in the sale of grocery products. Such specialization was hardly new—the Great American Tea Company (later A & P) had begun to modify the traditional general store as early as 1859, and even the practice of chain store ownership dated back into the 19th century. The chains did not formally begin until after 1912, however, when A & P introduced the ''economy store,'' using efficient management and smaller store size to offer lower prices on a cash-and-carry basis—no credit, and no home delivery. The idea rapidly caught on across the country, and it was this merchandising trend that Julius Robbins, his brother Joseph, and his nephew Sidney Rabb followed after the war. Sidney Rabb introduced self-service to its stores in 1918, which pioneered the concept of modern supermarket. Following a period of instability, their chain, Economy, righted itself and, buoyed by the surging economy of the 1920s, began a program of rapid growth through acquisition in Massachusetts.

As chain store operators gained in strength they were soon able to convince manufacturers to sell to them directly instead of through the usual wholesalers, thus vastly reducing their costs and increasing the competitive advantage they already enjoyed over the traditional independent owner. Consumers preferred the lower prices of the chains; by the mid-1920s, Economy had expanded to 262 stores. In 1925 Sidney Rabb was named chairman, a post he would hold for the next 60 years. In the same year, Economy issued its first shares of public stock, and Norman S. Rabb joined his brother Sidney in the business, now called Economy Grocery Stores Corporation. Ten years later, Irving Rabb, youngest of the brothers, also joined the company. Economy's operations continued to gain momentum; the brothers bought a chain of meat retailers and gave them space in each of their grocery stores.

Although the Great Depression brought many industries to a standstill, the resulting need for tight household budgeting was in many respects a boon to the Economy chain stores. The Rabbs continued to expand with the purchase in 1932 of 106 Grey United Stores located throughout northern New England. The supermarket, a concept that had originated in Southern California, based its customer appeal on rock-bottom prices, increased product selection, self-service (the customer roamed about the store while the clerk remained at a cash register), and intensive advertising. To the storeowner, the new format promised streamlined operation and excellent overall profit. In 1935 the Rabbs opened New England's first supermarket in Cambridge, Massachusetts, in a converted automobile assembly

Company Perspectives:

The Stop & Shop Supermarket Company is proud to partner with the communities in which we operate to provide support for thousands of local organizations throughout the region. In addition, Stop & Shop's charitable giving program includes a long standing commitment to supporting hunger relief efforts and cancer research and treatment.

plant. First-year sales were nearly $2 million, equivalent to the revenue of 45 conventional stores.

Full Conversion to Supermarkets after World War II

The Rabbs built more of the new stores as fast as they could, calling them Stop & Shop Supermarkets. The program continued to do well until the onset of World War II in 1941, when the food industry was swept up in the war effort and had little money or manpower with which to expand. The labor shortage during the war years, however, proved to be an unexpected boon to the supermarket business, as customers grew accustomed to serving themselves in all departments of the store, including the meat section. Such total self-service created lower labor costs and an increased number of purchases per customer. When the war ended, Economy was well positioned to proceed with the conversion of its entire chain to the supermarket format, effectively reducing its number of stores while increasing total sales and profits. By 1947 annual sales topped $47 million and the company had changed its name to Stop & Shop, Inc., signaling its total commitment to the supermarket concept.

The postwar boom years saw another period of tremendous growth for Stop & Shop. In order to distribute products more efficiently, between 1948 and 1960 the company built a central bakery, a perishable goods distribution warehouse, and a grocery distribution center, all in strategic Massachusetts locations. Stop & Shop also quickly established itself in Rhode Island and Connecticut, and by the end of the 1950s the company was nearing $200 million in sales. The company made an important decision in 1961 to diversify outside the food business with its purchase of Bradlees, a small chain of discount department stores operating largely in shopping centers that already featured a Stop & Shop supermarket. The Rabbs saw in Bradlees a company based on the same high-volume, low-margin marketing used in the food industry. Their expertise soon turned a few moribund stores into a thriving chain. With the addition of new outlets each year, Bradlees' sales increased from $5 million to $107 million between 1962 and 1968.

Over the years Stop & Shop tried to develop and maintain excellent relations with the communities in which it did business. The company was one of the first to unionize in the 1930s; it created the Stop & Shop Foundation in 1951 to support various civic and cultural projects; and in 1967 it initiated its Consumer Board Program in response to growing public concern about health and environmental issues. In a further move to accommodate changing customer demands, in 1971 the company gave far greater autonomy to each of its store managers, freeing them to respond more directly to the needs of local customers. On the other hand, the company was twice sued for allegedly conspiring to fix the prices of certain grocery, meat, and dairy products. Both suits were settled.

Both Stop & Shop and Bradlees continued their robust growth into the mid-1980s. Building on an ever more sophisticated network of warehouse distribution centers, the two chains expanded their geographic range, their total number of stores, and their total sales. In addition, in 1968 and 1969, respectively, the company established the Medi Mart Drug Store Company and acquired the Charles B. Perkins Company, a 21-unit New England retailer of tobacco and sundries. A year later all four retailing chains were brought together as divisions of a newly renamed The Stop & Shop Companies, Inc., which at that point included 150 supermarkets, 52 Bradlees Department Stores, 10 Medi Marts, and 25 Perkins Tobacco Shops, together totaling about $750 million in sales. Four years later the company celebrated its first $1 billion year; it had doubled that figure by 1980.

Other acquisitions were not as successful. In 1978 Stop & Shop bought Off the Rax, a discount women's clothing store chain, but sold it after six less than spectacular years. Similarly, a venture into a more upscale segment of the department store world ended in 1987 with the sale of Almys, a 19-store chain the company had purchased just two years before. Despite a history of steady growth and good profits, Medi Mart and Perkins were also put on the block in the mid-1980s as Stop & Shop decided to concentrate its resources on its two biggest and most lucrative divisions, supermarkets and Bradlees. Bradlees reached a high of 169 units in 1987, combining with the 113 supermarkets to bring in $4.34 billion in sales.

In 1985 Sidney R. Rabb died and was succeeded as chairman by his son-in-law, Avram J. Goldberg. Goldberg and his wife Carol, who became president of the company, moved decisively to keep pace with the trend toward the "superstore," a greatly enlarged and further diversified model of the traditional supermarket. Superstores typically combined a grocery store with a general merchandise store. Stop & Shop's superstores—known as Super Stop & Shops—were immense, averaging 55,000 to 60,000 square feet in size, and were planned around a "street of shops" concept in which each class of product received its own well-defined and suitably decorated segment of the store and was offered to the consumer in an ever-larger variety of brands and packaging. In 1982 Stop & Shop completed its first superstore—considered to be the first superstore in New England. In certain respects this development brought shopping full circle back to the pattern of 100 years ago, when families made their progress through a series of neighborhood stores, each specializing in a different product line. The "street of shops" had simply moved indoors.

Taken Private in 1988

Stop & Shop took another step reminiscent of its past when, for the first time since 1924, it once again became a privately owned corporation. Responding to a hostile 1988 takeover bid by corporate raider Herbert Haft, Stop & Shop's board of directors enlisted the aid of Kohlberg Kravis Roberts & Company (KKR) in forming a privately held acquisition company to buy all outstanding shares for approximately $1.23 billion. The acquisition company merged with Stop & Shop, whose top management was largely unaffected. To pay down some of its

Key Dates:

1914: The Rabinovitz family began operations of the Economy Grocery Stores Company.
1918: Sidney Rabb introduces self-service to the stores, pioneering the concept of modern supermarket.
1925: Known now as the Economy Grocery Stores Corporation, the company goes public.
1947: Company becomes Stop & Shop, Inc.
1951: The Stop & Shop Foundation is established.
1961: Diversification outside the food business begins.
1982: The first Super Stop & Shop is opened.
1988: The company is taken private.
1991: Once again, becomes publicly traded company.
1996: Stop & Shop is acquired by Ahold USA, a subsidiary of Royal Ahold N.V.

hefty debt, Stop & Shop sold 70 Bradlees stores and eliminated 450 positions. In November 1989 the Goldbergs suddenly quit their jobs, reportedly because of differences between them and KKR officials, ending more than 70 years of family management. Lewis Schaeneman took over as chairman and CEO.

Stop & Shop became a public company once again in late 1991 through a public offering that sold 41 percent of the company for $212.5 million, the bulk of which was used to reduce debt at the still highly leveraged company. KKR retained control of the business following the offering. At the time of the offering Stop & Shop operated 117 stores in Massachusetts, Connecticut, Rhode Island, and New York, 62 of which were Super Stop & Shop combination stores. The company also owned the 130-unit Bradlees chain, but it was spun off to the public in the summer of 1992 in order to further focus on the core supermarkets and to further reduce Stop & Shop's $1.1 billion debt load.

Robert G. Tobin, who had become president of Stop & Shop in March 1993, added the title of CEO in May 1994 and the title of chairman in January 1995, as Schaeneman gradually retired. One day before Schaeneman's last day in office, around 60 FBI agents raided the company headquarters as an outgrowth of an investigation of possible mishandling of merchandise incentive funds paid by manufacturers through brokers to retailers. In June 1997 Stop & Shop—without acknowledging guilt—agreed to pay $700,000 to settle allegations over vendor promotions and temporary price reductions.

As Stop & Shop continued to improve its financial health in the mid-1990s, expansion once again became the watchword. In mid-1995 the company made plans to enter the highly competitive, highly fragmented greater New York City area through the opening of superstores. In November 1995 Stop & Shop acquired Purity Supreme, a chain based in North Billerica, Massachusetts, for about $255 million. To satisfy regulators, the company had to divest 17 overlapping stores, meaning that it gained a net 38 stores through the deal. The purchase also temporarily extended Stop & Shop's territory into New Hampshire, but the units in that state were soon sold off. Also gained with Purity was a 64-unit chain of Li'l Peach convenience stores, but this noncore operation was quickly divested, in mid-1996, to Tedeschi Food Shops Inc. of Rockland, Massachusetts. In December 1995 Stop & Shop spent $87 million for Melmarkets, which ran a Foodtown chain with 17 units on Long Island, thereby gaining its first foothold in the New York region.

New Ownership in the Mid-1990s

By this time the expanding Stop & Shop had caught the eye of the highly acquisitive Dutch global food retailing giant Royal Ahold N.V., which acquired Stop & Shop in its entirety, including the KKR stake, in July 1996 for $2.9 billion. Stop & Shop thus became another in a string of eastern U.S. grocery subsidiaries of Ahold. The Dutch company had first gained a foothold in the United States in 1977 when it bought the Bi-Lo chain in North and South Carolina and Georgia. Ahold then purchased the Pennsylvania-based Giant Food Stores, which operated under the Giant, Edwards, and Martin's brands, in 1981. Finast Supermarkets, of Ohio, Connecticut, New York, and Massachusetts, was bought in 1988. To gain regulatory approval of its purchase of Stop & Shop, Ahold agreed to sell 29 stores in Massachusetts, Connecticut, and Rhode Island, states in which Stop & Shop and Edwards had overlapping operations. Also in July 1996, William J. Grize, who had joined the company in 1967, was named president of Stop & Shop; he added the CEO title as well in December 1997, with Tobin remaining chairman.

Within days of closing the Stop & Shop deal, Ahold reorganized its U.S. operations. The reorganization gave Stop & Shop 35 Edwards stores in Massachusetts, Connecticut, Rhode Island, and New York. The New York stores, however, were located in counties north of the New York City region, as Ahold had decided to halt Stop & Shop's expansion there, turning the Long Island locations acquired in the Melmarkets deal over to Edwards. As a result, Stop & Shop solidified its position as the largest supermarket chain in New England, with nearly 200 units by the end of 1996. The additional stores were expected to push the company's annual revenue to more than $5.3 billion, making Stop & Shop Ahold's largest unit worldwide.

In May 1998 Ahold agreed to acquire Landover, Maryland-based Giant Food Inc. for about $2.7 billion. The purchase of Giant Food Stores LLC—which operated 173 stores in Washington, D.C., Maryland, Virginia, Delaware, New Jersey, and Pennsylvania—made Ahold the fourth largest supermarket company in the United States and solidified its number one position on the East Coast. Stop & Shop, meanwhile, was concentrating on its core New England market and was expanding geographically only in three counties north of New York City: Westchester, Dutchess, and Putnam.

Integration Activities in the Early 2000s

During the year 2000, Stop & Shop purchased the Edwards chain, which previously was a part of Giant Food Stores, LLC (Giant-Carlisle), except for four stores that were transferred to Giant Food LLC (Giant-Lanover). In June 2000, international food retailing and foodservice company Royal Ahold N.V. took a 51 percent ownership of Peapod. Later, in August 2001, Royal Ahold bought the remaining shares of Peapod, making the online grocer a wholly owned subsidiary of the company. Stop & Shop and Peapod teamed up to provide an Internet-based home shopping and grocery delivery service under the name Peapod by Stop & Shop.

Further, in 2001, Stop & Shop aggressively expanded into the New York City metropolitan area, purchasing 36 supermarkets from C&S Wholesale Distributors, which previously acquired the stores from Grand Union, along with the 63 former Edwards stores. In November of that same year, Stop & Shop opened its first low-energy superstore in Foxboro, Massachusetts. The high-efficient store used 30 percent less energy than the average supermarket.

Twenty years after opening its first Super Stop & Shop and creating a new standard for one-stop shopping, Stop & Shop introduced its next-generation supermarkets. With new departments offering products such as party goods, toys, home accessories, and office supplies, Stop & Shop's new superstores offered customers an increased level of one-stop shopping convenience. For example, in early 2002, Stop & Shop partnered with Dunkin' Donuts (Dunkin' Brands Inc.), the world's largest coffee and baked goods chain. By 2003, Stop & Shop had more than 100 full-service Dunkin' Donuts restaurants in its stores.

In 2003, Stop & Shop expanded into the New Hampshire market, where it previously had three stores. Also, Stop & Shop completed the purchase of four store locations in the area of Boston, Massachusetts, from The Great Atlantic & Pacific Tea Company.

Financially troubled Royal Ahold N.V. announced in November 2003, that it would develop a three-year plan to rebuild the value of its global operations. As a result, in January 2004, Ahold began the integration of services within its two key U.S. store chains, Stop & Shop and Giant Food LLC (Giant-Landover), along with the alignment of its retail and corporate managerial and administrative functions. The process combined stores and functions only when it allowed a strong commitment to maintain the strength of each brand, and the knowledge and involvement of the local market and community. The integration and alignment, once complete, is expected to create a company with more than 500 stores, 84,000 employees, and an estimated $16.5 billion a year in sales.

The modern Super Stop & Shop averaged 65,000 square feet (generally between 55,000 to 75,000 square feet), combined specialty food shops with a wide selection of general merchandise, and offered the convenience of one-stop shopping. Stop & Shop stores provided an average of 52,000 items per superstore. Along with the traditional food products, Stop & Shop offers many full service departments such as Foods-To-Go, full-service pharmacy, florist, salad bar, full-service branch banking, bakery, delicatessen, and other services and products such as gas stations, photo processing (including one-hour photo developing), portrait studios, bookstores, and small appliances.

Stop & Shop announced that 2004 net sales growth would only be modest in the U.S. retail business as a result of competitive pressures. However, the continuing integration of Stop & Shop and Giant-Landover was expected to improve the long-term competitiveness and cost-effectiveness of these operations. Although this integration would require an initial investment in 2004, the result was expected to cause significant benefits in 2005 and beyond.

Principal Competitors

Big Y Foods, Inc.; Hannaford Bros. Company; Shaw's Supermarkets, Inc.

Further Reading

"Ahold Realigning Stores, Officials," *Supermarket News,* August 5, 1996, p. 4.

"Ahold USA Built on Strength, Diversity of Six Chains," *MMR*, March 25, 2002, p. 41(1)

"Ahold USA on Track with Plans," *MMR*, May 3, 2004, v. 21, i.8, p. 4(1).

Alaimo, Dan, "Stop & Shop to Open Separate Video Store," *Supermarket News*, July 19, 1993, p. 27.

Baljko, Jennifer L., "Ahold Closes Stop & Shop Deal," *Supermarket News,* July 29, 1996, p. 1.

Collins, Glenn, "Circling the Grocery Carts: Stop & Shop Plans a Foothold in the New York Region," *New York Times*, August 5, 1995, pp. 31, 33.

Emert, Carol, "Stop & Shop Completes Purity Deal by Agreeing to Sell Off 17 Stores," *Supermarket News*, November 6, 1995, p. 4.

Farnsworth, Steve, "Stop & Shop Going Public Again," *Supermarket News,* October 14, 1991, p. 1.

Fox, Bruce, "Stop & Shop Gets Stronger," *Chain Store Age Executive,* June 1992, p. 23.

Gold, Howard, "Learning the Hard Way," *Forbes*, May 19, 1986, p. 80.

Goldberg, Avram J., "Stop & Shop Chief Talks Business," *Progressive Grocer*, April 1984, p. 25.

Hirsch, James S., and Charles Goldsmith, "KKR's Dutch Treat: Stop & Shop Sold to Ahold NV for $1.8 Billion," *Wall Street Journal*, March 29, 1996, pp. A3, A8.

Peak, Hugh S., and Ellen F. Peak, *Supermarket Merchandising and Management, Englewood Cliffs,* New Jersey: Prentice-Hall, 1977.

Petreycik, Richard M., "Stop & Shop Comes Back in a Big Way," *Progressive Grocer*, March 1991, p. 104.

Schaeffer, Larry, "Tobin's Turn," *Progressive Grocer*, September 1994, p. 28.

"Stop & Shop's New Properties," *Supermarket News*, March 25, 1996, p. 1.

"Stop & Shop Opens 'Next Generation of Superstores'," *Food Institute Report*, November 11, 2002, p. 2.

"Stop & Shop Plans $176M Bradlees Public Offer," *Discount Store News*, May 18, 1992, p. 1.

"Stop & Shop Settles Billback, TPR Dispute," *Supermarket News*, June 16, 1997, p. 1.

"Stop & Shop Starts Internal Probe," *Supermarket News*, February 20, 1995, p. 42.

"Stop & Shop to Buy Purity Supreme Chain," *Supermarket News,* May 1, 1995, p. 1.

Zimmerman, M.A., *The Super Market: A Revolution in Distribution,* New York: McGraw Hill, 1955.

Zwiebach, Elliot, "FBI Raids Stop & Shop Main Office, Data Center," *Supermarket News*, February 6, 1995, p. 1.

—Jonathan Martin

—updates: David E. Salamie; William Arthur Atkins

Strauss-Elite Group

84 Arlozorov Street
Ramat Gan
52136
Israel
Telephone: (+972) 3 675 23 38
Fax: (+972) 3 675 22 79

Public Company
Incorporated: 1934 (Elite); 1936 (Strauss)
Employees: 6,700
Sales: $540 million (2003)
Stock Exchanges: Tel Aviv
Ticker Symbol: ELEI
NAIC: 311511 Fluid Milk Manufacturing; 311320 Chocolate and Confectionery Manufacturing from Cacao Beans; 311340 Non-Chocolate Confectionery Manufacturing; 311423 Dried and Dehydrated Food Manufacturing; 311520 Ice Cream and Frozen Dessert Manufacturing; 311812 Commercial Bakeries; 311821 Cookie and Cracker Manufacturing; 311911 Roasted Nuts and Peanut Butter Manufacturing; 311920 Coffee and Tea Manufacturing; 424410 General Line Grocery Merchant Wholesalers; 424490 Other Grocery and Related Product Merchant Wholesalers; 551112 Offices of Other Holding Companies; 722110 Full-Service Restaurants

Merging two of Israel's oldest and largest food companies in 2004, the Strauss-Elite Group has become that country's second-largest food company, behind Ofeh. Strauss-Elite produces and markets a full range of dairy products under the Strauss brand name, including yogurts, fresh and flavored milk, cheeses and dairy-based desert products. The company also remains a major shareholder in Strauss Ice Cream, alongside Unilever. The company's Elite coffee division is the world's eighth largest; the coffee division is also the company's most international division, with operations in 12 countries. Strauss-Elite is also well known for its Elite-branded chocolates and confectionery, including the company's flagship ''Cow'' chocolate, Elite's first product launched in 1934, and the Max Brenner premium chocolate brand acquired in 2001. Strauss-Elite also produces fruit juices, baked goods, salty snacks, salads, honey, olive oil, and cereals and cereal-based snacks. In addition to food products, Strauss-Elite is expanding into the café business with the launch of the Max Brenner chocolate bar. The company opened two cafés in Israel in 2004 and planned to open the first international Max Brenner café, most likely in the United States, in 2005. Strauss operates 22 production sites, including 14 in Israel, and the remainder primarily located in the Eastern European markets. The company has also entered South America through the purchase of a company in Brazil. Strauss acquired control of Elite in 1997; in 2004, under leadership of Ofra Strauss, granddaughter of Strauss's founder, the two companies were formally merged. Strauss-Elite is listed on the Tel Aviv Stock Exchange; Danone controls 20 percent of the group's shares.

Founding Israel's Food Industry in the 1930s

The origins of the Strauss-Elite Group reach back to the years before the founding of the Israeli state. Eliyahu Fromenchenko started making candies in his apartment kitchen in Russia, launching his own business in 1918. Fleeing the economic and political chaos of the early years of communism in the Soviet Union, Fromenchenko moved to Latvia, where he established a new confectionery business in Riga. That company, called Leema, quickly grew into the country's leading candy maker. Yet the rise of the Nazi Party in neighboring Germany, especially Hitler's election to the head of the German government in 1933, convinced Fromenchenko to leave Europe for Palestine.

Fromenchenko bought property in Ramat Gan, sold the Leema factory, and had a new factory constructed in Palestine. With backing from a number of investors, notably Ludwig Jesselson of the United States, Fromenchenko founded a new company—Elite. By spring of 1934, the company had launched production, and its first product reached the stores in time for Passover. That first product, ''Shamnonit,'' a sweet in the shape of a red cow, was an immediate success and remained one of the company's flagship products through the end of the 20th century.

Elite's candies were so successful that they drew attention from around the world. By 1938, the company had already begun

Company Perspectives:

A constant will to win describes the atmosphere that runs through our organization and this is what motivates us. We are committed to doing everything we can to maintain our preference with the consumer, beating our competitors and overcoming the obstacles, wherever they may be, while remaining dedicated to the values of trust, honesty, quality, cooperation and innovation. The Elite Vision:

"Our goals for the future are long-term targets of the organization that reflects our ambitions. Having courageous and challenging goals demand an exceptional effort in order to achieve them . . . their purpose is to serve us as milestones along the way".

exporting its products, and the Elite brand became well known among Jewish communities in the United States, South Africa, England, and elsewhere. Back in Palestine, Elite began scouting out new expansion opportunities. In 1940, the company made its first diversification, acquiring jam and canned goods producer Freiman. That company had primarily manufactured for the British army during the U.K.'s control of the region.

By then, the Strauss family was also enjoying success in Palestine. The husband and wife team of Richard and Hilda Strauss arrived in Israel from Germany in 1936. The Strauss's founded a dairy farm in Nahariya, and began producing milk, cheeses, and other dairy products. Yet it was under the leadership of their children, Michael and Hilda Strauss, that the company grew into Palestine's leading dairy products group and one of its leading food groups. In addition to developing the company's fresh dairy products business, the brother and sister team extended the company into prepared dairy products. A major success for the Strauss company was its Milky brand of puddings; the company also launched its own hummous and techina products, then found international success with the Strauss Ice Cream brand, launched in the 1951.

Expanding Israel's Food Industry in the 1950s

The creation of the State of Israel in 1948 brought a new expansion to Elite's operations. In that year, the company opened its new Schachal factory and began producing techina and other dairy products. The company also became the first in Israel to launch a fruit-flavored yogurt. The new factory was established in part to meet the rising demand brought on by the influx of new immigrants to the young country; at the same time, Elite was able to provide jobs to the growing population.

A major milestone in Elite's history came in 1956, when the company acquired a new factory site in Nazareth. That facility dedicated to the production of chocolates, confectionery, and baked goods, became the company's flagship site. Total production at the site later reached 120,000 tons per day. The company added a new wafers wing to the site in 1958.

The mid-1950s marked another major strategic move for the company. The invention of instant coffee had swept the coffee market elsewhere in the world. In the mid-1950s, Elite decided to bring instant coffee to Israel and began construction of a dedicated production facility in Safed. Production was launched in 1958, and the new coffee was immediately popular in Israel. The company's decision to enter instant coffee production led it to develop its interests into the wider coffee market. Over the next five decades, Elite grew into one of the world's top ten coffee companies.

Elite had a new hit product at the end of the 1960s with the launch of its Ta'ami puffed rice, caramel, and chocolate snack in 1969. In 1970, the company launched production of its first sugarless chewing gum products. Also in that year, Elite expanded its coffee business, acquiring Lieber. Elite then expanded the Lieber site, boosting production and adding new brands, including Karat, Classic, and Haag.

Elite went public in 1973, listing on the Tel Aviv Stock Exchange. Through the 1970s, the company continued to build its foods businesses and also entered the retail market, opening its first confectionery shops. During the 1980s, the store chain was expanded throughout Israel. In 1989, Elite launched a second retail concept, the Sweet Minute shop. By then, a controlling stake in Elite had been acquired by the ED&F Man company led by the Federman family. David Federman became Elite company chairman, while the Federman, Jesselson, and other families combined to control some 62 percent of Elite.

International Expansion in the 1990s

Under David Federman, Elite began to develop its international ambitions. On the one hand, the company sought to acquire licenses for producing foreign brands in Israel. Such was the case with the company's agreement with Pepsico to introduce the Cheet-os and Ruffles snack brands to the Israeli market. As part of that effort, in 1992 Elite added a new factory in Sderot.

Yet the company's primary international focus was to expand its own brands and operations overseas. In 1992, Elite bought its first foreign facility, Union Kaffee, in Poland. Elite then launched a chain of coffee shops in that county. Next, Elite turned to western Europe, buying the Excella chocolate factory in France. In order to develop its international operations, Elite established a new subsidiary that year, Elite International, and by the middle of the decade had built or acquired eight factories in Europe.

Elite went on to acquire a number of other operations in Europe, notably Fort, based in Belgium, and Klaverblad, in the Netherlands. Both companies produced coffee for the private label segment and were part of Elite's strategy to develop itself into one of the world's leading coffee concerns. During this time, Eastern Europe emerged as the company's fastest-growing international market, especially after Elite built a new coffee roasting and grinding facility in Romania in 1995. Later that year, Elite Romania launched three coffee brands for the market—Pedro's, Sahara, and Elita. By the end of 1996, the company had already claimed a 5 percent share of the market.

A repositioning of its branded line, notably with the introduction of the Elite brand there, enabled the company to capture a still more significant share of the Rumanian market. By 1998, the company claimed a 19 percent share, and by 2000 its share had risen to 45 percent, making Elite the leading coffee maker in the country. Elite quickly sought to capitalize on its success

Key Dates:

1934: Eliyahu Fromenchenko of Russia sets up a candy factory called Elite in Ramat Gan, Palestine.
1936: Richard and Hilda Strauss establish a dairy farm in Nahariya.
1940: Elite acquires Freiman jam and canned goods company.
1951: Strauss begins producing ice cream.
1958: Elite launches the first Israeli instant coffee.
1970: Elite acquires instant coffee manufacturer Lieber.
1973: Elite lists its stock on the Tel Aviv Stock Exchange.
1992: Elite signs a licensing agreement with Pepsico, launches Elite International, and acquires factories in France and Poland.
1995: Strauss sells 50 percent of its shares in Strauss Ice Cream to Unilever.
1996: Strauss sells 20 percent of its shares to Danone; Elite establishes operations in Rumania.
1999: Elite enters Bulgaria.
2000: Elite acquires Très Coracoes in Brazil.
2001: Max Brenner brand is acquired.
2004: Strauss and Elite complete merger to form the Strauss-Elite Group.

in Eastern Europe and entered new markets in other regions, including Bulgaria, Ukraine, Russia, Croatia, and Turkey.

Elite then sought to reproduce its success further abroad. In 2000, the company acquired Café Très Cuaracoes, based in Belo Horizonte, in Brazil. That purchase gave Elite its first foothold in South America and placed it closer to a primary source of raw materials. It also gave it a leading share in the state of Minas Gerais, and, on a national level, a 40 percent share of the country's large cappuccino segment.

Israeli Food Leader in the 2000s

Elite's international expansion came not without a great deal of criticism. As *The Marker* pointed out: "The main criticism is that the company has mortgaged its hard-earned profits and reputation in Israel for a fling overseas where it is has no real competitive advantage." Dissension among its shareholding families had also begun to grow during the early 1990s, especially after Ludwig Jesselson's sons backed a takeover attempt by Bino Zadik in 1995.

In response, the Federman family decided to exit the business and sold their stake to the Strauss family. Strauss quickly consolidated its control of Elite, and by 1998 the Jesselson brothers too sold most of their shares in Elite to the Strauss family. Michael Strauss took charge of restructuring Elite, notably by closing four of its eight production sites in Europe.

Under Strauss's ownership, Elite was restructured into four operating divisions, representing its candy, snacks, coffee, and sales operations. While Strauss and Elite themselves remained separate companies, the synergy between the two groups quickly became apparent with the 1998 acquisition of a 50 percent stake in kibbutz-based Yotvata Dairies, which specialized in dairy-based drinks. Under Strauss-Elite, the dairy introduced a new line of flavored milk drinks. The Yotvata acquisition also brought the company a 20 percent share of fruit juice producer Ganir-Primor, leading to the launch of a new line of fruit-based milk and juice blends.

Strauss too had undergone a number of changes in the mid-1990s. The company sold off a 50 percent stake in Strauss Ice Cream to Unilever in 1995 and spun off that operation as a separate business. The following year, Strauss sold a 20 percent stake to Danone. In both cases, Strauss gained licenses to introduce a number of Unilever and Danone brands into Israel.

After acquiring the Kfar Saba Biscuit Factory in 2000, Elite established a new bakery division the following year, launching a new brand, Chagiga, and acquiring the De La Paix bakery in Rishon Le Zion. In an extension of its chocolates activities, Elite bought the rights to the Max Brenner brand of premium chocolates. The company then reorganized the brand's chocolate range, which primarily focused on the premium and gift package segments, by adding new chocolate snacks and mid-range chocolate varieties.

The company continued to expand its food range toward mid-decade. In 2003, for example, it launched a line of soy-based desserts. That same year, Elite expanded into cereal products with the acquisition of the Energy brand of snack bars and cereals. In 2004, Elite launched a new café concept featuring the Max Brenner brand. The successful opening of the first two chocolate cafes quickly encouraged the company to make plans to expand the café network. The company also began preparations to launch the Max Brenner brand internationally, with the United States as its first target.

Elite and Strauss remained separate companies into the 2000s, although investments in new production facilities, distribution operations, and moving into new product categories and markets came generally through joint efforts. Much of the companies' growth since during this time had been guided by Ofra Strauss, daughter of Michael Strauss, who had joined the company after a stint working for Estée Lauder in the early 1980s. Ofra Strauss, acting as CEO, began lobbying to formally merge the two companies.

The merger of the two companies was carried out in 2004, creating the Strauss-Elite Group and marking Ofra Strauss's ascension to the head of the family business empire. Strauss-Elite listed its shares on the Tel Aviv Stock Exchange in March 2004, replacing the Elite's former listing. Danone, however, chose not to participate in the merger and held onto its 20 percent stake in Strauss. Under Ofra Strauss, described by *Fortune* as one of the world's 50 most powerful businesswomen, Strauss-Elite was poised for future growth in both the Israeli and global food industries.

Principal Divisions

Candy; Snacks; Coffee; Bakeries.

Principal Operating Units

Elite International; Elite Israel; Strauss Fresh Foods; Strauss Ice Cream.

Principal Competitors

Tnuva Central Cooperative for the Marketing of Agricultural Products; Unilever Israel Ltd.; Sunfrost Ltd.; Tara Agricultural Producers Cooperative Society in Nahalat Itzhak Ltd.; Soglowek Ltd.; Carmel Wineries.

Further Reading

Coren, Ora, ''Big Plans Abroad for Max Brenner Cafes,'' *Haaretz*, December 3, 2004.

Ginsburg, Ami, ''Bittersweet Quarter,'' December 2, 2003. Available from Marker.com.

Manor, Hadas, ''Groupe Danone Is Likely to Increase Its Stake in Strauss Dairies,'' *Globes*, March 16, 2004.

Rolnik, Guy, ''Strauss Hits the Market,'' March 23, 2004. Available from Marker.com.

Steinberg, Jessica, ''Milk and Money,'' *Jerusalem Post*, September 15, 2004.

—M.L. Cohen

SULZER

Sulzer Ltd.

Zürcher Strasse 12
CH-8401 Winterthur
Switzerland
Telephone: +41-52-262-11-22
Fax: +41-52-262-01-01
Web site: http://www.sulzer.com

Public Company
Incorporated: 1914 as Gebrüder Sulzer
Employees: 8,996
Sales: CHF 1.82 billion ($1.46 billion) (2003)
Stock Exchange: Swiss
Ticker Symbol: Sulzer N
NAIC: 325110 Petrochemical Manufacturing; 333610 Engine, Turbine, and Power Transmission Equipment Manufacturing; 332812 Metal Coating, Engraving (Except Jewelry and Silverware), and Allied Services

Sulzer Ltd. is an engineering firm with worldwide operations divided into five business divisions: Sulzer Metco, Sulzer Turbomachinery Services, Sulzer Pumps, Sulzer Chemtech, and Sulzer Hexis. Sulzer Metco produces surface technology coatings solutions that prolong the life and improve the performance of components treated with the division's products. Sulzer Metco sells its surface technology solutions to aerospace, power generation, and automotive industries. Sulzer Turbomachinery Services provides repair, overhaul, and maintenance services for thermal turbomachinery equipment. The division also makes replacement parts for compressors and gas and steam turbine engines, marketing its products and services to a broad range of industries. Sulzer Pumps, which represents the largest facet of the company's business, manufactures centrifugal pumps for industries such as oil and gas, pulp and paper, and power generation. Sulzer Chemtech serves the oil and gas, petrochemical, chemical, and plastics industries, supplying its customers with products that enhance the performance of industrial processes. Sulzer Hexis develops fuel cell units that are used for decentralized heat and power generation to meet residential needs.

18th Century Origins

The beginnings of Sulzer must rate among the most picturesque of any multinational company. The story began in a little shed in the dried-up town moat of Winterthur, near Zürich, in northeast Switzerland. The grandfather of the company's two official founders had been born in Winterthur in 1751. Salomon Sulzer was the son of the landlord of a coaching inn. Legend has it that Salomon Sulzer had studied theology, and was serving as pastor to a parish by the shores of Lake Zürich, when he developed an interest in the growing trade of brass foundry, and that he eventually abandoned his ministry in order to take up an apprenticeship as a brass founder in Schaffhausen. Documentary evidence is not so specific about his early career, but gives the impression that he was gifted, unorthodox, and adventurous, qualities that were to characterize the careers of his descendants and the development of the Sulzer enterprise.

At the age of 23, Sulzer returned to his home town of Winterthur. Realizing the economic potential, in those early days of Europe's industrial revolution, of a cheaper substitute for copper machinery and tools, he planned to set up his own brass foundry. This intention was opposed by the town council, ostensibly on the grounds that the foundry would constitute a fire hazard, but perhaps, in reality, out of a desire to protect the local coppersmiths from competition.

Eventually, Sulzer was permitted to set up his foundry in the disused moat beyond the town walls. Its early products included fire engines and presses. In the town itself Sulzer opened a turner's workshop for producing articles made of wood, horn, iron, and brass. A house called the Fig Tree accommodated this shop and, above the shop, a flat in which Sulzer and his family lived. The Fig Tree was located in the town's unused moat. At first business was good, and in due course Salomon Sulzer's only son, Johann Jakob Sulzer, born in 1782, began to learn both the foundry and turnery trades. Salomon Sulzer formed social and business contacts with his neighbors, through whom he acquired contacts in the fitting trade and the mining and salt-production industries. He predicted accurately that the future lay in cast iron, which would in its turn be a much cheaper substitute for brass. For the time being, however, the technology for casting iron was not available in Switzerland.

Company Perspectives:

Our primary goal is to create value by utilizing our engineering know-how in selected industrial markets.

Despite its auspicious start, as the 19th century approached, Salomon Sulzer's enterprise was beginning to suffer seriously from the effects of the Napoleonic Wars. From 1798 to 1799 Switzerland had been the scene of the struggle of the Russian and Austrian armies against the French. Troops were billeted in Winterthur and trade was next to impossible. Sulzer was forced to accept work at the Dieuze salt works in Lorraine, a job that he found through the good offices of a neighbor. Johann Jakob Sulzer-Neuffert—it was customary in Switzerland for a man to append his wife's surname to his own on marriage—took over the management of the family business, such as it was, in 1806. The following year, his father, Salomon Sulzer, died in Lorraine.

Under the management of Johann Jakob Sulzer, the fortunes of the business began to improve. Fire engines for neighboring villages, saucepans, and bells were the staple products. Salt works abroad also were beginning to buy Sulzer pumps. The foundry moved from the moat to a more prestigious site by the Holdertor, one of the town gates. Katherina Neuffert, Sulzer's wife, set the tone of the enterprise's treatment of its employees. She wrote that, if her vision of the company's future came true, ''the workers will be looked after better here than anywhere else.'' The Sulzers had two sons, Johann Jakob, born in 1806 and named after his father, and Salomon, born in 1809 and named after his grandfather.

Johann Jakob Sulzer-Neuffert agreed with his father's views about the importance of cast iron. The industrial revolution brought an ever-increasing demand for iron, especially in the form of machinery for cotton mills and the associated machine tools. Already iron foundries had sprung up in France, Germany, and—in particular—England; obviously these were not over-keen to share their expertise with possible competitors, but the Sulzer family connections opened doors.

After the two Sulzer-Neuffert sons had served their apprenticeships in the family firm, they set off, one after the other, to complete their engineering training with a period of travel abroad. Their travels were designed to give them the opportunity to discover all they could about iron, and also about mechanical engineering. Johann Jakob Sulzer, Jr., spent several semesters at the Paris Ecole des Arts et Métiers (School of Applied Arts and Crafts), as well as working at the important English-run iron foundry at Chaillot, France. Salomon Sulzer worked in a foundry in Munich.

In the meantime, Johann Jakob Sulzer performed his own experiments with iron, being keen to be among the first Swiss manufacturers of cast iron. When the two sons returned, the family felt confident enough to embark on the construction of an iron foundry. Overcoming the difficulties of finding investors prepared to risk their capital in a new type of venture, they opened their iron foundry on a new site in the Zürichstrasse in 1834. That is regarded as the year of the founding of the company, known thereafter as Gebrüder Sulzer (Sulzer Brothers) after young Johann Jakob and Salomon Sulzer.

The sons knew that to make a success of cast-iron manufacture they needed a new type of furnace, the so-called cupola. Their father was reluctant to make the additional investment, so the sons ordered it without his knowledge. After initial disapproval, the older man was forced to recognize the value of the acquisition in terms of both quality and productivity. Subsequent expansions followed a similar pattern, with the elder Johann Jakob being carried along in the wake of his more adventurous sons.

Also at this time there began a tradition of staff training that has persisted at Sulzer. The first workers were foreigners, mostly from Bavaria, but the Sulzer brothers realized that it would be more effective as well as more patriotic to use Swiss engineers. Accordingly, from 1834 onward Sulzer provided training courses for young apprentices. The system was later formalized, and in 1870, by which time there were as many as 95 apprentices, a works training college was founded. This institution continued to operate under Sulzer management until 1989, when it was handed over for management by the canton, though Sulzer still maintained a supervisory interest.

In 1836, the firm was expanding. In its first two years of trading it had acquired 12 skilled journeymen, all of whom lodged with the young Johann Jakob Sulzer-Hirzel and were provided with meals by his wife, Marie Louise Hirzel, in the forerunner of the works canteen that soon followed. The mortgage on the foundry site had already been repaid. In 1839 a new, larger foundry was built, and the original 1834 building, still in use to this day, became a workshop. The brothers continued to supervise the work in person and the company gained a reputation for quality cast-iron goods. Output grew from 400,000 pounds in 1837 to more than 1.6 million pounds after the new foundry began production, to 5 million pounds in 1884.

Johann Jakob Sulzer-Hirzel was always searching for new products, and during this period the company began to make boilers and stoves. A boiler made in 1841 for heating the Winterthur grammar school enhanced the company's reputation for quality and reliability; it remained in service for a century. Sulzer-Hirzel also tried to use the latest production techniques, and in at least one case a novel piece of equipment suggested a new product line. In 1839 the foundry acquired its first steam engine, four horsepower, to replace the two horses that formerly turned the capstan working the bellows. A steam engine was then such a novelty that the citizens of Winterthur paid to come and look at it. Soon it was to become one of Sulzer's main products.

Ten years later, Sulzer-Hirzel went on a trip to England where the manufacture of steam engines was at a more advanced stage. He brought back with him, together with his notebooks of research findings, a British steam engineer by the name of Charles Brown, who, as chief engineer, became the first Sulzer employee to hold a managerial position. Sulzer Brothers, now recognizably an industrial concern rather than a group of craftsmen, began to manufacture its own steam engines, most of them destined to power ships. Soon the engines became the mainstay of the enterprise, and Sulzer also went on to build some of the ships themselves. Steam railways were an

Key Dates:

1834: Johann Jakob Sulzer and his two sons open an iron foundry, marking the establishment of Sulzer Brothers.
1885: A plant is opened in Germany, the first Sulzer Bros. facility located outside Switzerland.
1914: Sulzer Brothers Ltd. is incorporated.
1930s: Sulzer Bros. begins to manufacture industrial looms and gas turbine engines.
1961: Sulzer Bros. acquires Swiss Locomotive and Machine Works.
1988: Sulzer Bros. embarks on a sweeping reorganization program.
1997: Sulzer Medica is spun off as an independent company.
1999: Management initiates a reorganization program that leads to numerous divestitures.
2002: Once the divestitures are completed, Sulzer is left with five divisions.

obvious progression, and in 1871 Charles Brown went on to found the Swiss Locomotive and Machine Works (SLM) as a parallel enterprise. Among its products was the steam railway on Mount Snowdon in Wales, completed in 1894 and still running. In years to come SLM was to become part of Sulzer, which also would have dealings with Brown Boveri, a company that Brown's son founded in Baden.

As the original brothers withdrew from the day-to-day running of Sulzer, retiring in 1860 and 1872, their sons Albert, Heinrich, and Edward Sulzer took over. They demonstrated the same spirit of innovation. In 1872 the company put on show a new steam engine, the first to incorporate valves, at the Vienna World Fair. After a slow start, due to the economic difficulties that beset Switzerland during the 1870s, this valve-based steam engine led to a period of dramatic growth for Sulzer. Between 1880 and 1895 the number of employees rose from 1,240 to 3,200. Despite the success of the latest engine, the quest for new products did not cease. In 1876 a patent was obtained for a rock-drilling device. From 1877 metal piping and tanks went into production, together with refrigeration equipment.

The first plant outside Winterthur was opened in 1885, at Ludwigshafen, Rhineland-Palatinate, Germany. The chief motivation for this new departure was the desire to circumvent import duties, but it was to be only the first of many foreign installations for Sulzer. The year after its opening, a new heating and ventilation division was added to the German works.

Expansion and Diversification in the Early 20th Century

The company continued to flourish through the early years of the 20th century. In 1909, the 75th anniversary of the company's founding, Winterthur and Ludwigshafen between them could boast a workforce of 5,500. A new plant had been built at Upper Winterthur. Output of heating systems had increased by a factor of six over the preceding quarter century. Overseas expansion was beginning in earnest; by 1914, sales offices had opened in Milan, Paris, London, Cairo, Moscow, Bucharest, and Kobe, Japan.

New products continued to appear. The company had been working for some years to realize the ideas of Rudolf Diesel, who had taken out patents in 1892 and 1893. Although Sulzer was not the first to build a diesel engine, it had spotted the marine applications of this form of propulsion before anyone else. The first diesel-powered oceangoing ship had been launched as far back as 1900, and the first diesel locomotive was to make its maiden run out of Winterthur in 1913; both had Sulzer engines. Sulzer also put the world's first reversible two-cycle marine diesel engine on the market in 1906.

Despite these technical triumphs, some challenging business problems faced the original brothers' grandchildren, who had assumed control during the first decade of the 20th century. Sales of the large steam engine, hitherto the firm's best-selling product, were suffering from the advent of the steam turbine and the electric motor. This threat to the company was mitigated by using the spare capacity arising from the dwindling demand for steam engines to step up output of the profitable new diesel engines.

Sulzer's management, however, felt that considerable capital investment was needed before the company's newer products could become as commercially viable as the old ones had been. In any case, the company was outgrowing its original structure—there were now eight partners. Consequently, on the eve of World War I Gebrüder Sulzer was incorporated and became a limited company, able to raise share capital. Its name appeared on the public register of companies for the first time in June 1914.

During World War I, demand for diesel engines soared. Diesels became the chosen power source for submarines, because of their fuel efficiency and the comparative safety of diesel fuel in storage. Sulzer supplied diesel engines for the submarines of the U.S. Navy, and in 1917 the company granted a license to the Japanese Navy allowing it to upgrade its diesels in accordance with design improvements developed at Winterthur.

All this time, the policy of staff care and training that went back to the days of Katherina Neuffert was sustained, in spite of the fact that employees now numbered more than 6,000. Canteens and recreational facilities were provided, and in 1918 a hostel for invalid employees was opened in the mountains. The following year saw Sulzer launch Switzerland's first regular house newspaper.

Some of Sulzer's research and development at this time was aimed at improving compression technology, essential to the diesel but also relevant to industrial evaporation processes. Sulzer installed the world's first thermo-compression plant for industrial evaporation in 1917. Innovations between the wars related not only to diesels and compressors but also to such diverse fields as turbines, funicular railways, and ship propellers.

The company was hit badly by the worldwide Depression of the 1930s. Sulzer's management implemented rigorous cost-saving measures and managed to reduce spending by around 22.5 percent in the three years from 1936. Staff numbers dropped back to 4,000. In spite of the cost-cutting measures, some assets also had to be sold. The Ludwigshafen works was sold off in 1940, though Sulzer was able to retain its heating and ventilation divisions.

Despite the Depression technical innovations and improvements continued. Industrial weaving machines and gas turbines were among the new products added to the range during this period. The firm also strengthened its overseas capacity, adding manufacturing plants in France and England, and a marketing operation in Argentina. The war years saw further overseas expansion, with the opening of offices in New York and Madrid.

The company's perseverance in the face of the adversity of the Depression and war stood it in good stead during the postwar boom. Subsidiaries were created in Brazil, Johannesburg, Vienna, and Norway during the 1940s and 1950s. During the 1950s, the workforce, already back to pre-Depression levels, grew from 6,200 to 10,400. In 1959 Sulzer celebrated its 125th anniversary with the opening of a new foundry at Winterthur, where its site now occupied an area of 330 kilometres square, three times as much as it had 25 years before.

Post-World War II Progress

The jubilee year of 1959 also saw the death of Hans Sulzer, who had been a cabinet minister, like his brother Carl Sulzer and uncle Edward Sulzer, as well as the chairman of Gebrüder Sulzer. He was succeeded by a new generation: Hans's son Georg Sulzer became chairman, and Hans's nephew Henry Sulzer also joined the board, along with Herbert Wolfer and Alfred Schaffner. Their aggressive approach to marketing and product development was rewarded in 1963, when Sulzer became worldwide market leader for the low-speed marine diesel engine. By 1966 Sulzer was providing one-third of engine capacity for newly launched oceangoing vessels, representing almost 2.5 million horsepower in total.

The 1960s saw Sulzer strengthening its competitive position through the acquisition of other Swiss firms operating in the same or similar markets. Notable examples included the acquisition in 1961 of the Swiss Locomotive and Machine Works of Winterthur, founded by Charles Brown 90 years previously, and—following the purchase three years earlier of a 50 percent share—the takeover in 1969 of the Zürich-based engineering firm of Escher Wyss. A temporary joint venture with Brown Boveri of Baden for the manufacture of turbo engines during the 1960s and 1970s ended when the two parent companies divided up the enterprise, with Sulzer retaining the capacity to manufacture the smaller turbines. By 1968 Sulzer had 32,500 workers and a turnover of CHF 1.68 billion. The large corporation known today was taking shape.

Although the company was hit by the 1973 oil crisis, its vigorous worldwide growth continued into the 1980s. Weaving machine plants were built in Japan and in the United States, and domestic output of these machines also grew. Also in Japan, a fruitful and enduring joint venture with Toyoda Automatic Loom Works was established in the 1970s. Plants for pump manufacture in The Netherlands, West Germany, Brazil, and South Africa enabled Sulzer to meet local requirements better.

The Sulzer family had been quick to realize the importance of computerization and was building the foundations for its current electronics division as early as 1962. In 1969 it acquired an interest in ELMA Electronic, later a wholly owned subsidiary of Sulzer. Industrial automation was the focus of its early work, although it now made electronic components as well as robotic systems, both for its own use and for sale to customers. A corporate computer center opened to serve the company's administrative functions in 1972.

Both in its product lines and in its production methods, Sulzer continued to innovate—its research-and-development budget was CHF 228 million in 1989. The company claimed to have the most advanced foundry in Europe; the forge was robotically controlled and casting was computerized also. The machine shop boasted the world's largest longitudinal milling machine.

In 1988 Sulzer undertook a radical review of its business situation and strategy. Despite its valuable asset base the company recognized the need to improve profitability. Three options were considered: reorganization, further diversification, or focusing on the strongest areas of the business. This third option was adopted as the one with the greatest long-term potential.

Accordingly, Sulzer began a period of reshaping, during which it began developing what it calls its pillar businesses, those in which profitability and market share were outstanding and where the company was highly regarded by its business partners. These pillar businesses consisted of construction services, such as air conditioning and refrigeration—represented by the building and construction service group with 1989 turnover of CHF 1.5 billion; weaving machines—led by the Sulzer Rüti Group, whose 1989 turnover was CHF 1.1 billion; and medical engineering—Sulzer Medica, with CHF 600 million in 1989 turnover. The area of medical engineering, with products such as pacemakers, defibrillators, and artificial heart valves and hip joints, was being expanded through acquisition. The year 1989 saw three important purchases in this field: Intermedics in the United States, and in Switzerland Allo Pro and a majority shareholding in Protek. Apart from the three existing pillar businesses, Sulzer planned to nurture certain promising divisions, in large part through internal growth, during the 1990s. These potential pillar businesses included chemical engineering, paper machinery, and surface technology.

Less profitable areas were under scrutiny and were to be sold off if they were not profitable within a time limit. Gas turbines, knitting machines, and the historic diesel engines were among the areas in which disinvestment took place. The pumps, refrigeration, and turbo compressor divisions showed signs of improving profitability, however.

This focus on profitable business areas was only one of five key objectives in Sulzer's strategy for the 1990s, as summarized by Fritz Fahrni—since 1988 president of corporate executive management. Other objectives were: improvement of the quality of the end product; a motivated workforce, both technical and managerial; satisfied shareholders, a corollary of a profitable portfolio; and a dynamic response to the requirements of a changing marketplace.

Sulzer believed that its key objectives would best be achieved through a decentralized company structure, which encouraged a spirit of entrepreneurship. Business units were to be strategically independent, but supported from the central organization in terms of the management of human and financial resources, research-and-development services, and international marketing.

Georg Sulzer retired as chairman in 1981. Although no longer family run, Gebrüder Sulzer continued to bear the hallmark of the Sulzer family, maintaining its position not only by research to ensure that it was at the leading edge of technology, but also by shrewdly assessing and quickly adapting to the changing marketplace, entering into alliances with other firms when necessary.

A demonstration of this policy came in July 1990 when Sulzer, as the world's second largest diesel manufacturer, announced the formation of New Sulzer Diesel, a cooperative venture with other companies from West and Eastern Europe to safeguard the European diesel industry against competition from the Far East. The chairman of the board and executive president of this company was Peter Sulzer.

A New Profile for the 21st Century

The reorganization of Sulzer begun in the late 1980s became a prevailing theme throughout the 1990s and into the 21st century. The process created a more sharply defined corporation, and one that was substantially smaller, as the company's revenue volume shrank by roughly 65 percent during the 1990s. One of the most significant events of the decade occurred in 1997, when Sulzer Medica—the company's medical engineering business—became a publicly traded company, with Sulzer retaining roughly 80 percent of the former subsidiary's shares. By this point, Sulzer's operations were divided into two distinct groups, medical technology and industrial, but the profile of the company soon changed after management initiated another sweeping reorganization program in 1999.

By the end of the 20th century, Sulzer's efforts to decentralize management led the company to distance itself from a number of its businesses. After its public offering, Sulzer Medica was assigned its own chief executive officer, giving the company considerable independence from Sulzer. In 1999, Sulzer Industries also was assigned its own chief executive officer. During the year, the water turbine and pump business operating within Sulzer Hydro was sold to VA TECH, an Austrian company. Against the backdrop of spinning off companies and divesting others, Sulzer bolstered the business of its largest division, Sulzer Pumps. In 1999, the division formed a joint venture with China-based Dalian Pumps, increasing its presence in China. In 2000, Sulzer Pumps acquired Ahlstrom Pumps, a Finnish company.

The reorganization plan developed in 1999 led to the divestiture of several divisions during the first years of the 21st century. Sulzer Turbo was sold at the end of 2000, followed by the divestiture of Sulzer Infra, Sulzer Textil, and all interests in Sulzer Medica in 2001 (Sulzer Medica became Centerpulse AG). The divestiture program was completed in 2002 with the sale of Sulzer Burckhardt to its management, leaving Sulzer trimmed and focused on five businesses.

Sulzer entered the 1990s as a more than $4 billion-in-sales conglomerate; it entered the mid-2000s generating slightly less than $1.5 billion in sales. Divestitures left the company with five divisions: Sulzer Metco, Sulzer Turbomachinery Services, Sulzer Pumps, Sulzer Chemtech, and Sulzer Hexis. To these divisions fell the responsibility of producing consistent profits and revenue growth, the objective of the decade-long restructuring program that drastically reduced the size of Sulzer. As the company prepared for the future, it rested its hopes on the performance of its newly aligned corporate structure, endeavoring to make Sulzer a commanding force in Swiss business and markets worldwide in the years ahead.

Principal Subsidiaries

Metaplas Ionon; Woka Gmbh (Germany); Sulzer Elbar (Netherlands); Sulzer Repco (Netherlands); PT Sulzer Hickham Indonesia; Sulzer Hickham; Sulzer Enpro; Sulzer Innotec; Johnston Pumps; PACO Pumps; Crown Pumps; Sulzer Process Pumps US Inc.; Sulzer Chemtech USA Inc.

Principal Divisions

Sulzer Metco; Sulzer Turbomachinery Services; Sulzer Pumps; Sulzer Chemtech; Sulzer Hexis.

Principal Competitors

GE Energy; ITT Industries, Inc.; Tecumseh Products Company.

Further Reading

Die Berufsschule Sulzer im Rahmen der Lehrlingsausbildung 1870–1989, Winterthur: Sulzer, 1989.

"Fortress Switzerland," *Business Week,* June 4, 2001, p. 56.

"Fuel Cell Future: The Sulzer Perspective," *Modern Power Systems,* May 2001, p. 69.

Das Jubiläumsiahr 1984 im Rückblick, Winterthur: Sulzer, 1984.

Knobel, Bruno, *A World-Wide Company Is Born,* Winterthur: Sulzer.

Labhart, Walter, *Schweizer Pioniere der Wirtschaft und Technik,* Zürich: Verein für wirtschaftshistorische Studien, 1984.

"Ein Technologiekonzern auf dem Weg in die 90er Jahre," Number 2, 1990.

—Alison Classe and Olive Classe
—update: Jeffrey L. Covell

APLICAÇÃO DO LOGO EM FUNDO BRANCO

TAM Linhas Aéreas S.A.

Hangar BRC – S/No. - Cabeceira da Pista – 35 R
Congonhas
CEP 04357-080
Sao Paulo
Brazil
Telephone: (+55) 11 5582 8811
Fax: (+55) 11 5071 1080
Web site: http://www.tam.com.br

Public Company
Incorporated: 1961 as Táxi Aéreos Marília
Employees: 7,625
Sales: $1.26 billion (2003)
Stock Exchanges: Sao Paulo
Ticker Symbol: TANC4.BR
NAIC: 481111 Scheduled Passenger Air Transportation; 481112 Scheduled Freight Air Transportation; 481212 Nonscheduled Chartered Freight Air Transportation; 481211 Nonscheduled Chartered Passenger Air Transportation; 488190 Other Support Activities for Air Transportation

TAM Linhas Aéreas S.A. is Brazil's leading domestic airline. TAM operates a fleet of about 50 Airbus jets and 40 Fokker 100 turboprops, which form a vital commercial air link in a country that takes four hours to cross by plane. The company's TAM Mercosur unit flies to neighboring countries. The family of the late Rolim Amaro owns most (69 percent) of the company's shares. Amaro is credited with building an air taxi operation into Brazil's strongest airline over the course of 30 years.

Origins

TAM was founded on January 7, 1961, as Táxi Aéreos Marília (TAM), named for a city in the state of Sao Paulo. It was a pilots' cooperative. TAM was eventually acquired by sugar producer Orlando Ometto.

Ommetto's right hand man was Rolim Adolfo Amaro, who joined TAM in 1963. Amaro soon after left to work for Viaçao Aérea Sao Paulo (VASP), according to a profile in *Airways* magazine. In 1968, he was flying for a farm owned by a bank, which financed the purchase of his own tiny Cessna 140.

Amaro and his brother Joao started another air taxi service, Araguaia Tàxi Aéreo (ATA), in 1971. It ferried laborers in the states of Goiás and Paraná. By 1973, notes *Airways,* the enterprise was operating ten planes.

Amaro became a half owner of his former employer, TAM, in 1971. Two years later, local farmer Sebastiano Maia bought in. TAM's fleet was soon upgraded with Cessna 409s and even Learjets, notes *Airways*. TAM carried 2,800 passengers in 1972 and 18,000 in 1975. Headquarters was relocated to Sao Paulo.

TAR Formed in 1976

Around this time, the Brazilian government began promoting air service to the small communities that had been abandoned by the major airlines in the age of the jet. Five smaller airlines were assigned exclusive rights to one of five regions, and TAM was earmarked for the wealthiest and most populous, the Regiao Centro-Oeste.

TAM Transportes Aéreos Regionais (TAR) was established on May 12, 1976. VASP received a holding in the company in exchange for contributing a fleet of six 160-seat EMB-110 Bandeirantes, plus facilities at seven local airports. In July 12, 1976, the new venture began flying its first route, Sao Paulo-Ourinhos-Maringá.

In November 1976, Amaro bought out his partners. Amaro, often called "Commandante," was known for his emphasis on customer service. "The customer is king," was his motto, notes *Air Transport World.* A red carpet was typically rolled out for passengers as they deplaned.

TAM replaced its fleet of Bandeirantes with 48-seat Fokker F27s turboprops in the early 1980s. In 1982, TAM Jatos Executivos was created to market Cessna Citation business jets.

A New Name in the Mid-1980s

TAM adopted the name TAM Linha Aérea Regional on August 1, 1986, reports *Airways* magazine. With a democratic

Key Dates:

1961: Táxi Aéreos Marília air taxi service is formed.
1971: Rolim Amaro becomes a partner in Táxi Aéreos Marília.
1976: TAM Transportes Aéreos Regionais (TAR) is formed; Amaro acquires the rest of air taxi service.
1986: TAM is renamed TAM Linha Aérea Regional.
1996: TAM acquires LAPSA.
1998: A Miami route is launched.
2000: TAM and TAR merge; sales exceed $1 billion.
2001: Amaro dies in midst of a major expansion program.
2003: TAM code shares with VARIG.

government in power, the air market was liberalized and TAM was free to begin connecting major cities via downtown airports, which business travelers found to be a great convenience. TAM was allowed to begin flying the Sao Paulo-Rio "Air Bridge" in 1989.

TAM bought an interest in the regional airline assets of VOTEC in 1986. A new company was formed around them called Viaçao Brasil Central. In 1996, it was renamed Transportes Aéreos Meridionais. TAM's Central operation connected some very remote spots in Brazil with a fleet of Cessna Caravans.

TAM began flying a pair of Fokker 100 twin-jets in October 1990. These allowed the airline to offer jet service from the downtown airports. The Brazilian aviation market was deregulated further in the early 1990s. This allowed for more growth, and TAM was soon operating 53 Fokker 100s.

Air Transport World named TAM its Regional Airline of the Year for 1995. However, with a route network of 2,140 miles, TAM stretched the definition of "regional airline," noted the magazine. The airline had revenues of about $330 million in the 1994 fiscal year, when it carried 1.6 million passengers (one-quarter of them on charter flights). The company then had 1,400 employees.

In September 1996, TAM acquired 80 percent of LAPSA, Paraguay's troubled national airline. Renamed Transportes Aéreos del Mercosur (or TAM Mercosur), it became the unit responsible for flights to countries neighboring Brazil.

On October 31, 1996, the company suffered its worst disaster when a Fokker 100 jet crash on takeoff, killing 90 people. This and later incidents would tarnish the jet's reputation in the eyes of the public, and they were eventually replaced.

In the late 1990s, TAM joined LAN Chile and TACA in the pooled purchase of 120 Airbus jets. TAM acquired 60 A320s and five of the larger A330s, one of which were used to open TAM's first international route to Miami in December 1998. Service to Paris was launched in the next year.

TAM and TAR Merge in 2000

Transportes Aéreos Meridionais and Transportes Aéreos Regionais were merged in late 2000 to form TAM Linhas Aéreas. The combined company had about 8,000 employees.

TAM was the only Brazilian airline to turn a profit in 2000, according to *Aviation Week & Space Technology.* After losing BRL 83.7 million in 1999, the carrier posted net income of BRL 41.4 million ($17.6 million) as passenger count rose from less than 8 million to 10.4 million. Sales were more than $1 billion. At the 2001 Paris Air Show, TAM announced orders for 20 Brazilian-made Embraer Regional Jets and 20 Airbus A318 airliners.

TAM launched a major international expansion in early 2001 by taking over routes to Buenos Aires and other destinations abandoned by VASP. TAM acquired Argentina's tiny Aerovip airline later in the year.

TAM's charismatic founder Rolim Amaro died in a helicopter crash on July 8, 2001. His widow, Noemy, headed the board of directors after his death. Amaro was succeeded as the company's president by his brother-in-law and longtime TAM employee Daniel Madelli Martin.

International services extended to Zürich and Frankfurt in May 2001. TAM also had marketing arrangements with American Airlines and Air France. Most of the international routes were cut after September 11, 2001, however. KLM Royal Dutch Airlines NV began a code-sharing arrangement with TAM on the Sao Paulo route in the winter of 2002–03. The flights were operated by TAM.

TAM lost BRL 607.5 million in 2002 on sales of $1.7 billion. Its passenger count was about 14 million. TAM was hurt by the devaluation of the Brazilian real. The cargo division, TAM Express, accounted for about 10 percent of sales. In the cost-cutting that followed, TAM began unloading its fleet of Fokker 100 jets and cut 524 jobs. The airline did take delivery of two new Airbus jets worth $71 million each.

VARIG Cooperation in 2003

TAM began merger talks with VARIG in February 2003 as both airlines struggled in a weakened Brazilian economy. They began selling seats on each other's aircraft through a code-sharing arrangement, which helped both of them gain more of the market.

TAM managed a net profit of BRL 173.8 million ($59 million) on sales of $1.26 billion in 2003. The company had focused on subsidiary TAM Mercosur's flights to neighboring countries—particularly Paraguay, Uruguay, and Bolivia—rather than long haul routes, reported *Aviation Daily.*

Company president Daniel Martin stepped down in August 2003 during merger negotiations with VARIG. He would be replaced by Marco Antonio Bologna.

In the summer of 2004, TAM added 15 new regional destinations to its offerings by partnering with local airlines Passaredo, Trip, and OceanAir. The airline was soon cleared to launch routes to Lima, Peru, and Santiago, Chile. Ten Airbus 320 jets were ordered to accommodate TAM's new growth. The company was considering an initial public offering for 2005 to raise at least $100 million. Only 0.5 percent of shares had been available on the Sao Paulo exchange.

By this time, merger talks with VARIG were no longer a priority, though the two airlines were continuing their code-sharing arrangement. TAM was leading Brazil's domestic aviation market with more than a one-third market share.

Principal Subsidiaries

TAM Jatos Executivos; TAM–Transportes Aereos Del Mercosur (Paraguay).

Principal Divisions

Centro Técnico TAM; Services Academy.

Principal Competitors

Gol Transportes Aereos SA; Viacao Aerea Rio Grandense SA (VARIG); Viacao Aerea Sao Paulo (VASP).

Further Reading

''Airlines Caught up in Price War—But VARIG Tries to Remain Aloof from Cutting Contest,'' *Latin American Newsletters*, April 24, 2001.

Beting, Gianfranco, ''TAM Has Reason to Smile,'' *Airways*, November 2004, pp. 8–17.

''Brazil Carrier TAM Hopes to Sell up to $200M in Stock—CEO,'' *Dow Jones International News*, July 14, 2004.

''Brazil TAM Authorised to Fly to Santiago, Lima,'' *Latin America News Digest*, October 1, 2004.

''Brazil TAM Has 36.17 PCT Domestic Air Traffic Share Aug 2004,'' *Latin America News Digest*, September 10, 2004.

''Brazil TAM Signs Partnership Agreements with Passaredo, OceanAir, Trip,'' *Latin America News Digest*, July 29, 2004.

''Brazil TAM Swings to All-Time High 2003 Profit,'' *Latin America News Digest*, March 30, 2004.

''Brazil's 2 Largest Airlines Deny Canceling Merger Plans,'' *Dow Jones International News*, March 17, 2004.

''Brazil's Biggest Airline to Buy 10 Airbus Passenger Jets,'' *Associated Press Newswires*, July 26, 2004.

''Brazil's TAM Airline Head Quits Amid Merger,'' *Reuters News*, August 14, 2003.

Flottau, Jens, ''TAM Brazil Regroups after Death of Founder,'' *Aviation Week & Space Technology*, July 30, 2001, p. 45.

Hay, Andrew, ''Brazilian Airlines Varig, TAM Delay Merger,'' *Reuters News*, February 10, 2004.

Lunda, Denise, and Carlos DeJuana, ''Brazil's Varig, TAM Commit to Airline Merger,'' *Reuters News*, September 17, 2003.

Manera, Roberto, ''TAM Bets on Rolim's Style to Stay on Top,'' *Gazeta Mercantil*, April 29, 2004.

Moorhouse, Neil, ''KLM Says Has Codeshare Deal with Tam,'' *Dow Jones International News*, October 4, 2002.

''Regional Airline of the Year: TAM,'' *Air Transport World*, February 1, 1996, p. 32.

''Rolim Amaro, Founder of TAM, Killed in Helicopter Crash in Brazil,'' *Weekly of Business Aviation*, July 16, 2001, p. 32.

''Serious Competition as Varig and TAM Merge,'' *Latin American Economic and Business Report*, March 27, 2003.

''TAM Brazil Begins Fokker Retirement, Fleet Renewal,'' *Aviation Daily*, October 1, 2002, p. 5.

''TAM Brazil to Increase Fleet for Domestic Flights,'' *Aviation Daily*, September 7, 2001, p. 8.

''TAM Brazil to Kick off Expansion with Brazil-Argentina Flights,'' *Aviation Daily*, February 20, 2001, p. 4.

''TAM Focus on Cargo Division,'' *Gazeta Mercantil*, December 26, 2002.

''TAM to Implement Cutbacks, As Varig Consolidates Fleet and Network,'' *Airclaims Airline News*, September 20, 2002.

''TAM's in the Black for 2003,'' *Valor Economico*, March 30, 2004.

Zalamea, Luis, ''Brazil's TAM Shows Net Profit for 2003,'' *Aviation Daily*, April 6, 2004, p. 6.

—Frederick C. Ingram

Tesco plc

Tesco House, Delamare Road
Cheshunt, Hertfordshire EN8 9SL
United Kingdom
Telephone: (+44) 1-992-632-222
Fax: (+44) 1-992-630-794
Web site: http://www.tesco.com

Public Company
Incorporated: 1932 as Tesco Stores Limited
Employees: 326,000
Sales: £30.81 billion ($54.44 billion) (2003)
Stock Exchanges: London
Ticker Symbol: TSCO
NAIC: 445110 Supermarkets and Other Grocery (except Convenience) Stores; 447110 Gasoline Stations with Convenience Stores; 524120 Direct Insurance (Except Life, Health, and Medical) Carriers

Tesco plc is one of the largest retailers in the world, operating more than 2,300 supermarkets and convenience stores and employing 326,000 people. Tesco's core business is in Britain, where the company ranks as the largest private sector employer in the United Kingdom and the largest food retailer, operating nearly 1,900 stores. In continental Europe, Tesco operates in the Czech Republic, Hungary, Poland, the Republic of Ireland, Slovakia, and Turkey. In Asia, the company operates in Japan, Malaysia, South Korea, Taiwan, and Thailand. Through Tesco.com, the company ranks as the largest online supermarket in the world. The company also offers financial services through Tesco Financial Services, which controls 4.6 million customer accounts roughly divided between credit cards and car insurance policies. Through the more than 100-unit Tesco Express chain, the company ranks as the largest seller of gasoline in the United Kingdom.

Early History

In John Edward (Jack) Cohen's day, a retailer's product line was comprised of whatever could be housed in a tiny stall. In 1919, Cohen invested his £30 stipend from his World War I service in the Royal Flying Corps in stock for his small grocery stall in the East End of London and began his career as a market trader. He soon became a successful trader in other London markets outside of the East End and also branched out into wholesaling for other market traders. In 1932, Cohen officially founded Tesco Stores Limited. The name was originally that of a private-label brand of tea Cohen sold, created from the initials of T.E. Stockwell, a merchant from whom he bought tea, and the first two letters of his last name.

Over the next eight years, the company grew rapidly, as Cohen opened more than 100 small stores, mainly in the London area. In 1935, Cohen was invited to the United States by several major American suppliers and became an eager student of the American food retailing system. His vision of taking the American self-service supermarket concept back to the United Kingdom was temporarily thwarted by World War II. Nevertheless, Cohen's dream became a reality in 1947 when Tesco opened its first self-service store, in St. Albans, Hertfordshire, the same year that shares in Tesco Stores (Holdings) Limited were first offered for sale to the public. Although the St. Albans store closed in 1948 after failing to capture the interest of British shoppers, it reopened one year later to a much warmer reception.

Over the next two decades, Tesco expanded quickly across the United Kingdom. This growth was accomplished almost exclusively by the acquisition of smaller grocery chains, including the 19-store Burnards chain in 1955, the 70-store Williamsons Ltd. in 1957, the 200-branch Harrow Stores Ltd. in 1959, the 97-unit Charles Phillips & Company Ltd. in 1964, and the 47-store Adsega chain in 1965. In 1956, the company opened its first supermarket, in Maldon, Essex, to carry fresh foods in addition to its traditional dry goods.

In 1960, Tesco established a special department in its larger stores called Home 'n' Wear to carry higher-margin, nonfood merchandise, including apparel and household items. Seven years later, the company completed construction on a 90,000-square-foot warehouse in Westbury, Wiltshire. The following year, Tesco opened its first 40,000-square-foot superstore at Crawley, Sussex. The term "superstore" referred not only to the store's size but also to its vast selection of inexpensive food and nonfood items.

Company Perspectives:

Our core purpose is "to create value for customers to earn their lifetime loyalty." We deliver this through our values—"No one tries harder for customers" and "Treat people how we like to be treated."

By 1976, Tesco operated nearly 900 supermarkets and superstores on the "pile it high, sell it cheap" formula that Cohen had imported from America. The firm's management found that the effectiveness of this strategy had deteriorated over time, however, leaving the company with uncomfortably slim margins and a serious image problem among consumers. While Tesco had been preoccupied with opening as many stores as possible and loading them with merchandise, the company had missed important signs that its market was changing and had come to value merchandise quality over quantity.

Turnaround in the Late 1970s

The task of turning the company around fell on the shoulders of Ian MacLaurin, who had risen through the Tesco ranks to become managing director in 1973. In the first phase of his rescue plan Tesco discontinued the use of Green Shield trading stamps (which had been introduced in 1963), an action that major stores in the United States had also taken. This was followed in 1977 by a controversial tactic dubbed Operation Checkout, in which Tesco cut prices across the board in an attempt to increase sales and market share during a period when consumers were spending less money on food purchases. Although the company accomplished these original objectives—market share rose from 7 to 12 percent in the span of a year—Operation Checkout did little to improve Tesco's sagging image among consumers. Most of Tesco's stores were cramped, difficult to operate, and even harder to staff. Customer service was poor and merchandise selection in many outlets was limited. Tesco also touched off a price war with J. Sainsbury plc, one of its major rivals, which ended up driving a number of smaller retailers and independent grocers out of business or into the arms of larger companies when they found themselves unable to compete with the prices offered by the two warring retailers.

Next, in order to reposition itself, Tesco embarked upon a massive modernization program intended in part to take the chain upmarket. It closed 500 unprofitable stores and extensively upgraded and enlarged others, including the installation of enhanced lighting and the widening of aisles. Tesco pursued the superstore concept much more aggressively than it had in the past in order to compete more successfully with other major retailers and be more responsive to consumers who preferred to shop where parking was convenient and the selection of goods was broad. The company made a significant investment not only in improving the physical appearance of its stores but also in providing the higher-quality merchandise consumers wanted. Superstores were also seen as a way to generate a higher volume of business at increased margins while reducing overhead.

In the beginning, the superstores averaged 25,000 square feet but eventually grew as large as 65,000 square feet. Each superstore functioned as a self-service department store coupled with a supermarket. The company placed a heavy emphasis on having a varied selection of fresh, high-quality foods available, as well as a wide range of general merchandise such as household items and clothing designed to appeal to more sophisticated tastes.

To the high-quality, service-oriented image of these stores, Tesco introduced its own private-label product lines, developed through an extensive research-and-development program. Tesco also restructured and computerized its distribution system, opening its own centralized warehouses for storing inventory which could then be supplied to its stores as needed, instead of having to rely on manufacturers' delivery schedules.

In 1979, in an attempt to increase its overall sales volume through larger stores, Tesco acquired 17 outlets affiliated with Cartiers Superfoods. This acquisition and another involving Ireland's Three Guys store chain, together with lower sales in nonfood merchandise than the company had expected, drained Tesco's profits the following year.

Battling for Market Share in the 1980s

By late 1981, food sales also appeared to be settling into another slump, placing additional pressure on Tesco's bottom line. In an effort to rekindle activity, MacLaurin initiated Checkout '82, cutting prices between 3 and 26 percent on approximately 1,500 food items. Like the strategy employed in 1977—but operating in an environment of smaller net profit margins—Checkout '82 touched off renewed price wars between Tesco and J. Sainsbury, in which each chain devoted all of its energies to outdoing the other to win customer loyalty.

In the midst of this ongoing battle, Tesco also established its Victor Value chain of discount stores. Growing over the next four years to a total of 45 outlets, the stores were sold to the Bejam Group plc in 1986, the same year in which the Three Guys chain, renamed Tesco Stores Ireland Ltd., was sold to H. Williams and Company, Ltd., a Dublin-based supermarket chain. This divestiture resulted primarily from the company's inability to operate effectively in Ireland from its home base in England.

In 1983, the company changed its name to Tesco plc. The following year, it joined forces with Marks & Spencer, the upscale British variety store, to develop shopping centers in areas outside the country's major cities. Their first venture, which became a model for subsequent centers, was established at Brookfield Centre, near Cheshunt, and placed a 65,000-square-foot Tesco superstore next to a 69,000-square-foot Marks & Spencer department store. Supported by 42 computerized checkout counters and 900 employees, the Tesco store offered a variety of food and nonfood departments, in addition to services ranging from a bank to a gas station to baby-care facilities to a consumer advisory kitchen staffed by home economists. The Marks & Spencer store featured mostly nonfood merchandise, though it devoted a small amount of space to the popular specialty food items it marketed under its own St. Michael label.

In 1985, Ian MacLaurin became chairman of Tesco, the same year that Tesco opened its 100th superstore in the United Kingdom. The construction of this outlet, located in Brent Park, Neasden, was a source of controversy between the company and the local governing council from the date Tesco first acquired

Key Dates:

1932: Tesco Stores Limited is founded.
1947: Tesco Stores (Holdings) Limited begins trading shares of its stock to the public.
1959: Tesco acquires the 200-store grocery chain Harrow Stores Ltd., one of numerous grocery chains the company acquired during the late 1950s.
1968: Tesco opens its first superstore, a 40,000-square-foot store in Sussex.
Late 1970s: As part of an extensive reorganization program, Tesco closes 500 stores.
1983: The company changes its name to Tesco plc.
1994: As part of a concerted push into continental Europe, Tesco acquires majority control of Global, a 43-store supermarket chain in Hungary.
1997: Terry Leahy is appointed chief executive officer.
2000: Tesco launches its e-commerce business, Tesco.com.
2003: Tesco acquires T&S Stores plc.

the 43-acre site in 1978. The council made a number of objections to the proposed development, maintaining that the store did not fit the planning needs of the area and did not make adequate allowances for future warehousing requirements. The council's greatest concern was the threat the Tesco store would pose to existing shopping centers and local merchants. Once Tesco's store finally opened for business it became London's largest food store.

Also in 1985, Tesco launched a major capital spending program for aggressive store and warehouse expansion and for more efficient technology in existing stores, both at the checkout counters and behind the scenes. Tesco's investment in the development of a sophisticated distribution system, together with other facility improvements, enabled the company to incorporate its 1987 acquisition of the 40-store Hillards plc chain easily. This expansion also gave Tesco increased visibility in Yorkshire. In 1988 and 1989, the company spent £500 million to build 29 new stores. In the late 1980s, Tesco also introduced a composite six-warehouse distribution system to serve its stores, resulting in increased efficiency and improved service.

Expansion Outside the United Kingdom in the 1990s

By the beginning of the 1990s, Tesco had 371 stores in England, Scotland, and Wales—150 of which were superstores—and the company had become one of the United Kingdom's top three food retailers. The early 1990s saw the culmination of Tesco's fight for market share fueled in part by a two-year £1 billion development program launched in 1990 which added about 60 new stores and more than 2.3 billion square feet of store space. By 1991, Tesco had become the largest independent gasoline retailer in Great Britain. Four years later, the company reached the number one spot among food retailers in terms of market share. This achievement was due in part to the 1992 introduction of the Tesco Metro format, which debuted at Covent Garden, London. The Metro stores were smaller outlets—10,000 square feet or so—designed for urban areas and offering a few thousand product lines tailored specifically for the local market. Whereas Tesco had typically concentrated its stores in suburbia, the Tesco Metro stores were slated for city neighborhoods and were intended to compete directly with Marks & Spencer's successful urban food-only stores. By 1997, Tesco had opened 40 Tesco Metro units.

Perhaps more important for Tesco in the long term, however, was the company's aggressive 1990s push outside of Great Britain. In 1993 Tesco paid £175 million ($282 million) to purchase Catteau S.A., a 92-store grocery chain in northern France. This first foray onto continental Europe proved ill-founded, however, as Catteau struggled to compete against discounters and larger chains such as Promodes and Carrefour. Lacking the critical mass needed to compete successfully, Tesco decided to exit from France four years after it had entered the country, selling Catteau to Promodes in December 1997 for £250 million ($416.9 million).

Other Tesco expansion moves in the 1990s were more successful. In August 1994, the company acquired William Low, gaining 57 stores in Scotland and northern England for £247 million. Also in 1994, Tesco moved into the burgeoning central European market for the first time through the £15 million purchase of a 51 percent stake in Global, a supermarket chain with 43 stores in northwest Hungary. The following year, Tesco acquired the 31-store Savia chain in Poland for £8 million. In 1996, the company spent £79 million for 13 Kmart stores in the Czech Republic and Slovakia, which it soon converted to the Tesco name. Initially, Tesco's central European operations suffered operating losses in large part because of hefty development costs, but the company announced in early 1998 that it aimed to be a major food retailer in the region, that it would spend £350 million through the year 2000 to expand its base, and that it expected to be making a profit there by the turn of the century. In 1997, Tesco acquired the Irish food retailing businesses of Associated British Food plc for £630 million ($1 billion), thereby gaining leading market share positions in both the Republic of Ireland (through 75 stores) and Northern Ireland (through 34 stores).

Meanwhile, back in Britain, Tesco was experimenting with additional new formats and introducing innovative new services. The year 1994 saw the opening of the first two Tesco Express gasoline stations, both located in London. The Express format was a combination filling station and convenience store; by late 1997, 15 of them had opened. In 1997, Tesco opened the first Tesco Extra unit in Pitsea, Essex. This store covered 102,000 square feet, with one-quarter of the sales area consisting of expanded nonfood departments. It soon became the company's number one store in terms of sales.

In February 1995, Tesco became the first British retailer with a loyalty card when it introduced the Tesco Clubcard. In 1997, the company created a new unit called Tesco Personal Finance in order to provide its customers with a wide array of financial services, including a Tesco Visa Card, a Tesco savings account, in-store bank branches, Tesco Travel Money and Insurance, and Clubcard Plus, a combination loyalty card and savings account.

The year 1997 also marked the end of an era for Tesco as MacLaurin retired, with John Gardiner taking over as chairman;

Gardiner had been appointed deputy chairman of Tesco in 1993 and also served as chairman of Larid Group plc. That same year, Terry Leahy was appointed chief executive. Leahy, who joined Tesco in 1979, had played a key role in Tesco's rise to the top of U.K. food retailing as the company's first marketing director. With a new management team in place, Tesco aimed to build upon its multiformat empire in the United Kingdom, to continue to develop innovative products and services (particularly financial services), to turn its central European operations into profitable ones, and to seek other overseas expansion opportunities, such as in the emerging markets of Asia.

Tesco in the 21st Century

Leahy emerged as the prominent figure guiding Tesco at the turn of the century. In 1997, the year Leahy was named chief executive officer, Tesco developed a four-pronged growth strategy, one that was ambitious in its design. In the coming years, the company directed its expansion efforts on its core U.K. business, retailing services, international operations, and nonfood business. The nonfood component of the company's growth strategy presented the most daunting challenge to Leahy because the company was essentially starting from scratch. Further, as Leahy's plans evolved, Tesco aimed to make its nonfood business as strong as its food business, which, considering the massive might of its food business, called for an enormous amount of growth. Leahy, during his first years in charge, did not disappoint, as Tesco recorded remarkable success on all four of its expansion fronts.

In 2000, Tesco launched its e-commerce business, Tesco .com, one of several new business developments that propelled the company's financial growth during the early years of the 21st century. The company's grocery home-shopping service quickly developed into the largest of its kind in the world. While its retailing services segment gathered steam, Tesco turned to developing its nonfood business. The company began stocking electronic products, toys, sports equipment, cookware, and home furnishings in its stores. In September 2002, the company added the Cherokee clothing brand to its U.K. stores, giving a substantial boost to the company's non-food business. On the international front, Tesco entered Thailand in 1998, South Korea in 1999, Taiwan in 2000, Malaysia in 2002, and China in 2004. The company's existing operations abroad were bolstered by several acquisitions, including the 2002 purchase of HIT, a 13-store chain located in Poland; the 2003 purchase of Kipa, a four-store chain in Turkey; and the 2003 acquisition of the C Two-Network, a chain of 78 food stores in Japan.

While great strides were being achieved in retailing services, international operations, and nonfood business, Leahy did not forget the heart of the company—its U.K. business. The company's market share in Britain increased steadily and impressively during Leahy's first decade in control. Tesco outperformed all its rivals, increasing its share of the market from 15.4 percent in 1998 to 28 percent in 2004. Highlights of the company's progress in its core business area included its rise to rank as the leading organics retailer in the U.K. in 2001 and the impressive strength of its brands, Value, Finest, and Tesco. Perhaps the most notable achievement in the company's core business area was its January 2003 acquisition of the convenience store chain T&S Stores plc, which owned 870 stores. Leahy planned to convert 450 of the units into Tesco Express stores by 2007.

As Tesco plotted further expansion in its four target areas, the company held considerably sway both in Britain and abroad. Leahy's achievements were applauded by many industry observers, who were hard pressed to find any weakness throughout the company's sprawling operations. Tesco stood as a genuine retail giant, one whose stature only promised to grow more intimidating to competitors as the decade progressed. In 2004, when one out every eight pounds spent in Britain went into Tesco's coffers, the company's expansion program represented more than half of all the new supermarket space planned for the United Kingdom.

Principal Subsidiaries

Tesco Capital Ltd.; Tesco Insurance Ltd.; Tesco Property Holdings Ltd.; Tesco Stores Hong Kong Ltd.; Tesco Stores Limited; Global TH (Hungary); Savia S.A. (Poland); Tesco.com; Tesco Personal Finance; GroceryWorks Holdings, Inc (35%).

Principal Competitors

ASDA Group Limited; Dunnes Stores; J Sainsbury plc.

Further Reading

Bird, Michael, "At Your Convenience," *In-Store Marketing*, December 2002, p. 9.

Board, Laura, "Tesco Offers to Acquire T&S," *Daily Deal*, October 31, 2002, p. 54.

"Brain Food: Speaking Out—Sir Terry Leahy, CEO, Tesco," *Management Today*, September 1, 2004, p. 19.

Church, Chris, "How Tesco Took the Low Road to Scotland," *Grocer*, September 30, 1995, p. 14.

Corina, Maurice, *Pile It High, Sell It Cheap: The Authorized Biography of Sir John Cohen*, London: Weidenfeld & Nicolson, 1971, 204 p.

Fallon, James, "Tesco Grows Restless," *Supermarket News*, August 10, 1992, pp. 1ff.

"The Grocer Focus on Tesco Supplement," *Grocer*, September 20, 1997.

Harrington, Sian, "On Top of the World," *Grocer*, June 19, 2004, p. 44.

Hollinger, Peggy, "The Skier Keeping Tesco away from Slippery Slopes," *Financial Times*, February 28, 1997, p. 25.

——, "Tesco Considers Expanding into South-East Asia," *Financial Times*, August 4, 1997, p. 1.

——, "A French Blot on Tesco's Copybook," *Financial Times*, December 10, 1997, p. 30.

Mills, Lauren, "Terry's All Gold at Tesco," *In-Store*, October 2004, p. 17.

Mitchell, Alan, "There Is More in Store for Tesco with T&S Buy," *Marketing Week*, November 14, 2002, p. 34.

Mowbray, Simon, "Spot the Difference Tesco Once Told Suppliers That Its Days of Copying Their Brands Were Over," *Grocer*, September 4, 2004, p. 36.

O'Connor, Robert, "Tesco, Safeway, Sainsbury Target Ireland," *Chain Store Age Executive*, December 1997, pp. 134ff.

Powell, David, *Counter Revolution: The Tesco Story*, London: Grafton, 1991.

Price, Chris, "Tesco Checks Out As Leader," *Financial Times*, September 21, 1996, p. WFT5.

Reier, Sharon, "Branding the Company," *Financial World*, November 26, 1991, pp. 32+.

''Tesco Makes Forey into China Market,'' *Asia Africa Intelligence Wire*, August 6, 2004, p. 34.

''Tesco's New Tricks: British Supermarkets,'' *Economist*, April 15, 1995, pp. 61ff.

''U.K. Grocer Expands RFID Initiative,'' *InternetWeek*, September 29, 2004, p. 43.

Voyle, Susanna, ''UK: Stepping Back Quietly from a Dream Spree,'' *Financial Times*, January 20, 2000, p. 22.

——, ''Tesco Planning to Create 20,000 Jobs,'' *Financial Times*, April 12, 2000, p. 25.

Wilsher, Peter, ''Housekeeping?,'' *Management Today*, December 1993, pp. 38ff.

—updates: David E. Salamie; Jeffrey L. Covell

Time Out Group Ltd.

Universal House
251 Tottenham Court
London W1T 7AT
United Kingdom
Telephone: (+44) 20 7813 3000
Fax: (+44) 20 7813 6001
Web site: http://www.timeout.co.uk

Private Company
Incorporated: 1968
Employees: 180
Sales: £20 million ($34.4 million) (2003 est.)
NAIC: 511140 Database and Directory Publishers

Time Out Group Ltd. is a leading London-based publisher of city guides, such as its flagship *Time Out London* magazine. Launched in 1968, *Time Out London* provides a comprehensive guide to that city's cultural events, as well as television listings, guides to shopping, and news features. The magazine's paid circulation stands at more than 85,000 (down from a peak of nearly 105,000 in the early 1990s) and reaches a total readership of nearly 290,000 each week. Time Out has built on the success of its flagship publication through diversification. The company produces a wide range of annual London-specific titles, including the *Student Guide, Eating & Drinking, Pubs & Bars, London for Children,* and the *Time Out Film Guide*. The company's latest annual publication, *Gay London,* is slated to be launched in 2005. In the early 2000s, Time Out has also moved to expand its coverage to include the wider U.K. market, in part through its successful Web sites. The company also produces a wide range of tourist guide books covering more than 40 cities worldwide, with a total circulation of more than 350,000. The *Time Out International Eating & Drinking Guides* series covers such markets as Barcelona, Rome, Edinburgh, Brussels, New York, and Istanbul. Other guides include *Cheap Eats in London, Europe by Air,* and *Eating & Drinking in Great Britain & Ireland.* Time Out has also expanded internationally, launching the English-language *Time Out Paris* in 1993, and forming a partnership to launch its *Time Out New York* edition in 1995. The company prepared to launch a Chicago edition in 2005, and editions for Los Angeles, San Francisco, and Toronto are planned. At the same time, Time Out has licensed its format for local language versions in foreign markets, including Beijing, Shanghai, Mumbai, Tel Aviv, Athens, Cyprus, Mexico City, St. Petersburg, Istanbul, Dubai, and Abu Dhabi. Time Out founder and owner Tony Elliott remains in control of the group, which posts sales of approximately £20 million ($34.4 million).

Listing Culture in the 1970s

While studying French at England's Keele University, Tony Elliott became involved in the campus arts newspaper, *Unit,* in the late 1960s. Elliott at first sold advertising for the paper but soon after took over as editor. He then quickly expanded the newspaper's scope. As he told *The Sunday Times:* "When I got my hands on *Unit,* I took the decision that I would be going nowhere fast if I just printed 500 copies to circulate around university, so I printed 4,000 copies. There were 20 places in London that I knew would take it on sale or return and I just persuaded people to take it. I knew I had to make it appeal beyond the student audience and secured interviews with Yoko Ono and Jimi Hendrix. I covered my costs out of cashflow and sold 2,000 copies of the first edition."

Elliott's experience with *Unit* not only convinced him to pursue a career in journalism, it also gave him an idea for a new magazine. During his trips to London, Elliott had discovered that there was no single publication covering the bustling cultural scene of London in the late 1960s with listings of political, cultural, and entertainment events, as well as film and concert reviews. As Elliott described it to *The Independent:* "I was interested in cataloguing what was going on in London—and the first issue of *Time Out* was born."

In 1968, Elliott left Keele to begin a required 12-month stay in France; instead, he stopped off in London. There, with several friends and a gift of £70 pounds from his aunt, he began preparing the first issue of his newsletter, originally titled "Where It's At," for August 1968. The fortuitous release of Dave Brubeck's landmark album, *Time Out,* provided Elliott with a new name for his magazine.

Time Out appeared as a single, fold-out sheet with a print run of 5,000 and a price of just one shilling. The paper quickly sold

Key Dates:

1968: Tony Elliott leads launch of *Time Out* magazine, which features listings for London cultural and entertainment events.
1972: *Time Out*'s circulation tops 30,000.
1981: After a staff strike, Elliott gains full control of the company.
1982: *Time Out Eating & Drinking Guide* is launched.
1984: Elliott acquires 51 percent of *I-D* magazine.
1988: Time Out acquires *Paris Passion* magazine in France.
1991: *Time Out Film Guide* begins publication.
1992: *Time Out Paris* supplement to *Pariscope* magazine is launched.
1995: *Time Out New York* partnership is formed.
1997: *Time Out Pub & Bar Guide* is added to the company's roster of publications.
2002: A partnership is formed with DatingDirect.com to add dating services to Time Out Web site.
2004: The company announces the launch of a Chicago edition of *Time Out* in 2005.

out, and a second number of *Time Out* appeared just three weeks later. By the end of the year, Elliott abandoned his plans to go to France and dropped out of Keele University in order to devote himself to his newspaper.

By 1972, *Time Out* had already claimed its place in London's cultural landscape, becoming the city's leading listings magazine. It switched to a fortnightly before becoming a glossy weekly magazine of some 72 pages. In addition to its listings, which remained Elliott's primary focus, the magazine established its reputation as a voice for radical politics. Indeed, *Time Out*'s penchant for agitprop prompted singer Mick Jagger to remark that getting to the listings section of the magazine was "like crossing a picket line."

At the start of the 1980s, a strike among the magazine's staff led to Elliott's gaining full control of the magazine. The pay structure at the company had from the outset been based on an egalitarian model in which all employees, apart from management, received the same £5,000 yearly salary. Decisions were also made on a collective basis, which often brought Elliot into conflict with the company's editorial staff. Toward the end of the 1970s, Elliott had recognized a change in the market that coincided with the end of the counter-counter movement and began seeking to attract new editorial talent to the magazine, in part to shift the magazine's focus away from its highly political content. In order to do this, Elliott began offering higher pay scales, a move that prompted a revolt among the company's staff, most of whom had become unionized over the previous decade.

By May 1981, the crisis had reached its peak, resulting in a walkout by company's staff. *Time Out* was forced to stop publication and disappeared from newsstands for some four months. In the end, Elliott forced his employees' hand, and all but 15 were dismissed. The disgruntled *Time Out* employees joined together to launch a rival listings magazine, *City Lights,* which, while providing cultural listings, focused strongly on political content.

As he prepared to relaunch *Time Out,* Elliott faced another threat in the form of former schoolmate and Virgin Records tycoon Richard Branson. With *Time Out*'s publication suspended, Branson launched his own listings magazine, *Event.* That magazine, however, failed to capture a readership and folded within a year. Branson then offered to buy out *Time Out* with an offer to Elliott of some £750,000. Elliott refused. Before long, *City Lights* also fell by the wayside, and *Time Out* saw its readership climb once again past its pre-strike peak of 85,000.

New Products in the 1990s

Time Out attempted to expand as a business during the 1980s, launching a second publication, *Sell Out,* which focused on shopping. That effort met with little success and was quickly shut down. Time Out also came into conflict with authorities when it attempted to begin publishing advance television listings, which remained controlled by the country's television stations. Originally thwarted by a court order in 1983, Elliott later found support from a number of other media groups, including News International, Emap, IPC, *The Daily Telegraph* and *The Independent.* As a result, *Time Out* added television listings in 1988.

Elliott toyed with the idea of taking his company public in the mid-1980s but ultimately proved unwilling to give up control of the group he had founded. This meant that Time Out's expansion would come slowly. The company explored a number of possibilities, including entering the radio market and launching Pathe News-style features for London movie theaters. However, none of these projects came to fruition.

More successful was the company's launch of the first *Eating & Drinking Guide* in 1982. Elliott himself purchased a 51 percent stake in the London style magazine *I-D* for £20,000 in 1984. In 1988, Elliott at last made it to Paris when the company bought the magazine *Paris Passion,* which was subsequently redesigned as a cultural guide for the city's English-speaking community.

Time Out further expanded in the 1990s when it began introducing a series of annual guides, such as *Time Out Film Guide,* launched in 1991. Other annual Time Out guides covered such themes as sex, drugs, and fashion. These were followed by a number of new magazines, including *Europe by Air* and *Pubs & Bars Guide,* both introduced in 1997. The company also launched a new series of Time Out city guides, first introduced in the early 1990s and published by Penguin. Meanwhile, *Time Out* magazine itself grew strongly, reaching a peak circulation of more than 104,000 during the decade.

Time Out first turned to the international market in the 1990s as well. The company launched the *Paris Free Guide,* a quarterly magazine with a circulation of 250,000. In 1992, it also began producing an English-language supplement for the popular Parisian listings magazine *Pariscope* called *Time Out Paris.* Neither operation provided the company with a financial bonanza, however, and by 2004 the company had decided to convert its Paris magazines to books that appeared on a yearly schedule.

More promising was the company's entry into New York, where it formed a partnership to launch *Time Out New York* in

1995. Despite competition from such rivals as *The Village Voice*, *Time Out New York* caught on quickly. By the end of the decade, the U.S. magazine had outpaced its London forerunner, with a circulation of more than 125,000.

Continuing International Growth in the 2000s

At the turn of the 21st century, Time Out found a new means of developing its international presence. The company began licensing the *Time Out* format to local groups in a number of markets. By 2004, the *Time Out* name was featured as weekly and monthly local language versions in such markets as Istanbul, Dubai, Tel Aviv, Beijing, Cyprus, Athens, Mumbai, and Saint Petersburg. Elliott was highly enthusiastic about the company's ''franchised'' versions, declaring to *The Evening Standard:* ''What's so exciting is that these guys go off and you think, 'F***, it's just like *Time Out*!' ''

Time Out continued to seek new markets as it approached mid-decade. The Internet became an obvious source for the group's development, with the launch of its first Web sites dating to the mid-1990s. The company joined with matchmaking site operator DatingDirect.com to create a dating service supplement for Time Out's timeout.com site in 2002. The company's Internet expansion was seen as playing a crucial role in the company's U.K. strategy, as a new wave of competitors succeeded in nibbling away at the company's readership. By the end of 2004, *Time Out London*'s total circulation had dropped down to just over 85,000.

In 2003, Time Out formed a 50–50 joint venture partnership with Morningstar Inc. founder Joe Mansueto to launch a Chicago edition of *Time Out* magazine. Each side contributed $4 million to the project, slated to be launched in early 2005. Time Out also began developing plans to roll out *Time Out* editions in other North American markets, including Los Angeles, San Francisco, and Toronto. Given the company's success in the New York market, Time Out appeared set to become an international listings leader in the new century.

Principal Subsidiaries

Time Out New York Partners LP.

Principal Competitors

Mindscape; Reed Elsevier N.V.; Michelin North America Inc.; Virgin Group Ltd.; R.R. Donnelley and Sons Co.; VNU N.V.; Guardian Group plc; Yell Group plc.

Further Reading

Aspden, Peter, ''The Timings, They Have A-Changed,'' *Financial Times*, October 3, 1998, p. 4.

Cohen, Nicole, ''The Windy City Gets a Time Out,'' *Mediaweek*, June 21, 2004, p. 10.

''Elliott Sells Magazine That Became the Face of Style,'' *Observer*, August 22, 2004, p. 2.

Grove, Valerie, ''Media Boy Makes Time to Branch Out,'' *Sunday Times*, October 2, 1998.

Mulliman, Jeremy, ''Urban Weekly on Local Lookout,'' *Crain's Chicago Business*, November 10, 2003, p. 4.

Neustatter, Angela, ''Really Valid for 20 Years,'' *Times*, April 13, 1988.

Oakes, Chris, ''Time Out Bids Adieu to Paris,'' *International Herald Tribune*, July 26, 2004, p. 9.

Rowan, David, ''Time Out Takes on the World,'' *Evening Standard*, July 14, 2004, p. 53.

Sabbagh, Dan, ''Time Out Owner Will Not Loosen Grip on the Reins,'' *Times*, October 15, 2004, p. 59.

Snoddy, Raymond, ''Listing But Not Sunk Yet,'' *Times*, February 22, 2002, p. 19.

Steiner, Rupert, ''Student's *Time Out* to Print a Listings Guide, *Sunday Times*, June 4, 2000, p. 19.

''Time for out with the Old, and in with the New,'' *Independent*, December 22, 1998, p. 12.

—M.L. Cohen

Trans World Entertainment Corporation

38 Corporate Circle
Albany, New York 12203
U.S.A.
Telephone: (518) 452-1242
Fax: (518) 862-9519
Web site: http://www.twec.com

Public Company
Incorporated: 1972 as Trans World Music Corporation
Employees: 8,200
Sales: $1.33 billion (2004)
Stock Exchanges: NASDAQ
Ticker Symbol: TWMC
NAIC: 451220 Prerecorded Tape, Compact Disc, and Record Stores

Trans World Entertainment Corporation is one of the country's largest specialty music retailers. Through such retail chains as F.Y.E. (For Your Entertainment), Spec's Music, and Camelot Music, the company sells compact discs, prerecorded audio cassettes, prerecorded videocassettes, and related merchandise in both mall outlets and stand-alone stores. Trans World operates the chains Coconuts Music & Movies, Strawberries, Planet Music, and Saturday Matinee. In 2003, the company acquired the financially beleaguered Wherehouse Entertainment. Trans World also operates a successful online shopping presence on the Web.

The Great Expansion of the Early Years: 1972–88

Prior to founding Trans World Music Corporation, Robert J. Higgins worked as the Eastern divisional sales manager for Trans Continental Music Corporation. There he gained important experience, and in 1972 he opened his own company, Trans World Music Corporation, with a $30,000 personal investment. Originally a wholesale music distributor, Trans World was headquartered in Albany primarily because Higgins, a native of Albany, recognized the city's advantage of having easy access to both the Northeast and Mid-Atlantic markets.

Although Trans World initially entered the profitable wholesale prerecorded music business, it did not take long for the company to take advantage of Higgins's experience and knowledge of the industry as a whole, and in 1973 it opened its first retail operation under the name Record Town. By the end of 1974, Trans World was a $5.5 million company. The following year Higgins and Trans World made another important foray into the retail field: recognizing that Americans were spending a great deal of time and money in malls, Trans World opened the first of many Record Town mall locations. Then, in 1979, the company made a further commitment to the malls, opening its first specialty mall store under the name Tape World, selling prerecorded music tapes rather than records. One of the presiding factors in the decision to open the Tape World stores—and in its eventual success—was that tapes were much smaller than records, allowing Tape World to fit more music titles into a smaller, less-expensive space.

By 1982 Trans World had sales of $25 million and was operating 38 retail units. That year the success of Record Town and Tape World encouraged Trans World to sell its wholesale business and to begin an aggressive expansion of its retail stores. At the time, most of Trans World's stores were clustered on the East Coast, but the expansion would eventually spread the company's stores throughout the United States.

Trans World made its initial public offering in 1986, trading shares on the NASDAQ with the ticker symbol TWMC. (The ticker symbol remained TWMC even after the name change to Trans World Entertainment Corporation in 1994). Higgins, president and chief executive officer, retained the majority of Trans World shares and also served as chairman of the board of directors. Trans World continued rapid expansion throughout the 1980s and early 1990s, mostly by opening stand-alone and mall stores associated with the company but also through acquisition of retail outlets. On June 1, 1985, Trans World acquired all outstanding stock of the B&B Record Corporation, and in 1988 the company acquired the 14 Great American Music Stores located primarily in the Minneapolis-St. Paul area. Trans World's rapid expansion eventually contributed to an oversaturation of the music and video retail market, and by 1990 company profits began to erode.

> **Company Perspectives:**
>
> *Generating a competitive return on investment for shareholders is Trans World Entertainment's foremost responsibility, and this is the principal goal that guides the board of directors and the entire management team.*

Legal and Financial Trouble in the Late 1980s and Early 1990s

In 1989 a judge ruled that Trans World had to pay $2.5 million in damages to Peaches Entertainment Corporation. Peaches had given Trans World a license to use its trademark, but when the license expired in August 1986, Trans World continued to use the trademark in three states. The charge put a dent in profits for 1989, but Higgins said of the award: ''We are happy to get this non-operating issue behind us so that we can turn our management focus back to . . . operating the business.''

In part because of the costs of its continued rapid expansion, the early 1990s saw declining profits for Trans World. In the third quarter of 1990, for example, the company's net income of $992,000 represented a drop of 47 percent compared with that in the same period of 1989. Though revenue was up 11 percent in the third quarter of 1990 to $74.4 million, costs associated with the opening of 40 new stores devoured Trans World's profits. These problems were reflected in the company's stock. Trans World had announced a plan in July 1990 to make a public offering of one million shares, 750,000 of which were owned by Higgins and 250,000 by the company. The offering was to be made at approximately the market value—at the time about $31.50 per share—but by November 1990 the price of Trans World stock had fallen to $14.00 per share, and the company withdrew its public offering registration, citing poor stock market conditions as the reason for withdrawal. By 1993 net income was $9.8 million, down from $14.5 million in 1990, and in 1994 Trans World operated at a net loss of $6.3 million.

Part of the reason for the company's poor returns was the increasing competition from stores such as Best Buy Co., Inc., and Circuit City Stores Inc., which would often sell its music recordings at or below cost in an effort to attract customers into their stores (customers who might then buy other items). In 1996 music companies attempted to discourage stores from this practice by establishing the Minimum Advertised Pricing (MAP) policies, which threatened to withhold marketing allowances to retailers that sold their product below MAP prices. But retailers seemed to ignore the MAP policies until it became apparent that their loss-leader practices were not helping their sales.

In May 1994 Higgins purchased 10,000 shares of Trans World stock at $11 per share. The price might have seemed like a bargain (down from $31.50 in July 1990), but Trans World shares would eventually trade at a low of $1.75 during the fourth quarter of 1995. Recognizing that the market was probably oversaturated with retail music and video stores and that something drastic had to be done to turn Trans World around, Higgins announced on February 2, 1995, that Trans World would close 143 stores. The move was to eliminate poor-performing stores and concentrate on a core group of productive stores. Though Trans World closed 180 outlets during the year (more than the 143 initially announced), sales declined only 3.7 percent. The company also reduced its inventory by $28 million while increasing the product mix available to stores. Trans World took a net loss for 1995 of $25.4 million, due in large part to the $35 million charge for restructuring and closing.

By 1996 the store closings were beginning to pay off, and net income had risen to $7.1 million. Trans World operated a total of 479 stores at the year's end, and by the third quarter of 1996, the share price had returned to $9.50. The positive income figure included a record single-quarter net income of $14.7 million for the fiscal 1996 fourth quarter, which meant fourth-quarter earnings of $1.51 per share.

Growth and Reorganization in the 1990s

On December 10, 1993, Trans World Music opened its first F.Y.E. (For Your Entertainment) store in Trumbull, Connecticut. F.Y.E. was to be Trans World's highest-volume mall operation. Billed in company literature as ''larger than life, bigger than anyone had imagined, with more store, more product, more of everything the customer wants,'' F.Y.E. was Trans World's prototype of a multimedia superstore where there is something to see, do, and ultimately buy for everyone in the family. ''This amazing superstore is about having a great time in the family game center, pulling up a chair in a reading nook, or celebrating a child's birthday or other event with an F.Y.E. party.'' Trans World was hoping to distinguish F.Y.E. from its competition by being one of the few family-oriented, multimedia retail superstores designed to fit in a mall environment.

Also important to the success of F.Y.E. and other Trans World retail outlets was the fact that by 1993 children ages four to 12 controlled or influenced as much as $132 billion a year in spending. The influence of children was particularly strong in the sales of movie videos. For example, the Walt Disney Company's *Beauty and the Beast* was not only the best-selling video of 1992 but the best-selling video ever. In 1993 *Aladdin*, also by the Walt Disney Company, outperformed *Beauty and the Beast*, becoming the best-selling video ever. Following *Aladdin* as top sellers for 1993 were *Pinocchio*, *Free Willy*, and *Homeward Bound*, all movies with children as the targeted audience. Recognizing this trend, Trans World Music made several moves in 1993 to take advantage of this huge source of sales. In their new F.Y.E. stores, a special department was set aside with children's music, books, and videos. Within the Saturday Matinee stores, a special section called Kids' Matinee was designed; called a ''store within a store'' by Trans World, Kids' Matinee offered similar merchandise as that found in their F.Y.E. children's section.

In 1992, when the Tandy Corporation was packaging its Incredible Universe electronic superstores, it turned to Trans World to supply the ''soft'' goods, such as compact discs and prerecorded videotapes, to accompany Tandy's electronic ''hard'' goods, such as compact discs and VCRs. Trans World agreed to supply the music and video products to the giant stores, some of which occupied nearly 200,000 square feet of retail space, of which 10,000 square feet on average was devoted to the music and video departments. At the launch of Incredible Universe in the fall of 1992, Tandy chairman John Roach predicted that the United States could accommodate up

Key Dates:

1972: Robert J. Higgins founds Trans World Music as a wholesale music distributor.
1982: The company begins focusing on retail rather than wholesale.
1986: Trans World goes public.
1994: Trans World Music becomes Trans World Entertainment to reflect the broadening range of its interests.
1999: The company acquires Camelot Music.
2003: The company acquires Wherehouse Entertainment Inc.

to 50 of these ''gigastores,'' with a total sales of $3 billion. Trans World hoped that the joint venture with Incredible Universe would provide a broader customer base with a lower capital investment, thus lowering overhead and start-up costs and increasing profitability.

Though initial response to the Incredible Universe stores had been positive, performance over a longer period was lackluster. In 1996, in an effort to increase plunging profits, Incredible Universe announced plans to promote Coconuts, Record Town, or F.Y.E.—depending upon the popularity and market recognition of the Trans World stores in the various Incredible Universe markets—as retail outlets inside the superstores. But it was already too late. In late 1996 Tandy Corporation announced that all its Incredible Universe stores were to be closed or sold. Retail analyst Lynn Detrick, of Williams MacKay Jordan & Co. in Houston, told Time magazine that ''maybe this does suggest that you can take it too far, that stores can be too big and inconvenient.'' Though not especially good news for Trans World, the closing losses were primarily Tandy's.

Once Trans World began to see consistently positive results from its restructuring, Higgins began again to turn his sights toward growth and expanding market share. Though Trans World was to close another 37 stores in 1997, it was also planning to open 70 new stores, 40 of which would be relocations.

Meanwhile, Higgins and John Sullivan, the chief financial officer, began to talk publicly about acquiring another company. A few companies that did not respond well to sluggish sales and market oversaturation in the 1990s—especially those that had filed for bankruptcy—seemed ripe for takeover. ''Due to the financial difficulties of our competitors,'' said Higgins, ''our acquisitions in real estate will be opportunistic. We will only acquire profitable stores and save them [with] economies of distribution.'' The reduction in the total number of music and video stores nationwide made it possible for Trans World to pursue exclusive operating agreements with shopping malls so that a Trans World retailer would be the only music and video store in the mall. The closing of hundreds of stores across the industry also made it possible for Trans World to expand again without falling into the same trap it had in the early 1990s. The company could rapidly pick up market share with relatively slow openings of new stores in strong sales areas and by making a few strategic acquisitions.

Adding to Trans World's good news, the company announced a new debt agreement to shareholders on June 5, 1997. The new refinancing agreement was reached with Congress Financial Corporation, a CoreStates Company, at interest rates averaging below the prime rate. ''This new debt agreement finalizes our successful restructuring efforts,'' said Higgins in a press statement. ''By offering such favorable rates, our lenders clearly recognize that we have effectively repositioned our company. Based on current borrowing levels, the company will save up to $2.5 million per year in interest charges alone.'' The company had previously obtained waivers from lenders to keep from being in default of two provisions of its loan agreements. The loans were initially made to finance store openings and relocations. The waivers had included agreements to pay higher interest rates.

Much of Trans World Entertainment Corporation's turnaround has been credited to Higgins. A majority shareholder with slightly more than 50 percent of shares, he continued to have a vested interest in the company performing well. In 1997, as a testament to Trans World's turnaround, Higgins received Billboard magazine's Video Person of the Year award.

Into the New Millennium

Although Trans World prospered in the late 1990s, many music stores did not do as well in the new, more competitive market. Increased competition in the business by home electronics marketers such as Best Buy drove many music specialty stores into bankruptcy. One of these was the Columbus, Ohio-based store Camelot Music. In October 1998 Trans World announced that it would purchase the nearly defunct music store chain for about $450 million.

However, the acquisition of Camelot proved to be a drag on Trans World's profits for a number of years. By the end of 1999, the stores that came with the purchase of the Ohio company still were losing money, with sales down 4 percent compared to those of the previous year. Part of the reason for this loss was due to the fact that Camelot had less inventory on hand than had been thought at the time of the sale. In addition, in 2000 Trans World was hit with the results of a federal investigation into a tax fraud that Camelot participated in between 1990 and 1993. Trans World, as the owner of Camelot, became liable for $14 million, including the unpaid tax and the interest due on it.

Despite the setbacks posed by its troubles with the Camelot acquisition, Trans World continued to expand in the early years of the 21st century. In spite of the fact that music sales continued to drop industry-wide through 2001, Trans World profited through sales of DVDs and video games. Although CDs and other music-delivery systems made up 64 percent of total sales—and thus still constituted Trans World's core business—sales of movies in electronic format and the gaming industry jumped 30 percent and 64 percent respectively. In 2003 Trans World made a successful bid for Wherehouse Entertainment Inc., a rival firm, which gave the corporation access to markets on the west coast.

Still more difficulties awaited the Albany, New York-based music retailer in 2003. One of its major suppliers of listening technology, Full-Play Media Systems, contracted with Best Buy to produce listening stations for use in Best Buy stores. Trans World claimed that Full-Play's action constituted a breach of contract, and the corporation sued the technology manufacturer to prevent the Best Buy deal. In addition, Trans World protested the decision by the classic rock band the Rolling Stones to release a new four-DVD set only through Best Buy by pulling Rolling Stones albums from their shelves. Through that action, executive vice-president Fred Fox told Alan Wechsler of the *Albany Times Union*, Trans World took a stand against the band's decision. ''It's just not right,'' he said. ''We believe it should be a level playing field.''

Principal Competitors

The Musicland Group Inc.; MTS Inc.; Amazon.com Inc.

Further Reading

Christman, Ed, ''Trans World Entertainment Corp.,'' *Billboard,* November 20, 1999, p. 127.

——, ''Trans World Losses Down; MCA Golden in 4th Quarter,'' *Billboard,* November 30, 1996, p. 68.

——, ''Trans World Unwraps Plan for 'Comeback' 4th Quarter,'' *Billboard,* October 7, 1995, pp. 83–84.

Fitzpatrick, Eileen, ''Trans World at 25,'' *Billboard,* July 5, 1997, pp. 68–75.

Frank, Stephen E., ''Insiders at Specialty Retailers Purchase Shares in Their Own Troubled Businesses,'' *Wall Street Journal,* August 3, 1994, pp. C23–24.

Furfaro, Danielle T., ''Guilderland, N.Y., Entertainment Firm Found Liable for Camelot Music Tax Scam,'' *Times Union* (Albany, New York) October 20, 2000.

Goldstein, Seth, ''Q&A: Bob Higgins,'' *Billboard,* July 5, 1997, pp. 65–72.

Jeffrey, Don, ''Falling Stocks Zap Retail; Ongoing Price War Hobbles Chains,'' *Billboard,* February 18, 1995, pp. 1–3.

Lanctot, Roger C., ''Data Points,'' *Computer Retail Week 1996*, April 15, 1996, p. 15.

Payne, Melanie, ''New York Entertainment Firm to Buy Ohio-Based Camelot Music,'' *Knight Ridder/Tribune Business News*, October 26, 1998.

''The Perils of Having Way More Than Enough,'' *Time*, January 13, 1997, p. 58.

Reilly, Patrick M., ''Music Retailer Trans World Reports Narrowed Loss for Fiscal Third Period,'' *Wall Street Journal*, November 19, 1996, p. B13.

Scally, Robert, ''Incredible Universe Comes to an End; Final Sales Over by Mid-March,'' *Discount Store News*, March 3, 1997, pp. 1–2.

''Trans World Music Plans Public Offering,'' *Wall Street Journal*, July 24, 1990, p. C21.

''Trans World Music's 1st-Period Net Slashed by Damages Liability,'' *Wall Street Journal*, May 9, 1989, p. C22.

Wechsler, Alan, ''Albany, N.Y.-Based Music Chain Pulls Rolling Stones Albums after Best Buy Deal,'' *Times Union* (Albany, New York), October 31, 2003.

—Terry Bain
—update: Kenneth R. Shepherd

Tutogen Medical, Inc.

1130 McBride Avenue, Third Floor
West Paterson, New Jersey 07424
U.S.A.
Telephone: (973) 785-0004
Fax: (973) 812-1722
Web site: http://www.tutogen.com

Public Company
Incorporated: 1984 as BGM Exploration Ltd.
Employees: 192
Sales: $30.3 million (2003)
Stock Exchanges: American Stock Exchange
Ticker Symbol: TTG
NAIC: 339113 Surgical Appliance and Supplies Manufacturing

Based in West Paterson, New Jersey, Tutogen Medical, Inc., is a publicly traded company that makes bio-implants and medical devices used primarily to repair tissue and bone. Its most important products are allografts, donated human tissues that the company subjects to a patented process called Tutoplast, which uses dehydration and sterilization to prevent infection or tissue rejection. Unlike autographs—tissues taken from a patient's own body—allografts are tissue and bone harvested from cadavers, a process that offers a number of advantages: less pain for patients, quicker and less expensive surgeries, and faster rehabilitation. Examples of allografts include the use of a cadaver's patella tendon to replace a patient's knee ligament, the brain sheathing used in pediatric brain surgery, or bone wedges as a replacement for surgically removed spinal discs. The company also makes wound dressings and materials used in dental implants. Tutogen maintains offices in Germany and France and production facilities in Alachua, Florida, and Neunkirchen, Germany. The company's products are available in 45 countries around the world.

1980s Origins

Technically, Tutogen was incorporated in April 1984 in Vancouver, Canada, as GBM Exploration Ltd., an oil exploration company. This may have been an ill-advised time to enter the oil business, which collapsed during this period and led to the ruin of countless energy companies, but it was an opportune moment to start a biotech venture. A more relevant date for the launch of Tutogen was October 1985 when Texas doctor Weldon S. Guest founded Biodynamics Inc. in Houston to develop medical and surgical products. In 1986 he attracted $2.6 million in Canadian venture capital money and a reverse merger was engineered with GBM Exploration, which served as little more than a shell in order to gain Canadian standing. The name was then changed to American Biodynamics Inc. and the headquarters was relocated to Houston. The seed money did not last long, however, and by late 1987 most of the funds were exhausted. To help establish the young company Guest brought in a seasoned executive, John Hargiss, from a San Antonio medical technology firm to serve as the chief executive.

Although Guest had several research projects under way, by 1988 American Biodynamics only had two major products—and just one that was bringing in any money. The company served as the exclusive distributor for a West German company, Viggo GmbH, which processed human connective tissue used in surgical transplants. American Biodynamics also was getting another product ready for the market, the Extracorporeal Circulation System (ECS). It was a proprietary blood transfusion device that collected, cleaned, and reintroduced a patient's own blood during surgery. In this way, the risk of contracting a transfusion-related disease such as AIDS or hepatitis was eliminated. The technology was promising enough that it attracted the interest of much larger corporations. Minneapolis-based Medtronic Inc. courted American Biodynamics in 1989, but its buyout offer for ECS was ultimately rejected. A subsidiary of Pfizer Inc., Shiley, Inc., stepped in with $200,000 in 1989 and provided technical assistance in developing the device, but when it also made a offer to buy the technology, American Biodynamics declined. Hargiss told *Houston Business Journal* that the offer "fell short of what we wanted—by a lot." Instead, the company elected to move forward on its own to complete the design work on the device, gain Food and Drug Administration approval, and find a way to get ECS on the market.

In 1989 Hargiss and Guest had a falling out over the direction of the company, after Hargiss pulled the plug on three of Guest's research projects that were draining resources. A battle

Company Perspectives:

Tutogen's mission is to become a world leader in creating and providing superior and safe biological implants for surgical solutions to surgeons for the benefit and health of patients worldwide.

for control of the company ensued, with Hargiss coming out on top. In November 1989 Guest sued the company, alleging that Hargiss required his approval before selling off assets, terminating research projects, and negotiating corporate partnerships. Hargiss responded by suing on behalf of the company alleging that Guest had failed to live up to his fiduciary responsibilities to shareholders. With the filing of additional lawsuits in both Canada and Texas, the matter lingered for three years. Because Guest owned a 15 percent stake in the company he was able to submit his own slate of directors to shareholders in an attempt to win back control of the board. Finally, in 1992 a settlement was reached between the two sides. A noncompete agreement was signed, Guest stayed in Texas, and American Biodynamics changed its name to Biodynamics International, Inc. and moved its headquarters to Tampa, Florida. The company also reincorporated in Florida, putting an end to its unusual Vancouver-Houston connection.

Steady Growth Marking the Early 1990s

While Hargiss and Guest fought for control, the company made advances on some fronts. In 1991 it formed an alliance with Surgimedics Inc. to market a new bone-graft product and other surgical products. A year later it established a German subsidiary, Biodynamics International GmbH, to produce allografts using the company's new Tutoplast sterilizing process. As Biodynamics made its move to Florida, it appeared positioned to enjoy steady growth. It also was involved in areas other than tissue and bone. It owned a 51 percent stake in Corin Othopedic Products, which served as the U.S. importer for British partner Corin Medical Ltd., maker of artificial hip and knee joints. Biodynamics also had forged a joint venture, Advance Haemotechnologies, with a subsidiary of Surgimedics to continue its long-term work on a blood autotransfusion system. Although ECS at one time held out great promise, it faced stiff competition and never did perform as well as management hoped. Rather, it was the Tutoplast technology that now offered the greatest promise. The company turned a profit in fiscal 1991, fiscal 1992, and fiscal 1993, altogether earning about $2.5 million during this stretch. In May 1993 Biodynamics was strong enough to acquire the Wound Care Division of Pfimmer-Viggo, but then events would now combine to stunt the company's growth.

In late 1993 the FDA refused to accept bone imports from the German subsidiary because the donors had not received serological testing from an FDA-approved laboratory. It was an impossible condition for the company to meet because there were no FDA-approved labs in Germany. Next, in May 1994 the FDA banned the importation of brain sheathing from the German plant. According to the company, the FDA never suggested that the products were unsafe; they merely forbade their sale in the United States. Because about one-third of Biodynamics' revenues resulted from these German imports, the company took a major hit to the balance sheet. It also had to invest money in order to ramp up production of hard and soft tissues in the United States. Because of these difficulties, the price of Biodynamics' stock sagged below $1 and was almost delisted by the NASDAQ. In 1994 the company posted revenues just shy of $12 million and lost $3.2 million.

Biodynamics took another blow in 1995 when France placed a moratorium on the importation of bone allografts. The country had been Biodynamics' best market for the product. In April 1995 Hargiss resigned as president, CEO, and a member of the board in order to ''pursue other interests.'' He was replaced on an interim basis by Chairman Charles C. Dragone. A permanent replacement was hired in March 1996, when Karl H. Meister took over as president and CEO. He brought more than 30 years of experience in the pharmaceutical and medical device field, including a five-year stint as the head of Carrington Laboratories and executive positions at Pfizer, Inc. and Schering-Plough Corporation. In 1997 Meister moved Biodynamics' headquarters to New Jersey, where he lived. More important, the area was home to all the major players in the pharmaceutical and medical device field.

As Meister attempted to turn around Biodynamics, he had to contend with the same kind of challenges that Hargiss faced. In March 1997 the Japanese Ministry of Health banned the company's brain sheath products. But during the same month, France also lifted its ban on bone allografts, a move that buoyed Biodynamics' business considerably. Meister also was able to reopen the U.S. market for the company's products. Another nettlesome problem he had to overcome was Biodynamics' high level of debt, taken on because the company in the past had relied on lines of credit and institutional investors to make up for a lack of cash flow. In order to shore up a shortage in working capital and gain some long-term flexibility, Meister in 1997 worked out an arrangement with the company's institutional investors to convert debt into equity. With the company on a better financial footing, he now began to pursue a growth strategy that banked the company's future on its Tutoplast technology, using it as a platform to develop tissue engineered products. In keeping with this concept, in 1998 Biodynamics changed its name to Tutogen Medical, Inc., an effort to more closely link the corporate name with the company's core technology.

The company also enjoyed positive developments on other fronts in 1998. It forged a strategic alliance with Regeneration Technologies, Inc., bringing technology transfers to Tutogen, and the two companies began to develop a European tissue banking program. Moreover, Tutogen received positive research results in 1998. In Germany a case study was conducted involving a jawbone with a malignant tumor that was removed from a body, the cancer destroyed, then the bone treated with the Tutoplast process and successfully reintroduced to the patient. It was the first published case of such a procedure, which offered a marked improvement over the traditional treatment in which part of the jaw is removed and replaced by bone from the patient's hip.

As a result of the steps Meister took, he was able to begin the process of restoring sales levels and returning the company to profitability. In fiscal 1997 sales totaled $8.9 million, resulting in a net loss of $5.2 million. A year later, sales grew by a modest 3 percent to $8.9 million but because interest payments dropped from $934,000 in 1997 to $362,000 in 1998, Tutogen was able

Key Dates:

1985: Dr. Weldon Guest launches American Biodynamics in Houston, Texas.
1986: Biodynamics merges with BGM Exploration Ltd.
1992: The company moves to Tampa, Florida, and changes its name to Biodynamics International, Inc.
1997: Headquarters is moved to New Jersey.
1998: The company's name is changed to Tutogen Medical, Inc.
2000: The company gains a listing on the American Stock Exchange.

to turn a profit of $122,000 on the year. A year later revenues improved 29 percent to $11.5 million, much of which came from the United States where the company was again able to market its products. Because domestic sales increased by 80 percent over the previous year, net income improved to $414,000. Having turned around the business in little more than three years, Meister elected to retire in 1999, and once again Dragone stepped in as interim CEO. Manfred Krueger, brought in earlier in 1999 as chief operating officer, was soon named as Meister's permanent replacement.

New Century Bringing New Research Development

In 2000 Tutogen gained a listing on the American Stock Exchange, a move that management hoped would boost the company's reputation with the investment community. The company's investment in research and development also was beginning to pay off in the form of new products. In late 1999 Tutogen introduced Tutofix pins, made from cow bone and used to help with fractured bones, especially forearms and small breaks in the hands and feet. Not only were Tutofix pins absorbed, eliminating a second surgery, they were replaced by bone during the healing process. In 2001 Tutogen introduced a Tutoplast Processed Dermis product that was used in a procedure that treated female incontinence, and Puros, a bone graft material used with dental implants. The company entered the sports medicine field in 2002 by offering the LigaTech line of products that repaired and replaced ligaments. Also in 2002 Tutogen began the European marketing of Tutomesh, a membrane used to repair abdominal walls damaged by hernias. In 2003 Tutogen introduced Cervical Space, a spinal product.

Sales grew steadily through the early years of the new century, increasing from $16.6 million in fiscal 2000 to $30.3 million in fiscal 2003, while net income improved to $2.3 million. But the company's small size limited its ability to fully realize the potential of its technologies. As a result, in 2003 the Tutogen board gave management permission to look for a strategic buyer, one with the resources to adequately market the company's products. Tutogen began the process of selling itself to a private equity firm but the negotiations were terminated at the close of 2003. The company remained independent in 2004, although it would change leadership. Krueger stayed on as president, but 55-year-old Roy D. Crowninshield now took over as CEO and chairman. Holding a doctorate from the University of Vermont, he was a former faculty member at the University of Iowa, where he headed the orthopedic biomechanics laboratory. He also had 21 years of experience at Zimmer Holdings, maker of orthopedic products. Crowninshield took over a company with a great deal of potential and unanswered questions about its future.

Principal Subsidiaries

Tutogen Medical GmbH; Tutogen Medical (United States) Inc.

Principal Competitors

CryoLife, Inc.; Osteotech, Inc.; Regeneration Technologies, Inc.

Further Reading

Marcial, Gene G., "Tutogen May Get a Facelift," *Business Week,* April 1, 2002, p. 91.

McNamara, Victoria, "Founder Files Suit, Delays Biotech Board Meeting," *Houston Business Journal,* June 10, 1991, p. 10.

——, "Small Biotech Firm Rebuffs Big Buyers," *Houston Business Journal,* April 2, 1999, p. 1.

Shepherd, Gary, "After Losses, Biodynamics Relies on Medical Miracles," *Tampa Bay Business Journal,* February 10, 1995, p. 17.

——, "Biodynamics Moves to N.J.," *Tampa Bay Business Journal,* May 16, 1997, p. 3.

—Ed Dinger

UnitedAuto

United Auto Group, Inc.

13400 Outer Drive West, Suite 36B
Detroit, Michigan 48239-4001
U.S.A.
Telephone: (313) 592-7311
Fax: (313)592-7340
Web site: http://www.unitedauto.com

Public Company
Incorporated: 1990
Employees: 13,000
Sales: $8.67 billion (2004)
Stock Exchanges: New York
Ticker Symbol: UAG
NAIC: 441110 New Car Dealers; 441120 Used Car Dealers

United Auto Group, Inc., is a leading acquirer, consolidator, and operator of franchised automobile and light-truck dealerships and related companies. In terms of total revenues, the company is the second largest publicly traded retailer of new motor vehicles in the United States. The company owns and operates nearly some 140 franchises in the United States and abroad, many of them focusing on the retail of foreign and luxury automobiles. United Auto Group's franchised dealerships include integrated service and parts operations. Subsidiaries engage in the purchase, sale, and servicing of automobile loans, as well as in marketing a complete line of aftermarket automotive products and services.

Selling the Concept: 1990–93

United Auto Group was founded in 1990 by Marshall S. Cogan, a New York City financier and investor who had amassed a fortune as a Wall Street dealmaker. Cogan, who owned the well-known midtown Manhattan restaurant "21" and controlled Foamex International Inc., a major automotive interiors supplier, traced his interest in consolidating the auto sales industry to a stint with his uncle's Chevrolet dealership in Cambridge, Massachusetts, when he was a teenager.

Cogan founded United Auto Group with two other investors: Apollo Advisors L.P. and Harvard Private Capital Group Inc., Harvard University's investment unit. Cogan invested $33 million and his partners, who came to include J.P. Morgan Capital Corporation, invested about $70 million in the enterprise. For $5.2 million, they bought a 70 percent interest in New Jersey-based DiFeo Automotive Group, the second largest dealer network in the New York City metropolitan area, with 1991 sales of $375 million, and later added other dealerships, including ones in Nyack, New York, and Danbury, Connecticut. By the end of 1993—United Auto's first full year in business—it was the eighth largest retail automotive dealer in the United States, with total revenues that year of $606.1 million. The company was employing 1,200 people and operating 41 franchises at seven sites in late 1994.

The purpose of the investors was to capitalize on consolidation opportunities within the highly fragmented automotive retailing industry by purchasing and operating family-owned auto dealerships and managing them professionally, controlling costs, and improving customer service. Other companies had begun doing the same in the 1980s, buying up smaller dealers, offering a wide variety of makes and models, and merging service and parts operations, but these efforts capsized in the junk-bond fiasco at the end of the decade. "This was an industry not well-regarded by Wall Street," Cogan recalled. "People avoid auto dealers like they avoid the dentist."

In spite of Wall Street's reluctance, Cogan felt that consolidation made sense, arguing that a big dealership franchiser could make money even during an economic downturn because most of the revenue would come from fixing and financing new cars, not selling them. He also argued that economy of scale would allow such a company to save money on advertising, credit lines, and computer processing. Carl Spielvogel, formerly head of the Bates Worldwide advertising agency, was brought in as United Auto Group's first chairman and chief executive. He said his mission was to turn the company's dealerships into supermarkets where customers could buy any car make, new or used, and get any kind of part or service. His strategy was to acquire dealerships in geographic clusters. "We try to surround a market," he told a reporter, "because it gives you the ability, in particular, to move used cars from one dealership to another."

Company Perspectives:

Friendly, courteous and forthright service. Fair competitive pricing. Accessible and flexible financing programs. Dependable, comprehensive care and protection plans. Welcome to United Auto. Come explore how our network of authorized dealers can make a difference in the way you find, purchase, finance and service a new or pre-owned car. United Auto. We're with you.

United Auto Group's courtship of the nation's 23,400 auto dealers, many of them approaching or already at retirement age, was being matched by other ventures, such as Asbury Group, Cross-Continent Auto Retailers, and AutoNation USA, a subsidiary of H. Wayne Huizenga's Republic Industries Inc. United Auto Group paid cash for acquired dealerships: an average of $12 million for each of the three suburban Atlanta dealerships it acquired in 1996. In return, the company wanted the dealer to stay on (at least until professional management was installed) and the business to keep its prior name.

Automakers traditionally had eschewed dealing with groups of dozens or hundreds of dealerships, opting instead to do business with small, often family-owned corporations tightly monitored under the franchise system. They were not sure they wanted to negotiate with megadealers who ordered cars by the tens of thousands, and they were especially resistant to the idea of selling to retailers who also offered rival car models. This unwillingness began to change in the mid-1990s, when automakers such as Ford and Chrysler began to feel that large companies could help them cut the cost of delivering cars to dealerships from the factory, which some experts estimated was accounting for up to 30 percent of the retail price of a new car. In 1997 Ford and Chrysler were creating or proposing their own auto superstores, grouping their brands under one roof.

United Auto Group made it clear that selling used cars, which yielded profit margins of up to 15 percent—far more than the 5 percent profit on a new car—was an essential part of its strategy. One of its innovations was the Security Blanket, a 15-day money-back guarantee—unique for the industry—on all of its used cars, which were being sold on a few of the company's lots. United Auto's used car lots also offered a 132-point car inspection and, unlike their main competitors, made prices negotiable. The vehicles were mostly two- or three-year-old off-lease vehicles, purchased at auction. The company's wholly owned subsidiary, Atlantic Auto Finance Corporation, made car loans at attractive interest rates. United Auto opened its first strictly used car outlets in 1996 and, as of early March 1997, had eight freestanding used car superstores in four states as well as 51 new car dealerships with used car areas in 11 states.

Broadening Its Base: 1994–98

After earning net income of $1.2 million in 1993, United Auto Group lost $245,000 in 1994 on revenues of $731.6 million and $3.7 million in 1995 on revenues of $805.6 million. The company's fortunes began to turn around in that year, when DiFeo Group eliminated 17 unprofitable franchises—almost half the total—and about 250 jobs and tied pay plans to net profits and customer satisfaction. In 1996 United Auto had net income of $3 million on revenues of $1.3 billion, with Cogan attributing the turnaround to used cars. The company went public in October 1996, raising $180 million in a sale of common stock at $30 a share.

In March 1997 United Auto Group bought nine auto dealerships with 1996 sales of $430 million from John Stalupp and John Stalupp, Jr. Five of them were in West Palm Beach, Florida, and the other four were located on Long Island, New York. The acquisition price was $53 million in a combination of cash, stock, and promissory notes. By the end of 1997 United Auto had acquired a number of other dealerships, all of them in the South or Puerto Rico, and was the nation's second largest publicly traded auto dealership. It was first in the New York metropolitan area, with 23 dealerships.

Despite the rapid growth of the company, all was not well with United Auto Group. The common stock, which peaked at $35.25 a share in November 1996, plunged to $16 in April 1997, soon after company executives told financial analysts that overhead costs would keep first-quarter earnings from reaching previous projections. Spielvogel resigned his post and was replaced by Cogan, who adopted a strategy of concentrating on the "aftercare" market of parts and services, where profit margins could run much higher than on sales of automobiles. AutoCare was the company's subsidiary for aftermarket products and services.

Typically, fewer than one-third of new car customers were going to their original dealership for service, but Cogan was trying to change that with sales training and a database sending customers reminders about tune-ups and oil changes. At some United Auto Group dealerships, the rate of customers coming back for service rose as high as 60 percent. Another goal that Cogan announced for 1998 was to have 90 percent of United Auto's finance originations, including the loans bought by other lenders, pass through Atlantic Auto Finance's hands and generate fees. In nearly every case customers would make their checks out to the subsidiary, even if another lender actually held the paper.

United Auto Group continued to broaden its base in 1998. In January of that year, for about $28 million, it acquired five franchises with estimated 1997 revenues of $320 million. The company also purchased, for $14.5 million, The Triangle Group, Puerto Rico's second largest auto retailer with estimated 1997 revenues of $160 million. In July United Auto announced it had purchased two San Diego dealerships and had agreed to buy two more. The four franchises had estimated annual revenues of $160 million. Their acquisition brought United Auto's total to 98 franchises nationwide.

Expansion was not coming cheaper, however, and United Auto Group's long-term debt rose from $11.1 million at the end of 1996 to $238.6 million at the end of 1997. Interest expenses of $14.1 million were one reason the company lost $10.1 million on $2.09 billion of revenues in 1997. The firm also suffered when the big U.S. automakers cut prices of new cars, which depressed used car sales and pushed used car prices lower. United Auto Group took a pretax charge of $31.7 million in late 1997, related to the realignment of operations, including

Key Dates:

1990: United Auto is established by entrepreneur Marshall Cogan and partners.
1996: United Auto goes public.
1998: Penske Corporation becomes a major investor in United Auto.
2002: Company expands into the United Kingdom with two Mercedes-Benz dealerships.

the divestiture of nine unprofitable franchises. Its stock fell as low as $9.50 a share in January 1998.

The Late 1990s

As of April 1998, United Auto Group was operating franchised dealerships in Arizona, Arkansas, Connecticut, Florida, Georgia, Illinois, Indiana, Louisiana, Nevada, New Jersey, New York, North Carolina, Puerto Rico, South Carolina, Tennessee, and Texas. The company was selling U.S., European, and Asian brands, ranging from economy cars to luxury automobiles and sports utility vehicles. Eight of its outlets were stand-alone used car retail centers. Vehicle sales accounted for 88 percent of total revenues in 1997. The company sold 50,985 new and 1,253 used vehicles.

United Auto Group had ready access to used vehicles through trade-ins for new cars, vehicles originally leased through its new vehicle dealerships, and used vehicle auctions only open to new vehicle dealers. In addition, only new vehicle franchises were able to sell used vehicles certified by manufacturers under a recently introduced program by which manufacturers supported specific high-quality used cars with extended warranties and attractive financing options.

Aftermarket products and service and parts operations accounted for 9 percent of total revenues. Aftermarket products included accessories such as radios, cellular phones, and alarms, as well as extended service contracts and credit insurance policies. Each of United Auto Group's new vehicle dealerships was offering a fully integrated service and parts department. Unlike independent service shops or used car dealerships with service operations, United Auto was qualified to perform work covered by manufacturer warranties. The company believed that its market share would grow at the expense of independent mechanics' shops, which might be unable to address the increased sophistication of motor vehicles and the increased expense of compliance with more stringent environmental regulations. It was actively marketing warranty-covered services to potential customers such as municipalities and corporations with large fleets of automobiles.

Atlantic Auto Finance was renamed UnitedAuto Finance in 1997. Based in Rochester, New York, UnitedAuto Finance accounted for 3 percent of the parent company's total revenues that year. It was the subsidiary for purchasing, selling, and servicing primarily prime-credit-quality automobile loans originated by both the parent company and third-party dealerships. UnitedAuto Finance also was receiving fees from financial institutions that purchased installment contracts from customers referred to them by UnitedAuto Finance. At the end of 1997 this subsidiary was serving about 250 dealerships in eight states.

In April 1998 Cogan was United Auto Group's largest stockholder, holding 20.5 percent of the common stock through Trace International Holdings, Inc. Aeneas Venture Corporation, an affiliate of Harvard Private Capital Group, held 14.5 percent, and a unit of Apollo Advisers L.P. held 9.4 percent.

Following news of continued business losses in 1998 (797,000 versus 10.1 million in 1997), United Auto Group announced that they were seeking new investors. News that Chairman Roger Penske of Penske Corporation in Detroit might be interested set the stock prices of United Auto Group soaring in March. By April 19th Penske was in place as the company's new CEO, having invested 83 million in the company. In return, Penske Corporation was given a majority of the United Auto's board seats. Penske, a former race car driver, had a reputation for taking over companies and improving them—in the 1980s he'd taken the reins of Detroit Diesel Corporation and turned it into a legitimate competitor among diesel engine makers.

Profits skyrocketed shortly after Penske's arrival. By May 1999 the company could claim a 245 percent increase in profits, and a 213 percent rise in net earnings. By March 2000 Penske had plans for expansion into Charlotte, North Carolina, a playing field that would set him directly against an old rival, Bruton Smith, owner of Sonic Automotive Inc. Industry sources said that Penske hoped to make Charlotte the hub of its new Southeastern operations, despite the fact that Smith already had several holdings in the same city. In May 2000 UnitedAuto Group launched into another industry first, and announced that they would be the primary source of automobiles for CarsDirect.com, an online firm that made it possible to buy cars directly off the Internet.

New Territories in the 2000s

In June 2000 United Auto acquired four Columbus Ohio dealerships and two Infiniti and Mercedes Benz showrooms. It also moved its corporate headquarters to Detroit, Michigan, amid news of other dealership acquisitions. The dealership acquisitions continued into the first of the year 2001, when Penske announced intentions to purchase at least 80 percent of UnitedAuto Group and possibly take it private. Penske's Investment company, Penske Capital Partners LLC, spent $64 million to increase the percentage of the company owned by Penske to 57.9 percent. Profits rose through the middle of the year, with the unexpected result that UnitedAuto squeezed from the third largest automotive retailer to become the second largest.

January 2002 saw a new first as United Auto Group expanded into the United Kingdom with two Mercedes-Benz dealerships, furthering the company's plans to become a global player in the auto retailing market. By May 2002 UnitedAuto Group had become joint owner of several automotive firms in Mexico, and partnered with German auto retailer Werner Nix to sell and service Toyota and Lexus automobiles in Germany. Profits continued to rise, up 19 percent in the first quarter of 2002. Record growth followed in the second quarter and retail sales rose 26 percent. In early 2003 UnitedAuto was able to announce continued double-digit profits, followed by another record first quarter. On the heels of consistently excellent financial news for several years running, Penske announced a stock dividend of ten cents per share for all investors in October 2003.

Stating that customers wanted ''a buying experience, a broader selection and great customer service,'' in November 2003 Penske oversaw the acquisition and construction of so-called auto malls in major cities of the United States so customers could compare makes and models of cars before buying. The year 2004 saw a continuation of the policies championed by Penske since his arrival—expansion into Europe continued alongside acquisitions throughout the United States. Profits continued their upward climb as additional record quarters followed.

Principal Subsidiaries

Synter Group plc; Atlantic Auto Funding Corporation; UAG Capital Management, Inc.; UAG Finance Company, Inc.; United Auto Enterprises, Inc.; United AutoCare, Inc.; United AutoCare Products, Inc.; UnitedAuto Finance Inc.; United Lenders, Inc.

Principal Competitors

Larry H. Miller Group; AutoNation Inc.

Further Reading

Armstrong, Julie, ''European Expansion Boosts UnitedAuto,'' *Automotive News,* July 19, 2004, p. 4.

Brown, Peter, ''Dealer Groups Enter on Exit Strategy,'' *Automotive News,* February 27, 1995, p. 14.

Halliday, Jean, ''For United Auto, Expansion Not As Important As Profits,'' *Advertising Age,* April 7, 1997, p. S10.

Harris, Donna, ''Empire Building,'' *Automotive News,* February 18, 2002, p. 1.

Henry, Jim, ''UAG's Cogan Leads Profit-Center Push,'' *Automotive News,* August 25, 1997, pp. 3, 9.

Incantalupo, Tom, ''Major Car Chain Buys 5 LI Dealers,'' *Newsday,* February 26, 1997, pp. A43–A44.

Messina, Judith, ''Spielvogel to Speed Auto Dealers' Growth,'' *Crain's New York Business,* November 28, 1994, pp. 3, 51.

Naughton, Keith, ''Demolition Derby on Wall Street?,'' *Business Week,* September 9, 1996, p. 48.

Temes, Judy, ''Dealer's Auto Motive,'' *Crain's New York Business,* March 31, 1997, pp. 1, 52.

''United Auto Expanding into California Market,'' *New York Times,* July 14, 1998, p. D3.

Wernle, Bradford, ''United Buys 9 More Stores; Stock Falls,'' *Automotive News,* March 3, 1997, pp. 1, 47.

''Who Will Deal in Dealerships?,'' *Economist,* February 14, 1998, pp. 61–63.

Yung, Katherine, ''Public Dealerships Shake Up Old-Line Auto Sales Industry,'' *Detroit News,* February 2, 1997, p. 1C+.

—Robert Halasz
—update: Howard A. Jones

United Industries Corporation

2150 Schuetz Road
St. Louis, Missouri 63146
U.S.A.
Telephone: (314) 427-0780
Fax: (314) 253-5978
Web site: http://www.spectrumbrands.com

Private Company
Incorporated: 1969
Employees: 900
Sales: $536.1 million (2003)
NAIC: 325320 Pesticide and Other Agricultural Chemical Manufacturing.

United Industries Corporation is a St. Louis, Missouri-based company with its business divided among three operating divisions. Operating under the Spectrum Brands name, the Home and Garden division offers household insecticide and insect repellent products, insect control products, and lawn and garden fertilizer and organic growing media products. The Canada division operates as Nu-Gro, offering a variety of home and garden products, including fertilizers and controlled nitrogen release products. United Pet Group, United Industries' pet division, offers a wide range of pet supplies for cats, dogs, birds, fish, and small animals. United Industries is highly dependent on three major customers—The Home Depot, Lowe's Home Improvement Warehouse, and Kmart—which account for nearly 75 percent of all sales. The private company is majority owned by The Thomas H. Lee Equity Fund IV, which has a 84.3 percent stake in the business, and is expected to eventually cash out through a sale or public offering of stock. Current management owns 7.9 percent and the previous owner and management 7.8 percent.

Late 1960s Origins

United Industries was founded in St. Louis in 1969 by David C. Pratt. The company started out as a bolt maker but switched gears starting in 1973 with the acquisition of a contract manufacturer of insecticides and herbicides called Spray Chem. Subsidiary Chemisco was formed to house the new business line. A dozen years would pass before the company moved beyond contract work to become involve in branded products, achieved through the 1985 acquisition of Real-Kill. Three years later, United Industries bolstered its portfolio of branded products considerably by buying lines from Unilever's U.S.A. subsidiary Chesebrough-Ponds, adding such brands as Hot Shot, No-Pest, Rid-a-Bug, and Spectracide. The next major pickup came in 1994 with the acquisition of the well known Cutter insect repellent, along with other lines, from Miles Laboratories of Akla-Seltzer fame. The product was developed in 1957 by physician Bob Cutter and grew to become one of the leading products in the insect control category, trailing only Off! in sales.

After being in business for a quarter-century, United Industries was now poised to enjoy dramatic growth, realized by making larger and more frequent acquisitions. In 1995, the company added a number of brands that enjoyed strong sales at Kmart, including plant products KRid, KGro, Shootout, and Gro Best. It also obtained an exclusive license on the Peters and Peters Professional brands of plant food from Scotts Co. The company's lawn and garden slate was so strong that Lowe's named United Industries its Supplier of the year for its products in this category in 1995. The company would also make inroads with Home Depot, which in 1997 began offering Real-Kill as it opening price point brand, as well as recognizing United Industries' lawn and garden offerings by naming the company its Partner of the Year.

In 1998, United Industries introduced what it called the first new do-it-yourself termite home defense system, an item that generated some controversy. Dubbed Terminate, the product relied on bait stakes that homeowners planted around the foundation of their houses. Although it was approved by the Environmental Protection Agency, Terminate came under fire from the Federal Trade Commission and eight state attorney generals, which went to federal court to halt the sale of the product, charging that United Industries' labels and advertising made unsubstantiated claims about its effectiveness. The FTC maintained that the Terminate did not kill drywood or Formosan termites, which only professional exterminators could eliminate. Moreover, the commission charged that United Industries

Key Dates:

1969: The company is founded by David C. Pratt.
1973: Spray Chem is acquired.
1985: Real-Kill is acquired.
1994: Cutter brand is acquired.
1999: The company sold to Thomas H. Lee Partners.
2004: Nu-Gro Corporation and United Pet Group, Inc., are acquired.

could not prove that Terminate by itself could prevent infestation, eliminate active infestations, or was more effective than chemical barriers and sprays already on the market. Far from being a no-maintenance system, according to the FTC, Terminate's bait stakes needed to be inspected periodically and replaced every 11 months. United Industries ultimately settled the matter in 1999 by agreeing to change its advertising and as a consequence escaped paying any fines.

Climbing Sales in the Mid- to Late 1990s

From 1995 to 1998, United Industries performed strongly. On average, revenues grew by 26 percent each year while profits increased at an even faster clip. By this stage, the company was generating annual sales in the $300 million range, and Pratt, who had become a minority owner of the St. Louis Cardinals baseball team, was ready to cash in after 30 years of effort. He found a willing buyer in Thomas H. Lee Partners L.P., a Boston-based leveraged buyout company. Lee Partners paid $620 million to acquire a 90 percent stake in United Industries. Pratt retained a 5 percent interest.

United Industries' new owner was founded by Thomas H. Lee in 1974. A 1965 Harvard graduate, Lee always wanted to own equities. He cut his teeth as a securities analyst in New York before returning to his native Boston, where he joined First National Bank of Boston's high-tech venture capital group. Lee eventually headed the unit while he simultaneously attempted to launch two of his own funds, neither of which caught on with investors. Finally, in 1974, he put up $100,000 of his own money and started Thomas H. Lee Co., which slowly began to attract outside funds. Lee was an earlier proponent of leveraged buyouts, but he took a far different approach from that of most corporate raiders of the 1980s. He was a little known practitioner of ''friendly takeovers,'' concentrating on companies that wanted to be bought and could be improved and later sold at a profit. Lee told *Forbes* in 1997, ''It's like buying an already nice house on a perfectly good lot and then improving it.'' Acquisitions made in the 1980s included SCOA Industries Inc., Playtex Products Inc., General Nutrition Inc., and Sterling Jewelers. Although Lee would attract such high-caliber investors as the State of Connecticut, Commonfund Capital, Duke University, Hamilton Lane Advisors, Liberty Mutual Group, and the PSR&G Master Retirement Fund, it was not until the 1992 purchase of soft-drink maker Snapple that his name became widely known. After buying Snapple for $140 million, he grew the company's revenues from $95 million to $750 million in just two years. He then sold the business to Quaker Oats for $1.7 billion. His funds had invested $28 million in Snapple and now reaped $927 million in return. As the reputation of Lee Partners grew, so did the size of his funds. In 1990, the firm raised a $568 million general buyout fund, followed by a $1.37 billion fund in 1995, and a $3.4 billion fund in 1998 that would provide the money to buy United Industries.

The number of companies interested in being acquired by Lee Partners also grew over the years. Tom Lee was willing to pay a high price if necessary to acquire a target company. He told *Money* in 2004 that what he bought was momentum: ''We look for kernels and gems and then we roll with it.'' To find such hidden treasures required a great deal of sifting. ''Of 1,000 deals that come in,'' he explained, ''probably 300, or a deal a day, actually fit what we're looking for. And we'll actually do only five or 10.'' Hence, his decision to acquire United Industries spoke volumes about the growth potential of the business.

In November 1999, United Industries installed a new management team headed by Robert L. Caulk, named president and chief executive officer. Two years later, Caulk would also assume the chairmanship. Like Tom Lee, Caulk was a Harvard graduate, earning a masters of business administration. In addition, he had experience in the insecticide industry, having worked ten years at S.C. Johnson & Johnson, which owned the Raid brand. He then spent five years at Clopay Building Products, a residential garage door manufacturer, where he rose to the level of president. His experience at Clopay was helpful because the company employed a marketing strategy similar to that of United Industries. They both sold to some of the same customers, such as The Home Depot.

The first order of business in taking United Industries to the next level was to pay down the company's $375 million debt load in order to improve the ratio of debt to earnings and prepare the ground for acquisitions. The plan was to achieve growth through acquisitions, with the goal of taking the company public, or, as was the case with Snapple, selling the business outright. The first significant acquisition under Lee Partners ownership did not take place until late 2001, when United Industries acquired several consumer fertilizer lines from Pursell Industries, Inc., expanding its presence in the lawn and garden category beyond insect control products. It was the first step in the company's strategy of becoming an industry consolidator in lawn-and-garden products. Brands acquired from Pursell included Vigoro, Sta-Green, and Bandini. In addition, United Industries added the rights to the Best brand of fertilizer as well as some intellectual property. Altogether, these branded products generated some $145 million in revenues for Pursell in 2001. As a result, United Industries now commanded the second largest market share in the lawn and garden fertilizer market in the United States.

More Acquisitions in the Early 21st Century

Several months later, in May 2002, United Industries added to its cache of lawn and garden products through the acquisition of Schultz Co., maker of consumer garden fertilizers, plant food, potting soils, soil conditioners, and an emerging line of organic pesticides sold under the Garden Safe brand. At a cost of $58 million in cash and stock, Schultz also brought with it exclusive supplier agreements with a number of retailers. Later in 2002, United Industries paid $19.5 million in cash to acquire

WPC Brands, a Wisconsin company that manufactured Repel, an insect repellent, as well as other outdoor health and safety products. United Industries now owned the second- and third-largest selling personal insect repellent brands in Cutter and Repel. Together they accounted for about one-third of all U.S. sales in this product area, while Off!, owned by Caulk's former employer S.C. Johnson, controlled about half of the market. Moreover, due to concerns about the West Nile Virus, which is spread by mosquitoes, all insect repellents experienced a bump in sales. As a result of its recent spate of acquisitions, United Industries grew its annual sales to $520 million, from $297 million in 2001.

Also of note in 2002 was an alliance forged with Bayer CropScience, a unit of the giant German healthcare and chemical concern Bayer AG. Bayer agreed to buy about 9 percent of United Industries over the course of seven years and allow United Industries to develop new products using current and future Bayer pesticide ingredients. Bayer also agreed to sell its Bayer Advanced line of lawn and garden care products through its partner's distribution network. There was some speculation that Bayer was taking the first steps in acquiring United Industries, but the relationship between the two companies would last no more than two years. Only months after establishing a strategic partnership with United Industries, Bayer sold much of its household insecticide business to S.C. Johnson, a sign that it was not likely in the market to buy United Industries. The distribution part of the alliance also proved to be a disappointment, since Bayer's distribution was reduced to a single retailer, Lowe's. In February 2004, United Industries terminated the relationship by canceling its distribution arrangement for Bayer products and buying back the stock Bayer had purchased to that point. United Industries would continue to purchase some of Bayer's products, but they accounted for only a small fraction of the company's revenues.

United Industries moved into a new 80,000-square-feet corporate headquarters in St. Louis in 2003. The company also paused in its acquisition efforts to digest what it had purchased in 2002. The next major acquisition came in April 2004 with the $143.8 million purchase of Nu-Gro Corporation, Canada's top manufacturer of consumer lawn and garden products. It also did a sizeable global business in controlled release nitrogen and other fertilizer technologies intended to keep lawns green over an extended period of time. Not only did the deal expand United Industries reach geographically, it added a number of brands, including CIL, Wilson, Vigro, Pickseed, So-Green, Plant-Pro, Greenleaf, and Green Earth. Nu-Gro had been a consolidator in the Canadian market, completing 13 acquisitions in the previous 15 years, but it had reached a crossroads, unable to grow much larger in Canada. The obvious next move was to enter the U.S. market, and merging with United Industries was the path chosen.

The addition of Nu-Gro was an important step in preparing United Industries for an eventual public offering or sale to a larger concern, but the composition of the company still required tweaking before investors or corporate suitors would express strong interest. Although United Industries offered a strong line of lawn-and-garden and insect-control products, it was very much a seasonal company. Over 70 percent of its sales came in the first six months of a given year, and its bottom line for that year depended to some extent on the vagaries of weather. Moreover, United Industries was highly dependent on three customers. Lowe's, The Home Depot, and Wal-Mart accounted for 71 percent of the company revenues in 2003. To help compensate for these factors, the company completed a second acquisition in 2004, paying $360 million to buy Cincinnati-based United Pet Group Inc., a pet supplies company with annual sales of $250 million. United Pet's top brands included Dingo rawhide-and-meat chew products for dogs, Nature's Miracle pet stain remover, and Marineland aquarium supplies. The pet supply industry was expected to grow at a 6 to 8 percent annual rate, making it a desirable market to enter. The acquisition also provided year-round sales and expanded United Industries' customer base. Combined sales were expected to reach the $1 billion mark.

To better manage its business lines, in September 2004 United Industries implemented a strategic realignment and established three divisions: Home and Garden, Canada, and Pet. Each group would be run by its own president and report to Caulk as CEO and chairman. The goal, however, remained the same: to grow the business to the point it could either be taken public or sold, thereby turning a profit for Lee Partners.

Principal Subsidiaries

The Nu-Gro Corporation; United Pet Group, Inc.

Principal Divisions

Home and Garden; Pet; Canada.

Principal Competitors

Bayer Group; S.C. Johnson & Sons, Inc.; The Scotts Company.

Further Reading

Berman, Phyllis, "Tom Lee Is on A Roll," *Forbes*, November 17, 1997, p. 126.

Holyoke, Larry, "United Industries Aims for IPO," *St. Louis Business Journal*, March 13, 2000, p. 1.

Melcer, Rachel, "St. Louis-Based Garden-Products Company Buys Cincinnati Pet Supplier," *St. Louis Post-Dispatch*, June 16, 2004.

Primack, Dan, "Up to Par: Is Thomas H. Lee Partners What Tom Lee Had in Mind All Along?," *Buyouts*, June 10, 2002.

Vise, Marilyn, and Julie Johnson, "Recession Doesn't Bug United Industries' Caulk," *St. Louis Business Journal*, December 21, 2001, p. 5.

—Ed Dinger

Verity Inc.

894 Ross Drive
Sunnyvale, California 94089
U.S.A.
Telephone: (408) 541-1500
Fax: (408) 511-1600
Web site: http://www.verity.com

Public Company
Incorporated: 1988
Employees: 524
Sales: $124.3 million
Stock Exchanges: NASDAQ
Ticker Symbol: VRTY
NAIC: 511210 Software Publishers

Based in Sunnyvale, California, Verity Inc. provides intellectual capital management (ICM) software to some 11,500 private and public organizations, including the U.S. Army, the U.S. Department of Energy, the U.S. Department of Justice, SAP, Hewlett-Packard, Cap Gemini Ernst & Young, Bristol-Myers Squibb, AT&T, and American Express. According to Verity, its solutions ''provide integrated search, classification, recommendation, monitoring and analytics across the real-time flow of enterprise information, along with question and answer interfaces for effective online self-service.'' In addition to its own ICM products, Verity's technology is included in more than 250 software applications from other vendors.

A New Way to Search: 1988–92

Verity was spun off from Advanced Decision Systems in 1988 by Dr. Michael S. Pliner and a group that included David Glazer, Phil Nelson, Andrew Leak, Abe Lederman, John Lehman, and Clifford A. Reid. Prior to joining Advanced Decision Systems and founding Verity, Pliner co-founded a company called Sytek, which invented the local area network protocol NetBIOS.

Glazer and Nelson were the key engineers behind Verity's first product, a full-text retrieval system called Topic. Pliner and his colleagues developed Topic so that users could search for electronic information based on concepts or ideas, as opposed to more limited keyword searching with the traditional Boolean operators AND, OR, and NOT. In the November 1998 issue of *Online*, Pliner commented on the state of search technology during the late 1980s: ''Searching out and retrieving the right documents using today's retrieval technology is like trying to eat spaghetti with a single chopstick. The second generation of products will give you a second chopstick.''

Topic users had the ability to rank searches by assigning weights to keywords and subtopics, with the goal of obtaining more relevant results. In addition, Topic was designed to be format and hardware platform independent, and was available for individual, multi-user, and networked environments. An unlimited multi-user Topic license cost $39,500. For a networked setup, clients paid $15,000 for server software and either $695 (DOS) or $2,500 (Sun) for each workstation.

Among Verity's first clients was the Strategic Air Command, which had begun beta testing Topic in July 1987. Profits were elusive for Verity during the company's early years. However, from its headquarters at 1550 Plymouth Street in Mountain View, California, Verity quickly began to evolve. In 1990 the company rolled out Topic Real-Time, which analyzed information such as market data, news wire content, and e-mail messages and then routed it to businesspeople in real time based on their interests. Verity partnered with Dow Jones & Co. to resell its DowVision news service with Topic Real-Time.

The type of technology used in Topic Real-Time was of interest to Verity's government clients, which accounted for some 30 percent of the company's business. With the advent of Operation Desert Shield in 1990, Verity was awarded a large percentage of a United States Air Force contract, valued at $40 million, to build a real-time automated system that scanned and routed messages to the right intelligence personnel.

Growth continued at a steady clip, and by November 1991 Verity's employee base reached the 100 mark. Around this time, the company's client base included Borland International Inc., Motorola Inc., the U.S. Department of Defense, and the White House.

Company Perspectives:

Verity provides software that enables organizations to maximize the return on their intellectual capital investment.

Striving for Profitability: 1993–99

In January 1993, San Jose, California-based Frame Technology Corporation signed a letter of intent to acquire Verity. At this time, Pliner announced that he would step down as president, chairman, and CEO, and would serve as a consultant to Frame Technology President and CEO Paul Robichaux. Although the planned merger fell apart in March 1993, after Frame suffered a first quarter loss of $3.9 million, Pliner moved forward with his decision to step down as the head of Verity, and Philippe F. Courtot became verity's new president and CEO. Prior to joining Verity, Courtot served as the CEO of cc:Mail, and also held positions with Thomson-CGR Medical Corporation, ADAC Laboratories, and Modular Computer Corporation.

By 1993, Verity's employee base had grown to 140 workers. While Pliner was gone, co-founders Glazer, Nelson, Leak, Lederman, and Lehman remained with the company. Courtot decreased the price of Verity's products in order to increase the company's customer base, and also ramped up spending on research and development by 30 percent. In addition, Courtot initiated a strategy to incorporate Verity's search technology in software applications from other vendors.

As part of Courtot's strategy, in April 1994 Verity unveiled its InfoAgent technology, which independent developers could include in their applications. The technology, which relied on so-called ''intelligent agents,'' benefited individuals, groups, and entire organizations with tools to filter, analyze, and retrieve all available information, regardless of operating system, application, database type, or source. By 1995 intelligent agents were part of Verity's Topic Information Server, a client-server text retrieval system that allowed users to look for information across many different types of documents residing in different databases.

While Verity's product offerings expanded during the early and mid-1990s, so did its losses. Shortfalls, which totaled less than $1 million in both 1992 and 1993, reached almost $6 million in 1995. Nevertheless, when company went public in the fall of 1995, it raised $40 million in its initial public offering—double what it initially anticipated.

By late 1995 Courtot's strategy to shift the company's focus away from the enterprise sector and toward a variety of other end markets had successfully materialized. By this time Verity had deals in place with most leading PC manufacturers and a number of online services for the use of its search technology. The company adapted its technology to meet the unique requirements of many different customers. Verity ended the year by announcing it would release an enhanced version of its Topic Search Engine in early 1996, which it planned to bundle with Netscape Communications' World Wide Web Server 2.0.

In mid-1996 Verity acquired InSite Computer Technology, a consultancy based in the United Kingdom that had made Verity's search products compatible with Microsoft Exchange and BackOffice. Driven by higher software sales, Verity's revenues mushroomed 93 percent that year, climbing from $15.9 million in 1995 to $30.7 million. At the end of fiscal year 1996, the company's revenues from software licenses had increased for seven consecutive quarters. In the fourth quarter of 1996 alone, Verity's new applications customers included Wells Fargo Bank, Nortel, MCI, Intel, and British Broadcasting Corporation. Although the company posted a net loss of $313,000, this was an improvement over 1995's loss of $5.8 million. Ending 1996 on a high note, *Database Programming and Design* magazine named Verity one of the database industry's leading 12 firms, along with heavyweights Hewlett-Packard, IBM, Microsoft, and Oracle.

In January 1997 Verity acquired Bellevue, Washington-Based Cognisoft for $10 million in cash. Cognisoft, which became Verity's business applications unit, was established in April of the previous year by five Microsoft employees. The acquisition gave Verity IntelliServ, a content delivery product that delivered ''customized content via the Internet or intranets from any data source—including file servers, Web servers, Microsoft Exchange, Lotus Notes and ODBC databases,'' according to the January 20, 1997, issue of *Computer Reseller News*. IntelliServ was a natural fit with Verity's Search '97 technology. Two other acquisitions in 1997 included the Keyview line of filtering products from FTP Software, and the database management firm 64K Inc.

In 1997, IDC reported that Verity's share of the text retrieval market was a leading 28 percent. Although revenues increased to $42.7 million that year, Verity's many acquisitions came at a price: a net loss of $17.9 million. This led the company's board to replace Courtot with a new CEO named Gary J. Sbona in July.

Verity began 1998 by winning a Market Recognition Award from Delphi Computing Group for offering the most popular information retrieval technology. Charged with making improvements, Sbona called for a 15 percent work force reduction, as well as a more streamlined product line and sales force. In an April 21, 1998, *Business Wire* release, Sbona explained: ''In recent months we've realigned our products, our sales force, our pricing, our support and our market message around the needs of enterprise knowledge and retrieval.''

In 1998 Verity sued IBM subsidiary Lotus Development Corporation, claiming that Lotus planned to use Verity's technology in a way that went beyond the scope of an existing licensing agreement. Specifically, the lawsuit charged ''copyright infringement, unfair competition, breach of contract, misappropriation of trade secrets, and unjust enrichment and conversion,'' according to the March 11, 1998, issue of *InfoWorld Daily News*. The companies settled the lawsuit in June 1998.

After investing some 40 percent of revenues into research and development initiatives during 1998, Verity registered a net loss of $16.5 million on revenues of $38.9 million. Late that year, two new products were introduced. As opposed to search technology, Verity HTML Export 2.0 and Key View Pro 6.5 were document management applications.

Key Dates:

1988: Dr. Michael S. Pliner and a group of researchers spin Verity off from Advanced Decision Systems; the company's first product, a full-text retrieval system called Topic, is introduced.
1990: Verity is awarded a large contract to build a real-time automated messaging system for the U.S. Air Force.
1995: Verity raises $40 million in its initial public offering.
1996: *Database Programming and Design Magazine* names Verity one of the database industry's leading 12 firms.
1999: Verity finally achieves profitability.
2001: *Fortune* ranks Verity 17th on its list of the 100 fastest-growing companies, and as the second-fastest growing software firm.

New Directions: 1999 and Beyond

Verity finally achieved profitability in 1999, recording a profit of $12.1 million on revenues of $64.4 million. That March, Sbona was named chairman in addition to his responsibilities as CEO. New product introductions in 1999 included Verity Profiler and Knowledge Organizer. In August, the company sold 1.78 million shares of common stock in a public offering valued at $79.9 million. The following month, Verity Senior Vice President Anthony J. Bettencourt III was promoted to president, with responsibilities for product development, professional services, marketing, and sales.

In 2000, Verity unveiled new software called Portal One, which allowed customers to access business information from a multitude of devices and locations. The company also expanded in Japan through a new distribution agreement with Toshiba. That year, Verity's revenues reached a record $96.1 million, up 49 percent from 1999. Of this amount, software revenues were $69.7 million. The company remained profitable, with net income of $33.0 million.

International expansion continued in 2001, when Verity announced that it would open regional offices in Sweden, Singapore, Brazil, Mexico, and South Africa. In a May 9, 2001, *PR Newswire* release, Bettencourt said: ''Verity's new offices will allow us to take greater advantage of the expanding market opportunities in these regions. However, we're not new to the international arena. Our business outside of North America generally accounts for about one-third of the company's revenue. International sales were strong before, but our direct sales presence in these areas will enhance our ability to make them even stronger.'' By this time, Verity's customer base had grown to include 80 percent of *Fortune* 50 companies.

In 2001 Verity remained focused on profitability. To this end, the company cut 13 percent of its work force in November to reduce expenses. Verity continued to work on substantial new projects, including a secure portal for the United States Air Force. Called My.AirForce, the portal used Verity's K2 portal infrastructure and provided a gateway to content from 1,500 different Air Force Web sites and 28,000 different legacy systems around the globe. Verity ended 2001 by receiving recognition from *Fortune* magazine, which ranked the company 17th on its list of the 100 fastest-growing companies, and as the second-fastest growing software firm. Additionally, *Software Magazine* included Verity on its Annual Software 500 list for the second consecutive year, naming it one of the leading portal vendors.

Sbona's efforts to remain profitable continued to pay off in 2002, as the company recorded its fourth consecutive year of profitability. At $93.8 million, revenues were down 35 percent from 2001 amidst weak economic conditions. However, the company's net income totaled $1.4 million. Verity's employee base reached 437 in 2002. That year, the company's technology was used by the Department of Defense as part of a message handling system that served some 40 different sites.

In 2003 Verity acquired the enterprise search software business of Inktomi Corporation for $25 million in cash. In addition to 44 new employees, the acquisition resulted in a newly branded search product called Ultraseek and gave Verity access to more ''department-level'' staff. In the March 2003 issue of *Econtent*, Bettencourt indicated that Verity's customer base grew to include 2,500 new department-level customers, in addition to its existing base of 1,500 corporate clients. Verity's revenues totaled $102 million in 2003, with net income of $11.6 million.

Another acquisition came in early 2004 when Verity obtained Cardiff Software, a developer of forms processing applications that was established in 1991, for $50 million in cash. With 185 employees and offices in California, Virginia, and London, Cardiff became a wholly owned subsidiary of Verity. True to its roots, Verity continued to strike new deals in the government sector. In April 2004 the Department of Homeland Security chose the company's K2 Enterprise software to power an intelligence-sharing network called the Joint Regional Information Exchange System. Verity's 2004 sales totaled $124.3 million, and net income remained unchanged from the previous year at $11.6 million.

Principal Competitors

Adobe Systems Inc.; Captiva Software Corporation; Documentum Inc.; Fast Search & Transfer ASA; IBM Software; Microsoft Corporation; Oracle Corporation; SAP AG.

Further Reading

Bigelow, Bruce V., ''Software Firm Is Bought by Sunnyvale, Calif., Company,'' *San Diego Union-Tribune*, February 3, 2004.

Blythen, Lloyd, ''Verity Is Still Searching for Success,'' *Computergram International*, May 22, 1997.

Cisler, Steve, ''Searching for a Better Way: Verity, Inc.'s Topic Software,'' *Online*, November 1988.

''Cognisoft Merges Into Verity for $10 Million,'' *Newsbytes*, January 14, 1997.

Ferranti, Marc, ''Verity Sues Lotus Over Search Software in Notes,'' *InfoWorld Daily News*, March 11, 1998.

Foley, Mary Jo, ''Verity Snaps Up Cognisoft for $10M,'' *Computer Reseller News*, January 20, 1997.

Krey, Michael, ''Verity Awarded Chunk of Large Defense Contract,'' *Business Journal*, October 29, 1990.

Mace, Scott, ''Text Retrieval System Based on Priorities,'' *InfoWorld*, June 20, 1988.

Manafy, Michelle, "The Low-End Theory: Verity Leverages Inktomi Acquisition to Open New Doors," *EContent*, March 2003.

Pallatto, John, "Verity System Offers Real-Time Data Retrieval," *PC Week*, May 7, 1990.

"Text Retrieval System Lets Users Fine-Tune Searches," *PC Week*, June 21, 1988.

"The Future's Bright and Well Sorted for Verity Inc.—Interview," *Telecomworldwire*, November 30, 1995.

"Verity Advances International Presence in Rapidly Expanding Markets," *PR Newswire*, May 9, 2001.

"Verity Launches Scaleable, Precision, Knowledge Retrieval Software; New Product Offerings are Result of Company's Intensified Focus on Enterprise Knowledge Retrieval," *Business Wire*, April 21, 1998.

"Verity Raises $79.9m in Stock Sale," *Computergram International*, August 6, 1999.

"Verity to Acquire Enterprise Search Software Business from Inktomi," *EContent*, January 2003.

"Verity Chosen as One of the Top 12 Companies That Define Direction of Database Industry," *M2 Presswire*, December 5, 1996.

—Paul R. Greenland

W.W. Grainger, Inc.

100 Grainger Parkway
Lake Forest, Illinois 60045-5201
U.S.A.
Telephone: (847) 793-9030
Fax: (847) 647-5669
Web site: http://www.grainger.com

Public Company
Incorporated: 1928
Employees: 14,701
Sales: $4.66 billion (2004)
Stock Exchanges: New York
Ticker Symbol: GWW
NAIC: 423610 Electrical Apparatus and Equipment, Wiring Supplies, and Related Equipment Merchant Wholesalers; 423830 Industrial Machinery and Equipment Merchant Wholesalers; 423840 Industrial Supplies Merchant Wholesalers; 423990 Other Miscellaneous Durable Goods Merchant Wholesalers

W.W. Grainger, Inc., is the largest distributor of maintenance, repair, and operating supplies to the commercial, industrial, contractor, and institutional markets in North America. As of 2004, the company held the largest worldwide percentage of market share—about 5 percent—of any corporation in its market. It has accomplished steady growth of 7 to 10 percent annually, not primarily through diversification but by expansion of its core business in terms of geographic scope and volume of its product line. Privately held until March 1967, the company finances most growth internally. The company has traditionally served small industrial contractors and institutions but expanded in the late 20th century to serve specialty markets for general industrial, replacement parts, and safety and sanitary products, and to supply large corporations with multiple locations. By the early 21st century the company had also expanded its order-processing system, featuring Internet-based ordering with same-day delivery and facilitated billing through electronic data interchange (EDI) and electronic funds transfer (EFT).

Early History

In the late 1920s, William W. Grainger—motor designer, salesman, and electrical engineer—sought to tap a segment of the market for wholesale electrical equipment sales. He set up an office in Chicago in 1927 and incorporated his business one year later. The company sold goods primarily through MotorBook, an eight-page catalog, which would become the backbone of the company's name recognition. It contained electrical motors that Grainger himself, his sister Margaret, and two employees would ship. By 1991 would Grainger publish two editions of its general catalog—the successor to MotorBook—offering more than 35,000 items. The catalog also included extensive technical and application data.

The market for electric motors was so expansive in the late 1920s and 1930s that many companies developed with it. In 1926 two of the ten largest U.S. corporations were electrical companies. City utilities made the switch from direct current (DC) to alternating current (AC) for nearly every apparatus driven by electricity. Manufacturers moved away from uniform, DC-driven assembly lines and toward separate work stations, each with individually driven AC motors. This development created a vast market, and distributors like Grainger could reach segments untapped by volume-minded manufacturers.

Grainger established its first branch in Philadelphia in 1933. Atlanta, Dallas, and San Francisco branches opened in 1934. Sales in 1932 fell below the previous year's, to $163,000—the first of only four years where sales would not increase. In 1937 Grainger had 16 branches and sales of more than $1 million.

The complexity of the industry allowed Grainger to decentralize marketing efforts and strengthen its regional presence by adding an outside sales force in 1939, but the company limited it to one sales representative for every branch for the first ten years. Branches opened around the country at a brisk pace, with 24 operating by 1942.

Yet Grainger did not expand solely through the number of outlets. In 1937 it began merchandising selected products under the Dayton trademark, Grainger's first private label. In order to stimulate summer business, a line of air circulators and

Company Perspectives:

The company has been successful since its founding in 1927. This success has been due in large part to a philosophy of management that will continue to guide us in the future: To be the leader in the distribution of maintenance, repair, and operating supplies and related information to commercial, industrial, contractor, and institutional customers.

ventilating fans was designed, assembled, and offered for sale by the company in 1938. Assembly operations continued to be performed by the company until it got out of manufacturing in the 1980s.

Grainger acted as a distributor of electric motors for government use during World War II. With its normal market disrupted, Grainger offered furniture, toys, and watches through MotorBook for a brief period. Grainger continued expansion during the war as sales grew from 1941's $2.6 million to $7.8 million in 1948, and earnings increased almost tenfold to $240,000 in 1948.

Postwar Growth

The rapid growth continued immediately after the war. Sales more than doubled from 1948 to 1952, calling for organizational adjustments. A single sales representative could no longer serve an entire branch, and in 1948 Grainger expanded the sales force for the first time. The postwar transition also required renewed efficiency, and in 1949 Grainger had a branch office built to its own specifications for the first time. Most new branches since have also been built specifically for Grainger.

Beginning in 1953 the company created a regional warehousing system that replenished branch stock and filled larger orders. Called regional distribution centers, they were eventually located in Chicago; Atlanta; Oakland, California; Ft. Worth, Texas; Memphis, Tennessee; and Cranford, New Jersey. This system operated until the mid-1970s.

As alternating current became standard in the United States, Grainger's market changed. No longer processing large orders, the company intensified its focus on the secondary market that existed throughout the country—small manufacturers, servicers, and dealers who purchased with high frequency but low volume. Grainger could anticipate the needs of this market and purchase from manufacturers in high volume. Grainger's distribution system, warehousing, and accounting allowed manufacturers to produce at low cost for Grainger's customers. These customers were otherwise difficult for manufacturers to reach.

Most of the increases in sales volume after World War II were due to large-scale geographic expansion. This expansion continued through the 1950s and 1960s at a consistent pace. By 1967 Grainger operated 92 branches. Branches built after 1949 were automated to keep administrative and personnel costs low. In 1962 sales were $43.5 million. In 1966 sales nearly doubled to $80.2 million. Automation helped build the company's reputation as a reliable supplier and brought in accounts with bigger clients. Average branch sales grew from $596,000 in 1962 to more than $2.1 million in 1974.

In 1966 Grainger acquired those shares of Dayton Electric Manufacturing Company that it did not already own. Also in the 1960s, Grainger acquired a producer of home accessories, which was divested in the 1970s. In 1967 the company went public.

In 1969 the company purchased Doerr Electric Corporation, a manufacturer of electric motors, and three Doerr affiliates. Two thirds of Doerr's sales volume was already to Grainger. In 1972 Grainger acquired McMillan Manufacturing, another maker of electric motors. By 1974—seven years after the company went public—sales had more than tripled.

Continued Expansion in the 1970s–80s

Brands exclusive to Grainger—Dayton, Teel, Demco, Dem-Kote, and Speedaire—accounted for about 65 percent of the company's 1975 sales. As Grainger's branches became larger, the need for a centralized stock diminished. The company eliminated the regional distribution centers by the mid-1970s. It discontinued its McMillan Manufacturing operations in 1975.

Grainger's prominence allowed it to count on sales increases due to population growth. In addition, the replacement market for small motors exceeded that of the repair market. Slimmed-down operations and reduced long-term debt, however, poised the company for more aggressive growth through the 1980s.

Unlike in the 1960s, the company saw no need to diversify during the 1980s, recognizing that the electrical industry itself could provide enough opportunity for growth. The transition from electromechanical equipment to electronics provided long-term growth during boom and bust periods—comparable to the motor market upgrades of the 1920s and 1930s. Growth in domestic business activity led to broad-scale upgrades and system replacements—resulting in increased orders for Grainger and more disposable cash for its own expansion. In 1986 the company sold Doerr to Emerson Electric Company for $24.3 million.

A study showed that while Grainger sold products in every county in the United States, it held less than a 2 percent share of a $70 billion to $90 billion industry. The study also indicated that most Grainger customers had fewer than 100 employees and valued immediacy over breadth of product line or price. In response, Grainger accelerated its decades-old expansion rate of six branches a year. It opened more than 100 new branches between 1987 and 1989, trying to bring a branch to within 20 minutes of every customer.

Investment in computer automation allowed Grainger to resurrect its centrally managed regional distribution centers. In 1983 the company opened a heavily automated distribution center in Kansas City, Missouri, and in 1989 opened a third such operation in Greenville County, South Carolina.

During the 1980s Grainger returned to its origins, trying to reach larger institutional customers. Although essentially the same business since its inception, Grainger expanded the scope of its services. Starting in 1986, through acquisition and internal development, the company began building specialty distribution businesses that were intended to complement the market position held by Grainger. These businesses included replacement parts, general industrial products, safety products, and sanitary supplies. Parts distribution continued to expand under

Key Dates:

1928: Company is incorporated as an electrical equipment wholesaler.
1937: Grainger has 16 branches and sales of more than $1 million.
1953: The company creates a regional warehousing system that replenishes branch stock and fills larger orders.
1967: Grainger goes public.
1969: Doerr Electric Corporation, a manufacturer of electric motors, is acquired.
1986: Doerr is sold to Emerson Electric for $24.3 million.
1990: The company enters the safety-products distribution business through the acquisition of Allied Safety, Inc.
1996: Grainger establishes presences in Mexico and Canada.
1999: Company adds three Internet businesses to facilitate ordering and help customers locate hard-to-find products.

the Parts Company of America (PCA) name. PCA provided parts service for more than 550 equipment manufacturers and offered 80,000 parts.

Acquisitions and Reorganization in the 1990s

General industrial distribution expanded in the late 1980s and early 1990s through a series of acquisitions. In 1989 Grainger purchased Vonnegut Industrial Products. The following year, the company acquired Bossert Industrial Supply, Inc. Bossert, positioned in the midwestern market, provided manufacturing and repair operations products, cutting tools and abrasives, and other supplies used in manufacturing processes. Also in 1990, the company entered into the safety-products distribution business through the acquisition of Allied Safety, Inc. The new safety products line included such items as respiratory systems, protective clothing, and other equipment used by individuals in the workplace and in environmental clean-up operations. Grainger added to the line in 1992 by purchasing Lab Safety Supply.

JANI-SERV Supply was created in 1990 to service the sanitary supply market. It offered more than 1,200 items, representing a full range of sanitary products. The subsidiary was expanded in 1991 with the purchase of Ball Industries, Inc., a distributor of sanitary and janitorial supplies based in California.

In 1993 Grainger began a three-year reorganization of the company and its subsidiaries with the goal of streamlining its sales force and eliminating redundant inventories. Grainger began by dismantling JANI-SERV Supply 1993 and incorporating its product line into its core business. The following year it began the same process with Allied Safety, the company's safety products subsidiary, and Bossert, finishing the integration in 1995. In addition to this streamlining, Grainger opened zone distribution centers in Dallas and Atlanta in 1994.

Costs related to the reorganization and upgrades to information systems contributed to lower gross margins in the mid-1990s. A more important factor in these lower margins was Grainger's decision to lower prices on some products to attract new customers and expand existing accounts. As part of the company's effort to return to national accounts and larger industrial customers, the strategic pricing helped expand Grainger's customer base. Although the stock price fell in response to the lower margins, this effect was temporary.

Leadership of the company left the hands of the Grainger family for the first time when David Grainger, son of the founder, retired as chief executive officer in 1995. He remained as chair of the board and was succeeded as CEO by Richard Keyser. In another change from the status quo, the company moved its headquarters to Lincolnshire, Illinois, the same year. By 1999, however, the company had shifted addresses once again, relocating to Lake Forest, Illinois outside of Chicago.

In the late 1990s, Grainger established operations outside the United States for the first time. In 1996 the company opened a branch in Monterrey, Mexico. The same year, Grainger purchased a division of Acklands, Ltd., a Canadian manufacturer of industrial safety and automotive aftermarket products.

The company made great strides in adding large national accounts in the mid- and late 1990s. In 1996 it signed supply agreements with several large companies, including Lockheed Martin, Procter & Gamble, and American Airlines. In 1998 it announced a materials management outsourcing agreement with Compaq Computer Corporation. With the addition of new accounts and new products, sales at Grainger almost quadrupled in a decade, growing from $1.3 billion in 1987 to $4.1 billion in 1997. In 1997 as well, the company was recognized by Industrial Distribution magazine as the number one industrial distributor in North America in terms of sales.

Strides into the New Millennium

In the 21st century W.W. Grainger became one of the first old-economy companies to use the power of the internet for direct business-to-business ordering. By 1999 Grainger had developed three separate internet businesses (Grainger.com, OrderZone.com, and FindMRO.com), all specifically designed to facilitate ordering and to help customers locate hard-to-find products. In that year the corporation also announced a deal with Netscape that would allow customers to access and order from Grainger's online catalogue using Netscape's Netcenter, one of the leading internet portal sites. Online resources gave Grainger about $160 million in sales in 1999.

However, the new Internet economy also created problems for Grainger. Although its Internet businesses exploded onto the market, they did not initially increase the value of the parent company's stock. While stock prices hit a high of $58 a share in 1999 shortly after the launch of OrderZone.com, by the following year stock had sunk to around $34. Existing customers loved the convenience that ordering through Grainger.com gave them, but OrderZone.com did not attract as many new paying customers as management had hoped it would. As a result, in 2000 Grainger announced a deal with Works.com, an e-commerce business based in Texas, that would expand the corporation's internet visibility by merging OrderZone into Works.com. In 2001 Grainger also announced that customers of FacilityPro would have access to the entire line of Grainger products through FacilityPro's own online market.

The economic slowdown of the early 21st century led Grainger to try to intensify its relationships with its existing customers. In February 2001 the corporation opened an on-site facility at Florida State University, and the following year it created a similar facility for the U.S. Armed Forces at Langley Air Force in Virginia. At the same time Grainger became one of several companies that supplied the U.S. Navy's Norfolk, Virginia, base with maintenance equipment and supplies.

As of 2004 W.W. Grainger's long-term plan was to focus on capturing a greater percentage of market share in North America, the site of its core business. The program began by increasing Grainger's presence in three selected metropolitan areas (Denver, Atlanta, and Seattle), increasing the size of existing branches and expanding their staff in order to make needed products and customer service more available. Grainger plans to expand this process to other, targeted metropolitan areas and a few selected secondary markets across North America. The company has also increased its ability to supply customers with needed supplies automatically by opening new distribution centers or redesigning old ones. The company projects that this streamlining of the distribution process will cut costs by about $20 million when the plan is fully realized.

Principal Subsidiaries

Grainger S.A. de C.V. (Mexico); Acklands-Grainger Inc. (Canada); Lab Safety Supply Inc.

Principal Divisions

Industrial Supply; Integrated Supply; FindMRO; Parts; Internet.

Further Reading

Cohen, Andy, "Practice Makes Profits: Sales Training Spurs Double-Digit Increases Every Year for W.W. Grainger," *Sales and Marketing Management*, July 1995, pp. 24–25.

"Compaq Signs Outsourcing Agreement with Grainger Integrated Supply," *PR Newswire*, July 28, 1998.

Daniels, Steve, "Old-Line Company Tangles with Net: Grainger's Dilemma: Float Stock in Online Venture?," *Crain's Chicago Business*, November 29, 1999, p. 1.

"Grainger: The Positive View," *Forbes*, November 21, 1994, pp. 248–49.

"How the Big Get Bigger," Industrial Distribution, February 1988.

60 Years of Growth, Skokie, Ill., W.W. Grainger, Inc., 1987.

Knapp, Kevin, "Grainger Defends Move; Says OrderZone Equity Swap a Wise Decision," *B to B*, July 3, 2000, p. 6.

Johnson, John R., "1997 Top 100 Distributor," *Industrial Distribution*, June, 1997, p. 50.

Maddox, Kate, "Growing Wiser," *B to B*, September 9 2002, p. 1.

"W.W. Grainger, Inc., 2-for-1 Stock Split Declared," *PR Newswire*, April 29, 1998.

—Ray Walsh
—updates: Susan Windisch Brown;
Kenneth R. Shepherd

Warrell Corporation

1250 Slate Hill Road
Camp Hill, Pennsylvania 17011
U.S.A.
Telephone: (717) 761-5440
Toll Free: (866) 736-6388
Fax: (717) 761-5702

Private Company
Founded: 1957
Employees: 200
Sales: $48 million (2004 est.)
NAIC: 311330 Confectionary Manufacturing from Purchased Chocolate

Warrell Corporation, based in Camp Hill, Pennsylvania, manufactures candy under the Pennsylvania Dutch and Katherine Beecher brand names as well as private labels. Approximately 75 percent of sales are generated from co-manufacturing and private-label confections. With a 200,000 square-foot plant, Warrell manufactures candy in several categories. Dutch Treats include crunchy peanut squares, honey nut crisps, and peanut butter pillows. Pennsylvania Dutch specialties include apple butter, peanut brittle, funnel cake mix, and salt water taffy. Warrel makes a variety of old fashioned sandy candy in such flavors as cherry, licorice, root beet, and horehound. Another Warrel specialty is Old Fashion Stick Candy. Finally, the company makes a number of nostalgic items, including cashew coconut pie, peanut coconut pie, coconut strips, coconut marshmallow toasties, and flat mountain taffy. An on-site gift shop is also operated at the company's facility. It serves as a showroom for gift shop owners, a sample room, and a freestanding gift shop. The company is privately owned and operated by the Warrell family.

1950s Origins

Founded in 1957 as Pennsylvania Dutch Candies Company, Warrell Corporation at first made butter mints but soon added licorice, lollipops, and milk chocolate items. The products were either manufactured by the company or bought from others and packaged under the Pennsylvania Dutch label. It was a niche business that relied on a wide range of outlets, such as tourist attraction gift shops, restaurant retail sections, roadside stands, and country stores. By 1965, the company was generating sales of about $1 million, and it was at this point that Jonas Warrell helped his two sons, Lincoln (Warrell Corporation's long-time chairman) and Carroll, to buy the business. ''Linc'' Warrell earned a degree in chemical engineering from Pennsylvania State University in 1953 and then went to work for the Aluminum Co. of America, better known as Alcoa, where he became a technical salesman. However, he longed to run his own company, just like his father, who was president and chief executive officer of Carlisle Tire and Rubber Corporation. Carroll began scouting around for a manufacturer for the family to buy and came upon Pennsylvania Dutch Candies. The brothers, with the financial backing of their father, made a buyout offer, it was accepted, and they now became involved in the candy business, which neither knew anything about.

Linc Warrell considered his lack of industry knowledge to be an advantage in some ways, since he came to it was no preconceived notions about the right way to do things. For instance, he applied his training in chemical engineering to discard long-held practices in the candy industry that simply had no scientific basis. He was also willing to listen and learn and, despite being a part-owner, to serve in a supporting capacity. In a 2004 profile in *Candy Industry,* he recalled his first day at work: ''They had brought up an old and quite dirty wooden desk, which had been in storage, and placed it in a shared office for me. Well, the first thing I did was to get some soap and water and clean that desk. I was then put in charge of purchasing janitorial supplies for the company, something that I also knew nothing about.''

The company's previous owner stayed on to teach Warrell the business, and the future chairman was soon moved into sales, where he possessed a solid foundation. He knew from his days at Alcoa how to deal with customers and the professional conduct expected of a reputable sales operation. He hit the road and soon received a number of complaints from gift shop brokers and customers. The brokers in particular were unhappy with the way Pennsylvania Dutch Candies's was often late in making deliveries and slow to pay. Warrell took steps to resolve these problems, and he also raised retail prices on the com-

Company Perspectives:

Although the company has achieved considerable growth over our 38 years, the Pennsylvania Dutch candies commitment to selling exclusively to the specialty retail trade, keeping very high consumer value in it products, offering products at a fair price, and providing unrivaled customer service remains unwavered.

pany's products, in this way improving profitability for both the company and its customers. As a result, after just a year under new ownership, Pennsylvania Dutch Candies doubled its sales.

Katherine Beecher Candies Acquired in the 1970s

The company enjoyed steady growth through the remainder of the 1960s and into the early 1970s, adding about $1 million in sales each year. In 1974, Pennsylvania Dutch Candies expanded through acquisition by purchasing Manchester, Pennsylvania-based Katharine Beecher Candies, Inc., which was on the verge of bankruptcy. Beecher produced more than just candy, targeting the upscale market including fancy food distributors, department stores, food shops, and gourmet shops. About 90 percent of its business came from private label work, but the company was selling its products at or below cost. It was an untenable situation, leading Warrell to sit down with the major clients to discuss the situation. He convinced them to accept a price increase, which allowed Beecher to get on a solid footing. However, as the gourmet market began to contract, the company eventually dropped gourmet food items, only keeping on such Pennsylvania Dutch items as apple butter and corn relish. To become more of a mass market business, Beecher concentrated on candy and expanded its offerings to include party mints and anise mints, as well as some snack items. It also installed hot panning for sugar toasted peanuts and, in general, upgraded to state-of-the-art equipment to increase volumes and remain competitive by becoming a low-cost producer. The strategy worked, and by the early 1980s Katherine Beecher had become a profitable concern.

With one successful turnaround project under its belt, in 1982 Pennsylvania Dutch Candies considered a new challenge: Melster Candies, a Cambridge, Wisconsin, company founded in 1919 by brothers Harvey and Arthur Melster, who had converted a tobacco warehouse into a candy factory. It specialized in seasonal candy such as grained marshmallows (circus peanuts), chocolate coated whipped marshmallows, peanut butter kisses, and salt water taffy. After learning the business was for sale, Warrell and long-time president Bill Billman took a trip to Wisconsin to inspect the facility. Although it was in rough condition, they decided the company's real problems lay in sales and marketing, areas they felt they could correct. They bought Melster but soon learned that the former tobacco facility itself was the major challenge. ''We didn't realize how naive we were in seeing what needed to be done in that plant,'' Warrell told *Candy Industry* in 1998. ''Sales was only a minor problem. Production in every department was a problem, efficiency was a problem, motivation was a problem. The easiest solution was the financial arrangements.''

As it had done with Beecher, Pennsylvania Dutch Companies gradually added state-of-the-art equipment to the Melster operation to make it a low-cost, quality producer that could operate a competitive player on the national stage. All told, Pennsylvania Dutch Candies estimated it spent about three times the original purchase price on upgrading the facilities. Warrell's scientific background was also helpful in turning around Melster. When he took over, the company was limiting the production on some of its items to a seasonal basis. For instance, circus peanuts were not made during the summer because of heat and humidity. Warrell realized that an open drying room window caused the problem and had air conditioning installed, thus allowing Melster to produce quality circus peanuts year-round and eventually become the country's largest producer of the candy. Despite all the money and effort, however, it was not until the early 1990s, almost a dozen years after Pennsylvania Dutch Candies bought the operation, that Melster finally turned the corner.

Warrell proved to be a tireless worker in all aspects of Pennsylvania Dutch Candies. He helped to expand the company's reach well beyond Pennsylvania Dutch country so that sales outside of Pennsylvania grew to 90 percent. According to son-in-law and vice-president of administration, logistics, and warehousing, Kevin Silva, ''Linc would ensure that Pennsylvania Dutch had a presence in any town that had a show or a fair. For him there was no market too small nor no rack too good for Pennsylvania Dutch candies. His daughters always talk about visiting their mother's family in St. Louis. It would take several days to make the drive since Dad would be stopping at every roadside outlet to find out if they sold Pennsylvania Dutch candies.'' In the spring of 1996, Warrell, upon reaching age 65, retired, staying on as chairman but turning over day-to-day responsibilities to Billman and his sons-in-law. Nevertheless, he continued to come into the office every day, and instead of working half-days as planned, he continued to put in long hours. Near the end of the year, a salesman suggested they award Warrell a plaque for perfect attendance, since he had not missed a day of work since entering retirement.

New Packaging Look in the Mid-1990s

In 1996, Pennsylvania Dutch Candies updated its look, replacing its yellow candy bags featuring a red-and-green hearts-and-flower logo with a clear package and a more modern looking logo that suggested the look of an Amish quilt, employing teals, burgundy, purples, and greens to accent a picture of an Amish horse and buggy. The packaging makeover was a success with retailers, who believed the look was more in keeping with their own image, and resulted in even more distribution opportunities.

Pennsylvania Dutch Candies generated some $30 million in sales in 1998. To keep growing and remain competitive, the company began looking to relocate to a larger facility where it could consolidate its Pennsylvania manufacturing operations as part of a strategic long-term plan. Because the cost of building a brand new plant was too high, management was in the market to buy an existing facility that could be renovated. There was some thought of moving to a new area but the state stepped in to persuade the company to stay close to home. A large plant, the Iceland Seafood building, located in Camp Hill near Harrisburg,

Key Dates:

1965: Warrell family acquires Pennsylvania Dutch Candies Company.
1974: Katherine Beecher Candies, Inc. is acquired.
1982: Melster Candies is acquired.
2000: The company's name is changed to Warrell Corporation.
2004: Melster Candies is sold.

was available, but initially Warrell did not like the former frozen food processing plant, which had been on the market for two years. After revisiting it, however, he and Billman began to see the benefits the facility had to offer. It was large, some 200,000 square feet in size, providing the company was ample room to grow. Moreover, it had plenty of warehousing space and offered a fully equipped research and development lab, a full-service cafeteria, a suitable food plant infrastructure, and access to a rail line.

Warrell and his team decided to buy the property, paying $3.9 million, with the intent of spending a similar amount on renovations. The Pennsylvania Industrial Development Authority chipped in with a low-interest loan of $1.25 million, and Pennsylvania's machine and equipment loan fund awarded the company an additional loan of $300,000. An engineering firm was hired to help develop the retrofit plans, and key co-manufacturing customers were also consulted about plant improvements they would like to see. They brought in their own engineering and quality control people to provide their input, in effect giving the company the advice of high-priced talent for free. In the end, the cost of retrofitting the building cost far more than expected, some $7 million, but management was pleased with the result. A plant built from scratch would have cost an estimated $30 million, making the final $11 million price tag seem reasonable. Moreover, the company was now better able to attract even more contracting and private label business.

The operations of Pennsylvania Dutch Candies and Beecher were consolidated in the new plant, which opened in 2000. In that same year the company became Warrell Corporation, a name management believed was more suitable for its national standing. The company was confident that the U.S. candy industry would continue to enjoy strong growth and that with its new plant it was well positioned to take advantage. However, the company's business was also being conducted in a changing landscape. Consolidation was a major factor, one that already resulted in the elimination of many niche and specialty candies. To remain competitive, Warrell Corporation elected in 2004 to consolidate its own operations and focus on co-manufacturing opportunities. As a consequence, management decided that after all the money, resources, and effort it had put in turning around Melster Candies, it was time to sell the subsidiary. A buyer was found in Colorado-based Impact Confections. Warrell's project revenues for 2004 were $48 million, and there was every reason to believe that the niche candy maker would continue to enjoy steady growth in the years to come.

Principal Subsidiaries

Pennsylvania Dutch Candies Company; Katherine Beecher Candies, Inc.

Principal Competitors

Hershey Foods Corporation; Mars, Inc.; Nestlé S.A.

Further Reading

''Inside Warrell,'' *Candy Business*, July–August 2002, p. 20.
''Linc Warrell Enjoying the Challenge,'' *Candy Business*, May–June 2002, p. 24.
''Melster Turnaround Proves a Success,'' *Candy Industry*, April 1998, p. 24.
Pacyniak, Bernard, ''Linc'ed to Leadership,'' *Candy Industry*, August 2004, p. 16.
Tiffany, Susan, ''The Nuts and Bolts of Pennsylvania Dutch Co.,'' *Candy Industry*, April 1998, p. 20.

—Ed Dinger

The Wawanesa Mutual Insurance Company

900-191 Broadway
Winnipeg, Manitoba R3C 3P1
Canada
Telephone: (204) 985-3923
Fax: (204) 942-7724
Web site: http://www.wawanesa.com

Private Company
Founded: 1896
Employees: 1,747
Total Assets: $1.39 billion (2003)
NAIC: 524126 Property and Casualty Insurance Carriers

The Wawanesa Mutual Insurance Company, based in Winnipeg, is Canada's largest mutual insurer. It also offers automobile insurance in California and Oregon through San Diego-based subsidiary Wawanesa General Insurance Company. Wawanesa Mutual offers personal, homeowners, business, farm, and automobile coverage through 1,300 independent insurance brokers spread across Canada, with the exception of Quebec, where it relies on company agents. A subsidiary, The Wawanesa Life Insurance Company, offers individual products, life insurance and investment products, as well as group products, including group life, disability, and health and dental products. Unlike its parent corporation, which is owned by policyholders, Wawanesa Life is a stock company.

19th Century Roots

Wawanesa Mutual takes its name from the small Canadian town of Wawanesa, located in southern Manitoba just north of where Minnesota and North Dakota meet. The insurer was founded in 1896 by friends Alonzo Kempton and Charles Kerr, but it was Kempton who was the driving force behind the venture. As a young man he moved from Nova Scotia with his parents to Manitoba in 1891. He wanted no part of the farm his father bought, preferring to find other work. A jovial, although sometimes gruff, man, he proved to be a natural salesman. He also developed a drinking problem that would plague him during his adult life. Selling out of a horse and buggy, Kempton peddled pots and pans and washing machines before turning to fire insurance, which he sold for an eastern stock insurance company. Farmers desperately needed fire insurance, due in large part to the wooden threshing machines in use during this period. They burned straw and threw off dangerous sparks. In addition, coal-oil lamps were a major fire hazard. But Kempton grew frustrated with the product, which was not tailored to the needs of western farmers. The insurance was expensive and required that the customer pay the premiums upfront, at the beginning of the year, several months before farmers were paid for their crops.

According to company lore, Kempton hatched the idea for organizing a mutual insurance company to serve farmers while sharing a jug of whiskey on a sales trip in 1895 with Kerr, another Manitoba transplant who became an accountant. The concept of a mutual company was not foreign to the men or their potential customers; it was the spirit behind the cooperative movement among farmers. By pooling their resources, Kempton reasoned, farmers would be able to obtain reasonably priced fire insurance. He and Kerr supposedly pitched their idea to an influential wheat farmer named Alexander Naismith, who agreed to participate but only if the two men took the ''Keeley'' cure for their drinking—referring to the Keeley Institute. The men agreed and took the cure, but according to a Keeley director quoted in *MacLean's Magazine* in a 1954 company profile, ''Kerr stayed with it for the rest of his life. Kempton stayed with it until he got home.''

Kempton planned to establish the new insurance company in the village of Glenboro, but cure or no cure, Kempton was not welcome, banned by the town's fervent temperance league. Instead, he traveled 19 miles to the west to the more accommodating town of Wawanesa, thus depriving Glenboro the honor of having a major insurance company named after it. Kempton spent the summer of 1896 visiting farmers, trying to convince them to contribute $20 a piece to start a mutual insurance company. Twenty signed on, and on September 25, 1896, a provincial charter was granted to establish The Wawanesa Mutual Insurance Company. Drawing on its modest funds, the company rented a room above a drugstore, which, ironically, was owned by a future managing director, Dr. C.M. Vanstone. Kempton was named the first managing director, with Kerr

Company Perspectives:

Since 1896, Wawanesa has insured people from all walks of life, in their work and in their play.

serving as accountant, and seven of the 20 original investors acting as directors. Just two weeks later Wawanesa wrote its first policy, covering a thresher for $600 for three years at a premium of $24.

Unlike the stock insurance companies, Kempton did not demand payment up front. Rather, farmers signed an assessment note, which was to be paid after they sold their crops in the fall. The note plan was a major factor in Wawanesa's early success and would be used by the insurer in one form or another for the next 75 years. Despite this innovation, however, Wawanesa struggled in the early years, forcing the directors to sometimes guarantee personal notes at the bank to meet claims. Changes were needed and in 1898 the company split the business into two branches: Thresher and Farm, the latter offering fire insurance for farm buildings. Wawanesa soon phased out coverage for threshers, which proved to be too risky a business, and started covering schools, churches, and other buildings. Wawanesa also looked westward to what would become the provinces of Saskatchewan and Alberta. By the start of the 1900s Wawanesa covered more than $1 million in property, and confidence in the future of the enterprise was strong enough that in 1901 the company bought a lot and erected a brick building for its new headquarters.

Steady Growth in the Early 1900s

Wawanesa grew at a rapid clip, so that by 1907 it was covering $20 million in property, and by 1910 it was claiming to be the largest mutual fire insurance company in Canada. An important step was taken in 1913 when the finance committee moved beyond bank deposits to begin investing in farm mortgages. Prudent investments would become an important component in the insurers' future growth. Wawanesa prospered during World War I, adding Victory Loan Bonds to is investment portfolio, and by the end of the war in 1918 the amount of insured property reached 75 million. To maintain the company's momentum, Kempton took Wawanesa into British Columbia in 1920. He also retained the company's independence. While a number of western mutual companies in 1918 formed an alliance, the Western Canada Mutual Fire Insurance Association, to reinsure one another's business, Wawanesa elected to go it alone. In the 1920s Wawanesa also displayed an innovative spirit in the area of fire prevention. It manufactured dry powder fire extinguishers and made them available to policyholders who lived far from a fire department, and later made a smaller version suitable for tractors. In addition, during these pre-electricity days, Wawanesa offered Little Wonder Lantern Snufflers and fireproof matchboxes.

Although Kempton had well served Wawanesa policyholders in many respects, he also ran the company with an autocratic hand, often fought with his directors, and insisted that his secretary type up his profanity-laced dictations verbatim. He also never lost sight of his own personal interests. In 1901 he launched the stock-owned Occidental Fire Insurance Company to reinsure Wawanesa policies. Occidental shared Wawanesa office space and personnel. Kempton was also involved in a number of outside business ventures, including a mortgage company (Occidental Trust), a land development company, The Wawanesa Wagon Seat Company, and the Canada Hone company, which made leather razor straps and a ''magnetized'' honing paste that was supposed to be just as useful in curing hemorrhoids as it was in sharpening razors. Kempton also lived large, building a massive house in town powered by an electric generator and staffed by a Chinese cook, who often served him raw oysters that he had shipped in from Nova Scotia by the barrel. He showed off his wealth by driving around in the town's largest car. His saving grace appeared to be a genuine fondness for children. He was quick to dispense nickels to them and often piled as many as would fit in his car for an excursion.

On occasion Kempton threatened to quit if the Wawanesa board did not accede to his plans, and although the board backed down, his manner created simmering animosity. After Kerr died in 1920, Kempton's drinking problem worsened, as he would be out of the office for days at a time engaged in one of his periodic drinking binges. Business began to suffer, so that when he threatened to quit in January 1922, the Wawanesa board promptly accepted his resignation, and when he tried to rescind his resignation at a subsequent meeting the directors reaffirmed their acceptance of it and asked him to immediately turn over the keys to the building and clear out. Enraged, Kempton moved to British Columbia where he would ultimately die a pauper in 1939, remembered by locals for his wild claims about having founded the great Wawanesa Mutual Insurance Company.

Taking over as managing director at Wawanesa was Dr. Charles Morley Vanstone, a man with a personality that was the mirror opposite of Kempton. He was disciplined and methodical, traits that would prove useful as Wawanesa dealt with a downturn in the Canadian economy in the early 1920s. He cut costs and diversified the company's business even further. Wawanesa began covering private buildings in towns and cities and in 1928 added automobile insurance. Other mutual insurers did not fare as well, however, and Wawanesa would absorb 11 struggling mutuals over the next decade. In 1930 Wawanesa received a Dominion of Canada charter, allowing it to operate in every province, leading to the opening of offices in Vancouver and Toronto in 1930. By 1935 additional offices would open in Montreal, Winnipeg, and Moncton. As a result of this expansion, Wawanesa was able to operate during the Depression years of the 1930s with little ill effect. All told, Vanstone's 21-year tenure as the head of Wawanesa was very successful, and left the organization financially sound and highly regarded in its field.

Adding Life Insurance in the 1950s

Due to poor health, Vanstone stepped down in 1943, replaced as managing director by H.E. Hemmons. During his five years at the top, Wawanesa decentralized its operations, granting branch managers a great deal of latitude to take advantage of local market conditions. This change would help spur even further growth. By the mid-1950s Wawanesa was Canada's fourth largest fire insurance company and the fourth largest automobile insurance company. Serving as general manager at

Key Dates:

1896: The company is founded by A.F. Kempton and Charles Kerr.
1922: Kempton is ousted as general manager.
1928: Auto insurance is added.
1961: A life insurance business is launched.
1975: A California auto insurance business is launched.
1992: Gregg Hanson is named chief executive.
1996: Wawanesa celebrates its 100th anniversary.

this stage was Milton C. Holden, a former school teacher and part-time Wawanesa salesman, who ascended to the top post in 1948. Under Holden, Wawanesa began charging drivers under the age of 25 a 30 percent premium while lowering the general rate. This change, Holden once told a reporter, "sweetened up our business." In the late 1950s Holden petitioned the government to engage in the life insurance business. The request was eventually granted and in 1961 The Wawanesa Mutual Life Insurance Company was launched. Because of the need for additional executive and technical staff, the move into the life insurance business also led the company to move its corporate offices from Wawanesa to Winnipeg.

But after granting the company a new business, a few years later the government took some away. A new government came into power in Manitoba in a 1969 election and created a public insurance corporation. As a result, Wawanesa lost two-thirds of its automobile business in the province. British Columbia followed suit in 1974. Holden stepped down as Wawanesa's president in 1971, stayed on as chairman, then passed away in 1975. His handpicked successor, Claude Trites, a 34-year veteran of the firm, had to deal with the loss of the automobile business. Wawanesa looked to the U.S. market. An initial impulse to move into nearby North Dakota was rejected in favor of the more lucrative California and New York markets. The company settled on California, and in 1975 Wawanesa was granted a license to sell insurance in the state and opened an office in San Diego. It proved to be a wise choice in location, as the population in the region grew 500 percent within 20 years. In Canada, Wawanesa made up for the loss in auto insurance premiums by expanding into other areas of property and casualty insurance. With this growth came the need for a new office building in Winnipeg, opening in 1976. By the end of the decade, Wawanesa also would launch a new branch office in Calgary and a second location in Alberta. Trites retired as president at the close of 1981, having played a crucial role during a transitional period in the company's history.

Selected as just the sixth person to head Wawanesa was Ivan Montgomery, who had been with the insurer for 23 years. During the 1980s he had to deal with unpredictable interest rates as well as intense competition, which forced Wawanesa to underprice its policies. Significant underwriting losses occurred throughout the industry. But because of the investment strategy instituted decades earlier, Wawanesa continued to grow its business and increase profits. Even while many firms struggled during the difficult economic conditions that prevailed in the late 1980s and early 1990s, Wawanesa was able to hold steady.

Montgomery stepped down as Wawanesa's president in 1992, replaced by Gregg J. Hanson, the company's current president. At age 41 he was the youngest person since Kempton to lead the company. An accountant by training, he joined Wawanesa in 1979, just four years after graduating from college, and quickly rose through the ranks. He tackled the problem of underwriting losses by raising deductibles, a change that cut down on the number of frivolous claims and resulted in a return to underwriting profits. He also oversaw the conversion of the life insurance company from mutual to stock ownership, making it a fully owned subsidiary. In addition, Hanson was responsible for converting Wawanesa from a mainframe computer environment to a personal computer-based network, a move that resulted in a significant increase in productivity. By the middle of the decade, Wawanesa had more than 1.2 million policies in force and its assets topped $1.5 billion.

Wawanesa celebrated its 100th anniversary in 1996. The company now faced new challenges, from Canadian banks, which were now allowed to sell insurance products, and from consolidation within the insurance industry. Nevertheless, Wawanesa was able to continue expanding its business into the new century and looked forward to ongoing growth. Wawanesa enjoyed the further advantage of having a seasoned, yet relatively young chief executive in Hanson, who recognized how to keep the company competitive. As he told *Manitoba Business* in 1999, "The status quo is never an option, you're either moving forward or you're being left behind."

Principal Subsidiaries

The Wawanesa Life Insurance Company; Wawanesa General Insurance Company.

Principal Competitors

The Economical Insurance Group; Fairfax Financial Holdings Ltd.; Power Corporation of Canada.

Further Reading

Collins, Robert, "The One-Horse Town," *MacLean's Magazine,* May 1, 1954, p. 30.

Nelson, Heather E., "Small Town Roots: A History of the Wawanesa Mutual Insurance Company," Winnipeg: University of Winnipeg, 2000.

Old Pathways, New Horizons: A History of The Wawanesa Mutual Insurance Company, Winnipeg: The Wawanesa Mutual Insurance Company, 1996.

—Ed Dinger

winterthur

Winterthur Group

Post Office Box 357
General Guisan-Strasse 40
CH-8401 Winterthur, Zurich
Switzerland
Telephone: +41-52-261-1111
Fax: +41-52-213-6620
Web site: http://www.winterthur.com

Wholly Owned Subsidiary of Credit Suisse Group
Incorporated: 1875 as Schweizerische Unfallversicherungs-Actiengesellschaft (Swiss Accident Insurance Joint-Stock Company)
Employees: 20,281
Sales: $25.56 billion (2003)
NAIC: 524114 Direct Health and Medical Insurance Carriers; 524126 Direct Property and Casualty Insurance Carriers

Winterthur Group is the largest life and nonlife insurance company in Switzerland, selling a broad range of insurance products. The company operates on a worldwide basis, selling life, pension, property, vehicle, disability, and numerous other types of insurance in more than 20 countries in Europe, North America, Asia, and South America.

19th Century Origins

The company takes its name from Winterthur, the industrial town in the Swiss canton of Zürich known not only as an important center of the engineering industry but also as the home of several major art collections. The founders of the company were well-known entrepreneurs and businessmen, responding to a need created by the increased risk of workplace accidents that had accompanied the industrialization process. The pattern for the company had been set principally by the workmen's compensation insurance available in Germany since the early 1870s. The founders were encouraged by the fact that Switzerland was about to introduce regulations, on the German model, governing legal liability for risks to railway and factory workers.

The man who took the initiative was Colonel Heinrich Rieter, member of the Swiss parliament and owner of the Winterthur spinning mill and engineering works Johann Jakob Rieter & Co. This company had pioneered the industrialization of Switzerland, equipping its factory, around 1800, with the first spinning plant in the country. Napoleon's continental blockade of English imports favored domestic Swiss production. Soon the mill acquired its own repair shop, which before long also was producing new machines. In 1832 Johann Jakob Rieter & Co. dispatched a complete set of spinning machinery to Austria. In due course the engineering works would include railway carriages and weaponry among its products.

On February 10, 1875, under the chairmanship of Heinrich Rieter, the heads of Winterthur's leading enterprises met to discuss the possibility of founding a Swiss accident insurance company. They agreed that such a company was needed, and as the result of Rieter's efforts the founding meeting of the Schweizerische Unfallversicherungs-Actiengesellschaft (Swiss Accident Insurance Joint-Stock Company) took place in Winterthur on March 2, 1875. The share capital, fixed at CHF 5 million, was subscribed by Swiss industrialists and businessmen, most from Winterthur. Three thousand shares were issued first, each with a nominal value of CHF 1,000, for a down payment of 20 percent; the remaining 2,000 shares were deferred to 1880, with a premium payable by other buyers.

From the outset Heinrich Rieter was the venture's driving force. He had made a close study of the problems of insurance and of the Swiss industry's need for Swiss insurance cover. Salomon Volkart and Heinrich Sulzer-Steiner also played leading roles in the founding of the company. In 1851 Salomon Volkart, together with his brother Johann Georg Volkart, had created the Winterthur firm Gebrüder Volkart (Volkart Brothers), producing Indian raw cotton and European manufactured goods. Heinrich Sulzer-Steiner was the true founder of Switzerland's engineering industry. In 1860 he had gone into the Winterthur engineering firm Gebrüder Sulzer (Sulzer Brothers) founded by his father Johann Jakob Sulzer and his uncle Salomon Sulzer. In 1856, with the English engineer Charles Brown, Sulzer-Steiner had developed the valve steam engine, and in 1866 he had introduced steam central heating. Heinrich

Company Perspectives:

The goal of Winterthur is to set the European benchmark for profitability, productivity and quality. Operational efficiency and client service are the most important priorities in this regard. The prospects are good, based on the company's excellent employees and strong brand. Premium growth is therefore not an immediate priority for Winterthur Group. Winterthur Group will focus more on markets where it has a strong position or can take advantage of opportunities for growth. The aim is to put a sustainable business model in place in all markets, one that promises to achieve a positive result.

Rieter was the first president of the Winterthur advisory board, with Salomon Volkart as vice-president. From 1884 until his death in 1906, Heinrich Sulzer-Steiner headed the body later designated the supervisory board. On many occasions members of the well-known industrialist family of Sulzer, serving on board and committee, have had a decisive influence on Winterthur's development.

The company's statutes had to be approved by the cantonal government of Zürich. The charter, dated March 27, 1875, bears the signature of the famous Swiss writer Gottfried Keller, who as clerk to the canton of Zürich drew up official documents. This document authorized the company to begin supplying individual and collective accident insurance. Around the same time, the firm later to be known as the Zürich Insurance Company, which had been founded in 1872 under the name of the Versicherungs-Verein to offer reinsurance and marine insurance, extended its activities to include accident insurance.

Winterthur's practical organization and its charges and conditions were taken in their essentials from those current in neighboring Germany. Accordingly the company chose as its first head not someone specializing in insurance, but the Winterthur town notary Friedrich Gysler, a distinguished lawyer and an acquaintance of the founders. He held office for only a year. In 1876 he was succeeded by C. Widmer-Kappeler of Zürich. The first people to be insured were the employees of the town of Winterthur's large industrial firms. From the beginning, a chain of agencies was built up in the individual Swiss cantons. When the Swiss Factory Act came into force in 1878 the company began selling liability insurance, and it promptly availed itself of the opportunities for foreign business provided by the regulations. This tendency to seek business abroad was shared by the Zürich Insurance Company. Both firms took the idea of accident and liability insurance from Germany, first introducing the two types of cover into Switzerland and then selling them worldwide. In 1875 Winterthur set up branches in Germany, Austria-Hungary, Belgium, Holland, Luxembourg, Denmark, and Norway. A year later it opened a general agency in Paris for France and the French colonies; it even established itself in Finland.

The rapid and large-scale spread of the company network in Switzerland and Austria entailed heavy expenses that could not at first be met by the volume of business achieved. In addition, premiums were clearly too low in some countries—tariffs cannot simply be transferred indiscriminately from one state to another—and liability insurance was hit by several exceptionally heavy compensation payments. The annual report for 1891 speaks of a marked disparity between premium income and the total disbursed in settlement of claims. In both the following years the figures were even worse, and in 1883 the managing director, C. Widmer-Kappeler, fled abroad. At the general meeting there was a proposal, later withdrawn, that the company go into liquidation. Under new management, however, the firm made a recovery without having to cut benefits. Premium rates were adjusted to actual costs, types of cover not in demand were withdrawn, and expenses were reduced by the adoption of appropriate economies.

Gradually the firm got back on an even keel. It owes its successful development from the dawn of the 20th century onward chiefly to the personality of Gottfried Bosshard. He came to Winterthur from the judiciary in 1898 and served the firm from then until 1940, ending up as delegate to the board of directors. It is in large part thanks to Bosshard that the company achieved its fine reputation. In a wider sphere, he played a major part in the evolution of insurance law in Switzerland; the University of Zürich recognized this achievement in 1929 by making him an honorary doctor of law.

At the same time that it was increasing its geographical spread—moving into Spain, for example, in 1910—the company was also anxious to introduce new lines of insurance and types of cover. In the field of accident insurance, provision was now offered against death from acute infectious illness; in liability insurance, cover for material damage was added to that hitherto available only for personal damage. Finally, Winterthur started offering burglary-and-guarantee insurance and, following a decision of the general meeting of 1900, extended its activities to the whole area of material damage insurance. With so much of its business in Switzerland, Winterthur suffered considerable losses as a result of the legal transfer, effective from April 1, 1918, of workmen's accident insurance into the Swiss state accident insurance scheme. The company was forced to rechannel its activities into individual accident and liability insurance and foreign business.

The balance was redressed mainly by the introduction of motor insurance. In 1918, when it took over the portfolio of the German firm of Agrippina, Winterthur started selling comprehensive motor insurance, which had been initiated by Agrippina in 1901. To this was added motor vehicle third-party insurance, which had been obligatory in some Swiss cantons since before World War I. In the 1920s Winterthur expanded considerably in this area, which today constitutes a basic component of its income.

Under Heinrich Fehlmann, who succeeded Bosshart, first in 1918 as director and then in 1921 as chairman of the board, the firm continued to grow and prosper. Premium income rose from CHF 4 million in 1890 to CHF 30 million in 1930 and CHF 69 million in 1940. When inflation brought about the decline of the German currency, German insurance companies—which at the time occupied an important position in the Swiss market—could no longer meet their commitments in Swiss francs and had to give up business. The resulting gaps in the market made way for the establishment of life insurance companies in Switzerland, notably, in 1923, the Winterthur Lebensversicherungs-Gesellschaft (Winterthur Life Assurance Company). Like its parent company, Winterthur Life soon turned its attention

Key Dates:

1875: The founding meeting of Schweizerische Unfallversicherungs-Actiengesellschaft (Swiss Accident Insurance Joint-Stock Company) is held in Winterthur, Switzerland.
1898: Gottfried Bosshard, arguably the company's most influential leader, begins a career at Winterthur that will last until 1940.
1918: Winterthur begins selling automobile insurance.
1936: Winterthur's first office in the United States is opened in New York.
1975: The company changes its name to Winterthur Schweizerische Versicherungs-Gesellschaft (Winterthur Swiss Insurance Company).
1997: Winterthur and Credit Suisse Group merge.
2001: Winterthur International is sold to XL Capital Ltd.
2002: Winterthur acquires Luxembourg-based Premier Life.

abroad, starting with Belgium, Germany, and France. It was now the second largest life assurance company in Switzerland.

The growth of the two companies found visible expression in new head office buildings, completed in 1931 and now quite a feature of the Winterthur scene. The most striking impact made by the complex on the townspeople was reflected in its nickname, ''Accident Tower.''

Post-World War II Expansion

Immediately after the end of World War II, Winterthur set about rebuilding its extensive foreign business. There were branches in most of the countries of Western Europe; to these were added property and life insurance acquisitions, beginning with Europeia in Portugal in 1958, followed by Union et Prévoyance of Belgium in 1964, and Heimat of Austria in 1966. In 1962 Winterthur had succeeded in taking over the Eidgenössische Versicherungs-Aktien- Gesellschaft (Federal Insurance Company Ltd.) of Zürich, founded in 1891 and steeped in Swiss tradition. In the same period Winterthur extended its own activities to include many new types of business, particularly in the area of engineering insurance. This process of expansion was taken into account in 1975, the year the company celebrated the centenary of its founding, when it changed its name to Winterthur Schweizerische Versicherungs-Gesellschaft (Winterthur Swiss Insurance Company). In 1978 the Winterthur Rechtsschutz-Versicherungs-Gesellschaft (Winterthur Legal Insurance Company) came into being.

During the 1970s and 1980s, under the leadership of Hans Braunschweiler, the Winterthur insurance group kept up and intensified its postwar policy of expansion through the purchase of other companies. In two decades these acquisitions led to an eightfold increase in Winterthur's gross premium income, which rose from CHF 1.3 billion in 1968 to CHF 10.4 billion in 1988. Two-thirds of these premiums came from foreign business, concentrated mainly in Western Europe and North America.

Winterthur already had explored the possibility of trading in the United States in the 19th century, but had been put off by the distance involved and the $100,000 security required. After much reflection and investigation, Winterthur opened a New York City branch in 1936. In 1950 Winterthur bought the American Casualty Company, to which it handed over its own existing U.S. insurance clientèle. After the sale of this company to the present Continental National American, Winterthur in the United States was left with only reinsurance. It came back into the U.S. direct insurance business in 1982, when it acquired the important, long-established Republic Insurance group of Dallas, Texas. In 1988 the Southern Guaranty Companies of Montgomery, Alabama, joined Winterthur, followed in 1990 by the General Casualty Group of Sun Prairie, Wisconsin. Its Canadian activities began with the acquisition of two companies now doing business under the name of Citadel General, Toronto.

At home in Switzerland, in 1987 Winterthur bought a majority holding in the Neuenberger Versicherungs-Gruppe (Neuchatel Insurance Group), founded in 1869. Winterthur always laid emphasis on its trade in Germany, centered in large part on insurance for the medical profession. In 1987 Winterthur took on a minority holding in the Nordstern insurance group. The Transatlantische Gruppe (Transatlantic), acquired in 1989, confined itself mainly to brokerage and direct marketing of motor insurance. In the United Kingdom, Winterthur sold life insurance through Provident Life, founded in 1877. In 1989 the Churchill Insurance Company Ltd., specializing in telephone sales of car insurance, started up. The acquisition of the Intercontinentale insurance group in 1988 tripled Winterthur's share of the Italian insurance market and secured its position there.

In addition to these successful exercises in partnership, since the beginning of the 1970s Winterthur has been arranging cooperation deals with well-known insurance companies for the purpose of protecting its clients' interests in areas where it had no branches or subsidiaries of its own. It was this kind of cooperation that led in 1976 to the establishment of the Norwich Winterthur Group, in which Winterthur and the U.K. firm Norwich Union each held 48.5 percent, and the Japanese Chiyoda Fire and Marine, the remaining 3 percent. The Norwich Winterthur Reinsurance Corporation Ltd., of Norwich, formed part of this cooperative venture. In 1979 Itaú Winterthur Seguradura S.A. (Itaú Winterthur Insurance Company Ltd.) was set up in Sao Paolo, Brazil, as a base from which to cover South America.

With its tight trading network Winterthur controlled a large share of the Swiss insurance market. In the 14 most important countries where it operated, it did so directly through its own branches and subsidiaries. In addition, cooperative ventures were opening up new insurance markets in the Middle and Far East and in Africa, Australia, and South America. With an eye to the European Common Market, Union et Prévoyance was rechristened Winterthur-Europe Assurance in 1989 and in 1990 provided with branches in four more countries; in addition, Winterthur-Europe Vie (Winterthur-Europe Life Assurance) was set up. These companies allowed Winterthur to extend its protection right across the frontiers of the European Community.

Winterthur and Credit Suisse in the 1990s

The 1990s was a decade of profound change for Winterthur. The agent of change was a corporate financier named Martin Ebner, whose interest in the company triggered a reaction that reverberated throughout the European financial community. Ebner, through his investment company, BK Vision, began building a stake in Winterthur during the mid-1990s, when the company ranked as the second largest insurer in Switzerland and the fourth largest insurer in Europe. Winterthur was a worthy investment in Ebner's mind, prompting him eventually to acquire a 30 percent interest in the company. When he revealed to the Swiss business press that he might support a foreign takeover of Winterthur, the news set in motion events that inaugurated a new era of existence for the company.

In 1996, Switzerland's oldest bank, Credit Suisse Group, formed a joint venture with Winterthur. The partnership sparked rumors of a potential merger, but such speculation was brushed aside by Credit Suisse's chief executive officer, Lukas Muhlemann. ''If you only need a glass of milk,'' Muhlemann remarked in an August 16, 1997 interview with the *Economist (US),* ''why buy the cow?'' Despite assurances to the contrary, Credit Suisse and Winterthur were holding secret talks about a merger—discussions codenamed ''Project Dupont''—but Ebner's pronouncement forced the two companies to make their plans public and greatly accelerate merger discussions. ''Somebody tried to steal the cow,'' Muhlemann explained, describing Credit Suisse's defensive posture. In August 1997, Credit Suisse acquired Winterthur in an all-stock transaction. The combination created a company with $465 billion in assets, 15 million clients, and a payroll of 60,000. Credit Suisse, with Winterthur operating as a fully autonomous subsidiary, turned into a financial giant overnight, ranking as one of the top ten financial companies in the world.

In the wake of this massive merger, Winterthur retained a separate identity from Credit Suisse, with little substantive change affecting the company. ''Apart from the name of the shares, practically nothing changes,'' a Winterthur executive said in the August 16, 1997 issue of the *Economist (US).* As the company entered the 21st century, its progress was highlighted by divestitures and acquisitions, as it stripped away parts of itself and expanded its holdings in other areas. In 2001, the company sold Winterthur International, a subsidiary with offices in 27 countries that sold primarily liability and property and fire insurance, to Bermuda-based XL Capital Ltd. The deal was valued at $405 million. In 2002, Winterthur acquired Premier Life, a life insurance company based in Luxembourg. Although some of Winterthur's business potentially was subject to change pending Credit Suisse's worldwide review of its operations midway through the decade, the Swiss insurer's ironclad foundation appeared immutable as it prepared for the future.

Principal Subsidiaries

Winterthur Life (Switzerland); Wincare Zusatzversicherungen (Switzerland); Winterthur-ARAG Legal Assistance (Switzerland); Credit Suisse Life & Pensions AG (Liechtenstein); Winterthur Beteiligungsgesellschaft GmbH (Germany); Medvantis Holding (Germany); Winterthur Insurance Health & Accident (Germany); Hispanowin S.A. (Spain); Winterthur-Europe Assurances (Belgium); Credit Suisse Life & Pensions (Luxembourg) S.A.; Winterthur-Europe Vie (Luxembourg); Winterthur (UK) Holdings Ltd.; Credit Suisse Life & Pensions Management GmbH (Austria); Rhodia Assurances (France); Credit Suisse Life & Pensions poistovna a.s. (Czech Republic; 65.1%); Credit Suisse Life & Pensions penzijini fond a.s. (Czech Republic; 79.97%); Credit Suisse Life & Pensions poistovna, a.s. (Slovakia); Credit Suisse Life & Pensions Slovensko (Slovakia; 50.99%); Credit Suisse Life & Pensions Pénztárszolgáltató Rt. (Hungary; 65%); Credit Suisse Life & Pensions, Biztositó Rt. (Hungary; 65%); Towarzystwo Ubezpieczeniowe Winterthur S.A. (Poland); Winterthur U.S. Holdings; Winterthur Canada Financial; Winterthur Holdings Australia; Winterthur Insurance Services Asia Ltd. (Hong Kong); PT. Credit Suisse Life Insurance Co. Ltd. (Japan); Credit Suisse Life & Pensions (Bermuda) Ltd.; Harrington International Insurance Ltd. (Bermuda); Winterthur Atlantic Ltd. (Bermuda); Winterthur Capital Ltd. (Bermuda); Winterthur Integra Ltd. (Bermuda); SRS Holdings Ltd. (Cayman Islands).

Principal Competitors

AXA; Swiss Life Holding; Zurich Financial Services.

Further Reading

Howard, Lisa S., ''Winterthur, Credit Suisse to Join,'' *National Underwriter Property & Casualty-Risk & Benefits Management,* August 18, 1997, p. 3.

''In the Land of Milk and Honey,'' *Economist (US),* August 16, 1997, p. 54.

''It's Got to Fit Somehow,'' *Economist (US),* August 16, 1997, p. 53.

Koch, Peter, ''Der schweizerische Beitrag zur Entwicklung des Versicherungswesens,'' *Schweizerische Versicherungs-Zeitschrift,* 1985.

——, ''Versicherer aus aller Welt in Deutschland,'' *Versicherungskaufmann,* July 1987.

Markun, Sylvia, ed., *Facetten Europas—100 Jahre Winterthur-Unfall, 50 Jahre Winterthur-Leben,* Mitteillungen Jubilee Edition, Winterthur: Winterthur Schweizerische Versicherungs-Gesellschaft, 1975.

Parry, John, ''Credit Suisse Insures Itself with Winterthur,'' *The European,* August 14, 1997, p. 28.

Souter, Gavin, ''XL Expands Business,'' *Business Insurance,* February 19, 2001, p. 1.

Von Winterthur in alle Welt, Winterthur: Winterthur Schweizerische Versicherungs-Gesellschaft, 1990.

''Winterthur Buys Luxembourg Company Premier Life,'' *European Report,* June 12, 2002, p. 600.

''Winterthur Future in Doubt Over Credit Suisse Review,'' *Money Marketing,* March 6, 2003, p. 5.

—Peter Koch. Translated from the German by Olive Classe.
—update: Jeffrey L. Covell

Zingerman's®

Zingerman's Community of Businesses

422 Detroit Street
Ann Arbor, Michigan 48104
U.S.A.
Telephone: (734) 477-5711
Toll Free: (888) 636-8162
Fax: (734) 477-6988
Web site: http://www.zingermans.com

Private Company
Incorporated: 1982
Employees: 400
Sales: $21 million (2004 est.)
NAIC: 722211 Limited-Service Restaurants; 722110 Full-Service Restaurants; 454110 Electronic Shopping and Mail-Order Houses; 611430 Professional and Management Development Training; 311812 Commercial Bakeries; 311510 Dairy Product (Except Frozen) Manufacturing; 722320 Caterers; 311920 Coffee and Tea Manufacturing

Zingerman's Community of Businesses encompasses a delicatessen, a full-service restaurant, a catering service, a bakery, a dairy, a coffee company, a mail order sales operation, and a training service, all based in or near Ann Arbor, Michigan. Zingerman's has gained a national reputation for offering specialty foods of the highest quality with matchless service, and under the guidance of founding partners Ari Weinzweig and Paul Saginaw it has grown from a single store into a $20 million operation.

Beginnings

Zingerman's was founded by a pair of young men who met in the late 1970s while both were employed at a restaurant in Ann Arbor, Michigan, called Maude's. Ari Weinzweig, from Chicago, was working as a dishwasher after having earned his bachelor's degree in Russian history from the University of Michigan, while Paul Saginaw, from Detroit, was a manager. Both had grown up in towns which had great delicatessens, and each lamented the fact that Ann Arbor did not offer one. The pair decided to join forces, and secured a $20,000 bank loan to start a delicatessen that would offer high quality traditional food products like corned beef, imported cheeses, and olive oils in an atmosphere of energy and abundance. The deli would also specialize in large sandwiches that contained only top quality ingredients and were memorably tasty.

The delicatessen opened in March of 1982 in an old brick building on Detroit Street in Ann Arbor, a cobblestone-paved historic area called Kerrytown near an indoor specialty-store mall a few blocks from downtown. It's name was an invention—there was no real ''Zingerman,'' but the moniker seemed to fit the traditional Jewish delicatessen the pair had in mind, while also sounding an upbeat note.

Soon after it opened, the deli's high-quality food and friendly service began to draw customers from Ann Arbor and Detroit who were eager to sample the many deli meats, cheeses, mustards, vinegars, olive oils, sandwiches, and deli salads. Over the next several years, the bustling Zingerman's established itself as one of the Midwest's finest delicatessens. To give back to the community, in 1988 the founding partners helped create a non-profit organization, Food Gatherers, which distributed donated food (mainly from local restaurants that included Zingerman's) to homeless shelters in the Ann Arbor area. In time, the original Zingerman's outlet was expanded to a house next door, which had more seating for customers, a coffee bar, desserts, and some packaged foods.

To highlight the deli's many specialty foods, a monthly newsletter was created as well as a newsletter for employees. In addition to introducing newly discovered food products, it also included recipes and articles (many written by Weinzweig) about the history of a particular food or culinary region. For his part, Weinzweig had begun to travel the world in search of the best foods, be they cheeses produced on a family farm in France, olive oil pressed in small batches in Italy, or chocolates made of the purest ingredients in Belgium. Zingerman's customers could always sample anything in the store, and the idea of tasting a dollop of imported olive oil on a wedge of handmade bread amid the bustle of the busy sandwich line led many an Ann Arborite to drop by Zingerman's often.

By the end of its first decade, Zingerman's had grown into a $5 million business with more than 100 employees. Frank

Company Perspectives:

Mission Statement: We share the Zingerman's experience. Selling food that makes you happy. Giving service that makes you smile. In passionate pursuit of our mission. Showing love and caring in all our actions. To enrich as many lives as we possibly can.

Carollo, one of the deli's managers, was now preparing to open an artisanal bakery offshoot, and catalog sales were starting up, but not much had changed in the two partners' basic game plan. If anything, the business seemed to be in a bit of a rut, with new deli rivals appearing on the scene with lower priced, if lesser-quality food, including one which Zingerman's sued over its apparent appropriation of the store's style.

Developing a New Approach in the Early 1990s

On a hot summer's day in 1992, as the usual lunchtime rush was backing up and a cooler was breaking down, Saginaw requested that Weinzweig accompany him outside to talk. Instead of mentioning a matter of extreme urgency, as Weinzweig was expecting, Saginaw simply asked, "Ari, where are we going to be in ten years?" Weinzweig was at first taken aback, but then admitted that Saginaw had a point. This moment of reflection initiated a two-year dialogue between the partners over the future of their business. For his part, Saginaw thought opening other Zingerman's delis was the solution, an idea which had often been suggested by patrons. Weinzweig disagreed strongly, unwilling to sanction watering down the unique quality and purpose of the original store. After spending much time researching, writing, and rewriting vision statements, and rejecting other ideas such as moving to larger quarters or acquiring other businesses, in 1994 Saginaw and Weinzweig settled on a plan to create a new entity, to be called Zingerman's Community of Businesses.

In an informal letter to the company's employees called "Zingerman's 2009: A Food Odyssey" (and in a similar one to customers), they laid out plans for a company that would grow to encompass twelve to fifteen separate businesses over the next fifteen years, each one small and located in the Ann Arbor area. Like Zingerman's Bakehouse, now in operation, each would have at least one managing partner who would do hands-on work and be a part owner. The businesses would all be food-related and serve to enhance the basic Zingerman's concept and bear its name. Funding would come from the two original partners (who would take a majority stake) and their new managing partner-owners and be designed to break even as quickly as possible based on cash flow.

The plan was met with a decidedly mixed response. The partners' legal and financial advisers thought the structure of separate businesses co-owned with new partners was a bad idea. Customers were concerned that the deli they loved would change in ways they did not like. In addition, the store's managers had the most negative reaction of all—within the next year and a half, more than four-fifths quit.

Unfazed, the partners proceeded to put the plan into action, first forming Zingerman's Service Network, or ZingNet, which would provide central administrative services to the new units. A Chief Financial Officer was hired, and new management practices were put into place. A new non-food unit, Zingerman's Training, Inc. (ZingTrain), was introduced next. Cofounded with University of Michigan MBA and former General Motors and SoHo Natural Soda executive Maggie Bayless, ZingTrain would offer training for both Zingerman's employees and outside firms that wanted to reach the high levels of quality for which Zingerman's had earned a reputation.

To facilitate training new employees, the company's principles and practices had already been codified in a series of multi-part plans with names like "Five Steps to Handling Customer Complaints" and "Four Steps to Order Accuracy." Building on these, Weinzweig did extensive research and wrote papers on other business philosophies, which were then broken down into straightforward sets of steps and points. In addition to forming the curriculum of ZingTrain, this work also helped the different units of Zingerman's learn a common corporate language. ZingTrain soon became known as the University of Zingerman's, with the firm's own staffers learning not just basic service techniques but food history and sociology, business practices, and other related information. ZingTrain would also come to serve a wide range of businesses from around the Midwest, including restaurants, banks, hospitals, and even a funeral home. Seminars on such topics as "Specialty Foods 101" and "The Art of Giving Great Service" cost $375 for a one-day session or $695 for two.

Growth in the Late 1990s

In 1996, Zingerman's Mail Order was founded to offer the deli's specialty foods around the globe. By the following year, the firm employed 270 full- and part-time workers and was taking in an estimated $10.5 million in annual sales. In 1998, Zingerman's Catering was introduced, offering high quality food for small and large events. The next year a Web site, Zingermans.com, gave the mail order unit an online presence.

On Labor Day weekend, 2001, Zingerman's Creamery opened, run by managing partner Dave Carson. Located southwest of Ann Arbor in Manchester, Michigan, the $520,000 facility began operations by producing small batches of cream cheese and gelato ice cream for use and sale at Zingerman's. After being road-tested in the deli and bakehouse, products from Zingerman's Creamery were later sold through other retailers.

By now it was clear that the firm had gotten over its growing pains, and it was attracting a new, highly skilled group of business professionals who were happy to be earning less than what the corporate world paid doing traditional "Slow Food" work such as baking bread and making cheese, while finding creative ways to market them. With a corporate culture drawn from the laid-back, hippie ethos of a classic college town, where a cheerfully pierced and green-haired employee might serve food to a suited corporate type, Zingerman's also had a goal of donating 10 percent of its operating profit to charitable causes.

During 2001, nearby Detroit Metropolitan Airport was undergoing major renovations, with a new terminal being built to house the hub operation of Northwest Airlines. Plans were in place to open a second Zingerman's Delicatessen in the concourse, but after the September 11 terrorist attacks, heightened

Key Dates:

1982: Zingerman's Delicatessen is founded by Ari Weinzweig and Paul Saginaw.
1988: Founding partners help create Food Gatherers to donate surplus food to the homeless.
1992: Zingerman's Bakehouse opens in conjunction with Frank Carollo.
1994: Zingerman's Service Network and Zingerman's Training Inc. (ZingTrain) are created.
1996: Zingerman's Mail Order is founded.
1998: Zingerman's Catering debuts.
1999: Online service Zingermans.com is introduced.
2001: Zingerman's Creamery opens in Manchester, Michigan.
2003: Full-service Zingerman's Roadhouse restaurant opens in Ann Arbor.
2004: Zingerman's Coffee Company is founded.

airline security caused the main food contractor to pull out of the project over concerns that fewer customers would be admitted past security gates. It was a rare setback for the firm, which had years earlier also given up on a short-lived produce business offshoot. For fiscal 2001, revenues hit an estimated $13 million.

Zingerman's was now known nationally as a purveyor of fine foods, as attested to by articles in *Saveur, Esquire, Eating Well, Bon Appetit,* and the *New York Times,* among others. The company's national presence helped boost its Internet sales, which in 2003 hit a peak of $1 million, up from $150,000 in 2000. The original deli operation continued to do strongly as well, pulling in $6.6 million.

In the fall of 2003, another new business made its debut. Zingerman's Roadhouse was a full-service restaurant offering ''down-home'' specialties like barbecue, grits, and greens, all made from the finest ingredients (and priced accordingly). Located on the west side of Ann Arbor at a busy intersection near two shopping malls, the operation employed 120 and was expected to bring in annual revenues of $4 million.

The spring of 2004 saw the introduction of a smaller offshoot called Zingerman's Coffee Company. Run by Allen Liebowitz, it would supply high-quality roasted coffee to Zingerman's Delicatessen, Roadhouse, and Mail Order. Other plans on the drawing board reportedly included a Mexican restaurant and a chocolatier. By now, cofounder Ari Weinzweig had published several books, most recently *Zingerman's Guide to Giving Great Service* and *Zingerman's Guide to Good Eating.* During the year, Zingerman's was named one of the world's 25 great markets by *Food & Wine* magazine.

After more than twenty years, Zingerman's Community of Businesses had grown into a thriving, multifaceted operation that brought great food and service to Ann Arbor and the world. With its founding partners still enthusiastically involved, and more new business ideas on the drawing board, the company's future looked bright.

Principal Subsidiaries

Zingerman's Creamery; Zingerman's Bakehouse; Zingerman's Mail Order LLC; Zingerman's Deli; Zingerman's Training, Inc.; Zingerman's Service Network, Inc.; Dancing Sandwiches, Inc.; Zingerman's Coffee Co.

Principal Competitors

Dean & Deluca Inc.; Harry & David; Balducci's.

Further Reading

Bayless, Maggie, ''Staff Training: Maintaining and Strengthening Culture as Your Organization Grows,'' *Gourmet Retailer*, August 1, 2003.

Burlingham, Bo, ''The Coolest Small Company in America,'' *Inc.*, January, 2003, p. 64.

Dietderich, Andrew, ''Not Just Window Shopping—Shoppers Blending Online Purchases with Trips to the Store,'' *Crain's Detroit Business*, November 17, 2003, p. 11.

Endelman, Michael, ''Small Midwestern Deli Has Big-City Charm,'' *Boston Globe*, April 3, 2002, p. E5.

Kiley, David, ''Zingerman's Took the Road Less Traveled to Success,'' *USA Today*, October 1, 2003, pg. 5B.

Kosdrosky, Terry, ''Zingerman's Plans to Milk Another Niche Biz: Dairy,'' *Crain's Detroit Business*, September 10, 2001, p. 10.

Moran, Tim, ''Deli's Extensive Biz Menu Began with Vision of 2 Men: 'Spirituality' Is a Key Ingredient to Zingerman's,'' *Crain's Detroit Business*, September 8, 1997, p. E-13.

''Restaurant Contractor Pulls out of New Terminal Project,'' *Associated Press State & Local Wire*, September 21, 2001.

Rueter, Anne, ''Growing Bakery Turns out Thousands of Loaves, Rolls and Pastries Daily,'' *Associated Press State & Local Wire*, May 15, 2000.

—Frank Uhle

INDEX TO COMPANIES

Index to Companies

Listings in this index are arranged in alphabetical order under the company name. Company names beginning with a letter or proper name such as Eli Lilly & Co. will be found under the first letter of the company name. Definite articles (The, Le, La) are ignored for alphabetical purposes as are forms of incorporation that precede the company name (AB, NV). Company names printed in bold type have full, historical essays on the page numbers appearing in bold. Updates to entries that appeared in earlier volumes are signified by the notation **(upd.)**. Company names in light type are references within an essay to that company, not full historical essays. This index is cumulative with volume numbers printed in bold type.

Xetra, **59** 151

INDEX TO INDUSTRIES

Index to Industries

ACCOUNTING

ADVERTISING & OTHER BUSINESS SERVICES

ADVERTISING & OTHER BUSINESS SERVICES *(continued)*

AEROSPACE

AIRLINES

AUTOMOTIVE

AUTOMOTIVE *(continued)*

BEVERAGES

BIOTECHNOLOGY

CHEMICALS

CHEMICALS *(continued)*

CONGLOMERATES

CONSTRUCTION

CONTAINERS

CONTAINERS *(continued)*

DRUGS/PHARMACEUTICALS

ELECTRICAL & ELECTRONICS

ELECTRICAL & ELECTRONICS *(continued)*

ENGINEERING & MANAGEMENT SERVICES

ENTERTAINMENT & LEISURE

ENTERTAINMENT & LEISURE *(continued)*

FINANCIAL SERVICES: BANKS

FINANCIAL SERVICES: NON-BANKS

FINANCIAL SERVICES: NON-BANKS *(continued)*

FOOD PRODUCTS

FOOD PRODUCTS *(continued)*

FOOD SERVICES & RETAILERS

FOOD SERVICES & RETAILERS *(continued)*

HEALTH & PERSONAL CARE PRODUCTS

HEALTH CARE SERVICES

HOTELS

HOTELS *(continued)*

INFORMATION TECHNOLOGY

INSURANCE

INSURANCE *(continued)*

LEGAL SERVICES

MANUFACTURING

MANUFACTURING *(continued)*

MANUFACTURING *(continued)*

MANUFACTURING *(continued)*

MATERIALS

MINING & METALS

MINING & METALS *(continued)*

PAPER & FORESTRY

PERSONAL SERVICES

PETROLEUM

PETROLEUM *(continued)*

PUBLISHING & PRINTING

REAL ESTATE

RETAIL & WHOLESALE

RETAIL & WHOLESALE *(continued)*

RUBBER & TIRE

TELECOMMUNICATIONS

TELECOMMUNICATIONS *(continued)*

TEXTILES & APPAREL

TEXTILES & APPAREL *(continued)*

TOBACCO

TRANSPORT SERVICES

UTILITIES

UTILITIES *(continued)*

WASTE SERVICES

GEOGRAPHIC INDEX

Geographic Index

Ecuador

Egypt

El Salvador

Finland

France

Ghana

Greece

Hong Kong

Hungary

Iceland

India

Indonesia

Iran

Ireland

Israel

Italy

Jamaica

Japan

Switzerland *(continued)*

Taiwan

Thailand

Tunisia

Turkey

Ukraine

United Arab Emirates

United Kingdom

United States *(continued)*

United States *(continued)*

United States *(continued)*

United States *(continued)*

United States *(continued)*

United States *(continued)*

Venezuela

Vietnam

Virgin Islands

Wales

Zambia

NOTES ON CONTRIBUTORS

Notes on Contributors

ATKINS, William Arthur. Illinois-based writer.

BRENNAN, Gerald E. California-based writer.

COHEN, M. L. Novelist and business writer living in Paris.

COVELL, Jeffrey L. Seattle-based writer.

DINGER, Ed. Bronx-based writer and editor.

GREENLAND, Paul R. Illinois-based writer and researcher; author of two books and former senior editor of a national business magazine; contributor to *The Encyclopedia of Chicago History* and *Company Profiles for Students.*

HAUSER, Evelyn. Researcher, writer and marketing specialist based in Arcata, California; expertise includes historical and trend research in such topics as globalization, emerging industries and lifestyles, future scenarios, biographies, and the history of organizations.

INGRAM, Frederick C. Utah-based business writer who has contributed to *GSA Business, Appalachian Trailway News,* the *Encyclopedia of Business,* the *Encyclopedia of Global Industries,* the *Encyclopedia of Consumer Brands,* and other regional and trade publications.

JONES, Howard A. Writer and editor.

LAZZARI, Marie. Writer and editor.

ROTHBURD, Carrie. Writer and editor specializing in corporate profiles, academic texts, and academic journal articles.

SHEPHERD, Kenneth R. Michigan-based writer and editor.

UHLE, Frank. Ann Arbor-based writer; movie projectionist, disc jockey, and staff member of *Psychotronic Video* magazine.